# NEW UNDERSTANDING

# BIOLOGY

## For Advanced Level

### Fourth Edition

Glenn Toole
Susan Toole

Originally published in 1987 by Hutchinson Education

Second edition published in 1991
Third edition published in 1995
Fourth edition published in 1999 by
Stanley Thornes (Publishers) Ltd
Delta Place
Cheltenham GL53 7TH
United Kingdom


01   02   03   04   /   10   9   8   7   6   5   4


A catalogue record of this book is available from the British
Library.

ISBN 0 7487 3957 2

**Book plus Course Study Guide**
ISBN 0 7487 3964 5

**Course Study Guide**
ISBN 0 7487 3963 7

**IMAGES of BIOLOGY for Advanced Level Version 2.0
CD-ROM**
Single- and Multi User Versions available.
Free sample available on request.
Please contact the publisher at the address given above or
telephone customer services on 01242 267273

Throughout this book a CD-ROM icon is used to indicate
where links exist to the CD-ROM. The CD-ROM provides
additional support described on the back cover of the book to
further aid your understanding of the topic.

Artwork by Oxford Designers & Illustrators, Peters & Zabransky,
Hardlines, Tech-Set Ltd, Geoff Jones, Annabel Milne,
Angela Lumley, Mark Dunn, Tim Smith and David Oliver
Typeset by Tech-Set Ltd, Gateshead, Tyne & Wear
Printed and bound in Spain by Graficas Estella S.A.

## Acknowledgements

To Annabel Milne for permission to reproduce artwork on pp. 55, 59,
480, 481, 509, 527.

The authors and publishers are grateful to the following examination bo
for kind permission to reproduce examination questions:
Associated Examining Board London Examinations, a division of Edexce
Northern Examinations and Assessment Board
Northern Ireland Council for the Curriculum Examinations and Assessme
University of Cambridge Local Examinations Syndicate (incorporating
University of Oxford Delegacy of Local Examinations)
Welsh Joint Education Committee

The authors and publishers are grateful to the following for permission to
reproduce photographs and other material as follows:

AEA Technology: 4; Ardea: 346 (bottom – John Mason); Biophoto Associates: 4
(top), 62, 64, 80 (bottom), 134 (left), 142 (eight photos), 151, 191, 201, 215
(bottom), 219 (top), 219 (bottom), 257, 272 (top right), 280, 288, 370 (bottom),
461, 463 (bottom), 500, 501, 510, 518, 571, 572, 617; Bruce Coleman: 9 (Kim
Taylor), 225 (Alain Compost), 272 (top left – Dr Freider Sauer), 311 (Gordon
Langsbury), 358 (Kim Taylor), 367 (bottom – John Murray), 371 (Gerald Cubitt),
374 (Dr Norman Myers), 386 (bottom – Adrian Davies), 461 (Dr Eckart Pott);
Colorific: 357 (Andrew Holbroke); Ecoscene: 38 (top – Frank Blackburn), 361
(Andrew Brown), 369 (top – D T Grewcock), 382 (bottom – Andrew D R
Brown), 384 (Nick Hawkes), 386 (bottom – Andrew Brown), 499 (top – Dr MP
Kahl), 614 (W Pierdon); Environmental Picture Library: 265 (Robert Brook);
Frank Lane Picture Agency: 8 (top – D P Wilson), 54 (top – Life Science Images),
65 (J C Allen), 89 (Mark Newman), 503 (Leonard Lee Rue); Garden Matters
Photolibrary: 86 (Colin Milkins); Gene Cox: 1, 312 (top); Geoscience Features
Picture Library: 276, 346 (bottom), 372 (D Hoffman), 396; Heather
Angel/Biofotos: 91, 258, 291, 354, 458, 359; Holt Studios International: 12, 94
(left – Nigel Cattlin), 205 (top), 337 (Inga Spence), 342 (Nigel Cattlin), 370 (top),
378 (top), 379 (bottom – Nigel Cattlin, top – Richard Antony), 578, 608 (Inga
Spence), 618; ICCE: 334 (Alain Compost); J and S Professional Photography:
607 (Jim Lowe); Martyn Chillmaid: 350, 556 (top); Oxford Scientific Films: 8
(bottom – London Scientific Films), 88 (Geoff Kidd), 94 (right four photos –
David Thompson), 205 (J K Burras), 226 (London Scientific Films), 283 (Tim De
Roy), 290 (David Fleetham) 305 (top – Scott Camazine), 305 (bottom – London
Scientific Films), 347 (K G Vock, Okapia), 353 (Laurence Gold), 358 (Marty
Stouffer), 369 (bottom – Kim Westerskov), 384 (bottom – Kathie Atkinson), 459
(C G Gardener), 477 (Fran Allen), 499 (bottom – Norbert Rosing), 503 (bottom –
M Austermann, Animals Animals), 556 (David Fox), 558 (bottom – G I
Bernard), 571 (David Thompson), 585 (Colin Milkins); Panos Pictures: 346 (top
– Robert Cousins), 367 (top – J Hartley), 613 (Sean Spragne); Philip Allen
Publishers: 595; Ralston Photography: 610; Robert Harding Picture Library:
165, 168, 386 (top – Ian Griffiths); Science Photolibrary: 7 (Dr Jeremy Burgess),
23 (Richard Kirby), 31 (Philippe Plailly), 36 (J C Revy), 49 (bottom – David
Scharf), 54 (bottom – Chris Priest), 56 (Biology Media), 58 (top – Professors P
Motta and T Naguro), (bottom – Secchi/Lecaque/Roussel/Uclaf/CNRI), 60
(Professors P Motta and T Naguro), 76 (Eye of Science), 77, 80 (top – CNRI), 84
(Biophoto Associates), 90 (top – Bruce Iverson) (bottom – Eye of Science), 101,
124 (Simon Fraser/RVI Newcastle upon Tyne), 126 (Phillipe Plailly/ Eurelios),
128 (David Parker), 134 (right), 138 (six photos – CNRI), 147 (Moredun Animal
Health), 163 (Dr Jeremy Burgess), 221 (middle), 223 (top and bottom), 232
(bottom), 235 (Professors PM Motta, G Macchiarelli and S A Nottola), 240
(bottom – Dr Yorgos Nikas) (top – Professors P M Motta and J V Blerkow), 289
(Dr Jeremy Burgess), 272 (bottom – Dr Jeremy Burgess), 298 (Professor P Motta,
Department of Anatomy, University La Sapienza, Rome), 304 (Manfred Kage),
317 (J C Revy), 325 (James Holmes/Cell Tech Ltd), 335 (Claude Nuridsary and
Marie Perennou), 340 (Martin Bond), 370 (bottom – NOVSTI), 375 (Simon
Fraser), 391 (A S A Thoresen), 392 (M I Walker), 393 (Claude Nuridsany and
Marie Perennou), 394 (John Mead), 399, 400 (Professors Motta, Correr and
Nottola, University La Sapienza, Rome), 401 (Alfred Pasieka), 405 (top – Astrid
and Hans-Frieder Michler, bottom – Manfred Kage), 412 (Biophoto Associates),
413, 420 (CNRI), 422 (Professor S H E Kaufmann and Dr J R Golecki), 425
(Martin Dohrn), 432 (Professors P Motta and S Correr), 437 (Eammon
McNulty), 439 (Biophoto Associates), 451 (Andrew Syred), 453 (Dr Jerermy
Burgess), 454 (Andrew Syred), 467 (top – Andrew Syred), 487 (Nancy
Kedersha, NUCLA), 511 (Prof. P Motta, Dept. of Anatomy, Univ. La Sapienza,
Rome), 530 (Dr Don Fawcett), 534 (CNRI), 541 (Dr Colin Chumbley), 546 (top –
Tim Beddows, middle – Catherine Pouedras, bottom), 551 (top – Bill Longcove,
bottom – Adam Hart-Davies) 553 (Astrid and Hanns-Frieder Michler), 558
(Claude Nuridsarry and Marie Perennou), 565 (Biology Media), 567 (Secchi-
Lecaque, Roussel – UCLAF, CNRI), 601 (James King-Homes), 616 (A B
Dowsett), 632 (Eye of Science), 633 (BSIP, VEM), 635 (Sinclair Stammers), 637
(CNRI), 645 (Clinique Sainte Catherine/CNRI); Science Pictures Limited: 70,
83, 92, 189, 216, 219 (middle), 224, 228, 232 (top), 234, 241, 271, 298 (bottom),
300, 302, 303, 309, 312 (middle and bottom), 447, 448, 454 (top), 456, 459
(bottom), 463 (top), 480, 481, 542, 550; Still Pictures: 430 (Thomas Raupach), 635
(Mark Edwards); Tony Stone Images: 51 (top – Newcomb and Wergin) (bottom
– Ron Boardman), 215 (top – Kevin Schafer), 239 (John Garrett), 268, 433 (G W
Willis/BPS), 455 (Andrew Syred); Topham Picturepoint: 348, 378 (Associate
Press); University of Manchester: 522 (Dr A Dickson).

Every effort has been made to contact copyright holders. The publishers
apologise to anyone whose rights have been overlooked and will be happy to
rectify any errors or omissions at the earliest opportunity.

# Contents

## Part V    Coordination, Response and Control

## Part VI    Microorganisms, Biotechnology, Health and Disease

# Preface

Advanced Level Biology specifications (previously called syllabuses), along with the Awarding Bodies that produce them, have changed over the past few years. One major change has been the introduction of Advanced Subsidiary (AS-level) and A2 specifications.

New Advanced Subsidiary specifications are examined at a standard expected of candidates who have completed the first half of a full Advanced Level course. As such, it occupies a place intermediate between GCSE and Advanced Level. It can either be a qualification in its own right or a stepping-stone towards a full Advanced Level. An AS-level can be obtained after one year of study with a further year (called A2) being required to convert it to the full A-level.

All biology specifications include a core of topics (called the Subject Criteria) which is common to all and which builds upon the knowledge and understanding of Science in the National Curriculum. All specifications are divided into units (modules) which can either be taken at intervals during the course or stacked together at the end. A practical investigation or project is also a common feature. Detailed analysis of all the AS-level and A2 specifications has ensured that this latest edition of **Understanding Biology for Advanced Level** gives a clear and comprehensive coverage of these topics and many others which may be optional in your AS-level or A2 specifications.

The book is primarily intended for students taking AS-level and A-level (A2) biology, but will also be valuable to students studying the Scottish Higher Grade examination, Advanced GNVQ Science and the International Baccalaureate.

Style and accessibility have always been a strong feature of this book and its numerous diagrams have been further enhanced by the introduction of many three-dimensional drawings which improve understanding. Likewise the frequently used tables have been supplemented by detailed charts which summarize the essential points of a particular topic. Many more photographs have been introduced to add interest, aid understanding and to add reality to the subject. The 'Notebooks', giving short explanatory sections on key topics which underpin biology, have been retained while the applications have been expanded in number and renamed 'Biology around us' to reflect their broader coverage of relevant materials.

To provide ideas for independent, practical work, 'Project suggestions' are also retained and the popular 'Did you knows' continue to provide those remarkable little snippets of information which not only put things into perspective but also provide interesting and worthwhile factual data.

Three major additions are, firstly, inclusion of a new chapter on Human Health and Disease which covers in detail this popular option in AS-level and A2 specifications. Although material on human health has been brought together in a single coherent unit to assist study of this topic, information is still integrated into the rest of the book either in its own right or by cross-referencing to the new chapter. Secondly, a new chapter on Food, diet and health has been added to meet the requirements of this increasingly common option. Finally, a 'Glossary' has been included to enable the reader to quickly research the definition of all the most commonly used biological terms in the book.

The transition from GCSE to AS-level is not an easy one and the book has been written in a manner which makes this process smoother. To further assist this change the authors have produced a **Course Study Guide,** which complements this core textbook. In addition to providing help on practical work and answering examination questions, it also includes most of the diagrams within the book which can then be annotated and labelled as you wish and included in your own notes.

A further exciting addition to this range of publications is **Images of Biology for Advanced Level CD-ROM**. Packed with light and scanning electron micrographs, as well as video clips, it is an interactive resource which runs on a PC. Written text, as well as a sound commentary, provide a wealth of emphasized key points and information. The user is able to tour around a specimen or magnify parts of it as they choose as if they had their own microscope. The resource brings biology to life in a way no textbook ever could.

All these linked resources and this core textbook in particular are intended to provide clear, highly readable and easily understood information to the average student. This textbook contains sufficient detail to satisfy the requirements of all the major specifications without the sometimes unnecessary detail which can cloud the underlying issues.

We trust that this book will contribute to examination success while engendering a genuine love of biology which will stimulate the reader to delve further and deeper into the subject. We would like to express our gratitude to Wilbert Garvin for compiling the project suggestions and to Adrian Wheaton, Simon Read, Malcolm Tomlin and all other at Stanley Thornes whose hard work and encouragement have made this fourth edition possible.

**Glenn and Susan Toole**

Transverse section through kidney tubules to show cellular organization *(opposite)*

# Part I

# LEVELS OF ORGANIZATION

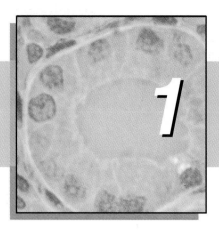

# 1 Size and complexity

Biology covers a wide field of information over a considerable size range. On the one hand it involves the movements of electrons in photosynthesis and on the other the migrations of individuals around the earth. Within this range it is possible to recognize seven levels of organization, each of which forms the basis of the next. The most fundamental unit is the **atom**; atoms group to form **molecules**, which in turn may be organized into **cells**. Cells are grouped into **tissues** which collectively form **organs**, which form **organisms**. A group of organisms of a single species may form a **population**.

TABLE 1.1 **Metric units**

| Units of size | | | |
|---|---|---|---|
| 1 kilometre | (km) | = | 1000 ($10^3$) metres |
| 1 metre | (m) | | |
| 1 centimetre | (cm) | = | 1/100 ($10^{-2}$) metre |
| 1 millimetre | (mm) | = | 1/1000 ($10^{-3}$) metre |
| 1 micrometre (micron) | ($\mu$m) | = | 1/1 000 000 ($10^{-6}$) metre |
| 1 nanometre | (nm) | = | 1/1 000 000 000 ($10^{-9}$) metre |
| 1 picometre | (pm) | = | 1/1 000 000 000 000 ($10^{-12}$) metre |

## 1.1 Atomic organization

Atoms are the smallest unit of a chemical element that can exist independently. They comprise a nucleus which contains positively charged particles called **protons**, the number of which is referred to as the **atomic number**. For each proton there is a particle of equal negative charge called an **electron**, so the atom has no overall charge. The electrons are not within the nucleus, but orbit in fixed quantum shells around it (see Fig. 1.1). There is a fixed limit to the number of electrons in any one shell. There may be up to seven such shells each with its own energy level; electrons in the shells nearest the nucleus have the least energy. The addition of energy, e.g. in the form of heat or light, may promote an electron to a higher energy level within a shell. Such an electron almost immediately returns to its original level, releasing its newly absorbed energy as it does so. This electron movement is important biologically in processes such as photosynthesis (Chapter 14).

| | HYDROGEN | CARBON | NITROGEN | OXYGEN |
|---|---|---|---|---|
| | | 6p 6n | 7p 7n | 8p 8n |
| Atomic number | 1 | 6 | 7 | 8 |
| Number of protons | 1 | 6 | 7 | 8 |
| Number of neutrons | 0 | 6 | 7 | 8 |
| Relative atomic mass | 1 | 12 | 14 | 16 |
| **Number of electrons** | | | | |
| First quantum shell | 1 | 2 | 2 | 2 |
| Second quantum shell | – | 4 | 5 | 6 |
| Total | 1 | 6 | 7 | 8 |

(Atomic nucleus; Proton (positively charged); Electron (negatively charged) in a 3-dimensional orbit around the nucleus; Electron shell)

*Fig. 1.1 Atomic structure of four commonly occurring biological elements*

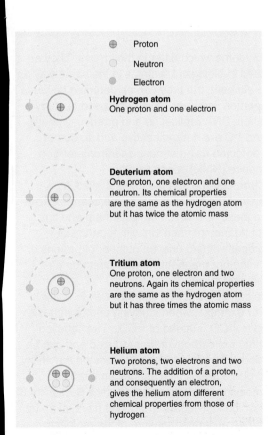

Proton
Neutron
Electron

**Hydrogen atom**
One proton and one electron

**Deuterium atom**
One proton, one electron and one neutron. Its chemical properties are the same as the hydrogen atom but it has twice the atomic mass

**Tritium atom**
One proton, one electron and two neutrons. Again its chemical properties are the same as the hydrogen atom but it has three times the atomic mass

**Helium atom**
Two protons, two electrons and two neutrons. The addition of a proton, and consequently an electron, gives the helium atom different chemical properties from those of hydrogen

*Fig. 1.2 Atomic structure of the atoms of hydrogen, deuterium, tritium and helium*

The nucleus of the atom also contains particles called **neutrons** which have no charge. Protons and neutrons contribute to the mass of an atom, but electrons have such a comparatively small mass that their contribution is negligible. However, the number of electrons determines the chemical properties of an atom. (See Fig. 1.2.)

### 1.1.1 Ions

As we have seen, atoms do not have any overall charge because the number of protons is always the same as the number of electrons and both have equal, but opposite, charges. If an atom loses or gains electrons it becomes an **ion**. The addition of electrons produces a negative ion while the loss of electrons gives rise to a positive ion. The loss of an electron is called **oxidation**, while the gain of an electron is called **reduction**. The atom losing an electron is said to be oxidized, while that gaining an electron is said to be reduced. The loss of an electron from a hydrogen atom, for instance, would leave a hydrogen ion, comprising just a single proton. Having an overall positive charge it is written as $H^+$. Where an atom, e.g. calcium, loses two electrons its overall charge is more positive and it is written $Ca^{2+}$. The process is similar where atoms gain electrons, except that the overall charge is negative, e.g. $Cl^-$. Ions may comprise more than one type of atom, e.g. the sulphate ion is formed from one sulphur and four oxygen atoms, with the addition of two electrons, $SO_4^{2-}$.

### 1.1.2 Isotopes

The properties of an element are determined by the number of protons and hence electrons it possesses. If protons (positively charged) are added to an element, then an equivalent number of electrons (negatively charged) must be added to maintain an overall neutral charge. The properties of the element would then change – indeed it now becomes a new element. For example, it can be seen from Fig. 1.1 that the addition of one proton, one electron and one neutron to the carbon atom, transforms it into a nitrogen atom.

If, however, a neutron (not charged) is added, there is no need for an additional electron and so its properties remain the same. As neutrons have mass, the element is heavier. Elements which have the same chemical properties as the normal element but have a different mass are called **isotopes**. Hydrogen normally comprises one proton and one electron and consequently has an atomic mass of one. The addition of a neutron doubles the atomic mass to two, without altering the element's chemical properties. This isotope is called **deuterium**. Similarly, the addition of a further neutron forms the isotope **tritium**, which has an atomic mass of three (Fig. 1.2).

Isotopes can be traced by various means, even when incorporated in living matter. This makes them exceedingly useful in tracing the route of certain elements in a variety of biological processes.

## NOTEBOOK

### Using isotopes as tracers

Autoradiograph of labelled leaves

Isotopes are varieties of atoms which differ in their mass. They are usually taken up and used in biological systems in the same way as the 'normal' form of the element, but they can be detected because they have different properties. Isotopes have been used to study photosynthesis, respiration, DNA replication and protein synthesis. Isotopes such as $^{15}C$ and $^{13}C$ are not radioactive and so do not decay but they can be detected using a mass spectrometer or a nuclear magnetic resonance (NMR) spectrometer.

To use a mass spectrometer the sample to be studied is vaporized is such a way that the molecules become charged. They then pass through a magnetic field which deflects them and the machine records the abundance of each ion with a particular charge : mass ratio. Isotopes with an uneven number of protons or electrons spin, like spinning bar magnets. A NMR spectrometer detects each type of spinning nucleus.

Radioactive isotopes can be used in a different way to follow biological processes. For example, when studying photosynthesis leaves may be exposed to $^{14}CO_2$ instead of $^{12}CO_2$. The 'labelled' carbon is incorporated into the carbohydrate produced and can be detected using autoradiography. This technique relies on the ability of radioisotopes to 'fog' photographic film as they emit radiation. When the process is combined with chromatography (see Section 14.3) it is possible to identify which individual compounds have taken up the radioactive carbon. If an accurate measure of the radioactivity in a sample is required, a scintillation counter can be used.

## BIOLOGY AROUND US

### Radioisotopes in medicine

Radioisotopes can be used both for diagnosis and treatment of disease as well as for research into possible causes. A particularly important isomer used to study lung and heart complaints is $^{99m}$technetium. It has a half life of only 6 hours and so decays very rapidly. It can be used as an aerosol, in very low concentrations, to show up available air spaces in patients' lungs. It may be used to label red blood cells so that the distribution of blood within the spaces of the heart or in deep veins can be shown. This is useful if there is a possibility of blood clots having formed.

The radiation emitted by a radioisotope can be used to destroy damaged tissue. For example $^{137}$caesium is inserted in a sealed probe to destroy cancerous cells in the cervix. $^{131}$Iodine is taken up selectively by the thyroid gland and can be used in carefully calculated doses to destroy a specific amount of that gland.

$^{90}$Yttrium in a silicate injection kills synovial tissues which are eroding the ends of the bones in sufferers of rheumatoid and osteo arthritis.

## 1.2  Molecular organization

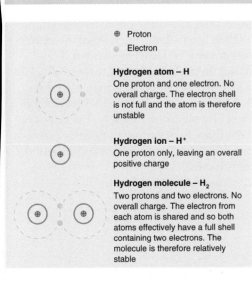

⊕ Proton
◦ Electron

**Hydrogen atom – H**
One proton and one electron. No overall charge. The electron shell is not full and the atom is therefore unstable

**Hydrogen ion – H⁺**
One proton only, leaving an overall positive charge

**Hydrogen molecule – H₂**
Two protons and two electrons. No overall charge. The electron from each atom is shared and so both atoms effectively have a full shell containing two electrons. The molecule is therefore relatively stable

*Fig. 1.3 Atomic structure of a hydrogen atom, a hydrogen ion and a hydrogen molecule*

We have seen that the electron shells around an atom may each contain a maximum number of electrons. The shell nearest the nucleus may possess a maximum of two electrons and the next shell a maximum of eight. An atom is most stable, i.e. least reactive, when its outer electron shell contains the maximum possible number of electrons. For example, helium, with a full complement of two electrons in its outer shell, is inert. In a hydrogen atom, the electron shell has a single electron and so the atom is unstable. If two hydrogen atoms share their electrons (Fig. 1.3), they form a hydrogen **molecule**, which is more stable. The two atoms are effectively combined and the molecule is written as $H_2$. The sharing of electrons in order to produce stable molecules is called **covalent bonding**.

The oxygen atom contains eight protons and eight neutrons in the nucleus with eight orbiting electrons. The inner quantum shell contains its maximum of two electrons, leaving six electrons in the second shell (Fig. 1.1). As this second shell may contain up to eight electrons, it requires two electrons to complete the shell and become stable. It may therefore combine with two hydrogen atoms by sharing electrons to form a water molecule (Fig. 1.4). In this way the outer shells of the oxygen atom and both hydrogen atoms are completed and a relatively stable molecule is formed.

Carbon with its six electrons (Fig. 1.1) has an inner shell containing two, leaving four in the outer shell. It requires four

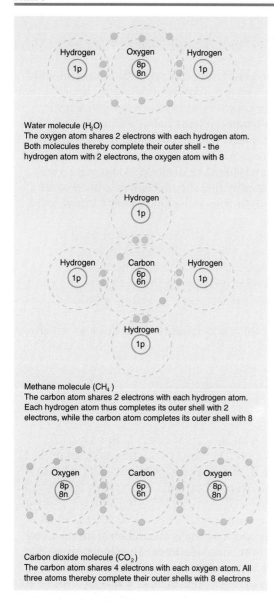

Water molecule (H₂O)
The oxygen atom shares 2 electrons with each hydrogen atom. Both molecules thereby complete their outer shell - the hydrogen atom with 2 electrons, the oxygen atom with 8

Methane molecule (CH₄)
The carbon atom shares 2 electrons with each hydrogen atom. Each hydrogen atom thus completes its outer shell with 2 electrons, while the carbon atom completes its outer shell with 8

Carbon dioxide molecule (CO₂)
The carbon atom shares 4 electrons with each oxygen atom. All three atoms thereby complete their outer shells with 8 electrons

*Fig. 1.4 Atomic models of the molecules of water, methane and carbon dioxide*

TABLE 1.2 **Relative abundance by weight of elements in humans compared to the earth's crust**

| Element | Human | Earth's crust |
|---|---|---|
| Oxygen | 63.0 | 46.5 |
| Carbon | 19.5 | 0.1 |
| Hydrogen | 9.5 | 0.2 |
| Nitrogen | 5.0 | 0.0001 |
| Phosphorus | 0.5 | 1.5 |

more electrons to fill this shell. It may therefore combine with four hydrogen atoms each of which shares its single electron. This molecule is called methane $CH_4$ (Fig. 1.4). It may also combine with two oxygen atoms, each of which shares two electrons. This molecule is carbon dioxide (Fig. 1.4).

When an atom, e.g. hydrogen, requires one electron to complete its outer shell it is said to have a **combining power (valency)** of one. Oxygen, which requires two electrons to complete its outer shell, has a combining power of two. Likewise nitrogen has a combining power of three and carbon of four.

When two atoms share a single electron, the bond is referred to as a **single bond** and is written with a single line, e.g. the hydrogen molecule is H—H and water may be represented as H—O—H. If two atoms share two electrons a **double bond** is formed. It is represented by a double line, e.g. carbon dioxide may be written as O=C=O. To form stable molecules, hydrogen must therefore have a single bond; oxygen two bonds (either two singles or one double); nitrogen must have three bonds (either three singles, or one single and one double); and carbon must have four bonds. It should now be apparent that these four atoms can combine in a number of different ways to form a variety of molecules. This partly explains the abundance of these elements in living organisms although some are relatively rare in the earth's crust (Table 1.2).

Carbon in particular can be seen to be almost 200 times more abundant in living organisms than in the earth's crust. Why should this be so? In the first place, carbon with its combining power of four can form molecules with a wide variety of other elements such as hydrogen, oxygen, nitrogen, sulphur, phosphorus and chlorine. This versatility allows great diversity in living organisms. More importantly, carbon can form long chains linked by single, double and triple bonds. These chains may be thousands of carbon atoms long. Such large molecules are essential to living organisms, not least as structural components. Furthermore, these chains have great stability – another essential feature. Carbon compounds may also form rings. These rings and chains may be combined with each other to give giant molecules of almost infinite variety. Examples of the size, diversity and complexity of carbon molecules can be found among the three major groups of biological compounds: carbohydrates, fats and proteins.

These are discussed in more detail in Chapter 2.

### 1.2.1 Ionic bonding

In addition to forming covalent bonds through the sharing of electrons, atoms may stabilize themselves by losing or gaining electrons to form ions. The loss of an electron (oxidation) leaves the atom positively charged (oxidized). The gain of an electron (reduction) leaves the atom negatively charged (reduced). Oppositely charged atoms attract one another forming **ionic bonds**. Sodium, for example, tends to lose an electron forming a $Na^+$ ion; chlorine tends to gain an electron forming a $Cl^-$ ion. These two oppositely charged ions form ionic bonds and form sodium chloride (common salt).

### 1.2.2 Hydrogen bonds

The electrons in a molecule do not distribute themselves evenly but tend to group at one position. This region will consequently be more negative than the rest of the molecule. The molecule is said to be **polarized**. The negative region of such a molecule will be attracted to the positive region of a similarly polarized molecule. A weak electrostatic bond between the two is formed. In biological systems this type of bond is frequently a hydrogen bond. These bonds are weak individually, but collectively form important forces which alter the physical properties of molecules. Water forms hydrogen bonds, which significantly affect its properties and hence its biological importance.

## 1.3    Cellular organization

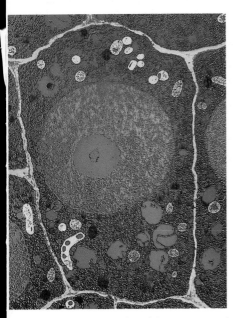

Root cell of a maize plant (TEM) ($\times$ 3000 approx.)

In 1665, Robert Hooke, using a compound microscope, discovered that cork was composed of numerous small units. He called these units **cells**. In the years that followed, Hooke and other researchers discovered that many other types of material were similarly composed of cells. By 1838, the amount of plant material shown to be composed of cells convinced Matthias Schleiden, a German botanist, that all plants were made up of cells. The following year, Theodor Schwann reached the same conclusion about the organization of animals. Their joint findings became known as the **cell theory**. It was of considerable biological significance as it suggested a common denominator for all living matter and so unified the nature of organisms. The theory makes the cell the fundamental unit of structure and function in living organisms. Hooke had originally thought the cell to be hollow, and that the wall represented the living portion. It soon became clear that cells were far from hollow. With the development of better light microscopes, first the nucleus and then organelles such as the chloroplasts became visible. One hundred years after Schleiden and Schwann put forward the cell theory, the development of the **electron microscope** revolutionized our understanding of cell structure. With its ability to magnify up to 500 times more than the light microscope, the electron microscope revealed the fine structure of cells including many new organelles. This detail is called the **ultrastructure** of the cell. The complexity of cellular structure so revealed led to the emergence of a new field of biology, **cytology** – the study of cell ultrastructure. This shows that while organisms are very diverse in their structures and cells vary considerably in size and shape, there is nevertheless a remarkable similarity in their basic structure and organization. This structure and organization is studied in Chapter 4.

## 1.4   Colonial organization

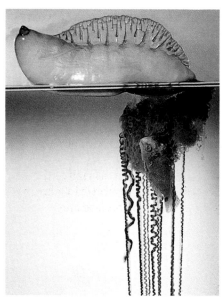

Portuguese man-of-war (*Physalia*) eating fish

The first colonies may have arisen when individual unicells failed to separate after cell division. Within colonies each cell is capable of carrying out all the essential life processes. Indeed, if separated from the colony, any cell is capable of surviving independently. The only advantage of a colonial grouping is that the size of the unit probably deters some predators and thus increases the group's survival prospects.

If one cell in a colony should lose the ability to carry out a vital process, it could only survive by relying on other cells in the colony to perform the process on its behalf. The loss of one function, however, might permit the cell to perform one or other of its functions more efficiently, because the energy and resources required by the missing function could be directed towards the remaining ones. In this way, the individual cells within a colony could have become different from one another in both structure and function, a process known as **differentiation**. Further changes of this type would finally result in cells performing a single function. This is known as **specialization**. Clearly specialization must be organized in such a way that all essential functions are still performed by the colony as a whole. With increasing specialization, and the consequent loss of more and more functions, any cell becomes increasingly dependent on others in the colony for its survival. This **interdependence** of cells must be highly organized. Groups of cells must be coordinated so that the colony carries out its activities efficiently. Such coordination between the different cells is called **integration**. Once the cells become so dependent on each other that they are no longer capable of surviving independently, then the structure is no longer a colony but a **multicellular organism**.

## 1.5   Tissue organization

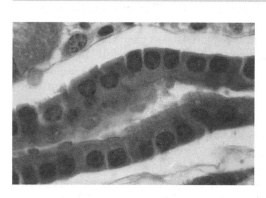

Kidney epithelium (TS) ($\times$ 350)

A tissue is a group of similar cells, along with any intercellular substance, which performs a particular function. Some cells, e.g. unicellular protozoans and algae, perform all functions which are essential to life. It is impossible for such cells to be efficient at all functions, because each function requires a different type of cellular organization. Whereas one function might require the cell to be long and thin, another might require it to be spherical. One function might require many mitochondria, another, very few. Acid conditions might suit one activity but not another. No one cell can possibly provide the optimum conditions for all activities. For this reason, cells are specialized to perform one, or at most a few, functions. To increase efficiency, cells performing the same functions are grouped together into a tissue. The study of tissues is called **histology**. Some organisms, e.g. cnidarians, are at the tissue level of organization. Their physiological activities are performed by tissues rather than organs. Examples of animal tissues include squamous and ciliated epithelium (Section 20.2.5). Examples of plant tissues include xylem (Section 22.4.3) and phloem (Section 22.8.2).

## 1.6 Organ level of organization

An organ is a structural and functional unit of a plant or animal. It comprises a number of tissues which are coordinated to perform a variety of functions, although one major function often predominates. The majority of plants and animals are composed of organs. Examples include the leaf of plants, and the liver in mammals. Most organs do not function independently but in groups called **organ systems**. A typical organ system is the digestive system which comprises organs such as the stomach, duodenum, ileum, liver and pancreas. Certain organs may belong to more than one system. The pancreas, for example, forms part of the **endocrine (hormone)** system as well as the digestive system, because it produces the hormones insulin and glucagon, as well as the digestive enzymes amylase and trypsinogen.

## 1.7 Social level of organization

Honey bee queen surrounded by workers

A **population** is a number of individuals of the same species which occupy a particular area at the same time. In itself, a population is not a level of organization as no organization exists between the individual members. In some species, however, the individuals do exhibit some organization in which they cooperate for their mutual benefit. Such a population is more accurately termed a **society**. It differs from a colony (although the term is often used) in that the individuals are not physically connected to one another, but totally separate. As with a colony, the individuals can survive independently of others in the society, although usually somewhat less successfully. Unlike most colonies, there is considerable coordination between the society members and communication forms an integral part of their organization. Societies may exist simply because there is safety in numbers, e.g. schools of fish. They may enable more successful hunting, as in wolves, or aid the successful rearing of young, as in baboons. In insects, however, the degree of organization is considerable. There is **division of labour** which leads to differentiation of individuals in order to perform specialized functions. In a bee society for instance, the queen is the only fertile female and has a purely reproductive role. The drones (males) also function reproductively while the workers (sterile females) perform a variety of tasks such as collecting food, feeding the larvae and guarding and cleaning the hive. Complex societies can readily be compared to an organism with its organs each specialized for a major function. Some account of the organization of a bee colony is given in Section 27.7.5.

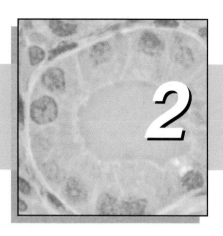

# 2 Molecular organization

## 2.1  Inorganic ions

Water is the most important inorganic molecule in biology. Dissolved in the water within living organisms are a large number of inorganic ions. Typically they constitute about 1% of an organism by weight, but they are nonetheless essential. They are divided into two groups: the **macronutrients** or **major elements** which are needed in very small quantities, and the **micronutrients** or **trace elements** which are needed in minute amounts (a few parts per million). Although the elements mostly fall into the same category for plants and animals, there are a few exceptions. Chlorine, for example, is a major element in animals but a trace element in plants. In addition to the essential elements listed in Table 2.1, some organisms also have specific requirements such as vanadium, chromium and silicon.

TABLE 2.1  **Inorganic ions and their functions in plants and animals**

| Macronutrients/ main elements | Functions | Notes |
|---|---|---|
| Nitrate $NO_3^-$ Ammonium $NH_4^+$ | Nitrogen is a component of amino acids, proteins, vitamins, coenzymes, nucleotides and chlorophyll. Some hormones contain nitrogen, e.g. auxins in plants and insulin in animals | A deficiency of nitrogen in plants causes chlorosis (yellowing of leaves) and stunted growth |
| Phosphate $PO_4^{3-}$ Orthophosphate $H_2PO_4^-$ | A component of nucleotides, ATP and some proteins. Used in the phosphorylation of sugars in respiration. A major constituent of bone and teeth. A component of cell membranes in the form of phospholipids | Deficiency of phosphates in plants leads to stunted growth, especially of roots, and the formation of dull, dark green leaves. In animals, deficiency can result in a form of bone malformation called rickets |
| Sulphate $SO_4^{2-}$ | Sulphur is a component of some proteins and certain coenzymes, e.g. acetyl coenzyme A | Sulphur forms important bridges between the polypeptide chains of some proteins, giving them their tertiary structure. A deficiency in plants causes chlorosis and poor root development |
| Potassium $K^+$ | Helps to maintain the electrical, osmotic and anion/cation balance across cell membranes. Assists active transport of certain materials across the cell membrane. Necessary for protein synthesis and is a co-factor in photosynthesis and respiration. A constituent of sap vacuoles in plants and so helps to maintain turgidity | Potassium plays an important role in the transmission of nerve impulses. A deficiency in plants leads to yellow-edged leaves and premature death |

*cont*

ABLE 2.1   *cont.*

| Macronutrients/main elements | Functions | Notes |
|---|---|---|
| Calcium $Ca^{2+}$ | In plants, calcium pectate is a major component of the middle lamella of cell walls and is therefore necessary for their proper development. It also aids the translocation of carbohydrates and amino acids. In animals, it is the main constituent of bones, teeth and shells. Needed for the clotting of blood and the contraction of muscle | In plants, deficiency causes the death of growing points and hence stunted growth. In animals, deficiency leads to rickets and delay in the clotting of blood |
| Sodium $Na^+$ | Helps to maintain the electrical, osmotic and anion/cation balance across cell membranes. Assists active transport of certain materials across the cell membrane. A constituent of the sap vacuole in plants and so helps maintain turgidity | In animals, it is necessary for the functioning of the kidney, nerves and muscles; deficiency may cause muscular cramps. Sodium is so common in soils that deficiency in plants is rare. Sodium ions have much the same function as potassium ions and may be exchanged for them |
| Chlorine $Cl^-$ | Helps to maintain the electrical, osmotic and anion/cation balance across cell membranes. Needed for the formation of hydrochloric acid in gastric juice. Assists in the transport of carbon dioxide by blood (chloride shift) | In animals, deficiency may cause muscular cramps. Its widespread availability in soils makes deficiency in plants practically unknown |
| Magnesium $Mg^{2+}$ | A constituent of chlorophyll. An activator for some enzymes, e.g. ATPase. A component of bone and teeth | Deficiency in plants leads to chlorosis |
| Iron $Fe^{2+}$ or $Fe^{3+}$ | A constituent of electron carriers, e.g. cytochromes, needed in respiration and photosynthesis. A constituent of certain enzymes, e.g. dehydrogenases, decarboxylases, peroxidases and catalase. Required in the synthesis of chlorophyll. Forms part of the haem group in respiratory pigments such as haemoglobin, haemoerythrin, myoglobin and chlorocruorin | Deficiency in plants leads to chlorosis and in animals to anaemia |
| **Micronutrients/trace elements** | | |
| Manganese $Mn^{2+}$ | An activator of certain enzymes, e.g. phosphatases. A growth factor in bone development | Deficiency in plants produces leaves mottled with grey and in animals, bone deformations |
| Copper $Cu^{2+}$ | A constituent of some enzymes, e.g. cytochrome oxidase and tyrosinase. A component of the respiratory pigment haemocyanin | Deficiency in plants causes young shoots to die back at an early stage |
| Iodine $I^-$ | A constituent of the hormone thyroxin, which controls metabolism in animals | Iodine is not required by higher plants. Deficiency in humans causes cretinism in children and goitre in adults; in some other vertebrates it is essential for metamorphic changes |
| Cobalt $Co^{2+}$ | Constituent of vitamin $B_{12}$, which is important in the synthesis of RNA, nucleoprotein and red blood cells | Deficiency in animals causes pernicious anaemia |
| Zinc $Zn^{2+}$ | An activator of certain enzymes, e.g. carbonic anhydrase. Required in plants for leaf formation, the synthesis of indole acetic acid (auxin) and anaerobic respiration (alcoholic fermentation) | Carbonic anhydrase is important in the transport of carbon dioxide in vertebrate blood. Deficiency in plants produces malformed, and sometimes mottled, leaves |
| Molybdenum $Mo^{4+}$ or $Mo^{5+}$ | Required by plants for the reduction of nitrate to nitrite in the formation of amino acids. Essential for nitrogen fixation by prokaryotes | Deficiency produces a reduction in crop yield. Not vital in most animals |
| Boron $BO_3^{3+}$ or $B_4O^{2+}$ | Required for the uptake of $Ca^{2+}$ by roots. Aids the germination of pollen grains and mitotic division in meristems | Boron is not required by animals. Deficiency in plants causes death of young shoots and abnormal growth. May cause specific diseases such as 'internal cork' of apples and 'heart rot' of beet and celery |
| Fluorine $F^-$ | A component of teeth and bones | Not required by most plants. Associates with calcium to form calcium fluoride which strengthens teeth and helps prevent decay |

Chlorosis (thistle) – with healthy plants shown for comparison

## 2.2   Carbohydrates

Carbohydrates comprise a large group of organic compounds which contain carbon, hydrogen and oxygen and which are either aldehydes or ketones. The word carbohydrate suggests that these organic compounds are hydrates of carbon. Their general formula is $C_x(H_2O)_y$. The word carbohydrate is convenient rather than exact, because while most examples do conform to the formula, e.g. glucose ($C_6H_{12}O_6$) and sucrose ($C_{12}H_{22}O_{11}$), a few do not, e.g. deoxyribose ($C_5H_{10}O_4$). Carbohydrates are divided into three groups: the **monosaccharides** ('single-sugars'), the **disaccharides** ('double-sugars') and the **polysaccharides** ('many-sugars'). This arrangement is typical of many organic molecules where single units, called **monomers**, are combined to form larger units, called **polymers**.

The functions of carbohydrates, although variable, are in the main concerned with storage and liberation of energy. A few, such as cellulose, have structural roles. A full list of individual carbohydrates and their functions is given in Table 2.3 on p. 19.

## 2.3   Monosaccharides

Monosaccharides are a group of sweet, soluble crystalline molecules of relatively low molecular mass. They are named with the suffix -ose. Monosaccharides contain either an aldehyde group (—CHO), in which case they are called **aldoses** or **aldo-sugars**, or they contain a ketone group (C=O), in which case they are termed **ketoses** or **keto-sugars**. The general formula for a monosaccharide is $(CH_2O)_n$. Where $n = 3$, the sugar is called a **triose** sugar, $n = 5$, a **pentose** sugar, and $n = 6$, a **hexose** sugar. Table 2.2 classifies some of the more important monosaccharides

TABLE 2.2   Classification of monosaccharides

|  | Trioses (C$_3$H$_6$O$_3$) | Pentoses (C$_5$H$_{10}$O$_5$) | Hexoses (C$_6$H$_{12}$O$_6$) |
|---|---|---|---|
| Aldoses (—CHO) (Aldo-sugars) | Glyceraldehyde | Ribose Arabinose Xylose | Glucose Galactose Mannose |
| Ketoses (C=O) (Keto-sugars) | Dihydroxyacetone | Ribulose Xylulose | Fructose Sorbose |

### 2.3.1 Structure of monosaccharides

Probably the best known monosaccharide, glucose, has the formula C$_6$H$_{12}$O$_6$. All but one of the six carbon atoms possesses an hydroxyl group (—OH). The remaining carbon atom forms part of the aldehyde group. Glucose may be represented by a straight chain of six carbon atoms. These are numbered beginning at the carbon of the aldehyde group. Glucose in common with other hexoses and pentoses easily forms stable ring structures. At any one time most molecules exist as rings rather than a chain. In the case of glucose, carbon atom number 1 may combine with the oxygen atom on carbon 5. This forms a six-sided structure known as a **pyranose** ring. In the case of fructose, it is carbon atom number 2 which links with the oxygen on carbon atom 5. This forms a five-sided structure called a **furanose** ring (Fig. 2.1). Both glucose and fructose can exist in both pyranose and furanose forms.

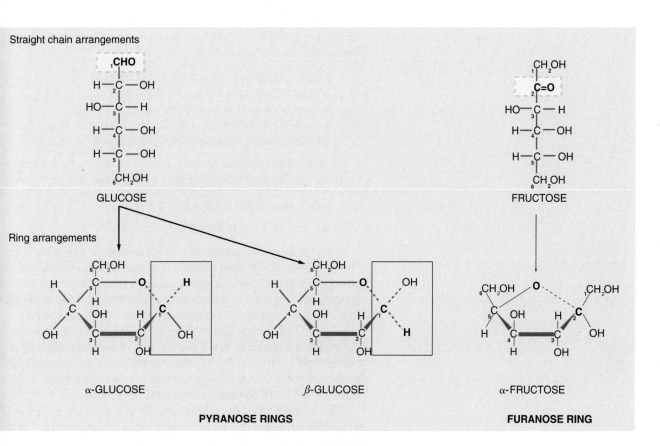

Fig. 2.1 Structure of various isomers of glucose and fructose

13

Glucose, in common with most carbohydrates, can exist as a number of **isomers** (they possess the same molecular formula but differ in the arrangement of their atoms). One type of isomerism, called **stereoisomerism**, occurs when the same atoms, or groups, are joined together but differ in their arrangement in space. One form of stereoisomerism, called **optical isomerism**, results in isomers which can rotate the plane of polarized light (light which is vibrating in one plane only). The isomer which rotates the plane of polarized light to the right is called the **+form**; the isomer rotating it to the left is called the **−form**.

## NOTEBOOK

### The mole

The mole is the scientific unit for the amount of a substance and is expressed as the symbol **mol**. 1 mol of any substance contains the same number of particles (atoms, molecules or ions). This number is known as **Avogadro's constant** and is equal to $6.023 \times 10^{23}$. To give you some idea of the vast size of this number, it is equal to the total human population of one hundred million million worlds identical to ours!

Different atoms (and therefore molecules and ions) have different masses. Chemists use the atomic weight of carbon, set at 12, as a standard against which to compare the weight of other atoms. Thus hydrogen, which has a mass one-twelfth that of carbon, is given the mass of 1. These are known as relative atomic masses. The relative atomic mass of an element in grams always contains 1 mol of its atoms (i.e. $6.023 \times 10^{23}$ atoms). The same is true of the relative **molecular** mass of a molecule. Thus:

a mole of hydrogen atoms (H) has a mass of 1 g
a mole of hydrogen molecules ($H_2$) has a mass of 2 g
a mole of oxygen atoms (O) has a mass of 16 g
a mole of oxygen molecules ($O_2$) has a mass of 32 g
a mole of water molecules ($H_2O$) has a mass of 18 g.

To find out the number of moles in a given mass of a substance we simply divide the mass (in grams) by the mass of 1 mol,

e.g. in 90 g of water there are $\frac{90}{18}$ mol

= 5 mol (or $5 \times 6.023 \times 10^{23}$ molecules)

When dealing with gases, we use volume rather than weight to measure amounts. A mole of any gas at standard temperature and pressure (0 °C and 1 atmosphere) occupies $22.4\,dm^3$ (litres). At room temperature (20 °C) this volume expands to $24\,dm^3$. That all gases, regardless of the mass of the molecules they comprise, should occupy the same volume may seem surprising. In a gas, however, the molecules are so far apart that the size of the molecule itself is unimportant in terms of the volume occupied. Imagine several balls bouncing around inside a large hall – they could all be fitted in whether they were golf balls, tennis balls or footballs.

The concentration of a solution can be expressed in moles. A $1\,mol\,dm^{-3}$ solution (1M solution) contains 1 mol in each $dm^3$ of the

Different isomers arise when a carbon atom has four different groups attached to it. This is called an **asymmetric carbon atom.** An asymmetric carbon atom arises when glucose forms a ring structure. This gives rise to two isomers, the *α*-**form** and the *β*-**form**. Both types occur naturally and, as we shall see later, result in considerable biological differences when they form polymers. Fig. 2.1 illustrates both types.

solution. In other words to make up a 1 mol dm$^{-3}$ (1 M) solution of a substance we add the relative molecular mass in grams of that substance to 1 dm$^3$ (litre) of water. In the case of sucrose ($C_{12}H_{22}O_{11}$) this is:

| Molecule | Number in sucrose | Relative atomic mass (g) | Total mass (g) |
|---|---|---|---|
| CARBON | 12 | 12 | $12 \times 12 = 144$ |
| HYDROGEN | 22 | 1 | $22 \times 1 = 22$ |
| OXYGEN | 11 | 16 | $11 \times 16 = 176$ |
| | | | Total 342 g |

Hence we dissolve 342 g of sucrose in 1 dm$^3$ of water

To convert moles into number of molecules, mass or volume and vice versa simply follow the scheme below.

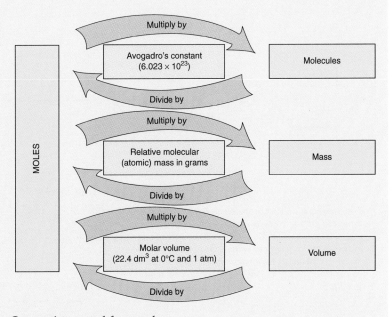

*Conversion to and from moles*

# 2.4   Disaccharides

Monosaccharides may combine together in pairs to give a **disaccharide** (double-sugar). The union involves the loss of a single water molecule and is therefore a **condensation reaction**. The bond which is formed is called a **glycosidic bond**. It is usually formed between carbon atom 1 of one monosaccharide and carbon atom 4 of the other, hence it is called a 1–4 glycosidic bond (see Fig. 2.2). Any two monosaccharides may be linked in this way to form a disaccharide, of which maltose, sucrose and lactose are the most common.

The addition of water, under suitable conditions, is necessary if the disaccharide is to be split into its constituent monosaccharides. This is called **hydrolysis** 'water-breakdown' or, more accurately, 'breakdown *by* water'.

Disaccharides, like monosaccharides, are sweet, soluble and crystalline. Maltose and lactose are reducing sugars, whereas sucrose is a non-reducing sugar. The significance of this is considered in Section 2.5.5.

maltose (malt sugar)= glucose + glucose

sucrose (cane sugar) = glucose + fructose

lactose (milk sugar)  = glucose + galactose

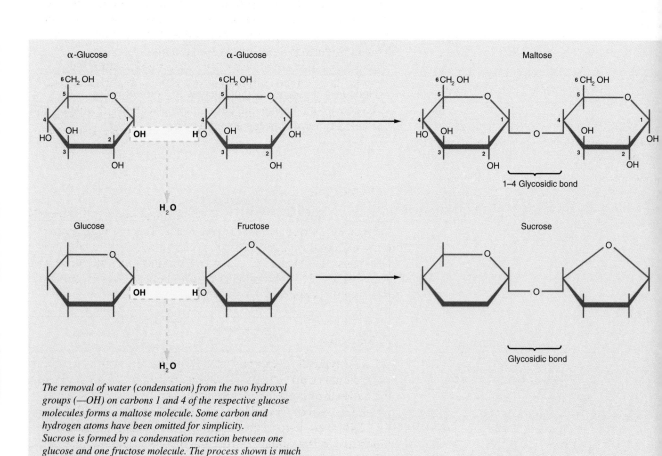

The removal of water (condensation) from the two hydroxyl groups (—OH) on carbons 1 and 4 of the respective glucose molecules forms a maltose molecule. Some carbon and hydrogen atoms have been omitted for simplicity.
Sucrose is formed by a condensation reaction between one glucose and one fructose molecule. The process shown is much simplified.

*Fig. 2.2 Formation of maltose and sucrose*

# 2.5 Polysaccharides

In the same way that two monosaccharides may combine in pairs to give a disaccharide, many monosaccharides may combine by condensation reactions to give a **polysaccharide**. The number of monosaccharides that combine is variable, and the chain produced can be branched or unbranched. The chains may be folded, thus making them compact and therefore ideal for storage. The size of the molecule makes them insoluble – another feature which suits them for storage as they exert no osmotic influence and do not easily diffuse out of the cell. Upon hydrolysis, polysaccharides can be converted to their constituent monosaccharides ready for use as respiratory substrates. Starch and glycogen are examples of storage polysaccharides. Not all polysaccharides are used for storage; cellulose, for example, is a structural polysaccharide giving strength and support to cell walls.

### 2.5.1 Starch

Starch is a polysaccharide which is found in most parts of the plant in the form of small granules. It is a reserve food formed from any excess glucose produced during photosynthesis. It is common in the seeds of some plants, e.g. maize, where it forms the food supply for germination. Indirectly these starch stores form an important food supply for animals.

Starch is a mixture of two substances: amylose and amylopectin. Starches differ slightly from one plant species to the next, but on the whole they comprise 20% amylose, 79% amylopectin, and 1% of other substances such as phosphates and fatty acids. A comparison of amylose and amylopectin is given in Fig. 2.3.

### 2.5.2 Glycogen

Glycogen is the major polysaccharide storage material in animals and fungi and is often called 'animal starch'. It is stored mainly in the liver and muscles. Like starch it is made up of $\alpha$-glucose molecules and exists as granules. It is similar to amylopectin in structure but it has shorter chains (10–20 glucose units) and is more highly branched.

### 2.5.3 Cellulose

Cellulose typically comprises up to 50% of a plant cell wall, and in cotton it makes up 90%. It is a polymer of around 10 000 $\beta$-glucose molecules forming a long unbranched chain. Many chains run parallel to each other and have cross linkages between them (Fig. 2.4). These help to give cellulose its considerable stability which makes it a valuable structural material. The stability of cellulose makes it difficult to digest and therefore not such a valuable food source to animals, which only rarely produce cellulose-digesting enzymes. Some, however, have formed symbiotic relationships with organisms which can digest cellulose. To these organisms it is the major component of their

*arch and glycogen are degraded in the digestive tract by ɑmylase, $\beta$-amylase and amylo-$\alpha$-(1→6)-glucosidase.*

**Amylase** *is an endoglucosidase which randomly ɖrolyses $\alpha$-(1→4) linkages of the side chains of glycogen ɖ amylopectin. It can cleave either side of a branch point ɕept in very highly branched regions.*

**Amylase**, *an exoglycosidase, sequentially removes ɱaltose from the ends of the outer branches but stops ɕavage before any branch points are reached.*

*ɛ structures remaining after hydrolysis by $\alpha$- and ɑmylase are called limit dextrins and comprise about ɼee dozen glucose residues.*

*ɱylo-$\alpha$-(1→6)-glucosidase, the debranching enzyme, ƚalyses the hydrolysis of the $\alpha$-(1→6) glycosidic bonds of ɛ limit dextrins, thereby permitting further breakdown by ɑnd $\beta$-amylase.*

## PROJECT

1. Put scrapings from round and wrinkled pea seeds on a microscope slide.

2. Stain with iodine/potassium iodide solution and cover with a cover slip.

3. Compare the starch grains from both types of seed.

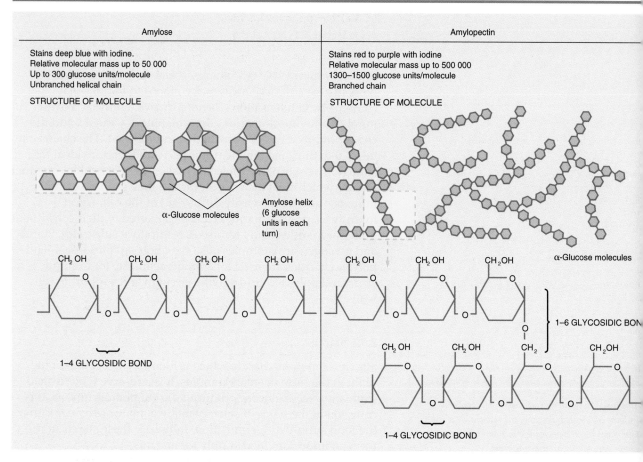

Fig. 2.3. Comparison of the properties and structures of amylose and amylopectin

diet. Cellulose's structural strength has long been recognized b
humans. Cotton is used in the manufacture of fabrics. Rayon is
produced from cellulose extracted from wood and its
remarkable tensile strength makes it especially useful in the
manufacture of tyre cords. Cellophane, used in packaging, and
celluloid, used in photographic film, are also cellulose
derivatives. Paper is perhaps the best known cellulose product.

*Being composed of β-glucose units, the chain, unlike that of
starch, has adjacent glucose molecules rotated by 180°. This
allows hydrogen bonds to be formed between the hydroxyl
(—OH) groups on adjacent parallel chains which help to
give cellulose its structural stability.*

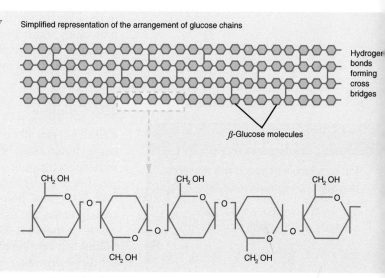

Fig. 2.4 Structure of the cellulose molecule

## 2.5.4 Other polysaccharides

*Chitin* – Chemically and structurally chitin resembles cellulose. It differs in possessing an acetyl-amino group ($NH.OCCH_3$) instead of one of the hydroxyl (—OH) groups. Like cellulose it has a structural function and is a major component of the exoskeleton of insects and crustacea. It is also found in fungal cell walls.

**TABLE 2.3   Carbohydrates and their functions**

| Group of carbohydrates | Name of carbohydrate | Type/composition | Function |
|---|---|---|---|
| Monosaccharides Trioses ($C_3H_6O_3$) | Glyceraldehyde | Aldose sugar | The phosphorylated form is the first formed sugar in photosynthesis, and as such may be used as a respiratory substrate or be converted to starch for storage. It is an intermediate in glycolysis |
| | Dihydroxyacetone | Ketose sugar | Respiratory substrate. Intermediate in glycolysis |
| Pentoses ($C_5H_{10}O_5$) | Ribose / deoxyribose | Aldose sugar | Makes up part of nucleotides and as such gives structural support to the nucleic acids RNA and DNA. Constituent of hydrogen carriers such as NAD, NADP and FAD. Constituent of ATP |
| | Ribulose | Ketose sugar | Carbon dioxide acceptor in photosynthesis |
| Hexoses ($C_6H_{12}O_6$) | Glucose | Aldose sugar | Major respiratory substrate in plants and animals. Synthesis of disaccharides and polysaccharides. Constituent of nectar |
| | Galactose | Aldose sugar | Respiratory substrate. Synthesis of lactose |
| | Mannose | Aldose sugar | Respiratory substrate |
| | Fructose | Ketose sugar | Respiratory substrate. Synthesis of inulin. Constituent of nectar. Sweetens fruits to attract animals to aid seed dispersal |
| Disaccharides | Sucrose | Glucose + fructose | Respiratory substrate. Form in which most carbohydrate is transported in plants. Storage material in some plants, e.g. *Allium* (onion) |
| | Lactose | Glucose + galactose | Respiratory substrate. Mammalian milk contains 5% lactose, therefore major carbohydrate source for sucklings |
| | Maltose | Glucose + glucose | Respiratory substrate |
| Polysaccharides | Amylose Amylopectin } starch | Unbranched chain of α-glucose with 1–4 glycosidic links + branched chain of α-glucose units with 1–4 and 1–6 glycosidic links | Major storage carbohydrate in plants |
| | Glycogen | Highly branched short chains of α-glucose units with 1–4 glycosidic links | Major storage carbohydrate in animals and fungi |
| | Cellulose | Unbranched chain of β-glucose units with 1–4 glycosidic links + cross bridges | Gives structural support to cell walls |
| | Inulin | Unbranched chain of fructose with 1–2 glycosidic links | Major storage carbohydrate in some plants, e.g. Jerusalem artichoke; *Dahlia* |
| | Chitin | Unbranched chain of β-acetylglucosamine units with 1–4 glycosidic links | Constituent of the exoskeleton of insects and crustacea |

TABLE 2.4 **Relationship between amount of reducing sugar and colour of precipitate on boiling with Benedict's reagent**

| Amount of reducing sugar | Colour of solution and precipitate |
|---|---|
| No reducing sugar | Blue |
| Increasing quantity of reducing sugar | Green |
| | Yellow |
| | Brown |
| | Red |

*Inulin* – This is a polymer of fructose found as a storage carbohydrate in some plants, e.g. *Dahlia* root tubers. *Mucopolysaccharides* – This group includes **hyaluronic acid**, which forms part of the matrix of vertebrate connective tissues. It is found in cartilage, bones, the vitreous humour of the eye and synovial fluid. The anticoagulant **heparin** is also a member of this group of polysaccharides.

### 2.5.5 Reducing and non-reducing sugars

All monosaccharides, whether aldo- or keto-sugars, are capable of reducing copper (II) sulphate in Benedict's reagent to copper (I) oxide (see Table 2.4). When monosaccharides combine to form disaccharides this reducing ability is often retained with the result that sugars such as lactose and maltose, although disaccharides, are still reducing sugars. In a few cases, however, the formation of a disaccharide results in the loss of this reducing ability. This is true of the formation of sucrose which is therefore a non-reducing sugar.

## 2.6 Lipids

Lipids are a large and varied group of organic compounds. Like carbohydrates, they contain carbon, hydrogen and oxygen, although the proportion of oxygen is much smaller in lipids. They are insoluble in water but dissolve readily in organic solvents such as acetone, alcohols and others. They are of two types: fats and oils. There is no basic difference between these two; fats are simply solid at room temperatures (10–20°C) whereas oils are liquid. The chemistry of lipids is very varied but they are all esters of **fatty acids** and an alcohol, of which **glycerol** is by far the most abundant. Glycerol has three hydroxyl (—OH) groups and each may combine by means of an **ester bond**, with a separate fatty acid, forming a **triglyceride** (Fig. 2.5). It is a condensation reaction and thus hydrolysis of the triglyceride will yield glycerol and three fatty acids.

*The three triglycerides may all be the same, thereby forming a simple triglyceride, or they may be different in which case a mixed triglyceride is produced. In either case it is a condensation reaction.*

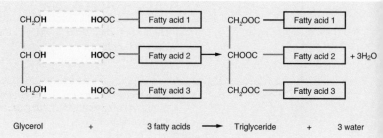

*Fig. 2.5 Formation of a triglyceride*

### 2.6.1 Fatty acids

As most naturally occurring lipids contain the same alcohol, namely glycerol, it is the nature of the fatty acids which determines the characteristics of any particular fat. All fatty acid contain a carboxyl group (—COOH). The remainder of the molecule is a hydrocarbon chain of varying length (examples are given in Table 2.5). This chain may possess one or more double bonds in which case it is said to be **unsaturated**. If, however, it possesses no double bonds it is said to be **saturated**.

It can be seen from Table 2.5 that the hydrocarbon chains may be very long. Within the fat they form long 'tails' which extend from the glycerol molecule. These 'tails' are **hydrophobic**, i.e. they repel water.

TABLE 2.5 **Nature and occurrence of some fatty acids**

| Name of fatty acid | General formula | Saturated/ unsaturated | Occurrence |
| --- | --- | --- | --- |
| Butyric | $C_3H_7COOH$ | Saturated | Butter fat |
| Linoleic | $C_{17}H_{31}COOH$ | Unsaturated | Linseed oil |
| Oleic | $C_{17}H_{33}COOH$ | Unsaturated | All fats |
| Palmitic | $C_{15}H_{31}COOH$ | Saturated | Animal and vegetable fats |
| Stearic | $C_{17}H_{35}COOH$ | Saturated | Animal and vegetable fats |
| Arachidic | $C_{19}H_{39}COOH$ | Saturated | Peanut oil |
| Cerotic | $C_{25}H_{51}COOH$ | Saturated | Wool oil |

### 2.6.2 Phospholipids

Phospholipids are lipids in which one of the fatty acid groups is replaced by phosphoric acid ($H_3PO_4$) (Fig. 2.6). The phosphoric acid is **hydrophilic** (attracts water) in contrast to the remainder of the molecule which is **hydrophobic** (repels water). Having one end of the phospholipid attracting water while the other end repels it affects its role in the cell membrane.

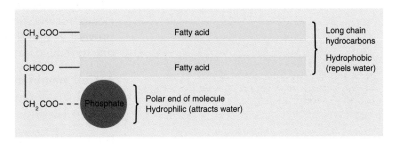

*Fig. 2.6 Structure of a phospholipid*

### 2.6.3 Waxes

Waxes are formed by combination of fatty acids with an alcohol other than glycerol. This alcohol is much larger than glycerol, and therefore waxes have a more complex chemical structure. Their main role is in waterproofing plants and animals, although they form storage compounds in a few organisms, e.g. castor oil and in fish.

### 2.6.4 Functions of lipids

1. **An energy source** – Upon breakdown they yield $38\,kJ\,g^{-1}$ of energy. This compares favourably with carbohydrates which yield $17\,kJ\,g^{-1}$ and means lipids are excellent energy stores. This makes them especially useful for animals where locomotion requires mass to be kept to a minimum. In plants they are useful in seeds where dispersal by wind or insects makes small mass a necessity. This explains the abundance of oils extracted from seeds and fruits, e.g. olive, linseed, castor, peanut, coconut and sunflower. Their insolubility is another advantage, as they are not easily dissolved out of cells.

2. **Insulation** – Fats conduct heat only slowly and so are useful insulators. In endothermic animals, such as mammals, fat is stored beneath the skin (subcutaneous fat) where it helps to retain body heat. In aquatic mammals, such as whales, seals and manatees, hair is ineffective as an insulator because it cannot trap water in the same way as it can air. These animals therefore have extremely thick subcutaneous fat, called blubber, which forms an effective insulator.

3. **Protection** – Another secondary use to which stored fat is put is as a packing material around delicate organs. Fat surrounding the kidneys, for instance, helps to protect them from physical damage.

4. **Buoyancy** – Being less dense than water, lipids aid buoyancy of aquatic vertebrates such as sharks, seals and whales. Sharks have extremely fatty livers which make up to 25% of their body volume and contain a lipid, squaline, with a specific gravity of only 0.86. Oils on bird feathers are especially important in keeping aquatic varieties afloat.

5. **Waterproofing** – Terrestrial plants and animals have a need to conserve water. Animal skins produce oil secretions, e.g. from the sebaceous glands in mammals, which waterproof the body. Oils also coat the fur, helping to repel water which would otherwise wet it and reduce its effectiveness as an insulator. Birds spread oil over their feathers, from a special gland near the cloaca, for the same purpose. Insects have a waxy cuticle to prevent evaporative loss in the same way that plant leaves have one to reduce transpiration.

6. **Cell membranes** – Phospholipids are major components of the cell membrane and contribute to many of its properties (see Section 4.2.2).

7. **Other functions** – Lipids perform a host of miscellaneous functions in different organisms. For example, plant scents are fatty acids (or their derivatives) and so aid the attraction of insects for pollination. Bees use wax in constructing their honeycombs.

### 2.6.5 Steroids

Steroids are related to lipids, and **cholesterol** is perhaps the best known. It is found in animals where it is important in the synthesis of steroid hormones, such as oestrogen and cortisone.

# Cholesterol

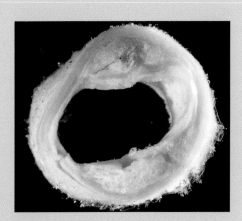

*Cholesterol*

Cholesterol is a lipid containing four rings of carbon and hydrogen atoms with a branched side chain. A single hydroxyl group (OH⁻) gives the molecule a small charge as the result of ionization. Cholesterol is very hydrophobic.

Most cholesterol in the body is found in the membranes of cells. The plasma membrane has the most, almost one cholesterol molecule for each phospholipid. In internal membranes the ratio is closer to 1:10.

Cholesterol is essential for the functioning of plasma membranes where it plays two main roles. Firstly it limits the uncontrolled leakage of small molecules (water and ions) in and out of the plasma membrane. The cell can thus control the passage of solutes and ions using specialized membrane proteins and without wasting energy counteracts their leakage. Cholesterol is an important constituent of myelin and helps to prevent the outward flow of ions which would 'short circuit' the movement of nerve impulses along the axon. The second role of cholesterol in membranes is to pull together the fatty acid chains in phospholipids, restricting their movement, but not making them solid. Cholesterol is also used by the liver for making bile salts and, in small quantities, is used to make steroids in the ovaries, testes and adrenal glands.

In total the body contains a pool of about 120–150 g of cholesterol which is maintained by biosynthesis in the liver and intestine and by ingestion of meat, seafood, eggs and dairy produce. Vegans take in no cholesterol but most other diets result in an intake of approximately 0.5 g, the body making a further 0.5 g, per day. Cholesterol is lost from the body mainly as bile salts, but also as bile, in cells from the lining of the intestine and a tiny percentage as steroid hormones in the urine.

Cholesterol is insoluble in water but can be carried in the blood plasma in the form of lipoproteins. The balance of these lipoproteins is usually maintained by special receptors in the liver cells but saturated fats in the diet decrease their activity and hence lead to a rise in plasma cholesterol. Deposits of crystalline cholesterol and droplets of cholesterol esters can cause thickening of the artery walls (atherosclerosis). This can lead to heart attacks (from blocking of coronary arteries), strokes (brain arteries blocked) or blockages of arteries in the legs. Atherosclerosis may follow damage caused to the artery walls by high blood pressure and smoking. Smoking considerably decreases the concentration of the antioxidant vitamins E and C in the blood resulting in the oxidation of some lipoproteins.

The products of oxidation are often toxic to the cells of the artery and cause them to behave abnormally. The damaged cells release substances which cause the blood to clot and the artery to contract. Macrophages which degrade the oxidized lipoproteins are unable to deal with the cholesterol it carries. Eventually they fill with cholesterol and die, depositing the cholesterol back into the artery.

T.S. human aorta with a fatty atheroma partially obstructing the interior

# 2.7 Proteins

Other important steroids include vitamin D and bile acids. Proteins are organic compounds of large molecular mass (up to 40 000 000 for some viral proteins but more typically several thousand, e.g. haemoglobin = 64 500). They are not truly soluble in water, but form colloidal suspensions. In addition to carbon, hydrogen and oxygen, they always contain nitrogen, usually sulphur and sometimes phosphorus. Whereas there are relatively few carbohydrates and fats, the number of proteins is almost limitless. A simple bacterium such as *Escherichia coli* has around 800, and humans have over 10 000. They are specific to each species. Glucose is glucose in whatever organism it occurs, but proteins vary from one species to another. Indeed, it is the proteins rather than the fats or carbohydrates that determine the characteristics of a species. Proteins are rarely stored in organisms, except in eggs or seeds where they are used to form the new tissue. The word protein (from the Greek) means 'of first importance' and was coined by a Dutch chemist, Mulder, because he thought they played a fundamental role in cells. We now know that proteins form the structural basis of all living cells and that Mulder's judgement was sound.

---

**PROJECT**

**Breakfast cereals have labels on the outside of the packet indicating the amounts of the various ingredients**

Use your knowledge of the various food tests to find out if the claims on the labels are correct.

---

### 2.7.1 Amino acids

Amino acids are a group of over a hundred chemicals of which around 20 commonly occur in proteins. They always contain a basic group, the amino group ($-NH_2$), and an acid group, the carboxyl group ($-COOH$). (See Fig. 2.7.) Most amino acids have one of each group and are therefore neutral, but a few have more amino groups than carboxyl ones (basic amino acids) while others have more carboxyl than amino groups (acidic amino acids). Histidine and arginine are examples of basic amino acids; aspartic acid and glutamic acid are examples of acidic amino acids.

Amino acids are soluble in water where they form ions. These ions are formed by the loss of a hydrogen atom from the carboxyl group, making it negatively charged. This hydrogen atom associates with the amino group, making it positively charged. The ion is therefore **dipolar** – having a positive and a negative pole. Such ions are called **zwitterions** (see Fig. 2.8). Amino acids therefore have both acidic and basic properties, i.e. they are **amphoteric**. Being amphoteric means that amino acids act as **buffer solutions**. A buffer solution is one which resists the tendency to alter its pH even when small amounts of acid or alkali are added to it. Such a property is essential in biological systems where any sudden change in pH could adversely affect the performance of enzymes.

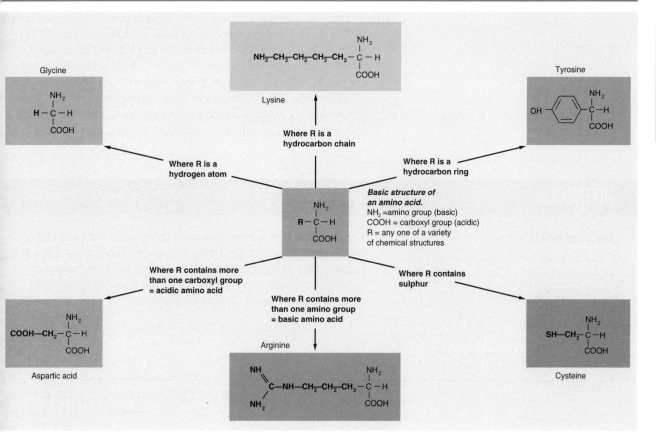

ig. 2.7 *Structure of a range of amino acids*

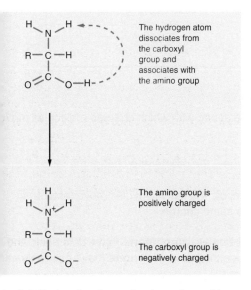

ig. 2.8 *Zwitterion formation in amino acids*

## 2.7.2 Formation of polypeptides

We have seen that monosaccharides may be linked to form disaccharides and polysaccharides by the loss of water (condensation reaction). Similarly, fats are formed from condensation reactions between fatty acids and glycerol. The formation of polypeptides follows the same pattern. A condensation reaction occurs between the amino group of one amino acid and the carboxyl group of another, to form a **dipeptide** (see Fig. 2.9). Further combinations of this type extend the length of the chain to form a **polypeptide** (see Fig. 2.10).

A polypeptide usually contains many hundreds of amino acids. Polypeptides may be linked by forces such as disulphide bridges to give proteins comprising thousands of amino acids.

## 2.7.3 Structure of polypeptides

The chains of amino acids which make up a polypeptide have a specific three-dimensional shape. This shape is important in the functioning of proteins, especially enzymes. The shape of a polypeptide molecule is due to four types of bonding which occur between various amino acids in the chain (see Fig. 2.11).

The first type of bond is called a **disulphide bond**. It arises between sulphur-containing groups on any two cysteine molecules. These bonds may arise between cysteine molecules in the same amino acid chain (intrachain) or between molecules in different chains (interchain).

25

The second type of bond is the **ionic bond**. We have seen that amino acids form zwitterions (Section 2.7.1) which have $NH_3^+$ and $COO^-$ groups. The formation of peptide bonds when making a polypeptide means that the COOH and $NH_2$ groups are not available to form ions. In the case of acidic amino acids, however, there are additional COOH groups which may ionize to give $COO^-$ groups. In the same way, basic amino acids may still retain $NH_3^+$ groups even when combined into the structure

## NOTEBOOK

**Electrophoresis**

Electrophoresis is a technique used to separate molecules of different electrical charge. Under the influence of an electrical field, **anions** (negatively charged ions) will move towards the **anode** (positive electrode) while **cations** (positively charged ions) are attracted to the cathode (negative electrode).

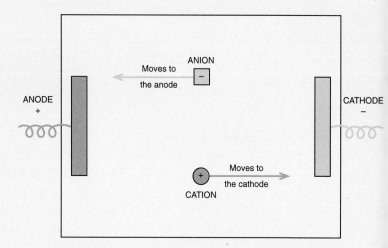

Two factors affect the speed with which charged molecules move towards an electrode:

1.  The amount of charge – the greater the charge the faster the molecule moves.
2.  The size of the molecule – small molecules move faster than larger ones with the same charge.

Amino acids and proteins are **amphoteric** (have both basic and acidic properties) because they are **zwitterions** (have positively and negatively charged groups).

The amount of positive or negative charge is affected by pH. Each molecule has a specific pH at which the total positive charge is exactly equal to the total negative charge, i.e. it is electrically neutral and has no tendency to move to either the anode or cathode of an electric field. This is known as the **isoelectric point**. At higher pH protein and amino acid molecules become more negatively charged while at lower pH they become more positively charged.

of a polypeptide. In addition $NH_3^+$ and $COO^-$ can occur at the ends of a polypeptide chain. Any of these available $NH_3^+$ and $COO^-$ groups may form ionic bonds which help to give a polypeptide molecule its particular shape. These ionic bonds are weak and may be broken by alterations in the pH of the medium around the polypeptide.

The third type of bond is the **hydrogen bond**. This occurs between certain hydrogen atoms and certain oxygen atoms

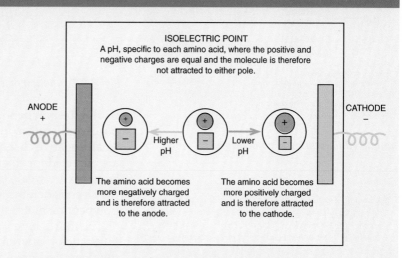

ISOELECTRIC POINT
A pH, specific to each amino acid, where the positive and negative charges are equal and the molecule is therefore not attracted to either pole.

ANODE +

CATHODE −

Higher pH

Lower pH

The amino acid becomes more negatively charged and is therefore attracted to the anode.

The amino acid becomes more positively charged and is therefore attracted to the cathode.

The molecules being separated have to be supported in an appropriate medium such as paper or a thin layer of gel.

Either end of a strip of the medium is dipped in a small reservoir of buffer solution of the appropriate pH. Each reservoir also contains an electrode.

The electrical field is applied for a specific period of time and then the position of the molecules is determined by adding a suitable stain to colour them. The molecules are separated according to their charges; the negatively charged ones moving to the anode with the most negatively charged ones moving furthest. The positively charged ones move to the cathode and again the more positive they are the closer they get to the cathode.

It is possible to treat the mixture being separated in such a way that all the molecules are equally negatively charged. These can then be loaded at the cathode end of the apparatus and will be attracted to the anode. The distance they travel in a given time will then depend not on their charge but their size, the smaller molecules moving further than the larger ones.

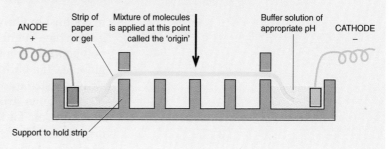

ANODE +

Strip of paper or gel

Mixture of molecules is applied at this point called the 'origin'

Buffer solution of appropriate pH

CATHODE −

*Typical apparatus for carrying out electrophoresis*

Support to hold strip

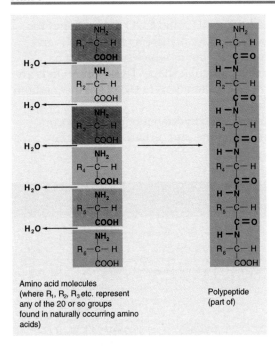

Amino acid molecules
(where $R_1$, $R_2$, $R_3$ etc. represent
any of the 20 or so groups
found in naturally occurring amino
acids)

Polypeptide
(part of)

*Fig. 2.10 Formation of a polypeptide*

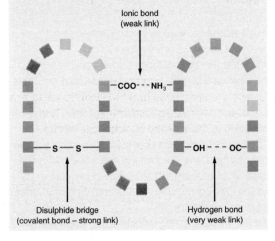

*A simplified representation of a polypeptide chain to show three types of bonding responsible for shaping the chain. In practice the polypeptide chains are longer, contain more of these three types of bond and have a three-dimensional shape.*

Ionic bond
(weak link)

—COO⁻ ⋯ NH₃—

—S—S—

—OH ⋯ OC—

Disulphide bridge
(covalent bond – strong link)

Hydrogen bond
(very weak link)

*Fig. 2.11 Types of bond in a polypeptide chain*

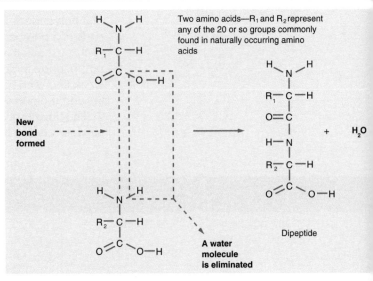

Two amino acids—$R_1$ and $R_2$ represent any of the 20 or so groups commonly found in naturally occurring amino acids

New bond formed

A water molecule is eliminated

Dipeptide

*Fig. 2.9 Formation of a dipeptide*

within the polypeptide chain. The hydrogen atoms have a small positive charge on them (electropositive) and the oxygen atoms small negative charge (electronegative). The two charged atoms are attracted together and form a hydrogen bond. While each bond is very weak, the sheer number of bonds means that they play a considerable role in the shape and stability of a polypeptide molecule.

The fourth type is **hydrophobic interactions** which are interactions between non-polar R groups. These cause the protein to fold as hydrophobic side groups are shielded from water.

### 2.7.4 Fibrous proteins

The fibrous proteins have a primary structure of regular repetitive sequences. They form long chains which may run parallel to one another, being linked by cross bridges. They are very stable molecules and have structural roles within organisms. Collagen (Fig. 2.12) is a good example. It is a common constituent of animal connective tissue, especially in structures requiring physical strength, e.g. tendons. It has a primary structure which is largely a repeat of the tripeptide sequence glycine–proline–alanine, and forms a long unbranched chain. Three such chains are wound into a triple helix, with cross bridges linking them to each other and providing additional structural support. (Compare the repeating glucose units, parallel chains and cross links of the structural carbohydrate cellulose.)

### 2.7.5 Globular proteins

In contrast to fibrous proteins, the globular proteins such as insulin have highly irregular sequences of amino acids in their polypeptide chains. Their shape is also different, being compact globules. If a fibrous protein is likened to a series of strands of string twisted into a rope, then a globular protein can be thought of as the same string rolled into a ball (see Fig. 2.13). These molecules are far less stable and have metabolic roles within organisms. All enzymes are globular proteins. Globular and fibrous proteins are compared in Table 2.6.

## BIOLOGY AROUND US

# Hair perming

The protein keratin, which makes up human hair, has a high percentage of the amino acid cysteine. The disulphide bridges formed between cysteine molecules are largely responsible for the shape of the hair. Hair is straight or curly because the keratin contains disulphide linkages that enable the molecules to hold their particular shapes. When hair is permed it is first treated with a reducing agent that breaks some of the —S—S— bonds.

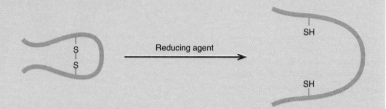

This allows the molecules to become more flexible and the hair is then set into the desired shape, using rollers or curlers. An oxidizing agent is then added which reverses the above reaction, forming new disulphide bonds, which now hold the molecules together in the desired positions. The straightening of curly hair is done in the same way. 'Perms' are not of course truly permanent. The hair keeps growing and the new hair has the same disulphide linkages as the original hair.

### 2.7.6 Conjugated proteins

Many proteins incorporate other chemicals within their structure. These proteins are called **conjugated proteins** and the non-protein part is referred to as the **prosthetic group**. The prosthetic group plays a vital role in the functioning of the protein. Some examples are given in Table 2.7.

*Fig. 2.12 Fine structure of the fibrous protein collagen*

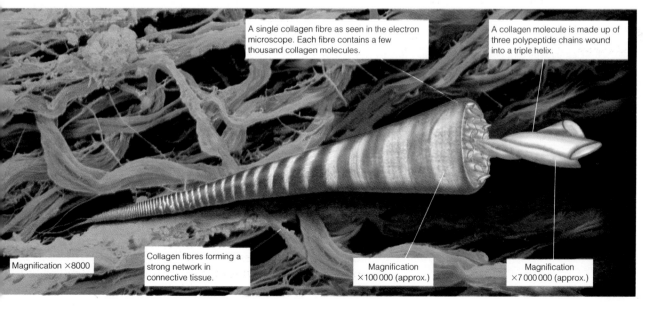

A single collagen fibre as seen in the electron microscope. Each fibre contains a few thousand collagen molecules.

A collagen molecule is made up of three polypeptide chains wound into a triple helix.

Magnification ×8000

Collagen fibres forming a strong network in connective tissue.

Magnification ×100 000 (approx.)

Magnification ×7 000 000 (approx.)

*(a)  The primary structure of a protein is the sequence of amino acids found in its polypeptide chains.  This sequence determines its properties and shape.  Following the elucidation of the amino acid sequence of the hormone insulin, by Frederick Sanger in 1954, the primary structure of many other proteins is now known.*

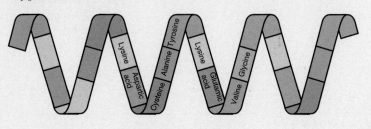

| | Lysine | Aspartic acid | Cysteine | Alanine | Tyrosine | Lysine | Glutamic acid | Valine | Glycine | |

*(b)  The secondary structure is the shape which the polypeptide chain forms as a result of hydrogen bonding.  This is most often a spiral known as the α-helix, although other configurations occur.*

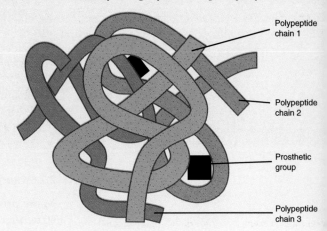

*(c)  The tertiary structure is due to the bending and twisting of the polypeptide helix into a compact structure. All three types of bond, disulphide, ionic and hydrogen, contribute to the maintenance of the tertiary structure.*

*(d)  The quaternary structure arises from the combination of a number of different polypeptide chains, and associated non-protein groups, into a large complex protein molecule.*

Polypeptide chain 1

Polypeptide chain 2

Prosthetic group

Polypeptide chain 3

*Fig. 2.13 Structure of proteins*

TABLE 2.6    **Comparison of globular and fibrous proteins**

| Fibrous proteins | Globular proteins |
| --- | --- |
| Repetitive regular sequences of amino acids | Irregular amino acid sequences |
| Actual sequences may vary slightly between two examples of the same protein | Sequence highly specific and never varies between two examples of the same protein |
| Polypeptide chains form long parallel strands | Polypeptide chains folded into a spherical shape |
| Length of chain may vary in two examples of the same protein | Length always identical in two examples of the same protein |
| Stable structure | Relatively unstable structure |
| Insoluble | Soluble – forms colloidal suspensions |
| Support and structural functions | Metabolic functions |
| Examples include collagen and keratin | Examples include all enzymes, some hormones (e.g. insulin) and haemoglobin |

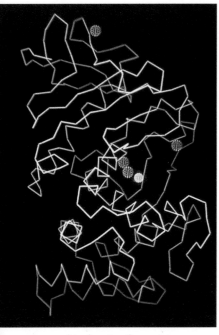

Computer graphic showing the protein
termolysine

TABLE 2.7   Examples of conjugated proteins

| Name of protein | Where found | Prosthetic group |
|---|---|---|
| Haemoglobin* | Blood | Haem (contains iron) |
| Mucin | Saliva | Carbohydrate |
| Casein | Milk | Phosphoric acid |
| Cytochrome oxidase | Electron carrier pathway of cells | Copper |
| Nucleoprotein | Ribosomes | Nucleic acid |

*Details of the molecular structure of haemoglobin are given in Section 21.2.1.

### 2.7.7 Denaturation of proteins

We have seen that the three-dimensional structure of a protein is, in part at least, due to fairly weak ionic and hydrogen bonds. Any agent which breaks these bonds will cause the three-dimensional shape to be changed. In many cases the globular proteins revert to a more fibrous form. This process is called **denaturation**. The actual sequence of amino acids is unaltered; only the overall shape of the molecule is changed. This is still sufficient to prevent the molecule from carrying out its usual functions within an organism.

Denaturation may be temporary or permanent and is due to a variety of factors as shown in Table 2.8.

TABLE 2.8   Factors causing protein denaturation

| Factor | Explanation | Example |
|---|---|---|
| Heat | Causes the atoms of the protein to vibrate more (increased kinetic energy), thus breaking hydrogen and ionic bonds | Coagulation of albumen (boiling eggs makes the white more fibrous and less soluble) |
| Acids | Additional $H^+$ ions in acids combine with $COO^-$ groups on amino acids and form COOH. Ionic bonds are hence broken | The souring of milk by acid (e.g. *Lactobacillus* bacterium produces lactic acid, lowering pH and causing it to denature the casein, making it insoluble and thus forming curds) |
| Alkalis | Reduced number of $H^+$ ions causes $NH_3^+$ groups to lose $H^+$ ions and form $NH_2$. Ionic bonds are hence broken | |
| Inorganic chemicals | The ions of heavy metals such as mercury and silver are highly electropositive. They combine with $COO^-$ groups and disrupt ionic bonds. Similarly, highly electronegative ions, e.g. cyanide ($CN^-$), combine with $NH_3^+$ groups and disrupt ionic bonds | Many enzymes are inhibited by being denatured in the presence of certain ions, e.g. cytochrome oxidase (respiratory enzyme) is inhibited by cyanide |
| Organic chemicals | Organic solvents alter hydrogen bonding within a protein | Alcohol denatures certain bacterial proteins. This is what makes it useful for sterilization |
| Mechanical force | Physical movement may break hydrogen bonds | Stretching a hair breaks the hydrogen bonds in the keratin helix. The helix is extended and the hair stretches. If released, the hair returns to its normal length. If, however, it is wetted and then dried under tension, it keeps its new length – the basis of hair styling |

TABLE 2.9 **Functions of proteins**

| Vital activity | Protein example | Function |
|---|---|---|
| Nutrition | Digestive enzymes, e.g. trypsin<br>amylase<br>lipase | Catalyses the hydrolysis of proteins to polypeptides<br>Catalyses the hydrolysis of starch to maltose<br>Catalyses the hydrolysis of fats to fatty acids and glycerol |
| | Fibrous proteins in granal lamellae | Help to arrange chlorophyll molecules in a position to receive maximum amount of light for photosynthesis |
| | Mucin | Assists trapping of food in filter feeders. Prevents autolysis. Lubricates gut wall |
| | Ovalbumin | Storage protein in egg white |
| | Casein | Storage protein in milk |
| Respiration and transport | Haemoglobin/haemoerythrin/haemocyanin/chlorocruorin | Transport of oxygen |
| | Myoglobin | Stores oxygen in muscle |
| | Prothrombin/fibrinogen | Required for the clotting of blood |
| | Mucin | Keeps respiratory surface moist |
| | Antibodies | Essential to the defence of the body, e.g. against bacterial invasion |
| Growth | Hormones, e.g. thyroxine | Controls growth and metabolism |
| Excretion | Enzymes, e.g. urease; arginase | Catalyse reactions in ornithine cycle and therefore help in protein breakdown and urea formation |
| Support and movement | Actin/myosin | Needed for muscle contraction |
| | Ossein | Structural support in bone |
| | Collagen | Gives strength with flexibility in tendons and cartilage |
| | Elastin | Gives strength and elasticity to ligaments |
| | Keratin | Tough for protection, e.g. in scales, claws, nails, hooves, skin |
| | Sclerotin | Provides strength in insect exoskeleton |
| | Lipoproteins | Structural components of all cell membranes |
| Sensitivity and coordination | Hormones, e.g. insulin/glucagon<br>adrenocorticotrophic hormone<br>vasopressin | Control blood sugar level<br>Controls the activity of the adrenal cortex<br>Controls blood pressure |
| | Rhodopsin/opsin | Visual pigments in the retina, sensitive to light |
| | Phytochromes | Plant pigments important in control of flowering, germination, etc. |
| Reproduction | Hormones, e.g. prolactin | Induces milk production in mammals |
| | Chromatin | Gives structural support to chromosomes |
| | Gluten | Storage protein in seeds – nourishes the embryo |
| | Keratin | Forms horns and antlers which may be used for sexual display |

## 2.8  Nucleic acids

Like proteins, nucleic acids are informational macromolecules. They are made up of chains of individual units called **nucleotides**. The structure of nucleic acids and their constituent nucleotides are closely related to their functions in heredity and protein synthesis. For this reason the details of their structure will be left until the nature of the genetic code is discussed in Chapter 7.

# 2.9   Questions

**1.** The diagrams below show part of the molecular structure of cellulose and starch (amylose). Both cellulose and starch are synthesized in plants from glucose.

*(a)* Describe the differences in molecular structure between cellulose and starch.
(2 marks)

Cellulose has a structural function in plants while starch has a storage function.

*(b)* Relate these functional differences to the differences in molecular structure of cellulose and starch.   (4 marks)

*(c)* Name the bond formed between adjacent glucose molecules in starch and cellulose.
(1 mark)

*(d)* Suggest why amylase, the enzyme that catalyses the hydrolysis of starch, will not catalyse the hydrolysis of cellulose.   (2 marks)
(Total 9 marks)

*UCLES June 1996, Paper 3, No. 2*

**2.** The table below refers to **two** organic molecules. Copy the table. If the statement is correct for the molecule, place a tick (✓) in the appropriate box. If it is incorrect, place a cross (✗) in the appropriate box.

| Statement | Triglyceride | Glycogen |
|---|---|---|
| Contains only carbon, hydrogen and oxygen | | |
| Glycosidic bonds present | | |
| Soluble in water | | |
| Provides storage of energy | | |
| Occurs in flowering plants and animals | | |

(Total 5 marks)
*Edexcel June 1998, B/HB1, No. 3*

**3.** The table below refers to some nutrients in the human diet. Copy and complete the table by writing **one** physiological function in humans of each nutrient in the spaces provided.

| Nutrient | *One* physiological function in humans |
|---|---|
| Calcium | |
| Iron | |
| Phosphate | |
| Nicotinic acid | |

(Total 4 marks)
*Edexcel June 1998, B2, No. 1*

**4.** The diagram below shows the structure of a lipid molecule.

*(a)* (i) Name the parts labelled **A** and **B**.
(2 marks)
(ii) Name this type of lipid.   (1 mark)
(iii) Name the chemical reaction used to form the bonds between **A** and **B**.
(1 mark)

*(b)* (i) State **one** function of this type of lipid in living organisms.   (1 mark)
(ii) State **one** feature of the molecules of this type of lipid which makes them suitable for the function you have given.
(1 mark)

(Total 6 marks)
*Edexcel June 1997, B/HB1, No. 2*

**5.** The statements in the table below refer to three polysaccharide molecules. Copy and complete the table. If the statement is correct, place a tick (✓) in the appropriate box and if the statement is incorrect, place a cross (✗) in the appropriate box.

| Statement | Starch | Glycogen | Cellulose |
|---|---|---|---|
| Polymer of $\alpha$-glucose | | | |
| Glycosidic bonds present | | | |
| Unbranched chains only | | | |
| Energy store in animal cells | | | |

(Total 4 marks)
*Edexcel June 1997, B/HB1, No. 4*

**6.** The diagrams below show the structure of two amino acids, **A** and **B**.

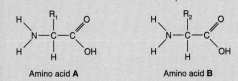

Amino acid **A**          Amino acid **B**

(a) Give **two** elements other than carbon, hydrogen and oxygen which could be present in the side groups $R_1$ and $R_2$. (*1 mark*)

(b) **A** and **B** can be linked together during protein synthesis.
  (i) What is the name given to this bond? (*1 mark*)
  (ii) Copy the diagrams and put a ring around the atoms which are removed when **A** and **B** are joined together. (*1 mark*)
  (iii) Draw a line connecting the atoms in **A** and **B** which are bonded. (*1 mark*)

(c) Describe how the properties of the side groups $R_1$ and $R_2$ may vary, and how these are involved in the structure of proteins. (*4 marks*)

(d) Copy and complete the table below giving a **named** example of a protein having the function indicated.

| Function | Example of protein |
|---|---|
| Contractile | |
| Enzyme | |
| Transport | |
| Structural | |
| Hormone | |
| Protection from disease | |

(*3 marks*)
(*Total 11 marks*)

*Oxford June 1997, Paper 1, No. 2*

**7.** (a) Copy and complete the following table with ticks (✓) to show which properties apply to each biochemical compound.

| | Biochemical compound | | | | |
|---|---|---|---|---|---|
| Property | Monosaccharide | Starch | Cellulose | Lipid | Protein |
| Is a polymer | | | | | |
| Contains nitrogen | | | | | |
| Is soluble in water | | | | | |

(*3 marks*)

(b) The diagram represents a small polypeptide consisting of eight amino acids, **s–z**.

$$H_2N - \boxed{s}\,\boxed{t}\,\boxed{u}\,\boxed{v}\,\boxed{w}\,\boxed{x}\,\boxed{y}\,\boxed{z} - \square$$

  (i) Give the formula of the chemical group which would appear at the end of amino acid **z**. (*1 mark*)
  (ii) Name the type of reaction by which amino acids are joined together. (*1 mark*)
  (iii) Name the reagent or reagents you would use to test for the presence of a protein. (*1 mark*)

(*Total 6 marks*)

*NEAB February 1997, Paper BY01, No. 1*

**8.** The following diagrams represent the structure of some common carbohydrates.

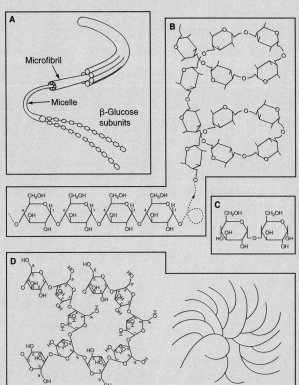

(a) Suggest a suitable name for each structure, **A–D**. (*4 marks*)

(b) Given that the chemical formula for glucose is $C_6H_{12}O_6$, write down the equation to show the production of the disaccharide maltose. (*2 marks*)

(c) Briefly explain how you could distinguish, using a practical technique, between the presence of a reducing sugar, such as maltose, and a non-reducing sugar, such as sucrose. (*3 marks*)

(*Total 9 marks*)

*Oxford February 1997, Paper 1, No.3*

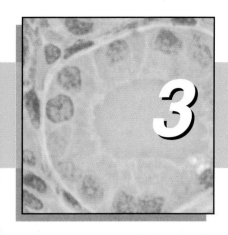

# 3 Enzymes

Until recently it was thought that all biological catalysts were enzymes. We now know that other substances may carry out catalytic functions in living organisms. **Abzymes** are antibodies with catalytic properties and **ribozymes** are molecules of RNA which act catalytically on themselves. Most biological catalysts however are globular proteins known as enzymes. A catalyst is a substance which alters the rate of a chemical reaction without itself undergoing a permanent change. As they are not altered by the reactions they catalyse, enzymes can be used over and over again. They are therefore effective in very small amounts. Enzymes cannot cause reactions to occur; they can only speed up reactions that would otherwise take place extremely slowly. The word 'enzyme' means 'in yeast', and was used because they were first discovered by Eduard Buchner in an extract of yeast.

## 3.1 Enzyme structure and function

Enzymes are complex three-dimensional globular proteins, some of which have other associated molecules. While the enzyme molecule is normally larger than the substrate molecule it acts upon, only a small part of the enzyme molecule actually comes into contact with the substrate. This region is called the **active site**. Only a few of the amino acids of the enzyme molecule make up the active site. These so-called **catalytic amino acids** are often some distance apart in the protein chain but are brought into close proximity by the folding of that chain (see Fig. 3.1).

*The catalytic amino acids A, B and C, although some distance apart in the chain, are close together when the protein is folded.*

Active site

A

C

B

Amino acid chain folded into its enzyme configuration

*Fig. 3.1 Catalytic amino acids forming the active site*

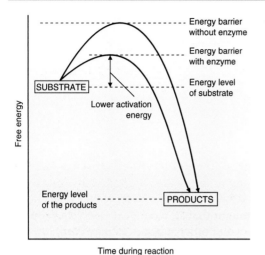

*Fig. 3.2 How enzymes lower the activation energy*

### 3.1.1 Enzymes and activation energy

Before a reaction can take place it must overcome an energy barrier by exceeding its activation energy. Enzymes operate by lowering this activation energy and thus permit the reaction to occur more readily (Fig. 3.2). As heat is often the source of activation energy, enzymes often dispense with the need for this heat and so allow reactions to take place at lower temperatures. Many reactions which would not ordinarily occur at the temperature of an organism do so readily in the presence of enzymes.

### 3.1.2 Mechanism of enzyme action

Enzymes are thought to operate on a **lock and key mechanism**. In the same way that a key fits a lock very precisely, so the substrate fits accurately into the active site of the enzyme molecule. The two molecules form a temporary structure called the **enzyme–substrate complex**. The products have a different shape from the substrate and so, once formed, they escape from the active site, leaving it free to become attached to another substrate molecule. The sequence is summarized in Fig. 3.3.

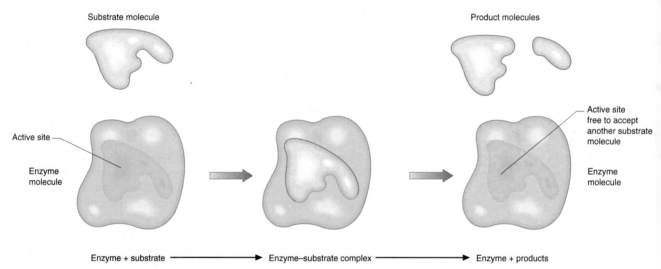

*Fig. 3.3 Mechanism of enzyme action*

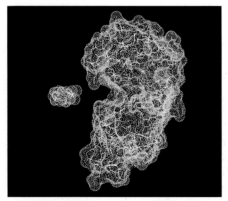

Computer graphic showing ribonuclease A enzyme and its substrate

Modern interpretations of the lock and key mechanism suggest that in the presence of the substrate the active site may change in order to suit the substrate's shape. The enzyme is flexible and moulds to fit the substrate molecule in the same way that clothing is flexible and can mould itself to fit the shape of the wearer. The enzyme initially has a binding configuration which attracts the substrate. On binding to the enzyme, the substrate disturbs the shape of the enzyme and causes it to assume a new configuration. It is this new configuration that is catalytically active and affects the shape of the substrate, thus lowering its activation energy. This is referred to as an **induced fit** of the substrate to the enzyme.

# 3.2 Properties of enzymes

The properties of enzymes can be explained in relation to the lock and key mechanism of enzyme action, and the theory of induced fit.

### 3.2.1 Specificity

All enzymes operate only on specific substrates. Just as a key has a specific shape and therefore fits only complementary locks, so only substrates of a particular shape will fit the active site of an enzyme. Some locks are highly specific and can only be opened with a single key. Others are opened by a number of similar keys; yet others may be opened by many different keys. In the same way, some enzymes will act only on one particular isomer. Others act only on similar molecules; yet others will break a particular chemical linkage, wherever it occurs.

### 3.2.2 Reversibility

Chemical reactions are reversible, and equations are therefore often represented by two arrows to indicate this reversibility. (See opposite.)

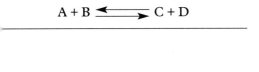

$$A + B \rightleftharpoons C + D$$

At any one moment the reaction (shown left) may be proceeding predominantly in one direction. If, however, the conditions are changed, the direction may be reversed. It may be that the reaction proceeds from left to right in acid conditions, but in alkaline conditions it goes from right to left. In time, reactions reach a point where the reactants and the product are in **equilibrium** with one another. Enzymes catalyse the forward and reverse reactions equally. They do not therefore alter the equilibrium itself, only the speed at which it is reached. Carbonic anhydrase is an enzyme which catalyses a reaction in either direction depending on the conditions at the time. In respiring tissues, where there is much carbon dioxide, it converts carbon dioxide and water into carbonic acid. In the lungs, however, the removal of carbon dioxide by diffusion means a low concentration of carbon dioxide, and hence the carbonic acid breaks down into carbon dioxide and water. Both reactions are catalysed by carbonic anhydrase, as shown opposite.

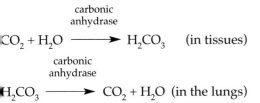

$$CO_2 + H_2O \xrightarrow{\text{carbonic anhydrase}} H_2CO_3 \quad \text{(in tissues)}$$

$$H_2CO_3 \xrightarrow{\text{carbonic anhydrase}} CO_2 + H_2O \quad \text{(in the lungs)}$$

### 3.2.3 Enzyme concentration

The active site of an enzyme may be used again and again. Enzymes therefore work efficiently at very low concentrations. The number of substrate molecules which an enzyme can act upon in a given time is called its **turnover number**. This varies from many millions of substrate molecules each minute, in the case of catalase, to a few hundred per minute for slow acting enzymes. Provided the temperature and other conditions are suitable for the reaction, and provided there are excess substrate molecules, the rate of a reaction is directly proportional to the enzyme concentration. If the amount of substrate is restricted, it may limit the rate of reaction. The addition of further enzyme cannot increase the rate and the graph therefore tails off (Fig. 3.4).

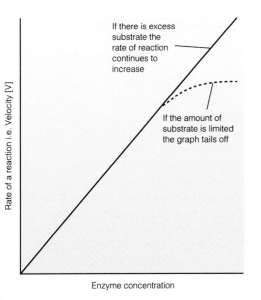

*Fig. 3.4 Graph to show the effect of enzyme concentration on the rate of an enzyme-controlled reaction*

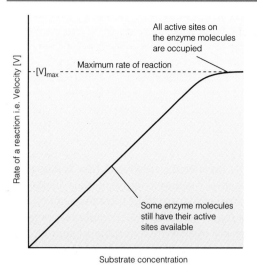

*Fig. 3.5 Graph to show the effect of substrate concentration on the rate of an enzyme-controlled reaction*

### 3.2.4 Substrate concentration

For a given amount of enzyme, the rate of an enzyme-controlled reaction increases with increasing substrate concentration – up to a point. At low substrate concentrations, the active sites of the enzyme molecules are not all used – there simply are not enough substrate molecules to occupy them all. As the substrate concentration increases, more and more sites come into use. A point is reached, however, where all sites are being used; increasing the substrate concentration further cannot therefore increase the rate of reaction, as the amount of enzyme is the limiting factor. At this point the graph tails off (Fig. 3.5).

### 3.2.5 Temperature

An increase in temperature affects the rate of an enzyme-controlled reaction in two ways:

**1.** As the temperature increases, the kinetic energy of the substrate and enzyme molecules increases and so they move faster. The faster these molecules move, the more often they collide with one another and the greater the rate of reaction.

**2.** As the temperature increases, the more the atoms which make up the enzyme molecules vibrate. This breaks the hydrogen bonds and other forces which hold the molecules in their precise shape. The three-dimensional shape of the enzyme molecules is altered to such an extent that their active sites no longer fit the substrate. The enzyme is said to be **denatured** and loses its catalytic properties. (See Section 2.7.7.)

The actual effect of temperature on the rate of reaction is the combined influence of these two factors and is illustrated in Fig. 3.6.

The optimum temperature for an enzyme varies considerably. Many arctic and alpine plants have enzymes which function efficiently at temperatures around 10 °C, whereas those in algae inhabiting some hot springs continue to function at temperatures around 80 °C. For many enzymes the optimum temperature lies around 40 °C and denaturation occurs at about 60 °C.

### 3.2.6 pH

The precise three-dimensional molecular shape which is vital to the functioning of enzymes is partly the result of hydrogen bonding. These bonds may be broken by the concentration of hydrogen ions ($H^+$) present. pH is a measure of hydrogen ion concentration. It is measured on a scale of 1–14, with pH 7 being the neutral point. A pH less than 7 is acid, one greater than 7 is alkaline.

By breaking the hydrogen bonds which give enzyme molecules their shape, any change in pH can effectively denature enzymes. Each enzyme works best at a particular pH, and deviations from this optimum may result in denaturation. Fig. 3.7 illustrates the different pH optima of four enzymes.

### 3.2.7 Inhibition

The rate of enzyme-controlled reactions may be decreased by the presence of inhibitors. They are of two types: **reversible inhibitors** and **non-reversible inhibitors**.

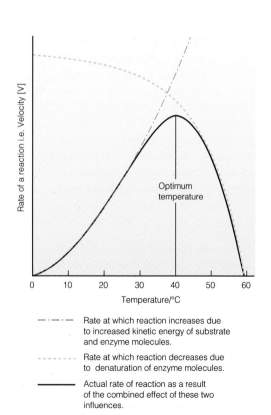

--- · — · — Rate at which reaction increases due to increased kinetic energy of substrate and enzyme molecules.

- - - - - - Rate at which reaction decreases due to denaturation of enzyme molecules.

——— Actual rate of reaction as a result of the combined effect of these two influences.

*Fig. 3.6 Graph to show the effect of temperature on the rate of an enzyme-controlled reaction*

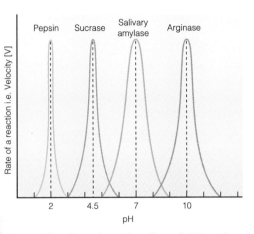

Fig. 3.7 Graph to show the effect of pH on the rate of reaction of four different enzymes

### Reversible inhibitors

The effect of this type of inhibitor is temporary and causes no permanent damage to the enzyme because the association of the inhibitor with the enzyme is a loose one and it can easily be removed. Removal of the inhibitor restores the activity of the enzyme to normal. There are two types: **competitive (active site-directed)** and **non-competitive (non-active site-directed)**.

**Competitive inhibitors** compete with the substrate for the active sites of enzyme molecules (Fig. 3.8). The inhibitor may have a structure which permits it to combine with the active site. While it remains bound to the active site, it prevents a substrate molecule from occupying that site and so reduces the rate of the reaction. The same quantity of product is formed, because the substrate continues to use any enzyme molecules that are unaffected by the inhibitor. It does, however, take longer to make the products. If the concentration of the substrate is increased, less inhibition occurs. This is because, as the substrate and inhibitor are in direct competition, the greater the proportion of substrate molecules the greater their chance of finding the active sites, leaving fewer to be occupied by the inhibitor.

Malonic acid is a competitive inhibitor. It competes with succinate for the active sites of succinic dehydrogenase, an important enzyme in the Krebs cycle (Section 16.3).

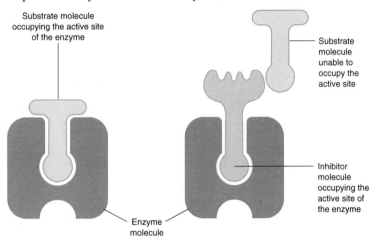

Fig. 3.8 Competitive inhibition

**Non-competitive inhibitors** attach themselves not to the active site of the enzyme but elsewhere on the enzyme molecule (Fig. 3.9). They alter the shape of the enzyme molecule in such a way that the active site can no longer properly accommodate the substrate. As the substrate and inhibitor molecules attach to different parts of the enzyme, they are not competing for the

1. *Inhibitor absent –*
   *The substrate attaches to the active site of the enzyme in the normal way. Reaction takes place as normal.*
2. *Inhibitor present –*
   *The inhibitor prevents the normal enzyme–substrate complex being formed. The reaction rate is reduced.*

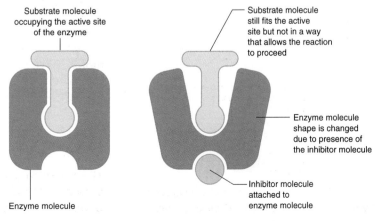

Fig. 3.9 Non-competitive inhibition

## PROJECT

Many different investigations into enzyme activity can be carried out using the digestion of starch by amylase, staining with iodine/potassium iodide solution, and a colorimeter, or using starch gels with wells. For example

(a) substrate concentration
(b) enzyme concentration
(c) temperature
(d) pH.

same sites. An increase in substrate concentration will not therefore reduce the effect of the inhibitor.

Cyanide is a non-competitive inhibitor. It attaches itself to the copper prosthetic group of cytochrome oxidase, thereby inhibiting respiration (Section 16.4).

*Non-reversible inhibitors*
Non-reversible inhibitors leave the enzyme permanently damaged and so unable to carry out its catalytic function. Heavy metal ions such as mercury ($Hg^{2+}$) and silver ($Ag^+$) cause disulphide bonds to break. These bonds help to maintain the shape of the enzyme molecule. Once broken the enzyme molecule's structure becomes irreversibly altered with the permanent loss of its catalytic properties.

## NOTEBOOK

### Why pH?

The term was first used by the Danish biochemist S.P.L. Sörenson when researching into the best conditions for brewing beer. Acidity is the result of free hydrogen ions ($H^+$) in a solution. The concentration is often very low, however. Vinegar, for example, typically has a concentration of 0.001 mol dm$^{-3}$. This is a rather long-winded way of expressing acid and base strength, especially when 1 M sodium hydroxide has a hydrogen ion concentration of 0.000 000 000 000 01 mol$^{-3}$. Sörenson appreciated that 0.001 can be written as $10^{-3}$ and 0.000 000 000 000 01 as $10^{-14}$. He then simply ignored the 10 and the minus sign to give values of 3 and 14 respectively. pH is therefore the negative power (p) of the hydrogen ion concentration (H).

| H⁺ concentration in mol dm⁻³ | $10^{-14}$ | $10^{-13}$ | $10^{-12}$ | $10^{-11}$ | $10^{-10}$ | $10^{-9}$ | $10^{-8}$ | $10^{-7}$ | $10^{-6}$ | $10^{-5}$ | $10^{-4}$ | $10^{-3}$ | $10^{-2}$ | $10^{-1}$ |
|---|---|---|---|---|---|---|---|---|---|---|---|---|---|---|
| pH | 14 | 13 | 12 | 11 | 10 | 9 | 8 | 7 | 6 | 5 | 4 | 3 | 2 | 1 |

## 3.3 Enzyme cofactors

A **cofactor** is a non-protein substance which is essential for some enzymes to function efficiently. There are three types: **activators**, **coenzymes** and **prosthetic groups**.

### 3.3.1 Activators

Activators are substances which are necessary for the functioning of certain enzymes. The enzyme thrombokinase, which converts prothrombin into thrombin during blood clotting, is activated by calcium ($Ca^{2+}$) ions. In the same way

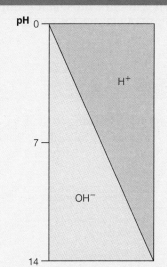

*Relative concentrations of $H^+$ and $OH^-$ ions at different pHs.*

### Why is water neutral at pH 7?

Some water molecules are always dissociated into hydrogen ($H^+$) and hydroxyl ($OH^-$) ions:

$$H_2O \rightleftharpoons H^+ + OH^-$$

At 25 °C, 1 $dm^3$ of water contains $10^{-7}$ moles of $H^+$ ions and therefore has a pH of 7. It follows from the equation above that there will also be $10^{-7}$ moles of $OH^-$ ions. As the concentration of $H^+$ ions increases, that of $OH^-$ ions decreases correspondingly. For example, where the concentration of $H^+$ ions is $10^{-5}$ mol $dm^{-3}$ that of $OH^-$ ions is $10^{-9}$ mol $dm^{-3}$. The two concentrations multiplied always give a value of $10^{-14}$. Hence the pH scale is 0–14. At pH 0 almost all the ions are $H^+$ whereas at pH 14 they are almost entirely $OH^-$.

The pH scale is not linear but is logarithmic, based on a factor of 10. pH 6 = 0.000 001 mol $dm^{-3}$ of $H^+$ and pH 5 = 0.000 01 mol $dm^{-3}$ of $H^+$, i.e. pH 5 is 10 times more acidic than pH 6. In the same way pH 3 is 10 times more acidic than pH 4 and 100 times more so than pH 5.

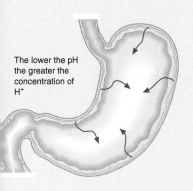

The lower the pH the greater the concentration of $H^+$

Gastric juice pH 1

Sweat is 1 000× more acid than water

Sweat pH 4

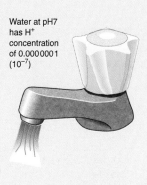

Water at pH 7 has $H^+$ concentration of 0.000 000 1 ($10^{-7}$)

Water pH 7

salivary amylase requires the presence of chloride ($Cl^-$) ions before it will efficiently convert starch into maltose. It is possible that these activators assist in forming the enzyme–substrate complex by moulding either the enzyme or substrate molecule into a more suitable shape.

### 3.3.2 Coenzymes

Coenzymes are non-protein organic substances which are essential to the efficient functioning of some enzymes, but are not themselves bound to the enzyme. Many coenzymes are derived from vitamins, e.g. **nicotinamide adenine dinucleotide (NAD)** is derived from nicotinic acid, a member of the vitamin B complex. NAD acts as a coenzyme to dehydrogenases by acting as a hydrogen acceptor.

### 3.3.3 Prosthetic groups

Like coenzymes, prosthetic groups are organic molecules, but unlike coenzymes they are bound to the enzyme itself. Perhaps the best known prosthetic group is **haem**. Haem is a ring-shaped organic molecule with iron at its centre. Apart from its role as an oxygen carrier in haemoglobin, it is also the prosthetic group of the electron carrier cytochrome and of the enzyme catalase.

## 3.4 Classification of enzymes

Enzymes are classified into six groups according to the type of reaction they catalyse. Table 3.1 summarizes this internationally accepted classification.

TABLE 3.1 **The classification of enzymes**

| Enzyme group | Type of reaction catalysed | Enzyme examples |
|---|---|---|
| 1. Oxidoreductases | Transfer of O and H atoms between substances, i.e. all oxidation–reduction reactions | Dehydrogenases Oxidases |
| 2. Transferases | Transfer of a chemical group from one substance to another | Transaminases Phosphorylases |
| 3. Hydrolases | Hydrolysis reactions | Peptidases Lipases Phosphatases |
| 4. Lyases | Addition or removal of a chemical group other than by hydrolysis | Decarboxylases |
| 5. Isomerases | The rearrangement of groups within a molecule | Isomerases Mutases |
| 6. Ligases | Formation of bonds between two molecules using energy derived from the breakdown of ATP | Synthetases |

Each enzyme is given two names:

A **systematic** name, based on the six classification groups. These names are often long and complicated.

A **trivial** name which is shorter and easier to use.
The trivial names are derived by following three procedures:

**1.** Start with the name of the substrate upon which the enzyme acts, e.g. succinate.

**2.** Add the name of the type of reaction which it catalyses, e.g. dehydrogenation.

**3.** Convert the end of the last word to an -ase suffix, e.g. dehydrogenase.

The example above gives succinic dehydrogenase. Another example would be DNA polymerase. This enzyme catalyses the formation (and breakdown) of the nucleic acid DNA by polymerization. Some of the commercial uses of enzymes are considered in Biology Around Us on pages 606 and 617.

## 3.5  Control of metabolic pathways

With many hundreds of reactions taking place in any single cell it is clear that a very structured system of control of metabolic pathways is essential. If the cell were merely a 'soup' of substrates, enzymes and products, the chances of particular reactants meeting would be small and the metabolic processes inefficient. In addition, different enzymes need different conditions, e.g. a particular pH, and it would be impossible to provide these in such an unstructured 'soup'. Cells contain organelles, and enzymes are often bound to these inner membranes in a precise order. This increases the chances of them coming into contact with their appropriate substrates, and leads to efficiency. The organelles may also have varying conditions to suit the specific enzymes they contain. By controlling these conditions, and the enzymes available, the cell can control the metabolic pathways within it.

Cells also make use of the enzyme's own properties to exercise control over metabolic pathways. The end-product of a pathway may inhibit the enzyme at the start (**end-product inhibition**).

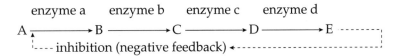

In the example above, the product E acts as an inhibitor to enzyme a. If the level of product E falls, this inhibition is reduced, and so more A is converted to B, and subsequently more E is produced. If the level of E rises above normal, inhibition of enzyme a increases and so the level of E is reduced. In this way homeostatic control of E is achieved, more details of which are given in Section 25.1. The mechanism is termed **negative feedback** because the information from the end of the pathway which is fed back to the start has a negative effect, i.e. a high concentration of E reduces its own production rate.

These forms of inhibition are, for obvious reasons, reversible, i.e. they do not permanently damage the enzymes. They frequently affect the nature of an enzyme's active site by binding with the enzyme at some point on the molecule remote from the active site. Such effects are termed **allosteric** and refer to the ability of the enzyme to have more than one shape. One shape renders the enzyme active, another renders it inactive.

# 3.6 Questions

**1.** The graph shows the results of an investigation into the effect of a competitive inhibitor on an enzyme-controlled reaction over a range of substrate concentrations.

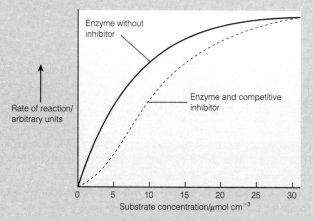

*(a)* Give **one** factor which would need to be kept constant in this investigation. *(1 mark)*

*(b)* (i) Explain the difference in the rates of reaction at the substrate concentration of 10 $\mu$mol cm$^{-3}$. *(2 marks)*

(ii) Explain why the rates of reaction are similar at the substrate concentration of 30 $\mu$mol cm$^{-3}$. *(1 mark)*

*(c)* The diagram represents a metabolic pathway controlled by enzymes.

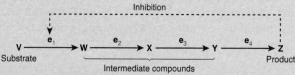

(i) Name the type of control mechanism which regulates production of compound **Z**. *(1 mark)*

(ii) Explain precisely how an excess of compound **Z** will inhibit its further production. *(2 marks)*

*(Total 7 marks)*

*NEAB February 1997, Paper BY01, No. 3*

**2.** *(a)* The diagram shows the structure of a dipeptide.

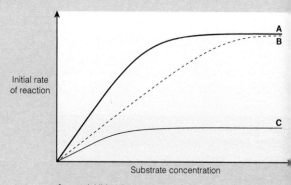

(i) With the aid of a similar diagram, show the reaction which breaks the dipeptide into its amino acids. *(2 marks)*

(ii) What type of enzyme catalyses the reaction you have shown? *(1 mark)*

The graph shows the relationship between substrate concentration and the initial rate of an enzyme-catalysed reaction under different conditions.

**A** — no inhibitor
**B** — competitive inhibitor
**C** — non-competitive inhibitor

*(b)* Suggest why the initial rate of the reaction was measured in each case. *(2 marks)*

*(c)* Explain:
(i) the shape of curve **A**; *(2 marks)*
(ii) the difference between the shapes of curve **B** and curve **C**. *(2 marks)*

*(d)* (i) Explain what is meant by the **induced fit** model of enzyme action. *(1 mark)*

(ii) Suggest how this may provide a better explanation for the effects of a non-competitive inhibitor than the **lock and key** model. *(1 mark)*

The thermostability of enzymes is important in industrial use. One such enzyme is papain. The table compares the thermostability of the enzyme papain in soluble and in immobilized forms.

| Temperature/°C | Rate of reaction compared with rate at 25°C/% | |
|---|---|---|
| | Soluble | Immobilized |
| 30 | 100 | 100 |
| 40 | 100 | 100 |
| 50 | 90 | 100 |
| 60 | 78 | 90 |
| 70 | 38 | 78 |
| 80 | 10 | 50 |

*(e)* Explain in terms of protein structure why enzymes are inactivated at high temperatures. *(3 marks)*

*(f)* Give evidence from the table which suggests that thermostability of papain is increased by immobilizing it. *(1 mark)*

(g) Briefly describe **one** method that might have been used to immobilize the enzyme. (*1 mark*)

(h) Briefly describe a method that you might use in the laboratory to measure the thermostability of a **named** enzyme. (*4 marks*)

(*Total 20 marks*)

*AEB Summer 1996, Module Paper 1, No. 4*

The effect of different concentrations of substrate the rate of an enzyme-catalysed reaction was vestigated. The experiment was then repeated using e same experimental conditions and substrate ncentrations but in the presence of a fixed amount compound **A** (0.2 mM). The results are shown in e following graph.

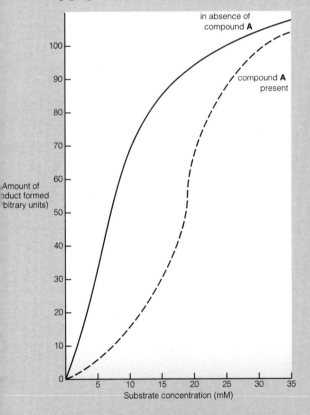

(a) Comment on the relationship between the reaction rate and substrate concentration when
   (i) no compound **A** was present, (*3 marks*)
   (ii) compound **A** was present. (*3 marks*)

(b) How may the experimental results be explained
   (i) in absence of compound **A**, (*4 marks*)
   (ii) when compound **A** is present? (*3 marks*)

(c) What might be the effect of using 0.4 mM of compound **A** in the investigation? (*2 marks*)

(d) Suggest why compounds with similar properties to compound **A** are often used to combat bacterial infections in the body. (*3 marks*)

(*Total 18 marks*)

*Oxford & Cambridge June 1996, Paper 1, No. 5*

4. Amylase is an enzyme which breaks down starch. The effect of pH on its activity can be investigated by using a starch agar plate as shown in the diagram. Circular wells were cut into the starch agar plate using a cork borer. Six outer wells were set up, each containing the same concentration and volume of amylase and a solution of different pH.

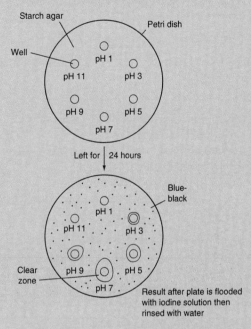

Result after plate is flooded with iodine solution then rinsed with water

(a) Explain how you could use these results to compare the activity of the enzyme at different pH values. (*1 mark*)

(b) Explain the result obtained at pH 7. (*1 mark*)

(c) Using your knowledge of enzyme structure, explain the result obtained at pH 11. (*2 marks*)

(d) Describe the control that would be necessary for this investigation. (*2 marks*)

(*Total 6 marks*)

*NEAB June 1995, BY01, No. 6*

5. The diagram shows the structure of the enzyme ribonuclease which breaks down RNA.

(a) List **three** structural features represented in the diagram that are common to all enzymes. *(3 marks)*

(b) Ribonuclease becomes inactivated when treated with mercaptoethanol solution. The diagram shows the effect of adding this solution to ribonuclease.

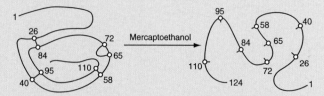

Use this information to describe why ribonuclease becomes inactive. *(3 marks)*

(c) What is meant by
   (i)   competitive inhibition:
   (ii)  non-competitive inhibition? *(4 marks)*
*(Total 10 marks)*

*NEAB June 1996, Paper 1, No. 12*

6. The graphs below show the relationship between pH and the relative activity of three different protein digesting enzymes: trypsin, pepsin and papain.

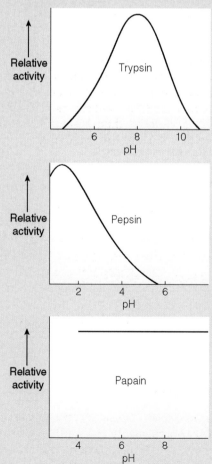

(a) Explain why changes in pH usually affect the activity of enzymes. *(3 marks)*

(b) Comment on the effects of changes in pH on the activity of trypsin, pepsin and papain. *(4 marks)*

(c) Which of these three enzymes would be most suitable to use as a meat tenderizer? Give an explanation for your answer. *(2 marks)*

(d) Rennin, an enzyme extracted from the stomach of calves, is used in the manufacture of cheese. Maxiren®, an enzyme similar to rennin, is produced by gene technology.

State **two** advantages of using Maxiren® instead of rennin in cheese manufacture. *(2 marks)*
*(Total 11 marks)*

*ULEAC, January 1996, B/HB1, No.*

7.  (a) Explain how the following are related to the protein structure of enzymes:
     (i)   the effect of high temperature on an enzyme-catalysed reaction;
     (ii)  substrate specificity;
     (iii) the effect of inhibitors. *(10 marks)*

   (b) Suggest a simple method by which you could find out whether an enzyme-catalysed reaction is being inhibited by a competitive or a non-competitive inhibitor. *(2 marks)*
*(Total 12 marks)*

*NEAB June 1997, Paper BY01, No.*

8. The diagram shows a metabolic pathway in which substrate **A** is converted, with the aid of enzymes, to the end-product **D**.

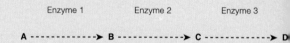

(a) Giving an explanation for your answers, suggest what would happen to the rate of production of the end-product **D** if:
     (i)   the concentration of substrate **A** were reduced; *(1 mark)*
     (ii)  the concentration of enzyme **1** were increased but the concentrations of the other enzymes remained constant. *(1 mark)*

(b) Suggest how molecule **D** could act as an **end-product inhibitor**. *(2 marks)*
*(Total 4 marks)*

*AEB June 1998, (AS) Paper 1, No.*

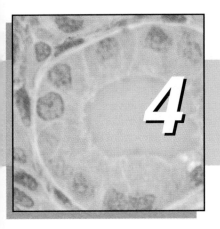

# 4 Cellular organization

The cell is the fundamental unit of life. All organisms, whatever their type or size, are composed of cells. The modern theory of cellular organization states that:

**1.** All living organisms are composed of cells.

**2.** All new cells are derived from other cells.

**3.** Cells contain the hereditary material of an organism which is passed from parent to daughter cells.

**4.** All metabolic processes take place within cells.

## 4.1 Cytology – the study of cells

All cells are self-contained and more or less self-sufficient units. They are surrounded by a cell membrane and have a nucleus, or a nuclear area, at some stage of their existence. Cells show remarkable diversity, both in structure and function. They are basically spherical in shape, although there is some variation where they are modified to suit their function. Cell sizes normally range from 10 to 30 $\mu$m.

### 4.1.1 The structure of prokaryotic cells

Prokaryotic cells (*pro* – 'before', *karyo* – 'nucleus') were probably the first forms of life on earth. Their hereditary material, DNA, is not enclosed within a nuclear membrane. This absence of a true nucleus only occurs in two groups, the bacteria and the blue-green bacteria (Section 5.3). There are no membrane-bound organelles within a prokaryotic cell, the structure of which is shown in Fig. 4.1.

### 4.1.2 Structure of the eukaryotic cell

Eukaryotic cells (*eu* – 'true', *karyo* – 'nucleus') probably arose a little over 1000 million years ago, nearly 2500 million years after their prokaryotic ancestors. The development of eukaryotic cells from prokaryotic ones involved considerable changes, as can be seen from Table 4.1. The essential change was the development of membrane-bound organelles, such as mitochondria and

**TABLE 4.1 Comparison of prokaryotic and eukaryotic cells**

| Prokaryotic cells | Eukaryotic cells |
| --- | --- |
| No distinct nucleus; only diffuse area(s) of nucleoplasm with no nuclear membrane | A distinct, membrane-bound nucleus |
| No chromosomes – circular strands of DNA | Chromosomes present on which DNA is located |
| No membrane-bound organelles such as chloroplasts and mitochondria | Chloroplasts and mitochondria may be present |
| Ribosomes are smaller | Ribosomes are larger |
| Flagella (if present) lack internal 9 + 2 fibril arrangement | Flagella have 9 + 2 internal fibril arrangement |
| No mitosis or meiosis occurs | Mitosis and/or meiosis occurs |

# NOTEBOOK

## Microscopy

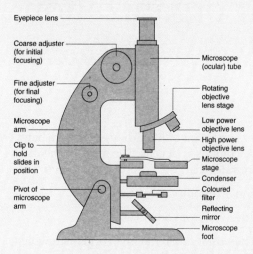

*Fig. 1 The compound light microscope*

Eyepiece lens

Coarse adjuster (for initial focusing)

Fine adjuster (for final focusing)

Microscope arm

Clip to hold slides in position

Pivot of microscope arm

Microscope (ocular) tube

Rotating objective lens stage

Low power objective lens

High power objective lens

Microscope stage

Condenser

Coloured filter

Reflecting mirror

Microscope foot

**Comparison of advantages and disadvantages of the light and electron microscopes**

| LIGHT MICROSCOPE | ELECTRON MICROSCOPE |
|---|---|
| **Advantages** | **Disadvantages** |
| Cheap to purchase and operate | Expensive to purchase and operate |
| Small and portable – can be used almost anywhere | Very large and must be operated in special rooms |
| Unaffected by magnetic fields | Affected by magnetic fields |
| Preparation of material is relatively quick and simple, requiring only a little expertise | Preparation of material is lengthy and requires considerable expertise and sometimes complex equipment |
| Material rarely distorted by preparation | Preparation of material may distort it |
| Natural colour of the material can be observed | All images are in black and white |
| **Disadvantages** | **Advantages** |
| Magnifies objects up to 2000× | Magnifies objects over 500 000× |
| The depth of field is restricted | It is possible to investigate a greater depth of field |

Have you ever wished you could see that little bit better – perhaps read what someone else is writing from a distance or to recognize who exactly it is in the crowd at a football match? How frustrating it can be when you can't quite make out the print of the newspaper of the person opposite you on the train. This is how early scientists must have felt when they strained their eyes to decipher the detailed structure of organisms. How they must have rejoiced at the development of first the glass lens and then the simple light microscope.

The light microscope (Fig. 1) opened up a new world of structural detail for biologists, but in time their curiosity again became thwarted because the wavelength of light limits the light microscope to distinguishing objects which are 0.2 $\mu$m or further from each other. This ability to distinguish two objects close together rather than to see them as a single image is called the resolving power or **resolution**. The poor resolving power of light microscopes could only be overcome by using a form of radiation which had a wavelength less than that of light. So in 1933 the electron microscope was developed. This instrument works on the same principles as the light microscope except that instead of light rays, with their wavelengths in the order of 500 nm, a beam of electrons wavelength 0.005 nm is used. This means that the electron microscope not only magnifies objects more, it also has a resolving power many thousands of times better than a light microscope.

Whereas the light microscope uses glass lenses to focus the light rays, the electron beam of the electron microscope is focused by means of powerful electromagnets. The image produced by the electron microscope cannot be detected directly by the naked eye. Instead, the electron beam is directed on to a screen from which black and white photographs, called **photoelectronmicrographs**, can be taken. A comparison of the radiation pathways in light and electron microscopes is given in Fig. 2.

There are two main types of electron microscope. In the **transmission electron microscope** (TEM), a beam of electrons is passed through thin, specially prepared slices of material. As the molecules in air would absorb the electrons, a vacuum has to be created within the instrument. Where electrons are absorbed by the material, and do not therefore reach the screen, the image is dark. Such areas are said to be **electron dense**. Where the electrons penetrate, the screen appears bright. These areas are termed **electron transparent**. As electrons have a very small mass, they do not easily penetrate materials and so sections need to be exceedingly thin. This sectioning creates a flat image and the natural contouring of a specimen cannot be seen. To overcome this problem, the **scanning electron microscope** (SEM) was developed. In this instrument a fine beam of electrons is passed to and fro across the specimen, beginning at one end and working across to the other. The specimen scatters many electrons, while others are absorbed. Low energy secondary electrons may be emitted by the specimen. The scattered electrons and the low energy secondary electrons are amplified and transmitted to a screen. The resultant image shows holes and depressions as dark areas and ridges and extensions of the surface as bright areas. In this way the natural contouring of the material may be observed.

ctron microscope

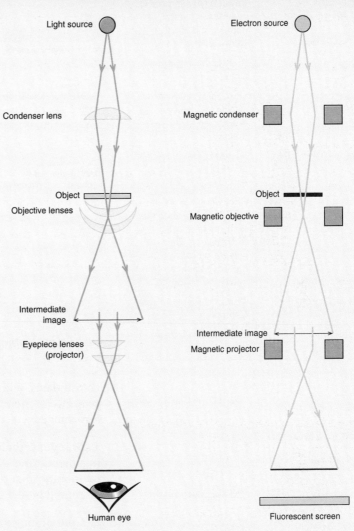

| | |
|---|---|
| Light source | Electron source |
| Condenser lens | Magnetic condenser |
| Object | Object |
| Objective lenses | Magnetic objective |
| Intermediate image | Intermediate image |
| Eyepiece lenses (projector) | Magnetic projector |
| Human eye | Fluorescent screen |

*Fig. 2 Comparison of radiation pathways in light and electron microscopes*

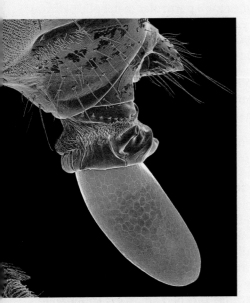

se-colour scanning electron micrograph of a fruit , *Drosophila sp.*, laying an egg. (Magnification ×80)

The problem with both these forms of electron microscope is that complex preparation techniques coupled with the need for a high vacuum means that not only must the material being observed be dehydrated and therefore dead, it is frequently considerably distorted; what you see may be very different from the original material. In response to this a new generation of electron microscopes has been developed – the environmental scanning electron microscope (ESEM). These microscopes allow the material on view to be kept at a low vacuum while the region around the electron gun is at a high vacuum. This is achieved by separating the microscope column into a series of chambers each with its own pressure. There is only a minute hole between chambers – wide enough to allow the tiny electron beam through. A special low voltage detector which can operate at low vacuums is used to detect the scattered electrons, secondary electrons and X-rays which provide the image.

TABLE 4.2  **Roles of bacterial cell components**

| Cell component | Role |
|---|---|
| Cell wall | Physical barrier, protects against mechanical damage and entry of some substances |
| Flagellum | Propels the bacterium along |
| Mesosome | Site of respiration. May also be involved in cell division and DNA uptake |
| Chromosome/DNA | Possesses the genetic information needed to replicate new cells |
| Plasmids | Circles of DNA able to replicate independently of the main circular chromosome. They possess genes which aid the survival of bacteria in adverse conditions |
| Glycogen granules | Store of carbohydrate for respiration |
| Lipid droplets | Concentrated store used in respiration |

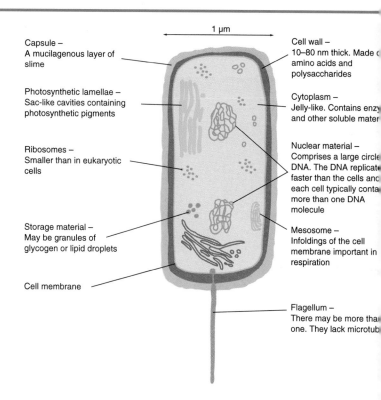

Capsule –
A mucilagenous layer of slime

Photosynthetic lamellae –
Sac-like cavities containing photosynthetic pigments

Ribosomes –
Smaller than in eukaryotic cells

Storage material –
May be granules of glycogen or lipid droplets

Cell membrane

Cell wall –
10–80 nm thick. Made o amino acids and polysaccharides

Cytoplasm –
Jelly-like. Contains enz and other soluble mater

Nuclear material –
Comprises a large circle DNA. The DNA replicate faster than the cells and each cell typically conta more than one DNA molecule

Mesosome –
Infoldings of the cell membrane important in respiration

Flagellum –
There may be more tha one. They lack microtub

*Fig. 4.1 Structure of the prokaryotic cell, e.g. a generalized bacterial c*

chloroplasts, within the outer plasma membrane of the cell. The presence of membrane-bound organelles confers four advantages:

**1.** Many metabolic processes involve enzymes being embedde in a membrane. As cells become larger, the proportion of membrane area to cell volume is reduced. This proportion is increased by the presence of organelle membranes.

**2.** Containing enzymes for a particular metabolic pathway within organelles means that the products of one reaction will always be in close proximity to the next enzyme in the sequenc The rate of metabolic reactions will thereby be increased.

**3.** The rate of any metabolic pathway inside an organelle can b controlled by regulating the rate at which the membrane surrounding the organelle allows the first reactant to enter.

**4.** Potentially harmful reactants and/or enzymes can be isolate inside an organelle so they won't damage the rest of the cell.

It is possible that such organelles arose as separate prokaryotic cells which developed a symbiotic relationship wit larger prokaryotic cells. This would explain the existence of one membraned structure inside another, the ability of mitochondri and chloroplasts to divide themselves (self-replication) and the presence of DNA within these two organelles. Alternatively, the organelles may have arisen by invaginations of the plasma membrane which became 'pinched off' to give a separate membrane-bound structure within the main cell. Although many variations of the eukaryotic cell exist, there are two main types, the plant cell and the animal cell. (See Figs. 4.2 and 4.3.)

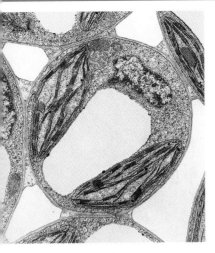

nt leaf cell (SEM) (×7700)

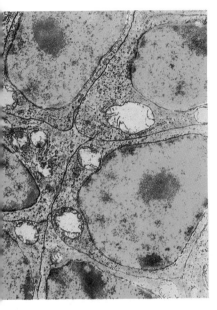

ammalian cells (SEM) (×2500)

### 4.1.3 Differences between plant and animal cells

The major differences between plant and animal cells are given in Table 4.2.

TABLE 4.3  **Differences between plant and animal cells**

| Plant cells | Animal cells |
| --- | --- |
| Tough, slightly elastic cellulose cell wall present (in addition to the cell membrane) | Cell wall absent – only a membrane surrounds the cell |
| Pits and plasmodesmata present in the cell wall | No cell wall and therefore no pits or plasmodesmata |
| Middle lamellae join cell walls of adjacent cells | Middle lamella absent – cells are joined by intercellular cement |
| Plastids, e.g. chloroplasts and leucoplasts, present in large numbers | Plastids absent |
| Mature cells normally have a large single, central vacuole filled with cell sap | Vacuoles, e.g. contractile vacuoles, if present, are small and scattered throughout the cell |
| Tonoplast present around vacuole | Tonoplast absent |
| Cytoplasm normally confined to a thin layer at the edge of the cell | Cytoplasm present throughout the cell |
| Nucleus at edge of the cell | Nucleus anywhere in the cell but often central |
| Lysosomes not normally present | Lysosomes almost always present |
| Centrioles absent in higher plants | Centrioles present |
| Cilia and flagella absent in higher plants | Cilia or flagella often present |
| Starch grains used for storage | Glycogen granules used for storage |
| Only some cells are capable of division | Almost all cells are capable of division |
| Few secretions are produced | A wide variety of secretions are produced |

# 4.2  Cell ultrastructure

### 4.2.1 Cytoplasmic matrix

All the cell organelles are contained within a cytoplasmic matrix, sometimes called the **hyaloplasm** or **cytosol**. It is an aqueous material which is a solution or colloidal suspension of many vital cellular chemicals. These include simple ions such as sodium, phosphates and chlorides, organic molecules such as amino acids, ATP and nucleotides, and storage material such as oil

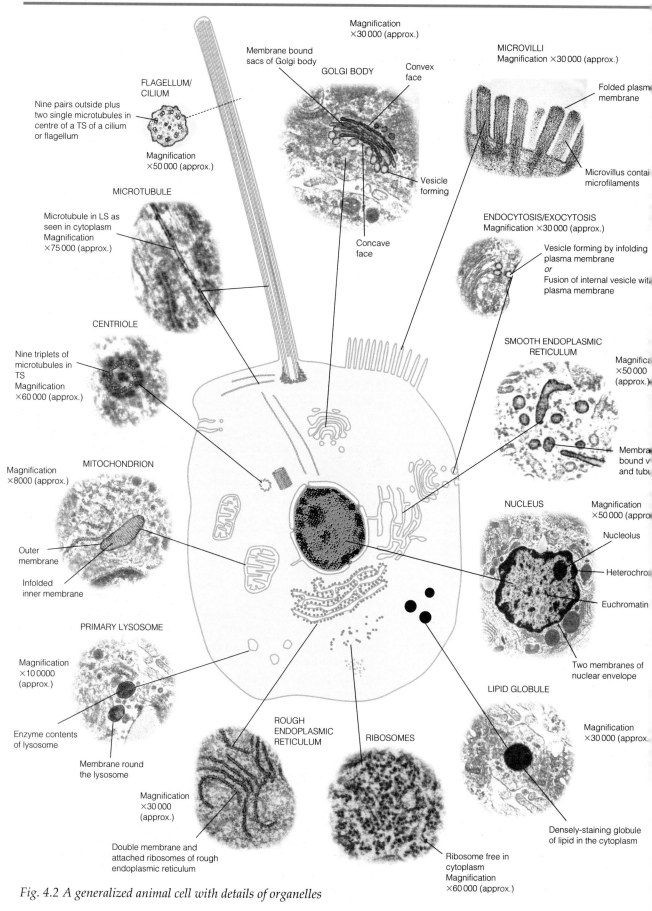

Magnification ×30 000 (approx.)

Membrane bound sacs of Golgi body

GOLGI BODY

Convex face

MICROVILLI
Magnification ×30 000 (approx.)

Folded plasma membrane

FLAGELLUM/ CILIUM

Nine pairs outside plus two single microtubules in centre of a TS of a cilium or flagellum

Magnification ×50 000 (approx.)

Vesicle forming

Microvillus contai microfilaments

Concave face

MICROTUBULE

Microtubule in LS as seen in cytoplasm Magnification ×75 000 (approx.)

ENDOCYTOSIS/EXOCYTOSIS
Magnification ×30 000 (approx.)

Vesicle forming by infolding plasma membrane
or
Fusion of internal vesicle wit plasma membrane

CENTRIOLE

Nine triplets of microtubules in TS Magnification ×60 000 (approx.)

SMOOTH ENDOPLASMIC RETICULUM

Magnifica ×50 000 (approx.)

Membra bound v and tubu

MITOCHONDRION

Magnification ×8000 (approx.)

NUCLEUS

Magnification ×50 000 (appro

Nucleolus

Outer membrane

Heterochro

Infolded inner membrane

Euchromatin

PRIMARY LYSOSOME

Two membranes of nuclear envelope

Magnification ×10 0000 (approx.)

LIPID GLOBULE

Enzyme contents of lysosome

ROUGH ENDOPLASMIC RETICULUM

RIBOSOMES

Magnification ×30 000 (approx.

Membrane round the lysosome

Magnification ×30 000 (approx.)

Densely-staining globule of lipid in the cytoplasm

Double membrane and attached ribosomes of rough endoplasmic reticulum

Ribosome free in cytoplasm Magnification ×60 000 (approx.)

*Fig. 4.2 A generalized animal cell with details of organelles*

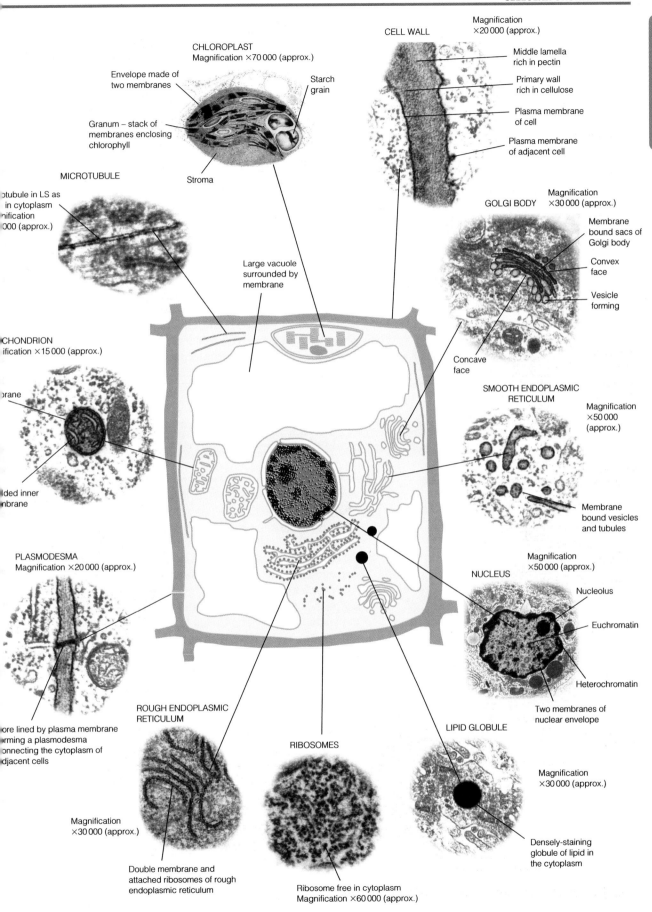

CHLOROPLAST
Magnification ×70 000 (approx.)

Envelope made of two membranes

Starch grain

Granum – stack of membranes enclosing chlorophyll

Stroma

CELL WALL

Magnification ×20 000 (approx.)

Middle lamella rich in pectin

Primary wall rich in cellulose

Plasma membrane of cell

Plasma membrane of adjacent cell

MICROTUBULE

...otubule in LS as ... in cytoplasm ...nification ...000 (approx.)

Large vacuole surrounded by membrane

GOLGI BODY

Magnification ×30 000 (approx.)

Membrane bound sacs of Golgi body

Convex face

Vesicle forming

Concave face

...CHONDRION
...ification ×15 000 (approx.)

SMOOTH ENDOPLASMIC RETICULUM

Magnification ×50 000 (approx.)

...brane

...ded inner ...nbrane

Membrane bound vesicles and tubules

PLASMODESMA
Magnification ×20 000 (approx.)

Magnification ×50 000 (approx.)

NUCLEUS

Nucleolus

Euchromatin

Heterochromatin

Two membranes of nuclear envelope

...ore lined by plasma membrane ...rming a plasmodesma ...onnecting the cytoplasm of ...djacent cells

ROUGH ENDOPLASMIC RETICULUM

RIBOSOMES

LIPID GLOBULE

Magnification ×30 000 (approx.)

Densely-staining globule of lipid in the cytoplasm

Magnification ×30 000 (approx.)

Double membrane and attached ribosomes of rough endoplasmic reticulum

Ribosome free in cytoplasm
Magnification ×60 000 (approx.)

*g. 4.3 A generalized plant cell with detail of organelles*

53

droplets. Many important biochemical processes, including glycolysis, occur within the cytoplasm. It is not static but capab of mass flow, which is called **cytoplasmic streaming**.

### 4.2.2 Cell membrane

The cell membrane's main function is to serve as a boundary between the cell and its environment. It is not, however, inert but a functional organelle. It may permanently exclude certain substances from the cell while permanently retaining others. Some substances may pass freely in and out through the membrane. Yet others may be excluded at one moment only to pass freely across the membrane on another occasion. On account of the membrane's ability to permit different substance to pass across it at different rates, it is said to be **partially permeable**.

There is little dispute that the cell membrane is made up almost entirely of two chemical groups – proteins and phospholipids. In 1972, J. J. Singer and G. L. Nicholson suggest a structure for the cell membrane. There is a bimolecular phospholipid layer with inwardly directed hydrophobic tails and a variety of protein molecules with an irregular arrangeme (Fig. 4.4). Some proteins occur on the surface of the phospholip

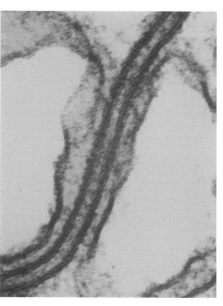

Cell membrane (×12000)

## NOTEBOOK

### Cell fractionation and centrifugation

A centrifuge used to separate blood components

If you shake up particles of different sizes within a liquid such as water and leave them to settle, they separate out – the largest and heaviest at the bottom and the smallest and lightest at the top. The same principle can be applied to separate out the various components of cells. Dividing the cell into its parts (or fractions) is called **cell fractionation** and is achieved by the process of **centrifugation** using a **centrifuge**.

A centrifuge is a machine which can spin tubes containing liqui suspensions at a very high speed. The effect is to exert a force on the contents of the tube similar to, but much greater than, that of gravity. The faster the speed and the longer the time for which the tubes are spun, the greater the force. At slower speeds (less force the larger fragments collect at the bottom of the tube and the smal ones remain in suspension in the liquid near the top of the tube – **supernatant liquid**. If the larger fragments are removed and the supernatant recentrifuged at a faster speed (more force), the large of these smaller fragments will collect at the bottom. By continuing this way, smaller and smaller fragments may be recovered. As the size of any organelle is relatively constant, each organelle will tend to separate from the supernatant at a specific speed of rotation. If the suspension of cell fragments is spun at a slower speed than tha required to separate out a particular organelle, all larger fragments and organelles can be collected and discarded. Spinning the supernatant at the appropriate speed will now cause a new fraction to be collected. This fraction will be a relatively pure sample of the required organelles. Since the process involves centrifuging at different speeds, it is called **differential centrifugation**.

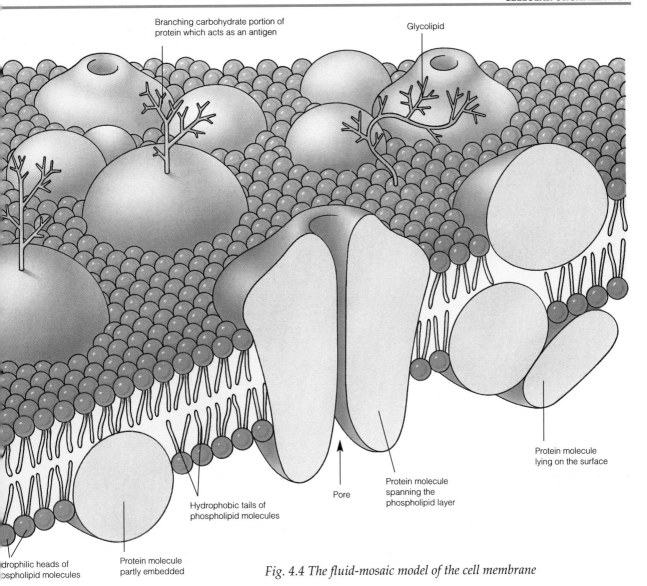

Branching carbohydrate portion of protein which acts as an antigen

Glycolipid

Protein molecule lying on the surface

Protein molecule spanning the phospholipid layer

Pore

Hydrophobic tails of phospholipid molecules

drophilic heads of ospholipid molecules

Protein molecule partly embedded

*Fig. 4.4 The fluid-mosaic model of the cell membrane*

BLE 4.4   **Functions of components of the cell embrane**

| Membrane component | Function |
|---|---|
| Phospholipids | Affect the fluidity and permeability of the membrane |
| Cholesterol | Make the membrane less fluid at higher temperatures but more fluid at lower ones |
| Glycolipids | Act as recognition sites, e.g. the human ABO blood system is the result of different glycolipids on the cell membrane of red blood cells. Also help to make the membrane more stable |
| Proteins | Provide structural support for the membrane. Assist the active transport of materials across the membrane. Act as recognition sites. Act as enzymes, energy transducers and electron carriers |
| Glycoproteins | Also act as recognition sites, e.g. for neurotransmitters and hormones |

layer (**peripheral** or **extrinsic proteins**) while others extend into it (**integral** or **intrinsic proteins**) and some even extend completely across (**transmembrane proteins**). Viewed from the surface, the proteins are dotted throughout the phospholipid layer in a mosaic arrangement. Other research suggests that the phospholipid layer is capable of much movement, i.e. is fluid. It was these facts that gave rise to its name, the **fluid-mosaic model**. Also present in the membrane is cholesterol, which interacts with the phospholipids to make the membrane less fluid.

The proteins in the membrane have a number of functions. Apart from giving structural support they are very specific, varying from cell to cell. It is this specificity which allows cells to be recognized by other agents in the body, e.g. enzymes, hormones and antibodies. In the fluid-mosaic model it is thought probable that the proteins also assist the active transport of materials across the membrane.

# MEMBRANOUS ORGANELLES

### 4.2.3 The nucleus

When viewed under a microscope, the most prominent feature of a cell is the nucleus. While its shape, size, position and chemical composition vary from cell to cell, its functions are always the same, namely, to control the cell's activity and to retain the organism's hereditary material, the chromosomes. It is bounded by a double membrane, the **nuclear envelope**, the outer membrane being continuous with the endoplasmic reticulum and often having ribosomes on its surface. The inner membrane has three proteins on its surface which act as anchoring points for chromosomes during interphase (see Section 8.2). It possesses many large pores (typically 3000 per nucleus) 40–100 nm in diameter, which permit the passage of large molecules, such as RNA, between it and the cytoplasm. The cytoplasm-like material within the nucleus is called **nucleoplasm**. It contains **chromatin** which is made up of coils of DNA bound to proteins. During division the chromatin condenses to form the chromosomes but these are rarely, if ever, visible in a non-dividing cell. The denser, more darkly staining areas of chromatin are called **heterochromatin**.

Within the nucleus are one or two small spherical bodies, each called a **nucleolus**. They are not distinct organelles as they are not bounded by a membrane. They manufacture ribosomal RNA, a substance in which they are especially rich, and assemble ribosomes.

The functions of a nucleus are:

**1.** To contain the genetic material of a cell in the form of chromosomes.

**2.** To act as a control centre for the activities of a cell.

**3.** To carry the instructions for the synthesis of proteins in the nuclear DNA.

**4.** To be involved in the production of ribosomes and RNA.

**5.** In cell division.

### 4.2.4 The chloroplast

Chloroplasts belong to a larger group of organelles known as **plastids**. In higher plants most chloroplasts are 5–10 $\mu$m long and are bounded by a double membrane, the **chloroplast envelope**, about 30 nm thick. While the outer membrane has a similar structure to the plasma membrane, the inner one is folded into a series of lamellae and is highly selective in what it allows in and out of the chloroplast.

Within the chloroplast envelope are two distinct regions. The **stroma** is a colourless, gelatinous matrix in which are embedded structures rather like stacks of coins in appearance. These are the **grana**. Each granum, and there may be around 50 in a chloroplast, is made up of between 2 and 100 closed flattened sacs called **thylakoids**. Within these are located the photosynthetic pigments such as chlorophyll, details of which are given in Section 14.2.2. Some thylakoids have tubular extensions which interconnect adjacent grana (Figs. 4.5 and 4.6).

Liver cell nucleus (TEM)

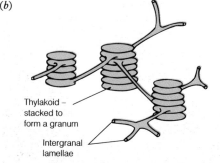

(*a*)

Chloroplast envelope comprising inner and outer membranes

Starch grain – stores photosynthetic products

Ribosomes – small (70S) type

Stroma

Oil droplet

Chloroplast DNA – circular formation

Large thylakoid, connecting grana (= intergranal lamellae)

Thylakoid – stacked together to form a granum. Containing photosynthetic pigments

(*b*)

Thylakoid – stacked to form a granum

Intergranal lamellae

*Fig. 4.5 Structure of the chloroplasts*

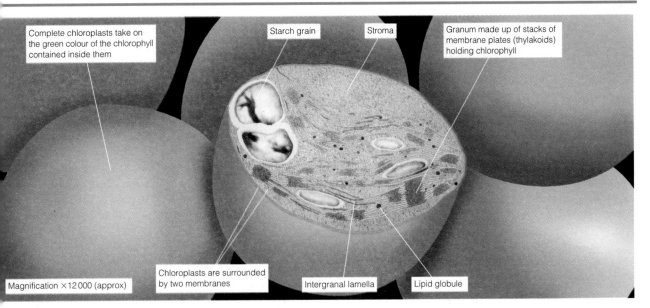

Complete chloroplasts take on the green colour of the chlorophyll contained inside them

Starch grain

Stroma

Granum made up of stacks of membrane plates (thylakoids) holding chlorophyll

Magnification ×12 000 (approx)

Chloroplasts are surrounded by two membranes

Intergranal lamella

Lipid globule

*ig. 4.6 Chloroplasts*

Also present within the stroma are a series of starch grains which act as temporary stores for the products of photosynthesis. A number of smaller granules within the stroma readily take up osmium salts during the preparation of material for the electron microscope. They are called **osmiophilic granules** (*osmio* – 'osmium', *philo* – 'liking') but their function is not yet clear. A small amount of DNA is always present within the stroma, as are oil droplets.

### 4.2.5 The mitochondrion

Mitochondria (Fig. 4.7) are found within the cytoplasm of all eukaryotic cells, although in highly specialized cells such as mature red blood cells they may be absent. They range in shape from spherical to highly elongated and are typically 5 $\mu$m in length and 0.2 $\mu$m across. They are bounded by a double membrane, the outer of which controls the entry and exit of chemicals. The inner membrane is folded inwards, giving rise to

*ig. 4.7 Mitochondria*

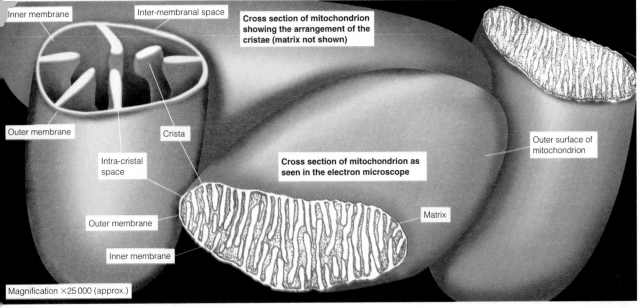

Inner membrane

Inter-membranal space

Cross section of mitochondrion showing the arrangement of the cristae (matrix not shown)

Outer membrane

Crista

Outer surface of mitochondrion

Intra-cristal space

Cross section of mitochondrion as seen in the electron microscope

Outer membrane

Matrix

Inner membrane

Magnification ×25 000 (approx.)

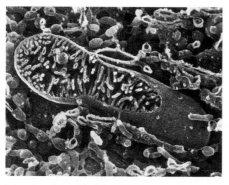

Mitochondrion (EM) (×15 000 approx.)

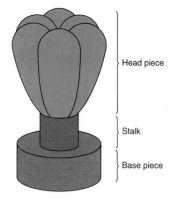

*Fig. 4.8 Structure of a stalked granule*

Head piece

Stalk

Base piece

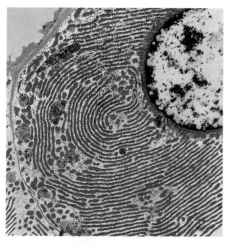

Endoplasmic reticulum (EM) (×94 000 approx.)

extensions called **cristae**, some of which extend across the entire organelle. They function to increase the surface area on which respiratory processes take place. The surface of these cristae has stalked granules along its length (Fig. 4.8).

The remainder of the mitochondrion is the **matrix**. It is a semi rigid material containing protein, lipids and traces of DNA. Electron-dense granules of 25 nm diameter also occur.

Mitochondria function as sites for certain stages of respiration details of which are given in Section 16.4.1. The number of mitochondria in a cell therefore varies with its metabolic activity Highly active cells may possess up to 1000. Similarly the number of cristae increases in metabolically active cells, giving weight to the proposition that respiratory enzymes are located on them.

### 4.2.6 Endoplasmic reticulum

The endoplasmic reticulum (ER) is an elaborate system of membranes found throughout the cell, forming a cytoplasmic skeleton. It is an extension of the outer nuclear membrane with which it is continuous. The membranes form a series of sheets which enclose flattened sacs called **cisternae** (Fig. 4.9). Its structure varies from cell to cell and can probably change its nature rapidly; the membranes of the ER may be loosely organized or tightly packed. Where the membranes are lined with ribosomes they are called **rough endoplasmic reticulum**. The rough ER is concerned with protein synthesis (Section 7.6) and is consequently most abundant in those cells which are rapidly growing or secrete enzymes. In the same way, damage to a cell often results in increased formation of ER in order to produce the proteins necessary for the cell's repair. Where the membranes lack ribosomes they are called **smooth endoplasmic reticulum**. The smooth ER is concerned with lipid synthesis and is consequently most abundant in those cells producing lipid-related secretions, e.g. the sebaceous glands of mammalian skin and cells secreting steroids.

The functions of the ER may thus be summarized as:

1. Providing a large surface area for chemical reactions.

2. Providing a pathway for the transport of materials through the cell.

3. Producing proteins, especially enzymes (rough ER).

4. Producing lipids and steroids (smooth ER).

5. Collecting and storing synthesized material.

6. Providing a structural skeleton to maintain cellular shape (e.g. the smooth ER of a rod cell from the retina of the eye).

### 4.2.7 Golgi apparatus (dictyosome)

The Golgi apparatus, named after its discoverer Camillo Golgi, has a similar structure to the smooth endoplasmic reticulum but is more compact. It is composed of stacks of flattened sacs made of membranes. The sacs are fluid-filled and pinch off smaller

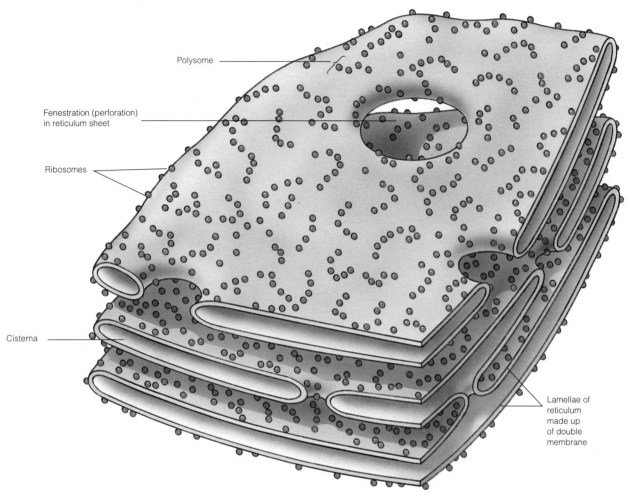

Polysome

Fenestration (perforation)
in reticulum sheet

Ribosomes

Cisterna

Lamellae of
reticulum
made up
of double
membrane

*Fig. 4.9 Structure of rough endoplasmic reticulum*

membranous sacs, called **vesicles**, at their ends. There is normally only one Golgi apparatus in each animal cell but in plant cells there may be a large number of stacks known as **dictyosomes**. The position and size of the Golgi apparatus varies from cell to cell but it is well developed in secretory cells and neurones and is small in muscle cells. All proteins produced by the endoplasmic reticulum are passed through the Golgi apparatus in a strict sequence (see Fig. 4.10). They pass first through the *cis*-Golgi network, which returns to the ER any proteins wrongly exported by it. They then pass through the stack of cisternae, which modify the proteins and lipids undergoing transport and add labels which allow them to be identified and sorted at the next stage, the *trans*-Golgi network. Here the proteins and lipids are sorted and sent to their final destinations. In general, the Golgi acts as the cell's post office, receiving, sorting and delivering proteins and lipids. More specifically its functions include:

**1.** Producing glycoproteins such as mucin required in secretions, by adding the carbohydrate part to the protein.

**2.** Producing secretory enzymes, e.g. the digestive enzymes of the pancreas.

**3.** Secreting carbohydrates such as those involved in the production of new cell walls.

4. Transporting and storing lipids.

5. Forming lysosomes as described in Section 4.2.8.

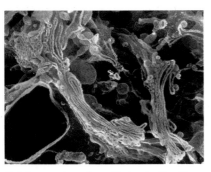

Golgi apparatus of an olfactory bulb cell

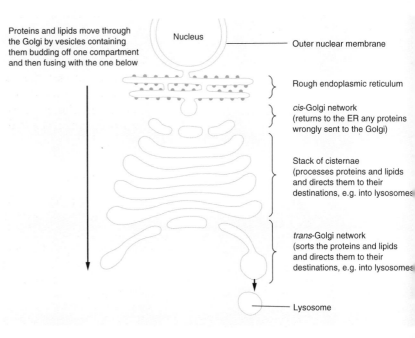

Proteins and lipids move through the Golgi by vesicles containing them budding off one compartment and then fusing with the one below

Nucleus

Outer nuclear membrane

Rough endoplasmic reticulum

*cis*-Golgi network
(returns to the ER any proteins wrongly sent to the Golgi)

Stack of cisternae
(processes proteins and lipids and directs them to their destinations, e.g. into lysosomes)

*trans*-Golgi network
(sorts the proteins and lipids and directs them to their destinations, e.g. into lysosomes)

Lysosome

*Fig. 4.10 The Golgi apparatus and its relationship to the nucleus, endoplasmic reticulum and lysosomes*

### 4.2.8 Lysosomes

Lysosomes (*lysis* – 'splitting', *soma* – 'body') are spherical bodies some 0.1–1.0 $\mu$m in diameter. They contain around 50 enzymes, mostly hydrolases, in acid solution. They isolate these enzymes from the remainder of the cell and by so doing prevent them from acting upon other chemicals and organelles within the cell.

The functions of lysosomes are:

1. To digest material which the cell consumes from the environment. In the case of white blood cells, this may be bacteria or other harmful material. In protozoa, it is the food which has been consumed by phagocytosis. In either case the material is broken down within the lysosome, useful chemicals are absorbed into the cytoplasm and any debris is egested by the cell by exocytosis (Fig. 4.11).

2. To digest parts of the cell, such as worn-out organelles, in a similar way to that described in 1. This is known as **autophagy**. After the death of the cell, the lysosomes are responsible for its complete breakdown, a process called **autolysis** (*auto* – 'self', *lysis* – 'splitting').

3. To release their enzymes outside the cell (**exocytosis**) in order to break down other cells, e.g. in the reabsorption of tadpole tail during metamorphosis.

In view of their functions, it is hardly surprising that lysosomes are especially abundant in secretory cells and in phagocytic white blood cells.

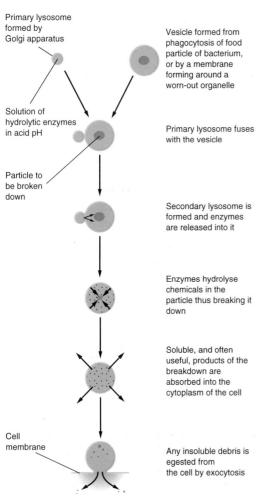

Primary lysosome formed by Golgi apparatus

Vesicle formed from phagocytosis of food particle of bacterium, or by a membrane forming around a worn-out organelle

Solution of hydrolytic enzymes in acid pH

Primary lysosome fuses with the vesicle

Particle to be broken down

Secondary lysosome is formed and enzymes are released into it

Enzymes hydrolyse chemicals in the particle thus breaking it down

Soluble, and often useful, products of the breakdown are absorbed into the cytoplasm of the cell

Cell membrane

Any insoluble debris is egested from the cell by exocytosis

*Fig. 4.11 The functioning of a lysosome*

### 4.2.9 Microbodies (peroxisomes)

Microbodies are small spherical membrane-bound bodies between 0.5 and 1.5 $\mu$m in diameter. Apart from being slightly granular, they have no internal structure. They contain a number of metabolically important enzymes, in particular the enzyme catalase, which catalyses the breakdown of hydrogen peroxide. Hence these microbodies are sometimes called peroxisomes.

Hydrogen peroxide is a potentially toxic by-product of many biochemical reactions within organisms. Peroxisomes containing catalase are therefore particularly numerous in actively metabolizing cells like those of the liver.

$$2H_2O_2 \xrightarrow{\text{catalase}} 2H_2O + O_2$$

Hydrogen peroxide      Water   Oxygen

### 4.2.10 Vacuoles

A fluid-filled sac bounded by a single membrane may be termed a vacuole. Within mature plant cells there is usually one large central vacuole. The single membrane around it is called the **tonoplast**. A plant vacuole contains a solution of mineral salts, sugars, amino acids, wastes (e.g. tannins) and sometimes also pigments such as **anthocyanins**.

Plant vacuoles serve a variety of functions:

1. The sugars and amino acids may act as a temporary food store.

2. The anthocyanins are of various colours and so may colour petals to attract pollinating insects, or fruits to attract animals for dispersal.

3. They act as temporary stores for organic wastes, such as tannins. These may accumulate in the vacuoles of leaf cells and are removed when the leaves fall.

4. They occasionally contain hydrolytic enzymes and so perform functions similar to those of lysosomes (Section 4.2.8).

5. They support herbaceous plants and herbaceous parts of woody plants by providing an osmotic system which creates a pressure potential (Section 22.3).

In animal cells, vacuoles are much smaller but may occur in larger numbers. Common types include food vacuoles, phagocytic vacuoles and contractile vacuoles. The latter are important in the osmoregulation of certain protozoans.

## NON-MEMBRANOUS STRUCTURES

### 4.2.11 Ribosomes

Ribosomes are small cytoplasmic granules found in all cells. They are around 20 nm in diameter in eukaryotic cells (80S type) but slightly smaller in prokaryotic cells (70S type). They may occur in groups called **polysomes** and may be associated with endoplasmic reticulum or occur freely within the cytoplasm. Despite their small size, their enormous numbers mean that they can account for up to 20% of the mass of a cell.

### PROJECT

1. Use eye-piece and stage micrometers to measure the thicknesses of various coloured hairs from the heads of your colleagues.

2. Examine a selection of light and electron micrographs of similar structures. List the similarities and differences.

3. (a) Examine electron micrographs of a selection of animal and plant cells where the magnifications are given.
   (b) Measure and calculate the mean sizes of a variety of organelles, e.g. nuclei, mitochondria, etc.
   (c) Are there any differences in the mean sizes of the organelles in animal and plant cells?

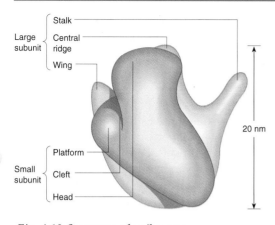

Fig. 4.12 Structure of a ribosome

Ribosomes are made up of one large and one small subunit (Fig. 4.12), and comprise RNA, known as **ribosomal RNA**, and protein. They are important in the synthesis of proteins, where they move along messenger RNA in succession (see Section 7.6).

### 4.2.12 Storage granules

Every cell contains a limited store of food energy. This store may be in the form of soluble material such as the sugar found in the vacuoles of plant cells. It may also occur in insoluble form, as grains or granules, within cells or organelles.

**Starch grains** occur within chloroplasts and the cytoplasm of plant cells. Starch may also be stored in specialized leucoplasts called amyloplasts. **Glycogen granules** occur throughout the cytoplasm of animal cells. They store animal starch or glycogen. **Oil or lipid droplets** are found within the cytoplasm of both plant and animal cells.

### 4.2.13 Microtubules

Microtubules occur widely throughout eukaryotic cells but are not found in prokaryotic ones. They are slender, unbranched tubes 24 nm in diameter and up to several microns in length. They are made of two similar proteins **alpha- and beta-tubulin**, each of which comprises 450 amino acids. The arrangement of these proteins is shown in Fig. 4.13.

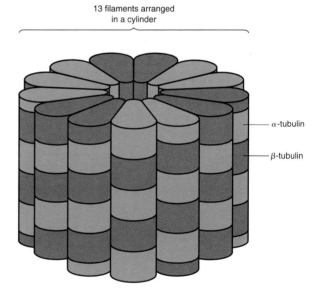

Fig. 4.13 Arrangement of alpha- and beta-tubulin within a microtubule

The functions of microtubules are:

**1.** To provide an internal skeleton (**cytoskeleton**) for cells and so help determine their shape.

**2.** To aid transport within cells by providing routes along which materials move.

**3.** To form a framework along which the cellulose cell wall of plants is laid down.

**4.** As major components of cilia and flagella. The microtubules are grouped in a very precise way (Fig. 4.14) and contribute to movement.

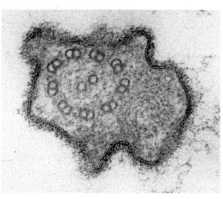

Flagellum (EM) (×90 000 approx.)

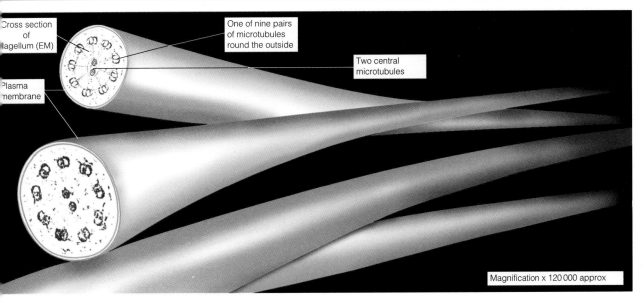

Cross section of flagellum (EM)

One of nine pairs of microtubules round the outside

Two central microtubules

Plasma membrane

Magnification x 120 000 approx

*g. 4.14 Flagella*

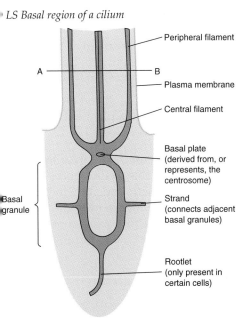

*LS Basal region of a cilium*

Peripheral filament

A — — B

Plasma membrane

Central filament

Basal plate (derived from, or represents, the centrosome)

Strand (connects adjacent basal granules)

Basal granule

Rootlet (only present in certain cells)

*TS Cilium (Section A/B)*

Extension of paired peripheral filaments – increasingly well developed towards the base of the cilium

One of nine paired peripheral filaments

Plasma membrane

One of two central filaments (present only in motile cilia)

*ig. 4.15 Structure of a cilium*

**5.** In the spindle during cell division and within the centrioles from which the spindle is formed, they help to draw chromosomes or chromatids to opposite poles (see Chapter 8).

### 4.2.14 Cilia and flagella

Cilia and flagella are almost identical, except that cilia are usually shorter and more numerous. Both are around 0.2 $\mu$m in diameter; cilia are up to 25 $\mu$m long whereas flagella may be 1000 $\mu$m long. They are found in a limited number of cells but are nevertheless of great importance. The structure of a cilium is shown in Fig. 4.15. They function to either move an entire organism, e.g. cilia on the protozoan *Paramecium*, or to move material within an organism, e.g. the cilia lining the respiratory tract move mucus towards the throat. In the human respiratory tract there are around 200 cilia (each 7 $\mu$m long) on each epithelial cell, giving a density of $10^9$ cilia per cm$^2$.

### 4.2.15 Centrioles

Centrioles have the same basic structure as the basal bodies of cilia. They are hollow cylinders about 0.2 $\mu$m in diameter. They arise in a distinct region of the cytoplasm known as the **centrosome**. It contains two centrioles. At cell division the centrioles migrate to opposite poles of the cell where they synthesize the microtubules of the spindle. Despite the absence of centrioles, the cells of higher plants do form spindles.

### 4.2.16 Microfilaments

Microfilaments are very thin strands about 6 nm in diameter. They are usually made up of the protein actin, although a smaller proportion are made of myosin. As these are the two proteins involved in muscle contraction, it seems probable that microfilaments play a role in movement within cells, and possibly of the cells as a whole in some cases.

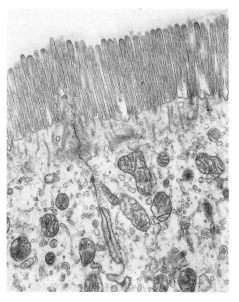

Microvilli (EM) (×10 000 approx.)

### 4.2.17 Microvilli

Microvilli are tiny finger-like projections about 0.6 $\mu$m in length on the membranes of certain cells, such as those of the intestinal epithelium and the kidney tubule. They should not be confused with the much larger villi which are multicellular structures. Microvilli massed together appear under a microscope similar to the bristles of a brush, hence the term **brush border** given to the edge of cells bearing microvilli. Actin filaments within the microvilli allow them to contract, which, along with their large surface area, facilitates absorption.

### 4.2.18 Cellulose cell wall

A cell wall is a characteristic feature of plant cells. It consists of cellulose microfibrils embedded in an amorphous polysaccharide matrix. The structure and properties of cellulose are discussed in Section 2.5.3 and the detailed structure of a cellulose microfibril is given in Fig. 4.16. The matrix is usually composed of polysaccharides, e.g. pectin or lignin. The microfibrils may be regular or irregular in arrangement.

The main functions of the cell wall are:

**1.** To provide support in herbaceous plants. As water enters the cell osmotically, the cell wall resists expansion and an internal pressure is created which provides turgidity for the plant.

**2.** To give direct support to the cell and the plant as a whole by providing mechanical strength. The strength may be increased by the presence of lignin in the matrix between the cellulose fibres.

**3.** To permit the movement of water through and along it and so contribute to the movement of water in the plant as a whole, in particular in the cortex of the root.

**4.** In some cell walls the presence of cutin, suberin or lignin in the matrix makes the cells less permeable to substances. Lignin helps to keep the water within the xylem, and cutin in the epidermis of leaves prevents water being lost from the plant. Suberin in root endodermal cells prevents movement of water across them, thus concentrating its movement through special passage cells.

*Fig. 4.16 Structure of a cellulose microfibril*

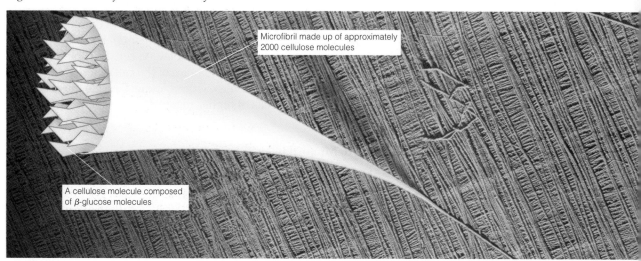

Microfibril made up of approximately 2000 cellulose molecules

A cellulose molecule composed of $\beta$-glucose molecules

## BIOLOGY AROUND US

# Cellulose and paper

Cotton plants ready for harvesting

Cellulose is a polysaccharide made up of several thousand glucose units linked together in long chains by $\beta$-1,4 links. As the major constituent of plant cell walls, cellulose is a readily available and renewable raw material. Although its most important use is in the manufacture of paper, cellulose is also the main component of many other household goods. The seed hairs of the cotton plant (*Gossypium*) are almost pure cellulose and their natural twist makes them easy to spin for use in a variety of textiles from clothes to curtains. Other products using cellulose are derived from various plants, e.g. linen from flax (*Linum usitatissimum*) and rattan furniture from the stems of an Asian climbing plant.

Cellulose can be processed to form an even wider range of products, such as thickeners in paints, stabilizers in foods and cosmetics, cellophane, adhesive tape and materials for dialysis membranes.

Paper making began in China in about AD 100 using hemp and flax but it was not until the eighteenth century that wood began to be used as a source of paper-making fibre. The properties of any paper depend on the plant fibres from which it is derived, as well as the processing techniques. The cellulose in fibres provides the necessary characteristics of chemical stability, flexibility, high tensile strength and good bonding ability.

The first stage in paper making is pulping. When only mechanical processes are used to heat and grind the wood chips, a high yield of relatively low grade pulp (suitable for newspaper) is produced. Chemical processes can also be employed to remove the lignin so that a better quality paper is produced which does not discolour. However, these chemical processes also remove some of the cellulose and a low yield is produced. Sometimes pure cellulose pulps are required, for example as a starting point for viscose or cellophane production.

High quality pulp, such as that produced from cotton, is used for the long-lasting paper required for bank notes or for specialist paper like filter paper. It is about seven or eight times more expensive than low grade pulp.

In Britain every person uses about 163 kg of paper per year but since 1981 over 50% of the fibre used by our paper industry has come from waste paper. Much of the rest comes from European forests which are carefully managed plantations, actually increasing in size by 3% per year. In recent years techniques have improved so that any grade of paper can be produced from waste fibre but it is still difficult to remove the inks and have a white product without the use of potentially harmful chemicals. Further recycling of waste paper would avoid the possible polluting effects of burning it (thus increasing atmospheric carbon dioxide levels) or burying it in landfill sites.

**5.** The arrangement of the cellulose fibrils in the cell wall can determine the pattern of growth and hence the overall shape of cell.

**6.** Occasionally cell walls act as food reserves.

# 4.3 Movement in and out of cells

The various organelles and structures within a cell require a variety of substances in order to carry out their functions. In tur they form products, some useful and some wastes. Most of thes substances must pass in and out of the cell. This they do by **diffusion, osmosis, active transport, phagocytosis** and **pinocytosis**.

### 4.3.1 Diffusion

**Diffusion is the process by which a substance moves from a region of high concentration of that substance to a region of low concentration of the same substance.** Diffusion occurs because the molecules of which substances are made are in random motion (kinetic theory). The process is explained in Fig. 4.17.

The rate of diffusion depends upon:

**1. The concentration gradient** – The greater the difference in concentration between two regions of a substance the greater th rate of diffusion. Organisms must therefore maintain a fresh supply of a substance to be absorbed by creating a stream over the diffusion surface. Equally, the substance, once absorbed, must be rapidly transported away.

**2. The distance over which diffusion takes place** – The shorter the distance between two regions of different concentration the greater the rate of diffusion. The rate is proportional to the reciprocal of the square of the distance (inverse square law). An structure in an organism across which diffusion regularly takes place must therefore be thin. Cell membranes for example are only 7.5 nm thick and even epithelial layers such as those lining the alveoli of the lungs are as thin as 0.3 $\mu$m across.

**3. The area over which diffusion takes place** – The larger the surface area the greater the rate of diffusion. Diffusion surfaces frequently have structures for increasing their surface area and hence the rate at which they exchange materials. These structures include villi and microvilli.

**4. The nature of any structure across which diffusion occurs** – Diffusion frequently takes place across epithelial layers or cell membranes. Variations in their structure may affect diffusion. For example, the greater the number and size of pores in cell membranes the greater the rate of diffusion.

**5. The size and nature of the diffusing molecule** – Small molecules diffuse faster than large ones. Fat-soluble molecules diffuse more rapidly through cell membranes than water-solubl molecules.

**1.** *If 10 particles occupying the left-hand side of a closed vessel are in random motion, they will collide with each other and the sides of the vessel. Some particles from the left-hand side move to the right, but initially there are no available particles to move in the opposite direction, so the movement is in one direction only. There is a large concentration gradient and diffusion is rapid.*

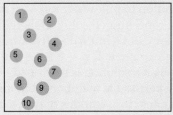

**2.** *After a short time the particles (still in random motion) have spread themselves more evenly. Particles can now move from right to left as well as from left to right. However, with a higher concentration of particles (7) on the left than on the right (3) there is a greater probability of a particle moving to the right than in the reverse direction. There is a smaller concentration gradient and diffusion is slower.*

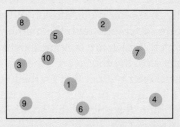

**3.** *Some time later, the particles will be evenly distributed throughout the vessel and the concentrations will be equal on each side. The system is in equilibrium. However, the particles are not static but remain in random motion. With equal concentrations on each side, the probability of a particle moving from left to right is equal to the probability of one moving in the opposite direction. There is no concentration gradient and no net diffusion.*

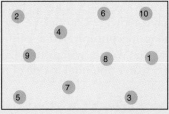

**4.** *At a later stage the particles remain evenly distributed and will continue to do so. Although the number of particles on each side remains the same, individual particles are continuously changing position. This situation is called **dynamic equilibrium**.*

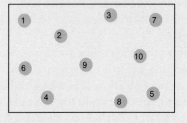

*Figure 4.17 Diffusion*

### 4.3.2 Facilitated diffusion

This special form of diffusion allows more rapid exchange. It may involve channels within a membrane which make diffusion of specific substances easier. These channels form water-filled connections across the lipid bilayer which allow water-soluble substances to move across. They are important therefore in transporting ions. The channels are selective in that they will open or close in response to certain signals such as a change in voltage or the binding of another molecule. In this way the cell can control the entry and exit of molecules and ions.

An alternative form of facilitated diffusion involves different protein molecules in the membrane called **carrier proteins**. These bind molecules to them and then change shape as a result of this binding in such a way that the molecules are released to the inside of the membrane (Fig. 4.18).

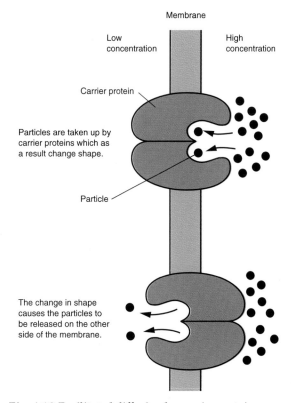

*Fig. 4.18 Facilitated diffusion by carrier proteins*

In all cases facilitated diffusion does not involve the use of energy (i.e. it is passive) and hence material is moved along a concentration gradient (i.e. from high to low concentration).

### 4.3.3 Osmosis

Osmosis is a special form of diffusion which involves the movement of solvent molecules. The solvent in biological systems is invariably water. Most cell membranes are permeable to water and certain solutes only. Such membranes are termed **partially permeable**. Osmosis in living organisms can therefore be defined as: **the passage of water from a region where it is highly concentrated to a region where its concentration is lower, through a partially permeable membrane**. The process is explained in Fig. 4.19.

If a solution is separated from its pure solvent, as in Fig 4.19, the pressure which must be applied to stop water entering that solution, and so prevent osmosis, is called the **osmotic pressure**. The more concentrated a solution the greater is its osmotic pressure. This is a hypothetical situation and, as a solution does not actually exert a pressure under normal circumstances, the term 'osmotic potential' is preferred. As the osmotic potential is in effect the potential of a solution to pull water into it, it always has a negative value. A more concentrated solution therefore has a more positive osmotic pressure but a more negative osmotic potential.

Osmosis occurs not only when a solution is separated from its pure solvent by a partially permeable membrane but also when such a membrane separates two solutions of different concentrations. In this case, water moves from the more dilute, or **hypotonic**, solution, to the more concentrated, or **hypertonic** solution. When a dynamic equilibrium is established and both solutions are of equal concentration they are said to be **isotonic**. The above terms should only be applied to animal cells. The osmotic relationships of plant cells should be described in terms of water potential (Section 22.3).

Consider Fig. 4.20. Initially the water molecules on the right of the partially permeable membrane collide with the membrane more often than those on the left, which are to some extent impeded by the glucose molecules. In other words the water on the right has a greater potential energy than that on the left of the membrane. The greater the number of collisions the water molecules make on the membrane, the greater the pressure on it. This pressure is called the **water potential** and is represented by the Greek letter psi ($\Psi$).

Under standard conditions of temperature and pressure (25 °C and 100 kPa) pure water is designated a water potential of zero. The addition of solute to pure water lowers its water potential because the solute molecules impede the water molecules, reducing the number of collisions they make with the membrane. It therefore exerts less pressure and has a lower water potential. Given that pure water has a water potential of zero, all solutions therefore have a lower potential, i.e. they have negative water potentials. The more concentrated a solution the more negative is its water potential. Water will diffuse from a region of less negative (higher) water potential to one of more negative (lower) water potential.

### 4.3.4 Active transport

Diffusion and osmosis are passive processes, i.e. they occur without the expenditure of energy. Some molecules are transported in and out of cells by active means, i.e. energy is required to drive the process.

The energy is necessary because molecules are transported against a **concentration gradient**, i.e. from a region of low concentration to one of high concentration. It is thought that the process occurs through the proteins that span the membrane. These accept the molecule to be transported on one side of the membrane and, by a change in the structure of the protein, convey it to the other side (see Fig. 4.21). A good example of

---

1. *Both solvent (water) and solute (glucose) molecules are in random motion, but only solvent (water) molecules are able to cross the partially permeable membrane. This they do until their concentration is equal on both sides of the membrane.*

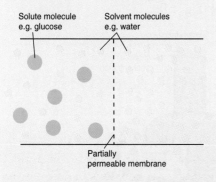

Solute molecule
e.g. glucose

Solvent molecules
e.g. water

Partially
permeable membrane

2. *Once the water molecules are evenly distributed, in theory a dynamic equilibrium should be established. However, the water molecules on the left of the membrane are impeded to some extent by the glucose molecules from crossing the membrane. With no glucose present on the right of the membrane, water molecules move more easily to the left than in reverse direction.*

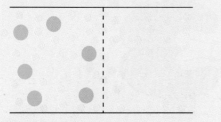

3. *A situation is reached whereby additional water molecules accumulate on the left of the membrane, until their greater concentration offsets the blocking effect of the glucose. The probability of water molecules moving in either direction is the same, and a dynamic equilibrium is established.*

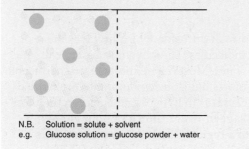

N.B.    Solution = solute + solvent
e.g.    Glucose solution = glucose powder + water

*Fig. 4.19 Osmosis*

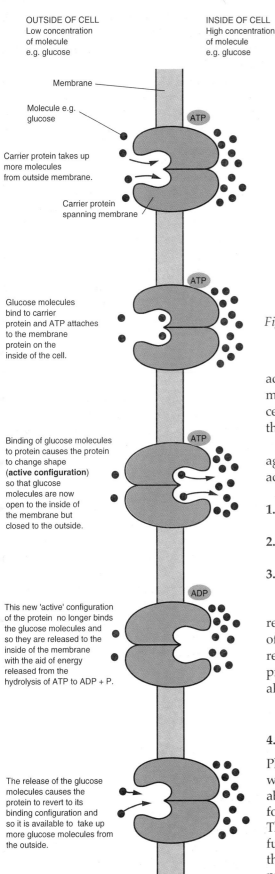

OUTSIDE OF CELL
Low concentration
of molecule
e.g. glucose

INSIDE OF CELL
High concentration
of molecule
e.g. glucose

Membrane

Molecule e.g.
glucose

Carrier protein takes up
more molecules
from outside membrane.

Carrier protein
spanning membrane

Glucose molecules
bind to carrier
protein and ATP attaches
to the membrane
protein on the
inside of the cell.

Binding of glucose molecules
to protein causes the protein
to change shape
(**active configuration**)
so that glucose
molecules are now
open to the inside of
the membrane but
closed to the outside.

This new 'active' configuration
of the protein no longer binds
the glucose molecules and
so they are released to the
inside of the membrane
with the aid of energy
released from the
hydrolysis of ATP to ADP + P.

The release of the glucose
molecules causes the
protein to revert to its
binding configuration and
so it is available to take up
more glucose molecules from
the outside.

Fig. 4.21 Active transport

---

Partially permeable membrane

Net flow of molecules

Solute molecule, e.g. glucose
Water molecule

Low concentration
of water molecules.
Low water potential

High concentration
of water molecules.
High water potential

High concentration
of solute molecules.
High osmotic pressure

Low concentration
of solute molecules.
Low osmotic pressure

*Fig. 4.20 Water potential and osmotic pressure*

active transport is the **sodium–potassium pump** which exists in most cell membranes. This actively removes sodium ions from cells while actively accumulating potassium ions into them from their surroundings.

Due to the energy expenditure necessary to move molecules against a concentration gradient, cells and tissues carrying out active transport are characterized by:

1. The presence of numerous mitochondria.

2. A high concentration of ATP.

3. A high respiratory rate.

As a consequence of **3**, any factor which increases the rate of respiration, e.g. a higher temperature or increased concentration of oxygen, will increase the rate of active transport. Any factor reducing the rate of respiration or causing it to cease, e.g. the presence of cyanide, will cause active transport to slow or stop altogether.

### 4.3.5 Phagocytosis

Phagocytosis (*phago* – 'feeding', *cyto* – 'cell') is the process by which the cell can obtain particles that are too large to be absorbed by diffusion or active transport. The cell invaginates to form a cup-shaped depression in which the particle is contained. The depression is then pinched off to form a vacuole. Lysosomes fuse with the vacuole and their enzymes break down the particle, the useful contents of which may be absorbed (Fig. 4.22). The process only occurs in a few specialized cells (called **phagocytes**), such as white blood cells where harmful bacteria can be ingested, or *Amoeba* where it is a means of feeding.

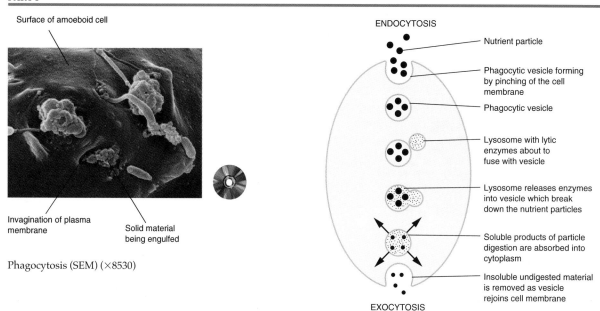

Surface of amoeboid cell

Invagination of plasma membrane

Solid material being engulfed

Phagocytosis (SEM) (×8530)

ENDOCYTOSIS

Nutrient particle

Phagocytic vesicle forming by pinching of the cell membrane

Phagocytic vesicle

Lysosome with lytic enzymes about to fuse with vesicle

Lysosome releases enzymes into vesicle which break down the nutrient particles

Soluble products of particle digestion are absorbed into cytoplasm

Insoluble undigested material is removed as vesicle rejoins cell membrane

EXOCYTOSIS

*Fig. 4.22 Endocytosis and exocytosis*

### 4.3.6 Pinocytosis

Pinocytosis or 'cell drinking' is very similar to phagocytosis except that the vesicles produced, called **pinocytic vesicles**, are smaller. The process is used for the intake of liquids rather than solids. Even smaller vesicles, called **micropinocytic vesicles**, may be pinched off in the same way.

Both pinocytosis and phagocytosis are methods by which materials are taken into the cell in bulk. This process is called **endocytosis**. By contrast, the reverse process, in which materials are removed from cells in bulk, is called **exocytosis** (Fig. 4.22).

# 4.4    Questions

. Most cells maintain different concentrations of ions
n either side of the cell membrane and usually there
s also a difference in electrical potential. The table
hows some typical concentrations for the principal
ons inside and outside mammalian cells.

| Ion | concentration inside cell /mM | concentration in blood plasma /mM |
|---|---|---|
| calcium | <0.0002 | 1.8 |
| chloride | 4.0 | 116.0 |
| potassium | 139.0 | 4.0 |
| sodium | 12.0 | 143.0 |

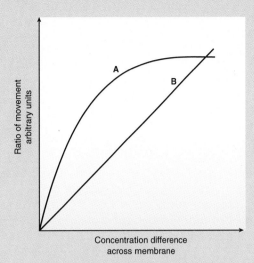

*(a)* (i) State the process by which these
unequal distributions are achieved
                                    *(1 mark)*

(ii) Why should this distribution of ions
result in a difference in electrical
potential across the membranes?
                                    *(1 mark)*

*(b)* Cell membranes from different cell types differ
considerably in their protein compositions.
Proteins are also distributed asymmetrically in
cell membranes; for example, intrinsic proteins
may have specific parts of their amino acid
sequences located on one side of the
membrane or the other. Some proteins are
localised in certain areas of the cell sueface.

(i) What is meant by the term *intrinsic
protein*?                        *(1 mark)*

(ii) Suggest why cell membranes differ in
protein composition.            *(2 marks)*

(iii) What is the significance of the
asymmetrical distribution of proteins in
cell membranes.                 *(2 marks)*

(iv) How is the localised distribution of
proteins at odds with the fluid mosaic
model of cell membrane structure?
                                    *(2 marks)*

The figure at the top of the next coloumn
shows the rate of movement of two
substance **A** amd **B** across a cell membrane.
Addition of a respiratory poison to prevent
ATP synthesis in the cell has no effect on the
rate of movement of either substance.

*(c)* (i) Name the processes involved in the
movement of substances **A** and **B** across
the cell membrane. Give an explanation
for each answer.               *(4 marks)*

(ii) Suggest what final concentration
differences across the cell membranes
would be achieved by processes **A**
and **B**.                      *(2 marks)*

(iii) Naturally occurring D-glucose
crosses some cell membranes several
times faster than another onosaccharide
called D-galactose. However, the non-
biological isomer (or mirror image
molecule) L-glucose hardly enters cells
at all. Explain these observations.
                                *(Total 17 marks)*

*Oxford and Cambridge Jan 1998, B1, No. 3*

**2.** Early research on the structure of the cell
membrane showed that lipid-soluble compounds
passed rapidly into cells. The membrane was found to
be selectively permeable to mineral ions, sugars and
amino acids. Further work demonstrated that all
membranes have the same basic structure but can
differ greatly in the types of lipid and protein they
contain. Many of the specialized proteins present
provide a means of communication between cells and
molecules in their environment.

*(a)* Apart from lipid solubility, suggest **two**
factors which could affect the rate of
penetration of a molecule through the
membrane.                       *(2 marks)*

*(b)* Describe how the structure of the cell
membrane is related to
(i) its selective permeability;   *(5 marks)*
(ii) its communication with molecules in
the cell's environment.       *(2 marks)*

*(c)* Describe how prokaryotes and eukaryotes
differ in terms of the membrane-bound
structures they contain.        *(3 marks)*
                                *(Total 12 marks)*

*NEAB June 1997, Paper BY01, No. 8*

3. The diagram shows a section of a cell surface membrane.

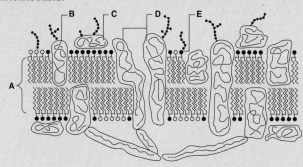

(a) Name the structures labelled **A** to **E**. (4 marks)
(b) Explain how proteins are held in the membrane. (2 marks)
(c) List **four** functions of proteins in membranes. (4 marks)
(Total 10 marks)

UCLES June 1997, Paper 3, No. 1

4. The diagram below shows the structure of a liver cell as seen using an electron microscope.

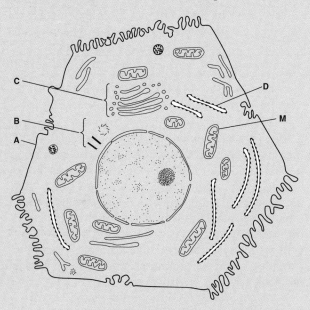

(a) Name the parts labelled **A**, **B**, **C** and **D**. (4 marks)
(b) The magnification of this diagram is ×12 000. Calculate the actual length of the mitochondrion labelled **M**, giving your answer in $\mu$m. Show your working. (2 marks)
(Total 6 marks)

Edexcel June 1997, B/HB1, No. 1

5. (a) Explain why it is possible to see cell structure in more detail with an electron microscope than with an optical microscope. (2 marks)

(b) The drawing shows a group of prokaryotic cells.

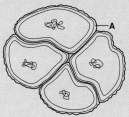

(i) Identify feature **A**. (1 mark)
(ii) Give **two** pieces of evidence from the drawing to support the fact that these are prokaryotic cells. (2 marks)
(Total 5 marks)

AEB January 1997, Module Paper 1, No.

6. The techniques of homogenizing and centrifugal fractionation (fractional sedimentation) have played an important part in our understanding of the nature and functions of cell organelles such as lysosomes, mitochondria, nuclei and ribosomes.

Usually mammalian tissue such as liver is chopped and homogenized in ice-cold sucrose solution and separated into different subcellular fractions by centrifuging successively at increasing speeds and for greater lengths of time. The diagrams shown below summarize the process. (Centrifugal force, ×$g$, measures the number of times that the force is greater than gravity.)

Five subcellular fractions (including the final resultant supernatant) can be obtained and are shown as **A**, **C**, **D**, **E** and **F** in the diagram. These fractions can then be investigated biochemically. For example, oxygen consumption or hydrolytic enzyme activity can be measured.

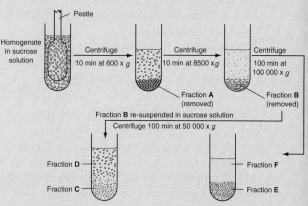

Differential Centrifugation (centrifugal fractionation) of Liver Tissue

(a) What is meant by **homogenized**? (1 mark)
(b) The concentration of the suspending sucrose medium is chosen with care. Briefly suggest why this is so. (1 mark)
(c) Suggest a reason for carrying out these procedures at ice-cold temperatures. (1 mark)

(d) Predict which one of the fractions **A, C, D, E** or **F** is most likely to contain mainly:

    (i) nuclei;

    (ii) ribosomes.         (2 marks)

(e) Supposing that lysosomes are marginally heavier than mitochondria, predict in which fraction the lysosomes would most probably be found.         (1 mark)

(f)  (i) Which fraction would show the highest rate of oxygen consumption? Give a reason for your answer.     (2 marks)

    (ii) Which fraction would you expect to produce most radioactively-labelled protein if 'labelled' amino acids were added? Give a reason for your answer.         (2 marks)

    (iii) Which fraction would probably show the greatest amount of hydrolytic enzyme activity? Give a reason for your answer.     (2 marks)

    (iv) Which fraction would probably show the most evidence of synthesis of messenger RNA? Give a reason for your answer.     (2 marks)

*(Total 14 marks)*

*Oxford June 1997, Paper 2, No. 6*

**7.** The generally agreed **fluid-mosaic model** of cell membrane structure is not immediately clear in electron micrographs. Normally, cell membranes appear in electron micrographs to have a structure which can be shown as on the diagram below.

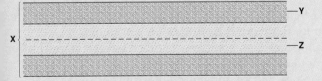

(a) Suggest a typical width for **X** (the complete cell surface membrane).     (1 mark)

(b) From your knowledge of the fluid-mosaic model of the membrane describe:

    (i) the likely composition of layer **Y**;     (2 marks)

    (ii) the likely composition of layer **Z**.     (2 marks)

(c) Some substances are said to pass across cell surface membranes by **facilitated diffusion**. Explain briefly what this term means.     (2 marks)

*(Total 7 marks)*

*Oxford February 1997, Paper 2, No. 1*

**8.** Liver cells were ground to produce an homogenate. The flow chart shows how centrifugation was used to separate organelles from liver cells.

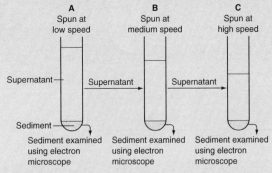

Drawings of electron micrographs of three organelles separated by the centrifugation are shown below. The drawings are **not** to the same scale.

(a) Copy and complete the table below.

| Electron micrograph | Name of organelle | Centrifuge tube in which the organelle would be the main constituent of the sediment |
|---|---|---|
| 1 | | |
| 2 | | |
| 3 | | |

*(2 marks)*

(b) Explain why it is possible to separate the organelles in this way.     (2 marks)

*(Total 4 marks)*

*NEAB February 1995, BY1, No. 2*

**9.** The diagram shows the fluid-mosaic model of the cell membrane structure.

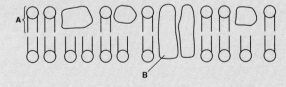

(a) Name the molecules labelled **A** and **B**.     (2 marks)

(b) Suggest **two** properties that drugs should possess if they are to enter a cell rapidly.     (2 marks)

(c) Explain why an electron microscope is useful in studying cell structure.     (2 marks)

*(Total 6 marks)*

*NEAB June 1995, BY01, No. 2*

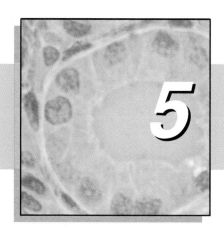

# 5 Biodiversity

## 5.1 Principles of classification

Before any study can be made of living organisms it is necessary to devise a scheme whereby their enormous diversity can be organized into manageable groups. This grouping of organisms is known as **classification** and the study of biological classification is called **taxonomy**. A good universal system of classification aids communication between scientists and allows information about a particular organism to be found more readily. There is no 'correct' scheme of classification since organisms form a continuum and any division of them into groups has been devised solely for human convenience.

During the eighteenth century, the Swedish botanist Linnaeus devised a scheme of classification which has become widely accepted. In this scheme organisms are grouped together according to their basic similarities. Relationships are based on homologous rather than analogous characteristics. **Homologous** characters are those that have a fundamental similarity of origin, structure and position, regardless of their function in the adult. **Analogous** characters are those that have a similar function in the adult but which are not homologous, i.e. they do not have the same origin. For example, wings of butterflies and birds are both used for flight but their origins are not similar. Classification based on homology is called **natural classification**. It now embraces biochemical and chromosome studies as well as the morphology and anatomy used by Linnaeus. A successful natural classification should reflect the true evolutionary relationships of organisms.

### 5.1.1 Taxonomic ranks

It is convenient to distinguish large groups of organisms from smaller subgroups and a series of rank names has been devised to identify the different levels within this hierarchy. The rank names used today are largely derived from those used by Linnaeus over 200 years ago. The largest groups are known as **phyla** and the organisms in each phylum have a body plan radically different from organisms in any other phylum. Diversity within each phylum allows it to be divided into **classes**. Each class is divided into **orders** of organisms which have additional features in common. Each order is divided into **families** and at this level differences are less obvious. Each family is divided into **genera** and each genus into **species**.

**TABLE 5.1 Classification of three organisms**

| Rank | Cabbage white butterfly | Human | Sweet pea |
|---|---|---|---|
| Phylum | Arthropoda | Chordata | Angiospermae |
| Class | Insecta | Mammalia | Dicotyledoneae |
| Order | Lepidoptera | Primates | Rosales |
| Family | Pieridae | Hominidae | Papilionaceae |
| Genus | *Pieris* | *Homo* | *Lathyrus* |
| Species | *brassica* | *sapiens* | *odoratus* |

With the gradual acceptance that all species arose by adaptation of existing forms, the basis of this hierarchy became evolutionary. Species are groups that have diverged most recently, genera somewhat earlier and so on up the taxonomic ranks.

Every organism is given a scientific name according to an internationally agreed system of nomenclature, first devised by Linnaeus. The name is always in Latin and is in two parts. The first name indicates the genus and is written with an initial capital letter; the second name indicates the species and is written with a small initial letter. These names are always distinguished in text by italics or underlining. This system of naming organisms is known as **binomial nomenclature**.

Table 5.1 shows the use of rank names in classifying a cabbage white butterfly, a human and a sweet pea. Only the obligate ranks of classification to which every organism must be assigned have been shown in the table. However, a taxonomist may use a large number of additional categories within this scheme as shown below:

kingdom, subkingdom, grade, **Phylum**, subphylum, superclass, **Class**, subclass, infraclass, superorder, **Order**, suborder, infraorder, superfamily, **Family**, subfamily, tribe, **Genus**, subgenus, **Species**, subspecies, variety.

Living organisms are divided into 5 kingdoms:

**Prokaryotae**, **Fungi**, **Protoctista**, **Plantae** and **Animalia**. It is difficult to fit viruses into this scheme of classification because they are on the border of living and non-living. For this reason they are dealt with separately.

## 5.2  Viruses

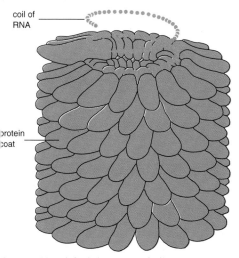

coil of RNA

protein coat

*Fig. 5.1 Simplified diagram of tobacco mosaic virus*

Viruses are smaller than bacteria, ranging in size from about 20 nm to 300 nm. They cannot be seen through a light microscope and pass through filters which retain bacteria. Many can be crystallized and they can only multiply inside living cells. They do, however, contain nucleic acids such as DNA or RNA and must therefore be considered as being on the border between living and non-living. Viruses are classified by their structure and nucleic acid types. They are made up of a nucleic acid core surrounded by a coat of protein; outside cells these inert particles are known as **virions**. Most viruses found in animal cells and those attacking bacteria (known as **bacteriophages**) have the nucleic acid DNA. Other animal viruses and plant viruses contain RNA. Electron microscopy and X-ray diffraction have shown viruses to be a variety of shapes such as spherical, e.g. poliomyelitis, straight rods, e.g. tobacco mosaic virus (Fig. 5.1), or flexible rods, e.g. potato virus X. Bacteriophages have a distinct 'head' and 'tail' (Fig. 5.2).

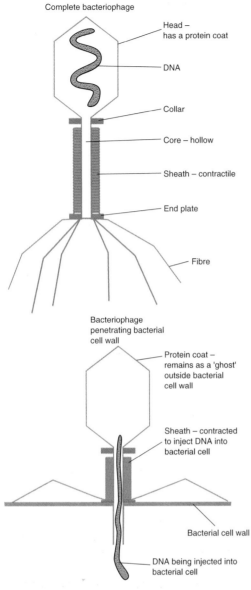

Complete bacteriophage

Head –
has a protein coat

DNA

Collar

Core – hollow

Sheath – contractile

End plate

Fibre

Bacteriophage
penetrating bacterial
cell wall

Protein coat –
remains as a 'ghost'
outside bacterial
cell wall

Sheath – contracted
to inject DNA into
bacterial cell

Bacterial cell wall

DNA being injected into
bacterial cell

*Fig. 5.2 Structure of a bacteriophage*

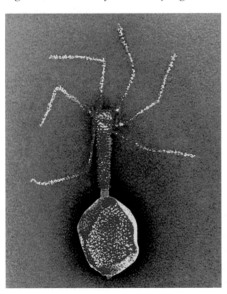

A bacteriophage (EM) (×135 000)

### 5.2.1 Transmission of viruses

Two viruses that have been widely studied are the **tobacco mosaic virus (TMV)**, which attacks tomato, blackcurrant, potato and orchid as well as tobacco itself, and the **T$_2$ phage**, a bacteriophage, which infects *Escherichia coli*. Tobacco mosaic virus is rod-shaped with a length of about 300 nm and a diameter of 15 nm. It comprises 94% protein and 6% RNA, the nucleic acid determining its characteristics. TMV is very infectious, being carried on seed coats, by grasshoppers and by mechanical means. The only effective way to limit its effect is to maintain virus-free stock.

T$_2$ phage is tadpole-shaped, the head having a diameter of about 70 nm and the tail a length of about 0.2 $\mu$m. The cycle of infection of this bacteriophage has been particularly well studied and is explained in Fig. 5.3.

T$_2$ phage immediately kills the bacterium it enters and is therefore known as a **lytic (virulent) phage**. In **lysogenic (temperate) phages**, such as the lambda ($\lambda$) virus, the process is much less rapid and the host and phage may exist together for many generations. Host DNA may become incorporated in the viral DNA, and this DNA is carried to the next host, thereby resulting in new characteristics. Details of the life-cycle of the lambda ($\lambda$) virus are given in Fig. 5.4. This process of **transduction** is an important method by which antibiotic resistance spreads throughout a population of bacteria.

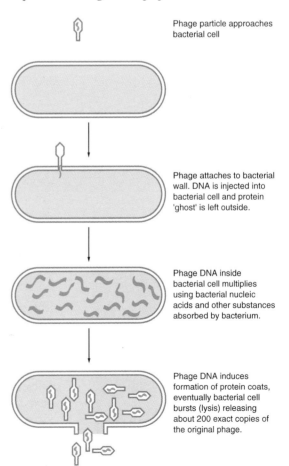

Phage particle approaches bacterial cell

Phage attaches to bacterial wall. DNA is injected into bacterial cell and protein 'ghost' is left outside.

Phage DNA inside bacterial cell multiplies using bacterial nucleic acids and other substances absorbed by bacterium.

Phage DNA induces formation of protein coats, eventually bacterial cell bursts (lysis) releasing about 200 exact copies of the original phage.

*Fig. 5.3 Life-cycle of a lytic (virulent) phage (e.g. T$_2$ phage)*

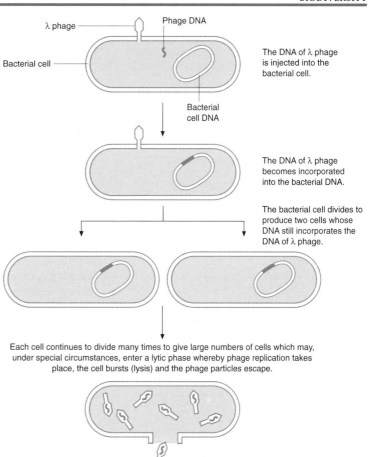

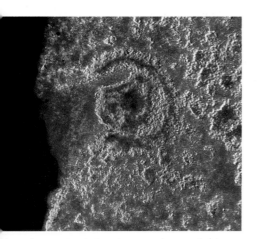

lse-colour transmission electron micrograph of a
uman Immunodeficiency Virus (HIV) – shown in
d – infecting a T-lymphocyte

*Fig. 5.4 Life-cycle of a lysogenic (temperate) phage (e.g. λ phage)*

### 5.2.2 Retroviruses

Probably the best known retrovirus is the Human
Immunodeficiency Virus (HIV) which causes AIDS (Acquired
Immune Deficiency Syndrome), further details of which are
given in Section 31.2.5.

The genetic information in a retrovirus is RNA. While many
viruses possess RNA, retroviruses are different in that they can
use it to synthesize DNA. This is a reversal of the usual genetic
process in which RNA is made from DNA and the reason
retroviruses are so called (*retro* = behind or backwards).

In 1970 the enzyme capable of synthesizing DNA from RNA
was discovered and given the name **reverse transcriptase** (as it
catalyses the opposite process to transcriptase which synthesizes
RNA from DNA). The discovery of this enzyme, more details of
which are given in Section 7.7.2, has considerable importance for
genetic engineering.

The DNA form of the retrovirus genes is called the **provirus**
and is significant in that it can be incorporated into the host's
DNA. Here it may remain latent for long periods before the
DNA of the provirus is again expressed and new viral RNA
produced. During this time any division of the host cell results in
the proviral DNA being duplicated as well. In this way the
number of potential retroviruses can proliferate considerably.
This explains why individuals infected with the HIV virus often
display no symptoms for many years before suddenly
developing full-blown AIDS.

When incorporated into the host DNA the provirus is capable of activating the host genes in its immediate vicinity. Where these genes are concerned with cell division or growth, and are 'switched off' at the time, their activation by the provirus can result in a malignant growth known as **cancer**. The RNA produced by these newly activated genes may become packaged inside new retrovirus particles being assembled inside the host cell. This RNA may then be delivered, along with the retroviral RNA, to the next cell the virus infects. This new cell will then become potentially cancerous.

Host genes which have been acquired by retroviruses in this way are called **oncogenes** (*oncos* = tumour). Very few human cancers are caused by retroviruses in this way but research into them has led to the discovery of similar genes found in human chromosomes. These genes can be activated by chemicals or forms of radiation rather than viruses, and their investigation has already helped to prevent some cancers and may, in time, provide a cure.

Retroviruses can cause diseases other than cancer, but most are harmless. Some proviral DNA has become such an integral part of the host-cell DNA that it is passed on from one generation to the next via the gametes and is, in effect, part of the host's genetic make-up. Such a virus is referred to as an **endogenous** virus.

The life-cycle of a retrovirus is shown in Fig. 5.5.

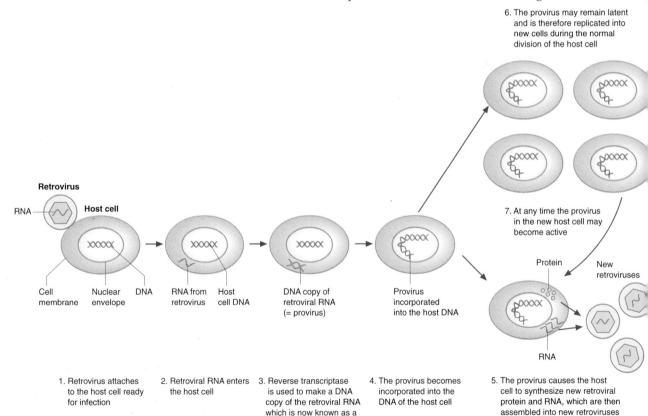

6. The provirus may remain latent and is therefore replicated into new cells during the normal division of the host cell

7. At any time the provirus in the new host cell may become active

1. Retrovirus attaches to the host cell ready for infection

2. Retroviral RNA enters the host cell

3. Reverse transcriptase is used to make a DNA copy of the retroviral RNA which is now known as a provirus

4. The provirus becomes incorporated into the DNA of the host cell

5. The provirus causes the host cell to synthesize new retroviral protein and RNA, which are then assembled into new retroviruses

*Fig. 5.5 Life-cycle of a retrovirus*

### 5.2.3 Economic importance of viruses

Viruses cause a variety of infectious diseases in humans, other animals and plants. The symptoms shown by plants may be localized or distributed throughout the plant. The same virus may have quite different effects in different hosts and these symptoms may be influenced by environmental conditions.

Viral diseases are often difficult to treat because antibiotics cannot be used. Vaccines may be produced but these are not always effective because one virus may exist in a variety of forms. Methods of control therefore depend primarily on prevention, such as breeding resistant species, removal of the source of infection and the protection of susceptible plants and animals.

Viral diseases of plants include those caused by TMV, potato virus X, barley yellow dwarf virus and turnip yellow mosaic virus.

Retroviruses cause a number of diseases including a degenerative brain disease in sheep, anaemia in cattle and some cancers, but by far the most important one is AIDS caused by the Human Immunodeficiency Virus. It may, however, prove possible to use retroviruses to cure diseases by utilizing them to insert useful genes into cells where particular genes are defective. Inherited diseases such as phenylketonuria and thalassaemia are the most likely to be cured by this means.

## 5.3   Prokaryotae

The cyanobacteria (blue-green bacteria) and bacteria which comprise the Prokaryotae are the only living prokaryotic organisms. As such they are the living organisms which most closely resemble the first forms of life. The differences between prokaryotic and eukaryotic cells are given in Section 4.1.2.

No Prokaryotae are truly multicellular although the blue-green bacteria are commonly found in filaments and clusters. This is either because their cell walls fail to separate completely at cell division or because they are held together by a mucilagenous sheath. Most blue-green bacteria can photosynthesize and many are capable of nitrogen fixation. They are important colonizers of bare land and were probably among the first organisms to evolve.

### 5.3.1 Bacteria

Bacteria are the smallest cellular organisms and are the most abundant.

The structure of a typical bacterial cell is shown in Fig. 4.1 on p. 50. Such cells may vary in the nature of the cell wall. In some forms the glycoprotein is supplemented by large molecules of lipopolysaccharide. Cells which lack the lipopolysaccharide combine with dyes like gentian violet and are said to be **gram positive**. Those with the lipopolysaccharide are not stained by gentian violet and are said to be **gram negative**. Gram positive bacteria are more susceptible to both antibiotics and lysozyme than are gram negative ones. Bacteria may be coated with a slime capsule which is thought to interfere with phagocytosis by the white blood cells. Bacteria are generally distinguished from each other by their shape. Spherical ones are known as **cocci** (singular – coccus), rod-shaped as **bacilli** (singular – bacillus) and spiral ones as **spirilla** (singular – spirillum).

### Did you know?

Each one of us has within our body 10 times as many bacterial cells as we have cells of our own.

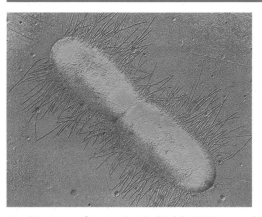

A rod bacterium showing flagella (EM) (×30 000 approx.)

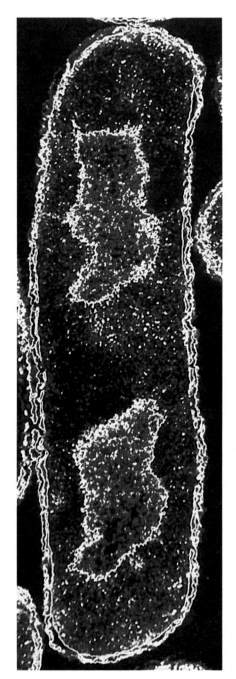

Cocci may stick together in chains, e.g. **streptococcus**, or in clusters, e.g. **staphylococcus**. Bacteria show considerable diversity in their metabolism. The majority are heterotrophic and most of these are saprobionts. They are responsible, with the Fungi, for decaying and recycling organic material in the soil. Others are parasitic, some causing disease but many having little effect on their host. Numerous gut bacteria have a symbiotic relationship with their host, for example helping to digest the cellulose ingested by ruminants.

Other bacteria are autotrophic. **Photosynthetic bacteria** are anaerobic and often use sulphur compounds as electron donors rather than the water used by higher plants.

$$CO_2 + 2H_2S \xrightarrow{\text{light}} (CH_2O) + H_2O + 2S$$

Some bacteria derive their energy from inorganic molecules such as ammonia, nitrite, sulphur or hydrogen sulphide. These are the **chemosynthetic bacteria**, some of which are essential links in the nitrogen cycle. For example, one group oxidizes ammonia or ammonium compounds to nitrites and energy, and another oxidizes nitrites to nitrates and energy.

$$2NH_4 + 3O_2 \longrightarrow 2NO_2^- + 4H^+ + 2H_2O + \text{energy } (Nitrosomonas)$$

$$2NO_2^- + O_2 \longrightarrow 2NO_3^- + \text{energy } (Nitrobacter)$$

Bacteria reproduce by binary fission, one cell being capable of giving rise to over $4 \times 10^{21}$ cells in 24 hours. Under certain circumstances conjugation occurs and new combinations of genetic material result. Bacteria may also produce thick-walled spores which are highly resistant, often surviving drought and extremes of temperature.

### 5.3.2 Economic importance of bacteria

It is easy to think of all bacteria as pathogens but it is important to remember that many are beneficial to humans. These benefits include:

**1.** The breakdown of plant and animal remains and the recycling of nitrogen, carbon and phosphorus.

**2.** Symbiotic relationships with other organisms. For example supplying vitamin K and some of the vitamin B complex in humans, breaking down cellulose in herbivores.

**3.** Food production, e.g. some cheeses, yoghurts, vinegar.

**4.** Manufacturing processes, e.g. making soap powders, tanning leather and retting flax to make linen.

**5.** They are easily cultured and may be used for research, particularly in genetics. They are also used for making antibiotics, amino acids, enzymes and SCP (single cell protein).

Further details of how humans exploit these beneficial uses of bacteria are given in Chapter 30.

Detrimental effects of bacteria include deterioration of stored food and damage to buried metal pipes caused by sulphuric acid production by *Thiobacillus* and *Desulphovibrio*.

*E. coli* (EM) (×90 000 approx.)

## 5.4  Fungi

The Fungi are a large group of organisms composed of about 80 000 named species. For many years they were classified with the plants but are now recognized as a separate kingdom. This separation is based on the presence of the polysaccharide chitin found in their cell walls, rather than the cellulose present in plant cell walls. Their bodies are usually a **mycelium** of thread-like multinucleate **hyphae** without distinct cell boundaries, i.e. they are **coenocytic**. The Fungi lack chlorophyll and are therefore unable to photosynthesize. They feed heterotrophically, generally as saprobionts or parasites, and details of these methods of feeding will be found in Chapter 15.

Within this kingdom there are three phyla, Zygomycota, Ascomycota and Basidiomycota (see Table 5.2).

TABLE 5.2  **Classification of the fungi**

| KINGDOM FUNGI | No chlorophyll; do not photosynthesize Heterotrophic Cell walls contain chitin rather than cellulose Body usually a mycelium Carbohydrate stored as glycogen Reproduce by means of spores without flagella | |
|---|---|---|
| **Zygomycota** | **Ascomycota** | **Basidiomycota** |
| No septa in hyphae; large branched mycelium formed | Septa in hyphae | Septa in hyphae; large three-dimensional structures often formed |
| Asexual reproduction by sporangia producing spores or by conidia | Asexual reproduction by conidia | Asexual reproduction unusual but spores formed |
| Conjugation gives rise to a zygospore | Sexual reproduction by ascospores forming in an ascus | Sexual reproduction by formation of basidiospores outside basidia |
| *e.g. Mucor* – pin mould *Rhizopus* – bread mould (See Fig. 5.6) | *e.g. Saccharomyces* – yeast *Erysiphe* – powdery mildew *Aspergillus* and *Penicillium* – saprophytic moulds (See Figs. 5.7 and 5.8) | *e.g. Agaricus campestris* – field mushroom *Coprinus* – ink cap toadstool (See Fig. 5.9) |

### 5.4.1 Economic importance of fungi

Many fungi are beneficial to humans. Examples include:

1. Decomposition of sewage and organic material in the soil.

2. Production of antibiotics, notably from *Penicillium* and *Aspergillus*.

3. Production of alcohol for drinking and industry.

4. Production of other foods. Citric acid for lemonade is produced by the fermentation of glucose by *Aspergillus*. Yeasts are used in bread production and the food yeast *Candida utilis* has been investigated as a source of single cell protein (SCP).

5. Experimental use, especially for genetic investigations.

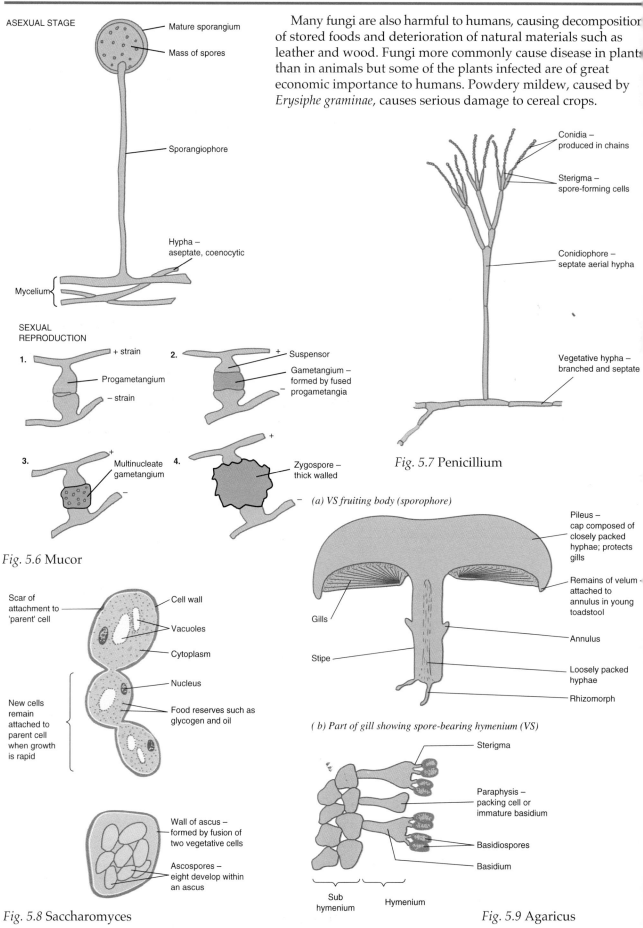

Many fungi are also harmful to humans, causing decomposition of stored foods and deterioration of natural materials such as leather and wood. Fungi more commonly cause disease in plants than in animals but some of the plants infected are of great economic importance to humans. Powdery mildew, caused by *Erysiphe graminae*, causes serious damage to cereal crops.

ASEXUAL STAGE

Mature sporangium

Mass of spores

Sporangiophore

Hypha – aseptate, coenocytic

Mycelium

SEXUAL REPRODUCTION

1. + strain
Progametangium
– strain

2. +
Suspensor
Gametangium – formed by fused progametangia
–

3. +
Multinucleate gametangium
–

4. +
Zygospore – thick walled
–

*Fig. 5.6 Mucor*

Conidia – produced in chains

Sterigma – spore-forming cells

Conidiophore – septate aerial hypha

Vegetative hypha – branched and septate

*Fig. 5.7 Penicillium*

*(a) VS fruiting body (sporophore)*

Pileus – cap composed of closely packed hyphae; protects gills

Remains of velum – attached to annulus in young toadstool

Gills

Stipe

Annulus

Loosely packed hyphae

Rhizomorph

Scar of attachment to 'parent' cell

Cell wall

Vacuoles

Cytoplasm

Nucleus

Food reserves such as glycogen and oil

New cells remain attached to parent cell when growth is rapid

Wall of ascus – formed by fusion of two vegetative cells

Ascospores – eight develop within an ascus

*Fig. 5.8 Saccharomyces*

*( b) Part of gill showing spore-bearing hymenium (VS)*

Sterigma

Paraphysis – packing cell or immature basidium

Basidiospores

Basidium

Sub hymenium

Hymenium

*Fig. 5.9 Agaricus*

# 5.5  Protoctista

The kingdom Protoctista is made up of single celled eukaryotic organisms or organisms which are assemblages of similar cells. Apart from this one common feature the kingdom is very varied and includes all nucleated algae, all protozoa and slime moulds. In this section the algae and Euglenophyta will be used to illustrate the group.

### 5.5.1 Algae

This is a collective name for a varied group of phyla with no one diagnostic feature. They are normally aquatic or live in damp terrestrial habitats. Subdivisions are mainly associated with biochemical differences related to photosynthesis.

The **Chlorophyta** are green algae which range in form from unicells such as *Chlamydomonas* (Fig. 5.10) and *Chlorella* through colonies like *Volvox* and filaments like *Spirogyra* (Fig. 5.11) to delicate thalloid genera like *Ulva*. They contain the same photosynthetic pigments as higher plants but the chloroplasts which contain them vary. *Chlamydomonas* has a single bowl-shaped chloroplast and that of *Spirogyra* is spiral. Both have starch deposits called **pyrenoids**. *Chlamydomonas* also has a light-sensitive spot and will swim, by means of flagella, towards the light. Both genera are capable of asexual and sexual reproduction.

Flagellum

Contractile vacuoles

Cytoplasm

Nucleus

Vacuoles

Cup-shaped chloroplast

Starch granule

Cell wall

*Fig. 5.10* Chlamydomonas

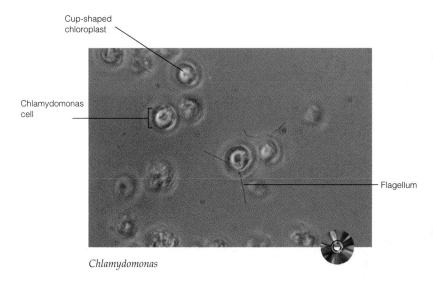

Cup-shaped chloroplast

Chlamydomonas cell

Flagellum

*Chlamydomonas*

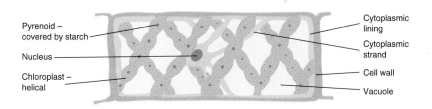

Pyrenoid – covered by starch

Nucleus

Chloroplast – helical

Cytoplasmic lining

Cytoplasmic strand

Cell wall

Vacuole

*Fig. 5.11* Spirogyra

TABLE 5.3  **Classification of the algae**

| ALGAE | No stems, roots or leaves<br>No sclerenchyma<br>No vascular tissue<br>No archegonia<br>Other photosynthetic pigments, in addition to chlorophyll a |
|---|---|
| **Chlorophyta (green algae)** | **Phaeophyta (brown algae)** |
| Chlorophyll a and b present | Chlorophyll a and c, xanthophylls (e.g. fucoxanthin) |
| Food reserve is starch | Food reserves include mannitol and laminarin |
| Cellulose cell walls | Cell wall includes alginic acid |
| Unicellular, filamentous or thalloid | No unicellular forms |
| Mostly freshwater | Almost entirely marine |
| e.g. Chlamydomonas<br>    Chlorella<br>    Pleurococcus<br>    Spirogyra | e.g. Ascophyllum<br>    Fucus |

The **Phaeophyta** is a phylum which shows great diversity in structure and method of reproduction. It includes all the larger seaweeds as well as small, branched filamentous ones such as *Ectocarpus*. Genera like *Fucus* (Fig. 5.12) are well adapted for life in the intertidal zone where they are frequently buffeted by waves and may be exposed at low tide. Both asexual and sexual reproduction are shown, although the latter is unusual in *Fucus*.

The classification of the algae is shown in Table 5.3.

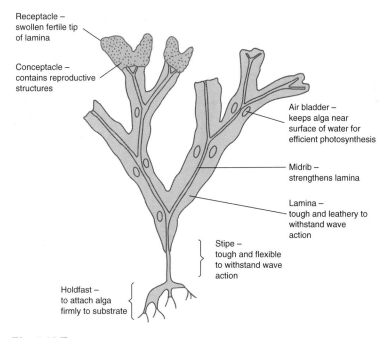

Receptacle – swollen fertile tip of lamina

Conceptacle – contains reproductive structures

Air bladder – keeps alga near surface of water for efficient photosynthesis

Midrib – strengthens lamina

Lamina – tough and leathery to withstand wave action

Stipe – tough and flexible to withstand wave action

Holdfast – to attach alga firmly to substrate

*Fig. 5.12* Fucus

### 5.5.2 Economic importance of algae

At least half the carbon fixation of the earth is carried out by algae in the surface layers of oceans. This primary production is at the base of all aquatic food chains. These algae are also responsible for half the oxygen released by plants into the atmosphere.

Algae can be used in some parts of the world as a direct food source for humans and they may be used as fertilizers on coastal farms. Unicellular green algae such as *Chlorella* are easy to cultivate and can be used as a source of a single cell protein (SCP) for human and animal consumption.

Green algae provide oxygen for the aerobic bacteria which break down sewage.

Derivatives of alginic acid found in the cell walls of many brown algae are non-toxic and readily form gels. These alginates are used as thickeners in many products including ice cream, hand cream, polish, medicine, paint, ceramic glazes and confectionery.

Excessive numbers of algae may develop in bodies of water following pollution by fertilizers or other chemicals. These 'blooms' cause the water to smell and taste unpleasant and may lead to oxygen depletion and the death of fish (Section 18.5.1).

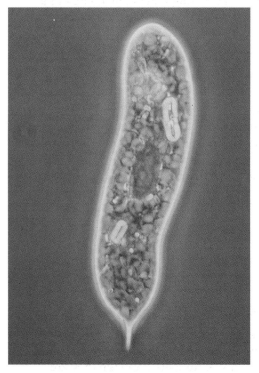

*Euglena*

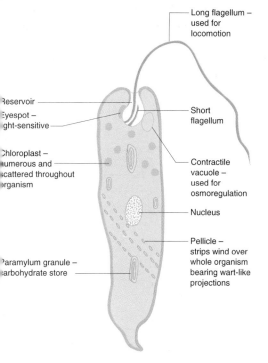

Fig. 5.13 Euglena

### 5.5.3 Euglenophyta

For many years, members of this phylum, such as *Euglena*, were classified by botanists as plants and by zoologists as animals. Their inclusion as a separate division of eukaryotic unicells avoids this dispute and recognizes their unique position on the boundary between plants and animals.

*Euglena* (Fig. 5.13) closely resembles the flagellate protozoa but its possession of numerous chloroplasts containing chlorophyll a and b means that it is able to photosynthesize. The rather animal-like possession of an eye-spot and flagella means that it is able to detect and swim towards light. It stores the products of photosynthesis as **paramylon**, a polysaccharide not found in any other group of organisms. *Euglena* does not have a cell wall but has strips of protein forming a pellicle inside the cell membrane. This pellicle is flexible and allows *Euglena* to change shape, providing an alternative means of locomotion in mud.

Osmoregulation is by means of a contractile vacuole, which opens into the reservoir at the base of the flagella. The cells reproduce by longitudinal binary fission.

## 5.6 Plantae

The organisms included in this kingdom are made up of more than one eukaryotic cell, have cell walls containing cellulose, and photosynthesize using chlorophyll as the main pigment.

### 5.6.1 Bryophyta

The mosses and liverworts which make up the Bryophyta are small plants generally found in moist terrestrial habitats. They have no roots and no vascular tissue. They all show alternation of generations in which the sporophyte and gametophyte are almost equally conspicuous, although the sporophyte is attached to, and dependent on, the gametophyte throughout its life. Although it is thought that bryophytes arose from green algae and colonized land over 400 million years ago, they are still very dependent on water for their existence. Fig. 5.14 shows the life-cycle of a moss.

### 5.6.2 Filicinophyta (ferns)

Ferns have large leaves called fronds which are coiled in bud (see Fig. 5.15). Most living ferns are quite small and have no direct economic importance to humans, although they are significant groundcover plants in moist areas. The larger ferns,

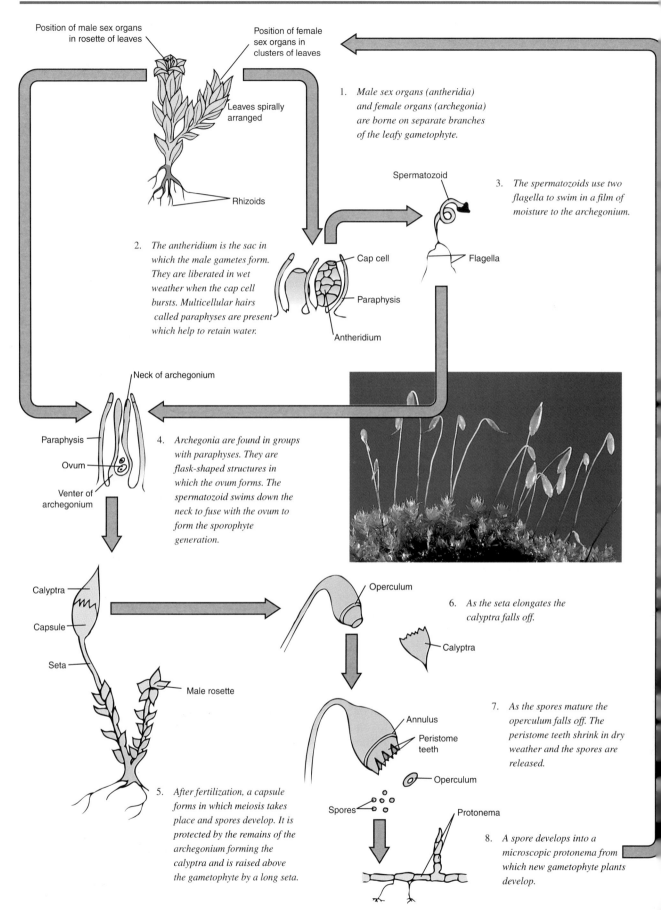

Position of male sex organs
in rosette of leaves

Position of female
sex organs in
clusters of leaves

Leaves spirally
arranged

Rhizoids

1. *Male sex organs (antheridia)
and female organs (archegonia)
are borne on separate branches
of the leafy gametophyte.*

Spermatozoid

3. *The spermatozoids use two
flagella to swim in a film of
moisture to the archegonium.*

Flagella

Cap cell

Paraphysis

Antheridium

2. *The antheridium is the sac in
which the male gametes form.
They are liberated in wet
weather when the cap cell
bursts. Multicellular hairs
called paraphyses are present
which help to retain water.*

Neck of archegonium

Paraphysis

Ovum

Venter of
archegonium

4. *Archegonia are found in groups
with paraphyses. They are
flask-shaped structures in
which the ovum forms. The
spermatozoid swims down the
neck to fuse with the ovum to
form the sporophyte
generation.*

Calyptra

Capsule

Seta

Male rosette

Operculum

6. *As the seta elongates the
calyptra falls off.*

Calyptra

Annulus

Peristome
teeth

Operculum

7. *As the spores mature the
operculum falls off. The
peristome teeth shrink in dry
weather and the spores are
released.*

Spores

Protonema

5. *After fertilization, a capsule
forms in which meiosis takes
place and spores develop. It is
protected by the remains of the
archegonium forming the
calyptra and is raised above
the gametophyte by a long seta.*

8. *A spore develops into a
microscopic protonema from
which new gametophyte plants
develop.*

*Fig. 5.14 Life-cycle of a moss*

1.  Dominant sporophyte is diploid. It consists of a number of fronds growing from an underground rhizome. It can photosynthesize, and the roots absorb water from the soil.

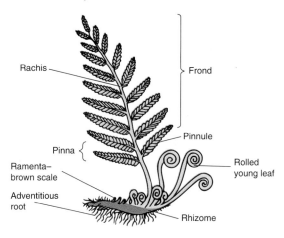

2.  In late summer, brown sori are visible on the underside of each pinnule. Each sorus is made up of a number of sporangia covered by the indusium.

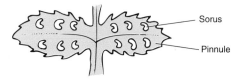

3.  The sporangia are found in groups. Within each sporangium, meiosis occurs to produce haploid spores.

VS Pinnule

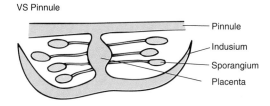

4.  As the spores mature the indusium falls off. The exposed sporangia dry out. The uneven thickening in the annulus sets up tension in the stomium whose cells rupture suddenly to release the spores.

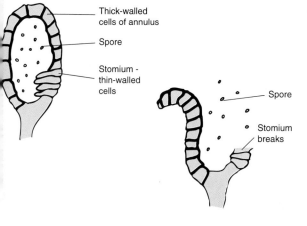

5.  The spores germinate in moist conditions and develop into a tiny plate of cells called the prothallus. This is the haploid gametophyte stage bearing archegonia and antheridia. It has rhizoids for anchorage and it is photosynthetic.

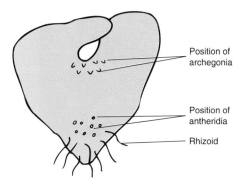

6.  Antheridia develop on the under-surface of the prothallus near the rhizoids. Within them, spiral, multiflagellate spermatozoids develop.

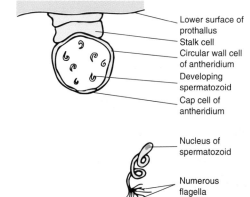

7.  The archegonia develop after the antheridia, so self-fertilization is rare. The venter of the archegonium is embedded in the prothallus and the neck is short.

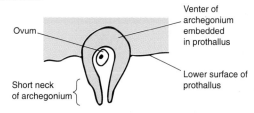

8.  Following fertilization, the young diploid sporophyte plant grows to become an independent plant. At first it has a foot which absorbs nutrients from the prothallus.

Fig. 5.15 Life-cycle of a fern

*Polystichum* (soft shield fern)

which formed the dominant terrestrial vegetation for about 70 million years from the Devonian to the Permian periods, contributed greatly to the coal measures now so useful to human

### 5.6.3 Angiospermophyta

Angiosperms form the dominant terrestrial vegetation today. They are found in a wide range of habitats and have even re-established themselves in freshwater and the sea. Their evolution has closely paralleled that of the insects on which many species depend for pollination. They are extremely well suited to life on land both in their morphology, e.g. efficient water-carrying xylem vessels, and in their reproduction, e.g. seeds enclosed in an ovary.

The two angiosperm classes, **monocotyledoneae** and **dicotyledoneae**, differ in a number of respects, the most significant of which are shown in Table 5.4.

TABLE 5.4 **Comparison of monocotyledoneae and dicotyledoneae**

| Monocotyledoneae | Dicotyledoneae |
|---|---|
| Embryo has one cotyledon | Embryo has two cotyledons |
| Narrow leaf with parallel venation | Broad leaf with net-like venation |
| Scattered vascular bundles in stem | Ring of vascular bundles in stem |
| Rarely vascular cambium present and normally no secondary growth | Vascular cambium present which can lead to secondary growth |
| Many xylem groups in root | Few xylem groups in root |
| Flower parts usually in threes | Flower parts usually in fours or fives |
| Calyx and corolla not easily distinguishable | Usually distinct calyx and corolla |
| Often wind pollinated | Often insect pollinated |
| *e.g. Avena* – oat  *Zea* – maize  *Triticum* – wheat  *Lilium* – lily | *e.g. Ranunculus* – buttercup  *Lamium* – dead-nettle  *Phaseolus* – bean  *Bellis* – daisy |

Asiatic lily

## 5.7    Animalia (animals)

The organisms included in this kingdom are non-photosynthetic multicellular organisms with nervous coordination.

### 5.7.1 Phylum Cnidaria

Animals in this phylum are all aquatic and predominantly marine. They are **diploblastic** with a body wall composed of two cell layers, an inner **gastrodermis** and an outer **epidermis**. Between these lies a jelly-like **mesogloea** which may contain cells derived from the other two layers. The body is organized around a central cavity, the **gastrovascular cavity**, which has one opening serving as both mouth and anus. This opening is surrounded by tentacles bearing specialized stinging cells or **nematocysts**. The main features of Cnidaria are summarized in Table 5.5.

### Did you know?

Ninety-nine per cent of all the animal species that have ever lived are now extinct.

The whole body is radially symmetrical and occurs in two main forms: a jellyfish-like medusoid phase and a hydroid or polyp phase (Fig. 5.16). When the same organism can exist in a number of morphologically distinct forms it is said to show **polymorphism**. Some species have both medusoid and polyp phases in their life history, others only one.

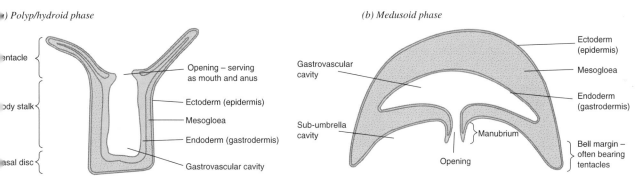

(a) Polyp/hydroid phase

tentacle
body stalk
basal disc

Opening – serving as mouth and anus
Ectoderm (epidermis)
Mesogloea
Endoderm (gastrodermis)
Gastrovascular cavity

(b) Medusoid phase

Gastrovascular cavity
Sub-umbrella cavity
Opening
Manubrium

Ectoderm (epidermis)
Mesogloea
Endoderm (gastrodermis)
Bell margin – often bearing tentacles

Fig. 5.16 A comparison of hydroid and medusoid phases

TABLE 5.5    **Classification of the Cnidaria**

| PHYLUM CNIDARIA | Diploblastic<br>Single body cavity with one opening surrounded by tentacles<br>Radial symmetry<br>Polymorphism with free-swimming medusoid and/or sedentary polyps<br>Nematocysts<br>Planula larva | | |
|---|---|---|---|
| **Class** | **Hydrozoa** | **Scyphozoa** | **Anthozoa** |
| | Dominant polyp | Reduced polyp | Only polyp |
| | Reduced medusa | Dominant medusa | No medusa |
| | No mesenteries (divisions in gastrovascular cavity) | Mesenteries in young polyp | Large mesenteries |
| Examples | *Obelia* – colonial; marine<br>*Hydra* – solitary; freshwater<br>*Physalia* – Portuguese man-of-war | *Aurelia* – solitary; free-swimming marine jellyfish<br>(See Fig. 5.17) | *Actinia* – solitary; marine sea anemone<br>(See Fig. 5.18)<br>*Corallium* – colonial; marine coral |

Aurelia aurita (jellyfish)

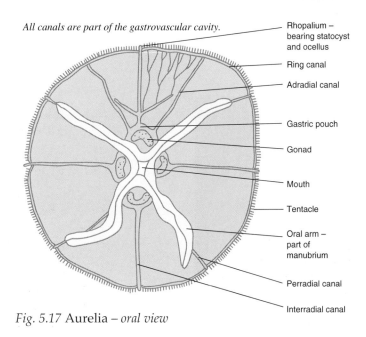

*All canals are part of the gastrovascular cavity.*

Rhopalium – bearing statocyst and ocellus
Ring canal
Adradial canal
Gastric pouch
Gonad
Mouth
Tentacle
Oral arm – part of manubrium
Perradial canal
Interradial canal

Fig. 5.17 Aurelia – *oral view*

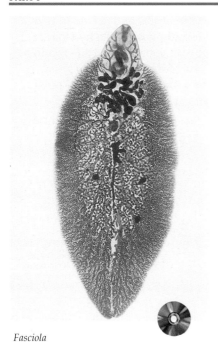

*Fasciola*

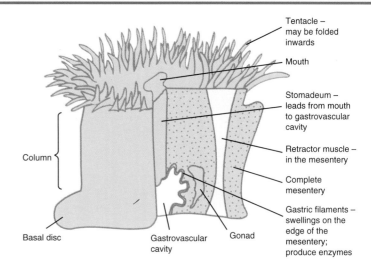

Fig. 5.18 Actinia – *cut to show part of the internal structure*

*The excretory and reproductive systems are very diffuse, and cover the digestive system.*

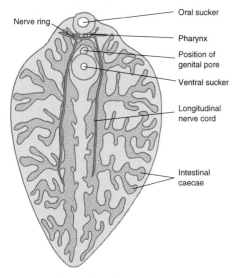

Fig. 5.19 Fasciola

### 5.7.2 Phylum Platyhelminthes

The Platyhelminthes are a group of flatworms with a definite head region and bilateral symmetry. They are **triploblastic** with a body wall composed of an outer epidermis and an inner gastrodermis separated by a relatively undifferentiated region of mesoderm called the **mesenchyme**. The phylum contains around 14 000 different species, many of which are parasitic and of great economic importance. (See Figs. 5.19 and 5.20, Table 5.6)

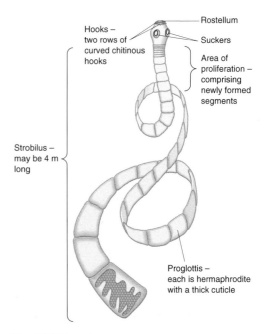

Fig. 5.20 Taenia

Scolex of *Taenia* (tapeworm)

BLE 5.6    **The parasitic flatworms**

| 'lass | Parasite | Primary host | Intermediate host | Harm caused to primary host |
|---|---|---|---|---|
| rematoda | *Fasciola hepatica* – liver-fluke | Sheep and cattle | Snails | Liver rot |
| | *Clonorchis sinensis* – Chinese liver-fluke | Humans | Aquatic snails and freshwater fish | Damage to liver where they feed on blood; large numbers block bile ducts |
| | *Schistosoma* – blood-fluke | Humans | Freshwater snails | Bilharzia (schistosomiasis); damage to lungs and liver and localized swellings; hepatitis |
| estoda | *Taenia solium* – pork tapeworm | Humans | Pig | Anaemia; diarrhoea; loss of weight; intestinal pains; heavy infestations may block gut and its associated ducts |
| | *Diphyllobothrium latum* – fish tapeworm | Humans and carnivores | Copepod (crustacean) and freshwater fish | |
| | *Echinococcus granulosus* | Humans, sheep and cattle | Dog | Hydatid cysts – 70% in liver, 20% in lungs and rest elsewhere |

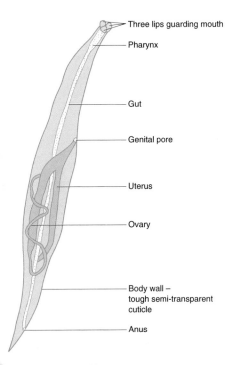

ig. 5.21 Ascaris *(female)*

*ereis*

### 5.7.3 Phylum Nematoda

Nematoda are found in very large numbers in a wide range of habitats. It is estimated that the 10 000 known species of nematodes represent only about 2% of their full number. Most are free-living, although the parasitic ones are best known. The animals are circular in cross-section, have very few cells in their structure and lack both cilia and flagella. (See Table 5.7 and Fig. 5.21.)

TABLE 5.7    **The Nematoda**

| PHYLUM NEMATODA | Unsegmented, cylindrical body<br>No cilia<br>Cuticle of protein<br>Pseudocoelom (body spaces but no true coelom)<br>Unbranched gut from mouth to anus |
|---|---|

### 5.7.4 Phylum Annelida

The annelids or 'true worms' are coelomate animals showing metameric segmentation. There are about 9000 species living in the sea, freshwater or moist soil.

Economically the most significant annelids are the earthworms which contribute to soil formation and improvement in the following ways:

1. Tunnels improve aeration and drainage.

2. Dead vegetation is pulled into the soil where decay by saprobionts takes place.

3. Mixing of soil layers.

4. Addition of organic matter by excretion and death.

5. Secretions of gut neutralize acid soils.

6. Improving tilth by passing soil through gut.

Annelids in general contribute to food chains and leeches used to be of medical importance. None of the parasites cause major infestations of humans or of domesticated animals. The classification of the annelids is summarized in Table 5.8.

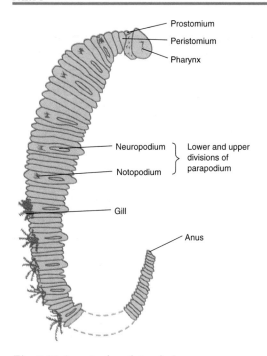

*Fig. 5.22* Arenicola – *lateral view*

TABLE 5.8   **Classification of the Annelida**

| PHYLUM ANNELIDA | | Metameric segmentation<br>Non-chitinous cuticle<br>Chaetae (bristles) | |
|---|---|---|---|
| **Class** | **Polychaeta** | **Oligochaeta** | **Hirudinea** |
| | Parapodia | No parapodia | No parapodia |
| | Many chaetae | Few chaetae | No chaetae |
| | Outer rings correspond to inner septa | Outer rings correspond to inner septa | Outer rings more numerous than inner septa |
| | Distinct head | No distinct head | No distinct head |
| | No suckers | No suckers | Suckers (ectoparasite) |
| | Separate sexes | Hermaphrodite | Hermaphrodite |
| | Larvae | No larvae | No larvae |
| Examples | *Nereis* – ragworm<br>*Arenicola* – lugworm<br>(See Fig. 5.22) | *Lumbricus* – earthworm<br>(See Fig. 5.23) | *Hirudo* – leech<br>(See Fig. 5.24) |

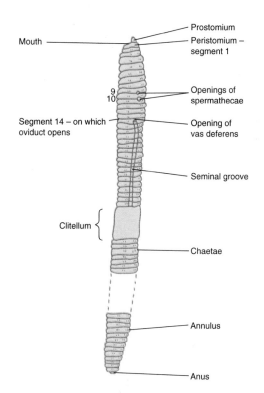

*Fig. 5.23* Lumbricus

TABLE 5.9   **Phylum Arthropoda**

| PHYLUM ARTHROPODA | Exoskeleton, mainly comprising a chitinous cuticle<br>Jointed appendages<br>Dorsal heart and open blood system<br>Growth in stages after moulting **(ecdysis)** |
|---|---|

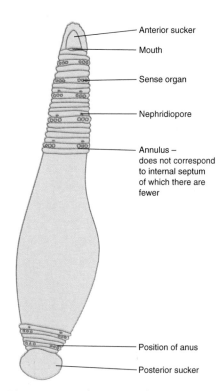

*Fig. 5.24* Hirudo – *ventral view*

### 5.7.5 Phylum Arthropoda

Arthropods (see Table 5.9) make up about three-quarters of living animal species. They have adapted to live successfully in both aquatic and terrestrial habitats and may be free-living or parasitic. **Trilobites** are an extinct group of arthropods, nearly 4000 species of which have been described from fossils. They became extinct at the end of the Palaeozoic era.

Because of the size and importance of this phylum we shall look at each class separately.

## Crustacea

There are about 26 000 species known. They are extremely abundant and many are relatively large. Table 5.10 gives the classification.

TABLE 5.10 **Classification of the Crustacea**

| **Superclass Crustacea** | Cephalothorax – formed by fusion of head and thorax<br>Strong exoskeleton – impregnated with calcium carbonate<br>Two pairs of antennae<br>Three pairs of mouthparts | |
|---|---|---|
| **Class** | **Branchiopoda** | **Malacostraca** |
| | One pair of compound eyes which may be fused to form a single eye | One pair of stalked compound eyes |
| | Thoracic appendages with bristles for filter feeding | Eight pairs of thoracic appendages for walking and feeding |
| | No abdomen | Abdomen with appendages for swimming |
| | Body enclosed in carapace of two pieces | Carapace covers thorax |
| Examples | *Daphnia* – water flea<br>(See Fig. 5.25) | *Carcinus* – crab<br>*Astacus* – crayfish<br>*Oniscus* – woodlouse<br>*Leander* – prawn |

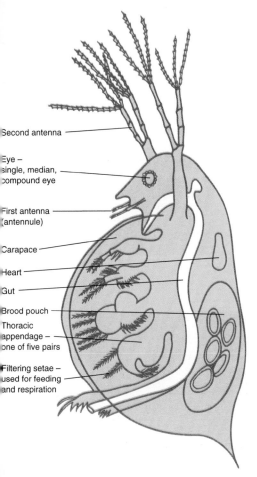

Second antenna

Eye – single, median, compound eye

First antenna (antennule)

Carapace

Heart

Gut

Brood pouch

Thoracic appendage – one of five pairs

Filtering setae – used for feeding and respiration

Fig. 5.25 Daphnia

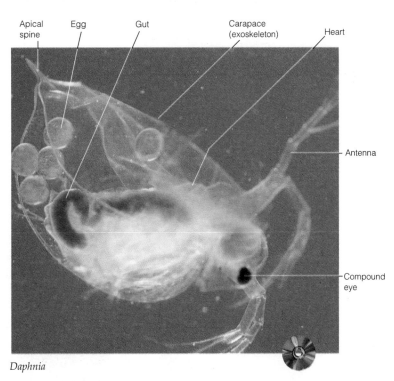

Apical spine    Egg    Gut    Carapace (exoskeleton)    Heart

Antenna

Compound eye

*Daphnia*

## Insecta

The Insecta (Table 5.11) comprise more than 750 000 species which show great diversity. They are extremely successful terrestrial animals in terms of numbers of species, individuals and habitats.

There are a few insects such as springtails and silverfish which do not develop wings. The remainder may be subdivided as shown in Table 5.12.

TABLE 5.11 **The Insecta**

| Class Insecta | Body comprises head, thorax and abdomen<br>Three pairs of thoracic legs<br>Two pairs of thoracic wings (except Apterygota) – sometimes modified<br>One pair of antennae<br>One pair of compound eyes<br>Respiration by tracheae |
|---|---|

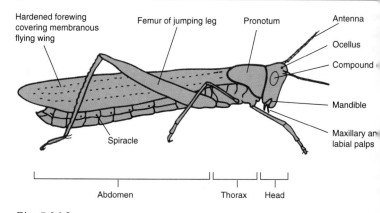

*Fig. 5.26 Locust*

TABLE 5.12 **The winged insects**

|  | Exopterygota | Endopterygota |
|---|---|---|
|  | Wings develop externally<br>Metamorphosis incomplete (**hemimetabolous**)<br>Egg → nymphal stages → adult | Wings develop internally<br>Metamorphosis complete (**holometabolous**)<br>Egg → larval stages → pupa → adult |
| Order | Orthoptera, e.g. *Locusta* – locust (See Fig. 5.26)<br>Odonata, e.g. *Libellula* – dragonfly<br>Dictyoptera, e.g. *Periplaneta* – cockroach | Lepidoptera, e.g. *Pieris* – cabbage white butterfly<br>Diptera, e.g. *Musca* – house-fly<br>Hymenoptera, e.g. *Apis* – honey-bee |

*Apis* (honey-bee), brood stages

### Did you know?

Scientists estimate that there may be as many as 40 000 different arthropod species in a single hectare of South American forest.

Cockroach

*Apis* adults – Queen (*top*), drone (*left*) and worker (*right*)

### 5.7.6 Phylum Mollusca

This phylum is the second largest in the animal kingdom, comprising about 100 000 living species. There is also a very long fossil record of molluscs stretching back to the Pre-Cambrian period. Most living species are marine and examples include octopus and squid as well as members of the classes shown in Table 5.13.

**TABLE 5.13  Classification of the Mollusca**

| PHYLUM MOLLUSCA | Body divided into head, muscular foot and visceral mass<br>Mantle may secrete a calcareous shell<br>Bilateral symmetry, but torsion may lead to asymmetry | |
|---|---|---|
| **Class** | **Gastropoda** | **Pelycopoda (Bivalves)** |
| | Asymmetrical (due to torsion of visceral mass) | Bilateral symmetry |
| | Single shell, usually coiled | Shell in two valves |
| | Well developed head with tentacles and eyes | Reduced head and no tentacles |
| | Radula (rasping tongue) for feeding | Gills with cilia used for filter feeding |
| Examples | *Littorina* – winkle<br>*Limax* – slug<br>*Helix* – snail<br>(See Fig. 5.27) | *Mytilus* – mussel<br>*Anodonta* – freshwater mussel<br>(See Fig. 5.28) |

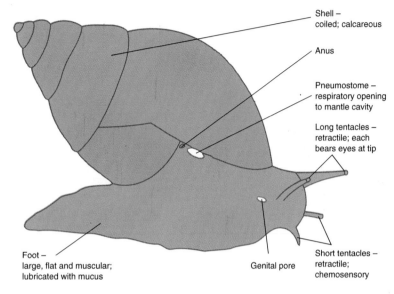

*Fig. 5.27 Land snail – gastropod*

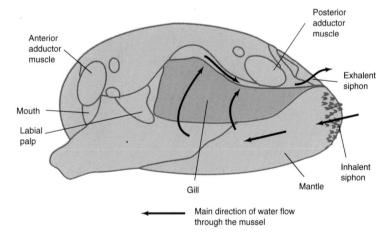

*Fig. 5.28 Anodonta – viewed from left side with left valve and one gill removed*

### 5.7.7 Phylum Chordata

This phylum (Table 5.14) includes the vertebrates which have evolved during the past 500 million years to become the dominant animals of land, sea and air. In number of species and individuals they do not rival the arthropods but their biomass and ecological dominance are much greater.

**TABLE 5.14 The chordata**

| PHYLUM CHORDATA | Gill-slits present in pharynx<br>Post-anal tail, at some stage in development<br>Notochord<br>Dorsal, tubular nerve cord |
|---|---|
| SUB-PHYLUM VERTEBRATA (Craniata) (See also Table 5.15) | Well developed head with brain encased in cranium<br>Vertebral column replaces notochord |

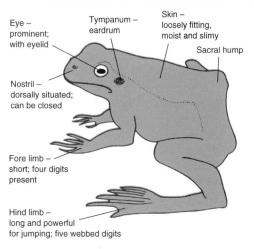

Eye – prominent; with eyelid

Tympanum – eardrum

Skin – loosely fitting, moist and slimy

Sacral hump

Nostril – dorsally situated; can be closed

Fore limb – short; four digits present

Hind limb – long and powerful for jumping; five webbed digits

Fig. 5.30 Class Amphibia, genus **Rana** – *frog*

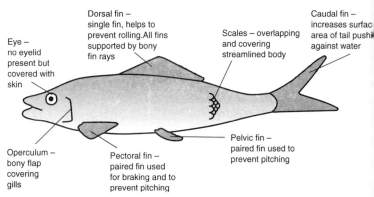

Eye – no eyelid present but covered with skin

Dorsal fin – single fin, helps to prevent rolling.All fins supported by bony fin rays

Scales – overlapping and covering streamlined body

Caudal fin – increases surface area of tail pushing against water

Operculum – bony flap covering gills

Pectoral fin – paired fin used for braking and to prevent pitching

Pelvic fin – paired fin used to prevent pitching

Fig. 5.29 Class Osteichthyes, genus **Clupea** – *herring*

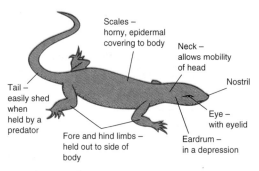

Scales – horny, epidermal covering to body

Neck – allows mobility of head

Nostril

Tail – easily shed when held by a predator

Fore and hind limbs – held out to side of body

Eye – with eyelid

Eardrum – in a depression

Fig. 5.31 Class Reptilia, genus **Lacerta** – *lizard*

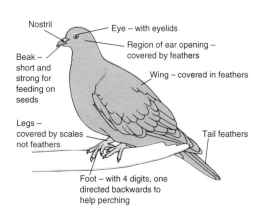

Nostril

Eye – with eyelids

Region of ear opening – covered by feathers

Beak – short and strong for feeding on seeds

Wing – covered in feathers

Legs – covered by scales not feathers

Tail feathers

Foot – with 4 digits, one directed backwards to help perching

Fig. 5.32 Class Aves, genus **Columba** – *pigeon*

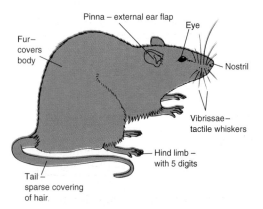

Pinna – external ear flap

Eye

Fur – covers body

Nostril

Vibrissae – tactile whiskers

Hind limb – with 5 digits

Tail – sparse covering of hair

Fig. 5.33 Class Mammalia, genus **Rattus** – *rat*

TABLE 5.15 **Classification of the vertebrata**

| Class | Characteristics | Examples | | |
|---|---|---|---|---|
| Chondrichthyes | Cartilaginous endoskeleton<br>No operculum<br>Heterocercal tail fin<br>No swim bladder | *Scyliorhinus* – dogfish<br>*Raja* – ray | | |
| Osteichthyes | Bony endoskeleton<br>Bony scales<br>Operculum over gills<br>Homocercal tail fin<br>Swim bladder present | *Clupea* – herring (Fig. 5.29)<br>*Gasterosteus* – stickleback<br>*Salmo* – salmon | | |
| Amphibia | No scales<br>Tympanum (eardrum) visible<br>Lungs in adult<br>Aquatic larvae<br>Metamorphosis | *Rana* – frog (Fig. 5.30)<br>*Bufo* – toad<br>*Triturus* – newt | | |
| Reptilia | Dry skin with horny scales<br>Teeth – all the same type (homodont)<br>Eggs with yolk and leathery shell<br>No gills<br>No larval stages | *Lacerta* – lizard (Fig. 5.31)<br>*Natrix* – grass snake<br>*Chelonia* – turtle<br>*Crocodilus* – crocodile | | |
| Aves | Endothermic (warm-blooded)<br>Feathers<br>Beak (no teeth)<br>Fore limbs modified into wings<br>Air sacs in light bones | *Columba* – pigeon (Fig. 5.32) | | |
| Mammalia | Endothermic<br>Hair<br>Sweat and sebaceous glands<br>Mammary glands<br>Pinna (external ear)<br>Heterodont (different types of teeth)<br>Diaphragm | Order | Insectivora<br>Carnivora<br>Cetacea<br><br>Chiroptera<br><br>Rodentia<br><br>Primates | *Talpa* – mole<br>*Canis* – dog<br>*Delphinus* – dolphin<br>*Desmodus* – vampire bat<br>*Rattus* – rat (Fig. 5.33)<br>*Pan* – chimpanzee |

# 5.8    Questions

The diagram illustrates a worm-like animal found in the damp tropical forests of South America, Australasia and South Africa. It belongs to the genus *Peripatus*.

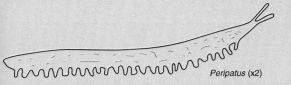

*Peripatus* (x2)

The table summarizes some of the features of *Peripatus* likely to be of interest to a taxonomist.

| Feature | Annelida | Arthropoda |
|---|---|---|
| 1. Body wall comprises both circular and longitudinal muscles | | |
| 2. Dry, chitinous cuticle present | | |
| 3. Limbs not jointed | | |
| 4. Excretory organs segmentally arranged, resembling nephridia | | |
| 5. Respiration by spiracles and branching tracheal tubes | | |
| 6. Open blood vascular system, not composed of closed blood vessels | | |

(a) Copy the table and place a tick (✓) in the appropriate column against each feature to indicate whether the feature concerned is regarded as being typical of either the phylum Annelida or the phylum Arthropoda. *(6 marks)*

(b) Adult cabbage white butterflies (*Pieris brassicae*) appear in May, feed only on nectar, and mate. Each female lays eggs in batches of 10 to 100 on the underside of *Brassica* leaves. After approximately ten days, larvae emerge from the eggs. These feed on the leaves, moult 5 or 6 times in the following three weeks and become pupae which exist for 2–3 weeks. During this time metamorphosis occurs and the next brood of adults emerges. These produce eggs in August which develop into larvae and in due course pupate and remain as pupae until adults emerge in the following May.

    (i) What do you understand by the term **moult**? *(2 marks)*

    (ii) The larvae differ greatly in structure and behaviour from the adults. Suggest **two** advantages of this. *(2 marks)*

    (iii) Define **metamorphosis**. *(2 marks)*

    (iv) Do you consider pupae to be in a resting stage? Explain your answer. *(2 marks)*

    (v) Suggest **two** environmental factors which may cause the difference in behaviour between summer pupae and autumn pupae. *(2 marks)*

(c) (i) How would development of a larva be altered if its corpus allatum was removed at an early stage? *(1 mark)*

    (ii) Explain your answer to (c)(i). *(2 marks)*

*(Total 19 marks)*

*Oxford & Cambridge June 1998, Paper B5, No. 2*

2. (a) The diagram represents the life-cycle of a moss plant. Fill in the empty boxes with an appropriate term.

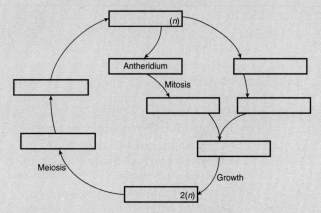

*(8 marks)*

(b) Suggest **two** reasons why water is important in this life-cycle. *(2 marks)*

*(Total 10 marks)*

*Oxford June 1994, Paper 1, No. 3*

3. The diagram shows one way of representing the classification of living organisms into five kingdoms. Box **A** has been drawn overlapping the other boxes since its members share characteristics with the other kingdoms.

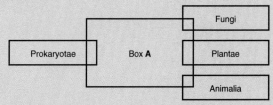

(a) Which kingdom is represented by the box labelled **A**? *(1 mark)*

(b) Give **one** structural characteristic that the members of the kingdom represented by box **A** may share with:
   (i) Fungi;                            (*1 mark*)
   (ii) Prokaryotae.                  (*1 mark*)

(c) Give **two** reasons why the Fungi are placed in a separate kingdom from the Plantae.
                                      (*2 marks*)
                              (*Total 5 marks*)

*AEB Summer 1995, Common Paper 1, No. 1*

**4.** The diagram below shows the structure of a typical bacterial cell as revealed by electron microscopy.

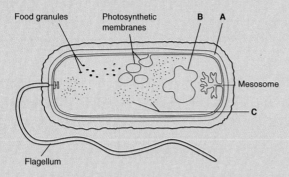

(a) Give **one** function for each of the structures labelled **A**, **B** and **C**.     (*3 marks*)

(b) Gram staining can be used in the identification of bacteria.
   (i) Explain the difference in appearance after staining between a sample of Gram negative bacteria and a sample of Gram positive bacteria.   (*2 marks*)
   (ii) Give **one** example of a genus of Gram negative bacteria.        (*1 mark*)
                           (*Total 6 marks*)

*Edexcel June 1997, B/HB4A, No. 2*

**5.** The diagrams below show **three** organisms. Each belongs to a different phylum (major group).

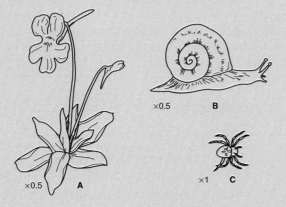

*The scale is indicated by each diagram.*

Copy and complete the table below. Fill in the name of the phylum to which each organism belongs and give **one** external feature, shown in the diagram, which is characteristic of this phylum.

| Organism | Phylum | **One** visible external feature |
|---|---|---|
| A | | |
| B | | |
| C | | |

(*Total 6 mark*)

*Edexcel January 1998, B2, No.*

**6.** The diagram below represents the structure of a bacteriophage virus.

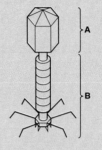

(a) Name and briefly describe the functions of the parts labelled **A** and **B**.   (*2 marks, 2 mark*)

(b) Suggest an approximate size (diameter) for such a virus.           (*1 mar*)

(c) Suggest **two** important reasons why such viruses are not referred to as living organisms.              (*2 mark*)
                        (*Total 7 mark*)

*Oxford November 1996, Paper 2, No.*

**7.** (a) The following is a list of organisms, labelled **A** to **E**.

**A** a protozoan   **B** a bacterium   **C** a mould fungu
     **D** a bryophyte    **E** a flowering plant

Answer questions (i)–(iv) using the appropriate letter(s).
   (i) In which organism(s) would reproductio be entirely asexual?    (*1 mar*)
   (ii) Which produce(s) spores at some stage in the life history?   (*2 mark*)
   (iii) Which possess(es) mitochondria?               (*2 mark*)
   (iv) Which may have the power to fix nitrogen?           (*1 mar*)
   (v) How many different kingdoms are represented by **A** to **E**?    (*1 mar*)

*(b)* Another organism, not included in the above list, is illustrated below.

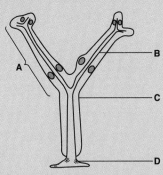

A thalloid brown alga

(i) Name the parts labelled **A** to **D**.
*(2 marks)*

(ii) List **three** ways in which this plant is suited for life on the rocky shore.
*(3 marks)*

(iii) Name the predominant photosynthetic pigment of this alga. *(1 mark)*
*(Total 13 marks)*

*Oxford & Cambridge June 1996, Unit 3, No. 1*

. *Testudo ephippium* is one of the species of giant tortoise found on the Galapagos Islands. Copy and complete the table to show its classification.

| Kingdom | Animalia |
|---|---|
| | Chordata |
| | Reptilia |
| | Chelonia |
| Family | Testudinidae |
| Genus | |

*(Total 3 marks)*

*NEAB June 1996, Paper 1, No. 5*

Copy and complete the table below by stating **one** external feature characteristic of the group.

| Group | Characteristic external feature |
|---|---|
| Cnidarians | |
| Mosses | |
| Arthropods | |
| Ferns | |

*(Total 4 marks)*

*ULEAC June 1996, B2, No. 2*

**10.** The table below refers to descriptions of some major groups of organisms. State the name of each group described.

| Features | Group |
|---|---|
| Heterotrophic organisms with rigid cell wall; body structure normally a mass of hyphae | |
| Photosynthetic organisms, with no flowers and no roots or stems or leaves, usually aquatic | |
| Photosynthetic non-flowering plants, with roots, stems and leaves | |
| Photosynthetic flowering plants, seeds enclosed in a fruit | |
| Heterotrophic, radially symmetrical, multicellular animals with nematocysts | |
| Heterotrophic, multicellular animals possessing a post anal tail and pharyngeal clefts at some stage of their life | |

*(Total 6 marks)*

*ULEAC June 1995, Paper 1, No. 4*

**11.** Hydra is a diploblastic, radially symmetrical animal. The diagram shows a longitudinal section of part of the body wall of a hydra.

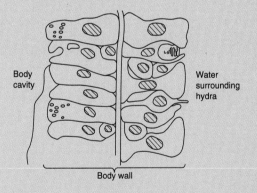

*(a)* Use information in the diagram to explain what is meant by the term **division of labour**.
*(1 mark)*

*(b)* Explain how radial symmetry may be an advantage to a sessile animal.
*(2 marks)*

*(c)* Larger animals, such as members of the phylum Chordata, possess blood systems while smaller animals, such as members of the phyla Platyhelminthes and Cnidaria, do not. Explain the link between body size and the possession of a blood system.
*(2 marks)*
*(Total 5 marks)*

*AEB June 1998, Paper 3, No. 2*

Computer representation of part of a DNA molecule (*opposite*)

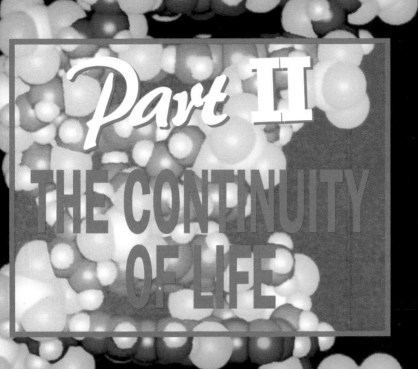

# Part **II**

# THE CONTINUITY OF LIFE

# 6 Inheritance in context

The obvious similarities between children and their parents, or sometimes their grandparents, have long been recognized. Despite many attempts to explain this phenomenon, it is only in recent years that our knowledge of the process of heredity has enabled us to understand the mechanism fully.

The fact that, in some species, both male and female are needed to produce offspring was realized from early times. The role each sex played was, however, a matter of argument. Aristotle believed that the male's semen was composed of an incomplete blend of ingredients, which upon mixing with the menstrual fluid of the female gained form and power and became the new organism. Apart from minor refinements, this belief was generally accepted until the seventeenth century. When Anton van Leeuwenhoek observed sperm in human semen, the idea arose that these contained a miniature human. When these sperm were introduced into the female, one would implant in the womb and develop there, the female's role being nothing more than a convenient incubator. Around this period, Regnier de Graaf discovered in ovaries what was later to be called the Graafian follicle. This was thought by another group of scientists to contain the miniature human, the sperm simply acting as a stimulus for its development.

The problem with both these beliefs was that it could easily be observed that any offspring tended to show characteristics of both parents rather than just one. This led, in the last century, to the idea that both parents contributed hereditary characteristics and the offspring was merely an intermediate blend of both. While closer to present thinking, it too had one flaw. Logically the offspring of a cross between a red flower and a white flower should have pink flowers and the children of a tall father and a short mother should be of medium height. It took the rediscovery of the work of Mendel at the beginning of this century to provide what is now an accepted explanation. Both parents do provide hereditary material, within the sperm and ovum. The offspring therefore has two sets of genetic information – one from the mother and one from the father. For any individual characteristic, e.g. eye colour, only one of the two factors expresses itself. An individual with one factor for blue eyes and one for brown eyes will always have brown eyes. A few characters do show an intermediate state between two contrasting factors, but this is relatively rare. Only one of each pair of factors will be present in any one gamete.

Alongside these changes in the last century, another development took place. It was originally believed that new species arose spontaneously in some manner. By the end of the

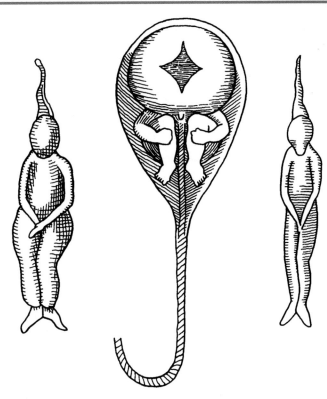

*Fig. 6.1 Observers in the seventeenth century believed the human sperm contained a tiny copy of the parent – they thought they could see these down the microscope and called them homunculi*

century it was more or less accepted that they were formed by adaptation of existing forms. Natural selection is considered to be the mechanism by which these changes arise and it depends upon there being much variety among individuals of a species. Without this variety and consequent selection of the types best suited to the present conditions, species could not adapt and evolve to meet the changing demands of the environment.

If this theory of evolution is accepted, then the process of inheritance must permit variety to occur. At the same time, if the offspring are to be supplied with the same genetic information as the parents, the genetic material must be extremely stable. This stability is especially important to ensure that favourable characteristics are passed on from one generation to the next. This then is the paradox of inheritance – how to reconcile the genetic stability needed to preserve useful characteristics with the genetic variability necessary for evolution. To satisfy both requirements it is necessary to have hereditary units which are in themselves exceedingly stable, which can be reassorted in an almost infinite variety of ways. The idea can be likened to a pack of playing cards. The cards themselves are stable, fixed units, but the number of different possible combinations in a typical hand of thirteen cards is immense. Imagine how much greater are the possible combinations of the thousands of hereditary units in a typical organism.

A summary of the historical events which contributed to our current understanding of heredity is given in Table 6.1.

TABLE 6.1 **Historical review of events leading to present-day knowledge of reproduction and heredity**

| Name | Date | Observation/discovery | Name | Date | Observation/discovery |
|------|------|----------------------|------|------|----------------------|
| Aristotle | 384–322 BC | Mixing of male semen and female semen (menstrual fluid) was like blending two sets of ingredients which gave 'life' | Morgan | early 1900s | Pioneered use of *Drosophila* in genetics experiments and described linkage |
| General scientific belief | Up to 17th century | Simple organisms arose spontaneously out of non-living material | Garrod | 1908 | Postulated mutations as sources of certain hereditary diseases |
| van Leeuwenhoek | 1677 | Discovered sperm – it was generally believed that these contained miniature organisms which only developed when introduced into a female | Johannsen | 1909 | Coined term 'gene' as hereditary unit |
| | | | Janssens | 1909 | Observed chiasmata and crossing over |
| de Graaf | 1670s | Described the ovarian follicle (later called Graafian follicle) | Sturtevant | 1913 | Mapped genes on chromosomes of *Drosophila* |
| Lamarck | 1809 | Proposed theory of evolution based on inheritance of acquired characteristics | Muller | 1920s | Observed mutagenic effect of X-rays |
| | | | Oparin | 1923 | Suggested theory of origin of life |
| Darwin | 1859 | *On the Origin of Species by Means of Natural Selection* published | Griffith | 1928 | Produced evidence suggesting that a chemical 'transforming principle' was responsible for carrying genetic information |
| Pasteur | 1864 | Experimentally disproved the theory of spontaneous generation | | | |
| Mendel | 1865 | Experiments on the genetics of peas and formulation of his two laws | Beadle and Tatum | 1941 | Produced evidence supporting the one gene, one enzyme hypothesis |
| Hertwig | 1875 | Witnessed fusion of nuclei during fertilization | Avery, McCarty and McCleod | 1944 | Showed nucleic acid to be the chemical which carried genetic information |
| Flemming | 1882 | Described all stages of mitosis | Hershey and Chase | 1952 | Showed DNA to be the hereditary material |
| de Vries | 1900 | Rediscovery of the significance of Mendel's 1865 experiment | Watson and Crick | 1953 | Formulated the detailed structure of DNA |
| Sutton | 1902 | Observed pairing of homologous chromosomes during meiosis and suggested these carried genetic information | Kornberg | 1956 | Produced DNA copies from single DNA template using DNA polymerase |
| | | | Meselsohn and Stahl | 1959 | Described mechanism of semi-conservative replication in DNA |
| | | | Jacob and Monod | 1961 | Postulated existence of mRNA in theory on control of protein synthesis |

# 7 DNA and the genetic code

## 7.1 Evidence that the nucleus contains the hereditary material

The universal occurrence of a nucleus at some stage of the life-cycle of cells suggests that it performs an essential role. The functions of the nucleus are listed in Section 4.2.3. The fundamental role of the nucleus in determining the features of a cell was established by Hämmerling. Working with individual cells is normally a difficult task, not least because of their small size. Hämmerling, however, used unusually large single-celled algae belonging to the genus *Acetabularia*. Each cell is up to 5 cm in length, making the sectioning of it relatively easy.

Fig. 7.1 gives a summary of the experiments using two species of *Acetabularia*, which show the nucleus to contain the hereditary material. The experiments are based on those of Hämmerling although they incorporate some refinements made possible by modern techniques.

## 7.2 Evidence that DNA is the hereditary material

### 7.2.1 Chromosome analysis

With the nucleus having been shown to contain the hereditary material, attention focused on determining the precise nature of this material. As **chromosomes** only become visible during cell division, it was hardly surprising that they quickly attracted attention. Chromosomes were shown to be made up of protein and DNA. Of the two, protein was thought a more likely candidate as it was known to be a complex molecule existing in an almost infinite number of forms – a necessary characteristic of a material which must carry an immense diversity of information. Later work showed this not to be the case and research centred on the DNA.

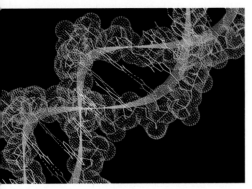

Computer representation of part of a DNA molecule

## 7.2.2 Metabolic stability of DNA

Any material which is responsible for transferring information from one generation to another must be extremely stable. If it were altered to any extent, imperfect copies would be made. Unlike protein, DNA shows remarkable metabolic stability. If DNA is labelled with a radioactive isotope, it can be shown that its rate of disappearance from the DNA is very slow. This suggests that, once formed, a DNA molecule undergoes little if any alteration.

| METHOD | RESULTS | CONCLUSION | EXPLANATION IN LIGHT OF PRESENT KNOWLEDGE |
|---|---|---|---|
| **Experiment 1**<br><br>*A. mediterranea* is cut into two approximately equal halves | The portion without the nucleus degenerates. The portion with the nucleus regenerates a new cap of the same type | The information for the regeneration of the cap is contained in, or produced by, the lower portion which contains the nucleus | The DNA in the nucleus produces mRNA which enters the cytoplasm where it provides the instructions for the formation of the enzymes needed in the production of a new cap. In the absence of a nucleus, the upper portion cannot do this |
| **Experiment 2**<br><br>*A. mediterranea* is cut to isolate the stalk section which does not contain the nucleus | A new cap is regenerated from the stalk section | The information on how to regenerate the cap is present in the stalk | As the nucleus produces a constant supply of mRNA there is sufficient in the cytoplasm of the stalk to provide instructions on how to form the enzymes necessary for the regeneration of the cap |
| **Experiment 3**<br><br>The regenerated cap from the previous experiment is again removed | The stalk does not regenerate a cap for a second time | The information on how to regenerate the cap, which is contained in the stalk, must be used up and so cannot effect a second regeneration | The mRNA is broken down once its role in regenerating the cap is complete. It is therefore not available for the cap to be generated a second time. In the absence of a nucleus, there is no new source of mRNA |
| **Experiment 4**<br><br>The stalk of *A. mediterranea* is grafted onto the base portion (which contains the nucleus) of *A.crenulata* – a species possessing a different shaped cap | The cap of *A.crenulata* is regenerated | The influence on cap regeneration of the base portion (with nucleus) is greater than the influence of the stalk portion (without the nucleus) | With the nucleus of *A. crenulata* present a constant supply of mRNA is available to regenerate this type of cap. The mRNA from *A.mediterranea* is limited to that present in the stalk when it was separated from its nucleus. The influence of the mRNA from *A. crenulata* is therefore greater |
| **Experiment 5**<br><br>The nucleus from a decapitated *A. crenulata* is removed and replaced with a transplanted nucleus from *A. mediterranea* | The cap regenerated is of the *A. mediterranea* type | As the only part of *A. mediterranea* which is present is the nucleus, it alone must contain the instruction on how to regenerate the cap | The situation is similar to that in experiment 4 except that it is the mRNA of *A. mediterranea* which is present in greater quantities, because its nucleus is present and forms a constant supply of mRNA |

*Fig. 7.1 Summary of experiments to show that the nucleus contains hereditary material*

### 7.2.3 Constancy of DNA within a cell

Almost all the DNA of a cell is associated with the chromosomes in the nucleus. Small amounts do occur in cytoplasmic organelles such as mitochondria, but this represents a small proportion of the total. Analysis shows that the amount of DNA remains constant for all cells within a species except for the gametes, which have almost exactly half the usual quantity. Prior to cell division the amount of DNA per cell doubles. This is shared equally between the two daughter cells which therefore have the usual quantity. These changes are consistent with those expected of hereditary material which is being transmitted from cell to cell during division.

### 7.2.4 Correlation between mutagens and their effects on DNA

**Mutagens** are agents which cause **mutations** in living organisms. A mutation is an alteration to an organism's characteristics which is inherited. Many agents are known mutagens; they include X-rays, nitrous acid and various dyes. It can be shown that these mutagens all alter the structure of DNA in some way. A typical example is ultra-violet light of wavelength 260 nm. It both causes mutations and alters the structure of the pyrimidine bases of which DNA is made. This suggests that it is this alteration of DNA which is the source of the mutation and DNA must therefore be the hereditary material.

### 7.2.5 Experiments on bacterial transformation

The most convincing evidence for the genetic role of DNA was provided by Griffith in 1928. He experimented on the bacterium *Pneumococcus* which causes pneumonia. It exists in two forms:

1. **The harmful form** – a virulent (disease-causing) type which has a gelatin coat. When grown on agar it produces **shiny, smooth** colonies and is therefore known as the S-strain.

2. **The safe form** – a non-virulent (does not cause disease) type which does not have a gelatin coat. When grown on agar it produces **dull, rough** colonies and is therefore known as the R-strain.

Griffith's experiments may be summarized thus:

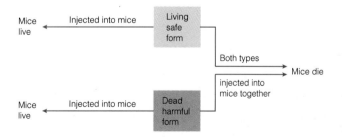

The living safe form and dead harmful form, while not causing pneumonia when injected separately, did so when injected together. The resulting dead mice were found to contain living harmful forms of *Pneumococcus*. If one discounts the improbable explanation that the dead harmful forms have been resurrected, how then could the living safe forms suddenly have acquired the ability to form a gelatin coat, produce smooth colonies and cause pneumonia? It is possible that the safe form had mutated into the harmful form, but this is unlikely. Furthermore, the experiment can be repeated with similar result and the likelihood of the same mutation arising each and every time is so improbable that it can be discounted.

If pneumonia is caused by some toxin produced by *Pneumococcus*, then the harmful type must have the ability to produce it, whereas the safe type does not. The explanation could therefore be that the dead harmful type has the information on how to make the toxin but, being dead, is unable to manufacture it. The safe type, being alive, is potentially able t make the toxin but lacks the information on how to go about it. then the recipe for the toxin can in some way be transferred from the dead harmful to the living safe variety, the toxin can be manufactured and pneumonia will result. As the substance was able to transform one strain of *Pneumococcus* into another, it became known as the **transforming principle**.

### 7.2.6 Experiments to identify the transforming principle

The identity of the transforming principle was determined by Avery, McCarty and McCleod in 1944. In a series of experiment they isolated and purified different substances from the dead harmful types of *Pneumococcus*. In turn they tested the ability of each to transform living safe types into harmful ones. Purified DNA was shown to be capable of bringing about transformation and this ability ceased when the enzyme which breaks down DNA (deoxyribonuclease) was added.

### 7.2.7 Transduction experiments

In 1952 Hershey and Chase performed a series of experiments involving the bacterium *Escherichia coli* and a bacteriophage ($T_2$ phage) which attacks it. (Details of a phage life-cycle are given in Section 5.2.1.) $T_2$ phage transfers to *E. coli* the necessary hereditar material needed to make it manufacture new $T_2$ phage viruses. As the $T_2$ phage virus is composed of just DNA and protein, one or the other must constitute the hereditary material. Hershey and Chase carefully labelled the protein of one phage sample with radioactive sulphur ($^{35}S$) and the DNA of another phage sample with radioactive phosphorus ($^{32}P$). They then separately introduced each sample into a culture of *E. coli* bacteria. At a critical stage, when the viruses had transferred their hereditary material into the bacterial cells, the two organisms were separated mechanically and each culture of bacteria was examined for radioactivity. The culture injected with radioactive DNA contained radioactive bacteria, while that injected with radioactive protein did not. The evidence was conclusive: DNA was the hereditary material; but if further proof were needed thi was provided by electron microscope studies which actually traced the movement of DNA from viruses into bacterial cells.

### Did you know?

Every cell contains all the DNA needed to make the entire organism from which it comes, and yet the DNA from a single cell of every human on earth would weigh a mere 0.024 g in total.

# 7.3 Nucleic acids

Adenosine monophosphate (adenylic acid)

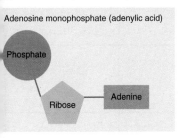

*Fig. 7.2 Structure of a typical nucleotide*

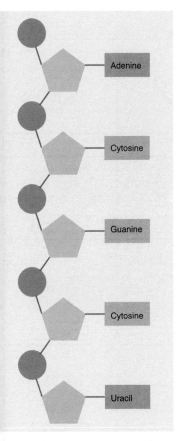

*Fig. 7.3 Structure of section of polynucleotide, e.g. RNA*

## 7.3.1 Structure of nucleotides

Individual nucleotides comprise three parts:

1. **Phosphoric acid** (phosphate $H_3PO_4$). This has the same structure in all nucleotides.

2. **Pentose sugar.** Two types occur, ribose ($C_5H_{10}O_5$) and deoxyribose ($C_5H_{10}O_4$).

3. **Organic base.** There are five different bases which are divided into two groups, described on the next page.

(a) **Pyrimidines** – these are single rings each with six sides. Examples found in nucleic acids are: **cytosine**, **thymine** and **uracil**.

(b) **Purines** – these are double rings comprising a six-sided and a five-sided ring. Two examples are found in nucleic acids: **adenine** and **guanine**.

The three components are combined by condensation reactions to give a nucleotide, the structure of which is shown in Fig. 7.2. By a similar condensation reaction between the sugar and phosphate groups of two nucleotides, a **dinucleotide** is formed. Continued condensation reactions lead to the formation of a **polynucleotide** (Fig. 7.3).

The main function of nucleotides is the formation of the nucleic acids **RNA** and **DNA** which play vital roles in protein synthesis and heredity. In addition they form part of other metabolically important molecules. Table 7.1 gives some examples.

TABLE 7.1 **Biologically important molecules containing nucleotides, and their functions**

| Molecule | Abbreviation | Function |
|---|---|---|
| Deoxyribonucleic acid | DNA | Contains the genetic information of cells |
| Ribonucleic acid | RNA | All three types play a vital role in protein synthesis |
| Adenosine monophosphate<br>Adenosine diphosphate<br>Adenosine triphosphate | AMP<br>ADP<br>ATP | Coenzymes important in making energy available to cells for metabolic activities, osmotic work, muscular contractions, etc. |
| Nicotinamide adenine dinucleotide<br>Flavine adenine dinucleotide | NAD<br>FAD | Electron (hydrogen) carriers important in respiration in transferring hydrogen atoms from the Krebs cycle along the respiratory chain |
| Nicotinamide adenine dinucleotide phosphate | NADP | Electron (hydrogen) carrier important in photosynthesis for accepting electrons from the chlorophyll molecule and making them available for the photolysis of water |
| Coenzyme A | CoA | Coenzyme important in respiration in combining with pyruvate to form acetyl coenzyme A and transferring the acetyl group into the Krebs cycle |

| NAME OF MOLECULE | CHEMICAL STRUCTURE | REPRESENTATIVE SHAPE |
|---|---|---|
| Phosphate | 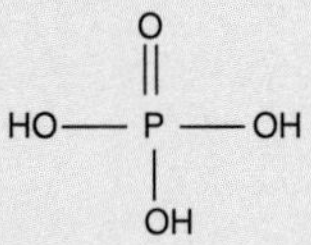 | |
| Ribose | 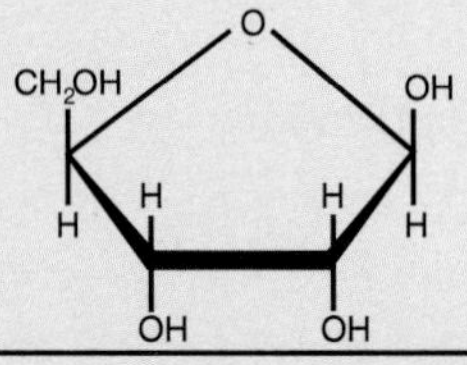 | |
| Deoxyribose | 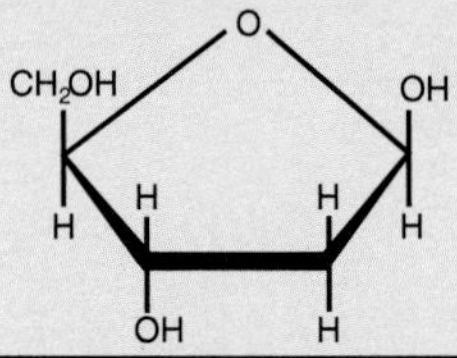 | |
| Adenine (a purine) | 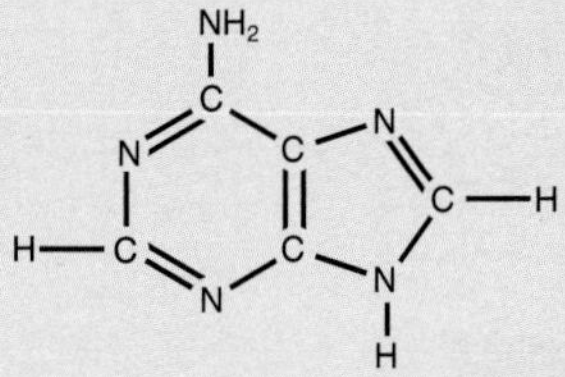 |  Adenine |
| Guanine (a purine) | 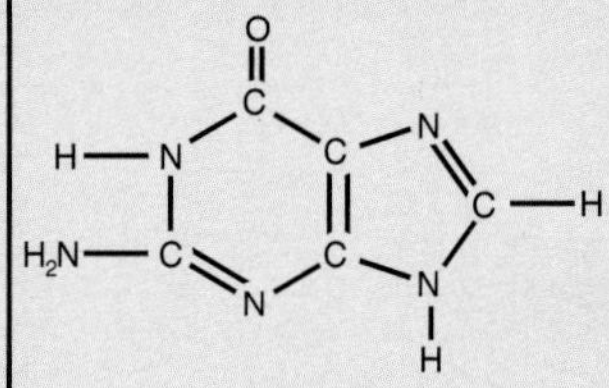 | Guanine |
| Cytosine (a pyrimidine) | 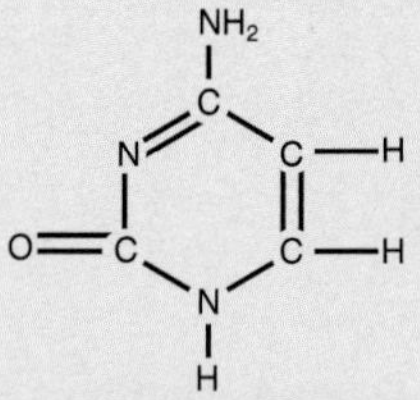 | 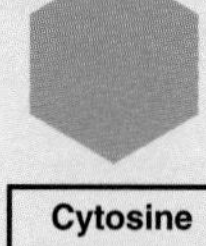 Cytosine |
| Thymine (a pyrimidine) | 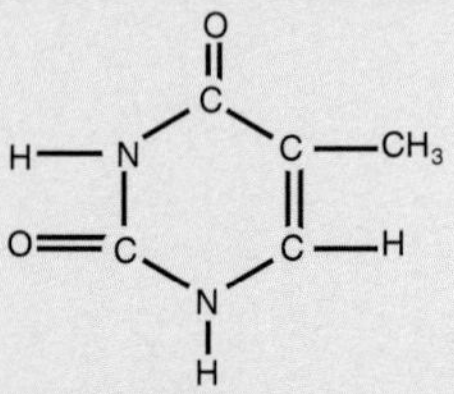 | Thymine |
| Uracil (a pyrimidine) | 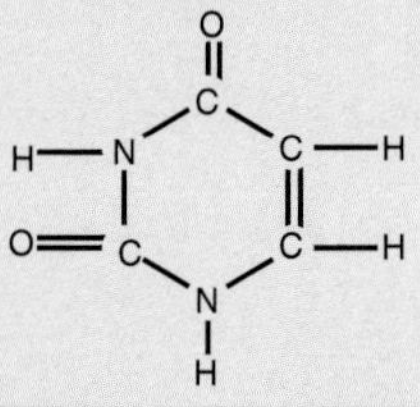 | Uracil |

*Fig. 7.4 Structure of molecules in a nucleotide*

## 7.3.2 Ribonucleic acid (RNA)

**RNA** is a single-stranded polymer of nucleotides where the pentose sugar is always ribose and the organic bases are adenine, guanine, cytosine and uracil. Its basic structure is given in Fig. 7.3. There are three types of RNA found in cells, all of which are involved in protein synthesis.

**Ribosomal RNA (rRNA)** is a large, complex molecule made up of both double and single helices. Although it is manufactured by the DNA of the nucleus, it is found in the cytoplasm where it makes up more than half the mass of the ribosomes. It comprises more than half the mass of the total RNA of a cell and its base sequence is similar in all organisms.

**Transfer RNA (tRNA)** is a small molecule (about 80 nucleotides) comprising a single strand. Again it is manufactured by nuclear DNA. It makes up 10–15% of the cell's RNA and all types are fundamentally similar. It forms a clover-leaf shape (Fig. 7.5), with one end of the chain ending in a cytosine–cytosine–adenine sequence. It is at this point that an amino acid attaches itself. There are at least 20 types of tRNA, each carrying a different amino acid. At an intermediate point along the chain is an important sequence of three bases, called the **anticodon**. These line up alongside the appropriate codon on the mRNA during protein synthesis (Section 7.6).

**Messenger RNA (mRNA)** is a long single-stranded molecule, of up to thousands of nucleotides, which is formed into a helix. Manufactured in the nucleus, it is a mirror copy of part of one strand of the DNA helix. There is hence an immense variety of types. It enters the cytoplasm where it associates with the ribosomes and acts as a template for protein synthesis (Section 7.6). It makes up less than 5% of the total cellular RNA. It is easily and quickly broken down, sometimes existing for only a matter of minutes.

## 7.3.3 Deoxyribonucleic acid (DNA)

DNA is a double-stranded polymer of nucleotides where the pentose sugar is always deoxyribose and the organic bases are adenine, guanine, cytosine and thymine, but never uracil. Each of these polynucleotide chains is extremely long and may contain many million nucleotide units.

By the early 1950s, information on DNA from a variety of sources had been collected, but no molecular structure had been agreed. The available facts about DNA included:

1. It is a very long, thin molecule made up of nucleotides.

2. It contains four organic bases: adenine, guanine, cytosine and thymine.

3. The amount of guanine is usually equal to that of cytosine.

4. The amount of adenine is usually equal to that of thymine.

5. It is probably in the form of a helix whose shape is maintained by hydrogen bonding.

Using the accumulated evidence, James Watson and Francis Crick in 1953 suggested a molecular structure which proved to be one of the greatest milestones in biology. They postulated a

ig. 7.5 Structure of transfer RNA

### Did you know?

Each cell in the body contains about 2 metres of DNA. If all the DNA in all the cells of a single human were stretched out, it would reach to the moon and back 8000 times.

TABLE 7.2    **Differences between RNA and DNA**

| RNA | DNA |
|---|---|
| Single polynucleotide chain | Double polynucleotide chain |
| Smaller molecular mass (20 000–2 000 000) | Larger molecular mass (100 000–150 000 000) |
| May have a single or double helix | Always a double helix |
| Pentose sugar is ribose | Pentose sugar is deoxyribose |
| Organic bases present are adenine, guanine, cytosine and uracil | Organic bases present are adenine, guanine, cytosine and thymine |
| Ratio of adenine and uracil to cytosine and guanine varies | Ratio of adenine and thymine to cytosine and guanine is one |
| Manufactured in the nucleus but found throughout the cell | Found almost entirely in the nucleus |
| Amount varies from cell to cell (and within a cell according to metabolic activity) | Amount is constant for all cells of a species (except gametes and spores) |
| Chemically less stable | Chemically very stable |
| May be temporary – existing for short periods only | Permanent |
| Three basic forms: messenger, transfer and ribosomal RNA | Only one basic form, but with an almost infinite variety within that form |

double helix of two nucleotide strands, each strand being linked to the other by pairs of organic bases which are themselves joined by hydrogen bonds. The pairings are always cytosine with guanine and adenine with thymine. This was not only consistent with the known ratio of the bases in the molecule, but also allowed for an identical separation of the strands throughout the molecule, a fact shown to be the case from X-ray diffraction patterns. As the purines, adenine and guanine, are double ringed structures (Fig. 7.4) they form much longer links paired together than the two single ringed pyrimidines, cytosine and thymine. Only by pairing one purine with one pyrimidine can a consistent separation of three rings' width be achieved. In effect, the structure is like a ladder where the deoxyribose and phosphate units form the uprights and the organic base pairings form the rungs. However, this is no ordinary ladder; instead it is twisted into a helix so that each upright winds around the other. The two chains that form the uprights run in opposite directions, i.e. are **antiparallel**. The structure of DNA is shown in Figs. 7.6–7.8.

The structure postulated both fitted the known facts about DNA and was consistent with its biological role. Its extreme length (around 2.5 billion base pairs in a typical mammalian cell) permitted a very long sequence of bases which could be almost infinitely various, thus providing an immense store of genetic information. In addition its structure allowed for its replication. The separation of the two strands would result in each half attracting its complementary nucleotide to itself. The subsequent joining of these nucleotides would form two identical DNA double helices. This fitted the observation that DNA content doubles prior to cell division. Each double helix could then enter one of the daughter cells and so restore the normal quantity of DNA.

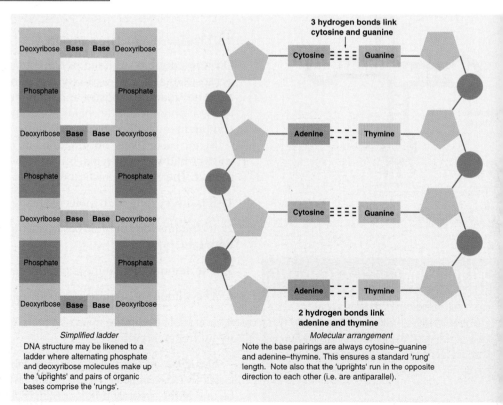

*Simplified ladder*

DNA structure may be likened to a ladder where alternating phosphate and deoxyribose molecules make up the 'uprights' and pairs of organic bases comprise the 'rungs'.

*Molecular arrangement*

Note the base pairings are always cytosine–guanine and adenine–thymine. This ensures a standard 'rung' length. Note also that the 'uprights' run in the opposite direction to each other (i.e. are antiparallel).

*Fig. 7.6 Basic structure of DNA*

### 7.3.4 Differences between RNA and DNA

Despite the obvious similarities between these two nucleic acids, a number of differences exist and these are listed in Table 7.2.

## 7.4　DNA replication

*The uprights are composed of deoxyribose–phosphate molecules, the rungs of pairs of bases*

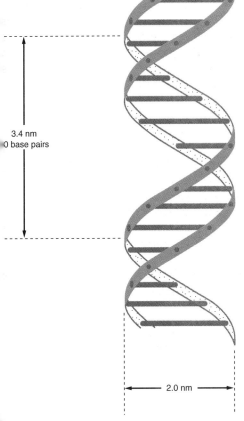

3.4 nm
0 base pairs

2.0 nm

*Fig. 7.7 The DNA double helix structure*

The Watson–Crick model for DNA allows for a relatively simple method by which the molecule can make exact copies of itself, something which must occur if genetic information is to be transmitted from cell to cell and from generation to generation. Replication is controlled by the enzyme DNA polymerase and an illustrated description is given in Fig. 7.9 on the next page.

Evidence for **semi-conservative replication** came from experiments by Meselsohn and Stahl. They grew successive generations of *Escherichia coli* in a medium where all the available nitrogen was in the form of the isotope $^{15}N$ (heavy nitrogen). In time, all the nitrogen in the DNA of *E. coli* was of the heavy nitrogen type. As DNA contains much nitrogen, the molecular weight of this DNA was measurably greater than that of DNA with normal nitrogen ($^{14}N$).

The *E. coli* containing the heavy DNA were then transferred into a medium containing normal nitrogen ($^{14}N$). Any new DNA produced would need to use this normal nitrogen in its manufacture. The question was, would the new DNA all be of the light type (contain only $^{14}N$) or would it, as the semi-conservative replication theory suggests, be made up of one original strand of heavy DNA and one new strand of light DNA? In the latter case its weight would be intermediate between the heavy and light types. To answer this they allowed *E. coli* to divide once and collected all the first generation cells. The DNA from them was then extracted and its relative weight determined by special techniques involving centrifugation with caesium chloride. As the results depicted in Fig. 7.10 show, the weight was indeed intermediate between the heavy and light DNA types, thus confirming the semi-conservative replication theory.

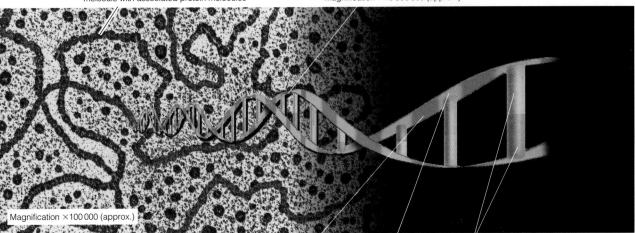

Electron micrograph of part of the long DNA molecule with associated protein molecules

Drawing of the DNA double helix without associated protein. Magnification ×13 000 000 (approx.)

Magnification ×100 000 (approx.)

*Fig. 7.8 Deoxyribonucleic acid*

Phosphate　　Deoxyribose sugar　　Complementary base pair

**1.** *A representative portion of DNA, which is about to undergo replication, is shown.*

**2.** *DNA polymerase causes the two strands of the DNA to separate.*

**3.** *The DNA polymerase completes the splittin of the strand. Meanwhile free nucleotides are attracted to their complementary bases.*

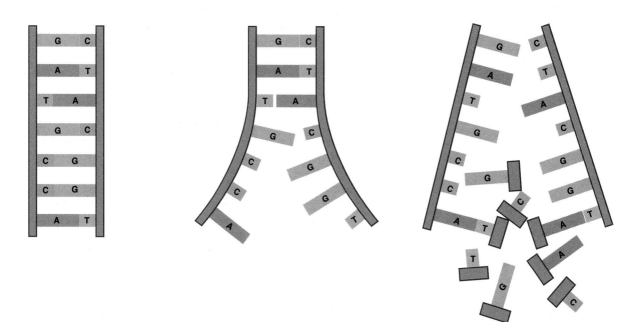

**4.** *Once the nucleotides are lined up they join together (bottom 3 nucleotides). The remaining unpaired bases continue to attract their complementary nucleotides.*

**5.** *Finally all the nucleotides are joined to form a complete polynucleotide chain. In this way two identical strands of DNA are formed. As each strand retains half of the original DNA material, this method of replication is called the semi-conservative method.*

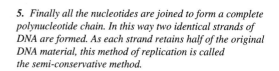

*Fig 7.9 The replication of DNA*

If a second generation of *E. coli* is grown from the first generation it is found to comprise half light and half intermediate weight DNA. Can you explain this?

Analysis shows that the replication of DNA takes place during interphase, shortly before cell division. Thus when the chromatids appear during prophase each has a double helix of DNA.

# 7.5  The genetic code

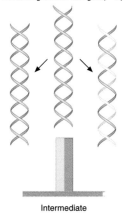

DNA made with $^{14}$N (normal nitrogen)
DNA made with $^{15}$N (heavy nitrogen)

DNA extracted from *E. coli* grown in a medium containing normal nitrogen ($^{14}$N)

All DNA is of the 'light' type

Light

DNA extracted from *E. coli* grown in a medium containing heavy nitrogen ($^{15}$N) and then transferred to a medium containing normal nitrogen ($^{14}$N)

Intermediate

DNA extracted from *E. coli* grown in a medium containing heavy nitrogen ($^{15}$N)

Heavy

Relative weight of DNA as determined by centifugation

*ig. 7.10 Interpretation of Meselsohn–Stahl xperiments on semi-conservative replication of DNA*

Once the structure of DNA had been elucidated and its mechanism of replication discovered, one important question remained: how exactly are the genetic instructions stored on the DNA in such a way that they can be used to mastermind the construction of new cells and organisms? Most chemicals within cells are similar regardless of the type of cell or species of organism. It is in their proteins and DNA that cells and organisms differ. It seems a reasonable starting point, therefore, to assume that the DNA in some way provides a 'code' for an organism's proteins. Moreover, most chemicals in cells are manufactured with the aid of enzymes, and all enzymes are proteins. Therefore by determining which enzymes are produced, the DNA can determine an organism's characteristics. Every species possesses different DNA and hence produces different enzymes. The DNA of different species differs not in the chemicals which it comprises, but in the sequence of base pairs along its length. This sequence must be a code that determines which proteins are manufactured.

Proteins show almost infinite variety. This variety likewise depends upon a sequence, in this instance the sequence of amino acids in the protein (Section 2.7.1). There are just 20 amino acids which regularly occur in proteins, and each must presumably have its own code of bases on the DNA. With only four different bases present in DNA, if each coded for a different amino acid, only four different amino acids could be coded for. Using a pair of bases, 16 different codes are possible – still inadequate. A triplet code of bases produces 64 codes, more than enough to satisfy the requirements of 20 amino acids. This is called the **triplet code**.

The next problem was to determine the precise codon for each amino acid. Nirenberg devised a series of experiments towards the end of the 1950s which allowed him to break the code. He synthesized mRNA which had a triplet of bases repeated many times, e.g. GUA, GUA, GUA etc. He prepared test tubes which contained cell-free extracts of *E. coli*, i.e. they possessed all the necessary biochemical requirements for protein synthesis. Twenty tubes were set up, each with a different radioactively labelled amino acid. His synthesized mRNA was added to each tube and the presence of a polypeptide was looked for. Only in the test tube containing valine was a polypeptide found, indicating that GUA codes for valine. By repeating the process for all 64 possible combinations of bases, Nirenberg was able to determine which amino acid each coded for.

In some cases only the first two bases of the codon are relevant. Valine for instance is coded for by GU*, where * can be any of the four bases. Some amino acids have up to six codons. Arginine, for example, has CGU, CGC, CGA, CGG, AGA and AGG. At the other extreme, methionine, with AUG, and tryptophan, with UGG, have only one codon each. As there is more than one triplet for most amino acids it is called a **degenerate code** (a term derived from cybernetics). There are three codons UAA, UAG and UGA which are not amino acid codes. These are **stop** or **nonsense codons** and their importance is discussed in Section 7.6.4

115

All the codons are **universal**, i.e. they are precisely the same for all organisms.

The code is also **non-overlapping** in that each triplet is read separately. For example, CUGAGCUAG is read as CUG–AGC–UAG and not CUG–UGA–GAG–AGC etc., where each triplet overlaps the previous one, in this case by two bases. Overlapping would allow more information to be provided by a given base sequence, but it limits flexibility. Some viruses, with limited amounts of DNA, may use overlapping codes, but this is very rare.

## 7.6    Protein synthesis

If the triplet code on the DNA molecule determines the sequence of amino acids in a given protein, how exactly is the information transferred from the DNA, and how is the protein assembled? There are four main stages in the formation of a protein:

1. Synthesis of amino acids.

2. Transcription (formation of mRNA).

3. Amino acid activation.

4. Translation.

### 7.6.1 Synthesis of amino acids

In plants, the formation of amino acids occurs in mitochondria and chloroplasts in a series of stages:

(a) absorption of nitrates from the soil (Section 22.7.1);

(b) reduction of these nitrates to the amino group ($NH_2$);

(c) combination of these amino groups with a carbohydrate skeleton (e.g. $\alpha$-ketoglutarate from Krebs cycle);

(d) transfer of the amino groups from one carbohydrate skeleton to another by a process called **transamination**. In this way all 20 amino acids can be formed.

Animals usually obtain their amino acids from the food they ingest, although they have some capacity to synthesize their own **non-essential amino acids**. The remaining nine – **essential amino acids** – must be provided in the diet.

### 7.6.2 Transcription (formation of messenger RNA)

Transcription is the process by which a complementary mRNA copy is made of the specific region of the DNA molecule which codes for a polypeptide (about 17 base pairs). A specific region of the DNA molecule, called a **cistron**, unwinds. This unwinding is the result of hydrogen bonds between base pairs in the DNA double helix being broken. This exposes the bases along each strand. Each base along one strand attracts its complementary RNA nucleotide, i.e. a free guanine base on the DNA will attract an RNA nucleotide with a cytosine base. It should be remembered, however, that uracil, and not thymine, is attracted to adenine (Fig. 7.11).

A portion of DNA, called a cistron, unwinds. One strand acts as a template for the formation of mRNA

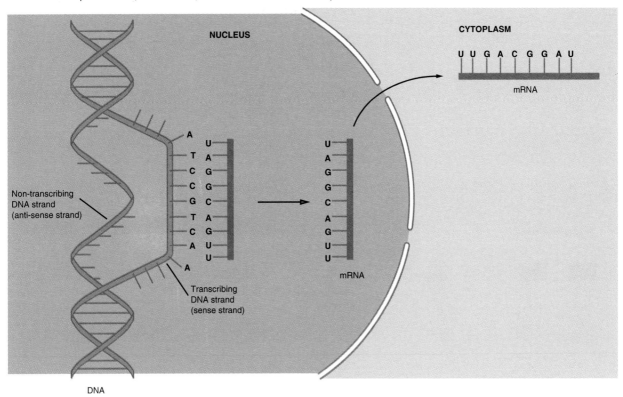

*Fig. 7.11 Transcription*

The enzyme **RNA polymerase** moves along the DNA adding one complementary RNA nucleotide at a time to the newly unwound portion of DNA. The region of base pairing between the DNA and the RNA is only around 12 base pairs at any one time as the DNA helix reforms behind the RNA polymerase. The DNA thus acts as a **template** against which mRNA is constructed. A number of mRNA molecules may be formed before the RNA polymerase leaves the DNA, which closes up reforming its double helix. Being too large to diffuse across the nuclear membrane, the mRNA leaves instead through the nuclear pores. In the cytoplasm it is attracted to the ribosomes. Along the mRNA is a sequence of triplet codes which have been determined by the DNA. Each triplet is called a **codon**.

### 7.6.3 Amino acid activation

**Activation** is the process by which amino acids combine with tRNA using energy from ATP. Fig. 7.5 shows the structure of a tRNA molecule. Each type of tRNA binds with a specific amino acid, which means there must be at least 20 types of tRNA. Each type differs, among other things, in the composition of a triplet of bases called the **anticodon**. What all tRNA molecules have in common is a free end which terminates in the triplet CCA. It is to this free end that the individual amino acids become attached, although how each specific amino acid is specified is not known (Fig. 7.12). The tRNA molecules with attached amino acids now move towards the ribosomes.

117

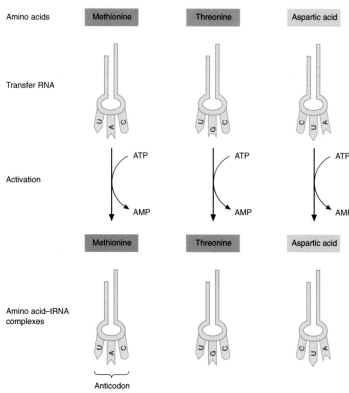

Fig. 7.12 Activation

### 7.6.4 Translation

Translation is the means by which a specific sequence of amino acids is formed in accordance with the codons on the mRNA. A group of ribosomes becomes attached to the mRNA to form a structure called a **polysome**. The complementary anticodon of a

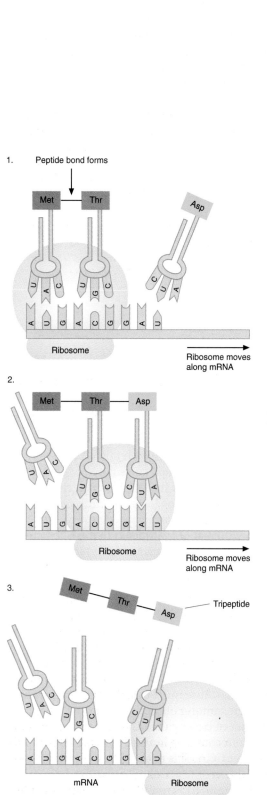

Fig. 7.13(a) Translation

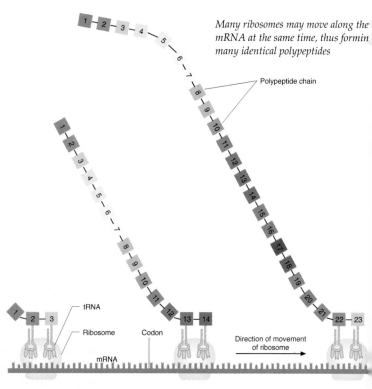

Fig. 7.13(b) Polypeptide formation

tRNA–amino acid complex is attracted to the first codon on the mRNA. The second codon likewise attracts its complementary anticodon. The ribosome acts as a framework which holds the mRNA and tRNA–amino acid complex together until the two amino acids form a peptide bond between each other. Once they have combined, the ribosome will move along the mRNA to hold the next codon–anticodon complex together until the third amino acid is linked with the second. In this way a polypeptide chain is assembled, by the addition of one amino acid at a time. Second and subsequent ribosomes may pass along the mRNA immediately behind the first. In this way many identical polypeptides are produced simultaneously.

Once each amino acid is linked, the tRNA which carried it to the mRNA is released back into the cytoplasm. It is again free to combine with its specific amino acid. The ribosome continues along the mRNA until it reaches one of the nonsense codes (Section 7.5) at which point the polypeptide is cast off. The process of translation is summarized in Fig. 7.13.

The polypeptides so formed must now be assembled into proteins. This may involve the spiralling of the polypeptide to give a secondary structure, its folding to give a tertiary structure and its combination with other polypeptides and/or prosthetic groups to give a quaternary structure (see Fig. 2.13 on p. 30).

## Did you know?

Eukaryotic genes contain regions called **introns** which do not code for amino acids. The parts of the gene that do code for amino acids are called **exons**.

## 7.7 Genetic engineering

The part of the DNA molecule which specifies a polypeptide is termed a gene.

Perhaps the most significant scientific advance in recent years has been the development of technology which allows genes to be manipulated, altered and transferred from organism to organism – even to transform DNA itself. This has enabled us to use rapidly reproducing organisms such as bacteria as chemical factories producing useful, often life-saving, substances. The list of these substances expands almost daily and includes hormones, antibiotics, interferon and vitamins. Details of the production of some of these chemicals are given in Chapter 30.

### 7.7.1 Recombinant DNA technology

A number of human diseases are the result of individuals being unable to produce for themselves chemicals which have a metabolic role. Many such chemicals, e.g. insulin and thyroxine, are proteins and therefore the product of a specific portion of DNA. The treatment of such deficiencies previously involved extracting the missing chemical from either an animal or human donor. This has presented problems. While the animal extracts may function effectively, subtle chemical differences in their composition have been detected by the human immune system, which has responded by producing antibodies which destroy the extract. Even chemically compatible extracts from human donors present a risk of infection from other diseases, as the transmission of the HIV virus to haemophiliacs illustrates only too well. Whether from animals or humans, the cost of such extracts is considerable.

It follows that there are advantages in producing large quantities of 'pure' chemicals from non-human sources. As a result, methods have been devised for isolating the portion of human DNA responsible for the production of insulin and combining it with bacterial DNA in such a way that the microorganism will continually produce the substance. This DNA, which results from the combination of fragments from two different organisms, is called **recombinant DNA**.

### 7.7.2 Techniques used to manipulate DNA

The manipulation of DNA involves three main techniques, each using a specific enzyme or group of enzymes:

### 1. Cutting of DNA into small sections using restriction endonucleases

These enzymes are used to cut DNA between specific base sequences which the enzyme recognizes. For example, Hae III nuclease recognizes a four base-pair sequence and cuts it as shown by the arrow:

```
G   G ↑ C   C ⎫
             ⎬   four complementary base-pairs
C   C ↓ G   G ⎭   on DNA double helix
```

The Hind III nuclease however recognizes a six base-pair sequence, cutting it as shown by the arrow below:

```
A ↑ A   G   C   T   T ⎫   six complementary base-
                     ⎬   pairs on DNA double helix
T   T   C   G   A ↓ A ⎭
```

As any sequence of four base-pairs is likely to occur more frequently than a six base-pair sequence, the nucleases recognizing four base-pairs cut DNA into smaller sections than those recognizing six base-pairs. The latter group are, however, more useful as the longer sections they produce are more likely to contain an intact gene.

### 2. Production of copies of DNA using either plasmids or reverse transcriptase

In bacterial cells there are small circular loops of DNA called **plasmids**. Plasmids are distinct from the larger circular portion of DNA which make up the bacterial chromosome. Bacteria replicate their plasmid DNA so that a single cell contains many copies. If a portion of DNA from, say, a human cell, is inserted into a plasmid and it is reintroduced into the bacterial cell, replication of the plasmid will result in up to 200 identical copies of the human DNA being made. A population of bacteria containing this human DNA can now be grown to provide a permanent source of it. By repeating the process for other DNA portions, a complete library of human DNA can be maintained. Geneticists can then select any gene they require for further investigation or use, in much the same way as a book is selected from a conventional library. Selection is, however, more complex, requiring the use of DNA probes or specific antibodies. This collection of genetic information is called a **genome library**.

A second method of duplicating particular portions of DNA is appropriate where the protein for which it codes is synthesized in a specific organ. Thyroxine, for example, is produced in the thyroid gland and therefore cells from this gland would be expected to contain a relatively large amount of messenger RNA which codes for thyroxine. Reverse transcriptase (Section 5.2.2) can be used to synthesize DNA, called **copy DNA (cDNA)**, from the mRNA in thyroid cells. A large proportion of the cDNA produced is likely to code for thyroxine, and it can be isolated using the techniques described in Section 7.7.3.

**3. Joining together portions of DNA using DNA ligase**
The recombination of pieces of DNA, e.g. the addition of cDNA into bacterial plasmid DNA, is carried out with the aid of the enzyme **DNA ligase**.

### 7.7.3 Gene cloning

The techniques described in the previous section are utilized in the process of gene cloning in which multiple copies of a specific gene are produced which may then be used to manufacture large quantities of valuable products.

Manufacture involves the following stages:

1. Identification of the required gene.

2. Isolation of that gene.

3. Copying of the gene. (See Biology Around Us – Polymerase chain reaction on the next page.)

4. Insertion of the gene into a vector.

5. Insertion of the vector into a host cell (see section 7.7.4).

6. Multiplication of the host cell.

7. Synthesis of the required product by the host cell.

8. Separation of the product from the host cell.

9. Purification of the product.

Figure 7.14 illustrates how gene cloning is used in the production of insulin. The bacteria produced in this way can be grown in industrial fermenters using a specific nutrient medium under strictly controlled conditions. The bacteria may then be collected and the insulin extracted from them by suitable means. Alternatively, it is possible to engineer bacteria which secrete the insulin and this can be extracted from the medium which is periodically drawn off. Details of these, and other, fermentation techniques are given in Chapter 30.

### 7.7.4 Insertion of vector into a host cell

The final destination of a particular gene is not always a bacterial cell as shown in Fig 7.14. It may be that the gene is to be transferred to another organism such as a crop plant. In this case the bacterium chosen to transfer the gene has to be one which readily infects the other plants. A common choice is *Agrobacterium tumefaciens*. This bacterium forms cancerous growths, called galls, when it invades plant cells by incorporating its large tumour-inducing plasmid into the genome of the host cells. As *Agrobacterium tumefaciens* has a number of different strains it therefore infects a wide variety of different plants making it especially useful in transferring genes into new organisms.

Since not all the bacteria will take up the plasmid containing the gene to be transferred it pays to be sure that *Agrobacterium* actually contains the desired gene before infecting a host plant

## BIOLOGY AROUND US

# Polymerase chain reaction (PCR)

The polymerase chain reaction is a process whereby a selected short length of DNA can be copied millions of times. In order to make these copies all that is required are

1. The length of double-stranded DNA to be copied.

2. DNA polymerase – an enzyme capable of adding 70 000 bases in just a few minutes.

3. Primers – short pieces of DNA complementary to the bases at each end of the DNA which is to be copied.

4. Thermocycler – a computer-controlled piece of apparatus programmed for the critical temperatures and appropriate times.

The DNA, excess primers and DNA polymerase are put into a microtube and placed in the thermocycler at 73°C. The temperature is then raised to 95°C, which separates the two strands of DNA. The mixture is then cooled slowly to 56°C, causing the primers to anneal (join) to their complementary areas. Reheating to 73°C promotes the formation of complementary DNA strands by DNA polymerase. There are then two pieces of the required length of DNA. The process can be repeated to give 4, 8, 16 and eventually millions of copies.

| At 73°C | At 95°C | At 56°C | At 73°C |
|---|---|---|---|
| • Piece of double-stranded DNA to be copied | • Strands separate<br><br>• Primers ( ) ready for next stage | • Primers anneal to complementary areas<br><br>• DNA polymerase ( ) ready for next stage | • Enzyme promotes formation of complementary strand<br><br>• There are now two copies of the original DNA |

*Polymerase chain reaction*

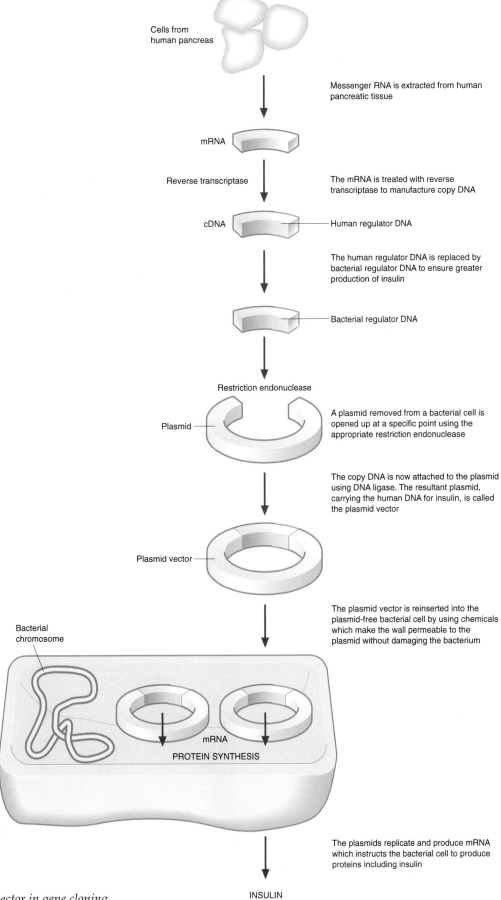

Cells from
human pancreas

Messenger RNA is extracted from human
pancreatic tissue

mRNA

Reverse transcriptase

The mRNA is treated with reverse
transcriptase to manufacture copy DNA

cDNA

Human regulator DNA

The human regulator DNA is replaced by
bacterial regulator DNA to ensure greater
production of insulin

Bacterial regulator DNA

Restriction endonuclease

Plasmid

A plasmid removed from a bacterial cell is
opened up at a specific point using the
appropriate restriction endonuclease

The copy DNA is now attached to the plasmid
using DNA ligase. The resultant plasmid,
carrying the human DNA for insulin, is called
the plasmid vector

Plasmid vector

The plasmid vector is reinserted into the
plasmid-free bacterial cell by using chemicals
which make the wall permeable to the
plasmid without damaging the bacterium

Bacterial
chromosome

mRNA
PROTEIN SYNTHESIS

The plasmids replicate and produce mRNA
which instructs the bacterial cell to produce
proteins including insulin

*ig. 7.14 Use of plasmid vector in gene cloning*

INSULIN

# BIOLOGY AROUND US

## Cystic fibrosis and gene therapy

One person in 2000 in Britain suffers from cystic fibrosis. CF patients produce mucus secretions which are too viscous. Thick, sticky mucus blocks the pancreatic duct and prevents pancreatic enzymes from reaching the duodenum; clogging up of the lungs leads to recurrent infections.

The long arm of chromosome 7 carries the CFTR (cystic fibrosis transmembrane conductance regulator) gene which codes for a protein which is essential for chloride transport. Everyone has two copies of this gene in every cell, one from the mother and one from the father. As long as one copy of the CFTR gene works correctly chloride transport is adequate but if two defective genes are present CF results.

Microbiologists have succeeded in isolating and cloning the CFTR gene and have found that 70% of its mutations consist of the same change to the normal DNA sequence. CFTR is a big gene, covering 250 000 base pairs of DNA and the commonest mutation is a small deletion in which three nucleotides are missing. After transcription and translation the CFTR gene lacks one amino acid, phenylalanine number 508, in the protein chain. People who have at least one chromosome bearing this mutation can be identified in the laboratory. This is done by using a blood sample or shed cells in a mouthwash to collect a DNA sample. DNA polymerase is used to make many copies of a 50 base-pair segment of both CFTR genes. The copies are then run on an electrophoretic gel (see Notebook, p. 26) in which small fragments move faster than big ones. If either of the CFTR genes has the three-base deletion it will move more quickly.

This test is quick and easy. A series of other, more expensive, tests would enable another 20% of CF carriers to be identified. But once a carrier for CF, or any other genetic disease, has been identified is it possible to replace the mutant gene with a normal version of the gene? Gene therapy is now becoming a realistic possibility, although there are many medical and ethical problems to be solved.

In **germ-line therapy** the approach could be to repair the gene in a fertilized egg so that the repaired gene would be

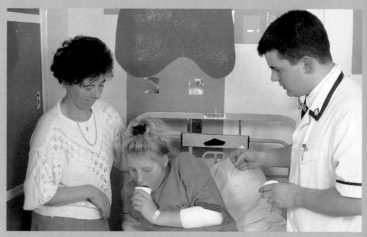

Cystic fibrosis patient coughing up mucus following treatment to loosen it

copied into each daughter cell at mitosis. In this way the mutant gene will not only have been eliminated from the person receiving treatment, but also from all his or her offspring. This raises the ethical question of whether we have the right to alter the genes of future generations, and following the report of the Warnock Committee such germ-line therapy is prohibited in Britain.

Research now centres on a different approach: **somatic cell gene therapy**. Although the mutated gene occurs in every cell of the patient's body, somatic cell gene therapy would target just the affected tissues, for example:

the lungs in cystic fibrosis;

the muscles in Duchenne muscular dystrophy;

blood cells or their precursors (reticulocytes in the bone marrow) in $\beta$-thalassaemia.

These tissues are fully differentiated and will eventually die, so treatments may have to be repeated as the treated cells die and are replaced. It has not yet been possible to isolate and treat the undifferentiated stem cells which give rise to the mature tissues. It is relatively easy to introduce large molecules of DNA into a cell nucleus using a fine glass needle or by subjecting cells in a test tube to an electric pulse which causes temporary holes in the plasma membrane and induces them to take up DNA. DNA can also be carried into the cell by a suitable virus.

There are two types of genetic disease: those due to loss of function and those due to gain of function. Gain-of-function diseases are normally dominant and the mutated gene which causes them is doing something positively bad. Such a gene would need to be removed or neutralized and this is proving a very difficult task. On the other hand gene supplementation treatment looks promising for CF sufferers. The CFTR gene could be introduced via a harmless viral vector, or by wrapping the gene in lipid molecules which can pass through the membranes of lung cells. This would leave patients with their digestive problems but would solve the problem of congested and infected lungs.

An example of successful treatment by gene supplementation is in Severe Combined Immunodeficiency Disease (SCID). The gene coding for adenosine deaminase is mutated and homozygotes are unable to deaminate adenosine. This leads to the death of lymphocytes and sufferers have no immunity at all. Since 1990 two affected children have had some of their lymphocyte precursor cells infected with a special virus carrying the missing gene. The treatment is repeated every month or so to replace the lymphocytes as they die and the two children now attend normal schools.

For many Mendelian recessive disorders in which the damage is confined to an accessible tissue, gene therapy by gene supplementation looks a promising way forward. Even cancer, where mutations are confined to tumour cells, may be a candidate for gene therapy in the future.

## BIOLOGY AROUND US

### Transgenic animals

While it is possible to clone plants from any differentiated plant cell, the same is not true of animals. It is however possible to mix together cells from two different embryos, such as a sheep and a goat, to produce a chimera, in this example called a geep.

The problem with chimeras is that no-one can predict which cells will form which part of the animal. A more precise method of producing desired characteristics is to augment traditional animal breeding by genetic engineering to make transgenic animals.

For a brief time following the fusion of a sperm and an ovum, the cell contains two pronuclei. Cloned DNA (Section 7.7.3) can be injected into one of these and in some cases it will integrate into one or more of the chromosomes. The manipulated offspring are then transferred to a foster mother and the resulting offspring screened for the presence of the introduced gene. A more recent approach which allows the gene to be positioned more precisely involves transferring the DNA into embryonic stem cells (cells from embryos prior to implantation). These cells can be grown indefinitely in a test tube and can be monitored to see if they produce the desired protein before they are injected into a normal embryo and transferred to a foster mother.

Genetic engineering may be used to improve animal health. For example, genes responsible for resistance to a particular disease could be introduced into otherwise vulnerable animals. Transgenic animals may also be used to produce rare and expensive proteins for use in human medicine. The genes coding for certain proteins may be expressed in a sheep's mammary glands and the protein recovered from the milk. Researchers have managed to insert the gene for a blood clotting protein known as factor IX alongside the regulator of the lactoglobulin gene which encodes for one of the proteins in sheep's milk. The transgenic ewes now produce factor IX in their milk and it can be used to treat one type of haemophilia. Some people suffer congenital emphysema (page 405) because they are unable to make a protein known as ATT (alpha-1-antitrypsin). This protein can also be extracted from the milk of transgenic ewes.

In transgenic animals the 'foreign' DNA has become stably integrated into the animal's own genome so that it can be passed from generation to generation, effectively giving rise to a new strain of the animal.

This transgenic ram has had a human gene incorporated into its DNA. This gene for the production of the protein alpha-1-antitrypsin (ATT) is inherited by the ram's offspring and the protein is secreted in the ewe's milk

with it. To achieve this, the desired gene is not transferred on its own, but along with a second gene, called a **marker gene**. Such marker gene codes for a distinctive characteristic such as the ability to break down antibiotics, i.e. an antibiotic resistant gene. To identify those bacteria which possess the gene we wish to transfer, we simply grow them on a media containing an antibiotic. Those *Agrobacterium* with the desired gene will survive because they also possess the marker gene (for antibiotic resistance) and so do not succumb to the antibiotic. Those *Agrobacterium* lacking the desired gene, also lack the antibiotic resistance gene and are destroyed by the antibiotic.

The *Agrobacterium* with the new gene can now be cultured to provide a large population. They may then be used to infect host plants which will incorporate the new gene into their own genome.

### 7.7.5 Applications of genetic engineering

The techniques illustrated above may be utilized to manufacture a range of materials that can be used to treat diseases and disorders. In addition to insulin, human growth hormone is now produced by bacteria in sufficient quantity to allow all children in this country requiring it to be treated. Among other hormones being produced in this manner are erythropoietin, which controls red blood cell production, and calcitonin, which regulates the levels of calcium in the blood (Section 26.4). Much research is taking place into the production of antibiotics and vaccines through recombinant DNA technology and already interferon, a chemical produced in response to viral infection, is in production.

A form of abnormal haemoglobin is produced by a defective gene causing a disease called **thalassaemia**. It is likely that genetic engineering will provide a cure for the disease, by the transference of a normal gene for haemoglobin into patients afflicted by the disease.

The scope of recombinant DNA technology is not restricted to the field of medicine. In agriculture, it is now possible to transfer genes which produce toxins with insecticidal properties from bacteria to higher plants such as potatoes and cotton. In this way these plants have 'built-in' resistance to certain insect pests. The saving in time and money by not having to spray such crops regularly with insecticides is obvious, to say nothing of avoiding killing harmless or beneficial insect species which inevitably happens however carefully spraying is carried out. It may prove possible to transfer genes from nitrogen-fixing bacteria to cereal crops, to enable them to fix their own nitrogen. There would then be less need to apply expensive nitrogen fertilizers, thus reducing the pollution problems of 'run-off' (Section 18.5.1).

There would seem to be no end of possibilities – transfer of genes conferring resistance to all manner of diseases, development of plants with more efficient rates of photosynthesis, the control of weeds and the development of oil-digesting bacteria to clear up oil spillages are just some of the potential uses of recombinant DNA technology. There are however ethical as well as practical problems to be overcome before many of these ideas can be brought to fruition. Some of these problems are discussed in the following section.

### 7.7.6 Implications of genetic engineering

The benefits of genetic engineering are obvious but it is not without its hazards. It is impossible to predict with complete accuracy what the ecological consequences might be of releasing genetically engineered organisms into the environment. It is always possible that the delicate balance that exists in any habitat may be irretrievably damaged by the introduction of organisms with new gene combinations. It is also possible that organisms designed for use in one environment may escape to other environments with harmful consequences. We know that viruses can transfer genes from one organism to another. Advantageous genes added to our domestic animals or crop plants may be transferred in this way to their competitors, making them even greater potential dangers. The escape of a single pathogenic bacterium into a susceptible population could result in considerable damage to a species. Perhaps more sinister is the fear that the ability to manipulate genes could allow human characteristics and behaviour to be modified. In the wrong hands this could be used by individuals, groups or governments in order to achieve certain goals, control opposition or gain ultimate power.

Even without these dangers there are still ethical issues which arise from the development of recombinant DNA technology. Is it right to replace a 'defective' gene with a 'normal' one? Is the answer the same for a gene which causes the bearer pain as it is where the gene has a merely cosmetic effect? Who decides what is 'defective' and what is 'normal'? A 'defective' gene may actually confer some other advantage, e.g. sickle-cell gene (Section 10.5.3). Is there a danger that we shall in time reduce the variety so essential to evolution by the progressive removal of unwanted genes or, by combining genes from different species, are we actually increasing variety and favouring evolution? Where a gene probe detects a fetal abnormality, what criteria, if any, should be applied before deciding whether to carry out an abortion?

It is inevitable that we shall remain inquisitive about the world in which we live and, in particular, about ourselves. Scientific research will therefore continue. The challenge is to develop regulations and safeguards within moral boundaries which permit genetic engineering to be used in a safe and effective way to the benefit of both individuals in particular and humans in general.

## 7.8   Genetic fingerprinting

The pattern of dermal ridges and furrows which constitute the fingerprint not only persist unchanged throughout our lives, but are also unique to each one of us (identical twins excepted). For this reason they have long been used to help solve crimes by comparing the fingerprint pattern of the suspect with the impressions left, as a result of the furrow's oily secretions, at the scene of the crime. To this well-tried and successful forensic technique has now been added another – **genetic fingerprinting**

While having nothing to do with either fingers or printing, the technique is equally, if not more, successful in identifying individuals from 'information' they provide. This 'information' is contained in a spot of blood, a sample of skin, a few sperm – in fact almost any cell of the body.

The technique, developed by Alec Jeffreys of Leicester University, takes around six days and involves the following stages

1. The DNA is separated from the sample.

2. Restriction endonucleases are used to cut the DNA into sections

3. The DNA fragments are separated in an agarose gel using electrophoresis.

4. The fragments are transferred to a nitrocellulose (or nylon) membrane – a process called **Southern Blotting** after its inventor, Professor Southern.

5. Radioactive DNA probes (**gene probes**) are used to bind to specific portions of the fragments known as the core sequences.

6. The portions of the DNA not bound to the radioactive probes are washed off.

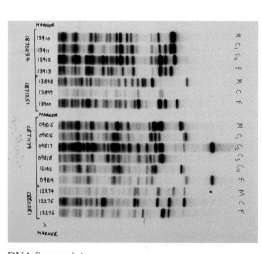

DNA fingerprint

**7.** The remaining DNA still attached to the nylon membrane is placed next to a sheet of X-ray film.

**8.** The radioactive probes on this DNA expose the film, revealing a pattern of light and dark bands when it is developed. The pattern makes up the genetic fingerprint.

The patterns, like fingerprints, are unique to each individual (except identical twins) and remain unchanged throughout life. Unlike fingerprints, however, the pattern is inherited from both parents. The scope for genetic fingerprinting, therefore, extends beyond catching criminals – it can also be used in paternity suits for example (Section 9.5.3). White blood cells are taken from the mother and the possible father. From the pattern of bands of the child are subtracted those bands which correspond to the mother's bands. If the man is truly the parent, he must possess all the remaining bands in the child's genetic fingerprint.

As sperm contain DNA, they too can be used to provide a genetic fingerprint, leading to a remarkably accurate method of determining guilt, or otherwise, of an accused rapist. The method has also been successfully applied in immigration cases where the relationship of an immigrant to someone already resident in a country is in dispute. Confirming the pedigree of animals, detecting some inherited diseases and monitoring bone-marrow transplants are other applications of the technique.

Despite the fact that we are, as yet, unclear as to what exactly the dark bands of the genetic fingerprint represent, the chances of two individuals (other than identical twins) having identical patterns is so small that the technique is widely used and its results accepted as accurate.

## BIOLOGY AROUND US

### Human Genome Project

The Human Genome Project is a massive international effort to identify and catalogue all the human genes and place them in their sequence along the 23 pairs of chromosomes. This will lay the foundations for finding out how genes function to cause disease and uncover new approaches to prevention and cure. There will develop an understanding of inherited disease and genetic aspects of chronic disease such as cancer and heart disease. Perhaps we will be able to identify genes responsible for schizophrenia and other forms of mental illness. Will we begin to understand what makes a genius and learn more about our evolution? Will we learn to adjust the human life span? The basic work on the Human Genome Project will be completed early in the 21st Century and then we will be faced with ethical concerns about what should be done with the information about an individual's genetic make-up. Should it be confidential or should the family, the employer or the life insurance company have the information? What are the implications for a National Health Service or a provider of private health insurance? Will DNA profiling lead to a bank of information that could be used maliciously and will people want 'designer babies'?

The benefits from the Human Genome Project could be enormous but all people, not just scientists, will need to be properly equipped to make the decisions that may face us in the future.

# 7.9 Questions

**1.** The following codon dictionary shows all 64 triplet codons which may occur in mRNA and the amino acids that are coded, as well as the chain termination codons which are labelled STOP.

| | | | | | | | |
|---|---|---|---|---|---|---|---|
| UUU | phe | UCU | ser | UAU | tyr | UGU | cys |
| UUC | phe | UCC | ser | UAC | tyr | UGC | cys |
| UUA | leu | UCA | ser | UAA | STOP | UGA | STOP |
| UUG | leu | UCG | ser | UAG | STOP | UGG | trp |
| CUU | leu | CCU | pro | CAU | his | CGU | arg |
| CUC | leu | CCC | pro | CAC | his | CGC | arg |
| CUA | leu | CCA | pro | CAA | gln | CGA | arg |
| CUG | leu | CCG | pro | CAG | gln | CGG | arg |
| AUU | ileu | ACU | thr | AAU | asn | AGU | ser |
| AUC | ileu | ACC | thr | AAC | asn | AGC | ser |
| AUA | ileu | ACA | thr | AAA | lys | AGA | arg |
| AUG | met | ACG | thr | AAG | lys | AGG | arg |
| GUU | val | GCU | ala | GAU | asp | GGU | gly |
| GUC | val | GCC | ala | GAC | asp | GGC | gly |
| GUA | val | GCA | ala | GAA | glu | GGA | gly |
| GUG | val | GCG | ala | GAG | glu | GGG | gly |

Use this dictionary to answer questions about the diagram below which summarises the processes of protein synthesis.

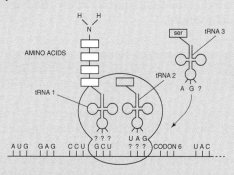

(a) Which is the first codon used in protein synthesis from this mRNA? *(1 mark)*

(b) What is the sequence of the first 4 amino acids from the amino terminal of the growing polypeptide? *(4 marks)*

(c) What is the anticodon sequence in tRNA 1? *(2 marks)*

(d) (i) Give the codon which is recognised by tRNA 2. *(1 mark)*

(ii) Give the amino acid carried by tRNA 2. *(1 mark)*

(e) (i) Explain what changes will occur in the translation apparatus to allow codon 6 to be translated. *(4 marks)*

(ii) What are the possible codon sequences for codon 6? *(1 mark)*

(f) The figure above gives information about the first 7 amino acids of an 80 amino acid polypeptide. What would be the effect on this polypeptide if there was a base

substitution mutation in the DNA sequence of the gene so that the UAC codon in the diagram became a UAG codon?

*(2 mark*

*(Total 16 mark*

*Oxford & Cambridge June 1998, Paper B2, No.*

**2.** (a) Explain why the genetic code for an amino acid is a 3 base code rather than a 2 base code

*(3 mark*

The table below shows some of the DNA triplet codes together with their corresponding amino acids.

| DNA triplet | Amino acid | Standard abbreviatio for amino acid |
|---|---|---|
| AAA | Phenylalanine | Phe |
| AAC | Leucine | Leu |
| AAG | Phenylalanine | Phe |
| AAT | Leucine | Leu |
| CAT | Valine | Val |
| CCA | Glycine | Gly |
| CCG | Glycine | Gly |
| CTT | Glutamic acid | Glu |
| GCC | Arginine | Arg |
| GTA | Histidine | His |
| TCG | Serine | Ser |
| TCT | Arginine | Arg |
| TGC | Threonine | Thr |
| TGT | Threonine | Thr |
| TTT | Lysine | Lys |
| ACT | Nonsense / stop | |

A section of the DNA template strand is represented below.

– C A T C C A A A T T G T T G C C C G

(b) (i) Write the mRNA codon for the first DNA triplet of this section of the strand. *(1 mar*

(ii) Using the standard abbreviations give in the table, write out the sequence of amino acids coded by this section of DNA. *(2 mark*

It is possible for the DNA template strand to become changed or mutated in various ways. Some of these mutations are shown below.

Original – C A T C C A A A T T G T T G C C C G

Mutation 1 – C A T C C A A A T T C T T G C C C G

Mutation 2 – C A T C C A A A T T T T G C C C G –

Mutation 3 – C A T C C A A C T T G T T G C C C G

*(c)* (i) Explain the effect of each of the mutations shown above. *(6 marks)*

(ii) State, with a reason, which of the three mutations would have the least effect on the primary sequence of the polypeptide formed. *(1 mark)*

*(d)* Explain the consequence of gene mutation, with reference to the condition known as phenylketonuria (PKU).

*(3 marks)*

*(Total 16 marks)*

*UCLES June 1998 (Central Concepts in Biology), No. 2*

. The following diagram represents part of a DNA molecule and a mRNA molecule.

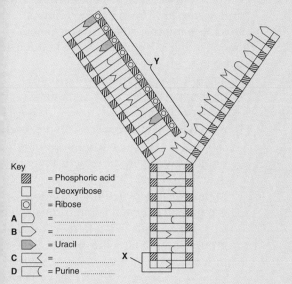

Key

| | |
|---|---|
| (hatched) | = Phosphoric acid |
| (square) | = Deoxyribose |
| (circle) | = Ribose |
| A | = ................................ |
| B | = ................................ |
| (shaded) | = Uracil |
| C | = ................................ |
| D | = Purine ................. |

*1)* Name molecules **A**, **B**, **C** and **D** in the spaces provided in the key. *(4 marks)*

*(b)* (i) What is the name given to the molecular subunit shown in the box **X**? *(1 mark)*

(ii) Give the names of the component molecules which make up this structure. *(3 marks)*

*(c)* On the diagram, use a **ruled guide line** and the letter **H** to show the position of a hydrogen bond. *(1 mark)*

*(d)* Condensation reactions are involved in the production of DNA. Give the names of **two pairs** of molecules which are linked in such a way. *(2 marks)*

*(e)* Give **two** pieces of evidence from the diagram which indicate that the molecule **Y** is RNA and not half a strand of DNA. *(2 marks)*

*(Total 13 marks)*

*Oxford February 1997, Paper 1, No. 1*

**4.** The flow chart below outlines stages in the process by which foreign DNA may be inserted into a bacterium.

*(a)* (i) Name the enzyme used to make single-stranded DNA in stage **A**. *(1 mark)*

(ii) The original mRNA contained the following base sequence:

U A A C U G C C G

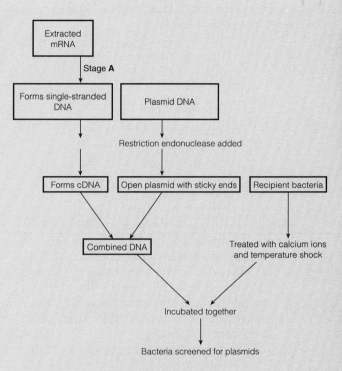

Write the corresponding sequence of bases in the single-stranded DNA made in stage **A**.

*(2 marks)*

*(b)* (i) Explain how the sticky ends allow a temporary link to be made between suitable pieces of DNA.

*(2 marks)*

(ii) Name the enzyme used to convert this temporary link into a permanent combined DNA.

*(1 mark)*

(iii) What name is usually given to this combined DNA?

*(1 mark)*

*(c)* Suggest why the bacteria were treated with calcium ions and subjected to temperature shock.

*(2 marks)*

*(d)* Describe **one** way in which bacteria can be screened for the presence of plasmids.

*(3 marks)*

*(Total 12 marks)*

*Edexcel June 1997, B/HB1, No. 7*

5. (a) Give:
   (i) **one** structural similarity between DNA and mRNA; (1 mark)
   (ii) **one** structural difference between DNA and mRNA. (1 mark)

In an investigation involving genetic fingerprinting, DNA was extracted from a virus and broken into fragments with the restriction enzyme *Eco*R1. The diagram shows the resulting separation of these fragments by electrophoresis.

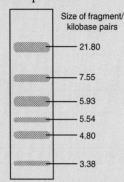

Size of fragment/ kilobase pairs

— 21.80

— 7.55

— 5.93

— 5.54

— 4.80

— 3.38

(b) (i) Add an arrow to the diagram to show the direction in which the fragments moved during electrophoresis.
    (ii) Give a reason for your answer. (1 mark)
(c) Assuming that the DNA in the virus is linear and not circular, how many times does the sequence of bases recognised by *Eco*R1 occur in this length of DNA? (1 mark)
(d) Give the sequence of nucleotide bases of the DNA probe that would be used to identify the sequence GCAT from the virus DNA.
(1 mark)
(Total 5 marks)

*AEB Summer 1996, Module Paper 2, No. 1*

6. (a) After DNA has been extracted from cells in order to carry out genetic fingerprint analysis, it is incubated with restriction enzymes and the resulting DNA fragments are separated on a gel using electrophoresis. The double helix structure of the DNA is then split by the addition of an alkali and the DNA is drawn from the gel onto a nitrocellulose membrane by a blotting process before radioactively labelled probes are added. The membrane is then placed next to a photographic film and the genetic fingerprint can be seen when the film is developed.
   (i) Why are **restriction enzymes** used in the procedure? (2 marks)
   (ii) Why do the DNA fragments separate out on the gel? (2 marks)
   (iii) Why is the DNA made single-stranded? (1 mark)

(iv) Explain why the **nitrocellulose membrane** is used. (1 mar[k])
(v) Explain what is meant by a **probe** in genetic fingerprinting. (1 mar[k])
(vi) What is the significance of the probes being **radioactively labelled**? (2 mark[s])

(b) A pet shop has several young parrots for sale. These parrots are an endangered specie[s] and may not now be imported into the country legally. However, the owner claims that all the parrots were bred from his own pet adult birds that he has kept for many years and so he has not broken the law. How could genetic fingerprinting be used to establish if the owner is telling the truth?
(2 mark[s])

(c) Comparisons of fingerprint patterns left at crime scenes have been used in criminal cases for many years. Nowadays, **genetic** fingerprinting is commonly used in forensic science.
   (i) Suggest **two** advantages of genetic fingerprints when used as criminal evidence in court cases. (2 mark[s])
   (ii) A conviction in a court case depends on the belief that a genetic fingerprint is unique. However, the genetic fingerprin[t] of an individual has a greater similarity to those of others in the same ethnic group than to genetic fingerprints take[n] from individuals in a different ethnic group. Suggest how this might result in miscarriage of justice. (2 mark[s])
(Total 15 mark[s])

*Oxford & Cambridge June 1997, Unit B10, No.*

7. Read the following passage and answer the questions which follow.

**The Polymerase Chain Reaction**

Until the late 1980s, cloning was the only means of obtaining a pure sample of an individual gene. This i[s] no longer the case as the revolutionary yet simple polymerase chain reaction (PCR) provides an alternative approach. It is less complicated than cloning and allows millions of copies of the gene to b[e] produced from a single molecule, allowing genes from a single cell to be isolated, or from traces of blood, or even Egyptian mummies!

PCR causes selective amplification of any region of a DNA molecule. So long as the borders of the chosen region are known, two short oligonucleotides can be attached to act as primers for the synthesis of DNA under the control of DNA polymerase I. The specific enzyme, Taq DNA polymerase I, is obtained from the bacterium *Thermus aquaticus* which lives in hot springs. The thermostability of its enzymes are essential to the PCR procedure.

DNA is primed by heating the DNA and primer mixture to 95°C. This separates the two DNA strands. When cooled to 37°C, the primers bind to the complementary strands of DNA.

Heating to 72°C, the optimum for Taq Polymerase I, causes new DNA strands to be formed alongside the separated template strands.

Reheating to 95°C separates the newly formed strands from their partners.

The process of cooling and heating is repeated. With each cycle the number of copies of template DNA is doubled. After 25 cycles, over a million copies of the DNA will have been made.

Adapted from *Gene Cloning*, T. A. Brown,
Chapman and Hall, 1995.

(a) Give **three** reasons why the PCR is considered to be a better process than cloning to obtain a pure sample of a gene. *(3 marks)*

(b) What is the function of DNA polymerase I? *(1 mark)*

(c) (i) What is the source of Taq polymerase I? *(1 mark)*

    (ii) Explain why Taq polymerase I is so suitable for catalysing the PCR. *(2 marks)*

(d) Explain the meaning of the following terms:
    (i) **oligonucleotide**; *(1 mark)*
    (ii) **selective amplification**. *(1 mark)*

*(Total 9 marks)*

*Oxford March 1997, Paper 41, No. 5*

---

8. The diagram shows the sequence of bases on one strand of a short length of DNA.

C G A C C C | C A G |

This sequence should be read from left to right.

(a) Give:
    (i) the base sequence that will be produced as a result of transcription of the complete length of DNA shown in the diagram. *(2 marks)*
    (ii) the three bases of the tRNA which will correspond to the sequence of bases shown in the box on the diagram. *(1 mark)*

The table shows some DNA base sequences and the amino acids for which they code.

| DNA base sequence | Amino acid |
|---|---|
| ACC | Tryptophan |
| CAG | Valine |
| CCA | Glycine |
| CCC | Glycine |
| CGA | Alanine |
| GAC | Leucine |

As a result of a mutation, the first base in the length of DNA shown in the diagram is lost (deleted).

(b) (i) Use the table to identify the first two amino acids for which the mutated DNA codes. *(1 mark)*

    (ii) Explain why mutations involving the deletion of a base may have greater effects than those involving substitution of one base for another. *(2 marks)*

*(Total 6 marks)*

*NEAB February 1995, BY2, No. 1*

9. The drawing shows a section of a DNA molecule.

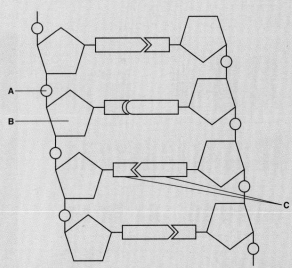

(a) Name the parts labelled **A**, **B**, and **C**. *(3 marks)*

(b) The mRNA code for the amino acid serine is UCA.
    (i) Give the DNA code for serine.
    (ii) Give the tRNA code for serine. *(2 marks)*

(c) (i) What type of molecule is the end product of translation? *(1 mark)*

    (ii) Describe the role of tRNA in the translation process. *(2 marks)*

*(Total 8 marks)*

*NEAB February 1997, Paper BY02, No. 2*

133

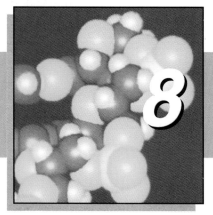

# 8

# Cell division

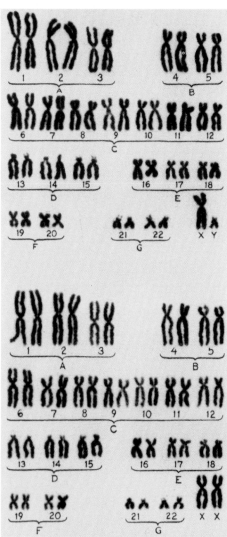

Human karyotypes (male and female)

Modern cell theory, as described in Chapter 4, states that 'all new cells are derived from other cells'. The process involved is **cell division**. All $10^{14}$ cells which comprise a human are derived, through cell division, from the single zygote formed by the fusion of two gametes. These gametes in turn were derived from the division of certain parental cells. It follows that all cells in all organisms have been formed from successive divisions of some original ancestral cell. The remarkable thing is that, while cells and organisms have diversified considerably over millions of years, the process of cell division has remained much the same.

There are two basic types:

**Mitosis** which results in all daughter cells having the same number of chromosomes as the parent.

**Meiosis** which results in the daughter cells having only half the number of chromosomes found in the parent cell.

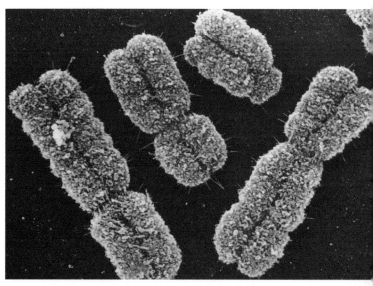

False-colour scanning electron micrograph (SEM) of a group of human chromosomes

## 8.1    Chromosomes

### 8.1.1 Chromosome structure

Chromosomes carry the hereditary material DNA (15%). In addition they are made up of protein (70%) and RNA (10%). Individual chromosomes are not visible in a non-dividing (resting) cell, but the chromosomal material can be seen,

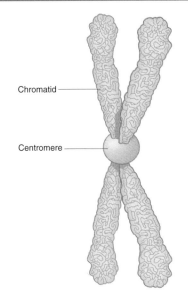

Chromatid

Centromere

*Fig. 8.1 Structure of a chromosome*

DNA molecule

Nucleosome

10 nm

Complex of histone molecules

*Fig. 8.2 Detailed structure of a chromosome*

especially if stained. This material is called **chromatin**. It is only at the onset of cell division that individual chromosomes become visible. They appear as long, thin threads between 0.25 $\mu$m and 50 $\mu$m in length. Each chromosome is seen to consist of two threads called **chromatids** joined at a point called the **centromere** (Fig. 8.1). Chromosomes vary in shape and size, both within and between species. The detailed structure of a chromosome is illustrated in Fig. 8.2.

### 8.1.2 Chromosome number

The number of chromosomes varies from one species to another but is always the same for normal individuals of one species. Table 8.1 gives some idea of the range of chromosome number in different species. It can be seen that the numbers are not related to either the size of the organism or to its evolutionary status; indeed it is quite without significance.

Although the chromosome number of a cell varies from two to 300 or more, the majority of organisms have between 10 and 40 chromosomes in each of their cells. With well over one million different species, it follows that many share the same chromosome number, 24 being the most common.

TABLE 8.1　**The chromosome number of a range of species**

| Species | Chromosome number |
|---|---|
| Certain roundworms | 2 |
| Crocus (*Crocus balansae*) | 6 |
| Fruit fly (*Drosophila melanogaster*) | 8 |
| Onion (*Allium cepa*) | 16 |
| Maize (*Zea mays*) | 20 |
| Locust (*Locusta migratoria*) | 24 |
| Lily (*Lilium longiflorum*) | 24 |
| Tomato (*Lycopersicon esculentum*) | 24 |
| Cat (*Felis cattus*) | 38 |
| Mouse (*Mus musculus*) | 40 |
| Human (*Homo sapiens*) | 46 |
| Potato (*Solanum tuberosum*) | 48 |
| Horse (*Equus caballus*) | 64 |
| Dog (*Canis familiaris*) | 78 |
| Certain protozoa | 300+ |

## 8.2　Mitosis

### Did you know?

Nerve cells may spend up to 60 years in interphase.

Dividing cells undergo a regular pattern of events, known as the **cell cycle** (Fig. 8.3). This cycle may be divided into two basic parts:

**Interphase** – when the cell undergoes a period of intense chemical activity. The amount of DNA is doubled during this

*Nuclear division, or mitosis, typically occupies 5–10% of the total cycle. The cycle may take as little as 20 minutes in a bacterial cell, although it typically takes 8–24 hours.*

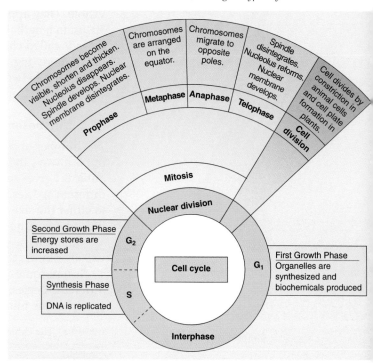

*Fig. 8.3 The cell cycle*

period. Interphase is divided into three phases: first growth phase ($G_1$) follows cell division and is the period where most ce organelles are synthesized and the cell grows rapidly. The synthesis (S) phase is next, during which DNA replication occurs, and finally the second growth phase ($G_2$) when the centrioles replicate and energy stores increase.

**Mitosis** – when the nucleus is mechanically active as it divides. The stages of mitosis are illustrated in Fig. 8.4.

*Interphase*
Although often termed the **resting phase** because the chromosomes are not visible, interphase is in fact a period of considerable metabolic activity. It is during this phase that the DNA content of the cell is doubled. Duplication of the cell organelles also takes place at this time.

*Prophase*
The chromosomes become visible as long, thin tangled threads. Gradually they shorten and thicken, and each is seen to compris two chromatids joined at the centromere. With the exception of higher plant cells which lack them, the centrioles migrate to opposite ends or **poles** of the cell. From each centriole, microtubules develop and form a star-shaped structure called a **aster**. Some of these microtubules, called **spindle fibres**, span the cell from pole to pole. Collectively they form the **spindle**. The nucleolus disappears and finally the nuclear envelope disintegrates, leaving the chromosomes within the cytoplasm of the cell.

## PROJECT

1. Examine longitudinal sections of bean root using a microscope. Locate the area just behind the tip of the root where mitosis is occurring.

2. Count the number of cells at interphase and at the various phases of mitosis and from this data determine the relative time taken for each phase.

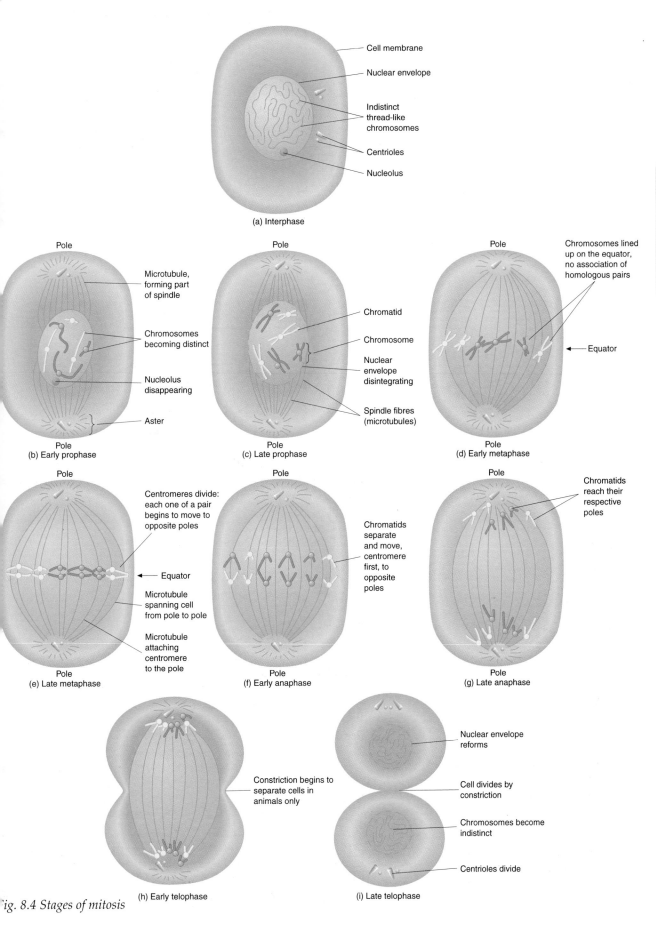

(a) Interphase

Cell membrane
Nuclear envelope
Indistinct thread-like chromosomes
Centrioles
Nucleolus

Pole
Microtubule, forming part of spindle
Chromosomes becoming distinct
Nucleolus disappearing
Aster
Pole
(b) Early prophase

Pole
Chromatid
Chromosome
Nuclear envelope disintegrating
Spindle fibres (microtubules)
Pole
(c) Late prophase

Pole
Chromosomes lined up on the equator, no association of homologous pairs
Equator
Pole
(d) Early metaphase

Pole
Centromeres divide: each one of a pair begins to move to opposite poles
Equator
Microtubule spanning cell from pole to pole
Microtubule attaching centromere to the pole
Pole
(e) Late metaphase

Pole
Chromatids separate and move, centromere first, to opposite poles
Pole
(f) Early anaphase

Pole
Chromatids reach their respective poles
Pole
(g) Late anaphase

Constriction begins to separate cells in animals only
(h) Early telophase

Nuclear envelope reforms
Cell divides by constriction
Chromosomes become indistinct
Centrioles divide
(i) Late telophase

Fig. 8.4 Stages of mitosis

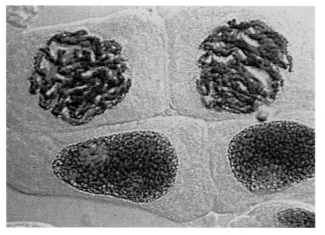

(i)

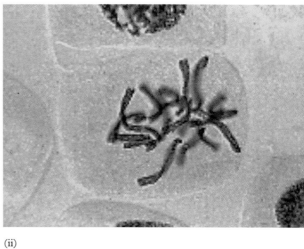

(ii)

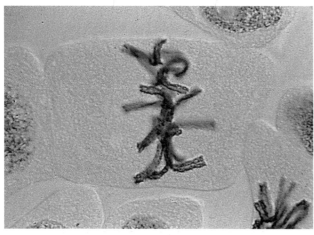

(iii)

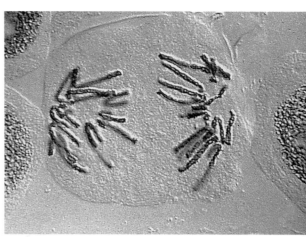

(iv)

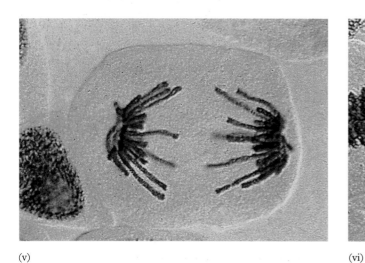

(v)

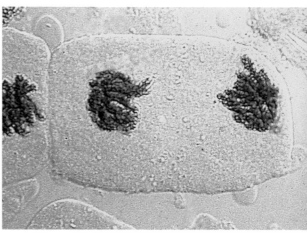

(vi)

The main stages of mitosis (×600 approx.):
(i) interphase
(ii) prophase – chromosomes become visible
(iii) metaphase – chromosomes line up on the equator

(iv) anaphase i ⎫
(v) anaphase ii ⎭ chromatids migrate to opposite poles
(vi) telophase – daughter nuclei form at opposite poles

*Metaphase*

The chromosomes arrange themselves at the centre or **equator** of the spindle, and become attached to certain spindle fibres at the centromere. Contraction of these fibres draws the individual chromatids slightly apart.

*Anaphase*

The centromeres split and further shortening of the spindle fibres causes the two chromatids of each chromosome to separate and migrate to opposite poles. The shortening of the spindle fibres is due to the progressive removal of the **tubulin** molecules of which they are made. The energy for this process is provided by mitochondria which are observed to collect around the spindle fibres.

*Telophase*

The chromatids reach their respective poles and a new nuclear envelope forms around each group. The chromatids uncoil and lengthen, thus becoming invisible again. The spindle fibres disintegrate and a nucleolus reforms in each new nucleus.

In single-celled organisms and actively dividing cells, the cycle is continuous, i.e. the cells continue to divide regularly. In some cells, like those of the liver, division ceases after a certain time and only resumes if damaged or lost tissue needs replacing. In specialized tissues, such as nerves, division ceases completely once the cells are mature.

### 8.2.1 Differences between mitosis in plant and animal cells

The cells of higher plants lack centrioles and do not form asters as in animal cells. Spindle formation still takes place, however, and therefore the centrioles would seem not to be the centre of spindle synthesis.

In animal cells, cell division or **cytokinesis** occurs by the constriction of the centre of the parent cell from the outside inwards (Fig. 8.4h). In plant cells, however, the process occurs by the growth of a **cell plate** across the equator of the parent cell from the centre outwards. The plate is formed from the fusion of vesicles produced by the dictyosome. Cellulose is laid down on this plate to form the cell wall.

Whereas most animals cells are, if the need arises, capable of mitosis, only a specialized group of plant cells, called **meristematic cells**, are able to do so.

## 8.3 Meiosis (reduction division)

Meiosis involves one division of the chromosomes followed by two divisions of the nucleus and cell. The result is that the number of chromosomes in each cell is reduced by half. The **diploid (2n)** parent cell gives rise to **four haploid (n)** daughter cells. Meiosis occurs in the formation of gametes, sperm and ova, in animals, and in the production of spores in most plants.

Meiosis comprises two divisions (Fig. 8.5):

1. **First meiotic division** – similar to mitosis except for a highly modified prophase stage.

2. **Second meiotic division** – a typically mitotic division.

The process is continuous but for convenience is divided into the same stages as mitosis, as illustrated in Fig. 8.6. The symbols I and II indicate the first and second meiotic divisions respectively.

*Interphase*
The cell is in the non-dividing condition during which it replicates its DNA and organelles.

*Prophase I*
Organisms have two sets of chromosomes, one derived from each parent. Any two chromosomes which determine the same characteristics, e.g. eye colour, blood groups, etc., are called an **homologous pair**. Although each chromosome of a pair determines the same characteristics, they need not be identical. For instance, while one of the pair may code for blue eyes, the other may code for brown eyes.

Prophase I of meiosis is similar to prophase in mitosis, in that the chromosomes become visible, shorten and fatten, but differs in that they associate in their homologous pairs. They come together by a process termed **synapsis** and each pair is called a **bivalent**.

Each chromosome of the pair is seen to comprise two chromatids. These chromatids wrap around each other. The chromatids of the pair partially repel one another although they remain joined at certain points called **chiasmata** (singular – **chiasma**). It is at these points that chromatids may break and recombine with a different chromatid. This swapping of portions of chromatids is termed **crossing over**. The chromatids continue to repel one another although at this stage they still remain attached at the chiasmata. The nucleolus disappears and the nuclear envelope breaks down. Where present, the centrioles migrate to the poles and the spindle forms.

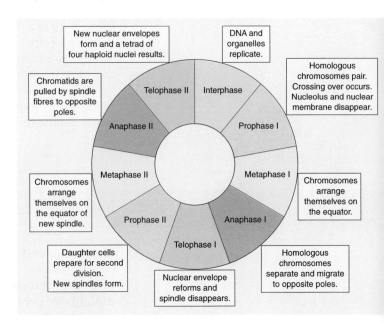

*Fig. 8.5 Meiosis*

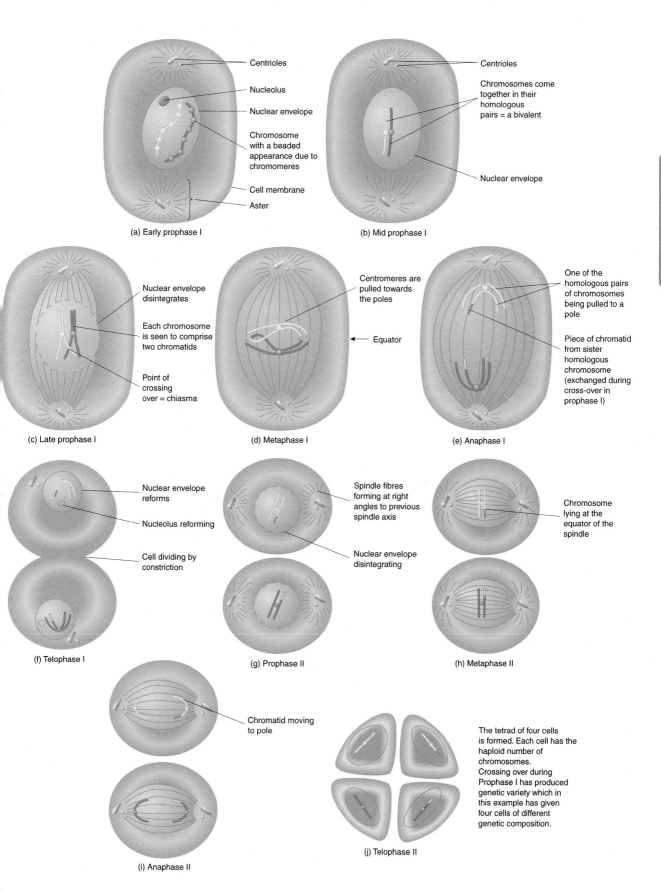

Fig. 8.6 Stages of meiosis (only one pair of chromosomes shown)

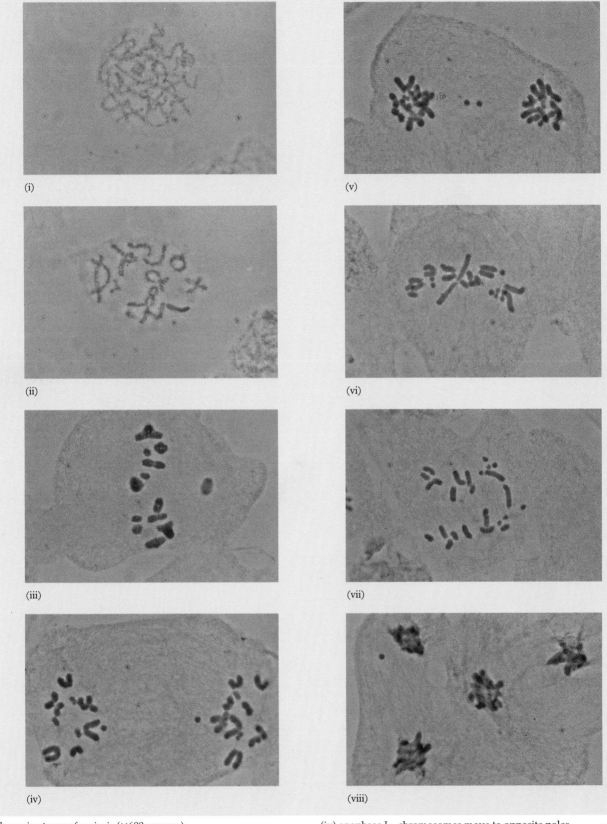

The main stages of meiosis (×600 approx.):
(i) prophase I (leptotene) – chromosomes become visible as long beaded structures
(ii) prophase I (diakinesis) – chiasmata and crossing over
(iii) metaphase I – homologous pairs of chromosomes line up on equator

(iv) anaphase I – chromosomes move to opposite poles
(v) telophase I – chromosomes reach poles
(vi) metaphase II – chromosomes line up on equator of daughter cell
(vii) anaphase II – chromatids move to opposite poles
(viii) telophase II – chromatids reach opposite poles

*Metaphase I*

The bivalents arrange themselves on the equator of the cell with each of a pair of homologous chromosomes orientated to opposite poles. This arrangement is completely random relative to the orientation of other bivalents. The genetic significance of this will be discussed later. The spindle fibres attached to the centromeres contract slightly, pulling the chromosomes apart as much as the chiasmata allow.

*Anaphase I*

The spindle fibres, which are attached to the centromeres, contract and pull the homologous chromosomes apart. One of each pair is pulled to one pole, its sister chromosome to the opposite one.

*Telophase I*

The chromosomes reach their opposite poles and a nuclear envelope forms around each group. In most cells the spindle fibres disappear and the chromatids uncoil. Cell division, or **cleavage**, may follow. The nucleus may enter interphase although no replication of the DNA takes place. In some cells this stage does not occur and the cell passes from anaphase I directly into prophase II.

*Prophase II*

In those cells where telophase and interphase take place, the nucleolus disappears and the nuclear envelope breaks down. Where centrioles are present these divide and move to opposite poles. The poles on this occasion are at right angles to the plane of the previous cell division and therefore the spindle fibres develop at right angles to the spindle axis of the first meiotic division.

*Metaphase II*

The chromosomes arrange themselves on the equator of the new spindle. The spindle fibres attach to the centromere of each chromosome.

*Anaphase II*

The centromeres divide and are pulled by the spindle fibres to opposite poles, carrying the chromatids with them.

*Telophase II*

Upon reaching their opposite poles, the chromatids unwind and become indistinct. The nuclear envelope and the nucleolus are reformed. The spindle disappears and the cells divide to give four cells, collectively called a **tetrad**.

## 8.4 Comparison of mitosis and meiosis

The process of nuclear division is basically the same in mitosis and meiosis. The appearance and behaviour of the chromosomes is similar, but there are nevertheless some differences. These are listed in Table 8.2.

# 8.5 The significance of cell division

TABLE 8.2 **Differences between mitosis and meiosis**

| Mitosis | Meiosis |
|---|---|
| A single division of the chromosomes and the nucleus | A single division of the chromosomes but a double division of the nucleus |
| The number of chromosomes remains the same | The number of chromosomes is halved |
| Homologous chromosomes do not associate | Homologous chromosomes associate to form bivalents in prophase I |
| Chiasmata are never formed | Chiasmata may be formed |
| Crossing over never occurs | Crossing over may occur |
| Daughter cells are identical to parent cells (in the absence of mutations) | Daughter cells are genetically different from parental ones |
| Two daughter cells are formed | Four daughter cells are formed, although in females only one is usually functional |
| Chromosomes shorten and thicken | Chromosomes coil but remain longer than in mitosis |
| Chromosomes form a single row at the equator of the spindle | Chromosomes form a double row at the equator of the spindle during metaphase I |
| Chromatids move to opposite poles | Chromosomes move to opposite poles during the first meiotic division |

## 8.5.1 Significance of mitosis

The significance of mitosis is its ability to produce daughter cell which are exact copies of the parental cell. It is important in three ways.

### (a) Growth

If a tissue is to extend by growth it is important that the new cells are identical to the existing cells. Cell division must therefore be by mitosis.

### (b) Repair

Damaged cells must be replaced by exact copies of the originals if the repair is to return a tissue to its former condition. Mitosis the means by which this is achieved.

### (c) Asexual reproduction

If a species is successful in colonizing a particular habitat, there is little advantage, in the short term, in producing offspring which differ from the parents, because these may be less successful. It is better to establish quickly a colony of individual which are similar to the parents. In simple animals and most plants this is achieved by mitotic divisions.

## 8.5.2 Significance of meiosis

The long-term survival of a species depends on its ability to adapt to a constantly changing environment. It should also be able to colonize a range of new environments. To achieve both these aims it is necessary for offspring to be different from their parents as well as different from each other.

There are three ways in which this variety is brought about with the aid of meiosis.

### (a) Production and fusion of haploid gametes

Variety of offspring is increased by mixing the genotype of one parent with that of the other. This is the basis of the sexual process in organisms. It involves the production of special sex cells, called gametes, which fuse together to produce a new organism. Each gamete must contain half the number of chromosomes of the adult if the chromosome number is not to double at each generation. It is therefore essential that meiosis, which halves the number of chromosomes in daughter cells, occurs at some stage in the life-cycle of a sexually reproducing organism. Meiosis is thus instrumental in permitting variety in organisms, and giving them the potential to evolve.

### (b) The creation of genetic variety by the random distribution of chromosomes during metaphase I

When the pairs of homologous chromosomes arrange themselves on the equator of the spindle during metaphase I of meiosis, they do so randomly. Although each one of the pair determines the same general features, they differ in the detail of these features. The random distribution and consequent independent assortment of these chromosomes produces new genetic combinations. A simple example is shown in Fig. 8.7.

In arrangement 1, the two pairs of homologous chromosomes orientate themselves on the equator in such a way that the chromosome carrying the allele for brown eyes and the one carrying the allele for blood group A migrate to the same pole. The alleles for blue eyes and blood group B migrate to the opposite pole. Cell 1 therefore carries the alleles for brown eyes and blood group A while cell 2 carries the alleles for blue eyes and blood group B.

In arrangement 2, the left hand homologous pair of chromosomes is shown orientated the opposite way around. As this orientation is random, this arrangement is equally as likely as the first. The result of this different arrangement is that cell 3 carries the alleles for blue eyes and blood group A whereas cell 4 carries the alleles for brown eyes and blood group B.

All four resultant cells are different from one another. With more homologous pairs the number of possible combinations becomes enormous. A human, with 23 such pairs, has the potential for $2^{23} = 8\,388\,608$ combinations.

## (c) The creation of genetic variety by crossing over between homologous chromosomes

During prophase I of meiosis, equivalent portions of homologous chromosomes may be exchanged. In this way new genetic combinations are produced and linked genes separated.

The variety which meiosis brings about is essential to the process of evolution. By providing a varied stock of individuals it permits the natural selection of those best suited to the existing conditions and so ensures that species constantly change and adapt when these conditions alter. This is the main significance of meiosis.

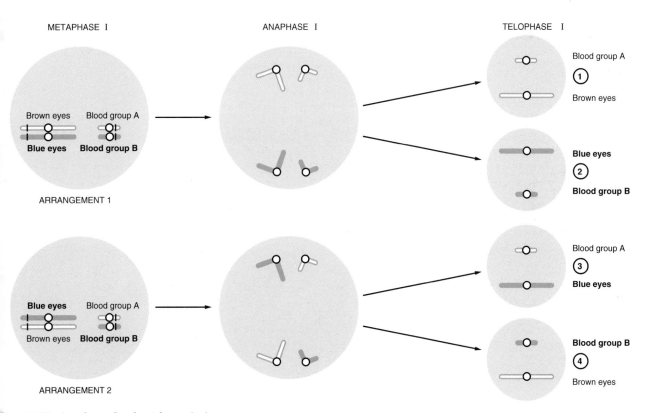

Fig. 8.7 Variety brought about by meiosis

# BIOLOGY AROUND US

## Cancer

Superficially, cancer seems to be a range of diseases in which tumours arise at different sites, grow at different rates and may be benign or lethal. However, in all cancers a population of cells multiplies in an unregulated manner independent of normal control mechanisms. Most cancers are believed to arise from single cells which transform from a normal into a malignant state. If the abnormal cell is not recognized and destroyed by the immune system, it multiplies into a small mass and then into a large primary tumour with its own blood supply. Primary tumours can be managed and patients are often cured. The more usual causes of death are the effects of secondary tumours, or metastases, in distant organs. Transport within the lymph duct will give rise to metastases in lymph nodes adjacent to the primary tumour while transport within the blood may give rise to more distant secondaries.

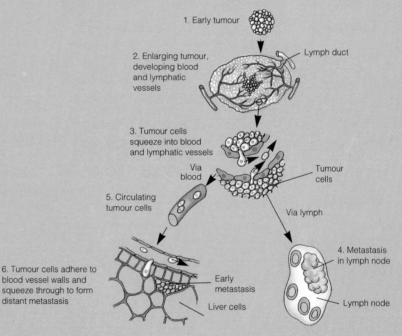

*The early development and spread of secondary tumour*

Cancers can occur at any age but overall incidence rises rapidly with age and they are a more prevalent cause of death in men than in women. Cancers which are clearly age-related are carcinomas of the gut, skin, urinary tract and some leukaemias. In breast cancer the incidence rises steeply up to menopause and then declines; cervical cancer peaks in the 30s.

It has been suggested that the cumulative effect of carcinogens in the environment may account for cancers whose incidence increases with age. The pattern of breast cancer suggests a hormonal link, and cervical cancer correlates with sexual behaviour, age at which intercourse began and possibly the number of sexual partners.

As a cause of death today, cancer is second only to diseases of the circulatory system. In terms of working years lost, it

## BIOLOGY AROUND US continued

exceeds all other diseases. In the western world, the commonest forms of cancer are those of the lung, breast, skin, gut and prostate gland. In men the greatest killer is lung cancer while in women it is breast cancer. There are, however, considerable national variations. Skin cancer is 200 times more prevalent in parts of Australia than in India – possibly linked to the long exposure of Caucasian skin to sunlight. Stomach cancer is 30 times more common in Japan than in parts of Britain – possibly due to dietary or genetic effects.

The transformation of a normal cell into a cancerous one may be brought about by exposure to certain chemicals, by radiation or by the action of retroviruses (see Section 5.2.2). Chemical carcinogens fall into several classes, including polycyclic hydrocarbons, nitrosamines, aromatics, amines and others. Polycyclic hydrocarbons are found in soot and cigarette smoke. It has been estimated that 25–30% of environmentally associated cancers can be attributed to smoking, and it is now the main cause of lung cancer which kills over 40 000 people a year in Britain.

Carcinogenic transformation may also be brought about by exposure to radiation, the most damaging being short wavelengths – X-rays, gamma rays and some ultra-violet rays. Ultra-violet rays do not penetrate beyond the superficial layers of the skin but they are responsible for a significant number of skin cancers.

Some cancers, including Burkitt's lymphoma and AIDS-related Kaposi's sarcoma, have been linked to viruses, namely EB virus and HIV-I respectively, but in general it is now recognized that the relationship involves certain cancer-causing genes, termed oncogenes, rather than the viruses themselves.

If cancer cannot be prevented, then early detection and diagnosis can at least improve the likelihood of a cure. Progress in this field has been rapid and now relies on specific biochemical and chemical reagents as well as sophisticated instruments such as ultrasound, computer tomography (CT) scanning and magnetic resonance imaging (MRI).

Once diagnosed, the choice of therapy will depend on the nature, site and extent of the tumours but may include surgery, radiotherapy, the use of drugs or immunotherapy. Surgery remains a major weapon in the fight against cancer although it is often used in association with radio- or chemotherapy. Radiotherapy has been used in cancer treatments for many years although many tumours respond poorly, especially those with low internal oxygen levels. There are many classes of anti-cancer drugs in use but the search still goes on for derivatives which retain their activity but have reduced toxicity.

It is generally accepted that the immune system plays an important role in preventing cancer and research is now centred on finding suitable molecules to stimulate the immune reaction. Such substances include interferons and interleukins, both produced by genetically engineered bacteria.

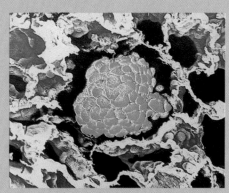

False-colour scanning electron micrograph (SEM) of a bronchial carcinoma (lung tumour) filling an alveolus

# 8.6   Questions

**1.** (a) Diagram **I** shows a three-dimensional view of one of the stages of mitosis in a typical animal cell. The chromosomes are shown lying in the same plane.

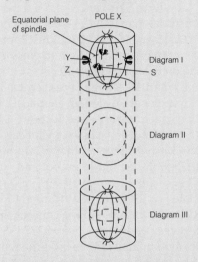

(i) Name the stage shown in the diagram **I**.
    *(1 mark)*
(ii) Name the structure labelled **Y**.    *(1 mark)*
(iii) What is the function of:
    1. structure **Z**?
    2. mitosis?    *(2 marks)*
(iv) Diagram **II** shows the outline of the equator of the cell. Draw **all** the chromosomes in diagram **I** as they would appear looking down from pole **X**.    *(4 marks)*
(v) Copy outline diagram **III** and draw the chromosomes labelled **S** and **T** as they would appear in the next stage of mitosis.    *(2 marks)*

(b) The details of mitosis vary in different organisms. The diagram shows nuclear division in a unicellular organism.

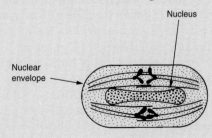

Use the information in the diagram to suggest **two** ways in which nuclear division in this species differs from that in an animal cell.    *(2 marks)*

*(Total 12 marks)*

*WJEC June 1994, Paper A2, No. 7*

**2.** (a) State **two** ways in which cancer cells differ from normal body cells.    *(2 marks)*
(b) State **three** factors which increase the chances of cancerous growth.    *(3 marks)*
(c) Suggest why cancerous growths are most likely to occur in tissues where cells normally divide at a higher rate, such as in epithelial tissues which line organs.
    *(2 marks)*

Chemotherapy is one of the methods used to treat cancerous growths. Drugs are administered which kill dividing cells. A typical chemotherapy drug programme is illustrated in the graph below. The drug is administered at 21-day intervals, as indicated on the graph by arrows. The effect of the treatment on the numbers of normal and tumour cells per unit volume is recorded.

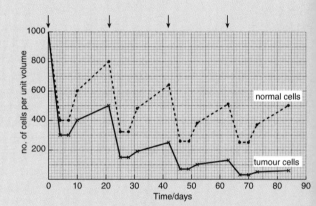

(d) With reference to the graph,
    (i) describe the way in which **both** types of cell respond during the first 30 days of treatment;    *(3 marks)*
    (ii) explain the difference between the responses of the normal and tumour cells over the period of the drug programme.    *(3 marks)*

The tumour cells could be destroyed more effectively if the amount of drug given each time was increased and if it was given at shorter time intervals.

(e) Suggest why
    (i) the amount of drug given on each occasion is not increased;    *(1 mark)*
    (ii) the drug is not given at shorter intervals (e.g. weekly).    *(1 mark)*

*(Total 15 marks)*

*UCLES March 1998, (Biology Foundation), No.*

**3.** *(a)* Explain why root tips are particularly suitable material to use for preparing slides to show mitosis. *(1 mark)*

*(b)* Give a reason for carrying out each of the following steps in preparing a slide showing mitosis in cells from a root tip.
  (i) The tissue should be stained. *(1 mark)*
  (ii) The stained material should be pulled apart with a needle and gentle pressure applied to the cover slip during mounting. *(1 mark)*

*(c)* The drawing has been made from a photograph showing a cell undergoing mitosis.

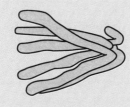

  (i) In which stage of mitosis is the cell shown in this drawing? *(1 mark)*
  (ii) Describe **one** piece of evidence, visible in the drawing, which could be used to confirm this cell is *not* in the first division of meiosis. *(1 mark)*
    *(Total 5 marks)*

*NEAB June 1998, Paper 1, No. 11*

*(a)* During which phase of the cell cycle do the following events take place:
  (i) the replication of DNA; *(1 mark)*
  (ii) the movement of daughter chromosomes to the poles of the cell? *(1 mark)*

*(b)* The diagram shows a section through an onion bulb which is starting to grow.

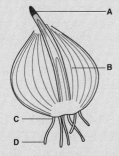

  (i) Which of the parts **A** to **D** of this bulb would you use in order to prepare a slide showing mitosis? *(1 mark)*
  (ii) Give the name of the stain you would use to make this preparation. *(1 mark)*
  (iii) Describe the effect that this stain would have on the cells. *(1 mark)*
    *(Total 5 marks)*

*AEB Summer 1996, Module Paper 2, No. 3*

**5.** The figure below shows a single pair of homologous chromosomes at two stages of meiosis.

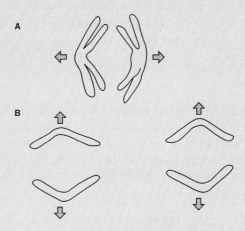

*(a)* (i) Name the stages **A** and **B**. *(2 marks)*
  (ii) Describe the differences between the two stages. *(3 marks)*

*(b)* List **three** differences in the behaviour of chromosomes in mitosis, compared with meiosis. *(3 marks)*

*(c)* Explain why two sister chromatids are genetically identical before crossing over, while a pair of homologous chromosomes are not. *(3 marks)*
  *(Total 11 marks)*

*UCLES June 1996, Paper 3, No. 3*

**6.** *(a)* Explain **two** ways in which meiosis contributes to genetic variation. *(4 marks)*

*(b)* The bar chart shows the amount of DNA present in one cell of an organism at different stages of mitosis.

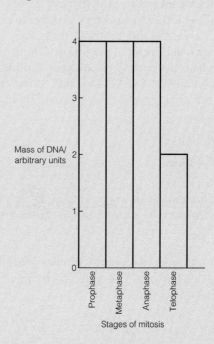

How many units of DNA would you expect to be present in one cell of this organism
  (i) during the first division of meiosis;
  (ii) in one of the gametes formed as a result of meiosis? *(2 marks)*
*(Total 6 marks)*

*NEAB June 1996, Paper 1, No. 13*

**7.** The following diagram shows the changes in the amount of DNA (arbitrary values) in the spermatogonia of a diploid organism as the spermatogonia undergo mitotic nuclear division, and then the amount of DNA in the primary and secondary spermatocytes as they undergo meiosis.

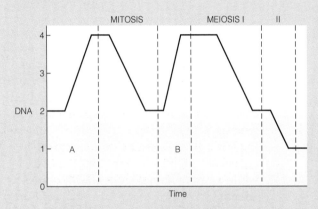

*(a)* Explain what process accounts for the change in DNA quantity during periods **A** and **B** in the diagram. *(2 marks)*

*(b)* Notice that the amount of DNA doubles before mitosis and meiosis. Does the number of chromosomes double? Explain your answer. *(2 marks)*

*(c)* If the diploid chromosome number in this organism is 8 and the haploid number is 4, what is the chromosome number of cells:
  (i) at the end of mitotic division?
  (ii) at the end of meiotic division? *(2 marks)*

*(d)* The DNA in the cells at the end of mitosis contains 56% G–C base-pairs. What are the percentages of the four bases in this DNA?

adenine    ...

guanine    ...

cytosine    ...

thymine    ... *(4 marks)*

*(e)* 20 amino acids are used to make up proteins. Explain why a minimum of three adjacent bases is needed to code for one amino acid. *(2 marks)*

*(f)* What is the maximum number of amino acids that could be coded by a triplet genetic code? *(1 mark)*

*(g)* Explain how the codons are used so that the code for only 20 amino acids. *(2 marks)*
*(Total 15 marks)*

*Oxford & Cambridge June 1997, Unit B2, No.*

**8.** The diagram shows the life-cycle of a water flea. In favourable conditions all the animals in a population are females (**A**). These females produce eggs (**B**), by mitosis, which develop into young females (**C**) without being fertilized. In unfavourable conditions, eggs produced by meiosis develop directly without fertilization into either males (**D**) or females (**E**). The eggs produced by females (**E**) are fertilized by sperm from the males, then released in a protective case (**F**) which enables them to survive unfavourable conditions. When favourable conditions return these eggs develop into young females (**G**).

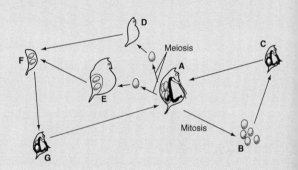

*(a)* (i) Explain why the eggs in female **E** must be produced by mitosis. *(1 mark)*
  (ii) Copy and complete the table to show the number of chromosomes at each stage in the life-cycle.

| Stage in life history | Chromosome number |
|---|---|
| A | $2n$ |
| C | |
| D | |
| E | |
| G | |

*(2 marks)*

*(b)* Explain why the females **G** are genetically different from each other but females **C** are genetically the same. *(3 marks)*

*(c)* Explain in terms of natural selection why it advantageous to an organism to have a sexual stage as well as an asexual stage in its life history. *(3 marks)*
*(Total 9 marks)*

*NEAB June 1997, Paper BY02, No*

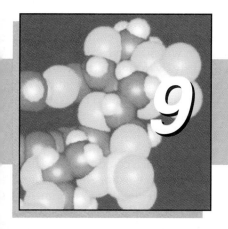

# 9

# Heredity and genetics

Gregor Mendel

It has been estimated that all the ova from which the present human population was derived could be contained within a 5-litre vessel. All the sperm that fertilized these ova could be contained within a thimble. Put another way, all the information necessary to produce in excess of 5 000 000 000 different humans can be stored within this relatively tiny volume. Indeed, we now know that the genetic information itself occupies only a small proportion of the ovum. Imagine the space occupied if all the characteristics of every living human being were printed in book form (see 'Did You Know?' on p. 116). Whatever else it may be, the genetic information is remarkably condensed. In Chapter 7 we described the chemical nature of this genetic information, namely DNA. In the present chapter we shall concern ourselves with the means by which it is transmitted from generation to generation.

**Genetics** is a fundamental and increasingly important branch of biology. Humans have unknowingly used genetic principles in the breeding of animals and plants for many thousands of years. An understanding of the underlying genetic principles is, however, fairly recent. In fact the term genetics was first used only at the beginning of this century. The understanding of the chemical foundations of heredity and genetics came even more recently with the discovery of the structure of DNA by Watson and Crick in 1953.

Observation of individuals of the same species shows them all to be recognizably similar. This is **heredity**. Closer inspection reveals minor differences by which each individual can be distinguished. This is **variation**.

The genetic composition of an organism is called the **genotype**. This often sets limits within which individual characteristics may vary. Such variation may be due to the effect of environmental influences, e.g. the genotype may determine a light-coloured skin, but the precise colour of any part of the skin will depend upon the extent to which it is exposed to sunlight. The **phenotype**, or set of characteristics, of an individual is therefore determined by the interaction between the genotype and the environment. Any change in the genotype is called a **mutation** and may be inherited. Any change in the phenotype only is called a **modification** and it is not inherited.

## 9.1  Mendel and the laws of inheritance

Gregor Mendel (1822–84) was an Austrian monk and teacher. He studied the process of heredity in selected features of the garden pea *Pisum sativum*. He was not the first scientist to study heredity, but he was the first to obtain sufficiently numerous, accurate and detailed data upon which sound scientific conclusions could be based. Partly by design and partly by luck, Mendel made a suitable choice of characteristics for study. He isolated pea plants which were **pure-breeding**. That is, when bred with each other, they produced consistently the same characteristics over many generations. He referred to each character as a **trait**. He chose traits which had two contrasting features, e.g. he chose stem length, which could be either long or short, and flower colour, which could be red or white. It must be remembered that Mendel began his 10-year-long experiments in 1856, when the nature of chromosomes and genes was yet to be discovered.

### 9.1.1 Monohybrid inheritance (Mendel's Law of Segregation)

Monohybrid inheritance refers to the inheritance of a single character only. One trait which Mendel studied was the shape of the seed produced by his pea plants. This showed two contrasting forms, round and wrinkled. When he crossed plants which were pure-breeding for round seed with ones pure-breeding for wrinkled seed, all the resulting plants produced round seed. The first generation of a cross is referred to as the **first filial generation ($F_1$)**. When individuals of the $F_1$ generation were intercrossed, the resulting **second filial generation ($F_2$)** produced 7324 seeds, 5474 of which were round and 1850 wrinkled. This is a ratio of $2.96 : 1$.

In all his crosses, Mendel found that one of the contrasting features of a pair was not represented in the $F_1$ generation. This feature reappeared in the $F_2$ generation where it was consistently outnumbered 3 to 1 by the contrasting feature.

The significance of these findings was that the $F_1$ seeds were not intermediate between the two parental types, i.e. partly wrinkled, partly smooth. This shows that there was no blending or mixing of the features. It also indicated that, as only one of the features expressed itself in the $F_1$, this feature was **dominant** to the other. The feature which does not express itself in the $F_1$ is said to be **recessive**. In the example given, round is dominant and wrinkled is recessive.

In interpreting his results, Mendel concluded that the features were passed on from one generation to the next via the gametes. The parents, he decided, must possess two pieces of information about each character. However, only one of these pieces of information was found in an individual gamete. On the basis of this he formulated his first law, the **Law of Segregation**, which states:

**The characteristics of an organism are determined by internal factors which occur in pairs. Only one of a pair of such factors can be represented in a single gamete.**

We know that Mendel's 'factors' are specific portions of a chromosome called **genes**. We also know that the process which produces gametes with only one of each pair of factors is meiosis. On the basis of his results, Mendel had effectively predicted the existence of genes and meiosis.

### 9.1.2 Representing genetic crosses

Genetic crosses are usually represented in a form of shorthand. There is more than one system of this shorthand, but the system outlined in Table 9.1 has been adopted here because it is quick and less liable to errors, especially under the pressures of an examination.

TABLE 9.1

| Instruction | Reason/notes | Example [round and wrinkled seed] |
|---|---|---|
| Choose a single letter to represent each characteristic | An easy form of shorthand. In some conventional genetic crosses, e.g. in *Drosophila*, there are set symbols, some of which use two letters | |
| Choose the first letter of one of the contrasting features | When more than one character is considered at one time, such a logical choice means it is easy to identify which letter refers to which character | Choose either R (round) or W (wrinkled) |
| If possible, choose the letter in which the upper and lower case forms differ in shape as well as size | If the upper and lower case forms differ, it is almost impossible to confuse them, regardless of their size | Choose R, because the upper case form (R) differs in shape from the lower case form (r), whereas W and w differ only in size, and are more likely to be confused. |
| Let the upper case letter represent the dominant feature and the lower case letter the recessive one. Never use two different letters where one character is dominant. Always state clearly what feature each symbol represents | The dominant and recessive features can easily be identified. Do *not* use two different letters as this indicates incomplete dominance or codominance | Let R = round and r = wrinkled Do *not* use R for round and W for wrinkled |
| Represent the parents with the appropriate pairs of letters. Label them clearly as 'parents' and state their phenotypes | This makes it clear to the reader what the symbols refer to | Parents: Round seed RR v Wrinkled seed rr |
| State the gametes produced by each parent. Label them clearly, and encircle them. Indicate that meiosis has occurred | This explains why the gametes only possess one of the two parental factors. Encircling them reinforces the idea that they are separate | Gametes: meiosis ↓ (R)   meiosis ↓ (r) |
| Use a type of chequerboard or matrix, called a **Punnett square**, to show the results of the random crossing of the gametes. Label male and female gametes even though this may not affect the results | This method is less liable to error than drawing lines between the gametes and the offspring. Labelling the sexes is a good habit to acquire – it has considerable relevance in certain types of crosses, e.g. sex-linked crosses | ♂ gametes: ♀ gametes (R) (R); (r) Rr Rr; (r) Rr Rr |
| State the phenotype of each different genotype and indicate the numbers of each type. Always put the upper case (dominant) letter first when writing out the genotype. | Always putting the dominant feature first can reduce errors in cases where it is not possible to avoid using symbols with the upper and lower case letters of the same shape | All offspring are plants producing round seed (Rr) |

NB Always carry out the above procedures in their entirety. Once you have practised a number of crosses, it is all too easy to miss out stages or explanations. Not only does this lead to errors, it often makes your explanations impossible for others to follow. *You* may understand what you are doing, but if the reader cannot follow it, it isn't much use, neither will it bring full credit in an examination.

### 9.1.3 Genetic representation of the monohybrid cross

Using the principles outlined in Table 9.1, the full genetic explanation of one of Mendel's experiments is shown below.

Let R = allele for round seed
    r = allele for wrinkled seed

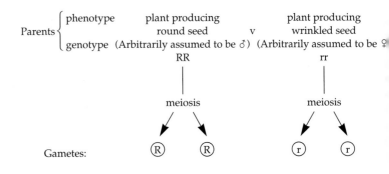

Gametes:

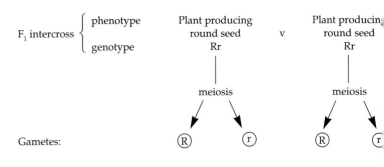

F₁ generation:

All offspring are plants producing round seed (Rr)

F₁ intercross

Gametes:

F₂ generation:

3 plants producing round seeds (1 × RR + 2 × Rr)
1 plant producing wrinkled seeds (rr)

Mendel's actual results gave a ratio of 2.96 : 1, a very good approximation to the 3 : 1 ratio which the theory suggests should be achieved. Any discrepancy is due to statistical error. Such errors are inevitable. Imagine, for instance, tossing a coin 10 times – it should in theory come down heads five times and tails five times. More often than not, some other ratio is achieved in practice. The actual results are rarely exactly the same as predicted by theory. The larger the sample, the more nearly the results approximate to the theoretical value. This was an essential aspect of Mendel's experiments. Probably because he was trained partly as a mathematician, he appreciated the need to collect large numbers of offspring if he was to draw meaningful conclusions from his experiments.

The use of '$F_1$ generation' should be limited to the offspring of homozygous parents. Similarly, '$F_2$ generation' should refer only to the offspring of the $F_1$ generation. In all other cases 'offspring (1)' should replace '$F_1$ generation', and 'offspring (2)' should replace '$F_2$ generation'. The complete set of headings in order therefore will be:

Parents: phenotypes

Parents: genotypes

Gametes

Offspring (1) genotypes

Offspring (1) phenotypes

Gametes

Offspring (2) genotypes

Offspring (2) phenotypes

Whether the variation from an expected ratio is the result of statistical chance or not can be tested mathematically using the chi-squared test. Details are given in Section 10.3.

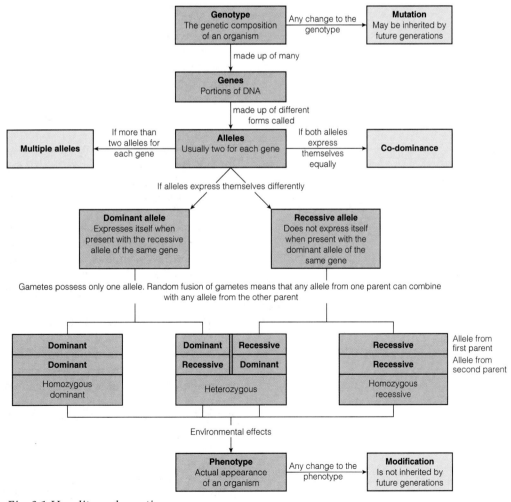

*Fig. 9.1 Heredity and genetics*

### 9.1.4 Genes and alleles

A character such as the shape of the seed coat in peas is determined by a single gene. The gene is therefore the basic unit of inheritance. It is a region of the chromosome or, more specifically, a length of the DNA molecule, which has a particular function. Each gene may have two, or occasionally more, alternative forms. Each form of the gene is called an **allele**. The gene for the shape of the seed coat in peas has two alleles, one determining round shape, the other wrinkled. The position of a gene within a DNA molecule is called the **locus**. When two identical alleles occur together at the same locus on a chromosome, they are said to be **homozygous**, e.g. when two alleles for round seeds occur together (RR) they are said to be **homozygous dominant**. Similarly, the two alleles for wrinkled seeds (rr) are referred to as **homozygous recessive**. Where the two alleles differ (Rr) they are termed **heterozygous**.

### 9.1.5 Dihybrid inheritance (Mendel's Law of Independent Assortment)

Dihybrid inheritance refers to the simultaneous inheritance of two characters. In one of his experiments Mendel investigated the inheritance of seed shape (round v. wrinkled) and seed colour (green v. yellow) at the same time. He knew from his monohybrid crosses that round seeds were dominant to wrinkled ones and yellow seeds were dominant to green. He chose to cross plants with both dominant features (round and yellow) with ones that were recessive for both (wrinkled and green). The $F_1$ generation yielded plants all of which produced round, yellow seeds – hardly surprising as these are the two dominant features.

Mendel planted the $F_1$ seeds, raised the plants and allowed them to self-pollinate. He then collected the seeds. Of the 556 seeds produced, the majority, 315, possessed the two dominant features – round and yellow. The smallest group, 32, possessed the two recessive features – wrinkled and green. The remaining 209 seeds were of types not previously found. They combined one dominant and one recessive feature; 108 were round (dominant) and green (recessive) and 101 were wrinkled (recessive) and yellow (dominant). At first inspection these results may appear to contradict those obtained in the monohybrid cross, but as Table 9.2 shows, the ratio of dominant to recessive for each feature is still 3 : 1, as expected.

The significance of these findings was that as the features of seed shape and colour had each produced a 3 : 1 ratio (dominant : recessive), the two features had behaved completely independently of one another. The presence of one had not affected the behaviour of the other. On the basis of these findings, Mendel formulated his second law, the **Law of Independent Assortment**, which states:

**Each of a pair of contrasted characters may be combined with either of another pair.**

With our present knowledge of genetics the law could now be rewritten as:

**Each member of an allelic pair may combine randomly with either of another pair.**

TABLE 9.2 **Results of Mendel's dihybrid cross**

Parents: round, yellow seeds v. wrinkled, green seeds

$F_1$ generation: all round, yellow seeds

$F_2$ generation:

| | | Seed shape | | | |
| --- | --- | --- | --- | --- | --- |
| | | Round | Wrinkled | Total | Approx. ratio |
| Seed colour | Yellow | 315 | 101 | 416 | 3 yellow |
| | Green | 108 | 32 | 140 | 1 green |
| | Total | 423 | 133 | | |
| | Approx. ratio | 3 round | 1 wrinkled | | |

Approx. ratio: 
round, yellow (2 dominants) : round, green (dominant + recessive) : wrinkled, yellow (recessive + dominant) : wrinkled, green (2 recessives)

9 : 3 : 3 : 1

### 9.1.6 Genetic representation of the dihybrid cross

Using the principles outlined in Table 9.1, the full genetic explanation of this dihybrid cross is shown below.

Let R = allele for round seed
r = allele for wrinkled seed
G = allele for yellow seed
g = allele for green seed

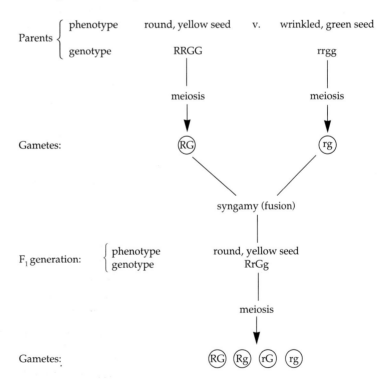

As the plants are self-pollinated the male and female gametes are of the same types. The offspring of this cross may therefore be represented in a Punnett square.

|  | ♂ gametes | | | |
|---|---|---|---|---|
| ♀ gametes | RG | Rg | rG | rg |
| RG | RRGG | RRGg | RrGG | RrGg |
| Rg | RRGg | RRgg | RrGg | Rrgg |
| rG | RrGG | RrGg | rrGG | rrGg |
| rg | RrGg | Rrgg | rrGg | rrgg |

In the following list, '–' represents either the dominant or recessive allele.

|  |  | Total |
|---|---|---|
| R–G– = round, yellow seed | | 9 (315) |
| R–gg = round, green seed | | 3 (108) |
| rrG– = wrinkled, yellow seed | | 3 (101) |
| rrgg = wrinkled, green seed | | 1 (32) |

Allowing for statistical error, Mendel's results (shown in brackets) were a reasonable approximation to the expected 9:3:3:1 ratio.

## 9.2 The test cross

One common genetic problem is that an organism which shows dominant character can have two possible genotypes. For example, a plant producing seeds with round coats could either be homozygous dominant (RR) or heterozygous (Rr). The appearance of the seeds (phenotype) is identical in both cases. It is often necessary, however, to determine the genotype accurately. This may be achieved by crossing the organism of unknown genotype with one whose genotype is accurately known. One genotype which can be positively identified from its phenotype alone is one which shows the recessive feature. In the case of the seed coat, any pea seed with a wrinkled coat must have the genotype rr. By crossing the dominant character, the unknown genotype can be identified. To take the above example

Let R = allele for round seeds
      r = allele for wrinkled seeds

If the plant producing round seed has the genotype RR:

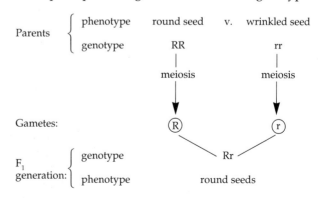

The only possible offspring are plants which produce round seed

If the plant producing round seeds has the genotype Rr:

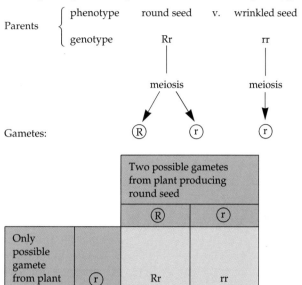

The offspring comprise equal numbers of plants producing round seeds and plants producing wrinkled seeds.

If some of the plants produce seeds with wrinkled coats (rr), then the unknown genotype must be Rr. An exact 1 : 1 ratio as above is not often achieved in practice, but this is unimportant as the presence of a single plant producing wrinkled seeds is proof enough (the possibility of a mutation must be discounted as it is highly unlikely and totally unpredictable). Such a plant with its rr genotype could only be produced if both parents donated an r gamete. The only way a plant which produces round seed can donate such a gamete is if it is heterozygous (Rr).

If all the offspring of our test cross were plants producing round seed, then no definite conclusions could be drawn, since both parental genotypes (Rr and RR) are capable of producing such offspring. However, provided a large number of offspring are produced, the absence of plants producing wrinkled seeds would strongly indicate that the unknown genotype was RR. Had it been Rr, half the offspring should have produced wrinkled seeds. While it would be theoretically possible for no wrinkled seeds to arise, this would be highly improbable where the sample was large.

It is possible to perform a dihybrid test cross. A plant which produces round, yellow seeds has four possible genotypes, namely: RRGG, RrGG, RRGg and RrGg. To determine the genotype of such a plant, it must be crossed with one producing wrinkled, green seeds. Such a plant has only one possible genotype, rrgg, and produces only one type of gamete, namely rg. The outcome of each of the crosses is shown in Table 9.3.

From the table it can be seen that the unknown genotypes can be identified from the results of the test cross as follows. If the offspring contain at least one plant producing wrinkled, yellow seeds, the unknown genotype is RrGG; if round, green seeds it is RRGg, and if wrinkled, green seeds it is RrGg. If the number of offspring is large and *all* produce round, yellow seeds it is highly probable that the genotype is RRGG.

**TABLE 9.3  Dihybrid backcross**

| Possible genotypes of plant producing round, yellow seeds | Possible gametes | Genotypes of offspring crossed with plant producing wrinkled, green seeds (gamete = rg) | Phenotype (type of seeds produced) |
|---|---|---|---|
| RRGG | RG | RrGg | All round and yellow |
| RrGG | RG | RrGg | ½ round and yellow |
| | rG | rrGg | ½ wrinkled and yellow |
| RRGg | RG | RrGg | ½ round and yellow |
| | Rg | Rrgg | ½ round and green |
| RrGg | RG | RrGg | ¼ round and yellow |
| | Rg | Rrgg | ¼ round and green |
| | rG | rrGg | ¼ wrinkled and yellow |
| | rg | rrgg | ¼ wrinkled and green |

## 9.3   Sex determination

In humans there are 23 pairs of chromosomes. Of these, 22 pairs are identical in both sexes. The 23rd pair, however, is different in the male from the female. The 22 identical pairs are called **autosomes**; the 23rd pair are referred to as **sex chromosomes** or **heterosomes**. In females, the two sex chromosomes are identical and are called **X chromosomes**. In males, an X chromosome is also present, but the other of the pair is smaller in size and called the **Y chromosome**. Unlike other features of an organism, sex is determined by chromosomes rather than genes.

Humans of the genotype XXY arise from time to time and are phenotypically male, while genotypes with just one X chromosome (XO) are phenotypically female. This suggests that it is the presence of the Y chromosome which makes a human male; in its absence the sex is female. How then does the Y chromosome determine maleness? The Y chromosome possesses several copies of a **testicular differentiating gene**, which codes for the production of a substance that causes the undifferentiated gonads to become testes. In the absence of this gene, and hence this substance, the gonads develop into ovaries.

It can be seen that in humans the female produces gametes which all contain an X chromosome and are therefore the same. She is called the **homogametic sex** ('same gametes'). The male, however, produces gametes of two genetic types: one which contains an X chromosome, the other a Y chromosome. The male is called the **heterogametic sex** ('different gametes').

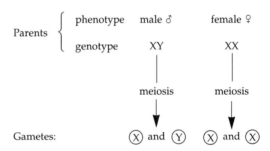

| Offspring | ♂ gametes | |
| --- | --- | --- |
| ♀ gametes | Ⓧ | Ⓨ |
| Ⓧ | XX | XY |
| Ⓧ | XX | XY |

Sex ratio   1 female : 1 male

Sex determination differs in other organisms. In birds, most reptiles, some fish and all butterflies, the male is the homogametic sex (XX) and the female is the heterogametic sex (XY). In some insects, while the female is XX, the Y chromosome is absent in the male, which is therefore XO. In the fruit fly *Drosophila*, the female is XX and the male XY; however, the Y chromosome is not smaller, as in humans, but simply a different shape.

# 9.4   Linkage

For just 23 pairs of chromosomes to determine the many thousands of different human characteristics, it follows that each chromosome must possess many different genes. Any two genes which occur on the same chromosome are said to be **linked**. All the genes on a single chromosome form a **linkage group**.

Under normal circumstances, all the linked genes remain together during cell division and so pass into the gamete, and hence the offspring, together. They do not therefore segregate in accordance with Mendel's Law of Independent Assortment. Fig. 9.2 shows the different gametes produced if a pair of genes A and B are linked rather than on separate chromosomes.

### 9.4.1 Crossing over and recombination

It is known that genes for flower colour and fruit colour in tomatoes are on the same chromosome. Plants with yellow flowers bear red fruit, those with white flowers bear yellow fruit. If the two types are crossed, the following results are obtained.

Let R = allele for red fruit (dominant) and

r = allele for yellow fruit (recessive)

W = allele for yellow flowers (dominant) and

w = allele for white flowers (recessive)

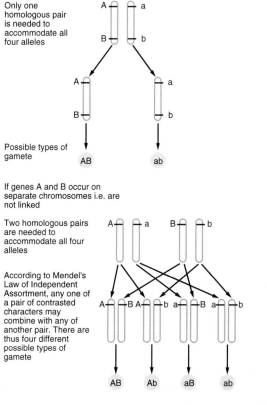

If genes A and B occur on the same chromosome i.e. are linked

Only one homologous pair is needed to accommodate all four alleles

Possible types of gamete    AB    ab

If genes A and B occur on separate chromosomes i.e. are not linked

Two homologous pairs are needed to accommodate all four alleles

According to Mendel's Law of Independent Assortment, any one of a pair of contrasted characters may combine with any of another pair. There are thus four different possible types of gamete

AB    Ab    aB    ab

*Fig. 9.2 Comparison of gametes produced by an organism heterozygous for two genes A and B, when they are linked and not linked.*

Parents
Phenotype    Yellow flowers +red fruit          White flowers +yellow fruit
Genotype

Meiosis          Meiosis

Gamete:

Syngamy

$F_1$ generation

All have yellow flowers and red fruit

If the F₁ generation is intercrossed (i.e. self-pollinated), the following results would be expected:

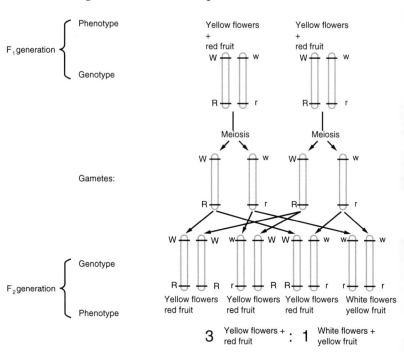

$$3 \quad \text{Yellow flowers + red fruit} \quad : \quad 1 \quad \text{White flowers + yellow fruit}$$

When the actual cross is performed, however, the following results are typical if 100 F₂ plants are produced:

| | |
|---|---|
| Yellow flowers and red fruit | 68 |
| Yellow flowers and yellow fruit | 7 |
| White flowers and red fruit | 7 |
| White flowers and yellow fruit | 18 |

What then is the explanation? Could it be that the two characters are not linked, but occur on separate chromosomes? If this were so, it would be a normal dihybrid cross, and a 9:3:3:1 ratio should be found. For 100 plants this would mean a 56:19:19:6 distribution. This is sufficiently different from the actual ratio of 68:7:7:18 which was obtained for it to be discounted. For the answer, we have to go back to Section 8.3 and the events in prophase I of meiosis. During this stage portions of the chromatids of homologous chromosomes were exchanged in the process called crossing over. Could this be the explanation as to how the two unexpected phenotypes (yellow flowers/yellow fruit and white flowers/red fruit) came about? To find out, let us consider the same F₁ intercross as before but assume that in one parent crossing over took place and this plant was subsequently self-pollinated (see left).

The new combinations are thus the result of crossing over in prophase I of meiosis. These new combinations are called **recombinants**. As shown, this cross produces a 9:3:3:1 ratio. However, in practice, crossing over will not always occur between the two genes. In some cases it may not occur at all; in others it may occur in such a way that the two genes are not separated. In these circumstances the only gametes are WR and wr. For this reason plants with yellow flowers and red fruit, and those with white flowers and yellow fruit, occur in greater numbers than expected.

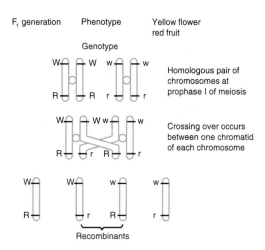

F₁ generation    Phenotype    Yellow flower red fruit

Genotype

Homologous pair of chromosomes at prophase I of meiosis

Crossing over occurs between one chromatid of each chromosome

Recombinants

If the plant is self-fertilized

| F₂ generation: | ♂ gametes | | | |
|---|---|---|---|---|
| ♀ gametes | WR | Wr | wR | wr |
| WR | WWRR | WWRr | WwRR | WwRr |
| Wr | WWRr | WWrr | WwRr | Wwrr |
| wR | WwRR | WwRr | wwRR | wwRr |
| wr | WwRr | Wwrr | wwRr | wwrr |

New combinations WWrr and Wwrr (yellow flowers, yellow fruit)
wwRR and wwRr (white flowers, red fruit)

### 9.4.2 Sex linkage

Sex linkage refers to the carrying of genes on the sex chromosomes. These genes determine body characters and have nothing to do with sex. The X chromosome carries many such genes, the Y chromosome has very few. Features linked on the Y chromosome will only arise in the heterogametic (XY) sex, i.e. males in mammals, females in birds. Features linked on the X chromosome may arise in either sex.

White eye colour is a sex-linked character in the fruit fly *Drosophila*. It is carried on the X chromosome and the male is the heterogametic sex. To represent sex-linked crosses, the same principles which were laid down in Table 9.1 should be followed. The letter representing each allele should, however, be attached to the letter X to indicate it is linked to it. No corresponding allele is found on the Y chromosomes, which therefore have no attached letter.

The expected results of a cross between a white-eyed male mutant and a **wild-type** (red-eyed) female are shown below. 'Wild-type' is a term used to describe an organism as it normally occurs in nature. The **reciprocal cross** is shown on the next page. A reciprocal cross is one where the same genetic features are used, but the sexes are reversed. In this case the reciprocal cross is between a white-eyed mutant female and a wild-type (red-eyed) male.

Red eyes are dominant over white eyes.

Therefore let R represent the allele for red eyes and
r represent the allele for white eyes

As the genes for eye colour are carried on the X chromosome the alleles are represented as $X^R$ and $X^r$ respectively. In *Drosophila* the male is the heterogametic sex (XY) and the female is the homogametic sex (XX).

Mutant and normal *Drosophila*

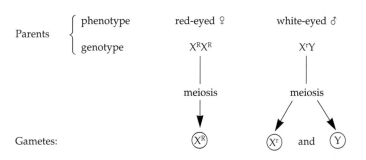

| Parents | phenotype | red-eyed ♀ | white-eyed ♂ |
|---|---|---|---|
| | genotype | $X^RX^R$ | $X^rY$ |

meiosis          meiosis

Gametes:          $X^R$          $X^r$   and   $Y$

F₁ generation:

| ♀ gametes | ♂ gametes | |
|---|---|---|
| | $X^r$ | $Y$ |
| $X^R$ | $X^RX^r$ | $X^RY$ |

50% red-eyed ♀ ($X^RX^r$)
50% red-eyed ♂ ($X^RY$)

*continued on next page*

*continued from previous page*

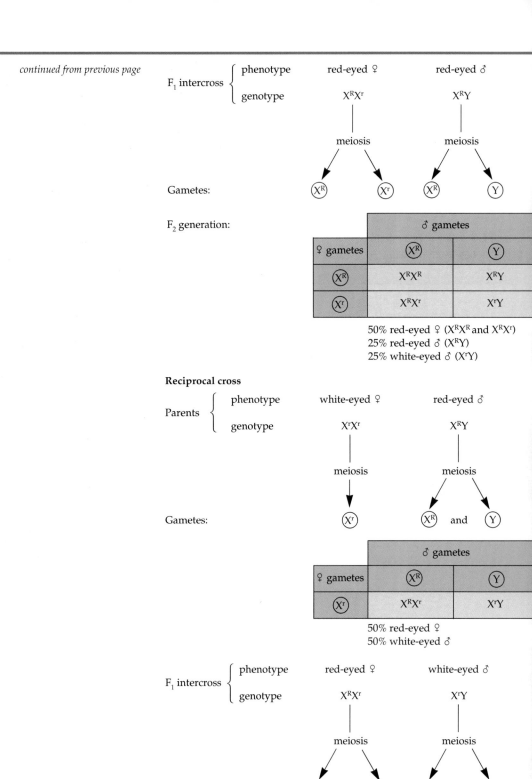

F₁ intercross
- phenotype: red-eyed ♀ — red-eyed ♂
- genotype: $X^R X^r$ — $X^R Y$

meiosis — meiosis

Gametes: $X^R$ — $X^r$ — $X^R$ — Y

F₂ generation:

| ♀ gametes | ♂ gametes | |
|---|---|---|
| | $X^R$ | Y |
| $X^R$ | $X^R X^R$ | $X^R Y$ |
| $X^r$ | $X^R X^r$ | $X^r Y$ |

50% red-eyed ♀ ($X^R X^R$ and $X^R X^r$)
25% red-eyed ♂ ($X^R Y$)
25% white-eyed ♂ ($X^r Y$)

**Reciprocal cross**

Parents
- phenotype: white-eyed ♀ — red-eyed ♂
- genotype: $X^r X^r$ — $X^R Y$

meiosis — meiosis

Gametes: $X^r$ — $X^R$ and Y

| ♀ gametes | ♂ gametes | |
|---|---|---|
| | $X^R$ | Y |
| $X^r$ | $X^R X^r$ | $X^r Y$ |

50% red-eyed ♀
50% white-eyed ♂

F₁ intercross
- phenotype: red-eyed ♀ — white-eyed ♂
- genotype: $X^R X^r$ — $X^r Y$

meiosis — meiosis

Gametes: $X^R$ and $X^r$ — $X^r$ — Y

F₂ generation:

| ♀ gametes | ♂ gametes | |
|---|---|---|
| | $X^r$ | Y |
| $X^R$ | $X^R X^r$ | $X^R Y$ |
| $X^r$ | $X^r X^r$ | $X^r Y$ |

25% red-eyed ♀ ($X^R X^r$)
25% red-eyed ♂ ($X^R Y$)
25% white-eyed ♂ ($X^r Y$)
25% white-eyed ♀ ($X^r X^r$)

Two well known sex-linked genes in humans are those causing haemophilia and red–green colour-blindness. Both are linked to the X chromosome and both occur almost exclusively in males. For the condition to arise in females requires the double recessive state and as the recessive allele is relatively rare in the population this is unlikely to occur. In females the recessive allele is normally masked by the appropriate dominant allele which occurs on the other X chromosome. These heterozygous females are not themselves affected but are capable of passing the recessive allele to their offspring. For this reason such females are termed **carriers**. When the recessive allele occurs in males it expresses itself because the Y chromosome cannot carry any corresponding dominant allele. The inheritance of red–green colour-blindness is illustrated below.

Normal sight is dominant over red–green colour-blindness. Therefore let B represent the allele for normal sight and
b represent the allele for colour-blindness

As this gene is carried on the X chromosome, its alleles are represented as $X^B$ and $X^b$ respectively. In humans the male is the heterogametic sex (XY) and the female is the homogametic sex (XX).

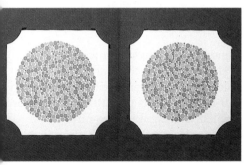

wo numbers from the Ishihara test

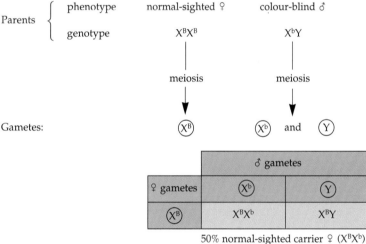

Parents
- phenotype: normal-sighted ♀     colour-blind ♂
- genotype: $X^BX^B$     $X^bY$

meiosis     meiosis

Gametes: $X^B$     $X^b$ and $Y$

|  | ♂ gametes | |
|---|---|---|
| ♀ gametes | $X^b$ | $Y$ |
| $X^B$ | $X^BX^b$ | $X^BY$ |

50% normal-sighted carrier ♀ ($X^BX^b$)
50% normal-sighted ♂ ($X^BY$)

$F_1$ intercross
- phenotype: normal-sighted carrier ♀     normal-sighted ♂
- genotype: $X^BX^b$     $X^BY$

meiosis     meiosis

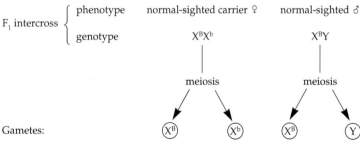

Gametes: $X^B$    $X^b$    $X^B$    $Y$

$F_2$ generation:

|  | ♂ gametes | |
|---|---|---|
| ♀ gametes | $X^B$ | $Y$ |
| $X^B$ | $X^BX^B$ | $X^BY$ |
| $X^b$ | $X^BX^b$ | $X^bY$ |

25% normal-sighted ♀ ($X^BX^B$)     25% normal-sighted ♂ ($X^BY$)
25% normal-sighted carrier ♀ ($X^BX^b$)     25% colour-blind ♂ ($X^bY$)

A study of the crosses reveals that the recessive gene causing colour-blindness is exchanged from one sex to the other at each generation. The father passes it to his daughters, who thus become carriers. The daughters in turn may pass it to their sons, who are thus colour-blind. This pattern of inheritance is perhaps more obvious when viewed another way. As the male is XY, his Y chromosome must have been inherited from his father as the mother does not possess a Y chromosome. The X chromosome and hence colour-blindness must therefore have been inherited from the mother. The colour-blind male can only donate his X chromosome to his daughters as it is bound to fuse with another X chromosome – the only type the mother produces. Colour-blind females can only arise from a cross between a carrier female and a colour-blind male. As both types are rare in the population, the chance of this happening is very small indeed. Even then, there is only a one in four chance of any single child of such a cross being a colour-blind female.

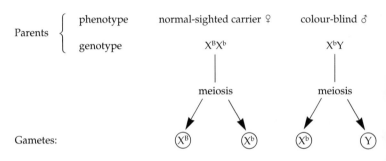

Parents
- phenotype: normal-sighted carrier ♀     colour-blind ♂
- genotype: $X^B X^b$     $X^b Y$

meiosis     meiosis

Gametes: $X^B$   $X^b$   $X^b$   Y

Offspring genotypes:

|  | ♂ gametes | |
|---|---|---|
| ♀ gametes | $X^b$ | Y |
| $X^B$ | $X^B X^b$ | $X^B Y$ |
| $X^b$ | $X^b X^b$ | $X^b Y$ |

25% normal-sighted carrier ♀ ($X^B X^b$)     25% colour-blind ♂ ($X^b Y$)
25% normal-sighted ♂ ($X^B Y$)     25% colour-blind ♀ ($X^b X^b$)

The inheritance of haemophilia follows a similar pattern to that of colour-blindness. Haemophilia is the inability of the blood to clot, leading to slow and persistent bleeding, especially in the joints. Unlike colour-blindness it is potentially lethal. For this reason, the recessive allele causing it is even rarer in the population. Haemophiliac females are thus highly improbable, and in any case are unlikely to have children as the onset of menstruation at puberty is often fatal. Haemophilia is the result of an individual being unable to produce one of the many clotting factors, namely **factor 8** or **anti-haemophiliac globulin (AHG)** (see Biology Around Us on page 126). The extraction of this factor from donated blood now permits haemophiliacs to lead near-normal lives, although they still run the same risk of conveying the disease to their children.

Any mutant recessive allele, such as that causing haemophilia, is normally rapidly diluted among the many normal alleles in a population. Its expression is thus a rare event. If, however, there is close breeding between members of a family in which a

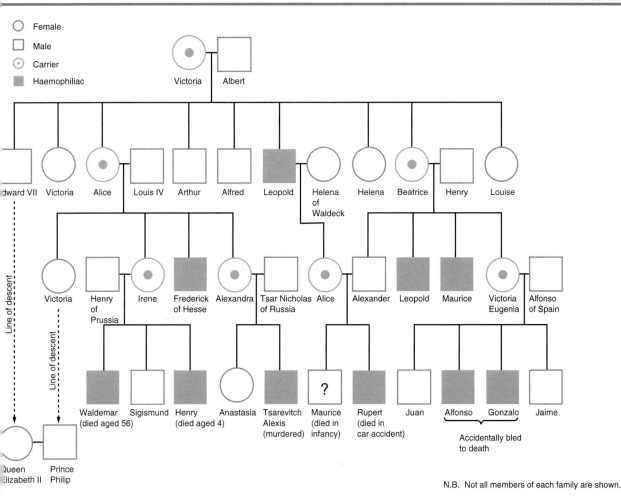

Key:
- ○ Female
- □ Male
- ◉ Carrier
- ▨ Haemophiliac

Victoria — Albert

Edward VII · Victoria · Alice · Louis IV · Arthur · Alfred · Leopold · Helena of Waldeck · Helena · Beatrice · Henry · Louise

Victoria · Henry of Prussia · Irene · Frederick of Hesse · Alexandra · Tsar Nicholas of Russia · Alice · Alexander · Leopold · Maurice · Victoria Eugenia · Alfonso of Spain

Waldemar (died aged 56) · Sigismund · Henry (died aged 4) · Anastasia · Tsarevitch Alexis (murdered) · Maurice (died in infancy) · Rupert (died in car accident) · Juan · Alfonso · Gonzalo · Jaime

?

Accidentally bled to death

Line of descent

Queen Elizabeth II — Prince Philip

N.B. Not all members of each family are shown.

*Fig. 9.3 Transmission of haemophilia from Queen Victoria*

mutant gene exists, the chances of it expressing itself are enhanced. This accounts for the higher than normal occurrence of the haemophiliac gene among members of various European royal families. The origin of this particular gene can be traced back to England's Queen Victoria, who had a haemophiliac son, Leopold Duke of Albany. Prior to this there was no history of the gene among the royal family, although it existed elsewhere in the population. In order to marry someone of similar status, members of the European royal families were limited in their choice of partners and tended to marry within a relatively small circle. In effect, the gene pool was very restricted. As a result there was a disproportionately large number of haemophiliacs in these families. Fig. 9.3 traces the inheritance of this gene. The present English royal family is unaffected, as it is descended from Edward VII who did not inherit the haemophilia gene. The chart also illustrates another method of representing sex-linked crosses.

It is unusual to find dominant mutant genes linked to the X chromosome in humans, but one example is the congenital absence of incisor teeth. These conditions occur in both sexes but are more common in females as they have two X chromosomes. Genes linked to the Y chromosome are very rare, but hairy ear rims are an example.

# 9.5 Allelic interaction

## PROJECT

**Surveys can be carried out among your fellow students to find, for example:**

1. The relationships between skin, hair and eye colour.

2. The proportions of tongue-rollers and non-rollers; ear-lobe types, etc.

3. If there are any correlations in laterality studies, for example, between handedness and
   (a) eye dominance
   (b) arm folding
   (c) volumes of hands
   (d) lengths of fingers, etc.

Up to now we have looked at inheritance in a straightforward way – the black and white of genetics so to speak. We now turn our attention to the less straightforward situations – the many shades of grey which exist when alleles interact in different ways.

### 9.5.1 Codominance

So far we have dealt with situations where one of the alleles of a gene is dominant and the other recessive. Sometimes however, alleles express themselves equally in the phenotype. Such a condition is called **codominance**.

One example of codominance occurs when a snapdragon (*Antirrhinum*) with red flowers is crossed with one with white flowers. All the $F_1$ generation produce flowers of intermediate colour, namely pink. The $F_2$ generation produces red, pink and white flowers in the ratio $1:2:1$. The cross may be represented by the procedure shown below:

**N.B.** Where codominance is involved, it is normal to use different letters to represent each allele, e.g. R to represent red flowers and W to represent white flowers. The use of upper and lower cases of one letter, e.g. R and r or W and w, would imply dominance and be confusing. It is also usual to assign the gene an upper case letter (in the above case C = colour) and use superscript upper case letters to designate the different alleles.

*Antirrhinum majus*

Let $C^R$ = the allele for red flowers

$C^W$ = the allele for white flowers

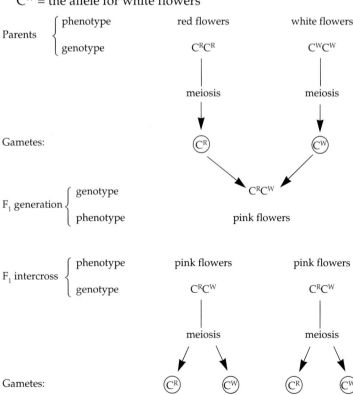

F$_2$ generation:

|  | $\male$ gametes | |
|---|---|---|
| $\female$ gametes | Ⓒᴿ | Ⓒᵂ |
| Ⓒᴿ | CᴿCᴿ | CᴿCᵂ |
| Ⓒᵂ | CᴿCᵂ | CᵂCᵂ |

25% red flowers (CᴿCᴿ)
50% pink flowers (CᴿCᵂ)
25% white flowers (CᵂCᵂ)

### 9.5.2 Partial dominance

Sometimes both alleles express themselves in the phenotype, but one more so than another. This is an intermediate stage between complete dominance and codominance. There are many blends of partial dominance which lead to a wide range of intermediate varieties between two extremes.

### 9.5.3 Multiple alleles

All examples so far studied have involved a gene having two alternative alleles. We now look at a situation where a gene has more than two possible alleles.

In humans, the inheritance of the ABO blood groups is determined by a gene, I, which has three different alleles. Any two of these can occur at a single locus at any one time (Table 9.4).

Allele A causes production of antigen A on red blood cells.

Allele B causes production of antigen B on red blood cells.

Allele O causes no production of antigens on red blood cells.

Alleles A and B are codominant and allele O is recessive to both.

The transmission of these alleles occurs in normal Mendelian fashion.

A cross between an individual of group AB and one of group O therefore gives rise to individuals none of whom possess either parental blood group.

**TABLE 9.4 Possible genotypes of blood groups in the ABO system**

| Blood group | Possible genotypes |
|---|---|
| A | IᴬIᴬ or IᴬIᴼ |
| B | IᴮIᴮ or IᴮIᴼ |
| AB | IᴬIᴮ |
| O | IᴼIᴼ |

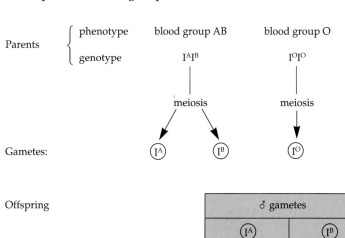

Parents { phenotype: blood group AB, blood group O; genotype: IᴬIᴮ, IᴼIᴼ }

meiosis    meiosis

Gametes: Ⓘᴬ  Ⓘᴮ   Ⓘᴼ

Offspring

|  | $\male$ gametes | |
|---|---|---|
|  | Ⓘᴬ | Ⓘᴮ |
| $\female$ gametes  Ⓘᴼ | IᴬIᴼ | IᴮIᴼ |

50% blood group A (IᴬIᴼ)
50% blood group B (IᴮIᴼ)

A cross between certain individuals of blood group A and certain individuals of blood group B may produce offspring with any one of the four blood groups.

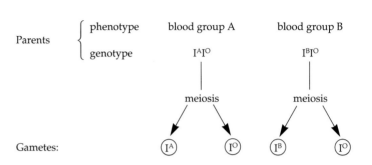

Offspring

|  |  | ♂ gametes | |
|---|---|---|---|
|  |  | $I^A$ | $I^O$ |
| ♀ gametes | $I^B$ | $I^A I^B$ | $I^B I^O$ |
|  | $I^O$ | $I^A I^O$ | $I^O I^O$ |

25% blood group A ($I^A I^O$)   25% blood group AB ($I^A I^B$)
25% blood group B ($I^B I^O$)   25% blood group O ($I^O I^O$)

*Paternity suits*

Although blood groups cannot prove who the father of a child is, it is possible to use inheritance to show that an individual could not possibly be the father. Imagine a mother who is blood group B having a child of blood group O. She claims the father is a man whose blood group is found to be AB. As the child is group O its only possible genotype is $I^O I^O$. It must therefore have inherited one $I^O$ allele from each parent. The mother, if $I^B I^O$, could donate such an allele. The man with blood group AB can only have the genotype $I^A I^B$. He is unable to donate an $I^O$ allele and cannot therefore be the father.

*Dominance series*

Coat colour in rabbits is determined by a gene C which has four possible alleles:

Allele $C^F$ determines full coat colour and is dominant to
Allele $C^{CH}$ which determines chinchilla coat and is in turn dominant to
Allele $C^H$ which determines Himalayan coat and is in turn dominant to
Allele $C^A$ which determines albino coat colour.

There is therefore a dominance series, and each type has a range of possible genotypes (see Table 9.5).

Inheritance is once again in normal Mendelian fashion.

TABLE 9.5   **Possible genotypes of rabbits with different coat colour**

| Coat colour | Possible genotypes |
|---|---|
| Full | $C^F C^F$ or $C^F C^{CH}$ or $C^F C^H$ or $C^F C^A$ |
| Chinchilla | $C^{CH} C^{CH}$ or $C^{CH} C^H$ or $C^{CH} C^A$ |
| Himalayan | $C^H C^H$ or $C^H C^A$ |
| Albino | $C^A C^A$ |

# 9.6    Gene interaction

### 9.6.1 Epistasis

Epistasis arises when the allele of one gene suppresses or masks the action of another. An example occurs in mice where three genes determine coat colour. However the absence of a dominant allele at one of the loci results in no pigment being produced and the coat being albino. This occurs regardless of the genes present at the other loci, even if these produce normal coat colour. The gene at the third locus clearly suppresses the action of the others.

### 9.6.2 Polygenes

Many genes acting together are referred to as polygenes. Imagine a character determined by five genes, each gene having a dominant or recessive allele. An organism inheriting five dominant alleles will lie at one end of the spectrum and one with five recessive alleles will lie at the other. Between these extremes will be a continuum of types depending on the relative proportions of dominant and recessive alleles. Polygenes give rise to continuous variation, which is discussed further in Section 10.2.1.

# 9.7   Questions

1. In tomatoes the allele for red fruit, **R**, is dominant to that for yellow fruit, **r**. The allele for tall plant, **T**, is dominant to that for short plant, **t**. The two genes concerned are on different chromosomes.

(a) A tomato plant is homozygous for allele **R**. Giving a reason for your answer in each case, how many copies of this allele would be found in
  (i) a male gamete produced by this plant,
  (ii) a leaf cell from this plant?         (2 marks)

(b) A cross was made between two tomato plants.
  (i) The possible genotypes of the gametes of the plant chosen as the male parent were **RT**, **Rt**, **rT** and **rt**. What was the genotype of this plant?         (1 mark)
  (ii) The possible genotypes of the gametes of the plant chosen as the female parent were **rt** and **rT**. What was the phenotype of this plant?         (1 mark)
  (iii) What proportion of the offspring of this cross would you expect to have red fruit? Use a genetic diagram to explain your answer.         (3 marks)
         (Total 7 marks)

*NEAB March 1998, Paper BY02, No. 5*

2. In humans, two genes affect the hands. One gene determines the ability to curve the thumb, the other controls the presence of hair on the middle segments of the fingers. The allele for curved thumb, **T**, is dominant to the allele for straight thumb, **t**. The allele for hair on the middle segment of the fingers, **H**, is dominant to that for an absence of hair, **h**.

(a) Give all the possible genotypes of individuals who are able to curve their thumbs but have no hair present on the middle segments of their fingers.         (1 mark)

(b) (i) Copy and complete the table to show the possible genotypes resulting from a cross between two individuals heterozygous for both of these genes.

| | Genotypes of female gametes | | | |
|---|---|---|---|---|
| Genotypes of male gametes | | | | |
| | | | | |
| | | | | |
| | | | | |

         (2 marks)

  (ii) What is the probability that one of the offspring of this cross would have hair on the middle segments of the fingers         (1 mark)

(iii) What is the probability that the first child born to this couple would be a girl with straight thumbs?         (1 mark)
         (Total 5 marks)

*AEB January 1998, Paper 2, No.*

3. The stems of tomato plants can be different colours (green or purple) and may be hairy or without hairs (hairless). Each character is controlled by a different gene. Each gene has two alleles.

The following symbols are used to represent the alleles involved.

**A**   dominant allele for colour

**a**   recessive allele for colour

**B**   dominant allele for hairiness of stem

**b**   recessive allele for hairiness of stem

In an experiment, a homozygous tomato plant with a green, hairless stem was crossed with a homozygous plant with a purple, hairy stem. The $F_1$ seeds were collected and grown. All the resulting $F_1$ seedlings had purple, hairy stems.

(a) State the genotypes of each of the parent plants and of the $F_1$ seedlings in this cross.

Parent with green, hairless stem

Parent with purple, hairy stem

$F_1$ seedlings
         (3 marks)

(b) The $F_1$ plants were self-pollinated (interbred). The phenotypes and numbers of offspring are given in the table below.

| Phenotypes | Number of offspring |
|---|---|
| Purple, hairy stem | 293 |
| Purple, hairless stem | 15 |
| Green, hairy stem | 12 |
| Green, hairless stem | 98 |

  (i) In this dihybrid cross, what would be the expected ratio of the phenotypes in the offspring?         (2 marks)
  (ii) Explain the difference between the expected ratio and the numbers shown in the table.         (3 marks)

(c) A tomato grower wants to find out which of the purple, hairy plants are homozygous for both characters.
  (i) State the genotype of the plant which should be crossed with the purple, hairy plants in this test cross.         (1 mark)

(ii) Explain why this genotype should be used. *(2 marks)*

*(Total 11 marks)*

*Edexcel January 1998, Paper, B/HB1, No. 6*

. The inheritance of colour in sweet peas is controlled y two pairs of alleles (**A** and **a**, and **B** and **b**) at two ifferent gene loci.

he diagram shows how the dominant alleles at these wo gene loci determine flower colour by controlling ne synthesis of a purple pigment.

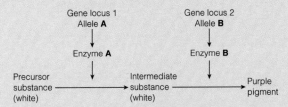

(a) Plants with the genotypes **aaBB**, **aaBb** and **aabb** all have white flowers. Use information in the diagram to explain why plants homozygous for the mutant allele, **a**, have white flowers. *(3 marks)*

(b) Use a genetic diagram to explain the genotypes and the expected ratio of phenotypes when plants with the genotypes **Aabb** and **aaBb** are crossed.

| | | |
|---|---|---|
| Parental phenotypes | White | White |
| Parental genotypes | **Aabb** | **aaBb** |
| Genotypes of gametes | | |
| Genotypes of offspring | | |
| Phenotypes of offspring | | |
| Ratio of phenotypes of offspring | | *(4 marks)* |

*(Total 7 marks)*

*NEAB June 1997, Paper BY02, No. 6*

. (a) What is meant by **epistasis**? *(1 mark)*

(b) How does epistasis differ from Mendelian dominance? *(1 mark)*

(c) In oats, the grain is enclosed by the dried remains of the outer parts of the flower, called the **hull**. In a cross between two pure-breeding varieties of oats, one with black-hulled grains, the other with white-hulled grains, the offspring ($F_1$) all had black-hulled grains. Allowing the $F_1$ plants to self-fertilize gave an $F_2$ with the phenotypes shown below.

| Phenotype | Number |
|---|---|
| Black-hulled grains | 418 |
| Grey-hulled grains | 106 |
| White-hulled grains | 36 |

These data show evidence of epistasis.

(i) What genetic ratio is suggested from the figures given? *(1 mark)*

(ii) Devise suitable symbols for the alleles involved. *(1 mark)*

(iii) Set out the crosses, using a Punnett square, to show the gametes, genotypes and phenotypes in each generation. *(5 marks)*

(d) Which statistical test might you use to confirm or reject the evidence for epistasis? *(1 mark)*

*(Total 10 marks)*

*Oxford June 1997, Paper 32, No. 3*

6. The way in which sex is determined in birds is different from that in mammals. In birds, the male has two X chromosomes while the female has one X and one Y chromosome. In poultry, the gene for chick colour is sex-linked and carried on the X chromosome. The allele for light colour is dominant to that for dark colour.

(a) Copy and complete the genetic diagram below to show the cross in which all the male chicks will be light coloured and all the female chicks will be dark coloured.

| | Male (XX) | Female (XY) |
|---|---|---|
| Phenotype of parents: | ................... | ................... |
| Genotype of parents: | ................... | ................... |
| Gametes: | ................... | ................... |
| Genotype of chicks: | ................... | ................... |
| Phenotype of chicks: | Light-coloured : male | Dark-coloured female |
| | 1:1 | |

*(3 marks)*

(b) Poultry farmers who keep hens for egg laying usually buy young chicks from a poultry breeder. Explain why sex linkage may be of practical use in poultry farming. *(1 mark)*

*(Total 4 marks)*

*AEB Summer 1997, Paper 1, No. 16*

**7.** A particular species of tropical beetle was maintained in a laboratory population. The beetles in this population had red, orange or yellow marks on their wing cases. This genetic polymorphism is known to be controlled at a single locus by three alleles.

    *(a)* What is meant by a **genetic polymorphism**?
                                       (*2 marks*)

    *(b)* The following controlled matings were carried out to produce the progeny shown.

| Cross | Parent colours | Progeny colours ratios |
|---|---|---|
| 1 | red × orange | 1 red : 1 orange |
| 2 | red × red | 3 red : 1 yellow |
| 3 | orange × orange | 3 orange : 1 yellow |
| 4 | red × yellow | 1 red : 1 yellow |
| 5 | red × red | 3 red : 1 orange |
| 6 | red × orange | 2 red : 1 orange : 1 yellow |

      (i) Which of the three wing colours is the most dominant character? (*1 mark*)

     (ii) If the letter **A** is used to represent the dominant form of the gene for wing case pigments, write down the symbols you would use to represent its other two alleles. (*2 marks*)

    (iii) Copy and complete the following table to show the genotypes of the parents, and the progeny genotypes with their ratios, in each of the above crosses.

| Cross | Parent genotypes | Progeny genotypes and ratios |
|---|---|---|
| 1 | | |
| 2 | | |
| 3 | | |
| 4 | | |
| 5 | | |
| 6 | | |

                                       (*12 marks*)

    *(c)* What is the dominance order of the alleles involved in these crosses? (*1 mark*)
                                    (*Total 18 marks*)

*Oxford & Cambridge January 1997, Unit B2, No. 2*

**8.** In mice, the dominant allele (**B**) of a gene for coat colour gives a black coat and the recessive allele (**b**) of this gene gives a brown coat. A second gene determines the density of the coat colour. The dominant allele (**D**) of this gene allows expression of coat colour, its recessive allele (**d**) dilutes the colour converting black to grey and brown to cream.

    *(a)* A breeder crossed a male black mouse with a female brown one. The offspring produced showed four different coat colours, black, grey, brown and cream.

      (i) State the genotypes for the black parent and the brown parent giving an explanation for your answer. (*5 marks*)

     (ii) Copy and complete the Punnett square below to show the genotypes of the gametes and the offspring.

| Genotypes of male gametes / Genotypes of female gametes | | | |
|---|---|---|---|
| | | | |
| | | | |

                                      (*2 marks*)

    (iii) State the expected phenotypic ratio. (*1 mark*)

    *(b)* With the aid of a genetic diagram, explain how the breeder could determine which of the black offspring were homozygous for the full colour allele (**D**). (*4 marks*)

    *(c)* Explain how events taking place during gametogenesis and fertilization lead to the production of variety in the offspring. (*3 marks*)
                                    (*Total 15 marks*)

*Edexcel June 1998, Paper HB6, No. 4*

**9.** Maize cobs may have purple or red grains. This character is controlled by a single pair of alleles. The dominant allele **A** gives a purple colour and the recessive allele **a** gives a red colour.

    *(a)* In an experiment, a heterozygous plant is crossed with a maize plant homozygous for allele **a**. State the genotypes of these two plants. (*1 mark*)

    *(b)* Grain colour is also affected by a second pair of alleles. The presence of the dominant allele **E** allows the purple or red colour to develop, but in the homozygous recessive (**ee**) no colour will develop (despite the presence of alleles **A** or **a**) and the grain will be white. A plant of genotype **AAEE** is crossed with a plant of genotype **aaee**.

      (i) State the genotype and phenotype of the offspring produced as a result of this cross. (*2 marks*)

     (ii) The plants of the offspring are allowed to self-fertilize. Draw a genetic diagram to show the possible genotypes produced as a result of this cross. (*3 marks*)

    (iii) Predict the phenotypic ratio that would be obtained from this cross. (*3 marks*)

(iv) Which genotypes, if allowed to self-fertilize, would produce pure-breeding lines containing white grains? *(3 marks)*

*(Total 12 marks)*

*ULEAC January 1996, B/HB1, No. 6*

In the broad bean, a pure-breeding variety with **green seeds** and **black hilums** (the point of attachment of the seed to the pod) was crossed with a pure-breeding variety with **yellow seeds** and **white hilums**. All the F$_1$ plants had yellow seeds and black hilums. When these were allowed to self-fertilize, the plants of the F$_2$ generation produced the following seeds.

| | |
|---|---|
| yellow seeds with white hilums | 31 |
| yellow seeds with black hilums | 93 |
| green seeds with white hilums | 8 |
| green seeds with black hilums | 28 |

*(a)* Which characteristics do you consider to be dominant and which recessive? *(1 mark)*

*(b)* Devise suitable symbols for the alleles of the genes involved. *(1 mark)*

*(c)* What genetic ratio is suggested by the numerical data in the experiment? *(1 mark)*

*(d)* Construct two suitable crossing diagrams to show the genotypes of the plants and their gametes in each generation. *(5 marks)*

*(Total 8 marks)*

*Oxford February 1997, Paper 31, No. 3*

*(a)* The nuclear divisions shown below are taking place in a heterozygote for **two** gene loci **A/a** and **B/b**. The chromosomes this organism inherited from a parent homozygous dominant at both loci are shown dark in the diagrams; those from the other, homozygous recessive parent are shown light. The **A/a** and **B/b** loci, which are positioned quite close to their centromeres, are **not** linked on the same chromosome.

The following diagrams show similar stages in two nuclear divisions. Name the type of division shown in each diagram. *(2 marks)*

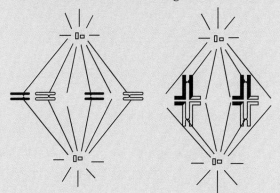

*(b)* Label the chromosomes in both diagrams with the letters **A/a** and **B/b** to indicate the genetic complement of each chromosome during the nuclear divisions. *(4 marks)*

*(c)* Use letters in the circles below to give the genetic makeup of the daughter cells produced by the **mitotic** division. *(2 marks)*

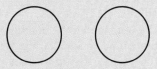

*(d)* In the circles below, give the genetic complement of the cells which would be produced at the end of the meiotic division shown in the diagram above. *(2 marks)*

*(e)* Mendel's law of independent assortment requires a double heterozygote **AaBb** to produce all four different haploid meiotic products (**AB**, **Ab**, **aB** and **ab**) at equal frequency. Explain this statement in terms of your answer to *(d)* above. *(5 marks)*

*(Total 15 marks)*

*Oxford & Cambridge June 1996, Unit B2, No. 1*

12. *(a)* Give **two** differences between the X and Y chromosomes of humans. *(2 marks)*

*(b)* The diagram below is a family tree showing the pattern of inheritance of a sex-linked genetic disorder through five generations.

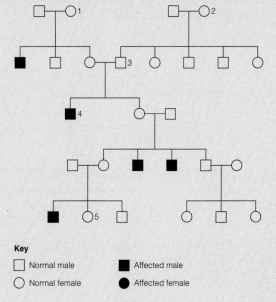

**Key**

☐ Normal male      ■ Affected male

○ Normal female      ● Affected female

175

(i) Identify **two** features of the inheritance of this disorder that are characteristic of sex-linked inheritance. *(2 marks)*

(ii) The disorder is caused by a recessive allele of a single gene. Using the symbol **A** to represent the normal allele and **a** to represent the recessive allele, write down the most likely genotypes of individuals 1, 2, 3 and 4. *(4 marks)*

(c) Individual 5 is engaged to be married. Her future partner comes from a family with no history of this genetic disorder. They plan to have several children.

(i) If individual 5's first child is a boy, what is the probability that he will have the disorder? *(1 mark)*

(ii) If individual 5's first child is a girl, what is the probability that she will have the disorder? *(1 mark)*

(d) The diagram below shows a small part of the same family tree, involving individuals 1 and 3. If this disorder had been caused by a dominant allele rather than a recessive allele, the pattern of inheritance would be different.

Using information in the complete tree, re-draw this part of the tree to show this different pattern of inheritance.

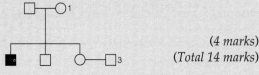

*(4 marks)*
*(Total 14 marks)*

ULEAC June 1995, Paper 3, No. 8

**13.** Cystic fibrosis is a condition in which affected people suffer from the accumulation of a thick, sticky mucus in their lungs.

The diagram shows part of a family tree in which some individuals have cystic fibrosis.

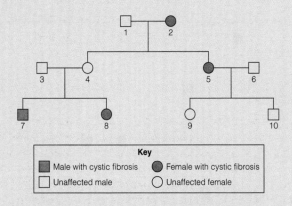

| Key | |
|---|---|
| ▪ Male with cystic fibrosis | ● Female with cystic fibrosis |
| □ Unaffected male | ○ Unaffected female |

(a) Explain the evidence from this family tree that cystic fibrosis is controlled by a recessive allele. *(2 marks)*

(b) What is the probability that the next child born to individuals **3** and **4** would have at least one allele for cystic fibrosis? Explain your answer. *(2 mark*

(c) In Britain, 1 in 2000 people are born with cystic fibrosis. What is the frequency of the cystic fibrosis allele in the British populatior *(1 mar*
*(Total 5 mark*

*AEB January 1996, Module Paper 2, No.*

**14.** In cats, sex is determined by X and Y chromosome in the same way as in humans.

One gene for coat colour in cats is present on the X chromosome but not on the Y chromosome. This gene has two alleles, orange (**B**) and black (**b**). An X chromosome bearing the **B** allele is represented by $X^B$ and one bearing the **b** allele by $X^b$.

Female cats that are homozygous for the $X^b$ allele have black coats; female cats that are heterozygous have tortoiseshell coats, that is, orange coats with dark patches.

(a) Give the genotype of:
(i) a female cat with a tortoiseshell coat.
(ii) a male cat with an orange coat.
(iii) a male cat with a black coat.
*(3 mark*

(b) A black-coated male cat is mated with a tortoiseshell-coated female cat.

Use a genetic diagram to explain what would be the expected ratios of the genotypes and th phenotypes of the kittens that could be produced by this cross.

| Parental phenotypes | Black-coated male | Tortoiseshell coated female |
|---|---|---|

Parental genotypes

Genotypes of gametes

Genotypes of kittens

Phenotypes of kittens

Ratio of phenotypes of kittens
*(4 mark*
*(Total 7 mark*

NEAB June 1995, Paper BY02, No.

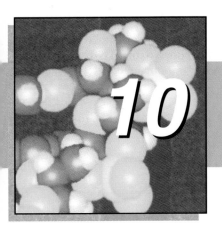

# 10 Genetic change and variation

Within any given population there are variations among individual organisms. It is this variation which forms the basis of the evolutionary theory of Darwin. There are two basic forms of variation: **continuous variation**, where the individuals in a population show a gradation from one extreme to the other, and **discontinuous (discrete) variation**, where there is a limited number of distinct forms within the population. Any study of variation inevitably involves the collection of large quantities of data.

## 10.1 Methods of recording variation

The investigation of variation within a population may involve recording the number of individuals that possess a particular feature, e.g. black fur. On the other hand, it may involve recording the number of individuals that fall within a set range of values, e.g. those weighing between 1 kg and 10 kg. What is being measured in both cases is the **frequency distribution**. This may be presented in a number of ways. To illustrate each method the same set of data is used throughout (Table 10.1), although it is not really suitable for some methods of presentation.

### 10.1.1 Table of data

Tabulation is the simplest means of presenting data. It is a useful method of recording information initially but is less useful for demonstrating the relationship between two variables.

### 10.1.2 Line graph

A graph typically has two axes, each of which measures a variable. One variable has fixed values which are selected by the experimenter. This is called the **independent variable**. The other variable is the measurement taken and as such is not selected by the experimenter. This is called the **dependent variable**. In Table 10.1, 'height' is the independent variable and 'frequency' the dependent variable. The values of the independent variable are plotted along the horizontal axis (also known as the *x* axis or abscissa) and the values of the dependent variable are plotted along the vertical axis (also known as the *y* axis or ordinate). The

TABLE 10.1   **Frequency of heights (measured to the nearest 2 cm) of a sample of humans**

| Height/cm | Frequency |
|-----------|-----------|
| 140 | 0 |
| 142 | 1 |
| 144 | 1 |
| 146 | 6 |
| 148 | 23 |
| 150 | 48 |
| 152 | 90 |
| 154 | 175 |
| 156 | 261 |
| 158 | 352 |
| 160 | 393 |
| 162 | 462 |
| 164 | 458 |
| 166 | 443 |
| 168 | 413 |
| 170 | 264 |
| 172 | 177 |
| 174 | 97 |
| 176 | 63 |
| 178 | 46 |
| 180 | 17 |
| 182 | 7 |
| 184 | 4 |
| 186 | 0 |
| 188 | 1 |
| 190 | 0 |

corresponding values of the two variables can be plotted as points on the graph known as **coordinates**. These points may then be joined to give a line or smooth curve, as in Fig. 10.1.

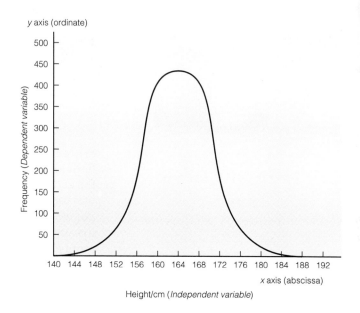

*Fig. 10.1 Graph of frequency against height/cm for a sample of humans*

### 10.1.3 Histogram

Axes are drawn in much the same way as for a line graph. The values for the independent variable on the $x$ axis are, however, normally reduced, often by grouping the data into convenient classes. For example, the 26 values for height used on the line graph may be reduced to 10 by grouping the heights into sets of 5 cm, e.g. 140–145, 145–150 etc. Instead of plotting points, vertical columns are drawn. The method is illustrated in Fig. 10.2.

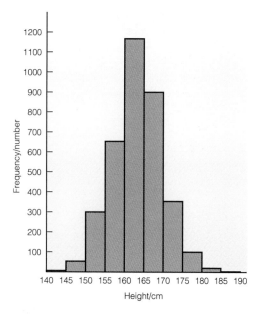

*Fig. 10.2 Histogram showing height frequencies in a sample human population*

### 10.1.4 Bar graph

This is similar to a histogram except that a non-numerical value is plotted on the $y$ axis. Let us suppose the sample population is divided into non-numerical sets such as racial groups and sex. These can be plotted along the $y$ axis, with average height being plotted along the $x$ axis. The resultant bar graph is shown in Fig. 10.3.

### 10.1.5 Kite graph

This is a form of bar graph, which gives more detailed information on the frequency of a non-numerical variable. To take the information given in Fig. 10.3, it simply reveals the average height of each group and not the frequency at different heights. In a kite graph, the frequency of particular heights is plotted vertically for certain non-numerical variables, e.g. males and females. A kite graph is shown in Fig. 10.4.

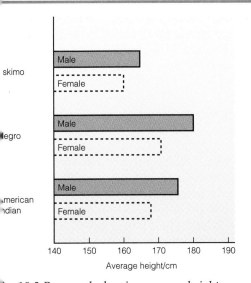

Fig. 10.3 Bar graph showing average height variation according to racial group and sex

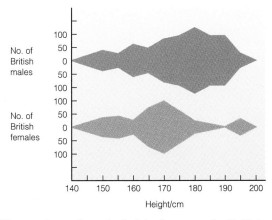

Fig. 10.4 Kite graphs to show the height frequency for British males and females in the population sample

### 10.1.6 Pie chart

Pie charts are a simple and clearly visible means of showing how a whole sample is divided up into specified parts. A circle (the pie) represents the whole and it is subdivided into different sized sections according to the relative proportions of each constituent part. To be effective the pie chart should not be divided into a large number of portions, nor should it be used when it is necessary to read off precise information from the chart. It is simply a means of giving an idea of relative proportions. Fig. 10.5 shows a pie chart depicting the proportions of our sample which fall within broad height ranges.

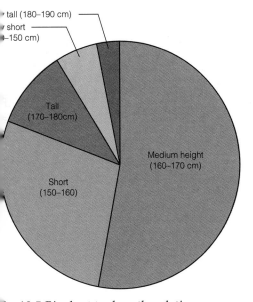

Fig. 10.5 Pie chart to show the relative proportions of five height categories in a population sample

## 10.2 Types of variation

### 10.2.1 Continuous variation

Certain characteristics within a population vary only very marginally between one individual and the next. This results in a gradation from one extreme to the other, called continuous variation. The height and weight of organisms are two

179

## PROJECT

Determine the distribution of characteristics of your fellow students. The list is endless, but examples would be:

(a) heights and weights of males and females of different ages
(b) lengths of middle fingers
(c) sizes of feet
(d) lengths or widths of ears etc.

characteristics which show such a gradation. If a frequency distribution for such a characteristic is plotted, a bell-shaped graph similar to that in Fig. 10.1 is obtained. This is called a **normal distribution curve** or **Gaussian curve** (after the mathematician Fredrick Gauss). It is discussed further in Section 10.2.2.

Characteristics which show continuous variation are controlled by the combined effect of a number of genes, called **polygenes**. Thus any character which results from the interaction of many genes is called a **polygenic character**. The effect of an individual gene is small, but their combined effect is marked. The random assortment of the genes during prophase of meiosis ensures that individuals possess a range of genes from any polygenic complex. Where a group of genes all favouring the development of a tall individual combine, a very tall individual results. A combination of genes favouring small size results in a very short individual. These extremes are rare because it is probable that an individual will possess genes from both extremes. The combined effect of these genes produces individuals of intermediate height.

### 10.2.2 The normal distribution (Gaussian) curve

Fig. 10.6 shows a normal distribution curve; its bell-shape is typical for a feature which shows continuous variation, e.g. height in humans. The graph is symmetrical about a central value. Occasionally the curve is shifted slightly to one side. This is called a skewed distribution and is illustrated in Fig. 10.7. There are three main terms used in association with normal distribution curves, whether skewed or not. To illustrate these terms, let us consider the values given in the table on the left for the number of children in 11 different families.

*The mean (arithmetic mean)*
This is the average of a group of values. In our example opposite this is found by totalling the number of children in all families and dividing it by the number of families.

Total children in all families
$$= 0+1+1+1+2+2+3+4+6+6+7 = 33$$
Total number of families A–K = 11

Mean = $33 \div 11 = 3$

*The mode*
This is the single value of a group which occurs most often. In our example more families have one child than any other number. The mode is therefore equal to 1.

*The median*
This is the central or middle value of a set of values. In our example the values are already arranged in ascending order of the number of children in each family. There are eleven families. The sixth family in the series (family F) is therefore the middle family of the group. There are five families (A–E) with the same number or fewer children, and five families (G–K) with more children. As family F has two children the median is 2.

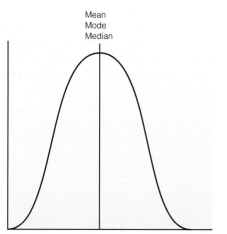

Mean
Mode
Median

*Fig. 10.6 A normal distribution curve where the mean, mode and median have the same value*

| Family | Number of children |
|--------|--------------------|
| A | 0 |
| B | 1 |
| C | 1 |
| D | 1 |
| E | 2 |
| F | 2 |
| G | 3 |
| H | 4 |
| I | 6 |
| J | 6 |
| K | 7 |

Fig 10.6 shows a typical symmetrical normal distribution curve in which the mean and mode (and often the median) have the same value.

Fig 10.7 shows a skewed distribution in which the mean, mode and median all have different values.

The mean height of a sample population gives a good indication of its relative height compared to other sample populations. It does not, however, give any indication of the distribution of height within the sample. Indeed, the mean can be misleading. A population made up of individuals who were either 140 or 180 cm tall would have a mean of 160 cm, and yet no single individual would be anywhere near this height. It is therefore useful to have a value which gives an indication of the range of height either side of the mean. This value is called the **standard deviation (SD)**. It is calculated as follows:

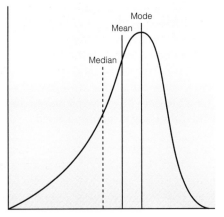

g. 10.7 A skewed distribution where the *ean, mode and median have different values*

$$SD = \sqrt{\frac{\Sigma d^2}{n}}$$

$\Sigma$ = the sum of
$d$ = difference between each value in the sample and the mean
$n$ = the total number of values in the sample

How then does the standard deviation provide information on the range within a sample? Let us suppose the mean height of a sample human population is 170 cm and its standard deviation is ±10 cm. This means that over two thirds (68%) of the sample have heights which are within 10 cm of 170 cm, i.e. 68% of the sample have heights between 160 cm and 180 cm. Furthermore we can say that 95% of the sample lie within two standard deviations of the mean. In our example two standard deviations = 2 × 10 = 20 cm. In other words, 95% of the sample have heights between 150 cm and 190 cm. Fig. 10.8 illustrates these values.

### 10.2.3 Discontinuous (discrete) variation

Certain features of individuals in a population do not show a gradation between extremes but instead fall into a limited number of distinct forms. There are no intermediate types. For example, humans may be separated into distinct sets according to their blood groups. In the ABO system there are just four groups: A, B, AB and O. Unlike continuous variation, which is controlled by many genes (polygenes), a feature which exhibits discontinuous variation is normally controlled by a single gene. This gene may have two or more alleles. Features exhibiting discontinuous variation are normally represented on histograms, bar graphs or pie charts.

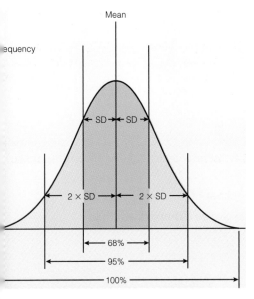

g. 10.8 The normal distribution curve *owing the values for standard deviation*

## 10.3   The chi-squared test

Imagine tossing a coin 100 times. It is reasonable to expect it to land heads on 50 occasions and tails on 50 occasions. In practice it would be unusual if these results were obtained (try it if you like!). If it lands heads 55 times and tails only 45 times, does this mean the coin is weighted or biased in some way, or is it purely a chance deviation from the expected result?

The **chi-squared test** is the means by which the statistical validity of results such as these can be tested. It measures the extent of any deviation between the expected and observed results. This measure of deviation is called the **chi-squared value** and is represented by the Greek letter chi, shown squared, i.e. $\chi^2$. To calculate this value the following equation is used:

$$\chi^2 = \sum \frac{d^2}{x}$$

where $\sum$ = the sum of

$d$ = difference between observed and expected result (the deviation)

$x$ = the expected result

Using our example of the coin tossed 100 times, we can calculate the chi-squared value. We must first calculate the deviation from the expected number of times the coin should land heads:

**Expected** number of heads in 100 tosses of the coin $(x) = 50$

**Actual** number of heads in 100 tosses of the coin $= 55$

Deviation $(d)$ $\quad$ 5

Therefore $\dfrac{d^2}{x} = \dfrac{5^2}{50} = \dfrac{25}{50} = 0.5$

We then make the same calculation for the coin landing tails.

**Expected** number of tails in 100 tosses of the coin $(x) = 50$

**Actual** number of tails in 100 tosses of the coin $= 45$

Deviation $(d)$ $\quad$ 5

Therefore $\dfrac{d^2}{x} = \dfrac{5^2}{50} = \dfrac{25}{50} = 0.5$

The chi-squared value can now be calculated by adding these values:

Therefore $\chi^2 = 0.5 + 0.5 = 1.0$.

The whole calculation can be summarized thus:

$$\chi^2 = \sum \frac{d^2}{x}$$

$$\chi^2 = \overset{\text{Heads}}{\left[\frac{(55-50)^2}{50}\right]} + \overset{\text{Tails}}{\left[\frac{(50-45)^2}{50}\right]}$$

$$= \left[\frac{(5)^2}{50}\right] + \left[\frac{(5)^2}{50}\right]$$

$$= \frac{1}{2} + \frac{1}{2}$$

$$= 1.0$$

To find out whether this value is significant or not we need to use a chi-squared table, part of which is given in Table 10.2. Before trying to read these tables it is necessary to decide how

TABLE 10.2  Part of a $\chi^2$ table (based on Fisher)

| Degrees of freedom | Number of classes | $\chi^2$ | | | | | | | |
|---|---|---|---|---|---|---|---|---|---|
| 1 | 2 | 0.00 | 0.10 | 0.45 | 1.32 | 2.71 | 3.84 | 5.41 | 6.64 |
| 2 | 3 | 0.02 | 0.58 | 1.39 | 2.77 | 4.61 | 5.99 | 7.82 | 9.21 |
| 3 | 4 | 0.12 | 1.21 | 2.37 | 4.11 | 6.25 | 7.82 | 9.84 | 11.34 |
| 4 | 5 | 0.30 | 1.92 | 3.36 | 5.39 | 7.78 | 9.49 | 11.67 | 13.28 |
| 5 | 6 | 0.55 | 2.67 | 4.35 | 6.63 | 9.24 | 11.07 | 13.39 | 15.09 |
| Probability that deviation is due to chance alone | | 0.99 (99%) | 0.75 (75%) | 0.50 (50%) | 0.25 (25%) | 0.10 (10%) | 0.05 (5%) | 0.02 (2%) | 0.01 (1%) |

many **classes of results** there are in the investigation being carried out. In our case there are two classes of results, 'heads' and 'tails'. This corresponds to one degree of freedom. We now look along the row showing 2 classes (i.e. one degree of freedom) for our calculated value of 1.0. This lies between the values of 0.45 and 1.32 on the table. Looking down this column we see that this corresponds to a probability between 0.50 (50%) and 0.25 (25%). This means that the probability that chance alone could have produced the deviation is between 0.50 (50%) and 0.25 (25%). If this probability is greater than 0.05 (5%), the deviation is said to be **not significant**. In other words the deviation is due to chance. If the deviation is less than 0.05 (5%), the deviation is said to be **significant**. In other words, some factor other than chance is affecting the results. In our example the value is greater than 0.05 (5%) and so we assume the deviation is due to chance. Had we obtained 60 heads and 40 tails, a chi-squared value of slightly less than 0.05 (5%) would be obtained, in which case we would question the validity of the results and assume the coin might be weighted or biased in some way. This test is especially useful in genetic experiments.

In *Drosophila*, normal (wild-type) wings are dominant to vestigial wings. Suppose we cross two normal-winged individuals both believed to be heterozygous for this character. We should expect a 3:1 ratio of normal wings to vestigial wings. In practice, of 48 offspring produced, 30 have normal wings and 18 have vestigial wings. Is this close enough to a 3:1 ratio to justify the view that both parents were heterozygous?

Applying the chi-squared test:

| | Normal wings | Vestigial wings |
|---|---|---|
| Expected number of *Drosophila* ($x$) | 36 | 12 |
| Actual number of *Drosophila* | 30 | 18 |
| Deviation ($d$) | 6 | 6 |
| $d^2 = 36$ | | 36 |

$$\chi^2 = \sum \frac{d^2}{x}$$
$$= \frac{36}{36} + \frac{36}{12}$$
$$= 1.0 + 3.0$$
$$= 4.0$$

With two classes of results (vestigial and normal wings) there is just one degree of freedom. Using the relevant row on the chi-squared table we find that the value of 4.0 lies between 3.84 and 5.41, i.e. 0.05 (5%) and 0.02 (2%), which means that the possibility that the deviation is due to chance is less than 5%. The deviation is therefore significant and we cannot assume the parents are heterozygous.

In another experiment domestic fowl with walnut combs were crossed with each other. The expected offspring ratio of comb types was 9 walnut, 3 rose, 3 pea and 1 single. In the event, the 160 offspring produced 93 walnut combs, 24 rose combs, 36 pea combs and 7 single combs. Applying the chi-squared test:

|  | Walnut | Rose | Pea | Single |
|---|---|---|---|---|
| Expected number of comb types ($x$) | 90 | 30 | 30 | 10 |
| Actual number of comb types | 93 | 24 | 36 | 7 |
| Deviation ($d$) | 3 | 6 | 6 | 3 |
| $d^2 =$ | 9 | 36 | 36 | 9 |

$$\chi^2 = \sum \frac{d^2}{x}$$

$$\therefore \chi^2 = \frac{9}{90} + \frac{36}{30} + \frac{36}{30} + \frac{9}{10}$$

$$= \frac{1}{10} + \frac{12}{10} + \frac{12}{10} + \frac{9}{10}$$

$$= \frac{34}{10}$$

$$= 3.4$$

In this instance there are four classes of results (walnut, rose, pea and single) and this is equivalent to three degrees of freedom. We must therefore use this row to determine whether the deviations are significant. The values lies between 2.37 and 4.11 which is equivalent to a probability of 0.5 (50%) to 0.25 (25%). This deviation is not significant and is simply the result of statistical chance.

## 10.4 The *t*-test

While the chi-squared test can be used to test the statistical significance of discontinuous (discrete) variables the *t*-test is used to test the statistical significance of continuous variables (see Section 10.2.1). The *t*-test therefore has less application in genetics and far more in other areas of biology, such as ecology. It is nevertheless dealt with here because of its statistical nature and the use it makes of standard deviations. The *t*-test is used when a sample size is relatively small, e.g. under 30 readings/figures. The mean and standard deviation of these small samples are prone to error since a single 'extreme' reading will have a disproportionate effect. The *t*-test accounts for this error. For the *t*-test to be of use, the data used have to conform to certain conditions, namely:

**TABLE 10.3  Yield of wheat for fertilizers 1 and 2**

| | Number of tonnes of wheat per plot | |
|---|---|---|
| | Fertilizer 1 | Fertilizer 2 |
| | 5 | 4 |
| | 9 | 3 |
| | 11 | 6 |
| | 9 | 7 |
| | 10 | 5 |
| | 7 | 3 |
| | 5 | 3 |
| | 8 | 5 |
| Total: | 64 | 36 |
| No. of plots: | 8 | 8 |
| Mean $\bar{x}$: | 8 | 4.5 |

1. They must be related to one another.
2. They must be normally distributed (Section 10.2.2).
3. They must have similar variances.
4. The sample size must be small.

The $t$-test can be expressed as:

$$t = \frac{\bar{x}_1 - \bar{x}_2}{\sqrt{\dfrac{s_1^2}{n_1} + \dfrac{s_2^2}{n_2}}}$$

where   $\bar{x}$ = mean of observations
   $n$ = number of observations (sample size)
   $s$ = standard deviation
(The suffixes 1 and 2 refer to samples 1 and 2 respectively.)

To take an example.  A farmer wishes to decide which of two fertilizers gives the best yield for her crop of wheat. She divides one of her fields into 16 plots, eight of which she treats with fertilizer 1 and eight with fertilizer 2. The number of tonnes of wheat obtained from each plot is given in Table 10.3.

The first stage of the $t$-test is to calculate the standard deviation for each sample (see Section 10.2.2). To do this we must calculate:

1. The mean of each sample (see Table 10.3)
2. The deviation of each reading from the mean (see Table 10.4)
3. The square of this deviation and the sum of the squares (see Table 10.4)

**TABLE 10.4**

| Fertilizer 1 | | | Fertilizer 2 | | |
|---|---|---|---|---|---|
| Observation ($x$) | Deviation from the mean ($x - \bar{x}_1$) | Square of the deviation ($x - \bar{x}_1)^2$ | Observation ($x$) | Deviation from the mean ($x - \bar{x}_2$) | Square of the deviation ($x - \bar{x}_2)^2$ |
| 5 | −3 | 9 | 4 | −0.5 | 0.25 |
| 9 | +1 | 1 | 3 | −1.5 | 2.25 |
| 11 | +3 | 9 | 6 | +1.5 | 2.25 |
| 9 | +1 | 1 | 7 | +2.5 | 6.25 |
| 10 | +2 | 4 | 5 | +0.5 | 0.25 |
| 7 | −1 | 1 | 3 | −1.5 | 2.25 |
| 5 | −3 | 9 | 3 | −1.5 | 2.25 |
| 8 | 0 | 0 | 5 | +0.5 | 0.25 |
| Sum of squares of deviation: | | 34 | Sum of squares of deviation: | | 16 |
| Standard deviation $\sqrt{\dfrac{\Sigma(x - \bar{x}_1)^2}{n-1}}$ | | $\sqrt{\dfrac{34}{7}} = 2.2$ | Standard deviation $\sqrt{\dfrac{\Sigma(x - \bar{x}_2)^2}{n-1}}$ | | $\sqrt{\dfrac{16}{7}} = 1.51$ |

To obtain the standard deviation, we saw in Section 10.2.2 that we divide the sum of the squares of deviation, $\Sigma(x - \bar{x})^2$, by the number of values in the sample ($n$) and then take the square root. However, it has been shown that when we use deviations from a sample mean, rather than a population mean, a better estimate of variance is given by dividing by $n - 1$ rather than $n$.

Thence we can now substitute in the equation:

$$t = \frac{\overline{x}_1 - \overline{x}_2}{\sqrt{\dfrac{s_1^2}{n_1} + \dfrac{s_2^2}{n_2}}}$$

$$t = \frac{8 - 4.5}{\sqrt{\dfrac{2.2^2}{8} + \dfrac{1.51^2}{8}}}$$

$$= \frac{3.5}{\sqrt{\dfrac{4.84}{8} + \dfrac{2.28}{8}}}$$

$$= \frac{3.5}{\sqrt{0.61 + 0.29}}$$

$$= \frac{3.5}{\sqrt{0.9}}$$

$$= \frac{3.5}{0.95}$$

$$= \mathbf{3.68}$$

Finally, to discover whether our value of 3.68 indicates whether the different readings are significant, or merely due to chance, we need to look up 3.68 on a statistical table called the $t$-table, part of which is reproduced as Table 10.5. To do this we need to know the degrees of freedom. This is calculated according to the formula:

Degrees of freedom $(v) = (n_1 + n_2) - 2$
In our example: $\quad v = (8 + 8) - 2$
$\qquad\qquad\qquad = 14$

We now find that looking along the row for 14 degrees of freedom our value of 3.68 lies between 2.98 and 4.14, which corresponds to a probability value of between 0.01 and 0.001. This refers to the probability that chance alone is the reason for the difference between our two sets of data. In our example, the probability that the different wheat yields when using our two fertilizers was pure chance is between one in 100 ($p = 0.01$) and one in 1000 ($p = 0.001$). In other words it is more than 99% certain that the different yields were the result of differences in the two fertilizers (assuming all other factors in the experiment were constant).

## 10.5    Origins of variation

Variation may be due to the effect of the environment on an organism. For example, the action of sunlight on a light-coloured skin may result in its becoming darker. Such changes have little evolutionary significance as they are not passed from one generation to the next. Much more important to evolution are the inherited forms of variation which result from genetic changes. These genetic changes may be the result of the normal and frequent reshuffling of genes which occurs during sexual reproduction, or as a consequence of mutations.

BLE 10.5

| Degrees of freedom | Rejection level probabilities | | | | |
|---|---|---|---|---|---|
| | $p = 0.1$ | $p = 0.05$ | $p = 0.02$ | $p = 0.01$ | $p = 0.001$ |
| 1 | 6.31 | 12.71 | 31.82 | 63.66 | 636.62 |
| 2 | 2.92 | 4.30 | 6.97 | 9.93 | 31.60 |
| 3 | 2.35 | 3.18 | 4.54 | 5.84 | 12.94 |
| 4 | 2.13 | 2.78 | 3.75 | 4.60 | 8.61 |
| 5 | 2.02 | 2.57 | 3.37 | 4.03 | 6.86 |
| 6 | 1.94 | 2.45 | 3.14 | 3.71 | 5.96 |
| 7 | 1.90 | 2.37 | 3.00 | 3.50 | 5.41 |
| 8 | 1.86 | 2.31 | 2.90 | 3.36 | 5.04 |
| 9 | 1.83 | 2.26 | 2.82 | 3.25 | 4.78 |
| 10 | 1.81 | 2.23 | 2.76 | 3.17 | 4.59 |
| 11 | 1.80 | 2.20 | 2.72 | 3.11 | 4.44 |
| 12 | 1.78 | 2.18 | 2.68 | 3.06 | 4.32 |
| 13 | 1.77 | 2.16 | 2.65 | 3.01 | 4.22 |
| 14 | 1.76 | 2.15 | 2.62 | 2.98 | 4.14 |
| 15 | 1.75 | 2.13 | 2.60 | 2.95 | 4.07 |
| 16 | 1.75 | 2.12 | 2.58 | 2.92 | 4.02 |
| 17 | 1.74 | 2.11 | 2.57 | 2.90 | 3.97 |
| 18 | 1.73 | 2.10 | 2.55 | 2.88 | 3.92 |
| 19 | 1.73 | 2.09 | 2.54 | 2.86 | 3.88 |
| 20 | 1.73 | 2.09 | 2.53 | 2.85 | 3.85 |
| 21 | 1.72 | 2.08 | 2.52 | 2.83 | 3.82 |
| 22 | 1.72 | 2.07 | 2.51 | 2.82 | 3.79 |
| 23 | 1.71 | 2.07 | 2.50 | 2.81 | 3.77 |
| 24 | 1.71 | 2.06 | 2.49 | 2.80 | 3.75 |
| 25 | 1.71 | 2.06 | 2.49 | 2.79 | 3.73 |
| 26 | 1.71 | 2.06 | 2.48 | 2.78 | 3.71 |
| 27 | 1.70 | 2.05 | 2.47 | 2.77 | 3.69 |
| 28 | 1.70 | 2.05 | 2.47 | 2.76 | 3.67 |
| 29 | 1.70 | 2.05 | 2.46 | 2.76 | 3.66 |
| 30 | 1.70 | 2.04 | 2.46 | 2.75 | 3.65 |
| 40 | 1.68 | 2.02 | 2.42 | 2.70 | 3.55 |
| 60 | 1.67 | 2.00 | 2.39 | 2.66 | 3.46 |
| | | | fairly confident | very confident | almost certain |

← **Results not significant**, i.e. is more and more likely to be due to chance

**Results increasingly significant**, i.e. more and more likely that the difference is **not** pure chance →

### 10.5.1 Environmental effects

We saw in the previous chapter that the final appearance of an organism (phenotype) is the result of its genotype and the effec of the environment upon it. If organisms of identical genotype are subject to different environmental influences, they show considerable variety. If one of a pair of genetically identical plants is grown in a soil deficient in nitrogen, it will not attain the height of the other plant grown in a soil with sufficient nitrogen. Because environmental influences are themselves ver various, and because they often form gradations, e.g. temperature, light intensity, they are largely responsible for continuous variation within a population.

### 10.5.2 Reshuffling of genes

The sexual process in organisms has three inbuilt methods of creating variety:

**1.** The mixing of two different parental genotypes where cross-fertilization occurs.

**2.** The random distribution of chromosomes during metaphase of meiosis.

**3.** The crossing over between homologous chromosomes durin prophase I of meiosis.

These changes, which were dealt with in more detail in Section 8.5.2, do not bring about major changes in features but rather create new combinations of existing features.

## MUTATIONS

Any change in the structure or the amount of DNA of an organism is called a **mutation**. Most mutations occur in somatic (body) cells and are not passed from one generation to the next. Only those mutations which occur in the formation of gametes can be inherited. These mutations produce sudden and distinct differences between individuals. They are therefore the basis of discontinuous variation.

### 10.5.3 Changes in gene structure (point mutations)

A change in the structure of DNA which occurs at a single locus on a chromosome is called a **gene mutation** or **point mutation**. In Section 7.5 we saw that the genetic code, which ultimately determines an organism's characteristics, is made up of a specific sequence of nucleotides on the DNA molecule. Any change to on or more of these nucleotides, or any rearrangement of the sequence, will produce the wrong sequence of amino acids in the protein it makes. This protein is often an enzyme, which may hav a different molecular shape and hence be unable to catalyse its reaction. The result will be that the end product of that reaction cannot be formed. This may have a profound effect on the

## Did you know?

The name 'malaria' comes from the Italian 'mal aria' meaning 'bad air'. Until the 20th century most people thought malaria was caused by bad air in the mist arising in marshes.

BLE 10.6

| Message on telegram | Equivalent form of gene mutation | Likely result of receiving the message |
| --- | --- | --- |
| Meet station 2100 hours today | Normal | Individuals meet as arranged |
| Meet Met station 2100 hours today | Duplication | Individuals arrive at correct time, one at the prearranged station, the other at the nearest station on the Metropolitan line (or London police station) |
| Met station 2100 hours today | Deletion | |
| Meet bus station 2100 hours today | Addition | Individuals arrive on time but one at the bus station, the other at the prearranged station |
| Meet station 1200 hours today | Inversion | Individuals arrive at correct place – but 9 hours apart |
| Meet station 1100 hours today | Substitution | Individuals arrive at correct place but 10 hours apart |
| Meet sat on it 2100 hours today | Inversion (including translocation) | Message incomprehensible |

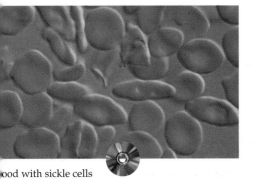

ood with sickle cells

organism. For example, a gene mutation may result in the absence of pigments such as melanin. The organism will be unpigmented, i.e. an albino. There are many forms of gene mutation.

1. **Duplication** – a portion of a nucleotide chain becomes repeated.

2. **Addition (insertion)** – an extra nucleotide sequence becomes inserted in the chain.

3. **Deletion** – a portion of the nucleotide chain is removed from the sequence.

4. **Inversion** – a nucleotide sequence becomes separated from the chain. It rejoins in its original position, only inverted. The nucleotide sequence of this portion is therefore reversed.

5. **Substitution** – one of the nucleotides is replaced by another which has a different organic base.

To illustrate these different types, let us imagine each nucleotide is equivalent to a letter of the alphabet. The sequence of nucleotides therefore makes up a sentence or groups of sentences which can be understood by the cell's chemical machinery as the instructions for making specific proteins. If a mutation results in the instructions being incomprehensible, the cell will be unable to make the appropriate protein. In most cases this will result in the death of the cell or organism at an early stage. Sometimes, however, the mutation will result in inaccurate, and yet comprehensible, instructions being given. A protein may well be produced, but it is the wrong one. The defect may create some phenotypic change, but not of sufficient importance to cause the death of the organism.

Imagine a telegram to confirm the details of an earlier arrangement to meet at a prearranged station. If we alter just one or two letters each time, either the message may be totally incomprehensible or it may be understood by the receiver but not in the way intended by the sender. Table 10.6, gives some examples.

A gene mutation in the gene producing haemoglobin results in a defect called **sickle-cell anaemia**. The replacement of just one base in the DNA molecule results in the wrong amino acid being incorporated into two of the polypeptide chains which make up the haemoglobin molecule. The abnormal haemoglobin causes red blood cells to become sickle-shaped, resulting in anaemia and possible death. The detailed events are illustrated in Fig. 10.9.

The mutant gene causing sickle-cell anaemia is codominant. In the homozygous state, the individual suffers the disease and frequently dies. In the heterozygous state, the individual has 30–40% sickle cells, the rest being normal. This is called the sickle-cell trait. These individuals suffer less severe anaemia and rarely die from the condition. As they still suffer some disability, it might be expected that the disease would be very rare, if not completely eliminated, by natural selection. In parts of Africa, however, it is very common. The reason is that the malarial parasite, *Plasmodium*, cannot easily invade sickle cells. Individuals with either sickle-cell condition are therefore more resistant to severe attacks of malaria. In the homozygous condition, this resistance is insufficient to offset the

**1.** *The DNA molecule which codes for the beta amino acid chain in haemoglobin has a mutation whereby the base adenine replaces thymine.*

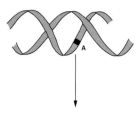

**2.** *The mRNA produced has the triplet codon GUA (for amino acid valine) rather than GAA (for amino acid glutamic acid).*

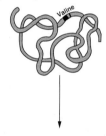

**3.** *The beta amino acid chain produced has one glutamic acid molecule replaced by a valine molecule.*

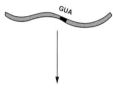

**4.** *The haemoglobin molecule containing the abnormal beta chains forms abnormal long fibres when the oxygen level of the blood is low. This haemoglobin is called haemoglobin-S.*

**5.** *Haemoglobin-S causes the shape of the red blood cell to become crescent (sickle) shaped.*

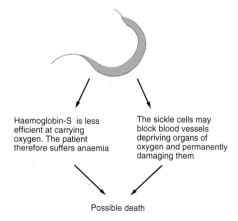

Haemoglobin-S is less efficient at carrying oxygen. The patient therefore suffers anaemia

The sickle cells may block blood vessels depriving organs of oxygen and permanently damaging them

Possible death

*Fig. 10.9 Sequence of events whereby a gene mutation causes sickle-cell anaemia*

considerable disadvantage of having sickle-cell anaemia. In the heterozygous condition (sickle-cell trait), however, the advantage of being resistant to severe malarial attacks outweigh the disadvantage of the mild anaemia the individual suffers. In malarial regions of the world the mutant gene is selected in favour of the one producing normal haemoglobin. Outside malarial regions, there is no advantage in being resistant to malaria, and the disadvantage of suffering anaemia results in selection *against* the mutant gene.

One relatively common gene mutation in European countries causes **cystic fibrosis**, which is the result of a recessive gene. Further details of this disorder are given on page 124.

Dominant gene mutations are rarer but include **Huntington's disease**. This is characterized by involuntary muscular movement and progressive mental deterioration. The mutant gene is so rare (around 1 in 100 000 people carry it) that it occurs almost exclusively in the heterozygous state.

### 10.5.4 Changes in whole sets of chromosomes

Sometimes organisms occur that have additional whole sets of chromosomes. Instead of having a haploid set in the sex cells and a diploid set in the body cells, they have several complete sets. This is known as **polyploidy**. Where three sets of chromosomes are present, the organism is said to be **triploid**. With four sets, it is said to be **tetraploid**.

Polyploidy can arise in several different ways. If gametes are produced which are diploid and these self-fertilize, a tetraploid is produced. If instead the diploid gamete fuses with a normal haploid gamete, a triploid results. Polyploidy can also occur when whole sets of chromosomes double after fertilization.

Tetraploid organisms have two complete sets of homologous chromosomes and can therefore form homologous pairings during gamete production by meiosis. Triploids, however, cannot form complete homologous pairings and are usually sterile. They can only be propagated by asexual means. The type of polyploidy whereby the increase in sets of chromosomes occurs within the same species is called **autopolyploidy**. The actual number of chromosomes in an autopolyploid is always an exact multiple of its haploid number. Autopolyploidy can be induced by a chemical called **colchicine** which is extracted from certain crocus corms. Colchicine inhibits spindle formation and so prevents chromosomes separating during anaphase.

Sometimes hybrids can be formed by combining sets of chromosomes from species with different chromosome numbers. These hybrids are ordinarily sterile because the total number of chromosomes does not allow full homologous pairing to take place. If, however, the hybrid has a chromosome number which is a multiple of the original chromosome number, a new fertile species is formed. The species of wheat used today to make bread was formed in this way. The basic haploid number of wild grasses is seven. A tetraploid with 28 chromosomes called emmer wheat was accidentally cross-fertilized with a wild grass with 14 chromosomes. The resultant wheat with 42 chromosomes is today the main cultivated variety. Having a chromosome number which is a multiple of the original haploid number of 7, it is fertile. This form of polyploidy is called **allopolyploidy**.

Polyploidy is rare in animals, but relatively common in plants. Almost half of all flowering plants (angiosperms) are polyploids, including many important food plants. Wheat, coffee, bananas, sugar cane, apples and tomatoes all have polyploid forms. The polyploid varieties often have some advantage. Tetraploid apples, for example, form larger fruits and tetraploid tomatoes produce more vitamin C.

### 10.5.5 Changes in chromosome number

Sometimes it is an individual chromosome, rather than a whole set, which fails to separate during anaphase. If, for example, in humans one of the 23 pairs of homologous chromosomes fails to segregate during meiosis, one of the gametes produced will contain 22 chromosomes and the other 24, rather than 23 each. This is known as **non-disjunction** and is often lethal. The condition where an organism possesses an additional chromosome is represented as $2n + 1$; where one is missing, $2n - 1$. Where two additional chromosomes are present it is represented as $2n + 2$ etc.

One frequent consequence of non-disjunction in humans is **Down's syndrome** (mongolism). In this case the 21st chromosome fails to segregate and the gamete produced possesses 24 chromosomes. The fusion of this gamete with a normal one with 23 chromosomes results in the offspring having 47 $(2n + 1)$ chromosomes. Non-disjunction does occur with other chromosomes but these normally result in the fetus aborting or the child dying soon after birth. The 21st chromosome is relatively small, and the offspring is therefore able to survive. Down's syndrome children have disabilities of varying magnitude. Typically they have a flat, broad face, squint eyes with a skin fold in the inner corner and a furrowed and protruding tongue. They have a low IQ and a short life expectancy.

Non-disjunction in the case of Down's syndrome appears to occur in the production of ova rather than sperm. Its incidence is related to the age of the mother. The chance of a teenage mother having a Down's syndrome child is only one in many thousands. A 40-year-old mother has a one in a hundred chance and by the age of 45 the risk is three times greater. The risk is unaffected by the age of the father.

Non-disjunction of the sex chromosomes can occur. One example is **Klinefelter's syndrome**. This may result in individuals who have the genetic constitution XXY, XXXY or XXXXY. These individuals are phenotypically male but have small testes and no sperm in the ejaculate. There may be abnormal breast development and the body proportions are generally female. The greater the number of Xs the more marked is the condition. As individuals are phenotypically male, this indicates that the presence of a Y chromosome is the cause of maleness. This is borne out by a second abnormality of the sex chromosomes. Individuals with **Turner's syndrome** have one missing X chromosome. Their genetic constitution is therefore

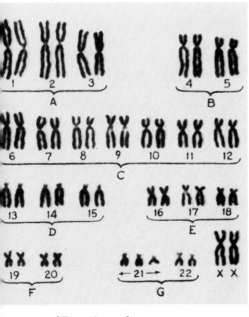

*...aryotype of Down's syndrome*

XO and they have only 45 $(2n - 1)$ chromosomes. Individuals with this condition often do not survive pregnancy and are aborted. Those that do survive are phenotypically female, but small in stature and sexually immature. Despite having a single X chromosome, like males, they are female, indicating again that the Y chromosome is the cause of maleness.

### 10.5.6 Changes in chromosome structure

During meiosis it is normal for homologous pairs of chromosomes to form chiasmata. The chromatids break at these points and rejoin with the corresponding portion of chromatid on its homologous partner. It is not surprising that from time to time mistakes arise during this process. Indeed, it is remarkable that these chromosome mutations do not occur more frequently. There are four types:

1. **Deletion** – a portion of a chromosome is lost (Fig. 10.10a). As this involves the loss of genes, it can have a significant effect on an organism's development, often proving lethal.

2. **Inversion** – a portion of chromosome becomes deleted, but becomes reattached in an inverted position. The sequence of genes on this portion are therefore reversed (Fig. 10.10b). The overall genotype is unchanged, but the phenotype may be altered. This indicates that the sequence of genes on the chromosome is important.

3. **Translocation** – a portion of chromosome becomes deleted and rejoins at a different point on the same chromosome or with a different chromosome (Fig. 10.10c). The latter is equivalent to crossing over except that it occurs between non-homologous chromosomes.

4. **Duplication** – a portion of chromosome is doubled, resulting in repetition of a gene sequence (Fig. 10.10d).

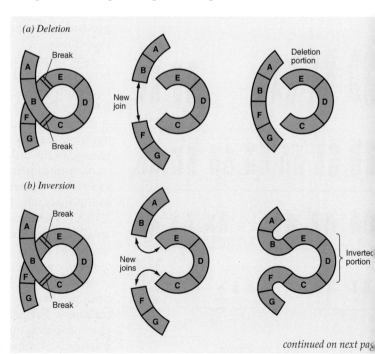

*Fig. 10.10 Diagrams illustrating the four types of chromosome mutation*

*continued on next page*

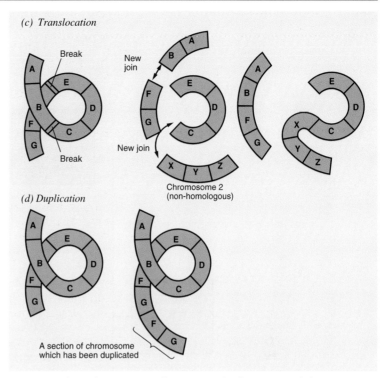

(c) Translocation

(d) Duplication

*Fig. 10.10 (cont.) Diagrams illustrating the four types of chromosome mutation*

## 10.6 Causes of mutations

Mutations occur continually. There is a natural mutation rate which varies from one species to another. In general, organisms with shorter life-cycles, and therefore more frequent meiosis, show a greater rate of mutation. A typical rate of mutation is one or two new mutations per 100 000 genes per generation.

This natural mutation rate can be increased artificially by certain chemicals or energy sources. Any agent which induces mutations is called a **mutagen**. Most forms of high energy radiation are capable of altering the structure of DNA and thereby causing mutations. These include ultra-violet light, X-rays and gamma rays. High energy particles such as $\alpha$ and $\beta$ particles and neutrons are even more dangerous mutagens.

A number of chemicals also cause mutations. We saw in Section 10.5.4 that colchicine inhibits spindle formation and so causes polyploidy. Other chemical mutagens include formaldehyde, nitrous acid and mustard gas.

## 10.7 Genetic screening and counselling

As our knowledge of inheritance has increased, more and more disabilities have been found to have genetic origins. Some of these disabilities cannot be predicted with complete accuracy. In Down's syndrome, for example, it is impossible to give a precise prediction of its occurrence for any individual. The risk for a mother of a particular age can, however, be calculated. Other

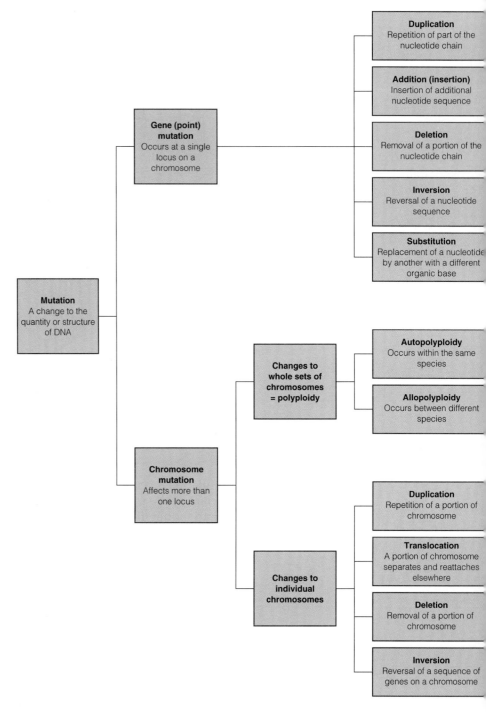

*Fig. 10.11 Mutations summary*

disabilities like haemophilia, cystic fibrosis, some forms of muscular dystrophy and Huntington's disease can be predicted fairly accurately, provided enough information on the history of the disease in the family is known. Genetic counselling has developed in order to research the family history of inherited disease and to advise parents on the likelihood of it arising in their children. Imagine a mother whose family has a history of cystic fibrosis. If she herself is unaffected but possesses the gene she can only be heterozygous for the condition. Suppose she wishes to produce children by a man with no history of the disease in his family. It must be assumed that he does not carry the gene for the disease and therefore none of the children will suffer from it, although they may be carriers. If, on the other hand, the potential father's family has a history of the disease, it is possible he too carries the gene. As we see from the genetic diagram above, it is possible to advise the parents that there is a one in four chance of their children being affected. The gene for cystic fibrosis is recessive and autosomal (i.e. not sex-linked).

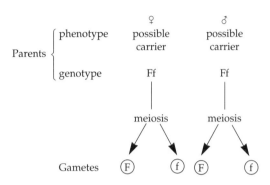

| F₁ generation | ♂ gametes | |
|---|---|---|
| | Ⓕ | ⓕ |
| ♀ gametes   Ⓕ | FF | Ff |
| ♀ gametes   ⓕ | Ff | ff |

25% normal children FF
50% normal children, but carriers of the gene Ff
25% children with cystic fibrosis ff

On the basis of this advice the parents can choose whether or not to have children. With a very detailed knowledge of the disease in each of the parent's families it may even be possible to establish for certain whether they are carriers or not. It is now possible to carry out tests to establish with some accuracy whether an individual is heterozygous for the gene, and so to make precise predictions about the likelihood of having a child with cystic fibrosis (see Biology Around Us on page 124).

What then of the parents who have children knowing that there is a greater than usual possibility of them inheriting a genetic defect? Is there any means of establishing whether a child is affected, before it is born? The answer is yes, for some defects at least. Doctors can now diagnose certain genetic defects in a fetus by studying samples of cells taken from the amniotic fluid which surrounds the fetus. The process is called **amniocentesis**. Certain genetic defects such as Down's syndrome can be detected directly as the additional chromosomes are easily seen. Biochemical tests on the cells, or even the amniotic fluid (which contains much fetal urine), may reveal other genetic defects. On the basis of these tests the parents can decide whether or not to have the pregnancy terminated. Details of the processes involved are given in Biology Around Us on page 244.

# 10.8   Questions

**1.** Read the following passage and then answer the questions below.

Much, but not all, of the variation to be found within a species results from gene (point) mutations. Such mutations are rare, with a frequency for each gene of the order, perhaps, of less than one per 100 000 ($10^5$) per gamete. A number of factors such as X-irradiation, ultra-violet light and mutagenic chemicals may increase the level above the so-called background rates. Gene mutations involve changes in the nucleotides on the DNA, resulting in a different sequence of bases. Such a change may alter the order of amino acids in the polypeptide for which the gene codes. A change in one base may change entirely the shape and function of the polypeptide in the organism. In those polypeptides which are constituents of enzymes, this may lead to inactivity of the enzyme concerned. Some mutations are capable of changing the entire sequence of amino acids for a part of the polypeptide. Mutations will only be inherited if they occur in cell lines leading to the formation of gametes.

    (a) Suggest **one** other source of variation apart from gene mutation. *(1 mark)*

    (b) Name **one** chemical mutagen. *(1 mark)*

    (c) Why are mutations not always inherited? *(1 mark)*

    (d) Why are some mutations more likely to be harmful to the organism than others? *(1 mark)*

    (e) If the human genome contains 50 000 genes, a conservative estimate, how many point mutations would be expected in a sample of 2 000 000 ($2 \times 10^6$) spermatozoa? Show your working. *(3 marks)*

    (f) A piece of DNA has the following base sequence.

        AATTCGCGATTC

    State the change (type of mutation) that has taken place in each of the following variants:

        (i)   ATTCGCGATTCC;
        (ii)  AATTCGAGCTTC;
        (iii) AACTCGCGATTC. *(3 marks)*

    (g) Give **one** example of a gene mutation you have studied. *(1 mark)*

    *(Total 11 marks)*

*Oxford February 1997, Paper 32, No. 1*

**2.** Beans collected from a pure-breeding variety showed a range of different masses which are tabulated at the top of the next column.

    (a) On graph paper, present these data in the form of a histogram. *(4 marks)*

    (b) What name is given to the type of variation shown by the data in (a)? *(1 mark)*

    (c) The heights of pea plants grown from the seeds of a particular plant gave a distribution histogram as shown in the next column.

| Mass/g | Number of beans of that mass |
|---|---|
| 1.5–2.0 | 1 |
| 2.0–2.5 | – |
| 2.5–3.0 | 1 |
| 3.0–3.5 | 7 |
| 3.5–4.0 | 25 |
| 4.0–4.5 | 45 |
| 4.5–5.0 | 46 |
| 5.0–5.5 | 22 |
| 5.5–6.0 | 8 |
| 6.0–6.5 | 2 |

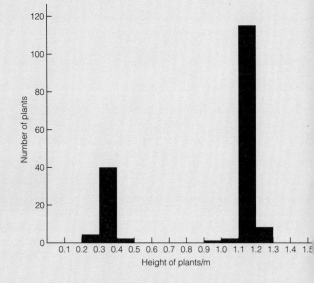

    (i) What name is given to the type of variation shown in this histogram? *(1 mar[k])*

    (ii) Suggest a possible cause of this variation. *(3 mark[s])*

    *(Total 9 mark[s])*

*Oxford February 1997, Paper 31, No.*

**3.** Down's syndrome is a condition in humans resulting from a major chromosomal defect; usually the presence of three copies of chromosome 21.

    (a) Explain, as far as you are able, how this may come about. *(3 mark[s])*

    (b) A rare form of Down's syndrome is found t[o] occur in some families. This has been show[n] to result from a chromosome translocation whereby individuals who carry the translocation are unaffected but may produc[e] offspring with Down's syndrome. Explain briefly what is meant by a **translocation** an[d] how it might come about. *(3 mark[s])*

(c) It is possible to detect Down's syndrome using amniocentesis or chorionic villus sampling. Describe how **one** of these procedures is carried out. *(3 marks)*

(d) Suggest **one** other characteristic that may be identified using this procedure. *(1 mark)*

*(Total 10 marks)*

*Oxford December 1996, Paper 32, No. 2*

. In the fruit fly, *Drosophila melanogaster*, the allele for rey body colour, **G**, is dominant to that for ebony ody body colour, **g**. The allele for normal wings, **N**, is ominant to that for curled wings, **n**. A student rossed a grey-bodied, normal-winged fly with an ebony-bodied, curled-winged fly. The offspring were s follows:

| Phenotype | Numbers |
|---|---|
| Grey body and normal wings | 33 |
| Grey body and curled wings | 23 |
| Ebony body and curled wings | 28 |
| Ebony body and normal wings | 16 |

(a) Show how this cross should have produced offspring in the ratio 1:1:1:1. *(2 marks)*

(b) (i) The chi-squared ($\chi^2$) test can be used to test whether the observed results fit the expectation. Copy and complete the table below in which $E$ represents the number of each type of fly expected in the above cross and $O$ represents the number actually observed.

| Phenotype | Number observed (O) | Number expected (E) | Difference (O–E) | Difference squared (O–E)² |
|---|---|---|---|---|
| Grey body, normal wings | 33 | | | |
| Grey body, curled wings | 23 | | | |
| Ebony body, curled wings | 28 | | | |
| Ebony body, normal wings | 16 | | | |

*(2 marks)*

(ii) Calculate the value of $\chi^2$ using the formula:

$$\chi^2 = \sum \frac{(O-E)^2}{E}$$

*(1 mark)*

(iii) Use the following extract from the $\chi^2$ table to decide whether the observed numbers of offspring are significantly different from those expected. Explain how you reached your answer.

| Degrees of freedom | Probability (*p*) | | | | | | |
|---|---|---|---|---|---|---|---|
| | 0.90 | 0.50 | 0.20 | 0.10 | 0.05 | 0.02 | 0.01 |
| 1 | 0.02 | 0.46 | 1.64 | 2.71 | 3.84 | 5.41 | 6.64 |
| 2 | 0.21 | 1.39 | 3.22 | 4.61 | 5.99 | 7.82 | 9.21 |
| 3 | 0.58 | 2.37 | 4.64 | 6.25 | 7.82 | 9.84 | 11.34 |
| 4 | 1.06 | 3.36 | 5.99 | 7.78 | 9.49 | 11.67 | 13.28 |

*(3 marks)*

*(Total 8 marks)*

*AEB Summer 1997, (AS) Paper 1, No. 8*

**5.** Leaves that are adapted to low light intensities are known as shade leaves, while those that function more efficiently in high light intensities are known as sun leaves.

An investigation was carried out to determine whether there was a significant difference in the surface area of shade and sun leaves of dog's mercury (*Mercurialis perennis*), a plant which grows in woodland and shady places.

17 leaves of dog's mercury were collected from plants growing in deep shade (Site A) and 17 leaves were collected from plants growing in a clearing open to sunlight (Site B). The surface area of each leaf was measured. The results are shown in the table below.

A *t*-test was carried out to determine whether the difference in mean surface areas was significance at the 5% level.

| Surface area of leaves/cm² | |
|---|---|
| **Deep shade (Site A)** | **Open clearing (Site B)** |
| 21 | 15 |
| 14 | 17 |
| 16 | 18 |
| 18 | 17 |
| 19 | 17 |
| 21 | 19 |
| 19 | 13 |
| 22 | 14 |
| 18 | 21 |
| 16 | 13 |
| 13 | 16 |
| 22 | 13 |
| 21 | 16 |
| 23 | 12 |
| 19 | 14 |
| 18 | 12 |
| 15 | 20 |
| Mean $\bar{x}_A = 18.53$ | Mean $\bar{x}_B =$ |
| Standard deviation (A) $s_A = 2.87$ | Standard deviation (B) $s_B = 2.70$ |

The formula used for the $t$-test was

$$t = \frac{(\bar{x}_A - \bar{x}_B)\sqrt{(n-1)}}{s}$$

where $\bar{x}_A$ is the mean surface area from Site A
$\bar{x}_B$ is the mean surface area from Site B
$n$ is 17, the number of leaves from each site
$s$ is found by the formula

$$s^2 = s_A{}^2 + s_B{}^2$$

(a) (i) The mean surface area ($\bar{x}_A$) of the leaves from Site A is given in the table. Calculate the mean surface area ($\bar{x}_B$) of the leaves from Site B. (1 mark)
(ii) Calculate the value of $s^2$ and of $s$. Show your working. (2 marks)
(iii) Use your values from (a) (i) and (a) (ii) to calculate the value of $t$. Show your working. (2 marks)
(b) A statistical table showed that the significance at the 5% level with 32 degrees of freedom required a $t$ value of at least 2.04. What does this indicate about the difference in mean surface areas between leaves from Site A and leaves from Site B? (1 mark)
(c) Suggest **one** reason for the differences in surface areas between leaves from the two sites. Explain your answer. (2 marks)
(d) Sun leaves are frequently thicker than shade leaves because they form longer palisade cells. The number of chloroplasts per cell is also greater in sun leaves than in shade leaves. Suggest how these features improve the efficiency of sun leaves. (2 marks)
(e) Suggest a simple method for determining the surface area of a leaf. (2 marks)

(Total 12 marks)

*Edexcel June 1997, (AS) B5/HB5, No. 2*

6. Electrophoresis is a process which can be used to separate and identify different proteins. Differences in the electrical charge on the proteins cause them to move at different rates in an electrical field. This technique can be used to identify the type of haemoglobin possessed by an individual. The figure shows the separation of haemoglobin from an individual who is homozygous normal ($\mathbf{Hb^A Hb^A}$) and that from an individual who is homozygous for the sickle-cell allele ($\mathbf{Hb^S Hb^S}$). The proteins have bee stained to show their positions after electrophoresis.

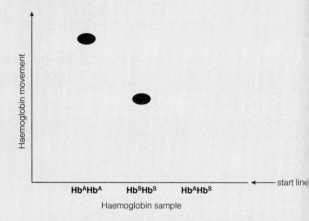

(a) Indicate the separation of the haemoglobin from an individual who is heterozygous for the sickle-cell allele ($\mathbf{Hb^A Hb^S}$). (1 mar
(b) Using the symbols given, illustrate by mean of a genetic diagram the probability of inheriting sickle-cell anaemia from parents who are heterozygous for the sickle-cell allele. (4 mark

Individuals who are homozygous for the $\mathbf{Hb^S}$ allele may have sickle-shaped red blood cells. This is caused by the substitution of the hydrophobic amin acid valine for the charged hydrophilic amino acid glutamic acid on the two beta chains in haemoglobin.

(c) Suggest why, and under what conditions, the red blood cells become sickle-shaped. (3 mark
(d) Explain briefly how the mutation which produces sickle-cell anaemia may occur. (3 mark

(Total 11 mark

*UCLES June 1997, Paper 3, No.*

# 11 Evolution

Evolution is the process by which new species are formed from pre-existing ones over a period of time. It is not the only explanation of the origins of the many species which exist on earth, but it is the one generally accepted by the scientific world at the present time.

## 11.1 Population genetics

To a geneticist, a population is an interbreeding group of organisms. In theory, any individual in the population is capable of breeding with any other. In other words, the genes of any individual organism are capable of being combined with the genes of any other. The genes of a population are therefore freely interchangeable. The total of all the alleles of all the genes in a population is called the **gene pool**. Within the gene pool the number of times any one allele occurs is referred to as its frequency.

### 11.1.1 Heterozygotes as reservoirs of genetic variation (the Hardy–Weinberg principle)

If one looks at a particular characteristic in a population, it is apparent that the dominant form expresses itself more often than the recessive form. In almost all human populations, for example, brown eyes occur more frequently than blue. It might be thought, therefore, that in time the dominant form would predominate to the point where the recessive type disappeared from the population completely. The proportion of dominant and recessive alleles of a particular gene remains the same, however. It is not altered by interbreeding. This phenomenon is known as the **Hardy–Weinberg principle**. It is a mathematical law which depends on four conditions being met:

1. No mutations arise.

2. The population is isolated, i.e. there is no flow of genes into, or out of, the population.

3. There is no natural selection.

4. The population is large and mating is random.

   While these conditions are probably never met in a natural population, the Hardy–Weinberg principle nonetheless forms a basis for the study of gene frequencies.

| 1st allele | 2nd allele | Frequency |
|---|---|---|
| A | A | $p \times p = p^2$ |
| A | a | $p \times q$ |
| a | A | $q \times p$ ⎫ $2pq$ |
| a | a | $q \times q = q^2$ |

To help understand the principle, consider a gene which has a dominant allele **A** and a recessive allele **a**.

Let $p$ = the frequency of allele **A** and
$q$ = the frequency of allele **a**

In diploid individuals these alleles occur in the combinations given on the left.

As the homozygous dominant (**AA**) combination is 1/4 of the total possible genotypes, there is a 1/4 (25%) chance of a single individual being of this type. Similarly, the chance of it being homozygous recessive (**aa**) is 1/4 (25%) whereas there is a 1/2 (50%) chance of it being heterozygous. There is a 1/1 (100%) chance of it being any one of these three types. In other words:

homozygous dominant (1/4) + heterozygous (1/2) + homozygous recessive (1/4) = 1.0 (100%)

thus $\quad$ **AA** + 2**Aa** + **aa** = 1.0 (100%)

and $\quad$ $p^2$ + $2pq$ + $q^2$ = 1.0 (100%)

The Hardy–Weinberg principle is expressed as:

$$p^2 + 2pq + q^2 = 1.0$$

(where $p$ and $q$ represent the respective frequencies of the dominant and recessive alleles of any particular gene).

The formula can be used to calculate the frequency of any allele in the population. For example, imagine that a particular mental defect is the result of a recessive allele. If the number of babies born with the defect is one in 25 000, the frequency of the allele can be calculated as follows:

The defect will only express itself in individuals who are homozygous recessive. Therefore the frequency of these individuals ($q^2$) = 1/25 000 or 0.000 04.
The frequency of the allele ($q$) is therefore $\sqrt{0.000\ 04}$
$$= 0.0063 \text{ approx.}$$
As the frequency of both alleles must be 1.0, i.e. $p + q = 1.0$, then the frequency of the dominant allele ($p$) can be calculated.

$$p + q = 1.0$$
$$\therefore p = 1.0 - q$$
$$\therefore p = 1.0 - 0.0063$$
$$\therefore p = 0.9937$$

The frequency of heterozygotes can now be calculated.

From the Hardy–Weinberg formula, the frequency of heterozygotes is $2pq$, i.e. $2 \times 0.9937 \times 0.0063 = 0.0125$.

In other words, 125 in 10 000 (or 313 in 25 000) are carriers (heterozygotes) of the allele.

This means that in a population of 25 000 individuals, just one individual will suffer the defect but around 313 will carry the allele. The heterozygotes are acting as a reservoir of the allele, maintaining it in the gene pool. As these heterozygotes are normal, they are not specifically selected against, and so the allele remains. Even if the defective individuals are selectively removed, the frequency of the allele will hardly be affected. In our population of 25 000, there is one individual who has two recessive alleles and 313 with one recessive allele – a total of 315. The removal of the defective individual will reduce the number of alleles in the population by just 2, to 313. Even with the removal of all defective individuals it would take thousands of years just to halve the allele's frequency.

Occasionally, as in sickle-cell anaemia (Section 10.5.3), the heterozygote individuals have a selective advantage. This is known as **heterozygote superiority**.

## 11.2 Evolution through natural selection (Darwin/Wallace)

Quite independently, Charles Darwin and Alfred Wallace developed the same theory on the mechanism of evolution. As a result, they jointly presented their findings to the Linnaean Society in 1858. The essential features of the theory Darwin put forward are:

### 1. Overproduction of offspring
All organisms produce large numbers of offspring which, if they survived, would lead to a geometric increase in the size of any population.

### 2. Constancy of numbers
Despite the tendency to increase numbers due to overproduction of offspring, most populations actually maintain relatively constant numbers.

### 3. Struggle for existence
Darwin deduced on the basis of **1** and **2** that members of the species were constantly competing with each other in an effort to survive. In this struggle for existence only a few would live long enough to breed.

### 4. Variation among offspring
The sexually produced offspring of any species show individual variations (Section 10.5) so that generally no two offspring are identical.

### 5. Survival of the fittest by natural selection
Among the offspring there will be some better able to withstand the prevailing conditions. That is, some will be better adapted ('fitter') to survive in the struggle for existence. These types are more likely to survive long enough to breed.

### 6. Like produces like
Those that survive to breed are likely to produce offspring similar to themselves. The advantageous characteristics that gave them the edge in the struggle for existence are likely to be passed on to the next generation.

### 7. Formation of new species
Over many generations, the individuals with favourable characteristics will breed, with consequent increase in their numbers. The development of a number of variations in a particular direction over many generations will gradually lead to the evolution of a new species.

harles Darwin

# 11.3    Natural selection

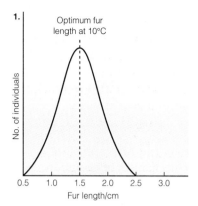

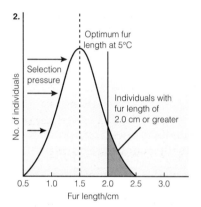

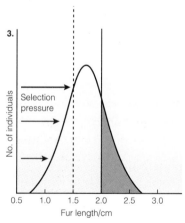

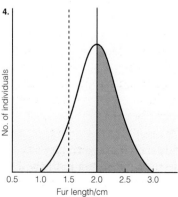

*Fig. 11.1 Directional selection*

The evolutionary theory of Darwin and Wallace is based on the mechanism of natural selection. Let us look more closely at exactly how this process operates.

Selection is the process by which organisms that are better adapted to their environment survive and breed, while those less well adapted fail to do so. The better adapted organisms are more likely to pass their characteristics to succeeding generations. Every organism is therefore subjected to a process of selection, based upon its suitability for survival given the conditions which exist at the time. The organism's environment exerts a **selection pressure**. The intensity and direction of this pressure varies in both time and space. Selection pressure determines the spread of any allele within the gene pool.

### 11.3.1 Types of selection

There are three types of selection which operate in a population of a given species.

*Directional selection*
When environmental conditions change, there is a selection pressure on a species causing it to adapt to the new conditions. Within a population there will be a range of individuals in respect of any one character. The continuous variation among individuals forms a normal distribution curve, with a mean which represents the optimum for the existing conditions. When these conditions change, so does the optimum necessary for survival. A few individuals will possess the new optimum and by selection these in time will predominate. The mean for this particular character will have shifted. An example is illustrated in Fig. 11.1.

*Stabilizing selection*
Stabilizing selection occurs in all populations and tends to eliminate the extremes within a group, thus reducing the variability of a population and hence the opportunity for evolutionary change.

In our earlier example, we see that at 10 °C there was an optimum coat length of 1.5 cm. Individuals within the population, however, had coats ranging in length from 0.5 cm to

*In a population of a particular mammal, fur length shows continuous variation.*

1. *When the average environmental temperature is 10 °C, the optimum fur length is 1.5 cm. This then represents the mean fur length of the population.*

2. *A few individuals in the population already have a fur length of 2.0 cm or greater. If the average environmental temperature falls to 5 °C, these individuals are better insulated and so are more likely to survive to breed. There is a selection pressure favouring individuals with longer fur.*

3. *The selection pressure causes a shift in the mean fur length towards longer fur over a number of generations. The selection pressure continues.*

4. *Over further generations the shift in the mean fur length continues until it reaches 2.0 cm – the optimum length for the prevailing average environmental temperature of 5 °C. The selection pressure now ceases.*

*Initially there is a wide range of fur length about the mean of 1.5 cm. The fur lengths of less than 1.0 cm or greater than 2.0 cm in individuals are maintained by rapid breeding in years when the average temperature is much warmer or colder than normal.*

*When the average environmental temperature is consistently around 10°C with little annual variation, individuals with very long or very short hair are eliminated from the population over a number of generations.*

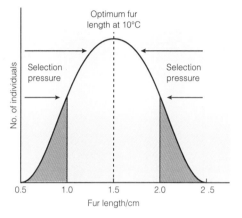

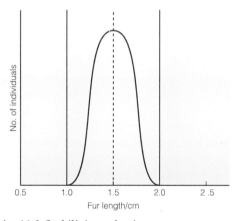

Fig. 11.2 Stabilizing selection

2.5 cm. Under normal climatic circumstances, the average temperature varies from one year to the next. In a warm year, with an average temperature of 15 °C, the individuals with shorter fur may be at an advantage as they can lose heat more quickly. In such years the numbers of individuals with short fur increase at the expense of those with long fur. In cold years, the reverse is true and numbers of individuals with long fur increase at the expense of their companions with shorter coats. The periodic fluctuations in environmental temperature thus help to maintain individuals with very long and very short fur.

Imagine that the average environmental temperature was 10 °C every year and there were no fluctuations. Without the warmer years to give them an advantage in the competition with others in the population, the individuals with short hair would decline in numbers. Likewise the absence of colder years would reduce the number of long-haired individuals. The mean fur length would remain at 1.5 cm but the distribution curve would show a much narrower range of lengths (Fig. 11.2).

*Disruptive selection*
Although much less common, this form of selection is important in achieving evolutionary change. Disruptive selection may occur when an environmental factor takes a number of distinct forms. To take our hypothetical example, suppose the environmental temperature alternated between 5 °C in the winter and 15 °C in the summer, with no intermediate temperatures occurring. These conditions would favour the development of two distinct phenotypes within the population: one with a fur length of 2.0 cm (the optimum for an environmental temperature of 5 °C); the other with a fur length of 1.0 cm (optimum length at 15 °C) (Fig. 11.3).

### 11.3.2 Drug and pesticide resistance

Following the production of antibiotics in the 1940s, it was noticed that certain bacterial cells developed resistance to these drugs, i.e. the antibiotics failed to kill them in the normal way. Experiments showed that this was not a cumulative tolerance to the drug, but the result of chance mutation. This mutation in some way allowed the bacteria to survive in the presence of drugs like penicillin, e.g. by producing an enzyme to break it down. In the presence of penicillin, non-resistant forms are destroyed. There is a selection pressure favouring the resistant types. The greater the quantity and frequency of penicillin use, the greater the selection pressure. The medical implications are obvious. Already the usefulness of many antibiotics has been destroyed by bacterial resistance to them. By 1950, the majority of staphylococcal infections were already penicillin-resistant.

The problem has been made more acute by the recent discovery that resistance can be transmitted between species. This means that disease-causing bacteria can become resistant to a given antibiotic even before the antibiotic is used against them. As a result, certain staphylococci are resistant to all major antibiotics.

## PROJECT

### The land snail *Cepaea nemoralis* possesses a shell with or without black bands

1. Collect data on land snails from two different localities, for example from a beech-wood and from under hedges, or from an oak-wood and from grassland.

2. Score the numbers of banded and unbanded snails from the two localities.

3. Analyse the data and suggest a hypothesis to explain the results.

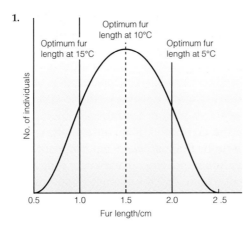

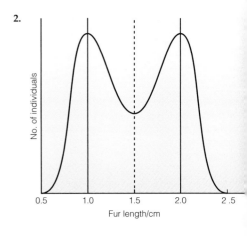

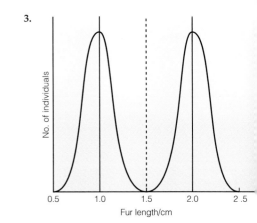

1. *When there is a wide range of temperatures throughout the year, there is continuous variation in fur length around a mean of 1.5 cm.*

2. *Where the summer temperature is static around 15°C and the winter temperature is static around 5°C, individuals with two distinct fur lengths predominate: 1.0 cm types which are active in summer and 2.0 cm types which are active in winter.*

3. *After many generations two distinct sub-populations are formed.*

*Fig. 11.3 Disruptive selection*

## PROJECT

### Any species of plant can exhibit polymorphism

Select examples of a particular species from two different localities and find out how they differ, for example, in

(a) height
(b) branching
(c) leaf shape
(d) numbers and colours of flowers, etc.

Resistance to insecticides has come about in a similar way. Within two years of using DDT, many insects had developed resistance to it, often independently in different parts of the world. Most common insect pests are now resistant to most insecticides. In many cases the presence of the insecticide switches on the gene present in the mutant varieties. This gene initiates the synthesis of enzymes which break down the insecticide. Apart from directly harmful insects, insect vectors have also acquired resistance. Examples include mosquitoes of the genus *Aedes*, which carry yellow fever, and of the genus *Anopheles* which carry malaria.

Resistance to myxomatosis in rabbits takes two forms. In one type a mutant gene renders the myxomatosis virus ineffective in some way. In the second form a mutant gene alters the rabbits' behaviour, in that they spend more time above ground and less in their burrows. The disease is spread by a vector, the rabbit flea. Normal rabbits live in crowded warrens underground where the flea can easily be transferred between individuals. The mutant variety, spending less time underground, has a reduced chance of being affected by fleas, and hence catching the myxomatosis virus. This variety is favourably selected whereas previously it was selected against because of the increased chance of predation due to its vulnerability when above ground.

### 11.3.3 Heavy metal tolerance in plants

Another example of natural selection occurs on spoil heaps, which contain the waste material from mining activities. Spoil heaps contain high concentrations of certain heavy metals, e.g. tin, lead, copper and nickel. In such high concentrations, these metals are toxic to most plants. Some varieties of grasses, e.g. *Festuca ovina* and *Agrostis tenuis*, have become genetically adapted to survive high levels of these metals. These plants are less competitive where the concentration of these metals is low and so do not always survive.

Disused spoil heap covered with grass re-growth on Dartmoor

## 11.4 Artificial selection

Humans have cultivated plants and kept animals for about 10 000 years. Over much of this time they have bred them selectively. There have been two basic methods, each with a particular aim:

1. **Inbreeding** – When, by chance, a variety of plant or animal arose which possessed some useful character, it was bred with its close relatives in the hope of retaining the character for future generations. Inbreeding is still widely practised today, especially with dogs and cats.

   One problem with inbreeding is that it increases the danger of a harmful recessive gene expressing itself, because there is greater risk of a double recessive individual arising (Section 9.4.2). As a result, inbreeding is not usually carried out indefinitely but new genes are introduced by outbreeding with other stock. While this makes consistent qualities harder to achieve, it can lead to stronger, healthier offspring.

2. **Outbreeding** – This is carried out in order to improve existing varieties. Where two individuals of a species each have their own beneficial feature they are often bred together in order to combine the two. A racehorse breeder, for example, might cross a fast mare with a strong stallion in the hope of attaining a strong, fast foal. Outbreeding frequently produces tougher individuals with a better chance of survival, especially where many generations of inbreeding have taken place. This is known as **hybrid vigour**.

   Extreme examples of outbreeding occur when individuals of different species are mated. Only rarely is this successful. When it is, the resulting offspring are normally sterile. These sterile hybrids may still be useful. Mules, produced from a cross between a horse and a donkey, have strength and endurance which make them useful beasts of burden.

The improvement of the human race by the selection or elimination of specific characters is called **eugenics**. To some, the idea of such selection is offensive but, as we saw in Section 10.7, genetic counselling is now fairly commonplace. Provided the individuals involved remain free to make their own choice about whether to have children, many see no harm in providing them with statistical information which might help them reach a decision.

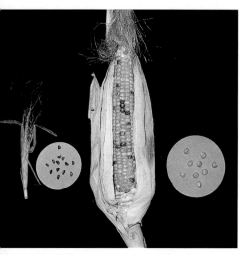

Selective breeding of corn. Note the small cob and seeds of the wild type (left) compared to the modern variety (right)

## BIOLOGY AROUND US

# Selective breeding

Selective breeding began many thousands of years ago as seeds saved from the best plants were sown the following year and animals with desired characteristics were chosen for breeding. Today, selective breeding programmes include the development of short-stemmed varieties of cereals, the selection of hens for increased egg production and development of different types of oilseed rape for industrial and domestic use.

### Selective breeding in maize
For many years maize plants with the desired characteristics were selected and self-pollinated. However, inbred lines tend to be weak and the 1930s saw the introduction of hybrid varieties derived from crossing two of the inbred lines. These hybrids are much stronger and forms have now been developed which can flourish in most soils and climates and which have a greatly increased grain yield. As well as these single-cross hybrids, commercial companies have also produced double-cross hybrids by crossing two of the single-cross varieties. The hybrids do not transmit their vigour to their offspring and so the parent stocks must be crossed each year to produce new hybrid seed for farmers.

### Selective breeding in wheat
Modern wheats are hexaploid ($6n$) and result from hybridization between emmer wheat ($4n$) and a $2n$ goat grass (see page 190). They generally have a high gluten content and are ideal for making bread. In recent years, varieties have been bred which have short stems and large grains. This means that farmers can increase their yield by the addition of fertilizers without the crop falling over. In addition, as concern grows over the excessive use of fungicides, new disease-resistant plants are being developed.

### Selective breeding in cattle
Many factors must be considered when selecting cattle for breeding. The choice is not as simple as choosing cows with a high milk yield for a dairy herd and those which grow most quickly or reach the largest size for a beef herd. Farmers also need to consider the nature of their land and the available feed, as well as market forces which might demand lean meat or low fat milk.

*Progeny testing.* In order to select suitable animals for breeding, it is necessary to assess their offspring, or progeny, under a variety of conditions. Since it takes a long time to rear a calf to an adult so that this testing can begin, and since a great deal of data are required, careful records must be kept of all the progeny of a certain bull. The higher the number of progeny showing the desired characteristics, the more valuable the bull will be.

*Artificial insemination.* Artificial insemination (AI) has been used in animal husbandry since the 1940s, and in the UK about 80% of matings are done by this means. It has many advantages: the sperm from a bull with desired characteristics can be used by many farmers so that these genetic features can be spread worldwide. Farmers can also get consistency within their herd and frozen semen can be used long after the death of the bull. Using AI enables farmers to move relatively easily between milk production and beef production as economic forces demand, without the need to keep several bulls. However, if we rely on only a small number of bulls, there is a danger of reducing the pool of genetic diversity; the establishment of gene banks are an important means of reducing this potential risk.

*Embryo transplantation.* Although this is not yet widely available, it has the potential to replace AI and it will certainly have at least as great an effect on selection. There are two main methods being developed. In the first, ova may be removed from cows at the abattoir, grown for about 5 days, and then fertilized *in vitro* with semen from a bull with the desired characteristics. After a further 5–6 days, the embryos can be frozen until required for transplantation into a recipient cow. Since it will be possible to sex these embryos, dairy farmers may choose to implant only females. In the second method, cows are treated with follicle stimulating hormone, which causes them to superovulate. Several ova are released and they are fertilized by AI with an increased number of sperm. In cattle there is a delay before embryos attach to the lining of the uterus and so the embryos may be grown for 6 days before being 'flushed out' and transferred to a culture medium and then to recipient cows either surgically or via the vagina.

## 11.5   Isolation mechanisms

Within a population of one species there are groups of individuals which breed with one another. Each of these breeding subunits is called a **deme**. Although individuals within the deme breed with each other most of the time, it is still possible for them to breed with individuals of separate demes. Therefore, a single gene pool remains. If demes become separated in some way, the flow of genes between them may cease. Each deme may then evolve along separate lines. The two demes may become so different that, even if reunited, they would be incapable of successfully breeding with each other. They would thus become separate species, each with its own gene pool. The process by which species, are formed is called **speciation** and depends on groups within a population becoming isolated in some way. There are two main forms of speciation:

### 11.5.1 Allopatric speciation

Allopatric speciation occurs as the result of two populations becoming geographically isolated. Any physical barrier which prevents two groups of the same species from meeting must

### Did you know?

The Arctic tern migrates about 35 000 kilometres each year.

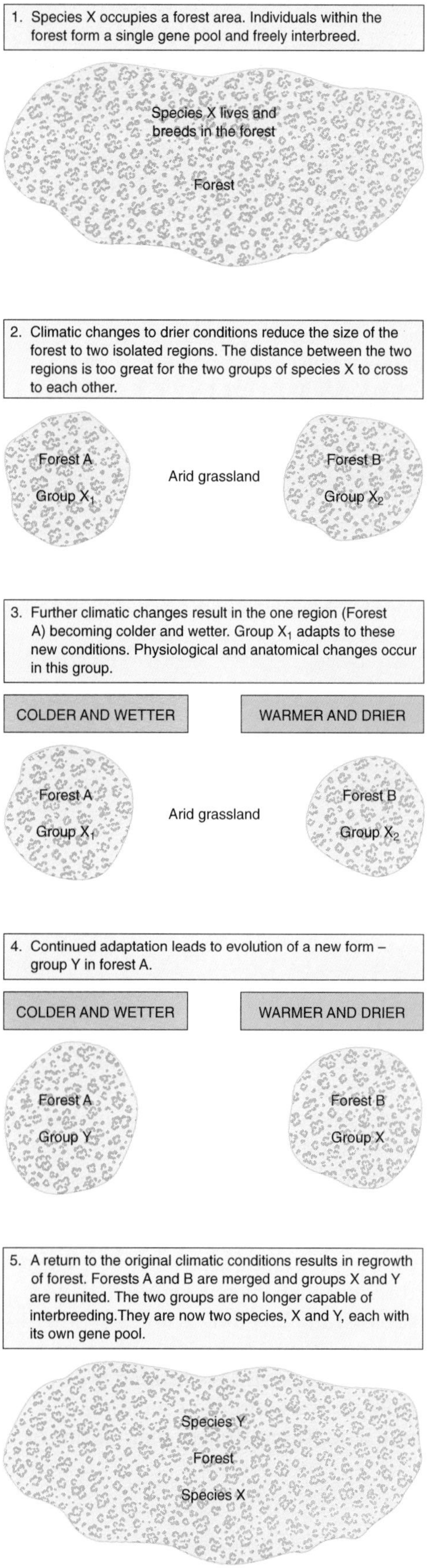

1. Species X occupies a forest area. Individuals within the forest form a single gene pool and freely interbreed.

Species X lives and breeds in the forest

Forest

2. Climatic changes to drier conditions reduce the size of the forest to two isolated regions. The distance between the two regions is too great for the two groups of species X to cross to each other.

Forest A

Group $X_1$

Arid grassland

Forest B

Group $X_2$

3. Further climatic changes result in the one region (Forest A) becoming colder and wetter. Group $X_1$ adapts to these new conditions. Physiological and anatomical changes occur in this group.

COLDER AND WETTER    WARMER AND DRIER

Forest A

Group $X_1$

Arid grassland

Forest B

Group $X_2$

4. Continued adaptation leads to evolution of a new form – group Y in forest A.

COLDER AND WETTER    WARMER AND DRIER

Forest A

Group Y

Forest B

Group X

5. A return to the original climatic conditions results in regrowth of forest. Forests A and B are merged and groups X and Y are reunited. The two groups are no longer capable of interbreeding. They are now two species, X and Y, each with its own gene pool.

Species Y

Forest

Species X

*Fig. 11.4 Speciation due to geographical isolation*

prevent them interbreeding. Such barriers include mountain ranges, deserts, oceans, rivers, etc. The effectiveness of any barrier varies from species to species. A small stream may separate two groups of woodlice, whereas the whole of the Pacific Ocean may fail to isolate some species of birds. A region of water may separate groups of terrestrial organisms, whereas land may isolate aquatic ones. The environmental conditions on either side of a barrier frequently differ. This leads to the group on each side adapting to suit its own environment – a process called **adaptive radiation**.

Imagine, for example, that climatic changes resulted in two areas becoming separated from one another by an area of arid grassland. A possible sequence of events which could lead to a new species being formed under these conditions is illustrated in Fig. 11.4.

### 11.5.2 Sympatric speciation

Sympatric speciation occurs when organisms inhabiting the same area become reproductively isolated into two groups for reasons other than geographical barriers. Such reasons might include:

**1. The genitalia of the two groups may be incompatible (mechanical isolation)** – It may be physically impossible for the penis of a male mammal to enter the female's vagina.

**2. The gametes may be prevented from meeting** – In animals, the sperm may not survive in the female's reproductive tract or, in plants, the pollen tube may fail to grow.

**3. Fusion of the gametes may not take place** – Despite the sperm reaching the ovum, or the pollen tube entering the micropyle, the gametes may be incompatible and so will not fuse.

**4. Development of the embryo may not occur (hybrid inviability)** – Despite fertilization taking place, further development may not occur, or fatal abnormalities may arise during early growth.

**5. Polyploidy (hybrid sterility)** – When individuals of different species breed, the sets of chromosomes from each parent are obviously different. These sets are unable to pair up during meiosis and so the offspring cannot produce gametes. For example, the cross between a horse ($2n = 60$) and an ass ($2n = 66$) results in a mule ($2n = 63$). It is impossible for 63 chromosomes to pair up during meiosis. More details of polyploidy are given in Section 10.5.4.

**6. Behavioural isolation** – Before copulation can take place, many animals undergo elaborate courtship behaviour. This behaviour is often stimulated by the colour and markings on members of the opposite sex, the call of a mate or particular actions of a partner. Small differences in any of these may prevent mating. If a female stickleback does not make an appropriate response to the actions of the male, he ceases to court her. The beak shape in many of Darwin's finches in the

The tambalacoque tree in Mauritius is threatened with extinction. It seems that its seeds only germinate if they have passed through the digestive system of a Dodo and the Dodo has been extinct for nearly 300 years. The seeds of the tree are being fed to turkeys in the hope that they will act as substitutes for the Dodo.

Galapagos Islands is the only feature that distinguishes the species. Individuals will only mate with partners having a beak similar to their own. The song of a bird or the call of a frog must be exact if it is to elicit the appropriate breeding response from the opposite sex. The timing of courtship behaviour and gamete production is also important. If the breeding season of two groups (demes) does not coincide, they cannot breed. Different flowering times in plants may mean that cross-pollination is impossible. These are both examples of **seasonal isolation**.

# 11.6   Questions

**1.** During meiosis the homologous chromosomes sometimes fail to separate, and the resulting gametes have two sets of chromosomes. When such a gamete takes part in fertilization, the offspring that is produced also has an extra set of chromosomes. In plants such offspring, even though they have increased numbers of chromosomes, are often viable. Having one or more extra sets of chromosomes is called polyploidy.

Einkorn wheat was first cultivated about 12 000 years ago. The diagram shows how modern bread wheat has been produced by a combination of polyploidy and hybridization. The figures in brackets show the number of chromosomes in the somatic (body) cells of each species.

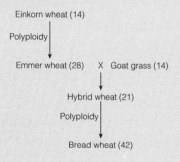

(a) How many chromosomes would there normally be in a gamete produced by
   (i)  goat grass;
   (ii)  emmer wheat?       *(1 mark)*
(b) Suggest why the hybrid wheat produced by crossing emmer wheat and goat grass was sterile.       *(1 mark)*
(c) Describe **two** advantages of the hybridization of emmer wheat with goat grass.   *(2 marks)*
(d) To make good bread, the wheat grains must contain a high proportion of the sticky and elastic protein gluten. Explain how selective breeding could be used to increase the gluten content of bread wheat.   *(3 marks)*
                            *(Total 7 marks)*

*NEAB February 1997, Paper BY07, No. 7*

**2.** Read the passage below and then answer the questions which follow.

1   Evolutionary change develops when a mutation occurs and survives the selective process (that is, when it is found to be either neutral or advantageous). For example, a GCT codon
5   might mutate to GAT and we would obtain leucine instead of arginine in the protein.

In about 20% of all mutations, because of the redundancy (degeneracy) of the code, a mutation might have no effect on protein
10  structure; thus a mutation from GCT to GCA would affect only the DNA and might well have no functional effects—no matter what the third base in the GC codon, we always obtain arginine in the protein.

15  The evolutionary process, then, involves a change (mutation) in the DNA which is incorporated into the ongoing gene pool of the evolving species and which can be reflected by a corresponding change in the amino acid
20  sequence of the particular protein coded for by that gene.

We might state as a basic rule that such a process will have to produce divergence when any two populations become isolated from one
25  another, as the relative rarity of mutations and the finite size of populations make it statistically improbable that identical changes will be available for natural selection to incorporate into the gene pools.

Adapted from V. Sarich
*A Molecular Approach to the Problem of Human Origins,* 197

(a) Explain what is meant by each of the following terms.
   (i)  A GCT codon (line 4)    *(1 mark)*
   (ii)  Redundancy (degeneracy) (line 8)
                            *(1 mark)*
   (iii)  Gene pool (line 17)    *(1 mark)*
   (iv)  Natural selection (line 28)   *(1 mark)*
(b)  (i)  Suggest **two** ways in which 'mutation from GCT to GCA' (line 10) might arise
                            *(2 marks)*
     (ii)  Explain why such a mutation 'might well have no functional effects' (line 12)
                            *(3 marks)*
(c)  (i)  State **two** ways in which 'populations become isolated from one another' (lines 24–25).   *(2 marks)*
     (ii)  Outline the possible consequences of the 'divergence' (line 23) which may result from such isolation.   *(3 marks)*
                            *(Total 14 marks*

*Edexcel June 1997, B6, No.*

**3.** Read the following passage.

**Shrimps Surface from Coal-Dust Soup in Min**

Fifty shrimps have been rescued from a colony living in a dark, sulphur-filled pool at the bottom of a 300 m mine shaft at Wearmouth Colliery, Tyne and Wear.

Dr Phil Gates of Durham University believes that they may even be a new species and has installed them in a laboratory aquarium in the 'coal-dust' soup in which they were found.

Dr Gates said, 'They've been isolated from other shrimps for most of this century and that makes them very interesting. The pool is full of sulphur, sulphur dioxide and hydrogen sulphide and we thought that if we put them straight into freshwater it would probably kill them.'

The shrimps are thought to have been feeding on sulphur-eating bacteria. 'It is possible that we have found an entirely new species,' he said, 'but more likely they are a subspecies which has evolved independently of ancestors in water at the surface. They will have been evolving in this extreme environment – total darkness, very acid water and living on sulphur-eating bacteria. In terms of evolutionary genetics, the mine shrimps are going to be fascinating. They'll be totally different from shrimps in pools on the surface.'

Adapted from *The Daily Telegraph*, 13 May 1994

(a) Dr Gates said, 'In terms of evolutionary genetics, the mine shrimps are going to be fascinating. They'll be totally different from shrimps in pools on the surface.' (lines 23–27). Explain how natural selection could account for the mine shrimps becoming genetically different from shrimps in pools on the surface. *(6 marks)*

(b) (i) What do you understand by the term 'species'? *(2 marks)*

(ii) Outline an experiment that you could carry out in a laboratory that would enable you to determine whether the mine shrimps were a different species from those in pools on the surface. Explain how you would interpret the results. *(4 marks)*

*(Total 12 marks)*

*NEAB February 1995, BY2, No. 8*

Rats and mice are common pests. Warfarin was developed as a poison to control rats and was very effective when first used in 1950.

Resistance to warfarin was first reported in British rats in 1958 and is now extremely common. Warfarin resistance in rats is determined by a single gene with two alleles, $W^S$ and $W^R$. Rats with the genotypes listed below have the characteristics shown.

$W^SW^S$  Normal rats susceptible to warfarin.

$W^SW^R$  Rats resistant to warfarin needing slightly more vitamin K than usual for full health.

$W^RW^R$  Rats resistant to warfarin but requiring very large amounts of vitamin K. They rarely survive.

(a) Explain why:
(i) there was a very high frequency of $W^S$ alleles in the British population of wild rats before 1950; *(1 mark)*
(ii) the frequency of $W^R$ alleles in the wild rat population rose rapidly from 1958. *(2 marks)*

(b) Explain what would be likely to happen to the frequency of $W^R$ alleles if warfarin were no longer used. *(2 marks)*

(c) Mice show continuous variation in their resistance to warfarin. What does this suggest about the genetic basis of warfarin resistance in mice? *(1 mark)*

In humans, deaths from conditions where blood clots form inside blood vessels occur frequently in adults over the age of 50. These conditions may be treated successfully with warfarin. However, some people possess a dominant allele which gives resistance to warfarin.

(d) Why would you not expect this allele to change in frequency? *(2 marks)*

*(Total 8 marks)*

*NEAB February 1995, BY2, No. 6*

5. (a) What is meant by the term **species**? *(1 mark)*
(b) Darwinian evolution depends on selection acting on the natural variation which exists within species. State the main source of such variation and briefly describe two ways in which this may occur. *(3 marks)*
(c) Powerful factors in the formation of new species are isolating mechanisms which prevent breeding between otherwise similar individuals. Give a brief account of **two** examples of such isolating mechanisms. *(4 marks)*

*(Total 8 marks)*

*Oxford June 1997, Paper 31, No. 4*

6. A single gene with two alleles controls variation in haemoglobin type in sheep. There are three different phenotypes, corresponding to genotypes $S^AS^A$, $S^AS^B$ and $S^BS^B$ respectively.

In a flock of 175 sheep the frequency of allele $S^A$ was found to be 0.6 and the frequency of allele $S^B$ was 0.4

  (a)  (i)  If the animals mated randomly, what frequencies of allele $S^A$ and allele $S^B$ would be expected in the next generation? *(1 mark)*

        (ii)  Using the Hardy–Weinberg equation, calculate the number of sheep with each phenotype in the flock. Show your working. *(4 marks)*

In humans, the phenotypes and genotypes with respect to the condition of sickle-cell anaemia are as follows:

| Phenotype | Genotype |
|---|---|
| Unaffected | $Hb^A Hb^A$ |
| Sickle-cell trait | $Hb^A Hb^S$ |
| Sickle-cell anaemia | $Hb^S Hb^S$ |

  (b)  Explain why:

      (i)  individuals with sickle-cell anaemia may be at a disadvantage; *(1 mark)*

      (ii)  the $Hb^S$ allele remains at a relatively high frequency in many populations. *(2 marks)*

The figure shows the length of cobs in two pure-breeding varieties of maize plant and the $F_1$ and $F_2$ generations derived from a cross between them.

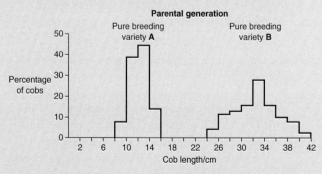

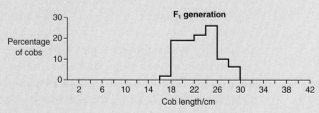

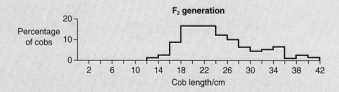

  (c)  Give the modal class for the $F_1$ generation. *(1 mark)*

  (d)  (i)  What is meant by polygenic inheritance? *(1 mark)*

      (ii)  Give evidence from the figure which suggests that inheritance of cob length is polygenic. *(1 mark)*

  (e)  What is the evidence that differences in cob length in the parental generation are partly due to:

      (i)  genetic differences; *(1 mark)*

      (ii)  environmental differences? *(1 mark)*

  (f)  Suggest a reason for the fact that although the mean values of the $F_1$ and $F_2$ generations are the same, the range of cob length is greater in the $F_2$. *(1 mark)*

  (g)  Explain briefly the part played by the following in genetic variation:

      (i)  mutation; *(1 mark)*

      (ii)  the behaviour of chromosomes during meiosis. *(3 marks)*

  (h)  The graph shows the frequency distribution of a continuous character.

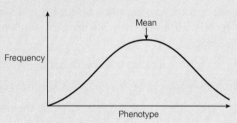

      (i)  Draw a line on the graph to represent changes that would occur under directional selection pressure. *(1 mark)*

      (ii)  Explain the shape of the line you have drawn. *(1 mark)*

*(Total 20 marks)*

*AEB Summer 1996, Module Paper 2, No.*

**7.** Give an account of the ways in which geographical isolation can lead to speciation.

*(Total 10 marks)*

*Edexcel January 1998, B2, No.*

# 12

# Reproduction, development and growth

No individual can live indefinitely. Some of its cells may be worn or damaged beyond repair or it may be killed by predators, disease or other environmental factors. If a species is to survive it must therefore produce new individuals. This is achieved in two ways:

**1. Asexual reproduction** – Rapidly produces large numbers of individuals, usually having an identical genetic composition to each other and to the single parent from which they are derived; gametes are never involved.

**2. Sexual reproduction** – Often less rapid, frequently involves two parents and produces offspring which are genetically different. The fusion of haploid nuclei is always involved. These nuclei are often contained in special cells called gametes.

Apart from purely increasing numbers, reproduction may involve one or more of the following:

**(a)** a means of increasing genetic variety and therefore helping a species adapt to changing environmental circumstances;

**(b)** the development of resistant stages in a life cycle which are capable of withstanding periods of drought, cold or other adverse conditions;

**(c)** the formation of spores, seeds or larvae which may be used to disperse offspring and so reduce intraspecific competition as well as capitalizing on any genetic variety among the offspring.

## 12.1 Comparison of asexual and sexual reproduction

Sexual reproduction always involves the fusion of nuclei which are often contained in special sex cells called gametes; asexual reproduction never does. If these gametes are produced by meiosis, they will show considerable genetic variety (Section 8.5.2). The offspring resulting from the fusion of gametes will likewise show genetic variability and therefore be better able to adapt to environmental change. In other words, they have the capacity to evolve to suit new conditions. As asexual reproduction rarely involves meiosis, the offspring are usually identical to each other and to their parents. While this lack of variety is a disadvantage in adapting to environmental change, it has one main advantage. If an individual has a genetic make-up

213

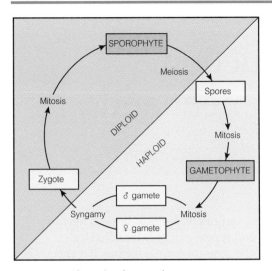

*Fig. 12.1 Life cycle of most plants*

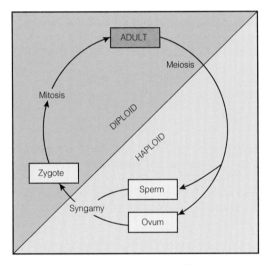

*Fig. 12.2 Life cycle of most animals*

which is suited to a particular set of conditions, asexual reproduction is a means by which large numbers of this successful type may be built up. A localized area can be rapidly colonized, something which is of particular advantage to plants.

It must be said that the differences in the variety of offspring resulting from sexual and asexual reproduction are not the same in all organisms. In mosses and ferns, for instance, the gametes are produced by a haploid gametophyte generation. Being haploid, its gametes can only be produced mitotically. Mitosis does not introduce genetic variety (Section 8.5.1) and these gametes are therefore identical. During asexual reproduction, mosses and ferns produce spores by meiosis. These spores show genetic variability. The usual differences between asexual and sexual reproduction are therefore reversed in mosses and ferns.

In all cases of asexual reproduction only one parent is involved but in sexual reproduction it may be one or two parents. If a species has male and female sex organs on separate individuals, it is said to be **dioecious**. In this case the male produces one gamete, the **sperm**, and the female another, the **ovum**. Only fusion between a sperm and an ovum can give rise to a new individual. Two parents are therefore always necessary for reproduction in these species. In some other species, one individual is capable of producing both male and female gametes. Such species are said to be **monoecious** or **hermaphrodite**. In most of these species the sperm from one individual fuses with the ovum from a separate individual. The fusion of gametes from two separate parents is called **cross-fertilization**. Provided the two parents are genetically different, greater variety of offspring results. In some species, however, sperm and ova from the same individual fuse. This is called **self fertilization** and involves a single parent; the degree of variety is therefore less. The process is nonetheless sexual, as fusion of gametes is involved, and, as these are produced by meiosis, some variety is still achieved.

It would be inaccurate to say that asexual reproduction always produces identical offspring. Mutations, although rare, nevertheless occur and so help create a little variety. Mutations also arise during sexual reproduction, indeed the greater complexity of the process means they arise more frequently.

To summarize, the main methods by which variety among offspring is achieved are:

1. The recombination of two different parental genotypes (genetic recombination).

2. During meiosis by:
   (a) random segregation of chromosomes on the metaphase plate (independent assortment);
   (b) crossing over during prophase I.

3. Mutations.

4. The effect of the environment on the genotype.

**1** and **2** apply only to sexual reproduction; **3** applies to both, although the frequency is usually greater in sexual reproduction and **4** applies equally to asexual and sexual reproduction. Overall the processes of sexual reproduction are more complex than those of asexual reproduction. The events of meiosis are

peror penguins in courtship

more complex than those of mitosis, and the processes of producing and transferring gametes are often complicated. Elaborate **courtship** and **mating rituals** are frequently part of sexual reproduction and serve to increase the likelihood of gametes successfully fusing (Section 12.7.1). These processes may take many months in some species and it is not therefore surprising that the offspring are often cared for by the parents. Where this is the case, the number of offspring is small to permit this parental care to be effective. By contrast, the process of asexual reproduction is normally more simple and straightforward. It is rapid and involves no parental care; the number of offspring is normally large.

On account of the variety of offspring produced and the consequent evolutionary potential, almost all organisms have a sexual phase at some stage in their life cycle. While simpler animals have retained the asexual process, most complex animals have abandoned it. A major disadvantage of being totally reliant on the sexual process is that it is difficult to maintain a favourable genotype. Once an organism has adapted to a particular set of conditions, sexual reproduction will tend to produce different offspring. These may not be as well adapted as identical copies of the parents would be. At least animals, with their ability to move from place to place, can search out conditions that suit any new variety. Plants do not exhibit locomotion and individuals must remain where they are. For this reason most have retained the asexual process as part of their life cycle. Hence, once a plant has successfully established itself in a suitable environment, it uses asexual means to rapidly establish a colony of identical, and therefore equally well-suited, individuals. Such a group has the advantage of reducing competition from other plant species, although with its identical genotypes it may be vulnerable to disease.

## 12.2 Asexual reproduction

As we have seen, asexual reproduction requires only a single parent and haploid gametes are not involved. There are seven major forms of asexual reproduction in organisms.

### 12.2.1 Binary or multiple fission

This occurs in single-celled organisms like bacteria and protozoans. The organism divides into two or more parts each of which leads a separate existence. Where the cell divides into two parts it is called binary fission and this typically occurs in bacteria.

The bacterial DNA replicates first and the nucleoplasm then divides into two, followed by the cell as a whole. Under favourable conditions (temperature around 20°C and an abundant supply of food) the daughter cells grow rapidly and may themselves divide within 20 minutes. Under unfavourable conditions some species develop a thick resistant wall around each daughter cell. The **endospore** thus formed is resistant to desiccation, extremes of temperature and toxic chemicals. Only

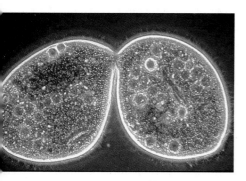

ary fission in *Paramecium*

Budding in *Hydra*

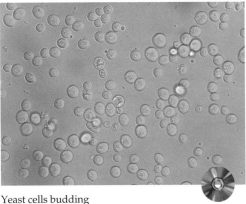

Yeast cells budding

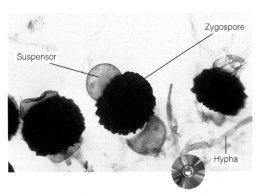

Zygospores of *Rhizopus nigra* germinate to form sporangia from which spores are released

when favourable conditions return does a vegetative cell emerge to continue binary fission as before. These endospores can survive certain forms of sterilization and so cause infection or disease. Multiple fission, or **schizogamy**, occurs when a cell divides into many parts rather than just two. In *Plasmodium*, the malarial parasite, for instance, the process occurs at a number of stages in the life cycle. These are described in Section 31.2.10.

### 12.2.2 Budding

An outgrowth develops on the parent and this later becomes detached and is then an independent organism. The process occurs in the Platyhelminthes (flatworms), some annelids (segmented worms) and cnidarians like *Hydra* and *Obelia*. In its simplest form it is little more than a type of binary fission, except that the two resultant cells are not of equal size but comprise a smaller bud cell, becoming detached from the larger parent cell. This occurs in *Saccharomyces* (yeast). In *Hydra* the buds arise near the centre of the parental column. They become highly differentiated, multicellular structures, and may develop their own buds before becoming detached.

### 12.2.3 Fragmentation

In one sense fragmentation is no more than a form of regeneration. If certain organisms are divided into sections, each portion will regenerate the missing parts, thus giving rise to new individuals. If the division occurs as a result of injury, then the process is regeneration. However, if an organism regularly and spontaneously divides itself up in this way, the process is fragmentation. Organisms exhibiting fragmentation must have relatively undifferentiated tissues and it is therefore limited to certain algae, sponges, cnidarians and flatworms. In *Spirogyra*, for example, portions of the filamentous alga break off when the filament reaches a certain length. These drift away, attach themselves elsewhere and begin vegetative growth again.

### 12.2.4 Sporulation

Sporulation is the formation of small unicellular bodies called **spores**, which detach from the parent and, given favourable conditions, grow into new organisms. Spores are usually small, light and easily dispersed. They are produced in vast numbers – a single mushroom for example may produce 500 000 spores a minute at the peak of its production. Sporulation occurs in bacteria, protozoans, algae, fungi, mosses and ferns (in one sense at least, all plants produce spores).

### 12.2.5 Vegetative propagation

In general, vegetative propagation involves the separation of a part of the parent plant which then develops into a new individual. Almost any part – root, stem, leaf or bud – may serve the purpose. These parts are often highly specialized for the task and bear little resemblance to the original plant organ from which they evolved; the potato, for instance, is actually a modified stem.

No plant is likely to survive long in a changing world if it relies exclusively on asexual reproduction. Plants exhibiting vegetative propagation have not therefore abandoned the sexual process but continue to produce flowers in the usual way.

In some plants, to ensure the continued survival of favourable genotypes, organs of vegetative propagation also act as **perennating organs** which lie in the soil over the winter. They are frequently swollen with excess food from the previous summer which is used to produce the new offspring the following year. One advantage is that growth can begin early in the spring using the stored food and the plant is therefore able to start photosynthesizing when there is little competition for light from other species. This is particularly important for small plants which live in deciduous woodland where they are subject to shading by their larger neighbours. Some organs of vegetative propagation are described in Table 12.1.

**TABLE 12.1  Organs of vegetative propagation and perennation**

| Name | Example | Description of organ | Mechanism of action | Perennating organ |
|---|---|---|---|---|
| Bulb | Onion Garlic Daffodil Tulip | Underground, swollen, fleshy leaf-bases closely packed on a short stem, i.e. a bud | Apical and axillary buds among the leaves each give rise to more new plants | Yes |
| Corm | Crocus Montbretia Gladiolus Cyclamen | Underground, vertical swollen base of main stem | Buds develop in the axils of the scale leaves surrounding the corm. Each may develop into a new plant | Yes |
| Rhizome | Solomon's seal Iris Couch grass Canna | Underground horizontal branching stem | Stem grows and branches. At the tip of each branch a bud produces new vertical growth which gives rise to a new plant | Yes |
| Stem tuber | Potato Artichoke | Swollen tip of slender rhizome | Many slender rhizomes arise from axil of scale leaf. The tips swell to form a stem tuber, each giving rise to a new plant | Yes |
| Suckers | Mint Pear | Underground horizontal branches | A number of underground branches radiate laterally from the parent plant. The tips ultimately turn upwards out of the soil and develop into new plants | Yes |
| Runner | Creeping buttercup Strawberry | Thin lateral stems on the soil surface | A number of stems radiate from the parent plant. Adventitious roots arise at points along the stem and new plants arise from these | No |
| Offset | Leek | A short, stout lateral stem on the soil surface | Stem grows laterally along the soil and a single plant arises from a bud at the top of each stem | No |
| Stolon | Blackberry | A long vertical stem with little structural support | The stem grows vertically at first but then bends over until the tip touches the soil. Adventitious roots develop and at this point a new plant arises from a nearby lateral bud | No |
| Root tuber | Dahlia | Swollen fibrous root | The tuber stores food but the new plant arises from an axillary bud at the base of the old stem | Yes |

### 12.2.6 Cloning

A group of genetically identical offspring produced by asexual reproduction is called a **clone**. The nucleus of every cell of an individual contains all the genetic information needed to develop the entire organism. It is therefore possible under suitable conditions to produce a whole organism from a single cell. If a cell divides mitotically it will produce a clone. If each cell of the clone is separated and allowed to develop into the complete organism, a group of genetically identical offspring is formed. This is known as cloning. (See Biology Around Us on micropropagation on page 615.)

### 12.2.7 Parthenogenesis

Parthenogenesis is the further development of a female gamete in the absence of fertilization. As a gamete is produced, the process is a modified form of sexual reproduction, even though only a single parent is involved. The parent is always diploid and the gametes are produced by mitosis or meiosis. In **diploid parthenogenesis** the gamete is produced by mitosis and therefore the offspring are likewise diploid. In aphids, diploid parthenogenesis is used as a means of rapidly building up numbers when conditions are favourable. During the summer, colonies of wingless females are formed by this means. In **haploid parthenogenesis** the gametes are produced by meiosis, giving rise to haploid eggs which may develop directly into haploid offspring. In the honey bee, unfertilized haploid eggs develop into males or drones, while fertilized eggs develop into female bees. If these females are fed honey and pollen they develop into workers. If they are fed a special food called royal jelly, produced by the workers, a queen results.

**Did you know?**

A pair of aphids could give rise to 800 million tonnes of aphids in a single year – assuming all the offspring of succeeding generations survived.

## 12.3 Reproduction in flowering plants

As plants have evolved they have reduced the water dependent phase of their life cycle – the gametophyte – and made the sporophyte generation totally dominant. This has allowed them to colonize land much more efficiently. They have also developed a unique reproductive structure – the flower – which has contributed to the undoubted success of this group.

### 12.3.1 Floral structure

Sexual reproduction confers on organisms the advantages of increased variety. This variety is achieved during meiosis by:

(i) the independent assortment of chromosomes on the metaphase plate;
(ii) exchange of genetic material due to crossing over between homologous chromosomes at prophase I.

Both processes achieve variety even when the offspring result from self-fertilization. Cross-fertilization confers an additional

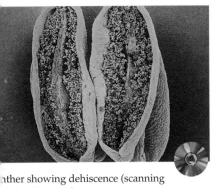

nther showing dehiscence (scanning
M) (×60 approx)

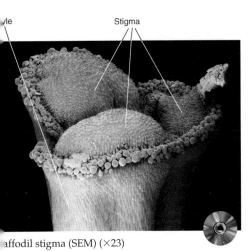

affodil stigma (SEM) (×23)

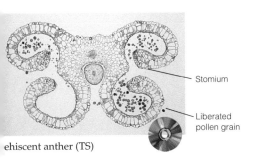

Stomium

Liberated
pollen grain

ehiscent anther (TS)

source of variety, that of mixing two parental genotypes. As terrestrial plants are incapable of moving from place to place in order to transfer genetic material between individuals, this third source of variety would be denied them but for the assistance of some external agent like insects or the wind. This, however, exposes the vulnerable gamete to dangers such as drying out during its transfer. To overcome this, the Angiospermaphyta have enclosed their male gamete within a spore, the **microspore** or **pollen grain**, a structure resistant to desiccation.

A typical flower is made up of four sets of modified leaves: **carpels**, **stamens**, **petals** and **sepals**, all attached to a modified stem, the **receptacle** (see Fig. 12.3).

In the centre are the carpels, which comprise a sticky **stigma** at the end of a slender stalk called the **style**. At the base of the carpel is the **ovary**, a hollow structure containing one or more **ovules**, each of which encloses the female gamete, the **egg nucleus**. The development of the ovule is illustrated in Fig. 12.4. The carpels may be separate as in *Ranunculus* (buttercup) or fused in groups as in *Tulipa* (tulip) where three carpels combine to give a single structure. Around the carpels are the **stamens**, each comprising a long stalk, the **filament**, at the end of which are the **anthers**. The anthers produce pollen grains which contain the male gametes. The development of the pollen grain is outlined in Fig. 12.5.

The stamens are surrounded by the petals, brightly coloured leaf-like structures which attract insects. They may produce **nectar** and be scented. The outer ring of structures is the sepals. These are usually green and may photosynthesize, but their main function is to protect the other floral parts when the flower is a bud.

Occasionally the sepals are brightly coloured, e.g. in lilies, and help to attract insects, or may later assist in dispersal, e.g. in mulberry, where they become juicy and attract animals.

The four sets of floral parts are given collective names as shown in Table 12.2.

Some flowers, like those of the buttercup, exhibit **radial symmetry (actinomorphic)** whereas the flowers of others, such as broad bean, are **bilaterally symmetrical (zygomorphic)**.

TABLE 12.2 **Some basic plant terminology**

| Floral part | Collective names of parts | Name given to flower if floral part is absent |
|---|---|---|
| Carpel | Gynoecium | Staminate, e.g. *Zea* |
| Stamen | Androecium | Carpellate, e.g. *Zea* |
| Petal | Corolla | Apetalous, e.g. *Clematis* |
| Sepal | Calyx | Asepalous, e.g. most of the Umbelliferae |
| Corolla + calyx | Perianth | e.g. wild arum |

### 12.3.2 Pollination

Pollination is the transfer of pollen from anthers to stigmas. If the transfer occurs between two plants of different genetic make-up, the process is **cross-pollination**. If the transfer takes place between flowers of identical genetic constitution, the process is

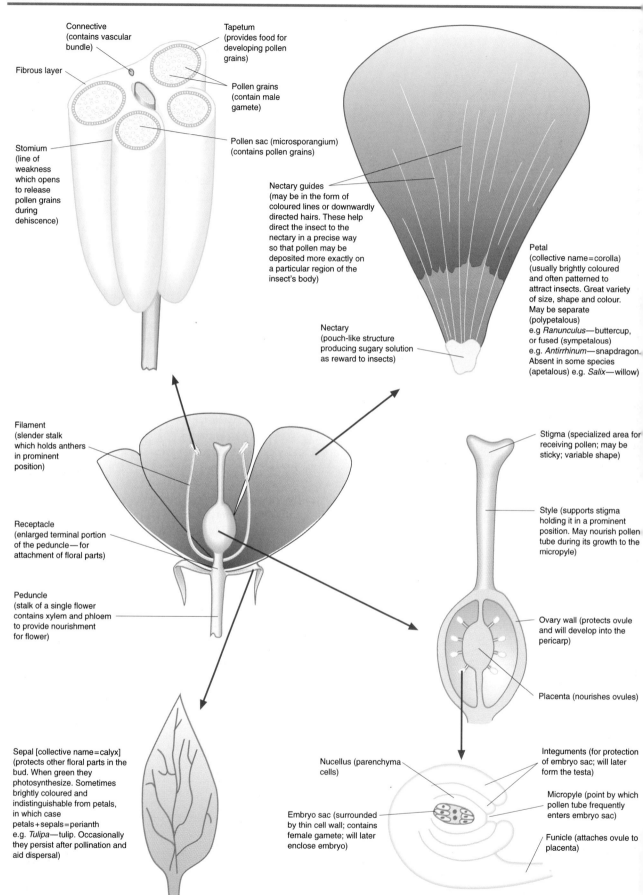

**Connective** (contains vascular bundle)

**Fibrous layer**

**Tapetum** (provides food for developing pollen grains)

**Pollen grains** (contain male gamete)

**Pollen sac (microsporangium)** (contains pollen grains)

**Stomium** (line of weakness which opens to release pollen grains during dehiscence)

**Nectary guides** (may be in the form of coloured lines or downwardly directed hairs. These help direct the insect to the nectary in a precise way so that pollen may be deposited more exactly on a particular region of the insect's body)

**Nectary** (pouch-like structure producing sugary solution as reward to insects)

**Petal** (collective name=corolla) (usually brightly coloured and often patterned to attract insects. Great variety of size, shape and colour. May be separate (polypetalous) e.g *Ranunculus*—buttercup, or fused (sympetalous) e.g. *Antirrhinum*—snapdragon. Absent in some species (apetalous) e.g. *Salix*—willow)

**Filament** (slender stalk which holds anthers in prominent position)

**Stigma** (specialized area for receiving pollen; may be sticky; variable shape)

**Style** (supports stigma holding it in a prominent position. May nourish pollen tube during its growth to the micropyle)

**Receptacle** (enlarged terminal portion of the peduncle—for attachment of floral parts)

**Peduncle** (stalk of a single flower contains xylem and phloem to provide nourishment for flower)

**Ovary wall** (protects ovule and will develop into the pericarp)

**Placenta** (nourishes ovules)

**Sepal [collective name=calyx]** (protects other floral parts in the bud. When green they photosynthesize. Sometimes brightly coloured and indistinguishable from petals, in which case petals+sepals=perianth e.g. *Tulipa*—tulip. Occasionally they persist after pollination and aid dispersal)

**Nucellus** (parenchyma cells)

**Embryo sac** (surrounded by thin cell wall; contains female gamete; will later enclose embryo)

**Integuments** (for protection of embryo sac; will later form the testa)

**Micropyle** (point by which pollen tube frequently enters embryo sac)

**Funicle** (attaches ovule to placenta)

*Fig. 12.3 Floral structure*

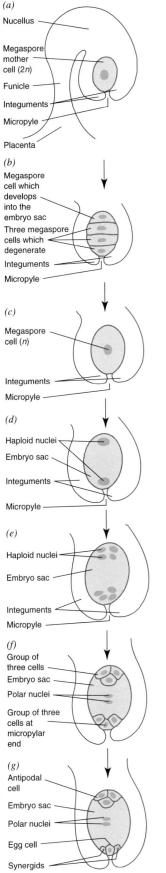

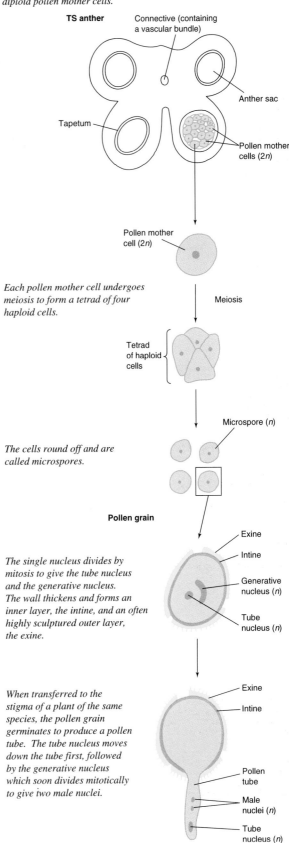

(a) The ovule consists of a mass of cells called the **nucellus** which is carried on a short stalk called the **funicle**. The nucellus is completely surrounded by two protective **integuments** except for a narrow channel at the tip called the **micropyle**. One cell of the nucellus becomes larger and more conspicuous than the rest. This is the **embryo sac mother cell.**

(b) The embryo sac mother cell divides meiotically to give four haploid **megaspore cells.**

(c) The three cells nearest the micropyle degenerate while the remaining one enlarges to form the **embryo sac.**

(d) The embryo sac nucleus divides by mitosis and the resultant nuclei migrate to opposite poles.

(e) Each nucleus undergoes two mitotic divisions to give a group of four haploid nuclei at each pole.

(f) One nucleus from each polar group moves to the centre of the embryo sac. These are the polar nuclei. The remaining nuclei develop cytoplasm around them and become separated by cell walls, leaving two groups of three cells at each pole.

(g) The three cells at the opposite end to the micropyle are called **antipodal cells** and play no further role in the process. Of the three cells at the micropyle end, one, the **egg cell** remains, the other two, the **synergids,** degenerate.

The anthers comprise pollen sacs (usually four) which contain a mass of diploid pollen mother cells.

Each pollen mother cell undergoes meiosis to form a tetrad of four haploid cells.

The cells round off and are called microspores.

The single nucleus divides by mitosis to give the tube nucleus and the generative nucleus. The wall thickens and forms an inner layer, the intine, and an often highly sculptured outer layer, the exine.

When transferred to the stigma of a plant of the same species, the pollen grain germinates to produce a pollen tube. The tube nucleus moves down the tube first, followed by the generative nucleus which soon divides mitotically to give two male nuclei.

*Fig. 12.4 Structure and development of the ovule*

*Fig. 12.5 Structure and development of the pollen grain*

221

**Pollen grains found in peat can tell us what types of vegetation were growing in the past**

1. Examine peat samples from different depths under the microscope.

2. Make drawings of the different kinds of pollen grains that you find.

3. Do the percentages of each type of pollen grain differ in the various samples?

4. Try to find out from the pollen grains what types of plants were growing when the peat was formed.

## Did you know?

In Australia when it is very hot the nectar in some flowers ferments and turns into alcohol. The bees get 'drunk' and are not allowed back into the hive.

self-pollination. It is common to think of self-pollination occurring within a single flower on a plant, such as garden peas, where the petals so enclose the stamens that the pollen has little chance of escaping. However, it also occurs if pollen is transferred between different flowers on the same plant. This may occur as an insect moves from flower to flower collecting nectar. A third type occurs when pollen is transferred between flowers on two separate plants which are genetically identical. This is most common where groups of plants have arisen as a result of asexual reproduction, e.g. groups of daffodils or irises. As members of a single clone, these groups have individuals with identical genotypes.

The design of any individual flower is related to the precise agent used to transfer pollen. If the plant is insect-pollinated (as in the sweet pea, Fig. 12.6) its bright colour, patterns and scent attract potential pollinating insects. The insects receive nectar or excess pollen, which encourages them to seek out a similar flower and thereby transfer more pollen.

As colour and scent have no bearing on wind direction, wind-pollinated flowers are dull, unattractive and without scent. Indeed, as petals may shelter the reproductive structures from the wind, they are frequently dispensed with altogether, leaving the anthers and stigmas exposed (see Fig. 12.7).

A comparison of wind-pollinated and insect-pollinated flowers is given in Table 12.3.

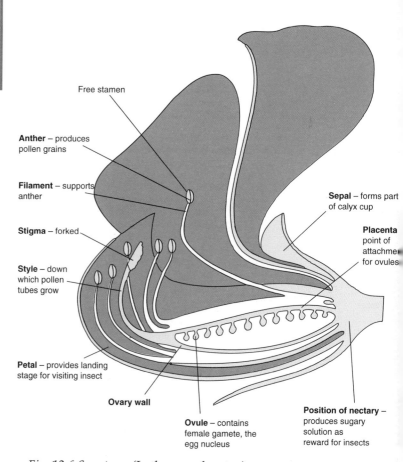

Free stamen

**Anther** – produces pollen grains

**Filament** – supports anther

**Stigma** – forked

**Style** – down which pollen tubes grow

**Petal** – provides landing stage for visiting insect

**Ovary wall**

**Sepal** – forms part of calyx cup

**Placenta** point of attachment for ovules

**Ovule** – contains female gamete, the egg nucleus

**Position of nectary** – produces sugary solution as reward for insects

*Fig. 12.6 Sweet pea* (Lathyrus odoratus)

ind dispersal of pollen from male tkins of alder tree

ild sage about to be pollinated by a bee

owering shoot of grass releasing its ollen

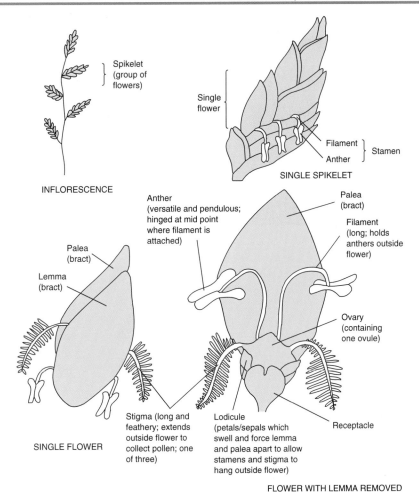

INFLORESCENCE

Spikelet (group of flowers)

Single flower

Filament
Anther
Stamen

SINGLE SPIKELET

Anther (versatile and pendulous; hinged at mid point where filament is attached)

Palea (bract)

Palea (bract)

Filament (long; holds anthers outside flower)

Lemma (bract)

Ovary (containing one ovule)

SINGLE FLOWER

Stigma (long and feathery; extends outside flower to collect pollen; one of three)

Lodicule (petals/sepals which swell and force lemma and palea apart to allow stamens and stigma to hang outside flower)

Receptacle

FLOWER WITH LEMMA REMOVED

*Fig. 12.7 Rye grass* (Lolium perenne)

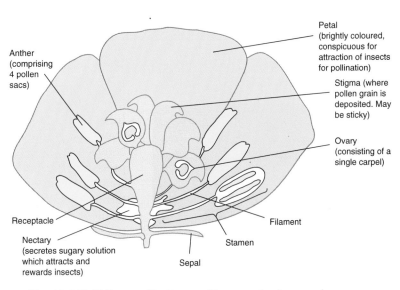

Petal (brightly coloured, conspicuous for attraction of insects for pollination)

Anther (comprising 4 pollen sacs)

Stigma (where pollen grain is deposited. May be sticky)

Ovary (consisting of a single carpel)

Receptacle

Filament

Nectary (secretes sugary solution which attracts and rewards insects)

Sepal

Stamen

*Fig. 12.8 Half-flower of buttercup* (Ranunculus), *a regular (actinomorphic) flower*

Highly sculptured exine

Groundsel pollen (SEM) (×370)

TABLE 12.3 Comparison of wind- and insect-pollinated flowers

| Wind-pollinated flowers (anemophilous) | Insect-pollinated flowers (entomophilous) |
|---|---|
| e.g. Rye grass (*Lolium perenne*) (Fig. 12.7) | e.g. Buttercup (*Ranunculus repens*) (Fig. 12.8) |
| Plants often occur in dense groups covering large areas | Plants often solitary or in small groups |
| Flowers occur in groups (inflorescences) on the plant (e.g. Graminae) | Flowers may occur on the plant as inflorescences (e.g. apple) but may also be solitary (e.g. tulip) |
| Flowers are often unisexual with an excess of male flowers | Mostly bisexual (hermaphrodite) flowers |
| Petals are dull and much reduced in size | Petals are large and brightly coloured to make them conspicuous to insects |
| No scent or nectar is produced | Flowers produce scent and/or nectar to attract insects |
| Stigmas often protrude outside the flower on long styles | Stigmas lie deep within the corolla |
| Stigmas are often feathery, giving them a large surface area to filter pollen from the air | Stigmas are relatively small as the pollen is deposited accurately by the pollinating insects |
| Anthers dangle outside the flower on long filaments so the pollen is easily released into the air | Anthers lie inside the corolla so the pollinating insect brushes against them when collecting the nectar |
| Enormous amounts of pollen are produced to offset the high degree of wastage during dispersal | Less pollen is produced as pollen transfer is more precise and so entails less wastage |
| Pollen is smooth, light and small and sometimes has 'wing-like' extensions to aid wind transport | Pollen is larger and often bears projections which help it adhere to the insect |

## 12.4 Fertilization and development in flowering plants

### 12.4.1 Fertilization

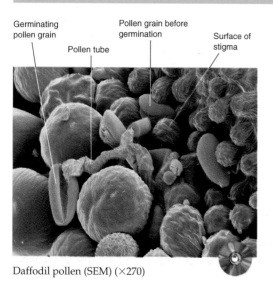

Germinating pollen grain

Pollen grain before germination

Pollen tube

Surface of stigma

Daffodil pollen (SEM) (×270)

In angiosperms the female gamete is protected within the carpel (Fig. 12.9) and the male gamete can only reach it via the **pollen tube**. On landing upon the stigma, the pollen grains absorb water and germinate to give the pollen tube. The tube pushes between the loosely packed cells of the style, the **tube nucleus** preceding the **male nuclei**. The role of the tube nucleus is to control the growth of the pollen tube and it plays no part in fertilization. While the initial growth into the style may be the result of a negative aerotropic response, it is thought that the tube then shows a positive chemotropic response to some substance produced in the embryo sac. The secretion of pectases by the pollen tube may soften the middle lamellae of the cells in the style and so assist its growth towards the micropyle – the usual point of entry to the embryo sac. Many tubes grow down the style simultaneously, and where an ovary has many ovules,

a separate pollen tube penetrates each. On entering the embryo sac, the tube nucleus, its work done, degenerates and the two male nuclei enter. One male nucleus fuses with the egg cell to give a diploid zygote; the other fuses with the two polar nuclei to form the primary endosperm nucleus, which is triploid. This double fertilization is peculiar to flowering plants.

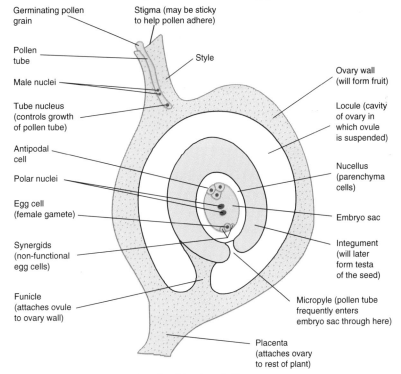

*Fig. 12.9 Mature carpel at fertilization (LS)*

### 12.4.2 Methods of preventing inbreeding

There can be no doubt that self-pollination occurs more or less regularly in some plants. However, there appears to be a general tendency to avoid self-pollination, since this is a form of inbreeding and would very quickly reduce the variability of a population and hence its potential for evolutionary change. There are four main methods of avoiding self-pollination and thereby promoting outbreeding.

**1.** The stamens and stigma of a flower mature at different times. If the stamens ripen before the stigma is in a condition to receive pollen, the flower is **protandrous**, e.g. white dead nettle (*Lamium*). If the stigma and ovule ripen before the stamens, the flower is **protogynous**, e.g. plantain (*Plantago*). Protandry is more common than protogyny.

**2.** If a plant has separate male and female flowers it is said to be **monoecious**, e.g. maize (*Zea*). This condition clearly limits the possibility of self-pollination and in *Zea* the number of seeds produced by self-pollination is reduced to less than 1%.

**3.** The structure of the flower itself makes self-pollination unlikely. Some flowers, e.g. *Iris*, have a stigmatic flap which is exposed to the pollen on the back of a visiting insect. The insect collects pollen from the stamens and closes the flap as it withdraws from the flower, thus protecting the stigmatic surface from its own pollen.

Pin-eyed and thrum-eyed *Primula* flowers (LS)

### Did you know?

The coco de mer palm of the Seychelles has the biggest seed in the plant kingdom. It weighs up to 27 kg.

| Before fertilization | After fertilization |
|---|---|
| Ovary and contents | Fruit |
| Ovary wall | Pericarp (wall of fruit) |
| Ovule | Seed |
| Integuments | Testa (seed coat) |

**4.** A **dioecious** species is one in which some individual plants have either all male or all female flowers. Completely dioecious plants are rare. It is more usual for a plant to be predominantly, although not completely, of one sex, e.g. plantain (*Plantago*) and ash (*Fraxinus*).

Preventing self-pollination is not the only means of preventing inbreeding. In many plants self-pollination occurs but there is a mechanism to prevent this leading to successful fertilization of the ovule and production of a seed. This is known as **incompatibility**. For example, in pears the pollen only becomes functional if the stigmatic surface on which it lands has a different genetic composition. *Primula vulgaris* (primrose) is a dimorphic plant in which there are two types of flower, pin-eyed and thrum-eyed. These differ in the length of the style (**heterostyly**) as well as in the size and chemical composition of their pollen.

These differences do not prevent self-pollination but the yield of seed produced by self-pollination is very poor.

### 12.4.3 Development of fruits and seeds

Following fertilization, the zygote divides rapidly by mitosis and develops into the embryo, which then differentiates into a young shoot, called the **plumule**, a young root, the **radicle**, and seed leaves known as **cotyledons**. The primary endosperm nucleus also divides mitotically to give a mass of cells, the **endosperm**. This forms the food source for the growing embryo. In some species, e.g. maize (*Zea mays*), the endosperm remains while in others, e.g. peas (*Pisum*), it is quickly absorbed by and stored in the cotyledons. Other parts develop as shown in the table on the left and in Fig. 12.10.

The most common food stored in seeds is carbohydrate. This is usually in the form of starch but some seeds, e.g. maize and

Endosperm – stores starch which provides an energy source for the growing embryo

Fused pericarp and testa – protects embryo

Cotyledon – stores food; only one present (monocotyledon)

Plumule – young shoot with apical meristem

Radicle – young root with apical meristem

*Fig. 12.10(a) Maize fruit (LS)*

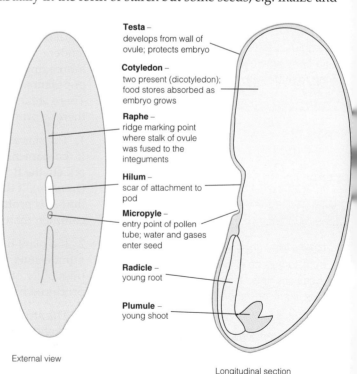

Testa – develops from wall of ovule; protects embryo

Cotyledon – two present (dicotyledon); food stores absorbed as embryo grows

Raphe – ridge marking point where stalk of ovule was fused to the integuments

Hilum – scar of attachment to pod

Micropyle – entry point of pollen tube; water and gases enter seed

Radicle – young root

Plumule – young shoot

External view

Longitudinal section

*Fig. 12.10(b) Broad bean*

## PROJECT

### Hawthorn seeds are dispersed by birds and have to pass through their intestines before they germinate

Test this statement by proposing a hypothesis and designing appropriate experiments.

(Hint: compare percentage germination of seeds soaked in different concentrations of hydrochloric acid, enzymes, etc.)

## PROJECT

### Gardening books often give the particular densities of sowing seeds which give the best yields

Investigate intraspecific competition by sowing cress seeds at different densities in trays and measuring their growth.

## PROJECT

Investigate the effect of any of a variety of substances on the germination of seeds like cress, mustard, etc.

peas, store quantities of sugar. Many young seeds store sugar but this changes to starch as they mature. Lipids are often stored in the cotyledons and may form a high percentage of the dry weight, e.g. 60% in walnuts and coconuts; 40% in sunflowers. Other economically important examples are peanuts, soya beans and castor oil seeds. Proteins are found to a lesser extent in seeds but wheat has an aleurone layer and protein is stored in the cotyledons of legumes and nuts.

### 12.4.4 Dormancy

The water content of seeds at between 5 and 10% is very low and is the major factor in preventing them germinating. As a rule, the addition of water in the presence of oxygen and a favourable temperature is enough to break this dormancy (Section 12.4.5). Some seeds, however, still fail to germinate for one reason or another:

1. Light is necessary for the germination of certain seeds, e.g. lettuce.

2. A sustained period of cold is needed to make some seeds of temperate climates germinate (Section 29.3). This helps to ensure that seeds do not germinate in late summer or during mild winter spells, thus making the young plant vulnerable to frosts at a later date.

3. Conversely a few seeds will not germinate unless subject to the heat of a flash-fire.

4. A period of time is necessary to permit internal chemical changes to take place before other seeds germinate.

5. The seed coat may be impermeable to water and/or gases and time may be needed for it to decay and break. In many seeds physical abrasion or partial digestion in the intestines of an animal help break dormancy by weakening the testa.

6. Another type of dormancy is brought about by the presence of natural chemical inhibitors.

### 12.4.5 Germination and early growth in flowering plants

Germination is the onset of growth of the embryo and requires water, oxygen and a temperature within a certain range (normally 5–40°C). In some seeds light is also required. Under these conditions the seed takes up water rapidly, initially by imbibition and later by osmosis. This water causes the seed contents to swell and so ruptures the **testa** (seed coat). At the same time the water activates enzymes in the seed which hydrolyse insoluble storage material into soluble substances which can be easily transported. In this way proteins are converted into amino acids, carbohydrates such as starch are converted into glucose, and fats are converted into fatty acids and glycerol. The soluble products of these conversions are transported to the growing point of the embryo. The glucose, fatty acids and glycerol provide respiratory substrates from which energy for growth is released. Glucose is also used in the formation of cellulose cell walls. The amino acids are used to form new enzymes and structural proteins within new cells.

Early growth results in the **plumule** and the **radicle** growing rapidly. The radicle grows downwards and the plumule upwards. In sunflowers the **cotyledons** may be carried up and out of the soil by this growth (**epigeal germination**), in which case they form the first photosynthetic structure. In some other plants, such as broad beans and wheat, the cotyledons remain below the soil surface (**hypogeal germination**).

## 12.5 Reproduction in mammals

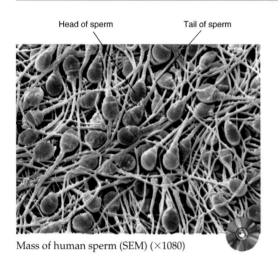

Head of sperm          Tail of sperm

Mass of human sperm (SEM) (×1080)

We saw earlier in this chapter that one major advantage of sexual reproduction is the genetic variety it creates, and that the extent of this variety is greater the more diverse the parental genotypes are. Animals, with their capacity for locomotion, are able to move far afield in their search for mates and so reproduce with individuals outside their family groups. This produces a greater degree of outbreeding, greater mixing of genes within the gene pool and hence greater variety. In mammals the gametes are differentiated into a small motile male gamete or **sperm** which is produced in vast numbers, and a larger, non-motile food-storing female gamete or **ovum** which is produced in much smaller numbers.

### 12.5.1 Gametogenesis

Gametogenesis is the formation of gametes. In the case of sperm production it is called **spermatogenesis** and where eggs are formed it is called **oogenesis**. Both types involve a multiplication phase, a growth phase and a maturation phase as depicted in Fig. 12.11. A human spermatozoan and an egg cell are illustrated in Fig. 12.12.

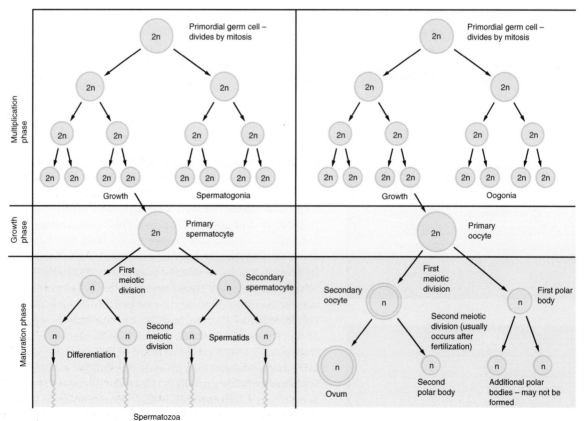

*Fig. 12.11(a) Spermatogenesis – formation of sperm*          *Fig. 12.11(b) Oogenesis – formation of ova*

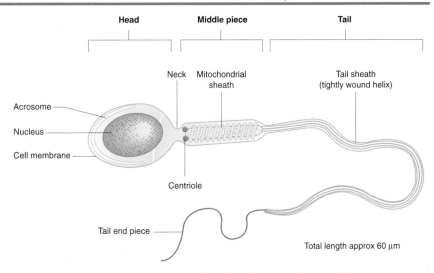

Fig. 12.12(a) Human spermatozoan based on electron micrograph

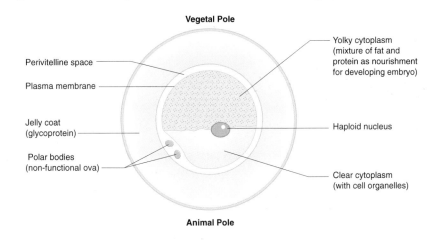

Fig. 12.12(b) A generalized egg cell

The organs which produce gametes are called **gonads** and are of two types: the ovaries which produce ova and the testes which produce sperm. In some animals, e.g. mammals, the reproductive and excretory systems are closely associated with one another; in such cases they are often represented together as the urinogenital system. (See Figs 12.13 and 12.17.)

### 12.5.2 Human male reproductive system

The male gonads, the **testes**, develop in the abdominal cavity and descend into an external sac, the **scrotum**, prior to birth. The optimum temperature for sperm development is around 35°C, about 2°C below normal human body temperature. The testes can be kept at this temperature by the contraction and relaxation of muscle in the scrotal wall. When the temperature of the testes exceeds 35°C the muscles relax, holding them away from the body to assist cooling. In colder conditions the muscles contract to bring the testes as close to the abdominal cavity as is necessary to maintain them at the optimum temperature. Each testis is suspended by a spermatic cord composed of the sperm duct or vas deferens, spermatic artery and vein, lymph vessels and

229

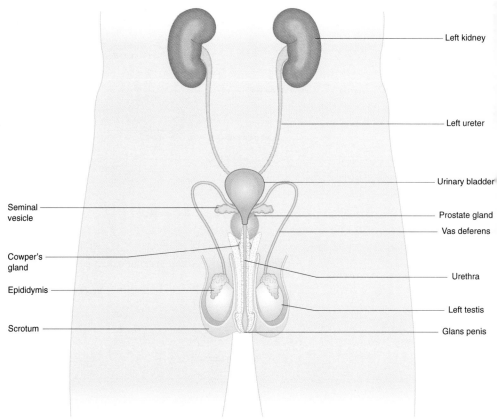

Left kidney

Left ureter

Urinary bladder

Seminal
vesicle

Prostate gland

Vas deferens

Cowper's
gland

Epididymis

Urethra

Left testis

Scrotum

Glans penis

*Male urinogenital system (simplified) – front view*

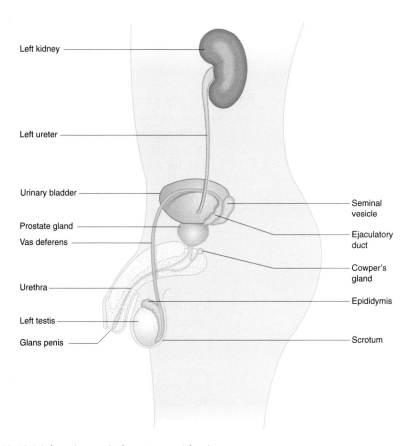

Left kidney

Left ureter

Urinary bladder

Prostate gland

Vas deferens

Urethra

Left testis

Glans penis

Seminal
vesicle

Ejaculatory
duct

Cowper's
gland

Epididymis

Scrotum

*Fig. 12.13 Male urinogenital system – side view*

nerves, bound together by connective tissue. A single testis is surrounded by a fibrous coat and is separated internally by septa into a series of lobules (Fig. 12.14).

Within each lobule are convoluted **seminiferous tubules**, the total length of which is over 1 km. Between the tubules are the **interstitial cells** which secrete the hormone **testosterone**. Each seminiferous tubule is lined by **germinal epithelium** which, by a series of divisions, gives rise to sperm, a process taking 8–9 weeks (Fig. 12.15).

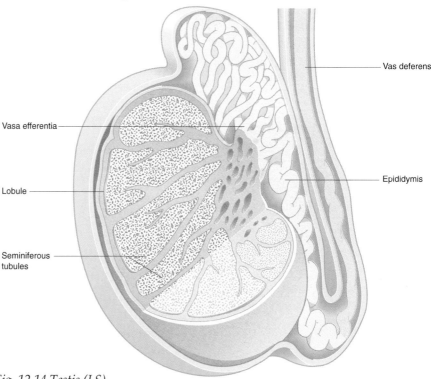

*Fig. 12.14 Testis (LS)*

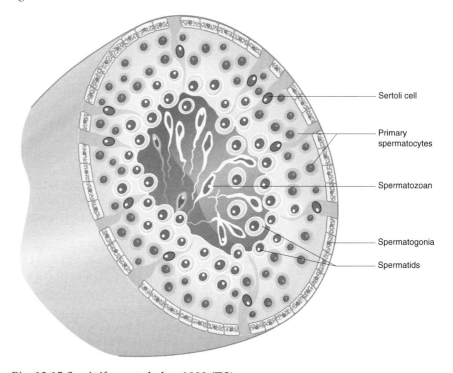

*Fig. 12.15 Seminiferous tubule ×1000 (TS)*

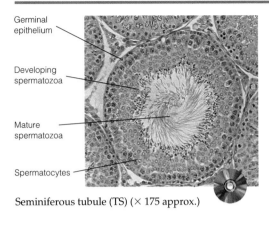

Germinal epithelium

Developing spermatozoa

Mature spermatozoa

Spermatocytes

Seminiferous tubule (TS) (× 175 approx.)

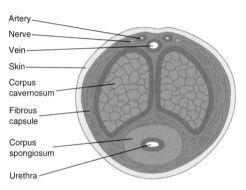

Artery
Nerve
Vein
Skin
Corpus cavernosum
Fibrous capsule
Corpus spongiosum
Urethra

*Fig. 12.16 Penis (TS)*

False–colour SEM of epithelium of Fallopian tube

The seminiferous tubules merge to form small ducts called the **vasa efferentia**, which in turn join up to form a 6 m-long coiled tube called the **epididymis**. The sperm are stored here, gaining motility over a period of 18 hours. From the epididymis leads another muscular tube, the **vas deferens**, which carries the sperm towards the urethra. Before it joins the urethra it combines with the duct leading from the **seminal vesicle**, forming the **ejaculatory duct**. The seminal vesicles produce a mucus secretion which aids sperm mobility. The ejaculatory duct then passes through the **prostate gland** which produces an alkaline secretion that neutralizes the acidity of any urine in the urethra as well as aiding sperm mobility. Below the prostate gland is a pair of **Cowper's glands** which secrete a sticky fluid into the urethra. The resultant combination of sperm and secretions is called **semen**. The semen passes along the **urethra**, a muscular tube running through the **penis**. The penis comprises three cylindrical masses of spongy tissue covered by an elastic skin (Fig. 12.16).

The end of the penis is expanded to form the **glans penis**, a sensitive region covered by loose retractable skin, the **prepuce** or **foreskin**. The foreskin is sometimes removed surgically, for medical or religious reasons, in a small operation called circumcision.

### 12.5.3 Human female reproductive system

The female gonads, the **ovaries**, lie suspended in the abdominal cavity by the ovarian ligaments. The external coat is made up of **germinal epithelium** which begins to divide to form ova while the female is still a fetus. At birth around 400 000 cells have reached prophase of the first meiotic division and are called **primary oocytes**. Each month after puberty, one of these cells completes its development into a secondary oocyte. As each cell takes some time to complete this change, the ovary consists of a number of oocytes at various stages of development. These oocytes lie in a region of fibrous tissue, the stroma, which fills the rest of the ovary. The largest and most mature of the cells are called **Graafian follicles** which are fluid-filled sacs each containing a secondary oocyte. A mature Graafian follicle can reach a diameter greater than 1 cm before it releases its secondary oocyte. Once the secondary oocyte is released, the empty follicle develops into a yellow body called the **corpus luteum** (Fig. 12.18).

Close to the ovary is the funnel-shaped opening of the **oviduct** or **Fallopian tube**. The opening has fringe-like edges called **fimbriae**. The oviducts are about 10 cm long and have a muscular wall lined with a mucus-secreting layer of ciliated epithelium. They open into the **uterus**, or womb, which is a pear-shaped body about 5 cm wide and 8 cm in length, held in position by ligaments joined to the pelvic girdle. It has walls of unstriated muscle and is lined internally by a mucus membrane called the **endometrium**. The uterus opens into the **vagina** through a ring of muscle, the **cervix**. The vagina has a wall of unstriated muscle with an inner mucus membrane lined by stratified epithelium. The vagina opens to the outside through the **vulva**, a collective name for the external genital organs. These consist of two outer

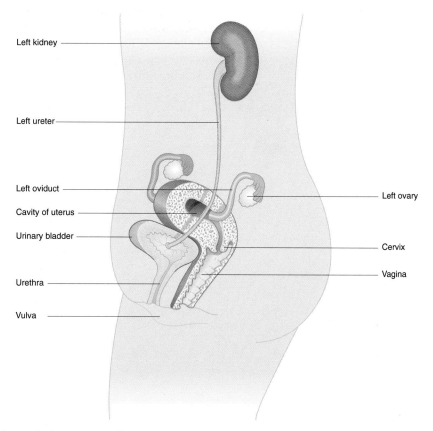

*Female urinogenital system – side view*

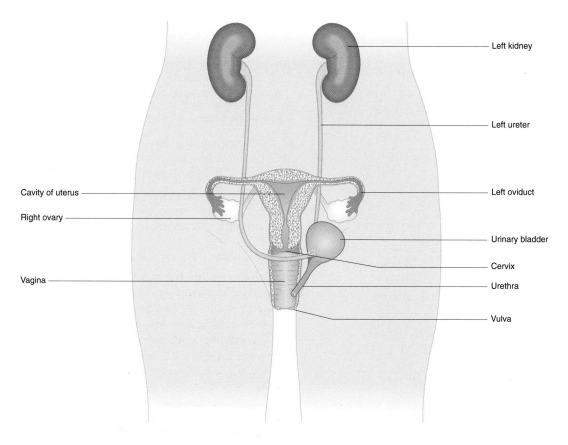

*Fig. 12.17 Female urinogenital system – front view*

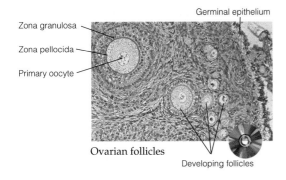

Zona granulosa
Zona pellocida
Primary oocyte
Germinal epithelium
Ovarian follicles
Developing follicles

folds of skin, the **labia majora**, covering two inner, more delicate folds, the **labia minora**. Anterior to the vaginal opening is a small body of erectile tissue, the **clitoris**, which is homologous to the penis of the male. Between the vaginal opening and the clitoris is the opening of the urethra.

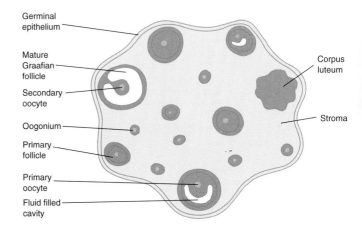

Germinal epithelium
Mature Graafian follicle
Secondary oocyte
Oogonium
Primary follicle
Primary oocyte
Fluid filled cavity
Corpus luteum
Stroma

*Fig. 12.18 Section through ovary*

## 12.6 Sexual cycles

Many animals have cycles of sexual activity in both males and females. These cycles often occur so that fertilization takes place at a time which gives the offspring the best chance of survival, e.g. the offspring are produced at a time when the climate and food availability are most favourable.

In mammals these cycles are of three main types:

**1.** The female undergoes a single period of sexual activity during the year, e.g. deer (**monoestrus**).

**2.** The female undergoes a number of periods of sexual activity during the year, each separated by a period of sexual inactivity, e.g. horses (**polyoestrus**).

**3.** The female has a more or less continuous cycle of activity where the end of one cycle is followed immediately by the start of the next, e.g. humans.

### 12.6.1 The menstrual cycle

In human females the onset of the first menstrual cycle is called **menarche** and represents the start of puberty. This takes place around the age of 12 years although the age varies widely between individuals. The menstrual cycle, which lasts about 28 days, continues until the **menopause** at the age of 45–50 years. The events of the cycle are controlled by hormones to ensure that the production of a secondary oocyte is synchronized with the readiness of the uterus to receive it, should it be fertilized. The start of the cycle is taken to be the initial discharge of blood known as **menstruation**, as this event can be easily identified. This flow of blood, which lasts about 5 days, is due to the lining of the uterus being shed, along with a little blood.

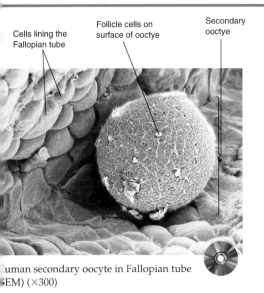

Cells lining the Fallopian tube

Follicle cells on surface of oocyte

Secondary oocyte

Human secondary oocyte in Fallopian tube (SEM) (×300)

During the following days the lining regenerates in readiness for a fertilized ovum. By day 14 it has thickened considerably and the Graafian follicle releases its secondary oocyte into the oviduct, the process being called **ovulation**. The secondary oocyte is moved down the oviduct mostly by muscular contractions of the oviduct wall, although the beating of the cilia may also assist. The journey to the uterus takes about 3 days, during which time the secondary oocyte may be fertilized. If it is not, it quickly dies and passes out via the vagina. The uterine lining is maintained for some time but finally breaks down again about 28 days after the start of the cycle (Fig. 12.19).

### 12.6.2 Hormonal control of the menstrual cycle

The control of the menstrual cycle is an excellent example of hormone interaction. The action of one hormone stimulates or inhibits the production of another. Four hormones are involved, two produced by the anterior lobe of the pituitary gland at the base of the brain, and two produced by the ovaries. The production of the hormones from the ovaries is stimulated by the pituitary hormones. These pituitary hormones are thus referred to as the gonadotrophic hormones. The two gonadotrophic hormones are **follicle stimulating hormone (FSH)** and **luteinizing hormone (LH)**. These stimulate the ovaries to produce **oestrogen** and **progesterone** respectively.

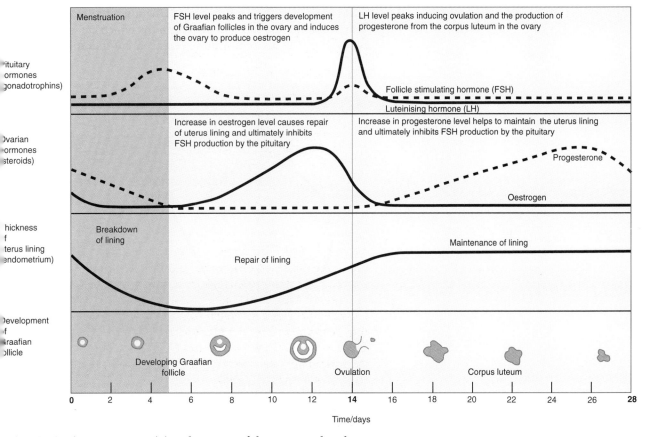

*Fig. 12.19 Diagram summarizing the events of the menstrual cycle*

The functions of these hormones are as follows:

*Follicle stimulating hormone*
1. Causes Graafian follicles to develop in the ovary.
2. Stimulates the ovary to produce oestrogen.

*Oestrogen*
1. Causes repair of the uterus lining following menstruation.
2. Stimulates the pituitary to produce luteinizing hormone.

*Luteinizing hormone*
1. Causes ovulation to take place.
2. Stimulates the ovary to produce progesterone from the corpus luteum.

*Progesterone*
1. Causes the uterus lining to be maintained in readiness for the blastocyst (young embryo).
2. Inhibits production of FSH by the pituitary.

The hormones are produced in the following sequence: FSH, oestrogen, LH, progesterone. Progesterone at the end of the sequence inhibits the production of FSH. In turn, the production of the other hormones stops, including progesterone itself. The absence of progesterone now means that the inhibition of FSH ceases and so oestrogen production commences again. In turn, all the other hormones are produced. This alternate switching on and off of the hormones produces a cycle of events – the menstrual cycle (see Fig. 12.20).

At the end of their fertile period, the **menopause**, women often experience a number of symptoms which can sometimes be relieved by the use of **hormone replacement therapy (HRT)**.

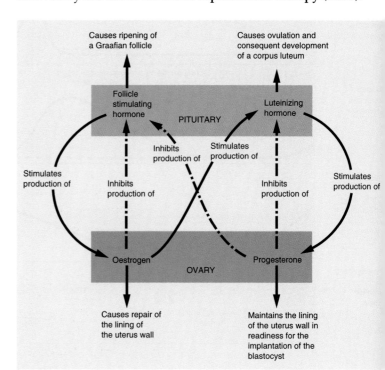

*Fig. 12.20 Hormone interaction in the menstrual cycle*

## BIOLOGY AROUND US

# Premenstrual syndrome

The natural fluctuation in sex hormone levels during the menstrual cycle produces a wide range of side effects, especially in the days leading up to the menstrual period. Over a hundred such effects have been identified, ranging from breast tenderness, bloating due to water retention, headache and pelvic pain through to irritability, depression, clumsiness and a craving for sweet foods. Such is the range of symptoms that the term premenstrual tension (PMT) is misleading and PMS is now preferred. It is estimated that 70% of fertile women suffer from PMS to a varying degree. A variety of drugs may be used to alleviate the symptoms but longer term treatment often involves providing oestrogen in patch, pill or implant form.

### 12.6.3 Artificial control of the menstrual cycle

The artificial control of the menstrual cycle has two main purposes: firstly as a contraceptive device by preventing ovulation and secondly as a fertility device by stimulating ovulation.

*The contraceptive Pill*

The Pill contains both oestrogen and progesterone and when taken daily it maintains high levels of these hormones in the blood. These high levels inhibit the production of the gonadotrophic hormones from the pituitary, and the absence of LH in particular prevents ovulation. The Pill is normally taken for 21 consecutive days followed by a period of 7 days without it, during which the uterus lining breaks down and a menstrual period occurs. The 'morning after' Pill contains the synthetic oestrogen diethylstibestrol, which is thought to prevent implantation of the fertilized ovum if it is present. Both types of Pill are very effective forms of contraception. These and other methods of contraception are reviewed in Table 12.4.

*Fertility drugs*

A fertility drug may induce ovulation in one of two ways:

**1.** It may increase gonadotrophin production which stimulates ovulation, e.g. **Clomiphene**.

**2.** It may provide some chemical which inhibits the natural production of oestrogen. As oestrogen normally inhibits FSH production, the level of FSH increases and Graafian follicles develop.

Fertility drugs frequently result in multiple births.

## 12.7  Fertilization and development in mammals

### 12.7.1 Courtship

In many species it is necessary for both partners to follow a specific pattern of behaviour before mating can occur. Courtship

TABLE 12.4   **Birth control**

| Method | How it works | Effectiveness | Advantages | Disadvantages |
|---|---|---|---|---|
| Sterilization | **Male (vasectomy)** – The vasa deferentia (the ducts carrying sperm from the testes to the urethra) are cut and tied off | 100% | No artificial appliance is involved. Once the operation has been performed there is no further cost | Irreversible in normal circumstances |
| | **Female (tubal ligation)** – The oviducts are cut and tied off | | | |
| Prevention of ovulation | **Oral contraceptive** – Contains artificial oestrogen and progesterone | 99% | Very reliable if taken regularly | A slightly higher than normal risk of thrombosis. Occasional side-effects e.g. nausea, breast tenderness and water retention |
| | **Injection contraceptive** (e.g. Depo-provera) – Injection given by doctor about every 3 months | 100% | Almost totally reliable | Hormonal surge on injection may produce side-effects e.g. irregular menstrual bleeding |
| | **Implant contraceptive** (e.g. Norplant) – Implant placed under the skin which releases artificial oestrogen and progesterone | 100% | Almost totally reliable. Each implant lasts 5 years | Can cause irregular menstrual bleeding |
| Prevention of implantation | **Morning-after Pill** – Contains high level of oestrogen. Taken orally | Not widely used but probably 99–100% | Can be used after rather than before intercourse | High dose of oestrogen can produce side-effects. Not suitable for regular use |
| | **Intra-Uterine Device (loop, coil)** – A device usually made of plastic and/or copper which is inserted into the womb by a doctor and which prevents implantation | 99–100% | Once fitted, no further action is required except for annual check-ups | Possible menstrual discomfort. The device may be displaced or rejected. Must be inserted by a trained practitioner. Only really suitable for women who have had children |
| | **Intra-vaginal ring** – Ring shaped device which releases artificial progesterone. Placed in vagina | Very reliable | Very reliable | Long term health effects yet to be assessed |
| Barriers which prevent sperm reaching an egg | **Female (diaphragm, cap)** – A dome-shaped sheet of thin rubber with a thicker spring rim which is inserted into the vagina, over the cervix. Best used with spermicide | Very reliable | Reliable. Available for use by all women | Must be inserted prior to intercourse and should be removed 8–24 hours after intercourse. Initial fitting must be by a trained practitioner |
| | **Female (condom)** – Sheath of thin rubber with two springy rings. Smaller inserted into vagina, larger remains outside | Very reliable | Readily available, quite easy to fit. Gives some protection against sexually transmitted diseases | May reduce enjoyment of intercourse |
| | **Male (condom, sheath)** – a sheath of thin rubber unrolled onto the erect penis prior to intercourse. Semen is collected in teat at the tip. Best used with a spermicide. | Very reliable | Easily available, no fitting or instruction by others needed. Available for use by all men. Gives some protection against sexually transmitted disease including AIDS | May reduce the sensitivity of the penis and so interfere with enjoyment |
| | **Spermicide** – Cream, jelly or foam inserted into vagina. Only effective with a mechanical barrier. Kills sperm | Not reliable alone | Easy to obtain and simple to use | Not effective on its own. May occasionally cause irritation |
| Natural method | **Rhythm method** – Refraining from intercourse during those times in the menstrual cycle when conception is most likely | Variable – not very reliable | No appliance required. Only acceptable method to some religious groups | Not reliable. Restricts times when intercourse can take place. Unsuitable for women with irregular cycles |

Peacock display

behaviour as it is called is developed in sexually mature individuals. In this way matings between sexually immature individuals, which cannot produce offspring, are avoided. This ensures that the often scarce sites for raising young are only occupied by pairs which have a good chance of producing offspring. On reaching sexual maturity many species develop easily recognizable features which are sexually attractive to a potential partner. These are referred to as the secondary sex characteristics. They take a variety of forms, including bright plumage in many birds, the mane of a lion, the comb and spurs of a cockerel and territory marking in dogs. In humans, secondary sex characteristics include the growth of pubic hair in both sexes, increased musculature, growth of facial hair and deepening of the voice in males and development of the breasts and broadening of the hips in females. Apart from preparing the female for child-bearing the changes in many animals help to distinguish males and females. In this way time and energy are not wasted on the fruitless courting of members of the same sex or sexually immature individuals of the opposite sex.

The females of many species undergo a cycle of sexual activity during which they are only capable of conceiving for a very brief period. Courtship behaviour is used by the male to determine whether the female is receptive or not. If she responds with the correct behavioural actions, courtship continues and is likely to result in fertilization. If she is not receptive, she exhibits a different pattern of behaviour and the male ceases to court her, turning his attentions elsewhere.

### 12.7.2 Mating

Under a variety of erotic conditions the blood supply to the genital regions increases. In females the process is slower than in males and results in the clitoris and labia becoming swollen with blood. At the same time the walls of the vagina secrete a lubricating fluid which assists the penetration of the penis. The fluid also neutralizes the acidity of the vagina which would otherwise kill the sperm. In males the increased blood supply results in the spongy tissues of the penis becoming swollen with blood, making it hard and erect. In this condition it more easily enters the vagina. By repeated thrusting of the penis within the vagina the sensory cells in the glans penis are stimulated. This leads to reflex contractions of muscles in the epididymis and vas deferens. The sperm are thus moved by peristalsis along the vas deferens and into the urethra. Here they mix with the secretions from the seminal vesicles, prostate and Cowper's glands. The resultant semen is forced out of the penis by powerful contractions of the urethra, a process called **ejaculation**. This is accompanied by **orgasm**, a sensation of extreme pleasure as a result of physiological and emotional release. The female orgasm is similarly intense, resulting from the contraction of the muscles of the vagina and uterus, although there is no associated expulsion of fluid. The process of mating, also known as **copulation** or **coitus**, results in internal fertilization and is an adaptation to life on land. The sperm, which require a liquid environment in which to swim, are never exposed to the drying effect of air.

239

Spermatozoa floating over the endometrium (SEM) (×2450)

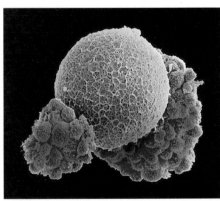

Human egg with cumulus corona cells (SEM) (×500 approx.)

### 12.7.3 Semen

In humans, each ejaculation consists of approximately 5 cm³ of semen. While it contains around 500 million sperm they comprise only a tiny percentage of the total volume, the majority being made up of the fluids secreted by the seminal vesicles, prostate and Cowper's glands. The semen therefore contains:

1. **Sperm**.

2. **Sugars** which nourish the sperm and help to make them mobile.

3. **Mucus** which forms a semi-viscous fluid in which the sperm swim.

4. **Alkaline chemicals** which neutralize the acid conditions encountered in the urethra and vagina, which could otherwise kill the sperm.

5. **Prostaglandins**, hormones which help sperm reach the ovum by causing muscular contractions of the uterus and oviducts.

### 12.7.4 Fertilization

The force of ejaculation of the semen from the penis is sufficient to propel some sperm through the cervix into the uterus, with the remainder being deposited at the top of the vagina. The sperm swim up through the uterus and into the oviducts by the lashing movements of their tails. The speed with which they reach the top of the oviducts indicates that muscular contraction of the uterus and oviduct are also involved. The egg or ovum released from the Graafian follicle of the ovary is metabolically inactive and dies within 24 hours unless fertilized. The ovum is surrounded by up to 2000 **cumulus cells**, which aid the movement of the ovum towards the uterus by giving the cilia which line the oviduct a large mass to 'grip'. The cumulus cells may also provide nutrients to the ovum. As the journey to the uterus takes 3 days in humans, it follows that fertilization must take place in the top third of the oviduct if the ovum is still to be alive when the sperm reaches it. In mammals there is no evidence that the ovum attracts the sperm in any way; their meeting would appear to be largely a matter of chance. Of the 500 million sperm in the ejaculate, only a few hundred reach the ovum, and only one actually fertilizes it.

The fertilized ovum is called a **zygote**. The fertilizing sperm firstly releases **acrosin**, a trypsin-like enzyme, from the acrosome. This softens the plasma membrane which covers the ovum. Inversion of the acrosome results in a fine needle-like filament developing at the tip of the sperm and this pierces the already softened portion of the plasma membrane. An immediate set of changes occurs which thickens the membrane and so ensures that no other sperm can penetrate the egg. This is essential to prevent a 'multinucleate' fertilized egg; such cells normally degenerate after a few divisions. The thickened membrane is now called the **fertilization membrane**. The sperm discards its tail, and the head and middle piece enter the cytoplasm. The second meiotic division of the ovum nucleus

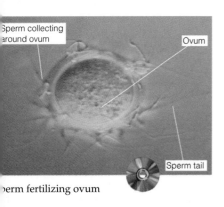

Sperm collecting around ovum

Ovum

Sperm tail

Sperm fertilizing ovum

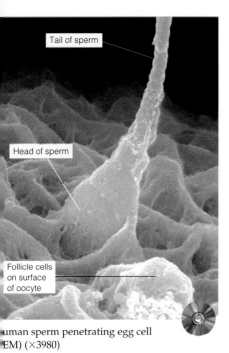

Tail of sperm

Head of sperm

Follicle cells on surface of oocyte

Human sperm penetrating egg cell (SEM) (×3980)

normally occurs immediately following the penetration of the sperm. The sperm and ovum nuclei fuse, restoring the diploid state. A spindle forms, the two sets of chromosomes line up and the cell undergoes mitotic division at once.

If the ovum is not fertilized it quickly dies and in humans the lining of the uterus is later shed to give the menstrual flow. In the female horseshoe bat, to achieve the earliest possible fertilization in spring, mating takes place in the autumn but the female stores the sperm in a thick plug of mucus. In spring the plug dissolves, releasing the sperm for fertilization. This is called **delayed fertilization** and depends on the sperm surviving considerably longer than the 2–3 days which is normal in a human.

### 12.7.5 Causes of infertility and its cures

There are a number of reasons why a couple may have difficulty conceiving a baby:

**1. Blocked oviducts** – These may prevent ova and sperm meeting, in which case an operation may be undertaken to unblock the tubes, or in-vitro fertilization can be attempted.

**2. An irregular menstrual cycle** – This may make the chance of fertilization remote, and hormone treatment may be necessary to regularize the cycle.

**3. Incorrect frequency and/or timing of intercourse** may make conception unlikely and couples may need to be counselled on the most appropriate time (the middle of the menstrual cycle) to have sexual intercourse in order to increase the possibility of fertilization.

**4. Non-production of ova** – This affects a few females, making it impossible for them to contribute genetically to their offspring. Adoption or the use of a donated ovum from another female for in-vitro fertilization are possible options. Artificial insemination of a surrogate mother with the potential father's sperm is another alternative.

**5. Non-production of sperm** – Some men produce no sperm, or so few that there is little realistic prospect of conception. Donated semen from another male can be used to artificially inseminate the woman.

**6. Impotence** – Some men are unable to erect the penis and/or ejaculate semen. The cause is often psychological, or the result of prolonged drug or alcohol abuse. In these cases counselling and guidance can sometimes remedy the problem. In other cases an implant may be used which can be pumped up as required. Alternatively an injection of a drug at the base of the penis will raise blood pressure within it and so create an erection. The drug Viagra can be taken orally and has a high success rate in curing impotence.

Some of the above causes of infertility may be the result of certain diseases or infections. Sexually transmitted diseases such as gonorrhoea can cause sterility, especially in females; mumps, if contracted in adult life, sometimes makes males infertile. Even when conception occurs, a few women are not able to sustain the pregnancy because either the embryo does not implant in the uterus lining, or having implanted, it is later miscarried. For some such women, the solution is to use in-vitro fertilization (see Biology Around Us, overleaf) but rather than implant the

# BIOLOGY AROUND US

## In-vitro fertilization and test tube babies

After first being achieved in rabbits in 1959, in-vitro fertilization, or IVF, was successfully performed between human sperm and ova by Drs Edwards, Bavister and Steptoe 10 years later. The development of these zygotes and their successful transfer into the uterus of the mother, called **embryo transfer** or **ET**, took a number of years but finally, in 1978, the first test tube baby was born.

The success of this technique owes as much to the development of a suitable medium in which the sperm, ova and embryo can survive and grow, as to the clinical techniques of obtaining ova and implanting the embryo. Such a medium must have a pH, osmotic potential and ionic concentration similar to that of blood and must also contain the patient's serum as a source of protein and other macromolecules. Glucose, lactate and pyruvate are other essential components.

The process begins with a fertility drug being administered to the potential mother to increase her ova production. Around six ova are collected using a fine needle, via the vagina. Some 100 000 sperm, collected from the potential father's semen sample by centrifugation, are added to the ova in a Petri dish. When the embryos are 2 days old, a few are transferred into the mother's uterus where, if all goes well, one will develop normally. More than one is used to guard against some not implanting successfully.

A major cause of infertility is blocked oviducts which therefore prevent ova and sperm meeting in natural circumstances. IVF has solved this problem in some cases, allowing both parents to contribute genetically to the offspring and almost all embryo development to take place inside the natural mother. IVF clinics are now common throughout the UK and despite their low success rate, at 10%, make a major contribution to providing otherwise childless couples with much wanted children. For those with other forms of infertility the technique is unsuitable.

embryo into the natural mother, it is transferred to a different female. The process whereby one woman carries a fertilized egg for another through to birth is known as **surrogacy**.

Surrogate motherhood, in-vitro fertilization and artificial insemination all raise complex legal and moral issues. Should the surrogate mother or sperm donor have any legal rights over the offspring they helped produce? To what extent should the natural mother be able to influence the behaviour of the surrogate mother during pregnancy – should she be able to insist on abstinence from smoking or drinking, both of which could damage the fetus? What details, if any, should a potential mother be entitled to know about the donor of the sperm to be used in artificial insemination? Should the excess embryos which result from in-vitro fertilization be used for the purposes of medical research? These are just a few of the issues which have been raised by recent scientific research into the causes of, and cures for, infertility.

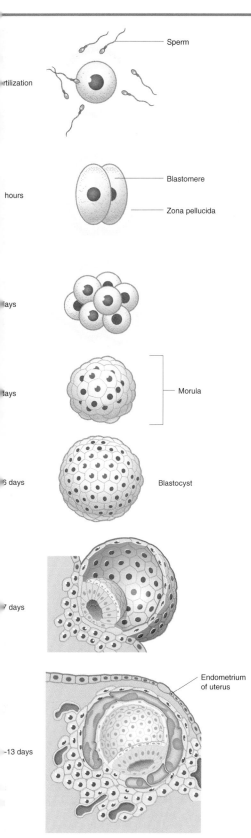

Sperm

rtilization

hours

Blastomere

Zona pellucida

lays

lays

Morula

6 days

Blastocyst

7 days

-13 days

Endometrium
of uterus

*g. 12.21 Embryo development*

### 12.7.6 Implantation

Following fertilization, the zygote divides (cleavage) mitotically until a hollow ball of cells, the **blastocyst**, is produced (Fig. 12.21). It takes 3 days to reach the uterus and a further 3–4 days to become implanted in the lining of the uterus. The outer layer of cells of the blastocyst, called the **trophoblast**, develops into the embryonic membranes, the **chorion** and the **amnion**. The chorion develops villi, which grow into the surrounding uterine tissue from which they absorb nutrients. These villi form part of the **placenta**, which is connected to the fetus by the **umbilical cord**. The amnion develops as a membrane around the fetus and encloses the amniotic fluid, a watery liquid which protects the fetus by cushioning it from physical damage. In badgers, mating and fertilization occur in midsummer and development takes place up to the blastocyst stage. However, the blastocyst does not become implanted until late winter or early spring, after which development proceeds normally. A similar process occurs in polar bears, allowing offspring to be weaned when food is plentiful, regardless of the time of fertilization. This is called **delayed implantation**.

### 12.7.7 The placenta

The chorionic villi develop about 14 days after fertilization and represent the beginning of the placenta. The placenta rapidly develops into a disc of tissue covering 20% of the uterus. The capillaries of the mother and fetus come into close contact without actually combining. (See Fig. 12.22.)

### 12.7.8 Functions of the placenta

**1.** The placenta allows exchange of materials between the mother and fetus without the two bloods mixing. This is necessary as the fetal blood may be different from that of the mother due to the influence of the father's genes. If incompatible bloods mix, they agglutinate (clot), causing blockage in vital organs such as the kidney, possibly resulting in death.

**2.** Oxygen, water, amino acids, glucose, essential minerals, etc. are transferred from maternal to fetal blood to nourish the developing fetus.

**3.** Carbon dioxide, urea and other wastes are transferred from fetal to maternal blood to allow their excretion by the mother and prevent harmful accumulation in the fetus.

**4.** The placenta allows certain maternal antibodies to pass into the fetus, providing the fetus with some immunity against disease. Such immunity is termed **passive natural immunity** as, while the antibodies are naturally produced, they are not formed by the fetus itself. The immunity only lasts for a few months after birth, although this period may be extended by antibodies provided in the mother's milk.

**5.** The placenta protects the fetus by preventing certain pathogens (disease-causing organisms) and their toxins from crossing it. This protection is by no means complete. Notable

243

# BIOLOGY AROUND US

## Screening in early pregnancy

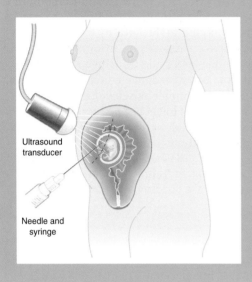

Ultrasound transducer

Needle and syringe

Screening is usually offered when a family has a history of an inherited disorder or when the mother is comparatively old and is therefore more likely to give birth to a child with Down's syndrome.

**Amniocentesis** is carried out from 10 weeks' gestation. A small quantity of amniotic fluid is taken through a hypodermic needle and the fetal cells contained in it are separated from the liquid by centrifugation. The cells are then cultured and their chromosomes examined.

**Chorionic villus sampling** is also carried out after 10 weeks' gestation. A sample of cells is taken from the chorion, the developing placenta, using a plastic catheter inserted through the vagina under ultrasound guidance. Preliminary results can be obtained within a day but the procedure is thought to increase the risk of miscarriage by about 4% (compared to a 1% increased risk with amniocentesis).

**Coelocentesis** is a new, relatively untried technique which involves the removal of cells from the coelomic cavity surrounding the amniotic sac. It can be carried out before 10 weeks' gestation and is thought to present less risk to the unborn child.

*The chorionic villi present a large surface area for the exchange of materials by diffusion across the chorionic membrane. In some mammals the maternal and fetal bloods flow in opposite directions. This counter-current flow leads to more efficient exchange as described in Section 20.2.4*

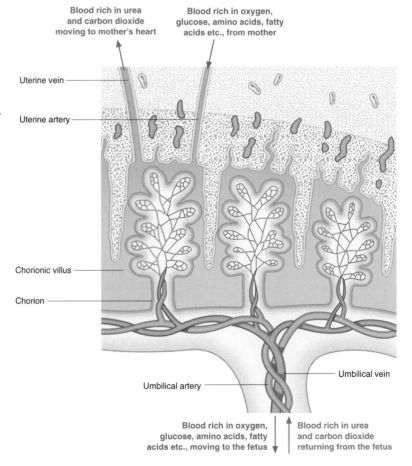

Blood rich in urea and carbon dioxide moving to mother's heart

Blood rich in oxygen, glucose, amino acids, fatty acids etc., from mother

Uterine vein

Uterine artery

Chorionic villus

Chorion

Umbilical vein

Umbilical artery

Blood rich in oxygen, glucose, amino acids, fatty acids etc., moving to the fetus

Blood rich in urea and carbon dioxide returning from the fetus

*Fig. 12.22 The mammalian placenta*

exceptions include toxins of the Rubella (German measles) virus which can cross the placenta causing physical and mental damage to the fetus, and the HIV virus which can also pass into the fetus.

**6.** In a similar way, the placenta acts as a barrier to the maternal hormones and other chemicals in the mother's blood which could adversely affect fetal development. Again, the protection is not complete and substances like nicotine, alcohol and heroin can all enter the fetus, causing lasting damage.

**7.** As the two blood systems are not directly connected, the placenta permits them to operate at different pressures without harm to mother or fetus.

**8.** As the pregnancy progresses, the placenta increasingly takes over the role of hormone production. In particular, it produces progesterone, which prevents ovulation and menstruation. It also secretes **human choriogonadotrophin** (HCG), a hormone whose presence in the urine of pregnant women is the basis of most pregnancy tests (see Biology Around Us, page 425).

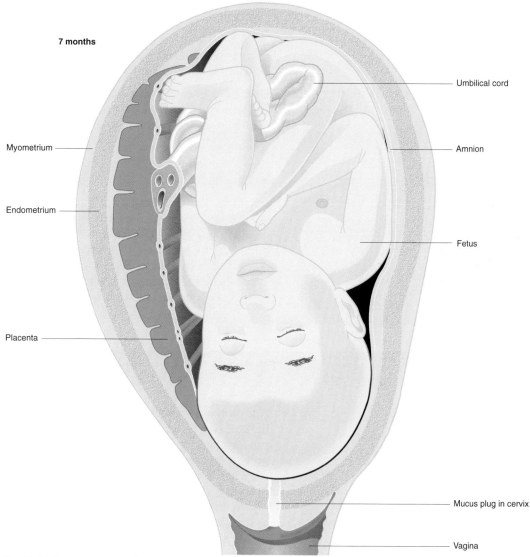

*Fig. 12.23 Fetus at 7 months*

# Drugs across the placenta

Drugs taken by a pregnant woman can cross the placenta if their molecules are small enough. The effect they have on the fetus depends on the nature of the drug, the dose taken and the stage of pregnancy. Obviously the best way to avoid damaging the unborn child is to avoid all drugs but this may not be possible if a serious condition needs treatment. The effects of a few legal and illegal drugs on the development of the fetus will be considered.

**Tetracyclines**: When given in early pregnancy these antibiotics may cause cataracts and bone abnormalities. Later on they are stored in the bones and also in the teeth where they cause yellow staining.

**Cytotoxic drugs**: These drugs are used in the treatment of cancers but they must be avoided during pregnancy because of their effect on dividing cells.

**Aspirin**: This rarely causes any harm but large doses towards the end of pregnancy interfere with the production of prostaglandins and thus delay the onset and progress of labour.

**Cannabis and LSD**: Both these drugs may cause growth retardation and LSD causes chromosome damage.

**Opiates**: Babies whose mothers are addicted to heroin become addicted in the uterus. They suffer withdrawal symptoms and growth retardation and may die of their addiction.

**Alcohol**: Alcohol abuse may lead to mid-term abortion and premature labour. Babies may be retarded both physically and mentally.

**Nicotine**: Smoke contains many substances which cross the placenta and damage the fetus. Even passive smoking causes an alteration in the heart rate and breathing pattern of the fetus and the constriction of blood vessels in the placenta leads to slower growth. Smoking leads to an increased risk of spontaneous abortion, congenital abnormalities, still birth and mental and physical retardation in later childhood.

# Abortion

Abortion is the premature termination of a pregnancy before the embryo/fetus is capable of surviving. It may be a natural process, perhaps the result of some genetic abnormality preventing normal development of the fetus, e.g. the absence of an X chromosome (see pages 191–192), or failure to implant properly. This is called **spontaneous abortion**. Abortion may also be brought on artificially by the use of suction or hormones. This is called **induced abortion**.

Abortion by suction takes place under general anaesthetic. The cervix is stretched open and the contents of the uterus are

## BIOLOGY AROUND US continued

# Abortion

sucked out through the vagina by machine. This is only feasible when the fetus/embryo is small as, even with stretching, the aperture of the cervix is small. The alternative is the introduction into the uterus of prostaglandins contained in a fluid. These cause dilation of the cervix and contraction of the uterus wall, and hence expulsion of the fetus/embryo.

In Britain, abortion is not available on demand: it is only permitted in certain circumstances and where two doctors agree. The circumstances are where continuing the pregnancy would cause greater damage to the woman's mental or physical health than if the pregnancy were terminated, or if there is a strong likelihood of severe handicap in the expected child. Abortion can also be legal if the two doctors agree that there is a risk to the health of the woman's existing children as a result of continuing the pregnancy.

Modern medical expertise has meant that premature babies can be kept alive at earlier stages of their development. As a result an amendment to the 1967 Abortion Act reduced the time limit for a legal termination from 28 weeks to 24 weeks.

Those in favour of abortion point out that prior to the 1967 Act almost 100 women a year died from having illegal 'back-street' abortions and many more were seriously injured; since the Act there have been few such deaths. They argue that there have always been abortions and always will be, and so it is better to make it safe and honest rather than potentially harmful and illegal. They also argue that the rights of the baby have to be weighed against those of the mother, who might otherwise suffer physical or psychological harm and who is, in any case, better suited than anyone to decide whether to have the child or not. It is each woman's right to decide her own fertility and as no method of contraception is foolproof, abortion will still be necessary. The pro-abortionists point out that the birth of a handicapped child can place an intolerable burden on the parents and may cause suffering to the child. Unwanted children, they feel, may well be neglected or even abandoned, and may create problems for society. Supporters of abortion say that in certain circumstances, e.g. rape resulting in pregnancy, abortion is the only practical and humane solution.

Arguments against abortion centre on the sanctity of life, which many opponents argue begins at conception. To destroy the embryo/fetus after this time they consider to be 'murder'. They point out that fewer than 10% of abortions are carried out for reasons of fetal handicap, the majority being for social reasons. In any case, new methods of detecting abnormalities (e.g. chorionic villus sampling) allow, in some cases, remedial measures to be undertaken while the fetus is still in the womb. Abortion, they contest, is the easy way out and more should be done to improve the quality of life rather than taking it away. Handicapped people can often lead happy, creative and fulfilling lives and any aborted fetus may have had the potential to be a great artist, scientist or world leader and hence of great value to mankind. When abortions go wrong they can leave physical and psychological scars.

## BIOLOGY AROUND US

## Infections across the placenta

The most significant infections which cross the placenta to affect the fetus are rubella and syphilis.

**Rubella**: If the rubella virus is contracted during the first 12 weeks of pregnancy, the risk of having a child with a congenital abnormality is between 5 and 12 times greater. Growth of the early fetal organs may be disorganized, leading to possible damage of the eyes, ears, heart and other organs.

**Syphilis**: The bacterium *Treponema pallida* which causes syphilis can only cross the placenta after the 20th week of pregnancy but it causes either death in the uterus or the birth of a child with congenital syphilis.

Babies are unable to manufacture **antibodies** in the uterus and for about 6 weeks after birth. Immunity to many diseases is transferred to them by the passage of the mother's antibodies across the placenta. However, the antibodies to tuberculosis and whooping cough cannot cross the placenta and young babies require protection against these two diseases.

## Did you know?

The sex of hatching sea turtles depends on their incubation temperature:

28°C – all male
30°C – equal numbers of male and female
32°C – all female

### 12.7.9 Birth (parturition)

During pregnancy the placenta continues to produce progesterone and small amounts of oestrogen. The amount of progesterone decreases during pregnancy while oestrogen increases. These changes help to trigger the onset of birth. As the end of the gestation period nears, the posterior lobe of the pituitary produces the hormone **oxytocin** which causes the uterus to contract. These contractions increase in force and frequency during labour.

The process of birth can be divided into three stages:

**1.** The dilation of the cervix, resulting in loss of the cervical plug ('the show') and the rupture of the embryonic membranes ('breaking of the waters').

**2.** The expulsion of the fetus.

**3.** The expulsion of the placenta ('afterbirth') which is eaten by most mammals.

### 12.7.10 Lactation

During pregnancy the hormones progesterone and oestrogen cause the development of lactiferous (milk) glands within the mammary glands. Following birth, the anterior lobe of the pituitary gland produces the hormone **prolactin** which causes the lactiferous glands to begin milk production. Suckling by the offspring causes the reflex expulsion of this milk from the nipple of the mammary glands. The first formed milk, called **colostrum**, is mildly laxative and helps the baby expel the bile which has accumulated in the intestines during fetal life. As well as essential nutrients, the milk contains antibodies which give some passive immunity to the newly born.

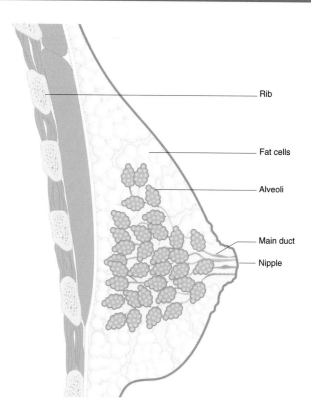

*Fig. 12.24  The human breast*

### 12.7.11 Parental care

Some organisms produce vast numbers of offspring, the cod (*Gadus gadus*), for example, may produce over one million eggs at a time. In such organisms there is little or no parental care and the majority of offspring fail to reach maturity, most being consumed by predators. In birds and mammals the tendency is to reduce the number of offspring but to expend much time and energy in caring for them in order to ensure a high survival rate. This is especially important in groups such as primates, where learning plays an important role in their development. Only through extended care of the young and close association with adults is there sufficient opportunity and time to acquire through learning the necessary skills for adult life. The onset of sexual maturity is often delayed in these species to allow time for learning to take place.

In mammals, the provision of milk is the most obvious example of parental care. As the offspring develop they are gradually introduced to other, more solid types of food, a process called weaning. In many animals the parents singly, or in pairs, collect the appropriate food for the offspring. This food may be partly digested, e.g. regurgitated from the crop in birds.

Many animals provide a nest in which to raise their young. Here the offspring may be raised in the relative safety of a warm, dry environment remote from predators.

# BIOLOGY AROUND US

## Embryo experimentation and its implications

Embryos developed from in-vitro fertilization can be used to achieve a successful pregnancy. However, the process usually produces more embryos than are needed for implantation and it is these surplus embryos which some scientists wish to use for research designed to improve our knowledge, for example about disease. Opponents argue that such research is improper because it leads to the death of the embryos, which they believe have a similar status to any fully developed human being. They argue that human life commences when a sperm fertilizes an egg, and to attempt to distinguish any later point in development where it becomes human is artificial. Those supporting embryo research contest that there are many benefits from the work, including improving ways of detecting genetic disorders and in the treatment of infertility. They believe that the alleviation of suffering that could follow is justification enough for research on human embryos.

In 1982 the Government set up a committee of inquiry under the now Baroness Warnock to 'consider recent and potential developments in medicine and science related to human fertilization and embryology'. One initial task was to define what is meant by an embryo. The committee chose to regard the 6 weeks immediately following fertilization as the embryonic stage. Others prefer to use the first 8 weeks after fertilization as their definition, with the first 2 weeks being regarded as the 'pro-embryo' stage. The committee recommended that there should be a legal time limit after which it would be a criminal offence to use an embryo for research purposes. The Government proposed this limit should be the point at which a feature called 'the primitive streak' appeared or 14 days after fertilization, whichever is earlier. Embryo research is now permitted in Britain only under licence from the Statutory Licensing Authority.

The committee also addressed concerns over the possible developments in human embryo research such as cloning, manipulation of the genetic make-up of an embryo, and keeping of embryos for progressively longer periods in the laboratory. As a result, the Government has legislated against such activities unless Parliament specifically makes exceptions, should this be felt appropriate in the future. The transfer of human embryos into the uterus of other species is also prohibited, as is any process which involves fusing human embryo cells with those of a different species to produce a hybrid organism (chimera).

# 12.8 Growth

## PROJECT

Investigations on fellow students, for example:

(a) Do finger and toe nails grow at the same rate?

(b) Is there any correlation between foot-size and height?

(c) Is there any difference in the lengths of the fingers of the right and left hands?

(d) Does red hair grow more quickly than black/blond hair?

(e) How does the growth of boys and girls at various ages differ?

(f) Do we get smaller as the day progresses?

The growth in size of an individual cell is limited by the distance over which the nucleus can exert its control. For this reason, when single-celled organisms reach a maximum size they divide to give two separate individuals. In order to attain greater size, organisms become multicellular. While being large and multicellular can present some problems, these are easily outweighed by the advantages conferred:

1. Cells may become differentiated in order to perform a particular function.

2. Specialized cells performing one particular function lead to greater efficiency.

3. It is possible to store more materials and so be better able to withstand periods when these are scarce.

4. If some cells are damaged, enough may still remain to carry out the repair.

5. Some processes require a range of conditions, e.g. digestion often has an acid and an alkaline phase. It is easier to separate regions of opposing conditions in a multicellular organism than it is in a single cell.

6. Larger organisms may have a competitive advantage, e.g. large plants compete better for light than small ones.

7. Large size may provide some protection from predators because the organisms are simply too large to ingest.

### 12.8.1 Measurement of growth

Growth is estimated by measuring some parameter (variable) over a period of time. The parameter chosen depends upon the organism whose growth is to be measured. It may be appropriate to measure the weight of a mouse; but this method would be impractical for an oak tree. Mass and length are most often used, but these may be misleading. A bush for example, while not increasing in height, may continue to grow in size by spreading sideways. Area or volume give a more accurate indication of growth but are often impractical to measure. The measurement of mass has its problems. If an organism takes in a large amount of water its mass may increase markedly, and yet such a temporary increase could not be considered as growth. For this reason two types of mass are recognized:

1. **Fresh mass** – This is the mass of the organism under normal conditions. It is easy to measure and doing so involves no damage to the organism. It may, however, be inaccurate due to temporary fluctuations in water content.

2. **Dry mass** – This involves removing all water by drying, before weighing. It is difficult to carry out and permanently destroys the organisms involved, but does give an accurate measure of growth.

It is sometimes possible to measure one part of an organism, e.g the girth of a tree; the length of the tail of a rat. Provided this part grows in proportion to the complete organism, increases in its size will reflect those of the individual as a whole. Groups of organisms are sometimes used rather than an individual. For instance, if the growth of peas was measured using dry mass, it would be necessary to grow a large population of the plants. Growth could be estimated by removing, say, 20 plants every day, drying and weighing them. Provided each sample is large enough to average out individual differences in growth, a good estimate of the growth rate can be found. The growth of a population of yeast can be measured by counting the number of cells in a known, and very small, volume of the medium in which the yeast is growing.

### 12.8.2 Growth patterns

When any parameter of growth is measured against set interval of time, **a growth curve** is produced. For many populations, organisms or organs, this curve is S-shaped and is called a **sigmoid curve** (Fig. 12.25). It represents slow growth at first, because there are so few cells initially that even when they are dividing rapidly the actual increase in size is small.

As the number of cells becomes greater the size increases more quickly because there are more cells carrying out division There is a limit to this rapid phase of growth. This limit may be

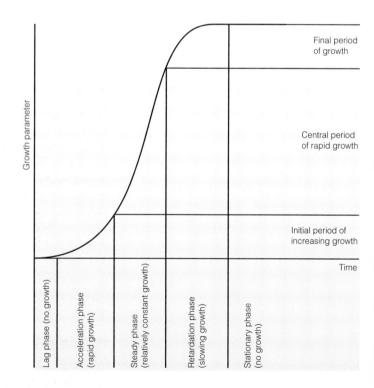

*Fig. 12.25 The sigmoid growth curve*

imposed by the genotype of the individual, which specifies a certain maximum size, or any external factors, such as shortage of food. Whatever the cause, the growth rate decreases until it ceases altogether. At this point cells are still dividing, but only at a rate which replaces those which have died. The size of the organism therefore remains constant.

While the sigmoid curve forms the basis of most growth curves, it may be modified in certain circumstances. In humans, for example, there are two phases of rapid growth; one during the early years of life, the other during adolescence. Between these two phases there is a period of relatively slow growth. The growth curve therefore resembles two sigmoid curves, one on top of the other (Fig. 12.26).

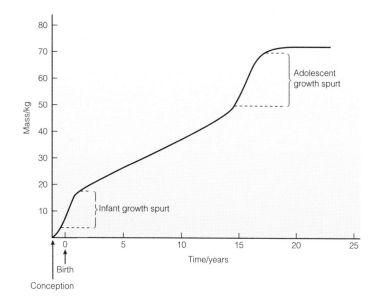

Fig. 12.26 Human growth curve

In annual plants, the growth curve is typically sigmoid, except there may be an initial decrease in mass during the early stages of germination (Fig. 12.27). This occurs as the food reserves in the seed are respired in order to produce the roots and leaves. Once the leaves begin to photosynthesize, growth proceeds in a sigmoid fashion. However, with the liberation of fruits and seeds at the end of the growing period, the mass of the plant may decrease prior to its death. When there is a natural limit on growth, as in annual plants, they are said to show **limited growth**. In these cases the growth curve flattens out, or even decreases prior to the organism's death.

In perennial plants, the growth pattern is an annual series of sigmoid curves (Fig. 12.28). During spring, when the temperature and light intensity are relatively low, there is less photosynthesis, and growth is slow. In summer, with higher temperatures and more light, the rate of photosynthesis increases and growth is rapid. The falling temperatures and lower light intensities of autumn again reduce the rate of photosynthesis and hence growth. During winter in temperate regions there is no growth in deciduous plants and so the curve flattens out. The following

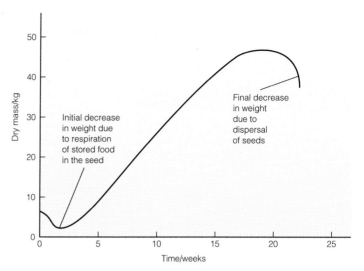

*Fig. 12.27 Annual plant growth curve, e.g. Pea plant (Pisum sativum*

*The annual growth follows a normal sigmoid curve. Variations occur from one year to the next according to environmental conditions. In a cold, dry year for example there will be less growth than in a mild, wet year.*

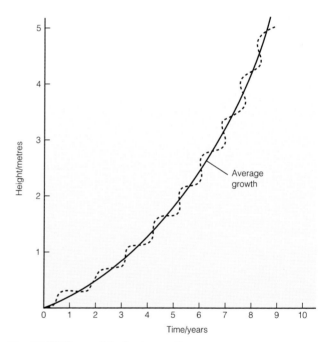

*Fig. 12.28 Perennial plant growth curve*

spring the process is repeated. The overall shape of these annual sigmoid curves is itself sigmoid, except that many perennial plants show **unlimited growth**, i.e. they grow continuously throughout their lives, and the curve therefore never flattens out.

A very different growth curve is exhibited by many arthropods. As their exoskeleton is incapable of expansion, they have to moult periodically during growth. Before a new exoskeleton has fully hardened it is capable of some expansion. During this time the insect may take up water in order to expand the exoskeleton as much as possible. This means that once it has hardened there is still some room for growth. Measuring the fresh mass as the growth parameter therefore gives the unusual growth pattern shown in Fig. 12.29. This type of growth is called **intermittent growth**. If dry mass is measured, a normal sigmoid curve is obtained.

Certain organs of an individual grow at the same rate as the organism as a whole. This is called **isometric growth**. Other organs grow at a different rate from the entire organism. This is called **allometric growth**. The leaves of most plants exhibit isometric growth and their growth curve is typically sigmoid (Fig. 12.30).

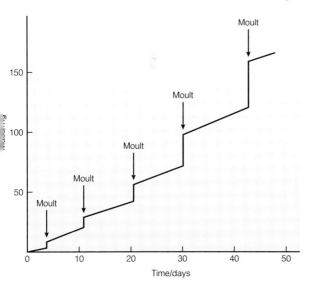

*ig. 12.29 Arthropod growth curve, e.g. Waterboatman Notonecta glauca)*

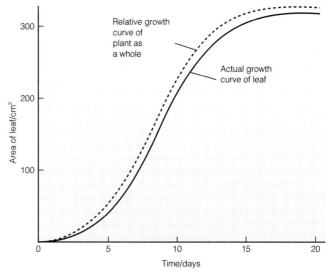

*Fig. 12.30 Isometric growth as shown by a cucumber leaf*

In animals, organs often exhibit allometric growth. Lymph tissue, which produces white blood cells to fight infection, grows rapidly in early life when the risk of disease is greater as immunity has not yet been acquired. By adult life the mass of lymph tissues is less than half of what it was in early adolescence. The reproductive organs grow very little in early life but develop rapidly with the onset of sexual maturity at puberty. Fig. 12.31 illustrates allometric growth in some human organs.

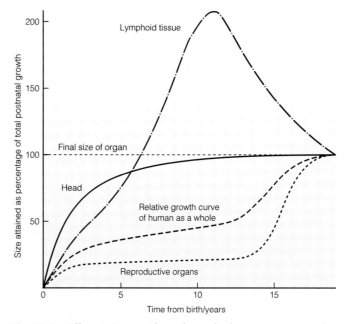

*Fig. 12.31 Allometric growth as shown by human organs and tissues*

### 12.8.3 Rate of growth

The actual growth of an organism is the cumulative increase in size over a period of time. A small annual plant, for example, might grow as shown in Fig. 12.32(a), in which case a typical sigmoid growth curve results. The rate of growth is a measure o size increase over a series of equal time intervals. If instead of measuring the actual height of the plant we measure the increas in height over each 3-day period, a set of results like that shown in Fig. 12.32(b) is obtained. These produce a bell-shaped graph a shown.

## PROJECT

A variety of investigations can be carried out, for example:

(a) Determine if the frequency of light has any effect on the growth of the coleoptile of oat seedlings.
(b) Is seedling growth affected by compaction of the soil?
(c) The effect of fertilizers on the growth of duckweed (*Lemna* spp.).
(d) Yield of vegetables in weeded and non-weeded plots.
(e) The number of roots formed on different angled cuts on stems of busy lizzie (*Impatiens balsamina*), etc.

| Time/ days | Height/ mm |
|---|---|
| 0 | 0 |
| 3 | 40 |
| 6 | 100 |
| 9 | 350 |
| 12 | 900 |
| 15 | 1600 |
| 18 | 2150 |
| 21 | 2400 |
| 24 | 2460 |
| 27 | 2500 |
| 30 | 2500 |

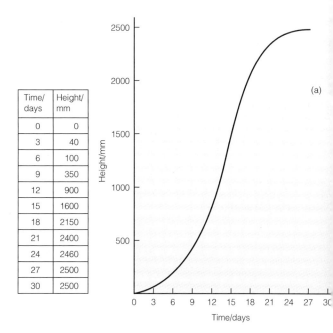

| Time/days interval | Height at start of time interval | Height at end of time interval | Height increase during the time interval |
|---|---|---|---|
| 0–3 | 0 | 40 | 40 |
| 3–6 | 40 | 100 | 60 |
| 6–9 | 100 | 350 | 250 |
| 9–12 | 350 | 900 | 550 |
| 12–15 | 900 | 1600 | 700 |
| 15–18 | 1600 | 2150 | 550 |
| 18–21 | 2150 | 2400 | 250 |
| 21–24 | 2400 | 2460 | 60 |
| 24–27 | 2460 | 2500 | 40 |
| 27–30 | 2500 | 2500 | 0 |

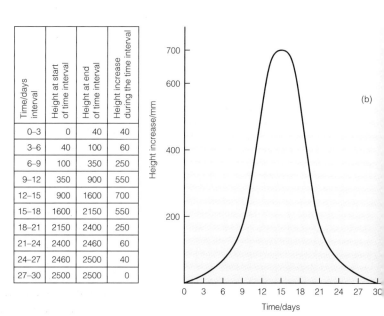

*Fig. 12.32 Comparison of (a) actual growth curve and (b) rate of growth curve*

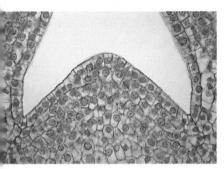

apical meristem of *Coleus*. (LS)

### 12.8.4 Meristems

The presence of a semi-rigid cell wall around plant cells effectively restricts their ability to divide and grow. For this reason, unlike animals, plants retain groups of immature cells which form the only actively growing tissues. These tissues are called **meristems**. Three types of meristems are generally recognized:

1. **Apical meristems** – These are found at the tips of roots and shoots and are responsible for primary growth of the plant. They increase its length.

2. **Lateral meristems** – These are found in a cylinder towards the outside of stems and roots. They are responsible for secondary growth and cause an increase in girth.

3. **Intercalary meristems** – These are found at the nodes in monocotyledonous plants. They allow an increase in length in positions other than the tip.

### 12.8.5 Growth and metamorphosis in insects

During their life cycles insects undergo **metamorphosis**. This is the series of changes which take place between larval and adult forms.

1. **Hemimetabolous (incomplete metamorphosis)** – The eggs hatch into **nymphs** which clearly resemble the adults except that they are smaller, lack wings and are sexually immature. There are a number of nymphal stages between which moulting occurs. Examples of hemimetabolous insects include locusts and cockroaches.

2. **Holometabolous (complete metamorphosis)** – The eggs hatch into **larvae** which differ considerably from the adults. Each larva undergoes a series of moults until it changes its appearance and becomes a dormant stage known as a **pupa**. After much reorganization of the tissues within the pupa, the adult **(imago)** emerges. Examples of holometabolous insects include moths, butterflies and flies.

Why have a larval form, such as a caterpillar, which is markedly different from an adult, such as a butterfly? One explanation is that it allows the species to exploit different food sources. Butterflies, for example, feed on nectar as adults. This is only plentiful in summer when flowers have developed, and even then the quantity in each flower is very small. If an animal is to complete its life cycle in 1 year, it needs to start as early as possible in the spring. At this time, flowers are likely to be in short supply and the total nectar available could not support the growth of offspring. In any case, nectar is almost exclusively carbohydrate and lacks the protein so essential to animal growth. The caterpillars (larvae) of butterflies are adapted to feed on foliage. This is plentiful in spring and contains some protein. Growth occurs rapidly and the caterpillar can pupate in time for adults to emerge in summer, when nectar is abundant. The mouthparts of the two stages are different as each is adapted to obtain a different food. The mandibles of the caterpillar are suited to biting the edges of leaves, while the long tube-like

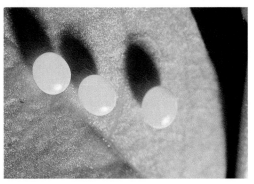

Eggs

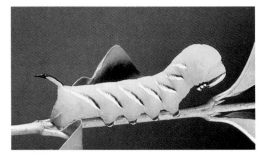

Larva (caterpillar)

Pupa in soil

Adult

Stages of development of privet hawk moth

proboscis of the butterfly is perfectly adapted to reaching deep down into flowers in order to suck up the liquid nectar. In the same way, the gut enzymes vary in the two stages, each being suited to its diet. Caterpillars produce protease, lipase, amylase, sucrase and maltase; butterflies produce only sucrase. The adult butterfly has wings, allowing it to disperse the species widely and to find a suitable mate. The further it disperses, the less likelihood there is of inbreeding and so its potential for evolutionary change is increased. Only the adult is capable of reproduction – the caterpillar lacking any sexual organs.

# 12.9    Questions

. The placenta forms a barrier between maternal and
etal blood.

   *(a)* State two reasons why a barrier between
maternal and fetal blood is necessary. *(2 marks)*

ig. 1 shows a diagram of the human placenta. Fig. 2
hows detail of the area on Fig. 1 marked **X**.

g. 1

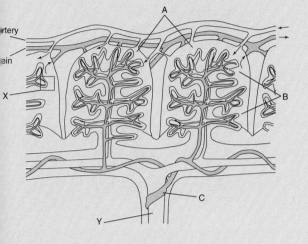

g. 2

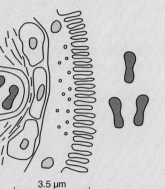

   *(b)*   (i)  Name the structures labelled A to D.
                            *(2 marks)*
         (ii)  On Fig. 1, what is the direction of blood
flow in C and Y?         *(1 mark)*

he table shows the rates of oxygen transfer across
he placenta just before birth and in the adult lung.

| | Rate of oxygen transfer/cm³min⁻¹ |
|---|---|
| Human placenta just before birth | 16 |
| Adult lung | 240 |

*(c)* Explain, in terms of **placental structure**,
why the rate of gas exchange in the
placenta is less than that in the adult lung.
                                  *(2 marks)*

*(d)* With reference to Figs 1 and 2 , explain how
the structure of the placenta allows efficient
transfer of substances between maternal and
fetal blood.            *(5 marks)*

Experiments show that the placenta metabolizes
about 60% of the glucose it absorbs from maternal
blood.

*(e)* Explain why the placenta metabolizes so
much glucose.            *(3 marks)*
                                *(Total 15 marks)*

*UCLES June 1998, Paper 1,
Option 3 (Social Biology), No. 1.*

**2.** The graph shows how the concentration of
progesterone changes during a normal menstrual
cycle.

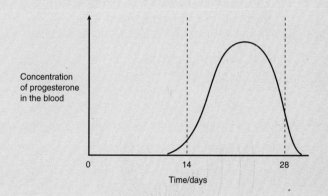

*(a)* Draw a line on the graph to show the
concentration of progesterone if pregnancy
occurs.                 *(1 mark)*
*(b)* Early in pregnancy a hormone, HCG, is
produced. Describe the role of this hormone.
                                  *(2 marks)*
*(c)* What causes some cells to respond to
progesterone whilst others do not?   *(2 marks)*
                                *(Total 5 marks)*

*NEAB June 1998, Paper BY10, No. 6*

259

**3.** The diagram below shows a germinating pollen grain and a mature ovule from a flower of Papilionaceae. Some nuclei have been labelled.

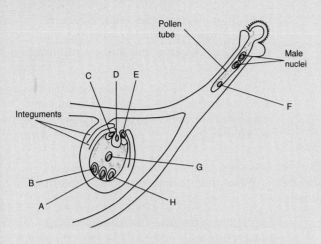

(a) Describe how pollination usually occurs in the Papillionaceae. (*2 marks*)

(b) Give the letter of the nucleus which fuses with a male nucleus to form
  (i) the zygote;
  (ii) the endosperm. (*2 marks*)

(c) Describe one mechanism which prevents self-fertilisation in flowering plants. (*2 marks*)
(*Total 6 marks*)

*Edexcel June 1998, Paper B3, No. 1*

**4.** (a) Describe the similarities and differences between male and female gametes (*3 marks*)

(b) The diagram shows a pollen tube entering the ovule of a flowering plant.

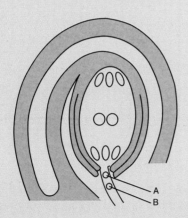

Explain why gametes **A** and **B** are genetically identical to each other but differ from other male gametes produced by this plant.
(*6 marks*)

(c) (i) Explain how a developing plant embryo gains its nutrients from the food reserve in the seed. (*4 marks*)

(ii) Explain **two** ways in which the placenta is adapted to provide a developing mammalian fetus with its nutrients.
(*4 marks*)
(*Quality of language 3 marks*)
(*Total 20 marks*)

*AEB June 1998, Paper 4, No. ?*

**5.** The diagram below shows some of the events which take place in the ovary and oviduct (Fallopian tube) around the time of fertilization.

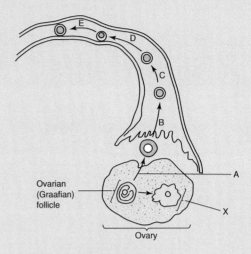

(a) Name the following.
  (i) The process labelled A. (*1 mark*)
  (ii) The type of nuclear division taking place at D and E. (*1 mark*)
  (iii) The structure labelled X. (*1 mark*)
  (iv) **One** hormone produced by structure X (*1 mark*)

(b) On the diagram, use the letter F to label the region where fertilization took place. (*1 mark*)
(*Total 5 marks*)

*Edexcel June 1998, Paper HB3, No. ?*

**6.** Read through the following passage on flowering plant reproduction then copy and complete the account using the most appropriate word or words.

The transfer of pollen grains from the ...................

of a flower on one plant to the ..................... of a

flower on another plant of the same species is known

as ..................... pollination. The pollen grains may

be carried from one plant to another by ...................

or ..................... . This type of pollination favours

..................... and flowers may have special

features to encourage it. Species in which there are

separate male and female plants are called

.................. . Where male and female reproductive structures are found in the same flower, they may mature at different times. In the condition known as .................... , the male reproductive structures ripen before the female.

*(Total 8 marks)*

*ULEAC June 1995, Paper 3, No. 2*

. Since seeds may not be sold for many months after they are harvested and packaged, seedsmen are required to stamp a 'sow by' date on their packets of seeds. Some seeds, such as beans, and peas, are simply enclosed in a paper envelope, but are often dusted with fungicide. Smaller seeds, such as carrots, parsley and many flower seeds are enclosed in a sealed, foiled, vacuum packed inner packet.

*(a)* Give biological reasons **related to germination** for each of the following procedures.
  (i) Dusting pea or bean seeds with fungicide before packing. *(1 mark)*
  (ii) Sealing small seeds in an inner packet. *(1 mark)*
  (iii) Printing a 'sow by' date on the packet. *(1 mark)*

*(b)* Some packets carry the instruction to place the seeds in a cold environment for a specified number of days or weeks before sowing them. Unless this is done, seeds which are otherwise viable will fail to germinate, even if placed in otherwise ideal conditions. Explain the biological basis of this instruction. *(2 marks)*

*(Total 5 marks)*

*Oxford June 1997, Paper 44, No. 4*

. The graph shows the changes in dry mass of a whole barley grain and of its endosperm and embryo during germination and the subsequent period of growth.

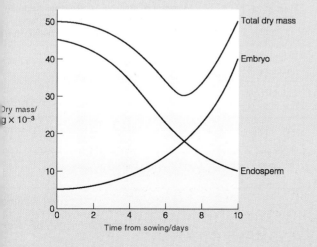

*(a)* Give **one** advantage and **one** disadvantage of using dry mass in this investigation. *(2 marks)*

*(b)* In terms of the events occurring within the grain, explain the change in total dry mass between:
  (i) days 0 and 6; *(2 marks)*
  (ii) days 7 and 10. *(2 marks)*

*(Total 6 marks)*

*AEB Summer 1994, Common Paper 1, No. 12*

**9.** The diagram shows the life cycle of a flowering plant.

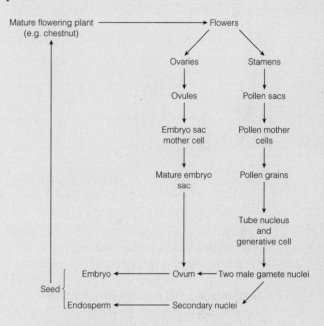

*(a)* Which stage(s) in the life cycle are the:
  (i) sporophyte? *(1 mark)*
  (ii) gametophytes? *(2 marks)*
  (iii) spores? *(3 marks)*

*(b)* How does this life cycle show alternation of generations? *(2 marks)*

*(c)* Indicate on the diagram, with the letter **M**, at which points meiosis occurs. *(2 marks)*

*(d)* In this life cycle there is said to be 'double fertilization'. What is meant by **double fertilization**? *(2 marks)*

*(e)* Name **two** organisms which exhibit alternation of generations in which the gametophyte generation is dominant. *(2 marks)*

*(Total 14 marks)*

*Oxford & Cambridge June 1997, Unit B5, No. 1*

**10.** *(a)* Make a fully labelled diagram to show the structure of a **named** insect-pollinated flower in longitudinal section. Include in your diagram the structure of the ovary in detail.

On your diagram indicate where **fertilization** takes place, by means of a label line and the letter 'F'. (7 *marks*)

(b) The pollen tube contains two haploid nuclei which enter the embryo sac. State what each nucleus fuses with and name the structure which results in each case. (4 *marks*)

(*Total 11 marks*)

*Oxford June 1997, Paper 44, No. 2*

**11.** Red campion has two distinct types of flower. All the flowers on a particular plant are of the same type.

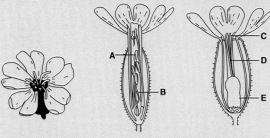

View of flower from above

Half-flower drawings of the two different flower types

(a) Give the letter of the part of the flower:
　(i) where fertilization takes place; (1 *mark*)
　(ii) which might contain the highest number of cells produced by meiosis. (1 *mark*)

(b) Give **one** piece of evidence from these drawings which suggests that:
　(i) red campion is a member of the Dicotyledones; (1 *mark*)
　(ii) cross-pollination is essential in this species. (1 *mark*)

(*Total 4 marks*)

*AEB Winter 1995, Paper 1, No. 6*

**12.** The diagram shows the process of sperm formation in a mammalian testis.

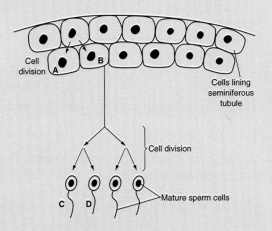

Cell division A B

Cells lining seminiferous tubule

Cell division

Mature sperm cells

C D

(a) Explain why cells **A** and **B** are genetically identical. (1 *mark*)

(b) Describe **two** ways in which cell division leads to cells **C** and **D** being genetically different. (2 *marks*)

(c) Briefly describe how the process of gamete formation in an ovary leads to a smaller number of larger gametes being produced in a female mammal. (1 *mark*)

(d) Both the testis and the ovary contain a large number of blood vessels. Other than cell division, what specific function of these organs is associated with these blood vessels? (1 *mark*)

(*Total 5 marks*)

*AEB Summer 1997, Paper 1, No. 1*

**13.** The table below refers to the hormones involved in human reproduction. Copy and complete the table by writing the appropriate words in the empty boxes.

| Hormone | Role |
| --- | --- |
|  | Repair of endometrium |
| Prolactin |  |
|  | Stimulates ovulation |
| Progesterone |  |
| Follicle stimulating hormone |  |

(*Total 5 marks*)

*ULEAC June 1995, Paper 3, No.*

**14.** The table below refers to four hormones associated with the human menstrual cycle. Copy and complete the table. If the statement is correct, place a tick (✓) in the appropriate box and if the statement is incorrect place a cross (✗) in the appropriate box.

| Hormone | Secreted by ovaries | Reaches highest level in blood before ovulation |
| --- | --- | --- |
| Follicle stimulating hormone (FSH) |  |  |
| Luteinizing hormone (LH) |  |  |
| Oestrogen |  |  |
| Progesterone |  |  |

(*Total 4 marks*)

*Edexcel June 1997, B3, No.*

**5.** In the process of sperm formation in a mammalian testis, cells divide by mitosis and by meiosis.

  (a) Explain the importance of mitosis in the process of sperm formation. *(2 marks)*

  (b) The diagram shows a mature mammalian sperm cell.

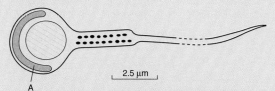

2.5 μm

A

   Describe the part played by structure **A** in the processes leading to fertilization. *(2 marks)*

  (c) Explain **one** advantage of internal fertilization to a terrestrial mammal. *(2 marks)*

*(Total 6 marks)*

*AEB Summer 1996, Paper 1, No. 6*

**6.      When the Pill gets under your skin**

When news of a new contraceptive method reached British women in 1993, family planning organizations were flooded with enquiries. The contraceptive is an implant called Norplant. Not everyone, however, is thrilled by Norplant. Organizations around the world are concerned that it might be used as a method of social control.

Norplant delivers in a new way. It consists of six capsules, each 34 mm long. Each capsule contains 38 mg of a synthetic progesterone hormone. This hormone thickens the mucus produced by the cervix (neck) of the uterus. It also inhibits the production of LH (luteinizing hormone).

A health worker inserts the contraceptive capsules through an incision on the inside of the upper arm and they remain under the skin for 5 years, steadily releasing progesterone into the bloodstream.

Adapted from an article in the *New Scientist*.

  (a) Suggest how the thickening of the mucus produced by the neck of the uterus might help to prevent conception. *(1 mark)*

  (b)  (i) Describe the role of LH in the menstrual cycle and then explain how the inhibition of LH production prevents conception. *(5 marks)*

      (ii) Hormone levels are often affected by negative feedback processes. Explain as fully as you can what is meant by negative feedback. *(2 marks)*

  (c) Suggest and explain the advantages and disadvantages of using Norplant as a contraceptive. *(4 marks)*

*(Total 12 marks)*

*NEAB February 1995, BY1, No. 8*

Power stations produce energy in many different forms. Some of it is wasted in the form of steam (opposite)

# Part III

## ENERGETICS

# 13 Energy and organisms

Energy is defined as the 'capacity to do work'. It exists in a number of different forms: heat, light, electrical, magnetic, chemical, atomic, mechanical and sound. The laws which apply to energy conversions are the **laws of thermodynamics**.

## 13.1 First law of thermodynamics

This states: **energy cannot be created or destroyed but may be converted from one form into another**. Energy may also be stored. Water in a lake high up on a mountain is an example of stored energy. The energy it possesses is called **potential energy**. If the water is released from the lake it begins to flow downhill, and the energy of its motion is called **kinetic energy**. The stream of moving water may be used to drive a turbine which produces electricity (hydroelectric power). The kinetic energy is thus converted to electricity. This electricity may in turn be converted into light (light bulb), heat (electric fire/cooker), sound (CD or cassette player) etc. During these changes not all the energy is converted into its intended form; some is lost as heat. By 'lost' we mean the energy is no longer available to do useful work because it is distributed evenly. Energy which is available to do work under conditions of constant temperature and pressure is called **free energy**. Reactions which liberate energy are termed **exothermic**, those which absorb free energy are termed **endothermic**.

## 13.2 Second law of thermodynamics

This states: **all natural processes tend to proceed in a direction which increases the randomness or disorder of a system**. The degree of randomness is called **entropy**. A highly ordered system has low entropy whereas a disordered one, with its high degree of randomness, has high entropy. Entropy and free energy are inversely related. Systems with high entropy have little free energy, those with low entropy have more free energy. The ability of living systems to maintain low entropy is what distinguishes them from non-living systems. The fact that living systems can decrease their entropy does not mean that they fail to obey the second law of thermodynamics. The reason that they are able to reduce their entropy is that they take in useful energy from their surroundings and release it in a less useful form. While the organism's entropy decreases, that of its surroundings increases to an even greater extent. The organism and its environment represent one system, the total entropy of which increases. The second law of thermodynamics is therefore not violated.

## 13.3 Energy and life

There are three stages to the flow of energy through living systems:

**1.** The conversion of the sun's light energy to chemical energy by plants during photosynthesis.

**2.** The conversion of the chemical energy from photosynthesis into ATP – the form in which cells can utilize it.

**3.** The utilization of ATP by cells in order to perform useful work.

The chemical reactions which occur within organisms are collectively known as **metabolism**. They are of two types:

**1.** The build-up of complex compounds from simple ones. These synthetic reactions are collectively known as **anabolism**.

**2.** The breakdown of complex compounds into simple ones. Such reactions are collectively known as **catabolism**.

A typical chemical reaction may be represented as:

$$A \rightarrow B + C$$

In this case A represents the **substrate** and B and C are the **products**. If the entropy of C and B is greater than A then the reaction will proceed naturally in the direction shown. A reaction which involves an increase in entropy is said to be **spontaneous**. The free energy of the products is less than that of the substrate. The word spontaneous could be misleading because the reaction is not instantaneous. Before any chemical reaction can proceed it must initially be activated, i.e. its energy must be increased. The energy required is called the **activation energy**. Once provided, the activation energy allows the products to be formed with a consequent loss of free energy and increase in entropy (Fig. 13.1). Chemical reactions are reversible and therefore C and B can be synthesized into A. Such a reaction is not, however, spontaneous and requires an external source of energy if it is to proceed. Most biological processes are in fact a cycle of reversible reactions. Photosynthesis and respiration, for example, are basically the same reaction going in opposite directions.

$$\text{Energy} + 6CO_2 + 6H_2O \underset{\text{respiration}}{\overset{\text{photosynthesis}}{\rightleftharpoons}} C_6H_{12}O_6 + 6O_2$$

As there is inevitably some loss of free energy in the form of heat each time the reaction is reversed, the process cannot

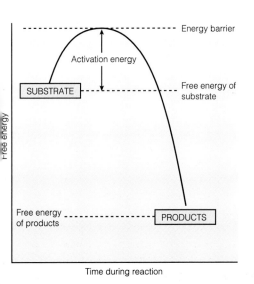

Fig. 13.1 Concept of activation energy

Dense jungle in Hawaii

continue without a substantial input of energy from outside the organisms. The ultimate source of this energy is the light radiation of the sun. The way in which organisms obtain their energy for metabolic and other processes is probably more important in determining their design than any other single factor. The fundamental differences between plants and animals are a result of their modes of nutrition.

Plants obtain their energy from the sun and use it to combine carbon dioxide and water in the synthesis of organic molecules. As the raw materials are readily available almost everywhere, there is no necessity for plants to move to obtain their nutrients. Indeed, in order to obtain sufficient light, plants need to have a large surface area. They therefore need to be as large as possible in order to compete with other plants for light. For this reason many plants are large. Locomotion for these plants would not only be difficult and slow, it would also be very energy-consuming. Plants therefore do not exhibit locomotion.

Animals obtain their energy from complex organic compounds. These occur in other organisms which must be sought. Most animals therefore exhibit locomotion in order to obtain their food. To help animals move from place to place they have developed a wide range of locomotory mechanisms. They are therefore more complex, and variable, in their design than plants. In carrying out locomotion, animals require a complex nervous system to coordinate their actions and a range of sense organs to help them to manoeuvre and to locate food.

Being sessile, plants do not require nervous systems and sense organs. Having a large surface area to obtain light energy means that plants have no need for separate specialized surfaces for obtaining respiratory gas. Any additional oxygen needed, over and above that produced in photosynthesis, can be obtained by diffusion through the leaves and roots which already provide a substantial surface area. Animals, by contrast, being compact to assist locomotion, require specialized respiratory surfaces with a large surface area to compensate for their small external area.

Even in reproduction, the differences between plants and animals can be related to the means by which they obtain energy. As their method of nutrition favours being stationary, plants have to use an external agent to transfer the male gametes from one individual to another during sexual reproduction. Insects and wind are the main agents of pollination. Animals, being capable of locomotion, utilize it in finding a mate and therefore male gametes are either introduced directly into the females, as in terrestrial organisms, or released in the vicinity of the female, as in some aquatic ones. In either case, male and female are in close proximity.

In this section of the book, we shall look at how energy is obtained and utilized by organisms.

# 14 Autotrophic nutrition (photosynthesis)

In Chapter 13 we saw that living systems differ from non-living ones in their ability to replace lost energy from the environment and so maintain themselves in an ordered condition (low entropy). Photosynthesis is the means by which this energy is initially obtained by living systems. All life is directly or indirectly dependent on this most fundamental process in living organisms. It provides part of the air we breathe, the food we eat and the fossil fuels we burn.

**Autotrophic** (*auto* – 'self'; *trophic* – 'feeding') organisms use an inorganic form of carbon, such as carbon dioxide, to make up complex organic compounds. These complex compounds are more ordered and so possess more energy. In autotrophs this energy is provided from two sources: light and chemicals. The processes involved are termed photosynthesis and chemosynthesis respectively.

Photosynthesis is much the more common of the two processes. It is principally important because:

**1.** It is the means by which the sun's energy is captured by plants for use by all organisms.

**2.** It provides a source of complex organic molecules for heterotrophic organisms.

**3.** It releases oxygen for use by aerobic organisms.

AUTOTROPHIC NUTRITION

light energy          chemical energy

PHOTOSYNTHESIS          CHEMOSYNTHESIS
All green plants          Certain bacteria

## 14.1    Leaf structure

The leaf is the main photosynthetic structure of a plant, although stems, sepals and other parts may also photosynthesize. The leaf is adapted to bring together the three raw materials, water, carbon dioxide and light, and to remove the products oxygen and glucose. The structure of a leaf is shown in Fig. 14.1.

Considering that all leaves carry out the same process, it is perhaps surprising that they show such a wide range of form. This range of form is often the consequence of different environmental conditions which have nothing directly to do with photosynthesis. In dry areas, for example, leaves may be small in size with thick cuticles and sunken stomata to help reduce water loss. The presence of spines to deter grazing by herbivores is not uncommon. Other differences in leaf shape are a result of the plant living in a sunny or shady situation.

**Did you know?**

Leaves of the Raphia palm found in tropical forests can be 22 metres long.

The equation for photosynthesis may be summarized as:

$$6CO_2 + 6H_2O + \text{sunlight} \xrightarrow{\text{chlorophyll}} C_6H_{12}O_6 + 6O_2$$

$$\text{carbon dioxide} + \text{water} + \text{sunlight} \xrightarrow{\text{chlorophyll}} \text{glucose} + \text{oxygen}$$

$$\text{gas} + \text{liquid} + \text{energy} \xrightarrow{\text{chlorophyll}} \text{liquid} + \text{gas (solution in water)}$$

The adaptations of the leaf to photosynthesis are therefore:

1. To obtain energy (sunlight).

2. To obtain and remove gases (carbon dioxide and oxygen).

3. To obtain and remove liquids (water and sugar solution).

### 14.1.1 Adaptations for obtaining energy (sunlight)

As sunlight is the energy source which drives the photosynthetic process, it is often the factor which determines the rate of photosynthesis. To ensure its efficient absorption the leaf shows many adaptations:

1. **Phototropism** causes shoots to grow towards the light in order to allow the attached leaves to receive maximum illumination.

2. **Etiolation** causes rapid elongation of shoots which are in the dark, to ensure that the leaves are brought up into the light as soon as possible.

3. **Leaves arrange themselves into a mosaic**, i.e. they are arranged on the plant in a way that minimizes overlapping and so reduces the degree of shading of one leaf by another.

4. **Leaves have a large surface area** to capture as much sunlight as possible. They are held at an angle perpendicular to the sun during the day to expose the maximum area to the light. Some plants, e.g. the compass plant, actually 'track' the sun by moving their leaves so they constantly face it during the day.

5. **Leaves are thin** – If they were thicker, the upper layers would filter out all the light and the lower layers would not then photosynthesize.

6. **The cuticle and epidermis are transparent** to allow light through to the photosynthetic mesophyll beneath.

7. **The palisade mesophyll cells are packed with chloroplasts** and arranged with their long axes perpendicular to the surface. Although there are some air spaces between them, they still form a continuous layer which traps most of the incoming light. In some plants this layer is more than one cell thick.

8. **The chloroplasts within the mesophyll cells can move** – This allows them to arrange themselves into the best positions within a cell for the efficient absorption of light.

9. **The chloroplasts hold chlorophyll in a structured way** – The chlorophyll within a chloroplast is contained within the grana, where it is arranged on the sides of a series of unit membranes. The ordered arrangement not only presents the maximum

*(a)*

A

B

*(b)*

Section A/B

*(c)*

Sclerenchyma

Palisade
mesophyll

Spongy
mesophyll

Xylem

Phloem

Cambial region

Dicotyledonous leaf (VS)

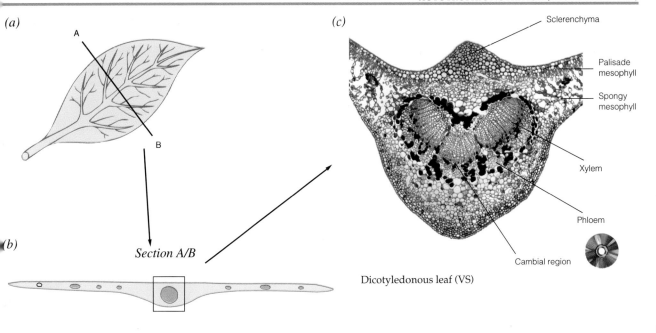

*(d) Dicotyledonous leaf (VS) (×40 approx.)*

*) Palisade cell*

ellulose cell wall

Chloroplasts

Cytoplasm

Vacuole

Nucleus

Tonoplast

Cell membrane

Cuticle

Upper (adaxial)
epidermis

Palisade mesophyll

Air space

Parenchyma

Xylem          Vein    Spongy
mesophyll

Phloem

Abaxial
epidermis

*) Stoma*

Stoma
(surface view)

Chloroplasts

Stomatal
aperture

Thick inner
wall of guard
cell

Nucleus

Guard cell

Nucleus

Vacuole of
epidermal cell

Chloroplasts

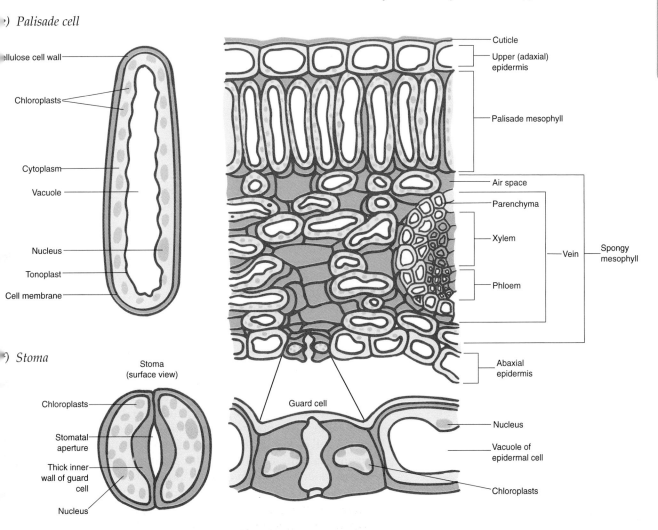

ig. 14.1 *The structure of the leaf (continued on next page)*

271

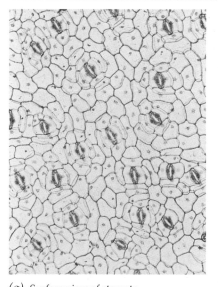

(g) Surface view of stomata

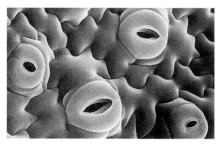

Stomata in surface view (scanning EM) (× 400 approx.)

(h)

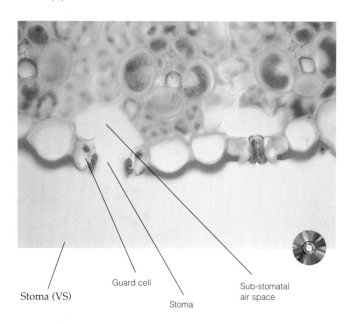

Stoma (VS)  Guard cell  Stoma  Sub-stomatal air space

Fig. 14.1 The structure of the leaf (continued)

amount of chlorophyll to the light but also brings it in close proximity to other pigments and substances which are necessary for its functioning. The structure of a chloroplast is shown in Fig. 4.5, Section 4.2.4.

### 14.1.2 Adaptations for obtaining and removing gases

As gases diffuse relatively rapidly, the leaf has no special transport mechanism for carbon dioxide and oxygen. The leaf does, however, show a number of adaptations which ensure rapid diffusion of these gases:

1. **Numerous stomata** are present in the epidermis of leaves. There may be tens of thousands per cm$^2$ of leaf surface, which itself represents a very considerable area. Stomata are minute pores in the epidermis which, when open, permit unrestricted diffusion into and out of the leaf.

2. **Stomata can be opened and closed** – Plants need to be relatively impermeable to gases in order to prevent water loss, and yet they need the free entry of carbon dioxide for photosynthesis. To overcome this problem, they have stomatal pores which are bounded by two **guard cells**. Alterations in the turgidity of these cells open and close the stomatal pore, thus controlling the uptake of carbon dioxide and the loss of water. The detail of stomatal control is given in Section 22.4.1. Stomata open in conditions which favour photosynthesis and at this time some water loss is unavoidable. When photosynthesis cannot take place, e.g. at night, they close, thus reducing considerably the loss of water. At times of considerable water loss, the stomata may close anyway, regardless of the demands for carbon dioxide.

**3. Spongy mesophyll possesses many air spaces** – The mesophyll layer on the underside of the leaf has many air spaces. These communicate with the palisade layer and the stomatal pores. There is hence an uninterrupted diffusion of gases between the atmosphere and the palisade mesophyll. During photosynthesis carbon dioxide diffuses in and oxygen out of this layer. The air spaces avoid the need for these gases to diffuse through the cells themselves, a process which would be much slower. The palisade mesophyll also possesses air spaces to permit rapid diffusion around the cells of which it is made.

### 14.1.3 Adaptations for obtaining and removing liquids

As water is a liquid raw material for photosynthesis and as the sugar produced is carried away in solution, the leaf has to be adapted for the efficient transport of liquids.

**1. A large central midrib** is possessed by most dicotyledonous leaves. This contains a large vascular bundle comprising xylem and phloem tissue. The xylem permits water and mineral salts to enter the leaf and the phloem carries away sugar solution, usually in the form of sucrose.

**2. A network of small veins** is found throughout the leaf. These ensure that no cell is ever far from a xylem vessel or phloem sieve tube, and hence all cells have a constant supply of water for photosynthesis and a means of removing the sugars they produce. The xylem and any sclerenchyma associated with the vascular bundle also provide a framework of support for the leaf, helping it to present maximum surface area to the light.

---

## PROJECT

1. Estimate the stomatal densities on the lower epidermis of a variety of plants.

2. Find out if the stomatal densities in the white and green parts of variegated leaves differ.

3. Determine if there are any differences in stomatal densities of leaves collected randomly from a tree.

---

## 14.2 Mechanism of light absorption

### 14.2.1 The nature of light

There are three features of light which make it biologically important:

**1.** Spectral quality (colour).

**2.** Intensity (brightness).

**3.** Duration (time).

To be of use as an energy source for organisms, light must first be converted to chemical energy. Radiant energy comes in discrete packets called **quanta** (Planck's quantum theory). A single quantum of light is called a **photon**. Light also has a **wave** nature and so forms a part of the electromagnetic spectrum. Visible light represents that part of this spectrum which has a wavelength between 400 nm (violet) and 700 nm (red).

The wavelength of light is the distance between successive peaks along a wave (Fig. 14.2) and this is inversely proportional to its frequency, i.e. the smaller the wavelength, the greater the frequency. The amount of energy is inversely proportional to the wavelength, i.e. light with a short wavelength has more energy than light with longer wavelengths. In other words, a photon of blue light (wavelength 400 nm) has more energy than a photon of red light (wavelength 700 nm).

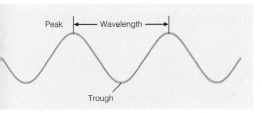

ig. 14.2 *Wave function of light*

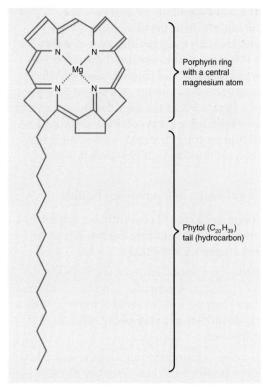

*Fig. 14.4 The general shape of the chlorophyll molecule*

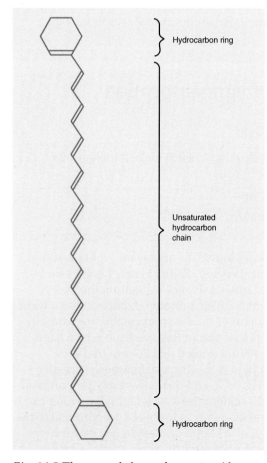

*Fig. 14.5 The general shape of a carotenoid molecule*

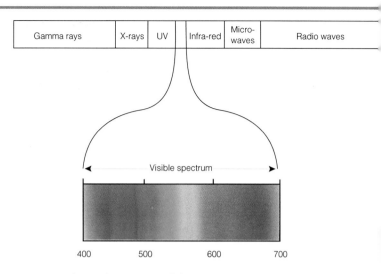

*Fig. 14.3 The visible section of the electromagnetic spectrum*

### 14.2.2 The photosynthetic pigments

A variety of pigments are involved in photosynthesis of which **chlorophyll** is by far the most important. There are a number of different chlorophylls, with chlorophylls *a* and *b* being the most common. Chlorophylls absorb light in the blue-violet and the red regions of the visible spectrum. The remaining light, in the green region of the spectrum, is reflected and gives chlorophyll its characteristic colour. All chlorophylls comprise a complex ring system called a **porphyrin ring** and a long hydrocarbon 'tail' (Fig. 14.4). This 'tail' is lipid soluble (hydrophobic) and is therefore embedded in the thylakoid membrane. The porphyrin ring is hydrophilic and lies on the membrane surface.

There is a second group of pigments involved in photosynthesis – the **carotenoids**. There are many types but their basic structure comprises two small rings linked by a long hydrocarbon chain (Fig. 14.5). The colour, which ranges from pale yellow through orange to red, depends upon the number of double bonds in the chain. The greater the number of double bonds, the deeper the colour.

The colour of carotenoids is normally masked in photosynthetic tissues by chlorophyll. Their colour does, however, become apparent when chlorophyll breaks down prior to leaf fall. The characteristic red, orange and yellow colours of leaves in the autumn are attributable to carotenoids as are many flower and fruit colours. They absorb light in the blue-violet range of the spectrum. There are two main types of carotenoids: the **carotenes** and the **xanthophylls**. A common example of a carotene is $\beta$-carotene which gives carrots their familiar orange colour. It is easily formed into two molecules of vitamin A, making carrots a useful source of this vitamin to animals.

### 14.2.3 Absorption and action spectra

If a pigment such as chlorophyll is subjected to different wavelengths of light, it absorbs some more than others. If the degree of absorption at each wavelength is plotted, an

**absorption spectrum** of that pigment is obtained. The absorption spectra for chlorophylls *a* and *b* are given in Fig. 14.6.

An **action spectrum** plots the biological effect of different wavelengths of light – in this case the effectiveness of different wavelengths of light in bringing about photosynthesis. As Fig. 14.6 shows, the action spectrum for photosynthesis is closely correlated to the absorption spectra for chlorophylls *a* and *b* and carotenoids. This suggests that these pigments are responsible for absorbing the light used in photosynthesis.

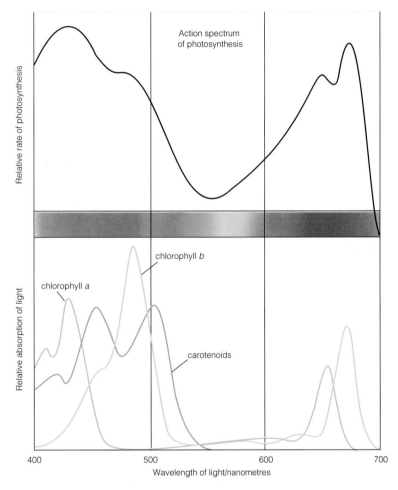

*Fig. 14.6 Action spectrum for photosynthesis and absorption spectra for common plant pigments*

## 14.3   Mechanism of photosynthesis

The overall equation for photosynthesis is:

$$6CO_2 + 6H_2O \xrightarrow[\text{chlorophyll}]{\text{sunlight}} C_6H_{12}O_6 + 6O_2$$

carbon dioxide + water $\longrightarrow$ glucose + oxygen

Photosynthesis is essentially a process of energy transduction. Light energy is firstly converted into electrical energy and finall into chemical energy. It has three main phases:

1. **Light harvesting**. Light energy is captured by the plant usin a mixture of pigments including chlorophyll.

2. **The light dependent stage (photolysis)** in which a flow of electrons results from the effect of light on chlorophyll and so causes the splitting of water into hydrogen ions and oxygen.

3. **The light independent stage** during which these hydrogen ions are used in the **reduction of carbon dioxide** and hence the manufacture of sugars.

### 14.3.1 Light harvesting

Within the thylakoid membranes of the chloroplast, chlorophyl molecules are arranged along with their accessory pigments int groups of several hundred molecules. Each group is called an **antenna complex**. Special proteins associated with these pigments help to funnel photons of light entering the chloropla

## NOTEBOOK

### Chromatography

Chromatography is a means of separating one type of molecule from another. It involves moving the mixture, normally as a liquid o a gas, over a stationary phase embedded in cellulose or silica. The separation may depend on a range of chemical and physical properties of the molecules such as solubility and molecular mass.

Essentially there are two basic ways of carrying out the separation. **Paper chromatography** is often used in schools and colleges to separate photosynthetic pigments, sugars or amino acids. The mixture is 'spotted' near one end of a paper strip and then dipped into a solvent which moves up the paper by capillarity, carrying the molecules with it.

Instead of using paper a thin layer of silica may be formed on an inert solid support. This is called **thin layer chromatography**.

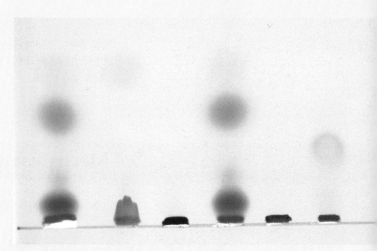

Chromatography plate at end of run

on to special molecules of chlorophyll *a*, known as the **reaction centre chlorophyll molecule**. When light strikes this molecule, an electron in its orbit is raised to a higher energy level, thus initiating a flow of electrons.

There are two types of reaction centre which differ in both their chlorophylls and their functions. These are known as **photosystem I (PSI)** and **photosystem II (PSII)**.

### 14.3.2 Light dependent stage (photolysis)

The light dependent stage of photosynthesis occurs in the thylakoids of the chloroplasts and involves the splitting of water by light – **photolysis of water**. In the process, ADP is converted to ATP. This addition of phosphorus is termed **phosphorylation** and as light is involved it is called **photophosphorylation**. These processes are brought about by two photochemical systems which are summarized in Figs. 14.7 and 14.8.

In the process summarized in Fig. 14.8, electrons from chlorophyll are passed into the light independent reaction via reduced nicotinamide adenine dinucleotide phosphate (NADPH + H+). They are replaced by electrons from another

olumn chromatography

The second, more commonly used method involves the mobile phase flowing over a supporting matrix held in a glass or metal tube. This is known as **column chromatography**. There have been many recent advances in the development of new matrices so that the liquid can now be pumped through under high pressure and very small fractions can be separated in miniature columns.

If chromatography is to be a really useful biochemical tool it is necessary to link separation to detection. This may be simply on the basis of colour, as with photosynthetic pigments.

Proteins, peptides and nucleic acids can be detected by their ability to absorb light in the ultra-violet region of the spectrum. Other molecules, such as amino acids, are colourless but can be made to form coloured derivatives if treated with particular chemicals, e.g. ninhydrin causes amino acids to form purple derivatives.

In paper chromatography the identification of a particular molecule is usually made on the basis of the distance travelled by the substance in relation to the distance moved by the solvent. Each molecule can then be referred to by its $R_f$ value (retardation factor) expressed as:

$$\frac{\text{Distance travelled by a compound}}{\text{Distance travelled by solvent front}}$$

If a mixture of radioactive compounds is separated, the molecules can be detected by their emission of radioactivity (see *Using isotopes as tracers* on p. 4). This was the basis of Calvin's work on the light independent stage of photosynthesis (p. 279).

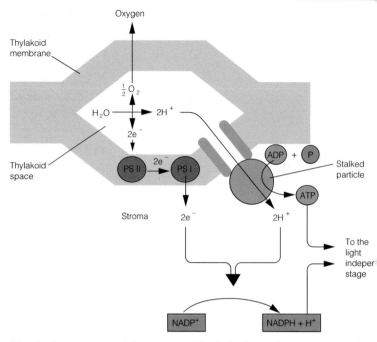

Fig. 14.7 Summary of the events of the light dependent stage and their locations within the chloroplast

source – the water molecule. The same electrons are *not* recycled back into the chlorophyll. This method of ATP production is thus called **non-cyclic photophosphorylation**. It is alternatively called the **Z-scheme** because the zig-zag route of the electrons in the diagram resembles a Z on its side.

There is a second method by which ATP can be generated. The electrons from the pigment system may return to the chlorophyll directly, via the electron carrier system, forming ATP in the process. Such electrons are recycled, harnessing energy from light and generating ATP. This is called **cyclic photophosphorylation** and involves only photosystem I. No reduced NADP is produced during cyclic photophosphorylation.

1. *Light energy is trapped in photosystem II and boosts electrons to a higher energy level.*
2. *The electrons are received by an electron acceptor.*
3. *The electrons are passed from the electron acceptor along a series of electron carriers to photosystem I. The energy lost by the electrons is captured by converting ADP to ATP. Light energy has thereby been converted to chemical energy.*
4. *Light energy absorbed by photosystem I boosts the electrons to an even higher energy level.*
5. *The electrons are received by another electron acceptor.*
6. *The electrons which have been removed from the chlorophyll are replaced by pulling in other electrons from a water molecule.*
7. *The loss of electrons from the water molecule causes it to dissociate into protons and oxygen gas.*
8. *The protons from the water molecule combine with the electrons from the second electron acceptor and these reduce **nicotinamide adenine dinucleotide phosphate**.*
9. *Some electrons from the second acceptor may pass back to the chlorophyll molecule by the electron carrier system, yielding ATP as they do so. This process is called **cyclic photophosphorylation.***

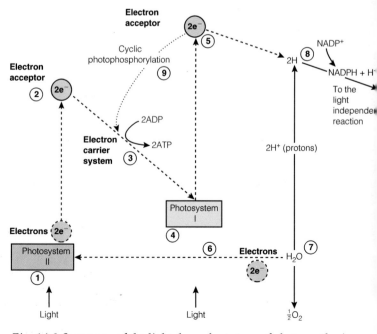

Fig. 14.8 Summary of the light dependent stage of photosynthesis

### 14.3.3 The light independent stage

The light independent stage of photosynthesis occurs in the stroma of the chloroplasts and it takes place whether or not light is present. The details of this stage were analysed by Melvin Calvin and his co-workers and the process is often called the **Calvin cycle** (Figs. 14.9 and 14.10). It is basically the reduction of carbon dioxide using the reduced nicotinamide adenine dinucleotide phosphate ($NADPH + H^+$) and ATP from the light dependent reaction. The carbon dioxide is initially fixed by combining it with a five-carbon compound – **ribulose bisphosphate** – with the aid of an enzyme called **ribulose bisphosphate carboxylase oxygenase**, thankfully abbreviated to **RUBISCO**.

*Carbon dioxide diffuses into the leaf through the stomata and dissolves in the moisture on the walls of the palisade cells. It diffuses through the cell membrane, cytoplasm and chloroplast membrane into the stroma of the chloroplast.*

*The carbon dioxide combines with a 5-carbon compound called **ribulose bisphosphate** to form an unstable 6-carbon intermediate.*

*The 6-carbon intermediate breaks down into two molecules of the 3-carbon **glycerate 3-phosphate (GP)**. Some of the ATP produced during the light dependent stage is used to help convert GP into **triose phosphate** (glyceraldehyde 3-phosphate – GALP).*

*The reduced nicotinamide adenine dinucleotide phosphate ($NADPH + H^+$) from the light dependent reaction is necessary for the reduction of the GP to triose phosphate. $NADP^+$ is regenerated and this returns to the light dependent stage to accept more hydrogen.*

*Pairs of triose phosphate molecules are combined to produce an intermediate hexose sugar.*

*The hexose sugar is polymerized to form starch which is stored by the plant.*

*Not all triose phosphate is combined to form starch. A portion of it is used to regenerate the original carbon dioxide acceptor, ribulose bisphosphate. Five molecules of the 3-carbon triose phosphate can regenerate three molecules of the 5-carbon ribulose bisphosphate. More of the ATP from the light dependent reaction is needed to provide the energy for this conversion.*

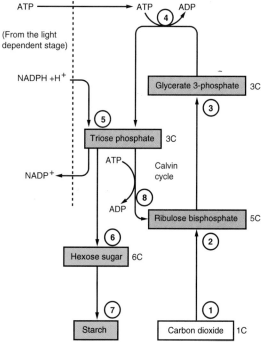

*Fig. 14.9 Summary of the light independent stage of photosynthesis*

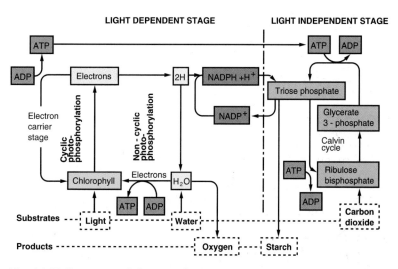

*Fig. 14.10 Summary of photosynthesis*

Some tropical plants such as maize use a specialized form of photosynthesis. Instead of the 3-carbon glycerate–3–phosphate, maize produces a 4-carbon intermediate called oxaloacetate. These plants are therefore called **C$_4$ plants**. High temperatures i the tropics mean that the rate of photosynthesis is high and carbon dioxide is rapidly used up during the day. C$_4$ plants like maize have the advantage of being more efficient at photosynthesis in these high temperatures and low carbon dioxide concentrations.

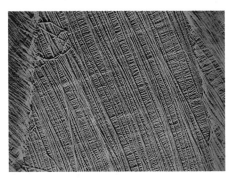

Cellulose fibres in plant cell wall (SEM) ($\times$8500)

### 14.3.4 Fate of photosynthetic products

*Synthesis of other carbohydrates*
The triose phosphate of the Calvin cycle can be synthesized int hexose sugars such as glucose and fructose by a reversal of the stages of glycolysis (Section 16.2). Glucose and fructose may be combined to give the disaccharide **sucrose** which is transported throughout the plant in the phloem. The glucose may, on the other hand, be polymerized into **starch** for storage, or polymerized into another polysaccharide, **cellulose**. This make up over 50% of plant cell walls.

*Synthesis of lipids*
Lipids are mostly esters of fatty acids and glycerol. Glycerate 3- phosphate (GP) may be converted to acetyl coenzyme A, which in turn is used to synthesize a variety of fatty acids. Triose phosphate is easily converted into glycerol. As well as being important storage substances, especially in seeds, lipids are a major constituent of cell membranes, and their waxy derivative make up the waterproofing cuticle. Fatty acids provide some flower scents, which are used to attract insects for pollination.

*Synthesis of proteins*
Conversion of the glycerate 3-phosphate of the Calvin cycle int acetyl coenzyme A is the starting point for amino acid synthesi The acetyl CoA enters the Krebs cycle and from its intermediat a wide variety of amino acids can be made by transamination reactions. The amino acids are polymerized into proteins. Detai are given in Section 7.6.

Proteins are essential for growth and development and make up a major structural component of the cell, especially the cell membrane. All enzymes are proteins, and they may also be use as storage material.

## 14.4    Factors affecting photosynthesis

The rate of photosynthesis is affected by a number of factors, th level of which determine the yield of material by a plant. Before reviewing these factors it is necessary to understand the principle of limiting factors.

### 14.4.1 Concept of limiting factors

In 1905, F. F. Blackman, a British plant physiologist, measured the rate of photosynthesis under varying conditions of light and carbon dioxide supply. As a result of his work he formulated the **principle of limiting factors**. It states: **At any given moment, the rate of a physiological process is limited by the one factor which is in shortest supply, and by that factor alone**.

In other words, it is the factor which is nearest its minimum value which determines the rate of a reaction. Any change in the level of this factor, called the **limiting factor**, will affect the rate of the reaction. Changes in the level of other factors have no effect. To take an extreme example, photosynthesis cannot proceed in the dark because the absence of light limits the process. The supply of light will alter the rate of photosynthesis – more light, more photosynthesis. If, however, more carbon dioxide or a higher temperature is supplied to a plant in the dark, there will be no change in the rate of photosynthesis. Light is the limiting factor, therefore only a change in its level can affect the rate.

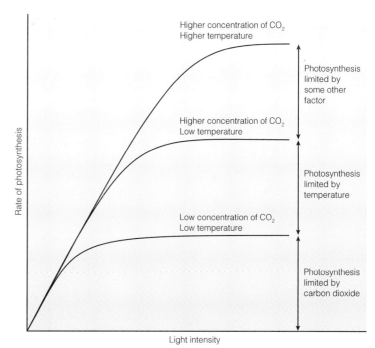

*Fig. 14.11 The concept of limiting factors as illustrated by the levels of different conditions on the rate of photosynthesis*

If the amount of light given to a plant is increased, the rate of photosynthesis increases up to a point and then tails off. At this point some other factor, such as the concentration of carbon dioxide, is in short supply and so limits the rate. An increase in carbon dioxide concentration again increases the amount of photosynthesis until some further factor, e.g. temperature, limits the process. These changes are illustrated in Fig. 14.11.

### 14.4.2 Effect of light intensity on the rate of photosynthesis

The rate of photosynthesis is often measured by the amount of carbon dioxide absorbed or oxygen evolved by a plant. These forms of measurement do not, however, give an absolute

281

measure of photosynthesis because oxygen is absorbed and carbon dioxide is evolved as a result of cellular respiration. As light intensity is increased, photosynthesis begins, and some carbon dioxide from respiration is utilized in photosynthesis and so less is evolved. With a continuing increase in light intensity a point is reached where carbon dioxide is neither evolved nor absorbed. At this point the carbon dioxide produced in respiration exactly balances that being used in photosynthesis. This is the **compensation point**. Further increases in light intensity result in a proportional increase in the rate of photosynthesis until **light saturation** is reached. Beyond this point further increases in light intensity have no effect on the rate of photosynthesis. If, however, more carbon dioxide is made available to the plant, further increases in light intensity do increase the rate of photosynthesis until light saturation is again reached, only this time at a higher light intensity. At this point the carbon dioxide concentration, or possibly some new factor such as temperature, is limiting the process. These relationships are represented graphically in Fig. 14.12.

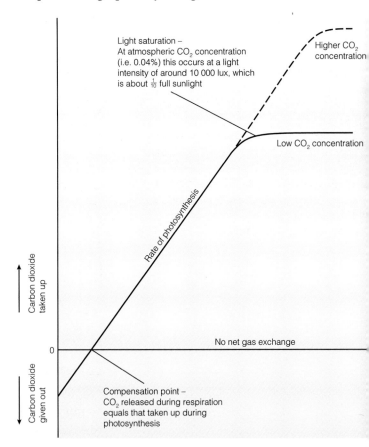

*Fig. 14.12 Graph showing the effect of light intensity on the rate of photosynthesis, as measured by the amount of $CO_2$ exchanged*

### 14.4.3 Effect of carbon dioxide concentration on the rate of photosynthesis

Carbon dioxide is one of the less abundant gases in the atmosphere. At its normal concentration of 0.04% it is present at only one-fifteenth of the concentration of argon, a so-called 'rare' gas. Despite occasional local fluctuations in carbon dioxide concentration, there is remarkable consistency in its concentration throughout the atmosphere at any one time. This consistency is the result of a fine balance between carbon dioxide taken up by green plants during photosynthesis and that released by all organisms during respiration. There has been a slight increase in the carbon dioxide concentration in the atmosphere in recent times and this has been attributed to the burning of fossil fuels. Coal and oil represent stores of carbon resulting from the fossilization of organisms. Burning these fuels oxidizes the carbon to carbon dioxide and so increases its concentration in the atmosphere.

The normally low atmospheric carbon dioxide concentration of 0.04% is a major limiting factor to photosynthesis. The optimum concentration for a sustained high rate of photosynthesis is 0.1% and some greenhouse crops like tomatoes are grown in carbon dioxide enriched environments to provide greater yields. The effect on the rate of photosynthesis of increasing the carbon dioxide concentration is illustrated in Figs. 14.11 and 14.12.

### 14.4.4 Effect of temperature on the rate of photosynthesis

We have seen that the photochemical reaction or light stage of photosynthesis is unaffected by temperature, but that the light independent stage (Calvin cycle) is temperature dependent. Provided the light intensity and concentration of carbon dioxide are not limiting, the rate of photosynthesis is found to increase proportionately with an increase in temperature. The minimum temperature at which photosynthesis can take place is 0 °C for most plants, although some arctic and alpine varieties continue to photosynthesize below this level. The rate of photosynthesis at these temperatures is very low. The rate approximately doubles for each rise of 10 °C up to an optimum temperature, which varies from species to species. Above the optimum temperature, the rate of increase is reduced until a point is reached above which there is no increase in photosynthesis. The optimum photosynthetic rate for most plants is around 25 °C. Above these levels further temperature increases lead to a levelling off and then a fall in the rate of photosynthesis. The fall occurs at temperatures too low for it to be entirely accounted for by the denaturation of enzymes.

### 14.4.5 Effect of inorganic ions on the rate of photosynthesis

In the absence of certain inorganic ions, such as iron, chlorophyll cannot be synthesized. Other ions, like nitrogen and magnesium, are an integral part of the chlorophyll molecule and their absence likewise prevents its formation. Where plants are grown on soils deficient in any one of these minerals, the chlorophyll concentration is reduced and the leaves become yellow, a condition called **chlorosis**. Under these circumstances the rate of photosynthesis is substantially reduced.

### 14.4.6 Other factors affecting the rate of photosynthesis

Of the other factors which may affect the rate of photosynthesis, water is by far the most important. As a substrate in the process its deficiency will clearly reduce the rate of photosynthesis. The

Purple saxifrage in flower during brief arctic summer

# Adaptations of cereals in different parts of the world

Cereals are among the most important food plants in the world, being grown for direct human consumption or to feed animals.

**Rice** – Rice provides the staple diet of about half the world's population. It is a partial hydrophyte, normally grown in paddy fields in 5–10 cm of water. Having the roots in water makes it difficult for them to obtain enough oxygen for respiration. This problem is overcome in two main ways. The cortex of the stem and root of rice is composed of chains of parenchyma cells separated by large air spaces. This tissue is called aerenchyma and it aids the diffusion of gases between the aerial and the submerged parts of the plant. However, the roots may still be short of oxygen at times and the tissues are therefore tolerant to the build-up of ethanol produced by anaerobic respiration.

**Sorghum** – Sorghum, a native grain of Africa and Asia, is a staple food in India, China and Africa. Elsewhere it is often used to feed livestock. It is one of the most heat and drought tolerant cereals, remaining dormant when conditions are most stressful and resuming growth when the climate improves. Both the embryo and the adult plants can tolerate high temperatures. Sorghum has a number of xerophytic modifications. To limit the rate of water loss by transpiration, the leaves have a thick cuticle and there is a reduced number of sunken stomata. In addition, water uptake is maximized by the presence of an extensive root system.

**Maize** – Along with wheat and rice, maize is one of the world's chief grain crops. It is a warm temperate and subtropical plant with a specialized method of photosynthesis known as the $C_4$ pathway. This uses a different carbon dioxide acceptor from that in the normal $C_3$ pathway, one which has a higher affinity for carbon dioxide and which is especially efficient at high temperatures. There are two further advantages of $C_4$ photosynthesis. It allows the plant to accumulate a store of carbon dioxide when it is in relative abundance and store it for later release when external supplies are reduced, for example during drought conditions when stomata may be closed. $C_4$ plants also avoid photorespiration. Like respiration, this process is the reverse of normal photosynthesis but, unlike respiration, it does not yield ATP.

problem is that water has so many functions in a plant that it is impossible to directly relate its availability to the rate of photosynthesis. There are many specific chemical compounds which prevent photosynthesis, often by inhibiting enzyme action. Examples include cyanide and dichlorophenyl dimethyl urea (DCMU). Even certain pollutants such as sulphur dioxide are known to reduce photosynthetic rate.

# 14.5  Questions

.. Read the following account of photosynthesis and hen write down the most appropriate word or words o complete the account.

There are four main pigments found in the chloroplasts of higher plants. These pigments are situated in the .................... of the chloroplast. Chlorophyll *a* absorbs mainly .................... and blue-violet light.

The pigments are organized into systems, the first of hese to be involved is .................... . The absorption of light causes the displacement of an electron from the chlorophyll *a* molecule. This electron nay be passed back to the chlorophyll via a series of .................... which are at progressively lower energy levels. Coupled with this electron transfer is the synthesis of .................... . This compound may be used in two stages of the light independent reactions of photosynthesis which occur in the .................... of he chloroplast. These two stages are the conversion of .................... to .................... and the resynthesis of the acceptor molecule .................... which combines with the carbon dioxide used in photosynthesis.

During non-cyclic photophosphorylation other important reactions take place. The electron is combined with .................... ions resulting from the photolysis of .................... to form the reduced coenzyme called .................... . This reduced coenzyme is also used in the .................... cycle. The electron emitted from the chlorophyll molecule is replaced by electrons from the .................... ions produced by the photolysis reaction. As a result .................... gas is given off.

In most plants carbohydrates are the main product of photosynthesis, but other important nutrients, namely .................... and .................... , are often produced in considerable quantities. Many crops are grown in order to harvest these products.

*(Total 17 marks)*

*Oxford & Cambridge January 1998, Paper B3, No. 4*

**2.** The statements in the table below refer to the light dependent and light independent (dark) reactions of photosynthesis. Copy and complete the table. If a statement is correct for the process, place a tick (✓) in the appropriate box and if it is incorrect, place a cross (✗) in the appropriate box.

| Statement | Light dependent reaction | Light independent reaction |
|---|---|---|
| Oxygen produced | | |
| Carbon dioxide fixed | | |
| Occurs in stroma | | |
| Uses NADPH and H⁺ | | |
| Produces ATP | | |

*(Total 5 marks)*

*ULEAC June 1996, B2, No. 4*

**3.** The diagram below represents the structure of a chloroplast.

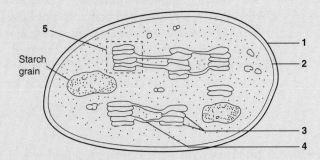

(a) Name the parts labelled **1–5**.     *(5 marks)*
(b) Explain how the structure of a chloroplast is related to its function.     *(5 marks)*
(c) Using only the following compounds, construct a **single** flow diagram to show the incorporation of carbon dioxide into carbohydrates, amino acids and fatty acids.

carbon dioxide, triose phosphate (glyceraldehyde 3-phosphate, GALP), acetyl CoA, ribulose bisphosphate, fatty acids, amino acids, glycerate 3-phosphate (phosphoglyceric acid, GP).     *(5 marks)*

*(Total 15 marks)*

*Oxford & Cambridge June 1996, Paper 1, No. 6*

**4.** The table below shows the effect of temperature on the rate of photosynthesis in two grasses, *Agropyron* and *Bouteloua*.

| Leaf temperature/ °C | Photosynthesis rate/ $\mu$mol $CO_2$ absorbed $m^{-2}\,s^{-1}$ | |
|---|---|---|
| | *Agropyron* | *Bouteloua* |
| 10 | 23 | 10 |
| 15 | 26 | 15 |
| 20 | 30 | 19 |
| 25 | 31 | 24 |
| 30 | 30 | 30 |
| 35 | 27 | 35 |
| 40 | 20 | 39 |
| 45 | 10 | 38 |

Adapted from Barber and Baker,
*Topics in Photosynthesis*, Vol. 6, 1985.

(a) Plot the data on graph paper. (*5 marks*)
(b) From your graph, find the rate of photosynthesis at 22 °C for each of the grasses. (*2 marks*)
(c) Suggest which of the two grasses is likely to grow faster in a tropical climate. Give a reason for your answer. (*2 marks*)
(d) (i) Suggest why the rate of photosynthesis declines at high temperatures. (*1 mark*)
    (ii) State **two** other factors which can be limiting in photosynthesis. (*2 marks*)
(e) Describe a simple method that you could use in the laboratory to investigate the effect of temperature on the rate of photosynthesis in an aquatic plant. (*4 marks*)
(*Total 16 marks*)

*ULEAC June 1995, Paper 1, No. 11*

**5.** (a) Briefly describe how ATP is produced as a result of light striking chlorophyll molecules. (*2 marks*)
(b) Although photosynthesis generates ATP, plants also generate ATP by respiration. Explain why this is necessary. (*2 marks*)
(c) The diagram shows the main steps in the light independent stage of photosynthesis.

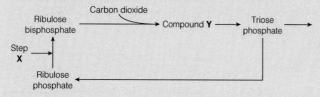

(i) For what is ATP used in step **X**? (*1 mark*)
(ii) Name compound **Y**. (*1 mark*)
(*Total 6 marks*)

*AEB Summer 1995, Common Paper 1, No. 6*

**6.** (a) (i) Where in the chloroplast does the light independent stage of photosynthesis occur?
    (ii) Describe briefly what happens in this stage of photosynthesis. (*4 marks*)

A sample of *Chlorella* (a unicellular organism) was allowed to photosynthesize at high and very low carbon dioxide levels. The graph shows the concentrations of glycerate 3-phosphate (GP) and ribulose bisphosphate (RuBP) during the investigation.

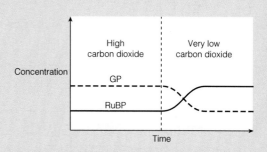

(b) Account for the different concentrations of RuBP during the whole course of the investigation. (*3 marks*)
(c) Explain why the concentration of GP falls when the level of carbon dioxide is reduced. (*1 mark*)
(d) Give **two** conditions which should be kept constant throughout the investigation. (*1 mark*)
(*Total 9 marks*)

*NEAB June 1996, Paper 1, No. 1.*

**7.** The graph shows the rate of photosynthesis of tomato plants under different environmental conditions

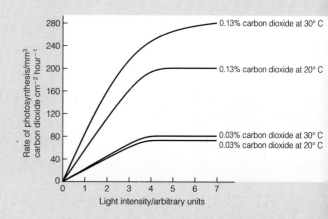

(a) (i) How is the carbon dioxide content of the air in a glasshouse usually increased? (*1 mark*)

(ii) Use the graph to help explain the environmental conditions under which it might be profitable to increase the carbon dioxide content of the air in the glasshouse in which the tomatoes were growing. *(3 marks)*

he table shows some effects of doubling the quantity f carbon dioxide in the air on plants growing in lasshouses.

| Plant | Percentage increase in total dry biomass |
|---|---|
| Tomato | 40 |
| Lettuce | 37 |
| Weeds | 34 |

(b) What is the advantage of giving these figures:
  (i)  as percentages; *(1 mark)*
  (ii) in terms of **dry** mass? *(1 mark)*
(c) Increasing the percentage of carbon dioxide to crops may not be economically sensible as the supply of other substances would also have to be increased. Using information in the table to help, suggest **two** such substances that would have to be increased. Give an explanation for your answer in **each** case.
*(2 marks)*
*(Total 8 marks)*

*NEAB June 1995, BY07, No. 7*

The diagram below shows the apparatus used to vestigate the rate of photosynthesis in *Elodea* Canadian pondweed) when exposed to different avelengths of light. Light was provided using a rojector with a coloured filter placed in front of the ght beam. The light source was fixed at 50 cm from e beaker containing the pondweed. The volume of xygen collected was recorded after 5 minutes' lumination using each of the coloured filters.

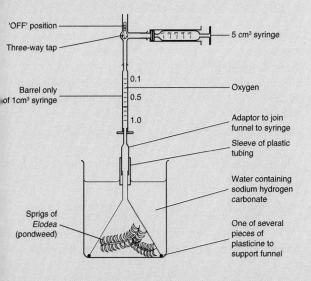

'OFF' position
Three-way tap
Barrel only of 1cm³ syringe
5 cm³ syringe
0.1
0.5 — Oxygen
1.0
Adaptor to join funnel to syringe
Sleeve of plastic tubing
Water containing sodium hydrogen carbonate
Sprigs of *Elodea* (pondweed)
One of several pieces of plasticine to support funnel

The following results were obtained.

| Colour of filter | Wavelength of light reaching the pondweed/nm | Volume of oxygen collected/cm³ |
|---|---|---|
| Violet | 400 | 0.80 |
| Indigo | 425 | 0.95 |
| Blue | 475 | 0.80 |
| Blue–green | 500 | 0.40 |
| Green | 550 | 0.20 |
| Yellow | 600 | 0.40 |
| Orange | 625 | 0.70 |
| Red | 675 | 0.90 |
| Far-red | 700 | 0.10 |

(a) Plot the data on graph paper. *(5 marks)*
(b) State the name of the process which occurs during photosynthesis to produce the oxygen which was collected. *(1 mark)*
(c)  (i) Calculate the relative amount of photosynthesis occurring in green light as a percentage of the maximum rate obtained in this investigation. Show your working. *(2 marks)*
  (ii) State a reason why, even though leaves reflect green light, some photosynthesis is still able to occur when green light falls on a leaf. *(1 mark)*
  (iii) Explain how the volume of oxygen collected over the same time period would alter if the light source with the green filter in place was placed 25 cm away from the beaker. *(2 marks)*
(d) Name the **two** compounds (other than oxygen) which are formed during the light dependent stage of photosynthesis, and state their use in the Calvin cycle (light independent stage). *(4 marks)*
*(Total 15 marks)*

*Oxford June 1997, Paper 44, No. 1*

9. Two groups of tomato plants were grown in atmospheres containing 350 vpm and 1000 vpm carbon dioxide respectively (vpm = volume parts per million). Other conditions were kept at a constant optimum level. The area of the seventh leaf of each plant was measured from 10 days after it first appeared. The table gives the mean leaf area for each group of plants.

| Time after leaf first appeared/days | Mean leaf area/dm² | |
|---|---|---|
| | 350 vpm CO₂ | 1000 vpm CO₂ |
| 10 | 0.35 | 0.50 |
| 18 | 1.00 | 1.80 |
| 25 | 2.60 | 4.25 |
| 32 | 4.20 | 5.45 |
| 39 | 5.00 | 6.05 |
| 50 | 5.40 | 6.30 |
| 65 | 5.60 | 6.35 |

(a) Plot the data in suitable form on graph
   paper. (5 marks)
(b) From the graph determine the rate of growth
   in area of the seventh leaf during the 22nd
   day after it first appeared, in an atmosphere
   of:
   (i) 350 vpm $CO_2$;
   (ii) 1000 vpm $CO_2$.
   Show your working. (2 marks)
(c) Briefly describe a method for measuring leaf
   area. (2 marks)
(d) Which treatment was the control?
   Explain your answer. (1 mark)
(e) (i) Identify **one** of the conditions that was
      kept at an optimum level.
   (ii) Explain the need for this precaution.
                                        (2 marks)
(f) Suggest why measurements were made
   on the seventh leaf rather than on an
   earlier leaf. (1 mark)
(g) Describe **one** difference shown in the graph,
   other than growth rate, between the leaves
   grown under different treatments. (1 mark)
(h) Use your biological knowledge to account
   for the results of the experiment. (2 marks)
   (Total 16 marks)

*AEB Summer 1995, (AS) Paper 1, No. 12*

**10.** A disaccharide is a carbohydrate with two sugar
units in its molecules. A particular disaccharide was
boiled with a dilute acid for 10 minutes.

The diagram shows the chromatogram that was
produced from the original disaccharide and after
treating it with the dilute acid.

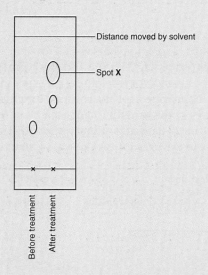

(a) (i) Calculate the $R_f$ value of spot **X**.
      Show your working. (2 marks)

(ii) Explain why, in order to identify a spot
   on the chromatogram, it is more useful
   to determine the $R_f$ value than the
   distance moved by the spot. (1 mark)
(b) Suggest an explanation for the presence of
   the three spots on this chromatogram.
                                        (2 marks)
   (Total 5 marks)

*AEB Summer 1997, Module Paper 1, No.*

**11.** The micrograph below shows the structure of a
leaf as seen in vertical section.

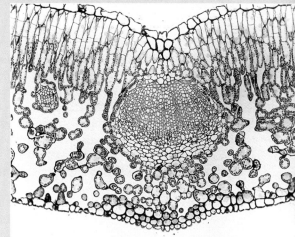

(a) Name the parts labelled **1–8**. (4 marks)
(b) List **four** anatomical features of a leaf which
   help to make photosynthesis possible.
                                        (4 marks)
(c) Copy and complete the following account of
   photosynthesis by selecting appropriate
   answers from the list below. Not all of the
   answers are needed. Each answer selected
   should be used once only.

ATP                            photosystem I
cyclic phosphorylation         photosystem II
hydrogen                       oxygen
light dependent                pyruvic acid
light independent              ribose bisphosphate
NAD                            ribulose bisphosphate
NADP                           water
non-cyclic phosphorylation     phosphoglyceraldehyde

Photosynthesis consists of two major stages. In the
initial stage known as the ......................... stage,
molecules of ......................... are broken down
liberating ......................... gas.
Photosynthetic pigments, collectively known as

..................... , absorb light at a wavelength of 80 nm and the energy is used to raise an electron to a higher energy level. This electron may be involved in the reduction of a carrier called ....................... or it may be involved in the synthesis of ....................... in a process called ....................... . These compounds are used in the second stage of photosynthesis called the ....................... stage. Carbon dioxide combines with ....................... to form ....................... and this is used to form sugars and starch.                  *(10 marks)*

*(Total 18 marks)*

*Oxford & Cambridge January 1997, Unit B3, No. 1*

**2.** The diagram below represents the structure of part of a chloroplast.

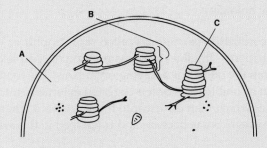

*(a)* Name the structures **A**, **B** and **C**.     *(3 marks)*
*(b)* Using accurate, ruled guide-lines and the letters given below, show on the diagram the area where:
   (i) ATP is produced (**X**);
   (ii) NADP is reduced (**Y**);
   (iii) ATP is broken down into ADP and inorganic phosphate (**Z**).     *(3 marks)*
*(c)* State which type of **molecule** in the chloroplast contains:
   (i) magnesium;
   (ii) iron.     *(2 marks)*
*(d)* (i) What is the name given to the substance which combines with $CO_2$ in the Calvin cycle?     *(1 mark)*
   (ii) What is the name given to the first stable product produced in the Calvin cycle (light independent stage of photosynthesis)?     *(1 mark)*

*(Total 10 marks)*

*Oxford February 1997, Paper 1, No. 4*

**13.** This is a transmission electron micrograph of a chloroplast.

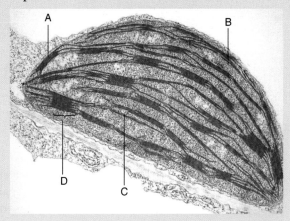

*(a)* (i) Name the parts labelled A to C.  *(3 marks)*
   (ii) What roles do parts B and D play in photosynthesis?     *(4 marks)*
*(b)* Explain how water molecules are utilized in the process of photosynthesis.     *(3 marks)*
*(c)* The graph shows the effect of temperature on the rates of photosynthesis and respiration in well-illuminated leaves (light and other variables kept constant).

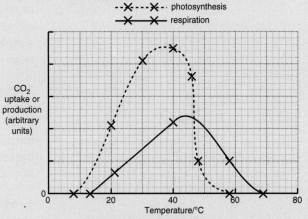

   (i) At what temperature was the net gas exchange zero?     *(1 mark)*
   (ii) Suggest a possible reason why the rate of respiration in the leaf is less affected by temperatures above 40°C than is the rate of photosynthesis.     *(1 mark)*
   (iii) What would be the effect of a rise in temperature on the rate of photosynthesis if the intensity of light falling on the leaf was very low? Explain your answer.     *(3 marks)*

*(Total 15 marks)*

*Oxford & Cambridge June 1998, Paper B3, No. 4*

# 15

# Heterotrophic nutrition

Heterotrophic organisms consume complex organic food material. This food originates with autotrophic organisms which synthesize it from simple inorganic raw materials. There are a number of forms of heterotrophic nutrition:

**1. Holozoic nutrition** – Involves the consumption of complex food which is broken down inside the organism into simple molecules which are then absorbed. Most animals feed in this way, utilizing a specialized digestive system. Insectivorous plants are partly holozoic.

**2. Saprobiontic nutrition** (sometimes called saprotrophic or saprophytic nutrition) – Involves the consumption of complex organic food from the bodies of decaying organisms. The food is either already in a soluble form or it is digested externally into simple molecules which then diffuse into the saprobiont. There is no digestive system. Some bacteria and fungi feed in this way.

**3. Parasitism** – Involves feeding on complex organic food derived from other living organisms. There is a close association between the parasite, which benefits, and the host, which is harmed. Food is usually obtained in soluble form and so if a digestive system is present it is very simple. A few parasites ingest solid food and therefore possess digestive systems.

**4. Mutualism** – Here again there is a close association between members of two species, but in this case both derive some benefit from the relationship.

**5. Commensalism** – In this close association, one member benefits while the other neither benefits nor is it harmed.

The term **symbiosis** is often used to describe two species which live together in an intimate relationship which entails one living in or on the body of another. As such the term is a general one covering the more specific associations of parasitism, mutualism and commensalism.

Associations between organisms are never static nor do they fall into clearly defined groups. It is often difficult to say to which category a relationship should be assigned – indeed a number of associations change in the course of time. The parasite *Armillaria mellea* (honey fungus) for example eventually kills the tree on which it lives but then continues to live as a saprobiont on its remains.

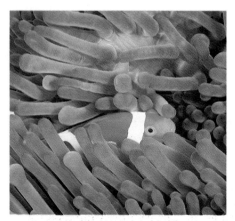

Clownfish on anemone

# 15.1 Holozoic nutrition

Holozoic organisms obtain their energy from the consumption of complex organic food which is digested within their bodies. Their nutrition involves most, if not all, of the following stages:

1. **Obtaining the food** – May involve movement of the organism to the food source.

2. **Ingestion** – Organisms use a variety of feeding mechanisms which depend upon the size and nature of the food.

3. **Physical (mechanical) digestion** – By means of a variety of structures including teeth, radula and gizzard.

4. **Chemical digestion** – A process largely carried out by enzymes.

5. **Absorption** – Useful soluble materials must be absorbed from the digestive system into the body tissues.

6. **Assimilation** – The materials absorbed must enter individual cells and be incorporated into them.

7. **Elimination (egestion)** – Unwanted material which has been ingested must be removed from the body.

Holozoic organisms can be classified according to the type of food ingested. Organisms which feed on living or recently dead plant material are called **herbivores**, while those feeding on living or recently dead animals are called **carnivores**. Organisms that feed on a diet combining plant and animal material are called **omnivores**. Some holozoic organisms consume liquid material (**liquid feeders**) but the majority take in particles of solid food and are known as **phagotrophs**. Phagotrophs may take in relatively large particles, in which case the organisms are called **macrophagous feeders**, or very small particles, in which case they are called **microphagous feeders**. Mussels are microphagous feeders; they use their sheet-like gills as a fine meshwork to strain tiny particles from the water. Cilia on these gills draw water across them and the particles become trapped on the mucus which covers the gills. This food-laden mucus is drawn to the mouth where it is ingested.

Mussels under water

# 15.2 Diet

All organisms require a constant supply of essential nutrients. What these nutrients are and the amounts of each required by an organism varies from species to species. In mammals **carbohydrates** and **fats** are needed in relatively large quantities as sources of energy, and **proteins** are needed in large amounts for growth and repair. **Vitamins** and **minerals** are required in much smaller quantities for a variety of specific functions. **Water** is a vital constituent of the diet and **dietary fibre (roughage)** is necessary for efficient digestion.

## 15.2.1 Carbohydrates and fats (energy requirements)

Details of the chemistry of carbohydrates and fats are given in Chapter 2. The main function of both is to provide energy. The amount of energy in food is expressed in **joules**. (It was previously measured in calories. In books and magazines concerned with diet the term calorie is still commonly used. One calorie is equal to 4.18 joules.) To measure the amount of energy in different foods, a given mass is burned in oxygen in a piece of apparatus called a **bomb calorimeter**. The total heat generated gives a measure of the food's energy content (also called its **calorific value**).

TABLE 15.1  **Recommended daily intake of energy according to age, activity and sex**

| Age/years | Average body weight/kg | Degree of activity/ circumstances | Energy requirement/kJ | |
|---|---|---|---|---|
| | | | Male | Female |
| 1 | 7 | Average | 3200 | 3200 |
| 5 | 20 | Average | 7500 | 7500 |
| 10 | 30 | Average | 9500 | 9500 |
| 15 | 45 | Average<br>Sedentary | 11 500<br>11 300 | 11 500<br>9000 |
| 25 | 65 (male)<br>55 (female) | Moderately active<br>Very active<br>Sedentary | 12 500<br>15 000<br>11 000 | 9500<br>10 500<br>9000 |
| 50 | 65 (male)<br>55 (female) | Moderately active<br>Very active | 12 000<br>15 000 | 9500<br>10 500 |
| 75 | 63 (male)<br>53 (female) | Sedentary | 9000 | 8000 |
| Any | – | During pregnancy | – | 10 000 |
| Any | – | Breast feeding | – | 11 500 |

The energy required by an organism varies with sex, size, age and activity. Table 15.1 provides examples of the recommended daily energy intake for humans of various ages. Ideally two-thirds of this should be derived from carbohydrates and the remainder from fats.

Much attention has been focused recently on the correlation between a high fat intake in the diet and heart disease. It is always difficult to draw relationships directly between one type of food and the incidence of a specific disease because foods contain a wide variety of substances. In addition, factors such as exercise, stress and smoking affect an individual's health and the way food is utilized. It does, however, seem that a high intake of fats, especially saturated fats (see Section 2.6.1), is a contributory factor in causing heart disease.

## 15.2.2 Proteins

The chemistry of proteins is given in Section 2.7. As a last resort the body may respire proteins to provide energy, but their main function is as a source of amino acids which are used to synthesize new proteins. These proteins are used in metabolism, growth and repair. Plants are able to synthesize all their own amino acids but animals are more limited. Humans, for example require nine amino acids, called **essential amino acids**, in the diet. Although plant food contains proportionately fewer proteins, a properly balanced vegetable diet can nevertheless provide all the essential amino acids. It is only where there is a dependence on just one or two plant foods as sources of proteins that malnutrition results.

### 15.2.3 Vitamins

Vitamins are a group of essential organic compounds which are needed in small amounts for normal growth and metabolism. If the diet lacks a particular vitamin, a disorder called a **deficiency disease** results. The vitamins required vary from species to species. Table 15.2 lists those needed in a human diet and the roles they play. Vitamins are normally classified as **water soluble** (vitamins C and the B complex) or **fat soluble** (vitamins

**BLE 15.2  Vitamins required in the human diet**

| Vitamin/name | Fat/water soluble | Major food sources | Function | Deficiency symptoms |
|---|---|---|---|---|
| $A_1$ Retinol | Fat soluble | Liver, vegetables, fruits, dairy foods | Maintains normal epithelial structure. Needed to form visual pigments | Dry skin. Poor night vision. Xerophthalmia |
| $B_1$ Thiamin | Water soluble | Liver, legumes, yeast, wheat and rice germ | Coenzyme in cellular respiration | Nervous disorder called beri-beri. Neuritis and mental disturbances. Heart failure |
| $B_2$ Riboflavin | Water soluble | Liver, yeast, dairy produce | Coenzymes (flavo-proteins) in cellular respiration | Soreness of the tongue and corners of the mouth |
| $B_3$ (pp factor) Niacin (nicotinic acid) | Water soluble | Liver, yeast, wholemeal bread | Coenzyme (NAD, NADP) in cellular metabolism | Skin lesions known as pellagra. Diarrhoea |
| $B_5$ Pantothenic acid | Water soluble | Liver, yeast, eggs | Forms part of acetyl coenzyme A in cellular respiration | Neuromotor disorders, fatigue and muscle cramps |
| $B_6$ Pyridoxine | Water soluble | Liver, kidney, fish | Coenzymes in amino acid metabolism | Dermatitis. Nervous disorders |
| $B_{12}$ Cyanocobalamine | Water soluble | Meat, eggs, dairy food | Nucleoprotein (RNA) synthesis. Needed in red blood cell formation | Pernicious anaemia. Malformation of red blood cells |
| Biotin | Water soluble | Liver, yeast. Synthesized by intestinal bacteria | Coenzymes in carboxylation reactions | Dermatitis and muscle pains |
| Folic acid | Water soluble | Liver, vegetables, fish | Nucleoprotein synthesis. Red blood cell synthesis | Anaemia |
| C Ascorbic acid | Water soluble | Citrus fruits, tomatoes, potatoes | Formation of connective tissues, especially collagen fibres | Non-formation of connective tissues. Bleeding gums – scurvy |
| D Calciferol | Fat soluble | Liver, fish oils, dairy produce. Action of sunlight on skin | Absorption and metabolism of calcium and phosphorus, therefore important in formation of teeth and bones | Defective bone formation known as rickets |
| E Tocopherol | Fat soluble | Liver, green vegetables | Function unclear in humans. In rats it prevents haemolysis of red blood cells | Anaemia |
| K Phylloquinone | Fat soluble | Green vegetables. Synthesized by intestinal bacteria | Blood clotting | Failure of blood to clot |

## Did you know?

A lifetime's supply of all vitamins for a human weigh just 250 g.

A, D, E and K). Whereas excess water-soluble vitamins are simply excreted in urine, fat-soluble vitamins tend to accumulat in fatty tissues of the body, and may even build up to lethal concentrations if taken in excess.

### 15.2.4 Minerals

The principal mineral ions required by plants and animals and their functions are listed in Chapter 2 in Table 2.1. The principal minerals required in the human diet, and their sources, are further summarized in Table 15.3.

### 15.2.5 Water

Water makes up about 70% of the total body weight of mamma and serves a wide variety of important functions which are discussed more fully in Section 22.1. Table 15.4 gives the daily water balance in a human not engaged in active work, i.e. there is no excessive sweating.

### 15.2.6 Dietary fibre (roughage)

Fibre is indigestible material which passes through the alimentary canal almost unchanged. As it does not cross an epithelial lining of the gut it never actually enters the body. It is

TABLE 15.3  **Some essential minerals required in the human diet**

| Mineral | Major food source | Function |
|---|---|---|
| **Macronutrients**<br>Calcium ($Ca^{2+}$) | Dairy foods, eggs, green vegetables | Constituent of bones and teeth, needed in blood clotting and muscle contraction. Enzyme activator |
| Chlorine ($Cl^-$) | Table salt | Maintenance of anion/cation balance. Formation of hydrochloric acid |
| Magnesium ($Mg^{2+}$) | Meat, green vegetables | Component of bones and teeth. Enzyme activator |
| Phosphate ($PO_4^{3-}$) | Dairy foods, eggs, meat, vegetables | Constituent of nucleic acids, ATP, phospholipids (in cell membranes), bones and teeth |
| Potassium ($K^+$) | Meat, fruit and vegetables | Needed for nerve and muscle action and in protein synthesis |
| Sodium ($Na^+$) | Table salt, dairy foods, meat, eggs, vegetables | Needed for nerve and muscle action. Maintenance of anion/cation balance |
| Sulphate ($SO_4^{2-}$) | Meat, eggs, dairy foods | Component of proteins and coenzymes |
| **Micronutrients (trace elements)**<br>Cobalt ($Co^{2+}$) | Meat | Component of vitamin $B_{12}$ and needed for the formation of red blood cells |
| Copper ($Cu^{2+}$) | Liver, meat, fish | Constituent of many enzymes. Needed for bone and haemoglobin formation |
| Fluorine ($F^-$) | Many water supplies | Improves resistance to tooth decay |
| Iodine ($I^-$) | Fish, shellfish, iodized salt | Component of the growth hormone, thyroxin |
| Iron ($Fe^{2+}$ or $Fe^{3+}$) | Liver, meat, green vegetables | Constituent of many enzymes, electron carriers, haemoglobi and myoglobin |
| Manganese ($Mn^{2+}$) | Liver, kidney, tea and coffee | Enzyme activator and growth factor in bone development |
| Molybdenum ($Mo^{4+}$) | Liver, kidney, green vegetables | Required by some enzymes |
| Zinc ($Zn^{2+}$) | Liver, fish, shellfish | Enzyme activator, involved in the physiology of insulin |

**TABLE 15.4  Human daily water balance**

| Process | Water uptake /cm³ | Water output /cm³ |
|---|---|---|
| Drinking | 1450 | – |
| In food | 800 | – |
| From respiration | 350 | – |
| In urine | – | 1500 |
| In sweat | – | 600 |
| Evaporation from lungs | – | 400 |
| In faeces | – | 100 |
| TOTAL | 2600 | 2600 |

not a metabolic product and its removal from the body is therefore called **egestion** or **elimination** and not excretion. Although it does not have a metabolic function, fibre is essential to the efficient working of the alimentary canal. It gives bulk to the material within the intestines, absorbing water and making the contents much more solid. In this form it stimulates peristalsis and is easier to move along the intestines. It thus helps prevent constipation and other intestinal disorders. Fibre consists mostly of the cellulose cell walls of plants. In humans, the removal of much fibre from processed food has led to an increase in intestinal disorders. This has shown the value of fibre and led to an emphasis on high-fibre diets as an aid to healthy living.

## 15.3  Principles of digestion

Food must be small enough to be ingested by holozoic organisms. This may involve the use of teeth or other organs designed to break up food into small pieces. This **mechanical breakdown** also has the effect of giving the food a larger surface area, which aids later digestion.

Food comprises relatively few building blocks, largely monosaccharides, amino acids, fatty acids and glycerol, arranged in an almost infinite variety of macromolecules, which meet the needs of the organism they make up. What suits one organism, however, does not necessarily suit another. The food ingested must therefore be broken down further into its component parts so that they can be rebuilt into the macromolecules and structures of the organism ingesting them. The food must, in any case, be made small enough to pass across cell membranes. This breakdown is mainly achieved through hydrolysis reactions speeded up by enzymes and is termed **chemical digestion**.

As we have seen in Section 3.2.1 enzymes are specific in the reactions they accelerate and therefore many are needed to completely break down a large macromolecule. Typically one enzyme breaks up a molecule into smaller sections and then others reduce these parts to their basic components. The carbohydrate starch, for example, has alternate glycosidic bonds, which may be hydrolysed by **amylase** to yield the disaccharide maltose, which may then be further hydrolysed to its glucose monosaccharides by the enzyme **maltase**. Protein molecules, being larger and more varied, require groups of enzymes to digest them. These are called **peptidases**. One group hydrolyses the peptide bonds between amino acids in the central region of molecules; these are called **endopeptidases**. Another group then hydrolyses the peptide bonds on the terminal amino acids of these portions, progressively reducing them to their individual amino acids. These are called **exopeptidases** and are of two types. The **aminopeptidases** work at the end of the chain that has an amino acid with a free amino ($-NH_2$) group whereas the **carboxypeptidases** work at the opposite end where the amino

## Did you know?

The average person consumes about 5 kg of food additives per year.

acid has a free carboxyl (−COOH) group (see Fig. 15.1). Fats, being smaller molecules, can be broken down into fatty acids and monoglycerides (a single fatty acid linked to a glycerol) by the one enzyme **lipase**.

As we also saw in Section 3.2.6, enzymes differ in the conditions under which they operate most efficiently, not least in their optimum pH. Clearly it is impossible for one region of the digestive system to be both acid and alkaline at the same time, and so an alimentary canal evolved, a tube which is long enough to possess different regions, each with its own set of conditions. To pass through each region food has to be moved along the alimentary canal by **peristalsis**. Digestion complete, **absorption** of the useful products must take place and the undigested food, dead cells and bacteria which aid digestion must be eliminated – a process called **egestion**.

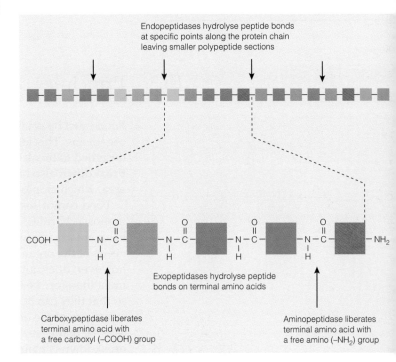

*Fig. 15.1 Action of endo- and exopeptidases*

## 15.4 Digestion in humans

Digestion in humans takes place along a muscular tube which measures around 10 m in length in adults. Associated with it are a variety of secretory glands, some of which are embedded in the wall of the alimentary canal, others are separate from it but connected to it by a duct.

### 15.4.1 Digestion in the mouth

Mechanical breakdown of food begins in the mouth or **buccal cavity**. Humans are omnivores and hence have an unspecialized diet of mixed animal and plant origin. Their teeth reflect this lack of specialization, all types being present and developed to a similar extent. Apart from assisting speech, the tongue also manipulates the food during chewing and so ensures it is well mixed with **saliva** produced from three pairs of **salivary glands** (Fig. 15.2). Around 1.0–1.5 dm$^3$ of saliva are produced daily. Saliva contains:

1. **Water** – Over 99% of saliva is water.

2. **Salivary amylase** – A digestive enzyme which hydrolyses starch to maltose.

3. **Mineral salts** (e.g. sodium hydrogen carbonate) – This helps to maintain a pH of around 6.5–7.5, which is the optimum for the action of salivary amylase.

4. **Mucin** – A sticky material which helps to bind food particles together and lubricate them to assist swallowing.

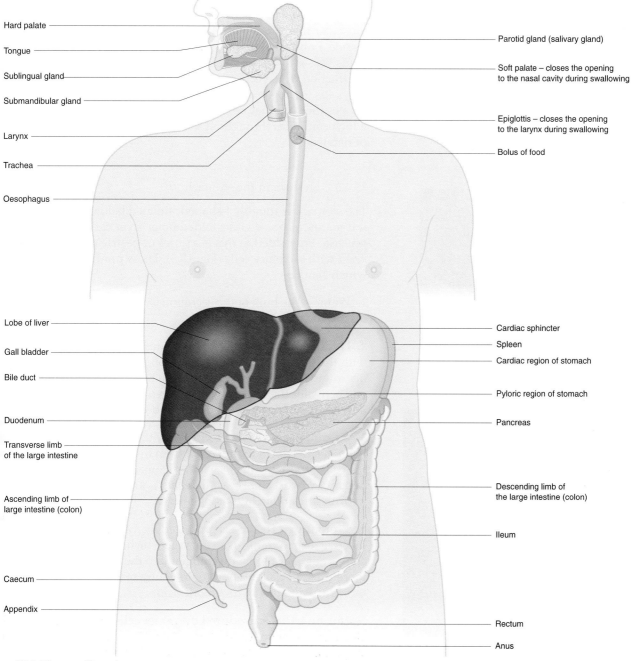

*g. 15.2 Human digestive system*

Taste buds on the tongue allow food to be selected – unpleasant tasting food being rejected. The thoroughly chewed food is rolled into a **bolus** and passed to the back of the mouth for swallowing.

### 15.4.2 Swallowing and peristalsis

The bolus is pushed by the tongue to the back of the mouth and then into the **pharynx** where the **oesophagus** (leading to the stomach) meets with the trachea (which leads to the lungs). A variety of reflexes ensure that food when swallowed passes down the oesophagus and not the trachea. One such reflex is the closure of the opening into the larynx (which leads to the trachea). This opening, called the **glottis**, is covered by a structure known as the **epiglottis** when food is passed to the back of the mouth. The opening to the nasal cavity is closed by the **soft palate**. In this way the bolus enters the oesophagus, a muscular tube lined with stratified epithelium and mucus glands. Lubricated by the mucus secreted by these glands, the bolus passes to the stomach by means of a wave of muscular contraction which causes constriction of the oesophagus behind the bolus. As this constriction passes along the oesophagus it pushes the bolus before it, down to the stomach. This process, which continues throughout the alimentary canal, is called **peristalsis**.

### 15.4.3 Digestion in the stomach

The stomach is roughly J-shaped, situated below the diaphragm. It is a muscular sac with a folded inner layer called the **gastric mucosa**. Embedded in this is a series of **gastric pits** which are lined with secretory cells (Fig. 15.3). These produce **gastric juice** which contains:

1. **Water** – The bulk of the secretion is water in which are dissolved the other constituents.

2. **Hydrochloric acid** – This is produced by **oxyntic cells** and with the water forms a dilute solution giving gastric juice its pH of around 2.0. It helps to kill bacteria brought in with the food and activates the enzymes pepsinogen and prorennin. It also initiates the hydrolysis of sucrose and nucleoproteins.

3. **Pepsinogen** – This is produced by the **zymogen** or **chief cells** in an inactive form to prevent it from hydrolysing the proteins of the cells producing it. Once in the stomach it is activated to **pepsin** by hydrochloric acid. Pepsin is an endopeptidase which hydrolyses protein into polypeptides.

4. **Prorennin** – This too is produced by zymogen cells and is an inactive form of **rennin**, an enzyme which coagulates milk by converting the soluble **caseinogen** into the insoluble **casein**. It is therefore especially important in young mammals. Prorennin, too, is activated by hydrochloric acid.

5. **Mucus** – This is produced by **goblet cells** and forms a protective layer on the stomach wall, thus preventing pepsin and hydrochloric acid from breaking down the gastric mucosa (i.e. prevents autolysis). If the protection is not effective and the

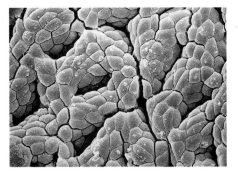

Gastric mucosa of the stomach (SEM) (×450 approx.)

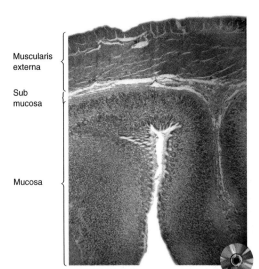

Muscularis externa

Sub mucosa

Mucosa

Stomach wall (×130)

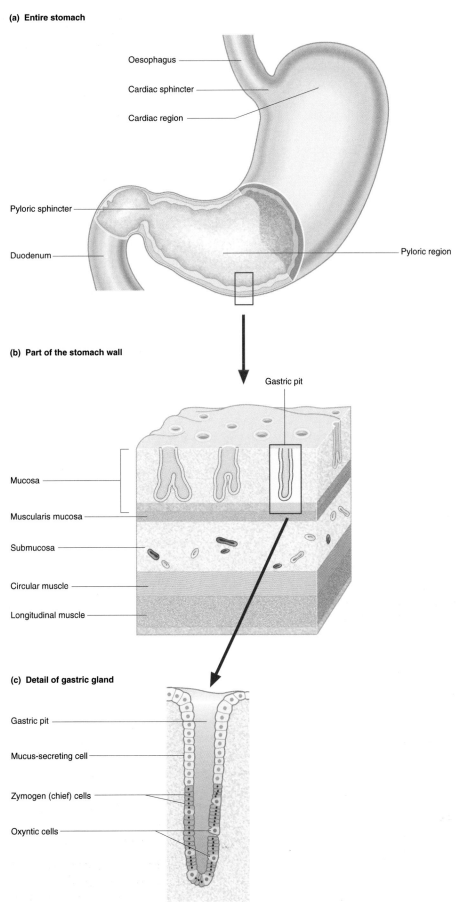

**(a) Entire stomach**

Oesophagus

Cardiac sphincter

Cardiac region

Pyloric sphincter

Duodenum

Pyloric region

**(b) Part of the stomach wall**

Gastric pit

Mucosa

Muscularis mucosa

Submucosa

Circular muscle

Longitudinal muscle

**(c) Detail of gastric gland**

Gastric pit

Mucus-secreting cell

Zymogen (chief) cells

Oxyntic cells

*Fig. 15.3 Structure of the human stomach*

gastric juice attacks the mucosa, an ulcer results. Mucus also helps lubricate movement of food within the stomach.

During its stay in the stomach, food is thoroughly churned and mixed with gastric juice by periodic contractions of the muscular stomach wall. In this way a creamy fluid called **chyme** is produced. Relaxation of the pyloric sphincter and contraction of the stomach allow the chyme to enter the duodenum. The chyme from any one meal is released gradually over a period of 3–4 hours. This enables the small intestine to work on a little material at a time and provides a continuous supply of food for absorption throughout the period between meals.

### 15.4.4 Digestion in the small intestine

In humans the small intestine is over 6 m in length and its coils fill much of the lower abdominal cavity. It consists of two main parts: the much shorter **duodenum** where most digestion occurs and the longer **ileum** which is largely concerned with absorption. The walls of the small intestine are folded and possess finger-like projections called **villi**. The villi contain fibres of smooth muscle and regularly contract and relax. This helps to mix the food with the enzyme secretions and keep fresh supplies in contact with the villi, for absorption. The digestive juices which operate in the small intestine come from three sources: the liver, the pancreas and the intestinal wall.

*Bile juice*
Bile juice is a complex green fluid produced by the liver. It contains no enzymes but possesses two other substances important to digestion.

1. **Mineral salts (e.g. sodium hydrogen carbonate)** – These help to neutralize the acid chyme from the stomach and so create a more neutral pH for the enzymes of the small intestine to work in.

2. **Bile salts – sodium and potassium glycocholate and taurocholate** – They **emulsify** lipids, breaking them down into minute droplets. This is a physical, not a chemical change, which provides a greater surface area for pancreatic lipase to work on.

The liver performs other functions, some associated with digestion, and these are detailed in Section 25.6.2.

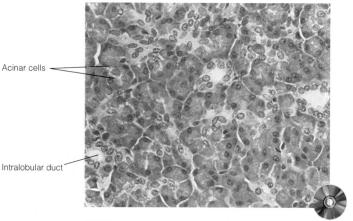

Acinar cells

Intralobular duct

Cellular structure of pancreas showing intralobular ducts

*Pancreatic juice*

The pancreas is situated below the stomach and is unusual in that it produces both an exocrine secretion, the pancreatic juice, and an endocrine secretion, the hormone insulin. The endocrine function is not directly concerned with digestion and is described in Section 25.3. Pancreatic juice, in addition to water, contains:

1. **Mineral salts (e.g. sodium hydrogen carbonate)** – Help to neutralize acid chyme from the stomach and so provide a more neutral pH in which the intestinal enzymes can operate.

2. **Proteases** – These include **trypsinogen** which, when activated by enterokinase from the intestinal wall, forms the endopeptidase called **trypsin** which hydrolyses proteins into peptides. Trypsin also activates another protease in the secretion, chymotrypsinogen into **chymotrypsin**; this too converts proteins into peptides. Also present is the exopeptidase called **carboxypeptidase** which converts peptides into smaller peptides and some amino acids.

3. **Pancreatic amylase** – Completes the hydrolysis of starch to maltose which began in the mouth.

4. **Lipase** – Breaks down fats into fatty acids and monoglycerides (glycerol + one fatty acid) by hydrolysis.

5. **Nuclease** – Converts nucleic acids into their constituent nucleotides.

*Intestinal juice (succus entericus)*

The mucus and sodium hydrogen carbonate in intestinal juice are made by coiled **Brunner's glands** whereas the enzymes are produced by the breakdown (lysis) of cells at the tips of the villi.

1. **Mucus** – Helps to lubricate the intestinal walls and prevent autolysis.

2. **Mineral salts (e.g. sodium hydrogen carbonate)** – Produced by the Brunner's glands in order to neutralize the acid chyme from the stomach and so provide a more suitable pH for the action of enzymes in the intestine.

3. **Proteases (erepsin)** – These include the exopeptidase called **aminopeptidase**, which converts peptides into smaller peptides and amino acids, and **dipeptidase**, which hydrolyses dipeptides into amino acids.

4. **Enterokinase** – A non-digestive enzyme which activates the trypsinogen produced by the pancreas.

5. **Nucleotidase** – Converts nucleotides into pentose sugars, phosphoric acid and organic bases.

6. **Carbohydrases** – These include **amylase**, which helps complete the hydrolysis of starch to maltose; **maltase**, which hydrolyses maltose to glucose; **lactase**, which hydrolyses the milk sugar lactose into glucose and galactose; and **sucrase**, which hydrolyses sucrose into glucose and fructose.

## BIOLOGY AROUND US

# Lactose intolerance and galactosaemia

In early life, humans feed exclusively on milk, whether breast milk or a substitute formulated from the milk of other mammals such as a cow. Milk contains the disaccharide lactose as its main sugar and so young babies produce the enzyme lactase to digest it into its component monosaccharides, glucose and galactose, which are readily absorbed in the intestines.

Lactose is not a component of other food and our distant ancestors did not drink milk as adults. As a consequence, the production of lactose was unnecessary and wasteful in adult life and so humans have evolved a system whereby the gene for lactase production is normally switched off in late childhood. Only in areas where milk continues to be consumed by adults is the production of lactase continued. These areas include much of Europe and some populations of West Africa, such as the Fulani who keep cattle whose milk they use to supplement their diet. Elsewhere the adult population is unable to digest lactose: a condition known as **lactose intolerance**.

Lactose intolerance in infants is rare but can be life-threatening. These infants cannot produce lactase and so cannot obtain their glucose from lactose digestion. One remedy is to feed these babies a milk substitute made from soy or other plants where sugars are in the form of glucose rather than lactose.

Another problem arises in babies who suffer from **galactosaemia**. About one in every 40 000 babies suffer from this inherited condition which prevents them producing the enzyme **galactose transferase (GALT)**. This enzyme converts the galactose absorbed into the bloodstream from lactose digestion into glucose, which is then used as an energy source. Without the enzyme, galactose accumulates, causing sickness. Once again the remedy is a lactose-free diet.

### 15.4.5 Absorption and assimilation

Digestion results in the formation of relatively small, soluble molecules which, provided there is a concentration gradient, could be absorbed into the body through the intestinal wall by diffusion. This, however, would be slow and wasteful and in any case, if the epithelial lining were permeable to molecules such as glucose, it could just as easily result in it diffusing out of the body when the concentration in the intestines was too low. For these reasons most substances are absorbed by **active transport** (Section 4.3.4) which only allows inward movement. Efficient uptake is often dependent on the presence of other factors. For example, glucose and amino acid absorption appear to be linked to the movement of sodium ions across the membranes of epithelial cells; calcium ion absorption requires the presence of vitamin D.

Villi

Lining of ileum (SEM) (×250)

Efficient absorption is also dependent on a large surface area being available. The wall of the ileum achieves this in four ways:

1. It is very long – almost 6 m in humans and up to 45 m in cattle.

2. Its walls are folded (**folds of Kerkring**) to provide large internal projections.

3. The folds themselves have numerous tiny finger-like projections called **villi** (Fig. 15.4).

4. The epithelial cells lining the villi are covered with minute projections about 0.6 $\mu$m in length, called **microvilli** (not to be confused with cilia). These collectively form a **brush border**.

Sugars, amino acids and other water-soluble materials such as minerals enter the blood capillaries of the villi. From here they enter arterioles, which later merge to form the hepatic portal vein which carries blood to the liver. In general, the level of different absorbed foods in the hepatic portal vein varies, depending on the type of food eaten and the interval since ingestion. It is the main role of the liver to regulate these variations – by storing excess where the level of a substance is above normal, and by releasing its store when the level in the hepatic portal vein is low. For this reason, blood from the intestines is sent to the liver for homeostatic regulation before it passes to other organs where fluctuations in blood composition could be damaging. The liver is also able to break down any harmful substances absorbed, a process called **detoxification**. The fatty acids and glycerol from lipid digestion enter the epithelial cells lining the villi, where

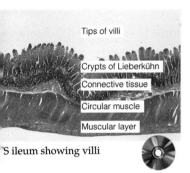

Tips of villi

Crypts of Lieberkühn

Connective tissue

Circular muscle

Muscular layer

'S ileum showing villi

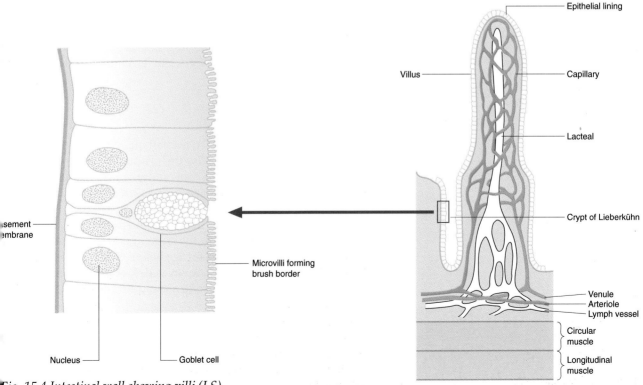

Fig. 15.4 Intestinal wall showing villi (LS)

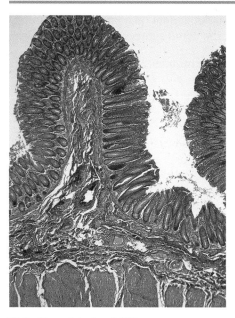

Wall of large intestine (×20)

they recombine into lipids. These then enter the lacteals rather than the blood capillaries. From here they are transported in the lymph vessels before later joining the venous system of the blood near the heart.

The passage of food from the ileum into the large intestine or colon is controlled by the **ileo-caecal valve**. The caecum in humans is little more than a slight expansion between the small and large intestine and the appendix is a small blind-ending sac leading from the caecum. In humans neither structure performs any important digestive function but, as we shall see in Section 15.9.1, they are of considerable importance to herbivorous mammals.

### 15.4.6 Water reabsorption in the large intestine

Most of the water drunk by humans is absorbed by the stomach. The large intestine or **colon** is partly responsible for reabsorbing the water from digestive secretions. With the gastric and intestinal juices each producing up to $3\,dm^3$ (litre) of secretion every day and the saliva, pancreatic and bile juices each adding a further $1.5\,dm^3$, the total volume of digestive secretions may exceed $10\,dm^3$. As most of this volume is water, it follows that the body cannot afford to allow it simply to pass out with the faeces. While most water is absorbed in the ileum, the large intestine plays an important role in reabsorbing the remainder. In doing so it changes the consistency of the faeces from liquid to semi-solid.

Within the large intestine live a huge population of bacteria, such as *Escherichia coli*, which in humans synthesize a number of vitamins including biotin and vitamin K. Deficiency of these vitamins is therefore rare, although orally administered antibiotics may destroy most of the bacteria and so create a temporary shortage. The vitamins produced are absorbed by the wall of the large intestine with water and some mineral salts. This wall is folded to increase the surface area available for absorption. Excess calcium and iron salts are actively transported from the blood into the large intestine for removal with the faeces.

### 15.4.7 Elimination (egestion)

The semi-solid faeces consist of a small quantity of indigestible food (fibre) but mostly comprise the residual material from the bile juice and other secretions, cells sloughed off the intestinal wall, a little water and immense numbers of bacteria. The wall of the large intestine produces mucus which, in addition to lubricating the movement of the faeces, helps to bind them together. After 24–36 hours in the large intestine the faeces pass to the rectum for temporary storage before they are removed through the anus, a process known as **defaecation**. Control of this removal is by two sphincters around the **anus**, the opening of the rectum to the outside.

As much of the material making up the faeces is not the result of metabolic reactions within the body, it is said to be eliminated or egested rather than excreted. However, cholesterol and bile pigments from the breakdown of haemoglobin are metabolic products and are therefore excretory.

# 15.5 Adaptations to diet

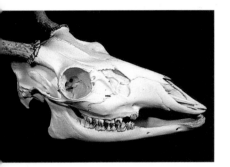

eer skull

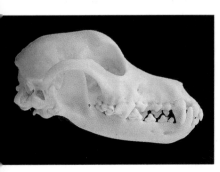

og skull

### 15.5.1 Adaptations of a herbivore to its diet

Plant material is relatively tough and largely indigestible by mammals without the aid of microorganisms. The first essential of its digestion is to grind up the vegetation, so disrupting the tissues and increasing its surface area. Animals such as cattle which consume predominantly plant material are called **herbivores** and they possess specialized dentition which may include the following features:

1. A horny pad which replaces the upper front teeth (incisors and canines).

2. A pronounced gap, the **diastema**, between the incisors and premolars. This provides a space in which newly nibbled food can be kept separate from that being ground down at the back of the mouth.

3. The **cheek teeth** (molars and premolars) have ridged surfaces which form an effective grinding surface not dissimilar to that of a coarse file.

4. The jaws easily move from side to side to allow food to be broken down between the ridged teeth.

5. The teeth grow continuously throughout the herbivore's life. This is essential as the grinding action of the teeth wears them away.

6. The alimentary canal is relatively long because digestion of plant material is difficult.

7. The stomach is divided into a number of chambers, some of which produce digestive enzymes to break down the food. Others, including the **rumen**, house bacteria and protozoa which produce the enzyme cellulase – essential to break down the cellulose which constitutes the bulk of the food ingested. Herbivores with these multichambered stomachs are called **ruminants**. Details of how ruminants digest cellulose are given in Section 15.9.1.

### 15.5.2 Adaptations of a carnivore to its diet

Carnivores such as a dog eat meat, which is mainly the muscle of another animal. This is rich in nutrients and therefore a much more concentrated source of food than plant material. Once captured and ingested, the digestion of meat presents little problem. Adaptations of a typical carnivorous mammal such as a dog include:

1. The incisor teeth are sharp and used for nipping and biting.

2. The canines are long and pointed. They are used for piercing and killing the prey and tearing flesh from the body.

3. The molars and premolars have a number of sharp pointed cusps. The last upper premolar and the first lower molar on each side of the mouth are particularly large and known as **carnassial teeth**.

4. The teeth of the upper jaw tend to overlap those of the lower jaw. The carnassial teeth therefore slide past one another, in the same way that two blades of a pair of scissors do, in order to slice the meat into manageable pieces.

5. The muscles of the jaw are well developed and powerful. This enables carnivores to grip the prey firmly during the kill and helps in crushing bone.

6. There is no lateral jaw movement as in herbivores. Such movement leads to easier dislocation of the jaw, a distinct disadvantage when trying to grip struggling prey.

7. Vertical movement of the jaw is less restricted, allowing a wide gape for capturing and killing prey.

8. The alimentary canal is short, reflecting the relative ease with which meat can be chemically digested.

## 15.6 Nervous and hormonal control of secretions

The production of a digestive secretion must be timed to coincide with the presence of food in the appropriate region of the gut. In mammals the production of digestive secretions is under both nervous and hormonal control.

Nervous stimulation occurs even before the food reaches the mouth. The sight, smell or even the mere thought of food is sufficient to cause the salivary glands to produce saliva. This response is a conditioned reflex and is explained more fully in Section 27.7.3. Once in the mouth, contact of food with the tongue causes nervous impulses to be transmitted to the brain. The brain in turn sends impulses which stimulate the salivary glands to secrete saliva. This is an unconditioned reflex response. At the same time the brain stimulates the stomach wall to secrete gastric juice, a response reinforced by nervous impulses transmitted as the food is swallowed. The stomach is thus prepared for digestion even before the food reaches it. Once initiated, the response will continue for up to an hour. The stretching of the stomach due to the presence of food within it stimulates production of gastric juice after this time.

Hormonal control of secretions begins with the presence of food in the stomach. This stimulates the stomach wall to produce a hormone called **gastrin** which passes into the bloodstream. Gastrin continues to stimulate the production of gastric juice for up to 4 hours. Because fat digestion takes longer and requires less acidic conditions, its presence in the stomach initiates the production of **enterogasterone** from the stomach wall. This hormone reduces the churning motions of the stomach and decreases the flow of the acid gastric juice. As stomach ulcers are irritated by gastric juice, sufferers are often urged to drink milk. Being rich in fat, it reduces the production of gastric juice.

ABLE 15.5    Summary of digestion

| Organ/ secretion | Production induced by | Site of action | pH of secretion | Contents | Effect |
|---|---|---|---|---|---|
| Salivary glands produce saliva | Visual or olfactory expectation and reflex stimulation | Mouth | About neutral | Salivary amylase | Amylose (starch) → maltose |
| | | | | Mineral salts | Produce optimum pH for amylase action |
| | | | | Mucin | Binds food particles into a bolus |
| Gastric glands in stomach wall produce gastric juice | Presence of food in mouth and swallowing. Presence of food in stomach. Hormones – gastrin and enterogasterone from stomach wall | Stomach | Very acid | Pepsin(ogen) | Proteins → peptides |
| | | | | (Pro)rennin | Caseinogen → casein |
| | | | | Hydrochloric acid | Activates pepsinogen and prorennin. Produces optimum pH for action of these enzymes |
| | | | | Mucus | Lubrication and prevention of autolysis |
| Liver produces bile juice | Secretin stimulates production of bile and cholecystokinin causes it to be released | Duodenum | Neutral | Bile salts | Emulsify fats |
| | | | | Mineral salts | Neutralize acid chyme |
| | | | | Bile pigments | Excretory products from breakdown of haemoglobin |
| | | | | Cholesterol | Excretory product |
| Pancreas produces pancreatic juice | Secretin stimulates production of mineral salts and pancreozymin production of enzymes | Duodenum | Neutral | Trypsin(ogen) | Protein → peptides + amino acids Activates chymotrypsinogen |
| | | | | Chymotrypsin(ogen) | Peptides → smaller peptides + amino acids |
| | | | | Carboxypeptidase | Peptides → smaller peptides + amino acids |
| | | | | Amylase | Amylose (starch) → maltose |
| | | | | Lipase | Fats → fatty acids + glycerol |
| | | | | Nuclease | Nucleic acids → nucleotides |
| | | | | Mineral salts | Neutralize acid chyme |
| Wall of small intestine produces intestinal juice (succus entericus) | Presence of food stimulates the intestinal lining | Duodenum and ileum | Alkaline | Aminopeptidase | Peptides → amino acids |
| | | | | Dipeptidase | Dipeptides → amino acids |
| | | | | Enterokinase | Activates trypsinogen |
| | | | | Nucleotidase | Nucleotides → organic base + pentose sugar + phosphate |
| | | | | Maltase | Maltose → glucose |
| | | | | Lactase | Lactose → glucose + galactose |
| | | | | Sucrase | Sucrose → glucose + fructose |
| | | | | Mineral salts | Neutralize acid chyme |

When food leaves the stomach and enters the duodenum, it stimulates the production of two hormones from the duodenal wall. **Secretin**, via the bloodstream, travels to the liver where it causes the production of bile and to the pancreas, where it stimulates the secretion of mineral salts. **Cholecystokinin–pancreozymin** causes the gall bladder to contract (releasing the bile juice into the duodenum) and stimulates the pancreas to secrete its enzymes.

# 15.7 Parasitism

## PROJECT

**Students who are involved in sport are more likely to suffer from athlete's foot**

Test this hypothesis.

Parasitism is an association between two organisms in which one, the parasite, is metabolically dependent on the other, the host. This is invariably a nutritional dependence, the parasite absorbing either host tissues and fluids, or the contents of the host's intestine. In this relationship the host is harmed in some way. It is often difficult to distinguish between parasitism and predation or scavenging. However, most parasitologists feel that a parasitic relationship is one in which the parasite spends a significant length of time feeding on the host. A biting fly would not be considered a parasite by most biologists, but a leech would.

Another difference between a parasite and a predator is that the host can produce an immune response to a parasite but not to a predator. A parasite's success may be measured by its ability to resist this immune reaction.

There are two main categories of parasites: **endoparasites** which live inside the body of the host and **ectoparasites** which live on the outside. In both cases the parasite needs to be able to maintain its position in or on the host. Any organism must be able to reproduce and the offspring must be able to find a suitable habitat in which to develop. This is a particular problem for parasites which often need to produce large numbers of eggs or spores in order to ensure the success of a few. Parasitic life cycles may include elaborate mechanisms for successful transmission, often with several larval stages.

Plant parasites are sometimes divided into two groups according to the way they obtain their energy from cells. **Biotrophs** (living feeders) obtain their energy only from living host cells, whereas **necrotrophs** (dead feeders) can obtain their energy from cells which they have killed.

Parasites display most, but not necessarily all, of the following features:

1.  They have agents for penetration of the host.

2.  They have a means of attachment to the host.

3.  They have protection against the host's immune responses.

4.  They show degeneration of unnecessary organ systems.

5.  They produce many eggs, seeds or spores.

6.  They have a vector or intermediate host.

7.  They produce resistant stages to overcome the period spent away from the host.

Some parasitic diseases are listed in Table 15.6. Let us now look at some examples of parasites to illustrate these features.

### 15.7.1 *Plasmodium* (malarial parasite)

*Plasmodium* is a protoctistan of the phylum Apicomplexa. Four species are parasitic in humans, all causing forms of malaria. Malaria is a debilitating fever and *Plasmodium falciparum* probably causes more human deaths in the tropics than any other organism. The malarial parasite has a very complex life cycle involving an asexual stage in the liver and red blood cells of humans and a sexual stage which begins in humans and continues in mosquitoes of the genus *Anopheles*. Full details of the malarial life cycle are given in Section 31.2.10.

## 15.7.2 Parasitic flatworms

Two groups of Platyhelminthes (flatworms) are parasitic: the Cestoda, or tapeworms, and the Trematoda, or flukes. The parasitic features of *Fasciola* (liver fluke) and *Taenia* (tapeworm) will be considered in this section.

Both have complex life cycles, that of *Fasciola* involving a vertebrate primary host and an invertebrate secondary host. The many eggs which are produced inside the primary host give rise to a series of larval stages, one of which enters the secondary host where its development continues. *Fasciola hepatica* is found in sheep and cattle worldwide and may cause epidemics of 'liver rot'. The life cycle of *Taenia* involves two vertebrate hosts (Fig. 15.5).

### The tapeworm *(Taenia)*

The adults of *Taenia solium*, the pork tapeworm, live attached to the intestinal mucosa of humans. The intermediate host is a pig. Tapeworms consist of a **scolex** followed by a series of segments known as **proglottids**. The scolex bears four suckers at the sides and a crown of hooks at the top. Although it is small, the scolex provides a firm attachment to the wall of the intestine and prevents the worm from being dislodged by the host's peristaltic movements.

Behind the scolex the narrow neck region gives rise to proglottids by a continuous process of budding. As the individual segments grow and mature they are pushed back from the scolex. The adult worm may be over 3 metres long.

Tapeworms are highly specialized endoparasites and neither scolex nor proglottids contain a mouth or alimentary canal. Predigested food can be absorbed over the entire body surface, facilitated by the worm's large surface-area to volume ratio; each proglottis is no more than 1 mm thick. The worms have a thick cuticle and produce inhibitory substances to prevent their digestion by the host's enzymes. Simple nerve fibres and a pair of excretory canals run the length of the worm but most of its anatomy is concerned with reproduction. Each mature proglottis contains both male and female reproductive organs and, following fertilization, eggs develop shells and yolk before passing to the uterus where they accumulate. The sex organs degenerate leaving an egg-packed uterus which fills the proglottis. At intervals these segments, known as **gravid proglottids**, break off the chain and are expelled with the host's

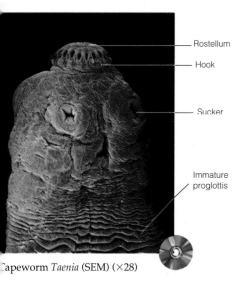

- Rostellum
- Hook
- Sucker
- Immature proglottis

Tapeworm *Taenia* (SEM) (×28)

TABLE 15.6 **Parasitic diseases**

| Parasite | Major group | Primary host | Disease caused | Secondary host, if any |
|---|---|---|---|---|
| *Phytophthora infestans* | Fungi | Potato | Potato blight | – |
| *Puccinia graminis* | Fungi | Wheat | Black stem rust | – |
| *Eimeria* | Apicomplexa | Poultry | Coccidiosis | – |
| *Plasmodium* | Apicomplexa | Humans | Malaria | *Anopheles* mosquito |
| *Schistosoma* | Platyhelminthes | Humans | Bilharzia (schistosomiasis) | Freshwater snail |
| *Fasciola* | Platyhelminthes | Sheep | Liver rot | Snail |
| *Taenia solium* | Platyhelminthes | Humans | Occasionally cysticercosis | Pig |
| *Wucheria bancrofti* | Nematoda | Humans | Elephantiasis | Mosquito |
| *Oncocerca volvulus* | Nematoda | Humans | River blindness | Blackfly |

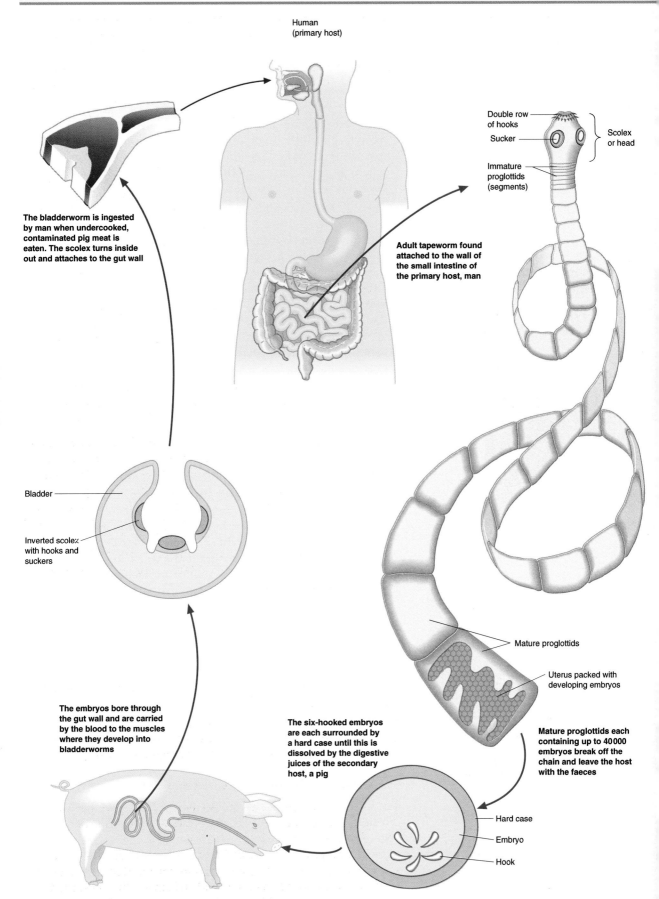

Human
(primary host)

Double row
of hooks

Sucker

Scolex
or head

Immature
proglottids
(segments)

The bladderworm is ingested
by man when undercooked,
contaminated pig meat is
eaten. The scolex turns inside
out and attaches to the gut wall

Adult tapeworm found
attached to the wall of
the small intestine of
the primary host, man

Bladder

Inverted scolex
with hooks and
suckers

Mature proglottids

Uterus packed with
developing embryos

The embryos bore through
the gut wall and are carried
by the blood to the muscles
where they develop into
bladderworms

The six-hooked embryos
are each surrounded by
a hard case until this is
dissolved by the digestive
juices of the secondary
host, a pig

Mature proglottids each
containing up to 40000
embryos break off the
chain and leave the host
with the faeces

Hard case

Embryo

Hook

*Fig. 15.5  Life cycle of the tapeworm* Taenia solium

**BLE 15.7  Blood fluke – another parasitic tworm**

| Name | Schistosoma mansoni |
|---|---|
| Disease caused | Bilharzia |
| Primary host | Human |
| Secondary host | Fresh water snail |
| Adults | Female always carried in a groove on the larger male |
| Eggs | Have spines; cause considerable damage as they bore out of the narrow blood vessels to reach the intestine; deposited in faeces. |
| Larval stages | Miracidium penetrates snail and encysts. Cercariae leave snail and penetrate human skin. Carried in blood to mature in hepatic portal vessels. |
| Other features | Miracidia and cercariae free swimming; adults move in large blood vessels. Adults have suckers for attachment and a body covering which protects them from the host's immune responses. Feed on blood, tissue fluid and cells, mainly extracellularly. |

faeces. Each segment may contain up to 40 000 eggs which survive until eaten by the secondary host because they have resistant shells. Further development only takes place when the eggs are consumed by pigs. Embryos then emerge and move into the animal's muscles where they remain dormant until the 'meat' is eaten by humans and the worm once again becomes active. Tapeworms are contracted by eating undercooked, infected meat.

The adult worms cause little discomfort in a human, who is usually aware of the parasite only by the presence of creamy-white segments in the faeces. However, pork tapeworm has a unique feature in its life history which makes its eradication essential. If the eggs are eaten by a human, they develop in just the same way as if they were eaten by a pig. This causes human **cysticercosis** with the dormant embryos encysting in various organs and damaging the surrounding tissue. The adult worms can be eradicated from humans by the use of appropriate drugs and this should reduce the frequency of cysticercosis. Treatment must also be accompanied by thorough meat inspection and public health measures. There must be adequate sewage treatment and the prohibition of the discharge of raw sewage into inland waters or the sea.

Beef tapeworm (*T. saginata*) has a similar life cycle to *T. solium* but with cattle as the intermediate host. *T. saginata* is more widespread worldwide but it is less serious because human cysticercosis does not arise in infections with this species.

Both *Fasciola* and *Taenia* have structural modifications for their parasitic mode of life. They have suckers for attachment and a body covering which helps protect them from the host's immune responses or digestive enzymes. *Fasciola* has a relatively well developed gut, and feeds on cells predominantly by extracellular digestion. *Taenia*, having no gut, absorbs predigested food. Most parasitic Platyhelminthes are hermaphrodite and all have systems capable of producing large numbers of eggs. A combination of sexual and asexual stages in order to multiply rapidly is ideal for a parasite.

## 15.8  Saprobiontism

Saprobionts are heterotrophic organisms which obtain carbon by absorption from dead organisms or organic wastes. True saprobionts do not invade living tissues but some parasitic fungi, e.g. *Ceratocystis ulmi* which causes Dutch elm disease, are able to feed saprobiontically when they have killed their host.

### 15.8.1 Extracellular digestion by saprobionts

The majority of saprobionts are bacteria or fungi and they carry out their digestion by secreting enzymes to the outside of their cells. These enzymes, which include amylases, cellulases, lignases and proteases, break down the material on which the saprobiont grows. The organism is thus surrounded by a solution of monosaccharides and amino acids which are then absorbed. An example of a saprobiont feeding in this way is the fungus *Rhizopus* which secretes enzymes from the tips of its hyphae.

ects of Dutch elm disease

### 15.8.2 Economic importance of saprobionts

If nutrients are not to become exhausted, carbon, nitrogen and other elements contained in dead organisms must be made available to living plants and animals. Saprobiontic bacteria and fungi play an essential role in recycling these chemicals as they break down dead organic material (Section 17.2).

Similar organisms cause spoilage of food as they utilize the organic compounds in such things as stored fruit and grain. Both recycling and food spoilage involve a large number of different saprobionts.

As saprobionts break down organic materials to obtain carbon, they form a number of by-products many of which can be used by humans as the basis for various industrial processes such as brewing, baking and cheese-making (Section 30.3).

## 15.9  Mutualism

Lichen (*Xanthoria*)

*Hydra* with *Chlorella* algae

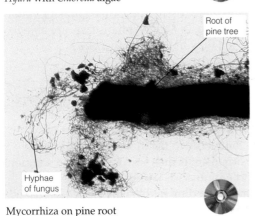

Root of pine tree

Hyphae of fungus

Mycorrhiza on pine root

Mutualism is an association between two different organisms in which neither is harmed and both may benefit in some way. Examples of mutualism include:

1.  **Lichen** – This is an association between an alga, usually *Trebouxia*, and a fungus, usually an ascomycete. The benefit to the alga is not clear but the fungus receives and uses the products of algal photosynthesis.

2.  **Hydra–Chlorella symbiosis** – *Chlorella* are unicellular green algae found in the endoderm of the cnidarian *Hydra*. They are able to photosynthesize and supply *Hydra* with maltose. Where one organism lives symbiotically inside the cells of another, the relationship is referred to as **endosymbiosis**.

3.  **Mycorrhizas** – These are structures formed by the association of roots of plants with fungi. They are common in many higher plants, including pine, oak, beech and birch. The fungus is dependent on symbiosis for carbon nutrition and the higher plant for inorganic nutrients.

### 15.9.1 Digestion of cellulose by microorganisms

Lacking the ability to produce their own cellulase, herbivorous mammals are reliant upon bacteria and protoctista to carry out cellulose breakdown for them. The herbivore must provide a region of the alimentary canal for these microorganisms to inhabit. This region must be separate from the main canal in order that food can be kept there long enough for the microorganisms to carry out the breakdown. Being separate, the compartment can also be kept free of the mammal's own digestive enzymes, which might otherwise destroy the microorganisms, and at a suitable pH for their activity. The accommodation for these cellulose-digesting bacteria and protoctista takes two main forms in mammals.

In **ruminants**, e.g. cattle, sheep and deer, a complex four-chambered stomach is present (Fig. 15.6). When swallowed, the food enters the first two chambers, the **rumen** and **reticulum**. It is here that the microorganisms carry out extracellular digestion

## Did you know?

Some living rock-encrusting lichens in the Arctic may be up to 4500 years old.

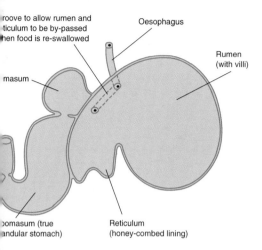

roove to allow rumen and ticulum to be by-passed hen food is re-swallowed

Oesophagus

Rumen (with villi)

masum

omasum (true andular stomach)

Reticulum (honey-combed lining)

*ig. 15.6 The ruminant stomach*

of the cellulose by secreting cellulase. The products of this digestion are either absorbed by the walls of the rumen and reticulum which have villi or honey-combed ridges for this purpose, or are absorbed by the microorganisms and digested later. The waste gases, largely carbon dioxide and methane, are expelled via the mouth.

The relationship between the mammal and microorganisms is **mutualistic** as both gain benefit. The mammal acquires the products of cellulose breakdown which it could not obtain alone, and the microorganisms receive a constant supply of food and a warm, sheltered environment in which to live. After some hours, and usually in the relative safety of some sheltered position, the herbivore regurgitates the food into the mouth, where it thoroughly chews it – 'chewing the cud'. On being re-swallowed, the food enters the final two chambers of the stomach, the **omasum** and the **abomasum** (true stomach) where the usual process of protein digestion in acid conditions takes place.

Also present in the rumen are protein-synthesizing bacteria which use ammonia as their source of nitrogen. These protein-rich bacteria are engulfed by the protoctista which in turn are digested by the ruminant's enzymes further along the alimentary canal. In this way ruminants are able to obtain a valuable source of protein, allowing them to survive on a diet which might otherwise prove too low in protein for a healthy existence.

In rabbits and horses, the **caecum** and **appendix** are much enlarged and accommodate the microorganisms. Some absorption of the products of this digestion takes place through the walls of the caecum. In rabbits the yield is improved by the re-swallowing of the material from the caecum after it has left the anus – a process known as **coprophagy**.

### 15.9.2 Mutualism and the nitrogen cycle

Many angiosperms and a few conifers form swellings called **nodules** on their stems, roots or leaves. These nodules contain microorganisms which are capable of **nitrogen fixation**. The best known examples are the root nodules formed in plants belonging to the Papilionaceae (Leguminosae) such as peas, beans and clover. In this case the nitrogen-fixing microorganism is the bacterium *Rhizobium*. This association provides the bacteria with a carbon source and the plant with a source of nitrates, independent of the nitrate abundance in the soil. The development of a nodule is similar to the development of a lateral root except that at an early stage the central cells are filled with bacterial cells enclosed in a membrane. *Rhizobium* thus remains extracellular.

It has been estimated that mutualistic organisms fix about 100 million tonnes of nitrogen per year. Without this recycling of atmospheric nitrogen the level of soil nitrates would be far too low to support the present vegetation cover. Leguminous crops improve soil fertility and, in terms of efficiency of fixation, the biological process compares favourably with the commercial manufacture of nitrogenous fertilizer.

The exact site of nitrogen fixation has been the subject of much research. Neither the plant nor *Rhizobium* alone are capable of nitrogen fixation. Fixation depends on the mutualistic relationship, and a possible site for it is the membrane which separates the two organisms. The nitrogen cycle is considered in more detail in Section 17.2.2.

# 15.10    Questions

1.  (a) What is a parasite?                     (2 marks)
    (b) Using a **named** example, describe how a
        **parasitic mode** of nutrition is:
        (i)  similar to a carnivorous mode of
             nutrition;                          (2 marks)
        (ii) dissimilar from a carnivorous mode of
             nutrition.                          (2 marks)
    (c) How does a herbivore obtain sufficient
        protein in its diet?                    (2 marks)
                                        (Total 8 marks)

*Oxford March 1997, Paper 45, No. 2*

2.  The diagram below shows part of the beef
tapeworm *Taenia saginata*.

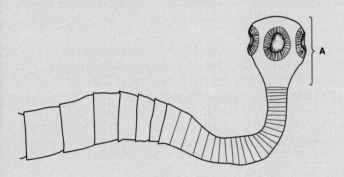

    (a) Explain the importance of the part labelled **A**
        in the life of the tapeworm.           (2 marks)
    (b) (i)  Describe how the tapeworm obtains its
             nutrition.                          (2 marks)
        (ii) How does the nutrition of *Rhizopus*
             differ from that of the tapeworm?
                                                 (2 marks)
                                        (Total 6 marks)

*Edexcel June 1997, B2, No. 5*

3.  An experiment was carried out to investigate the
effect on the growth of rats of including milk in the
diet.

Two groups (**A** and **B**), each consisting of eight
young rats, were fed on a synthetic diet consisting of
purified casein (a milk protein), sucrose, fat,
inorganic salts and water. Group **A** received a
supplement of $3\,cm^3$ of milk per day for the first 18
days then received no further milk. Group **B** was
given no milk for the first 18 days, then received a
supplement of $3\,cm^3$ of milk per day. The results are
shown in the graph at the top of the next column.

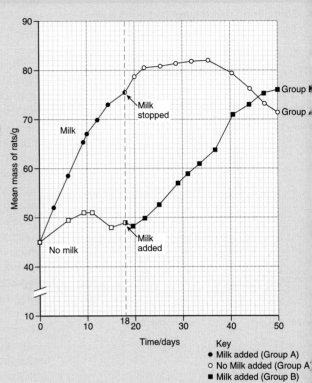

Key
● Milk added (Group A)
○ No Milk added (Group A)
■ Milk added (Group B)
□ No Milk added (Group B)

(a) (i)  From the graph, find the mean mass of
         each group of rats at day 10.     (2 marks)
    (ii) Describe the changes in mean mass up
         to day 18, for the rats which received no
         milk (Group **B**).               (2 marks)
    (iii) Compare the changes in mean mass of
         both groups of rats during the whole
         experiment.                       (3 marks)
(b) Suggest why the growth of the rats was
    faster when they received the milk than
    when they received no milk.            (2 marks)
(c) The inorganic salts provided in the diet
    included calcium. Describe the importance of
    calcium to growing rats.               (3 marks)
                                     (Total 12 marks)

*ULEAC June 1996, B2, No. 4*

4.  The diagram at the top of the next page represents
a small part of the duodenum wall seen in section
using a microscope.

(a) (i)  How is the epithelium (inner surface) of
         the duodenum adapted for absorption
         of soluble products of digestion?
                                             (2 marks)
    (ii) Suggest **two** other functions of the
         epithelium layer.                   (2 marks)
(b) What is the importance of the muscle in the
    duodenum wall?                           (1 mark)

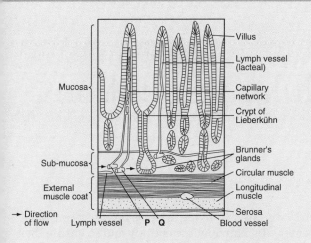

Mucosa
Villus
Lymph vessel (lacteal)
Capillary network
Crypt of Lieberkühn
Brunner's glands
Sub-mucosa
Circular muscle
External muscle coat
Longitudinal muscle
Serosa
→ Direction of flow
Lymph vessel  P  Q
Blood vessel

(c) Briefly give **four** ways in which the blood composition at **P** differs from the blood composition at **Q**. *(2 marks)*

(d) Along which vessel will blood at **Q** pass on leaving the duodenum? *(1 mark)*

*(Total 8 marks)*

*Oxford February 1997, Paper 2, No. 5*

. The graph shows how an injection of secretin ffects the secretion of pancreatic juice by the ancreas.

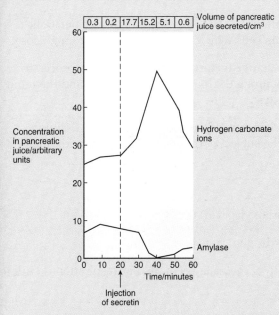

| 0.3 | 0.2 | 17.7 | 15.2 | 5.1 | 0.6 |

Volume of pancreatic juice secreted/cm³

Concentration in pancreatic juice/arbitrary units

Hydrogen carbonate ions

Amylase

Time/minutes

Injection of secretin

(a) (i) Use the graph to describe the effect of secretin on the pancreas.

(ii) Explain why the **concentration** of amylase in the pancreatic juice decreased shortly after the injection of secretin. *(3 marks)*

(b) What other digestive secretion is stimulated by secretin? *(1 mark)*

(c) Certain types of ulcer are thought to be made worse by the production of too much acid from the stomach. Doctors have used a number of different methods to treat these ulcers. Suggest how the following treatments might reduce the amount of acid secreted by the stomach.

(i) cutting the vagus nerve to the stomach, *(1 mark)*

(ii) giving the patient atropine, a drug which blocks the action of acetylcholine. *(2 marks)*

*(Total 7 marks)*

*NEAB June 1997, Paper BY10, No. 4*

**6.** The diagram below shows the mean volumes of water ingested, secreted, absorbed and egested by the human digestive system in one day (24 hours).

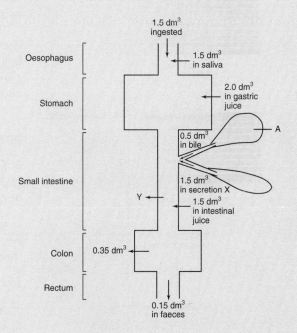

1.5 dm³ ingested

Oesophagus
1.5 dm³ in saliva

Stomach
2.0 dm³ in gastric juice

0.5 dm³ in bile
A

Small intestine
1.5 dm³ in secretion X
Y
1.5 dm³ in intestinal juice

Colon
0.35 dm³

Rectum
0.15 dm³ in faeces

(a) (i) Name the gland labelled A. *(1 mark)*

(ii) Name secretion X. *(1 mark)*

(b) Calculate the mean volume of water absorbed by the small intestine in one day, represented by Y on the diagram. Show your working. *(2 marks)*

(c) Comment on the mean volumes of water absorbed each day by the small intestine and the colon. *(3 marks)*

*(Total 7 marks)*

*Edexcel Jan 1998, HB3, No. 3*

# 16 Cellular respiration

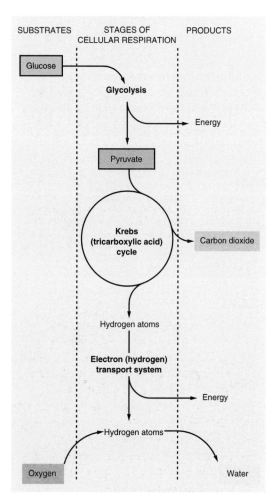

| SUBSTRATES | STAGES OF CELLULAR RESPIRATION | PRODUCTS |

Glucose

Glycolysis

Energy

Pyruvate

Krebs (tricarboxylic acid) cycle

Carbon dioxide

Hydrogen atoms

Electron (hydrogen) transport system

Energy

Hydrogen atoms

Oxygen

Water

*Fig. 16.1 Outline of cellular respiration*

In Chapter 13 we saw that living systems require a constant supply of energy to maintain low entropy and so ensure their survival. This energy initially comes from the sun and is captured in chemical form by autotrophic organisms during the process of photosynthesis (Chapter 14). While the carbohydrate, fats and proteins so produced are useful for storage and other purposes, they cannot be directly used by cells to provide the required energy. The conversion of these chemicals into forms like adenosine triphosphate, which can be utilized by cells, occurs during respiration.

Whatever form the food of an organism initially takes, it is converted into carbohydrate, usually the hexose sugar glucose, before being respired. Most respiration is the oxidation of this glucose to carbon dioxide and water with the release of energy, and the process can be conveniently divided into two parts:

1. **Cellular (internal or tissue) respiration** – the metabolic processes within cells which release the energy from glucose.

2. **Gaseous exchange (external respiration)** – the processes involved in obtaining the oxygen for respiration and the removal of gaseous wastes.

Gaseous exchange is dealt with in Chapter 20. Cellular respiration is the subject of this chapter and can be divided into three stages:

1. Glycolysis

2. Krebs (tricarboxylic acid) cycle

3. Electron (hydrogen) transport system.

The relationship of these stages in cellular respiration is outlined in Fig. 16.1.

## 16.1 Adenosine triphosphate (ATP)

Adenosine triphosphate (ATP) is the short-term energy store of all cells. It is easily transported and is therefore the universal energy carrier.

### 16.1.1 Structure of ATP

ATP is formed from the nucleotide adenosine monophosphate by the addition of two further phosphate molecules. Its structure is shown in Fig. 16.2.

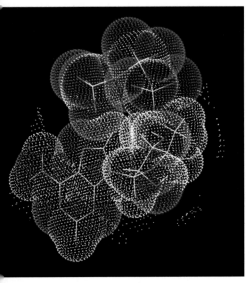

Computer graphics representation of ATP

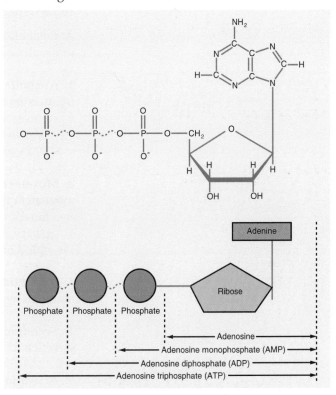

Fig. 16.2 Structure of adenosine triphosphate

### 16.1.2 Importance of ATP

The hydrolysis of ATP to ADP is catalysed by the enzyme ATPase, and the removal of the terminal phosphate yields $30.6 \, kJ \, mol^{-1}$ of free energy. Further hydrolysis of ADP to AMP yields a similar quantity of energy, but the removal of the last phosphate to give adenosine produces less than half this quantity of energy. For this reason the first two phosphate bonds are often termed high energy bonds on account of the relatively large quantity of energy they yield on hydrolysis. This is misleading in that it implies that all the energy is stored in these bonds. The energy is in fact stored in the molecule as a whole, although the breaking of the bonds initiates its release.

AMP and ADP may be reconverted to ATP by the addition of phosphate molecules in a process called **phosphorylation**, of which there are two main forms:

**1. Photosynthetic phosphorylation** – occurs during photosynthesis in chlorophyll-containing cells (Chapter 14).

**2. Oxidative phosphorylation** – occurs during cellular respiration in all aerobic cells.

The addition of each phosphate molecule requires 30.6 kJ of energy. If the energy released from any reaction is less than this, it cannot be stored as ATP and is lost as heat. The importance of ATP is therefore as a means of transferring free energy from energy-rich compounds to cellular reactions requiring it. While not the only substance to transfer energy in this way, it is by far the most abundant and hence the most important.

### 16.1.3 Uses of ATP

A metabolically active cell may require up to two million ATP molecules every second. ATP is the source of energy for:

1. **Anabolic processes** – It provides the energy needed to build up macromolecules from their component units, e.g.
   – polysaccharide synthesis from monosaccharides
   – protein synthesis from amino acids
   – DNA replication.

2. **Movement** – It provides the energy for many forms of cellular movement including:
   – muscle contraction
   – ciliary action
   – spindle action in cell division.

3. **Active transport** – It provides the energy necessary to move materials against a concentration gradient, e.g. ion pumps.

4. **Secretion** – It is needed to form the vesicles necessary in the secretion of cell products.

5. **Activation of chemicals** – It makes chemicals more reactive, enabling them to react more readily, e.g. the phosphorylation of glucose at the start of glycolysis.

## 16.2   Glycolysis

Glycolysis (*glyco* – 'sugar'; *lyso* – 'breakdown') is the breakdown of a hexose sugar, usually glucose, into two molecules of the three-carbon compound **pyruvate (pyruvic acid)**. It occurs in all cells; in anaerobic organisms it is the only stage of respiration. Initially the glucose is insufficiently reactive and so it is phosphorylated prior to being split into two triose sugar molecules. These molecules yield some hydrogen atoms which may be used to give energy (ATP) before being converted into pyruvate. During pyruvate formation, the ATP used in phosphorylating the glucose is regenerated. Glycolysis takes place in the cytoplasm of the cell and its main stages are outlined opposite.

Each glucose molecule produces two molecules of glycerate 3-phosphate and there is therefore a pair of every subsequent molecule for each glucose molecule. The energy yield is a net gain of two molecules of ATP (Stage 7). The two pairs of hydrogen atoms produced (Stage 5) may yield a further six ATP (see Section 16.4), giving an overall total of eight ATPs.

*Stages of glycolysis*

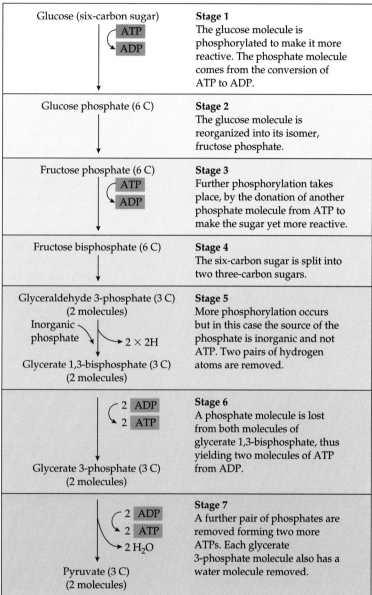

## 16.3    Krebs (tricarboxylic acid) cycle

Although glycolysis releases a little of the energy from the glucose molecule, the majority still remains 'locked-up' in the pyruvate. These pyruvate molecules enter the mitochondria and, in the presence of oxygen, are broken down to carbon dioxide and hydrogen atoms. The process is called the **Krebs cycle**, after its discoverer Hans Krebs. There are a number of alternative names, notably the **tricarboxylic acid cycle (TCA cycle)** and **citric acid cycle**. While the carbon dioxide produced is removed as a waste product, the hydrogen atoms are oxidized to water in order to yield a substantial amount of free energy. Before pyruvate enters the Krebs cycle it combines with a compound called coenzyme A to form **acetyl coenzyme A**. In the process, a molecule of carbon dioxide and a pair of hydrogen atoms are removed. The 2-carbon

319

acetyl coenzyme A now enters the Krebs cycle (Fig. 16.3) by combining with the 4-carbon **oxaloacetate (oxaloacetic acid)** to give the 6-carbon **citrate (citric acid)**. Coenzyme A is reformed and may be used to combine with a further pyruvate molecule. The citrate is degraded to a 5-carbon **α-ketoglutarate (α-ketoglutaric acid)** and then the 4-carbon oxaloacetate by the progressive loss of two carbon dioxide molecules, thus completing the cycle. For each turn of the cycle, a total of four pairs of hydrogen atoms are also formed. Of these, three pairs are combined with the hydrogen carrier **nicotinamide adenine dinucleotide (NAD)** and yield three ATPs for each pair of hydrogen atoms. The remaining pair combines with a different hydrogen carrier, **flavine adenine dinucleotide (FAD)** and yields only two ATPs. In addition, each turn of the cycle produces sufficient energy to form a single molecule of ATP. It must be remembered that all these products are formed from a single pyruvate molecule of which two are produced from each glucose molecule. The total yields from a single glucose molecule are thus double those stated. The significance of this will become apparent when considering the total quantity of energy released (Section 16.6).

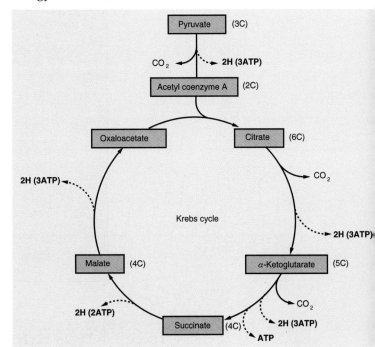

*Fig. 16.3 Summary of Krebs cycle*

### 16.3.1 Importance of Krebs cycle

The Krebs cycle plays an important role in the biochemistry of a cell for three main reasons:

**1. It brings about the degradation of macromolecules** – The 3-carbon pyruvate is broken down to carbon dioxide.

**2. It provides the reducing power for the electron (hydrogen) transport system** – It produces pairs of hydrogen atoms which are ultimately the source of metabolic energy for the cell.

**3. It is an interconversion centre** – It is a valuable source of intermediate compounds used in the manufacture of other substances, e.g. fatty acids, amino acids, chlorophyll (Section 16.7

# 16.4    Electron transport system

The electron transport system is the means by which the energy from the Krebs cycle, in the form of hydrogen atoms, is converted to ATP. The hydrogen atoms attached to the hydrogen carriers NAD and FAD are transferred to a chain of other carriers at progressively lower energy levels (Fig. 16.4). As the hydrogens pass from one carrier to the next, the energy released is harnessed to produce ATP. The series of carriers is termed the **respiratory chain**. The carriers in the chain include **NAD**, **flavoprotein**, **coenzyme Q** and iron-containing proteins called **cytochromes**. Initially hydrogen atoms are passed along the chain, but these later split into their protons and electrons, and only the electrons pass from carrier to carrier. For this reason, the pathway can be called the electron, or hydrogen, transport system. At the end of the chain the protons and electrons recombine, and the hydrogen atoms created link with oxygen to form water. This formation of ATP through the oxidation of the hydrogen atoms is called **oxidative phosphorylation**. It occurs in the mitochondria.

The role of oxygen is to act as the final acceptor of the hydrogen atoms. While it only performs this function at the end of the many stages in respiration, oxygen is nevertheless vital as it drives the whole process. In its absence, only the anaerobic glycolysis stage can continue. The transfer of hydrogen atoms to oxygen is catalysed by the enzyme **cytochrome oxidase**. This enzyme is inhibited by cyanide, so preventing the removal of hydrogen atoms at the end of the respiratory chain. In these circumstances the hydrogen atoms accumulate and aerobic respiration ceases, making cyanide a most effective respiratory inhibitor.

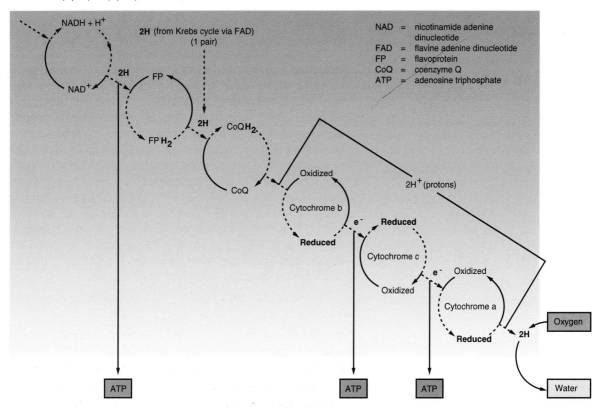

Fig. 16.4 Summary of the electron transport system

### 16.4.1 Mitochondria and oxidative phosphorylation

Mitochondria are present in all eukaryotic cells where they are the main sites of respiratory activity. Highly active cells requiring much energy characteristically have numerous large mitochondria packed with cristae. Such cells include:

**Liver cells** – Energy is required to drive the large and varied number of biochemical reactions taking place there.

**Striated muscle cells** – Energy is needed for muscle contraction especially where this is rapid, e.g. flight muscle of insects.

**Sperm tails** – These provide energy to propel the sperm.

**Nerve cells** – Mitochondria are especially numerous adjacent to synapses where they provide the energy needed for the production and release of transmitter substances.

## NOTEBOOK

**Oxidation, reduction and energy**

Many everyday processes such as burning, rusting and respiration are the result of substances combining with oxygen. These reactions also release energy. Fuel in a car engine – for example, petrol (made almost entirely of hydrogen and carbon) – is mixed with air in the carburettor, the oxygen of which combines with the petrol to form oxides of both hydrogen and carbon when ignited by spark. The reaction is **exothermic**, i.e. it releases much energy, which is used to propel the car.

Hydrocarbon + Oxygen $\longrightarrow$ Carbon dioxide + Water + Energy
(Petrol)    (From          (Oxide of   (Oxide of
          air)           carbon)  hydrogen)

Respiration is essentially the same process, with the carbon and hydrogen in our food being substituted for the petrol.

The process by which substances combine with oxygen is called **oxidation** and the substances to which oxygen is added are said to be **oxidized**. However, as one substance gains oxygen another must lose it. We call the process by which oxygen is lost **reduction** and say that the substance losing oxygen has been **reduced**. Just as oxidation involves energy being given out, so reduction involves being taken in.

Oxidation and reduction therefore always take place together; as one substance is oxidized so another must be reduced. We call these chemical reactions **redox** reactions (**red**uction + **ox**idation).

In many redox reactions oxygen is reduced by the addition of hydrogen to make water, e.g. in respiration. For this reason reduction is sometimes described as the **gain** of hydrogen and oxidation as the **loss** of hydrogen.

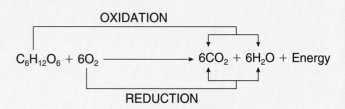

**Intestinal epithelial cells** – Many mitochondria occur beneath the microvilli on these cells to provide energy for the absorption of digested food by active transport.

We saw in Section 4.2.5 that mitochondria have an inner membrane which is folded to form cristae in order to increase its surface-area. The cristae are lined with stalked particles. Within the inner mitochondrial membrane there appears to be a mechanism which actively transports protons ($H^+$) from the matrix into the space between the inner and outer membranes of the organelle. This creates an electrochemical gradient of hydrogen ions across the inner membrane. According to the **chemi-osmotic theory** put forward by the British biochemist Peter Mitchell, in 1961, it is the energy of this 'charged' membrane which is used to synthesize ATP. Basically the

A closer investigation of redox reactions shows that when a substance is oxidized it **loses electrons** and when it is reduced it **gains electrons**. This is the modern definition of the two processes.

|  | Reduction | Oxidation |
|---|---|---|
| Oxygen | lost | gained |
| Hydrogen | gained | lost |
| Electrons | gained | lost |
| Energy | absorbed | released |

We can now see a pattern emerging which is helpful when considering the biochemical reactions of metabolism. The build up or synthesis of substances (**anabolism**) involves the reduction of molecules and hence an intake of energy, whereas the breakdown or degradation of substances (**catabolism**) involves the oxidation of molecules and a consequent release of energy. How then does this help our understanding of biological molecules? Clearly substances rich in hydrogen or electrons have more to lose, i.e. they can more easily become oxidized and since oxidation involves the release of energy these substances are more 'energy rich'. Conversely substances rich in oxygen are more likely to be reduced – a process involving the absorption of energy. From the point of view of our food, molecules with much hydrogen and little oxygen have the greatest potential to provide energy. So which foods are these? Let us consider two types: fats and carbohydrates. Typical examples are given in the table, left.

| Typical fat | Typical carbohydrate |
|---|---|
| Stearic acid | Glucose |
| Formula: $C_{17}H_{35}COOH$ | Formula: $C_6H_{12}O_6$ |

While the ratio of hydrogen to carbon is about 2:1 in both cases, there is proportionally more oxygen in the carbohydrates. This is because they comprise many H—C—OH groups whereas fats have H—C—H groups. In other words the carbohydrates are already partially oxidized and therefore can undergo less further oxidation than fats. Since oxidation releases energy, carbohydrates have less to release – typically 17 kJ per gram compared to 38 kJ for one gram of fat. In terms of energy then, it is the relative amount of hydrogen and oxygen a food molecule contains which is important; the carbon simply acts as a 'skeleton' to which these atoms are attached.

hydrogen atoms are picked up by NAD in the matrix and later split into protons and electrons. The protons enter the space between the inner and outer membrane of the mitochondrion while the electrons pass along the cytochromes located within the inner membrane (Fig. 16.5). The protons flow back to the matrix via the stalked granules owing to their high concentration in the intermembrane space. This flow acts as the driving force to combine ADP with inorganic phosphate and so synthesize ATP. ATPase associated with the stalked granules catalyses this reaction. These protons then recombine in the matrix with the electrons, and the hydrogen atoms so formed then combine with oxygen to form water.

In addition to carrying out oxidative phosphorylation, the mitochondria perform the reactions of the Krebs cycle. The enzymes for these reactions are mostly found within the matrix, with a few, like succinic dehydrogenase, attached to the inner mitochondrial membrane.

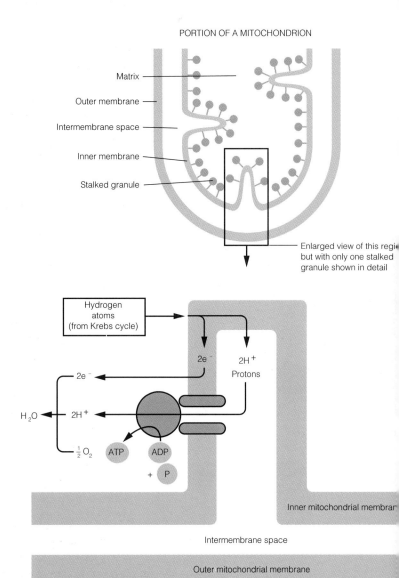

Fig. 16.5 The synthesis of ATP according to the chemi-osmotic theory of Mitchell

# 16.5 Anaerobic respiration (anaerobiosis)

Present thinking suggests that life originated in an atmosphere without oxygen and the first forms of life were therefore anaerobic. Many organisms today are also anaerobic; indeed, some find oxygen toxic. These forms are termed **obligate anaerobes**. Most anaerobic organisms will, however, respire aerobically in the presence of oxygen, only resorting to anaerobiosis in its absence. These forms are **facultative anaerobes**. The cells of almost all organisms are capable of carrying out anaerobic respiration, for a short time at least. From what we have so far learnt it is clear that, in the absence of oxygen, the Krebs cycle and electron transport system cannot operate. Only glycolysis can take place. This yields a little ATP directly (two molecules for each glucose molecule) and a total of two pairs of hydrogen ions. In the previous section we saw that these hydrogen ions possess much free energy. In the absence of oxygen, however, this energy cannot be released. Nevertheless, these hydrogen ions must be removed if glycolysis is to continue. They are accepted by the pyruvate formed at the end of glycolysis, to give either ethanol (alcohol) or lactate, in a process called **fermentation**. Neither process yields any additional energy; both are merely mechanisms for 'mopping-up' the hydrogen ions.

## 16.5.1 Alcoholic fermentation

In alcoholic fermentation the pyruvate from glycolysis is first converted to ethanal (acetaldehyde) through the removal of a carbon dioxide molecule.

$$\underset{\text{pyruvate}}{CH_3COCOOH} \longrightarrow \underset{\text{ethanal}}{CH_3CHO} + \underset{\text{carbon dioxide}}{CO_2}$$

The ethanal then combines with the hydrogen ions, which are transported by the hydrogen carrier NAD, to form the alcohol ethanol.

$$\underset{\text{ethanal}}{CH_3CHO} \xrightarrow{\quad NADH + H^+ \qquad NAD^+ \quad} \underset{\text{ethanol}}{CH_3CH_2OH}$$

This form of fermentation occurs in yeast, where the alcohol produced may accumulate in the medium around the cells until its concentration rises to a level which prevents further fermentation, and so kills the yeast. The ethanol cannot be further broken down to yield additional energy.

The overall equation is:

$$\underset{\text{glucose}}{C_6H_{12}O_6} \longrightarrow \underset{\text{ethanol}}{2CH_3CH_2OH} + \underset{\text{carbon dioxide}}{2CO_2}$$

Under anaerobic conditions, e.g. waterlogging of plant roots, the cells of higher plants may temporarily undergo this form of fermentation. Alcoholic fermentation is of considerable economic importance to humans. It is the basis of the brewing industry, where the ethanol is the important product, and of the baking industry, where the carbon dioxide is of greater value (Section 30.4).

n industrial fermenter

### 16.5.2 Lactate fermentation

In lactate fermentation the pyruvate from glycolysis accepts the hydrogen atoms from $NADH + H^+$ directly.

$$CH_3COCOOH \xrightarrow{\quad NADH + H^+ \quad NAD^+ \quad} CH_3CHOHCOOH$$

pyruvate · · · · · · · · · · · · · · · · · · · · · · · · · lactate
· · · · · · · · · · · · · · · · · · · · · · · · · · · · · · (2-hydroxypropanoic acid)

Unlike alcoholic fermentation, the lactate can be further broken down, should oxygen be made available again, thus releasing its remaining energy. Alternatively it may be resynthesized into carbohydrate, or excreted.

This form of fermentation is common in animals. Clearly any mechanism which allows an animal to withstand short periods without oxygen (anoxia) has great survival value. Animals living in environments of fluctuating oxygen levels, such as a pond or river, may benefit from the temporary use of it, as might a baby in the period during and immediately following birth. A more common occurrence of lactate fermentation is in a muscle during strenuous exercise. During this period, the circulatory system may be incapable of supplying the muscle with its oxygen requirements. Lactate fermentation not only yields a little energy, but removes the pyruvate which would otherwise accumulate. Instead lactate accumulates, and while this in time will cause cramp and so prevent the muscle operating, tissues have a relatively high tolerance to it.

In the process of lactate fermentation, the organism accumulates an **oxygen debt**. This is repaid as soon as possible after the activity, by continued deep and rapid breathing following the exertion. The oxygen absorbed is used to oxidize the lactate to carbon dioxide and water, thereby removing it, and at the same time replenishing the depleted stores of ATP and oxygen in the tissue. In some organisms such as parasitic worms, where the food supply is abundant, the lactate is simply excreted, obviating the need to repay an oxygen debt.

## 16.6  Comparison of energy yields

Let us now compare the total quantity of ATP produced by the aerobic and anaerobic pathways.

*Aerobic respiration*
The ATP is derived from two sources: directly by phosphorylation of ADP and indirectly by oxidative phosphorylation using the hydrogen ions generated during glucose breakdown.

The figures given in Table 16.1 represent the yield for each pyruvate molecule which subsequently enters the Krebs (TCA) cycle. As there are two pyruvate molecules formed for each glucose molecule (Section 16.3), all these figures must be doubled ($\times 2$) to give the quantities formed per glucose molecule.

The energy yield for each molecule of $NADH + H^+$ is three ATPs whereas for $FADH_2$ it is only two ATPs (Section 16.3).

TABLE 16.1  ATP yield during aerobic respiration of one molecule of glucose

| Respiratory process | Number of reduced hydrogen carrier molecules formed | Number of ATP molecules formed from reduced hydrogen carriers | Number of ATP molecules formed directly | Total number of ATP molecules |
|---|---|---|---|---|
| Glycolysis (glucose → pyruvate) | $2 \times (NADH + H^+)$ | $2 \times 3 = 6$ | 2 | 8 |
| pyruvate → acetyl CoA | $1 \times (NADH + H^+)(\times 2)$ | $2 \times 3 = 6$ | 0 | 6 |
| Krebs (TCA) cycle | $3 \times (NADH + H^+)(\times 2)$ $1 \times FADH_2 (\times 2)$ | $6 \times 3 = 18$ $2 \times 2 = 4$ | $1(\times 2) = 2$ | 24 |
| | | Total ATP = | | 38 |

The total of 38 ATPs produced represents the maximum possible yield; the actual yield may be different depending upon the conditions in any one cell at the time. For example, the two $NADH + H^+$ may enter the mitochondria in two different, indirect ways. Depending on the route taken, they may yield only four ATPs, rather than six ATPs as shown in Table 16.1.

Each ATP molecule will yield 30.6 kJ of energy. The total energy available from aerobic respiration is $38 \times 30.6 = 1162.8$ kJ. Compared to the total energy available from the complete oxidation of glucose of 2880 kJ, this represents an efficiency of slightly over 40%. This may not appear very remarkable, but it compares very favourably with machines – the efficiency of a car engine is around 25%.

*Anaerobic respiration*
We have seen in the previous section that only glycolysis occurs during anaerobiosis and that the $NADH + H^+$ it yields is not available for oxidative phosphorylation. The total energy released is therefore restricted to the two ATPs formed directly. With each providing 30.6 kJ of energy, the total yield is a mere 61.2 kJ. Compared to the 2880 kJ potentially available from a molecule of glucose, the process is a little over 2% efficient. It must, however, be borne in mind that in lactate fermentation all is not lost, and the lactate may be reconverted to pyruvate by the liver, and so enter the Krebs cycle, thus releasing its remaining energy.

## 16.7  Alternative respiratory substrates

Sugars are not the only material which can be oxidized by cells to release energy. Both fats and protein may, in certain circumstances, be used as respiratory substrates, without first being converted to carbohydrate. The alternative pathways are shown in Fig. 16.6.

### 16.7.1 Respiration of fat

The oxidation of fat is preceded by its hydrolysis to glycerol and fatty acids. The glycerol may then be phosphorylated and converted into the triose phosphate glyceraldehyde 3-phosphate. This can then be incorporated into the glycolysis pathway and subsequently the Krebs cycle. The fatty acid component is progressively broken down in the matrix of the mitochondria into 2-carbon fragments which are converted to acetyl coenzyme A. This then enters the Krebs cycle with consequent release of its energy. The oxidation of fats has the advantage of producing a large quantity of hydrogen ions. These can be transported by hydrogen carriers and used to produce ATP in the electron (hydrogen) transport system. For this reason, fats liberate more than double the energy of the same quantity of carbohydrate.

### 16.7.2 Respiration of protein

Protein is another potential source of energy but is only used in cases of starvation. It must first be hydrolysed to its constituent amino acids which then have their amino ($NH_2$) group(s) removed in the liver – a process called **deamination**. The remaining portions of the amino acids then enter the respiratory pathway at a number of points depending on their carbon content: 5-carbon amino acids (e.g. glutamate) and 4-carbon amino acids (e.g. aspartate) are converted into the Krebs cycle intermediates, $\alpha$-ketoglutarate and oxaloacetate respectively; 3-carbon amino acids like alanine are converted to pyruvate ready for conversion to acetyl coenzyme A. Other amino acids with larger quantities of carbon undergo transamination reactions to convert them into 3, 4 or 5-carbon amino acids.

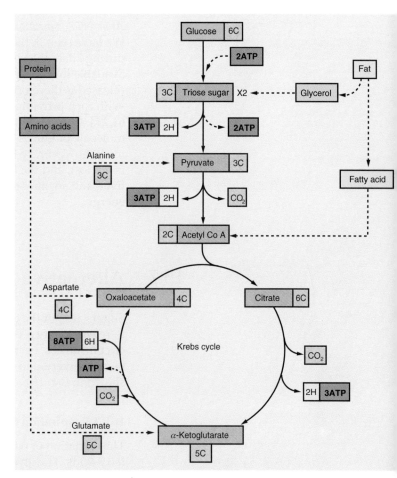

*Fig. 16.6 Summary of respiratory pathways*

## 16.8 Respiratory quotients

The **respiratory quotient (RQ)** is a measure of the ratio of carbon dioxide evolved by an organism to the oxygen consumed, over a certain period.

$$RQ = \frac{CO_2 \text{ evolved}}{O_2 \text{ consumed}}$$

For a hexose sugar like glucose, the equation for its complete oxidation is:

$$C_6H_{12}O_6 + 6O_2 \longrightarrow 6CO_2 + 6H_2O$$

The RQ is hence:

$$\frac{6CO_2}{6O_2} = 1.0$$

In fats, the ratio of oxygen to carbon is far smaller than in a carbohydrate. A fat therefore requires a greater quantity of oxygen for its complete oxidation and thus has a RQ less than one.

$$C_{18}H_{36}O_2 + 26O_2 \longrightarrow 18CO_2 + 18H_2O$$

stearic acid

$$RQ = \frac{18CO_2}{26O_2} = 0.7$$

The composition of proteins is too varied for them to give the same RQ, but most have values around 0.9.

Organisms rarely, if ever, respire a single food substance, nor are substances always completely oxidized. Experimental RQ values therefore do not give the exact nature of the material being respired. Most resting animals have RQs between 0.8 and 0.9. With protein only respired during starvation, this must be taken to indicate a mixture of fat and carbohydrate as the respiratory substrates.

# 16.9   Questions

**1.** The diagram below represents the hydrogen and electron transport chain (respiratory chain).

2H
↘
NADH + H⁺

NAD⁺  2H
↘  FAD
Flavoprotein
FADH₂  2H
↘ CoQH₂

CoQ  2e⁻
↘ 2Fe³⁺
Cytochrome b
2Fe²⁺  2e⁻
↘ 2Fe²⁺
2H⁺
Cytochrome c
2Fe³⁺  2e⁻
↘ 2Cu²⁺
Cytochrome a
2Cu⁺
2e⁻

*(a)* (i) Where precisely in the cell would the sequence of reactions take place?
*(1 mark)*

(ii) Give an example of a coenzyme shown in the sequence. *(1 mark)*

(iii) What is the name given to the prosthetic group found in the cytochromes? *(1 mark)*

(iv) Which vitamin forms the prosthetic group of the flavoproteins? *(1 mark)*

(v) Give **one** example of an oxidation reaction and **one** example of a reduction reaction shown in the diagram. *(2 marks)*

*(b)* (i) Energy is released during the electron transfer. What is the general name given to chemical reactions in which energy is released? *(1 mark)*

(ii) State concisely what will happen to the energy 'released' in these reactions. *(2 marks)*

*(c)* What eventually happens to the electrons which have been passed down the chain? *(2 marks)*

*(d)* Cyanide is an inhibitor of the enzyme involved in the final reaction in the sequence. Briefly explain some of the effects that will occur as a result of this terminal enzyme being inhibited. *(2 marks)*

*(Total 13 marks)*

*Oxford June 1997, Paper 1, No. 3*

**2.** The diagram below shows some of the stages of anaerobic respiration in a yeast cell.

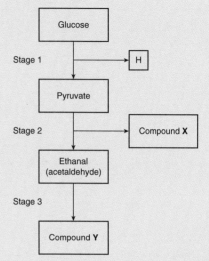

*(a)* (i) Identify compound **X**, produced at stage 2. *(1 mark*

(ii) Identify compound **Y**, produced by stage 3. *(1 mark*

*(b)* State what happens to the hydrogen atoms produced by stage 1. *(2 marks*

*(c)* Name **two** products of anaerobic respiration in muscle. *(2 marks*

*(Total 6 marks*

*ULEAC June 1995, Paper 1, No.*

**3.** The breakdown of glucose, to release energy, involves several linked metabolic pathways which take place in precise areas within the cell. Copy and complete the table.

| Metabolic pathway | Precise location | Substrate | Products |
|---|---|---|---|
| Glycolysis | | | |
| Krebs cycle | | | $CO_2$; ATP; NADH + H⁺ FADH₂ Oxaloacetate |
| Oxidative phosphorylation | | NADH + H⁺ FADH₂ | |
| Alcoholic fermentation | | Pyruvic acid Sugar/glucose | |

*(Total 9 marks*

*Oxford November 1996, Paper 1, No.*

. A preparation of mitochondria was made from ver tissue. Substances were added to this preparation nd the amount of oxygen remaining in the preparation 'as monitored over a period of time. The diagram hows the trace obtained and the times when the ifferent substances were added.

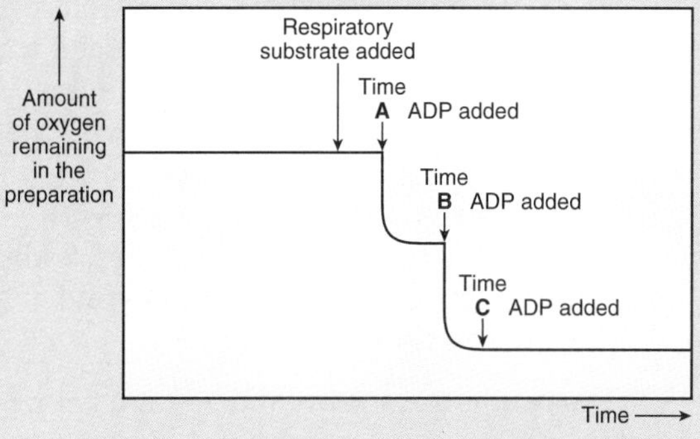


(*a*) Suggest why the respiratory substrate added to this preparation was a molecule from the Krebs cycle and not glucose. (*1 mark*)

(*b*) What additional substance, other than those mentioned on the diagram, would need to be added to this preparation in order to get the results shown? (*1 mark*)

(*c*) Explain:

(i) why the amount of oxygen fell between times **A** and **B**; (*2 marks*)

(ii) the shape of the trace after time **C**. (*1 mark*)

(*Total 5 marks*)

*AEB January 1996, Module Paper 1, No. 3*

. An experiment was carried out to investigate the ffect of three carbohydrates (glucose, sucrose and ctose) on the rate of respiration of yeast cells. Iethylene blue is an artificial hydrogen acceptor 'hich is blue in the oxidized form and colourless 'hen reduced. A colorimeter is an instrument 'hich can be used to measure the intensity of light assing through a liquid. In this experiment, 100% 'ansmission of blue light means that the methylene lue remains fully oxidized.

. tube was set up containing 10 $cm^3$ of a ispension of yeast cells in 0.5% glucose solution. $cm^3$ of 0.1% methylene blue solution was added to ie tube. The tube was covered and placed in a 'ater bath at 30 °C for 20 minutes. During this me, at 2-minute intervals, the percentage of blue ght transmitted through the tube was measured in colorimeter.

he experiment was repeated, first using the same olume of yeast in 0.5% sucrose solution and then 0.5% lactose solution.

The results of the experiment are given in the graph on the following page.

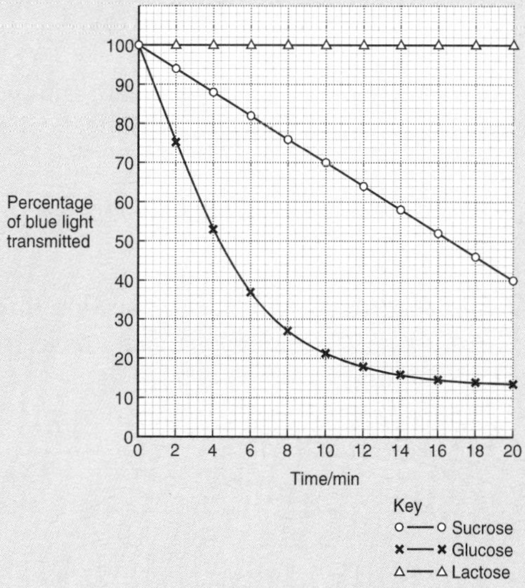


(*a*) What causes the methylene blue to lose its blue colour during this experiment? (*1 mark*)

(*b*) (i) Calculate the rate of respiration for the yeast in glucose solution during the first 4 minutes. Give your answer as % transmission $min^{-1}$. Show your working. (*3 marks*)

(ii) Comment on the rate of respiration of yeast in glucose during the 20 minutes of the experiment. (*3 marks*)

(iii) State **one** way in which the rate of respiration of yeast in sucrose solution differs from the rate in glucose solution. (*1 mark*)

(*c*) Suggest **one** reason for the shape of the lactose curve. (*1 mark*)

(*d*) Explain why the tubes were kept covered during the experiment. (*2 marks*)

(*Total 11 marks*)

*Edexcel June 1997, B/HB1, No. 6*

**6.** The diagram shows some of the processes that occur within a mitochondrion and some of the substances that enter and leave it.

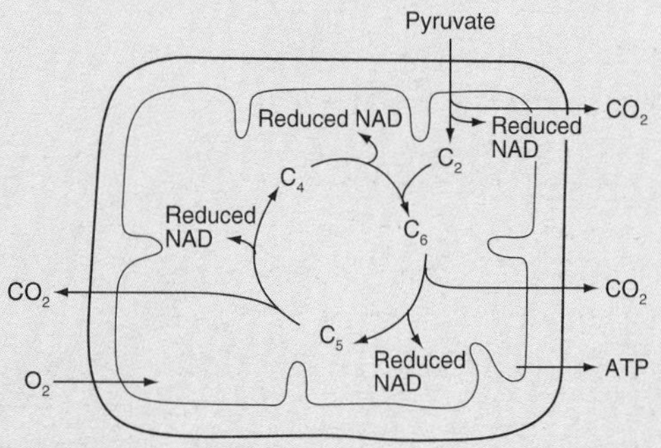

(a) Name the process that
  (i) produces pyruvate in the cytoplasm;
  (ii) produces reduced NAD and carbon dioxide in the matrix of the mitochondrion. *(2 marks)*
(b) Describe how ATP is produced from reduced NAD within the mitochondrion. *(3 marks)*
*(Total 5 marks)*

*NEAB June 1997, Paper 1, No. 3*

7.  (a) The diagram below shows a section through a mitochondrion as seen using an electron microscope.

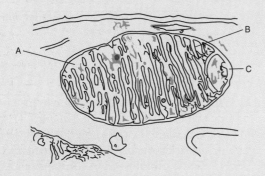

  (i) Name the parts labelled A, B and C *(3 marks)*
  (ii) On the diagram, by means of an arrow, show the location of the electron transport system. *(1 mark)*
  (iii) The magnification of this diagram is x 34 000. Calculate the actual length of the mitochondrion, giving your answer in suitable units. Show your working. *(2 marks)*

(b) Active mitochondria can be isolated from liver cells. If these mitochondria are then incubated in a buffer solution containing a substrate, such as dissolved succinate, dissolved oxygen will be used by the mitochondria. The concentration of dissolved oxygen in the buffer solution can be measured using an electrode.

An experiment was carried out in which a suspension of active mitochondria was incubated in a buffer solution containing succinate, an intermediate of the Krebs cycle. The concentration of dissolved oxygen was measured every minute for five minutes. A solution containing sodium azide was then added to this preparation and the concentration of dissolved oxygen was measured for a further five minutes. Sodium azide combines with cytochromes and prevents electron transport.

The results are shown in the graph below.

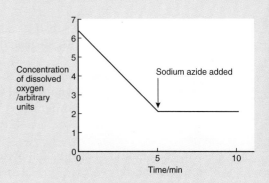

  (i) Explain why the concentration of oxygen decreased during the first five minutes. *(2 marks)*
  (ii) Suggest what effect the addition of sodium azide will have on the production of ATP and give an explanation for your answer. *(3 marks)*
*(Total 11 marks)*

*Edexcel June 1998, Paper B/HB1, No.*

# Energy and the ecosystem

Organisms live within a relatively narrow sphere over the earth's surface; it is less than 20 km thick, extending about 8 km above sea level and 10 km below it. The total volume of this thin film of land, water and air around the earth's surface is called the **biosphere**. It consists of two major divisions, the aquatic and terrestrial environments, with the aquatic environment being subdivided into freshwater, marine and estuarine. The terrestrial portion of the biosphere is subdivided into **biomes**, which are determined by the dominant plants found in them. It is, of course, largely climatic conditions that determine the dominant plant type of a region, and hence the biome. Tropical rain forests, for example, occur where the climate is hot and wet all through the year and are characterized by dense, lush vegetation and an immense variety of species. By contrast tundra occurs where the ground is frozen for much of the year and hence the vegetation is sparse with little variety of species. Deserts are the result of a lack of usable water, either because rain falls all too rarely and soon evaporates in the heat (hot deserts) or because the water is permanently frozen (cold deserts). Temperate deciduous forests occur where the rain is intermittent, the winters are cold and the summers are warm. It is equally possible to subdivide the terrestrial biosphere into **geographical zones**, e.g. Africa, Australia, North America, South America, Antarctica, etc. In this case the divisions are made by barriers like oceans or mountain ranges.

A biome can be further divided into **zones** which consist of a series of small areas called **habitats**. Examples of habitats include a rocky shore, a freshwater pond and a beech wood.

Within each habitat there are **populations** of individuals which collectively form a **community** (see Section 17.6). An individual member of the community is usually confined to a particular region of the habitat, called the **microhabitat**. The position any species occupies within its habitat is referred to as its **ecological niche**. It represents more than a physical area within the habitat as it includes an organism's behaviour and interactions with its living and non-living environment. As Section 17.6.8 shows, no two species can occupy the same ecological niche.

The inter-relationship of the living **(biotic)** and non-living **(abiotic)** elements in any biological system is called the **ecosystem**. There are two major factors within an ecosystem:

1. The flow of energy through the system.

2. The cycling of matter within the system.

## BIOLOGY AROUND US

### Tropical rain forests

Erosion after logging

Tropical rain forests have been estimated to contain 50% of the world's standing timber. They represent a huge store for carbon and sink for carbon dioxide and their destruction may increase atmospheric concentrations of carbon dioxide by 50%. They are important in conserving soil nutrients and preventing large-scale erosion in regions of high rainfall. They contain a large gene pool of plant resources and their potential for the production of food, fibre and pharmaceutical products is not known. At present rates of destruction, all tropical rain forest, except that in reserves, will have disappeared by the middle of the twenty-first century.

The traditional small-scale slash-and-burn agriculture of the hunter–gatherer cultures caused few environmental problems but attempts to exploit the forest on a large scale have been disastrous. The problems have been most apparent in the rain forests of Brazil and other countries of the Amazon basin. The forest has been cleared for rubber plantations, timber extraction, planting of cash crops like cocoa, coffee and oil palm, extraction of minerals, especially bauxite, and for pulp and paper manufacture. The consequences of deforestation have been soil infertility, floods, soil erosion and increased sediment in rivers. The scale of the problem is huge and there seems to be no decrease in the rate of deforestation as yet. However, some areas are being set aside as reserves and some attempts have been made at replanting.

It is feasible to consider the biosphere as a single ecosystem because, in theory at least, energy flows through it and nutrients may be recycled within it. However, in practice there are much smaller units which are more or less self-contained in terms of energy and matter. A freshwater pond, for example, has its own community of plants to capture the solar energy necessary to supply all organisms within the habitat, and matter such as nitrogen and phosphorus is recycled within the pond with little or no loss or gain between it and other habitats. It is often easier to consider these smaller units as single ecosystems.

## 17.1    Energy flow through the ecosystem

The study of the flow of energy through the ecosystem is known as **ecological energetics**. All the energy utilized by living organisms is ultimately derived from the sun but as little as 1% of its total radiant energy is actually captured by green plants for distribution throughout the ecosystem. This relatively small amount is nonetheless sufficient to support all life on earth. It may at first glance appear inefficient, but it must be remembered that factors other than light intensity often limit photosynthesis carbon dioxide, temperature, water and mineral availability, to name a few.

adybird feeding on aphids

### 17.1.1 Food chains

Because green plants manufacture sugars from simple raw materials utilizing solar energy, they are called **primary producers**. All primary producers are autotrophic and they include some bacteria as well as green plants.

Organisms that are unable to utilize light energy for the synthesis of food must obtain it by consuming other organisms. These are heterotrophs and include all animals as well as fungi and some bacteria. If they feed off the primary producers they are called **primary consumers**. These are typically herbivores but also include plant parasites.

Some heterotrophs, the carnivores, feed on other heterotrophs. These are called **secondary consumers** if they feed on a herbivore, and **tertiary consumers** if they feed on other carnivores. There is hence a type of feeding hierarchy with the primary producers at the bottom and the consumers at the top. The energy is therefore passed along a chain of organisms, known as a **food chain**. Each feeding level in the chain is called a **trophic level** (Table 17.1). Only a small proportion of the available energy is transferred from one trophic level to the next. Much energy is lost as heat during the respiratory processes of each organism in the chain. It is this loss of energy at each stage which limits the length of food chains. For this reason, it is rare to find chains with more than six different trophic levels.

On the death of the producers and consumers, some energy remains locked up in the complex organic compounds of which they are made. This is utilized by further groups of organisms which break down these complex materials into simple components again and in doing so contribute to the recycling of nutrients. The majority of this work is achieved by the saprobiontic fungi and bacteria, called **decomposers**, and to a lesser extent by certain animals called **detritivores**. The trophic relationships of these groups are shown in Fig. 17.1.

*Trophic efficiency*
This is the percentage of the energy at one trophic level which is incorporated into the next trophic level. The values differ from one ecosystem to another, with some of the highest values, around 40%, occurring in oceanic food chains. At the other

**ABLE 17.1    Trophic levels of a food chain in each of 5 different habitats**

| | Habitat | | | | |
|---|---|---|---|---|---|
| **Trophic level** | **Grassland** | **Woodland** | **Freshwater pond** | **Rocky marine shore** | **Ocean** |
| Quaternary consumers 3° carnivores) | Mammal e.g. stoat | Bird e.g. thrush | Large fish e.g. pike | Bird e.g. gull | Marine mammal e.g. seal |
| Tertiary consumers 2° carnivores) | Reptile e.g. grass snake | Arachnid e.g. spider | Small fish e.g. stickleback | Crustacean e.g. crab | Large fish e.g. herring |
| Secondary consumers 1° carnivores) | Amphibian e.g. toad | Carnivorous insect e.g. ladybird | Annelid e.g. leech | Carnivorous mollusc e.g. whelk | Small fish e.g. sand eel larvae |
| Primary consumers herbivores) | Insect larva e.g. caterpillar | Herbivorous insect e.g. aphid | Mollusc e.g. freshwater snail | Herbivorous mollusc e.g. limpet | Zooplankton e.g. copepods |
| Primary producers e.g. photosynthetic organisms) | Grass e.g. *Festuca* | Tree e.g. oak leaves | Aquatic plant e.g. *Elodea* | Seaweed e.g. sea lettuce | Phytoplankton e.g. diatom |

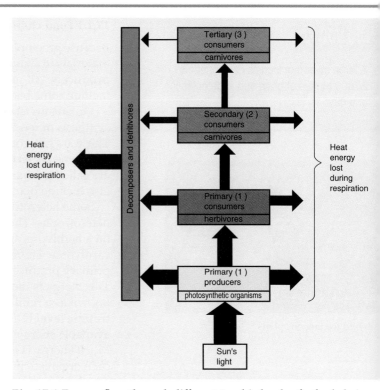

*Fig. 17.1 Energy flow through different trophic levels of a food chain*

extreme, values under 1% have been calculated for small mammals at the top of food chains, e.g. the shrew.

A classic piece of research carried out by Odum at Silver Spring in Florida provided the following figures for trophic efficiency:

Photosynthesis – 1.2%
Primary consumers (herbivores) – 15.9%
Secondary consumers (1st level carnivores) – 4.5%
Tertiary consumers (2nd level carnivores) – 6.7%.

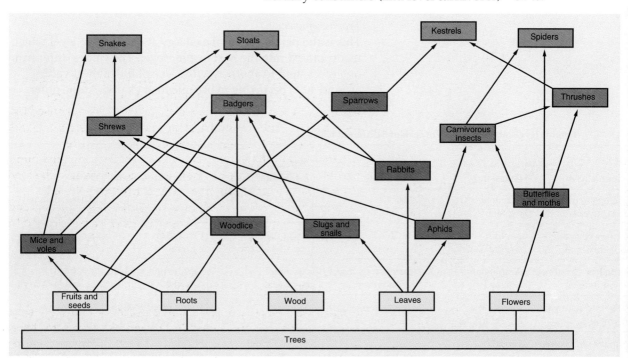

*Fig. 17.2 Simplified food web based on a woodland habitat*

## 17.1.2 Food webs

With rare exceptions, the diet of an individual is not restricted to a single food. Most animals feed on many different types. In the same way, an individual is normally a potential meal for many different species. The idea of a food chain as a sequence of species which feed exclusively off the individuals below them in the series is clearly oversimplified. Individual food chains interconnect in an intricate and complex way. A single species may form part of many different chains, not always occupying the same trophic level in each chain. Fig. 17.2 gives an example of a simplified food web for a woodland habitat.

## 17.1.3 Primary producers

It is the role of the photosynthetic organisms that make up the primary producers to manufacture organic substances using light, water and carbon dioxide. The rate at which they produce this organic food per unit area, per unit time, is called **gross primary productivity**. Not all this food is stored; around 20% is utilized by the plant, mainly during respiration. The remainder is called **net primary productivity**. It is this food which is available to the next link in the food chain, namely the primary consumers (herbivores). The net primary productivity depends upon climatic and other factors which affect photosynthesis. It is reduced in certain conditions such as cold, drought, absence of essential minerals, low light intensity, etc. The type of primary producer varies from habitat to habitat and some examples are given in Table 17.1. Chemosynthetic bacteria must be considered as primary producers because they provide energy for ecosystems, although from inorganic chemicals rather than light. Their overall contribution to the provision of the energy in a given ecosystem is very small compared to that provided by photosynthetic organisms.

## 17.1.4 Consumers

Those consumers which feed on the primary producers are called **primary consumers** or **herbivores**. Of the energy absorbed by a herbivore, only around 30% is actually used by the organism, the remainder being lost as urine and faeces. Some of this 30% is lost as heat, leaving even less of the net productivity of the primary producer to be incorporated into the herbivore and so made available to the next animal in the food chain – the **secondary consumers** or **carnivores**. Not all secondary and tertiary consumers are predators; parasites and scavengers may also fall into these categories depending on the nature of their food.

## 17.1.5 Decomposers and detritivores

A dead organism contains not only a potential source of energy but also many valuable minerals. Decomposers **(lysotrophs)** are saprobiontic microorganisms which exploit this energy source by breaking down the organic compounds that the organism is made of. In so doing they release valuable nutrients like carbon,

aprobiontic fungi are important decomposers of
ood

nitrogen and phosphorus, which may then be recycled (Section 17.2). Apart from dead organisms, they also decompose the organic chemicals in urine, faeces and other wastes.

**Detritus** is the organic debris from decomposing plants and animals and is normally in the form of small fragments. It forms the diet of a group of animals called **detritivores**. They usually differ from decomposers in being larger and in digesting food internally rather than externally. Examples of detritivores include earthworms, woodlice, maggots, dog whelks and sea cucumbers.

### 17.1.6 Ecological pyramids

*Pyramids of numbers*

If a bar diagram is drawn to indicate the relative numbers of individuals at each trophic level in a food chain, a diagram similar to that shown in Fig. 17.3(a) is produced. The length of each bar gives a measure of the relative numbers of each organism. The overall shape is roughly that of a pyramid, with primary producers outnumbering the primary consumers which in turn outnumber secondary consumers. Accepting that there is inevitably some loss when energy is transferred from one trophic level to the next in a food chain, it follows that to support an individual at one level requires more energy from the individual at the level below to compensate for this loss. In most instances this can only be achieved by having more individuals at the lower level (Fig. 17.3(a)).

The use of pyramids of numbers has drawbacks, however:

**1.** All organisms are equated, regardless of their size. An oak tree is counted as one individual in the same way as an aphid.

**2.** No account is made for juveniles and other immature forms of a species whose diet and energy requirements may differ from those of the adult.

**3.** The numbers of some individuals are so great that it is impossible to represent them accurately on the same scale as other species in the food chain. For example, millions of blackfly may feed on a single rose-bush and this relationship cannot be effectively drawn to scale on a pyramid of numbers.

These problems may create some different shaped 'pyramids'. Take for example the food chain:

oak tree → aphid → ladybird

The pyramid of numbers produced is illustrated in Fig. 17.3(b). It clearly bulges in the middle.

The food chain:

sycamore → caterpillar → protozoan parasites (of the caterpillar)

produces a complete inversion of the pyramid as illustrated in Fig. 17.3(c).

These difficulties are partly overcome by the use of a pyramid of biomass, instead of one of numbers.

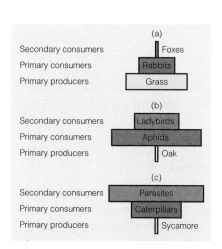

*Fig 17.3 Pyramids of numbers*

*Pyramids of biomass*

To overcome some of the problems of using pyramids of numbers, the dry mass of all the organisms at each trophic level may instead be estimated. The relative biomass is represented by bars of proportionate length. While this method is an improvement, it too has its drawbacks:

**1.** It is impossible to measure exactly the biomass of all individuals in a population. A small sample is normally taken and measured. This sample may not be representative.

**2.** The time at which a sample is taken may affect the result. Figures for a deciduous tree in summer may be very different from those in winter. What the sample measures is only the amount of material present at a particular instant. This is called the **standing crop** and gives no indication of total productivity. A young tree, for example, is the result of the accumulation of many years' growth, but it may not yet have seeded and produced offspring. A diatom, itself much smaller than the tree, may however have produced many times the tree's biomass in the same period of time. Such anomalies can occasionally lead to inverted pyramids of biomass, e.g. in oceans at certain times of the year zooplankton biomass exceeds phytoplankton biomass, although over the year as a whole the reverse is true.

*Pyramids of energy*

An energy pyramid overcomes the main drawbacks of the other forms of ecological pyramid. Here the bar is drawn in proportion to the total energy utilized at each trophic level. The total productivity of the primary producers of a given area (e.g. 1 square metre) can be measured for a given period (e.g. 1 year). From this, the proportion of it utilized by the primary consumer can be calculated, and so on up the food chain. The pyramids produced do not show any anomalies, but obtaining the necessary data can be a complex and difficult affair. Once again the unifying nature of energy in ecology is apparent.

## 17.2 The cycling of nutrients

Energy exists in a number of forms, only some of which can be utilized by living organisms. In an ecosystem, energy is obtained almost entirely as light and this is converted to chemical energy which then passes along the food chain. During chemical reactions in living organisms some of this energy is lost as heat – 'lost', because heat is a form of energy which is dissipated to the environment and cannot be re-used by organisms. It is exactly because this heat cannot be recycled that energy flows through ecosystems in one direction only. Like energy, minerals such as carbon, nitrogen and phosphorus exist in different forms. Unlike energy in ecosystems, these forms can be continuously recycled and so used repeatedly by organisms. Most nutrient or mineral cycles have two components:

1. **A geological component** – This includes rock and other deposits in the oceans and the atmosphere. These form the majo reservoirs of the mineral.

2. **A biological component** – This includes those organisms which in some way help to convert one form of the mineral into another and so recycle it. It therefore includes the producers, the consumers and especially the decomposers.

### 17.2.1 The carbon cycle (Fig. 17.4)

Despite containing less than 0.04% carbon dioxide, the atmosphere acts as the major pool of carbon. The turnover of thi carbon dioxide is considerable. It is removed from the air by the photosynthetic activities of green plants and returned as a result of the respiration of all organisms. This may lead to short-term fluctuations in the proportions of oxygen and carbon dioxide in the atmosphere. For example the concentration of $CO_2$ varies daily, being up to 40 parts per million (ppm) higher at night, and seasonally – it is around 16 ppm lower in summer than in winter These differences are accounted for by changes in the rate of photosynthesis. Overall however there is a long-term global balance between the two gases. Heterotrophic organisms (animals and fungi) obtain their carbon by eating plants, directly or indirectly. At times in the past, large quantities of dead organisms accumulated in anaerobic conditions and so were prevented from decaying. In time they formed coal, oil and other fossil fuels. The combustion of these fuels returns more carbon dioxide to the atmosphere and has resulted in a rise in its level from an estimated 265 parts per million (ppm) in 1600 to 315 ppm in 1958 and to 350 ppm today. Another factor contributing to a rise in atmospheric carbon dioxide has been the clearance of forests. As net users of carbon dioxide trees make a major contribution to the reduction of atmospheric carbon dioxide, especially in tropical rain forests where wet, hot conditions

Fiddlers Ferry coal-fired power station

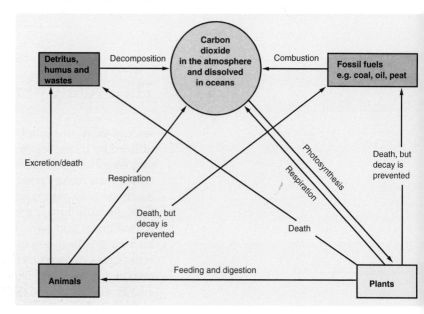

*Fig. 17.4 The carbon cycle*

throughout the year favour rapid photosynthesis. It has been estimated that removal of these trees has produced 30% of the increase in atmospheric carbon dioxide which, as a 'greenhouse gas', contributes to global warming (see Section 18.4.3).

### 17.2.2 The nitrogen cycle (Fig. 17.5)

In Chapter 2 (Table 2.1) we saw the range of biologically important chemicals which contain nitrogen, and it is clear from these just how essential a mineral it is to all organisms. Although the atmosphere contains 78% nitrogen, very few organisms can use this gaseous nitrogen directly. Instead they depend upon soil minerals, especially nitrates, as their source of nitrogen. The supply of these nitrates is variable, not least because they are soluble and therefore easily leached from the soil. For this reason a deficiency of nitrates is often the limiting factor to plant growth, and hence the size of the ecosystem it supports. Surrounded by an atmosphere abundant in nitrogen, the growth of many plants is stunted by a lack of it. This is the main reason that nitrogen is commonly applied in the form of artificial fertilizers.

Deforestation, especially of tropical rain forests, has also led to nitrate deficiency. With the trees gone there has been large scale erosion due to the high rainfall in these areas washing away the soil. Previously the trees acted as a canopy, preventing the rain beating directly on the soil, but they also absorbed much of the water, which otherwise washes off the surface taking the soil with it. Their roots, in addition, helped to bind the soil particles together. The combination of soil erosion and leaching of nitrates in these areas has impoverished the land, making it unfit for vegetation.

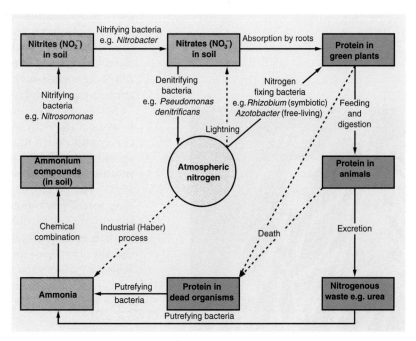

*Fig. 17.5 The nitrogen cycle*

*Nitrification*
This is the name given to the series of reactions involved in the oxidation of ammonia to nitrates. The process is carried out in two stages:

**1.** The oxidation of ammonia or ammonium compounds to nitrites by free-living bacteria e.g. *Nitrosomonas*.

$$2NH_3 + 3O_2 \longrightarrow 2NO_2^- + 2H^+ + 2H_2O$$

ammonia  oxygen  nitrite  hydrogen ions  water

**2.** The oxidation of the nitrite by other free-living bacteria e.g. *Nitrobacter* and *Nitrococcus*.

$$2NO_2^- + O_2 \longrightarrow 2NO_3^-$$

nitrite  oxygen  nitrate

In both cases these chemosynthetic bacteria carry out these processes as a means of obtaining their respiratory energy.

*Denitrification*
This is the process by which nitrate in the soil is converted into gaseous nitrogen, and thereby made unavailable to the majority of plants. It is carried out by anaerobic bacteria like *Pseudomonas denitrificans* and *Thiobacillus denitrificans*. The necessary anaerobic conditions are more likely in waterlogged soil. Where this occurs, denitrifying bacteria thrive and by converting nitrates to atmospheric nitrogen they reduce soil fertility. Farmers and gardeners plough or dig their land to improve drainage and aeration, so avoiding anaerobic conditions.

*Nitrogen fixation*
Nitrogen fixation is the opposite to denitrification in that it converts gaseous nitrogen into a form that can be utilized by plants, usually organic nitrogen-containing chemicals. Nitrogen fixation is carried out by free-living organisms and organisms living in symbiotic association with leguminous plants.

Free-living **nitrogen-fixing bacteria** include *Azotobacter* and *Clostridium* and **nitrogen-fixing blue-green bacteria** include *Nostoc*. Both types reduce gaseous nitrogen to ammonia which they then use to manufacture their amino acids. Around 90% of the total nitrogen fixation is carried out by free-living microorganisms such as these and they make a worthwhile contribution to soil fertility.

Symbiotic nitrogen-fixing bacteria like *Rhizobium* live mostly in association with leguminous plants such as beans, peas and clover although a few types associate with non-leguminous species. They live in special swollen areas on roots, known as **root nodules**. Details of this relationship are given in Section 15.9.2. The raising of an appropriate leguminous crop as part of crop rotation scheme has long been used as a means of improving soil fertility. The crop fixes nitrogen during its growth and may later be ploughed into the soil so that its decay can slowly release much needed nitrogen for use by later crops. Soils may alternatively be enriched by use of nitrogen fertilizers.

Legume with root nodules

# 17.3 Ecological factors and their effects on distribution

An organism's environment may be divided into two main parts: the non-living or **abiotic** component and the living or **biotic** component. They work both separately and jointly to influence the distribution and behaviour of organisms in the ecosystem. To help consider these influences we shall examine both components although, for convenience, the abiotic portion will be divided into **climatic** factors and **edaphic** (soil) factors.

## 17.3.1 Edaphic factors

Soil possesses both living and non-living components. The living portion comprises plant roots and an immense population of microorganisms and small animals. The non-living portion includes particles ranging in size from boulders to fine clay. In addition, there are minerals, water, organic matter and gases. Soil is the result of the weathering of rock which takes two forms:

1. **Physical weathering** – the mechanical breakdown of rock as a result of the action of water, frost, ice, wind and other rocks.

2. **Chemical weathering** – the chemical breakdown as a result of water, acids, alkalis and minerals attacking certain rock types.

The general appearance of a soil seen in vertical section and called a **soil profile** is given in Fig. 17.6.

We have seen that the nature of any ecosystem is dependent upon the type of primary producer and its productivity. Both these factors are, in turn, largely determined by the properties of the soil on which the producer grows. The factors which determine a soil's properties are briefly described below.

*Particle size and nature*

The size of the constituent mineral particles of soil probably affects its properties, and hence the type of plant which grows on it, more than any other single factor. Soils are classified according to the size of their particles as shown in Table 17.2.

The **texture** of a soil is determined by the relative proportions of sand, silt and clay particles and this affects the agricultural potential of a soil. A clay soil, with its many tiny particles, has the advantage over a sandy soil, with its coarse particles, in holding water more readily and being less likely to have its minerals leached. On the other hand, it may easily become compacted, reducing its air content; it is slower to drain, colder and more difficult to work, especially when wet. A fuller comparison of clay and sandy soils is given in Table 17.3.

The nature of the particles as well as their size affects soil properties. Sand and silt are mainly silica ($SiO_2$) which is inert. Clay particles, however, have negative charges and these react with minerals in the soil, especially cations. This helps to prevent these nutrient minerals from being leached.

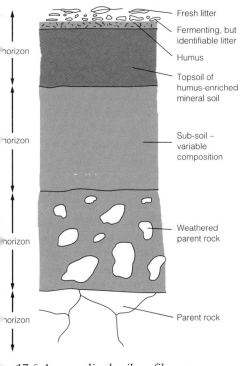

horizon — Fresh litter
— Fermenting, but identifiable litter
— Humus
horizon — Topsoil of humus-enriched mineral soil
horizon — Sub-soil – variable composition
horizon — Weathered parent rock
horizon — Parent rock

*Fig. 17.6 A generalized soil profile*

**TABLE 17.2  Classification of soil particles according to size**

| Particle size (diameter in mm) | Particle type |
| --- | --- |
| 2.00–0.200 | Coarse sand |
| 0.20–0.020 | Fine sand |
| 0.02–0.002 | Silt |
| <0.002 | Clay |

TABLE 17.3 **A comparison of clay and sandy soils**

| Clay soil | Sandy soil |
|---|---|
| Particle size is less than 0.002 mm (2 μm) | Particle size from 0.02 mm to 2.0 mm |
| Small air spaces between particles giving poor aeration | Large air spaces between particles giving good aeration |
| Poor drainage; soil easily compacted | Good drainage; soil not compacted |
| Good water retention leading to possible waterlogging | Poor water retention and no waterlogging |
| Being a wet soil, evaporation of water causes it to be cold | Less water evaporation and therefore warmer |
| Particles attract many mineral ions and so nutrient content is high | Minerals are easily leached and so mineral content is low |
| Particles aggregate together to form clods, making the soil heavy and difficult to work | Particles remain separate, making the soil light and easy to work |

### Did you know?

The number of dormant seeds found in 2.4 ha of soil at Rothampstead Horticultural Research Centre was 300 million.

*Organic (humus) content*

This includes all dead plant and animal material as well as some animal waste products. Dead animals, leaves, twigs, roots and faeces are broken down by the decomposers and detritivores into a black, amorphous material called **humus**. It has a complicated and variable chemical make-up and is often acidic. Humus acts rather like a sponge in retaining water and in this way improves the structure of sandy soils. It is equally beneficial to a clay soil where it helps to lighten the soil by breaking up the clods and thereby improving aeration and drainage. The slow breakdown of humus releases valuable minerals in both types of soil. This breakdown is carried out by aerobic decomposers and thereby ceases in waterlogged conditions due to the lack of oxygen. In these circumstances the partly decomposed detritus accumulates as **peat**.

*Water content*

The water content of any well-drained soil varies markedly. A freely drained soil which holds as much water as possible is said to be at **field capacity**. The addition of more water which cannot drain away leads to waterlogging and anaerobic conditions. Plants able to tolerate these conditions include the rushes (*Juncus* spp.), sedges (*Carex* spp.) and rice. They have air spaces among the root tissues which allow some diffusion of oxygen from the aerial parts to help supply the roots.

*Air content*

The space between soil particles is filled with air, from which the roots obtain their respiratory oxygen by direct diffusion. It is equally essential to the aerobic microorganisms in the soil which decompose the humus. They make heavy demands upon the available oxygen and may create anaerobic conditions.

*Mineral content*

As shown in Chapter 2 (Table 2.1), a wide variety of minerals is necessary to support healthy plant growth. Different species make different mineral demands and therefore the distribution of plants depends to some extent on the mineral balance of a particular soil. Some plants have particular nutrient requirements; the desert shrub, *Atriplex*, for example, requires sodium, a mineral not essential to most species.

*Biotic content*

Soils contain vast numbers of living organisms. They include bacteria, fungi and algae as well as animals like protozoans, nematodes, earthworms, insects and burrowing mammals. Bacteria and fungi carry out decomposition, while burrowing animals such as earthworms improve drainage and aeration by forming air passages in the soil. Earthworms also improve fertility by their thorough mixing of the soil which helps to bring leached minerals from lower layers within reach of plant roots. Earthworms improve the humus content through their practice of pulling leaves into their burrows. By passing soil through their bodies they may make its texture finer.

*pH*

The pH of a soil influences its physical properties and the availability of certain minerals to plants. Plants such as heathers, azaleas and camelias grow best in acid soils, while dog's mercury and stonewort prefer alkaline ones. Species which are tolerant to extremes of pH can become dominant in certain areas because competing species find it hard to survive in these extreme conditions. The dominance of heathers on upland moors is, in part, due to their ability to withstand very low soil pH. Most plants, however, grow best in an optimum pH close to neutral.

*Temperature*

All chemical and biological activities of a soil are influenced by temperature. The temperature of a soil may be different from that of the air above it. Evaporation of water from a soil may cool it to below that of the air whereas solar radiation may raise the soil temperature above that of the air. Germination and growth depend on suitable temperatures and the optimum varies from species to species. The activity of soil organisms is likewise affected by changes in temperature, earthworms becoming dormant at low temperatures, for example.

*Topography*

Three features of topography may influence the distribution of organisms:

**1. Aspect** (slope) – South-facing slopes receive more sunlight, and are therefore warmer, than north-facing ones (in the northern hemisphere).

**2. Inclination** (steepness) – Water drains more readily from steep slopes and these therefore dry more quickly than slopes with a shallower gradient.

**3. Altitude** (height) – At higher altitudes the temperature is lower, the wind speed is greater and there is more rainfall.

## BIOLOGY AROUND US

# Our disappearing soil

The soil available for agriculture is diminishing. Apart from land that is used to accommodate our ever-expanding cities, extra is lost as a consequence of pollution. Much more disappears as a result of poor management of farmland or its wasteful use. Badly designed irrigation schemes have increased salt levels of some soils to the point where they can no longer support plant growth. Water extracted from rivers and lakes has lowered their levels to such an extent that the surrounding land has been turned into deserts. The Aral Sea in the former USSR is a case in point.

Perhaps the biggest pollution problem is that of soil erosion. It is estimated that, each year, 75 billion tonnes of soil worldwide are either washed or blown away. In parts of Jamaica, up to 400 tonnes are lost from each hectare of land each year. Even in the UK the average figure is 17 tonnes per hectare per year .

Tropical rain forest

Tundra

Wind-trimmed Hawthorn

## 17.3.2 Climatic factors

The world's major biomes are largely differentiated on the basis of climate. From the warm, humid tropical rain forest to the cold arctic tundra it is the prevailing weather conditions which determine the predominant flora and hence its attendant fauna. Each climatic zone has its own community of plants and animals which are suited to the conditions. The adaptations of plants and animals to these conditions are dealt with elsewhere in this book and what follows is merely a general review of the major climatic variables within ecosystems.

*Light*
As the ultimate source of energy for ecosystems, light is a fundamental necessity. Light is not only needed for photosynthesis, however. It plays a role in such photoperiodic behaviour as flowering in plants, and reproduction, hibernation and migration in animals. Phototaxis and phototropism in plants as well as visual perception in animals require light. There are three aspects to light – its wavelength, its intensity and its duration. The influence of these on photosynthesis is dealt with in Chapter 14, and on photoperiodism in Chapter 29.

*Temperature*
Just as the sun is the only source of light for an ecosystem, so it is the main source of heat. The temperature range within which life exists is relatively small. At low temperatures ice crystals may form within cells, causing physical disruption, and at high temperatures enzymes are denatured. Fluctuation in environmental temperature is more extreme in terrestrial habitats than aquatic ones because the high heat capacity of water effectively buffers the temperature changes in aquatic habitats. The actual temperature of any habitat may differ in time according to the season and time of day, and in space according to latitude, slope, degree of shading or exposure, etc.

*Water*
Water is essential to all life and its availability determines the distribution of terrestrial organisms. The adaptations of terrestrial organisms to conserve water are discussed in Chapter 22 and 23. Even aquatic organisms do not escape problems of water shortage. In saline conditions water may be withdrawn from organisms osmotically, thus necessitating adaptations to conserve it. The salinity of water is a major factor in determining the distribution of aquatic organisms. Some fish, e.g. roach and perch, live exclusively in fresh water; others, like cod and herring, are entirely marine. A few fish, like salmon and eels, are capable of tolerating both extremes during their life.

*Air and water currents*
Air movements may affect organisms indirectly, for example by evaporative cooling or by a change in humidity. They may also affect them directly by determining their shape; the development of branches and roots of trees in exposed situations is an example. Wind is an important mechanism for dispersing seeds and spores. In the same way that the air currents determine the distribution of certain species in terrestrial habitats, so too do water currents determine species distribution in aquatic habitats.

*Humidity*
Humidity has a major bearing on the rate of transpiration in plants and so affects their distribution. To a lesser degree, it affects the distribution of some animals by affecting the rate of evaporation from their bodies.

### 17.3.3 Biotic factors

Relationships between organisms are obviously varied and complex and are detailed throughout the book, but a brief outline of a few major biotic factors which affect organisms' distribution is given below.

*Competition*
Organisms compete with each other for food, water, light, minerals, shelter and a mate. They compete not only with members of other species – **interspecific competition** – but also with members of their own species – **intraspecific competition**. Where two species occupy the same ecological niche, the interspecific competition leads to the extinction of one or the other – the **competitive exclusion principle** (Section 17.6.8).

*Predation*
The distribution of a species is determined by the presence or absence of its prey and/or predators. The predator–prey relationship is an important aspect in determining population size (Section 17.6.7).

*Antibiosis*
Organisms sometimes produce chemicals which repel other organisms. These may be directed against members of their own species. Many mammals, for example, use chemicals to mark their territories, with the intention of deterring other members of the species from entering. Some ants produce a type of external hormone called a **pheromone** when they are in danger and, in sufficient concentrations, this warns off other members of the species. The chemicals may also be directed against different species. Many fungi, e.g. *Penicillium*, produce **antibiotics** to prevent bacterial growth in their vicinity.

*Dispersal*
Many organisms depend upon another species to disperse them. Plants in particular use a wide variety of animal species to disperse their seeds.

*Pollination*
Angiosperms utilize insects to transfer their pollen from one member of a species to another, and a highly complex form of interdependence between these two groups has developed. This is discussed in Section 12.3.2.

*Mimicry*
Many organisms, for a variety of reasons, seek to resemble other living organisms. Warning mimicry is used by certain flies which resemble wasps. Potential predators are warned off the harmless flies, fearing they may be stung.

*Human influence*
Humans influence the distribution of other organisms more than any other single species. As hunters, fishers, farmers, developers and polluters, to name a few activities, they dictate which organisms grow where. Some aspects of these influences are considered in Chapter 18.

Hoverfly mimicking a wasp

### 17.3.4 Species diversity (richness) index

The number and range of different species found in an ecosystem is called its **species diversity (richness)**. A measure of species diversity is helpful when considering the interaction of the edaphic, climatic and biotic factors which influence an ecosystem. In general, a stable ecosystem has a wide range of different species, each with a similar population size. Such populations are dominated by biotic factors. A less stable ecosystem, i.e. one which is under stress due to pollution or extreme climatic conditions, has just a few species with very large populations and is dominated by abiotic factors.

One method of measuring species diversity is the **Simpson index**. It is most often used to estimate plant diversity and involves counting the numbers of each type found in a given area. The diversity is then calculated using the formula:

$$D = \frac{N(N-1)}{\Sigma n(n-1)}$$

where   $D$ = diversity index
$N$ = total number of plants
$n$ = total number of species
$\Sigma$ = sum of.

## 17.4   Ecological techniques

### 17.4.1 Measurement of environmental parameters

It is essential in any ecological study to be able to measure variations in environmental conditions both in time and space. The main parameters which the ecologist measures are:

*Temperature*
In ecological studies the precise temperature at any one moment is of little value. Of much greater significance are the **diurnal (daily)** and **seasonal** temperature variations. These variations can be measured using a mercury thermometer by taking readings at regular intervals. The best method of determining the highest and lowest temperature over a period of time is to use a maximum–minimum thermometer which leaves a marker at the highest temperature recorded and another at the lowest. For relatively inaccessible positions, e.g. under small stones, at different depths in a lake, a miniaturized **thermistor** may be used. This electrical instrument measures resistance, which changes with temperature. Using calibration scales it is possible to determine the actual temperature which corresponds to a given resistance.

*pH*
pH is a measure of the acidity or alkalinity of a solution. It is most easily determined by use of **universal indicator**, either as liquid or impregnated on test paper. More accurate is the use of a **pH meter**. The probe of the instrument is rinsed in distilled water (pH 7 – neutral) before being placed in the test solution. The reading is noted. A calibration graph or scale must be made by taking readings of a series of buffer solutions of known pH. From this calibration graph the pH corresponding to any reading can be determined.

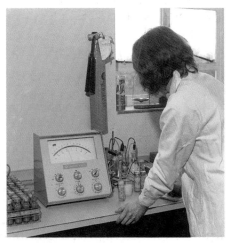
pH meter in use

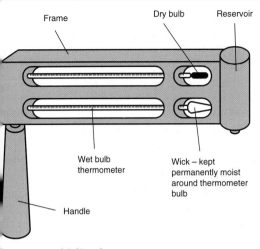

Frame — Dry bulb — Reservoir

Wet bulb thermometer

Wick – kept permanently moist around thermometer bulb

Handle

*Fig. 17.7 Whirling hygrometer*

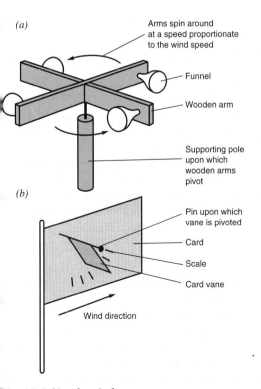

(a)

Arms spin around at a speed proportionate to the wind speed

Funnel

Wooden arm

Supporting pole upon which wooden arms pivot

(b)

Pin upon which vane is pivoted

Card

Scale

Card vane

Wind direction

*Fig. 17.8 Simple wind gauges*

## Light

Two aspects of light, its duration and intensity, are generally important to ecological studies. The duration of daylight hours can be determined astronomically and is predictable for any location. The values are available for any given day, from most diaries. The intensity of light is most easily measured by use of an ordinary photographic light meter.

## Humidity

Atmospheric humidity is normally expressed as **relative humidity**, i.e. the water content of a given volume of air relative to the same volume of fully saturated air. It is measured using a **whirling hygrometer**. This has two thermometers, the bulb of one being kept dry while the other is permanently wet. Both are mounted in a frame (Fig. 17.7). The hygrometer is rotated in the air until both thermometers give a constant reading. The wet bulb thermometer will always give a lower reading than the dry bulb one, due to the cooling effect of the evaporating water – the less humid the air, the more evaporation and the greater the temperature difference between the two thermometers. The actual humidity is determined by reading off the temperatures on a special scale.

## Wind and water speed

Wind speed is measured by an instrument called an **anemometer**. Simple, but effective, wind gauges can be improvised and two examples are given in Fig. 17.8. These may not provide a direct measure of wind speed but will give comparative readings, e.g. inside and outside a wood, or at various vertical heights.

The easiest method of determining water speed is to time the movement of a floating object over a measured distance. To avoid inaccuracies caused by the wind blowing the portion floating above the water, it should be weighted so that it hardly breaks the surface. A specimen tube partly filled with water works admirably.

## Salinity

The salinity of a water sample is best measured using a **conductivity meter**. This instrument measures the conductivity between two probes; the greater the salinity the greater the conductivity. It is also possible to determine the concentration of a particular ion. For example, chloride concentration can be determined by titration against silver nitrate solution, using potassium chromate as an indicator.

## Oxygen level

An instrument known as an **oxygen meter** can be used to give a measurement of the oxygen concentration in a water sample. This has now largely replaced the chemical technique involving titration, known as the Winkler method.

### 17.4.2 Sampling methods

It is virtually impossible to identify and count every organism in a habitat. For this reason only small sections of the habitat are usually studied in detail. Provided these are representative of an area as a whole, any conclusions drawn from the findings will be valid. There are four basic sampling techniques.

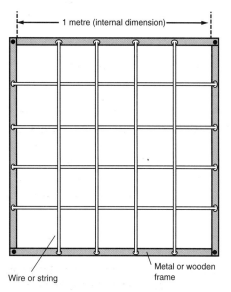

Fig. 17.9 A quadrat frame

Using a quadrat along a belt transect

*Quadrats*

A quadrat (Fig. 17.9) is a sturdily built wooden frame, often designed so it can be folded to make it more compact for storage and transport. It is placed on the ground and the species present within the frame are identified and their abundance recorded. Where the species are small and/or densely packed, one or more of the smaller squares within the frame may be used rather than the quadrat as a whole.

Sampling with a quadrat may be random or systematic. **Random sampling** can be as simple as throwing a quadrat over one's shoulder and counting the species within it wherever it falls. Even with the best of intentions it is difficult not to introduce an element of personal bias using this method. A better form of random sampling is to lay out two long tape measures at right angles to each other, along two sides of the study area. Using random numbers generated on a computer or certain calculators, a series of coordinates can be obtained. The quadrat is placed at the intersection of each pair of coordinates and the species within it recorded. **Systematic sampling** involves placing the quadrat at regular intervals, for example, along a transect. It is sometimes necessary to sample the same area over many years in order to investigate seasonal changes or monitor ecological succession. In these circumstances a rectangular area of ground may be marked out by boundary stakes which are connected by rope. This is known as a **permanent quadrat**.

*Point frames*

A point frame, or point quadrat (Fig. 17.10), consists of vertical legs across which is fixed a horizontal bar with small holes along it. A long metal pin, resembling a knitting needle, is placed in each of the holes in turn. Each time the pin touches a species, it is recorded. The point frame is especially useful where there is dense vegetation as it can sample at many different levels.

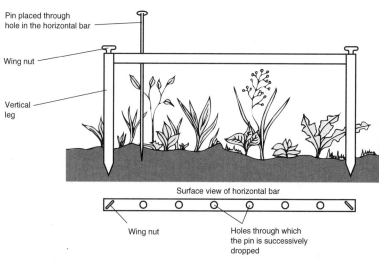

Fig. 17.10 Point frame (point quadrat)

*Line transect*

A line transect is used so that systematic sampling of an area can be carried out. A string or tape is stretched out along the ground in a straight line. A record is made of the organisms touching or covering the line all along its length, or at regular intervals. This

**TABLE 17.4  Collecting apparatus of general use**

| Apparatus | Purpose |
|---|---|
| Specimen tube (small) | With tight-fitting caps and of varying sizes, these can be used to contain small organisms while they are identified, or used to transport them |
| Screw-topped jars (large) | To collect and transport smaller organisms. Also useful for aquatic organisms |
| Polythene bags (various sizes) | To collect plant material, soil samples and other non-living material |
| Forceps | For transferring plants and hard-bodied animals as well as non-living materials, e.g. stones |
| Paint brush | For transferring small, delicate or soft-bodied organisms, e.g. aphids |
| Bulb pipette | For transferring small aquatic organisms |
| Pooter (aspirator) Fig. 17.11 | For collecting and transferring small animals, e.g. insects and spiders |
| Widger | A useful all-purpose tool, similar to a spatula, used for digging, levering and transferring material |
| Sieve | For sifting sand, soil, mud and pond-water for small organisms |
| Hand lens | To magnify features of organisms to help in their identification |
| Enamel dish | For sorting specimens |

technique is particularly useful where there is a transition of flora and/or fauna across an area, down a seashore for example. If there is any appreciable height change along the transect, it is advisable to construct a profile of the transect to indicate the changes in level. This is especially important where vertical height is a major factor in determining the distribution of species. On a seashore, for example, the height above the sea affects the duration of time any point is submerged by the tide. This has a considerable bearing on the species that can survive at that level. So, the distribution of species is related to the vertical height on the shore rather than the horizontal distance along it. This form of transect is called a **profile transect**.

*Belt transect*
A belt transect is a strip, usually a metre wide, marked by putting a second line transect parallel to the other. The species between the lines are carefully recorded, working a metre at a time. Another method is to use a frame quadrat in conjunction with a single line transect. In this case the quadrat is laid down alongside the line transect and the species within it recorded. It is then moved its own length along the line and the process repeated. This gives a record of species in a continuous belt, but the quadrat may also be used at regular intervals, e.g. every 5 m, along the line (a **ladder transect**).

### 17.4.3 Collecting methods

Reliable methods of collecting organisms are an essential part of ecology. Because they photosynthesize, plants always occur in the light and are hence visible and usually large and stationary. All these factors make them easy to find and collect. Animals by contrast may live underground, in crevices, or simply be camouflaged; this makes them less conspicuous. Even when seen, the animal's ability to move from place to place presents problems of capture. Collecting all organisms within a habitat is normally impractical and therefore small areas are selected. Organisms should be identified on site, but if removing them is unavoidable, as few as possible should be taken and for as short a time as possible and always returned to the same location. When collecting specimens, as much information as possible should be recorded at the time. This should include details of the time, date, location, substrate, climate and any other relevant data.

In addition to collecting specimens by hand or with the use of a pooter (Table 17.4), there are other pieces of apparatus of varying degrees of complexity which may be used to lure and trap animals.

*Beating tray*
This is a fabric sheet on a collapsible frame. It is held under a part of a bush or a tree which is then shaken or disturbed with a stick. The organisms which are dislodged are collected by hand or with the aid of a pooter (Fig. 17.11). It is used to collect small non-flying terrestrial organisms, e.g. beetles, spiders, caterpillars.

*Light traps*
Any light source will attract certain nocturnal flying insects. A very simple light trap may be made by placing a vertical sheet at the side of a light source, and a horizontal one beneath it. This is

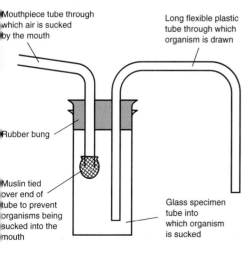

Mouthpiece tube through which air is sucked by the mouth

Long flexible plastic tube through which organism is drawn

Rubber bung

Muslin tied over end of tube to prevent organisms being sucked into the mouth

Glass specimen tube into which organism is sucked

*Fig. 17.11 Pooter (aspirator)*

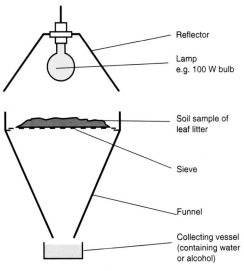

*Fig. 17.12(a) Tullgren funnel*

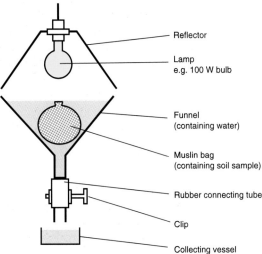

*Fig. 17.12(b) Baermann funnel*

necessary as some insects prefer to rest vertically and others horizontally. More effective traps involve **mercury vapour lamps**. These emit much ultra-violet light which is particularly attractive to nocturnal insects such as moths.

### Tullgren funnel

This is used to extract small animals from a sample of soil or leaf litter. The soil sample is placed on a coarse sieve and light and moderate heat are used to drive the animals downwards through the sieve (Fig. 17.12(a)). They fall into a funnel which directs them into a collecting vessel.

### Baermann funnel

This is again used to extract soil animals and is particularly effective for worms, especially nematodes. The soil sample is contained within a muslin bag which is then submerged in water in a funnel (Fig. 17.12(b)). A tungsten bulb may be used as a source of heat which, along with the water, induces the organisms to leave the sample. They collect in the neck of the funnel from where they can be periodically removed.

### Mammal traps

The best live trap is the **Longworth trap**. It is placed in situations which small mammals such as mice and voles frequent, like a runway. It comprises a metal box with a single entrance which closes firmly behind the mammal when it enters. The box is baited with bedding and the appropriate food to entice the animal to enter. The behaviour of many small mammals creates problems when this trap is used to assess population sizes, because some individuals, called 'trap-shy', never enter the trap while others, called 'trap-happy', actively seek them out for the meal and bed they provide.

### Pitfall traps

A jam-jar or similar vessel is sunk into the ground with its rim level with the soil. It is baited with the appropriate food, e.g. decaying meat to attract scavenging insects such as beetles, or honey to attract ants. Having fallen in, the insects are unable to climb the smooth walls of the jar to escape.

### Netting

This is a popular method of capture and takes many forms. Hand-held nets with short handles give greater precision for catching insects in flight. With some insects it is better to stalk them until they settle before netting them. These nets are called **kite nets**. A more robust form, called the **sweep net**, is used to collect insects from foliage. It is swept along grass or through bushes, dislodging insects which fall into the net. This net may also be used to collect aquatic animals by sweeping it through streams or ponds. A **plankton net** is made of bolting silk because its fine mesh, while allowing water through, traps even microscopic organisms. It has a wide mouth held open by a circular metal frame and narrows down to a small collecting jar at the other end in which the plankton accumulate. The net is towed slowly through the water, usually behind a small boat.

# 17.5 Estimating population size

To count accurately every individual of any species within a habitat is clearly impractical, and yet much applied ecology requires information on the size of animal and plant populations. It is necessary therefore to use sampling techniques in particular ways in order to make estimates of the size of any population. The exact methods used depend not only on the nature of the habitat but also on the organism involved. Whereas, for example, it may be useful to know the number of individuals in an animal population, this may be misleading for a plant species, where the percentage cover may be more relevant.

## 17.5.1 Using quadrats

By sampling an area using quadrats and counting the number of individuals within each quadrat, it is possible to estimate the total number of individuals within the area. If, for example, an area of $1000 \text{ m}^2$ is studied and 100 quadrats, each $1 \text{ m}^2$, are sampled, it follows that a total of $100 \text{ m}^2$ of the area has been sampled. This represents one-tenth of the total. The total number of individuals of a species in all 100 quadrats must therefore be multiplied by ten to give an estimate of the total population of that species in the area. The use of quadrats in estimating population size is largely confined to plants and sessile or very slow-moving animals. Faster-moving animals would simply disperse upon being disturbed.

## 17.5.2 Capture–recapture techniques

The capture–recapture method of estimating the size of a population is useful for mobile animals which can be tagged or in some other way marked. A known number of animals are caught, clearly marked and then released into the population again. Some time later, a given number of individuals is collected randomly and the number of marked individuals recorded. The size of the population is calculated on the assumption that the proportion of marked to unmarked individuals in this second sample is the same as the proportion of marked to unmarked individuals in the population as a whole. This, of course, assumes that the marked individuals released from the first sample distribute themselves evenly among the remainder of the population and have sufficient time to do so. This may not be the case, due to deaths, migrations and other factors. Another problem is that while the tag or label may not itself be toxic, it often renders the individual more conspicuous and so more liable to predation. In this case the number of marked individuals surviving long enough to be recaptured is reduced and the size of the population will consequently be over-estimated. 'Trap-shy' and 'trap-happy' individuals (see Section 17.4.3) will also adversely influence the estimate. The population size can be estimated using the calculation below:

quadrat in use

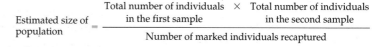

$$\text{Estimated size of population} = \frac{\substack{\text{Total number of individuals} \\ \text{in the first sample}} \times \substack{\text{Total number of individuals} \\ \text{in the second sample}}}{\text{Number of marked individuals recaptured}}$$

The estimate calculated is called the **Lincoln index**.

The method can be used on a variety of animals; arthropods may be marked on their backs with dabs of non-toxic paint, fish can have tags attached to their opercula, mammals may have tags clipped to their ears and birds can have their legs ringed.

### 17.5.3 Abundance scales

The population size may be fairly accurately determined by making some form of **frequency assessment**. These methods are subjective and involve an experimenter making some estimate of the number of individuals in a given area, or the percentage cover of a particular species. This is especially useful where individuals are very numerous, e.g. barnacles on a rocky shore, or where it is difficult to distinguish individuals, e.g. grass plants in a meadow. The assessments are usually made on an abundance scale of five categories. These are given, with two examples of how they are used for different species, in Table 17.5.

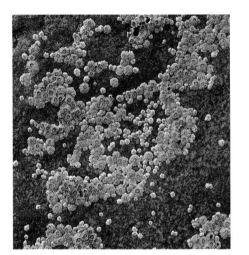

Barnacles exposed at low water

TABLE 17.5 **Abundance scales for two rocky shore species as devised by Crisp and Southward (1958)**

| Abundance group | Symbol | Scale used for the limpet (*Patella*) | Scale used for barnacles e.g. *Chthamalus stellatu* |
|---|---|---|---|
| Abundant | A | Over $50\,m^{-2}$ | Over $1\,cm^{-2}$ (rocks well covered) |
| Common | C | $10\text{–}50\,m^{-2}$ | $10\text{–}100\,dm^{-2}$ (up to one-third of rock covered) |
| Frequent | F | $1\text{–}10\,m^{-2}$ | $1\text{–}10\,dm^{-2}$ (never less than $10\,cm$ apart) |
| Occasional | O | Less than $1\,m^{-2}$ | $10\text{–}100\,m^{-2}$ (few less than $10\,cm$ apart) |
| Rare | R | Only a few found in 30 minutes' searching | Less than $1\,m^{-2}$ (only a few found in 30 minutes searching) |

# 17.6   Populations and communities

In previous chapters we reviewed the variety of organisms. These organisms do not live in isolation but as part of populations and communities.

A **population** is a group of individuals of the same species, all occupying a particular area at the same time.

A **community** comprises all the plants and animals which occupy a particular area. Communities therefore consist of a number of populations.

### 17.6.1 Population growth

Provided the birth rate exceeds the death rate, a population will grow in size. If only a few individuals are present initially, the rate of growth will be very slow. This is called the **lag phase** (Fig. 17.13). As numbers increase, more individuals become available for reproduction and the population grows at an ever increasing rate, provided no factor limits growth. This is called

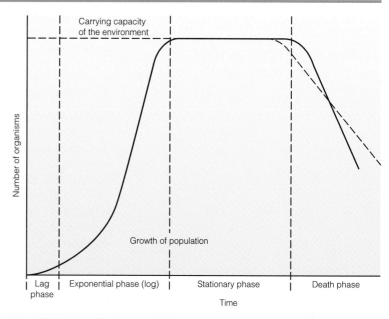

*Fig. 17.13 Growth of a population*

the **exponential phase**. Growth cannot continue indefinitely because there is a limit to the number of individuals any area can support. This limit is called the **carrying capacity** of the area. Beyond this point certain factors limit further population growth. The size of the population may then stabilize at a particular level. This is called the **stationary phase**. The high population level may, however, cause the carrying capacity of the environment to decline. In these circumstances the population level falls. This is called the **death phase**.

The factors which limit the growth of a particular population are collectively called the **environmental resistance**. Such factors include predation, disease, the availability of light, food, water, oxygen and shelter, the accumulation of toxic waste and even the size of the population itself.

### 17.6.2 Density-dependent growth

In this type of growth a population reaches a certain size and then remains stable. It is referred to as density-dependent because the size (or density) of the population affects its growth rate. Typical density-dependent factors are food availability and toxic waste accumulation. In a small population, little food is used up and only small amounts of waste are produced. The population can continue to grow. At high population densities the availability of food is reduced and toxic wastes build up. These cause the growth of the population to slow, and eventually stabilize at a particular level.

### 17.6.3 Density-independent growth

In this type of growth a population increases until some factor causes a sudden reduction in its size. Its effect is the same regardless of the size of the population, i.e. it is independent of the population density. A typical density-independent factor is temperature. A sudden fall in temperature may kill large numbers of organisms regardless of whether the population is large or small at the time. Environmental catastrophes such as fires, floods or storms are other density-independent factors.

### 17.6.4 Regulation of population size

The maximum possible number of offspring varies considerably from species to species. It may be as little as one offspring in 2 years in some mammals, or as great as one million eggs in a single laying in certain molluscs like the oyster. The term **fecundity** is used to describe the reproductive capacity of individual females of a species. In mammals the **birth rate** or **natality** is used to measure the fecundity. On the other hand, the number of individuals of a species that die from whatever cause is called the **death rate** or **mortality**. Clearly the size of a population is regulated by the balance between its fecundity and its mortality. However, there are other influences on the size of population. Two such influences are immigration and emigration.

**Immigration** occurs when individuals join a population from neighbouring ones. **Emigration** occurs when individuals depart from a population. The emigrants may either enter an existing neighbouring population or, as in the swarming of locusts and bees, they may form a new population. Factors such as overcrowding often act as a stimulus for emigration. Unlike the periodic seasonal movements which occur in migration, emigration is a non-reversible, one-way process.

The size of a population may fluctuate on a regular basis, called a **cycle**. These fluctuations are normally the consequence of regular seasonal changes, such as temperature or rainfall. At other times the population may be subject to sudden and unexpected fluctuations. While both types of fluctuation are usually due to a number of factors, there is often one, called the **key factor**, which is paramount in bringing about the change.

### 17.6.5 Control of human populations

Most animal populations are kept in check by food availability, climate, disease or predators. Populations frequently increase in size rapidly and then undergo a sudden 'crash' during which there is a dramatic reduction in numbers.

In increasingly more regions of the world human knowledge, expertise and technology are succeeding in reducing the impact of the climate and disease. As the top organism in many food chains, humans have little to fear from predators. Even in food production humans have made considerable advances, although in parts of South America, Asia and Africa famine remains a major check to population growth. As a result, the human population as a whole has grown virtually unchecked in recent times. Figures for the past rate of increase in human population can only be estimated, but it seems probable that prior to 1600 it had taken around 2000 years to double the world's population. By 1850, it had doubled again. It took just 80 years to complete the next doubling in 1939 and a mere 50 years to double again. At present the world population increases by about 1 500 000 every week, equivalent to about 150 people every minute (Fig. 17.14).

### Did you know?

The world's population is growing each year by more than the total population of Britain.

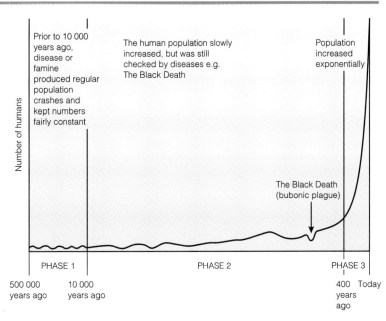

*Fig. 17.14 The growth of the human population*

In 1798, Thomas Robert Malthus, an English economist, published an essay on population in which he suggested that while the world's food supply would increase arithmetically, the human population would do so geometrically. The so-called **Malthusian principle** suggested famine as the inevitable consequence of this state of affairs. Despite many important agricultural advances, much of the world's population is still undernourished. It is inconceivable that the present rate of population growth can be sustained for much longer. War, famine or disease will inevitably curb further increases unless humans reduce their birth rate by appropriate forms of birth control. The variety of birth control methods available are given in Chapter 12 (Table 12.4). The solution may seem simple enough, but opposition to birth control is often deeply rooted in personal, social, religious or traditional belief.

### 17.6.6 Competition

Individuals of species in a population are continually competing with each other, not only for nutrients but also for mates and breeding sites. This competition between individuals of the same species is called **intraspecific competition**. Individuals are also in continual competition with members of different species for such factors as nutrients, space and shelter. Competition between individuals of different species is called **interspecific competition**.

### 17.6.7 Predation

Predator–prey relationships are important in producing cyclic change in the size of a population. By eating their prey, predators remove certain members of a population and so reduce their numbers. As the size of the prey population diminishes, the predators experience greater competition with each other for the remaining prey. The predator population therefore diminishes as some individuals are unable to obtain

e effects of famine in Somalia

357

enough food to sustain them. The reduction in the predator population results in fewer prey being taken and so allows their numbers to increase again. This increase in its turn leads to an increase in the predator population.

*The number of predators is usually less than the number of prey.*

*The shape of the two curves is similar, but there is a time lag between the two; the curve for the predators lags behind that of the prey.*

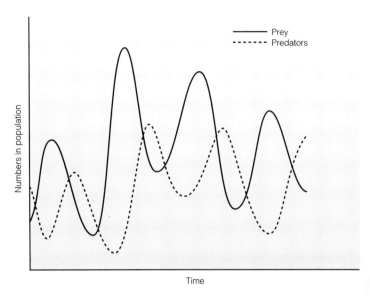

*Fig. 17.15 Relationship between prey and predator populations*

Bobcat catching Snowshoe hare

Typical examples of the relationship shown in Fig. 17.15 include the lynx preying upon the Canadian snowshoe hare and *Hydra* preying upon the water flea *Daphnia.* It must be said that predator–prey relationships alone are not responsible for fluctuations in the numbers in a population; disease and climatic factors also play a role. Nevertheless, predation is significant in the regulation of natural populations. The type of cyclic fluctuation shown in Fig. 17.15 plays an important role in evolution. The periodic population crashes create selection pressure whereby only those individuals who are able to escape predation, or withstand disease or adverse climatic conditions, will survive to reproduce. The population thereby evolves to be better adapted to the prevailing conditions.

### 17.6.8 Competitive exclusion principle

In 1934, a Russian biologist, C. F. Gause, experimented on two species of *Paramecium*. He grew *P. caudatum* and *P. aurelia* both separately and together. When grown together, the two species competed for the available food. After a few days the population of *P. caudatum* began to decline, and after 3 weeks all its members had died. It seemed that the two species were in such close competition that only one could survive. This became known as the **competitive exclusion principle** or **Gause's principle**. It states that only one species (population) in a given community can occupy a given ecological niche at any one time. Fig. 17.16 summarizes the results of Gause's experiments with *Paramecium*. Although *P. aurelia* survives, its population is reduced in the presence of *P. caudatum*, compared to its population when grown alone.

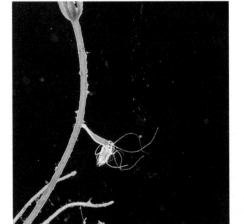

Hydra capturing Daphnia

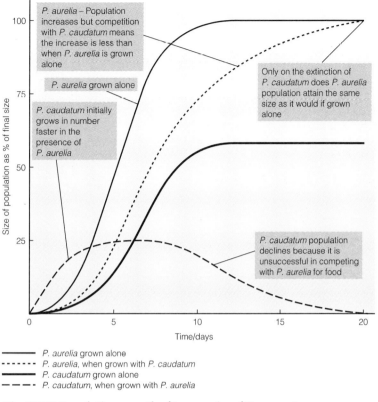

The following labels appear on the graph:

*P. aurelia* – Population increases but competition with *P. caudatum* means the increase is less than when *P. aurelia* is grown alone

*P. aurelia* grown alone

*P. caudatum* initially grows in number faster in the presence of *P. aurelia*

Only on the extinction of *P. caudatum* does *P. aurelia* population attain the same size as it would if grown alone

*P. caudatum* population declines because it is unsuccessful in competing with *P. aurelia* for food

Size of population as % of final size

Time/days

———— *P. aurelia* grown alone
------ *P. aurelia*, when grown with *P. caudatum*
▬▬▬ *P. caudatum* grown alone
– – – *P. caudatum*, when grown with *P. aurelia*

Fig. 17.16 *Population growth of two species of* Paramecium *grown separately and together*

Why *P. aurelia* is more successful in the long term may be because of its smaller size. Being smaller, it requires less food and is better able to survive when food is scarce. Its success may, however, be due to a faster reproductive rate or greater efficiency in obtaining its food. The reasons for success are hard enough to isolate in the laboratory; it is considerably more difficult to do so for a wild population.

### 17.6.9 Biological control

The effect of the predator–prey relationship in regulating populations has been exploited by humans as a method of controlling various pests. Biological control is a means of managing populations of organisms which compete for human food or damage the health of humans or livestock. The aim is to bring the population of a pest down to a tolerable level by use of its natural enemies. A beneficial organism (the **agent**) is deployed against an undesirable one (the **target**). A typical situation is where a natural predator of a harmful organism is introduced in order to reduce its numbers to a level where they are no longer harmful. The aim is not to eradicate the pest; indeed, this could be counter-productive. If the pest was reduced to such an extent that it no longer provided an adequate food source for the predator, then the predator in its turn would be eradicated. The few remaining pests could then increase their population rapidly, in the absence of the controlling agent. The ideal situation is where the controlling agent and the pest exist in balance with one another, but at a level where the pest has no major detrimental effect (Fig. 17.17).

innabar moth caterpillars feeding on ragwort

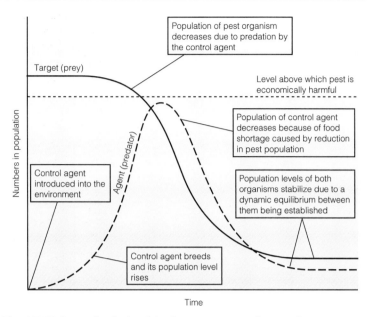

*Fig. 17.17 General relationships between pest and control agent populations in biological control*

TABLE 17.6   **Some examples of biological control**

| Target (pest) | Harmful effects of pest | Control agent | Method of action |
|---|---|---|---|
| Scale insect (*Icerya*) | Kills citrus fruit trees | Ladybird (*Rodolia*) | Ladybird uses scale insect as a food source |
| Codling moth (*Crypto-phlebia*) | Ruins orange crop | African wasp (*Tricho-gamatoidea*) | Wasp parasitizes moth eggs |
| Mosquito (*Anopheles*) | Vector of malarial parasite (*Plasmo-dium*) | Hydra (*Chloro-hydra*) | Hydra is a predator of mosquito larvae |
| Snail (*Biomphal-aria*) | Vector of *Schistosoma* which causes bilharzia | Snail (*Marisa*) | Control agent snail is predatory on the snail vector |
| Prickly pear (*Opuntia*) | Makes land difficult to farm by restricting access | Cochineal insect (*Dactylo-pius*) | *Opuntia* is a food source for the insect |
| Larvae of many butterflies and moths | Consume the foliage of many economic-ally important plants | Bacterium (HD-1 strain of *Bacillus thuringien-sis*) | Bacterium parasitizes the larvae of moths and butterflies |

Biological control was originally used against insect and weed pests of economically important crops. In more recent times its use has broadened to include medically important pests such as snails and even vertebrate pests. In the same way the type of controlling agent has become more diverse and the following are now employed: bacteria, viruses, fungi, protozoans, nematodes, insects and even amphibians and birds. These agents are sometimes used in combination. Certain nematodes carry bacteria which are deadly to many insects and their larvae. These nematodes have been nicknamed 'biological exocets' because of their ability to seek out their insect larvae hosts. The nematodes enter the insects' bodies releasing a fatal cargo of bacteria. Insects controlled in this way include the black vine weevil. Table 17.6 lists some examples of biological control.

One interesting and unusual form of biological control takes place in Australia. Cattle dung there presents a problem because two major pests, the bush fly and buffalo fly, lay their eggs in it. In addition, the dung carries the eggs of worms which parasitize the cattle. The indigenous dung beetles which are adapted to coping with the fibrous wastes of marsupials are ineffective in burying the soft dung of cattle. The introduction of an African species of dung beetle, which bury the dung within 48 hours, has been effective in controlling the flies. By burying the dung before the flies can mature, or before the parasitic worm can develop and reinfect cattle, they have controlled the populations of these pests.

### 17.6.10 Communities and succession

A community is all the plants and animals which occupy a particular area. The individual populations within the community interact with one another. The community is a constantly changing dynamic unit, which passes through a number of stages from its origin to its climax. The transition from one stage to the next is called **succession**.

Imagine an area of bare rock. One of the few kinds of organisms capable of surviving on such an inhospitable area is lichen. The symbiotic relationship between an alga and a fungus, which makes up a lichen, allows it to survive considerable drying out. As the first organisms to bring about **colonization** of a new area, the lichens are called **pioneers** or the **pioneer community**.

The weathering of any rock produces a sand or soil, but in itself this is inadequate to support other plants. With the decomposing remains of any dead lichen, however, sufficient nutrients are made available to support a community of small plants. Mosses are typically the next stages in the succession, followed by ferns. With the continuing erosion of the rock and the increasing amounts of organic material available from these plants, a thicker layer of soil is built up. This will then support smaller flowering plants such as grasses and, by turn, shrubs and trees. In Britain the ultimate community is most likely to be deciduous oak woodland. The stable state thus formed comprises a balanced equilibrium of species with few, if any, new varieties replacing those established. This is called the **climax community**. This community consists of animals as well as plants. The animals have undergone a similar series of successional stages, largely dictated by the plant types available. Within the climax community there is normally a **dominant** plant and animal species, or sometimes two or three **co-dominant** species. The dominant species is normally very prominent and has the greatest biomass.

The succession described above, where bare rock or some other barren terrain is first colonized, is called **primary succession**. If, however, an area previously supporting life is made barren, the subsequent recolonization is called **secondary succession**. Secondary succession occurs after a forest fire or the clearing of agricultural land. Spores, seeds and organs of vegetative propagation may remain viable in the soil, and there will be an influx of animals and plants through dispersal and migration from the surrounding area. In these circumstances the succession will not begin with pioneer species but with organisms from subsequent successional stages.

Around 4000 years ago much of lowland Britain was a climax community of oak woodland, but most of this forest was cleared to allow grazing and cultivation. The many heaths and grasslands which we now refer to as 'natural' are the result of this clearance and subsequent grazing by animals. These are not true climax communities but sub-climax ones resulting from human activities. Because the normal succession has been artificially changed it is often referred to as a **deflected succession** and the resultant sub-climax is called a **plagioclimax**.

A series of successional stages is called a **sere**. There are a number of different seres according to the environment being colonized. A **hydrosere** refers to a series of successions in an aquatic environment and a **halosere** to one in a saltmarsh.

n oak wood is a climax community

# 17.7 Questions

**1.** *(a)* State **two** ways in which the presence of weeds can reduce crop yields. *(2 marks)*

Partial control of weeds can be achieved using cultivation methods, but herbicides (weedkillers) are necessary in order to achieve full control of weeds in winter wheat. Selective herbicides alter growth regulation control in weed species, and have a slight, but less harmful effect on the crop. The table shows the effects of six common weed species on yields of winter wheat.

| Species | Number of weed plants per m² causing 2% yield loss |
|---------|-----------------------------------------------------|
| Cleavers | 1 |
| Wild oats | 2 |
| Poppy | 8 |
| Blackgrass | 10 |
| Speedwell | 17 |
| Pansy | 51 |

*(b)* With reference to the table,
  (i) explain why a farmer is more likely to need herbicides to control cleavers than to control pansies; *(2 marks)*
  (ii) suggest why wild oats and blackgrass are more difficult to control than poppies. *(1 mark)*

Cleavers usually grows along field boundaries and can be controlled by hedgerow removal.
*(c)* State **two** benefits of **not** removing hedgerows on a farm. *(2 marks)*

Some crop plants have been genetically engineered, making them completely resistant to the effects of a particular herbicide.
*(d)* Explain how wheat plants which have been genetically engineered to be resistant to herbicides could help to increase grain yields. *(2 marks)*
*(e)* For each of the following, explain one way in which a farmer, using organic methods only, could
  (i) control weeds; *(2 marks)*
  (ii) maintain soil fertility. *(2 marks)*
      *(Total 13 marks)*

*UCLES June 1998, (Human Ecology), No. 3*

**2.** In South Australia, carnivorous dingo dogs prey on red kangaroos.
*(a)* Copy the axes at the top of the next column; sketch graphs to show how the relative numbers of dingo dogs and red kangaroos might be expected to fluctuate over a period of several years. *(2 marks)*

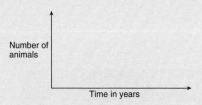

*(b)* An area was enclosed by a fence some 10 000 km long and **all** the dingo dogs were then killed inside the fence. The number of kangaroos inside the fenced area increased rapidly for several years but over time still showed a fluctuation in numbers

Suggest **three** factors that might account for these fluctuations. *(3 marks)*
*(c)* (i) Sheep have been introduced into areas where kangaroos occur. Suggest reasons why the introduction of sheep might affect kangaroo populations. *(2 marks)*
   (ii) Suggest **one** reason why the introduction of sheep could lead to an increase in the kangaroo population even when dingoes are present. *(1 mark)*
*(d)* The graphs below show two types of population growth curve.

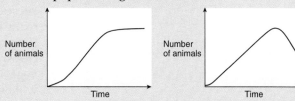

   (i) Add a line to the left-hand graph to indicate the carrying capacity of the environment. *(1 mark)*
   (ii) What is meant by the **carrying capacity** of the environment? *(2 marks)*
   (iii) How do you account for the population changes shown in the right-hand graph? *(2 marks)*
      *(Total 13 marks)*

*Oxford & Cambridge January 1997, Unit B3, No.*

**3.** The diagram shows a number of stages in an ecological succession in a lake.

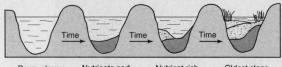

| Deep, clear, nutrient-poor water with very little aquatic life. | Nutrients and sediment begin to accumulate; increasing populations of aquatic life appear. | Nutrient rich, relatively shallow water with much plant growth and many other aquatic organisms. | Oldest stage of a lake, very shallow, overgrown with emerging rooted plant life. |

(a) Use information in this diagram to help explain what is meant by an ecological succession.
(2 marks)

(b) Give **two** general features which this succession has in common with other ecological successions. (2 marks)

(c) A number of small rivers normally flow into this lake. These rivers flow through forested areas. Explain how deforestation of the area might affect the process of succession in the lake. (2 marks)

hytoplankton consists of single-celled photosynthetic rganisms which are suspended in the surface water. he graphs show the relationship between the biomass f phytoplankton and the depth at which it is found in wo different lakes. Lake **A** has a low nutrient oncentration. Lake **B** has a high nutrient concentration.

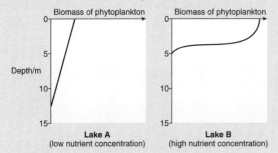

(d) Briefly describe a method by which you could measure the biomass of the phytoplankton. (2 marks)

(e) (i) Describe the effect of different nutrient concentrations on the distribution of phytoplankton in the two lakes. (2 marks)

(ii) The rate of biomass production at a depth of 5 metres was much higher in Lake **A** than in Lake **B**. Explain why. (2 marks)

(f) Phytoplanktonic organisms do not live for long. After a short period of time, they die and their remains decay.
(i) Use this information to explain how application of large amounts of nitrate fertilizer to the land surrounding a lake might affect other organisms living in the lake. (3 marks)

(ii) Suggest why a period of drought might increase the effect described in your answer to (f)(i). (1 mark)

(g) Biological techniques may be used to monitor water pollution such as that caused by the addition of fertilizer. Explain why each of the following may be used to monitor water pollution:
(i) the presence or absence of indicator species; (2 marks)
(ii) an index of diversity. (2 marks)
(Total 20 marks)

*AEB June 1998, Paper 2, No. 4*

4. (a) Briefly explain **two** examples of **edaphic** factors which could affect living organisms or ecosystems. (2 marks)

(b) Explain what is meant by:
(i) climax community;
(ii) ecological succession. (2 marks)

(c) (i) For the carbon (C) cycle, suggest which **one** of the sequences **I, II, III, IV** or **V** shown below, best represents the processes that occur. (1 mark)

I. atmospheric C ⟶ plant C ⟶ respiration and decay ⟶ atmospheric C

II. atmospheric C ⟶ respiration ⟶ animal C ⟶ plant C ⟶ decay ⟶ atmospheric C

III. atmospheric C ⟶ animal C ⟶ respiration and decay ⟶ atmospheric C

IV. atmospheric C ⟶ plant C ⟶ animal C ⟶ respiration and decay ⟶ atmospheric C

V. atmospheric C ⟶ plant C ⟶ photosynthesis ⟶ animal C ⟶ atmospheric C

(ii) Suggest a reason for the gradual increase annually in atmospheric carbon indicated by all measurements taken in recent decades. (1 mark)
(Total 6 marks)

*Oxford March 1997, Paper 43, No. 2*

5. (a) Consider a **named** ecosystem which you have studied. Copy the boxes below, and insert the name of an organism (scientific or common name) to illustrate four possible trophic levels occurring in a food chain appropriate to that ecosystem. (4 marks)

(b) The number of links in a food chain hardly ever exceeds six and often is only three. Briefly explain the reasons why this is so. (3 marks)

(c) A study was made of the plankton biomass in a lake at two different times of the year. The results are shown as pyramids of biomass **X** and **Y** below.

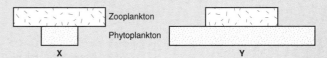

Suggest explanations for the different pyramids and explain why both results can be correct. *(4 marks)*

*(Total 11 marks)*

*Oxford March 1997, Paper 43, No. 1*

**6.** Sugar cane is not native to Australia. Soon after it was introduced it became severely affected by beetles which damaged the plants by eating through the base of the stems.

In South America, the native cane toad keeps down the number of beetles in sugar cane fields. In an attempt to control the beetle in Australia, a small number of cane toads was introduced into one location. The toads soon underwent an explosion in population growth which is still continuing. Cane toads are now a problem in their own right.

(a) Suggest **two** reasons why the cane toad underwent a population explosion when introduced into Australia. *(2 marks)*

(b) Suggest **two** reasons why cane toads might prove a threat to native Australian species. *(2 marks)*

(c) Describe how **one** parasite or predator is used successfully in the biological control of a pest. *(3 marks)*

*(Total 7 marks)*

*NEAB June 1995, BY02, No. 5*

**7.** Computer modelling is being used increasingly to represent individual aspects of the nitrogen cycle. One program describes average fluxes of nitrogen in grazed grassland according to fertilizer input, soil type, drainage, age of plants, previous management and climate. A copy of a computer screen display simulating annual nitrogen fluxes for permanent grassland is shown below. Study the diagram and answer the questions which follow.

(**Volatilization** is the natural loss of ammonia gas derived from faeces and urine to the atmosphere.)

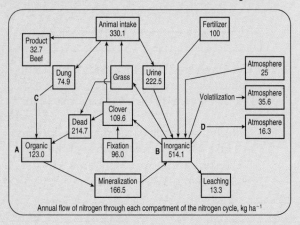

Annual flow of nitrogen through each compartment of the nitrogen cycle, kg ha$^{-1}$

Adapted from *Research on the Nitrogen Cycle,*
AFRC News Supplement

*(a)* (i) Give **two** examples of organic nitrogen and **two** examples of inorganic nitrogen which could be referred to in boxes **A** and **B**. *(2 marks)*

(ii) Name the process referred to by arrow **C** and the process referred to by arrow **D**. *(2 marks)*

*(b)* (i) Calculate the percentage of the inorganic nitrogen which would **not** be available to the organisms in the system. Show your working. *(2 marks)*

(ii) Calculate the annual flow of nitrogen through grass. Give your result in a kg ha$^{-1}$ and show all your working. *(4 marks)*

*(c)* The average application of nitrogen to winter wheat in the UK is 190 kg N ha$^{-1}$, but dairy grassland farmers need to add less (about 170 kg N ha$^{-1}$). Suggest three reasons to account for the difference. *(3 marks)*

*(Total 13 marks)*

*Oxford November 1996, Paper 1, No.*

*ULEAC June 1996, B2, No.*

**8.** An experiment was carried out to compare the uptake of nitrogen in soyabean seedlings grown in an atmosphere enriched with carbon dioxide with that of seedlings grown in a normal atmosphere (control plants). Soyabeans belong to Papilionaceae (legumes) and all the experimental plants had root nodules containing *Rhizobium*.

At the beginning of the experiment, the seedlings were 25 days old. The total amount of nitrogen incorporated into compounds in the plants was then measured at intervals until the plants were 100 days old.

The results of the experiment are shown in the graph below.

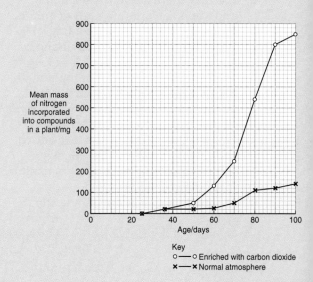

(a) (i) Of the nitrogen incorporated into compounds in the control plants, 75% was taken up from the soil. State the form in which this nitrogen was taken up by the plants. *(1 mark)*

(ii) Explain how the control plants obtained the remaining 25% of their nitrogen. *(2 marks)*

(b) (i) Compare the effect of the atmosphere enriched with carbon dioxide with that of the normal atmosphere on the mass of nitrogen incorporated into the seedlings. *(3 marks)*

(ii) Suggest **one** reason for any differences you observe. *(1 mark)*

(c) A possible application of gene technology would be to incorporate genes for nitrogen fixation into cereal plants. Suggest possible benefits of such an application. *(2 marks)*

*(Total 9 marks)*

*Edexcel June 1997, HB6, No. 1*

(a) In an investigation into seashore ecology, a group of students estimated the biomass of the producers, primary consumers and secondary consumers in three areas of a rocky shore.

The results are shown in the diagram.

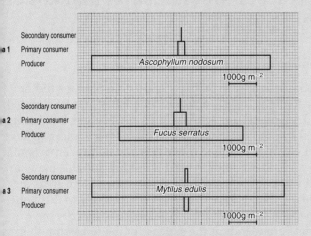

(i) Suggest how the students may have obtained the data shown. *(4 marks)*

(ii) Estimate the biomass of the primary consumers in area **1**. *(1 mark)*

(iii) In which of the areas, **1** or **2**, does the primary consumer make most efficient use of the producer? Explain your answer. *(1 mark)*

(iv) In area **3** the biomass of the primary consumers is greater than that of the producers. Suggest how a pyramid of biomass of this shape is possible. *(2 marks)*

(b) The diagram below represents how energy flows through each of the communities investigated.

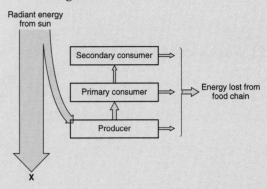

(i) Suggest **two** reasons why the energy labelled **X** does not enter the food chain. *(2 marks)*

(ii) Explain **two** ways in which energy can be lost from the food chain. *(4 marks)*

(c) *Mytilus edulis* (a species of edible mussel) is a marine mollusc. It has two shells which enclose its body. These animals attach themselves to rocky surfaces under the sea by means of sticky threads and feed by filtering plankton from the water. They have the potential to be an important source of protein for humans as each mussel is 40% flesh of which 11% is protein.

(i) Calculate the amount of protein which could be obtained from 1 tonne (1000 kg) of entire mussels (i.e. mussels with their shells). Show your working. *(2 marks)*

(ii) Assuming a daily requirement of protein of 50 g per person, calculate how many people could receive a day's ration of protein from 1 tonne of entire mussels. Show your working. *(2 marks)*

(iii) Sometimes, apparently suitable rocky surfaces are never colonized by *Mytilus edulis*. Suggest **two** reasons why not. *(2 marks)*

*(Total 20 marks)*

*AEB Summer 1997, (H. Biology) Paper 2, No. 4*

# 18 Human activities and the ecosystem

The effect of human activities on the environment is proportional to the size of the human population. As we saw in Section 17.6.5, the size of the human population has been rising exponentially and is presently increasing at the rate of one and a half million people each week, equivalent to 150 people per minute. The reasons for this increase are many but include more intensive forms of food production and better medical care. The latter has given many individuals a greater life expectancy and, more importantly, reduced child mortality. Reducing the mortality of individuals who have passed child-bearing age has little significance on the population, but reducing mortality among children means more people reach sexual maturity and so are able to produce offspring. The effect of this on the population is significant.

## 18.1 The impact of pre-industrial humans on the environment

### 18.1.1 Humans as hunters

As their population was small, pre-industrial humans did not have a great impact on the environment. Early humans hunted, fished and removed trees to make fires and shelters but, being nomadic, they did not remain in one place long enough to have significant effect. When they moved on, the natural environment rapidly recovered. Early humans did use fire and this may have accidentally got out of hand and burned down large areas of forest. Equally it may have been used deliberately to flush out prey to enable it to be captured. Humans may thereby have created some grasslands at the expense of the forest, but their total impact was small.

### 18.1.2 Humans as shepherds

In time, humans domesticated animals such as sheep, cattle, goats, llamas and alpacas. These herbivorous species required large areas of grassland on which to graze. To extend the grasslands, humans deliberately burnt large areas of trees causing **deforestation**. Domesticated species like cattle became symbols of wealth and power, as well as suppliers of milk and meat. This led to the build-up of large herds and subsequent overgrazing, with resultant loss of soil fertility leading to

## BIOLOGY AROUND US

# Desertification

Grazing in a desertified area

Desertification is the term used to describe severe land degradation which turns semi-arid areas into deserts. There are many possible causes but they normally involve climatic changes and/or an increase in the human population above the carrying capacity (Section 17.6.1) of the land. Extended periods of drought make plant regeneration difficult and bare soils are exposed to erosion. Increased human populations put additional pressures on the vegetation as shrubs and trees are cut for fuel and the land is overgrazed. The further loss of ground vegetation allows wind erosion to remove the soil and makes replanting difficult. Little can be done to combat these problems in the short term if there is not adequate water, although there is evidence of recovery in the longer term. In the more favourable semi-arid areas with sufficient water, skilful engineering schemes and a thorough knowledge of plant nutrition and soil structure have enabled some tree planting programmes to be successful in halting the spread of desertification.

Effect of irrigation from the Nile

erosion. These activities, which began in the Mediterranean and Near East, may have contributed to the development of many of the desert regions of these areas. Animal domestication also led to the extinction of their wild ancestors, probably through competition. Aurochs and European bison may have suffered this fate.

### 18.1.3 Humans as farmers

The advent of agriculture marked the most significant event of pre-industrial human impact on the environment. It probably originated in the Near East and involved the deliberate sowing of seeds to produce a crop. If humans were to enjoy the fruits of this labour, they needed to harvest the crop at some later date. They therefore had to remain in one place or risk losing the crop to other animals. For the first time humans formed permanent

367

settlements. They built shelters for themselves and their animals and barns to store their crops. This required much wood and led to further deforestation. More importantly, humans cleared much forest to provide a greater area for sowing crops. With no knowledge of minerals, they continued to grow the same crop on the same piece of land for many years, thus depleting it of essential nutrients. The soil could no longer support life, and this was a major factor in the formation of desert areas.

The extent of deforestation caused by humans is clearly illustrated in the United States of America. When first settled by Europeans in the early seventeenth century, there were an estimated 170 million hectares of forest. Now there are eight million. Most of this clearance was carried out to permit the cultivation of corn and wheat in the north, and tobacco and cotton in the south.

## 18.2    Exploitation of natural resources

Prior to the industrial revolution, the energy expended in the production of food by humans and their beasts of burden came from the food itself. Much of the crop therefore went into producing the next one. With the industrial revolution came machines which carried out ploughing, sowing, harvesting, etc. Instead of food, these machines used fossil fuels like coal, and more recently oil, as energy sources. A very much smaller proportion of the crop harvested was therefore needed to produce the next one. More food was left and a larger population could be supported. This partly explains the exponential rise in the size of the human population since the industrial revolution. The use of fertilizers, pesticides and better crops are other significant factors.

Humans are dependent for their survival on the earth's resources, and these take two forms: renewable and non-renewable.

### 18.2.1 Renewable resources

Renewable resources, as the name suggests, can be replaced. They are things which grow, and are materials based on plants or animals, e.g. trees and fish. They are not, however, produced in limitless quantities and their supply is ultimately exhausted if the rate at which they are removed exceeds that at which they have been produced. Renewable resources have a **sustainable yield**. This means that the amount removed (yield) is equal to, or less than, the rate of production. If the trees in a forest take 100 years to mature, then one-hundredth of the forest may be felled each year without the forest becoming smaller. A sustainable yield can be taken indefinitely.

Whilst wood is a renewable resource, its production is not without ecological problems. Trees grow relatively slowly and so give a small yield for a given area of land. For this reason, it is not economic to use fertile farmland for their cultivation. Instead, poorer quality land typical of upland areas is often used. As conifers grow more rapidly, these softwood species are more often cultivated than indigenous hardwoods such as elm, oak, ash and beech. Large areas in Scotland, Wales and the Lake

ows of larch planted on a hillside

hirty-tonne catch of fish by deep-sea trawler

District have become **afforested**. The trees are often grown in rows and many square miles are covered by the same species. Not only does this arrangement have an unnatural appearance, but the density of the trees permits little, if anything, to grow beneath them and the forest floor is a barren place. There is little diversity of animal life within these forests. The demand for wood, not only for construction but also for paper, necessitates this intensive form of wood production.

Another renewable resource is fish. Unlike many renewable resources used by humans, fish are not generally farmed. For the most part humans remove them from the seas with no attempt to replace stocks by breeding. The replacement is left to nature. As the seas are considered a common resource for all, no previous attempt has been made to control the amount of fish removed by each country. While fishing was carried out by small boats, working locally, its impact on stocks was negligible because a sustainable yield was removed. Modern fishing methods involve large factory ships, capable of travelling thousands of miles and catching huge hauls of fish, which can be processed and frozen on board. Sonar equipment, echo sounders and even helicopters may be used in locating shoals. These methods have led to **over-fishing**, because sustainable yields have been exceeded and stocks depleted. It takes many years for such stocks to recover. Some controls now exist and international agreement has been reached on **quotas** of fish which each country can take. These quotas are often bitterly disputed and the difficulty of enforcement has led to many being ignored. There are regulations concerning the **mesh size of nets**. If the mesh is sufficiently large, younger, and therefore smaller, fish escape capture. These survive to grow larger and, more importantly, are able to reach sexual maturity. These fish can then spawn, thus ensuring some replenishment of the stock. Other methods of control include **close seasons** for fishing (usually during a particular species' breeding season) and **exclusion zones** where fishing is banned completely. One species to have suffered from over-fishing is the North Sea herring. Depletion of its stocks have made fishing it practically uneconomic in recent years.

### 18.2.2 Non-renewable resources

These are resources which, for all practical purposes, are not replaced as they are used. Minerals such as iron and fuels like coal and oil are non-renewable. There is a fixed quantity of these resources on the planet and in time they will be exhausted. Oil and natural gas supplies are unlikely to last more than 50 years, although much depends upon the rate at which they are burned.

**Mineral and ore extraction** have been carried out for a considerable time with important metals such as iron, copper, lead, tin and aluminium being mined. In theory these metals can be recycled, but in practice this is often difficult or impossible for various reasons:

1. The metal may be oxidized or otherwise converted into a form unsuitable for recycling. Iron for example rusts.

2. The quantities of the metal within a material may be so small that it is not worthwhile recovering it. The thin layer of tin on most metal cans is not economically worth recovering.

## BIOLOGY AROUND US

### Fuel from oilseed rape

Oilseed rape in flower

Over a million tonnes of rapeseed are grown in Britain each year, almost all of it for processing into consumer goods. Rapeseed oil, from *Brassica napus* has, in the past, been turned into soap, lubricants and synthetic rubber. It can be used as a heating oil and, as rape methyl ester (RME), is now a renewable replacement for diesel. Most RME is manufactured by the Italian company Novamont and it has been used to run taxis, lorries, ferries and public transport in Italy and other parts of Europe. The production of biodiesel from rapeseed is expected to rise as it provides an environmentally friendly alternative to diesel. It emits fewer sooty particles and no sulphur dioxide. Recently an English farmer claimed to get 60 miles to the gallon using refined rapeseed oil in his unadapted Opel Ascona car.

Part of the Chernobyl nuclear reactor after the explosion in April 1986

**3.** The metal is often combined with many other materials, including other metals, which make it difficult to separate. A motor car may contain small amounts of many metals including zinc, lead, tin, copper and aluminium.

The supply of many ores is becoming more scarce and the belief that supply would satisfy demand for the foreseeable future is being questioned. The lead, tin, copper, gold and silver mines of Wales, Cornwall and the Lake District have almost entirely ceased their activities. As the supply is reduced, the price increases and it could be that sources previously considered uneconomic may prove worthwhile exploiting again.

**Fossil fuels** are continually being formed, but the process is so slow compared to their rate of consumption that for all practical purposes they may be considered as a non-renewable resource. Over 80% of the world's consumption of fossil fuels occurs in developed countries, where only 25% of its population lives. The burning of fossil fuels produces a range of pollutants and even their extraction is not without its hazards. As the supply of these fuels is becoming rapidly depleted, humans have sought alternative energy sources. Nuclear power is a potentially long-term supplier of energy, but it has inherent dangers as the accident at Chernobyl in Russia in April 1986 illustrated. It is therefore treated by the public with some suspicion. Attempts continue to be made to harness wind, wave and solar energy effectively. In the end it could be **biological fuels** that humans may have to look to to supply their growing energy needs. The energy content of the organic matter produced annually by photosynthesis exceeds annual human energy consumption by 200 times. The main end-product of this photosynthesis is cellulose, most of which is unused by humans. Some of it can be burnt as wood or straw to provide heat or electricity. Much can be converted to other fuels like methane ($CH_4$), methanol ($CH_3OH$), ethanol ($C_2H_5OH$) and other gases. These processes need not use valuable food resources; the energy may be obtained from plants with no food value or from the discarded parts of food plants, estimated to total 20 million tonnes dry mass year$^{-1}$ in the UK alone. The gasohol programme in Brazil, where sugar cane wastes are used to produce a motor vehicle fuel, is an example of this (Section 30.6.1). Wastes such as animal manure (45 million tonnes dry mass year$^{-1}$ in the UK), human sewage (6 million tonnes dry mass year$^{-1}$ in the UK) and other domestic and industrial wastes (30 million tonnes dry mass year$^{-1}$ in the UK) could be converted to useful fuels like methane by biogas digesters (Section 30.6.2). These conversions can be carried out by bacteria, often as part of fermentation reactions. The day may not be far away when large industrial plants convert these wastes into useful fuels and energy forms and where crops cultivated entirely for conversion to fuels are commonplace.

## 18.3 Pollution

Pollution is a difficult term to define. It has its origins in the Latin word *polluere* which means 'contamination of any feature of the environment'. Any definition of pollution should take account of the fact that:

**1.** It is not merely the addition of a substance to the environment but its addition at a rate faster than the environment can accommodate it. There are natural levels of chemicals such as arsenic and mercury in the environment, but only if these levels exceed certain critical values can they be considered pollutants.

**2.** Pollutants are not only chemicals; forms of energy like heat, sound, $\alpha$-particles, $\beta$-particles and X-rays may also be pollutants.

**3.** To be a pollutant, a material has to be potentially harmful to life. In other words, some harmful effect must be recognized.

Using the above criteria, it is arguable that there is such a thing as natural pollution. We know for example that sulphur dioxide, one product of the combustion of fossil fuels, is a pollutant, and yet 70% of the world's sulphur dioxide is the result of volcanic activity. To avoid 'natural pollution' some scientists like to add a fourth criterion, namely that pollution is only the result of human activities.

Mt. Semeru erupting in Indonesia

## 18.4 Air pollution

The layer of air which supports life extends about 8 km above the earth's surface and is known as the **troposphere**. While there may be small localized variations in the levels of gases in air, its composition overall remains remarkably constant. Almost all air pollutants are gases added to this mixture. Air pollution has existed since humans first used fire but it is only since the industrial revolution in the nineteenth century that its effects have become significant. Almost all air pollution is the result of burning fossil fuels, either in the home, by industry or in the internal combustion engine.

Air pollution from a coking plant

TABLE 18.1 **Tolerance of moss and lichen species to sulphur dioxide**

| Annual average sulphur dioxide concentration in $\mu g\,m^{-3}$ | Species tolerant and therefore able to survive |
| --- | --- |
| Greater than 60 | *Lecanora conizaeoides* (lichen) *Lecanora dispersa* (lichen) *Ceratodon purpureus* (moss) *Funaria hygrometrica* (moss) |
| Less than 60 | *Parmelia saxatilis* (lichen) *Parmelia fulginosa* (lichen) |
| Less than 45 | *Grimma pulvinata* (lichen) *Hypnum cupressiforme* (moss) |

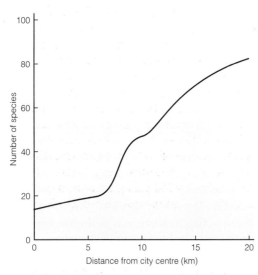

*Fig. 18.1 Number of lichen species as one moves from the centre of Newcastle upon Tyne*

### 18.4.1 Smoke

Smoke is tiny particles of soot (carbon) suspended in the air, which are produced as a result of burning fossil fuels, particularly coal and oil. It has a number of harmful effects:

**1.** When breathed in, smoke may blacken the alveoli, causing damage to their delicate epithelial linings. It also aggravates respiratory ailments, e.g. bronchitis.

**2.** While it remains suspended in the air, it can reduce the light intensity at ground level. This may lower the overall rate of photosynthesis.

**3.** Deposits of smoke, or more particularly soot and ash, may coat plant leaves, reducing photosynthesis by preventing the light penetrating or by blocking stomata.

**4.** Smoke, soot and ash become deposited on clothes, cars and buildings. These are costly to clean.

### 18.4.2 Sulphur dioxide

Fossil fuels contain between 1 and 4% sulphur and as a result around 30 million tonnes of sulphur dioxide is emitted from the chimneys of Europe each year. Much of this combines readily with other chemicals like water and ammonia and is quickly deposited. Sulphur dioxide may increase soil fertility in areas where sulphates are deficient, or even help to control diseases such as blackspot of roses by acting as a fungicide. Nevertheless its effects, especially in high concentrations, are largely harmful.

**1.** It causes irritation of the respiratory system and damage to the epithelial lining of the alveoli. It can also irritate the conjunctiva of the eye.

**2.** It reduces the growth of many plants, e.g. barley, wheat, lettuce, while others such as lichens may be killed.

The tolerance of lichen and moss species to sulphur dioxide is very variable and makes them useful **indicator species** for measuring sulphur dioxide pollution. Table 18.1 shows the tolerance of some mosses and lichen species to sulphur dioxide.

As one moves from the centre of a major industrial city like Newcastle upon Tyne, the concentration of sulphur dioxide falls rapidly. At the same time the number of species of lichen and moss increases. In the centre only the most tolerant species are found, whereas on the outskirts less tolerant species also occur (Fig. 18.1). Using Table 18.1, we can see that if an area of a city possesses *Lecanora dispersa* and *Funaria hygrometrica* but none of the other species, then the levels of sulphur dioxide must exceed $60\,\mu g\,m^{-3}$.

If all species in the table are present, the sulphur dioxide level must be less than $45\,\mu g\,m^{-3}$.

Much of the sulphur dioxide released into the atmosphere returns to earth as gas or minute particles (dry deposition) but about one-third dissolves in rain water. The sulphur dioxide and water combine to form sulphurous and sulphuric acids. The rain therefore has a low pH and is known as **acid rain**. The oxides of nitrogen are other pollutants which contribute to acid rain. Indeed, while the contribution of sulphur dioxide has

ABLE 18.2   Sources of acidifying gases

| Source | Percentage contribution | |
|---|---|---|
| | Nitrogen oxides | Sulphur dioxide |
| Motor vehicles | 45 | 1 |
| Power stations | 37 | 71 |
| Industry | 12 | 19 |
| Domestic | 3 | 5 |
| Other sources | 3 | 4 |

## Did you know?

The earth's protective ozone layer at the south pole recently fell to less than one-third of its historic level.

ABLE 18.3   Estimated relative importance of arious gases to the greenhouse effect

| Gas | % contribution |
|---|---|
| Carbon dioxide | 71 |
| CFCs | 10 |
| Methane | 9 |
| Carbon monoxide | 7 |
| Oxides of nitrogen | 3 |

diminished due to the industrial recession, that from nitrogen oxides has increased due to the increase in motor vehicle use. Table 18.2 shows the relative amounts of acidifying gases from different sources. Due to the prevailing winds, much of the sulphur dioxide from Europe, including that from Britain, is carried over Scandinavia. It is here that acid rain causes the greatest problems. Coniferous trees are particularly vulnerable and considerable damage has been caused to some forests. Lakes in the region are extremely acid and many species within them have been killed, largely as a result of the accumulation of aluminium leached from soils as a result of acid rain. This affects aquatic organisms' gills and their osmoregulatory mechanisms. Many countries have committed themselves to reducing the level of sulphur dioxide emissions, largely through changing to 'cleaner' fuels such as natural gas or by fitting desulphurization units to remove sulphur dioxide from the flue gases at power stations.

### 18.4.3 Carbon dioxide

Carbon dioxide is formed during the respiration of organisms, and by the burning of fossil fuels. That produced as a result of respiration is taken up by plants during photosynthesis, ensuring it does not accumulate. The additional carbon dioxide produced in the burning of fossil fuels has caused a rise in atmospheric carbon dioxide concentration. Scientists believe that this change in air composition prevents more of the sun's heat escaping from the earth, much in the way the glass in a greenhouse does. They argue that the rise in temperature that this so-called **greenhouse effect** produces will cause expansion of the oceans and the gradual melting of the polar ice caps with a consequent rise in sea level. This would in turn cause flooding of low-lying land, upon which, as it happens, many of the world's capital cities lie. The greenhouse effect is neither new, nor all bad. Indeed it is the greenhouse effect that maintains the earth's surface at an average of 15 °C rather than −18 °C which would be the case in the absence of greenhouse gases. The problem lies in the additional greenhouse gases which have been released over the past 200 years. While water vapour, methane and nitrogen oxides are all greenhouse gases (Table 18.3), it is the influence of carbon dioxide that has been most significant in contributing to global warming. Estimates of the warming attributable to carbon dioxide vary from 50–70%. While the other greenhouse gases are present in much lower concentrations than carbon dioxide they are much more efficient at absorbing infrared radiation and hence have a potentially greater influence on the greenhouse effect. Carbon dioxide however remains the greatest influence, not just because of its higher concentration but also the fact that it remains in the atmosphere longer – on average each molecule remains for 100 years, compared to 10 years for methane and a few months for carbon monoxide.

### 18.4.4 Carbon monoxide

Carbon monoxide occurs in exhaust emissions from cars and other vehicles. It is poisonous on account of having an affinity for haemoglobin some 250 times greater than that of oxygen.

Photochemical smog in Rio de Janeiro

Upon combining with haemoglobin, carbon monoxide forms a stable compound and prevents oxygen combining with the haemoglobin. Continued inhalation leads to death, as all haemoglobin becomes combined with carbon monoxide, leaving none to transport oxygen. In small concentrations it may cause dizziness and headache. Even on busy roads, however, levels of carbon monoxide rarely exceed 4%, and it does not accumulate due to the action of certain bacteria and algae which break it down, according to the equation:

$$4CO + 4H_2O \rightarrow 4CO_2 + 8H^+ + 8e^-$$

| carbon monoxide | water | carbon dioxide | protons | electrons |

hydrogen

Cigarette smoking is known to increase the carbon monoxide concentration of the blood; up to 10% of a smoker's haemoglobin may be combined with carbon monoxide at any one time.

### 18.4.5 Ozone depletion

Between 15 and 40 kilometres above the earth is a layer of ozone which is formed by the effect of ultra-violet radiation on oxygen molecules. In this way, a large amount of the potentially harmful ultra-violet radiation is absorbed and so prevented from reaching the earth's surface. There is evidence that this beneficial ozone layer is being damaged by atmospheric pollution, to the point where a hole in it has appeared over the Antarctic and possibly the Arctic too.

A number of pollutants can affect the ozone layer, the **chlorofluorocarbons (CFCs)** being the best known. CFCs are used in refrigerators, as propellants in aerosol sprays, and make up the bubbles in many plastic foams, e.g. expanded polystyrene. They are remarkably inert and therefore reach the upper stratosphere unchanged. Along with other ozone depleting gases such as **nitrous oxide** (NO), CFCs are contributing to global warming – the so-called 'greenhouse effect' (Section 18.4.3). In addition, the ultra-violet radiation causes skin cancer: an increase in the incidence of this disease is already evident.

## 18.5 Water pollution

Pure water rarely, if ever, exists naturally. Rain water picks up additives as it passes through the air, not least sulphur dioxide (Section 18.4.2). Even where there is little air pollution, chlorides and other substances are found in rain water. As water flows from tributaries into rivers it increasingly picks up minerals, organic matter and silt. If not the result of human activities, these may be considered as natural additives and therefore not pollutants. For domestic use alone, each individual in Britain uses an average of 150 litres of water each day.

### 18.5.1 Eutrophication by sewage and fertilizer

Eutrophication is a natural process during which the concentration of salts builds up in bodies of water. It occurs largely in lakes and the lower reaches of rivers. The salts accumulate until an equilibrium is reached where they are exactly counterbalanced by the rate at which they are removed. Lakes and rivers with low salt concentrations are termed **oligotrophic** and the salts are frequently the factor limiting plant growth. Waters with high concentrations of salts are termed **eutrophic** and here there is much less limitation on growth. **Algal blooms** occur where the waters become densely populated with species of blue-green bacteria in particular. The density of these blooms increases to a point where light is unable to penetrate to any depth. The algae in the deeper regions of the lake are therefore unable to photosynthesize, and die. Decomposition of these dead organisms by saprobiontic bacteria creates a considerable **biochemical oxygen demand (BOD)** resulting in deoxygenation of all but the very upper layers of the water. As a consequence all aerobic life in the lower regions dies.

The salts necessary for eutrophication of lakes and rivers are largely nitrates and phosphates from three sources:

1. **Leaching from the surrounding land** – This natural process is slow and is offset by the removal of salts as water drains from lakes or rivers.

2. **Sewage** – Even when treated, sewage effluent contains much phosphate. While some is the result of the breakdown of human organic waste, about half comes from detergents, which typically contain 5–10% phosphate by weight. This **detergent pollution** not only leads to unsightly foam on the rivers into which the treated sewage is discharged, but also to eutrophication as a consequence of the soluble phosphate. Solutions to the problem include the use of detergents with a lower phosphate concentration and removal of phosphate during sewage treatment.

3. **Fertilizers** – An increasing quantity of inorganic fertilizer is now applied to farmland to increase crop yield. A major constituent of these fertilizers is nitrate. As this is highly soluble it is readily leached and quickly runs off into lakes and rivers.

### 18.5.2 Oil

The effects of oil pollution are localized, but nonetheless serious. Oil is readily broken down by bacteria, especially when it is thoroughly dispersed. Most oil pollution is either the result of illegal washing at sea of storage tanks of oil tankers or accidental spillage. The first major oil pollution incident in Great Britain occurred in 1967 when the Torrey Canyon went aground off Land's End. It released 120 000 tonnes of crude oil which was washed up on many Cornish beaches. Sea birds are particularly at risk because the oil coats their feathers, preventing them from flying; it also reduces their insulatory properties, causing death by hypothermia. The Torrey Canyon incident alone is estimated to have killed 100 000 birds. On shores, the oil coats seaweed, preventing photosynthesis, and covers the gills of shellfish, interfering with feeding and respiration. However, the effects are temporary and shores commonly recover within 2 years. Detergents used to disperse oil can increase the ecological

...rmorant killed by the *Braer* oil spill

damage as they are toxic. With larger 'supertankers', the potential danger from oil pollution is increased. The wrecking of the Amoco Cadiz off the Brittany coast in 1978 with the release of 200 000 tonnes of crude oil made the Torrey Canyon incident appear small by comparison. In 1989 Exxon Valdez spilt 38 000 tonnes in Prince William Sound, Alaska and in 1993 the Braer spilt 84 000 tonnes in the Shetlands. The long-term effects of these spills in such environmentally sensitive areas are yet to be seen.

### 18.5.3 Thermal pollution

All organisms live within a relatively narrow range of temperature. Wide fluctuations in temperature occur more often in terrestrial environments as the high specific heat of water buffers temperature changes. For this reason aquatic organisms are less tolerant of temperature fluctuations. Most thermal pollution of water is the result of electricity generation in power stations. The steam used to drive the turbines in these stations is condensed back to water in large cooling towers. The water used in the cooling process is consequently warmed, being discharged at a temperature some 10–15 °C higher than when removed from the river. Although warmer water normally contains less dissolved oxygen, the spraying of water in cooling towers increases its surface area and thereby actually increases its oxygen content. The main effect of thermal pollution is to alter the ecological balance of a river by favouring warm-water species at the expense of cold-water ones. Coarse fish such as roach and perch may, for example, replace salmon and trout.

## 18.6 Terrestrial pollution

### 18.6.1 Pesticides

It is difficult to define exactly what a 'pest' is, but it is generally accepted to be an organism which is in competition with humans for food or soil space, or is potentially hazardous to health. It may even be an organism which is simply a nuisance and so causes annoyance. Pesticides are poisonous chemicals which kill pests, and they are named after the pests they destroy; hence insecticides kill insects, fungicides kill moulds and other fungi, rodenticides kill rodents such as rats and mice, and herbicides kill weeds. Unlike other pollutants, where their poisonous nature is an unfortunate and unwanted property, pesticides are quite deliberately produced and dispersed in order to exploit their toxicity.

An ideal pesticide should have the following properties:

**1.** It should be **specific**, in that it is toxic only to the organisms which it is directed and harmless to all others.

**2.** It should **not persist** but be unstable enough to break down into harmless substances. It is therefore temporary and has no long-term effect.

**3.** It should **not accumulate** either in specific parts of an organism or as it passes along food chains.

TABLE 18.4   Some major pesticides

| Name of pesticide | Type of pesticide | Additional information |
|---|---|---|
| **Inorganic pesticides**<br>Calomel (mercuric chloride) | Fungicide | Used for dusting seeds to control transmission of fungal diseases |
| Copper compounds (e.g. copper sulphate) | Fungicide and algicide | One of the first pesticides ever used was Bordeaux mixture (copper sulphate + lime) |
| Sodium chlorate | Herbicide | Used to clear paths of weeds. Persistent, although not very poisonous |
| **Organic pesticides**<br>Organo-phosphorus compounds (e.g. malathion and parathion) | Insecticides | Although very toxic they are not persistent and therefore not harmful to other animals if used responsibly. May kill useful insects such as bees, however |
| Organo-chlorine compounds (e.g. DDT, BHC, dieldrin, aldrin) | Insecticides | DDT is fairly persistent and accumulates in fatty tissue as well as along food chains. Aldrin may persist for more than 10 years. Resistance to them is now common. Most kill by inhibiting the action of cholinesterase |
| Hormones (e.g. 2,4-D, 2,4,5-T) | Herbicides | Selective weedkillers which kill broad-leaved species. Stimulate auxin production and so disrupt plant growth. May contain a dangerous impurity – dioxin |

| This most effective way to control insect pests is achieved by a combination of | |
|---|---|
| 1 | Chemical control:<br>Use of toxic chemicals to kill pests. |
| 2 | Biological control:<br>Deliberately increasing the numbers of predators or parasites of the insect pest. |
| 3 | Management techniques:<br>Providing suitable habitats for natural predators close to the crops |

The pest may not be eliminated but its numbers are kept below the economical damage threshold.

Pesticides have been used for some time. A mixture of copper sulphate and lime, called Bordeaux mixture, was used over 100 years ago to control fungal diseases of vines. The problem is that in an attempt to produce food more economically and control human disease, pesticides have been used in large amounts in most regions of the world. A summary of some major pesticides is given in Table 18.4.

Most pesticides are not persistent. Warfarin, for example, readily kills any rodent which eats it, but as it is quickly broken down inside the rodent's body, it is harmless to anything which eats the corpse, e.g. maggots. Some pesticides, dichlorodiphenyl-trichlorethane (DDT), for example, are unfortunately persistent. First synthesized in 1874, its insecticidal properties were not appreciated until 1939. It was used extensively during the Second World War, in which it played a vital role in controlling lice, fleas and other carriers of disease. It was subsequently used to kill mosquitoes, and so helped control malaria. Not only is DDT persistent, it also accumulates along food chains. If, for example, garden plants are sprayed with it in order to control greenfly, some of the flies will survive despite absorbing the DDT. These may then be eaten by tits who further concentrate the chemical in their bodies, especially in the fat tissues where it accumulates. If a number of tits, each containing DDT, are consumed by a predator, e.g. a sparrowhawk, the DDT builds up in high enough concentrations to kill the bird. Even where the concentrations are not sufficient to kill, they may still cause harm. It is known that DDT can alter the behaviour of birds, sometimes preventing them building proper nests. It may cause them to become infertile and can result in the egg shells being so thin that they break when the parent bird sits on them during

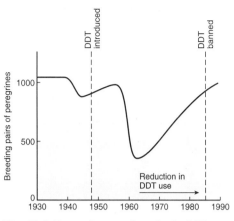

Fig. 18.2 *Peregrine numbers in the UK*

Weed control. Sugar beet crop in which weeds on the right have been controlled by chemicals and those on the left are untreated

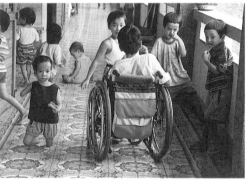

The effects of Agent Orange

incubation. In Britain these effects led to a marked decline in the 1950s and 60s of populations of peregrine falcons (Fig. 18.2), sparrowhawks, golden eagles and other predatory birds. As a consequence, Britain, along with many other countries, restricted the use of DDT with the result that populations of these birds have now recovered.

Owing to the persistence of DDT, it remains in the environment despite the death of the organism containing it. With over one million tonnes of the chemical having already been used it now occurs in all parts of the globe and is found in almost all animals. Indeed, many humans contain more DDT than is permitted by many countries in food for human consumption.

With such widespread use of DDT, it is not surprising that selection pressure has resulted in insect varieties which are able to break it down and so render it useless. The development of **resistance** is now common among insect disease vectors like mosquitoes, and has set back prospects of eradicating malaria.

Herbicides make up 40% of the world's total pesticide production, and in developed countries the figure exceeds 60%. Some herbicides like paraquat kill all vegetation. While paraquat is highly poisonous it is rapidly broken down by bacteria and rendered harmless. Other weedkillers are selective, destroying broad-leaved plants (mostly dicotyledons) but not narrow-leaved ones (mostly monocotyledons). As most cereal crops are narrow-leaved and the weeds that compete with them are broad-leaved, such selective weedkillers are extensively used. They are similar to the plant's natural hormones, auxins, and as such are quickly broken down and rendered harmless. The two best known examples are 2,4-dichlorophenoxyacetic acid (2,4-D) and 2,4,5-trichlorophenoxyacetic acid (2,4,5-T). In the production of 2,4,5-T an impurity called **dioxin** is formed. Dioxin is one of the most toxic compounds known, a single gram being sufficient to kill in excess of 5000 humans. Even in minute quantities it may cause cancer, a skin disorder called chloracne and abnormalities in unborn babies. The chemical gained notoriety when used as a defoliant by the US army during the Vietnam war in the 1970s. It was a constituent of 'Agent Orange', 50 million dm³ (litres) of which were sprayed over jungle areas to cause the leaves to drop so that enemy camps could be revealed. The dioxin produced physical and mental defects in children born in the area, as well as in children born to American servicemen working in the region. In 1976, an accident at a factory in Seveso, Italy, resulted in the release of dioxin into the atmosphere. Despite evacuation of the area, thousands of people suffered with chloracne, miscarriages, cancer and fetal abnormalities.

## 18.7 The impact of agriculture on the environment

We all need to eat to live and with an ever increasing population the need to produce sufficient food to meet the growing needs of the world's population has led to intensification of agricultural practices. Land is artificially prevented from reaching its climax vegetation through regular grazing, ploughing and the use of fertilizers and pesticides. In the United Kingdom agricultural food production has been doubled over the last 40 years. This has been achieved in a number of ways:

1. **Improved strains of plant and animal species** – Through artificial selection and genetic engineering the productivity of most crop plants and livestock animals has been increased.

2. **Greater use of fertilizers and pesticides** – There has been almost a ten fold increase in the use of artificial fertilizers over the past 50 years.

3. **Increased mechanization and use of biotechnology** – There have been major technological advances in machines used to sow, fertilize, harvest and transport crops as well as advances in the use of technology in controlling the harvesting and the conditions under which crops are stored. Animals are often reared under the optimum conditions for growth which are carefully controlled. There has been a consequent reduction in the number of farm labourers employed.

4. **Changes in farm practices and consequent increase in farm size** – There has been a trend to arable, rather than pastoral, farming. Sugar beet and oilseeds are increasingly grown instead of turnips and rye. Fields have become larger to accommodate modern machinery and so hedgerows have increasingly been removed. Wetland areas and ponds have been drained to increase the area of productive land.

Such has been the success of agricultural production in Europe that there are now surpluses of foods such as beef, dairy products and cereals. To reduce these surpluses farmers may, if they choose, be paid to **set-aside** up to 20% of their land for purposes other than food production, e.g. for planting woodland.

The demands of agriculture often conflict with the need for conservation. One example is **hedgerow removal**. It has been estimated that each year in the UK some 8000 km of hedgerows are removed. On the one hand the farmer may seek to remove hedges because:

1. They harbour pests, diseases and weeds, especially over winter.
2. They take up space which could otherwise be used to cultivate a crop.
3. They impede use of and accessibility for large machinery.
4. They reduce crop yields by absorbing moisture and nutrients.

On the other hand the hedges have conservation value:

1. They are a habitat for a rich and diverse variety of plant and animal species.
2. They produce food for many birds and other animals which do not actually live in the hedgerows.
3. They act as corridors along which many species move and disperse themselves.
4. They act as wind-breaks, often preventing soil erosion by the wind.
5. They add diversity and interest to the landscape.

rmland with small fields and many hedgerows

rge area of arable land without hedgerows

# 18.8  Conservation

TABLE 18.6  **The advantages and disadvantages of using organic and inorganic fertilizers**

| ADVANTAGES | |
|---|---|
| Organic | Supply all the necessary nutrients for growth |
| | Increase water retention of the soil |
| | Maintain the air content of the soil both directly and by encouraging earthworms |
| | Effective over a long period |
| | Improve the crumb structure of the soil |
| | Improve drainage and so help prevent waterlogging |
| Inorganic | Relatively light and therefore easy to transport and apply |
| | Quick acting |
| | Easy to handle |
| | Relatively cheap |
| | Easily obtained |

| DISADVANTAGES | |
|---|---|
| Organic | Not easily obtained |
| | Bulky and therefore expensive to transport and apply |
| | Slow acting and therefore not effective in a single season |
| | Difficult to handle |
| | Relatively expensive |
| Inorganic | Do not improve the physical characteristics of the soil |
| | Can be easily removed by leaching |
| | Need to be regularly applied |
| | Run-off can cause pollution of water courses |

There has been a growing interest in conservation as a result of increasing pressures placed upon the natural environment, the widespread loss of natural habitats, and the growing numbers extinct and endangered species. As early as 1872, the Yellowstone National Park in the USA was established in order to protect a particularly valuable natural environment. Australia (1886) and New Zealand (1894) established national parks soon after. It was not until 1949 that the first national park in Britain was established, but prior to that many societies such as the Royal Society for the Protection of Birds (1889) and the National Trust (1895) had been set up to promote conservation. There are now a large number of agencies responsible for conservation in one form or another. These include international groups like the World Wide Fund for Nature; large national bodies such as the Department of the Environment (DoE), Nature Conservancy Council (NCC), and the National Trust (NT); commercial organizations like the water authorities and the Forestry Commission; charitable groups like the Royal Society for the Protection of Birds (RSPB); as well as County Trusts for Nature Conservation and Farming and Wildlife Advisory Groups. The main impetus for conservation has come as a result of the pressures created by an ever-increasing human population – likely to be 6000 million before the end of the century.

There is often a conflict between the needs of a country to produce enough food to feed its inhabitants and the need to conserve natural habitats; this can be illustrated by the use of nitrogen-containing fertilizers. There is no doubt that the use of chemical fertilizers containing nitrogen increases the crop yield from a given area of land and so helps to feed the populus. Equally there is no doubt that some of this fertilizer runs off into watercourses causing eutrophication (see Section 18.5.1). Conservationists argue that there are viable non-polluting alternatives to the use of chemical fertilizers. For example, crop rotation or intercropping with nitrogen-fixing leguminous species will improve the nitrogen content of soils. Alternatively organic manures, which release their nitrogen too slowly to create pollution problems, could be used. These manures can be added to the surface in a layer thick enough to prevent weed growth – a process called **mulching** – so preventing additional loss of nitrogen from the soil into the weeds.

Conservation is more than preservation. The latter seeks to maintain individuals, populations and ecosystems in their current state without the capacity for change. Conservation, however, seeks not to keep things as they are indefinitely but rather to allow them to evolve naturally, much as they may have done without our presence. Why conserve at all? There are two basic reasons. Ethically many feel mankind has a duty to allow all species, most of which have occupied the earth far longer, to continue to exist in the same balance that existed before human evolution. Economically the long-term productivity of natural ecosystems is greater if they are maintained in their naturally balanced state; the richness and variety are not only aesthetically pleasing but retain the potential to provide natural products to satisfy not only mankind's present needs but also solutions to problems we have yet to encounter.

### 18.8.1 Endangered species

Many species have become **extinct**, i.e. they have not been definitely located in the wild during the past 50 years. Others are **endangered**, i.e. they are likely to become extinct if the factors causing their numbers to decline continue to operate. At least 25 000 plant species are considered to be endangered.

There are a number of reasons why organisms become endangered:

1. **Natural selection** – It is, and always has been, part of the normal process of evolution that organisms which are genetically better adapted replace those less well adapted.

2. **Habitat destruction** – Humans exploit many natural habitats, destroying them in the process. Timber cutting destroys forests and endangers species like the orang-utan. Industrial and agricultural development threaten many plant species of the Amazon forest. Clearing of river banks destroys the natural habitat of the otter, and modern farming methods remove hedgerows and drain wetlands, endangering the species which live and breed there. Maintaining the diversity of organisms in a habitat is important as species may have economic importance outside their habitat, e.g. pollinating insects. They may also possess undiscovered chemicals and/or genes with future medicinal or other importance.

3. **Competition from humans and their animals** – Where a species is restricted to a small area, e.g. the giant tortoises in the Galapagos Islands, they are often unable to compete with the influx of humans and their animals. Because their habitat is restricted, in this case by water, they cannot escape.

4. **Hunting and collecting** – Humans hunt tigers for sport, crocodiles for their skins, oryx as trophies, elephants for ivory, whales for oil and rhinoceros for their horn. Other organisms are collected for the pet trade, e.g. tamarins and parrots; and for research purposes, e.g. frogs. These are in addition to the numerous species hunted purely as food.

5. **Destroyed by humans as being a health risk** – Many species are persecuted because they carry diseases of domesticated species, e.g. badgers (tuberculosis of cattle) and eland (various cattle diseases).

6. **Pollution** – Oil pollution threatens some rare species of sea birds. The build-up of certain insecticides along food chains endangers predatory birds like the peregrine falcon and the golden eagle (Section 18.6.1).

### 18.8.2 Conservation methods

To combat the pressures listed above a number of conservation techniques are used:

1. **Development of national parks and nature reserves** – These are habitats legally safeguarded and patrolled by wardens. They may preserve a vulnerable food source, e.g. in China areas of bamboo forest are protected to help conserve the giant panda. In Africa game parks help to conserve endangered species such as the African elephant. Efforts are being made to conserve the

# BIOLOGY AROUND US

## Coppicing

Coppiced trees

Coppicing is an ancient technique for obtaining long, flexible lengths of wood of small diameter. Traditionally these were used to make fences known as **hurdles**, in furniture making, buildings, or just as firewood. The technique relies upon the fact that if a tree, even a mature one, is cut back near to the ground, many new shoots will develop from the remaining stump. If allowed to grow for a few years, these new stems can be harvested. The length of time they are permitted to grow depends on the species involved and the purpose to which the wood is to be put. Varieties of tree involved include ash, oak, hazel, lime and hornbeam.

Coppicing provides a good example of taking a sustainable yield because the stems quickly regrow in readiness for the next harvest. It is also an excellent conservation technique in the management of deciduous woodland, because coppicing provides a variety of habitats, especially when done in conjunction with the maintenance of larger trees around. In this way, areas of woodland are opened up to more light than would be the case if all trees were permitted to reach maturity. Plants which would normally only grow on the periphery of the wood can now thrive within it, attracting as they do associated insects and birds. The coppices themselves prove excellent nesting sites for birds such as nightingales, dunnocks and nuthatches.

dwindling areas of tropical rainforest. Planning authorities have greater powers to control developments and activities within these areas. Even so there are problems. In the Dartmoor National Park, for example, there is soil erosion caused by walkers and ponies which regularly use the area. Rare species such as the merlin and peregrine falcon are also disturbed by these groups. The difficulty is in trying to balance the increasing wish of people to escape to the solitude of National Parks such as Dartmoor with the need for conservation.

**2. Planned land use** – On a smaller scale, specific areas of land may be set aside for a designated use. The types of activities permitted on the land are carefully controlled by legislation. Such areas include Green Belts, Areas of Outstanding Natural Beauty, Sites of Special Scientific Interest, and country parks. Some places are designated as Environmentally Sensitive Areas (ESAs) and farmers or other landowners may be compensated for restricting activities which might conflict with conserving the natural habitats in the region. In addition to statutory bodies, many volunteer organizations protect habitats. The Royal Society for the Protection of Birds (RSPB), for example, is the largest volunteer conservation organization in Europe. By acquiring and managing land, the RSPB conserves and expands habitats important to birds. Its 100 and more reserves extend across Britain and provide appropriate breeding areas for rare species like ospreys (Loch Garten, Speyside), gannets (Grassholm, Dyfed) and avocets (Minsmere, Suffolk).

Heather moorland in Dartmoor National Park, Devon

## BIOLOGY AROUND US

### Conservation of grasslands

Much of Britain is prevented from reaching its natural woodland climax vegetation type as a result of agricultural practices such as mowing and grazing. Together these maintain a grassland vegetation. Traditionally these grasslands were grazed by animals such as sheep and/or were mowed annually for hay. The fertility of the soil was maintained by the addition of animal manure with little, or no, chemical fertilizers or pesticides. A rich and diverse flora of meadow plants resulted, partly because the overall fertility of the soil was relatively low and partly as a result of the meadow being cropped very close to the ground. Intensive farming and the use of herbicides, fertilizers and machine cutting rather than grazing has led to higher productivity but a much reduced diversity of species because a few grass varieties are favoured.

The conservation of species-rich grassland meadows is best achieved by grazing sheep on them because sheep leave a very short turf which favours a range of small perennial herbs rather than grasses. Trampling by the sheep also encourages new plant arrivals because it creates bare patches of disturbed ground on which they can establish themselves. The lower soil fertility as a result of natural manuring rather than artificial fertilizers also favours a variety of broad leaved species in preference to grasses. Hay making with a single cut each year, rather than multiple cuts for silage, helps to conserve species diversity. The nearer the mowing mimics the grazing of sheep, i.e. a low cut, the more effective it is in conserving the meadow. The richer the diversity of plants, the greater the variety of insects and other invertebrates that occur, which in turn encourages a greater number of vertebrate species, especially birds.

### Did you know?

For every human killed by a shark, 4.5 million sharks are killed by humans.

3. **Legal protection for endangered species** – It is illegal to collect or kill certain species, e.g. the koala in Australia. In Britain, the Wildlife and Countryside Act gives legal protection to many plants and animals. Even legislation such as the Clean Air Act may indirectly protect some species from extinction. Despite stiff penalties, such laws are violated because of the difficulty of enforcing them.

4. **Commercial farming** – The development of farms which produce sought-after goods, e.g. mink farming, deer farming, may produce enough material to satisfy the market and so remove the necessity to kill these animals in the wild.

5. **Breeding in zoos and botanical gardens** – Endangered species may be bred in the protected environment of a zoo and when numbers have been sufficiently increased they may be reintroduced into the wild. One species conserved in this way has been the Hawaiian Goose or Ne-Ne. Its population in the wild fell to around 20 pairs before being supplemented by thousands of birds bred in captivity and released in Hawaii.

# BIOLOGY AROUND US

## Conservation of fenlands

Wicken Fen

Surrounding the Wash in eastern England there was once a huge area of waterlogged marsh and peatland supporting a rich and unique flora. This fenland has been systematically drained to be used for farming, resulting in a shrinkage of the soil so that the level has fallen about 4.5 metres. For some years now attempts have been made to conserve the remaining patches of undrained land but it is difficult to maintain, or reintroduce if necessary, the original varieties of plants. The fen is now higher than the surrounding farmland and is becoming acidic as the topsoil is leached. This leads to invasion by untypical acid-loving species like *Sphagnum* and the bog myrtle. As water drains off the fen, more has to be pumped on to it along special channels to maintain the correct conditions for the vegetation. Typical fenland plants are the sedge, *Cladium mariscus*, and the reed, *Phragmites communis*, and these must be cut back every 4 years in the spring or summer to prevent invasion by scrub such as buckthorn and willows.

Despite being less adapted to feeding and more prone to predators, these introduced pairs have stabilized the falling population.

In addition to captive-breeding programmes, zoos often 'freeze' ova, sperm and embryos for later use when natural habitats become available and finances permit. Using embryo transfer and surrogacy, these 'frozen genes' can be later employed to yield additional individuals of endangered species. In the same way, plant species may be protected in botanical gardens, either as adult individuals or their genetic material temporarily preserved in seed banks.

Cane toad eating pygmy possum. Introduced as a means of biological control the cane toad is now a predator of native species.

**6. Removal of animals from threatened areas** – Organisms in habitats threatened by humans, or by natural disasters such as floods, may be removed and resettled in more secure habitats.

**7. Control of introduced species** – Organisms introduced into country by humans often require strict control if they are not to out-compete the indigenous species. Feral animals (domesticated individuals which escape into the wild) must be similarly controlled.

**8. Ecological study of threatened habitats** – Careful analysis of all natural habitats is essential if they are to be managed in a way that permits conservation of a maximum number of species.

**9. Pollution control** – Measures to control pollution such as smoke emissions, oil spillage, over-use of pesticides, fertilizer run-off, etc., all help to prevent habitat and species destruction. This is especially important in sensitive and vulnerable areas such as river estuaries and salt marshes.

## BIOLOGY AROUND US

# Reclamation of derelict land

### Did you know?

Removing a year's worth of waste generated by modern Britons would require a nose-to-tail queue of juggernauts stretching six times round the world.

### Did you know?

Four out of five new aluminium cans are dumped on the landscape.

### Did you know?

A year of Europe's junked aerosol cans could stack to the moon.

### Did you know?

At least four juggernauts would be required to transport the mercury in British adults' teeth to a toxic waste incinerator.

As Britain's economic base has shifted from heavy industrial and manufacturing processes to high technology and service industries, more and more land, once occupied by large factories, industries and mines, has been left derelict, some of it heavily polluted. Large volumes of waste associated with these industries have been dumped in spoil and slag heaps. These heaps may be toxic with high levels of heavy metal ions, making it difficult for vegetation to grow on them. Without vegetation they can become unstable and liable to slip. One such slip in the Welsh village of Aberfan in 1966 engulfed a primary school and nearby houses, killing 116 children and 28 adults.

The reclamation of this land is designed to make it safer, aesthetically more pleasing and, if possible, to bring it back into productive use. The establishment of vegetation is vital to this process but is often hampered by the toxicity of the material, its unfavourable pH, a lack of suitable plant nutrients or the absence of organic matter. In addition, the particle size of the material is often unsuitable, being too coarse, too fine, or simply so compacted that growth is impossible.

The reclamation of any one site involves finding out which factors are preventing plant growth and then remedying them. This may require draining the site, incorporating organic material, levelling the ground, ploughing, adding fertilizers and/or lime, and sowing the seeds of appropriate species which can tolerate the conditions. Let us look at two specific examples of reclamation, namely land contaminated by heavy metal ions and by china clay wastes.

Pollution of land by **heavy metal ions** is often the result of the mining of ores to extract metals such as tin, silver, nickel, lead, iron, zinc, chromium and copper. Most of these metals occur naturally as ions in soils. Indeed some, such as copper, iron and zinc, are necessary for plant growth. It is the high concentration of these ions that renders the land unsuitable for plant growth. Reclamation can take a number of forms. Where the degree of pollution is relatively small, natural leaching may, over time, reduce the concentration of heavy metal ions to a tolerable level. Alternatively, the area may be covered by unpolluted top soil which will support vegetation. The process is costly and the metal ions may migrate upwards, a process accelerated by the activities of earthworms. Another remedial measure is to treat the affected land chemically in order to precipitate-out the toxic ions into a form which cannot be taken up by plants, e.g. iron(II) sulphate may be used to precipitate-out chromium ions as chromium(III) sulphate. Lime is used to increase the pH of very acidic land. A further strategy is to establish plants which can tolerate the particular metal ions. A few species of plants have varieties which can tolerate high concentrations of one particular metal ion. For example, *Agrostis capillaris* – cultivar *Parys* can tolerate soils heavily polluted with copper ions. In combination with suitable fertilizers and other

## BIOLOGY AROUND US continued

China clay spoil heap

Reclaimed landscaped china clay spoil heap

after-care methods, these species can be successfully established. Further work is then needed to increase the variety of species and so establish a balanced ecosystem.

**China clay** has been mined in Cornwall since the eighteenth century and this mining has produced large pits, often now flooded, and associated spoil heaps. The fine clay particles in the flooded pits prevent organisms establishing themselves, while the spoil heaps are equally inhospitable owing to their low pH, large particle size and deficiency of nitrogen. Reclamation of the spoil heaps has entailed landscaping the contours by redistributing the waste with machinery and adding peat or other organic material to improve water retention and provide a longer-term supply of nutrients. A mixture of different plant seeds is then sown, including perennial grasses such as *Lolium perenne* (to establish vegetation quickly and stabilize the land), *Festuca rubra* (a species tolerant of acid conditions and which can survive on soils with poor nutrient levels) and *Trifolium pretense* (a clover which fixes nitrogen and so helps to fertilize the impoverished land naturally). Chemical fertilizers, rich in phosphates and potassium, are applied. If too much fertilizer is added initially, nitrogen fixation by the clover may be inhibited, although once the grasses are firmly established the amount of nitrate can be safely increased.

By these methods, the land can be reclaimed much more rapidly than by natural regeneration and can then be used for low intensity agriculture such as the grazing of Soay sheep – a variety which survives well on low grade pasture.

Bins for waste recycling

**10. Recycling** – The more material that is recycled, the less need there is to obtain that material from natural sources, e.g. through mining. These activities often destroy sensitive habitats, either directly or indirectly through the dumping of waste which is toxic or the development of roads to transport the products. This can be especially true of metal ores which are often found in mountainous regions, many of which are home to rare species.

**11. Education** – It is of paramount importance to educate people in ways of preventing habitat destruction and encouraging the conservation of organisms.

## Did you know?

It takes 15 000 recycled sheets of A4 paper to save a tree.

# 18.9 Questions

. A factory sited in a rural district was known to be emitting smoke containing sulphur dioxide ($SO_2$). A study was made of the numbers of lichen species and the $SO_2$ concentration at various sites in two directions leading away from the factory. The table below gives the distance and directions of (i) number of lichen species and (ii) sulphur dioxide concentration in the atmosphere in the two different directions from the factory chimney.

| Distance (kilometres) from factory in a south-west direction | 1.5 | 6.5 | 12.5 | 25 | 40 |
|---|---|---|---|---|---|
| Number of lichen species | 0 | 2 | 3 | 9 | 14 |
| Sulphur dioxide concentration/ parts per million | 28 | 26 | 23 | 16 | 2 |
| Distance (kilometres) from factory in a north-east direction | 1.5 | 6.5 | 12.5 | 25 | 40 |
| Number of lichen species | 1 | 3 | 4 | 5 | 5 |
| Sulphur dioxide concentration/ parts per million | 27 | 25 | 24 | 22 | 19 |

(a) On squared paper, plot the information to show the relationships between the lichen distribution and the sulphur dioxide concentration using the same $x$ axis and two $y$ axes, one on the right for $SO_2$ concentration and one on the left for the number of species. (8 marks)

(b) Discuss and suggest explanations for the differences in the results between those obtained for the south-west direction and those obtained for the north-east direction. (4 marks)

(Total 12 marks)

*Oxford March 1997, Paper 43, No. 5*

. Russia is due to decommission (take out of use and scrap) its fleet of nuclear submarines. In the interim, these and other radioactive wastes are being kept at Murmansk, on the north coast of Russia, inside the Arctic Circle.

(a) Give one possible reason for the choice of nuclear fuel for submarines. (1 mark)

(b) State two problems likely to be encountered during the decommissioning process. (2 marks)

(c) State two effects which exposure to radiation may have on living tissues. (2 marks)

(Total 5 marks)

*Oxford June 1997, Paper 43, No. 7*

. Acid rain is a matter of serious environmental concern. Sulphuric acid is present in acid rain and has adverse effects on both plants and animals.

(a) (i) Name two acidic components of acid rain other than sulphuric acid. (2 marks)

(ii) Describe how acid rain is formed. (3 marks)

(b) An experiment was carried out to investigate the effect of dilute sulphuric acid on the growth of cress seedlings. Batches of seeds were sown in glass dishes on filter paper to which dilute sulphuric acid was added. The dishes were then incubated. The root and shoot lengths were measured after 65 hours. The results are shown in the table below.

| Sulphuric acid concentration/mol dm$^{-3}$ | Mean root length/mm | Mean shoot length/mm |
|---|---|---|
| 0 | 55.5 | 25.2 |
| $1 \times 10^{-3}$ | 63.4 | 18.4 |
| $3 \times 10^{-3}$ | 6.5 | 9.5 |
| $4 \times 10^{-3}$ | 2.0 | 4.6 |
| $6 \times 10^{-3}$ | 2.8 | 0.8 |
| $7 \times 10^{-3}$ | 1.5 | 0.5 |
| $8 \times 10^{-3}$ | 1.3 | 0.3 |
| $9 \times 10^{-3}$ | 1.3 | 0.0 |
| $1 \times 10^{-2}$ | 1.0 | 0.0 |

Adapted from Fleet, Jones and Petter, *J.B.E.*, 1987.

(i) Describe the relationship between the concentration of sulphuric acid and the growth of roots as shown by the results in the table. (2 marks)

(ii) Compare the effects of sulphuric acid on the growth of roots and shoots. (3 marks)

(iii) Suggest two reasons why cress seedlings are suitable for investigating the effect of acid rain on plants. (2 marks)

(Total 12 marks)

*Edexcel January 1998, Paper HB2, No. 6*

4. In 1945, a report was published which laid down the concept of a National Park.

'A National Park may be defined, in application to Great Britain, as an extensive area of beautiful and relatively wild country in which, for the nation's benefit and by appropriate national decision and action:

A. the characteristic landscape beauty is strictly preserved;

B. access and facilities for public open air enjoyment are amply provided;

C. wildlife and buildings and places of architectural and historic interest are suitably protected while,

D. established farming is maintained.'

(a) (i) State **four** ways in which the **landscape beauty** of National Parks is preserved.
(4 marks)

(ii) Explain how part **B** in the passage may conflict with part **A**. (3 marks)

(b) Explain how wildlife may be protected within a National Park. (3 marks)

(c) Explain the environmental damage **each** of the following activities may cause within a National Park.

(i) Softwood afforestation (2 marks)

(ii) Quarrying (1 mark)

(iii) Hedgerow clearance (2 marks)

(Total 15 marks)

*Oxford & Cambridge June 1997, Unit B9, No. 1*

---

**5.** The Norfolk Broads is an area of rivers and lakes in East Anglia. It is surrounded by farmland and has become a popular area for boating. During the course of this century the water has been polluted by the addition of sewage, animal wastes and fertilizers. This pollution has had a major effect on the ecology of the area.

(a) Explain the part played by bacteria in converting organic matter in sewage to nitrate. (4 marks)

Algae are small, chlorophyll-containing organisms that live in the surface waters of lakes and rivers. One way of estimating the numbers of algae present is to measure the maximum depth of water through which a white disc can be seen. The table shows some measurements taken with different numbers of algae present in the water.

| Maximum depth of water through which white disc can be seen/m | Number of algae present measured as chlorophyll concentration/$\mu g\,dm^{-3}$ |
|---|---|
| 8.3 | 0.8 |
| 5.9 | 1.3 |
| 3.8 | 1.6 |
| 2.2 | 4.8 |
| 1.3 | 9.5 |
| 1.2 | 14.8 |
| 1.2 | 19.7 |

(b) (i) Plot the data in the table as a suitable graph. (4 marks)

(ii) Over what range of chlorophyll concentration would you consider this method to be a reliable way of estimating the number of algae present? Give a reason for your answer. (1 mark)

(c) The graphs show how the cloudiness of the water at two different sites varied over a period of one year. Site A had a low nitrate concentration. Site B had a high nitrate concentration.

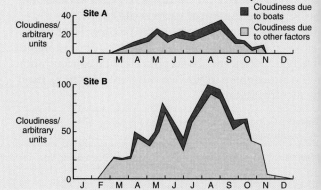

(i) Describe and explain the effect of increased nitrate concentration on algal growth. (2 marks)

(ii) Algae do not live long. Explain why the presence of large numbers of algae results in a fall in the amount of oxygen dissolved in the water. (2 marks)

(iii) There are very few submerged water plants at Site B. Use the graphs to suggest how placing a speed limit on boats might allow submerged water plants to become re-established at Site B. (2 marks)

(d) An electro-plating factory discharged its waste into one of the rivers. Cages containing fresh water mussels were placed at different distances above and below the discharge point. The concentration of copper in their tissues was measured after 14 and 45 days. The results are shown in the graph.

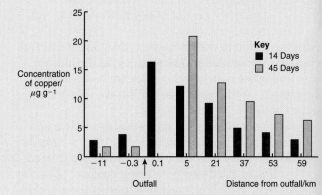

(i) A concentration of $23\mu g\,g^{-1}$ of copper in their tissues will kill fresh-water mussels. The mussels placed at 0.1km below the discharge point died before 45 days. What is the evidence from the data which suggests that they were killed by the copper? (1 mark)

(ii) The concentration of copper in the tissues of the mussels was higher than in the surrounding water. Suggest why.
*(2 marks)*

(iii) Mussels are primary consumers. Explain why heavy metal ions such as copper may have a much greater effect on secondary consumers than they do on primary consumers. *(2 marks)*
*(Total 20 marks)*

*AEB June 1998, (Human Biology), Paper 2, No. 4*

In the late 1970s and early 1980s, new international gislation regarding fishing came into force which eant that many countries adopted 200 mile fishing mits around their coasts. Later, as more countries ined what is now known as the European Union, rther agreements regarding fishing came into effect. od has always been a popular fish with consumers the United Kingdom and supplies have been fected by these events. Interestingly, between 1973 d 1984, cod landed in the United Kingdom from the orth Sea increased by 84%.

e table shows the mean annual mass of North Sea d landed in selected countries as officially reported tween 1981 and 1985.

| Country | tonnes |
|---|---|
| Belgium | 6 534 |
| Denmark | 52 748 |
| France | 7 978 |
| Germany (West) | 17 945 |
| Netherlands | 35 637 |
| Norway | 7 665 |
| United Kingdom | 103 678 |
| Others | 641 |

*(a)* (i) Calculate the percentage of the total catch that was landed in the United Kingdom between 1981 and 1985. Show your working. *(2 marks)*

(ii) Suggest why the heading for the table includes the words 'officially reported'.
*(1 mark)*

(iii) Suggest why the catch landed in the United Kingdom rose so dramatically between 1973 and 1984. *(2 marks)*

(iv) Since 1985, there have been significant changes in the relative **proportions** of the catches in the different countries. Outline the general trend of these changes and suggest why they have occurred. *(2 marks)*

*(b)* In order to estimate the **size** of a population of wild animals, appropriate data must be collected. Briefly outline one method by which this can be done in a sea fishery. *(4 marks)*

The graphs illustrate important changes in two measurements related to the growth of cod in the North Sea.

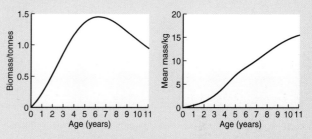

*(c)* (i) Using these data, deduce the optimum age for the commercial exploitation of the fish stock. Explain your answer.
*(2 marks)*

(ii) State **two** ways in which legislation is used to control the age at which most fish are caught. *(2 marks)*
*(Total 15 marks)*

*Oxford & Cambridge June 1997, Unit B9, No. 2*

7. *(a)* Explain briefly some of the problems which may arise from the excessive use of chemicals to control the plant and animal pests of crop plants. *(4 marks)*

*(b)* Biological pest control avoids some of the problems of chemical control.

(i) Explain what is meant by the term **biological pest control**. *(1 mark)*

(ii) Suggest **one** of the possible risks of biological pest control. *(2 marks)*

*(c)* (i) Explain how the release of chlorofluorocarbons (CFCs) into the atmosphere can damage ecosystems.
*(2 marks)*

(ii) What measures are being taken to minimize the problem? *(2 marks)*
*(Total 11 marks)*

*Oxford & Cambridge June 1996, Unit B9, No. 4*

False-colour SEM of ciliated epithelium lining the trachea of a rat (opposite)

# Part IV

# TRANSPORT AND EXCHANGE MECHANISMS

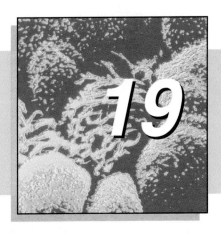

# Why organisms need transport and exchange mechanisms

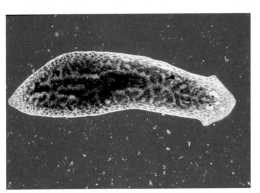

*Dugesia* – free-living cold water flatworm

All organisms need to exchange materials between themselves and their environment. Respiratory gases and the raw materials for growth must pass into an organism and waste products must be removed. This exchange is carried out passively by diffusion and osmosis and actively by active transport, pinocytosis and phagocytosis (Section 4.3). To be efficient, exchange mechanisms require the surface-area over which transfer occurs to be large when compared to the volume of the organism. Where diffusion is involved the exchange surface needs to be moist and the distance across which diffusion occurs must be as small as possible. In small organisms such as protozoans and unicellular algae their surface-area is sufficiently large compared with their volume to allow efficient exchange of most materials over the whole surface of their bodies.

When organisms became multicellular and so grew in size, they could only meet their exchange demands by simple diffusion if their requirements were very modest, for example if they had a very low metabolic rate. An increase in size inevitably meant an increased distance from the surface to the centre of the organism. Even if sufficient exchange occurred at the surface, the centre could still be starved of raw materials, because the rate of delivery was inadequate to supply the demand, if it was dependent on diffusion alone. One means of overcoming this problem is to become flattened in shape, so ensuring that no part of the body is far from the surface which supplies its nutrients. This explains the shape of the flatworms (Platyhelminthes). A further solution is to leave the central region of the organism hollow, or fill it with non-metabolizing material.

Further increases in size and/or metabolic rate necessitated the development of specialized exchange surfaces to compensate for a smaller surface-area to volume ratio and/or an increased oxygen demand. In insects, flight necessitated a high metabolic rate and hence a more efficient delivery of oxygen to the tissues and subsequent removal of carbon dioxide. To achieve this they developed tubular ingrowths, the tracheae, which carried the air directly to the respiring tissues. These have the advantage of allowing oxygen and carbon dioxide to diffuse through a gaseous medium, rather than through the aqueous medium of cells – a much slower process. In addition, mass flow of the air is possible and this too speeds the movement of gases. With tracheae there is no need for a circulatory system to carry respiratory gases. While a blood system is present in insects, it possesses no respiratory pigments and its purpose is to carry nutrients, wastes and phagocytic cells.

## Did you know?

The largest mammal is 70 million times bigger than the smallest (mass of the smallest shrew is 2 g; the largest whale is 140 tonnes)

bino axolotl (*Ambystoma mexicanum*)

Where large size is combined with a high metabolic rate, both specialized exchange surfaces and an efficient means of transport become essential. In water the exchange surfaces for respiratory gases take the form of gills. In their simplest forms these are branched external outpushings of the body wall, as in amphibians like the axolotl. When covered, gills require a means of ventilation to supply them with fresh respiratory medium. This ventilation may be carried out by muscular action or by cilia. In fish, gills form highly branched, blood-filled extensions around gill slits which lead from the pharynx. A regular current of water is pumped over these internal gills. While gills are in principle adequate exchange surfaces for terrestrial organisms, they suffer the disadvantage of lacking support in the less dense medium of air. They therefore collapse, reducing their surface-area and making them inefficient. An additional problem is that respiratory surfaces need to be kept moist to allow efficient diffusion. Gills could be kept moist, but due to their positions they would lose intolerably large quantities of water through evaporation. The solution for large, highly metabolizing, terrestrial organisms was to develop lungs. These comprise tiny elastic sacs, the alveoli, which are supported by connective tissue. The tubes, called bronchi, leading to these sacs are supported by cartilagenous rings to prevent collapse and the lungs as a whole are supported and protected by a bony cage of ribs. Being located deep within the body and communicating to the outside only by means of a narrow tube, the trachea, evaporative losses are kept to a minimum. The linings of the alveoli are thin and well supplied with blood. Muscular action ensures constant ventilation of the lungs.

With increasing size and specialization of organisms, tissues and organs became increasingly dependent upon one another. Materials needed to be exchanged not only between organs and the environment, but also between different organs. To this end, animals developed circulatory systems. These comprise a fluid which either flows freely over all cells (open system) or is confined to special vessels which communicate within diffusing distance of cells (closed system). The fluid is circulated by cilia, body muscle or a specialized pump (the heart) or some combination of these mechanisms. Closed blood systems are used by the larger, more highly evolved animals as they allow greater control of the distribution of the blood, making them more efficient at meeting changes in the demands of different tissues. Control of the heart beat assists this process.

The blood itself must be adapted to transport a wide variety of substances. Many are simply dissolved in a watery solution (the plasma), but others like oxygen are carried by special chemicals (respiratory pigments); these may be contained in specialized cells (red blood cells). Being distributed to all parts of the body, the blood is ideally situated to convey the body's defence and immune system (the white blood cells). The liquid nature of blood, so necessary for rapid transport around the body, suffers the disadvantage that it leaks away when damage is caused to the cavities or vessels containing it. Consequently a mechanism has evolved to ensure rapid clotting in these circumstances.

In plants their method of nutrition, necessitating as it does the need to capture light, means that they have an exceedingly large surface-area for this purpose. This same surface therefore serves

Giant redwoods (*Sequoiadendron giganteum*)

for the exchange of gases. As plants do not carry out locomotion their metabolic rate is relatively low compared to most animals and therefore diffusion suffices. In addition, all respiring tissues are near to the surface of the plant. Large trees, for example, possess dead xylem tissue at the centre of their trunks and large branches. Respiratory gases therefore need only be conveyed very short distances and there is no specialized system for their transport – diffusion suffices. The same is not true of water and photosynthetic products. These often need to be transported the total length of the plant, 100 m or more in some cases.

In an attempt to gain a competitive advantage in the struggle for light, many plants have evolved to be very tall. The water required for photosynthesis is, however, obtained from the root which are firmly anchored in the soil. A transport system is therefore necessary to convey water from the roots to the leaves. At the same time, the sugars manufactured in the leaves must b transported in the opposite direction to sustain their respiration.

Plants, unlike animals, do not possess contractile cells like muscles. They therefore depend largely upon passive rather tha active mechanisms for transporting materials. The evaporation of water from stomata creates an osmotic gradient across the lea which draws in water from the xylem. Xylem forms a continuous unimpeded column of narrow tubes from the roots to the leaves. Owing to its cohesive properties, removal of wate at the top of this column pulls up water from the bottom in a continuous stream. An osmotic gradient is responsible for the movement of water from the soil into the roots and across the cortex to the xylem. Only in the process of getting water into the xylem in the root is energy expended by the plant. The flow of sugars from the leaves to the roots is less clearly understood. Theories like 'mass flow' involve a passive movement; others, such as the 'transcellular strand theory', suggest an active mechanism.

## BIOLOGY AROUND US

# Adaptations to varying oxygen concentrations in fresh water

Water contains far less oxygen per unit volume than air and it is further reduced if the temperature increases, the concentration of dissolved salts increases or if the water is slow moving or contains high levels of decomposing material. Fresh water invertebrates show various adaptations to enable them to obtain as much of this dissolved oxygen as possible.

Presence of a respiratory pigment, e.g. *Tubifex*
- Lives in mud of stagnant water.
- Ventilation by waving posterior end out of mud.
- Haemoglobin saturated with oxygen at low oxygen levels.
- No Bohr effect.
- Respires glycogen anaerobically in absence of oxygen.

Direct exposure to air, e.g. great diving beetle (*Dytiscus*)
- Lives in ponds with plenty of weeds.
- Carries a store of air among hairs along abdomen, under wing covers.
- Air collected on visits to the surface and absorbed by spiracles when the beetle is submerged.

External gills, e.g. nymph of small mayfly (*Cloeon*)
- Has 7 pairs of oval, plate-like gills down the sides of the body.
- The anterior six pairs vibrate to bring fresh supplies of dissolved oxygen for absorption.
- The rate of vibration is faster when the oxygen supply is low.

# 20 Gaseous exchange

## 20.1 Respiratory surfaces

All aerobic organisms must obtain regular supplies of oxygen from their environment and return to it the waste gas carbon dioxide. The movement of these gases between the organism and its environment is called **gaseous exchange**. Gaseous exchange always occurs by **diffusion** over part or all of the body surface. This is called a **respiratory surface** and in order to maintain the maximum possible rate of diffusion respiratory surfaces have a number of characteristics.

1. **Large surface-area to volume ratio** – This may be the body surface in small organisms or infoldings of the surface such as lungs and gills in larger organisms.

2. **Permeable**

3. **Thin** – Diffusion is only efficient over distances up to 1 mm since the rate of diffusion is inversely proportional to the square of the distance between the concentrations on the two sides of the respiratory surface.

4. **Moist** – since oxygen and carbon dioxide diffuse in solution.

5. **Efficient transport system** – This is necessary to maintain a diffusion gradient and may involve a vascular system.

The relationship between some of these factors is expressed as **Fick's law** which states:

Diffusion is proportional to

$$\frac{\text{surface area} \times \text{difference in concentration}}{\text{thickness of membrane}}$$

Organisms can obtain their gases from the air or from water. The oxygen content of a given volume of water is lower than that of air (Table 20.1); therefore an aquatic organism must pass a greater volume of the medium over its respiratory surface in order to obtain enough oxygen.

TABLE 20.1  **Water and air as respiratory media**

| Property | Water | Air |
|---|---|---|
| Oxygen content | Less than 1% | 21% |
| Oxygen diffusion rate | Low | High |
| Density | Relative density of water about 1000 times greater than that of air at the same temperature | |
| Viscosity | Water much greater, about 1000 times that of air | |

## 20.2 Mechanisms of gaseous exchange

As animals increase in size most of their cells are some distance from the surface and cannot receive adequate oxygen by diffusion. Many larger animals also have an increased metabolic rate, which increases their oxygen demand. These organisms need specialized respiratory surfaces such as gills or lungs. These surfaces allow gases to enter and leave the body more rapidly. There remains the problem of transporting the gases between the respiring cells and the respiratory surface. Generally the gases are carried by the blood vascular system. The presence of respiratory pigments like haemoglobin increases the oxygen-carrying capacity of the blood (Section 21.2.1). Diffusion gradients may be further maintained by ventilation movements, e.g. breathing.

Gaseous exchange will be considered in detail for a number of different organisms. They will serve to demonstrate the differences between aquatic and terrestrial organisms and also show the problems associated with increased size.

### 20.2.1 Small organisms

Small organisms have a large surface-area to volume ratio and do not require specialized structures for gaseous exchange. Protozoans such as *Amoeba* are less than 1 mm in diameter and gases diffuse over their whole surface. Cnidarians, like the sea anemone *Actinia*, are hollow and have all their cells in contact with the water which surrounds them. Platyhelminthes (flatworms) also rely on diffusion over the whole body surface and this is facilitated by their flattened shape which considerably increases their surface-area to volume ratio. All these organisms must live in water from which they obtain dissolved oxygen; they would rapidly desiccate in a terrestrial environment.

### 20.2.2 Flowering plants

Plants have a low metabolic rate, requiring less energy per unit volume than animals. Unicellular algae employ the whole surface of the cell for gaseous exchange. In the larger flowering plants this is not possible because their outer surfaces are waterproof to prevent the desiccation which results from living on land. Gases pass through small pores in the leaves and green stems. These pores are the **stomata** whose structure is illustrated in Section 14.1 and the mechanisms of which are described in Chapter 22. Woody plants still have stomata in the leaves but the stems have small areas of loosely packed bark cells called **lenticels**. Gases diffuse through the stomata and lenticels. Within the plant, oxygen moves through the intercellular air spaces to the respiring cells. Carbon dioxide moves in the reverse direction. Both gases move by diffusion through the spaces and then through the moist cell walls into the respiring cells themselves. Cells which contain chloroplasts have a further source of oxygen because it is released as a waste product of photosynthesis and immediately taken up by the mitochondria. Similarly, the carbon dioxide released from the mitochondria can be used by the chloroplasts for photosynthesis. The rate of photosynthesis is affected by the intensity of light and so the carbon dioxide used and oxygen released by this process vary considerably during the day. The balance of respiratory and photosynthetic gases therefore changes. This is referred to in Section 14.4.2 and also in Fig. 14.12.

Elongated lenticels

Bark of silver birch showing lenticels

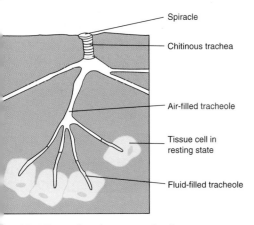

Spiracle

Chitinous trachea

Air-filled tracheole

Tissue cell in resting state

Fluid-filled tracheole

Fig. 20.1 Part of an insect tracheal system

## PROJECT

Measure the abdominal movements of locusts under varying concentrations of carbon dioxide.

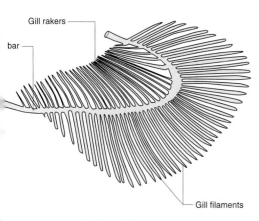

Gill rakers

bar

Gill filaments

Fig. 20.2  A single fish gill

### 20.2.3 Insects

For insects, diffusion of gases over the whole body surface is no longer possible. This is because they are predominantly a terrestrial group and therefore need to conserve water. This they do by having an exoskeleton and waterproof cuticle which are largely impermeable to gases. There is also a conflict between the requirement of a large surface-area for gaseous exchange and the need to conserve water. Gases enter and leave through pores called **spiracles**. Spiracles are usually found in pairs in ten of the body segments and are not just simple holes. Each spiracle is surrounded by hairs, which help to retain water vapour, and may be closed by a system of valves operated by tiny muscles. Respiring cells inside the insect release carbon dioxide and as this accumulates it is detected by chemoreceptors and the spiracles open.

The spiracles open into a complex series of tubes, the **tracheae** (Fig. 20.1) running throughout the body. These tracheae are supported by rings of chitin which prevent their collapse when the pressure inside them falls. The tracheae divide to form smaller **tracheoles** extending right into the tissues. Respiratory gases are carried in the **tracheal system** between the environment and the respiring cells; they are not transported by the blood. The tracheal system carries oxygen rapidly to the cells and allows the insects to develop high metabolic rates. The ends of the fine tracheoles are fluid-filled. At rest the tissue cells have a lower solute concentration than the fluid in the tracheoles. As activity increases the muscles respire anaerobically and lactic acid accumulates. This raises the solute concentration of these cells above that of the fluid in the tracheoles. Water therefore moves out of the tracheoles into the muscle cells by osmosis. As water is lost, air is drawn further into the tracheoles, making more oxygen available for cellular respiration. When activity ceases the metabolites are oxidized, the solute concentration of the muscle cells is lowered and the water re-enters the tracheoles. The system is ventilated by contraction of the abdominal muscles of the insect flattening the body. This reduces the volume of the tracheal system. The volume increases again as the elastic nature of the body returns the insect and tracheal system to their original shape. Larger insects, such as locusts, have some of the tracheae expanded to form air-sacs which act as bellows.

The tracheal system provides an extremely efficient means of gaseous exchange, but it does have its limitations. Since it relies entirely on diffusion for the gases to move from the environment to the respiring cells, insects are not able to attain a large size. In addition, the chitinous linings of the tracheae must be moulted with the rest of the exoskeleton.

### 20.2.4 Bony fish

Bony fish have four pairs of bony branchial arches supporting gill lamellae. These lamellae form a double row arranged in a V-shape and bear gill plates at right angles to their surface. There are no branchial valves but the gill slits are covered by a bony flap called an **operculum**. This helps to protect the delicate gills (Fig. 20.2) and also plays a part in their ventilation.

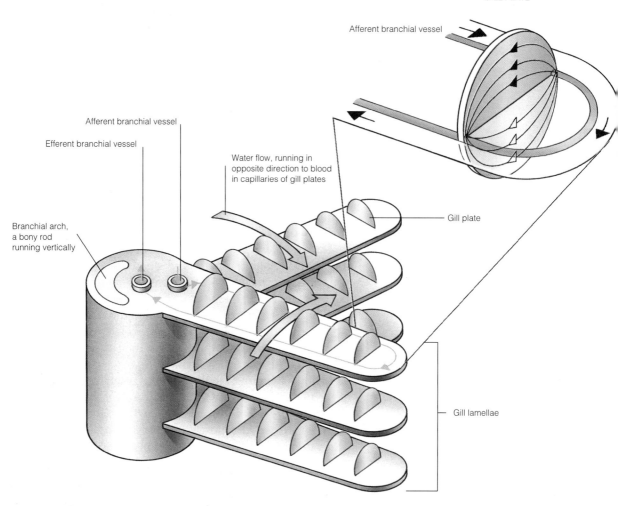

GILL PLATE

Afferent branchial vessel

Afferent branchial vessel

Efferent branchial vessel

Water flow, running in
opposite direction to blood
in capillaries of gill plates

Branchial arch,
a bony rod
running vertically

Gill plate

Gill lamellae

*Fig. 20.3 Water flow over gill lamellae in a bony fish*

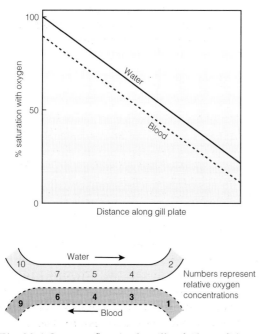

Numbers represent
relative oxygen
concentrations

*Fig. 20.4 Counter-flow in the gills of a bony fish*

Deoxygenated blood enters the gill capillaries via the afferent branchial vessels (Fig. 20.3). Oxygenated blood leaves in the efferent branchial artery to join the dorsal aorta along which blood passes to the rest of the body.

The gills of bony fish demonstrate extremely well the **counter current principle**. The essential feature of this is that the blood and water flow over the gill plates in opposite directions. This allows a fairly constant diffusion gradient to be maintained between the blood and the water, right across the gill. It ensures that blood which is already partly loaded with oxygen meets water which has had very little oxygen removed from it. Similarly blood with very low oxygen saturation meets water which has already had much of its oxygen removed. (See Fig. 20.4.)

This mechanism allows bony fish to achieve 80% absorption of oxygen, compared to about 50% in the parallel flow system of a dogfish. The overlapping ends of the gill lamellae also slow down the passage of the water so that there is a greater time for diffusion to occur. Alternation of a buccal pressure pump and an opercular suction pump allows water to be drawn over and between the gills more or less continuously. To take in water, the floor of the buccal cavity is lowered (Fig. 20.5); this increases its

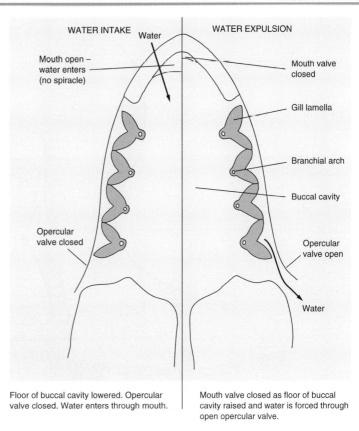

Fig. 20.5 Ventilation of gills in a bony fish

Trachea

Pulmonary artery

esin cast of pulmonary arteries (red) and trachea
nd bronchi (clear)

volume and the pressure within it decreases. Water enters through the mouth. At the same time the operculum is pressed close to the body and tiny opercular muscles increase the volume of the opercular cavity slightly. This causes some water to move out of the buccal cavity and into the opercular region, bathing the gills. Water is expelled by raising the floor of the buccal cavity. As pressure inside the buccal cavity increases, flaps of skin close the mouth and the water is forced over the gills and out of the body under the free edge of the operculum.

### 20.2.5 Mammals

**Lungs** are the site of gaseous exchange in mammals. They are found deep inside the thorax of the body and so their efficient ventilation is essential. The lungs are delicate structures and, together with the heart, are enclosed in a protective bony case, the **rib cage**. There are twelve pairs of ribs in humans, all attached dorsally to the thoracic vertebrae. The anterior ten pairs are attached ventrally to the sternum. The remaining ribs are said to be 'floating'. The ribs may be moved by a series of intercostal muscles. The thorax is separated from the abdomen by a muscular sheet, the **diaphragm**.

Air flow in mammals is **tidal**, air entering and leaving along the same route. It enters the nostrils and mouth and passes down the **trachea**. It enters the lungs via two **bronchi** which divide into smaller **bronchioles** and end in air-sacs called **alveoli**. These regions are illustrated in Fig. 20.6.

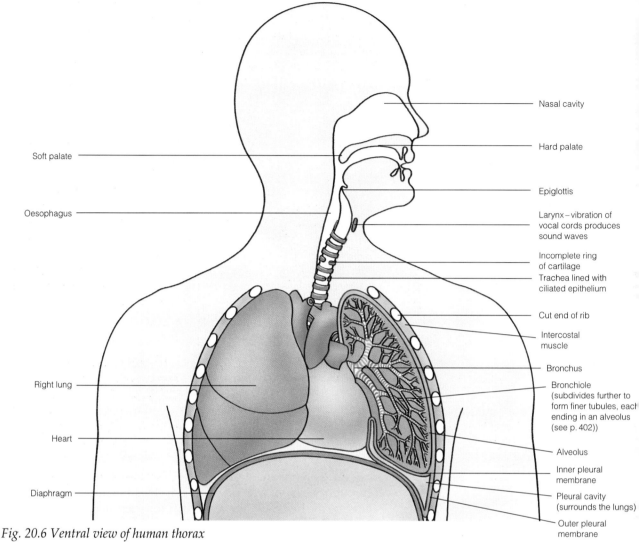

Fig. 20.6 Ventral view of human thorax

Labels (from top):
- Nasal cavity
- Hard palate
- Epiglottis
- Larynx – vibration of vocal cords produces sound waves
- Incomplete ring of cartilage
- Trachea lined with ciliated epithelium
- Cut end of rib
- Intercostal muscle
- Bronchus
- Bronchiole (subdivides further to form finer tubules, each ending in an alveolus (see p. 402))
- Alveolus
- Inner pleural membrane
- Pleural cavity (surrounds the lungs)
- Outer pleural membrane
- Soft palate
- Oesophagus
- Right lung
- Heart
- Diaphragm

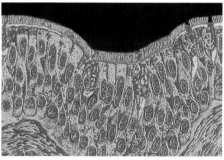

Trachea epithelium (×600)

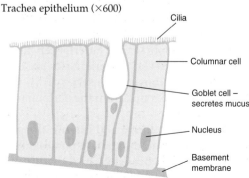

Labels:
- Cilia
- Columnar cell
- Goblet cell – secretes mucus
- Nucleus
- Basement membrane

Fig. 20.7 Ciliated epithelium (LS)

*Regions of the respiratory system*

Within the nasal channels mucus is secreted by goblet cells in the ciliated epithelium (Fig. 20.7). This mucus traps particles and the cilia move them to the back of the buccal cavity where they are swallowed. The mucus also serves to moisten the incoming air and it is warmed by superficial blood vessels. Within this region there are also olfactory cells which detect odours.

Air then passes through the pharynx and past the **epiglottis**, a flap of cartilage which prevents food entering the trachea. The **larynx**, or voice box, at the anterior end of the trachea is a box-like, cartilagenous structure with a number of ligaments, the **vocal cords**, stretched across it. Vibration of these cords when air is expired produces sound waves. The trachea is lined with ciliated epithelium and goblet cells. The mucus traps particles and the cilia move them to the back of the pharynx to be swallowed. The trachea is supported by incomplete rings of cartilage which prevent the tube collapsing when the pressure inside it falls.

The trachea divides into two **bronchi**, one entering each lung. The bronchi are also supported by cartilage. The **bronchioles** branch throughout the lung; as the tubes get finer cartilagenous support gradually ceases. These eventually end in alveoli. Each

ction of human trachea showing ciliated epithelium
3570 approx.)

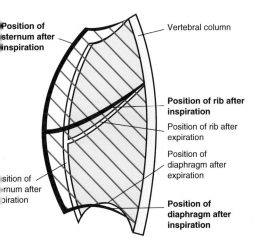

Position of
sternum after
inspiration

Vertebral column

Position of rib after
inspiration

Position of rib after
expiration

Position of
diaphragm after
expiration

sition of
rnum after
piration

Position of
diaphragm after
inspiration

g. 20.8 Relative positions of ribs, diaphragm
d sternum after breathing in and out

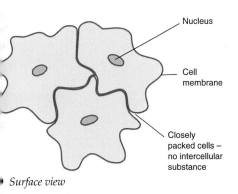

Nucleus

Cell
membrane

Closely
packed cells –
no intercellular
substance

Surface view

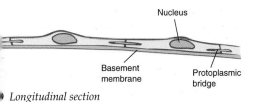

Nucleus

Basement
membrane

Protoplasmic
bridge

Longitudinal section

g. 20.9 Squamous epithelium

lung is surrounded by an air-tight cavity called the **pleural cavity**. This is bounded by two membranes, or **pleura**, which secrete **pleural fluid** into the cavity. The fluid is a lubricant, preventing friction when the lungs expand at inspiration. Pressure in the pleural cavity is always about 500 Pa lower than in the lungs and this allows them to expand and fill the thorax.

*Breathing in (inspiration) in humans*
In order for air to enter the lungs from the exterior, the pressure inside the lungs must be lower than that of the atmosphere. This lowering of pressure is brought about as follows.

When the external intercostal muscles contract and the internal intercostal muscles relax, the ribs move upwards and outwards (anteriorly and ventrally, see Fig. 20.8). The diaphragm muscle contracts and flattens. These two movements cause the volume of the thorax to increase and therefore the pressure inside it falls. The elastic lungs expand to fill the available space and so their volume increases and the pressure within them falls. This causes air to rush into the lungs from the exterior.

*Breathing out (expiration) in humans*
Breathing in is an active process but breathing out is largely passive. The volume of the thorax is decreased as the diaphragm muscle relaxes and resumes its dome-shape (Fig. 20.8). The external intercostal muscles also relax, allowing the ribs to move downwards (posteriorly) and inwards (dorsally). They may be assisted by contraction of the internal intercostal muscles. As the volume of the thorax decreases, the pressure inside it increases and air is forced out of the lungs as their elastic walls recoil.

*Exchange at the alveoli*
Each minute alveolus (diameter 100 $\mu$m) comprises **squamous epithelium** and some elastic and collagen fibres. Squamous epithelial cells form a single layer attached to a basement membrane. In surface view the cell outlines are irregular and closely packed (Fig. 20.9). The cells are shallow, the central nucleus often forming a bump in the surface. Adjacent cells may be joined by strands of cytoplasm. Such epithelia form ideal surfaces over which diffusion can occur and so are important not only in the alveoli of the lungs, but also in the Bowman's capsule and in capillary walls. Each alveolus is surrounded by a network of blood capillaries (Fig. 20.10) which come from the pulmonary artery and unite to form the pulmonary vein. These capillaries are extremely narrow and the red corpuscles (erythrocytes) are squeezed as they pass through. This not only slows down the passage of the blood, allowing more time for diffusion, but also results in a larger surface-area of the red blood cell touching the endothelium and thus facilitates the diffusion of oxygen. The oxygen in the inspired air dissolves in the moisture of the alveolar epithelium and diffuses across this and the endothelium of the capillary into the erythrocyte. Inside the red blood cell, the oxygen combines with the respiratory pigment **haemoglobin** to form **oxyhaemoglobin** (Section 21.2.1). Carbon dioxide diffuses from the blood into the alveolus to leave the lungs in the expired air.

## Did you know?

The 700 million alveoli in both human lungs cover an area of 90 m$^2$ – almost the size of a tennis court.

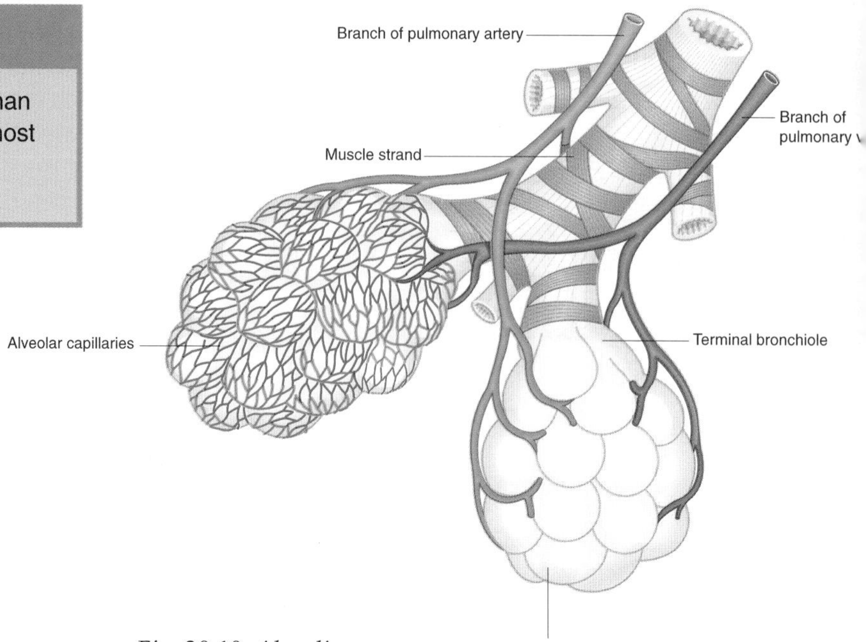

Branch of pulmonary artery
Branch of pulmonary v
Muscle strand
Alveolar capillaries
Terminal bronchiole
Alveolus


*Fig. 20.10 Alveoli*

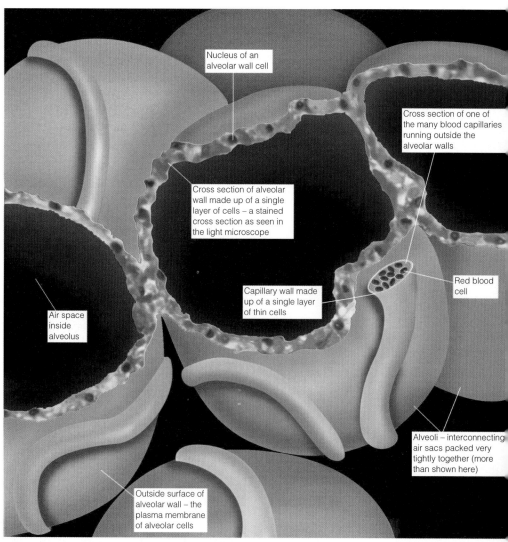

Nucleus of an alveolar wall cell
Cross section of one of the many blood capillaries running outside the alveolar walls
Cross section of alveolar wall made up of a single layer of cells – a stained cross section as seen in the light microscope
Red blood cell
Capillary wall made up of a single layer of thin cells
Air space inside alveolus
Alveoli – interconnecting air sacs packed very tightly together (more than shown here)
Outside surface of alveolar wall – the plasma membrane of alveolar cells


*Fig. 20.11 External appearance of a group of alveoli*

Magnification ×300 (approx

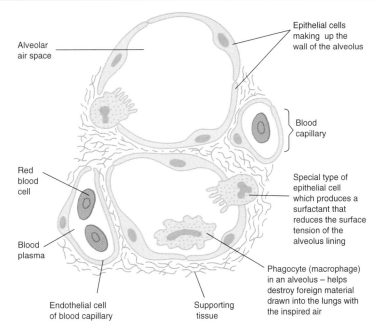

*Fig. 20.12 Arrangement of cells and tissues in mammalian lung alveoli*

## 20.3 Control of ventilation in humans

Ventilation of the respiratory system in humans is primarily controlled by the **breathing centre** in a region of the hindbrain called the medulla oblongata. The ventral portion of this centre controls inspiratory movements and is called the **inspiratory centre**; the remainder controls breathing out and is called the **expiratory centre**. Control also relies on **chemoreceptors** in the **carotid and aortic bodies** of the blood system. These are sensitive to minute changes in the concentration of carbon dioxide in the blood. When the carbon dioxide level rises, increased ventilation of the respiratory surfaces is required. Nerve impulses from the chemoreceptors stimulate the inspiratory centre in the medulla. Nerve impulses pass along the phrenic and thoracic nerves to the diaphragm and intercostal muscles. Their increased rate of contraction causes faster inspiration. As the lungs expand, **stretch receptors** in their walls are stimulated and impulses pass along the vagus nerve to the expiratory centre in the medulla. This automatically 'switches off' the inspiratory centre, the muscles relax and expiration takes place. The stretch receptors are no longer stimulated, the expiratory centre is 'switched off' and the inspiratory centre 'switched on'. Inspiration takes place again. This complex example of a feedback mechanism is illustrated in Fig. 20.13 and further examples of homeostatic control are considered in Chapter 25.

The breathing centre may also be stimulated by impulses from the forebrain resulting in a conscious increase or decrease in breathing rate.

The main stimulus for ventilation is therefore the change in carbon dioxide concentration and stimulation of stretch receptors in the lungs; changes in oxygen concentration have relatively little effect. At high altitudes the reduced atmospheric

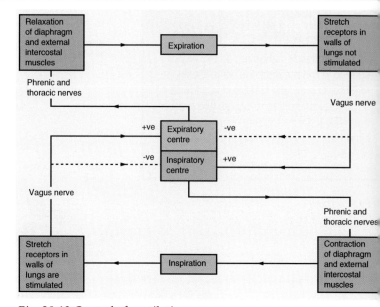

Fig. 20.13 Control of ventilation

pressure makes it more difficult to load the haemoglobin with oxygen. In an attempt to obtain sufficient oxygen a mountaineer takes very deep breaths. This forces more carbon dioxide out of the body and the level of carbon dioxide in the blood therefore falls. The inspiratory centre is no longer stimulated and breathing becomes increasingly laboured, causing great fatigue. Given time, humans can adapt to these conditions by excreting more alkaline urine. This causes the pH of the blood to fall, the chemoreceptors are stimulated and so is the inspiratory centre.

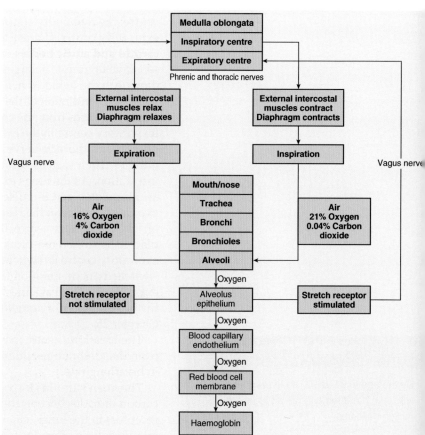

Fig. 20.14 Summary of ventilation

# BIOLOGY AROUND US

## Emphysema

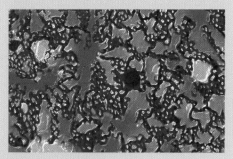

Normal healthy lung tissue

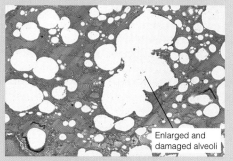

Enlarged and
damaged alveoli

Lung tissue damaged by emphysema

One in every five smokers will develop the crippling lung disease called emphysema which, together with other related obstructive lung disorders, kills 20 000 people a year in Britain alone. The disease develops over a period of 20 or so years and it is impossible to diagnose until the lungs have been irreversibly damaged. In its early stages the only symptom is a slight breathlessness but as this gets progressively worse many people are so disabled that they cannot even get out of bed. People with emphysema usually die of respiratory failure, often accompanied by infection. A small number die of heart failure as the heart becomes enlarged and overworked trying to pump blood through arteries which have become constricted as a result of lack of oxygen.

Healthy lungs contain large quantities of elastic connective tissue comprising predominantly the protein elastin. This tissue expands when we breathe in and returns to its former size when we breathe out. In emphysematous lungs the elastin has become permanently stretched and the lungs are no longer able to force out all the air from the alveoli. Little if any exchange of gases can take place across the stretched and damaged air sacs.

The damage is brought about by abnormally high levels of elastase, an enzyme formed in some of the white blood cells, which breaks down elastin. Elastase also degrades other proteins so that, in the latter stages of the disease, breakdown of lung tissue results in large, non-functional holes in the lung.

In healthy lungs elastin is not broken down because a protein inhibitor (PI) inhibits the action of the enzyme elastase. However, in smokers it has been suggested that the oxidants in cigarette smoke inactivate PI, resulting in greater elastase activity and hence a breakdown of elastin.

Elastase is produced by phagocytes which need it so they can migrate through tissue to reach sites of infection. This is part of the body's normal inflammatory response. In smokers, where a large number of phagocytic cells are attracted to the lungs by the particulate materials in smoke, a combination of the release of elastase and a low level of its natural inhibitor leads to a lot of tissue degradation.

Smoking obviously causes much of the damage associated with emphysema but why is it that not all smokers suffer to the same extent? It is possible that the one in five who develop emphysema do so because they have defective repair mechanisms and are unable to counteract the considerable cell damage which occurs during the development of the disease. This may be the result of a genetic defect which limits cell division or production of abnormal connective tissue proteins during smoke-induced stress.

Emphysema cannot be cured and the disease cannot be reversed. The only way to minimize the chance of getting it is not to smoke at all, or to give up – the function cannot be restored to smoke-damaged lungs but giving up can significantly reduce the rate of further deterioration.

# Asthma

Asthma is the name given to a group of long-lasting (chronic) disorders which are characterized by some restriction of the airways of the lungs due to muscular spasms, inflammation, excess mucus production, or a combination of all three. As a result breathing becomes difficult. Across the world asthma affects around 10% of people. It has increased dramatically in Britain over the past decade where it now accounts for around 2000 deaths each year and is the most frequent cause of children being away sick from school. Many factors may trigger an asthma attack, including anxiety, stress, infection, cold-air, exercise and specific substances to which an individual is allergic.

Why some individuals are allergic to certain substances while others are not is not clearly understood but there may be a genetic predisposition to an allergic response, or the condition may be acquired during early childhood or even when still in the womb. Dietary or environmental factors commonly trigger an attack in a vulnerable individual, with certain foods (e.g. milk or eggs), pollen grains, fungal spores and animal hair commonly provoking an attack. One of the most common **allergens** (particles which trigger an attack) are proteases found in the faeces of the house dust mite. Air pollution can make the situation worse; sulphur dioxide and soot particles with a diameter of 10 $\mu$m or less have all been shown to provoke an attack. Passive cigarette smoking is also closely linked to the development of asthma and the children of mothers who smoke during pregnancy display a higher than average incidence of the disorder.

Whatever the cause, the reaction to an allergen has two parts: **Sensitization** arises first, as a result of the substance being engulfed by phagocytic blood cells which then produce antibodies to the allergen. These antibodies circulate in the blood before becoming attached to a type of white blood cell called **mast cells**. The patient suffers no symptoms at this stage. **Activation** occurs when the individual is re-exposed to the same allergen, which now binds to the antibodies on the mast cells, causing the release of a range of chemicals. Some of these chemicals cause spasms of the smooth muscle in the bronchial passages, causing them to constrict, while others, e.g. histamines, lead to inflammation of the lungs. Together these restrict the air-flow to the alveoli and cause the asthma attack.

As would be expected with a complex disorder such as asthma, the treatment is varied, and can include any combination of the following drugs:

1. Agents which block the synthesis or release of the chemicals which cause inflammation.
2. Antihistamines to counteract histamines – chemicals which cause inflammation.
3. Agents which block inflammatory molecules other than histamines.
4. Agents which prevent cells accumulating at inflammatory sites by blocking the formation of the chemicals which attract the cells.
5. Medicines which block the actions of Platelet Activating Factor (PAF), a chemical which leads to congestion in the small blood vessels of the lung.
6. Agents which act as broncho-dilators and so open up the constricted airways of the lung.

# 20.4 Measurements of lung capacity

**TABLE 20.2 Comparison of inspired, alveolar and expired air**

| Gas | % Composition by volume | | |
|---|---|---|---|
| | Inspired air | Alveolar air | Expired air |
| Oxygen | 20.95 | 13.8 | 16.4 |
| Carbon dioxide | 0.04 | 5.5 | 4.0 |
| Nitrogen | 79.01 | 80.7 | 79.6 |

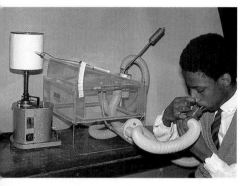

Spirometer attached to a kymograph

Human lungs have a volume of about $5\,dm^3$ but in a normal breath only about $0.45\,dm^3$ of this will be exchanged (**tidal volume**). During forced breathing the total exchanged may rise to $3.5\,dm^3$ (**vital capacity**) which leaves a **residual volume** of about $1.5\,dm^3$. These terms, and others associated with lung capacity, are illustrated in Fig. 20.15.

Air that reaches the lungs on inspiration mixes with the residual air so that it does not 'stagnate' but is gradually changed. This mixing of relatively small volumes of fresh air with a much larger volume of residual air keeps the level of gases in the alveoli more or less constant.

Measurements of respiratory activity may be made using a spirometer attached to a kymograph which records all its movements.

The ventilation rate is calculated as the number of breaths per minute × tidal volume.

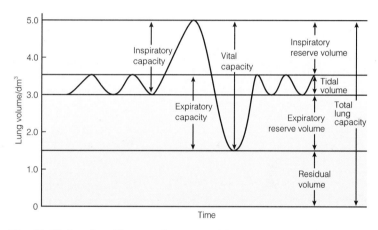

*Fig. 20.15 Graph to illustrate lung capacities*

# 20.5 Effects of exercise on breathing and gaseous exchange

Exercise entails muscular movement and hence the need for an adequate supply of oxygen to release the energy required for the contraction of muscle fibres. To increase the oxygen supply, the rate of gas exchange at the lungs must be increased. This is achieved firstly by increasing the number of breaths per minute from an average of 15 at rest to 45 at the peak of strenuous exercise. Secondly the amount of air exchanged at each breath is increased from $0.45\,dm^3$ at rest to a maximum of $3.5\,dm^3$ during exercise. These changes help to increase the oxygen consumption of the body to around $4\,dm^3\,min^{-1}$ from the normal resting value of $0.3\,dm^3\,min^{-1}$. This is a 13-fold increase, although values of up to 20 times are possible in well-trained athletes. This is partly because, with fitness training, the normally passive (and

## BIOLOGY AROUND US

# Smoking

Tobacco is responsible for 15–20% of all deaths in Britain, amounting to about 100 000 people every year. The three main diseases closely linked with smoking are:

*Coronary heart disease*
Smoking increases the likelihood of fatty deposits arising on the inner lining of the arteries (atherosclerosis), which cause the lumen to narrow, so restricting the movement of blood through them. Where this narrowing occurs in the coronary artery it can lead to a heart attack; narrowing in the carotid artery may result in a stroke.

*Lung cancer*
Cancer is described on pages 146–147. There is more than one type of lung cancer but bronchial carcinoma is by far the most common. The tars in tobacco smoke may induce the epithelial cells lining the bronchial tubes to become cancerous. If not treated, the tumour may completely disrupt the functioning of the lung, leaving surgical removal as the only effective treatment. A highly persistent cough, blood in the sputum and chest pains are all symptoms of lung cancer.

*Chronic bronchitis*
The tars in tobacco irritate the epithelial lining of the bronchial tubes causing it to produce excess mucus. The cilia lining the tubes become damaged and unable to remove this mucus in the usual manner. Only by coughing can the mucus be expelled and in time this leads to scarring and narrowing of the bronchial tubes, causing breathlessness.

Other smoking-related conditions include:
- emphysema (see page 405)
- cancer of the mouth, throat, bladder and pancreas
- other cardiovascular diseases
- peptic ulcers
- narrowing of blood vessels in limbs
- damage to the unborn child

Tobacco smoke is a mixture of chemicals, a number of which interact with each other, multiplying their effects. The three constituents which do most harm are nicotine, carbon monoxide and tars.

Nicotine:
- is quickly absorbed into the blood, reaching the brain in 30 seconds
- causes the platelets to become sticky, leading to clotting
- stimulates production of adrenaline, leading to increased heart rate and raised blood pressure, which puts an extra strain on the heart.

Carbon monoxide:
- combines with haemoglobin to form carboxyhaemoglobin, therefore lowering the oxygen-carrying capacity of the blood
- may aggravate angina
- seems to slow growth of the fetus.

Tars:
- form an aerosol of minute droplets which enter the respiratory system causing thickening of the epithelium and leading to chronic bronchitis
- paralyse cilia so dust, germs and mucus accumulate in the lungs, leading to infection and damage
- contain carcinogens – heavy smokers have a 25% greater risk of cancer than non-smokers.

therefore relatively slow) process of expiration is accelerated because both the internal intercostal and abdominal muscles contract forcefully to pull the ribs inwards and the diaphragm upwards. This results in a much more rapid expulsion of air than occurs in an unfit individual, thus allowing more breaths to be taken in a given period of time. Dilation of the bronchioles helps to increase the flow of air down to the alveoli.

Getting more air into the lungs more rapidly would be pointless unless the rate at which oxygen is absorbed from the lungs into the blood is also increased. This is largely achieved by the hormone adrenaline acting on the smooth muscle of the arterioles which supply blood to the capillary network around the alveoli. Dilation of these arterioles improves the blood flow to the  lungs and increases the uptake of oxygen into the blood three-fold. The way in which the circulatory system increases the rate of delivery of oxygenated blood to the muscles during exercise is dealt with in Section 21.5.5.

# 20.6 Questions

**1.** The drawing shows structures in the breathing system of an insect.

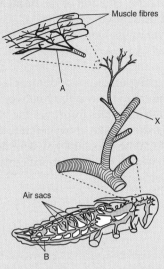

Muscle fibres

A

X

Air sacs

B

(a) Name the structures labelled **A** and **B**.
(2 marks)

(b) Describe the mechanism by which the respiratory surfaces of an insect are ventilated. (2 marks)

(c) Structure **X** has bands of thickening. Suggest the function of these. (1 mark)

(d) Give **two** features which the respiratory surfaces of an insect and a mammal have in common. (2 marks)
(Total 7 marks)

NEAB March 1998, Paper BY03, No. 1

**2.** Fig. 1 shows the position of the human rib-cage, external intercostal muscles and diaphragm at the end of expiration.

(a) (i) State **one** chordate feature shown in Fig. 1. (1 mark)

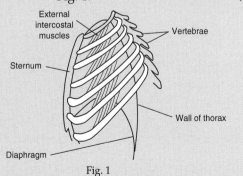

External intercostal muscles

Vertebrae

Sternum

Wall of thorax

Diaphragm

Fig. 1

(ii) State **one** chordate feature associated with gas exchange, which is present in the embryo but absent from adult humans. (1 mark)

Fig. 2 shows the position of the rib-cage at the end of inspiration.

(b) Draw lines to show the position of the external intercostal muscles and the diaphragm at the end of inspiration. (2 marks)

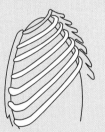

Fig. 2

Mountaineers often experience problems with gaseous exchange when they climb to high altitudes, due to the low pressure, low temperature and low humidity of the air.

(c) Outline how the diameter of the trachea is maintained at low pressures.
(1 mark)

Air is inhaled through the trachea, bronchi and bronchioles. As it passes along these tubes it is warmed and humidified, unless it is already at body temperature and saturated with water vapour. Fig. 3 shows the partial pressures of oxygen, water vapour and other gases entering the lungs at sea level and 8000 m above sea level.

(d) With reference to Fig. 3, comment on the differences in the air entering the lungs at sea level with that at 8000 m above sea level.
(3 marks)

(e) Predict, with a reason in each case, the difference between

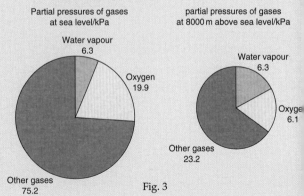

Partial pressures of gases at sea level/kPa

Water vapour 6.3

Oxygen 19.9

Other gases 75.2

partial pressures of gases at 8000 m above sea level/kPa

Water vapour 6.3

Oxygen 6.1

Other gases 23.2

Fig. 3

(i) oxygen absorption by the lungs at sea level and at 8000 m above sea level;
(2 marks)

(ii) blood carbon dioxide concentrations at sea level and at 8000 m above sea level.
(2 marks)

(f) Suggest **three** ways in which the gaseous exchange system could contribute to problems of dehydration and hypothermia (low body temperature) in mountaineers.

(3 marks)

(Total 15 marks)

*UCLES June 1998, Paper 1, No. 2*

(a) (i) Give **one** similarity between the way in which oxygen from the atmosphere reaches a muscle in an insect and the way it reaches a mesophyll cell in a leaf. (1 mark)

(ii) Give **one** difference in the way in which carbon dioxide is removed from a muscle in an insect and the way in which it is removed from a muscle in a fish. (1 mark)

The diagram shows the way in which water flows over the gills of a fish. The graph shows the changes in pressure in the buccal cavity and in the opercular cavity during a ventilation cycle.

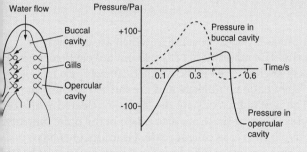

(b) Use the graph to calculate the rate of ventilation in cycles per minute. (1 mark)

(c) For most of this ventilation cycle, water will be flowing in one direction over the gills. Explain the evidence from the graph that supports this. (2 marks)

(d) Explain how the fish increases pressure in the buccal cavity. (2 marks)

(Total 7 marks)

*NEAB June 1997, Paper BY03, No. 4*

(a) The figure at the top of the next column shows part of the human airway system.

(i) Name the parts labelled **A**, **B** and **C**. (3 marks)

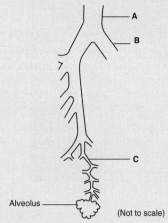

(ii) Give a distinctive feature of each of the parts labelled **A**, **B** and **C**. (3 marks)

(b) The table shows the effect of different types of breathing on ventilation.

(i) Suggest what is meant by the term **dead space volume**. (1 mark)

(ii) **Pulmonary ventilation = Tidal volume × Respiratory rate**

Using the data in the table, derive a similar word equation to show how the rate of alveolar ventilation has been calculated. (1 mark)

(iii) Explain why alveolar ventilation decreases with shallow rapid breathing. (1 mark)

(iv) What will happen to a person who continues to ventilate by shallow, rapid breathing? (2 marks)

(c) Three types of cells are found in the alveolus. Type 1 cells are thin and flat. Type 2 cells are secretory and first activated in the fetus, late in pregnancy. Finally, the alveoli also contain some white blood cells called macrophages.

(i) Using the information above and your own knowledge, explain the roles of the three cell types in the alveolus. (6 marks)

(ii) Sometimes babies born prematurely display breathing difficulties, a condition known as Respiratory Distress Syndrome (RDS). Without treatment they may become exhausted and die. Suggest the cause of this condition and explain why they become exhausted. (2 marks)

(Total 19 marks)

*Oxford & Cambridge January 1997, Unit B4, No. 1*

| Breathing type (all at rest) | Tidal volume /cm³ breath⁻¹ | Respiratory rate /breaths min⁻¹ | Dead space volume/cm³ | Pulmonary ventilation /cm³ min⁻¹ | Alveolar ventilation /cm³ min⁻¹ |
|---|---|---|---|---|---|
| Quiet | 500 | 12 | 150 | 6 000 | 4 200 |
| Deep, slow | 1 200 | 5 | 150 | 6 000 | 5 250 |
| Shallow, rapid | 150 | 40 | 150 | 6 000 | 0 |

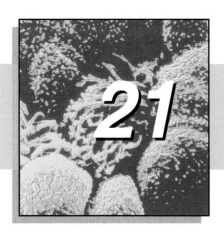

# 21 Blood and circulation (transport in animals)

As all cells are bathed in an aqueous medium, the delivery of materials to and from these cells is carried out largely in solution. The fluid in which the materials are dissolved or suspended is blood. The cellular components of mammalian blood are described in Section 21.1. While a number of ideas on blood were put forward by Greek and Roman scientists, it was the English physician William Harvey (1578–1657) who first showed that it was pumped into arteries by the heart, circulated around the body and returned via veins.

## 21.1 Structure of blood

Blood comprises a watery **plasma** in which are a variety of different cells. The majority of cells present are **erythrocytes** or red blood cells which are biconcave discs about 7 $\mu$m in diameter. They have no nucleus and are formed in the bone marrow. The remaining cells are the larger, nucleated white cells or **leucocytes**. Most of these are also made in the bone marrow. There are two basic types of leucocyte. **Granulocytes** have granular cytoplasm and a lobed nucleus; they can engulf bacteria by phagocytosis. Some of them are also thought to have antihistamine properties. **Agranulocytes** have a non-granular cytoplasm and a compact nucleus. Some of these also ingest bacteria but the **lymphocytes**, made mainly in the thymus gland and lymphoid tissues, produce **antibodies**. More sparsely distributed in the plasma are tiny cell fragments called **platelets**. These are important in the process of blood clotting.

Red blood cells

Plasma

White blood cell

Blood

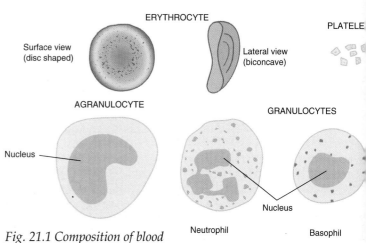

*Fig. 21.1 Composition of blood*

*Formation of blood*

In the fetus red blood cells are formed in the liver, but in adults production moves to bones, such as the cranium, sternum, vertebrae and ribs, which have red bone marrow. White cells like lymphocytes are formed in the thymus gland and lymph nodes whereas other types are formed in bones, e.g. the long bones of the limbs, which have white bone marrow.

# 21.2 Functions of blood

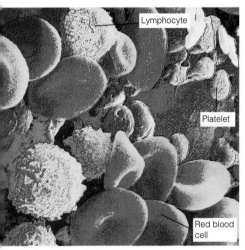

Lymphocyte

Platelet

Red blood cell

lse-colour SEM of human blood cells

Blood performs two distinct functions: the transport of materials (summarized in Table 21.1) and defence against disease.

### 21.2.1 Respiratory pigment – haemoglobin

The solubility of oxygen is low, with only $0.58\,cm^3$ dissolving in $100\,cm^3$ of water at $25\,°C$. At human body temperature ($37\,°C$) the quantity is even less, just $0.46\,cm^3$, because the solubility decreases as the temperature increases. Vertebrates, and many invertebrates, have evolved a group of coloured proteins capable of loosely combining with oxygen, in order to increase the oxygen-carrying capacity of the blood. These are known as **respiratory pigments**. With a few exceptions, the pigments with large relative molecular mass (RMM) are found in the plasma while those of smaller RMM occur within cells to prevent them being lost by ultrafiltration in the kidneys.

The important property of respiratory pigments is their ability to combine readily with oxygen where its concentration is high, i.e. at the respiratory surface, and to release it as readily where its concentration is low, i.e. in the tissues.

BLE 21.1   **Summary of the transport functions of blood**

| Materials transported | Examples | Transported from | Transported to | Transported in |
|---|---|---|---|---|
| Respiratory gases | Oxygen | Lungs | Respiring tissues | Haemoglobin in red blood cells |
| | Carbon dioxide | Respiring tissues | Lungs | Haemoglobin in red blood cells. Hydrogen carbonate ions in plasma |
| Organic digestive products | Glucose | Intestines | Respiring tissues/liver | Plasma |
| | Amino acids | Intestines | Liver/body tissues | Plasma |
| | Vitamins | Intestines | Liver/body tissues | Plasma |
| Mineral salts | Calcium | Intestines | Bones/teeth | Plasma |
| | Iodine | Intestines | Thyroid gland | Plasma |
| | Iron | Intestines/liver | Bone marrow | Plasma |
| Excretory products | Urea | Liver | Kidney | Plasma |
| Hormones | Insulin | Pancreas | Liver | Plasma |
| | Anti-diuretic hormone | Pituitary gland | Kidney | Plasma |
| Heat | Metabolic heat | Liver and muscle | All parts of the body | All parts of the blood |

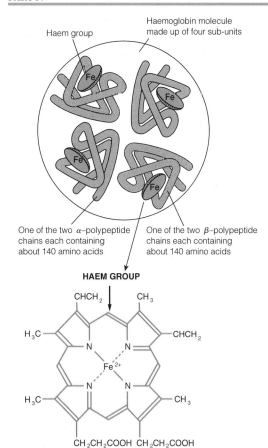

Fig. 21.2 The structure of haemoglobin

The best known and most efficient respiratory pigment is **haemoglobin**. It occurs in most animal phyla, protozoans and even a few plants. The haemoglobin molecule is made up of an iron porphyrin compound – the **haem** group – and a protein – **globin**. The haem group contains a ferrous iron atom, which is capable of carrying a single oxygen molecule. Different haemoglobins have a different number of haem groups and so vary in their ability to carry oxygen. A single molecule of human haemoglobin, for example, has a RMM of 68 000 and possesses four haem groups. Therefore it is capable of carrying four molecules of oxygen. The arrangement of the haemoglobin molecule is given in Fig. 21.2.

### 21.2.2 Transport of oxygen

An efficient respiratory pigment readily picks up oxygen at the respiratory surface and releases it on arrival at tissues. This may appear contradictory as a substance with a high affinity for oxygen is unlikely to release it easily. Respiratory pigments overcome the problem by having a high affinity for oxygen when its concentration is high, but this is reduced when the oxygen concentration is low. Oxygen concentration is measured by partial pressure, otherwise called the **oxygen tension**. Normal atmospheric pressure is approximately 100 kiloPascals. As oxygen makes up around 21% of the atmosphere, the oxygen tension (partial pressure) of the atmosphere is around 21 kPa.

When a respiratory pigment such as haemoglobin is exposed to a gradual increase in oxygen tension it absorbs oxygen easily at first, but less readily as the tension continues to rise. This relationship between the oxygen tension and the saturation of haemoglobin is called the **oxygen dissociation curve** and is illustrated in Fig. 21.3.

### Did you know?

Ice fish which live in the Antarctic are the only vertebrates on earth to completely lack haemoglobin. They survive because at low water temperatures oxygen is much more soluble and their metabolic rate, and hence their oxygen demand, is very low.

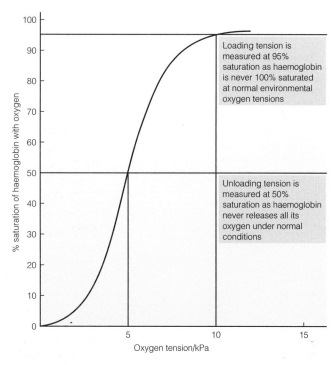

Fig. 21.3 Oxygen dissociation curve for adult human haemoglobin

The different haemoglobins found in animals vary in their affinity for oxygen. The oxygen dissociation curves for a number of animals are given in Figs. 21.4 and 21.5. Before attempting to explain the significance of these differences, it should be noted that:

**1.** The more the dissociation curve of a particular pigment is displaced to the right, the less readily it picks up oxygen, but the more easily it releases it.

**2.** The more the dissociation curve of a particular pigment is displaced to the left, the more readily it picks up oxygen, but the less readily it releases it.

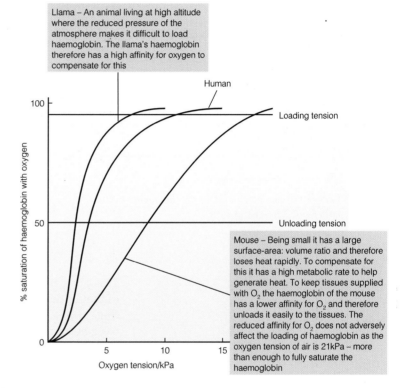

*Fig. 21.4 Oxygen dissociation curves for the haemoglobin of three mammals*

The release of oxygen from haemoglobin is facilitated by the presence of carbon dioxide – a phenomenon known as the **Bohr effect**. Where carbon dioxide concentration is high, i.e. in respiring tissues, oxygen is released readily; where carbon dioxide concentration is low, i.e. at the respiratory surface, oxygen is taken up readily. These effects are shown in Fig. 21.6.

The Bohr effect is not shown by the haemoglobin of animals like *Arenicola* which live in environments with low oxygen tensions. As the habitat of these animals frequently has a high level of carbon dioxide, the Bohr effect would cause the dissociation curve to shift to the right, reducing the haemoglobin's affinity for oxygen. As the environment contains little oxygen, this reduced affinity for it would prevent them taking it up in sufficient quantities for their survival.

Not only do respiratory pigments vary between species, there are often different types in the same species. In humans, for example, the fetus has a haemoglobin which differs in two of the four polypeptide chains from the haemoglobin of an adult.

415

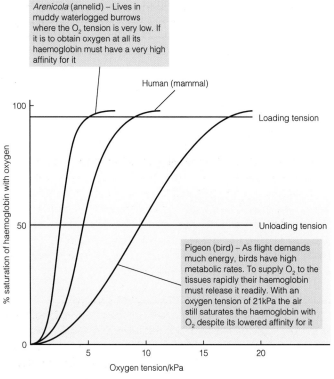

Fig. 21.5 Oxygen dissociation curves for the haemoglobin of three animals from different groups

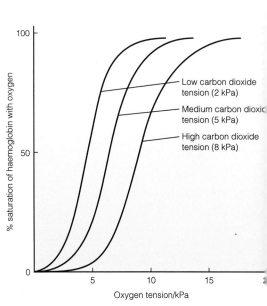

Fig. 21.6 Oxygen dissociation curve of human haemoglobin, illustrating the Bohr effect

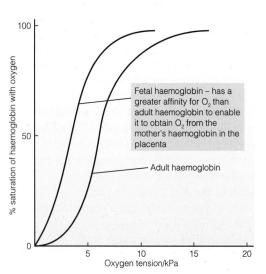

Fig. 21.7 Comparison of the oxygen dissociation curves of adult and fetal haemoglobin

This gives the fetal haemoglobin a dissociation curve to the left of that of the adult and therefore a greater affinity for oxygen (Fig. 21.7). Only in this way can the fetal haemoglobin absorb oxygen from the maternal haemoglobin in the placenta. At birth the production of fetal haemoglobin gives way to that of the adult type.

Another respiratory pigment in vertebrates is **myoglobin**. It consists of a single polypeptide chain and a single haem group, rather than the four found in haemoglobin. Like fetal haemoglobin, myoglobin has a greater affinity for oxygen than adult haemoglobin, and the dissociation curve is therefore displaced to the left (Fig. 21.8). Myoglobin occurs in the muscles of all vertebrates, where it acts as a store of oxygen. In periods of extreme exertion, when the supply of oxygen by the blood is insufficient to keep pace with demand, the oxygen tension of muscle falls to a very low level. At these very low oxygen tensions, myoglobin releases its oxygen to keep the muscles working efficiently. Once exercise has ceased the myoglobin store is replenished from the haemoglobin in the blood. Being red, myoglobin is largely responsible for the red colour of meat. The breast meat of much poultry is white as it is made up of the muscles which operate the wings. As most poultry is non-flying these muscles are relatively inactive and so have no need of an oxygen-storing pigment like myoglobin. By contrast, the breast meat of flighted birds is very dark.

Haemoglobin has a greater affinity for carbon monoxide than it does for oxygen. When carbon monoxide is inhaled, even in small quantities, it combines with haemoglobin in preference to

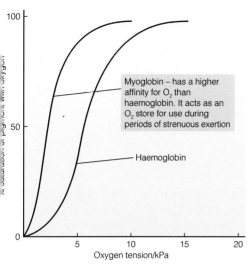

Fig. 21.8 Comparison of the oxygen dissociation curves of human haemoglobin and myoglobin

oxygen to form a stable compound, **carboxyhaemoglobin**. The carbon monoxide is not released at normal atmospheric oxygen tensions and the haemoglobin is therefore permanently prevented from transporting oxygen. Obviously, if sufficient carbon monoxide is inhaled, vital tissues become deprived of oxygen, resulting in death from **asphyxia**.

### 21.2 3 Living at high altitude

The amount of oxygen in the atmosphere is the same at high altitudes as it is at sea level, namely 21%. The respiratory problems associated with living at high altitude are a result of the reduced atmospheric pressure. The reduced pressure means that it is more difficult to load haemoglobin with oxygen. Above about 6000 m the pressure is inadequate to load haemoglobin effectively. Some human settlements exist at these altitudes and the inhabitants have become **acclimatized**. Acclimatization involves:

1. **Adjustment of blood pH** – The reduced loading of haemoglobin leads to deeper breathing – **hyperventilation** – in an attempt to compensate for lack of oxygen in the blood. This leads to excessive removal of carbon dioxide and a raised blood pH. Nervous responses are triggered, causing reduced depth of breathing - undesirable in the circumstances. In acclimatized individuals the hydrogen carbonate ions are removed by the kidney, restoring blood pH to normal.

2. **Increased oxygen uptake** – More oxygen is absorbed by the lungs as a result of an improved capillary network in the lungs, and deeper breathing.

3. **Improved transport of oxygen to the tissues** – This is the result of:
   (a) **increased red blood cell concentration** – this may rise from 45% to 60% of the total blood volume;
   (b) **increased haemoglobin concentration in red blood cells** – this may rise by 20%.

4. **Changes in haemoglobin affinity for oxygen** – The oxygen dissociation curve is shifted to the right to facilitate release of oxygen to the tissues. Above 3500 m this advantage is offset by the reduced affinity of haemoglobin for oxygen in the lungs and so is not shown by those living at these altitudes, where a shift to the left favours survival.

5. **Increased myoglobin levels in muscles** – With its higher affinity for oxygen this facilitates the exchange of oxygen from the blood to the tissues.

### 21.2.4 Transport of carbon dioxide

Carbon dioxide is more soluble than oxygen in water, but its transport in solution is still inadequate to meet the needs of most organisms. There are three methods of carrying carbon dioxide from the tissues to the respiratory surface.

1. **In aqueous solution** – A small amount, around 5% of carbon dioxide, is transported in physical solution in blood plasma.

# BIOLOGY AROUND US

## Mountain sickness

Although the proportion of oxygen remains the same anywhere in the atmosphere, the pressure of the atmosphere falls as we ascend from the surface of the earth. Atmospheric pressure at Everest Base Camp (5500 m; 18 000 feet), for example, is about half that at sea level. Reduced pressure means there is less oxygen available to the tissues, a condition called **hypoxia**. Both cold and exercise have effects on the body which, added to the effects of hypoxia, may contribute to the illness known as mountain sickness. Speed of ascent is a greater risk factor for mountain sickness than the absolute altitude reached. Those who drive, ride or fly to a high altitude are more at risk than those who walk, and those who climb more rapidly are more at risk than those who take their time. Commonly the symptoms of Acute Mountain Sickness (AMS) appear within 2–4 days of exposure to altitude.

**Benign AMS** is a fairly harmless form of mountain sickness in which sufferers may experience loss of appetite, headache, nausea, vomiting, sleeplessness and chest discomfort. Some people also develop swelling of the body as fluid accumulates under the skin. These symptoms may be considered an important warning of the more serious form of mountain sickness. **Malignant AMS** may be fatal, affecting the lungs and/or the brain. **Pulmonary AMS** leads to a build up of fluid in the lungs, causing breathlessness and blueness of the lips (cyanosis). **Cerebral AMS** causes sufferers to develop headaches, drowsiness, unsteadiness on the feet, abnormal behaviour, impaired consciousness and often coma. Both conditions may occur simultaneously.

There is no general agreement on how AMS is caused but an important factor appears to be the increased blood pressure that results from hypoxia. This may damage capillaries in the brain, eyes and lungs. The small blood vessels in the lungs also show an increased permeability to water, which leads to oedema. An increased level of antidiuretic hormone (ADH) secretion would explain why those suffering from mountain sickness generally pass less urine and retain more water in their body than those people at altitude who do not suffer.

In the event of benign AMS, sufferers should remain at the same altitude for a few days and then, if they recover, proceed cautiously. Malignant AMS sufferers are often in no condition to make decisions for themselves, both their judgement and their physical state being impaired. They should be brought down to lower altitudes at once. Patients with pulmonary AMS will usually improve rapidly after a descent of 2000–3000 feet. Those with cerebral AMS may not regain consciousness for days or even weeks but recovery, when it occurs, is usually complete.

**2. In combination with haemoglobin** – A little carbon dioxide, around 10%, will combine with the amino groups ($-NH_2$) in the four polypeptide chains which make up each haemoglobin molecule (Hb).

$$Hb-N\begin{array}{c}H\\\\H\end{array} + CO_2 \rightleftharpoons Hb-N\begin{array}{c}H\\\\COO^-\end{array} + H^+$$

| haemoglobin | + | carbon dioxide | carbamino haemoglobin | + | hydrogen ion |

**3. In the form of hydrogen carbonate** – The majority of the carbon dioxide (85%) produced by the tissues combines with water to form carbonic acid. This reaction is catalysed by the zinc-containing enzyme **carbonic anhydrase**. The carbonic acid dissociates into hydrogen and hydrogen carbonate ions.

$$H_2O + CO_2 \underset{\text{anhydrase}}{\overset{\text{carbonic}}{\rightleftharpoons}} H_2CO_3 \rightleftharpoons H^+ + HCO_3^-$$

| water | carbon dioxide | | carbonic acid | hydrogen ion | hydrogen carbonate ion |

The above reactions take place in red blood cells. The hydrogen ions produced combine with haemoglobin which loses its oxygen. The oxygen so released diffuses out of the red blood cell, through the capillary wall and tissue fluid into a respiring tissue cell. The hydrogen carbonate ions diffuse out of the red blood cell into the plasma where they combine with sodium ions from the dissociation of sodium chloride to form sodium hydrogen carbonate. It is largely in this form that the carbon dioxide is carried to the respiratory surface where the processes are reversed, releasing carbon dioxide which diffuses out of the body. The loss of negatively charged hydrogen carbonate ions from the red blood cells is balanced by the inward diffusion of negative chloride ions from the dissociation of the sodium chloride. In this way the electrochemical neutrality of the red blood cell is restored. This is known as the **chloride shift** and is illustrated in Fig. 21.9.

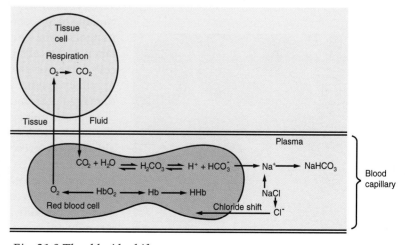

*Fig. 21.9 The chloride shift*

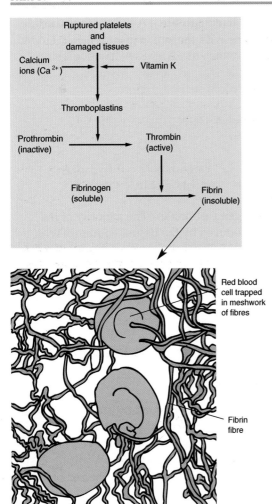

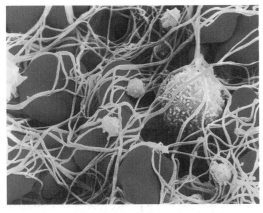

Fig. 21.10 *The clotting process – a summary of the main stages*

### 21.2.5 Clotting of the blood

If a blood vessel is ruptured it is important that the resultant loss of blood is quickly arrested. If not, the pressure of the blood in the circulatory system could fall dangerously low. At the same time it is important that clotting does not occur during the normal circulation of blood. If it does, the clot might lodge in some blood vessel, cutting off the blood supply to a vital organ and possibly resulting in death from **thrombosis**. For this reason the clotting process is very complex, involving a large number of stages. Only under the very specific conditions of injury are all stages completed and clotting occurs. In this way the chances of clotting taking place in other circumstances is reduced. The following account includes only the major stages of what is a more complex process.

Cellular fragments in the blood called **platelets (thrombocytes)** are involved in the clotting or **coagulation** of the blood. At the site of a wound the damaged cells and ruptured platelets release **thromboplastins**. The platelets attract **clotting factors** which create a cascade effect whereby each activates the next in the chain. Amongst these is factor VIII, the absence of which, due to a sex-linked genetic defect, is the cause of haemophilia (Section 9.4.2). At the end of these chain reactions factor X is produced which in the presence of calcium ions and vitamin K causes the inactive plasma protein, **prothrombin**, to become converted to its active form, **thrombin**. This in turn converts another plasma protein, the soluble **fibrinogen**, to **fibrin**, its insoluble form. The fibrin forms a meshwork of threads in which red blood cells become trapped. These dry to form a clot beneath which repair of the wound takes place. The clot not only prevents further blood loss, it also prevents entry of bacteria which might otherwise cause infection. The clotting process is summarized in Fig. 21.10.

Clotting of blood is prevented by substances such as oxalic acid, which precipitates out the calcium ions as calcium oxalate, and heparin, which inhibits the conversion of prothrombin to thrombin. These substances are known as **anticoagulants**.

### 21.2.6 Defence against infection – phagocytosis

Two types of white cell, the neutrophils and monocytes, are capable of amoeboid movement. Both types carry out **phagocytosis**. This is the process by which large particles are taken up by cells via plasma membrane-derived vesicles. White cells carry out phagocytosis for two reasons: to protect the organism against pathogens and to dispose of dead, dying or damaged cells and cellular debris.

In protecting against infection the phagocyte is attracted to chemicals produced naturally by bacteria. The recognition is aided by the presence of **opsonins** – plasma proteins which attach themselves to the surface of the bacteria. The phagocytes have specific proteins on their surface that bind to these chemo-attractants. This causes the phagocyte to move towards the bacteria, possibly along a concentration gradient. The phagocyte strongly adheres to a bacterium on reaching it. This stimulates the formation of pseudopodia which envelop the bacterium,

The clotting process (scanning EM) (× 4200 approx.)

1. The neutrophil is attracted to the bacterium by chemoattractants. It moves towards the bacterium along a concentration gradient

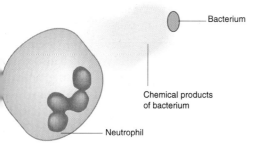

2. The neutrophil binds to the bacterium

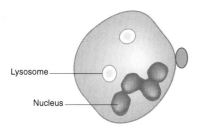

3. Lysosomes within the neutrophil migrate towards the phagosome formed by pseudopodia engulfing the bacterium

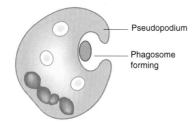

forming a vacuole called a **phagosome**. **Lysosomes** within the phagocyte migrate towards the phagosome into which they release lytic enzymes that break down the bacterium. The breakdown products are finally absorbed by the phagocyte. Fig. 21.11 summarizes the process.

Some phagocytic cells called **macrophages** are found throughout body tissues. They are part of the **reticulo-endothelial system** and are mostly concentrated in lymph nodes and in the liver.

Phagocytosis causes **inflammation** at the site of infection. The hot and swollen area contains many dead bacteria and phagocytes which are known as **pus**. Inflammation results when **histamine** is released as a result of injury or infection. This causes dilation of blood capillaries from which plasma, containing antibodies, escapes into the tissues. Neutrophils also pass through the capillary walls in a process called **diapedesis**.

4. The lysosomes release their lytic enzymes into the phagosome where they break down the bacterium

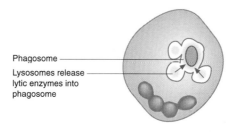

5. The breakdown products of the bacterium are absorbed by the neutrophil

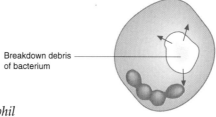

*Fig. 21.11 Summary of phagocytosis of a bacterium by a neutrophil*

## 21.3 The immune system

**Immunity** is the ability of an organism to resist disease. It involves the recognition of foreign material and the production of chemicals which help to destroy it. These chemicals, called antibodies, are produced by lymphocytes of which there are two types: **T-lymphocytes**, which are formed in bone marrow but mature in the thymus gland, and **B-lymphocytes**, which are formed and mature in the bone marrow.

### 21.3.1 Self and non-self antigens

Effective defence of the body against infection lies in the ability of the lymphocyte to recognize its own cells and chemicals (self) and to distinguish these from cells and chemicals which are foreign to it (non-self). Therefore the lymphocyte must be able to recognize everything which exists in nature, as any chemical or

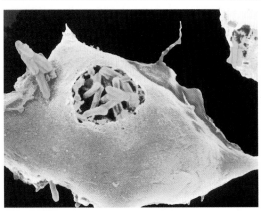

Phagocytosis of bacteria (SEM)
(see video sequence)

cell can potentially invade the body. Cell surfaces are complicated three-dimensional structures. Each lymphocyte has somewhere on its surface, receptors which fit exactly into one small part (perhaps only a few amino acids) of every cell. Clearly there are many different types of lymphocyte.

The different types of lymphocyte are derived from **stem cells** in the bone marrow, special cells in the embryo which also make red blood cells and platelets. The stem cells, on dividing, actually lose most of their DNA to the lymphocytes, i.e. they donate their genes to the lymphocytes. This they do randomly – dealing out genes in a way similar to dealing a hand of cards. Consider the vast number of combinations of cards in a typical hand. Clearly with hundreds of genes, rather than 52 cards, being randomly distributed there are at least 100 million different types of receptors that can be generated – each one able to fit a different chemical shape.

How then do lymphocytes distinguish between their own cell and those that are foreign? In the embryo the lymphocytes are constantly colliding with their own cells' shapes. Since infection in the uterus is rare, any lymphocytes whose receptors exactly fit cells must be the ones that recognize their own cells. These lymphocytes then either die or are suppressed, ensuring that the body's own cells will not be attacked. The body has thus become **self-tolerant**. The remaining lymphocytes have receptors which fit chemical shapes of non-self material. Any material with one of these shapes to which lymphocyte receptors adhere is called an **antigen**.

*Immune responses*

Once a lymphocyte has become attached to its complementary antigen it multiplies rapidly by mitosis to give a clone of identical lymphocytes. This is known as the **primary immune response** and typically takes a few days, during which time the invading pathogen often multiplies and so gives rise to the symptoms of the disease it causes. Some of the lymphocytes in this clone change into cells known as **memory cells**. Unlike the other lymphocytes from the clone, which die within a few days, these memory cells survive much longer – often for years. Further infections by the same pathogen cause these memory cells to divide immediately. Their numbers therefore build up as fast, if not faster, than those of the invader and so the pathogen is repelled before it can induce the symptoms of the disease. This is called the **secondary immune response** and explains why we only suffer some diseases once in a lifetime, despite frequent exposure to them. Each time a pathogen enters the body more and more memory cells are built up, making future infection even less likely. This progressive increase in the level of immunity to a disease is known as **adaptive** or **acquired immunity**.

*B-lymphocytes and humoral immunity*

B-lymphocytes are so called because they originate and mature the bone marrow. When a B-lymphocyte recognizes an antigen divides to form a clone. As most microorganisms possess more than one antigen, many lymphocytes are activated to produce

*The variable region differs with each antibody. It has a shape which exactly fits an antigen. Each antibody therefore can bind to two antigens.*

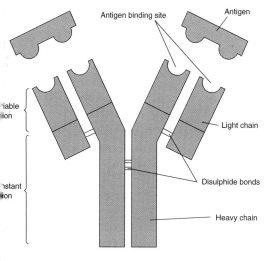

Fig. 21.12 Structure of an antibody

clones in a process known as **polyclonal activation**. Most of the cells in these clones are plasma cells which begin to secrete **antibodies** at the rate of thousands each second.

Antibodies are large protein molecules which comprise four polypeptide chains. One pair of chains is long – **heavy chains**; the other pair is shorter – **light chains**. They are arranged in a Y-shape and have two sites called **binding sites** which fit exactly into the antigen.

There are a number of different antibodies each performing a different function:

**1. Agglutination** – Because each antibody has two different binding sites it can join to two antigens on two different pathogens. In this way the pathogens can be joined together in clumps making them more vulnerable to attack from other types of antibody.

**2. Precipitation** – Some antibodies bind together soluble antigens into large units which are thus precipitated out of solution. As such they are more easily ingested by phagocytes.

**3. Neutralization** – Certain antibodies bind to toxic molecules produced by a pathogen and in doing so neutralize their harmful effects.

**4. Lysis** – Antibodies which are attached to a pathogen act as binding sites for a number of blood proteins which are collectively known as the **complement system**. Some of these proteins are enzymes which cause the breakdown of the pathogen.

*T-lymphocytes and cell-mediated immunity*
T-lymphocytes are so called because, while produced in bone marrow, they mature in the thymus gland. Once attached to their antigen, T-lymphocytes divide to form a clone, the cells of which then differentiate into different cell types:

**1. T-helper cells** – These produce chemicals which activate other white cells such as phagocytes to engulf harmful material. The chemicals attach themselves to the foreign material and so label them as requiring phagocytosis. These labelled chemicals are called **opsonins** (from the Greek meaning 'ready for the table'). The T-helper cells also activate B-lymphocytes to divide to produce plasma cells, as well as assisting the T-killer cells to destroy pathogens. Clearly they are essential to a successful immune response – a fact borne out by the consequences of their being rendered inoperable by the Human Immunodeficiency Virus (HIV) leading to AIDS.

**2. T-cytotoxic cells (killer cells)** – These kill body cells which have become invaded by viruses. They force cylindrical proteins through the cell membrane causing the cell to burst. Since viruses require host cells to reproduce, this sacrifice effectively prevents multiplication of the virus.

**3. T-suppressor cells** – Once an infection has been eliminated these cells suppress the activities of the lymphocytes and so maintain control of the immune system.

423

## 21.3.2 Monoclonal antibodies and their applications

We have seen in Section 21.3.1 that foreign material entering the body will possess more than one antigen and so induces a number of different B-lymphocytes to multiply, producing clones of themselves. The many clones then produce a range of antibodies known as **polyclonal antibodies**.

It is obviously of considerable therapeutic value to be able to produce antibodies outside the body, but until recently the inability to sustain the growth of B-lymphocytes prevented this. However, a cancer of B-lymphocytes produces myeloma cells which continue to divide indefinitely. These can be fused in the laboratory, using polyethylene glycol, with each specific B-lymphocyte to produce cells, called **hybridoma cells**, which produce antibodies of one type only – **monoclonal antibodies**.

The large scale production of antibodies using hybridoma cells is used medically to treat a range of infections. This is not their only application, however. Because they are specific to a single chemical (antigen), to which they become attached, they can be used to separate a particular chemical from a complex mixture. To do this, the monoclonal antibody for the required chemical is immobilized on resin beads which are then packed in a column. The mixture is passed over the beads and only the required chemical becomes attached to the antibodies. The chemical may then be obtained in a pure state by washing the beads with a solution which causes the antibodies to release it.

Monoclonal antibodies are also used in **immunoassays**. Here, the antibody is labelled in some way, e.g. radioactively or by a fluorescent dye, so that it can easily be detected. When added to a test sample, the antibodies attach to their specific antigen. Washing in solutions which remove only unattached antibodies leaves only those attached to the antigen. The amount of these attached antibodies in the sample is then apparent from the degree of radioactivity or fluorescence. For example, the presence of a particular pathogen in a blood sample can be detected by use of the appropriate monoclonal antibody tagged with a fluorescent dye.

Another technique is to immobilize the antibodies and pass the solution under test over them. Suppose we are testing for chemical X. If it is present in the solution it will attach to the antibody. A second type of antibody which has an enzyme attached is then added. It combines only with those original antibodies which are linked to chemical X. By adding a substrate which the enzyme causes to change colour, the amount of chemical X will be apparent by the extent of any colour change. This technique, called **Enzyme Linked Immunosorbant Assay (ELISA)**, has many uses including detecting drugs in athletes' urine, pregnancy testing kits and detecting the Human Immunodeficiency Virus (the AIDS test). It is also possible to link anti-cancer drugs to monoclonal antibodies which are attracted to cancer cells – the so-called '**magic bullets**'. An even more sophisticated technique is to tag monoclonal antibodies with an enzyme which converts an inactive form of the cytotoxic drug (the **prodrug**) into an active form. Once injected these antibodies link to the cancer cells. The prodrug is then administered in a relatively high dose as it is harmless in its inactive state. In the vicinity of normal cells the drug remains ineffective but in the presence of the cancer cells the enzyme on the attached antibody activates the drug which acts upon the cells, killing them. The technique is called **ADEPT (Antibody Direct Enzyme Prodrug Therapy)**.

# Pregnancy testing

Home pregnancy testing kits make use of immobilized antibodies on a urine dipstick to detect traces of human chorionic gonadotrophin (hCG), a hormone released from the placenta. Antibodies 'tagged' with blue latex combine with the hormone to produce a readily visible result.

5. Further row of antibodies which combine with latex-tagged antibodies *without* hCG attached

Negative result (blue line in this position)

4. Complex held by immobilized antibodies to form a blue line

Positive result (blue line in this position)

3. hCG bound to antibody to form a complex

2. Antibody tagged with blue latex particle

1. Urine sample containing hCG

Home pregnancy testing kit

### 21.3.3 Types of immunity and immunization

There are two basic types of immunity, passive and active.

**Passive immunity** is the result of antibodies being passed into an individual in some way, rather than being produced by the individual itself. This passive immunity may occur naturally in mammals when, for example, antibodies pass across the placenta from a mother to her fetus or are passed to the newborn baby in the mother's milk. In both cases the young developing mammal is afforded some protection from disease until its own immune system is fully functional.

Alternatively, passive immunity may be acquired artificially by the injection of antibodies from another individual. This occurs in the treatment of tetanus and diphtheria in humans, although the antibodies are acquired from other mammals, e.g. horses. In all cases, passive immunity is only temporary.

**Active immunity** occurs when an organism manufactures its own antibodies. Active immunity may be the natural result of an infection. Once the body has started to manufacture antibodies in response to a disease-causing agent, it may continue to do so for a long time after, sometimes permanently. It is for this reason that most people suffer diseases such as mumps and measles only once. It is possible to induce an individual to produce antibodies even without them suffering disease. To achieve this, the appropriate antigen must be injected in some way. This is the basis of **immunization (vaccination)** of which there are a number of different types depending on the form the antigen takes.

## BIOLOGY AROUND US

# Allergies

An excessive reaction of the body's immune system to certain substances is known as an allergy. When a foreign substance is detected for the first time lymphocytes produce antibodies, some of which bind to the surface of other white cells called mast cells. If the same substance is encountered again it binds to the antibodies on the mast cells causing the release of chemicals called mediators. The most important mediator is **histamine**. This chemical can produce rash, swelling, narrowing of the airways and a drop in blood pressure. These effects are important in protecting against infection but they may also be triggered inappropriately in allergy. One of the most common allergic disorders, hayfever, is caused by an allergic reaction to inhaled grass pollen leading to allergic rhinitis – swelling and irritation of the nasal passages and watering of the nose and eyes. Another common allergy, asthma, is covered in Biology Around Us on page 406.

**Antihistamines** are the most widely used drugs in the treatment of allergic reactions of all kinds. Their main action is to counter the effects of histamine by blocking its action on $H_1$ receptors. These receptors are found in various body tissues, particularly the small blood vessels in the skin, nose and eyes. This helps prevent the dilation of the vessels, thus reducing redness and swelling. Antihistamines pass from the blood into the brain where their blocking action on histamine activity produces general sedation, and repression of various brain functions, including the vomiting and coughing mechanisms.

1. **Living attenuated microorganisms** – Living pathogens which have been treated, e.g. by heating, so that they multiply but are unable to cause the symptoms of the disease. They are therefore harmless but nonetheless induce the body to produce appropriate antibodies. Living attenuated microorganisms are used to immunize against measles, tuberculosis, poliomyelitis and rubella (German measles).

2. **Dead microorganisms** – Pathogens are killed by some means and then injected. Although harmless they again induce the body to produce antibodies in the same way it would had they been living. Typhoid, cholera and whooping cough are controlled by this means.

3. **Toxoids** – The toxins produced by some diseases, e.g. diphtheria and tetanus, are sufficient to induce antibody production by an individual. To avoid these toxins causing the symptoms of the disease they are first detoxified in some way, e.g. by treatment with formaldehyde, and then injected.

4. **Extracted antigens** – The chemicals with antigenic properties may be extracted from the pathogenic organisms and injected. Influenza vaccine is produced in this way.

5. **Artificial antigens** – Through genetic engineering it is now possible to transfer the genes producing antigens from a pathogenic organism to a harmless one which can easily be

grown in a laboratory. Mass production of the antigen is then possible in a fermenter ready for separation and purification before use. Vaccines used in the treatment of hepatitis B can be produced in this way.

### 21.3.4 Acquired Immune Deficiency Syndrome (AIDS)

Acquired Immune Deficiency Syndrome or AIDS is caused by the **Human Immunodeficiency Virus (HIV)** – a retrovirus, more details of which are given in Section 5.2.2. HIV infects T-helper cells (Section 21.3.1) which are essential to cell mediated immunity and so the body's immune system is rendered ineffective, not only against HIV but against other infections too. Hence AIDS victims frequently die, usually within 2 years of developing the disease, due to opportunist pathogens which take advantage of the impaired resistance. Full details on AIDS are given in Section 31.2.5.

### 21.3.5 Blood groups

| Blood group | Antigens present |
|---|---|
| A | A |
| B | B |
| AB | A and B |
| O | None |

| Blood group | Antigen | Antibodies |
|---|---|---|
| A | A | b |
| B | B | a |
| AB | A and B | None |
| O | None | a and b |

Blood groups are an example of an antigen–antibody system. The membrane of red blood cells contains polysaccharides which act as antigens. They may induce the production of antibodies when introduced into another individual. While there are over 20 different blood grouping methods, the ABO system, first discovered by Landsteiner in 1900, is the best known. In this system there are just two antigens, A and B, which determine the blood group (see left). For each of these antigens there is an antibody, which is given the corresponding lower case letter. The presence of an antigen and its corresponding antibody together causes an immune response resulting in the clumping together of red cells (**agglutination**) and their ultimate breakdown (**haemolysis**). For this reason, an individual does not produce antibodies corresponding to the antigens present but produces all others as a matter of course. These antibodies are present in the plasma. The composition of each blood group is therefore as given opposite.

In transfusing blood from one person, the **donor**, to another, the **recipient**, it is necessary to avoid bringing together corresponding antigens and antibodies. However, if only a small quantity of blood is to be transfused, then it is possible to add the antibody to the antigen, because the donor's antibodies become so diluted in the recipient's plasma that they are ineffective. It is not, however, feasible to add small quantities of antigen to the corresponding antibody as even a tiny amount of antigen will cause an immune response. This, after all, is why small numbers of invading bacteria are immediately destroyed as part of the body's defence mechanism. It is therefore possible to safely add antibody a to antigen A and antibody b to antigen B, in small quantities, but not the reverse. For this reason, blood group O, with no antigens present, may be given in small amounts to individuals of all other blood groups. Group O is therefore referred to as the **universal donor**. Individuals of this group are, however, restricted to receiving blood from their own group. In the same way group AB, with no antibodies, may receive blood with either antigen. In other words, group AB can receive blood from all groups, and is therefore termed the universal recipient. They can, however, only donate to their own group. When agglutination occurs between two groups, they are said to be **incompatible**. Table 21.2 shows the compatibility of blood groups in the ABO system.

TABLE 21.2   **Compatibility of blood groups in the ABO system**

| | | | Recipient's blood group | | | |
|---|---|---|---|---|---|---|
| Group | | | A | B | AB | O |
| | Group | Antigens | A | B | A and B | None |
| | | Antigens / Antibodies | b | a | None | a and b |
| Donor's blood group | A — A — b | | ✓ | ✗ | ✓ | ✗ |
| | B — B — a | | ✗ | ✓ | ✓ | ✗ |
| | AB — A and B — None | | ✗ | ✗ | ✓ | ✗ |
| | O — None — a and b | | ✓ | ✓ | ✓ | ✓ |

✓ Compatible – bloods do not clot          ✗ Incompatible – bloods clot

Despite this knowledge and careful matching of blood groups there continued to be inexplicable failures of transfusions up to 1940. It was then that Landsteiner discovered a new antigen (actually a system of antigens) in rhesus monkeys, which was also present in humans. This became known as the **rhesus system** and the antigen as **antigen D**. Where an individual possesses the antigen he or she is said to be **rhesus positive**; where it is absent he or she is **rhesus negative**. There is no naturally occurring antibody to antigen D, but if blood with the antigen is transfused into a person without it (rhesus negative), antibody d production is induced in line with the usual immune response. For this reason, before transfusion, blood is matched with respect to the rhesus factor as well as the ABO system.

One problem associated with the rhesus system arises in pregnancy. As blood groups are genetically determined (Section 9.5.3), it is possible for the fetus to inherit from the father a blood group different from that of the mother. The fetus may, for example, be rhesus positive while the mother is rhesus negative. Towards the end of pregnancy, and especially around birth, fragments of blood cells may cross from the fetus to the mother. The mother responds by producing the rhesus antibody (d) in response to the rhesus antigen (D) on the fetal red blood cells. These antibodies are able to cross the placenta. As the build-up and transfer of rhesus antibodies takes some time, and as the problem only arises during the latter stages of pregnancy, their concentration is rarely sufficient to have any effect on the first child. The production of rhesus antibodies by the mother continues for only a few months, but subsequent fetuses may again induce production and are therefore subject to a greater influx of rhesus antibodies. These break down the fetal red blood cells – a condition known as **haemolytic disease of the newborn**. It requires a number of fetal blood transfusions throughout the pregnancy if it is not to prove fatal. Knowledge that the mother is rhesus negative can, however, avert the danger. If this is the case, and the father is known to be rhesus positive, a potential problem exists. In this event rhesus antibodies (d) from blood donors, are injected into the mother immediately after the first birth. These destroy any fetal cell

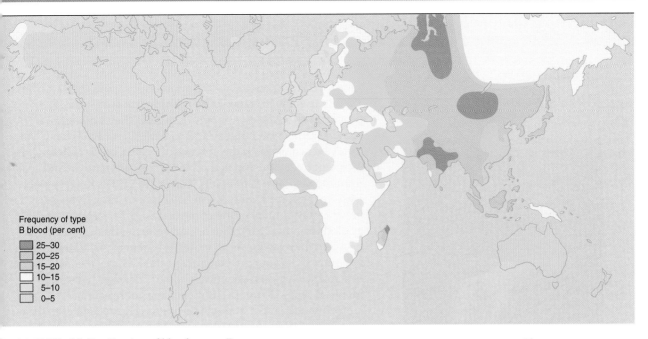

Fig. 21.13 World distribution of blood group B

Frequency of type
B blood (per cent)

- 25–30
- 20–25
- 15–20
- 10–15
- 5–10
- 0–5

fragments with antigen D, which may have entered her blood, before they induce the mother to manufacture her own antibodies. The injected antibodies are soon broken down by the mother, and in the absence of new ones being produced subsequent fetuses are not at risk.

The proportion of different blood groups varies throughout the world. In the British population the proportions are O–46%, A–42%, B–9%, AB–3%, although there are variations between different areas. In England, for example, numbers with group A slightly exceed group O. Some South American tribes are exclusively group O whereas some North American Indian tribes are three-quarters group A. Over a third of European gypsies have group B. The proportion of rhesus positive individuals in most groups is between 75% and 85%.

## 21.4    The circulatory system

### Did you know?

The entire length of arteries, veins and capillaries in the human body is estimated to be 80 000 miles – more than three times the distance around the world.

Only very small animals, where cells are never far from the outside, exist without a specialized transport system. The larger and more active an animal, the more extensive and efficient is its transport system. These systems frequently incorporate a pump, valves and an elaborate means of controlling distribution of the blood. Very simple animals have an **open blood system**. Here the blood moves freely over the tissues, through a series of spaces known collectively as the **haemocoel**. The blood is not confined to vessels. In its simplest form, e.g. in nematodes, the blood is transported haphazardly by the muscular movements of the body as it moves around. In most arthropods, including insects, there is some circulation of the blood by a tubular heart, which pumps it into the haemocoel. In all open blood systems the blood is moved at very low pressure and there is little control over its distribution.

To allow more rapid transport and greater control of distribution, larger and more active organisms have evolved

## BIOLOGY AROUND US

### Tissue compatibility and rejection

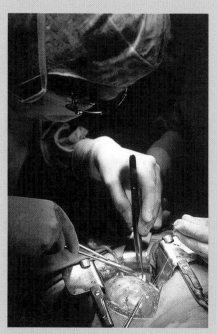

Kidney transplant operation

We have seen that blood, if adequately matched, can be transfused from one person to another. It should therefore be equally feasible to transplant organs in the same way. The problem lies in the complexity of organs; they possess a far greater number of antigens and so perfect cross-matching can rarely be achieved. In the absence of perfect cross-matching the recipient treats the donated organ as foreign material and so an immune response is initiated. The organ is therefore rejected. Despite these difficulties there have been major advances in the grafting and transplanting of tissues. Clearly if a tissue is grafted from one part of an organism to another, there are no problems of rejection as all material is genetically identical and so compatible. Skin is frequently grafted by this means. Equally transplants between genetically identical individuals like identical twins do not present problems of rejection. Unfortunately, most humans do not have genetically identical brothers or sisters and so depend upon organs from others when the need for a transplant arises. To minimize the chances of rejection, careful matching takes place, to find tissues which are as nearly compatible as possible. This minimizes the extent of the immune response, reducing the risk of rejection. Such compatible tissues are often, but not always, found in close relatives. In addition the recipient is treated with **immunosuppressant drugs** which lower the activity of their natural immune response, so delaying rejection long enough for the transplanted tissue to be accepted. The problem with these drugs is that the recipient is vulnerable to other infections and even minor ones can prove fatal.

More recently two techniques have been developed which suppress the T-lymphocytes responsible for the rejection response while having little effect on the B-cells which produce antibodies. This helps the patient to maintain a resistance to infection. The first technique employs Orthoclone OKT-3, a monoclonal antibody (see Section 21.3.2). Although this has some side effects they are reversible and the antibody has been used successfully to combat kidney rejection. In the second technique human T-lymphocytes are injected into a horse which then produces antibodies to them, known as anti-lymphocyte immunoglobulin (ALG). This is purified and, when injected into a transplant patient, is effective at combating rejection.

closed blood systems. Here blood is confined to vessels. The pumping action of the heart sustains high pressure within these vessels and a combination of vasodilation, vasoconstriction and valves ensures a much more controlled distribution of blood. Closed systems occur in cephalopod molluscs, echinoderms, annelids and vertebrates.

Within vertebrates, there are two different systems of circulating the blood. In fish, the blood passes from the heart, over the gills and then to the rest of the body before returning to the heart. As the blood passes only once through the heart during a complete circulation of the body it is called a single

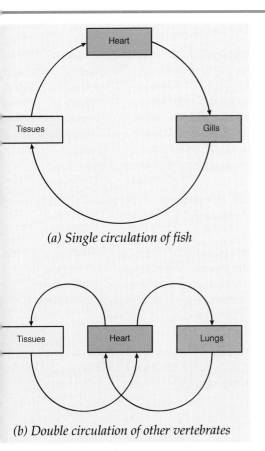

*(a) Single circulation of fish*

*(b) Double circulation of other vertebrates*

*Fig. 21.14 Single and double circulations*

**circulation** (Fig. 21.14a). The disadvantage of this system is that the resistance created by the fine network of blood capillaries in the gills causes the blood pressure to drop from around 11 kPa as it leaves the heart to 7 kPa as it leaves the gills. This blood then meets more resistance as it passes through the capillaries of the body tissues and its pressure is even further reduced. The flow is therefore rather sluggish. To overcome this problem, other vertebrates have developed a **double circulation** (Fig. 21.14b). Here the blood is returned to the heart after passing over the respiratory surface and before it is pumped over the body tissues. This helps to sustain a high blood pressure and so allows more rapid circulation. In mammals and birds the complete separation of the heart into two halves allows oxygenated and deoxygenated blood to be kept separate. This improves the efficiency of oxygen distribution, something which is essential to sustain the higher metabolic rate of these endothermic animals.

### 21.4.1 Blood vessels

In a closed circulation there are three types of vessel. **Arteries** carry blood away from the heart ('a' for 'artery' = 'a' for 'away' from the heart), **veins** carry blood to the heart whereas the much smaller **capillaries** link arteries to veins. A comparison of the structure of these three vessels is given in Table 21.3.

The diameter of arteries and veins gradually diminishes as they get further from the heart. The smaller arteries are called **arterioles** and the smaller veins are called **venules**.

TABLE 21.3   **A comparison of arteries, veins and capillaries**

| Artery | Vein | Capillary |
|---|---|---|
| Lumen<br>Endothelium<br>Elastic fibres<br>Smooth muscle<br>Collagen fibres | Lumen<br>Endothelium<br>Elastic fibres<br>Smooth muscle<br>Collagen fibres | Lumen<br>Endothelium |
| Thick muscular wall<br>Much elastic tissue<br>Small lumen relative to diameter<br>Capable of constriction<br>Not permeable<br>Valves in aorta and pulmonary artery only<br>Transports blood from the heart<br>Oxygenated blood except in pulmonary artery<br>Blood under high pressure (10–16 kPa)<br>Blood moves in pulses<br>Blood flows rapidly | Thin muscular wall<br>Little elastic tissue<br>Large lumen relative to diameter<br>Not capable of constriction<br>Not permeable<br>Valves throughout all veins<br>Transports blood to heart<br>Deoxygenated blood except in pulmonary vein<br>Blood under low pressure (1 kPa)<br>No pulses<br>Blood flows slowly | No muscle<br>No elastic tissue<br>Large lumen relative to diameter<br>Not capable of constriction<br>Permeable<br>No valves<br>Links arteries to veins<br>Blood changes from oxygenated to deoxygenated<br>Blood pressure reducing (4–1 kPa)<br>No pulses<br>Blood flow slowing |

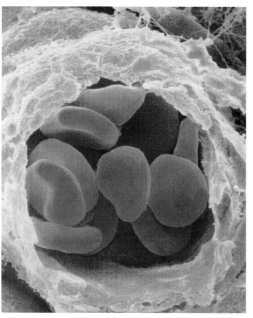

SEM of red blood cells in an arteriole

### 21.4.2 Mammalian circulatory system

The purpose of the mammalian circulatory system is to carry blood between various parts of the body. To this end, each organ has a major artery supplying it with blood from the heart and a major vein which returns it. These arteries and veins are usually named by preceding them with the adjective appropriate to that organ, e.g. each kidney has a renal artery and a renal vein. A general plan of the mammalian circulation is given in Fig. 21.15.

The flow of blood is maintained in three ways:

1. **The pumping action of the heart** – This forces blood through the arteries into the capillaries.

2. **Contraction of skeletal muscle** – The contraction of muscles during the normal movements of a mammal squeeze the thin-walled veins, increasing the pressure of blood within them. Pocket valves in the veins ensure that this pressure directs the blood back to the heart.

3. **Inspiratory movements** – When breathing in, the pressure in the thorax is reduced. This helps to draw blood towards the heart, which is within the thorax.

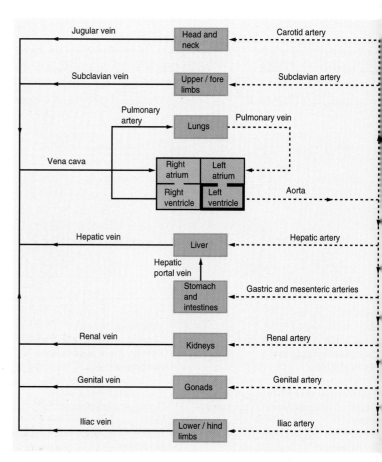

*Fig. 21.15 General plan of the mammalian circulatory system*

## 21.5    Heart structure and action

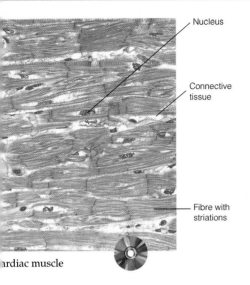

Nucleus

Connective tissue

Fibre with striations

Cardiac muscle

A pump to circulate the blood is an essential feature of most circulatory systems. These pumps or hearts generally consist of a thin-walled collection chamber – the **atrium** or **auricle** – and a thick-walled pumping chamber – the **ventricle**. Between the two are valves to ensure the blood flows in one direction, namely, from the atrium to the ventricle. In fish, with their single circulation, the heart has two chambers only. With the evolution of a double circulation came the development of two atria, one to receive blood from the systemic (body) circulation and the other to receive it from the pulmonary (lungs) circulation. In amphibia and most reptiles there is a three-chambered heart – two atria and a single ventricle. This has the disadvantage of allowing oxygenated blood from the pulmonary system to mix with deoxygenated blood from the systemic system. Ridges within the ventricle minimize this mixing so that in frogs, for example, three-quarters of the oxygenated blood from the pulmonary system is pumped into the systemic system. Being ectothermic, and therefore usually having a lower metabolic rate, allows this inefficiency to be tolerated. In the endothermic mammals and birds, however, the ventricle is completely partitioned into two, allowing complete separation of oxygenated and deoxygenated blood. This four-chambered heart is really two two-chambered hearts side by side.

### Did you know?

The heart pumps out 13 000 litres of blood each day – enough to fill a small road tanker.

### 21.5.1 Structure of the mammalian heart

The mammalian heart consists largely of **cardiac muscle**, a specialized tissue which is capable of rhythmical contraction and relaxation over a long period without fatigue. Its structure is shown in Fig. 21.16. The muscle is richly supplied with blood vessels and also contains connective tissue which gives strength and helps to prevent the muscle tearing.

The mammalian heart is made up of two thin-walled atria which are elastic and distend as blood enters them. The left atrium receives oxygenated blood from the pulmonary veins while the right atrium receives deoxygenated blood from the venae cavae. When full, the atria contract together, forcing the remaining blood into their respective ventricles (Fig. 21.17). The right ventricle then pumps blood to the lungs. Owing to the close proximity of the lungs to the heart, the right ventricle does not need to force blood far and is much less muscular than the left ventricle which has to pump blood to the extremities of the body. To prevent backflow of blood into the atria when the ventricles contract, there are valves between the atria and ventricles. On the right side of the heart these comprise three cup-shaped flaps, the **tricuspid valves**. On the left side of the heart only two cup-shaped flaps are present; these are the **bicuspid** or **mitral valves**. To prevent these valves inverting under the pressure of blood, they are attached to papillary muscles of the ventricular wall by fibres known as the **chordae tendinae**. Fig. 21.18 illustrates the structure of the heart.

Blood leaving the ventricle is prevented from returning by pocket valves in the aorta and pulmonary artery. These close when the ventricles relax.

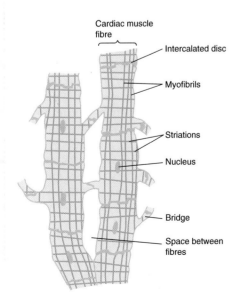

Cardiac muscle fibre

Intercalated disc

Myofibrils

Striations

Nucleus

Bridge

Space between fibres

*Fig. 21.16 Cardiac muscle (LS)*

**1.**

Blood enters atria and ventricles from pulmonary veins and venae cavae

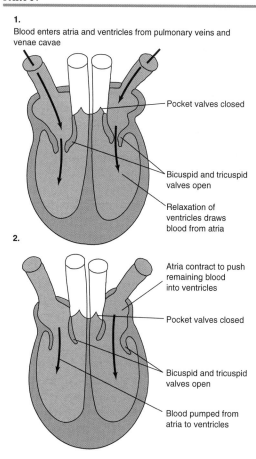

Pocket valves closed

Bicuspid and tricuspid valves open

Relaxation of ventricles draws blood from atria

**2.**

Atria contract to push remaining blood into ventricles

Pocket valves closed

Bicuspid and tricuspid valves open

Blood pumped from atria to ventricles

**3.**

Blood pumped into pulmonary arteries and the aorta

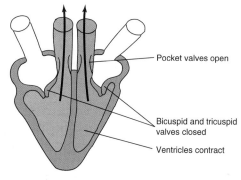

Pocket valves open

Bicuspid and tricuspid valves closed

Ventricles contract

1.  *Diastole*
    *Atria are relaxed and fill with blood. Ventricles are also relaxed.*
2.  *Atrial systole*
    *Atria contract pushing blood into the ventricles. Ventricles remain relaxed.*
3.  *Ventricular systole*
    *Atria relax. Ventricles contract pushing blood away from heart through pulmonary arteries and the aorta.*

*Fig. 21.17 The cardiac cycle*

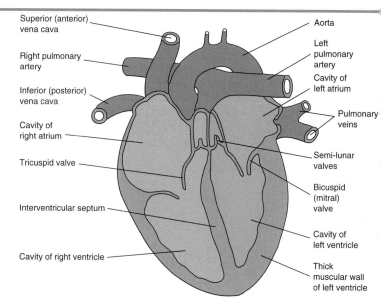

*Fig. 21.18 The structure of the mammalian heart as seen in vertical section from the ventral side*

### 21.5.2 Control of heart beat (cardiac cycle)

All vertebrate hearts are **myogenic**, that is, the heart beat is initiated from within the heart muscle itself rather than by a nervous impulse from outside it. Where it is initiated by nerves, as in insects, the heart is said to be **neurogenic**.

The initial stimulus for a heart beat originates in a group of histologically different cardiac muscle cells known as the **sino-atrial node (SA node)**. This is located in the wall of the right atrium near where the venae cavae enter (see Fig. 21.19). The SA node determines the basic rate of heart beat and is therefore known as the **pacemaker**. In humans, this basic rate is 70 beats/minute but can be adjusted according to demand by stimulation from the autonomic nervous system. A wave of excitation spreads out from the SA node across both atria, causing them to contract more or less at the same time.

The wave of excitation reaches a similar group of cells known as the **atrio-ventricular node (AV node)** which lies between the two atria. To allow blood to be forced upwards into the arteries, the ventricles need to contract from the apex upwards. To achieve this, the new wave of excitation from the AV node is conducted along **Purkyne fibres,** which collectively make up the **bundle of His**. These fibres lead along the interventricular septum to the apex of the ventricles, from where they radiate upwards. The wave of excitation travels along these fibres, only being released to effect muscle contraction at the apex. The ventricles contract simultaneously from the apex upwards. These events are known as the **cardiac cycle** and are summarized in Fig. 21.17.

### 21.5.3 Factors modifying heart beat

The human heart normally contracts 70 times a minute, but this can be varied from 50 to 200 times a minute. The volume of blood pumped at each beat can also be varied. The volume pumped multiplied by the number of beats in a given time is

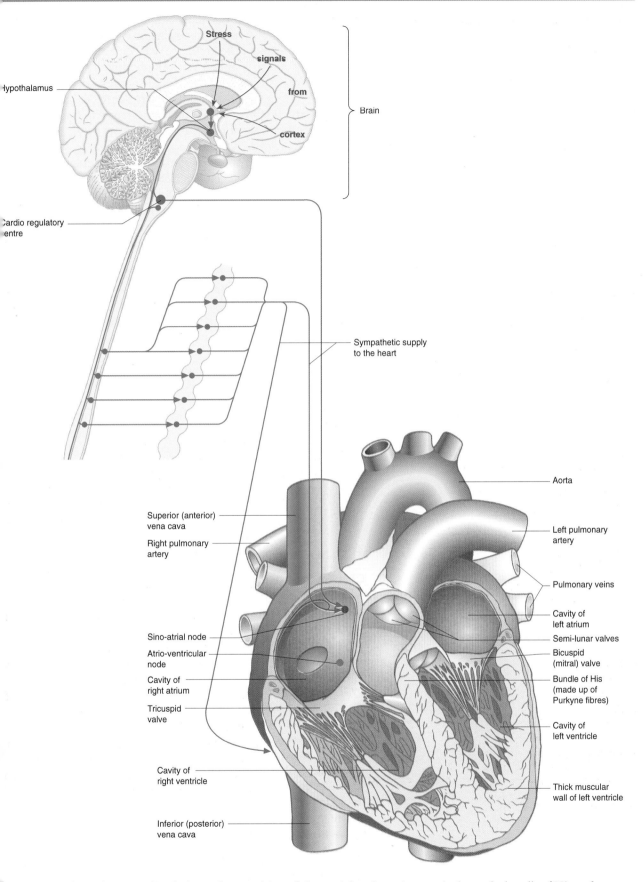

Stress

signals

from

cortex

Brain

Hypothalamus

Cardio regulatory
centre

Sympathetic supply
to the heart

Aorta

Superior (anterior)
vena cava

Left pulmonary
artery

Right pulmonary
artery

Pulmonary veins

Cavity of
left atrium

Sino-atrial node

Semi-lunar valves

Atrio-ventricular
node

Bicuspid
(mitral) valve

Cavity of
right atrium

Bundle of His
(made up of
Purkyne fibres)

Tricuspid
valve

Cavity of
left ventricle

Cavity of
right ventricle

Thick muscular
wall of left ventricle

Inferior (posterior)
vena cava

Fig. 21.19 VS through mammalian heart to show position of sino-atrial node, atrio-ventricular node, bundle of His and
nervous connections to the brain

TABLE 21.4   **Some uses and effects of beta blockers**
Signals from the sympathetic nervous system are carried by the neurotransmitter, noradrenaline, produced in the adrenal glands and at the ends of the sympathetic nerve fibres. Beta blockers interrupt the signals from the neurotransmitter by blocking the receptor sites.

| Effect | Consequence |
|---|---|
| Inhibits dilation of blood vessels around the brain. | Prevents migraine. |
| Reduces fluid production in eyes. | Lowers pressure inside eye. |
| Slows heart rate and reduces stroke volume. | Helps prevent angina and abnormal heart rhythms; reduces hypertension. |
| Airways constrict. | May cause breathlessness |

called the **cardiac output**. Changes to the cardiac output are effected through the autonomic nervous system. Within the medulla oblongata of the brain are two centres. The **cardio-acceleratory centre** is linked by the sympathetic nervous system to the SA node. When stimulated these nerves cause an increase in cardiac output. The **cardio-inhibitory centre** is linked by parasympathetic fibres within the vagus nerve to the SA node, AV node and bundle of His. Stimulation from these nerves decreases the cardiac output.

Which of these centres stimulates the heart depends on factors like the pH of the blood. This in turn depends upon its carbon dioxide concentration. Under conditions of strenuous exercise, the carbon dioxide concentration of the blood increases as a consequence of the greater respiratory rate. The pH of the blood is therefore lowered. Receptors in a swelling of the carotid artery, called the **carotid body**, detect this change and send nervous impulses to the cardio-acceleratory centre which increases the heart beat, thereby increasing the rate at which carbon dioxide is delivered to the lungs for removal. A fall in carbon dioxide level (rise in pH) of blood causes the carotid receptors to stimulate the cardio-inhibitory centre, thus reducing the heart beat.

Another means of control is by stretch receptors in the aorta, carotid artery and vena cava. When the receptors in the aorta and carotid artery are stimulated, it indicates that there is distension of these vessels as a result of increased blood flow in them. This causes the cardio-inhibitory centre to stimulate the heart to reduce cardiac output. Stimulation of receptors in the vena cava indicates increased blood in this vessel, probably as a result of muscular activity increasing the rate at which blood is returned from the tissues. Under these conditions the cardiac centres in the brain increase the cardiac output.

### 21.5.4 Maintenance and control of blood pressure

Changes in cardiac output will alter blood pressure (Fig. 21.20), which must always be maintained at a sufficiently high level to permit blood to reach all tissues requiring it. Another important factor in controlling blood pressure is the diameter of the blood vessels. When narrowed – **vasoconstriction** – blood pressure rises; when widened – **vasodilation** – it falls. Vasoconstriction and vasodilation are also controlled by the medulla oblongata, this time by the **vasomotor centre**. From this centre nerves run to the smooth muscles of arterioles throughout the body. Pressure receptors, known as **baroreceptors**, in the carotid artery detect blood pressure changes and relay impulses to the vasomotor centre. If blood pressure falls, the vasomotor centre sends impulses along sympathetic nerves to the arterioles. The muscles in the arterioles contract, causing vasoconstriction and a consequent rise in blood pressure. A rise in blood pressure causes the vasomotor centre to send messages via the parasympathetic system to the arterioles, causing them to dilate and so reduce blood pressure.

A rise in blood carbon dioxide concentration also causes a rise in blood pressure. This increases the speed with which blood is delivered to the lungs and so helps remove the carbon dioxide more quickly. Hormones like adrenaline similarly raise blood pressure.

## BIOLOGY AROUND US

### Artificial pacemakers

In Britain about 10 000 people a year receive an artificial pacemaker. The operation takes less than an hour and is performed under local anaesthetic.

Pacemakers are made up of a pulse generator and two electrodes. The pulse generator is about the size of a thin matchbox and weighs 20 – 60 g. It is powered by a lithium battery and is implanted under the patient's skin. The electrodes are placed intravenously into the right atrium and the right ventricle. Disease or ageing can damage the heart's natural pacemaker and the conduction of impulses through the heart, causing an abnormally slow heart beat. The artificial pacemaker overcomes this by generating electrical impulses artificially and conducting them to the muscles of the heart on demand or when the heart misses a beat.

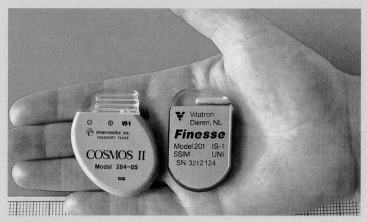

Pacemakers

## PROJECT

1. Compare mean blood pressures/heart rates of smokers and non-smokers.

2. Compare blood pressures/heart rates when listening to loud and quiet music, etc.

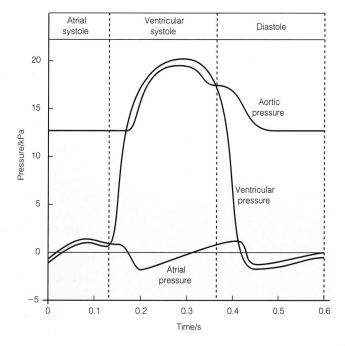

g. 21.20 Pressure changes in the atria, ntricles and aorta during one cardiac cycle

## BIOLOGY AROUND US

## Electrocardiogram

An ECG (electrocardiogram) trace follows the electrical activity of nerves and muscles in the heart. There are various characteristic patterns or waves. For diagnostic purposes doctors use three of the waves.

**Normal ECG**
Recorded on a chart running at 25 mm s$^{-1}$

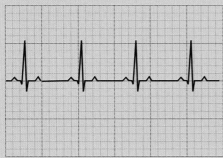

**Normal ECG**

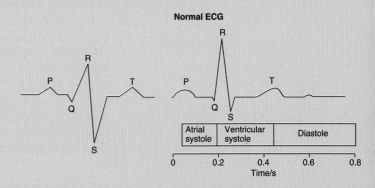

Myocardial Infarction
Heart attack

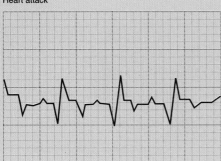

The P wave charts current flow through the atria from the SA node to the AV node. The QRS complex follows the spread of depolarization through the ventricles. Finally the T wave results from currents generated during ventricular repolarization.

Various waves can be picked up as electrical echoes from the heart by connecting the ECG machine's leads to the skin at different sites on the body. By fixing two or three electrodes to the wrists and ankles, doctors get a frontal view of the heart's activity by charting the direction of current flow in two dimensions. Together with horizontal-plane electrodes (six ECG leads strapped across the chest), the ECG can give a three-dimensional picture of the heart's electrical activity, and hence its health.

### 21.5.5 Effects of exercise on the heart and circulatory system

We saw in Section 20.5 that exercise increases the demand of muscles for oxygen and that to supply this demand, the ventilation rate increases. It follows that if the supply of oxygen to the blood is increased, then to be effective, so must the supply of blood to the muscles. Accordingly, the cardiac output must rise from around 5 dm$^3$ min$^{-1}$ at rest to a maximum of 30 dm$^3$ min$^{-1}$ during strenuous exertion, although a four-fold increase to 20 dm$^3$ min$^{-1}$ is more normal. This rise is achieved by increasing the heart rate from around 70 beats min$^{-1}$ to 190 beats min$^{-1}$ and the stroke volume from 80 cm$^3$ at each beat to 110 cm$^3$. A well-trained athlete has a greater cardiac output although the heart rate is normally less than that of an untrained person. This is achieved by repeated exercise increasing the amount of heart muscle and the size of the heart chambers. As a result the stroke volume of a well-trained athlete is as much as 50% greater than that of an untrained person.

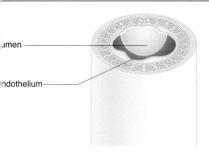

lumen

endothelium

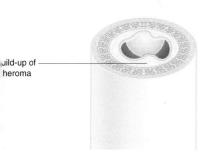

build-up of
atheroma

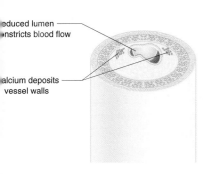

reduced lumen
constricts blood flow

calcium deposits
in vessel walls

*Fig. 21.21 Build-up of atheroma*

## 21.5.6 Heart disease

As the organ pumping blood around the body, any interruption to the heart's ceaseless beating can have serious, often fatal, consequences. There are many defects and disorders, some acquired, like atherosclerosis, others congenital, such as a hole-in-the-heart. Some affect the pacemaker, leading to an irregular heart rhythm; others affect the valves, allowing blood to 'leak' back into the atria when the ventricles contract. By far the most common is **coronary heart disease,** which affects the pair of blood vessels – the coronary arteries – which serve the heart muscle itself. There are three ways in which blood flow in these arteries may be impeded:

**Coronary thrombosis** – a blood clot which becomes lodged in a coronary vessel.

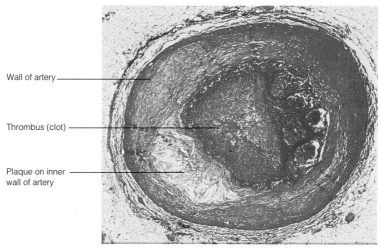

Wall of artery

Thrombus (clot)

Plaque on inner
wall of artery

Human coronary artery containing a thrombus

**Atherosclerosis** – narrowing of the arteries due to thickening of the arterial wall caused by fat, fibrous tissue and salts being deposited on it (Fig. 21.21). The condition is sometimes referred to as hardening of the arteries.

**Spasm** – repeated contractions of the muscle in the coronary artery wall.

It is often a combination of these factors, rather than one in isolation, which results in a **heart attack** or **myocardial infarction**. If the main coronary artery is blocked, the whole of the heart muscle or **myocardium** may be deprived of blood, resulting in death. If only a branch vessel is affected, the loss of blood supply affects only a portion of the myocardium and, after a period of severe chest pain and temporary incapacitation, followed by a number of days of complete rest, recovery normally takes place. **Angina** is the result of reduced blood flow in the coronary arteries due to atherosclerosis or sometimes the result of thrombosis or spasm. Chest pain and breathlessness often occur when an angina sufferer is undertaking strenuous physical effort.

Many factors are known to increase the risk of coronary heart disease. Smoking is a major contributor, increasing the likelihood of both thrombosis and atherosclerosis. A raised level of fat, especially cholesterol, in the blood is a major cause of atherosclerosis. Saturated fat of the type found in most meat an animal products, such as milk, is particularly dangerous. High blood pressure or **hypertension**, a high level of salt in the diet and diabetes are other factors which contribute to atheroscleros and hence coronary heart disease. Stress is suspected of increasing the risk of heart disease, but scientific evidence is hard to come by as it is difficult to measure stress levels accurately. There appears to be an inherited factor, individuals with a family history of heart disease being more susceptible to heart attacks. Older people are more at risk than younger ones, males more at risk than females. One thing generally accepted i that exercise can reduce the risk of coronary heart disease.

## 21.6    Lymphatic system

The lymphatic system consists of widely distributed **lymph capillaries** which are found in all tissues of the body. These capillaries merge to form **lymph vessels** which possess valves and whose structure is similar to that of veins. The fluid within these vessels, the **lymph**, is therefore carried in one direction only, namely, away from the tissues. The lymph vessels from th right side of the head and thorax and the right arm combine to form the **right lymphatic duct** which drains into the right subclavian vein near the heart. The lymph vessels from the rest of the body form the **thoracic duct** which drains into the left subclavian vein (Fig. 21.22).

Along the lymph vessels are series of **lymph nodes**. These contain a population of phagocytic cells, e.g. lymphocytes, whi remove bacteria and other foreign material from the lymph. During infection these nodes frequently swell. Lymph nodes ar the major sites of lymphocyte production.

The movement of lymph through the lymphatic system is achieved in three ways:

**1. Hydrostatic pressure** – The pressure of tissue fluid leaving the arterioles helps push the lymph along the lymph system.

**2. Muscle contraction** – The contraction of skeletal muscle compresses the lymph vessels, exerting a pressure on the lymp within them. The valves in the vessels ensure that this pressure pushes the lymph in the direction of the heart.

**3. Inspiratory movements** – On breathing in, pressure in the thorax is decreased. This helps to draw lymph towards the vessels in the thorax.

Lymph is a milky liquid derived from tissue fluid. It contain lymphocytes and is rich in fats obtained from the lacteals of the small intestines. These fats might damage red blood cells and s are carried separately, until they are later added to the general circulation in safe quantities.

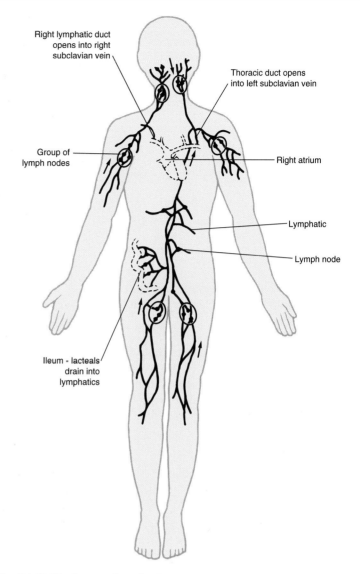

Right lymphatic duct
opens into right
subclavian vein

Thoracic duct opens
into left subclavian vein

Group of
lymph nodes

Right atrium

Lymphatic

Lymph node

Ileum - lacteals
drain into
lymphatics

*Fig. 21.22 The human lymphatic system*

### 21.6.1 Tissue fluid and its formation

As blood passes from arterioles into the narrow capillaries, a hydrostatic pressure is created which helps fluid escape through the capillary walls. This fluid is called **tissue (intercellular) fluid** and it bathes all cells of the body (Fig. 21.23). Tissue fluid contains glucose, amino acids, fatty acids, salts and oxygen, which it supplies to the tissues; from the tissues it obtains carbon dioxide and other excretory material. Tissue fluid is thus the means by which materials are exchanged between blood and tissues.

The majority of this tissue fluid passes back into the venules by osmosis. The plasma proteins, which did not leave the blood, exert an osmotic pressure which draws much of the tissue fluid back into the blood. The fluid which does not return by this means passes into the open-ended lymph capillaries, from which point it becomes known as lymph.

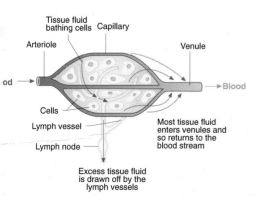

Tissue fluid
bathing cells   Capillary

Arteriole

Venule

od

Blood

Cells

Lymph vessel

Lymph node

Most tissue fluid
enters venules and
so returns to the
blood stream

Excess tissue fluid
is drawn off by the
lymph vessels

*ig. 21.23 Formation and destination of tissue
uid*

# 21.7   Questions

**1.** The diagram shows some nerves associated with the heart and the blood system.

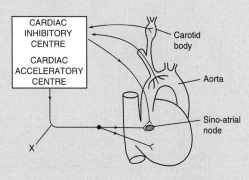

*(a)* In which part of the brain are the cardiac inhibitory and acceleratory centres found?
*(1 mark)*

*(b)* Give **two** stimuli detected in the aorta and the carotid body that may result in a change of heart rate. *(2 marks)*

*(c)* Suggest **two** ways in which stimulation of the heart by nerve **X** leads to an increase in the amount of blood pumped out by the ventricles. *(2 marks)*
*(Total 5 marks)*

*NEAB June 1998, Paper 1, No.5*

**2.** *(a)* Which body system is depicted below? *(1 mark)*

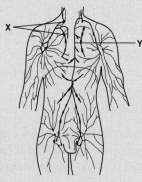

Adapted from *Human Biology*, J. K. Inglis, Pergamon

*(b)* Briefly explain how the fluid content of this network is formed. *(2 marks)*

*(c)* (i) Name the swellings labelled **X**. *(1 mark)*

(ii) Which structures in the pharynx (lower head–neck) region are related functionally to the swellings **X**? *(1 mark)*

(iii) Draw an arrow on the diagram alongside the structure labelled **Y** to indicate direction of flow in this system. *(1 mark)*

*(d)* Outline the functions of this system. *(4 mark*
*(Total 10 mark*

*Oxford June 1997, Paper 42, No.*

**3.** The graph shows the oxygen dissociation curves fo two species of fish, the carp and the mackerel.

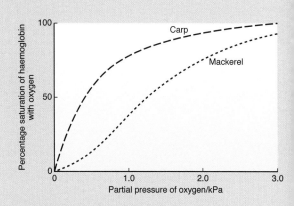

*(a)* Explain what is meant by the partial pressui of oxygen. *(1 mar*

*(b)* Explain how the oxygen dissociation curve of:

(i) carp haemoglobin is related to the fact that carp may be found in ponds containing large amounts of decomposing vegetation; *(2 mark*

(ii) mackerel haemoglobin is related to the fact that the mackerel is a very active species found in the surface waters of the sea. *(2 mark*

*(c)* Both of these fish have a single circulation.

(i) Explain what is meant by a single circulation. *(1 mar*

(ii) Give **one** disadvantage of a single circulation compared with a double circulation. *(1 mar*
*(Total 7 mark*

*AEB Summer 1996, Paper 1, No.*

**4.** Read the following passage on monoclonal antibodies and then write on the dotted lines the mo: appropriate word or words to complete the passage.

Monoclonal antibodies are produced by cells called hybridomas. First, a mouse is exposed to a particular ........., which stimulates the production of large numbers of ......... cells which secrete a particular antibody. These mouse cells are then fused with ......... to produce hybridomas. The hybridomas

vide to produce a culture of identical cells, thus
rming a ………. The monoclonal antibodies
roduced by these cells are collected and
ncentrated before being used, for example, in
agnosing ……….

*(Total 5 marks)*

*Edexcel June 1997, B/HB4A, No. 3*

(a) Describe how active immunity to a viral
infection can be acquired naturally. *(3 marks)*
(b) State **two** ways in which passive immunity
may be acquired naturally by a young child
*(2 marks)*
*(Total 5 marks)*

*Edexcel June 1997, B/HB4A, No. 4*

The diagram shows a wireframe model of a
molecule of haemoglobin.

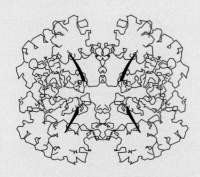

(a)  (i) On a copy of the diagram, indicate
clearly, using arrows, the positions of
iron in the molecule. *(1 mark)*
(ii) State **two** other features of the molecular
structure of haemoglobin that are visible
in the diagram. *(2 marks)*

he graph shows the oxygen dissociation curves for
aemoglobin at two concentrations of carbon dioxide
CO₂).

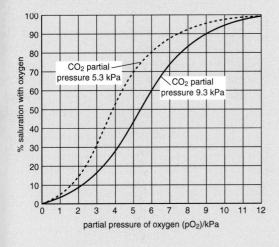

The partial pressure of oxygen ($pO_2$) in the tissues is
approximately 3.5 kPa.

(b) With reference to the graph,
(i) state the difference in % saturation of
haemoglobin between the two
concentrations of $CO_2$ at this partial
pressure of oxygen; *(1 mark)*
(ii) explain the physiological importance of
this difference in the % saturation of
haemoglobin. *(3 marks)*
*(Total 7 marks)*

*UCLES June 1998, Paper 3, No. 5*

7. The figure shows the changes in blood pressure (**A**),
velocity (**B**) and cross-sectional area (**C**) of the blood
vessels of the systemic circulation as blood flows and
returns to the heart.

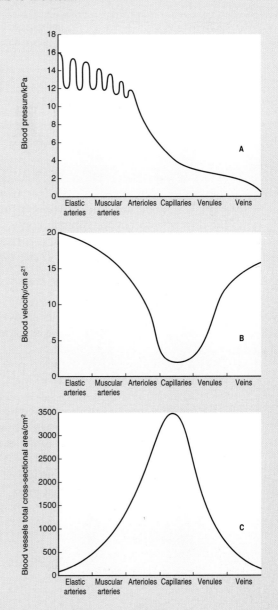

(a) State the relationship between the velocity of the blood and the total cross-sectional area of the blood vessels. *(1 mark)*

(b) (i) Comment on the rate of blood flow through the capillaries. *(1 mark)*

   (ii) Explain the importance of this in relation to the function of the capillaries. *(1 mark)*

(c) Explain how the velocity of the blood is maintained in the arteries, despite fluctuations in blood pressure. *(2 marks)*

(d) Explain how the velocity of blood in the veins increases, while the blood pressure continues to fall. *(2 marks)*

*(Total 7 marks)*

*UCLES June 1997, Paper 3, No. 3*

**8.** The bar chart shows the relative thickness of parts of the walls of two blood vessels, **A** and **B**. One of these blood vessels is an artery, the other is a vein.

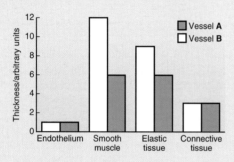

(a) Which blood vessel is the artery? Explain the reasons for your answer. *(2 marks)*

(b) Explain how the structure of veins ensures the flow of blood in one direction only. *(2 marks)*

*(Total 4 marks)*

*NEAB June 1996, Paper 1, No. 7*

**9.** The graph at the top of the next column shows the changes in pressure that take place in the left side of the heart.

(a) Use the graph to calculate the heart rate in beats per minute. Show your working. *(1 mark)*

(b) (i) Explain, in terms of pressure, why the valve between the left ventricle and the aorta opens at time **T**. *(1 mark)*

   (ii) For how long is the valve between the left atrium and the left ventricle closed? Explain how you arrived at your answer. *(2 marks)*

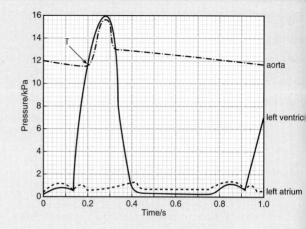

(c) (i) How would you expect the pressure in the right ventricle to differ from that in the left ventricle? *(1 mark)*

   (ii) Explain what causes this difference in pressure. *(1 mark)*

*(Total 6 marks)*

*NEAB February 1997, Paper BY10, No.*

**10.** The diagram shows a section through a healthy artery and a section through an artery with atheroma

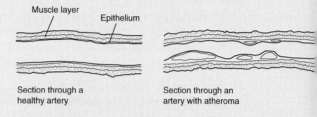

Section through a healthy artery

Section through an artery with atheroma

*Reproduced from GCSE Biology, by permission of D.G. Mackea*

(a) Give **one** way in which the atheroma has changed the structure of the artery wall. *(1 mark)*

(b) (i) Atheroma may lead to damage to red blood cells. Describe how this could lead to the formation of a blood clot. *(2 marks)*

   (ii) Explain the effects of a blood clot in the coronary artery. *(2 marks)*

(c) Give **two** ways in which changes in diet could reduce the risk of cardiovascular disease. *(2 marks)*

*(Total 7 marks)*

*NEAB June 1997, Paper BY08, No.*

# 22 Uptake and transport in plants

For plants there are certain advantages in large size. They can, for example, compete more readily for light. As a result, many trees are tall, some exceeding 100 m. The leaves, as the sites of photosynthesis, must be in these aerial parts to obtain light. The water so essential to photosynthesis is, however, collected by the roots which may be some considerable distance beneath the soil surface. An efficient means of transporting this water, and certain minerals, to the leaves is necessary. The sugars formed as a result of photosynthesis in the leaves must be transported in the opposite direction to sustain respiration in the roots. In the absence of muscle or other contractile cells, plants depend to a large extent on passive rather than active means of transport.

## 22.1 The importance of water to living organisms

Life arose in water and many organisms still live surrounded by it. Those that left water to colonize land nonetheless keep their cells bathed in it. Water is therefore the main constituent of all organisms – in jellyfish up to 98% and in most herbaceous plants 90%. Even mammals consist of around 65% water. The unique properties of the water molecule are given in the Appendix on page 681.

### 22.1.1 Metabolic role of water

1.  **Hydrolysis** – Water is used to hydrolyse many substances, e.g. proteins to amino acids, fats to fatty acids and glycerol, and polysaccharides to monosaccharides.

2.  **Medium for chemical reactions** – All chemical reactions in cells take place in an aqueous medium.

3.  **Diffusion and osmosis** – Water is essential to the diffusion of materials across surfaces such as the lungs or alimentary canal.

4.  **Photosynthetic substrate** – Water is a major raw material in photosynthesis.

### 22.1.2 Water as a solvent

Water readily dissolves other substances and therefore is used for:

1. **Transport** – Blood plasma, tissue fluid and lymph are all predominantly water and are used to dissolve a wide range of substances which can then be easily transported.

2. **Removal of wastes** – Metabolic wastes like ammonia and urea are removed from the body in solution in water.

3. **Secretions** – Most secretions comprise substances in aqueous solution. Most digestive juices have salts and enzymes in solution; tears consist largely of water and snake venoms have toxins in suspension in water.

### 22.1.3 Water as a lubricant

Water's properties, especially its viscosity, make it a useful lubricant. Lubricating fluids which are mostly water include:

1. **Mucus** – used externally to aid movement in animals, e.g. snail and earthworm; or internally in the vagina and gut wall.

2. **Synovial fluid** – lubricates movement in many vertebrate joints.

3. **Pleural fluid** – lubricates movement of the lungs during breathing.

4. **Pericardial fluid** – lubricates movement of the heart.

5. **Perivisceral fluid** – lubricates movement of internal organs, e.g. the peristaltic motions of the alimentary canal.

### 22.1.4 Supporting role of water

With its large cohesive forces, water molecules lie close together. Water is therefore not easily compressed, making it a useful means of supporting organisms. Examples include:

1. **Hydrostatic skeleton** – Animals like the earthworm are supported by the pressure of the aqueous medium within them.

2. **Turgor pressure** – Herbaceous plants and the herbaceous parts of woody ones are supported by the osmotic influx of water into their cells.

3. **Humours of the eye** – The shape of the eye in vertebrates is maintained by the aqueous and vitreous humours within them. Both are largely water.

4. **Amniotic fluid** – This supports and protects the mammalian fetus during development.

5. **Erection of the penis** – The pressure of blood, a largely aqueous fluid, makes the penis erect so that it can be introduced into the vagina during copulation.

6. **Medium in which to live** – Water provides support to the organisms that live within it. Very large organisms, e.g. whales, returned to water as their sheer size made movement on land difficult.

### 22.1.5 Miscellaneous functions of water

**1. Temperature control** – Evaporation of water during sweating and panting is used to cool the body.

**2. Medium for dispersal** – Water may be used to disperse the larval stages of some terrestrial organisms. In mosses and ferns, water is the medium in which sperm are transferred. The build-up of osmotic pressure helps to disperse the seeds of the squirting cucumber.

**3. Hearing and balance** – In the mammalian ear the watery endolymph and perilymph play a role in hearing and balance.

## 22.2    Simple plant tissues

Simple plant tissues each consist of only one type of cell. They are normally grouped according to the degree of thickening present in the cell wall.

### 22.2.1 Parenchyma

Parenchyma cells are usually spherical although their shape may be distorted by pressure from adjacent cells. These unspecialized living cells form the bulk of packing tissue within the plant. Parenchyma cells are metabolically active and may also store food. When tightly packed and turgid they provide support for herbaceous plants. Air spaces around parenchyma cells allow exchange of gases to take place. (See Fig. 22.1.)

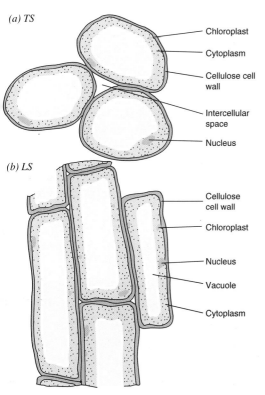

*(a) TS*

- Chloroplast
- Cytoplasm
- Cellulose cell wall
- Intercellular space
- Nucleus

*(b) LS*

- Cellulose cell wall
- Chloroplast
- Nucleus
- Vacuole
- Cytoplasm

*ig. 22.1 Parenchyma*

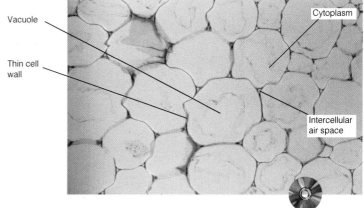

Vacuole

Thin cell wall

Cytoplasm

Intercellular air space

Parenchyma cells (TS) (×200 approx.)

### 22.2.2 Collenchyma

Collenchyma cells are living and have cell walls with additional cellulose deposited in the corners. This provides them with extra mechanical strength. They are elongated and important in growing stems since they are able to stretch. They are often found just under the epidermis of a stem or in the corners of angular stems. (See Fig. 22.2.)

447

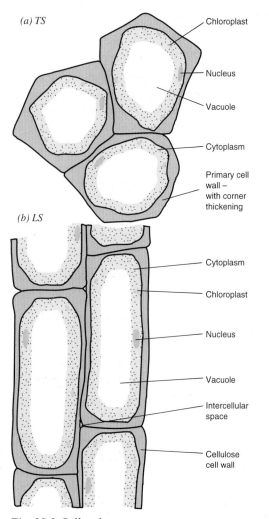

*(a) TS*

Chloroplast

Nucleus

Vacuole

Cytoplasm

Primary cell wall – with corner thickening

*(b) LS*

Cytoplasm

Chloroplast

Nucleus

Vacuole

Intercellular space

Cellulose cell wall

*Fig. 22.2 Collenchyma*

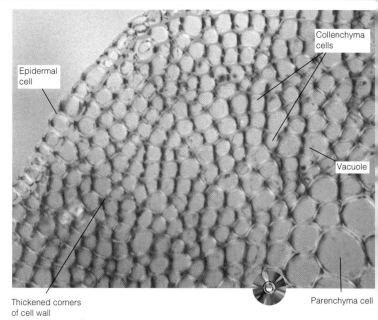

Collenchyma cells

Epidermal cell

Vacuole

Parenchyma cell

Thickened corners of cell wall

Collenchyma cells (TS) (×450 approx.)

### 22.2.3 Sclerenchyma

Mature sclerenchyma cells are dead and therefore incapable of growth. They develop fully when the growth of surrounding tissues is complete. Sclerenchyma cells have large deposits of lignin on the primary cell wall and the cell contents are lost. In places, lignin is not deposited due to the presence of **plasmodesmata** in the primary cell wall; such regions are called **pits**. (See Fig. 22.3.)

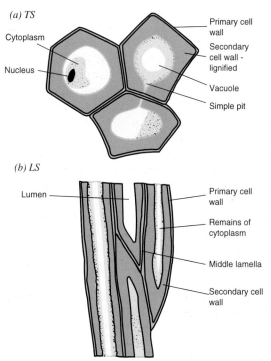

*(a) TS*

Cytoplasm

Nucleus

Primary cell wall

Secondary cell wall - lignified

Vacuole

Simple pit

*(b) LS*

Lumen

Primary cell wall

Remains of cytoplasm

Middle lamella

Secondary cell wall

*Fig. 22.3 Sclerenchyma*

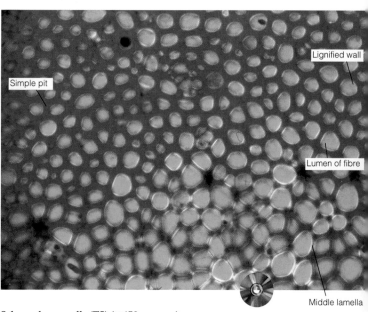

Lignified wall

Simple pit

Lumen of fibre

Middle lamella

Sclerenchyma cells (TS) (×450 approx.)

Some sclerenchyma cells are roughly spherical and are known as **sclereids**. These are usually found in small groups in fruits and seeds, cortex, pith and phloem.

Elongated sclerenchyma cells are called **fibres** and they provide the main supporting tissue of many mature stems. They may form a cylinder below the epidermis, are found in xylem and phloem and sometimes as masses associated with vascular bundles.

## 22.3    Water relations of a plant cell

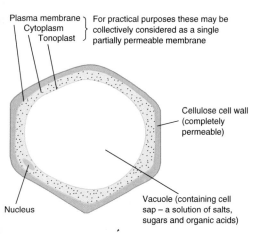

Plasma membrane ⎤
Cytoplasm    ⎬ For practical purposes these may be
Tonoplast    ⎦ collectively considered as a single
              partially permeable membrane

Cellulose cell wall (completely permeable)

Nucleus

Vacuole (containing cell sap – a solution of salts, sugars and organic acids)

*Fig. 22.4 Typical plant cell showing osmotically important structures*

For practical purposes the plant cell can be divided into three parts (Fig. 22.4):

1. **The vacuole** – This contains an aqueous solution of salts, sugars and organic acids.

2. **The cytoplasm surrounded by membranes** – The inner membrane is called the **tonoplast** and the outer one, the **plasma membrane**; both are partially permeable.

3. **The cell wall** – This is made of cellulose fibres and is completely permeable to even large molecules. It may be impregnated with substances like lignin, in which case it is impermeable to molecules.

We saw in Section 4.3.3 that **water potential ($\Psi$)** is the capacity of a system to lose water. The water potential of pure water at standard temperature and pressure (25 °C and 100 kPa) is zero.

The presence of solute molecules in the vacuole of a plant cell makes its water potential more negative (lower). The greater the concentration of solutes, the more negative is the water potential. This change in water potential as a consequence of the presence of solute molecules is called the **solute potential ($\Psi_s$)**. (This was previously called 'osmotic potential'.) As the solute molecules always lower the water potential, the value of the solute potential is always negative.

If a plant cell is surrounded by pure water, the water potential of the vacuole, containing solute molecules as it does, will be more negative than the surrounding medium. Water therefore enters by osmosis, thus creating a hydrostatic pressure which pushes outwards on the cell wall. This is known as the **pressure potential ($\Psi_p$)**. In this instance, as in most plant cells, the pressure potential is positive. In xylem vessels, however, where transpiration is pulling water up the plant, the pressure potential is negative.

The relationship between water potential, solute potential and pressure potential is shown in the equation:

$$\Psi = \Psi_s + \Psi_p$$

water        solute       pressure
potential    potential    potential

449

*Fig. 22.5 Chart to show differences between cells placed in external solutions of different water potential*

If the same cell is placed in a solution which has a more negative solute potential than that of its cell sap, it will lose water by osmosis. In this case the external solution has a more negative water potential than the internal solution of the cell sap. As a result, water is drawn out of the cell by osmosis and the protoplast (the living part of the cell) shrinks. As it does so the

| Water potential ($\psi$) of external solution compared to internal solution | Less negative (higher) | Equal | More negative (lower) |
|---|---|---|---|
| Net movement of water | Enters cell | Neither enters nor leaves cell | Leaves cell |
| Protoplast | Swells | No change | Shrinks |
| Condition of cell | Turgid | Incipient plasmolysis | Plasmolysed (flaccid) |

# NOTEBOOK

## Negative values for water potential – designed to confuse?

Not really – consider this:

The highest possible value of water potential is that of pure water – namely zero. Add solute to the water and its water potential is lowered, i.e. it has a negative value. All solutions therefore have negative water potentials. A somewhat crazy situation you may think until you understand that water potential is actually the capacity of a system to lose water.

Think of it as a person gambling at a casino with no money (not that many casinos would tolerate the idea!). If the gambler loses £5 he is in debt to the casino, i.e. he has −£5. The more he loses the higher is his debt and the lower is the level of his money. In terms of the level of his money −£10 is lower than −£5 (although the number 10 is actually bigger than 5). The bigger the debt, the lower the level of his money. At the same time the bigger the gambler's debt, the greater need he has for money to flow into his account. So it is with water potential (except that water is the currency rather than pound coins!). The more negative the water potential the greater the water 'debt' and the more readily water flows into the system.

A water potential of −20 kPa is lower than one of −10 kPa and therefore water moves from the solution at −10 kPa to that at −20 kPa just as a temperature of −20 °C is lower than one of −10 °C and heat will move from a system at −10 °C to one at −20 °C.

pressure potential decreases. A point is reached where the protoplast no longer presses on the cell wall, and hence the pressure potential falls to zero. This point is termed **incipient plasmolysis**. Any further loss of water causes the protoplast to shrink more and so pull away from the cell wall. This condition is called **plasmolysis** and the cell is said to be **flaccid** (see Fig. 22.5). It is important to remember that water will always move from a less negative (higher) water potential to a more negative (lower) one. Pure water has a water potential of zero.

## 22.4 Transpiration

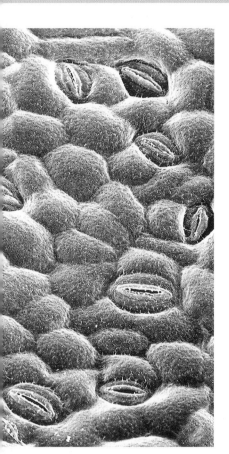

tomata on a rose leaf (SEM) (×500)

The evaporation of water from plants is called **transpiration**. This evaporation takes place at three sites:

**1. Stomata** – Most water loss, up to 90%, takes place through these minute pores which occur mostly, but not exclusively, on leaves. Some are found on herbaceous stems.

**2. Cuticle** – A little water, perhaps 10%, is lost through the cuticle, which is not completely impermeable to gases. The thicker the cuticle the smaller the water loss.

**3. Lenticels** – Woody stems have a superficial layer of cork which considerably reduces gas exchange over their surface. At intervals the cells of this layer are loosely packed, appearing externally as raised dots. These are the lenticels through which gaseous exchange, and hence water loss, may occur. The amount of transpiration through these is relatively insignificant.

Transpiration would appear to be the inevitable, if undesirable, consequence of having leaves punctured with stomata. The necessity of stomata for photosynthesis is obvious. It is unfortunate that any opening in a leaf which allows gases in will inevitably allow water out. The plant has to balance carefully the conflicting needs of obtaining carbon dioxide for photosynthesis with the inevitable loss of water this creates. We shall see in the next section how this is achieved by controlling the opening and closing of stomata. Transpiration is not essential as a means of bringing water to the leaves. This could occur by purely osmotic means. As water is used for photosynthesis in a leaf mesophyll cell, its water potential becomes more negative (lower). Water could then enter this cell from adjacent cells whose water potential would also become more negative (lower). They in turn would draw it from adjacent cells and so on down to the root hair cells of the plant, which would draw their water from the soil solution. While mineral salts are drawn up the plant in the transpiration stream, these could be diffused, or actively transported, in the absence of transpiration. Mineral uptake from the soil is largely independent of the rate of transpiration and could certainly occur in its absence. The cooling effect of transpiration is only beneficial when environmental temperatures are high, and even then its effects are insignificant. The definition of transpiration as a 'necessary evil' is therefore not without some justification.

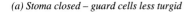

*(a) Stoma closed – guard cells less turgid*

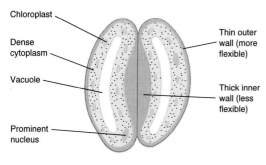

Chloroplast

Dense cytoplasm

Vacuole

Prominent nucleus

Thin outer wall (more flexible)

Thick inner wall (less flexible)

*(b) Stoma open – guard cells more turgid*

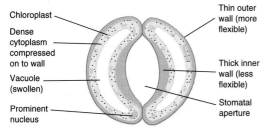

Chloroplast

Dense cytoplasm compressed on to wall

Vacuole (swollen)

Prominent nucleus

Thin outer wall (more flexible)

Thick inner wall (less flexible)

Stomatal aperture

*Fig. 22.7 Surface view of stoma*

Stoma is closed in the dark, but in the presence of light ATPase is stimulated to convert ATP to ADP and so provide the energy to pump out hydrogen ions (protons) from the guard cells. These protons return on a carrier which also brings chloride ions (Cl⁻) with it. At the same time potassium ions (K⁺) also enter guard cells.

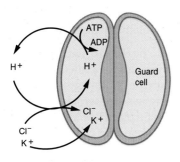

ATP
ADP
H⁺
H⁺
Guard cell
Cl⁻
K⁺
Cl⁻
K⁺

As a result of this influx of ions, the water potential of the guard cells becomes more negative (lower) causing water to pass in by osmosis. The resultant increase in pressure potential causes the stoma to open.

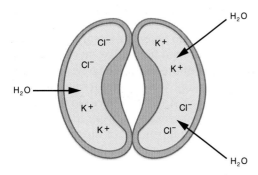

H₂O
Cl⁻
Cl⁻
K⁺
K⁺
H₂O
K⁺
K⁺
Cl⁻
Cl⁻
H₂O

In the dark, the movement of ions and water is reversed.

*Fig. 22.8 Mechanism of stomatal opening*

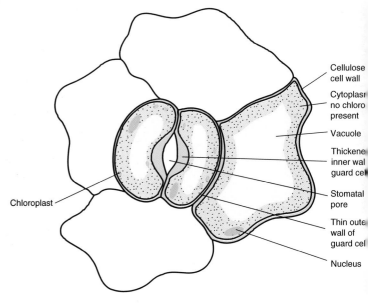

Cellulose cell wall

Cytoplasm no chloro present

Vacuole

Thickene inner wal guard cel

Stomatal pore

Thin oute wall of guard cel

Nucleus

Chloroplast

*Fig. 22.6 Epidermis and stoma*

### 22.4.1 Stomatal mechanism

Stomata occur primarily on leaves. They are normally more abundant on the abaxial (lower) surface, where there are typically around 180 per mm². They may even be entirely absent on the adaxial (upper) surface. The structure of a stoma is given in Chapter 14, Fig. 14.1. It consists of a pair of specialized epidermal cells, the **guard cells**, which surround a small pore a few microns wide known as the **stomatal aperture**. Guard cells are different from normal epidermal cells in being kidney-shaped (see Fig. 22.6). Unlike other epidermal cells, they possess chloroplasts and have denser cytoplasm with a more prominent nucleus. The inner walls of guard cells are thicker and less elastic than the outer ones. It is this which makes the inner wall less able to stretch and results in the typical kidney shape. Moreover any increase in the volume of a guard cell, owing, for example, to the osmotic uptake of water, causes increased bowing of the cell owing to the greatest expansion occurring in the outer wall. When this occurs in the two guard cells of a stoma, the stomatal aperture enlarges (Fig. 22.7).

Even when all stomata on a leaf are fully open, the total area of the apertures rarely exceeds 2% of the leaf area.

It is possible to show that opening of a stoma is the result of pressure potential changes within the guard cells by puncturing turgid guard cells using a micro-needle. This releases the pressure potential and the cells collapse, closing the stoma.

What exactly causes changes in pressure potential within guard cells? While there are a number of factors which influence pressure potential, they all operate through changes in the water potential. It has long been observed that stomata open in the light and close in the dark. In the light it is thought that potassium ions (K⁺) and chloride ions (Cl⁻) enter the guard cells lowering their water potential and so causing water to enter by osmosis. As a result the stoma opens. The mechanism involves a proton pump and is described in more detail in Fig. 22.8.

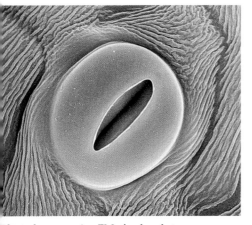

alse-colour scanning EM of a closed stoma

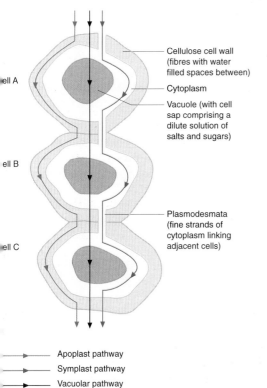

Cellulose cell wall (fibres with water filled spaces between)

Cytoplasm

Vacuole (with cell sap comprising a dilute solution of salts and sugars)

Plasmodesmata (fine strands of cytoplasm linking adjacent cells)

→ Apoplast pathway
→ Symplast pathway
→ Vacuolar pathway

Fig. 22.9 Alternative routes for water transport across cells

## 22.4.2 Movement of water across the leaf

Under normal circumstances the humidity of the atmosphere is less than that in the sub-stomatal air-space. Provided the stomata are open (see Section 22.4.1) the less negative (higher) water potential in the sub-stomatal air-space causes water vapour to diffuse out into the atmosphere through the stomatal aperture. Provided there is some air movement around the leaf, the water vapour is swept away once it leaves the stomata. The water lost from the sub-stomatal air-space is replaced by more evaporating from the spongy mesophyll cells surrounding the space. The water is brought to the spongy mesophyll cells from xylem in the leaf – in three ways:

**1. The apoplast pathway** – Most water travels from cell to cell via the cell wall, which is made up of cellulose fibres, between which are water-filled spaces. As the water evaporates into the sub-stomatal air-space from the wall of one cell, it creates a tension which pulls in water from the spaces in the walls of surrounding cells. The pull is transmitted through the plant by the cohesive forces between the water molecules which, due to hydrogen bonding, are particularly strong.

**2. The symplast pathway** – Some water is lost to the sub-stomatal air-space from the cytoplasm of cells surrounding it. The water potential of this cytoplasm is thereby made more negative (lower). Between adjacent cells are tiny strands of cytoplasm, known as **plasmodesmata**, which link the cytoplasm of one cell to that of the next. Water may pass along these plasmodesmata from adjacent cells with a less negative (higher) water potential. This loss of water makes the water potential of this second cell more negative (lower), which may in turn replace it with water from other cells with less negative (higher) water potentials. In this way a water potential gradient is established between the sub-stomatal space and the xylem vessels of the leaf. The symplast pathway carries less water than the apoplast pathway, but is of greater importance than the vacuolar pathway.

**3. The vacuolar pathway** – A little water passes by osmosis from the vacuole of one cell to the next, through the cell wall, membranes and cytoplasm of adjacent cells. In the same way as the symplast pathway, a water potential gradient between the xylem and the sub-stomatal air-space exists. It is along this gradient that the water passes.

In Fig. 22.9 water leaving cell C causes its water potential to become more negative. Assuming all three cells were originally of equal water potential, then, compared to cell C, cell B now has a less negative water potential. Water therefore flows from cell B to cell C. In the same way, loss of water from B to C causes water to enter B from A. Remember that this mechanism applies only to the symplast and vacuolar pathways. The apoplast pathway is due to cohesion tension and is independent of a water potential gradient.

## 22.4.3 Structure of xylem

Xylem consists of parenchyma cells and fibres together with two specialized types of cells: vessels and tracheids. These tissues are

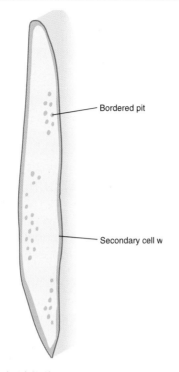

Bordered pit

Secondary cell w

*Fig. 22.10 Tracheid (LS)*

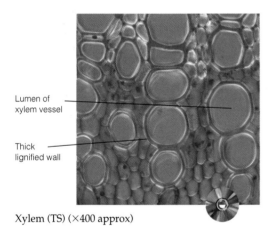

Lumen of
xylem vessel

Thick
lignified wall

Xylem (TS) (×400 approx)

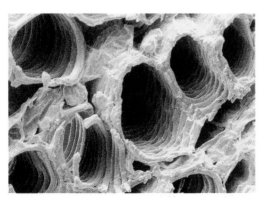

Leaf of tobacco showing xylem vessels
(scanning EM) (× 500 approx.)

both dead and serve the dual role of support and water transport. The types of **vessel** found depend upon the degree and nature of the cell wall thickening. In the **protoxylem** the lignin is deposited in rings or spirals, so the cell is still capable o expansion. In **metaxylem** there is more extensive lignification arranged in patterns known as **reticulate**, **scalariform** or **pitted**. All vessels are made up of cells whose cross walls have broken down, resulting in long tubes ideal for carrying water.

**Tracheids** are spindle-shaped cells arranged in rows with the ends of the cells overlapping. The cells have heavily lignified walls and so there are no cell contents. They provide mechanica strength and support to the plant. (See Fig. 22.10.)

### 22.4.4 Movement of water up the stem

Water moves up the stem and into the leaves through xylem vessels and tracheids. Xylem and phloem together form **vascular bundles** which are arranged mostly towards the outside of the stem. The reason for this is that the vascular bundles, along with associated sclerenchyma, give support to the stems of herbaceou plants. The main forces acting on stems are lateral ones, owing largely to the wind. These forces are best resisted by an outer cylinder of supporting tissue. Hence the vascular bundles are predominantly at the periphery of stems as shown in Fig. 22.11.

The evidence supporting the view that xylem carries water u the stem includes:

**1.** A leafy shoot is cut under water containing a dye, e.g. eosin. The cut end is kept in the solution of the dye and left for a few hours. The shoot is removed and cut at various levels up the stem. Only the xylem is found to be stained red, indicating that alone transports water. If left long enough in the dye, the veins of the leaves also become stained.

**2.** A ring of tissue removed from the outside of a woody stem does not affect the flow of water up the stem, provided only the bark, including the phloem, are removed. If, however, the outer layers of xylem are also removed, upward transport ceases and the leaves wilt.

**3.** If the cut end of a shoot is placed in a solution of a metabolic poison, the uptake of the solution continues as normal. If the process were an active one, it would be expected that the poison would kill the cells in which it travelled and so prevent water transport. As the process continues, it must be assumed that it occurs passively. As xylem cells are dead, these would seem the most likely sites of this passive process.

**4.** Plants which are allowed to draw up fatty solutions soon wil It is found by staining and microscopic examination that these fats have blocked the lumina of the xylem cells. The wilting mus therefore be the result of this blockage and hence xylem must be the route by which water rises up the stem.

The theory of the mechanism by which water moves up the xylem is known as the **cohesion–tension theory**. The transpiration of water from the leaves draws water across the leaf (Section 22.4.2). This water is replaced by that entering the mesophyll cells from the xylem by osmosis. As water molecules leave xylem cells in the leaf, they pull up other water molecules.

ylem macerate ($\times$ 200 approx.)

This pulling effect, known as the **transpiration pull**, is possible because of the large cohesive forces between water molecules. The pull creates a tension in the xylem cells which, if cut, draw in air rather than exude water. Such is the cohesive force of this column of liquid that it is sufficient to raise water to heights in excess of 100 m, i.e. large enough to supply water to the top of the tallest known trees, the Californian redwoods.

Other forces may contribute to the movement of water up the stems of plants. These make only a small contribution to transport in large trees but may be significant in smaller herbaceous plants. **Adhesion forces** between the water molecules and the walls of xylem vessels help water to rise in xylem – a phenomenon known as **capillarity**. This force can cause water to rise to a height of 3 m. Adhesion however also causes a frictional drag on the upward flow of water in the xylem. Its overall influence is therefore minimal and may even be detrimental in a large tree.

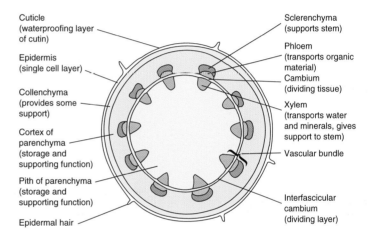

Fig. 22.11 (a) TS through a typical dicotyledonous stem

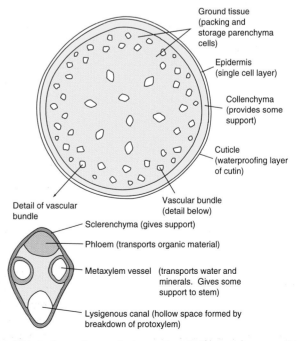

Fig. 22.11 (b) TS through a typical monocotyledonous stem

455

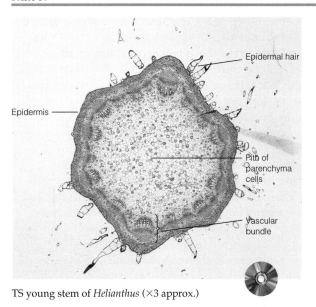

TS young stem of *Helianthus* (×3 approx.)

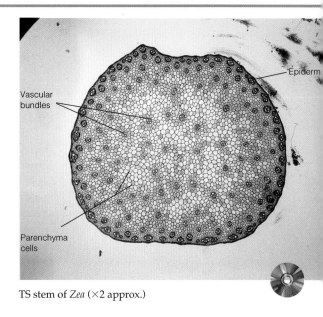

TS stem of *Zea* (×2 approx.)

### 22.4.5 Xylem structure related to its role of water transport

The relationship between structure and function is always a close one and this is especially true of xylem vessels and tracheids. The structure of xylem is given in Section 22.4.3. Correlations between xylem structure and its function of water transport include the six points below.

**1.** Both vessels and tracheids consist of long cells (up to 5 mm in length) joined end to end. This allows water to flow in a continuous column.

**2.** The end walls of xylem vessels have broken down to give an uninterrupted flow of water from the roots to the leaves. Even in tracheids where end walls are present, large bordered pits reduce the resistance to flow caused by the presence of these walls.

**3.** There are pits at particular points in the lignified wall which permit lateral flow of water where this is necessary.

**4.** The walls are impregnated with lignin, making them especially rigid to prevent them collapsing under the large tension forces set up by the transpiration pull.

**5.** The impregnation of the cellulose walls with lignin increases the adhesion of water molecules and helps the water to rise by capillarity.

**6.** The narrowness of the lumina of vessels and tracheids (0.01–0.2 mm in diameter) increases the capillarity forces.

### 22.4.6 Measurement of transpiration

Transpiration in a cut leafy shoot can be measured using a potometer, a diagram of which is given in Fig. 22.12. To be strictly accurate, the instrument measures the rate of water uptake of a shoot, but in practice this is almost exactly the same as the rate of transpiration. A little of the water taken up may be used in photosynthesis and other metabolic processes, but the vast majority is transpired. The experiment is carried out as follows:

**1.** Cut a leafy shoot off a plant. As it is under tension, cutting the shoot will cause air to enter the xylem so, if possible, firstly hold the part where the cut is to be made under water. If this is not feasible, it will be necessary to trim back the cut shoot a few centimetres to remove the xylem containing air.

**2.** Submerging the potometer, fill it with water, using the syringe to help pump out any air bubbles. Fit the leafy shoot to the rubber tube, ensuring a tight fit.

**3.** Remove the apparatus from the water and allow excess water to drain off. Gently shake the shoot to remove as much water as possible.

**4.** Seal joints around the rubber tube with vaseline to keep the apparatus watertight.

**5.** Introduce an air bubble into the water column by using the syringe to push the water almost to the end of the capillary tube. Leave a small air-space. Place the open end of the capillary tube in a vessel of water and draw up more water behind the air-space.

**6.** When the shoot is dry, the syringe may be depressed with the tap open until the air bubble in the capillary tube is pushed back to the zero mark. The tap should then be turned to close off the syringe.

**7.** Measure the distance moved by the air bubble in the calibrated capillary tube in a given time. Repeat the procedure a number of times, using the syringe to return the air bubble to zero each time.

**8.** Calculate the water uptake in $mm^3\ min^{-1}$ using the average of the results obtained.

**9.** The experiment can be repeated under differing conditions, e.g. in light and dark, at different air temperatures and humidities, in still and moving air.

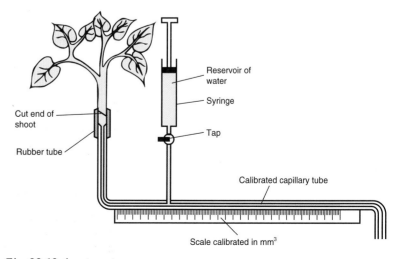

*Fig. 22.12 A potometer*

# 22.5 Factors affecting transpiration

A number of factors influence the rate of transpiration. These may be divided for convenience into external (environmental) factors and internal ones related to the structure of the plant itself.

### 22.5.1 External factors affecting transpiration

External factors include all aspects of the environment which alter the diffusion gradient between the transpiring surface and the atmosphere. Among these are:

**1. Humidity** – The humidity, or vapour pressure, of the air affects the water potential gradient between the atmosphere within the leaf and that outside. When the external air has a high humidity, the gradient is reduced and less water is transpired. Conversely, low humidities increase the transpiration rate.

**2. Temperature** – A change in temperature affects both the kinetic movement of water molecules and the relative humidity of air. A rise in temperature increases the kinetic energy of water molecules and so increases the rate of evaporation of water. At the same time it lowers the relative humidity of the air. Both changes increase the rate of transpiration. A fall in temperature has the reverse effect, namely, a reduction in the amount of water transpired.

**3. Wind speed** – In the absence of any air movement the water vapour which diffuses from stomata accumulates near the leaf surface. This reduces the water potential gradient between the moist atmosphere in the stomata and the drier air outside. The transpiration rate is thus reduced. Any movement of air tends to disperse the humid layer at the leaf surface, thus increasing the transpiration rate. The faster the wind speed, the more rapidly the moist air is removed and the greater the rate of transpiration.

**4. Light** – The stomata of most plants open in light and close in the dark. The suggested mechanism by which these changes are brought about is given in Section 22.4.1. It follows that, up to a point, an increase in light intensity increases the transpiration rate and vice versa.

**5. Water availability** – A reduction in the availability of water to the plant, for example as the result of a dry soil, means there is a reduced water potential gradient between the soil and the leaf. The transpiration rate is reduced as a result.

### 22.5.2 Internal factors affecting transpiration

There are a number of anatomical and morphological features of plants which also influence the transpiration rate. Many specific adaptations of plants designed to reduce water loss are dealt with in Section 22.5.3. Only general features applicable to all plants are dealt with here.

**1. Leaf area** – As a proportion of water loss occurs through the cuticle, the greater the total leaf area of a plant, the greater the rate of transpiration regardless of the number of stomata present. In addition, any reduction in leaf area inevitably involves a reduction in the total number of stomata.

Norway spruce needles

**2. Cuticle** – The cuticle is a waxy covering over the leaf surface which reduces water loss. The thicker this cuticle is, the lower the rate of cuticular transpiration.

**3. Density of stomata** – The greater the number of stomata for a given area, the higher the transpiration rate. Stomatal density on the abaxial (lower) epidermis of plants may vary from around 2000 cm$^{-2}$ in an oat (*Avena sativa*) leaf to 45 000 cm$^{-2}$ on an oak (*Quercus* spp.) leaf.

**4. Distribution of stomata** – In most dicotyledonous plants the leaves are positioned with their adaxial (upper) surfaces towards the light. The upper surfaces are subject to greater temperature rises than the lower ones owing to the warming effect of the sun. Transpiration is therefore potentially greater from the upper surface. Many plants, like the oak (*Quercus* spp.) and the apple (*Malus* spp.) limit their stomata entirely to the abaxial (lower) surface to reduce their overall water loss.

### 22.5.3 Xerophytic adaptations

**Xerophytes** are plants which have adapted to conditions of unfavourable water balance, i.e. conditions where the rate of loss is potentially greater than the availability of water. Most plants live in areas where ample water is available. These are known as **mesophytes**. Xerophytic plants have evolved a wide range of features designed to reduce the rate of transpiration. These are known as **xeromorphic** features. These adaptations are not confined to xerophytic plants but may also occur in mesophytes. By no means all xeromorphic adaptations occur in plants of hot, dry desert regions. Many species in cold regions cannot supply adequate water to the leaves as the soil water is frozen, and so unobtainable, for much of the year. Other species with a reasonable supply of water may suffer excessive loss from the leaves as a result of living in exposed, windy situations. These too exhibit xeromorphic features. Other plants live in salt marshes where the concentration of salts in the soil make it difficult to obtain water. These **halophytes**, as they are called, also exhibit xeromorphic features.

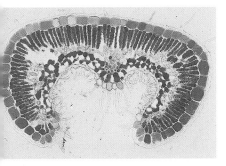

S leaf of *Erica* (heather)

**ABLE 22.1 Xerophytic modifications of sorghum**

| Sorghum is an important cereal in hot, dry areas of Africa and China |
|---|
| Extensive root system – to absorb available water from a large area. |
| Thick cuticle – to reduce evaporation. |
| Reduced number of sunken stomata – to reduce water loss by transpiration. |
| Adults and embryos tolerate high temperatures – to aid survival in hot environments. |

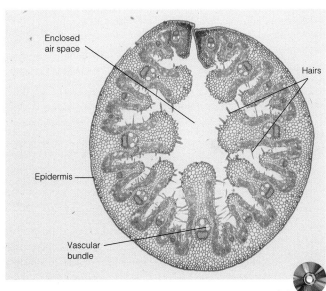

TS leaf of *Ammophila*, showing xerophytic features (×3 approx.)

The xeromorphic adaptations of plants are summarized in Table 22.1. These take three general forms:

**1. Reduction in the transpiration rate** – Clearly anything which lowers the rate at which the plant loses water helps to conserve when in short supply.

**2. Storage of water** – In plants living where water supply is intermittent, e.g. in the desert, there is considerable advantage i

TABLE 22.2 **Xeromorphic adaptations of plants**

| General form | Specific adaptation | Examples | Mechanism by which adaptation functions |
|---|---|---|---|
| Reduction of the transpiration rate | Thick cuticle | Evergreens, especially gymnosperms | Reduces cuticular transpiration by forming a waxy barrier preventing water loss |
| | Rolling of leaves | *Ammophila* (marram grass); *Calluna* (ling) | Moist air is trapped within the leaf, preventing water diffusing out through stomata which are confined to the inner surface |
| | Layer of protective hairs on leaf (pubescence) | *Ammophila* (marram grass); *Calluna* (ling) | Moist air is trapped in the hair layer, increasing the length of the diffusion path, so reducing transpiration |
| | Depression of stomata | *Pinus* (pine); *Ilex* (holly) | Lengthens the diffusion path by trapping still, moist air above the stomata, so reducing transpiration |
| | Reduction of surface-area/volume ratio of leaves | *Pinus* (pine) | The leaves are small and circular in cross-section to reduce the transpiration area. The shape also gives structural rigidity to help prevent wilting |
| | Absence of leaves | Most cacti, e.g. *Opuntia* (prickly pear) | Dispensing with leaves altogether limits water loss to the stems, which have considerably fewer stomata. These stems are flattened to provide an adequate area for photosynthesis |
| | Orientation of leaves | *Lactuca* (compass plant) | The positions of the leaves are constantly changed so that the sun strikes them obliquely. This reduces their temperature and hence the transpiration rate |
| | More negative (lower) water potential of cell sap | Many xerophytes and most halophytes, e.g. *Salicornia* (glasswort) | The cells accumulate salts which make their water potential more negative (lower). This makes it more difficult for water to be drawn from them |
| Succulence | Succulent leaves | *Bryophyllum* | Stores water |
| | Succulent stems | Most cacti, e.g. *Opuntia* (prickly pear) | Stores water |
| | Closing of stomata during daylight | Most cacti and other $C_4$ plants | The more efficient use of carbon dioxide by $C_4$ plants allows them to keep stomata closed during much of the day, so reducing transpiration |
| | Shallow but extensive root systems | Most succulents | Allows efficient absorption of water over a wide area when the upper layers of the soil are moistened by rain |
| Resistance to desiccation | Reduction of transpiration surface through loss or adaptation of leaves | *Berberis* (barberry); many cacti | Leaves reduced to spines to protect plant from grazing. Flattene stems perform photosynthesis |
| | | *Ruscus* (butcher's broom) | Leaves are lost and photosynthesis is performed by a flattened stem known as a cladode |
| | | *Acacia* | The lamina of the leaf is lost and the petiole becomes flattened to carry out photosynthesis |
| | Lignification of leaves | *Hakea* | Lignified tissue supports the leaf, preventing it wilting in times of drought and thereby allowing it to continue photosynthesis |
| | Reduction in cell size | Many xerophytes | The proportion of cell wall material is greater with many small cells. This gives additional support, making the plant less liable to wilt |

rapidly absorbing the water when available and storing it for use during periods of drought. Plants which store water are termed **succulents**. The adaptations of these plants are not limited to specialized water storage tissue but include mechanisms for rapid water absorption, and reducing the rate at which it is lost.

**3. Resistance to desiccation** – Some species exhibit a remarkable tolerance to water loss and resistance to wilting.

### 22.5.4 Hydrophytic adaptations

Plants that live wholly or partly submerged in water are called hydrophytes.

ater-lily (*Nymphaea*)

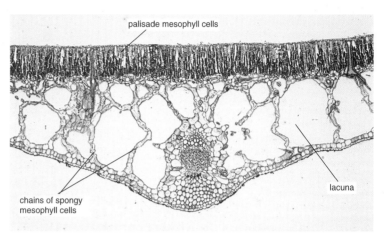

*Nymphaea* leaf (TS)

The greatest problem for hydrophytes is obtaining oxygen for respiration. Waterlogged soil has no air-spaces and the water in the soil spaces contains very little oxygen because it is not very soluble in water, and bacterial decay of organic material in the soil uses up any oxygen that is available. Most waterlogged soils are therefore anaerobic.

One common feature of hydrophytes is the presence of **aeration tissue (aerenchyma)**. This comprises large air-spaces, called **lacunae**, between the cells of the stems and leaves. These form an extensive communicating network which stores oxygen produced by photosynthesis, from where it can diffuse towards the roots for use in respiration. The economically important cereal rice has both aerenchyma and a tolerance to ethanol which is the product of the anaerobic respiration which takes place as a result of the low oxygen levels in waterlogged soil in which it grows. Aerating tissue also confers buoyancy, raising leaves to the surface where they can take maximum advantage of the light.

Hydrophytes, show a marked absence of supporting tissues like sclerenchyma. Not only is such tissue unnecessary as the water provides support, it would make the plant more rigid, rendering it liable to breakage by water currents. Xylem is poorly developed, because support is unnecessary and water transport is less important. Where leaves are submerged, stomata are absent or non-functional. Where leaves float, as in water lilies (*Nymphaea* spp.), only the upper surface possesses stomata.

461

# 22.6    Uptake of water by roots

If a plant is to survive, the large quantities of water lost through transpiration must be replaced. Water absorption is largely carried out by the younger parts of roots which bear extensions of the epidermal cells, known as **root hairs**. These root hairs only remain functional for a few weeks, being replaced by others formed on the younger regions nearer the growing apex. As the root becomes older the epidermis is replaced by a layer known as the **exodermis** through which some water absorption takes place.

### 22.6.1 Root structure

Beneath the epidermis of a young root is a broad cortex of parenchyma cells. The vascular tissue occurs as a central column rather than a peripheral cylinder as in stems. The reason is that roots are subject to pulling forces in a vertical direction rather than the lateral forces experienced by stems. Vertical forces are better resisted by a central column of supporting tissue such as xylem. As roots, embedded as they are in soil, are subject to fewer stresses and strains than aerial parts of the plant, the other major supporting tissue, sclerenchyma, is reduced or absent.

Around the central vascular tissue is a ring, one cell thick, known as the **endodermis**. These living cells are elongated vertically. Part of the wall is impregnated with **suberin**. This forms a distinctive band known as the **Casparian strip**. Inside the endodermis is the **pericycle**, a layer of parenchyma cells between the endodermis and the vascular tissue. It is from the pericycle that lateral roots originate. The internal structure of roots is shown in Fig. 22.13.

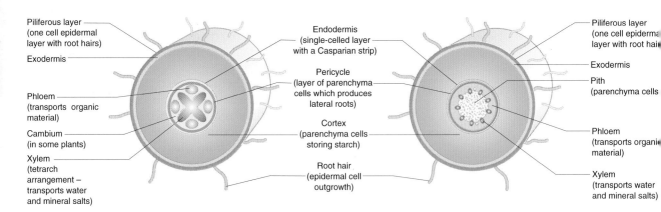

*Fig. 22.13 (a) TS through a typical dicotyledonous root, as seen under a microscope (100×)*

*Fig. 22.13 (b) TS through a typical monocotyledonous root, as seen under a microscope (100×)*

### 22.6.2 Mechanisms of uptake

The same three pathways that are responsible for movement of water across the leaf also bring about its movement in the root:

**1.  The apoplast pathway** – Compared to the leaf (Section 22.4.2) this pathway has one major difference in the root. Movement through the cell walls is prevented by the suberin of the

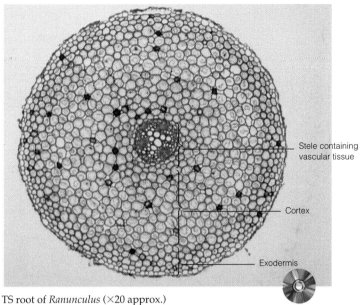

Stele containing vascular tissue

Cortex

Exodermis

TS root of *Ranunculus* (×20 approx.)

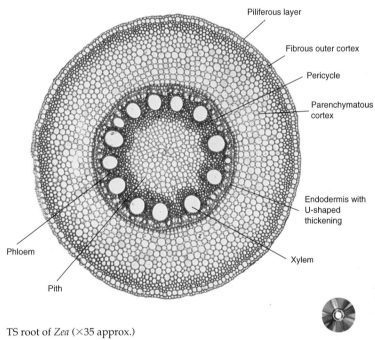

Piliferous layer

Fibrous outer cortex

Pericycle

Parenchymatous cortex

Endodermis with U-shaped thickening

Xylem

Phloem

Pith

TS root of *Zea* (×35 approx.)

Casparian strip in the endodermis. The water is thereby forced to enter the living protoplast of the endodermal cell, as the only available route to the xylem (Fig. 22.14).

The significance of this is that salts may then be actively secreted into the vascular tissue from the endodermal cells. This makes the water potential in the xylem more negative (lower), causing water to be drawn in from the endodermis. While the mechanism has yet to be proven scientifically, there is some circumstantial evidence supporting this view:

**(a)** There are numerous starch grains in endodermal cells which could act as an energy source for the process.

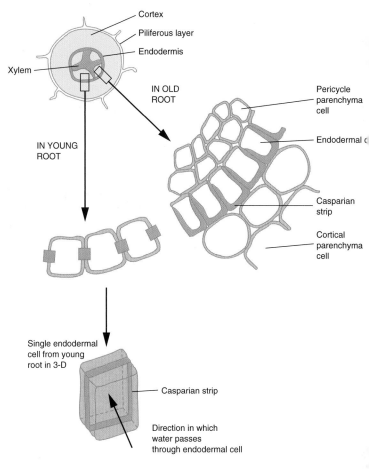

*Fig. 22.14 Water transport in the root*

**(b)** Depriving roots of oxygen prevents water being exuded from cut stems. Lowering the temperature reduces the rate of exudation.

**(c)** Treating roots with metabolic poisons like cyanide also prevents water being exuded from cut stems.

Whatever the process, it is clearly an active one.

**2. The symplast pathway** — This operates in the same way as in the leaf (Section 22.4.2). Water leaving the pericycle cells to enter the xylem causes the water potential of the pericycle cells to become more negative (lower). These therefore draw in water from adjacent cells, which in turn have a more negative (lower) water potential. In this way a water potential gradient is established across the root from the xylem to the root hair cells, which draws water across it.

**3. The vacuolar pathway** — This operates in the same way as in the leaf (Section 22.4.2), using the same water potential gradient described above.

A summary diagram of the passage of water throughout the plant is given in Fig. 22.15.

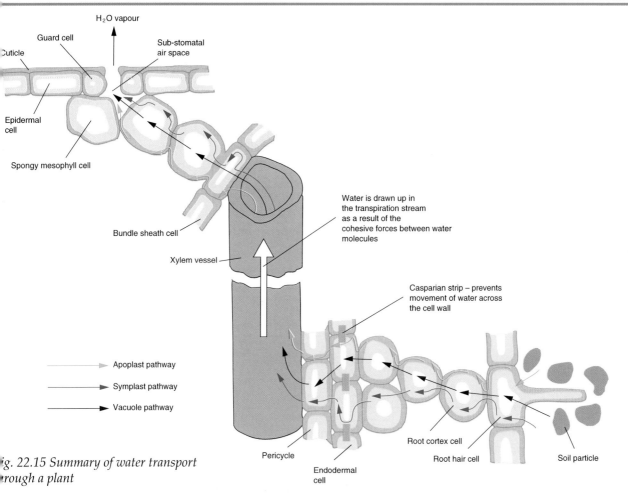

H₂O vapour

Guard cell

Cuticle

Sub-stomatal
air space

Epidermal
cell

Spongy mesophyll cell

Bundle sheath cell

Xylem vessel

Water is drawn up in
the transpiration stream
as a result of the
cohesive forces between water
molecules

Casparian strip – prevents
movement of water across
the cell wall

Apoplast pathway

Symplast pathway

Vacuole pathway

Pericycle

Endodermal
cell

Root cortex cell

Root hair cell

Soil particle

Fig. 22.15 Summary of water transport through a plant

## 22.7  Uptake and translocation of minerals

All plants require a supply of minerals, the functions of which are summarized in Chapter 2, Table 2.1. These minerals are largely absorbed by roots through root hairs, although leaves can also absorb them if sprayed with a suitable solution. Such sprays are called **foliar feeds**.

### 22.7.1 Mechanisms of mineral uptake

Minerals may be absorbed either passively or actively:

**1. Passive absorption** – If the concentration of a mineral in the soil solution is greater than its concentration in a root hair cell, the mineral may enter the root hair cell by **diffusion**.

**2. Active absorption** – If the concentration of a mineral in the soil solution is less than that in a root hair cell it may be absorbed by active transport, details of which are given in Section 4.3.4. Most minerals are absorbed in this way. The process is selective. Because active absorption requires energy, the rate of absorption is dependent upon respiration.

Fig. 22.16 shows that when salts are added to plants growing in water, the respiration rate of the plants increases, presumably in order to provide the energy for the mineral absorption. The addition of the respiratory inhibitor potassium cyanide prevents active mineral uptake, leaving only absorption by passive means

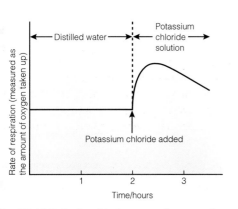

Distilled water

Potassium
chloride
solution

Rate of respiration (measured as
the amount of oxygen taken up)

Potassium chloride added

1          2          3

Time/hours

Fig. 22.16 Relationship between the rate of respiration and mineral uptake

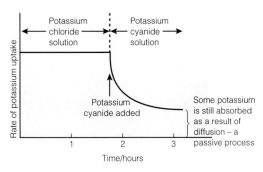

Fig. 22.17 *Effect of the respiratory inhibitor cyanide on mineral uptake*

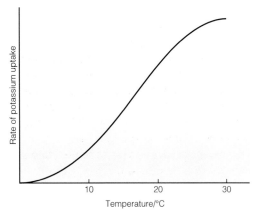

Fig. 22.18 *Effect of temperature on the rate of potassium uptake in plants*

(Fig. 22.17). Increases in temperature increase the rate of respiration and hence the rate of mineral uptake (Fig. 22.18).

Once absorbed, the mineral ions may move along the cell walls (apoplast pathway) by either diffusion or mass flow. In the latter case they are carried along in solution by the water being pulled up the plant in the transpiration stream. When these minerals reach the endodermis the Casparian strip prevents further movement along the cell walls. Instead, the ions enter the cytoplasm of the cell from where they diffuse or are actively transported into the xylem. Minerals may alternatively pass through the cytoplasm of cortical cells (symplast pathway) to the xylem into which they diffuse or are actively pumped.

### 22.7.2 Transport of minerals in the xylem

Analysis of the contents of xylem vessels reveals the presence of mineral salts and water, although sugars and amino acids may also be present. The evidence supporting the role of xylem in transporting minerals includes:

1.  The presence of mineral ions in xylem sap.

2.  A similarity between the rate of mineral transport and the rate of transpiration.

3.  Evidence that other solutes, e.g. the dye eosin, are carried in the xylem (Section 22.4.4).

4.  Experiments using radioactive tracers (Fig. 22.19). The interpretation of the experiments is that where lateral transfer of minerals can take place, minerals pass from the xylem to the phloem. Where it is prevented, the transport of minerals takes place almost exclusively in the xylem.

Once in the xylem, minerals are carried up the plant by the mass flow of the transpiration stream. Once they reach the place where they will be utilized, called **sinks**, they either diffuse or are actively transported into the cells requiring them.

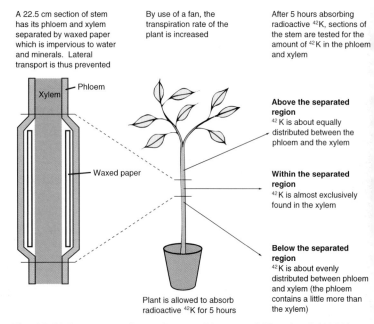

Fig. 22.19 *Summary of experiment of Stout and Hoagland (1939) to demonstrate that minerals are translocated up the plant in the xylem*

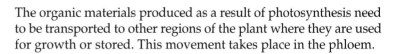

# 22.8   Translocation of organic molecules

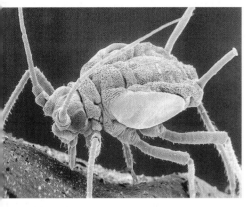

phid feeding showing needle-like mouthparts
enetrating phloem

The organic materials produced as a result of photosynthesis need to be transported to other regions of the plant where they are used for growth or stored. This movement takes place in the phloem.

### 22.8.1 Evidence for transport of organic material in the phloem

The evidence supporting the view that organic material formed as a result of photosynthesis is carried in the phloem includes:

**1.** When phloem is cut, the sap which exudes is rich in organic materials such as carbohydrates. The fact that sap is exuded suggests the contents of the phloem are under pressure.

**2.** The sugar content of phloem varies in relation to environmental conditions. Where conditions favour photosynthesis, the concentration of sugar in phloem increases. There is also a diurnal variation in the sugar content of phloem, which reflects the diurnal variation in the rate of photosynthesis in relation to light intensity. Fig. 22.20 shows how the sucrose content of leaves increases to a maximum around 15.00 hours, as a result of the high light intensity and temperature favouring photosynthesis at this time. This peak of sugar concentration is reflected in the phloem of the stem a little time later. Little variation of sucrose concentration in the xylem takes place.

**3.** Removal of a complete ring of phloem from around a stem causes an accumulation of sugars above the ring, indicating that their downward progress has been interrupted.

**4.** If radioactive $^{14}CO_2$ is given to plants as a photosynthetic substrate, the sugars later found in the phloem contain $^{14}C$. When phloem and xylem are separated by waxed paper, the $^{14}C$ is almost entirely found in the phloem.

**5.** Aphids have needle-like mouthparts with which they penetrate phloem in order to obtain sugars. If a feeding aphid is anaesthetized and then the mouthparts cut from the body, they

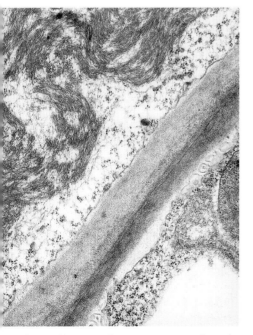

eve plate, at the junction between two sieve elements,
leaf of *Zinnia elegans* (EM) (× 31 000 approx.)

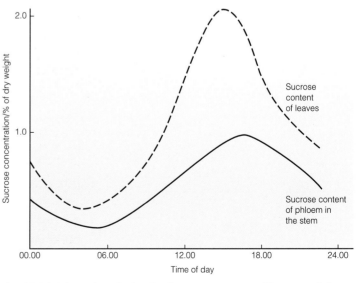

*Fig. 22.20 Diurnal variation in the sugar content of leaves and the phloem in stems*

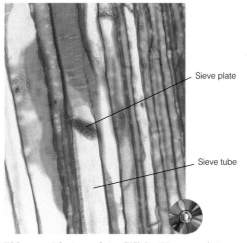

Phloem, with sieve plates (TS) (×400 approx.)

remain as tiny tubes from which samples of the phloem content exude. Analyses of these exudates confirm the presence of carbohydrates and amino acids, and a diurnal variation in their concentrations.

### 22.8.2 Structure of phloem sieve tubes

Phloem tissue is living and comprises **sieve tubes** (or sieve elements), phloem parenchyma and phloem fibres. In angiosperms specialized parenchyma cells known as **companion cells** are always found associated with sieve tube cells. (See Fig. 22.21.)

The sieve tube cells are the only components of phloem obviously adapted for the longitudinal flow of material. They are elongated with a characteristic series of pores 2–6 $\mu$m in diameter in the end walls. These are lined with the polysaccharide **callose** and form a **sieve plate**. The sieve tube cells have a well defined plasma membrane and their cytoplasm contains numerous plastids and mitochondria. Within the lumen of the cells are longitudinal strands of cytoplasm 1–7 $\mu$m wide. They are made up of **phloem protein**. The strands are continuous from cell to cell through the pores of the sieve plate and are known as **transcellular strands**. There is some question as to the existence of these strands, as some researchers believe them to be no more than artefacts. Mature sieve tube cells lack a nucleus and are called **sieve tube elements**.

The companion cells have a thin cellulose cell wall and dense cytoplasm. Within the cytoplasm is a large nucleus, numerous mitochondria, plastids, small vacuoles and an extensive rough endoplasmic reticulum. Companion cells are metabolically active. They are closely associated with the sieve tube element with which they communicate by means of numerous plasmodesmata.

The structure of a sieve tube element and companion cell as seen under an electron microscope is given in Fig. 22.22.

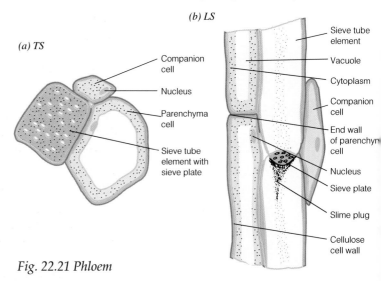

Fig. 22.21 Phloem

### 22.8.3 Mechanisms of translocation in phloem

There is much controversy regarding the mechanism by which materials are translocated in phloem. One thing, however, is agreed: the observed rate of flow is much too fast for diffusion to be the cause. The theories put forward include the following hypotheses.

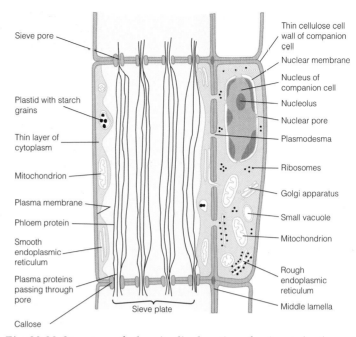

Fig. 22.22 *Structure of a longitudinal section of a sieve tube element and companion cell, as seen by an electron microscope*

*Mass flow (pressure flow) hypothesis*

Photosynthesis forms soluble carbohydrates like sucrose. Photosynthesizing cells in the leaf therefore have their water potentials made more negative (lower) by the accumulation of this sucrose. As a result, water that has been transported up the stem in the xylem enters these cells. This causes an increase in their pressure potential. At the other end of the plant, in the roots, sucrose is either being utilized as a respiratory substrate or is being converted to starch for storage. The sucrose content of these cells is therefore low, giving them a less negative (higher) water potential and a consequently lower pressure potential. There is therefore a gradient of pressure potential between *the source* of sucrose (the leaves) and its point of utilization – *the sink* (the roots and other tissues). The two are linked by the phloem and as a result liquid flows from the leaves to other tissues along the sieve tube elements. A simple physical model to illustrate this mechanism is given in Fig. 22.23.

Evidence supporting the mass flow theory includes:

**1.** There is a flow of solution from phloem when it is cut or punctured by the stylet of an aphid.

**2.** There is some evidence of concentration gradients of sucrose and other materials, with high concentrations in the leaves and lower concentrations in roots.

**3.** Some researchers have observed mass flow in microscopic sections of living sieve elements.

**4.** Viruses or growth chemicals applied to leaves are only translocated downwards to the roots when the leaf to which they are applied is well illuminated and therefore photosynthesizing. When applied to shaded leaves, no downward translocation occurs.

It is likely that the sucrose produced in mesophyll cells as a result of photosynthesis needs to be actively transported against a concentration gradient into the sieve elements. The energy for this process is provided by ATP.

One criticism of the mass flow theory is that it offers no explanation for the existence of sieve plates which act as a series of barriers impeding flow. Indeed, as the process is passive after the initial stage, there is no necessity for the phloem to be a living tissue at all. One suggested function of the sieve plates is a means of sealing off damaged sieve tube elements. As the material within the elements is under pressure, any damage could lead to wasteful loss of sugar solution. It has been observed that once an element is damaged the sieve plate is quickly sealed by deposition of callose across the pores. Another criticism is that while the theory would *suggest* that all material being transported in the phloem would travel at the same speed, in practice sugars and amino acids move at different rates.

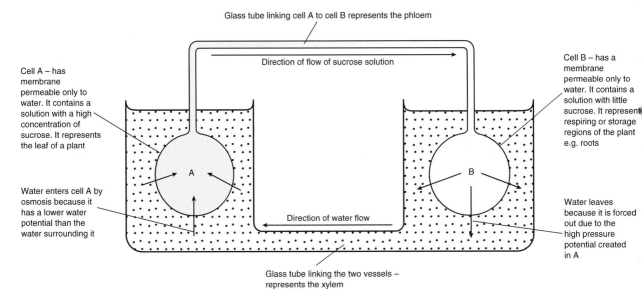

Fig. 22.23 Physical model to illustrate the mass flow theory of translocation in phloem

### Electro-osmosis hypothesis
Originally put forward by Spanner in 1958, and since modified on several occasions, the theory proposes that potassium ions are actively transported by companion cells, across the sieve plate. The movement of these ions draws polar water molecules across the plate. The movement is still one of mass flow, but the theory at least offers some function for the sieve plates and explains the high metabolic rate observed in companion cells. However, there is no consistent evidence of a potential difference existing across sieve plates.

### Transcellular strand hypothesis – cytoplasmic streaming
Thaine in 1962 proposed that transcellular strands, which extend from cell to cell via pores in the sieve plate, carry out a form of cytoplasmic streaming. The solutes move in this cytoplasmic stream which can occur between the strands or through them as they are in fact tiny tubules about 20 nm in diameter. The process, being active, accounts for the many mitochondria in both sieve tube elements and companion cells. It will, however, require more positive proof of the existence of the actual process before it becomes widely accepted.

# 22.9    Questions

*(a)* State what is meant by the term **water potential**. *(1 mark)*

This is a simplified diagram of cells in the root of a plant.

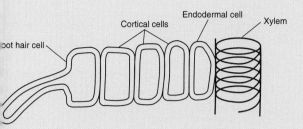

Root hair cell, Cortical cells, Endodermal cell, Xylem

*(b)*  (i)  If the water potential ($\Psi$) of the root hair cell is $-2000\,\text{kPa}$ and the pressure potential ($\Psi_P$) is $400\,\text{kPa}$, calculate the solute potential ($\Psi_S$) of the cell. Show your working. *(2 marks)*

(ii)  If $\Psi_P$ of a cell is $500\,\text{kPa}$ and its solute potential is $-4900\,\text{kPa}$, what is the water potential ($\Psi$) of the cell? Show your working. *(2 marks)*

(iii)  What is meant by **plasmolysis**? *(1 mark)*

(iv)  Incipient plasmolysis means the point at which plasmolysis is about to happen. At incipient plasmolysis:
1.  state the value of the $\Psi_P$ of the cell;
2.  comment on the values of $\Psi$ and $\Psi_S$. *(2 marks)*

(v)  Explain how the water potential of the root hair cell would be affected if water movement in the xylem ceases. *(3 marks)*

(vi)  Explain, giving your reasons, the effect on the solute and water potentials of the root hair cells, if ions were taken up activity by these cells. *(2 marks)*

(vii)  In what ways does active uptake of ions differ from passive uptake? *(3 marks)*

*(Total 16 marks)*

*Oxford & Cambridge January 1998, Paper B4, No. 1*

The diagram below shows two adjacent plant cells, A and B. The values of their pressure potentials ($\Psi_P$) and solute potentials ($\Psi_S$) are given in kPa.

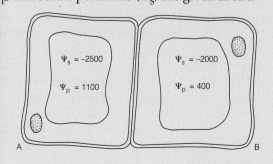

$\Psi_S = -2500$    $\Psi_S = -2000$

$\Psi_P = 1100$    $\Psi_P = 400$

A    B

*(a)* In which direction would water flow between the two cells? Give a reason for your answer. *(2 marks)*

*(b)* Complete the table below to show the values of the pressure potential $\Psi_P$ and the water potential $\Psi$ of each of the cells when equilibrium has been reached. Assume that changes in the value of $\Psi_S$ are negligible. *(4 marks)*

| Potential | Cell A | Cell B |
|---|---|---|
| Pressure potential $\Psi_P$ | | |
| Water potential $\Psi$ | | |

*(c)* The cells are then immersed in distilled water and again allowed to reach equilibrium. Assume that changes in the value of $\Psi_S$ are negligible.
(i)  State the new value of the water potential $\Psi$ of the two cells. *(1 mark)*
(ii)  State the new value of the pressure potential $\Psi_P$ of cell A. *(1 mark)*

*(Total 8 marks)*

*ULEAC January 1993, Paper III, No. 1*

**3.** The diagram shows two cells from the root of a plant.

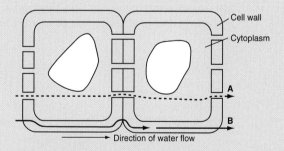

Cell wall, Cytoplasm, A, B, Direction of water flow

*(a)* What is the name given to the pathway represented by the arrow labelled **A**? *(1 mark)*

*(b)* The table gives some information about the uptake of nitrate and calcium ions by plant roots.

| Ion | Pathway by which ion travels across the root | Concentration difference |
|---|---|---|
| Nitrate | A | Higher concentration inside plant than in soil |
| Calcium | B | Higher concentration in soil than in plant |

(i) Name the process by which you would expect each ion to enter the root from the soil. *(2 marks)*

(ii) Suggest an explanation for the link between the pathway by which an ion travels across the root and the direction of the concentration gradient. *(2 marks)*

*(Total 5 marks)*

*NEAB February 1997, Paper BY03, No. 7*

**4.** The table records the transpiration rates of a group of plants under different environmental conditions of temperature and relative humidity.

| Air temperature/ °C | Transpiration rate/ mg water m$^{-2}$ min$^{-1}$ | | |
|---|---|---|---|
| | 20% relative humidity | 50% relative humidity | 70% relative humidity |
| 5 | 15.0 | 8.5 | 5.0 |
| 11 | 18.5 | 11.0 | 7.0 |
| 18 | 22.5 | 13.0 | 7.5 |
| 25 | 26.0 | 16.5 | 9.5 |
| 29 | 29.0 | 18.5 | 11.0 |

*(a)* Plot the data on a single pair of axes on graph paper. *(4 marks)*

*(b)* (i) What general relation is shown by the graph between relative humidity and transpiration rate? *(1 mark)*

(ii) At which relative humidity does a change in temperature have the greatest effect on transpiration rate? Give quantitative evidence from the graph to support your answer. *(2 marks)*

The diagram shows a transverse section through a leaf. This leaf transpires at a lower rate than a typical mesophyte leaf.

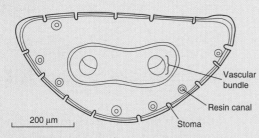

*(c)* Describe **three** features shown in the diagram that contribute to a lower transpiration rate. *(3 marks)*

The apoplast (cell wall system) is the main pathway followed by water across the cortex of the root of a terrestrial flowering plant on its way to the xylem.

*(d)* Explain briefly how the structure of the endodermis causes it to form a barrier to the passage of water by this route. *(2 marks)*

*(Total 12 marks)*

*AEB Summer 1994, (AS) Paper 1, No. 12*

**5.** Observe the drawings **A–F** of different types of plant cells.

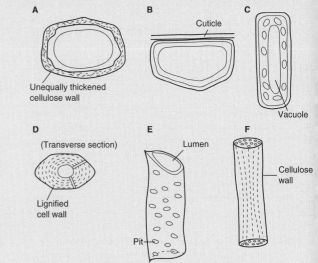

*(a)* Identify the cell types **A–F**. *(3 mark*

*(b)* (i) Make a line diagram ('low power plan of a dicotyledon leaf as seen in transverse section, to indicate the tissu areas. *(2 mark*

(ii) Using **only** the letters **A–F**, label your diagram to indicate where you would expect to find the cell types referred to in *(a)* above. *(3 mark*

*(c)* When cells such as **A–F** are mature and full functional, state:

(i) which cells would contain a nucleus;

(ii) which three cells could contain plastid

(iii) which 'cells' are dead;

(iv) which cell has a protective function.

*(4 mark*

*(Total 12 mark*

*Oxford June 1997, Paper 2, No.*

**6.** Scientists have concluded that there is little chance of life on Mars or any of the other planets in the sola system because they do not have any liquid water.

*(a)* Suggest a **chemical** test which could be used to show that more water is lost from the under surface of a leaf than the top surface. Indicate any change of colour which you might expect. *(2 mark*

*(b)* (i) Briefly state why water is described as **polar** molecule. *(1 mar*

(ii) Water molecules are attracted to each other by weak electrical charges. Wha is the name given to these weak bonds *(1 mar*

*(c)* The solvent properties of water are a result of its polar nature, and this enables life to exist on this planet. Give **two** other properties of water which are influenced by its polar nature. *(2 mark*

(d) Use a simple chemical **or** word equation to show a biological example of:
  (i) hydrolysis;
  (ii) condensation. *(2 marks)*
  *(Total 8 marks)*

*Oxford November 1996, Paper 1, No. 3*

Fresh green pepper strips were placed in sucrose solutions of varying concentrations to investigate changes in mass. Strips of pepper, each measuring cm × 0.5 cm, were cut from the wall of the fruit. The uit wall was 0.4 cm thick. This is illustrated in the iagram below.

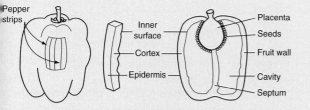

total of 18 strips were cut and their individual asses determined. Three strips were then placed in ich of the following sucrose solutions: 0.2, 0.4, 0.6, 8 and 1.0 mol dm$^{-3}$ respectively. The remaining ree were placed in distilled water. All were left for ) minutes then re-weighed. The mean mass of each roup of three strips was calculated; these are shown the table below.

| Molarity of sucrose/ mol dm$^{-3}$ | Mean mass/g | |
|---|---|---|
| | At start | After 30 minutes |
| 0.0 | 1.74 | 1.83 |
| 0.2 | 1.47 | 1.46 |
| 0.4 | 1.45 | 1.35 |
| 0.6 | 1.52 | 1.34 |
| 0.8 | 1.80 | 1.53 |
| 1.0 | 1.38 | 1.15 |

(a) Calculate the percentage change in mass for each group of strips. *(2 marks)*
(b) Plot these data using percentage change in mass on graph paper. *(5 marks)*
(c) From your graph determine the molarity of sucrose solution which has the same water potential as the pepper tissue. Mark this point **on the graph** with an arrow and state the molarity. *(2 marks)*
  *(Total 9 marks)*

*Oxford March 1997, Paper 44, No. 3*

The diagram at the top of the next column shows me of the cells involved in the loss of water from irt of a leaf.
  (a) Name the tissues labelled P and Q on the diagram. *(2 marks)*

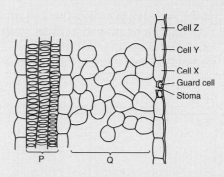

(b) The table below shows the concentrations of potassium ions in some of the cells shown in the diagram when the stoma is open and when the stoma is closed.

| Cell | Concentration of potassium ions/arbitrary units | |
|---|---|---|
| | Stoma closed | Stoma open |
| Guard cell | 95 | 448 |
| Cell X | 156 | 293 |
| Cell Y | 199 | 98 |
| Cell Z | 448 | 73 |

  (i) Describe the changes that take place in the concentrations of potassium ions in cells X , Y and Z when the stoma opens. *(2 marks)*
  (ii) Explain how these changes in potassium ion concentration are related to the mechanism for the opening of the stoma. *(3 marks)*
  *(Total 7 marks)*

*Edexcel January 1998, Paper B3, No. 3*

9. (a) Describe the processes by which carbohydrates are transported through a plant. *(4 marks)*
(b) The drawing shows an outline of a young morning glory plant.

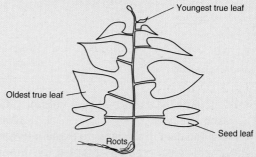

Reproduced from *Plant Physiology*, Salisbury and Ross, by permission of Wadsworth Publishing Co.

Autoradiograms are images produced on X-ray film. In six different morning glory plants, **A–F**, identical to the plant above, the leaf marked **a** was allowed to photosynthesize in the presence of radioactive carbon dioxide ($^{14}CO_2$) prior to autoradiograms being produced. Drawings **A-F** show autoradiograms of the six plants. The shaded area on each autoradiogram indicates radioactivity.

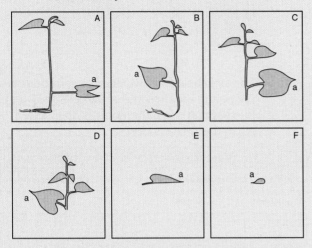

Give **two** conclusions that can be drawn from the autoradiograms about the transport of the carbohydrates produced by photosynthesizing leaves in the morning glory plant.　　　　　(2 marks)
　　　　　　　　　　　(Total 6 marks)

*NEAB March 1998, Paper BY03, No. 4*

**10.** The 'Two-leaf Hakea' is a plant found in south-west Australia, where the spring is relatively cool and wet but the summer is very hot and dry. The plant produces one type of leaf in spring and a different type in the summer. The table shows the average values of a range of measurements taken from the leaves.

| Characteristic of leaf | Type of leaf | |
| --- | --- | --- |
| | **A** | **B** |
| Length/mm | 33 | 55 |
| Maximum width/mm | 10 | 0.8 |
| Surface-area/mm$^2$ | 292 | 144 |
| Volume/mm$^3$ | 64 | 63 |
| Cuticle thickness/$\mu$m | 14 | 24 |

(a) Calculate the surface-area to volume ratio for **each** leaf type.　　　　　(2 marks)
(b) Use the data in the table to explain **two** ways in which leaf type **B** is adapted to summer conditions in south-west Australia.　(2 marks)
(c) Suggest and explain the advantages to the plant of producing leaf type **A** in spring.
　　　　　　　　　　　(2 marks)
　　　　　　　　　　　(Total 6 marks)

*NEAB June 1996, Paper 1, No. 18*

**11.** The diagrams at the top of the next column show some cells of a transport tissue found in flowering plants.

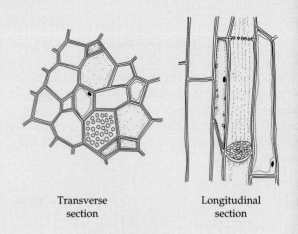

| Transverse section | Longitudinal section |

(a)　(i)　Name the tissue shown in the diagrams.　　　　(1 mar

　　(ii)　Name **two** types of cell shown in the drawing which are characteristic of thi tissue.　　　　(2 mark

(b)　(i)　State **two** substances which are normally transported in this tissue.
　　　　　　　　　(2 mark

　　(ii)　Describe a technique which could be used to show that **one** of the substance you have stated in (i) is transported in this tissue.　　(3 mark
　　　　　　　　(Total 8 mark

*ULEAC June 1995, Paper 3, No.*

**12.** The diagram below represents the mass flow hypothesis which explains the movement of substances in the phloem.

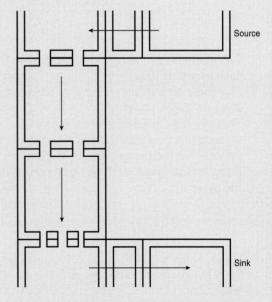

(a) Suggest a plant organ which is a sink.
　　　　　　　　　(1 mar

*(b)* There are companion cells alongside the phloem sieve tubes in a stem. Explain why this does **not** support the mass flow hypothesis. *(2 marks)*

*(c)* Radioactively labelled molecules applied to illuminated leaves were rapidly transported out of the leaves by the phloem. Radioactively labelled molecules applied to shaded leaves were not transported. Explain how the mass flow hypothesis accounts for these observations. *(2 marks)*

*(Total 5 marks)*

*AEB Summer 1997, Module Paper 3, No. 3*

**3.** The diagram below shows a section through a leaf, showing the pathways followed by water molecules, as black arrows, and passage of sugar molecules manufactured during photosynthesis, as white arrows.

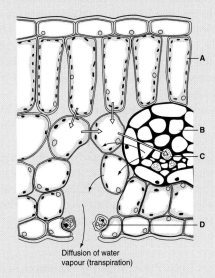

Diffusion of water vapour (transpiration)

*(a)* Identify cells **A** to **D**. *(2 marks)*

*(b)* Describe the methods by which water moves in the direction shown by the black arrows. *(4 marks)*

*(c)* Outline how sucrose is loaded into the cell **C**. *(2 marks)*

*(Total 8 marks)*

*UCLES June 1997, Paper 3, No. 2*

**5.** The potometer shown in the diagram was used to investigate transpiration in a willow herb shoot, by monitoring water uptake.

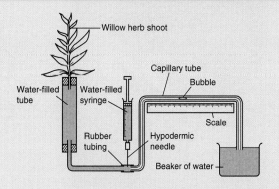

*(a)* Give **two** precautions that should be taken when obtaining the willow herb shoot and assembling the apparatus. *(2 marks)*

*(b)* Uptake of water by the willow herb shoot would cause a bubble introduced into the capillary to move. Briefly describe how you would make a series of measurements of the rate of movement of the bubble over a 1-hour period. *(3 marks)*

*(c)* How could a value for the total volume of water taken up by the willow herb shoot during the 1-hour period be easily obtained? *(1 mark)*

The results of exposing the willow herb shoot to a variety of environmental conditions are shown in the table.

| Environmental conditions | Mean rate of bubble movement/cm min$^{-1}$ |
| --- | --- |
| In natural light and still air | 6.1 |
| Completely enclosed inside a black plastic bag | 1.7 |
| Illuminated by three 40-watt tungsten-filament light bulbs, each placed 10 cm from the shoot | 8.3 |
| In natural light and an air current from an electric fan | 10.4 |

*(d)* Suggest **two** reasons for the reduction in water uptake by the willow herb shoot when enclosed in the black plastic bag. *(2 marks)*

*(e)* Explain why the mean rate of bubble movement for the willow herb shoot illuminated by the three light bulbs is **unlikely** to give an accurate indication of actual water uptake by the shoot. *(2 marks)*

*(Total 10 marks)*

*NEAB June 1997, Paper 1, No. 1*

# 23 Osmoregulation and excretion

## 23.1 Introduction

Animals living under terrestrial conditions tend to lose water by evaporation. Aquatic animals living in surroundings more concentrated (hypertonic) than their tissue fluids lose water by osmosis. Animals living in a hypotonic environment face the problem of water flooding into the body by osmosis. These problems have led to structural and physiological adaptations in order to maintain the balance of water and solutes. These homeostatic processes are termed **osmoregulation**. Homeostasis is the subject of Chapter 25.

The complex chemical reactions which occur in all living cells produce a range of waste products which must be eliminated from the body in a process known as **excretion**. Most nitrogenous waste comes from the breakdown of excess protein which cannot be stored in the body. The form of these excretory products is influenced partly by the availability of water for their excretion. Animals living under conditions of water shortage cannot afford to lose large volumes of water in order to remove their nitrogenous waste. If water is plentiful it may be used to facilitate excretion.

It is important not to confuse the terms excretion, secretion and elimination. **Excretion** is the expulsion from the body of the waste products of metabolism. **Secretion** is the production by the cells of substances useful to the body, such as digestive juice or hormones. **Elimination**, or **egestion** (see Section 15.4.7), is the removal of undigested food and other substances which have never been involved in the metabolic activities of cells.

## 23.2 Excretory products

All animals produce carbon dioxide as a waste product of aerobic respiration and the elimination of this is dealt with in Chapters 20 and 21. Other excretory products include bile pigments, water and mineral salts. However, in this section we shall concentrate on the variety of nitrogenous excretory products released by animals. There are three main waste products of nitrogenous metabolism: ammonia, urea and uric acid. No animal excretes one of these to the exclusion of the others but the predominance of one over the others is determined by three factors:

1. The production of enzymes necessary to convert ammonia into either urea or uric acid.

2. The availability of water in the habitat for the removal of the nitrogenous excretory material.

3. The animal's ability to control water loss or uptake by the body.

Many aquatic animals excrete mainly ammonia and are called **ammoniotelic**. Other aquatic animals and some terrestrial forms excrete predominantly urea and are said to be **ureotelic**. The remaining terrestrial animals are **uricotelic**, excreting mainly uric acid.

### 23.2.1 Ammonia

Ammonia is derived from the breakdown of proteins and nucleic acids in the body. Ammonia is very toxic and is never allowed to accumulate within the body tissues or fluids. It is extremely soluble and diffuses readily across cell membranes. In spite of its toxicity it is the main excretory product of marine invertebrates and all freshwater animals.

### 23.2.2 Urea

Urea, $CO(NH_2)_2$, is formed by the combination of two molecules of ammonia with one of carbon dioxide.

However, its synthesis in living tissues is much more complex than this simple equation suggests. Urea is produced by a cyclic process known as the **urea** or **ornithine cycle**, details of which are given in Section 25.6.2. Urea is much less toxic than ammonia and, although it is less soluble, less water is needed for its elimination because the tissues can tolerate higher concentrations of it.

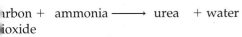
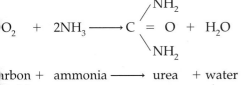

### 23.2.3 Uric acid

Uric acid is a more complex molecule than urea; it is a purine in the same group as adenine and guanine. Like urea, it involves the expenditure of quite considerable energy in its formation, but this is outweighed by the advantages it confers. Uric acid is virtually insoluble in water and is non-toxic. It requires very little water for its removal from the body and it is therefore a suitable product for animals living in arid conditions, e.g. terrestrial reptiles and insects. Containing little, if any, water, its storage within organisms does not greatly increase their mass. This is an advantage to flying organisms, e.g. birds and insects. It is removed as a solid pellet or thick paste.

lungfish, *Protopterus*, dormant in a cocoon of dried ud – all its nitrogenous waste is urea. When the ins return it excretes mainly ammonia

## 23.3    Osmoregulation and excretion in animals

### 23.3.1 Insects

Insects are among the most successful terrestrial animals. The problem of preventing water loss by evaporation is overcome by the waterproof waxy cuticle on the exoskeleton and a tracheal

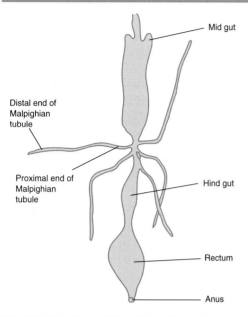

*Fig. 23.1 Position of the Malpighian tubules*

respiratory system (Chapter 20). The problem of water loss by excretion is overcome by the production of uric acid. Uric acid is concentrated in the **Malpighian tubules**. These form a bunch of blind-ending tubes which project into the blood-filled body cavity (haemocoel) from the junction of the mid gut and hind gut (see Fig. 23.1).

Insect cells release uric acid into the blood where it combines with potassium and sodium hydrogen carbonates and water to form potassium and sodium urate, carbon dioxide and water. Potassium and sodium urate are actively taken up by the Malpighian tubules and the water then enters by osmosis. As the soluble potassium and sodium urate pass down the tubules, they combine with carbon dioxide and water (from respiration) to form hydrogen carbonates and uric acid. At the proximal end of the Malpighian tubule the walls have many microvilli and it is here that hydrogen carbonates are actively reabsorbed into the haemocoel, lowering the osmotic pressure within the Malpighian tubule, so that water passes out by osmosis. There is a subsequent lowering of pH and concentration of the uric acid which precipitates out as crystals. These crystals pass into the rectum where they mix with the waste materials from the digestive system. Further water reabsorption takes place through the rectal epithelium, so that a very concentrated excretory product is eliminated from the body. These processes are illustrated in Fig. 23.2.

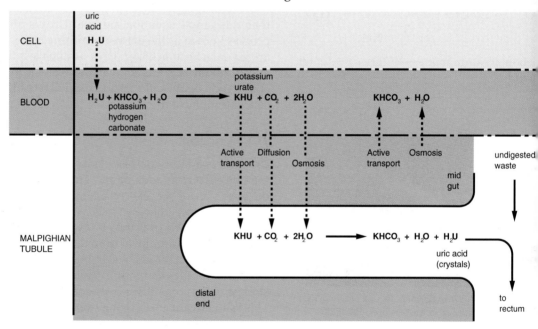

*Fig. 23.2 Functioning of the Malpighian tubule*

### 23.3.2 Fish

Freshwater fish have body fluids which are hypertonic to their surroundings and they are therefore subject to the osmotic uptake of water. Most of this water enters the fish through the highly permeable gills, the body itself being covered with impermeable scales and mucus. The excess water is removed from the body by the kidneys which have many large glomeruli. A large volume of glomerular filtrate is produced from which salts are selectively reabsorbed into the blood, resulting in the

Do smaller woodlice lose water more quickly than larger woodlice?

production of copious amounts of very dilute urine. Since water is plentiful, the nitrogenous excretory product is ammonia. Some of this ammonia is excreted by the kidneys, but as it is so soluble and diffuses readily, most of it is expelled by the gills.

Marine bony fish have body fluids which are hypotonic to sea water. There is little movement of water through the scale-covered body but the fish is liable to water loss by osmosis across the highly permeable gills. In order to maintain sufficient water inside the body these fish drink sea water and secretory cells in the gut actively absorb the salts and transfer them to the blood. The chloride secretory cells in the gills remove the sodium and chloride ions from the blood and other ions like sulphate and magnesium are removed by the kidney. The kidneys of marine bony fish are adapted to produce very small amounts of urine since the animal already has a problem of excessive water loss.

## 23.4　The mammalian kidney

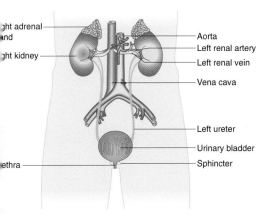

Fig. 23.3 Position of the kidneys in humans

In all vertebrates the main organ of nitrogenous excretion is the kidney. Kidneys are composed of a number of basic units called **nephrons**. In mammals, these nephrons are particularly numerous, with long tubules for water reabsorption.

### 23.4.1 Gross structure of the kidney

The paired kidneys are held in position in the abdominal cavity (Fig. 23.3) by a thin layer of tissue called the peritoneum and they are usually surrounded by fat. In humans, each kidney is about 7–10 cm long and 2.5–4.0 cm wide, packed with blood vessels and an estimated one million nephrons. Each kidney is supplied with blood from the renal artery and drained by a renal vein. The urine which is produced by the kidney is removed by a ureter for temporary storage in the urinary bladder. A ring of muscle called a sphincter closes the exit from the bladder. Sense cells in the bladder wall are stimulated as the bladder fills, triggering a reflex action which results in relaxation of the bladder sphincter and simultaneous contraction of the smooth muscle in the bladder wall. The expulsion of urine from the body via the urethra is known as **micturition**. Although micturition is controlled by the autonomic nervous system, humans learn to control it by voluntary nervous activity.

Within each kidney there are a number of clearly defined regions (Fig. 23.4). The outer region, or **cortex**, mainly comprises Bowman's capsules and convoluted tubules with their associated blood supply. This gives the cortex a different appearance from the inner **medulla** with its loops of Henle, collecting ducts and blood vessels. These structures in the medulla are in groups known as **renal pyramids** and they project into the **pelvis** which is the expanded portion of the ureter.

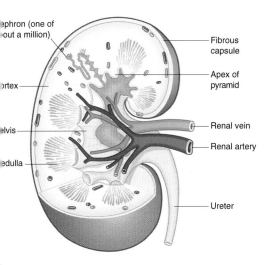

Fig. 23.4 Mammalian kidney to show position of a nephron (LS)

### 23.4.2 Structure of the nephron

The main regions of the mammalian nephron are shown in Fig. 23.5, with details in Figs. 23.6 and 23.7. Basically it comprises a

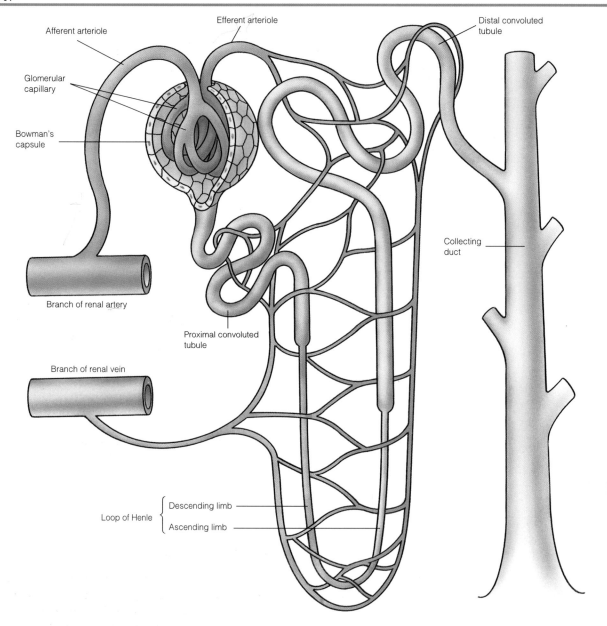

Fig. 23.5 Regions of the nephron

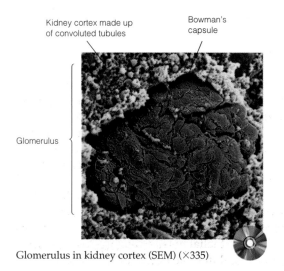

Glomerulus in kidney cortex (SEM) (×335)

glomerulus and a long tubule with several clearly defined regions. The **glomerulus** is a mass of blood capillaries which are partially enclosed by the blind-ending region of the tubule called the **Bowman's capsule**. The blood supply to the glomerulus is from the afferent arteriole of the renal artery; blood leaves the glomerulus via the narrower efferent arteriole. The inner, or visceral, layer of the Bowman's capsule is made up of unusual cells called **podocytes** (see Fig. 23.6), while the outer layer is unspecialized squamous epithelial cells. The remaining regions of the nephron are the proximal convoluted tubule, whose surface-area is increased by the presence of microvilli, the descending and ascending limbs of the loop of Henle, which function as a counter-current multiplier, the distal convoluted tubule and the collecting duct.

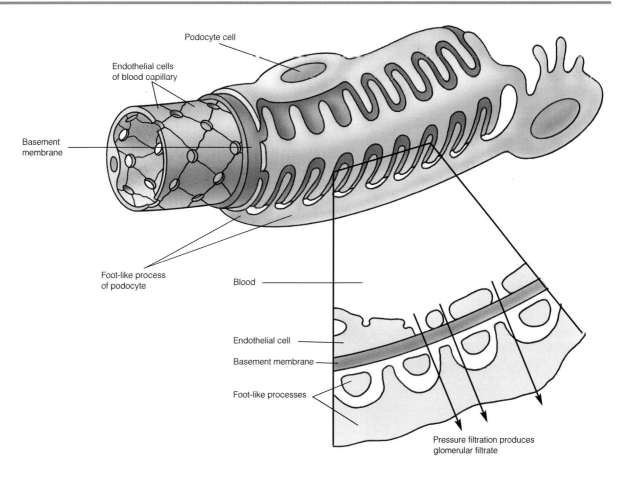

Fig. 23.6 Podocyte

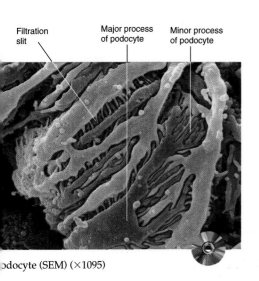

Podocyte (SEM) (×1095)

### 23.4.3 Functions of the nephron

Apart from being organs of nitrogenous excretion, the kidneys also play a major role in maintaining the composition of the body fluids in a more or less steady state, in spite of wide fluctuations in water and salt uptake. This dual function of excretion and osmoregulation is best studied by a detailed consideration of the functioning of one nephron, the main regions of which are shown in Fig. 23.5.

*Ultrafiltration in the Bowman's capsule*

The cup-shaped Bowman's capsule encloses a mass of capillaries, the **glomerulus**, originating from the afferent arteriole of the renal artery. The capillary walls are made up of a single layer of endothelial cells perforated by pores about 0.1 $\mu$m in diameter. The endothelium is closely pressed against the basement membrane, which in places is the only membrane between the blood and the cavity of the Bowman's capsule (see Fig. 23.5). The blood pressure in the kidneys is higher than in other organs. This high pressure is maintained because in each Bowman's capsule the afferent arteriole has a larger diameter than the efferent arteriole. As a result of this pressure, substances are forced through the endothelial pores of the capillary, across the basement membrane and into the Bowman's capsule by

481

**ultrafiltration**. The glomerular filtrate contains substances with a relative molecular mass (RMM) less than 68 000, e.g. glucose, amino acids, vitamins, some hormones, urea, uric acid, creatinine, ions and water. Remaining in the blood, along with some water, are red blood cells, white cells, platelets and plasma proteins which are too large to pass the filter provided by the basement membrane. Further constriction of the efferent arteriole in response to hormonal and nervous signals results in an increased hydrostatic pressure in the glomerulus and substances with an RMM greater than 68 000 may pass into the glomerular filtrate. This filtering process is extremely efficient. The glomerular filtrate passes from the Bowman's capsule along the kidney tubule (nephron). As it does so, the fluid undergoes number of changes, since the urine excreted has a very different composition from the glomerular filtrate. These differences are brought about primarily by selective reabsorption of substances useful to the body. The urine when compared with the glomerular filtrate will contain, for example, less glucose, amino acids and water and a relatively higher percentage of urea and other nitrogenous waste products.

Ultrafiltration is a passive process and selection of substance passing from the blood into the glomerular filtrate is made entirely according to relative molecular mass. Both passive and active processes are involved in the selective reabsorption of substances from the nephron. The composition is further altered by the active secretion of substances, such as creatinine, from the blood into the tubule. Without selective reabsorption humans would produce about 180 dm$^3$ of urine per day whereas the actual volume produced is approximately 1.5 dm$^3$.

### Proximal convoluted tubule

This is the longest region of the nephron. It comprises a single layer of epithelial cells, with numerous microvilli forming a brush border (see Fig. 23.7). The base of each cell is convoluted where it is adjacent to a blood capillary, and there are numerous intercellular spaces. Another notable feature of these cells is the presence of large numbers of mitochondria, providing the ATP necessary for active transport. These cells are ideally adapted fo

Lumen of proximal convoluted tubule

Reabsorption of material by diffusion, active transport and pinocytosis

- Microvillus
- Pinocytic vesicle
- Nuclear envelope
- Nucleoplasm
- Intercellular space
- Mitochondrion
- Infolding of basal membrane
- Basal channel
- Basement membrane
- Endothelial cell

Lumen of blood capillary

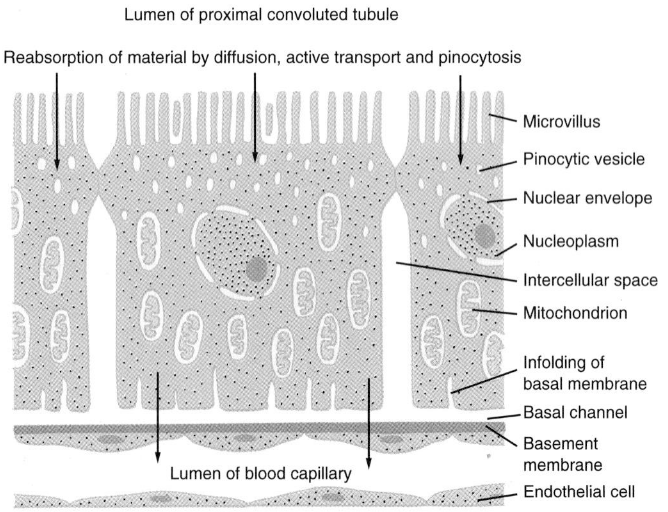

*Fig. 23.7 Detail of cells from the wall of the proximal convoluted tubu*

reabsorption and over 80% of the glomerular filtrate is reabsorbed here, including all the food substances and most of the sodium chloride and water. Amino acids, glucose and ions diffuse into the cells of the proximal convoluted tubule and these are actively transported into the intercellular spaces from where they diffuse into the surrounding capillaries. The constant removal of these substances from the cells of the convoluted tubule causes others to enter from the lumen of the tubule by diffusion. The active uptake of sodium accompanied by appropriate anions, e.g. chloride, raises the osmotic pressure in the cells and water enters them by osmosis. About half the urea present in the tubular filtrate also returns to the blood by diffusion. Proteins of small molecular mass which may have been forced out of the blood in the Bowman's capsule are taken up at the base of the microvilli by pinocytosis. As a result of all this activity, the tubular filtrate is isotonic with blood in the surrounding capillaries.

*Loop of Henle*

It is the presence of the loop of Henle that enables birds and mammals to produce urine which is hypertonic to the blood. The concentration of the urine is directly related to the length of the loop of Henle. It is short in semi-aquatic mammals, which have a correspondingly narrow medulla, and extremely long in desert-dwelling mammals such as the desert rat *Dipodomys,* which therefore has a wide medulla. *Dipodomys* produces a small volume of urine, ten times more concentrated than that produced in large volumes by a beaver. The loop of Henle is made up of two regions, the descending limb which has narrow walls readily permeable to water and the wider ascending limb with thick walls which are far less permeable to water.

The loop of Henle operates as a **counter-current multiplier** system. So how exactly does this work? Consider Fig. 23.8. Sodium and chloride ions are actively pumped out of the ascending limb creating a high solute concentration in the interstitial region. Normally water would follow, being drawn out osmotically. However the walls of the ascending limb are relatively impermeable to water and so little if any escapes. On the other hand the descending loop is highly permeable to water and so water is drawn from it osmotically. This water is carried away by the blood in the vasa recta. As glomerular filtrate enters the descending loop it progressively loses water and so becomes more concentrated. It reaches its maximum concentration at the tip of the loop because as it moves up the ascending limb, ions are removed making it less concentrated.

It might be thought that as the filtrate in the descending limb becomes more concentrated due to the reabsorption of water, osmosis might cease. However the surrounding fluid also becomes more concentrated, ensuring that an osmotic gradient is maintained right down to the tip of the loop of Henle.

In the same way as water is drawn from the descending limb, so it is too from the collecting duct, which runs alongside the loop in the medulla of the kidney. In this way the urine becomes progressively more concentrated (hypertonic) as it moves out of the nephron. The water which is drawn out passes into the blood of the vasa recta which is both slow-flowing and freely permeable, two factors which aid the uptake of water.

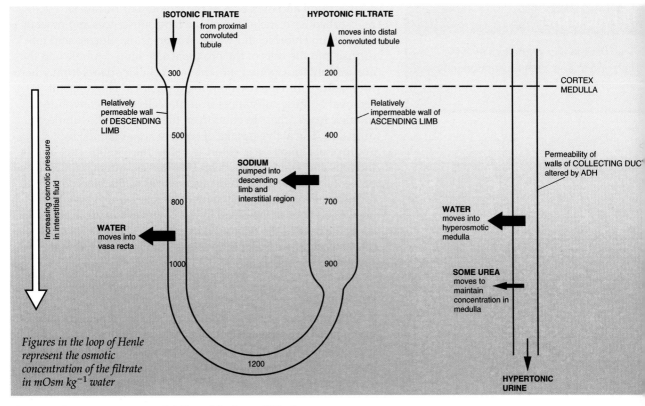

Fig. 23.8 Counter-current multiplier of the loop of Henle

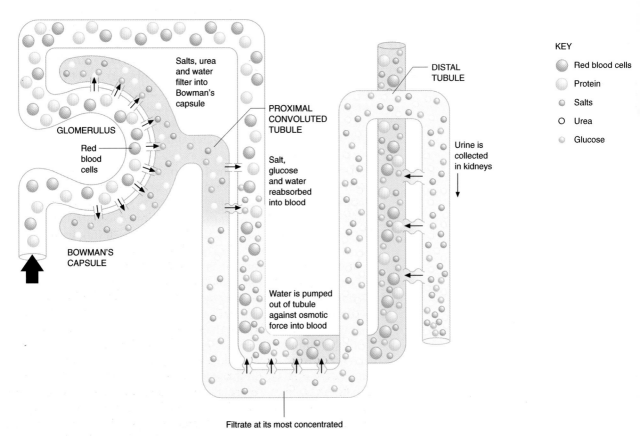

Fig. 23.9 Summary of nephron function

## BIOLOGY AROUND US

# Dialysis

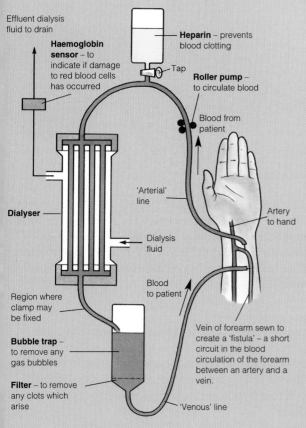

Effluent dialysis fluid to drain

**Haemoglobin sensor** – to indicate if damage to red blood cells has occurred

**Heparin** – prevents blood clotting

Tap

**Roller pump** – to circulate blood

Blood from patient

'Arterial' line

**Dialyser**

Dialysis fluid

Artery to hand

Blood to patient

Region where clamp may be fixed

**Bubble trap** – to remove any gas bubbles

**Filter** – to remove any clots which arise

Vein of forearm sewn to create a 'fistula' – a short circuit in the blood circulation of the forearm between an artery and a vein.

'Venous' line

*The mechanism of kidney dialysis*

Kidneys may fail as a result of damage or infection. Upon the loss of one kidney the remaining one will adapt to undertake the work of its partner, but the loss of both is inevitably fatal. Survival depends upon either regular treatment on a kidney machine or a transplant. A kidney machine carries out **dialysis**, a process in which the patient's blood flows on one side of a thin membrane while a solution, called the dialysate, flows in the opposite direction on the other side. This counter-current flow ensures the most efficient exchange of material across the membrane (Section 20.2.4). As the membrane is permeable to small molecules such as urea, this waste product will diffuse from the blood, where it is relatively highly concentrated, to the dialysate, where its concentration is lower. To prevent useful substances like glucose and salts, which are also highly concentrated in blood, diffusing out, the dialysate's composition is the same as that of normal blood. This means that any substance which is in excess, e.g. salts, will also diffuse out until they are in equilibrium with the dialysate. Large molecules such as blood proteins are too large to cross the membrane and there is therefore no risk of them being lost to the dialysate.

A patient's blood needs to pass through the kidney machine many times to ensure the removal of all wastes. Thus, it is necessary for dialysis to take place for up to 10 hours every few days. While wastes accumulate in the blood when the patient is away from the machine, adherence to a strict diet ensures they do not build up to a dangerous level before the next treatment.

*Distal convoluted tubule*

The cells in this region are very similar to those of the proximal convoluted tubule, having a brush border and numerous mitochondria. The permeability of their membranes is affected by hormones (see Section 23.5) and so precise control of the salt and water balance of the blood is possible. The distal convoluted tubule also controls the pH of the blood, maintaining it at 7.4. The cells of the tubule combine water and carbon dioxide to form carbonic acid. This then dissociates into hydrogen ions and hydrogen carbonate ions. The absorption of these hydrogen carbonate ions into the blood raises its pH to compensate for the lowering which results from the production of hydrogen ions during metabolic processes. The hydrogen ions from the dissociation of carbonic acid are pumped into the lumen of the distal tubule. In the lumen, hydrogen phosphate ions ($HPO_4^{2-}$) combine with these hydrogen ions to form dihydrogen phosphate ions ($H_2PO_4^{-}$) which are then excreted in the urine. The acidic effect of the hydrogen ions is therefore buffered by these hydrogen phosphate ions. The events are summarized in Fig. 23.10.

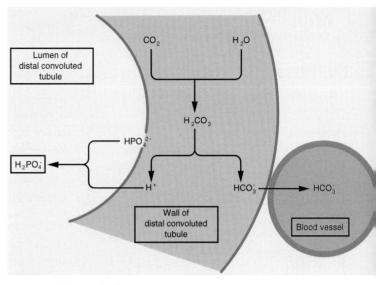

*Fig. 23.10 Control of pH*

Not only are hydrogen ions (protons) pumped into the tubule, potassium ions ($K^+$), ammonium ions ($NH_4^-$) and certain drugs are also pumped in as a means of controlling blood pH or removing unwanted material. This active removal of substances also takes place in the proximal convoluted tubule and is called **tubular secretion**.

*Collecting duct*
The permeability of the walls of the collecting duct, like the permeability of the distal convoluted tubule, is affected by hormones. This hormonal effect, together with the hypertonic interstitial fluids built up by the loop of Henle in the medulla, determine whether hypotonic or hypertonic urine is released from the kidney.

If the walls of the collecting duct are water-permeable, water leaves the ducts to pass into the hyperosmotic surroundings and concentrated urine is produced. If the ducts are impermeable to water the final urine will be less concentrated. Hormonal control of the permeability of the walls of the collecting duct to water will be considered in the next section.

The mechanism by which urine is concentrated is illustrated in Fig. 23.8.

## Did you know?

During our lifetime we expel 40 000 litres of urine.

## 23.5 Hormonal control of osmoregulation and excretion

If the kidney is to regulate the amount of water and salts present in the body, very precise monitoring systems are required. The two hormones ADH and aldosterone are particularly important in this respect.

### 23.5.1 Antidiuretic hormone (ADH)

Antidiuretic hormone (ADH) affects the permeability of the distal convoluted tubule and collecting duct.

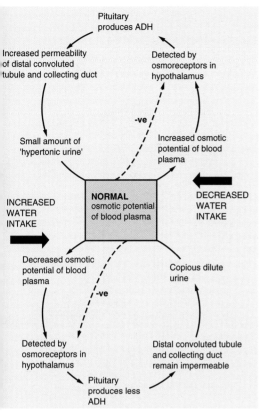

*Fig. 23.11 Regulation of ADH production*

A rise in blood osmotic pressure may be caused by any one of, or combination of, three factors:

1. Little water is ingested.

2. Much sweating occurs.

3. Large amounts of salt are ingested.

The rise in blood osmotic pressure is detected by **osmoreceptors** in the hypothalamus and results in nerve impulses passing to the posterior pituitary gland which releases ADH. ADH increases the permeability of the distal convoluted tubule and collecting duct to water. This water passes into the hyperosmotic medulla and a more concentrated (hypertonic) urine is released from the kidney.

ADH also increases the permeability of the collecting duct to urea which passes into the medulla, increasing the osmotic concentration and causing more water to be lost from the descending loop of Henle. If the osmotic pressure of the blood falls owing to

1. large volumes of water being ingested

2. little sweating

3. low salt intake

then ADH production is inhibited and the walls of the distal convoluted tubule and collecting duct remain impermeable to water and urea. As a result, less water is reabsorbed and hypotonic urine is released. Anyone who is unable to produce sufficient levels of ADH will produce large volumes of very dilute urine, whatever their diet. This condition is termed **diabetes insipidus**. ADH is also referred to in Section 26.2. Fig. 23.11 illustrates the regulation of ADH production.

### 23.5.2 Aldosterone

Aldosterone is the hormone responsible for maintaining a more or less constant sodium level in the plasma and it has a secondary effect on water reabsorption. The control of aldosterone production is very complex.

Any loss of sodium which causes a decrease in blood volume causes a group of secretory cells lying between the afferent arteriole and the distal convoluted tubule to release an enzyme. These cells are known as the **juxtaglomerular complex** and the enzyme they release is **renin**. Renin causes a plasma globulin produced by the liver to form the hormone **angiotensin**. It is this hormone which stimulates the release of aldosterone from the adrenal cortex.

Aldosterone causes sodium ions to be actively taken up from the glomerular filtrate into the capillaries which surround the tubule. This uptake will be accompanied by an osmotically equivalent volume of water, thus restoring the sodium level of the plasma and the volume of the blood.

Further details of aldosterone are given in Section 26.5.

# 23.6 Questions

1. The diagram shows the main functions of the different parts of a kidney tubule.

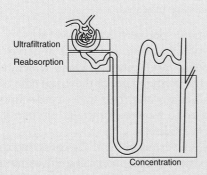

Kidney failure may result in a build up of urea in the blood, protein in the urine and retention of tissue fluid. Patients with kidney failure may need a transplant.

Recipients of transplanted kidneys are treated with drugs that suppress their immune system.

(a) Explain how ultrafiltration and reabsorption remove urea from the blood without losing essential nutrients such as protein and glucose. *(5 marks)*

(b) Explain the part played by the loop of Henle and the collecting duct in concentrating urine in a healthy individual. *(6 marks)*

(c) Explain the link between protein in the urine and retention of tissue fluid in patients with kidney failure. *(3 marks)*

(d) If not treated with drugs, explain how the recipient's immune system would reject a transplanted kidney. *(3 marks)*

*(Quality of language: 3 marks)*

*(Total 20 marks)*

*AEB June 1998, Paper 5, No. 5*

2. The diagram at the top of the next column is of a kidney tubule showing some of the pressure gradients that are involved in the movement of fluids from blood to the glomerular filtrate within the Bowman's capsule. The numbers represent hydrostatic pressure in kPa.

(a) From the figures given, calculate the *filtration pressure* i.e. the net force moving fluid out of the glomerulus. Show your working.

*(2 marks)*

Filtration pressure, and therefore the rate at which fluid passes from the glomerulus into Bowman's capsule, varies with blood pressure.

(b) If the renal artery was restricted with a clamp so that the blood pressure in the

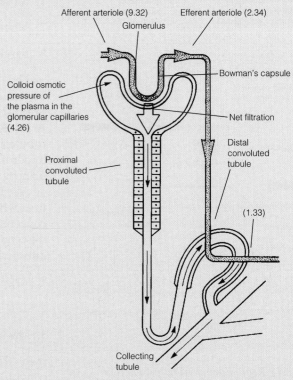

afferent artery fell to about 5.3 kPa, what would happen to the production of urine? Explain your answer. *(3 mark.*

Caffeine causes vasodilation of the afferent arterioles

(c) What effect would caffeine have on the rate at which fluid passes from the glomerulus into the Bowman's capsule? *(2 mark.*

The table shows the percentage composition of blood plasma and urine for four substances.

| Component | Blood plasma/% | Urine/% |
|---|---|---|
| Water | 90 | 90 |
| Plasma proteins | 8 | 0 |
| Glucose | 0.1 | 0 |
| Urea | 0.03 | 2 |

(d) Explain why
(i) there are no plasma proteins in urine;
(ii) there is no glucose in urine;
(iii) urea concentration is greater in urine than in blood plasma. *(6 mark.*

(e) The relative length of the loop of Henle differs greatly between different species of mammals. State the type of environment in which you might expect to find species with relatively long loops, giving reasons for you answer. *(3 mark.*

*(Total 16 mark.*

*UCLES (Modular) June 1992, (Transport, regulatio and control), No.*

(a) Outline the main features of the kidney nephron. Include in your account structural details of the regions of ultrafiltration and selective reabsorption. *(8 marks)*

(b) Explain how the mammalian kidney produces urine that is hypertonic to the blood. *(6 marks)*

(c) Describe how the nephron regulates the pH of the blood. *(4 marks)*

*(Total 18 marks)*

*UCLES June 1994, Paper 2, No. 7*

(a) The diagram shows the structure of an amino acid molecule.

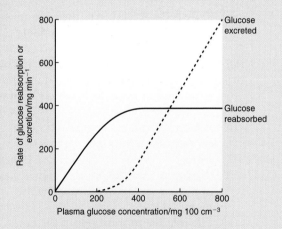

Explain how urea may be formed from this molecule. *(2 marks)*

(b) Explain how an increase in the level of the hormone ADH could lead to an increase in the concentration of urea in the urine. *(3 marks)*

*(Total 5 marks)*

*AEB Summer 1997, Module Paper 3, No. 1*

The graph shows the rate of glucose reabsorption a, and excretion from, a mammalian kidney in relation to the glucose concentration in the plasma.

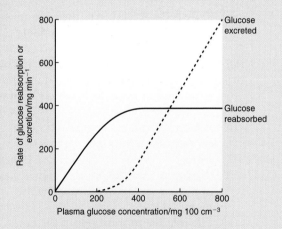

(a) In which part of the nephron is glucose reabsorbed? *(1 mark)*

(b) Explain the shape of the glucose reabsorption curve when the plasma glucose concentration is:
   (i) between 0 and 200 mg 100 cm$^{-3}$; *(1 mark)*
   (ii) over 400 mg 100 cm$^{-3}$. *(1 mark)*

(c) Use the graph to explain why glucose may occur in the urine of diabetics. *(2 marks)*

*(Total 5 marks)*

*AEB Summer 1995, Common Paper 1, No. 15*

6. Nephrosis is a kidney condition in which damage to the glomeruli results in large quantities of protein passing into the glomerular filtrate. This protein finally appears in the urine.

(a) Suggest why this protein is not reabsorbed into the blood in the proximal convoluted tubule of the nephron. *(1 mark)*

(b) As a result of nephrosis large amounts of tissue fluid accumulate in the body, especially in the ankles and feet.
   (i) Explain why the loss of protein from the blood results in the accumulation of tissue fluid. *(2 marks)*
   (ii) Suggest why this fluid accumulates especially in the ankles and the feet. *(2 marks)*

(c) (i) Explain how the action in the kidney of the hormone aldosterone controls the sodium content of the blood. *(2 marks)*
   (ii) Suggest why little aldosterone is produced by a person suffering from nephrosis. *(2 marks)*

*(Total 9 marks)*

*NEAB June 1995, BY03, No. 6*

7. (a) Copy and complete the table below with the appropriate letter, using **A** = Hypotonic; **B** = Hypertonic; **C** = Isotonic. *(3 marks)*

|  | Blood concentration relative to concentration of medium | Urine concentration relative to blood concentration |  |
| --- | --- | --- | --- |
| Dogfish | C |  | Does not drink sea water |
| Sea water teleost |  | C | Drinks sea water |
| Freshwater teleost |  |  | Water enters via gut and gills |
| Whale |  | B | Does not drink sea water |
| Seagull | A |  | Drinks sea water |

Eels are teleost fish which hatch from eggs in the sea but migrate to freshwater rivers to mature and then return to the sea to breed. It has been shown that eels lose 40% of their fresh body weight within 10 hours of migrating from the river back to the sea.

(b) How can you account for this decrease? *(1 mark)*

(c) What immediate effect is this change likely to have on the salt concentration of body fluids? *(1 mark)*

(d) How might the fish then compensate for this tendency in order to keep the salt concentration of its body fluids more or less constant? *(2 marks) (e)* On migrating from the sea back into freshwater, what would you expect to happen to its body mass and how might the fish continue to maintain osmotic equilibrium? *(2 marks)*

*(Total 9 marks)*

*Oxford & Cambridge June 1994, Paper 2/4 Option 2, No. 2*

**8.** *(a)* The following structures or areas occur within one nephron of the mammalian kidney:

Bowman's capsule; collecting duct, distal convoluted tubule; glomerulus; loop of Henle; proximal convoluted tubule.

List the sequence of structures through which a molecule of urea could pass on leaving the blood. *(3 marks)*

*(b)* (i) What is the **structural** relationship between the glomerulus and Bowman's capsule? *(1 mark)*

(ii) What is the **functional** relationship between the glomerulus and Bowman's capsule? *(1 mark)*

*(c)* Summarize the role of the brain and the pituitary gland in osmoregulation. *(4 marks)*

*(Total 9 marks)*

*Oxford June 1997, Paper 45, No. 6*

**9.** Diuretics are substances which increase urine production by the kidneys.

*(a)* Copy and complete the flow chart to show how ethanol acts as a diuretic. *(2 marks)*

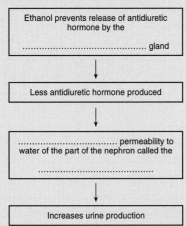

```
┌─────────────────────────────────────┐
│ Ethanol prevents release of antidiuretic │
│            hormone by the            │
│ ............................... gland │
└─────────────────────────────────────┘
                  │
                  ▼
┌─────────────────────────────────────┐
│ Less antidiuretic hormone produced   │
└─────────────────────────────────────┘
                  │
                  ▼
┌─────────────────────────────────────┐
│ ................... permeability to    │
│ water of the part of the nephron called the │
│ ...............................      │
└─────────────────────────────────────┘
                  │
                  ▼
┌─────────────────────────────────────┐
│      Increases urine production       │
└─────────────────────────────────────┘
```

*(b)* (i) Explain why eating large amounts of glucose can lead to an increase in urine production.

(ii) Some diuretics used in medicine inhibit the reabsorption of chloride ions in the loop of Henle. Explain how this would lead to an increase in urine production. *(3 marks)*

*(Total 5 marks)*

*AEB Summer 1997, Paper 1, No. 13*

**10.** The diagrams show the relative sizes of the parts o different vertebrate kidney tubules together with the amounts and concentrations of urine that are produced ($\Delta_i$ = ionic concentration inside the organism; $\Delta_o$ = ioni concentration of the environment.)

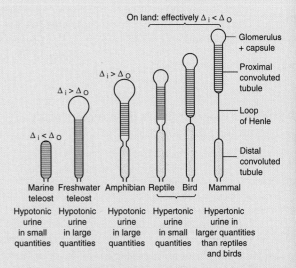

On land: effectively $\Delta_i < \Delta_o$

$\Delta_i > \Delta_o$

$\Delta_i > \Delta_o$

$\Delta_i < \Delta_o$

Glomerulus + capsule

Proximal convoluted tubule

Loop of Henle

Distal convoluted tubule

| Marine teleost | Freshwater teleost | Amphibian | Reptile | Bird | Mammal |
|---|---|---|---|---|---|
| Hypotonic urine in small quantities | Hypotonic urine in large quantities | Hypotonic urine in large quantities | Hypertonic urine in small quantities | | Hypertonic urine in larger quantities than reptiles and birds |

*(a)* (i) What effect will the difference between internal and external concentrations have on the transfer of water between a marine teleost and its environment? *(1 mark)*

(ii) Through which surfaces will most of this transfer occur? *(2 marks)*

*(b)* (i) What osmotic and ionic problems do freshwater teleosts and amphibia have *(1 mark)*

(ii) How is the structure of their kidneys adapted to deal with such problems? *(2 marks)*

*(c)* Reptiles and birds have similar kidneys whic produce hypertonic urine in small quantities.

(i) How are the structures of their kidneys adapted to do this? *(2 marks)*

(ii) What nitrogenous compound do they excrete that minimizes the loss of water? *(1 mark)*

*(d)* (i) What part does the loop of Henle play in the conservation of water by the mammal? *(3 marks)*

(ii) The relative proportions of the parts, shown in the diagram, of mammalian kidney tubules are typical for man. Suggest what the proportions might be for a freshwater mammal such as an otter. Explain your answer. *(2 marks)*

*(e)* Cartilaginous marine fishes, such as sharks, retain urea in the blood. How does this assist them in maintaining their internal ionic concentration? *(2 marks)*

*(Total 16 marks)*

*Oxford & Cambridge June 1997, Unit B6, No.*

1. Read through the following account of kidney function, then write the most appropriate word or words to complete the account.

In the kidney, the renal artery branches to form many smaller arterioles, each of which divides further to form a knot of capillaries called a ......... Here, small molecules such as ......... and ......... are forced into the cavity of the Bowman's (renal) capsule by the process of ......... Selective reabsorption takes place in the nephron. In the proximal convoluted tubule all the ......... is reabsorbed. In the ascending limb of the loop of Henle, ions are actively pumped out of the nephron. This causes ......... to be drawn out of the collecting duct.

*(Total 6 marks)*

*Edexcel January 1998, Paper HB3, No. 2*

12. The graph shows the concentration of the solutes in the fluid in the different regions of a nephron from a human kidney. Curve **A** shows the concentration in the presence of the hormone ADH. Curve **B** shows the concentration when no ADH is present.

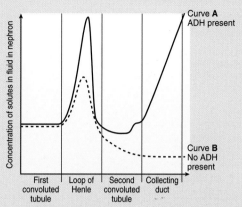

(a) Although solutes such as glucose are reabsorbed in the first convoluted tubule, the concentration of these solutes does not change as the fluid flows along this part. Explain why. *(1 mark)*
(b) What causes the concentration of the solutes to increase then decrease as the fluid flows through the loop of Henle? *(4 marks)*
(c) Explain the difference in concentration of the fluid in the collecting duct in curves **A** and **B**. *(2 marks)*
*(Total 7 marks)*

*NEAB February 1997, Paper BY10, No. 2*

Immunofluorescent light micrograph of neurones and asterocytes in mammalian spinal cord (*opposite*)

# Part V
## COORDINATION, RESPONSE AND CONTROL

# 24 How control systems developed

The ability to respond to stimuli is a characteristic of all living organisms. While many stimuli originate from outside, it is also necessary to respond to internal changes. In a single-celled organism, such responses are relatively simple. No part of it is far from the medium in which it lives and so it can respond directly to environmental changes. The inside of a single cell does not vary considerably from one part to another and so there are few internal differences to respond to.

With the development of multicellular organisms came the differentiation of cells which specialized in particular functions. With specialization in one function came the loss of the ability to perform others. This division of labour, whereby different groups of cells each carried out their own function, made the cells dependent upon one another. Cells specializing in reproduction, for example, depend on other cells to obtain oxygen for their respiration, yet others to provide glucose and others to remove waste products. These different functional systems must be coordinated if they are to perform efficiently. If, for example, an animal needs to exert itself in order to capture its food, the muscular activity involved must itself be coordinated. The locomotory organs need to operate smoothly and efficiently with each muscle contracting at exactly the correct time. In addition, more oxygen and glucose will be required and an increased amount of carbon dioxide will need to be removed from the tissues. If breathing is increased so that the oxygen concentration of the blood rises, it is essential that the heart increases its output accordingly. Without coordination between the two systems an increased effort by one could be neutralized by the other. No bodily system can work in isolation, but all must be integrated in a coordinated fashion.

There are two forms of integration in most multicellular animals: nervous and hormonal. The nervous system permits rapid communication between one part of an organism and another, in much the same way as a telephone system does in human society. The hormonal system provides a slower form of communication and can be likened to the postal system. Both systems need to work together. A predator, for example, may be detected by the sense organs, which belong to the nervous system, but in turn cause the production of adrenalin, a hormone. While the nervous system coordinates the animal's locomotion as it makes its escape, the adrenaline ensures that an increased breathing rate and heart beat supply adequate oxygen and glucose to allow the muscles to operate efficiently. The link between these two coordinating systems is achieved by the **hypothalamus**. It is here that the nervous and hormonal systems interact.

All organisms, plant and animal, must respond to environmental changes if they are to survive. To detect these changes requires sense organs. Those detecting external changes are located on the surface of the body and act as a vital link between the internal and external environments. Many other sense cells are located internally to provide information on a constantly changing internal environment. In responding to stimuli, an organism usually modifies some aspect of its functioning. It may need to produce enzymes in response to the presence of food, become sexually aroused in response to certain behaviour by a member of the opposite sex or move away from an unpleasant stimulus. In most cases the organ effecting the change is some distance away from the sense cell detecting the stimulus. A rapid means of communication between the sense cell and the effector organ is essential. In animals the nerves perform this function.

The stimuli received by many sense organs, e.g. the eyes, are very complex and require widely differing responses. The sight of a female of the same species may elicit a totally different response from the sight of a male of the same species. Each response involves different effector organs. The sense organs must therefore be connected by nerves to all effector organs, in much the same way as a telephone subscriber is connected to all other subscribers. One method is to have an individual nerve running from the sense organ to all effectors. Clearly this is only possible in very simple organisms where the sense organs respond to a limited number of stimuli and the number of effectors is small. The nerve nets of cnidarians work in this way.

Large, complex organisms require a different system, because the number of sense organs and effectors is so great that individual links between all of them is not feasible. Imagine having a separate telephone cable leading from a house to every other subscriber's house in Britain, let alone the world. Animals developed a **central nervous system** to which every effector and sense organ has at least one nerve connection. The central nervous system (brain and spinal cord) acts like a switchboard in connecting each incoming stimulus to the appropriate effector. It works in much the same way as a telephone exchange, where a single cable from a home allows a subscriber to be connected to any other simply by making the correct connections at various exchanges.

Where then should the brain be located? The development of locomotion in animals usually resulted in a particular part of the animal leading the way. This anterior region was much more likely to encounter environmental changes first, e.g. changes in light intensity, temperature, pH, etc. It was obvious that most sense organs should be located on this anterior portion. There would be little point locating them in the posterior region, as a harmful substance would not be detected until it had already caused damage to the anterior of the animal. Most sensory information therefore originated at the front. To allow a rapid response, the 'brain' was located in this region. This led, in many animals, to the formation of a distinct head, **cephalization**, concerned primarily with detection and interpretation of stimuli. It was still essential for the brain to receive stimuli from the rest of the animal and to communicate with effector organs throughout the body. An elongated portion of the central nervous system therefore extends the length of most animals. In vertebrates this is the spinal cord.

With increasingly complex stimuli being received, the brain developed greater powers of interpretation. In particular it developed the ability to store information about previous experiences in order to assist it in deciding on the appropriate response to a future situation. With this ability to learn came the capacity to use previous experience and even to make responses to situations never previously encountered. Thus intelligence developed.

The hormone or endocrine system is concerned with longer-term changes, especially in response to the internal environment. It is an advantage to maintain a relatively constant internal environment. Not only can chemical reactions take place at a predictable rate, but the organism also acquires a degree of independence from the environment. It is no longer restricted to certain regions of the earth but can increase its geographical range. It does not have to restrict its activities to particular periods of the day, or seasons, when conditions are suitable. The maintenance of a constant internal environment is called **homeostasis** and is largely controlled by hormones. In the same way that the brain coordinates the nervous system, the activities of the endocrine system are controlled by the **pituitary gland**.

Responding to changes in the internal and external environments is no less important to survival in plants. Because they lack contractile tissue and do not move from place to place independently, they have no need for very rapid responses. There is therefore no nervous system or anything equivalent to it. Plant responses are hormonal. Their movements are as a result of growth, rather than contractions, and as a consequence are much slower than those of animals.

# 25 Homeostasis

We have seen that matter tends to assume its lowest energy state. It tends to change from an ordered state to a disordered one, i.e. tends towards high entropy. The survival of biological organisms depends on their ability to overcome this tendency to disorderliness. They must remain stable. This need for constancy was recognized in the nineteenth century by Claude Bernard. He contrasted the constancy of the fluid which surrounds all cells (*milieu interieur*) with the ever changing external environment (*milieu exterieur*). Bernard concluded: *'La fixité du milieu interieur est la condition de la vie libre.'* (The constancy of the internal environment is the condition of the free life.)

By bathing cells in a fluid, the tissue fluid, whose composition remains constant, the chemical reactions within these cells can take place at a predictable rate. Not only are the cells able to survive but they can also function efficiently. The whole organism thus becomes more independent of its environment.

The term **homeostasis** (*homoio* = 'same'; *stasis* = 'standing') was not coined until 1932. It is used to describe all the mechanisms by which a constant environment is maintained. Some examples of homeostatic control have already been discussed, for example osmoregulation in Chapter 23. Further examples are examined in this chapter and the following one.

## 25.1 Principles of homeostasis

Before examining the detailed operation of homeostatic systems, it is necessary to look at the fundamental principles common to them. Organisms are examples of open systems, since there is exchange of materials between themselves and the environment. Not least, they require a constant input of energy to maintain themselves in a stable condition against the natural tendency to disorder. The maintenance of this stability requires control systems capable of detecting any deviation from the usual and making the necessary adjustments to return to the normal condition.

### 25.1.1 Control mechanisms and feedback

**Cybernetics** (*cybernos* = 'steersman') is the science of control systems, i.e. self-regulating systems which operate by means of feedback mechanisms.

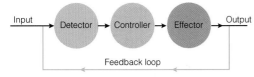

Fig. 25.1 Principal components of a typical control system

The essential components of a control system are:

1. **Reference point** – the set level at which the system operates.

2. **Detector** – signals the extent of any deviation from the reference point.

3. **Controller** – coordinates the information from various detectors and sends out instructions which will correct the deviation.

4. **Effector** – brings about the necessary change needed to return the system to the reference point.

5. **Feedback loop** – informs the detector of any change in the system as a result of action by the effector.

The relationship between these components is given in Fig. 25.1.

An everyday example of such a control system occurs in the regulation of a central heating system in a home, where the various components are:

1. **Reference point** – temperature determined by the occupant, e.g. 20 °C, and set on the thermostat.

2. **Detector** – the thermostat which constantly monitors the temperature of the room in which it is situated.

3. **Controller** – the programmer which can be set to turn the heating on and off at set times. It is connected to the boiler, hot water cylinder, circulation pump and thermostat.

4. **Effector** – the boiler, circulation pump, radiators and associated pipework.

5. **Feedback loop** – the movement of air within the room.

If the temperature of the room falls below 20 °C, the thermostat sends an electrical message to the programmer. The programmer coordinates this information with that in its own programme, i.e. whether the heating is set to operate at this particular time of day. If it is set to operate, it sends appropriate electrical messages which turn on the boiler and the circulation pump. Hot water flows around the central heating system to the radiator in the room. The heat from this radiator warms the air in the room which circulates until it reaches the thermostat. Once the temperature of this air reaches 20 °C, the thermostat ceases to send information to the programmer which then turns off the circulation pump. As the feedback causes the system to be turned off, it is called **negative feedback**. It is possible to have positive feedback systems. Although these are rare in living organisms one example is described in Section 27.1.3.

A similar system operates to control body temperature in birds and mammals. Temperature detectors in the skin provide information on changes in the external temperature which is conveyed to the hypothalamus of the brain, which acts as the controller. This initiates appropriate corrective responses in effectors, such as the skin and blood vessels, in order to maintain a constant body temperature. Details of these processes are given in the following section.

# 25.2   Temperature control

extremes of temperature such as those found in
~lar regions it is the endothermic birds and
~ammals which are most successful.

The temperature of environments inhabited by living organisms
ranges from 90 °C in hot springs to − 40 °C in the Arctic. Most
organisms, however, live in the narrow range of temperature
10–30 °C. To survive, most animals need to exert some control
over their body temperature. This regulation of body
temperature is called **thermoregulation**. In all organisms heat
may be gained in two main ways.

1.  **Metabolism of food.**

2.  **Absorption of solar energy** – This may be absorbed directly
or indirectly from

    (a)  heat reflected from objects;
    (b)  heat convected from the warming of the ground;
    (c)  heat conducted from the ground.

Heat may be lost in four main ways:

1.  **Evaporation of water**, e.g. during sweating.

2.  **Conduction from the body** to the ground or other objects.

3.  **Convection from the body** to the air or water.

4.  **Radiation from the body** to the air, water or ground.

### 25.2.1 Ectothermy and endothermy

The majority of animals obtain most of their heat from sources
outside the body. These are termed **ectotherms**. The body
temperature of these animals frequently fluctuates in line with
environmental temperature. Animals whose temperature varies
in this way are called **poikilotherms** (*Poikilos* = 'various'; *thermo* =
'heat'). While most ectotherms have a body temperature
approaching that of the environment, it is rarely equal to it.
During exercise, for example, the metabolic heat produced may
raise the body temperature above that of the environment.
Moist-bodied ectotherms frequently have temperatures a little
below that of the environment owing to the cooling effect of
evaporation. Ectotherms do attempt to regulate their
temperatures within broad limits. The methods used are largely
behavioural.

Mammals and birds maintain constant body temperatures
irrespective of the environmental temperature. As their heat is
derived internally, by metabolic activities, they are called
**endotherms**. As the temperature of the body remains the same,
they are sometimes called **homoiotherms** (*homoio* = 'same';
*thermo* = 'heat'). The body temperature of endotherms is usually
in the range 35–44 °C.

The higher the body temperature the higher the metabolic rate
of the animal. This is especially important for birds where the
energy demands of flight make a high metabolic rate an
advantage. Most birds therefore have body temperatures in the
range 40–44 °C. The problem with a high body temperature is
that the environment is usually cooler, and heat is therefore
continually lost to it. The higher the body temperature, the
greater the gradient between internal and external temperatures

and so the more heat is lost. Mammals, with less dependence on a very high metabolic rate than birds, therefore have body temperatures in the range 35–40 °C to minimize their total heat loss. The body temperatures of all endotherms are something of a compromise, balancing the advantage of a high temperature, in increasing metabolic activity, and the disadvantage of increased heat loss due to a greater temperature gradient between the internal and external environments. The evolutionary advantage of being endothermic is that it gives much more environmental independence. It is no coincidence that the most successful animals in the extremes of temperatures found in deserts and at the poles are mammals and birds. The independence that a constant high body temperature brings allows these groups to extend their geographical range considerably.

### 25.2.2 Structure of the skin

Most heat exchange occurs through the skin, as it is the barrier between the internal and external environments. It is in mammals that the skin plays the most important role in thermoregulation. Mammalian skin has two main layers, an outer epidermis and an inner dermis.

*The epidermis*
This comprises three regions:

1. **The Malpighian layer (germinative layer)** – The deepest layer made up of actively dividing cells. The pigment **melanin**, which determines the skin colour, is produced here. Melanin absorbs ultra-violet light and so helps to protect the tissues beneath from its damaging effects. The Malpighian layer has numerous infoldings which extend deep into the dermis, producing sweat glands, sebaceous glands and hair follicles. There are no blood vessels in the epidermis and so the cells of this layer obtain food and oxygen by diffusion and active transport from capillaries in the dermis.

2. **Stratum granulosum (granular layer)** – This is made up of living cells which have been produced by the Malpighian layer. As they are pushed towards the skin surface by new cells produced beneath, they accumulate the fibrous protein **keratin**, lose their nuclei and die.

3. **Stratum corneum (cornified layer)** – This is the surface layer of the skin and comprises flattened, dead cells impregnated with keratin. The stratum corneum forms a tough, resistant, waterproof layer which is constantly replaced as it is worn away. It is thickest where there is greatest wear, i.e. on the palms of the hands and the soles of the feet. Sweat ducts and hair extend through this layer.

*The dermis*
The dermis is largely made up of connective tissue consisting of collagen and elastic fibres. It possesses:

1. **Blood capillaries** – These supply both the epidermis and dermis with food and oxygen. Special networks supply the sweat glands and hair follicles. They play an important role in thermoregulation.

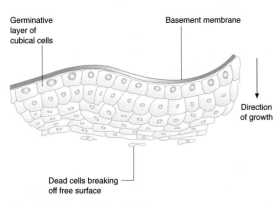

Fig. 25.2 Stratified epithelium

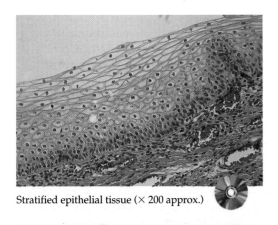

Stratified epithelial tissue (× 200 approx.)

### Did you know?

Skin cells form most rapidly in the four hours after midnight when the body's metabolism has slowed down and there is energy available.

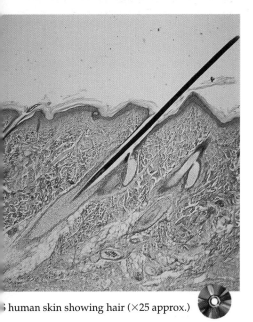

human skin showing hair (×25 approx.)

**2. Hair follicles** – These are formed by inpushings of the Malpighian layer. Cells at the base multiply to produce a long cylindrical hair, the cells of which become impregnated with keratin and die. The more melanin in the hair, the darker its colour. Attached to it is a small bundle of smooth muscle, contraction of which causes the hair to become erect.

**3. Sebaceous glands** – Situated at the side of the hair follicle these produce an oily secretion called **sebum** which waterproofs the hair and epidermis. It also keeps the epidermis supple and protects against bacteria.

**4. Sweat glands** – These are coiled tubes made up of cells which absorb fluid from surrounding capillaries and secrete it into the tube, from where it passes to the skin surface via the sweat duct. Sweat has a variable composition, consisting mainly of water in which mineral salts and urea are dissolved. Evaporation of sweat from the skin surface helps to cool the body.

**5. Sensory nerve endings** – There is a variety of different sensory cells concerned with providing information on the external environment. These include:

    **(a)** touch receptors (Meissner's corpuscles);
    **(b)** pressure receptors (Pacinian corpuscles);
    **(c)** pain receptors;
    **(d)** temperature receptors.

**6. Subcutaneous fat** – Beneath the dermis is a layer of fat (adipose) tissue. This acts both as a long-term food reserve and as an insulating layer.

The structure of human skin is shown in Fig. 25.3.

### 25.2.3 Maintenance of a constant body temperature in warm environments

Endothermic organisms which live permanently in warm climates have developed a range of adaptations to help them maintain a constant body temperature. These adaptations may be anatomical, physiological or behavioural, and include the following.

**1. Vasodilation** – Blood in the network of capillaries in the skin may take three alternative routes. It can pass through capillaries close to the skin surface, through others deeper in the dermis or it may pass beneath the layer of subcutaneous fat. In warm climates, superficial arterioles dilate in order to allow blood close to the skin surface. Heat from this blood is rapidly conducted through the epidermis to the skin surface from where it is radiated away from the body (Fig. 25.4).

**2. Sweating** – The evaporation of each gram of water requires 2.5 kJ of energy. Being furless, humans have sweat glands over the whole body, making them efficient at cooling by this means. Animals with fur generally have sweat glands confined to areas of the skin where fur is absent, e.g. pads of the feet in dogs. Sweating beneath a covering of thick fur is inefficient as the fur

501

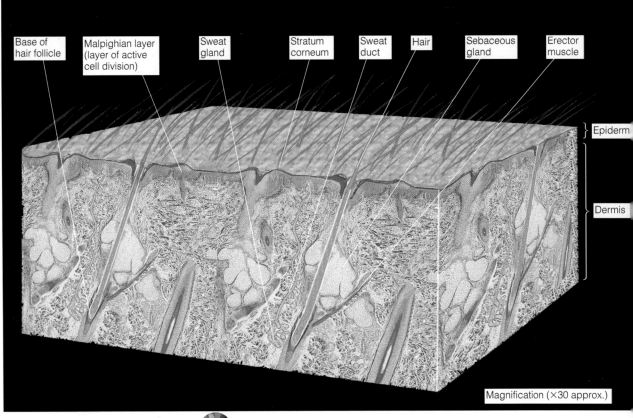

| Base of hair follicle | Malpighian layer (layer of active cell division) | Sweat gland | Stratum corneum | Sweat duct | Hair | Sebaceous gland | Erector muscle |

Epiderm

Dermis

Magnification (×30 approx.)

*Fig. 25.3 VS through human skin*

prevents air movements which would otherwise evaporate the sweat. Birds lack sweat glands altogether as their covering of feathers makes evaporation almost impossible. Humans, on the other hand, may produce up to 1000 cm³ of sweat per hour.

**3. Panting and licking** – Where animals have few or no sweat glands, cooling by evaporation of water nonetheless takes place from the mouth and nose. Panting in dogs may result in the breathing rate increasing from 30 to 300 breaths min$^{-1}$. This results in excessive removal of carbon dioxide from the blood which is partly offset by a reduction in the depth of breathing. Even so, dogs are able to tolerate a depletion of carbon dioxide which would prove fatal to other organisms. Panting is common in birds. Licking, while not as effective as sweating, may help cool the body. It has been reported in kangaroos, cats and rabbits.

**4. Insulation** – A layer of fur or fat may help prevent heat gain when external temperatures exceed those of the body. In warm climates the fur is usually light in colour to help reflect the sun radiation. At high environmental temperatures the hair erector muscles are relaxed and the elasticity of the skin causes the fur lie closer to its surface. The thickness of insulatory warm air trapped is thus reduced (Fig. 25.5) and body heat is more readi dissipated.

**5. Large surface-area to volume ratio** – Animals in warm climates frequently have large extremities, such as ears, when compared to related species from cold climates. Fennec foxes have much longer ears than their European counterparts which in turn have longer ears than the Arctic fox. Being well supplie with blood vessels and covered with relatively short hair, ears make especially good radiators of heat.

**6. Variation in body temperature** – Some desert animals allow their body temperatures to fluctuate within a specific range. In camels this range is 34–41 °C. By allowing their body temperature to rise during the day, they reduce the temperature gradient between the body and the environment and so reduce heat gain. In addition, the onset of sweating is delayed, so conserving water.

**7. Behavioural mechanisms** – Many desert animals avoid the period of greatest heat stress by being nocturnal. Some hibernate during the hottest months. This summer hibernation is known as **aestivation**. Other animals avoid the sun by sheltering under rocks or burrowing beneath the surface.

### 25.2.4 Maintenance of a constant body temperature in cold environments

Endothermic animals living in cold environments show adaptations to the climate. These include:

**1. Vasoconstriction** – In cold conditions, the superficial arterioles contract, so reducing the quantity of blood reaching the skin surface. Blood largely passes beneath the insulating layer of subcutaneous fat and so loses little heat to the outside. Both vasodilation and vasoconstriction are illustrated in Fig. 25.4.

rctic fox (*top*) and fennec fox (*bottom*) showing fferences in lengths of ears

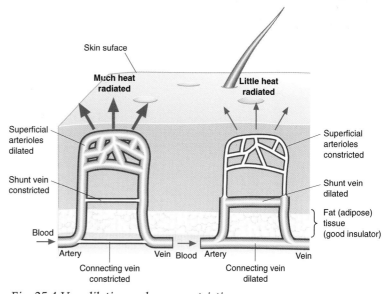

*Fig. 25.4 Vasodilation and vasoconstriction*

**2. Shivering** – At low environmental temperatures, the skeletal muscle of the body may undergo rhythmic, involuntary contractions which produce metabolic heat. This shivering may be preceded by asynchronous twitching of groups of muscle.

**3. Insulation** – Insulation is an effective means of reducing heat loss from the body. It may be achieved by an external covering of fur or feathers and/or an internal layer of subcutaneous fat. The thickness of the fur is related to the environmental temperature, with animals in cold regions having denser and thicker fur. One problem with effective insulation is that it prevents the rapid heat loss necessary during strenuous exercise.

## PROJECT

**A small organism has a relatively small surface-area to volume ratio and this reduces the rate at which heat is lost**

1. Translate this statement into a hypothesis which could be tested.

2. Test your hypothesis by comparing heat loss from round-bottomed flasks of different sizes, using temperature sensors and data-logging equipment if possible.

For this reason the fur on the underside of the body may be thinner to facilitate heat loss. In birds, specialized down feather provide particularly efficient insulation. Both fur and feathers function by trapping warm air next to the body. In cold conditions, the hair erector muscles contract to pull up the hairs and so increase the thickness of the layer of air trapped, improving insulation (Fig. 25.5).

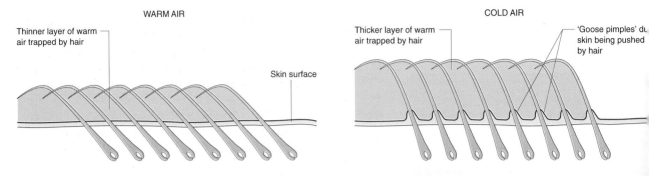

**WARM AIR**

Thinner layer of warm air trapped by hair

Skin surface

**COLD AIR**

Thicker layer of warm air trapped by hair

'Goose pimples' du skin being pushed by hair

*Fig. 25.5 Lowering and raising of hair in controlling heat loss*

Subcutaneous fat alone is only half as effective as fur but makes a useful additional contribution. In aquatic mammals (whales, dolphins, seals) fur would be ineffective and has therefore all but disappeared. To compensate for this loss the subcutaneous fat is extremely thick and forms an effective insulating layer, known as **blubber**.

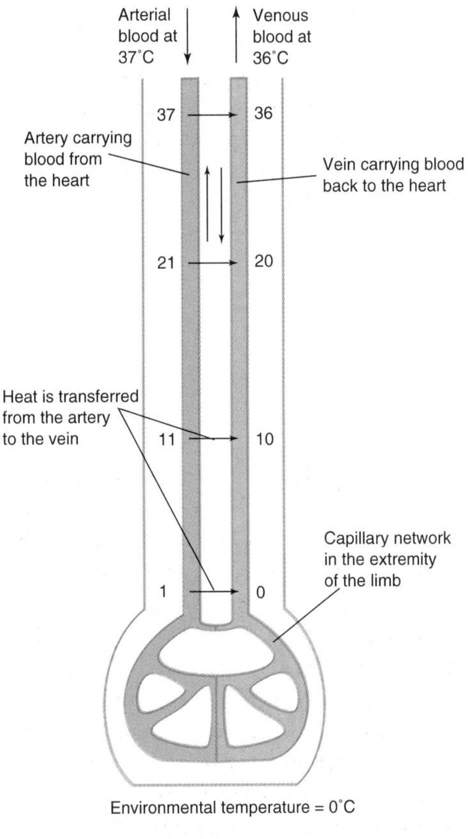

**4. Small surface-area to volume ratio** – Animals in colder climates have a tendency to be more compact, with smaller extremities, than related species in warm climates. In this way heat loss is reduced.

**5. Variations between superficial and core temperature** – The extremities of animals in cold regions are maintained at lower temperatures than the core body temperature. This reduces the temperature gradient between them and the environment. This is especially important in order to reduce heat loss from the fee which are in contact with the cold ground. The reduction of he loss from these extremities is achieved by **counter-current heat exchangers** found in the limbs of certain birds and mammals. Blood in veins returning from the limbs passes alongside blood in arteries. Heat from the warm blood entering the limb is transferred to cold blood in the vein returning from it. The limb is thereby kept at a lower temperature and cold blood is prevented from entering the core of the body. This system is illustrated in Fig. 25.6.

**6. Increased metabolic rate** – In addition to an increase in heat produced by muscles during shivering, the liver may also increase its metabolic rate during cold conditions. Low temperatures induce increased activity of the adrenal, thyroid and pituitary glands. All these produce hormones which help increase the body's metabolic rate and so produce additional heat. This requires increased consumption of food, arctic anima consuming more food per gram of body weight than their tropical relatives. Rats kept at 3 °C take in 50% more food than rats kept at 20 °C.

Arterial blood at 37°C

Venous blood at 36°C

Artery carrying blood from the heart

Vein carrying blood back to the heart

37 → 36

21 → 20

Heat is transferred from the artery to the vein

11 → 10

1 → 0

Capillary network in the extremity of the limb

Environmental temperature = 0°C

*Fig. 25.6 Counter-current heat exchange system* (rete mirabilis)

7. **Behavioural mechanisms** – In cold regions, animals are usually active during the day (diurnal). Huddling of groups of individuals is a common way of reducing heat loss. Reproductive behaviour is adapted to allow the young to be born at a time when food is available by the time they are weaned. Delayed fertilization and implantation of the embryo may occur (Sections 12.7.4–6).

8. **Hibernation** – One special behavioural mechanism utilized by endothermic animals in cold climates is hibernation. During times of greatest cold and hence shortest supply of food, mammals like squirrels and dormice may undergo a period of long sleep. During this time the metabolic rate is reduced 20–100 times below that of normal with a consequent reduction in food and oxygen consumption. The hibernation may last several months, during which time fat reserves accumulated during the summer are used. These reserves take the form of **brown adipose tissue** which is easily metabolized at low temperatures. Breathing and heart beat become slow and irregular. The body temperature falls close to that of the environment, being 1–4 °C higher. To prevent the body freezing at temperatures of − 4 °C and below, well insulated and sheltered nests are essential, often underground. For this reason hibernation is virtually impossible in areas of permafrost.

### 25.2.5 Role of the hypothalamus in the control of body temperature

Control of body temperature is effected by the **hypothalamus**, a small body at the base of the brain. Within the hypothalamus is the thermoregulatory centre which has two parts: a heat gain and a heat loss centre. The hypothalamus monitors the temperature of blood passing through it and in addition receives nervous information from receptors in the skin about external temperature changes. Any reduction in blood temperature will bring about changes which conserve heat. A rise in blood temperature has the opposite effect. These effects are summarized in Fig. 25.7.

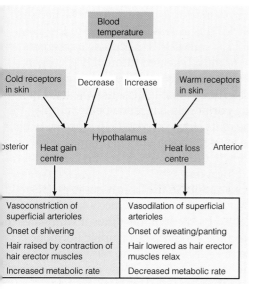

*Fig. 25.7 Summary of body temperature control by the hypothalamus*

## 25.3 Control of blood sugar

All metabolizing cells require a supply of glucose in order to continue functioning. The nervous system is especially sensitive to any reduction in the normal glucose level of 90 mg glucose in 100 cm³ blood. A rise in blood sugar level can be equally dangerous. The supply of carbohydrate in mammals fluctuates because they do not eat continuously throughout the day and the quantity of carbohydrate varies from meal to meal. There may be long periods when no carbohydrate is absorbed from the intestines. Cells, however, metabolize continuously and need a constant supply of glucose to sustain them. A system which maintains a constant glucose level in the blood, despite intermittent supplies from the intestine, is essential. The liver plays a key role in glucose homeostasis. It can add glucose to the blood in two ways:

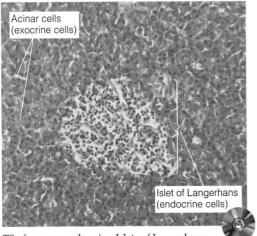

TS of pancreas, showing Islets of Langerhans (×200 approx.)

**(i)** by the breakdown of glycogen (**glycogenolysis**);

**(ii)** by converting protein into glucose (**gluconeogenesis**).

The liver can remove glucose from the blood by converting it into glycogen (**glycogenesis**) which is then stored. A normal liver stores around 75 g of glycogen, sufficient to maintain the body's supply of glucose for about 12 hours. The interconversion of glucose and glycogen is largely under the control of two hormones produced by the pancreas. In addition to being an exocrine gland producing pancreatic juice, the pancreas is also an endocrine gland. Throughout the pancreas are groups of histologically different cells known as the **Islets of Langerhans**. The cells within them are of two types: α-cells, which produce the hormone **glucagon**, and β-cells, which produce the hormone **insulin**. Both hormones are discharged directly into the blood. Some hours after a meal, the glucose formed as a result of carbohydrate breakdown is absorbed by the intestines. The blood capillaries from the intestine unite to form the hepatic portal vein which carries this glucose-rich blood to the liver. Insulin from the pancreas causes excess glucose to become converted to glucose-6-phosphate and ultimately glycogen which the liver stores. The same process can occur in many body cells, especially muscle. Some time later, when the level of glucose in the hepatic portal vein has fallen below normal, the liver reconverts some of its stored glycogen to glucose, to help maintain the glucose level of the blood. This change involves a phosphorylase enzyme in the liver which is activated by the pancreatic hormone glucagon.

Should the glycogen supply in the liver become exhausted, glucose may be formed by other means. Once a low level of blood glucose is detected by the hypothalamus it stimulates the pituitary gland to produce adrenocorticotrophic hormones (ACTH) which cause the adrenal glands to release the glucocorticoid hormones, e.g. cortisol. These cause the liver to convert amino acids and glycerol into glucose. In times of stress another hormone from the adrenal glands, **adrenaline**, causes the breakdown of glycogen in the liver and so helps to raise the blood sugar level. Further details of these effects are given in Section 26.5.

The control of blood sugar level is summarized in Fig. 25.8.

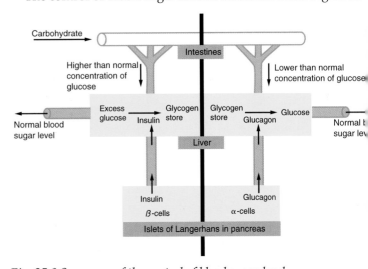

*Fig. 25.8 Summary of the control of blood sugar level*

## 25.4   Control of respiratory gases

Metabolizing cells all require a continuous supply of oxygen sufficient to satisfy their respiratory needs. The homeostatic control of both oxygen and carbon dioxide levels in the blood is achieved by the breathing (respiratory) centres in the medulla oblongata of the brain. Details of the mechanisms of control are given in Section 20.3

## 25.5   Control of blood pressure

Having achieved homeostatic control of the composition of respiratory gases, sugar and other metabolites in the blood, it is clearly essential for a mammal to control the distribution of this blood. It is essential that blood pressure be kept above a certain minimum level if the supply of essential materials to cells is to be maintained. This is achieved by controlling the rate at which the heart pumps blood and by the vasoconstriction or vasodilation of blood vessels. The mechanisms by which these are controlled are detailed in Sections 21.5.3 and 21.5.4 respectively.

## 25.6   The liver

The liver, weighing as it does up to 1.5 kg, makes up 3–5% of the body weight. It probably originated as a digestive organ but its functions are now much more diverse, many being concerned with homeostasis.

### 25.6.1 Structure of the liver

In an adult human, the liver is typically 28 cm × 16 cm × 9 cm although its exact size varies considerably according to the quantity of blood stored within it. It is found immediately below the diaphragm, to which it is attached. Blood is supplied to the liver by two vessels: the hepatic artery, which carries 30% of the liver's total blood supply, brings oxygenated blood from the aorta; the hepatic portal vein supplies 70% of the liver's blood and is rich in soluble digested food from the intestines. A single vessel, the hepatic vein, drains blood from the liver. In addition, the bile duct carries bile produced in the liver to the duodenum. The relationship of these structures is shown in Fig. 25.9.

The branches of the hepatic artery and those of the hepatic portal vein combine within the liver to form common venules which lead into a series of channels called **sinusoids**. These are lined with liver cells or **hepatocytes**. The sinusoids eventually drain into a branch of the hepatic vein called the **central vein**. Between the hepatocytes are fine tubes called **canaliculi** in which bile is secreted. The canaliculi combine to form bile ducts which drain into the gall bladder where the bile is stored before being periodically released into the duodenum. The structure of the liver is shown in Fig. 25.10.

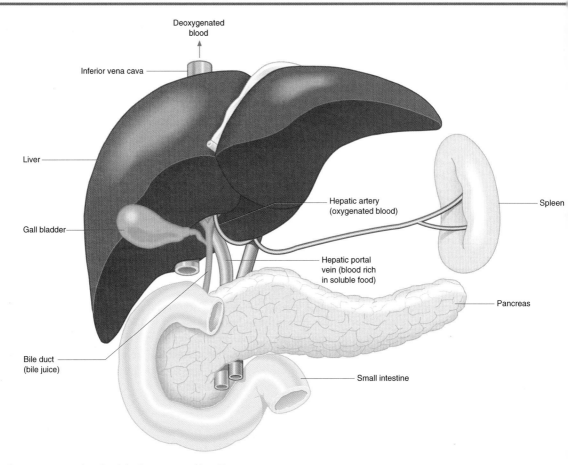

*Fig. 25.9 Blood system associated with the mammalian liver*

The functional unit of the liver is the **acinus**. As blood from the hepatic portal vein and hepatic artery mixes it passes along the sinusoids which are lined with hepatocytes. Materials are exchanged between these cells and the blood. To facilitate this exchange, the hepatocytes have microvilli to increase their surface area. They also possess a large nucleus, many mitochondria, lysosomes and glycogen granules – all indicate a highly metabolic role for these cells. The canaliculi are also lined with microvilli and these appear to remove bile from the hepatocytes by active transport.

The sinusoids are lined with flattened **endothelial cells**. Their structure is similar to that in many other organs except for the presence of pores up to 10 nm in diameter. In addition, there are specialized cells lining the sinusoid. These are **Kupffer** cells. They are highly phagocytic and form part of the **reticulo-endothelial system**. They are ideally situated for ingesting any foreign organisms or particulate matter which enter the body from the intestines. They also engulf damaged and worn out blood cells, producing the bile pigment bilirubin as a by-product of this process. The bilirubin is passed into the canaliculi for excretion in the bile.

### 25.6.2 Functions of the liver

The liver is the body's chemical workshop and has an estimated 500 individual functions. Some of these have been grouped under the following twelve headings:

Liver lobule

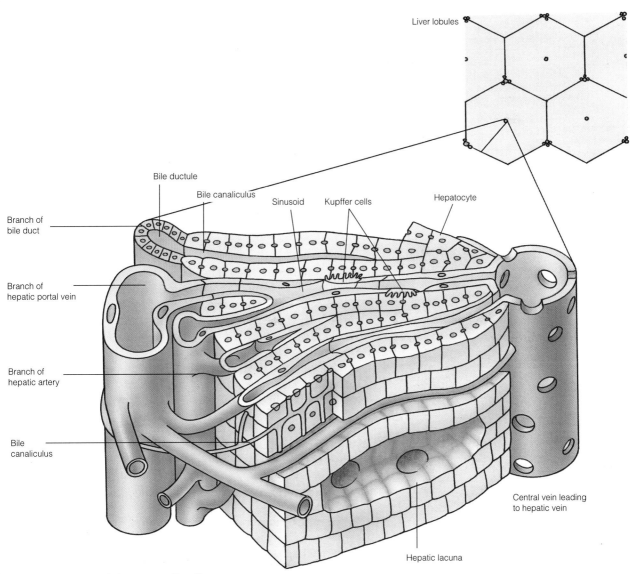

Fig. 25.10 Structure of the mammalian liver

**1. Carbohydrate metabolism** – The liver's major role in the metabolism of carbohydrates is to convert excess glucose absorbed from the intestine into glycogen. This stored glycogen can later be reconverted to glucose when the blood sugar level falls. This interconversion is under the control of the hormones insulin and glucagon produced by the Islets of Langerhans in the pancreas (Section 25.3).

**2. Lipid metabolism** – Lipids entering the liver may either be broken down or modified for transport to storage areas elsewhere in the body. Once the glycogen store in the liver is full, excess carbohydrate will be converted to fat by the liver. Excess cholesterol in the blood is excreted into the bile by the liver, which conversely can synthesize cholesterol when that absorbed by the intestines is inadequate for the body's need. The removal of excess cholesterol is essential as its accumulation may cause atherosclerosis (narrowing of the arteries) leading to thrombosis. If in considerable excess, its presence in bile may lead to the formation of **gall stones** which can block the bile duct.

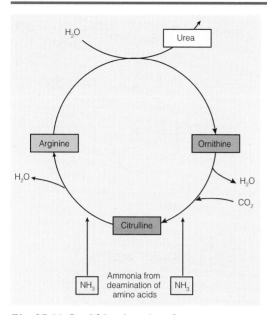

*Fig. 25.11 Ornithine (urea) cycle*

3. **Protein metabolism** – Proteins are not stored by the body and so excess amino acids are broken down in the liver by a process called **deamination**. As the name suggests, this is the removal of the amino group (–$NH_2$) to form ammonia ($NH_3$) which in mammals is converted to the less toxic urea ($CO(NH_2)_2$). This occurs in the ornithine cycle, the main stages of which are shown in Fig. 25.11.

**Transamination** reactions, whereby one amino acid is converted to another, are also performed by the liver. All non-essential amino acids may be synthesized in this way, should they be temporarily deficient in the diet.

4. **Synthesis of plasma proteins** – The liver is responsible for the production of vital proteins found in blood plasma. These include albumins and globulins as well as the clotting factors prothrombin and fibrinogen.

5. **Production of bile** – The liver produces bile salts and adds to them the bile pigment bilirubin from the breakdown of red blood cells. With sodium chloride and sodium hydrogen carbonate, cholesterol and water, this forms the green–yellow fluid known as bile. Up to $1\,dm^3$ of bile may be produced daily. It is temporarily stored in the gall bladder before being discharged into the duodenum. The bile pigments are purely excretory. The remaining contents have digestive functions and are described in Section 15.4.4.

6. **Storage of vitamins** – The liver will store a number of vitamins which can later be released if deficient in the diet. It stores mainly the fat-soluble vitamins A, D, E and K, although the water-soluble vitamins B and C are also stored. The functions of these vitamins are given in Chapter 2, Table 2.1.

7. **Storage of minerals** – The liver stores minerals, e.g. iron, potassium, copper and zinc, the functions of which are dealt with in Chapter 2, Table 2.1. It is the liver's stores of these minerals, along with vitamins, which makes it such a nutritious food.

8. **Formation and breakdown of red blood cells** – The fetus relies solely on the liver for the production of red blood cells. In an adult, this role is transferred to the bone marrow. The adult liver, however, continues to break down red blood cells at the end of their 120-day life span. The Kupffer cells lining the sinusoids carry out this breakdown, producing the bile pigment bilirubin which is excreted in the bile. The iron is either stored in the liver or used in the formation of new red blood cells by the bone marrow. The liver produces **haematinic principle**, a substance needed in the formation of red blood cells. Vitamin B is necessary for the production of this principle, and its deficiency results in pernicious anaemia.

9. **Storage of blood** – The liver, with its vast complex of blood vessels, forms a large store of blood with a capacity of up to $1500\,cm^3$. In the event of haemorrhage, constriction of these vessels forces blood into the general circulation to replace that lost and so helps to maintain blood pressure. In stressful situations, adrenaline also causes constriction of these vessels, creating a rise in blood pressure.

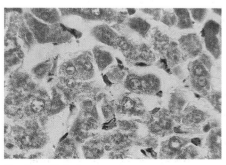

Kupffer cells in liver

## BIOLOGY AROUND US

# Cirrhosis of the liver

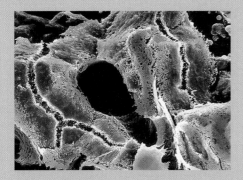

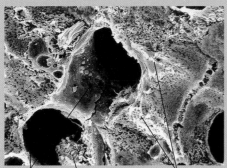

Sinusoids    Phagocytes associated with tissue damage    Connective tissue invading liver

False-colour scanning EMs of cell structure within (top) a healthy liver and (above) one affected by cirrhosis

Worldwide the main cause of the severe liver disease cirrhosis is infection with the hepatitis B virus but in the western world the commonest cause is alcohol abuse. The chance of developing cirrhosis is related to the amount of alcohol consumed daily. The risks are significantly increased in men with an intake greater than seven units (56 g absolute alcohol) per day and in women exceeding five units (40 g) per day. There is also some evidence that some people are genetically predisposed to develop cirrhosis. Although ethanol itself is toxic, the main liver damage is thought to occur as a result of ethanal produced during ethanol metabolism. Ethanal binds to proteins, altering the liver structure and function. It inhibits protein secretion from hepatocytes, decreases the activity of many enzymes, encourages cell destruction and stimulates collagen production. The extra collagen produced is responsible for the fibrous scars typical of cirrhosis and has a profound effect on liver function. The collagen deposits in the liver sinusoids, depriving the hepatocytes of nutrients. The hepatocytes are therefore unable to produce essential proteins like albumin. The low serum albumin level causes fluid to leak into the tissues and accumulate causing swelling. There is a decreased production of clotting factors leading to a tendency to bleed easily. The liver is unable to carry out its usual functions of dealing with ammonia and other nitrogenous compounds and their accumulation progressively poisons the brain, causing confusion and eventually coma.

Many of the severe and irreversible effects of liver damage are preventable if alcohol consumption is reduced and vaccinations against hepatitis viruses are given.

**10. Hormone breakdown** – To varying degrees, the liver breaks down all hormones. Some, such as testosterone, are rapidly broken down whereas others, like insulin, are destroyed more slowly.

**11. Detoxification** – The liver is ideally situated to remove, or render harmless, toxic material absorbed by the intestines. Foreign organisms or material are ingested by the Kupffer cells while toxic chemicals are made safe by chemical conversions within hepatocytes. Alcohol and nicotine are two substances dealt with in this way.

**12. Production of heat** – The liver, with its considerable metabolic activity, can be used to produce heat in order to combat a fall in body temperature. This reaction, triggered by the hypothalamus, is in response to adrenaline, thyroxine and nervous stimulation. Whether the liver's activities produce excess heat under ordinary circumstances is a matter of some debate.

# 25.7    Questions

**1.**    *(a)* The graph shows changes in blood glucose concentration after a meal.

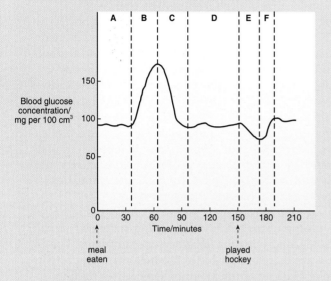

Explain the changes in blood glucose concentration in **each** of the stages **A** to **F** in the graph.    *(8 marks)*

*(b)* Explain why it is an advantage for humans to have a constant body temperature.

*(4 marks)*
*(Total 12 marks)*

*NEAB June 1998, Paper BY10, No. 8*

**2.** The diagram summarizes the mechanism of temperature regulation in a mammal.

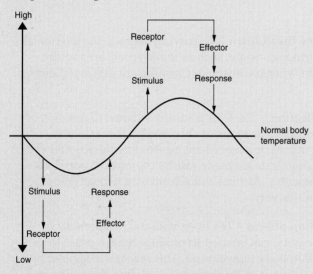

*(a)* Use the information in this diagram to explain what is meant by **negative feedback**.

*(1 mark)*

*(b)* Where are the receptors which detect a rise in the temperature of the blood?    *(1 mar)*
*(c)* Describe the part played by the blood vesse in the skin in returning a high body temperature to its normal value.    *(2 mark)*
*(d)* Give **one** advantage to the body of possessing separate mechanisms to return high and low body temperatures to their normal value.    *(1 mar)*
*(Total 5 mark)*

*AEB January 1996, Module Paper 1, No.*

**3.** The oryx is a mammal which lives in hot deserts. The diagram below shows the blood circulation in th head of an oryx and the temperature of the blood at certain points. The external temperature was 40.0 °C.

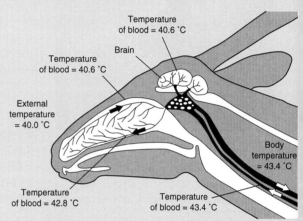

*(a)* Suggest why the body temperature of the oryx was higher than the external temperature.    *(1 mar)*
*(b)* Panting involves breathing in and out very rapidly with the mouth open.
Explain:
   (i)  how panting would help the oryx to lose heat;    *(1 mar)*
   (ii) why the blood reaching the brain has lower temperature than that of the body core.    *(1 mar)*
*(c)* Suggest an advantage to a desert mammal c panting rather than sweating.    *(2 mark)*
*(Total 5 mark)*

*AEB Summer 1997, Module Paper 4, No.*

**4.**    *(a)* What is meant by the term **homeostasis**?
*(1 mar)*

*(b)* With reference to suitable examples, distinguish between **endothermy** and **ectothermy**.    *(4 mark)*
*(Total 5 mark)*

*Edexcel January 1998, B2, No.*

The diagram below represents the structure of a transverse section of mammalian (pig) liver as seen using a microscope.

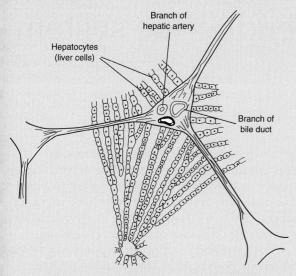

(a) Rule accurate guide lines and, using the initial letters indicated below, label the diagram to identify the following:
   (i) a branch of the hepatic vein (**HV**);
   (ii) a branch of the hepatic portal vein (**HPV**);
   (iii) a liver sinusoid (**S**);
   (iv) a site where the storage carbohydrate glycogen would be present (**G**);
   (v) a portion of connective tissue (Glisson's capsule) (**CT**).    (*5 marks*)

(b) The liver is an important organ of homeostasis. Excluding changes in concentration of oxygen and carbon dioxide, list **four different** ways in which blood composition could be changed as a result of homeostatic activity in the liver.
                                (*4 marks*)

(c) The rate of blood flow in the hepatic vein is approximately four times greater than the rate of blood flow in the hepatic artery. Briefly explain the reason why this is so.
                                (*2 marks*)
                            (*Total 11 marks*)

*Oxford November 1996, Paper 2, No. 6*

(a) Name a polymer that is formed from amino acids by condensation reactions.   (*1 mark*)
(b) The diagram shows part of the structural formula of an amino acid.

(i) Complete the structural formula of the amino acid.          (*1 mark*)
(ii) With reference to the diagram, explain what is meant by deamination.  (*1 mark*)
(iii) Describe what happens, in the liver, to the products of the deamination process.           (*3 marks*)
                            (*Total 6 marks*)

*NEAB February 1995, BY3, No. 6*

7. The following observations were made during studies on temperature control in animals. Use your knowledge of thermoregulation to provide an explanation for each of these observations.
(a) On a hot day a kangaroo rat produces a lot of saliva which it then licks over its body.
                            (*2 marks*)
(b) A mouse exposed to low environmental temperatures
   (i) lies curled up in a ball;      (*1 mark*)
   (ii) has pale ears and feet.      (*3 marks*)
                            (*Total 6 marks*)

*NEAB June 1997, Paper BY01, No. 3*

8. The diagrams show the difference between negative feedback and positive feedback.

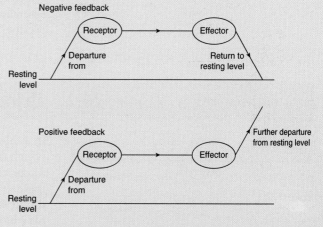

(a) Suggest why negative feedback is frequently involved in homeostasis.   (*1 mark*)
(b) Explain how negative feedback enables the carotid and aortic bodies and the medulla to maintain a constant blood carbon dioxide level.               (*3 marks*)
(c) Explain why the mechanism involved in the initiation of an action potential is an example of positive feedback.   (*2 marks*)
                            (*Total 6 marks*)

*NEAB February 1997, Paper BY10, No. 7*

# The endocrine system

Animals possess two principal coordinating systems, the **nervous system** and the **endocrine system**. The nervous system gives rapid control and details of its functioning are provided in Chapter 27. The endocrine system on the other hand regulates long-term changes. The two systems interact in a dynamic way in order to maintain the constancy of the animal's internal environment, while permitting changes in response to a varying external environment. Both systems secrete chemicals, the nervous system as a transmitter between neurones and the endocrine system as its sole means of communication between various organs and tissues in the body. It is worth noting that adrenaline may act both as a hormone and as a nervous transmitter.

This chapter discusses the principles of the endocrine system, the nature of hormones and the activities of specific endocrine glands. Because of their close association with particular organ systems, the activities of certain endocrine glands are dealt with elsewhere in this book. Reproductive hormones are described in Section 12.6 and digestive hormones in Section 15.6.

## 26.1 Principles of endocrine control

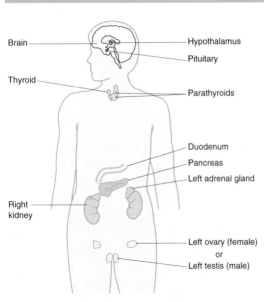

*Fig. 26.1 Location of major endocrine glands in humans*

In animals, two types of gland are recognized: **exocrine glands**, which convey their secretions to the site of action by special ducts, and **endocrine glands**, which lack ducts and transport their secretions instead by the blood. For this reason, the term **ductless glands** is often applied to endocrine glands. The glands may be discrete organs or cells within other organs.

The secretions of these glands are called **hormones**. Derived from the Greek word *hormon*, which means 'to excite', hormones often inhibit actions as well as excite them. All hormones are effective in small quantities. Most act on specific organs, called **target organs**, although some have diffuse effects on all body cells.

Most, but not all, endocrine glands work under the influence of a single master gland, the **pituitary**. In this way the actions of individual glands can be coordinated. Such coordination is essential as hormones work not in isolation, but interacting with each other. Most organs are influenced by a number of different hormones. If the pituitary is considered to be the master of the endocrine system then the **hypothalamus** can be thought of as the manager. It not only assists in directing the activities of endocrine glands, it also acts as the all-important link between the endocrine and nervous systems.

The positions of the major endocrine organs in humans are shown in Fig. 26.1.

## 26.2    The pituitary gland

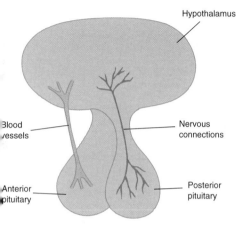

*Fig. 26.2 Structure of the pituitary gland and its relationship to the hypothalamus*

Situated at the base of the brain and immediately above the roof of your mouth is the pituitary. Despite its small size (about the dimensions of a pea) it controls, either directly or indirectly, many of your features – your size, sex, metabolism and the rate at which you age. The pituitary depends to a large extent upon information received from the nearby hypothalamus to determine which hormones to produce and when. The pituitary is sometimes referred to as the master gland because it orchestrates the production of hormones from other endocrine glands. In fact it works not in isolation, but in a complex interrelationship with the brain whose messages are filtered and refined by the hypothalamus. The pituitary gland itself has two distinct portions. The **anterior pituitary** is a region of glandular tissue which communicates with the hypothalamus by means of tiny blood vessels. The **posterior pituitary** is of nervous origin and is in effect an outgrowth of the hypothalamus. Communication with the hypothalamus is by nerves rather than blood vessels. The structure is shown in Fig. 26.2.

### 26.2.1 The anterior pituitary

This portion of the pituitary gland produces six hormones. Most have other endocrine glands as their target organs. These hormones, called **trophic hormones**, stimulate the activity of their respective endocrine glands. The only non-trophic hormone is growth hormone which, rather than influencing other endocrine glands, affects body tissues in general. The production of all these hormones is determined by small peptide molecules produced by the hypothalamus and passed to the pituitary via small connecting blood vessels. The functions of the hormones produced are given in Table 26.1.

### 26.2.2 The posterior pituitary

This portion of the pituitary gland stores two hormones: **anti-diuretic hormone (ADH)** or **vasopressin** and **oxytocin**. Both have remarkably similar chemical structures, differing in just one of their nine amino acids. Despite this they exert very different influences, as detailed in Table 26.1.

### 26.2.3 Release of pituitary hormones

The release of pituitary hormones is controlled by a combination of cells within the pituitary itself, neurosecretory cells in the hypothalamus and the endocrine secretions of the target organs of the pituitary hormones. Hormones are released rhythmically – each one having a different periodicity. Gonadotrophins have a monthly pattern of release while luteinizing hormone is produced in pulses about every 2 hours.

TABLE 26.1    Functions of hormones secreted by the pituitary

| Hormone | Abbreviation | Function |
|---|---|---|
| **Anterior pituitary**<br>Thyroid stimulating hormone<br>(thyrotrophic hormone, thyrotrophin) | TSH | 1. Stimulates the growth of the thyroid gland<br>2. Stimulates the thyroid gland to produce its hormones, e.g. thyroxin |
| Adrenocorticotrophic hormone | ACTH | 1. Regulates the growth of the adrenal cortex<br>2. Stimulates the adrenal cortex to produce its hormones, e.g. cortison |
| Follicle stimulating hormone | FSH | 1. Initiates cyclic changes in the ovaries, e.g. development of the Graafian follicles<br>2. Initiates sperm formation in the testes |
| Luteinizing hormone<br>(interstitial cell stimulating hormone) | LH (ICSH) | 1. Causes release of the ovum from the ovary and consequent development of the follicle into the corpus luteum<br>2. Stimulates secretion of testosterone from interstitial cells in the test |
| Prolactin<br>(luteotrophic hormone, luteotrophin) | LTH | 1. Maintains progesterone production from the corpus luteum<br>2. Induces milk production in pregnant females |
| Growth hormone | GH | 1. Promotes growth of skeleton and muscles<br>2. Controls protein synthesis and general body metabolism |
| **Posterior pituitary**<br>Antidiuretic hormone (vasopressin) | ADH | 1. Reduces the quantity of water lost from the kidney as urine<br>2. Raises the blood pressure by constricting arterioles |
| Oxytocin | | 1. Induces parturition (birth) by causing uterine contractions<br>2. Induces lactation (secretion of milk from the nipple) |

## 26.3    The hypothalamus

Lying at the base of the brain to which it is attached by numerous nerves, the hypothalamus in humans weighs a mere 4 g. Despite its small size it performs many vital functions.

**1.** It regulates activities such as thirst, sleep and temperature control.

**2.** It monitors the level of hormones and other chemicals in the blood passing through it.

**3.** It controls the functioning of the anterior pituitary gland.

**4.** It produces antidiuretic hormone and oxytocin which are stored in the posterior pituitary gland.

The hypothalamus is the link between the nervous and endocrine systems, as illustrated in Fig. 26.3. By monitoring the level of hormones in the blood, the hypothalamus is able to

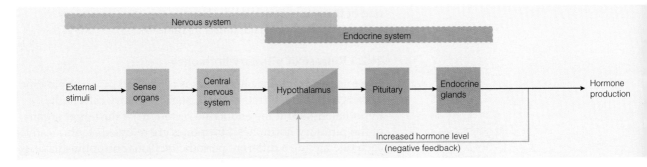

Fig. 26.3 Role of the hypothalamus as the link between the nervous and the endocrine systems

exercise homeostatic control of them. For example, the control of thyroxine production by the thyroid gland is achieved by this means:

**1.** The hypothalamus produces **thyrotrophin releasing factor (TRF)** which passes to the pituitary along blood vessels.

**2.** TRF stimulates the anterior pituitary gland to produce **thyroid stimulating hormone (TSH)**.

**3.** TSH stimulates the thyroid gland to produce thyroxine.

**4.** As the level of thyroxine builds up in the blood it suppresses TRF production from the hypothalamus and TSH production by the anterior pituitary gland. By this form of negative feedback the level of thyroxine in the blood is maintained at a constant level.

Fig. 26.4 summarizes these effects.

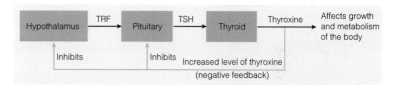

Fig. 26.4 Homeostatic control of thyroxine production

# 26.4 The thyroid gland

Found in the neck close to the larynx, the thyroid gland, which weighs around 25 g and whose structure is shown in Fig. 26.5, produces three hormones: **triiodothyronin (T$_3$)**, **thyroxine (T$_4$)** and **calcitonin**.

Triiodothyronin and thyroxine are very similar chemically and functionally. They regulate the growth and development of cells. In this respect they are especially important in young mammals. In addition, these hormones increase the rate at which glucose is oxidized by cells. One consequence of this is the production of

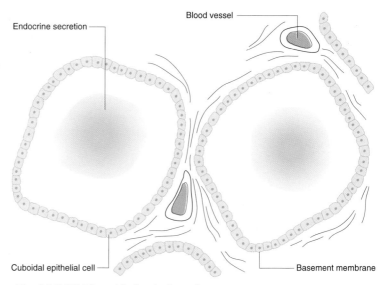

Fig. 26.5 TS Thyroid gland of monkey

## BIOLOGY AROUND US

# Abnormalities of the thyroid

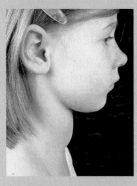

A goitre

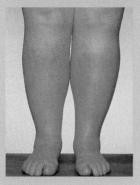

Symptoms of myxoedema

The two main thyroid abnormalities are underactivity (**hypothyroidism**) and overactivity (**hyperthyroidism**).

Underactivity (hypothyroidism) has a more marked effect on immature mammals as mental and physical retardation occur in addition to general sluggishness. The condition is known as **cretinism**. In adults, where mental, physical and sexual development is already complete, underactivity of the thyroid causes mental and physical sluggishness as well as a reduced metabolic rate. The latter leads to a reduced heart and ventilation rate, a lowered body temperature and obesity. The condition is known as **myxoedema**. As a result of underactivity, a swelling called a **goitre** may arise in the throat. The cause of underactivity is often the result of an insufficient supply of thyroid stimulating hormone (TSH). The symptoms of underactivity can be eliminated by taking thyroxine orally.

Overactivity (hyperthyroidism) leads to an increased metabolic rate. This results in an increased heart and ventilation rate and a raised body temperature. Nervousness, restlessness and irritability are other symptoms. A goitre may also be apparent. Extreme cases may result in such overactivity that heart failure occurs. This condition is called **thyrotoxicosis**. One main cause of overactivity is a blood protein which stimulates the thyroid to increase its production of triiodothyronin and thyroxine. Controlling overactivity is achieved by the surgical removal of part of the thyroid gland or the destruction of part of the gland by some means, e.g. administration of radioactive iodine.

heat and these hormones are therefore produced when an organism is exposed to severe cold. Emotional stress and hunger may elicit a similar production of these hormones. The overall effect is to control the metabolic rate of cells and in so doing the hormones work in close conjunction with insulin, adrenaline and cortisone.

Both triiodothyronin and thyroxine are derivatives of the amino acid tyrosine and both contain iodine. Thyroxine possesses four iodine molecules while triiodothyronin has only three. In times of iodine shortage the latter is produced in preference to the former in order to make maximum use of the limited iodine. If the iodine supply is severely reduced, the thyroid is unable to make adequate supplies of these hormones and underactivity of the thyroid results.

### Calcitonin

Calcitonin is concerned with calcium metabolism. Calcium, in addition to being a major constituent of bones and teeth, is essential for blood clotting and the normal functioning of muscles and nerves. In conjunction with parathormone from the parathyroid gland, calcitonin controls the level of calcium ions ($Ca^{2+}$) in the blood. A peptide of 32 amino acids, calcitonin is produced in response to high levels of $Ca^{2+}$ in the blood and it causes a reduction in the $Ca^{2+}$ concentration. (See Fig. 26.6).

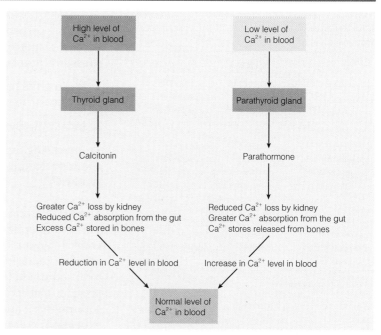

*Fig. 26.6 Summary of the control of calcium in the blood*

## 26.5 The adrenal glands

Situated above each kidney in humans is a collection of cells weighing about 5 g. These are the adrenal glands. They have two separate and independent parts:

**1. The adrenal cortex** consisting of the outer region of the glands.

**2. The adrenal medulla** consisting of the inner region of the glands.

### 26.5.1 The adrenal cortex

Making up around 80% of the adrenal gland, the cortex produces a number of hormones which have relatively slow, long-lasting effects on body metabolism, kidney function, salt balance and blood pressure. All the hormones produced are **steroids** formed from **cholesterol**. Being lipid-soluble they are able to pass across cell membranes. Hormones from the adrenal cortex are collectively called **corticoids** and fall into two groups:

**1. Glucocorticoids** which are concerned with glucose metabolism.

**2. Mineralocorticoids** which are concerned with mineral metabolism.

*Glucocorticoid hormones*
This group of hormones includes **cortisol** which is produced in response to stress. In stressful situations like shock, pain, emotional distress, extreme cold or infection, the hypothalamus induces the anterior pituitary gland to produce adrenocorticotrophic hormone (ACTH). This in turn causes the

TABLE 26.2 **Effects of the hormones adrenaline and noradrenaline on the body and the purpose of these responses**

| Effect | Purpose |
|---|---|
| Bronchioles dilated | Air is more easily inhaled into the lungs. More oxygen is therefore made available for the production of energy by glucose oxidation |
| Smooth muscle of the gut relaxed | The diaphragm can be lowered further, increasing the amount of air inhaled at each breath, making more oxygen available for the oxidation of glucose |
| Glycogen in the liver converted to glucose | Increases blood sugar level, making more glucose available for oxidation |
| Heart rate increased | |
| Volume of blood pumped at each beat increased | Increase the rate at which oxygen and glucose are distributed to the tissues |
| Blood pressure increased | |
| Blood diverted from digestive and reproductive systems to muscles, lungs and liver | Blood rich in glucose and oxygen is diverted from tissues which have less urgent need of it to those more immediately involved in producing energy |
| Peristalsis and digestion inhibited | Reduction of these processes allows blood to be diverted to muscle and other tissues directly involved in exertion |
| Sensory perception increased | Heightened sensitivity produces a more rapid reaction to external stimuli |
| Mental awareness increased | Allows more rapid response to stimuli received |
| Pupils of the eyes dilated | Increases range of vision and allows increased perception of visual stimuli |
| Hair erector muscles contract | Hair stands upright. In many mammals this gives the impression of increased size and may be sufficient to frighten away an enemy |

adrenal cortex to increase its production of glucocorticoids, including cortisol. Where stress is prolonged, the size of the adrenal glands increases. The glucocorticoid hormones combat stress in a number of ways:

1. Raising the blood sugar level, partly by inhibiting insulin and partly by the formation of glucose from fats and proteins.

2. Increasing the rate of glycogen formation in the liver.

3. Increasing the uptake of amino acids by the liver. These may either be deaminated to form more glucose or used in enzyme synthesis.

*Mineralocorticoid hormones*
This group of hormones includes **aldosterone** which regulates water retention by controlling the distribution of sodium and other minerals in the tissues. Aldosterone cannot increase the total sodium in the body, but it can conserve that already present. This it achieves by increasing the reabsorption of sodium ($Na^+$) and chloride ($Cl^-$) ions by the kidney, at the expense of potassium ions which are lost in urine. Control of aldosterone production is complex. In response to a low level of sodium ions in the blood, or a reduction in the total volume of blood, special cells in the kidney produce **renin** which in turn activates a plasma protein called **angiotensin**. It is angiotensin which stimulates production of aldosterone from the adrenal cortex. This causes the kidney to conserve both water and sodium ions. Angiotensin also affects centres in the brain, creating a sensation of thirst, in response to which the organism seeks and drinks water, thus helping to restore the blood volume to normal.

## 26.5.2 The adrenal medulla

The central portion of the adrenal gland is called the **adrenal medulla**. It produces two hormones, **adrenaline** (epinephrine) and **noradrenaline** (norepinephrine). Both are important in preparing the body for action. The cells producing them are modified neurones, and noradrenaline is produced by the neurones of the sympathetic nervous system. These hormones therefore link the nervous and endocrine systems. They are sometimes called the 'flight or fight hormones' as they prepare an organism to either flee from or face an enemy or stressful situation. The effects of both hormones are to prepare the body for exertion and to heighten its responses to stimuli. These effects and their purposes are summarized in Table 26.2.

At a cellular level, adrenaline acts as the first messenger and combines with receptors on the membrane of liver and muscle cells. The hormone–receptor complex on the outer face of the membrane activates the enzyme **adenylate cyclase** which is on the inner face of the membrane. The adenylate cyclase causes the conversion of ATP to cyclic AMP. The cyclic AMP acts as a **second messenger** (intracellular mediator) in that it moves within the cell to activate enzymes such as those involved in glycogen breakdown. The process is a complex series of enzyme reactions in a chain reaction known as a **cascade effect**. The cascade effect amplifies the response. Fig. 26.7 illustrates the mechanism of adrenaline action.

## BIOLOGY AROUND US

### Imbalance of adrenal hormones

Where the production of glucocorticoids is deficient, a condition known as **Addison's disease** occurs. Symptoms include a low blood sugar level, reduced blood pressure and fatigue. The condition of the body deteriorates when stresses such as extreme temperatures and infection are experienced. Over-production of glucocorticoids causes **Cushing's syndrome** where there is a high blood sugar level mainly due to excessive breakdown of protein. This breakdown causes wasting of tissues, especially muscle. There is high blood pressure and symptoms of diabetes.

Over-production of aldosterone, often as a result of a tumour, leads to excessive sodium retention by tissues; high blood pressure and headaches then arise. The retention of sodium leads to a consequent fall in potassium levels leading to muscular weakness. Under-production of aldosterone leads to a fall in the level of sodium in the tissues. In extreme cases this is fatal.

*Use of second messenger, e.g. protein and polypeptide hormones such as adrenaline*

- *Hormone approaches receptor site.*

- *Hormone fuses to receptor site, and in doing so activates adenylate cyclase inside the membrane.*

- *The activated adenylate cyclase converts ATP to cyclic AMP which acts as a second messenger that activates other enzymes.*

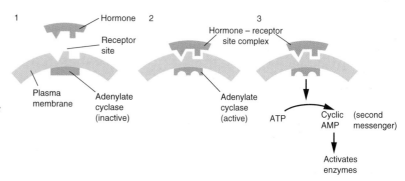

*Fig. 26.7 Mechanism of hormone action*

In one respect adrenaline and noradrenaline differ. Whereas adrenaline dilates blood vessels, noradrenaline constricts them. This difference explains the constriction of blood vessels around the gut while those supplying muscles, lungs and liver are dilated. It appears that receptors on some blood vessels are sensitive to noradrenaline and so constrict while others are sensitive to adrenaline and so dilate.

## 26.6   The pancreas

The structure of the pancreas and its role as an exocrine gland are considered in Section 15.4.4. At intervals within the exocrine cells are the **Islets of Langerhans,** which are part of the endocrine system. Cells known as $\alpha$-cells produce the hormone **glucagon** whereas $\beta$-cells secrete the hormone **insulin**. The two operate antagonistically, with glucagon stimulating the

## BIOLOGY AROUND US

# Diabetes

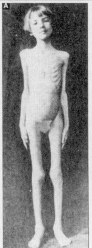
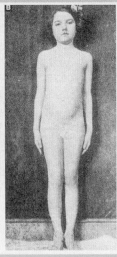

Improvement of health of diabetic child in response to insulin treatment

There are two medical conditions known as 'diabetes'. **Diabetes insipidus** is rare and results from a deficiency of ADH, the hormone which controls urine production. **Diabetes mellitus**, or 'sugar diabetes', is much more common and occurs in two forms: insulin-dependent, or type 1 diabetes, which usually develops before the age of 20, and non-insulin-dependent, or type 2 diabetes, which often comes on in later life and may be associated with obesity. Insulin-dependent diabetes usually results from a massive loss of insulin-secreting $\beta$-cells from the pancreas. The lack of insulin means that the uptake of glucose from the blood after a meal is not promoted. Glucagon continues to convert glycogen to glucose, and proteins and lipids are broken down to release even more glucose. This leads untreated sufferers to have a thin, wasted appearance.

Excess blood glucose is excreted via the kidneys and is associated with a considerable loss of water resulting in thirst. The fatty acids from lipid breakdown form ketone bodies which may build up in the blood, lowering its pH and leading to coma. Diabetes was a fatal disease until in 1921 Banting and Best succeeded in isolating insulin from the pancreas of pigs and cows. Insulin is a small protein comprising a total of 51 amino acids in two chains. The sequence of amino acids in insulin was determined by Sanger in the 1950s and more recently the gene for human insulin has been isolated and inserted into the DNA of *E. coli* so that the bacteria can make 'human' insulin on a large scale. This has the advantage of producing fewer side effects than the insulin extracted from pigs or cattle pancreases, and is acceptable to vegetarians.

Diabetics must regulate their carbohydrate intake, test their blood glucose level and have regular injections of insulin if they are to lead a normal life and avoid some of the longer-term complications of the disease. Such complications include atherosclerosis and degeneration of the kidney, nerves and retina. Insulin cannot be taken orally because, as a protein, it would be broken down by digestive enzymes.

About 90% of diabetics are non-insulin-dependent diabetics. There seems to be some evidence for a genetic predisposition to this form of diabetes and it may be associated with obesity. Other mature-onset diabetics who secrete low amounts of insulin may be helped by drugs such as sulphonylureas which can be used to stimulate insulin production.

## Did you know?

In 1995 there were 123 million people in the world with diabetes. By 2010 it is estimated that this will rise to 220 million.

breakdown of glycogen to glucose while insulin initiates the conversion of glucose to glycogen. The mechanism by which these two control the level of sugar in blood is described in Section 25.3.

A summary of the major endocrine glands and the functions of the hormones they produce is given in Fig. 26.8.

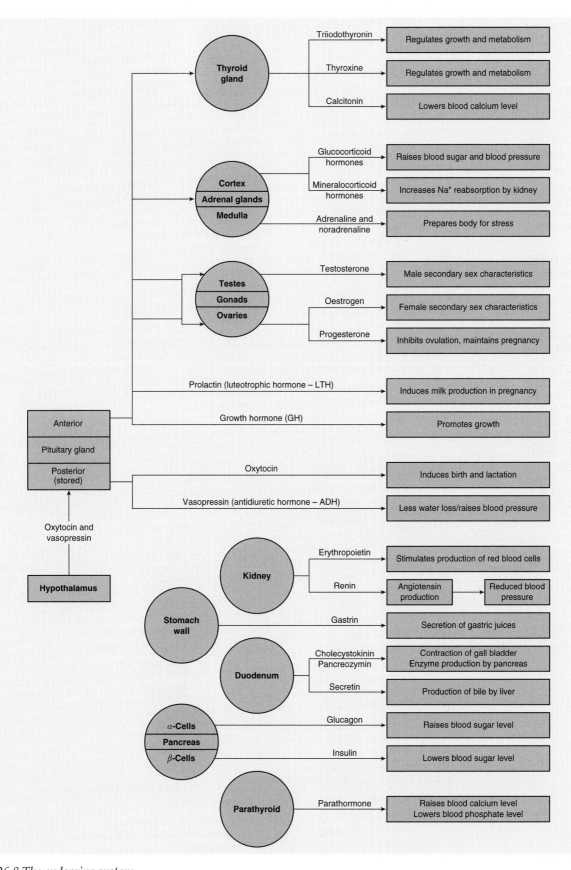

*Fig. 26.8 The endocrine system*

# 26.7    Questions

1. Discuss the principles and functions of chemical coordination in living organisms.    (*Total 30 marks*)

*ULEAC January 1994, Paper 3, No. 9(b)*

2. Read the extract about the drug *Ecstasy* and then answer the questions which follow.

A few deaths have been due to drinking too much water. This occurred either because people thought that water was an antidote to Ecstasy (it is only an antidote to dehydration) or because the drug induced repetitive behaviour. Under the influence of *Ecstasy* people have been known to drink 20 litres of fluid and smoke 100 cigarettes within three hours. Drinking pure water to replace the fluid lost in sweating is dangerous because it does not put back the sodium ions and so dilutes the blood. This makes the cells of the body swell up, which is particularly lethal in the brain which can expand and be crushed against the skull. The centres in the brain that regulate breathing and the heart can be irreversibly damaged, and the person dies. *Ecstasy* increases the risk of brain damage by triggering the release of antidiuretic hormone (ADH).

(Reproduced by permission of *The Guardian*)

(*a*)  (i)  Explain in terms of water potential why the drinking of large amounts of pure water after copious sweating may lead to swelling of cells in the brain.
(*4 marks*)

(ii)  Explain how '*Ecstasy* increases the risk of brain damage by triggering the release of antidiuretic hormone (ADH)'.
(*4 marks*)

(*b*) Describe the role of aldosterone in the control of the mineral salt content of blood.
(*4 marks*)
(*Total 12 marks*)

*NEAB June 1998, Paper BY03, No.8*

3.    (*a*) Various activities in the body are controlled by hormones. Complete the following table by writing the name of a hormone involved in the activity described and the name of the gland which produces it.    (*20 marks*)
(*b*) State **two** advantages in the body of controlling physiological processes by the action of hormones compared with nervous control.    (*2 marks*)

| Function | Hormone | Gland |
|---|---|---|
| 1. decreases blood sugar levels | | |
| 2. controls the basal metabolic rate | | |
| 3. controls secretion of gastric juice | | |
| 4. increases rate of heart beat | | |
| 5. controls retention of sodium ions in kidney | | |
| 6. alters permeability of distal convoluted tubule | | |
| 7. controls growth of the ovarian follicle | | |
| 8. controls uterine growth and development | | |
| 9. involved in ovulation and maintenance of the corpus luteum | | |
| 10. controls male secondary characteristics | | |

(*c*) A small patch of tissue in a mammal is known to be secretory in function. Outline an investigation to discover whether the secretion acts as a hormone.    (*3 mark*
(*Total 25 mark*

*O&CSEB June 1991, Paper I, No.*

4. The diagram summarizes the way in which adrenaline can control a chemical reaction in a liver cell.

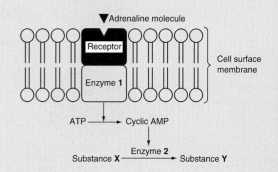

(*a*) Describe the function of cyclic AMP in this process.    (*1 mar*
(*b*) Give **one** example of a chemical reaction in a liver cell which is controlled by adrenaline by naming:

(i) substance **X**; *(1 mark)*

(ii) substance **Y**. *(1 mark)*

*(c)* Use the diagram to explain:

(i) why adrenaline may affect some cells and not others; *(1 mark)*

(ii) how a single molecule of adrenaline may cause this cell to produce a large amount of substance **Y**. *(2 marks)*

*(Total 6 marks)*

*AEB Summer 1997, Paper 1, No. 9*

*(a)* The table shows some of the hormones produced by the pituitary gland, the organ or gland which they affect, and the effect they produce on this organ or gland. Copy and complete the table.

| Pituitary hormone | Target organ/gland | Effect on organ/gland |
|---|---|---|
|  | Adrenal cortex | Secretes cortisol |
|  |  | Increased secretion of thyroxine |
| Luteinizing hormone (LH) | Ovary |  |

*(4 marks)*

*(b)* Somatotropic hormone is also a pituitary hormone. It plays an important part in normal growth. Suggest:

(i) how somatotropic hormone may increase growth; *(1 mark)*

(ii) how it acts to oppose the action of insulin. *(1 mark)*

*(Total 6 marks)*

*AEB Summer 1995, (H. Biology) Paper 1, No. 13*

*(a)* Describe briefly what is meant by the term **endocrine system**. *(2 marks)*

*(b)* Explain why the pancreas is described as both an exocrine **and** an endocrine gland. *(3 marks)*

*(c)* In each case, state **two** likely effects on a mammal of:

(i) **over-production** of thyroxine; *(2 marks)*

(ii) **under-production** of insulin. *(2 marks)*

*(Total 9 marks)*

*Oxford June 1997, Paper 45, No. 8*

Diabetes mellitus is a complex disease which occurs in two main forms, insulin-dependent (type I) and non-insulin-dependent (type II). Type I diabetes is sometimes called juvenile onset diabetes and people affected require frequent injections of insulin. The cells which produce the insulin appear to have been destroyed by the body's immune system. Type II diabetes can occur at any age but characteristically in adulthood. It can often be found in people who are obese from over-eating. Type II diabetes appears to be the result of a failure to respond to insulin, which may be the result of reduced numbers of insulin receptors. In many cases this form of the disease may be controlled by dietary means. For both types of diabetes, exercise is also often beneficial.

*(a)* Which cells are destroyed in **type I diabetes**? *(1 mark)*

*(b)* Outline the role of insulin in the control of blood glucose levels. *(3 marks)*

*(c)* Why does insulin have to be taken by injection rather than by swallowing a tablet? *(1 mark)*

*(d)* Suggest what sort of molecules **insulin receptors** are and state where they would be found. *(2 marks)*

*(e)* (i) Suggest why dietary management might be used for patients with **type II diabetes**. *(2 marks)*

(ii) Suggest why exercise may be beneficial for both types of diabetes. *(1 mark)*

*(Total 10 marks)*

*Oxford & Cambridge January 1997, Unit B4, No. 4*

8. The table shows how the concentrations of insulin and glucose in the plasma vary at different times.

| When measurement taken | Plasma insulin concentration/ units per cm³ | Plasma glucose concentration/ mg per 100 cm³ |
|---|---|---|
| During overnight fast | 10 | 60–100 |
| During a meal | 70 | 110–180 |
| After a meal | 10 | 60–100 |
| During prolonged fasting | 5 | 50–70 |

*(a)* Describe the relationship between glucose concentration and insulin concentration in the plasma. *(1 mark)*

*(b)* Explain the rise in plasma glucose and insulin levels that occurs during the meal. *(3 marks)*

*(c)* Use information from the table to explain how the control of insulin production is an example of negative feedback. *(2 marks)*

*(d)* The plasma glucose level is maintained at a minimum of $50\,mg$ per $100\,cm^3$ during prolonged fasting. Suggest how this might be achieved. *(2 marks)*

*(Total 8 marks)*

*NEAB February 1995, Paper BY3, No. 4*

# 27      The nervous system

The ability to respond to stimuli is a fundamental characteristic of living organisms. While all cells of multicellular organisms are able to perceive stimuli, the cells of the nervous system are specifically adapted to this purpose.

The nervous system has three functions:

**1.** To collect information about the internal and external environment.

**2.** To process and integrate the information, often in relation to previous experience.

**3.** To act upon the information, usually by coordinating the organism's activities.

One remarkable feature of the way in which these functions are performed is the speed with which the information is transmitted from one part of the body to another. In contrast to the endocrine system (Chapter 26), the nervous system responds virtually instantaneously to a stimulus. The cells which transmit nerve impulses are called **neurones**.

The nervous system may be sub-divided into a number of parts. The collecting of information from the internal and external environment is carried out by **receptors**. Along with the neurones which transmit this information, the receptors form the **sensory system**. The processing and integration of this information is performed by the **central nervous system (CNS)**. The final function whereby information is transmitted to **effectors**, which act upon it, is carried out by the **effector (motor) system**, which has two parts. The portion which activates involuntary responses is known as the **autonomic nervous system** whereas that activating voluntary responses is termed the **somatic system** (Fig. 27.1). The sensory and effector (motor) neurones are sometimes collectively called the **peripheral nervous system (PNS)**.

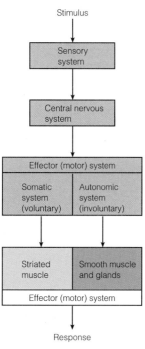

*Fig. 27.1 Interrelationships of the various components of the nervous system*

## 27.1    Nervous tissue and the nerve impulse

Nervous tissue comprises closely packed nerve cells or **neurones** with little intercellular space. The neurones are bound together by connective tissue.

All neurones have a cell body containing a nucleus. This cell body has a number of processes called **dendrites** which transmit impulses to the cell body. Impulses leave via the **axon** which

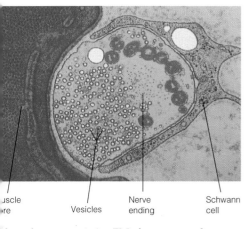

uscle
re

Vesicles    Nerve    Schwann
              ending    cell

ulse-colour transmission EM of neuromuscular
nction (×18 500 approx.)

may be several metres in length. Some axons are covered by a fatty **myelin sheath** formed by **Schwann cells**. (See Fig. 27.2).

Nerve fibres may be bundled together and wrapped in connective tissue to form **nerves**. Nerves may be **sensory**, comprising sensory neurones, **effector (motor)**, comprising effector (motor) neurones, or **mixed**, with both types present.

### 27.1.1 Resting potential

In its normal state, the membrane of a neurone is negatively charged internally with respect to the outside. The potential difference varies somewhat depending on the neurone but lies in the range 50–90 mV, most usually around 70 mV. This is known as the **resting potential** and in this condition the membrane is said to be **polarized**. The resting potential is the result of the distribution of four ions: potassium ($K^+$), sodium ($Na^+$), chloride ($Cl^-$) and organic anions ($COO^-$). Initially the concentration of

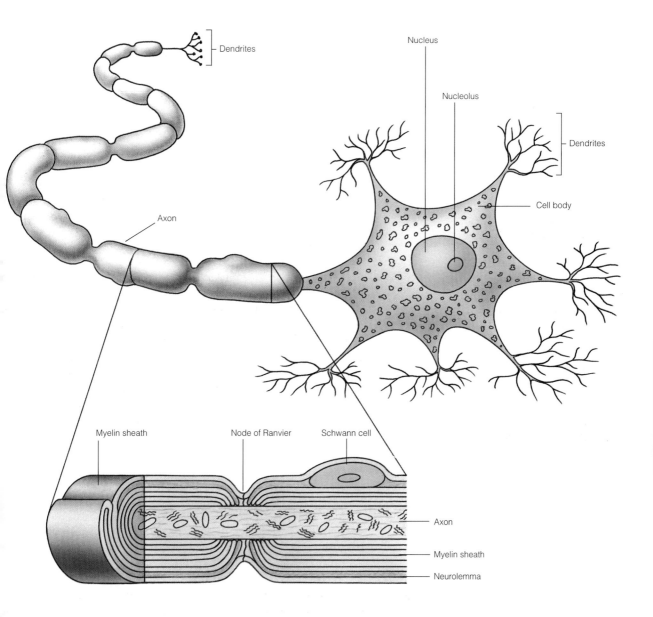

ig. 27.2 Effector (motor) neurone

# BIOLOGY AROUND US

## Multiple sclerosis and the myelin sheath

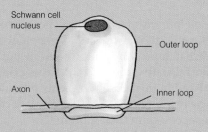

The myelin sheath is produced by the Schwann cell and is rolled around the nerve axon for insulation.

*Fig. 1 Schwann cell and axon*

On neurones a specialized cell, the **Schwann cell**, wraps itself around the nerve axon to form the numerous concentric layers which comprise the myelin sheath (Fig. 1). This sheath consists of 70% lipid and 30% proteins in the usual bilipid structure; it provides insulation and allows the rapid conduction of electrical signals.

In multiple sclerosis (MS) gradual degradation of the myelin sheath takes place leaving areas of bare, demyelinated axons which cannot conduct impulses (Fig. 2). These regions, known as **plaques**, are approximately 2–10 mm in size and most commonly affect the optic nerve, cerebellum, cervical spinal cord and the area around the ventricles of the brain. Peripheral nerves are unaffected. The most well known symptoms of MS are a weakness of the limbs, 'pins and needles' and numbness, but damage to the optic nerve also results in blurring of the vision and pains in the eyes.

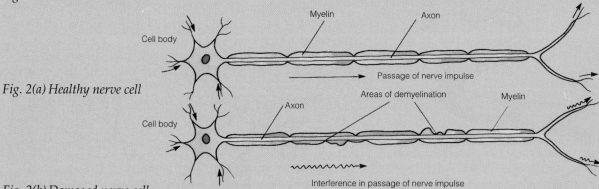

*Fig. 2(a) Healthy nerve cell*

*Fig. 2(b) Damaged nerve cell in multiple sclerosis*

MS has two main patterns of disease development. In some people the condition is progressive and unrelenting, leading to severe crippling, but in most there are periods of relapse followed by spells of remission which may last several years. Although in the later stages there is often progressive disability, only about 1 in 10 MS sufferers end up in a wheelchair.

Multiple sclerosis is one of the commonest diseases of the central nervous system in Europe and yet its cause is still unknown. It affects more women than men, in a ratio of 3 : 2 , and there is a high prevalence in countries with a temperate climate; it is uncommon in tropical countries. It has been suggested that possibly diet, lifestyle and physical environment have some influence but no theory has yet been proved. There are approximately 80 000 people with MS in the United Kingdom and 250 000 in the USA. The range of onset of the disease varies from 12 years old to 50 years old but the average age of diagnosis is late 20s to mid 30s.

As yet multiple sclerosis cannot be cured and treatment is very limited. Steroids and ACTH (adrenocorticotrophic hormone) are prescribed during relapse to reduce inflammation and promote a remission but otherwise treatment is supportive in the form of pain relievers, muscle relaxants, occupational therapy and physiotherapy, as well as counselling for the individuals and their families.

(a) Unipolar neurone,
   e.g arthropod motor neurone

(b) Bipolar neurone,
   e.g from mammalian retina

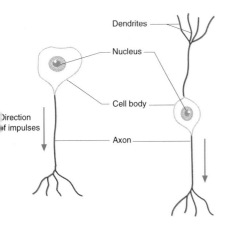

Dendrites

Nucleus

Cell body

Direction of impulses

Axon

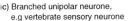

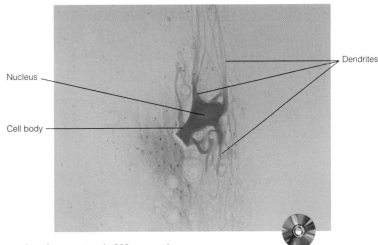

Nucleus

Cell body

Dendrites

Multipolar neurone (×200 approx.)

(c) Branched unipolar neurone,
   e.g vertebrate sensory neurone

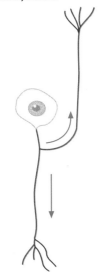

(d) Multipolar neurone,
   e.g from the mammalian spinal cord

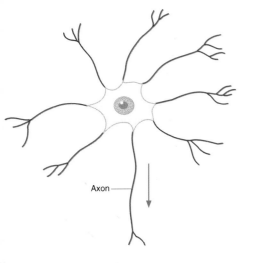

Axon

Fig. 27.3 Types of neurone

potassium ($K^+$) and organic anions ($COO^-$) is higher inside the neurone, while the concentration of sodium ($Na^+$) and chloride ($Cl^-$) is higher outside. The membrane, however, is considerably more permeable to potassium ions ($K^+$) than any of the others. As the potassium ion ($K^+$) concentration inside the neurone is 20 times greater than that outside, potassium ions ($K^+$) rapidly diffuse out. This outward movement of positive ions means that the inside becomes slightly negative relative to the outside. As more potassium ions move out, the less able they are to do so. In time an equilibrium is reached whereby the rate at which they leave is exactly balanced by the rate of entry. It is therefore the electrochemical gradient of potassium ions which largely creates the resting potential.

The differences in concentration of ions across the membrane are maintained by the active transport of the ions against the concentration gradients. The mechanisms by which these ions are transported are called pumps. As sodium ions ($Na^+$) are moved in this way they are often referred to as **sodium pumps**. However, as potassium ions are also actively transported they are more accurately **cation pumps**. These cation pumps exchange sodium and potassium ions by actively transporting in potassium ions and removing sodium ions. Being active, this transport requires ATP.

### 27.1.2 Action potential

By appropriate stimulation, the charge on a neurone can be reversed. As a result, the negative charge inside the membrane of $-70\,mV$ changes to a positive charge of around $+40\,mV$. This is known as the **action potential** and in this condition the membrane is said to be **depolarized**. Within about 2 ms (two thousandths of a second) the same portion of the membrane returns to resting potential ($-70\,mV$ inside). This is known as **repolarization**. These changes are illustrated graphically in Fig. 27.4.

Provided the stimulus exceeds a certain value, called the **threshold value**, an action potential results. Above the threshold value the size of the action potential remains constant, regardless of the size of the stimulus. In other words, the action potential is

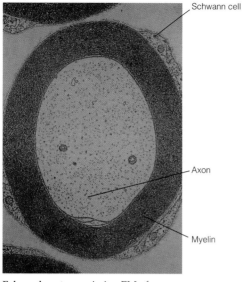

False-colour transmission EM of
myelinated nerve fibre

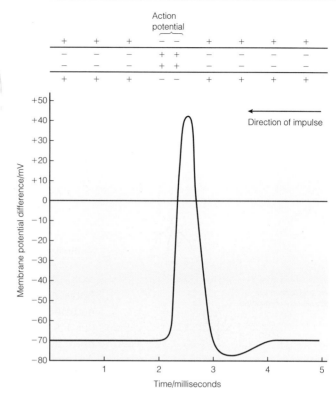

*Fig. 27.4 The action potential*

either generated, in which case it is always the same, or it is not. This is called an **all or nothing** response. The size of the action potential does not decrease as it is transmitted along the neurone but always remains the same.

### 27.1.3 Ion movement

The action potential is the result of a sudden increase in the permeability of the membrane to sodium. This allows a sudden influx of sodium ions because there is a high concentration outside the neurone which has been maintained by the sodium pump. The influx of sodium ions begins to depolarize the membrane and this depolarization in turn increases the membrane's permeability to sodium, leading to greater influx and further depolarization. This runaway influx of sodium ions is an example of **positive feedback**. When sufficient sodium ions have entered to create a positive charge inside the membrane, the permeability of the membrane to sodium starts to decrease.

At the same time as the sodium ions begin to move inward, so potassium ions start to move in the opposite direction along a diffusion gradient. This outward movement of potassium is, however, much less rapid than the inward movement of sodium. It nevertheless continues until the membrane is repolarized. The changes are summarized in Fig. 27.5.

So why is the movement of ions so rapid? We saw in Section 4.2.2 that some protein molecules span membranes and these have a fine pore or channel through the middle of them. In a neurone membrane some of these channels allow sodium ions ($Na^+$) to pass through while others permit the movement of potassium ($K^+$). In the resting state these channels are closed, but they open when the membrane is depolarized by a stimulus such

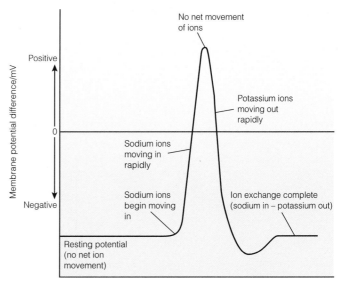

*Fig. 27.5 Ion movements during an action potential*

as pressure on the **Pacinian corpuscles** deep in the skin. They act rather like an entry with a closed gate which can be unlatched. For this reason they are sometimes called **voltage-gated channels**. The gates to the sodium channel open more quickly than those to the potassium channel. This explains why sodium ions entering the neurone cause depolarization followed by the potassium ions leaving which cause repolarization.

### 27.1.4 Refractory period

Following an action potential, the outward movement of potassium ions quickly restores the resting potential. However, for about 1 ms after an action potential the inward movement of sodium is prevented in that region of the neurone. This means that a further action potential cannot be generated for at least 1 ms. This is called the **refractory period**.

The refractory period is important for two reasons:

**1.** It means the action potential can only be propagated in the region which is not refractory, i.e. in a forward direction. The action potential is thus prevented from spreading out in both directions until it occupies the whole neurone.

**2.** By the end of the refractory period the action potential has passed further down the nerve. A second action potential will thus be separated from the first one by the refractory period, which therefore sets an upper limit to the frequency of impulses along a neurone.

The refractory period can be divided into two portions:

**1.** The **absolute refractory period** lasts around 1 ms and during this period no new impulses can be propagated, however intense the stimulus.

**2.** The **relative refractory period** lasts around 5 ms and during this period new impulses can be propagated only if the stimulus is more intense than the normal threshold level.

Fig. 27.6 illustrates the refractory period in graph form, while Fig. 27.7 demonstrates how the refractory period determines the frequency of impulses along a neurone.

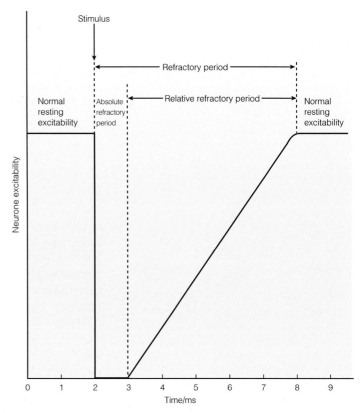

*Fig. 27.6 Graph illustrating neurone excitability before and after a nerve impulse*

*Where the stimulus is at the threshold value the excitability of the neurone must return to normal before a new action potential can be formed. In the time interval shown, this allows just two action potentials to pass, i.e. a low frequency of impulses. Where the stimulus exceeds the threshold value, a new action potential can be created before neurone excitability returns to normal. In the time interval shown, this allows six action potentials to pass, i.e. a high frequency of impulses.*

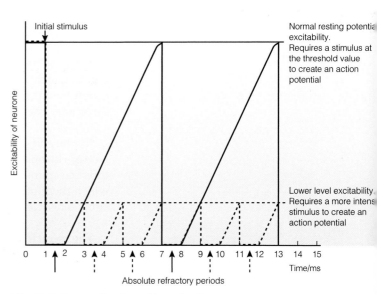

*Fig. 27.7 Determination of impulse frequency*

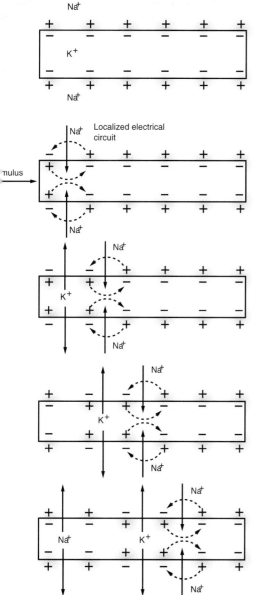

1. *At resting potential there is a high concentration of sodium ions outside and a high concentration of potassium ions inside the neurone.*
2. *When the neurone is stimulated sodium ions rush into the axon along a concentration gradient. This causes depolarization of the membrane.*
3. *Localized electrical circuits are established which cause further influx of sodium ions and so progression of the impulse. Behind the impulse, potassium ions begin to leave the axon along a concentration gradient.*
4. *As the impulse progresses, the outflux of potassium ions causes the neurone to become repolarized behind the impulse.*
5. *After the impulse has passed and the neurone is repolarized, sodium is once again actively expelled in order to increase the external concentration and so allow the passage of another impulse.*

### 27.1.5 Transmission of the nerve impulse

Once an action potential has been set up, it moves rapidly from one end of the neurone to the other. This is the nerve impulse and is described in Fig. 27.8.

According to the precise nature of a neurone, transmission speeds vary from 0.5 metres ms$^{-1}$ to over 100 metres ms$^{-1}$. Two factors are important in determining the speed of conduction:

**(a) The diameter of the axon**: the greater the diameter the faster the speed of transmission.

**(b) The myelin sheath**: myelinated neurones conduct impulses faster than non-myelinated ones.

The myelin sheath, which is produced by the **Schwann cells**, is not continuous along the axon, but is absent at points called **nodes of Ranvier** which arise every millimetre or so along the neurone's length. As the fatty myelin acts as an electrical insulator, an action potential cannot form in the part of the axon covered with myelin. It can, however, form at the nodes. The action potentials therefore jump from node to node (**saltatory conduction**), increasing the speed with which they are transmitted (Fig. 27.9).

*Fig. 27.8 Transmission of an impulse along an unmyelinated neurone*

*The insulating myelin causes ion exchange to occur at the nodes of Ranvier. The impulse therefore jumps from node to node.*

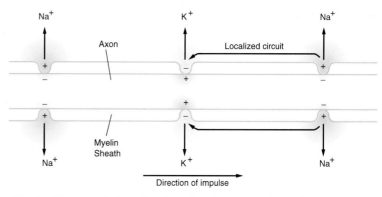

*Fig. 27.9 Transmission of an impulse along a myelinated neurone*

533

# 27.2    The synapse

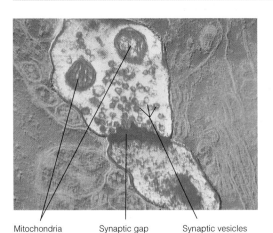

Mitochondria        Synaptic gap        Synaptic vesicles

False-colour transmission EM of synapse
(×34 000 approx.)

The word synapse (*syn* = 'with'; *apsis* = 'knot') means 'to clasp'. It is the point where the axon of one neurone clasps or joins the dendrite or cell body of another. The gap between the two is around 20 nm in width. The synapse must in some way pass information across itself from one neurone to the next. This is achieved in the vast majority of synapses by **chemical** transmission, although at some synapses the transmission is **electrical**. Chemicals which transmit messages across the synapse are called **neurotransmitter substances**. The two main ones in the peripheral nervous system are **acetylcholine** and **noradrenaline,** although others include dopamine and serotonin. Neurones using acetylcholine as a neurotransmitter are termed **cholinergic neurones** whereas those using noradrenaline are called **adrenergic neurones**. Amino acids, e.g. L-glutamate, are thought to be the most widely used neurotransmitters in the brain. In all over 40 substances with a wide variety of chemical structures act as neurotransmitters.

## Did you know?

An average motor neurone may have as many as 15 000 synapses.

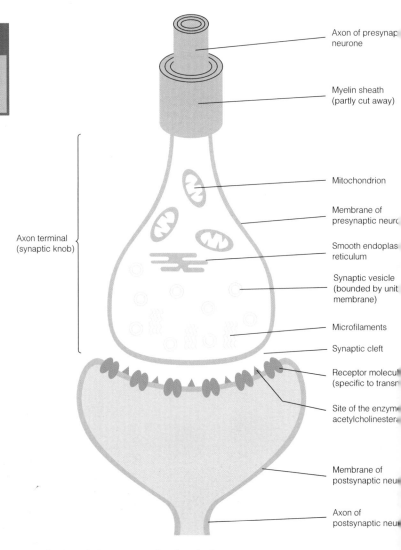

Axon of presynap
neurone

Myelin sheath
(partly cut away)

Axon terminal
(synaptic knob)

Mitochondrion

Membrane of
presynaptic neuro

Smooth endoplas
reticulum

Synaptic vesicle
(bounded by unit
membrane)

Microfilaments

Synaptic cleft

Receptor molecu
(specific to transm

Site of the enzyme
acetylcholinestera

Membrane of
postsynaptic neur

Axon of
postsynaptic neur

*Fig. 27.10 Structure of a chemical synapse*

### 27.2.1 Structure of the synapse

As it is the most frequently occurring type, we shall deal here with the structure of the chemical synapse.

At the synapse the nerve axon is expanded to form a bulbous ending called the **axon terminal (bouton terminale)** or **synaptic knob**. This contains many mitochondria, microfilaments and structures called **synaptic vesicles**. The vesicles contain a neurotransmitter substance such as acetylcholine or noradrenaline. The neurone immediately before the synapse is known as the **presynaptic neurone** and is bounded by the presynaptic membrane. The neurone after the synapse is the **postsynaptic neurone** and is bounded by the postsynaptic membrane. Between the two is a narrow gap, 20 nm wide, called the **synaptic cleft**. The postsynaptic membrane possesses a number of large protein molecules known as **receptor molecules**. The structure of the synapse is illustrated in Fig. 27.10.

### 27.2.2 Synaptic transmission

When a nerve impulse arrives at the synaptic knob it alters the permeability of the presynaptic membrane to calcium, which therefore enters. This causes the synaptic vesicles to fuse with the membrane and discharge their neurotransmitter substance which, for the purposes of this account, will be taken to be acetylcholine. The empty vesicles move back into the cytoplasm where they are later refilled with acetylcholine.

The acetylcholine diffuses across the synaptic cleft, a process which takes 0.5 ms. Upon reaching the postsynaptic membrane it fuses with the receptor molecules. In **excitatory synapses** this opens ion channels on the postsynaptic membrane allowing sodium ions to enter and thus creating a new potential known as the **excitatory postsynaptic potential** in the postsynaptic neurone. These events are detailed in Fig. 27.11.

Once acetylcholine has depolarized the postsynaptic neurone, it is hydrolysed by the enzyme **acetylcholinesterase** which is found on the postsynaptic membrane. This breakdown of acetylcholine is essential to prevent successive impulses merging at the synapse. The resulting choline and ethanoic acid (acetyl) diffuse across the synaptic cleft and are actively transported into the synaptic knob of the presynaptic neurone into which they diffuse. Here they are coupled together again and stored inside synaptic vesicles ready for further use. This recoupling requires energy which is provided by the numerous mitochondria found in the synaptic knob.

The excitatory postsynaptic potentials build up as more neurotransmitter substance arrives until sufficient depolarization occurs to exceed the threshold value and so generate an action potential in the postsynaptic neurone. This additive effect is known as **temporal summation**.

All events so far described relate to an **excitatory synapse**, but not all synapses operate in this way. Some, known as **inhibitory synapses**, respond to the neurotransmitter by opening potassium ion channels and leaving the sodium ion channels closed. Potassium therefore moves out, causing the postsynaptic membrane to become more polarized. It is thus more difficult for the threshold value to be exceeded and therefore less likely that a new action potential will be created.

## Did you know?

The fugu fish is considered a culinary delicacy in Japan. However, it contains a highly toxic chemical which kills by blocking the sodium ion channels in nerve membranes. As a result only a few chefs are licenced to prepare this dish – even so some deaths have resulted from eating this fish.

**1** The arrival of impulses at the synaptic knob alters its permeability, allowing calcium ions to enter.

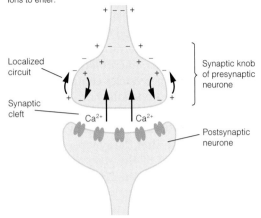

Localized circuit

Synaptic cleft

$Ca^{2+}$   $Ca^{2+}$

Synaptic knob of presynaptic neurone

Postsynaptic neurone

**2** The influx of calcium ions causes the synaptic vesicles to fuse with the presynaptic membrane, so releasing acetylcholine into the synaptic cleft.

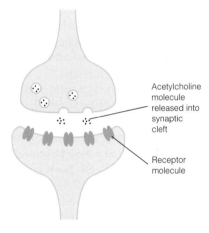

Acetylcholine molecule released into synaptic cleft

Receptor molecule

**3** Acetylcholine fuses with receptor molecules on the postsynaptic membrane. This causes ion channels to open allowing sodium ions to rush in.

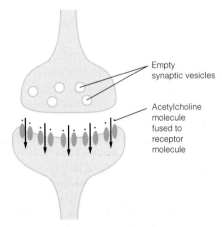

Empty synaptic vesicles

Acetylcholine molecule fused to receptor molecule

**4** The influx of sodium ions generates a new impulse in the postsynaptic neurone.

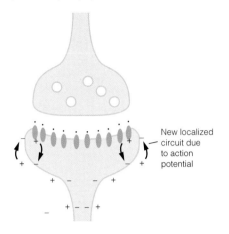

New localized circuit due to action potential

**5** Acetylcholinesterase on the postsynaptic membrane hydrolyses acetylcholine into choline and ethanoic acid (acetyl). These two components then diffuse back across the synaptic cleft into the presynaptic neurone.

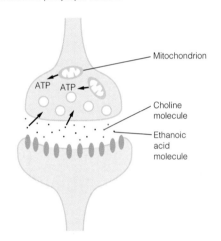

Mitochondrion

ATP   ATP

Choline molecule

Ethanoic acid molecule

**6** ATP released by the mitochondria is used to recombine choline and ethanoic acid (acetyl) molecules to form acetylcholine. This is stored in synaptic vesicles for future use.

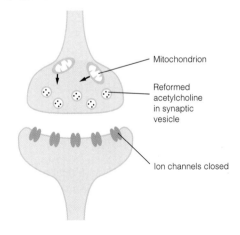

Mitochondrion

Reformed acetylcholine in synaptic vesicle

Ion channels closed

*Fig. 27.11 Sequence of diagrams to illustrate synaptic transmission (only relevant detail is included in each drawing)*

## Drugs and the synapse

There are many different neurotransmitters responsible for information exchange across synapses. Most of the psychoactive drugs available in society today, such as **ecstasy**, **cannabis** and **cocaine**, cause their effects by interfering with the synaptic transmission of one of these messengers. Those drugs which amplify the process of synaptic transmission are called **excitatory** or **agonistic** drugs, while those which inhibit synaptic transmission are known as **inhibitory** or **antagonistic** drugs.

Narcotics such as **heroin** and **morphine** mimic the actions of the neurotransmitters known as endorphins, binding to their specific receptors and blocking sensations of pain. **Nicotine** similarly mimics natural transmitters.

The presence of **caffeine** in the body raises cell metabolism, leading to the release of more neurotransmitters. **Amphetamines** cause increased release of noradrenaline by interfering with storage mechanisms. This leads to excessive activation of neurones and extra information is transmitted around the brain. A user will feel highly aroused but may also suffer damage to organs including the heart.

Some drugs affect the body by interacting with natural neurotransmitters. The **benzodiazepine tranquillizers**, such as Valium, increase the effect of the inhibitory transmitter GABA in the brain, resulting in less transfer of information between neurones. In contrast phencyclidine, the active ingredient in **magic mushrooms**, interacts with excitatory transmitters in the brain and inappropriate information is passed between neurones, leading to hallucinations.

It is important to remember that neurotransmitters are rapidly absorbed or broken down. **Cocaine** causes noradrenaline to 'linger' in the synapse, producing effects similar to those from amphetamines.

£2m Cocaine Seizure

CRACK BARONS TARGET UK

Drugs 'cocktail' caused teenager's death hears court

### 27.2.3 Functions of synapses

Synapses have a number of functions:

1.  **Transmit information between neurones** – The main function of synapses is to convey information between neurones. It is from this basic function that the others arise.

2.  **Pass impulses in one direction only** – As the neurotransmitter substance can only be released from one side of a synapse, it ensures that nerve impulses only pass in one direction along a given pathway.

3. **Act as junctions** – Neurones may converge at a synapse. In th[is] way a number of impulses passing along different neurones may between them release sufficient neurotransmitter to generate a new action potential in a single postsynaptic neurone whereas individually they would not. This is known as **spatial summatio[n]**. In this way responses to a single stimulus may be coordinated.

4. **Filter out low level stimuli** – Background stimuli at a constantly low level, e.g. the drone of machinery, produce a lo[w] frequency of impulses and so cause the release of only small amounts of neurotransmitter at the synapse. This is insufficient to create a new impulse in the postsynaptic neurone and so the impulses are carried no further than the synapse. Such low leve[l] stimuli are of little importance and the absence of a response to them is rarely, if ever, harmful. Any change in the level of the stimulus will be responded to in the usual way.

5. **Allow adaptation to intense stimulation** – In response to a powerful stimulus, the high frequency of impulses in the presynaptic neurone causes considerable release of neurotransmitter into the synaptic cleft. Continued high-level stimulation may result in the rate of release of neurotransmitte[r] exceeding the rate at which it can be reformed. In these circumstances the release of neurotransmitter ceases and hence also any response to the stimulus. The synapse is said to be **fatigued**. The purpose of such a response is to prevent overstimulation which might otherwise damage an effector.

## 27.3   The reflex arc

A **reflex** is an automatic response which follows a sensory stimulus. It is not under conscious control and is therefore involuntary. The pathway of neurones involved in a reflex action known as a **reflex arc**. The simplest forms of reflex in vertebrates include those concerned with muscle tone. An example of this is the **knee jerk reflex** which may be separated into six parts:

1. **Stimulus** – A blow to the tendon situated below the patella (knee cap). This tendon is connected to the muscles that extend the leg, and hitting it causes these muscles to become stretched.

2. **Receptor** – Specialized sensory structures, called **muscle spindles**, situated in the muscle detect the stretching and produce a nervous signal.

3. **Sensory neurone** – The signal from the muscle spindles is conveyed as a nervous impulse along a sensory neurone to the spinal cord.

4. **Effector (motor) neurone** – The sensory neurone forms a synapse inside the spinal cord with a second neurone called an effector neurone. This effector neurone conveys a nervous impulse back to the muscle responsible for extending the leg.

5. **Effector** – This is the muscle responsible for extending the le[g]. When the impulse from the effector neurone is received, the muscle contracts.

6. **Response** – The lower leg jerks upwards as a consequence o[f] the muscle contraction.

This reflex arc has only one synapse, that between the sensory and effector neurone in the spinal cord. Such reflex arcs are therefore termed **monosynaptic**. These reflexes do not involve any neurones connected to the brain which therefore plays no part in the response. As the reaction is routine and predictable, not requiring any analysis, it would be wasteful of the brain's capacity to burden it with the millions of such responses that are required each day. Any reflex arc which is localized within the spinal cord and does not involve the brain is called a **spinal reflex**.

Reflexes involving two or more synapses are termed **polysynaptic**. Typical polysynaptic spinal reflexes include the withdrawal of parts of the body from painful stimuli, e.g. removal of the hand or foot from a hot or sharp object. Due to the response involved, such an action is called a **withdrawal reflex**. Fig. 27.12 illustrates a withdrawal reflex where the hand is placed on a hot object. This reflex involves an additional stage, namely the **connector (intermediate, internuncial** or **relay) neurone**, within the spinal cord.

These simple reflexes are important in making involuntary responses to various changes in both the internal and external environment. In this way homeostatic control of things like body posture may be maintained. Control of breathing, blood pressure and other systems are likewise effected through a series of reflex responses. Another example is the reflex constriction or dilation of the iris diaphragm of the eye in

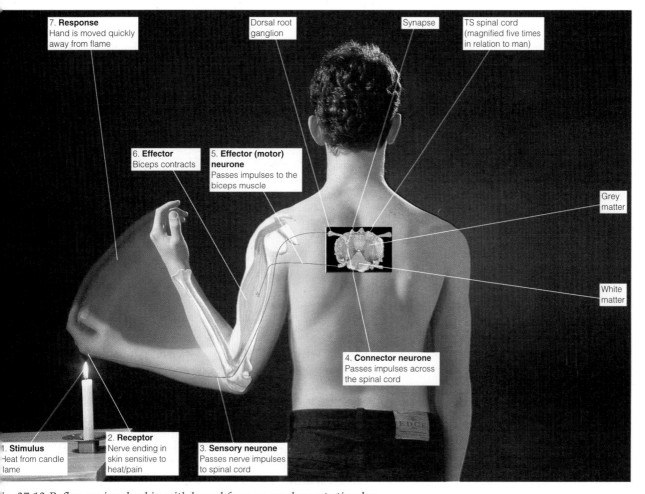

Fig. 27.12 *Reflex arc involved in withdrawal from an unpleasant stimulus*

response to changes in light intensity. Details of this are given in Section 27.6.1.

**Brain reflexes** have neurone connections with the brain and are usually far more complex, involving multiple responses to a stimulus. While reflexes are themselves involuntary, they may be modified in the light of previous experience. These are called **conditioned reflexes** and are discussed in Section 27.7.3.

## 27.4   The autonomic nervous system

The autonomic (*auto* = 'self'; *nomo* = 'govern') nervous system controls the involuntary activities of smooth muscle and certain glands. It forms a part of the peripheral nervous system and can be sub-divided into two parts: the **sympathetic nervous system** and the **parasympathetic nervous system**. Both systems comprise effector neurones, which connect the central nervous system to their effector organs. Each pathway consists of a **preganglionic neurone** and a **postganglionic neurone**. In the sympathetic system the synapses between the two are located near the spinal cord whereas in the parasympathetic system they are found near to, or within, the effector organ. This, and other differences, are illustrated in Fig. 27.13.

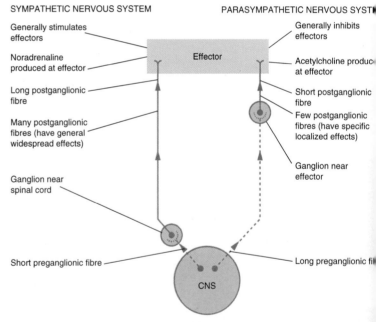

*Fig. 27.13 Comparison of the sympathetic and parasympathetic nervous systems*

The effects of the sympathetic and parasympathetic nervous systems normally oppose one another, i.e. they are **antagonistic**. If one system contracts a muscle, the other usually relaxes it. The balance between the two systems accurately regulates the involuntary activities of glands and organs. It is possible to control consciously certain activities of the autonomic nervous system through training. Control of the anal and bladder sphincters are examples of this.

Table 27.1 lists some of the effects of the sympathetic and parasympathetic nervous systems.

TABLE 27.1   **Comparison of some effects of the sympathetic and parasympathetic nervous systems**

| Sympathetic nervous system | Parasympathetic nervous system |
|---|---|
| Increases cardiac output | Decreases cardiac output |
| Increases blood pressure | Decreases blood pressure |
| Dilates bronchioles | Constricts bronchioles |
| Increases ventilation rate | Decreases ventilation rate |
| Dilates pupils of the eyes | Constricts pupils of the eyes |
| Contracts anal and bladder sphincters | Relaxes anal and bladder sphincters |
| Contracts erector pili muscles, so raising hair | No comparable effect |
| Increases sweat production | No comparable effect |
| No comparable effect | Increases secretion of tears |

# 27.5   The central nervous system

The central nervous system (CNS) acts as the coordinator of the nervous system. It comprises a long, approximately cylindrical structure – the **spinal cord** – and its anterior expansion – the **brain**.

## 27.5.1 The spinal cord

The spinal cord is a dorsal cylinder of nervous tissue running within the vertebrae which therefore protect it. It possesses a thick membranous wall and has a small canal, the **spinal canal**, running through the centre. The central area is made up of nerve cell bodies, synapses and unmyelinated connector neurones. This is called **grey matter** on account of its appearance. Around the grey matter is a region largely composed of longitudinal axons which connect different parts of the body. The myelin sheath around these axons give this region a lighter appearance, hence it is called **white matter**.

At intervals along the length of the spinal cord there extend spinal nerves. There are 31 pairs of these nerves in humans. They separate into two close to the spinal cord. The uppermost (dorsal) of these is called the **dorsal root**, while the lower (ventral) one is called the **ventral root**. The dorsal root carries only sensory neurones while the ventral root possesses only effector neurones; a sort of spinal nerve one-way system. The cell bodies of the sensory neurones occur within the dorsal root, forming a swelling called the **dorsal root ganglion**. The structure of the spinal cord is illustrated in Fig 27.14.

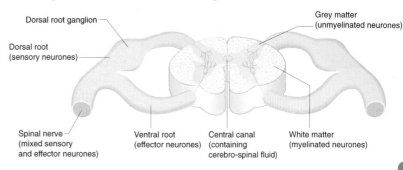

Dorsal root ganglion

Grey matter
(unmyelinated neurones)

Dorsal root
(sensory neurones)

Spinal nerve
(mixed sensory
and effector neurones)

Ventral root
(effector neurones)

Central canal
(containing
cerebro-spinal fluid)

White matter
(myelinated neurones)

*Fig. 27.14 TS through the spinal cord*

## 27.5.2 Structure of the brain

As an elaboration of the anterior region of the spinal cord, the brain has a basically similar structure. Both grey and white matter are present, as is the spinal canal although it is expanded to form larger cavities called **ventricles**. Broadly speaking, the brain has three regions: the **forebrain**, **midbrain** and **hindbrain**.

In common with the entire central nervous system, the brain is surrounded by protective membranes called **meninges**. There are three in all and the space between the inner two is filled with **cerebro-spinal fluid**, which also fills the ventricles referred to above. The cerebro-spinal fluid supplies the neurones in the brain with respiratory gases and nutrients and removes wastes. To achieve this, it must first exchange these materials with the blood. This it does within the ventricles which are richly supplied with capillaries. Having exchanged materials, the fluid must be

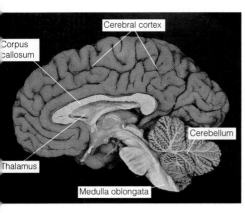

Cerebral cortex

Corpus callosum

Cerebellum

Thalamus

Medulla oblongata

ongitudinal section through a human brain

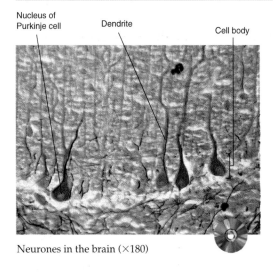

Neurones in the brain (×180)

circulated throughout the CNS in order that it may be distributed to the neurones. This function is performed by cilia found on the epithelial lining of the ventricles and central canal of the spinal cord. The structure of the brain is illustrated in Fig. 27.15.

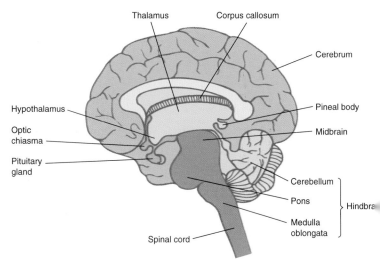

Fig. 27.15 VS through the centre of the human brain

### 27.5.3 Functions of the brain

*The hindbrain*

**Medulla oblongata**
This region of the brain contains many important centres of the autonomic nervous system. These centres control reflex activities like ventilation rate (Section 20.3), heart rate (Section 21.5.3) and blood pressure (Section 21.5.4). Other activities controlled by the medulla are swallowing, coughing and the production of saliva.

**Cerebellum**
This is a large and complex association area concerned with the control of muscular movement and body posture. It receives sensory information relating to the tone of muscles and tendons as well as information from the organs of balance in the ears. Its role is not to initiate movement but to coordinate it. Any damage to the cerebellum not surprisingly results in jerky and uncoordinated movement.

*The midbrain*
The midbrain acts as an important link between the hindbrain and the forebrain. In addition it houses both visual and auditory reflex centres. The reflexes they control include the movement of the head to fix on an object or locate a sound.

*The forebrain*

**The thalamus**
Lying as it does at the middle of the brain, the thalamus forms an important relay centre, connecting other regions of the brain. It assists in the integration of sensory information. Much of the sensory input received by the brain must be compared to previously stored information before it can be made sense of. It is the thalamus which conveys the information received to the appropriate areas of the cerebrum. Pain and pleasure appear to be perceived by the thalamus.

### The hypothalamus

This is the main controlling region for the autonomic nervous system. It has two centres, one for the sympathetic nervous system and the other for the parasympathetic nervous system. At the same time it controls such complex patterns of behaviour as feeding, sleeping and aggression. Another of its roles is to monitor the composition of the blood, in particular the plasma solute concentration, and not surprisingly therefore, it has a very rich supply of blood vessels. It is also an endocrine gland and details of this function are given in Section 26.3.

### The cerebrum

In vertebrates, the size of the cerebrum relative to the body increases from fish, through amphibians and reptiles, to mammals. Even with mammals there is a graded increase in this relative size, with humans having by far the largest. The cerebrum is highly convoluted in humans, considerably increasing its surface area and hence its capacity for complex activity.

The cerebrum is divided into left and right halves known as **cerebral hemispheres**. The two halves are joined by the **corpus callosum**. In general terms, the cerebrum performs the functions of receiving sensory information, interpreting it with respect to that stored from previous experiences and transmitting impulses along motor neurones to allow effectors to make appropriate responses. In this way, the cerebrum coordinates all the body's voluntary activities as well as some involuntary ones. In addition, it carries out complex activities like learning, reasoning and memory.

The outer 3 mm of the cerebral hemispheres is known as the **cerebral cortex** and in humans this covers an especially large area. Within this area the functions are localized, a fact verified in two ways. Firstly, if an electrode is used to stimulate a particular region of the cortex, the patient's response indicates the part of the body controlled by that region. For example, if a sensation in the hand is felt, then it is assumed that the area receives sensory information from the hand. Equally, if the hand moves, this must be the effector centre for the hand. The second method involves patients who have suffered brain damage by accidental means. If the injured person is unable to move his arm, then the damaged portion is assumed to be the effector centre for that arm.

The association areas of the cerebral cortex help an individual to interpret the information received in the light of previous experience. The **visual association area**, for example, allows objects to be recognized, and the **auditory association area** performs the same function for sounds. In humans, there are similar areas which permit understanding of speech and the written word. Yet another centre, the **speech effector centre**, coordinates the movement of the lips and tongue as well as breathing, in order to allow a person to speak coherently. The functions of the brain are summarized in Fig. 27.16.

Despite the methods outlined above that are used to investigate the functions of the brain, certain areas at the front of the cerebral cortex produce neither sensation nor response when stimulated. These are aptly termed **silent areas**. It is possible that they determine certain aspects of personality as their surgical removal has been known to relieve anxiety. The patients, while tranquil, become rather irresponsible and careless, however. The major localized regions of the cerebral cortex are outlined in Fig. 27.17.

## Did you know?

Public funding for medical research on Alzheimer's disease has gone down by a fifth.

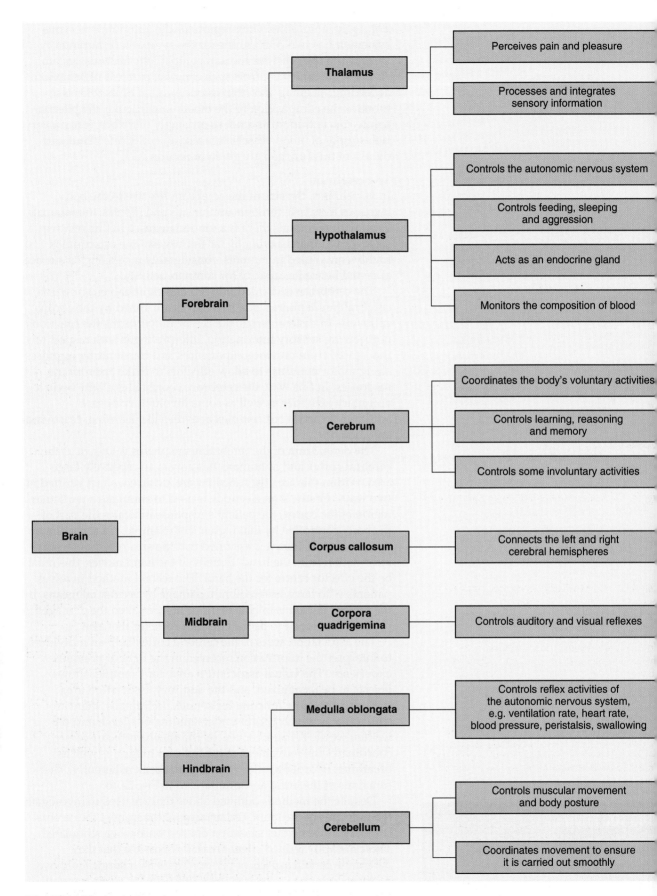

*Fig. 27.16 The brain functions*

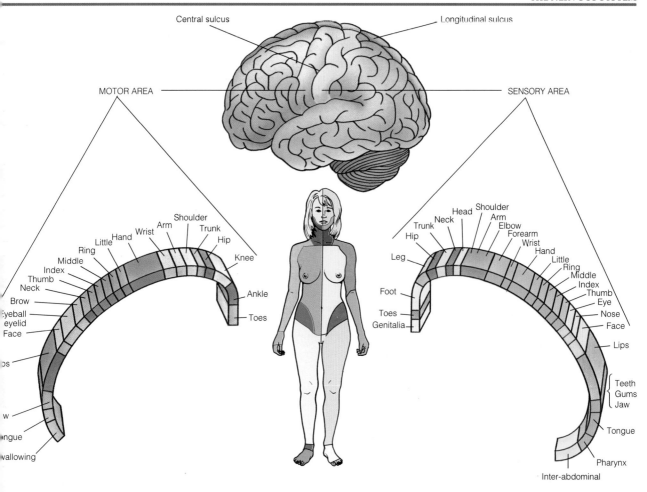

Fig. 27.17 Map of the major regions of the cerebral cortex and their functions

TABLE 27.2    Comparison of endocrine and nervous systems

| Endocrine system | Nervous system |
|---|---|
| Communication is by chemical messengers – hormones | Communication is by nervous impulses |
| Transmission is by the blood system | Transmission is by nerve fibres |
| Target organ receives message | Effector (muscle or gland) receives message |
| Transmission is relatively slow | Transmission is very rapid |
| Effects are widespread | Effects are localized |
| Response is slow | Response is rapid |
| Response is often long-lasting | Response is short-lived |
| Effect may be permanent and irreversible | Effect is temporary and reversible |

Diffusely situated throughout the brain stem is a system called the **reticular activating system**. It is used to stimulate the cerebral cortex and so rouse the body from sleep. The system is therefore responsible for maintaining wakefulness. The reticular activating system also appears to monitor impulses reaching and leaving the brain. It stimulates some and inhibits others. By doing so it is likely that the system concentrates the brain's activity upon the issues of most importance at any one time. For example, if searching avidly for a lost contact lens, the visual sense may be enhanced. On the other hand, if straining to hear a distant voice, the system may shift the emphasis to increase auditory awareness.

### 27.5.4 Comparison of endocrine and nervous systems

Both endocrine and nervous systems are concerned with coordination and in performing this function they inevitably operate together. At the same time the systems operate independently and therefore display differences. A comparison of the two systems is given in Table 27.2.

545

# BIOLOGY AROUND US

## Alzheimer's disease

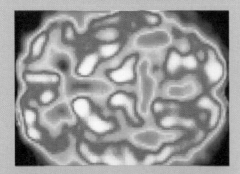

Colour-coded scans of (top) a normal brain and (above) the brain of an Alzheimer's patient, where the pattern of activity is less symmetrical

Alzheimer's disease now afflicts more than 600 000 people in the United Kingdom and every day on average a further 42 people develop it. The disease is usually associated with old age, affecting 5% of people over 65 and 20% of those over 80. Sadly it can also affect those as young as 40.

Alzheimer's is a disease which leads to dementia, a term used to describe all illnesses which cause a progressive loss of mental function.

People with dementia have reduced abilities to think and reason; they may not remember people or events, who or where they are. They have difficulty communicating and become increasingly dependent on carers for their every need. Although there are some treatments available which may slow down the progress of the disease, there are no cures. No-one even knows exactly what causes Alzheimer's disease.

There is evidence that patients with Alzheimer's have significantly diminished acetylcholine transferase activity in their brains. This enzyme synthesizes acetylcholine by transferring the acetyl group from acetyl CoA to choline:

$$CH_3\overset{O}{\overset{\|}{C}}-S-CoA + HO-CH_2CH_2-\overset{CH_3}{\overset{|}{\underset{CH_3}{N^+}}}-CH_3 \longrightarrow$$

$$CH_3\overset{O}{\overset{\|}{C}}-O-CH_2CH_2-\overset{CH_3}{\overset{|}{\underset{CH_3}{N^+}}}-CH_3 + CoA-SH$$

The cause of the disease may also lie in a defect in the neurotransmitter receptors.

Analyses of diseased human brains demonstrate abnormalities in the neurones of various regions, such as the cerebral cortex, the location of many complex mental processes and an area which plays a vital role in memory. In particular the diseased neurones contain accumulations of filaments known as neurofibrillar tangles and areas of the brain are replaced by extracellular deposits called plaques.

These plaques contain aggregates of protein called amyloid which derives from a normal membrane protein (APP – amyloid precursor protein) found in neurones and other cells. Abnormal catabolism of APP results in the production of insoluble fragments which accumulate outside the neurones and form the plaques. Mutations of the APP gene have been shown to be associated with the early onset of Alzheimer's.

Lysosomes may also play some role in the degeneration of neurones. APP and similar hydrophobic proteins are difficult to degrade and their accumulation within cells may cause lysosomes to burst and release their hydrolytic enzymes into the cytoplasm of the neurone. This leads to neuronal death and an aggregation of the proteins in the extracellular space.

By the year 2020 about 40% of the population of Britain, North America and Japan will be over 65 years old. This makes research into the dementing illnesses associated with ageing vital to ensure quality of life for sufferers and their carers.

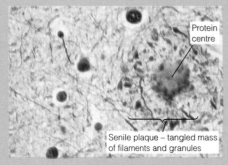

Protein centre

Senile plaque – tangled mass of filaments and granules

LM of brain tissue of an Alzheimer's patient showing a plaque (×250 approx.)

# 27.6    Sensory perception

All organisms experience changes in both their internal and external environments. Their survival depends upon responding in an appropriate way to these changes, and they have therefore developed elaborate means of detecting stimuli. To some degree, all cells are sensitive to stimuli, but some have become highly specialized to detect a particular form of energy. These are **receptor** cells. In general terms, these receptors convert whichever form of energy it is that they respond to into a nervous impulse, i.e. they act as **biological transducers**.

### 27.6.1 The mammalian eye

That part of the electromagnetic spectrum which can be detected by the mammalian eye lies in the range 400–700 nm. The eye acts like a television camera in producing an ever-changing image of the visual field at which it is directed.

Each eye is a spherical structure located in a bony socket of the skull called the **orbit**. It may be rotated within its orbit by **rectus muscles** which attach it to the skull. The external covering of the eye is the **sclera**. It contains many collagen fibres and helps to maintain the shape of the eyeball. The sclera is transparent over the anterior portion of the eyeball where it is called the **cornea**. It is the cornea that carries out most refraction of light entering the eye. A thin transparent layer of living cells, the **conjunctiva**, overlies and protects much of the cornea. The conjunctiva is an extension of the epithelium of the eyelid. Tears from **lachrymal glands** lubricate and nourish the conjunctiva and cornea.

Inside the sclera lies a layer of pigmented cells, the **choroid**, which prevents internal reflection of light. It is rich in blood capillaries which supply the innermost layer, the **retina**. This contains the light-sensitive **rods and cones** which convert the light waves they receive into nerve impulses which pass along neurones to the **optic nerve** and hence to the brain. There is an especially light-sensitive spot on the retina which contains only cones. This is the **fovea centralis**. The amount of light entering the eye is controlled by the **iris**. This is a heavily pigmented diaphragm of circular and radial muscle whose contractions alter the diameter of the aperture at its centre, called the **pupil**, through which light enters. Just behind the pupil lies the transparent, biconvex **lens**. It controls the final focusing of light onto the retina. It is flexible and elastic, capable of having its shape altered by the **ciliary muscles** which surround it. These are arranged circularly and radially and work antagonistically to focus incoming light on the retina by altering the lens' shape and hence its focal length. The region in front of the lens is called the **anterior chamber** and contains a transparent liquid called **aqueous humour**. Behind the lens is the much larger **posterior chamber** which contains the transparent jelly-like **vitreous humour** which helps to maintain the eyeball's shape. The structure of the eye is illustrated in Fig. 27.18.

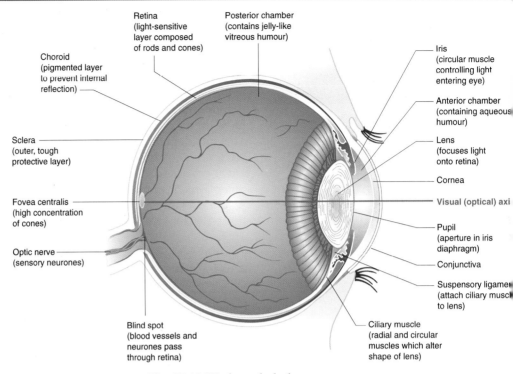

Fig. 27.18 VS through the human eye

*Control of the amount of light entering the eye*
Controlling the amount of light entering the eye is important because if too little light reaches the retina the cones may not be stimulated at all. Alternatively, if the quantity of light is too great the retinal cells may be overstimulated, causing dazzling. Contr is exercised by the iris diaphragm as outlined in Fig. 27.19.

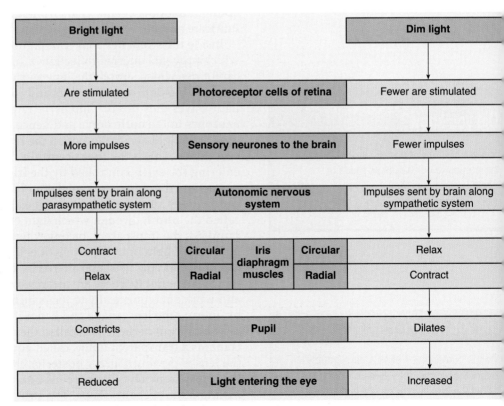

| Bright light | | | | Dim light |
|---|---|---|---|---|
| Are stimulated | **Photoreceptor cells of retina** | | | Fewer are stimulated |
| More impulses | **Sensory neurones to the brain** | | | Fewer impulses |
| Impulses sent by brain along parasympathetic system | **Autonomic nervous system** | | | Impulses sent by brain along sympathetic system |
| Contract | **Circular** | **Iris diaphragm muscles** | **Circular** | Relax |
| Relax | **Radial** | | **Radial** | Contract |
| Constricts | **Pupil** | | | Dilates |
| Reduced | **Light entering the eye** | | | Increased |

Fig. 27.19 Control of light entering the eye

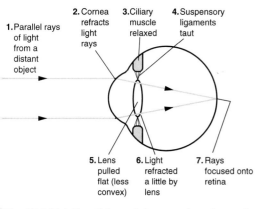

1. Parallel rays of light from a distant object

2. Cornea refracts light rays
3. Ciliary muscle relaxed
4. Suspensory ligaments taut
5. Lens pulled flat (less convex)
6. Light refracted a little by lens
7. Rays focused onto retina

*Fig. 27.20(a) Condition of the eye when focused on a distant object*

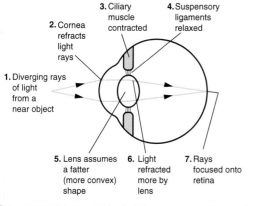

1. Diverging rays of light from a near object

2. Cornea refracts light rays
3. Ciliary muscle contracted
4. Suspensory ligaments relaxed
5. Lens assumes a fatter (more convex) shape
6. Light refracted more by lens
7. Rays focused onto retina

*Fig. 27.20(b) Condition of the eye when focused on a near object*

*Focusing of light rays onto the retina*

Light rays entering the eye must be **refracted** (bent) in order to focus them onto the retina and so give a clear image. Most refraction is achieved by the cornea. However, the degree of refraction needed to focus light rays onto the retina varies according to the distance from the eye of the object being viewed. Light rays from objects close to the eye need more refraction to focus them on the retina than rays from more distant objects. The cornea is unable to make these adjustments and so the lens has become adapted to this purpose. Being elastic, it can be made to change shape by the ciliary muscle which encircles it. The muscle fibres are arranged circularly and the lens is supported by **suspensory ligaments** (Fig. 27.18). When the circular ciliary muscle contracts, the tension on the suspensory ligaments is reduced and the natural elasticity of the lens causes it to assume a fatter (more convex) shape. In this position it increases the degree of refraction of light. When the circular ciliary muscle is relaxed, the suspensory ligaments are stretched taut, thus pulling the lens outwards and making it thinner (less convex). In this position it decreases the degree of light refraction. By changing its shape in this manner the lens can focus light rays from near and distant objects on the retina. The process is called **accommodation**. How the eye accommodates for distant and near objects is shown in Fig. 27.20(a) and (b).

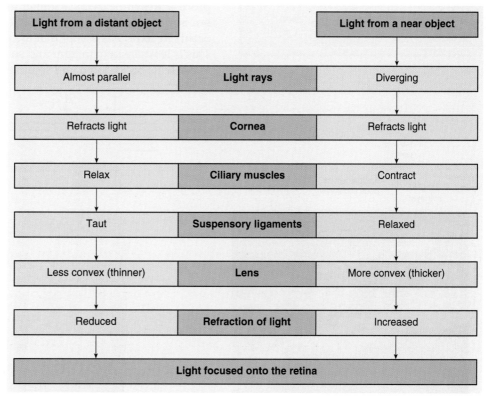

| Light from a distant object | | Light from a near object |
|---|---|---|
| Almost parallel | Light rays | Diverging |
| Refracts light | Cornea | Refracts light |
| Relax | Ciliary muscles | Contract |
| Taut | Suspensory ligaments | Relaxed |
| Less convex (thinner) | Lens | More convex (thicker) |
| Reduced | Refraction of light | Increased |
| | Light focused onto the retina | |

*Fig. 27.21 Accommodation (focusing) of objects by the eye*

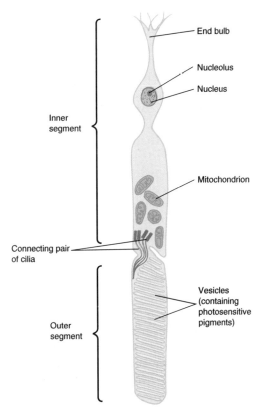

Fig. 27.22 *Structure of a single rod cell*

## Did you know?

In a lifetime a human blinks 415 million times

### The retina

The retina possesses the **photoreceptor** cells. These are of two types, **rods** and **cones**. Both act as transducers in that they convert light energy into the electrical energy of a nerve impulse. Both cell types are partly embedded in the pigmented epithelial cells of the choroid. The microscopic structure of the retina is shown in Figs. 27.22 and 27.23. In cats and some other nocturnal mammals, there exists a reflecting layer, called the **tapetum**, behind the retina. This reflects light back into the eye and so affords further opportunities for rod cells to absorb it. This greatly improves vision in dim light and is why cats' eyes give bright reflections when light shines into them – it is light reflected from the tapetum which is seen.

As Figs. 27.22 and 27.23 show, the basic structure of rods and cones is similar. However, there are both structural and functional differences and these are detailed in Table 27.3.

Each rod possesses up to a thousand vesicles in its outer segment. These contain the photosensitive pigment **rhodopsin** or **visual purple**. Rhodopsin is made up of the protein **opsin** and a derivative of vitamin A, **retinal**. Retinal normally exists in its *cis* isomer form, but light causes it to become converted to its *trans* isomer form. This change initiates reactions which lead to the splitting of rhodopsin into opsin and retinal – a process known as **bleaching**. This splitting in turn leads to the creation of a generator potential in the rod cell which, if sufficiently large, generates an action potential along the neurones leading from the cell to the brain.

Before the rod cell can be activated again in the same way, the opsin and retinal must first be resynthesized into rhodopsin. This resynthesis is carried out by the mitochondria found in the inner segment of the rod cell, which provide ATP for the process. Resynthesis takes longer than the splitting of rhodopsin but is more rapid in lower light intensity. A similar process occurs in cone cells except that the pigment here is **iodopsin**. This is less sensitive to light and so a greater intensity is required to cause its breakdown and so initiate a nerve impulse.

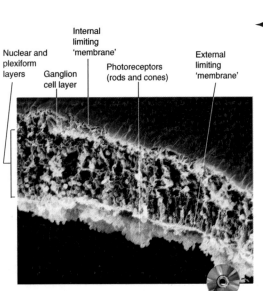

Human retina (TS) (SEM) (×255)

Fig. 27.23 *Microscopic structure of the retina*

TABLE 27.3    Differences between rods and cones

| Rods | Cones |
|---|---|
| Outer segment is rod-shaped | Outer segment is cone-shaped |
| Occur in greater numbers in the retina – being 20 times more common than cones | Fewer are found in the retina – being one-twentieth as common as rods |
| Distributed more or less evenly over the retina | Much more concentrated in and around the fovea centralis |
| None found at the fovea centralis | Greatest concentration occurs at the fovea centralis |
| Give poor visual acuity because many rods share a single neurone connection to the brain | Give good visual acuity because each cone has its own neurone connection to the brain |
| Sensitive to low-intensity light, therefore mostly used for night vision | Sensitive to high-intensity light, therefore mostly used for day vision |
| Do not discriminate between light of different wavelengths, i.e. not sensitive to colour | Discriminate between light of different wavelengths, i.e. sensitive to colour |
| Contain the visual pigment rhodopsin which has a single form | Contain the visual pigment iodopsin which occurs in three forms |

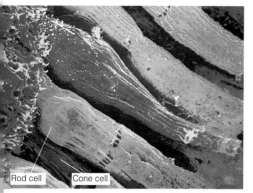

Rod cell    Cone cell

False-colour scanning EM of rod and cone cells

## Did you know?

Your eyes are able to see 8 million shades of colour.

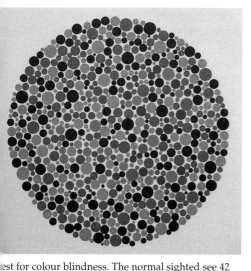

Test for colour blindness. The normal sighted see 42 while those with red–green colour blindness see either just a 4 or a 2 depending on the type of deficiency

*Colour vision*

It is thought that there are three forms of iodopsin, each responding to light of a different wavelength. Each form of iodopsin occurs in a different cone and the relative stimulation of each type is interpreted by the brain as a particular colour. This system is known as the **trichromatic theory** because there are three distinct types of cone, each responding to a different colour of light: blue, green or red. Other colours are perceived by combined stimulation of these three. Equal stimulation of red and green cones, for example, is perceived as yellow. Fig. 27.24 shows the extent of stimulation of each type of cone at different wavelengths of light.

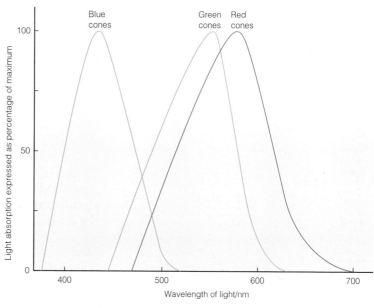

Fig. 27.24 *Absorption spectra for the three types of cone occurring in the retina as proposed in the trichromatic theory of colour vision*

Colour blindness can be explained in terms of some deficiency in one or more cone type. Deficiencies in the red and green cones, for example, give rise to the relatively common **red–green** colour blindness. The condition is due to a defect on a gene which is linked to the X chromosome (Section 9.4.2). Alternative theories to the trichromatic theory have been put forward in recent years but these have yet to achieve general acclaim.

### 27.6.2 Role of the brain in vision

All light, of whatever colour, intensity or pattern, which enters the eye is transformed into nerve impulses, all of which are the same. It is up to the brain to visualize these impulses into meaningful shapes. This it does by analysing and interpreting the frequency of impulses and the origins of the neurones which carry them, e.g. from a red cone or green cone. The visual association areas in the cerebral cortex of the brain are especially important here as they match the incoming information with images already stored in these areas. Hence a corgi would be recognized as a dog even if an individual's previous experience of the species was restricted to labradors.

### 27.6.3 The mammalian ear

The mammalian ear performs both as an organ of hearing and one of balance. It is broadly divided into three regions: the **outer ear**, the **middle ear** and the **inner ear**.

The outer ear comprises an external flap of skin-covered elastic cartilage, known as the **pinna**. The pinna collects and focuses sound waves and directs them along the **ear canal (external auditory meatus)**. Across the inner end of the ear canal is stretched the **tympanic membrane (eardrum)**, which separates the outer ear from the middle ear.

Within the middle ear are three connected bones called the ear **ossicles**, which are held in position by muscles. The bones are the **malleus** (hammer), the **incus** (anvil) and the **stapes** (stirrup). The middle ear is air-filled and so it is important that the pressure within it is kept equal to that of the atmosphere. Failure to do so causes the tympanic membrane to be stretched, so reducing the amplitude of its vibration and dulling the sense of hearing. The equalization of pressure within the middle ear with that of the atmosphere is achieved through a narrow tube called the **Eustachian tube**, which connects the middle ear to the pharynx. It is usually during swallowing that air enters or leaves the middle ear.

The inner ear comprises a complex of fluid-filled tubes. Certain of these tubes form a coil known as the **cochlea**, which is concerned with hearing, while the remainder form the **semi-circular canals**, which are organs of balance. The full structure of the ear is illustrated in Fig. 27.25.

*Mechanism of hearing*
Sound travels as waves and the distance between identical points on these waves is known as the wavelength. The longer the wavelength, the lower the frequency. The human ear can detect wavelengths which range from 40 to 16 000 Hz (cycles s$^{-1}$) but is most sensitive to the range 800–8500 Hz. The frequency of sound waves is known as **pitch** whereas its loudness is referred to as **intensity**.

Sound waves are collected by the pinna and focused into the ear canal down which they travel until they meet the tympanic

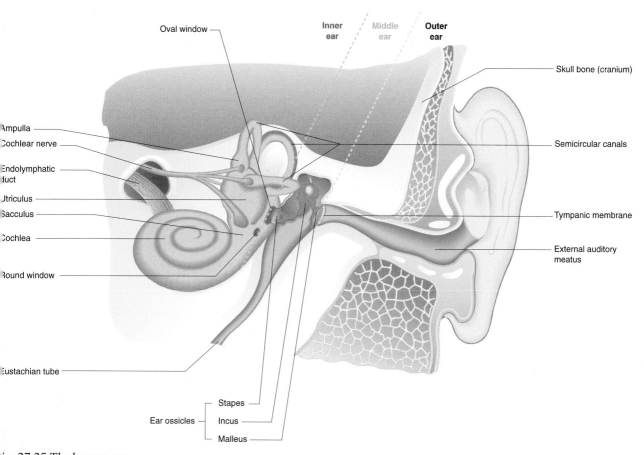

Fig. 27.25 The human ear

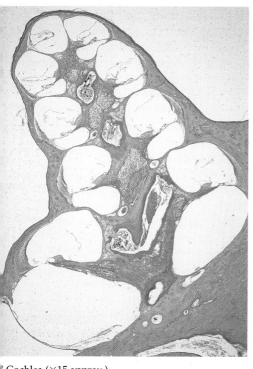

Cochlea (×15 approx.)

membrane (eardrum). They cause the tympanic membrane to vibrate and these vibrations are transmitted to the oval window by the ear ossicles. As the area of the oval window is only about one-twentieth that of the tympanic membrane, the vibrations are amplified over 20 times. In other words, relatively small movements of the tympanic membrane produce relatively large displacements of the oval window.

The oval window lies at one end of a long, hair-pin canal filled with perilymph (Fig. 27.26 (b)). Between the upper and lower portions of the hair-pin is another canal containing endolymph which communicates with the semi-circular canals. The hair-pin is 35 mm long in humans, but to economize on space it is coiled (Fig. 27.26 (a)). As the last of the ear ossicles, the stapes, vibrates, it pushes the oval window in and out in a piston-like manner. Being a liquid, the perilymph behind the oval window cannot be compressed or expanded and so movements of the oval window cause similar movements of the perilymph. These displacements of perilymph cause similar displacements of the round window, so as the oval window moves inwards the perilymph displaced causes the round window to bulge outwards into the middle ear (Fig. 27.26 (b)). This is possible because the middle ear is air-filled and the displacement of the round window simply compresses the air.

How then does this arrangement detect sound? It is thought that the pressure waves set up as a result of the piston-like action of the stapes on the oval window lead to displacements of **Reissner's membrane** (between the upper and middle

(a) Side view to illustrate spiral shape of the cochlea

(b) Diagrammatic section through an 'unwound' cochlea showing the relationship between displacements of the round and oval windows

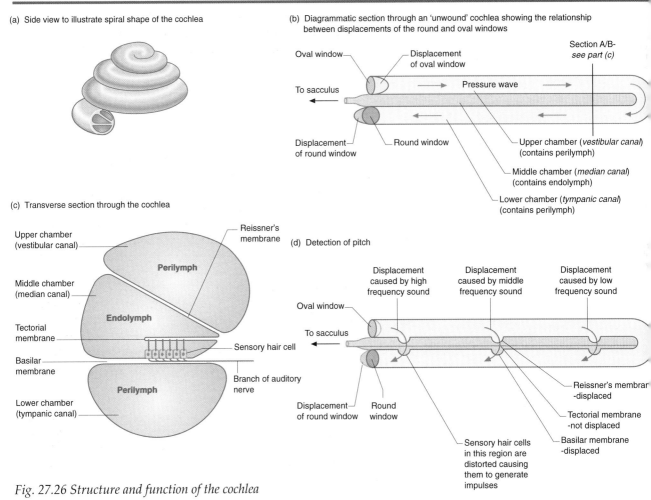

(c) Transverse section through the cochlea

(d) Detection of pitch

Fig. 27.26 Structure and function of the cochlea

chambers), which in turn displace endolymph in the middle chamber). Being incompressible, the endolymph displaces the basilar membrane. As the basilar membrane is quite elastic but the tectorial membrane is more rigid, this leads to movements o the basilar membrane while the tectorial membrane remains relatively fixed. Strung between these two membranes are sensory hair cells (Fig. 27.26 (c)). As the basilar membrane is displaced relative to the tectorial membrane, the sensory hair cells become distorted. This distortion sets up an action potentia which is conveyed to the CNS along a branch of the auditory nerve. In this way the brain is made aware that a sound stimulu has reached the ear. The tectorial and basilar membranes along with the sensory hair cells make up a special structure called th **organ of Corti**.

How is the pitch of the sound determined? The basilar membrane broadens and thickens the further away it is from th round window. Microscope observations have shown that the basilar membrane nearest to the round window vibrates more when a sound is of high frequency, while the region of the basilar membrane closest to the apex of the cochlea vibrates mos when stimulated by low frequency sound. It seems therefore tha different frequency sound waves stimulate different regions of the cochlea. By determining which region of the cochlea is sending impulses, the brain can interpret the pitch of sound entering the ear. These events are summarized in Fig. 27.26(d).

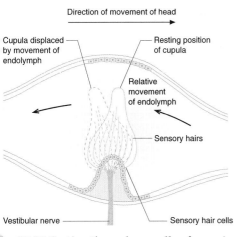

Fig. 27.27 Section through ampulla of a semi-circular canal

Finally, how is the intensity of sound determined? It seems likely that at any point along the basilar membrane there are a number of different sensory hair cells each with a different threshold at which it is stimulated. The louder the sound at any one frequency, the greater the number of sensory hair cells which will be stimulated at any one point on the basilar membrane.

*Maintenance of balance*
The parts of the ear concerned with balance are the **semi-circular canals**. These are three curved canals containing endolymph, which communicate with the middle chamber of the cochlea via the **utriculus** and **sacculus**. Each of the three canals is arranged in a plane at right angles to the other two. A movement in any one plane will result in movement of the canals in the same direction as the head. However, the inertia of the endolymph within the canals means that the endolymph remains more or less stationary. There is therefore relative movement between the canals and endolymph within them, in the same way that there is between a bottle and the liquid within it when the bottle is shaken. The movement of the endolymph is much greater in the canal which is in the same plane as the plane of movement.

Each of the three canals possesses a swollen portion, the **ampulla**, within which there is a flat gelatinous plate, the **cupula**. The movement of endolymph displaces this cupula in the opposite direction to that of the head movement (Fig. 27.27). Sensory hairs at the base of the cupula detect the displacement and send impulses to the brain via the **vestibular nerve**. The brain can then initiate motor impulses to various muscles to correct the imbalance.

The utriculus and sacculus also aid balance by providing information on the position of the body relative to gravity as well as changes in position due to acceleration and deceleration. The information is provided by chalk granules known as **otoliths** which are embedded in a jelly-like material. Various movements of the head cause these otoliths to displace sensory hair cells on regions of the walls of the utriculus and sacculus which respond to vertical and lateral movements respectively. The sensory hair cells thus send appropriate sensory impulses to the brain.

## 27.7  Behaviour

In order to survive, organisms must respond appropriately to changes in their environment. Broadly speaking, behaviour is the response of an organism to these changes and it involves both endocrine and nervous systems. Behaviour has a genetic basis and is unique to each species. It is often adapted, however, in the light of previous experience. The study of behaviour is called **ethology**.

Although both plants and animals exhibit behaviour, that of animals is considerably more complex. This section deals only with animal behaviour; plant behaviour is covered in Chapter 29.

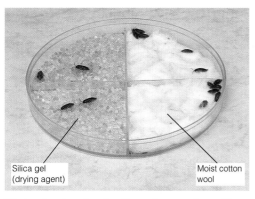

Silica gel
(drying agent)

Moist cotton
wool

Choice chamber showing the preference of woodlice for a moist environment

### 27.7.1 Reflexes, kineses and taxes

Reflexes are the simplest form of behavioural response. Section 27.3 describes a simple reflex response to a stimulus. These reflexes are involuntary responses which follow an inherited pattern of behaviour. How then do these responses improve an animal's chance of survival? The **withdrawal reflex** illustrates their importance. If the hand is placed on a hot object, the reflex response causes it to be immediately withdrawn. In this way damage is avoided. Invertebrate animals have a similar **escape reflex**. An earthworm, for example, withdraws down its burrow in response to vibrations of the ground. By behaving in this way the earthworm is less likely to be captured by a predator and so improves its chances of survival.

A more complex form of behaviour is a **kinesis**. This is a form of orientation behaviour. The response is non-directional, i.e. the animal does not move towards or away from the stimulus. Instead it simply moves faster, and changes direction more frequently when subjected to an unpleasant stimulus. The greater the intensity of the stimulus the faster it moves and the more often it changes direction. This is known as **orthokinesis**. is exhibited by woodlice which prefer damp situations. If a woodlouse finds itself in a dry area, it simply moves faster and keeps changing its direction. It thereby increases the speed with which it is likely to move out of the dry area. If this brings it into a more moist situation its movement slows, indeed it may cease altogether. It therefore spends a much longer period of time in the more humid conditions. Naturally it cannot remain stationary indefinitely, and factors such as hunger will ultimately cause it to move in search of food.

A **taxis** involves the movement of a whole organism in response to a stimulus, where the direction of the movement is related to the direction of the stimulus, usually towards it (positive +), or away from it (negative −). Tactic responses are classified according to the nature of the stimulus, e.g. light – **phototaxis**; chemicals – **chemotaxis**. The flatworm, *Planaria*, shows a positively chemotactic response to the presence of food. By moving its head from side to side it can detect the relative intensity of chemical stimulation experienced on each side of the head. This allows it to locate the source of food. Other examples of taxes are given in Section 29.1.2.

### 27.7.2 Innate behaviour

**Innate** or **instinctive** behaviour is inherited and is highly specific. It is normally an inborn pattern of behaviour which cannot be altered. In practice almost all instincts can be modified to some degree in response to experiences. However, innate behaviour is relatively inflexible when compared to learning. Much instinctive behaviour is highly complex and consists of a chain of actions, the completion of each stage in the chain acting as the stimulus for the commencement of the next stage.

This pattern of events is illustrated by a species of digger wasp. As its parents die long before each wasp hatches, there is no opportunity for it to learn from its parents and it must rely on inherited patterns of behaviour. When the time comes to lay

Digger wasp

eggs, a female digger wasp digs a nest hole and in it constructs small cells, each of which it provisions with a paralysed caterpillar to act as a food source for its offspring. The wasp then lays a single egg on the roof of each cell and seals the cell. If upon sealing the cell another caterpillar is placed where it is visible to the wasp, the wasp opens the cell, adds the caterpillar, lays another egg and seals the cell. It will repeat this many times, to the point where the cell is so crammed with caterpillars that there is insufficient air or space for the eggs to develop. It is obvious that the wasp has no appreciation of the purpose of its actions. If it had it would surely not pursue its pattern of behaviour to the point of jeopardizing the survival of its eggs. Instead the wasp reacts automatically, responding to the sight of a caterpillar, which acts as a **sign stimulus**, by carrying out the next stage in its inherited pattern of events. Removal of the roof of the cell where the egg is normally laid causes the wasp some agitation. However, it continues to lay the egg as if the cell roof was still intact, rather than adapt its behaviour to lay it elsewhere. This illustrates the relative inflexibility of innate behaviour.

The characteristics of innate behaviour are:

**1.** It is inherited and not acquired, although some modifications may result from experience.

**2.** It is similar among all members of a species and there are no individual differences other than those between males and females of the species.

**3.** It is unintelligent and often accompanied by no appreciation of the purposes it serves.

**4.** It often comprises a chain of reflexes. Completion of each link in the chain provides the stimulus for the commencement of the next link.

### 27.7.3 Learned behaviour

Learned behaviour is behaviour which is acquired and modified in response to experience. As such it takes time to refine and so is of greatest benefit to animals with relatively long life spans. The chief advantage of learning over innate behaviour is its adaptability; learned behaviour can be modified to meet changing circumstances. The simplest form of learned behaviour is **habituation**. This involves learning to ignore stimuli because they are followed by neither reward nor punishment. A snail crawling across a board can be made to withdraw into its shell by hitting the board firmly. Repetition of this action results in the snail taking no notice of the stimulus, i.e. it has learnt to ignore the stimulus as it is neither beneficial nor harmful.

**Associative learning** involves the association of two or more stimuli. One form of associative learning is the **conditioned reflex** exemplified by the classic experiments performed on dogs by the Russian physiologist I. P. Pavlov:

**1.** He allowed dogs to hear the ticking of a metronome and observed no change in the quantity of saliva produced.

**2.** He presented the dogs with the taste of powdered meat and measured the quantity of saliva produced.

Swallow tail caterpillar

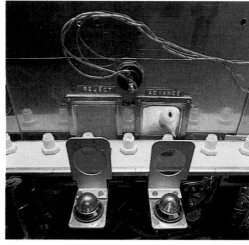

Pigeon choosing in a Skinner box

---

**PROJECT**

**Students often express the view that they can study better if there is background music going on at the same time**

Find out if they are right or not.

---

**3.** He presented the powdered meat and the noise of the metronome simultaneously on five or six occasions.

**4.** He presented the noise of a ticking metronome *only* and observed that the dogs salivated in response to it whereas previously they had not done so (Stage **1**).

**5.** Repetition of Stage **4** leads to a reduction in the quantity of saliva produced until the stimulus fails to produce any response

This association of one stimulus with another is the basis upon which birds reject certain caterpillars. If a caterpillar is distasteful it is in its interests to advertise itself by being brightl patterned. This is known as **aposematic** colouration (*apo* = awa* *sema* = sign; therefore 'keep away sign'). Having associated a particular pattern with the unpleasant memory of eating such a caterpillar, the bird ignores it as a potential source of food. This often leads to mimicry by otherwise edible insects, which thereby avoid being eaten.

The features of a conditioned reflex are:

**1.** It is the association of two stimuli presented together.

**2.** It is a temporary condition.

**3.** The response is involuntary.

**4.** It is reinforced by repetition.

**5.** Removal of the cerebral cortex causes loss of the response.

A second form of associative learning is **operant conditionin (trial and error learning)**. This form of learning, studied by Skinner, differs from the conditioned reflex in the way it becomes established. Animals learn by trial and error. If mistakes are followed by an unpleasant stimulus while correct responses are followed by a pleasant one, the animal learns a particular pattern of behaviour.

The features of operant learning are:

**1.** The associative stimulus *follows* the action, i.e. it does not nee to be simultaneous with it.

**2.** Repetition improves the response.

**3.** The action is involuntary.

**4.** While temporary, the association is less easily removed than in a conditioned reflex.

**5.** Removal of the cerebral cortex does *not* cause loss of the response.

**Latent learning** arises when an animal stores information while exploring its environment, and uses it at some later time. A rat placed in a maze with no reward as a stimulus will later complete the maze, when a reward is present, more rapidly tha a rat which has never been in the maze.

The highest form of learning is **insight** or **intelligent behaviour**. It involves the recall of previous experiences and their adaptation to help solve a new problem. The rapidity with which a solution is achieved excludes any possibility of trial and error. Kohler showed that chimpanzees will acquire bananas fixed to the roof of their cage by piling up boxes upon which they climb to reach them. In the same way sticks may be joined together to form a long pole which is used to obtain bananas which are out of reach outside the cage. Chimpanzees may even chew the ends of the sticks so they can be made to fit one another.

**Imprinting** is a simple but specialized form of learning. Unlike other forms of learning, imprinted behaviour is fixed and not easily adapted. Newly hatched geese will follow the first thing they see. Ordinarily this would be their mother and the significance of this behaviour is therefore obvious. However, as shown by the Austrian behaviourist, Konrad Lorenz, they will follow humans or other objects should these be seen first. This principle is often used in training circus animals. If a trainer becomes imprinted in an animal's mind, it becomes much easier to train.

### 27.7.4 Reproductive behaviour

For successful reproduction it is essential that an individual finds a mate who is of the opposite sex, sexually mature and prepared to copulate. **Courtship** is largely geared to achieving this end, and some details are given in Section 12.7.1. The preparedness of an individual to copulate is often controlled by hormones which can be affected by a number of factors (Section 12.6). In female mammals for example there may be behavioural patterns associated with the oestrous cycle. Parental care (Section 12.7.11) is a further example of reproductive behaviour, in this case designed to improve the probability of the young surviving to independence and sexual maturity.

### 27.7.5 Social behaviour

Even individuals of solitary species interact, if only to bring their gametes together. At the opposite end of the spectrum, the individuals of some species are completely dependent on one another for their survival. It is vital that these social groupings adapt their behaviour so that it is directed towards the interests of the group rather than the individual.

The advantages of a social group include greater opportunities for locating food and better protection against predators. To achieve this there needs to be efficient communication between individuals and an appreciation of each individual's role within the community. Frequently there is a **social hierarchy** or **pecking order**, with each individual having its own fixed status within the group. Examples occur in domestic animals such as chickens and cattle. In much the same way there is a dominance hierarchy in human organizations and institutions.

Social behaviour may be illustrated by a honey-bee colony. Here there is a **caste system** where there are distinct types, each with a specified role in the group. The **queen** is the single fertile female; the remaining females, the **workers**, are sterile as a result of licking a pheromone off the body of the queen. In this way the caste system is maintained. All males, called **drones**, are fertile. It is particularly in foraging for food that the honey-bees demonstrate complex social cooperation. This form of social

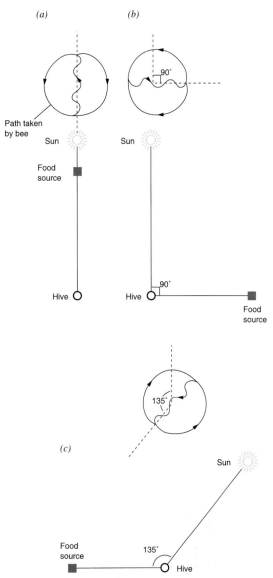

*(a)*  *(b)*

Path taken by bee

Sun

Food source

Hive

90°

Sun

Hive

90°

Food source

135°

*(c)*

Sun

Food source

135°

Hive

Fig. 27.28 Waggle dance of the honey-bee

behaviour was studied in detail by the German zoologist, Karl von Frisch. He discovered that worker bees returning from foraging missions reveal the location of food sources to other workers using a special **bee dance**. These dances communicate the direction of the food source from the hive and its distance away.

There are two forms of the dance: if the food source is within 100 m of the hive, a **round dance** is performed; if greater than 100 m, a **waggle dance** is carried out. In both dances, the speed a which it is performed is inversely proportional to the distance away from the hive that the food lies. The round dance does not indicate the direction of the food from the hive, but as it lies within 100 m the other workers easily locate it after a brief search

The waggle dance is more complex. The worker bee moves in a figure-of-eight pattern, waggling its abdomen as it does so. Th waggle part of the dance occurs as it moves along the line between the two loops of the figure-of-eight. The number of waggles gives some indication of the quantity of food discovered. The angle of this waggle relative to the vertical is the same as the angle relative to the sun which the other bees should take on leaving the hive, if they are to locate the food. Examples to illustrate this are shown in Fig. 27.28.

The obvious question arises – how do bees locate food source on cloudy days? They seem able to determine the plane of polarized light, which penetrates the cloud cover, and so are abl to locate the sun. To navigate accurately the bees must be able to make allowances for movements in the position of the sun according to the time of day. Honey-bees achieve this with the aid of an internal biological clock, which permits them to have a continually changing picture of the sun's movement during the day. Further information on the nature of the food source may be provided by samples of the nectar and/or pollen brought back to the hive by the foraging worker bee.

These complex bee dances serve to illustrate the importance c social behaviour in communicating valuable information quickl and accurately between individuals in the colony.

### 27.7.6 Migratory behaviour

The main reason that birds migrate is to find food. Birds which breed in the far north in summer come to spend winter in Britai because there is no food available in their Arctic breeding grounds. In the same way, there is not enough food in Britain in winter to supply most of our insect-eating birds. These birds therefore move south to winter in the tropics.

*Some birds that come to Britain in summer*

| | |
|---|---|
| Swallows | from South Africa |
| Swifts | from Malawi |
| Whitethroats | from West Africa |

*Some birds that come to Britain in winter*

| | |
|---|---|
| Redwings | from Iceland and Siberia |
| Wigeons | from Scandinavia |
| Brent Geese | from Siberia |

Migrations are triggered by behavioural cycles, changes in day length, temperature and a shortage of food.

# 27.8   Questions

Write an essay on how living organisms detect changes in their environment.

(*Total 24 marks*)

*AEB November 1992, Paper II, No. 5A*

The diagram below shows a single rod from a mammalian retina.

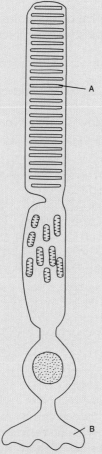

(a) Name the parts labelled A and B and give **one** function of each. (*4 marks*)

(b) Draw an arrow next to the diagram to indicate the direction in which light passes through this cell. (*1 mark*)

(c) State **two** ways in which vision using cones differs from vision using rods. (*2 marks*)

(*Total 7 marks*)

*ULEAC January 1993, Paper 3, No. 4*

(a) What are the **two** main functions of the mammalian ear? (*2 marks*)

(b) Give a description of the method of functioning of **one** of the functions in part (a). (*5 marks*)

(*Total 7 marks*)

*Oxford March 1997, Paper 45, No. 3*

4.  (a) Explain how light energy falling on a rod cell in the retina of the eye is converted to electrical energy. (*2 marks*)

(b) Suggest why rod cells contain large numbers of mitochondria. (*2 marks*)

(c) Explain how the possession of different types of cone cell helps us to see:

　　(i)   blue light; (*1 mark*)

　　(ii)  white light. (*1 mark*)

(*Total 6 marks*)

*AEB Summer 1996, Module Paper 4, No. 1*

5. The diagram shows rod cells and neurones from the retina of an eye.

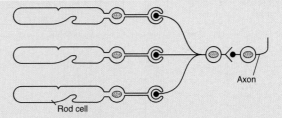

(a) Describe how light falling on a rod cell can give rise to a generator potential. (*5 marks*)

(b) Explain how an action potential is produced and a nerve impulse transmitted along an axon. (*6 marks*)

(c) With reference to the diagram, explain the following properties of a synapse;

　　(i)   summation; (*3 marks*)

　　(ii)  transmission across a synapse will only occur in one direction. (*3 marks*)

(*Quality of language: 3 marks*)

(*Total 20 marks*)

*AEB Summer 1997, Module Paper 4, No. 5*

6. The diagram below shows a human brain seen from the right side.

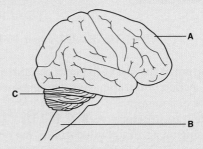

(a) Name the parts labelled **A**, **B** and **C**. (*3 marks*)

(b) Give **two** functions of the part labelled **B**.

(*2 marks*)

(*Total 5 marks*)

*Edexcel June 1997, B3, No. 1*

**7.** A neurone was suspended in a suitable solution and connected both to an electrical stimulator and to an oscilloscope. The intensity of the stimulus could be varied. The oscilloscope produced a visual record of the action potentials in the neurone.
The diagrams show the apparatus and a summary of the results of the experiment.

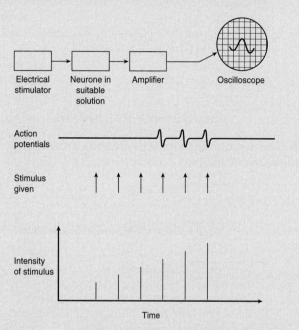

(a)  (i)  What sort of solution would be suitable to use in this experiment? *(1 mark)*
   (ii) Explain why this solution is used.
        *(1 mark)*
(b) Explain why the first three stimuli do not produce action potentials. *(1 mark)*
(c)  (i)  Give **two** similarities between the action potentials. *(2 marks)*
   (ii) Sense organs receive stimuli at different intensities. Explain how the neurones transmit this information. *(1 mark)*
(d) Explain what happens at a point on a neurone when an action potential is generated and a resting potential is re-established. *(4 marks)*
*(Total 10 marks)*

*NEAB March 1998, Paper BY10, No. 6*

**8.** The diagram at the top of the next column shows a transverse section of the spinal cord and associated spinal nerve of a mammal.
(a) Identify structures **A**, **B**, **C** and **D**. *(2 marks)*
(b) Using an accurate, ruled guide line on the diagram, clearly label the position of a postsynaptic membrane. *(1 mark)*
(c) Briefly explain, quoting a named example, what would be found at the commencement of structure **C** (not shown on the diagram). *(2 marks)*

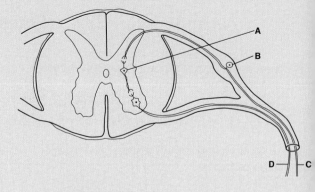

(d) Explain what occurs at the synapse when a nerve impulse (action potential) arrives.
*(4 marks)*
*(Total 9 marks)*

*Oxford June 1997, Paper 2, No.*

**9.** The diagram below shows a synapse as seen with the electron microscope.

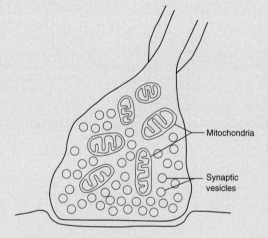

(a) Explain the function of each of the following
   (i)  The mitochondria. *(2 marks)*
   (ii) The synaptic vesicles. *(2 marks)*
(b) The graphs below show the effect of adding acetylcholine to skeletal muscle and heart muscle.

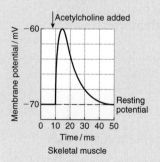
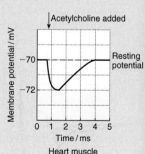

   (i)  Describe the effect of acetylcholine on skeletal muscle. *(2 marks)*
   (ii) State how the effects of acetylcholine on heart muscle differ from its effects on skeletal muscle. *(2 marks)*

(iii) Suggest how these differences may be related to the functions of the two types of muscle. *(2 marks)*

(c) (i) Suggest why it is important that acetylcholine is rapidly hydrolysed after its release. *(2 marks)*

(ii) Some organophosphate insecticides work by inhibiting the enzyme that catalyses the hydrolysis of acetylcholine. Suggest what effects this will have in the body of the insect. *(2 marks)*

*(Total 14 marks)*

*Edexcel June 1997, B6, No. 5*

**0.** (a) State **two** functions of synapses. *(2 marks)*

Calcium ions enter neurones through presynaptic membranes when action potentials arrive.

(b) (i) Explain how these ions enter the neurones. *(2 marks)*

(ii) Describe the events which follow the entry of these ions until the depolarization of the postsynaptic membrane. *(5 marks)*

(iii) Explain the importance of acetylcholinesterase at synapses *(2 marks)*

The functioning of the synapse can be affected by the presence of drugs, as shown in the table.

| Drug | Effect at synapse |
|------|-------------------|
| Curare | Blocks the receptors on the postsynaptic membrane of a motor neurone muscle junction |
| Morphine | Activates inhibitory receptors in the presynaptic membrane of sensory neurones. |

(c) Suggest the consequences, on the action of the synapse, of

(i) curare; *(2 marks)*

(ii) morphine. *(2 marks)*

*(Total 15 marks)*

*UCLES June 1998, (Biology Foundation), No. 4*

**1.** The graph shows the changes in permeability of an axon membrane to sodium and potassium ions during an action potential in a neurone.

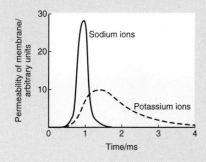

(a) Use information in the graph to explain why, at the start of an action potential, the potential difference across the membrane rapidly changes from negative to positive. *(2 marks)*

(b) Suggest why, during a period of intense nervous activity, the metabolic rate of a nerve cell increases. *(2 marks)*

(c) Predict the effect on an action potential of lowering the external concentration of sodium ions. Explain your answer. *(2 marks)*

*(Total 6 marks)*

*AEB Summer 1996, Paper 1, No. 10*

**12.** In a series of experiments on ducklings, the effectiveness of imprinting was measured at various times after hatching. In each of these experiments, the ducklings had the opportunity to follow a model duck. The figure represents the percentage of ducklings at a particular age which followed the model.

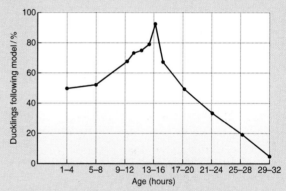

(a) Explain what is meant by **imprinting**. *(2 marks)*

(b) What conclusions can be drawn from these results? *(2 marks)*

(c) What will happen if the ducklings have no adult to imprint on? *(1 mark)*

*(Total 5 marks)*

*Oxford & Cambridge June 1997, Unit B8, No. 6*

**13.** The results on the next page were recorded from an experiment in which 10 blowfly larvae (maggots) were released at the centre of a paper circle divided into sectors. A light was shone from the side of each sector of the circle in a darkened room. The sectors from which the maggots left the circle and the position of the lamp were recorded for each of eight trials.

(a) State a suitable hypothesis for this experiment. *(1 mark)*

(b) (i) Why should the light be moved round the circle of paper? *(2 marks)*

(ii) Why should the experiment be conducted in a darkened room? *(2 marks)*

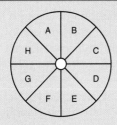

| Trial | Position of light | Sector from which the maggots left the circle | | | | | | | |
|-------|-------------------|---|---|---|---|---|---|---|---|
| | | A | B | C | D | E | F | G | H |
| 1 | Sector A | 1 | 0 | 0 | 2 | 7 | 0 | 0 | 0 |
| 2 | Sector B | 1 | 0 | 0 | 0 | 3 | 5 | 1 | 0 |
| 3 | Sector C | 0 | 0 | 0 | 0 | 0 | 2 | 8 | 0 |
| 4 | Sector D | 0 | 0 | 2 | 0 | 0 | 0 | 1 | 7 |
| 5 | Sector E | 7 | 2 | 0 | 0 | 0 | 0 | 0 | 1 |
| 6 | Sector F | 1 | 6 | 3 | 0 | 0 | 0 | 0 | 0 |
| 7 | Sector G | 1 | 1 | 8 | 0 | 0 | 0 | 0 | 0 |
| 8 | Sector H | 1 | 0 | 3 | 6 | 0 | 0 | 0 | 0 |

*(c)* What general conclusions can you make from these results about the response of maggots to light? *(2 marks)*

*(d)* (i) Explain the term **innate** behaviour. *(2 marks)*

(ii) What type of innate behaviour are these maggots showing? *(1 mark)*

(iii) Explain how this behaviour increases the survival advantage of the maggots. *(2 marks)*

*(Total 12 marks)*

*Oxford & Cambridge June 1997, Unit B8, No. 2*

**14.** The diagram shows some of the events that occur in a synapse after the arrival of an impulse at the presynaptic membrane.

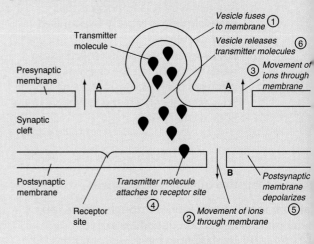

*(a)* (i) Put the events **1–6** in the correct sequence. *(1 mark)*

(ii) Name the ions labelled **A** and **B**. *(2 marks)*

(iii) By what process do transmitter molecules move across the synaptic cleft?. *(1 mark)*

(iv) Name **one** transmitter molecule released by synaptic vesicles. *(1 mark)*

*(b)* One impulse arriving at the presynaptic membrane does not produce an action potential in the postsynaptic neurone, but several impulses arriving in close succession do.

(i) Explain this observation. *(2 marks)*

(ii) What name is given to the process described? *(1 mark)*

*(Total 8 marks)*

*NEAB June 1997, Paper BY04, No.*

# 28 Muscular movement and support

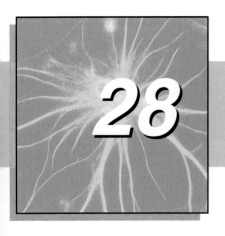

## 28.1 Structure of skeletal muscle

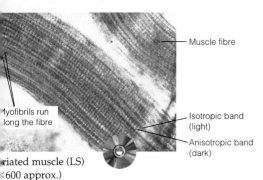

Muscle fibre

Myofibrils run along the fibre

Isotropic band (light)

Anisotropic band (dark)

Striated muscle (LS) (×600 approx.)

An individual muscle is made up of hundreds of **muscle fibres**. These fibres are cylindrical in shape with a diameter of around 50 $\mu$m. They vary in length from a few millimetres to several centimetres. Each fibre has many nuclei and a distinctive pattern of bands or cross striations. It is bounded by a membrane – the **sarcolemma**. The fibres are composed of numerous **myofibrils** arranged parallel to one another. Each repeating unit of cross striations is called a **sarcomere** and in mammals has a length of 2.5–3.0 $\mu$m. The cytoplasm of the myofibril is known as **sarcoplasm** and possesses a system of membranes called the **sarcoplasmic reticulum**.

The myofibril has alternating dark and light bands known as the **anisotropic** and **isotropic** bands respectively. Confusion between their names can be avoided by reference to the following:

| D | L |
|---|---|
| **A**nisotropic band | **I**sotropic band |
| R | G |
| K | H |
|   | T |

Each isotropic (light) band possesses a central line called the **Z line** and the distance between adjacent Z lines is a **sarcomere**. Each anisotropic (dark) band has at its centre a lighter region called the **H zone**, which may itself have a central dark line – the **M line**. This pattern of bands is the result of the arrangement of the two types of protein found in a myofibril. **Myosin** is made up of thick filaments and **actin** of thin ones. Where the two types overlap, the appearance of the muscle fibre is much darker. Anisotropic bands are therefore made up of both actin and myosin filaments whereas the isotropic band is made up solely of actin filaments. These arrangements and the overall structure of skeletal muscle are shown in Fig. 28.1.

Myosin filaments are approximately 10 nm in diameter and 2.5 $\mu$m long. They consist of a long rod-shaped fibre and a bulbous head which projects to the side of the fibre. These heads are of major significance in the contraction of muscle (Section 28.2.1). Actin filaments are thinner and slightly shorter than those of myosin being approximately 5 nm in diameter and

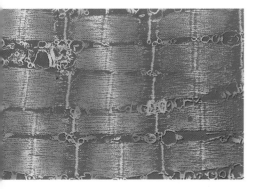

Striated muscle (EM)

565

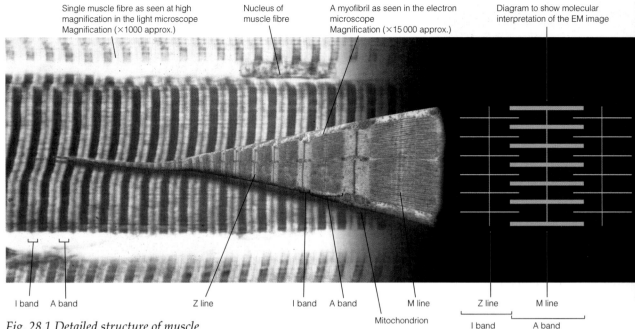

Single muscle fibre as seen at high magnification in the light microscope Magnification (×1000 approx.)

Nucleus of muscle fibre

A myofibril as seen in the electron microscope Magnification (×15 000 approx.)

Diagram to show molecular interpretation of the EM image

I band  A band                    Z line

I band  A band          M line

Mitochondrion

Z line        M line

I band      A band

*Fig. 28.1 Detailed structure of muscle*

2.0 $\mu$m long. The filaments comprise two different strands of actin molecules twisted around one another. Associated with these filaments are two other proteins: **tropomyosin**, which forms a fibrous strand around the actin filament, and **troponin**, globular protein vital to contraction of muscle fibre.

### 28.1.1 The neuromuscular junction

Skeletal muscle will not contract of its own accord but must be stimulated to do so by an impulse from an effector nerve. The point where the effector nerve meets a skeletal muscle is called the **neuromuscular junction** or **end plate**. If there were only one junction of this type it would take time for a wave of contraction to travel across the muscle and so not all the fibres would contract simultaneously and the movement would be slow. As rapid contraction is frequently essential for survival, animals have evolved a system whereby there are many end plates spread throughout a muscle. These simultaneously stimulate a group of fibres known as an **effector (motor) unit**; contraction of the muscle is thus rapid and powerful. This arrangement also gives control over the force generated by a muscle as not all the units need be stimulated at one time. If only slight force is needed only a few units will be stimulated. The structure of an end plate is shown in Fig. 28.2.

When a nerve impulse is received at the end plate, synaptic vesicles fuse with the end plate membrane and release their acetylcholine. The transmitter diffuses across to the sarcolemma altering the permeability of the sarcolemma to sodium ions, which now rapidly enter, depolarizing the membrane. Provided the threshold value is exceeded, an action potential is fired in the muscle fibre and the effector (motor) unit served by the end plate contracts. Breakdown of the acetylcholine by acetylcholinesterase ensures that the muscle is not over-stimulated and the sarcolemma becomes repolarized. This sequence of events is much the same as the mechanism of synaptic transmission (Section 27.2.2).

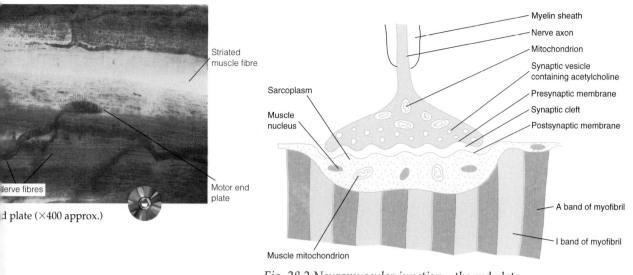

Striated muscle fibre

Nerve fibres

Motor end plate

d plate (×400 approx.)

Sarcoplasm

Muscle nucleus

Muscle mitochondrion

Myelin sheath

Nerve axon

Mitochondrion

Synaptic vesicle containing acetylcholine

Presynaptic membrane

Synaptic cleft

Postsynaptic membrane

A band of myofibril

I band of myofibril

*Fig. 28.2 Neuromuscular junction – the end plate*

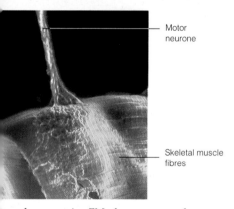

Motor neurone

Skeletal muscle fibres

se-colour scanning EM of a neuromuscular ction (×3600 approx.)

## Did you know?

There are more than 600 voluntary muscles in the human body.

LE 28.1 **Antagonistic pairs of muscles and the** vements they perform

| uscle action | Opposing muscle action |
|---|---|
| exor – bends a limb | **Extensor** – straightens a limb |
| ·ductor – moves a limb erally away from the dy | **Adductor** – moves a limb from a lateral position in towards the body |
| ·tractor – moves a limb wards | **Retractor** – moves a limb backwards |

# 28.2 Muscular contraction

Muscle cells have the ability to contract when stimulated and are therefore able to exert a force in one direction. Before a muscle can be contracted a second time, it must relax and be extended by the action of another muscle. This means that muscles operate in pairs with each member of the pair acting in the opposite direction to the other. These muscle pairs are termed **antagonistic**. Muscles may be classified according to the type of movement they bring about. For example, a **flexor** muscle bends a limb, whereas an **extensor** straightens it. Flexors and extensors therefore form an antagonistic pair. These and other types of skeletal muscle are listed in Table 28.1.

Skeletal muscle, as the name suggests, is attached to bone. This attachment is by means of **tendons** which are connective tissue made up largely of **collagen fibres**. Collagen is relatively inelastic and extremely tough. When a muscle is contracted, the tendons do not stretch and so the force is entirely transmitted to the bone. Each muscle is attached to a bone at both ends. One attachment, called the **origin**, is fixed to a rigid part of the skeleton, while the other, the **insertion**, is attached to a moveable part. There may be a number of points of insertion and/or origin. For example, two antagonistic muscles which bend the arm about the elbow are the **biceps** (flexor) and **triceps** (extensor). The biceps has two origins both on the scapula (shoulder blade) and a single insertion on the radius. The triceps has three origins, two on the humerus and one on the scapula and a single insertion on the ulna. These arrangements are illustrated in Fig. 28.3.

### 28.2.1 Mechanism of muscular contraction – the sliding filament theory

Much of our present knowledge about the mechanism of muscular contraction has its origins in the work of H. E. Huxley and J. Hanson in 1954. They compared the appearance of striated muscle when contracted and relaxed, observing that the length

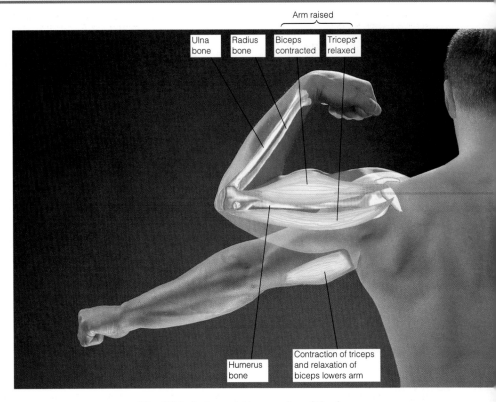

Fig. 28.3 Antagonistic muscles of the forearm

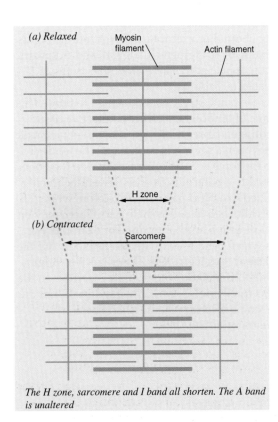

*(a) Relaxed*    Myosin filament    Actin filament

H zone

*(b) Contracted*

Sarcomere

The H zone, sarcomere and I band all shorten. The A band is unaltered

Fig. 28.4 Changes in appearance of a sarcomere during muscle contraction

of the anisotropic band (A band) remained unaltered. They concluded that the filaments of actin and myosin must in some way slide past one another – the **sliding filament theory**. It appears that the actin filaments, and hence the Z lines to which they are attached, are pulled towards each other, sliding as they do over the myosin filaments. No shortening of either type of filament occurs. These changes are illustrated in Fig. 28.4. From this diagram it should be clear that upon contraction the following can be observed in the appearance of a muscle fibre:

1. The isotropic band (I band) becomes shorter.

2. The anisotropic band (A band) does not change in length.

3. The Z lines become closer together, i.e. the sarcomere shortens.

4. The H zone shortens.

How exactly do the actin and myosin filaments slide past one another? The explanation seems to be related to cross bridges between the two types of filament, which can be observed in photoelectronmicrographs of muscle fibres. The bulbous heads along the myosin filaments form these bridges, and they appear to carry out a type of 'rowing' action along the actin filaments. The sequence of events involved in these movements is shown in Fig. 28.5.

Each myosin filament has a number of these bulbous heads and each progressively moves the actin filament along, as it becomes attached and reattached. This process is similar to the way in which a ratchet operates and for this reason it is often termed a **ratchet mechanism**. The result of this process is the contraction of a muscle or **twitch**. Having contracted, the muscle then relaxes. In this condition the myosin heads are drawn back towards the myosin filament and the fibrous tropomyosin blocks the

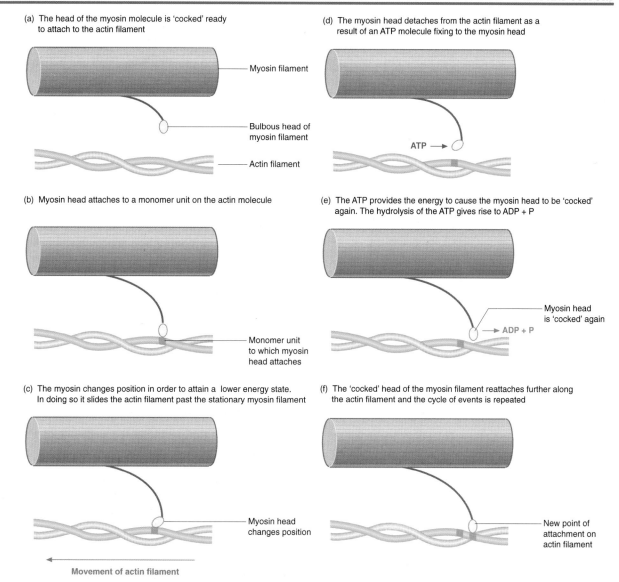

(a) The head of the myosin molecule is 'cocked' ready to attach to the actin filament

Myosin filament

Bulbous head of myosin filament

Actin filament

(b) Myosin head attaches to a monomer unit on the actin molecule

Monomer unit to which myosin head attaches

(c) The myosin changes position in order to attain a lower energy state. In doing so it slides the actin filament past the stationary myosin filament

Myosin head changes position

Movement of actin filament

(d) The myosin head detaches from the actin filament as a result of an ATP molecule fixing to the myosin head

ATP →

(e) The ATP provides the energy to cause the myosin head to be 'cocked' again. The hydrolysis of the ATP gives rise to ADP + P

Myosin head is 'cocked' again

→ ADP + P

(f) The 'cocked' head of the myosin filament reattaches further along the actin filament and the cycle of events is repeated

New point of attachment on actin filament

Fig. 28.5 Sliding filament mechanism of muscle contraction

attachment sites of the actin filament (Fig. 28.6). This prevents linking of myosin to actin and so stops further muscle contraction.

As the separation of the myosin and actin requires the binding of ATP to the myosin head, and as this can only be produced in a living organism, the muscles at death remain contracted. This results in a stiffening of the body known as **rigor mortis**.

Before a relaxed muscle may be contracted again, the actin filament must be unblocked by somehow moving the tropomyosin, so that the myosin heads may once again bind with an actin molecule. When a muscle is stimulated the wave of depolarization created spreads, not only along the sarcolemma but also throughout a series of small tubes known as the **T-system**. The T-system is in contact with the sarcoplasmic reticulum, and both are rich in calcium ions ($Ca^{2+}$). On depolarization they both release these ions. The calcium released binds to part of a protein molecule called **troponin**. This causes the troponin to change shape and in so doing move the tropomyosin molecule away from the actin filament. This unblocks the actin and so allows the myosin head to become

## Did you know?

When walking you use 200 different muscles.

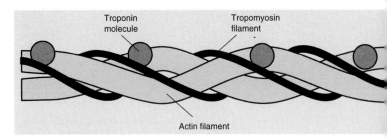

*Fig. 28.6 Relationship of tropomyosin and troponin to the actin filament*

attached to it, causing the muscle to contract. The calcium ions are then actively pumped back into the sarcoplasmic reticulum and T-system ready for use in initiating further muscle contractions.

The energy for muscle contraction is provided by ATP which is formed by oxidative phosphorylation during the respiratory breakdown of glucose. The supply of glucose is provided from the store of glycogen found in muscles. The resynthesis of ATP after its hydrolysis requires a substance called **phosphocreatine**.

### 28.2.2 Summary of muscle contraction

The events described fit the observed facts of muscle contraction. Further research may reveal additional detail, but the basic mechanism is unlikely to be modified. In view of the complexity of the process, a summary of the main stages is given below:

**1.** Impulse reaches the neuromuscular junction (end plate).

**2.** Synaptic vesicles fuse with the end-plate membrane and release a transmitter (e.g. acetylcholine).

**3.** Acetylcholine depolarizes the sarcolemma.

**4.** Acetylcholine is hydrolysed by acetylcholinesterase.

**5.** Provided the threshold value is exceeded, an action potential (wave of depolarization) is created in the muscle fibre.

**6.** Calcium ions ($Ca^{2+}$) are released from the T-system and sarcoplasmic reticulum.

**7.** Calcium ions bind to troponin, changing its shape.

**8.** Troponin displaces tropomyosin which has been blocking the actin filament.

**9.** The myosin heads now become attached to the actin filament.

**10.** The myosin head changes position, causing the actin filaments to slide past the stationary myosin filaments.

**11.** An ATP molecule becomes fixed to the myosin head, causing it to become detached from the actin.

**12.** Hydrolysis of ATP provides energy for the myosin head to be 'cocked'.

**13.** The myosin head becomes reattached further along the actin filament.

**14.** The muscle contracts by means of this ratchet mechanism.

**15.** The following changes in the muscle fibre occur:
  (a) I band shortens;
  (b) Z lines move closer together (i.e. sarcomere shortens);
  (c) H zone shortens.

**16.** Calcium ions are actively absorbed back into the T-system.

**17.** Troponin reverts to its original shape, allowing tropomyosin to again block the actin filament.

**18.** Phosphocreatine is used to regenerate ATP.

## 28.3    Skeleton and locomotion

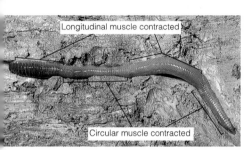

earthworm (*Lumbricus terrestris*) – waves of contraction of the two types of muscle bring about movement

Organisms originally evolved in water which gave support. Nevertheless some skeletal system was still necessary for most aquatic organisms, either as a rigid framework for the attachment of muscles or for protection. When organisms colonized land, where air provides little support, a skeleton was also necessary to support them against the pull of gravity. Skeletons therefore fulfil three main functions: support, locomotion and protection.

### 28.3.1 Types of skeleton

Skeletons take a wide variety of forms but they are generally classified into three main types: **hydrostatic**, **exoskeleton** and **endoskeleton**.

*Hydrostatic skeleton*
As liquids are incompressible they can form a resilient structure against which muscles are able to contract. This type of skeleton is typical of soft-bodied organisms such as annelids where liquid is secreted and trapped within body cavities. Around the liquid, muscles are arranged segmentally. They are not attached to any part of the body but simply contract against one another. The antagonistic arrangement involves circular muscles, whose contraction makes the body longer and thinner, and longitudinal muscles, whose contraction makes it shorter and thicker. In an earthworm (*Lumbricus terrestris*), chaetae on each segment anchor it to the substrate, so that alternate contractions of the two types of muscle bring about movement. Not all circular or longitudinal muscles contract together; instead, waves of contraction pass along the body.

*Exoskeleton*
An exoskeleton is a more or less complete external covering which provides protection for internal organs and a rigid attachment for muscles. It is characteristic of arthropods where it comprises a three-layered cuticle secreted by epidermal cells beneath it. The outer layer, the **epicuticle**, is thin and waxy and so forms a waterproof covering. Beneath this is a rigid layer of **chitin** (Section 2.5.4) impregnated with tanned proteins. This is the **exocuticle**. The inner layer, or **endocuticle**, is a more flexible layer of chitin. The exoskeleton may be impregnated with salts, e.g. calcium carbonate, which give it additional strength. This is frequently the case in crustacean exoskeletons.

    To permit uninhibited movement, the inflexible parts of the exoskeleton are separated by flexible regions where the rigid exocuticle is absent. Openings to glands and the digestive, respiratory and reproductive systems puncture the exoskeleton

stag beetle exoskeleton

571

as do sensory hairs. Since the exoskeleton cannot expand, it imposes a limit on growth. To overcome this, it is periodically shed by a process known as moulting or **ecdysis** (Section 12.8.5).

*Endoskeleton*

An endoskeleton forms an internal framework within an organism. Endoskeletons occur in certain protozoans, molluscs (cephalophods) and vertebrates. In the vertebrates, the skeleton is cellular although the bulk of it is a non-cellular matrix secreted by the cells. In the Chondrichthyes (sharks and rays), cartilage forms the entire skeleton. This has the advantage of combining rigidity with a degree of flexibility. Most vertebrates have a skeleton made up of bone which provides a strong, rigid framework. This, however, needs special articulating points known as **joints** if movement is to be possible.

### 28.3.2 Structure of bone

As bones are usually observed in their dried state, they often give the impression of dead, immutable structures. In fact they are living tissue which is very plastic; capable of moulding itself to meet the mechanical requirements demanded of it. The matrix of compact bone is made up of collagen together with inorganic substances such as calcium, magnesium and phosphorus. These components are arranged in concentric circles, called **lamellae**, around an **Haversian canal** containing an artery, a vein, lymph vessels and nerve fibres. Bone cells, or **osteocytes**, are found in spaces in the lamellae known as **lacunae** and fine channels called **canaliculi** link lacunae. The system of lamellae around one Haversian canal is called an **Haversian system**. Bone is an extremely important and strong skeletal material. It is not static. Its various inorganic components may be deposited or absorbed at different times to meet new stresses put upon the tissue.

When a bone, e.g. the femur, is examined in detail, it is found to have a complex internal structure. There is a hollow shaft, the **diaphysis**, which contains **marrow**, a tissue producing various kinds of blood cell. At each end is an expanded head, the **epiphysis** which articulates with other bones or to which tendons are attached. While the diaphysis and epiphysis are composed of

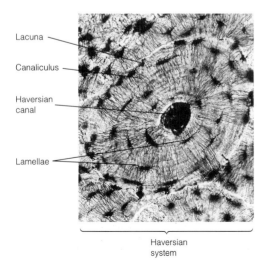

Compact bone (TS) (×400 approx.)

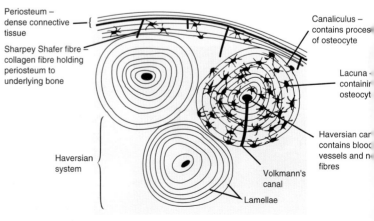

*Fig. 28.7 Compact bone (TS)*

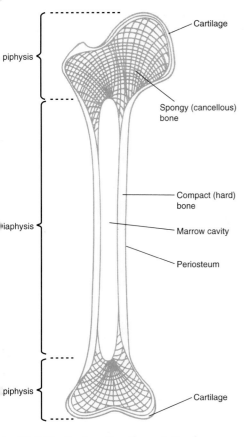

Cartilage

piphysis

Spongy (cancellous) bone

Compact (hard) bone

iaphysis

Marrow cavity

Periosteum

piphysis

Cartilage

*ig. 28.8 Vertical section through the femur*

**hard (compact) bone**, the remainder of the structure is made up of **spongy (cancellous) bone**. This has a honeycomb appearance and provides strength with a minimum of additional mass. A tough, fibrous membrane, the **periosteum**, surrounds the bone. The structure of the femur is shown in Fig. 28.8.

Bone has a number of functions:

1. Providing a framework for supporting the body.

2. Providing a means of attachment for muscles which then operate the bones as a system of levers for locomotion.

3. Protecting delicate parts of the body, e.g. the rib cage protects the heart and lungs; the cranium protects the brain.

4. Acting as a reservoir for calcium and phosphorus salts, helping to maintain a constant level in the bloodstream.

5. Producing red blood cells and certain white cells, e.g. granulocytes.

### 28.3.3 Joints

The skeleton has to fulfil two conflicting functions. On the one hand, it needs to be rigid in order to provide support and attachment for muscles; on the other hand, it needs to be flexible in order to permit movement. In the case of bony endoskeletons this paradox is overcome by having a series of flexible joints between the individual bones of the skeleton. The various types of joint found in a mammalian skeleton can be classified into three groups according to the degree of movement possible:

1. **Immoveable (suture) joints** – No movement is possible between the bones.

2. **Partly moveable (gliding) joints** – Only a little movement is possible between individual bones.

3. **Moveable (synovial) joints** – There is considerable freedom of movement between bones; the actual amount depends upon the precise nature of the joint.

The different joints found in mammals are described in Table 28.2.

TABLE 28.2 **Joints of the mammalian skeleton**

| Name of joint | Type of joint | Example |
|---|---|---|
| Suture | Immoveable | Between the bones of the cranium<br>Between the sacrum and ilia of the pelvic girdle |
| Gliding | Partly moveable | Between adjacent vertebrae<br>In the wrist and ankle |
| Pivot | Partly moveable | Between the axis and atlas vertebrae |
| Hinge | Synovial | In the elbow and knee<br>In the fingers and toes |
| Ball and socket | Synovial | At the shoulder and hip |

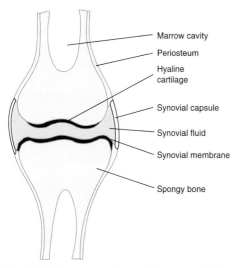

Fig. 28.9 Structure of a typical synovial joint

In moveable joints, the ends of the bones are covered with a layer of **cartilage**. This prevents damage to the articulating surfaces of bones as a result of friction between them. The joint surrounded by a fibrous covering called the **synovial capsule**. The inner lining of this capsule is known as the **synovial membrane**. It secretes a mucus-containing lubricant fluid called **synovial fluid** which also provides nutrients for the cartilage at the ends of the bones. The structure of a typical synovial joint is illustrated in Fig. 28.9.

The bones of a joint are held together by means of strong, but elastic, **ligaments**.

### 28.3.4 Locomotion in fish

Water has a greater relative density than air and so, at the same time as lending support to organisms within it, it also offers considerable resistance to their movement. This resistance make streamlining essential if rapid progress is to be achieved. It does however, provide a sufficiently dense medium against which muscles can push

The propulsive force in a fish is provided by blocks of muscle segmentally arranged on either side of the vertebral column. These blocks are called **myotomes**. The myotomes contract and relax alternately on each side of the flexible vertebral column. The fish is thereby bent into a series of waves which create a side-to-side lashing of the tail. This creates a forward and sideways thrust, which is greatly increased in magnitude by the broad caudal fin which presents a large surface area with which to push against the water. As the sideways thrust alternates between left and right, the forces cancel one another out. This leaves an overall forward thrust, with little sideways motion. These events are summarized in Fig. 28.10.

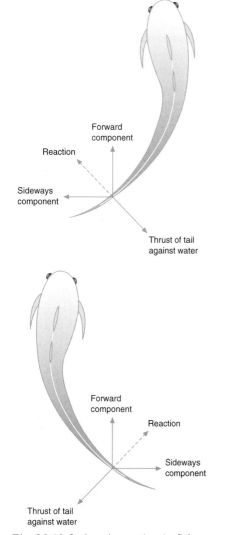

Fig. 28.10 Swimming action in fish

# 28.4   Questions

. The diagrams below (labelled 1, 2, 3, 4 and 5) show
ve possible states of a sarcomere from striated
muscle. The relative positions of some actin and
myosin filaments are shown.

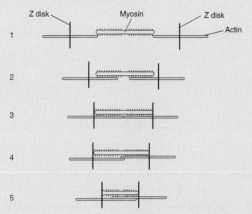

he graph below shows the relationship between
arcomere length and the amount of tension
enerated during the contraction. The letters A, B, C,
) and E on the graph correspond to the different
ositions of the actin and myosin filaments, shown on
he diagrams above, during the contraction.

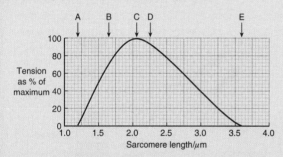

(a)  (i)  State the letter of the stage on the graph
which corresponds to the greatest
length of the sarcomere shown in the
diagrams.                    (1 mark)
(ii)  State the length of the sarcomere when
the maximum tension is generated
during contraction.          (1 mark)
(iii)  Which diagram of the sarcomere shows
the position of the actin and myosin
filaments when the maximum tension
is generated?                (1 mark)
(b)  (i)  Describe **two** ways in which the
positions of structures in the sarcomere
you have identified in (a)(iii) differ
from those in the sarcomere at its
greatest length.             (2 marks)
(ii)  Explain how a sarcomere in a
contracting muscle would change
between the state shown in diagram 1
and that in diagram 3.       (4 marks)

(iii)  Suggest why the maximum tension is
not achieved when the sarcomere
length is at its shortest.       (2 marks)
(Total 11 marks)

*Edexcel January 1998, Paper HB3, No. 6*

2.  The diagram represents a longitudinal section
through part of a striated muscle.

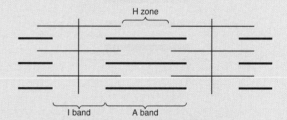

(a)  The diagram shows the **A** band, the **I** band
and the **H** zone. Which one or more of these:
(i)  contains actin but not myosin;   (1 mark)
(ii)  shortens when the muscle contracts?
(1 mark)
(b)  Describe the part played by each of the
following in muscle contraction:
(i)  ATP;                     (2 marks)
(ii)  calcium ions.             (1 mark)
(Total 5 marks)

*AEB Summer 1997, Module Paper 4, No. 2*

3.  The diagram shows a motor end plate.

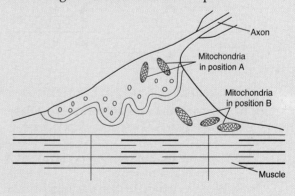

(a)  What is the name of the biochemical
pathway in the matrix of a mitochondrion
that produces ATP?              (1 mark)
(b)  Give **one** function of the ATP produced by
the mitochondria shown in the diagram in:
(i)  position **A**;              (1 mark)
(ii)  position **B**.             (1 mark)
(c)  Describe **one** function of calcium ions in the
structures shown in the diagram.   (1 mark)

575

(d) ATP present in a muscle is used during muscle contraction. Complete the equation to show how it is rapidly restored.

ADP + ..................... → ATP + .....................

*(1 mark)*

*(Total 5 marks)*

*AEB Summer 1996, (H. Biology) Module Paper 5, No. 3*

**4.** The figure below represents part of a skeletal muscle fibril.

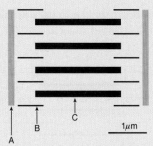

(a) (i) What term is used to describe the complete structure shown above?

*(1 mark)*

(ii) Identify the parts labelled **A**, **B** and **C**.

*(3 marks)*

(iii) By means of simple diagrams show how the interaction of **myosin** and **actin** molecules produces movement in a muscle cell. *(2 marks)*

(b) The following diagram represents the cycle of the proteins actin and myosin in a muscle cell as it contracts and relaxes (Pi represents phosphate).

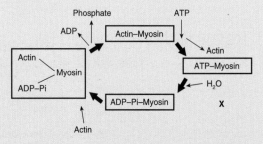

(i) Myosin can be described as an **ATPase**. What is an **ATPase** and what does it do? *(2 marks)*

(ii) State the type of reaction occurring at **X** in the diagram above. *(1 mark)*

(iii) When an organism dies, the muscles soon become contracted, a condition called **rigor mortis**. Indicate on the diagram, using the letter **Y**, the point where rigor mortis probably occurs. *(1 mark)*

(iv) Outline the way in which calcium is used to activate muscle contraction.

*(5 marks)*

*(Total 15 marks)*

*Oxford & Cambridge June 1996, Unit B4, No. 1*

**5.** The diagram shows the main muscles in a human leg.

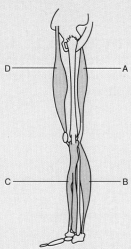

Which of muscles **A** to **D** on the diagram

(a) must contract to raise the heel from the ground;

(b) is antagonistic to this muscle?

*(Total 2 marks)*

*NEAB June 1996, Paper 1, No.*

**6.** The diagram shows the structure of a nerve–muscle junction together with part of the associated muscle.

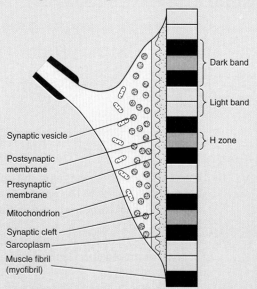

(a) Describe how transmission of information occurs across the nerve–muscle junction when an impulse arrives at the presynaptic membrane. *(5 marks)*

(b) (i) What causes the banding pattern seen in the muscle fibril? *(3 marks)*

(ii) How and why will the banding pattern change when the muscle fibril contracts? *(4 marks)*

*(Total 12 marks)*

*NEAB February 1997, Paper BY04, No.*

# 29 Control systems in plants

The ordered growth and development of plants shows that, like animals, they are capable of coordinating their activities. Unlike animals, they possess no nervous system and so plant coordination is achieved almost entirely by hormones. These hormones are similar to those of animals in being organic substances which in low concentrations cause changes in other parts of the organism. Unlike animal hormones, plant hormones almost always affect some aspect of growth.

## 29.1 Plant responses

Plants do not possess any contractile tissue with which to move. Their survival may, however, depend on their ability to move towards certain stimuli such as light and water. These movements are usually performed by growth responses.

### 29.1.1 Tropisms

A tropism is a growth movement of part of a plant in response to a directional stimulus. The direction of the response is related to that of the stimulus and in almost all cases the plant part moves

TABLE 29.1   **Examples of tropic responses**

| Stimulus | Name of response | Examples |
|---|---|---|
| Light | Phototropism | In almost all plants, shoots bend towards a directional light source (i.e. are positively phototropic), some roots bend away (i.e. are negatively phototropic) while leaves position themselves at right angles (i.e. are diaphototropic) |
| Gravity | Geotropism | In almost all plants, shoots bend away from gravity (i.e. are negatively geotropic) and roots bend towards it (i.e. are positively geotropic). The leaves of dicotyledonous plants position themselves at right angles (i.e. are diageotropic) |
| Water | Hydrotropism | Almost all plant roots bend towards moisture (i.e. are positively hydrotropic) while stems and leaves show no response |
| Chemicals | Chemotropism | Some fungal hyphae grow away from the products of their metabolism (i.e. are negatively chemotropic). Pollen tubes grow towards chemicals produced at the micropyle (i.e. are positively chemotropic) |
| Touch | Thigmotropism | The tendrils of peas (*Pisum*) twine around supports. The shoots of beans (*Phaseolus*) spiral around supports |
| Air | Aerotropism | Pollen tubes grow away from air (i.e. are negatively aerotropic) |

Phototropism – the cress seedlings in the pot on the left have been grown in all-round light while those on the right have been subject to unilateral light

towards or away from the stimulus. Each response is named according to the nature of the stimulus, e.g. a response to light is termed phototropism. The direction of the response is described as positive, if movement is towards the stimulus, or negative if movement is away from it. Some examples of tropisms are given in Table 29.1.

### 29.1.2 Taxes

A taxis is the movement of a freely motile organism, or a freely motile part of an organism, in response to a directional stimulus. The direction of the response is related to that of the stimulus, being towards it (positive) or away from it (negative). Taxes occur in both plants and animals. As with tropisms, the type of stimulus determines the name of a tactic response. Examples are given in Table 29.2.

TABLE 29.2  **Examples of tactic responses**

| Stimulus | Name of response | Examples | |
|---|---|---|---|
| | | Plants | Animals |
| Light | Phototaxis | *Euglena* swims towards light provided it is not too intense (i.e. is positively phototactic) | Earthworms (*Lumbricus*) and woodlice (*Oniscus*) move away from light (i.e. are negatively phototactic) |
| Temperature | Thermotaxis | The green alga, *Chlamydomonas*, will swim to regions of optimum temperature. Motile bacteria behave in a similar way | Blowfly larvae and many other small animals move away from extremes of temperature |
| Chemicals | Chemotaxis | Antherozooids (sperm) of mosses, liverworts and ferns, are attracted to chemicals produced by the archegonium (i.e. they are positively chemotactic) | Many show negative chemotactic responses to specific chemicals – a fact exploited in the use of insect repellents |

## 29.2   Plant hormones

Plant hormones, or **plant growth substances** as they are often called, are chemical substances produced in plants which accelerate, inhibit or otherwise modify growth. Growth at the apices of plants occurs in three stages: cell division, cell elongation and cell differentiation. Plant hormones may affect any, or all, of these processes. There are five groups of growth substances generally recognized: **auxins, gibberellins, cytokinins, abscisic acid (inhibitor)** and **ethene** (ethylene). Sometimes two hormones act together to reinforce an effect, e.g. auxins and gibberellins both increase cell elongation. This is known as **synergism**. Alternatively, two hormones may have opposing actions, e.g. auxins induce apical dominance whereas cytokinins prevent it. This is known as **antagonism**.

### 29.2.1 Auxins

Auxins are a group of chemical substances of which **indoleaceti acid (IAA)** is the most common. They have been isolated from a large number of plants. Charles Darwin was one of the earliest investigate the response of plant shoots to light (phototropism) which eventually led to the discovery and isolation of auxins. The historical record of these developments is traced in Fig. 29.

The auxin indoleacetic acid, a derivative of the amino acid tryptophane, is largely produced at the apices of shoots and roots. Fig. 29.2 outlines its chemical structure.

The transport of auxin occurs in one direction, namely away from the tip, i.e. its movement is **polar**. Short distance movement from cell to cell occurs by diffusion, but long distance transport is possible via phloem.

The role of auxin in producing a phototropic response is shown in Fig. 29.1. It appears that unilateral light causes a redistribution

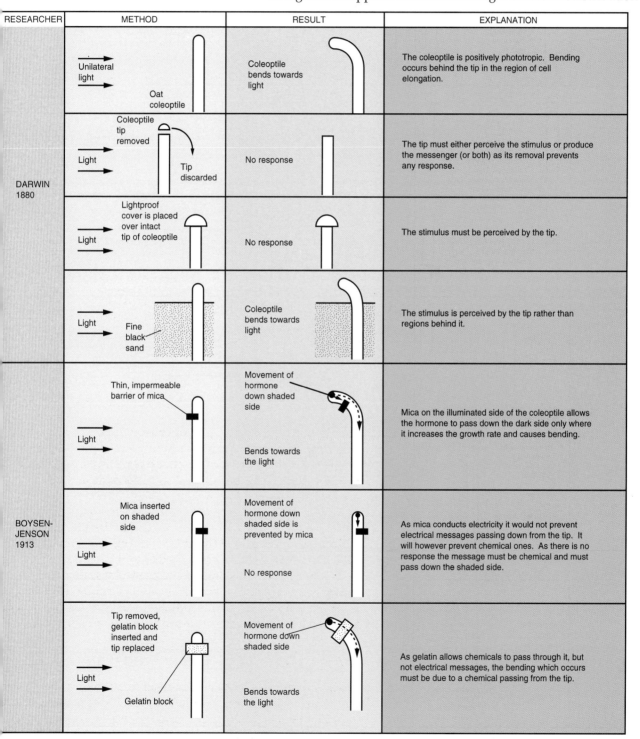

| RESEARCHER | METHOD | RESULT | EXPLANATION |
|---|---|---|---|
| DARWIN 1880 | Unilateral light — Oat coleoptile | Coleoptile bends towards light | The coleoptile is positively phototropic. Bending occurs behind the tip in the region of cell elongation. |
| | Coleoptile tip removed — Light — Tip discarded | No response | The tip must either perceive the stimulus or produce the messenger (or both) as its removal prevents any response. |
| | Lightproof cover is placed over intact tip of coleoptile — Light | No response | The stimulus must be perceived by the tip. |
| | Light — Fine black sand | Coleoptile bends towards light | The stimulus is perceived by the tip rather than regions behind it. |
| BOYSEN-JENSON 1913 | Thin, impermeable barrier of mica — Light | Movement of hormone down shaded side — Bends towards the light | Mica on the illuminated side of the coleoptile allows the hormone to pass down the dark side only where it increases the growth rate and causes bending. |
| | Mica inserted on shaded side — Light | Movement of hormone down shaded side is prevented by mica — No response | As mica conducts electricity it would not prevent electrical messages passing down from the tip. It will however prevent chemical ones. As there is no response the message must be chemical and must pass down the shaded side. |
| | Tip removed, gelatin block inserted and tip replaced — Light — Gelatin block | Movement of hormone down shaded side — Bends towards the light | As gelatin allows chemicals to pass through it, but not electrical messages, the bending which occurs must be due to a chemical passing from the tip. |

Fig. 29.1 Diagrammatic summary of the historical events leading to the discovery of auxin and an understanding of its mechanism of action (cont.)

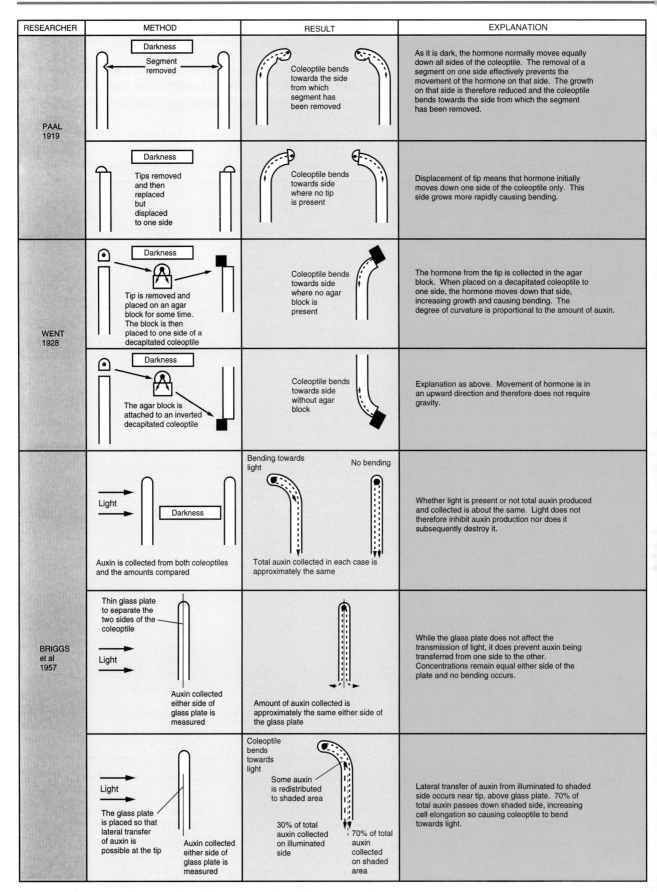

*Fig. 29.1 (cont.) Diagrammatic summary of the historical events leading to the discovery of auxin and an understanding of its mechanism of action*

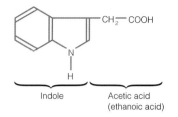

*Fig. 29.2 Structure of indoleacetic acid (IAA)*

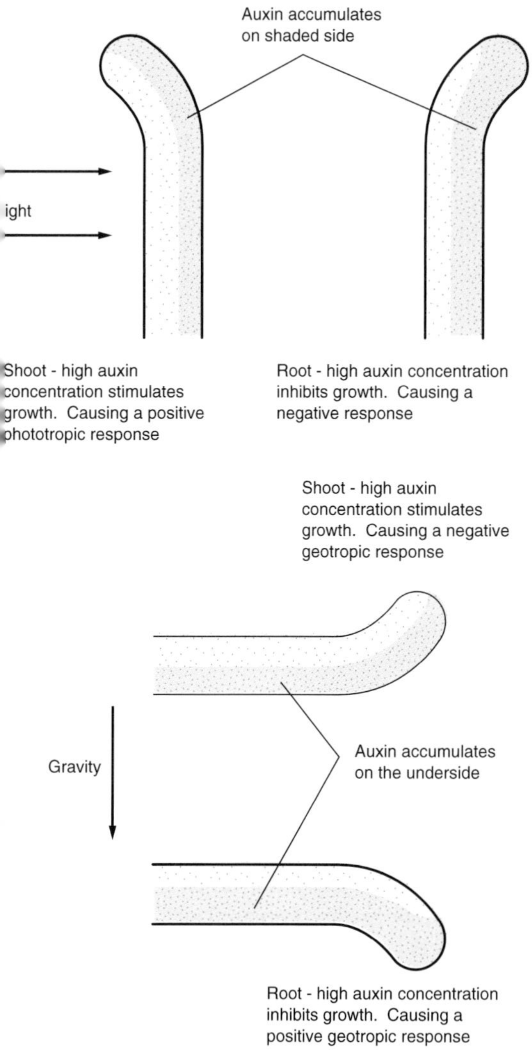

of auxin so that a greater amount travels down the shaded side. As one effect of auxin is to cause cell elongation, the cells on the shaded side elongate more than those on the illuminated side. The shoot therefore bends towards the light. Exactly how unilateral light effects a redistribution is not clear.

The redistribution theory may seem plausible but does not immediately explain why many roots are negatively phototropic. If the same arguments are used, it follows that a root exposed to unilateral light should accumulate auxin on its shaded side. This side should elongate more rapidly and the root bend towards the light. Why then does it bend in the opposite direction? Experiments have revealed that roots are more sensitive to auxin than stems, i.e. they respond to lower concentrations of auxins. As the concentration of auxin increases, the growth of roots, far from being stimulated, becomes inhibited. At a concentration of auxin of 1 part per million, for example, the growth of roots is reduced while that of stems is considerably increased (see Fig. 29.3). If the effect of unilateral light is to redistribute the auxin so that a concentration of 1 part per million passes down the shaded side, then in a stem, growth will increase on that side and it will bend towards the light, while in a root, growth will be inhibited on that side and it will bend away from the light.

Auxin accumulates on shaded side

Light

Shoot - high auxin concentration stimulates growth. Causing a positive phototropic response

Root - high auxin concentration inhibits growth. Causing a negative response

Shoot - high auxin concentration stimulates growth. Causing a negative geotropic response

Gravity

Auxin accumulates on the underside

Root - high auxin concentration inhibits growth. Causing a positive geotropic response

*Fig. 29.4 Mechanism of auxin action in phototropic and geotropic responses of shoots and roots*

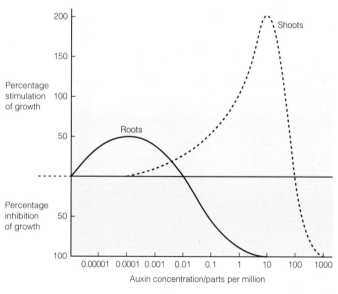

*Fig. 29.3 Relationship between growth and auxin concentration in roots and shoots*

Similar redistribution of auxins could account for the responses of shoots and roots to gravity. It can be shown experimentally that a higher concentration of auxin occurs on the underside of horizontal roots and shoots. The concentrations found inhibit root growth, causing it to bend downwards, i.e. a positive geotropic response. The same concentrations stimulate stem growth, causing it to bend upwards, i.e. a negative geotropic response. However the differences in concentration of auxin are small – smaller in fact than those of another plant hormone – gibberellin. Clearly the process is complex, probably involving a number of hormones. Indeed some theories suggest other factors such as pH or water potential differences are responsible. One mechanism to explain these differences is the **statolith theory**. This suggests that starch grains (or statoliths) fall within the cytoplasm of a cell under the influence of gravity. Their accumulation on the lower side of the cell is responsible for many of the physiological differences between the upper and lower sides of a cell. Both phototropic and geotropic responses of stems and roots are summarized in Fig. 29.4. Phototropic and geotropic responses are due to auxins promoting cell elongation. Auxins, however, have other influences in plants. They stimulate cell division, help to maintain the structure of cell walls and, in high concentrations, inhibit growth. Their ability to stimulate cell division is most easily observed by treating the cut end of plant parts with auxins. Often, an area of disorganized and largely undifferentiated tissue results. The large swellings so produced are called **calluses**. By a similar means, auxins may stimulate fruit development without fertilization (**parthenocarpy**). The maintenance of the structure of cell walls by auxins inhibits **abscission**. This is the separation of leaves, flowers and fruits from a plant as the result of the middle lamellae between cell walls, at the base of a petiole, pedicel or peduncle, weakening to such an extent that small mechanical disturbances, e.g. wind, cause them to fall. Auxin prevents the formation of this abscission layer and so inhibits abscission.

The inhibition of growth by high concentrations of auxin results in **apical dominance**. This is where the bud at the apex of a shoot produces auxin in sufficient concentration to inhibit growth of the lateral buds further down the shoot. These lateral buds remain dormant unless the apical bud is removed, in which case one or more of them develops into side branches. This is the principle behind the pruning of many plants as a means of producing a more bushy form of growth. The effects of auxins are summarized at the end of this section, in Table 29.3.

### 29.2.2 Gibberellins

The name **gibberellins** was derived from the fungus *Gibberella* (since renamed *Fusarium*). This fungus was shown by Japanese scientists in the 1920s to be the cause of 'foolish seedling disease', a disorder which resulted in rice seedlings growing considerably taller than their healthy counterparts. An extract from this fungus produced an increase in growth when applied to other plants. A group of active substances was finally isolated from the extract; these were called gibberellins. The number of gibberellins now isolated exceeds 50, but all have a similar chemical make-up.

The main influence of gibberellins on plants is to promote cell elongation and so increase growth. Unlike auxins, however, gibberellins can stimulate growth in dwarf varieties, thus restoring them to normal size. These dwarf varieties are thought to result from a genetic mutation which prevents them producing gibberellins naturally. They therefore require an external supply to make them grow to normal size. While the main effect of gibberellins is to cause elongation of the stem, they also influence cell division and differentiation to some extent. Their varied effects sometimes complement those of auxins, e.g. in promoting growth, but at other times they have antagonistic effects, e.g. while auxins promote the growth of adventitious roots, gibberellins inhibit their formation. Gibberellins play a role in breaking dormancy in seeds such as wheat and barley.

Effect of gibberellins on plant growth

They mobilize food reserves in readiness for germination by stimulating the synthesis of enzymes such as $\alpha$-amylase. It is likely that gibberellins operate by switching genes on and off. Their varied effects are summarized in Table 29.3.

### 29.2.3 Cytokinins

Plant cells grown in synthetic nutrient media were found to remain alive but did not undergo cell division. Division only occurred if malt extract or coconut milk was added to the culture. It was later found that autoclaved samples of DNA also induced cell division and from these **kinetin**, a substance similar to adenine, was isolated. Partly as a consequence of their effects in promoting cell division (**cytokinesis**), substances like kinetin were termed **cytokinins**. A number of cytokinins are produced naturally by many plants; all are derivatives of adenine. This suggests that they operate through some role in nucleic acid metabolism, most probably being involved in tRNA synthesis. They are found largely in actively dividing tissues, especially fruits and seeds, where they promote cell division in the presence of auxins.

One interesting effect of cytokinins is their ability to delay **senescence** (ageing) in leaves. In the presence of cytokinins, leaves removed from a plant remain green and active, rather than turning yellow and dying. Further effects are summarized in Table 29.3.

### 29.2.4 Abscisic acid

Abscisic acid inhibits growth and so works antagonistically to auxins, gibberellins and cytokinins. Its main effect, as its name suggests, is on abscission (leaf and fruit fall). The process results from a balance between the production of auxin and abscisic acid. As a fruit ripens, the level of auxin (which inhibits abscission) falls, while that of abscisic acid (which promotes abscission) increases. This leads to the formation of an abscission layer which causes the fruit to fall. Other influences of abscisic acid are listed in Table 29.3.

### 29.2.5 Ethene

Unlike the other hormones, **ethene** (ethylene) has a relatively simple chemical structure. It is produced as a metabolic by-product of most plant organs, especially fruits. Its main effect is in stimulating the ripening of fruits, but it also influences many auxin-induced responses. Other effects are summarized in Table 29.3.

## 29.3  Control of flowering

Plants flower at different times of the year, daffodils and snowdrops appearing in early spring, roses in summer and chrysanthemums in autumn. The seasonal differences in the time of flowering are related to two main climatic factors: day length and temperature.

TABLE 29.3   **A summary of the effects of plant hormones**

| Hormone | Effects | | Examples |
|---|---|---|---|
| Auxins | Promote cell elongation | Phototropic responses | Shoots bend towards light |
| | | Geotropic responses | Roots grow down into the soil |
| | Stimulate cell division | Promote development of roots | Hormone rooting powders are used to help strike cuttings |
| | | Stimulate cambial activity | Callus development at the site of wounds |
| | | Stimulate development of fruits | Natural fruit setting may be improved by spraying with synthetic auxins, or fruits may develop parthenocarpically, e.g. in apples |
| | Maintain cell wall structure | Inhibit leaf abscission | If the supply of auxin from leaves exceeds that from the stem, the leaf remains intact |
| | | Inhibit fruit abscission | If the supply of auxin from the fruit exceeds that from the stem, the fruit remains intact |
| | Inhibit growth in high concentrations | Apical dominance | Lateral buds remain dormant under the influence of auxin from the apical bud |
| | | Disruption of growth | Synthetic auxins, e.g. 2,4-D and 2,4,5-T, are used as selective weedkillers |
| Gibberellins | Reverse genetic dwarfism | | Dwarf varieties of peas and maize grow to normal size when gibberellin is applied |
| | Promote cell elongation | | Increase the length of internodes |
| | Break dormancy of buds | | Dormancy of many buds, e.g. birch (*Betula*), is broken by the addition of gibberellin |
| | Break dormancy of seeds | | Ash, wheat and barley seed dormancy may be broken as a result of mobilizing food reserves, leading to germination |
| | Stimulate fruit development | | Cherry and peach fruits develop more readily after application of gibberellins |
| | Remove need for cold period in vernalization | | Carrots can be induced to flower without first being subjected to a period of cold |
| | Affect flowering | | Promote flowering in some long-day plants and inhibit flowering in some short-day plants |
| Cytokinins | Promote cell division | | Increase growth rate in many plants, e.g. sunflower (*Helianthus*) |
| | Delay leaf senescence | | Maintain leaf for some time once detached from plant |
| | Stimulate bud development | | Promote development of buds on cuttings of African violet (*Saintpaulia*) and protonemata of some mosses |
| | Break dormancy | | Break dormancy in both seeds and buds |
| Abscisic acid | Inhibits growth | | Retards growth in most plant parts |
| | Promotes abscission | | Causes the formation of an abscission layer in the petioles and pedicels of leaves, flowers and fruits |
| | Induces dormancy | | Promotes dormancy in the seeds and buds of many plants, e.g. birch (*Betula*) and sycamore (*Acer*) |
| | Closes stomata | | Promotes stomatal closure under conditions of water stress |
| Ethene | Ripens fruit | | Most citrus fruits ripen more rapidly in the presence of ethene |
| | Breaks dormancy | | Ends dormancy of buds in some plants |
| | Induces flowering | | Promotes flowering in pineapples |

## BIOLOGY AROUND US

# Commercial applications of synthetic growth regulators

Normal seed – normal auxin production

Aborted seed – reduced auxin production

Apple sectioned to show effects of auxin production

As the main function of plant hormones is to control growth, it is hardly surprising that they, or rather their synthetic derivatives, have been extensively used in crop production.

Synthetic auxins such as 2,4-dichlorophenoxyacetic acid (2,4-D) and 2,4,5-trichlorophenoxyacetic acid (2,4,5-T) are used as **selective weedkillers**. When sprayed on crops, they have a more significant effect on broad-leaved (dicotyledonous) plants than on narrow-leaved (monocotyledonous) ones. They so completely disrupt the growth of broad-leaved plants that the plants die, while narrow-leaved plants at most suffer a temporary reduction in growth. As cereal crops are narrow-leaved and most of their competing weeds are broad-leaved, the application of these hormone weedkillers is of much commercial value. They are also extensively used domestically for controlling weeds in lawns. Other details of these weedkillers are given in Section 18.6.1. Another synthetic auxin, naphthaleneacetic acid (NAA), is used to increase fruit yields. If sprayed on trees, it helps the fruit to set naturally, or in some species causes fruit to set without the initial stimulus of fertilization (parthenocarpy). This usually results in seedless fruits which may be a commercial advantage. Gibberellins extracted from fungal cultures are used commercially in the same way.

Auxins are the active constituent of rooting powders. The development of roots is initiated when the ends of cuttings are dipped in these compounds. As we have seen, cytokinins will delay leaf senescence. They are therefore sometimes used commercially to keep the leaves of crops, like lettuce, fresh and free from yellowing after they have been picked. Both gibberellins and cytokinins are sometimes applied to seeds to help break dormancy and so initiate rapid germination. The longer a seed remains ungerminated in the soil, the more vulnerable it is to being eaten, e.g. by birds.

Abscisic acid may be sprayed on fruit crops to induce the fruits to fall so they can be harvested together. Ethene is applied to tomatoes and citrus fruits in order to stimulate ripening.

### 29.3.1 The phytochrome system

Many plant processes are influenced by light. Before a plant can respond to variations in light intensity, duration or wavelength it must first detect these changes. Some form of photoreceptor is necessary. In Section 14.2.3 we discussed the relationships between the absorption spectrum for chlorophyll and the action spectrum for photosynthesis. A similar relationship can be established between a pigment called **phytochrome** and a number of light-induced plant responses (see Fig. 29.5).

Phytochrome, isolated in 1960, exists in two interconvertible forms:

1. **Phytochrome 660 ($P_{660}$)** – This absorbs red light (peak absorption at a wavelength of 660 nm).

2. **Phytochrome 730 ($P_{730}$)** – This absorbs light in the far-red region of the spectrum (peak absorption at 730 nm).

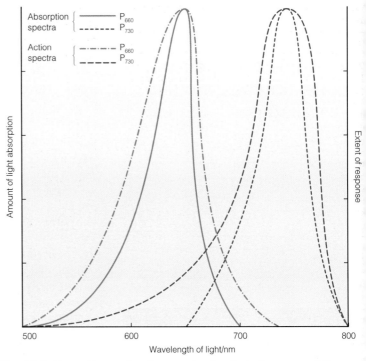

*Fig. 29.5 Absorption and action spectra for phytochromes and the responses they control*

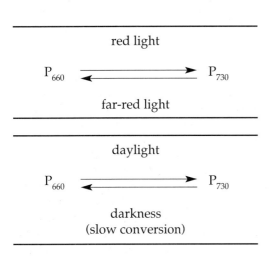

Even a short exposure to the appropriate light wavelength causes the conversion of one form into the other, as shown on the left. These conversions may also be brought about by daylight and darkness. During daylight, $P_{660}$ is converted to $P_{730}$ while in the dark, a rather slower conversion of $P_{730}$ to $P_{660}$ occurs

Phytochrome comprises a protein and a pigment. It is distributed throughout the plant in minute quantities, being most concentrated in growing tips. The actions of the two forms are usually antagonistic, i.e. where $P_{660}$ induces a response, $P_{730}$ inhibits it. The various effects of the two forms are listed in Table 29.4.

### 29.3.2 Photoperiodism

One major influence on the timing of flowering is the length of the day or **photoperiod**. The effects of the photoperiod on flowering differ from species to species but plants fall into three basic categories:

**1. Long-day plants (LDP)** – These only flower when the period of daylight exceeds a critical minimum length. Examples of long day plants include radish, clover, barley and petunia.

**2. Short-day plants (SDP)** – These only flower when the period of daylight is shorter than a critical maximum length. Examples of short-day plants include chrysanthemum, poinsettia, cocklebur and tobacco.

**3. Day-neutral plants** – These plants flower regardless of the length of daylight. Examples of day-neutral plants include cucumber, begonia, violet and carrot.

Intermediate varieties exist. For example, **short-long-day plants** only flower after a sequence of short days is followed by long days. These plants will flower naturally in mid-summer when

**TABLE 29.4   Summary of the effects of red light and far-red light**

| Red light effects | Far-red light effects |
| --- | --- |
| Phytochrome 660 changes to phytochrome 730 | Phytochrome 730 changes to phytochrome 660 |
| Stimulates germination of some seeds, e.g. lettuce (*Lactuca*) | Inhibits germination of some seeds, e.g. lettuce (*Lactuca*) |
| Induces formation of anthocyanins (plant pigments) | Inhibits formation of anthocyanins |
| Stimulates flowering in long-day plants | Inhibits flowering in long-day plants |
| Inhibits flowering in short-day plants | Stimulates flowering in short-day plants |
| Elongation of internodes is inhibited | Elongation of internodes is promoted |
| Induces increase in leaf area | Prevents increase in leaf area |
| Causes epicotyl (plumule) hook to unbend | Maintains epicotyl (plumule) hook bent |

the days are long following the shorter days of spring. **Long-short-day plants** flower after a sequence of long days is followed by short days. These will flower naturally in the autumn after the long days of summer are followed by the shorter days of early autumn.

It is rather unfortunate that historically plants were categorized as short-day or long-day, as it is the length of the dark period which is crucial in determining flowering. Short-day plants require a long dark period, whereas long-day plants require a short dark period. This fact was established by a series of experiments summarized in Fig. 29.6.

Interrupting a long dark period with red light is as effective as daylight in stopping short-day plants flowering. Far-red light, however, has no effect and short-day plants flower as if the dark period had been continuous. These and other experiments suggest that phytochrome is the photoreceptor detecting different light wavelengths and ultimately determining whether or not a plant flowers.

Although flowers are formed at the apex, experiments confirm that the light stimulus is detected by the leaves. In some cases only a single leaf needs to be subjected to the appropriate stimulus to induce flowering. A message must therefore pass from the leaves to the apex. As plants coordinate by chemical means, this message is assumed to be a hormone and has been called **florigen**, even though it has not yet been isolated. It is thought to be transported within phloem. Understanding of the mechanism by which phytochrome initiates flowering is poor. The process is clearly complex and, because they can have similar effects to red light, gibberellins may be involved. One possible mechanism is summarized in Fig. 29.7. As long-day plants are known to flower after a short exposure to red light, it is possible that red light (wavelength 660 nm) is absorbed by phytochrome 660 which is rapidly converted to phytochrome 730 which then induces flowering. Short-day plants by contrast flower in response to phytochrome 660. This is formed by absorption of far-red light (wavelength 730 nm) by phytochrome 730 which is then converted to phytochrome 660. This rapid conversion by far-red light can also take place, although far more slowly, in darkness. Hence a long dark period induces flowering in these short-day plants. One postulated mechanism by which

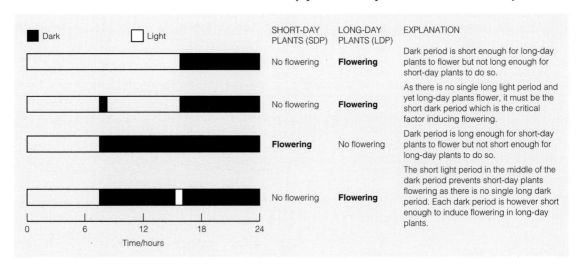

*Fig. 29.6 Flowering related to the length of dark period*

florigen is produced suggests that there are two inactive forms of the hormone, one of which is converted to the hormone by $P_{660}$ the other by $P_{730}$. These events are summarized in Fig. 29.7

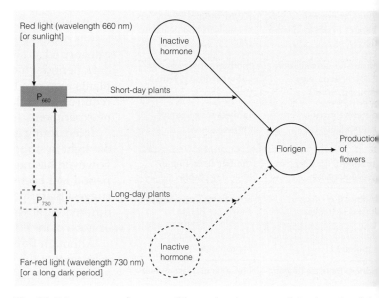

*Fig. 29.7 Summary of one possible mechanism to explain the role of the phytochrome system in flowering*

# 29.4　Questions

*(a)* State **two** roles of cytokinins in regulating plant growth　*(2 marks)*

The shoots of germinating cereals, such as wheat, maize and oats, are protected by a sheath of cells known as a coleoptile.

Some oat seeds were germinated in the dark. Segments, each 10 mm in length, were cut from the coleoptiles. 60 of these segments were divided into six batches. These were placed into petri dishes containing a solution of sucrose and mineral salts. Different concentrations of an auxin, indole-3-acetic acid (IAA), were added to five of the dishes. The coleoptile segments were left in the dark for 20 hours at 25°C and then remeasured. The results are shown in the graph below.

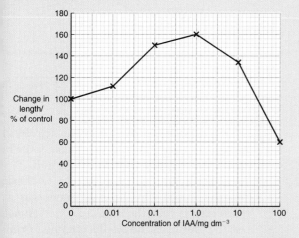

*(b)* (i) Explain why sucrose was used in the experiment.　*(1 mark)*

(ii) Explain how the results, plotted on the graph, were calculated.　*(2 marks)*

Tomato fruits swell in response to IAA produced by the seeds inside.

*(c)* Suggest how the oat coleoptile experiment described above could be used to measure the concentration of IAA at several different stages in the development of tomato fruits.　*(3 marks)*

One extract from a developing tomato fruit gave an average percentage change in length of the coleoptile segments of 120%.

*(d)* (i) Explain why it is difficult to state the concentration of IAA in this tomato fruit.　*(2 marks)*

(ii) Suggest a way in which the method described in *(c)* could be modified to find the IAA concentration in this fruit.　*(2 marks)*

*(e)* Describe the use of plant growth regulators, such as auxins, in the production of seedless fruits.　*(3 marks)*

*(Total 15 marks)*

*UCLES June 1997, Paper 1, Option 2, No. 2*

**2.** During germination, the leaves that emerge from cereal grains are protected by coleoptiles. These coleoptiles produce indole-3-acetic acid (IAA) which can be collected by placing cut coleoptiles on to blocks of agar.

*(a)* An experiment was carried out to compare the amount of IAA produced by maize coleoptile tips in light and in dark conditions. Tips were removed from coleoptiles of maize seedlings and placed on blocks of agar. Some of these were left in the light and some in the dark.

The diagram below shows how the experiment was set up and the relative amounts of IAA collected in the agar blocks at the end of the experiment.

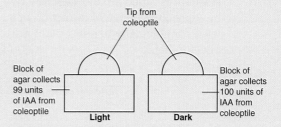

What do the results of this experiment suggest about the production of IAA?　*(2 marks)*

*(b)* The diagram below shows a second experiment carried out to investigate the movement of IAA through maize coleoptiles. Short lengths of coleoptiles were cut from maize seedlings and further cuts were made in their sides to remove a small section from each coleoptile. Agar blocks containing IAA were placed on the upper cut surfaces of these coleoptiles (block **A**). IAA that had travelled through the coleoptiles was collected in agar blocks that had been placed on their lower cut surfaces (block **B**) and in the cut sides (block **C**).

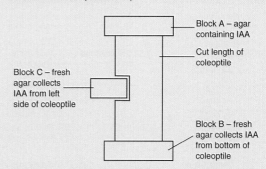

The table overleaf shows the relative amounts of IAA collected at the side and lower surface of a group of coleoptiles that have been in dark conditions and a second group that have been illuminated from the right.

589

| Agar blocks | Relative amounts of IAA collected | |
| --- | --- | --- |
| | Dark | Light from right side |
| Block **A** | 100 | 100 |
| Block **B** | 73 | 65 |
| Block **C** | 27 | 35 |

(i) Describe what the results of this investigation show about the movement of IAA through coleoptiles.
(*4 marks*)

(ii) IAA stimulates elongation of cells in the stem and coleoptile of maize. Explain how the movement of IAA helps the maize plant to carry out photosynthesis efficiently. (*2 marks*)

(c) IAA is one of a group of plant growth substances called auxins. Describe **two** ways in which knowledge of the action of auxins is used commercially to affect plant growth or development. (*4 marks*)

(*Total 12 marks*)

*Edexcel June 1997, B3, No. 6*

**3.** Many experiments have investigated the mode of action of auxins, e.g. IAA, in affecting plant growth, often using the coleoptile (shoot) tips of oat or maize seedlings. One such experiment (Experiment 1) involved cutting off a number of coleoptile tips and placing them on a layer of agar for several hours (Diagram A). These tips were then discarded and the agar cut into equal sized blocks, each of which was placed **asymmetrically** on a freshly decapitated coleoptile. The experiment was kept in total darkness for 12 hours. The angle of curvature of each coleoptile was measured as shown in Diagram B, and the mean calculated. The procedure was repeated using different numbers of coleoptile tips placed on the same area of agar.

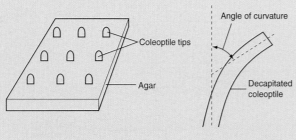

Diagram A          Diagram B

A further experiment (Experiment 2) was carried out, in which agar blocks containing a range of auxin concentrations were used instead of the coleoptile tips.

The results of both experiments are shown graphically below.

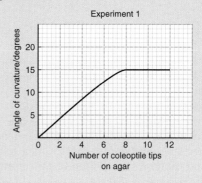

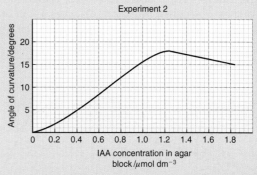

(a) Draw a diagram to show how the agar block would have been placed on the coleoptile to obtain the results shown in Diagram B.
(*1 mark*)

(b) Give the reason why the experiment was conducted in total darkness. (*1 mark*)

(c) Use the graphs of the results obtained from the two experiments to:
   (i) determine the maximum curvature obtained with
      1. coleoptile tips,
      2. auxin (IAA); (*1 mark*)
   (ii) suggest an explanation to account for the difference in results. (*2 marks*)

(d) Give explanations to account for the results of Experiment 2:
   (i) between 0 and 1.3 $\mu$mol dm$^{-3}$ IAA;
(*2 marks*)
   (ii) between 1.3 and 1.8 $\mu$mol dm$^{-3}$ IAA.
(*2 marks*)

(e) Name **two** regions of a plant other than shoot tips where auxins are produced. (*2 marks*)

(f) Although auxin is produced in shoot tips, it exerts its effect elsewhere in the plant.
   (i) Which region of the shoot is most affected by the auxin? (*1 mark*)
   (ii) How does the auxin reach this region?
(*1 mark*)
   (iii) State *two* effects auxin has on the cell in order to promote growth. (*2 marks*)

(*Total 15 marks*)

*Oxford March 1997, Paper 44, No.*

An experiment was carried out to investigate the [ef]fect of an auxin, indole acetic acid (IAA), and [gi]bberellic acid (GA₃) on the elongation of segments [of] pea stem.

[A] control group of pea segments received no added [IA]A or GA₃; other groups of pea segments were [tr]eated with equivalent quantities of IAA only, GA₃ [on]ly or both IAA and GA₃. The results are shown in [th]e graph below.

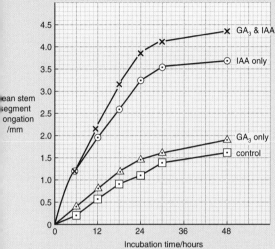

(a) Calculate the percentage increase in the mean length of the stem segments between 12 hours and 24 hours in the control. Show your working. *(2 marks)*

(b) Comment on the growth of the stem segments over 48 hours:
   (i) when IAA only was added; *(2 marks)*
   (ii) when GA₃ only was added; *(2 marks)*
   (iii) when IAA and GA₃ were added together. *(4 marks)*

(c) Explain how IAA causes stem elongation. *(3 marks)*

(d) Explain the part played by GA₃ in seed germination. *(3 marks)*

(e) IAA related substances are often used in gardening. State **one** such use. *(1 mark)*
*(Total 17 marks)*

*Oxford & Cambridge June 1997, Unit B3, No. 3*

(a) State what is meant by the term **photoperiodism**. *(2 marks)*

(b) The graphs below indicate the responses to daylength of two flowering plants.

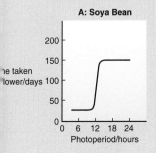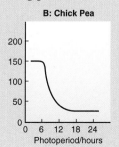

(i) Which of these plants will flower under long-day conditions? *(1 mark)*
(ii) Give a reason for your answer. *(1 mark)*

(c) (i) Where is phytochrome produced? *(1 mark)*
   (ii) Briefly describe the role of phytochrome in the flowering process. *(4 marks)*
   (iii) How does the response to phytochrome differ in short-day and long-day plants? *(2 marks)*

(d) Chrysanthemum plants in flower are produced commercially under glass throughout the year. At certain times of the year growers cover the greenhouse with black polythene for part of the day. Account for this in terms of photoperiodism. *(3 marks)*
*(Total 14 marks)*

*Oxford & Cambridge January 1998, Paper B3, No. 3*

6. (a) Ethene is produced in the tissues of fruits such as tomatoes and bananas. What is the effect of ethene on the fruit? *(1 mark)*

Ethene is synthesized from an amino acid, methionine, by a pathway involving two intermediate compounds, SAM and ACC.

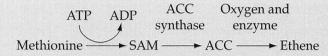

(b) Explain each of the following.
   (i) Fruits kept in an atmosphere of nitrogen gas accumulate ACC in their tissues. *(1 mark)*
   (ii) When these fruits are then brought out into the air, ethene is produced much more rapidly than in fruit that has been kept in air all the time. *(1 mark)*

(c) What would be the effect on tomatoes of treating them with a specific inhibitor of the enzyme ACC synthase? Explain your answer. *(2 marks)*

(d) Suggest why, when a ripe banana is put in the same container as green tomatoes, the tomatoes turn red. *(1 mark)*
*(Total 6 marks)*

*NEAB June 1997, Paper BY07, No. 5*

Testing the purity of water

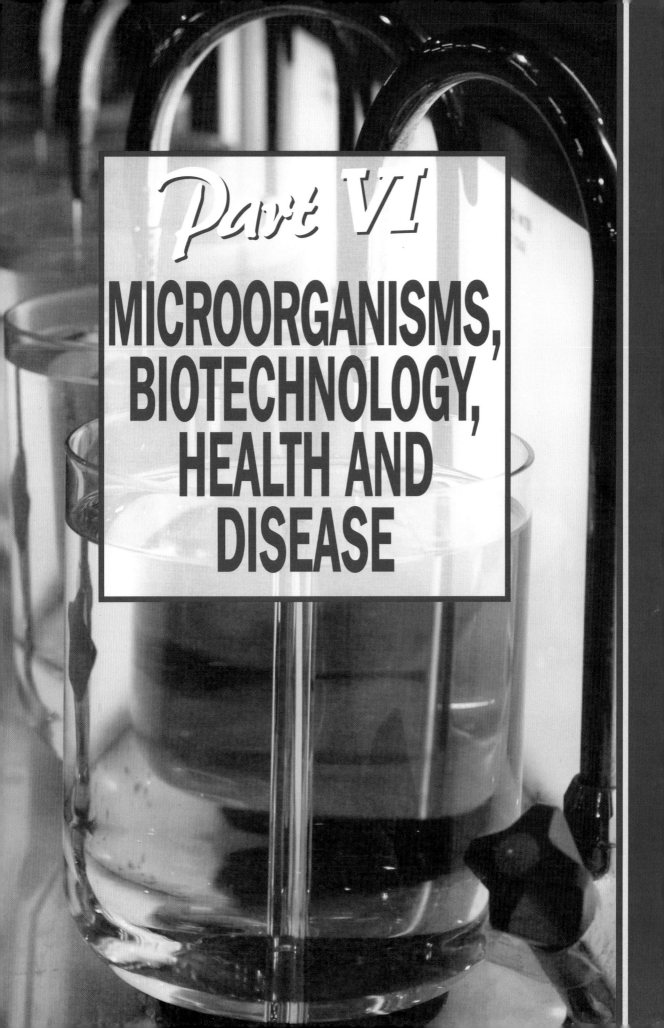

# Part VI

# MICROORGANISMS, BIOTECHNOLOGY, HEALTH AND DISEASE

# 30 Biotechnology

Biotechnology is the application of scientific and engineering principles to the production of materials by biological agents. Given its recent wide publicity, one could be forgiven for thinking it was a new branch of science. While there is no doubt that recent technological and biochemical advances have led to considerable developments in biotechnology, its origins go back a long way. Food for human consumption has always been vulnerable to spoilage by microorganisms. Ancient civilizations probably found that normally detrimental microbial contamination occasionally conferred some benefit: improved flavour or better preservation for instance. In this way beers would have been developed from 'spoilt' grain and wine from 'spoilt' fruit. Contamination of the alcohol by a different agent led to the production of vinegar which was then used to preserve food. Cheese, butter and yoghurt all resulted from various microbial contaminations of milk.

The modern biotechnology industry had its origins in the First World War. A naval blockade deprived Germany of the supply of vegetable fats necessary for the production of glycerol from which explosives were made. They turned to the fermentation of plant material by yeast as an alternative source. At the same time, the British were using *Clostridium acetobutylicum* to produce acetone and butanol as part of their war effort. In a similar way, the Second World War prompted the mass production of the antibiotic penicillin (discovered by Alexander Fleming in 1929) using *Penicillium notatum*.

Many other chemicals were produced thereafter by use of fermentation techniques, but it was in the 1980s that biotechnology underwent major expansion. This was almost entirely due to the development of **recombinant DNA technology** (Section 7.7.1).

## 30.1 Microorganisms

The name 'microorganism' is a general descriptive term rather than a specific scientific one. It refers to those organisms which are not clearly visible to the naked eye. As such it includes representatives from three of the biological kingdoms, namely all the Prokaryotae, and some members of the Protoctista and the Fungi, as well as all viruses whose place in biological classification is still somewhat uncertain. If microorganisms share the feature of small size, they have little else in common,

594

being very varied in structure and function. Despite the lack of any real biological coherence, the term is nevertheless a convenient, and well-understood, one.

If the structure and functions of microorganisms are diverse, so too are their effects. On the one hand, they are beneficial, indeed essential, to our continued existence; on the other hand they are frequently the cause of our demise. Their role in decomposition and recycling is essential to life, while their use in the production of bread, wine, beer and cheese has benefited mankind since ancient times. More recently humans have utilized microorganisms in the production of antibiotics, hormones, fuels and other materials. Their role in genetic engineering may yet prove to be their most significant.

On the other hand, microorganisms are the cause of fatal diseases such as cholera, typhoid, malaria, tuberculosis, influenza and AIDS. They are also a major contributor to famine through being agents of plant disease – the Irish potato famine of 1845–7 (caused by the fungus *Phytophthora infestans*) killed one million people through starvation. Their role in spoiling stored food further exacerbates the problem of feeding the world's population.

Our love–hate relationship with microorganisms may have become more affectionate in recent years as we have developed the biotechnology to exploit the activities of these minute life forms, but the capacity of most microorganisms to evolve rapidly and so thwart our attempts to eradicate the diseases they cause may prevent us becoming completely won over by them. The structure and classification of microorganisms is detailed in chapter 5.

## 30.2   Growth of microorganisms

Microorganisms (microbes) are found in every ecological niche – from deepest ocean to the limits of the stratosphere, from hot springs to the frozen poles. They are small, easily dispersed and quickly multiply given a suitable environment. They grow on a wide diversity of substrates making them ideal subjects for commercial application. Each species has its own optimum conditions within which it grows best.

### 30.2.1 Factors affecting growth

The factors which affect the growth of microorganisms are equally applicable to the growth of plant and animal cell cultures.

*Nutrients*
Growth depends upon both the types of nutrients available and their concentration. Cells are largely made up of the four elements carbon, hydrogen, oxygen and nitrogen with smaller, but significant, quantities of phosphorus and sulphur. Accounting as they do for 90% of the cell's dry mass, all six elements are essential for growth.

Needed in smaller quantities, but no less important, are the metallic elements calcium, potassium, magnesium and iron, sometimes known as **macronutrients**. Required in smaller

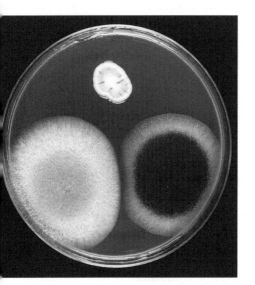
icroorganisms growing on a nutrient media

amounts still are the **micronutrients (trace elements)**: manganese, cobalt, zinc, copper and molybdenum – indeed not all may be essential to some species. A further group of chemicals, loosely termed **growth factors**, are also needed. These fall into three categories:

1. Vitamins

2. Amino acids

3. Purines and pyrimidines

Up to a point, the more concentrated a nutrient the greater the rate of growth, but as other factors become limiting the addition of further nutrients has no beneficial effect. More details of the nutrients used in culturing cells are given in Section 30.2.4.

*Temperature*
As all growth is governed by enzymes and these operate only within a relatively narrow range of temperature, cells are similarly affected by it. If the temperature falls too low, the rate of enzyme-catalysed reactions becomes too slow to sustain growth; if too high, the denaturation of enzymes causes death. Most cells grow best within the range 20–45 °C although some species can grow at temperatures as low as − 5 °C, while others do so at 90 °C. Three groups are recognized according to their preferred temperature range:

1. **Psychrophiles** (e.g. *Bacillus globisporus*) – These have optimum growth temperatures below 20 °C, many continuing to grow at temperatures down to 0 °C.

2. **Mesophiles** (e.g. *Escherichia coli*) – These have optimum growth temperatures in the range 20–40 °C.

3. **Thermophiles** (e.g. the alga *Cyanidium caldarium*) – These have optimum growth temperatures in excess of 45 °C, a few surviving in temperatures as high as 90 °C. These cells have enzymes which are unusual in not being denatured at high temperatures.

*pH*
Microorganisms are able to tolerate a wider range of pH than plant and animal cells, some species growing in an environment as acid as pH 2.5, others in one as alkaline as pH 9. Microorganisms preferring acid conditions, e.g. *Thiobacillus thio oxidans*, are termed **acidophiles**.

*Oxygen*
Many microorganisms are aerobic, requiring molecular oxygen for growth at all times: these are termed **obligate aerobes**. Some while growing better in the presence of oxygen, can nevertheless survive in its absence; these are called **facultative anaerobes**. Others find oxygen toxic and do not grow well in its presence: these are the **obligate anaerobes**. Some microorganisms, while tolerating oxygen, nevertheless grow better when its concentration is very low. These are termed **microaerophiles**.

*Osmotic factors*
All microorganisms require water for growth. In most cases this is absorbed osmotically from the environment, although pinocytosis is used in certain protozoa and all groups produce a

## PROJECT

We are advised to keep sugar-reduced jam in the fridge once it has been opened. Investigate the keeping qualities of various preserves.

little water as a product of aerobic respiration. To ensure absorption, the water potential of the external environment must be less negative (higher) than the cell contents. For this reason most microorganisms cannot grow in environments with a high solute concentration – a fact made use of in preserving foods, e.g. salting of meat and fish, bottling of jam and fruit in sugar. A few, called **halophiles**, can survive, however, in conditions of high salt concentration.

*Pressure*
Although pressure is not a major factor affecting growth in most microorganisms, a few species inhabiting the ocean depths can grow under immense pressure. Some of these **barophiles** cannot grow in surface waters where the pressure is too low for their survival.

*Light*
Photosynthetic microorganisms require an adequate supply of light to sustain growth.

*Water*
In common with all organisms, microorganisms require water for a variety of functions. In addition, photosynthetic microorganisms use it as a source of hydrogen to reduce carbon dioxide. Chemoautotrophs may use alternative inorganic hydrogen sources, e.g. hydrogen sulphide, for this purpose.

### 30.2.2 Measurement of growth

The growth rate of microorganisms in liquid culture (broth) can be estimated in a number of ways. A **haemocytometer** (so-called because it was originally used to count blood cells) is a large microscope slide on the surface of which is etched one or more grids of known dimensions (usually 25 squares each of side 0.2 mm). A coverslip is placed over the centre part of the slide and supported in such a way that there is a set depth (usually 0.1 mm) between it and the portion of the slide on which the grid is marked. The volume of liquid above one small square can thus be calculated (0.2 mm × 0.2 mm × 0.1 mm = 0.004 mm$^3$). If a drop of culture containing the cells is placed on the haemocytometer and the coverslip is properly positioned, the number of cells in 0.004 mm$^3$ of broth can be counted. Many squares should be counted and the average found to obtain more reliable results. The number of cells in 1 mm$^3$ or 1 cm$^3$ can be found by multiplying by an appropriate factor (in our example 250 × and 250 000 × respectively). Where the number of cells is too large to count effectively, the broth should first be diluted by a suitable amount. The final estimate can then be calculated by multiplying the average count by the dilution factor used.

The haemocytometer provides a **total count** of all cells, whether living or dead. Often it is more useful to be able to estimate only the number of living cells in a culture. A technique known as **dilution plating** is adopted for this. Firstly a set of **serial dilutions** are made up. This is done by taking 1 cm$^3$ of the original culture broth and placing it into 9 cm$^3$ of distilled water in a second tube and mixing it thoroughly. This solution is now one-tenth of the concentration of the original. Adding 1 cm$^3$ of this diluted solution to 9 cm$^3$ of distilled water and mixing gives a one-hundredth concentration. Continuing this five or six more time provides a range of dilutions. 1 cm$^3$ of each dilution is then added to a separate agar plate, spread evenly over it, and left to incubate at a suitable temperature for a few days. Each living ce (but only living cells), will give rise to a visible colony growing on the agar plate. Some plates will have so many colonies that separate ones cannot be identified, others will have no colonies at all. At one dilution, however, the number of colonies will number 5–50. The actual number is counted and multiplied by the dilution factor to give the number of **living** cells in 1 cm$^3$ of the original culture. This is called a **viable count**.

The more a broth culture of microorganisms grows, the more turbid (cloudy) it becomes owing to the density of cells in it. Culture growth can hence be measured by a **photometric method** using a colorimeter – an instrument which measures the **optical density** (amount of light absorbed) of a solution. This method provides a measure of the relative growth rate of different solutions. The **actual** growth can be calculated using a calibration graph of a known mass/number of microorganisms in a given volume of water against optical density.

The most accurate method of estimating growth rate is to remove samples from a large broth culture at regular intervals. These samples are filtered, dried and then weighed. The mass of each sample can then be plotted against time to give a graph of growth rate.

A simple, but far less accurate, method is to measure the diameter of a fungal or bacterial colony growing on a solid medium at regular time intervals.

### 30.2.3 Growth patterns

The growth of a culture of individual cells, e.g. of unicellular yeasts, protozoa or bacteria is, in effect, the growth of a population and follows the pattern described in Section 12.8.2. The typical bacterial growth curve for a batch culture, illustrate in Fig. 30.1, consists of four phases:

1. **The lag phase** – This is the period after **inoculation** (the addition of cells to the nutrient medium) during which the growth rate increases towards its maximum. Growth during th time is slow initially as the bacteria adapt to produce the necessary enzymes needed to utilize the nutrient medium. The rate of cell division gradually increases during this phase.

2. **The exponential (logarithmic) phase** – During this period, with nutrients in good supply and few waste products being produced, the rate of cell division is at its maximum, cells sometimes dividing as frequently as every 10 minutes. The culture is in a state of **balanced growth** with the doubling time, cell protein content and cell size all remaining constant.

3. **The stationary phase** – As nutrients are used up and toxic waste products accumulate, the rate of growth slows. The changed composition of the medium results in the production of cells of various sizes with a different chemical make-up. They are in a state of **unbalanced growth**. For the total count, this section of the graph is horizontal because the rate at which new cells are produced is equal to the rate at which dead ones are broken down.

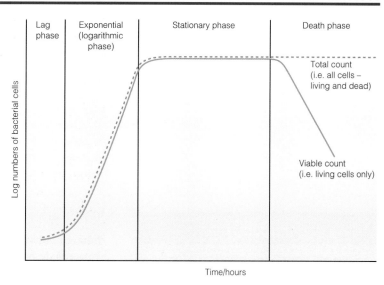

Fig. 30.1 Bacterial growth curve

**4. The death phase** – While the total number of cells remains constant, the number of living ones diminishes as an ever-increasing number die from a lack of the nutrients necessary to produce cellular energy, or because of poisoning by their own toxic wastes.

### 30.2.4 Culture media

The correct balance of nutrients, an appropriate pH and a suitable medium are essential to microbial growth.

The medium itself may be liquid (broth) or solid. Solid media are usually based upon **agar**, a seaweed extract which is metabolically inert and which dissolves in hot water but solidifies upon cooling. The more agar, the more solid is the resulting jelly. Any medium composed to satisfy the demands of a single species is called a **minimal medium**. One which provides the nutrients for a small group of microorganisms with similar requirements, e.g. acidophiles, is known as a **narrow spectrum medium**, whereas a medium for general purposes, designed to grow as wide a range of microorganisms as possible, is called a **broad spectrum medium**. It is possible to select for the growth of specific types of organisms by use of **selective media,** which permit growth of only a single species. The composition of a typical broad spectrum medium is given in Table 30.1.

### 30.2.5 Aseptic conditions

Both in the laboratory and on an industrial scale, pure cultures of a single type of microorganism need to be grown free from contamination with others.

A number of techniques are used to sterilize equipment, instruments, media and other materials. Heat, either passing through a flame, dry heating in an oven, or using water in an autoclave (a type of pressure cooker) is effective in sterilizing instruments, small vessels and culture media. Where heating may affect the medium, it may be filtered free of microorganisms using especially fine filters. Ultra-violet light can be used on equipment or even whole rooms. Certain other equipment may be sterilized using a suitable disinfectant, e.g. hypochlorite.

TABLE 30.1 **A typical broad spectrum medium**

| Ingredient | Quantity | Source of |
|---|---|---|
| Water | 1.0 dm³ | Metabolic and osmotic water, hydrogen and oxygen |
| Glucose | 5 g | Carbohydrate energy source |
| Yeast extract | 5 g | Organic nitrogen, organic growth factors |
| Dipotassium hydrogen phosphate | 1 g | Potassium and phosphorus |
| Magnesium sulphate | 250 mg | Magnesium and sulphur |
| Iron (II) sulphate | 10 mg | Iron and sulphur |
| Calcium chloride | 10 mg | Calcium and chloride |
| Cobalt, copper, manganese, molybdenum and zinc salts | trace | Metallic ion trace elements |

## 30.3 Industrial fermenters and fermentation

Much of modern biotechnology involves the large-scale production of substances by growing specific microorganisms in a large container known as a fermenter. Fermentation should strictly refer to a biological process which occurs in the absence of oxygen. However, the word is taken to include aerobic processes – indeed the supply of adequate oxygen is a major design feature of the modern fermenter.

### 30.3.1 Batch versus continuous cultivation

In **batch cultivation**, the necessary nutrient medium and the appropriate microorganisms are added to the fermenter and the process allowed to proceed. During the fermentation, air is added if it is needed and waste gases are removed. Growth is allowed to continue up to a specific point at which the fermenter is emptied and the product extracted. The fermenter is then cleaned and sterilized in readiness for the next batch.

With **continuous cultivation**, once the fermenter is set up, the used medium and products are continuously removed. The raw materials are also added throughout and the process can therefore continue, sometimes for many weeks.

The continuous process has the advantage of being quicker because it removes the need to empty, clean and refill the fermenter as regularly and hence ensures an almost continuous yield. In addition, by adjusting the nutrients added, the rate of growth can be maintained at the constant level which provides the maximum yield of product. Continuous cultivation is, however, only suited to the production of biomass or metabolites which are associated with growth. **Secondary metabolites**, like antibiotics, which are produced when growth is past its maximum, need to be manufactured by the batch process. The organisms used to produce antibiotics are in any case too unstable for growth by continuous fermentation. In addition, continuous fermentation requires sophisticated monitoring technology and highly trained staff to operate efficiently.

### 30.3.2 Fermenter design

The basic design of a **stirred-tank fermenter** is shown in Fig. 30.2. It consists of a large stainless steel vessel with a capacity of up to 500 000 dm$^3$ around which is a jacket of circulating water used to control the temperature within the fermenter. An agitator, comprising a series of flat blades which can be rotated is incorporated. This ensures that the contents are thoroughly mixed, thus bringing nutrients into contact with the microorganisms and preventing the cells settling out at the bottom.

Where oxygen is required, air is forced in at the bottom of the tank through a ring containing many small holes – a process known as **sparging**. To assist aeration, increased turbulence may be achieved by adding baffles to the walls of the fermentation vessel. A series of openings, or **ports**, through which materials can be introduced or withdrawn, is provided. The **harvest line**

rmenter for cloned protein

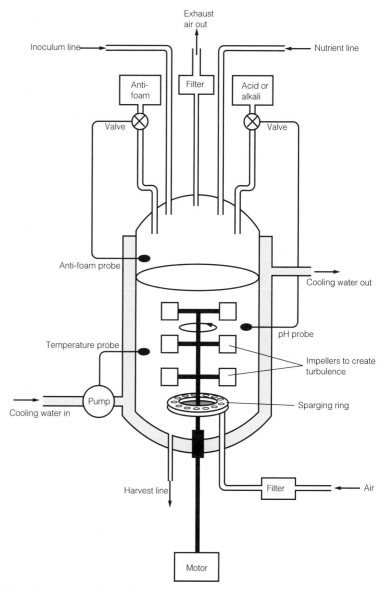

Fig. 30.2 A stirred-tank fermenter

used to extract culture medium. An outlet to remove air and waste gases is needed, as well as one to allow small samples of the culture medium to be removed for analysis. Inlet tubes permit nutrients to be provided and, as the pH changes during fermentation, allow acid or base to be added to maintain the optimum pH. With air being forced into the medium, chemicals often need to be added to reduce foaming. Finally, it is essential to have an **inoculation port** through which the initial inoculum of cells can be introduced once the required conditions in the fermenter are achieved. **Probes**, which constantly register the temperature and pH within the vessel, are used to indicate when adjustments to these factors are necessary.

The stirred-tank fermenter is a well-tried and tested design used extensively in the fermentation industry. It is, however, relatively costly to run, largely as a consequence of the energy needed to drive the agitators and introduce the compressed air.

Alternatives have therefore been designed where the air forced into the vessel to provide oxygen is used to circulate the contents, thus making an agitator unnecessary.

One such design, the **pressure-cycle fermenter**, is of two types. In the **air-lift type** the air is introduced centrally at the bottom making the medium less dense. It therefore rises throug a central column in the vessel to the top where it escapes. The now more dense medium descends around the sides of the vessel to complete the cycle (Fig. 30.3a). Higher pressure at the bottom of the vessel increases solubility of oxygen, while lower pressure at the top decreases solubility of carbon dioxide, whic as a consequence comes out of solution. In the **deep-shaft type**, the principle is similar but the air is introduced at the top (Fig. 30.3b). This has the advantage of giving a more even delivery o oxygen to the microorganisms.

The **tower-** or **bubble-column** (a variety of the air-lift fermenter) has horizontal rather than vertical divisions (Fig. 30.3c). This allows conditions in each section to be maintained a different levels if necessary. A microorganism being carried up from the bottom may therefore pass from a high pH and low temperature to a lower pH and higher temperature to suit each phase of its growth.

While all three types can be used continuously, only the air-lift fermenter is used for batch processing. All types must be taller than the conventional stirred-tank vessel to operate effectively.

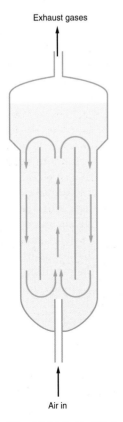

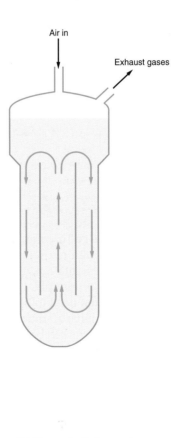

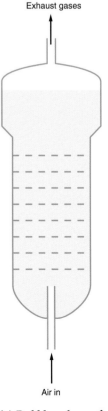

*Fig. 30.3(a) Air-lift fermenter*       *(b) Deep-shaft fermenter*       *(c) Bubble-column fermente*

### 30.3.3 The operation and control of fermenters

There are two main problems associated with setting up a large-scale fermentation process. Firstly, the inoculum containing the desired strain of microorganism has to be obtained in sufficient quantity; if too little is added to the fermenter, the lag phase is unacceptably long, making the process uneconomic. A small-scale fermentation is set up in a vessel as small as $10 \, cm^3$, using frozen culture stock. This is then added to flasks, containing the appropriate nutrient medium, of increasing capacity, e.g. $300 \, cm^3$, $3000 \, cm^3$, $30 \, 000$ $cm^3$, etc., until the final capacity of the end fermentation vessel is reached. This is known as the **fermenter train**. The problem is that the operational conditions that give the optimum yield in a $300 \, cm^3$ fermentation flask are often very different from those for a $300 \, 000 \, cm^3$ vessel.

The other main problem arises from the fact that the microorganisms used in fermenters have been genetically selected for the properties (e.g. a high product yield) which make them suitable for use in a large-scale fermenter. They are often enfeebled mutant strains which have resulted from deliberately induced mutanogenesis. As efficient production depends upon rapid growth, i.e. many generations of the microorganism in a short period, there is a tendency for the strain to mutate naturally, often reverting to the parent type which has less desirable properties. One way around the problem is to prevent the microorganism producing the desired product until the final fermentation. This reduces the selection pressure which might alter the gene responsible for the product, but is not always feasible. The use of genetically engineered stock (Section 7.7) has the advantage that it is much easier to express ('switch on') the desired gene at the appropriate time by use of chemical triggers called **promoters**.

Once a sufficient quantity of the inoculum has been produced, usually between 1% and 10% of the total medium, it is added to the fermenter only after the medium within it is of the correct composition and at the desired temperature and pH. The problem now is to maintain all conditions throughout the fermentation. To achieve this the levels of various nutrients, oxygen, pH and temperature are constantly monitored using probes and the information is fed to a computer for analysis, along with information on the composition of the exhaust gases. The necessary corrective changes can then be made. These may be complex – for example, an increase in oxygen uptake could be countered by reducing the air supply, the pressure within the vessel, the nutrient levels or the agitator speed. Which one is selected has implications for other factors and the choice therefore needs to be made advisedly. While the temperature of the medium may need to be increased initially by piping steam through it, once fermentation is under way the heat generated by the microorganisms necessitates continuous cooling by the water jacket around the vessel.

The processes involved in recovering the product are called **downstream processing**. This often involves separation of the cells from the medium which may be achieved in a number of ways:

1. **Settlement** – The cells may readily settle once agitation and sparging cease. The process can be accelerated by the addition of **flocculating agents**, many of which work by neutralizing the charges on the cells which otherwise keep them in suspension by electrostatic repulsion.

2. **Centrifugation** – The contents of the fermenter are spun at high speed in a centrifuge causing the cells to settle out. Continuous centrifugation is now possible.

3. **Ultrafiltration** – The fermenter contents are forced through filters with a pore size less than $0.5\mu m$ which thereby trap cells, allowing only liquid through. Some extracellular protein may also be retained.

Where the desired products are the entire cells themselves, these need only be washed, dried and compacted to complete the process. Where the product is contained within the cells, these must be disrupted by some means, the cell debris removed (e.g. by centrifugation or ultrafiltration), and the desired chemical recovered using precipitation, chromatographic or solvent extraction techniques. Where the product lies in the fermentation liquor rather than the cells, this is separated from unwanted enzymes and metabolites, again by precipitation, chromatography or solvent extraction as appropriate.

### 30.3.4 Sterilization during and after fermentation

The need for aseptic conditions and the basic mechanisms for achieving them were discussed in Section 30.2.5. In industrial fermentation this presents many practical problems considering that not only a very large vessel needs to be sterilized, but also all associated pipework and probes as well as the nutrients, air-supply, and other agents added during the process.

The equipment is designed so that any nooks and crannies which might harbour microorganisms are minimized. The vessel is highly polished, for example, and all components are designed to allow easy access by sterilizing agents. Having been thoroughly washed all equipment is steam sterilized.

The initial nutrient medium may be sterilized in the fermenter by heating it; any added later may be sterilized by heating *en route* to the vessel, as can all other liquid additions. Concentrated acids and alkalis used to adjust the pH may be so inhospitable to contaminating organisms as not to warrant sterilization.

Filtration is used to remove potential contaminants from the air supply although bacteriophages are small enough to pass through – with disastrous consequences. Heat treatment of incoming air can alleviate this problem. The exhaust air is also sterilized to prevent potentially harmful microorganisms being introduced into the atmosphere.

### 30.3.5 Immobilization of cells and enzymes

One problem with the fermentation processes described so far is that at some point the cell culture is removed and discarded. This is fine when the cells are the desired product, but if it is a

## PROJECT

**When enzymes are immobilized by entrapment they appear to be less prone to denaturing at high temperatures**

1. From this statement suggest a testable hypothesis.

2. Test your hypothesis by comparing the activity of an enzyme under normal and immobilized conditions.

metabolite they produce that is required, their removal takes away the manufacturing source, which then needs to be replaced. Any mechanism for immobilizing the microorganism and/or the enzymes they produce improves the economics of the process. The idea is not a new one – vinegar manufacture and some stages of sewage treatment have used the technique for a century or more.

There are three basic methods of immobilization:

**1. Entrapment** – Cells or enzyme molecules are trapped in a suitable meshwork of inert material, e.g. collagen, cellulose, carrageenan, agar, gelatin, polystyrene.

**2. Binding** – Cells or enzyme molecules become physically attached to the surface of a suitable material, e.g. sand or gravel.

**3. Cross-linking** – Cells or enzyme molecules are chemically bonded to a suitable chemical matrix, e.g. glutaraldehyde.

However immobilized, the cells or enzymes are made into small beads which are then either packed into columns or kept in the nutrient medium. The nutrient can be continually added and the product removed without frequent removal of the microorganisms/enzymes. Although the process cannot be continued indefinitely as impurities may accumulate, the semi-continuous nature of the process is a major advantage.

Other advantages include:

**1.** With whole cell immobilization, a number of enzymes can act together at the same time in a single process.

**2.** With enzyme immobilization, the enzyme can be used repeatedly as it is not lost in the process making it more economic, especially where the enzyme is expensive.

**3.** Enzymes are vulnerable to changes in temperature and pH. The matrix on/in which they are trapped can buffer them against such fluctuations.

**4.** The immobilized enzymes and cells, being held in place, cannot contaminate the substance being produced leading to a purer product.

## 30.4 Biotechnology and food production

### Did you know?

The total bread market in Britain is worth about £3000 million a year.

## PROJECT

Investigate the effect of Vitamin C on the expansion of bread dough.

Until Louis Pasteur showed in 1857 that wine fermentation was the consequence of microbial activity, no one had been aware of the role that microorganisms played in the manufacture of some foods. With Pasteur's discovery came further development of the use of microorganisms in food production, an expansion which continues today.

### 30.4.1 Baking

The use of yeasts in food production is the oldest and most extensive contribution made by any group of microorganisms. In bread-making, cereal grain is crushed to form flour, thus exposing the stored starch. Water is added (making a dough) to

# BIOLOGY AROUND US

## Commercial uses of enzymes

Immobilised microbial cell pellets in a packed reactor column used to carry out biotransformations

For many years humans have used enzymes to produce bread, cheese, wine, beer and yoghurts but now they have more diverse commercial applications and the sale of enzymes is a multi-billion pound industry.

The commonest sources of these enzymes are bacteria, yeasts and other fungi. The enzymes may be released from the microbial cell, extracted from it when it is broken or the whole cell may be used. Enzymes or whole cells are usually used in an immobilized form so that the enzyme can be reused many times.

Enzymes are very specific and can be used to produce pure products, often more cheaply than by traditional methods. They may also require less energy and result in less pollution.

The specificity of enzymes enables them to be used for sensitive analytical techniques, such as detecting glucose or cholesterol in blood and the enzyme thermolysin is used to produce aspartame, a sweetener sold as *Canderel* and *Nutrasweet*, much more cheaply than by chemical processes.

There is a great demand by the food industry for high fructose syrups which are as sweet as sucrose and which contain glucose and fructose in approximately equal amounts. These syrups are now produced from starch (itself often a waste product of the food industry) using a combination of four enzymes: α-amylase, glucoamylase, pullulanase and glucose isomerase. The first three catalyze the conversion of starch to glucose and then the glucose isomerase converts the glucose to a 50 : 50 mixture of glucose and fructose.

On a commercial scale enzymes are now providing products for pharmaceutical, agrochemical, food, cosmetic and analytical uses. They are used to manufacture semi-synthetic antibiotics, to degrade wastes and in genetic engineering.

activate the natural enzymes, e.g. amylases, in the flour, which then hydrolyse the starch via maltose into glucose. Yeast, *Saccharomyces cerevisiae*, is added which uses the glucose as a respiratory substrate, producing carbon dioxide. This carbon dioxide forms small bubbles which become trapped in the dough; upon baking in an oven these expand giving the bread a light texture. Dough is often kneaded – a process which traps air within it. This not only helps to lighten the bread directly but also provides a source of oxygen so that the yeast can respire aerobically, producing a greater quantity of carbon dioxide. Some anaerobic respiration nevertheless takes place and the alcohol produced is evaporated during baking.

### 30.4.2 Beer and wine production

Fermentation by yeasts produces alcohol according to the equation:

$$C_6H_{12}O_6 \longrightarrow 2C_2H_5OH + 2CO_2$$

hexose sugar    ethanol    carbon dioxide

Some alcohol produced in this way is for industrial use, but much goes to make beverages like beers and wines which may then be

rewing beer

distilled to form spirits. The variety of such beverages is immense and depends largely on the source of the sugar and the type of yeast used to ferment it. Various additives further increase the diversity of alcoholic drinks.

To make wine, the sugar fermented is glucose obtained directly from grapes, whereas beers are made by fermenting glucose obtained from cereal grain (usually barley) which results from the breakdown of starch in the grain. The yeast used in wine production is often *Saccharomyces ellipsoideus* as this variety can tolerate the higher alcohol levels encountered in wines. Even more tolerant to high alcohol levels are *S. fermentati* and *S. beticus* and these are primarily used in making sherry. Beers are of two basic types – top fermenting varieties of yeast such as *S. cerevisiae* produce a typical British 'bitter' while *S. carlsbergensis*, a bottom fermenting variety, is used to make lager. In beer production, the barley grain is first malted by soaking it in water for 2–3 days. The grain is then spread on concrete floors and allowed to germinate (about 10 days), during which time the natural amylases and maltases in the grain start to convert starch to glucose. This process is stopped by drying the grain and storing it – a process called **kilning** or **roasting**. The higher the temperature during this process, the darker the resulting beer. The germinated grain is often crushed during this stage. The dried, crushed germinated grain is now added to water and heated to the desired temperature – **mashing**. During mashing the remaining starch is converted to sugar to produce a liquid called **wort**. Yeast is added to the wort to convert it to alcohol, as well as hops and other additives, e.g. caramel, which are used to give each beer its characteristic flavour and colour.

The fermentation itself takes place in large deep tanks of around 500 000 dm³ capacity. No air is introduced as anaerobic respiration is the aim. Although traditionally a batch process, beer production can also be carried out using continuous fermentation. This is more economic and it also allows the carbon dioxide to be collected – a valuable by-product when converted to dry-ice.

The beer is finally separated from the yeast and clarified, and carbon dioxide is added. Sometimes the beer is pasteurized to extend its shelf-life. A good traditional beer, however, retains some yeast in the enclosed barrel which produces the carbon dioxide naturally. Such beers are, for obvious reasons, termed 'live' beers.

### 30.4.3 Dairy products

Microorganisms have long been exploited in the dairy industry as a means of preserving milk. A large number of different products are manufactured, which fall into three main categories: cheese, yoghurt and butter.

*Cheese manufacture*
An ancient process, cheese-making has altered little over the years. A group of bacteria known as **lactic acid bacteria** are used to ferment the lactose in milk to lactic acid according to the equation:

$$C_{12}H_{22}O_{11} + H_2O \longrightarrow 4CH_3CHOHCOOH$$
lactose　　　　water　　　　　　　　　　lactic acid

Cheese making

Most commercially used lactic acid bacteria are species of two genera – *Lactobacillus* and *Streptococcus*.

Cheese production begins with the pasteurization of raw milk which is then cooled to around 30 °C before a starter culture of the required lactic acid bacteria is added. The resultant fall in pH due to the bacterial activity causes the milk to separate into a solid **curd** and a liquid **whey** in a process called **curdling**. The addition of **rennet** at this stage encourages the casein in the milk to coagulate, aiding curd formation. Originally extracted from the stomachs of calves slaughtered for food, rennet has now largely been replaced by **chymosin**, a similar enzyme produced by genetically engineered yeast. The whey is drained off and may be used to feed animals. The curd is heated in the range 32–42 °C and some salt added before being pressed into moulds for a period of time which varies according to cheese type.

The ripening of the cheese allows flavour to develop as a result of the action of other milk enzymes or deliberately introduced microorganisms. In blue cheese, for example, *Penicillium* spp. are added. The duration of ripening varies, with Caerphilly taking just a fortnight in contrast to a year required for mature Cheddar. Whereas hard cheeses ripen owing to the activity of lactic acid bacteria throughout the cheese, in soft cheeses it is fungi growing on the surface which are responsible.

*Yoghurt manufacture*
Yoghurt is made from pasteurized milk with much of the fat removed, and its production also depends on lactic acid bacteria in particular *Lactobacillus bulgaricus* and *Streptococcus thermophilus*. These are added to the milk in equal quantity and incubated at around 45 °C for 5 hours, during which time the pH falls to around 4.0. Cooling prevents further fermentation and fruit or flavourings can then be added as required.

*Butter manufacture*
Not essentially a process requiring microorganisms, butter production is nevertheless frequently assisted by the addition to cream of *Streptococcus lactis* and *Leuconostoc cremoris* which help to sour it, give flavour and aid the separation of the butterfat. Churning of this butterfat produces the final product.

### 30.4.4 Production of mycoprotein

Mycoprotein is produced from the fungus *Fusarium graminearum* which is grown by continuous culture techniques in 1300 litre fermenters in aerobic conditions at 30 °C and pH 6. The fungus requires a carbon and nitrogen source as well as other substances such as salts and vitamins. The carbon source is glucose syrup often derived from wheat or maize starch; gaseous ammonia provides the nitrogen. Choline is added to increase the length of the hyphae and various salts and vitamins such as biotin are also required. The mycelium which is produced has a high RNA content of around 10% which would make it unsuitable for consumption by humans and other animals. The content may be reduced to about 2% by heat treatment and the use of ribonucleases. The mycelium is then filtered to form a 'filter cake' which may be stored at 18 °C for long periods.

## BIOLOGY AROUND US

# Enzymes and fruit juice production

Pectin is a substance which helps to hold plant cell walls together. As a fruit ripens the plant produces proteolytic enzymes which convert the insoluble protopectin of the unripe fruit into more soluble forms, causing the fruit to soften. When fruits are mashed and pressed to form juices these more soluble forms of pectin enter the juice, making it cloudy and causing the colour and flavour to deteriorate. They also increase the viscosity of the juice itself, making it difficult to obtain optimal yields. For fruit juice manufacturers the addition of industrial pectinases between mashing and pressing causes complete depectinization so that a good quality, clear juice is obtained which retains its stability when concentrated. Producers may also use other enzymes such as starch-splitting enzymes to reduce cloudiness, especially with apples, cellulases to improve juice yield and colour, and arabanase to reduce the haze caused by the polysaccharide araban passing from the cell walls into the extracted juice.

## PROJECT

### The production of fruit juices has been greatly improved by the addition of pectinase

1. Compare the yields of fruit juice from apples with and without the addition of pectinase.

2. Determine the optimum, and thus the most economical, concentration of pectinase.

Although mycoprotein itself has little flavour its hyphae give it a fibrous texture, similar to meat, and it can be easily flavoured to resemble, for example, chicken. Since mycoprotein contains fibre and only about half the fat content of meat it might be considered to be a healthy alternative.

### 30.4.5 Enzymes associated with the food industry

Many enzymes used in the food industry are produced by microorganisms. Some examples are given in Table 30.2.

TABLE 30.2 **Some enzymes produced by microorganisms used in the food industry**

| Enzyme | Examples of microorganisms involved | Application |
|---|---|---|
| $\alpha$-Amylases | *Aspergillus oryzae* | Breakdown of starch in beer production<br>Improving of flour<br>Preparation of glucose syrup<br>Thickening of canned sauces |
| $\beta$-Glucanase | *Bacillus subtilis* | Beer production |
| Glucose isomerase | *Bacillus coagulans* | Sweetener for soft drinks<br>Cake fillings |
| Lactase | *Kluyveromyces* spp. | Lactose removal from whey<br>Sweetener for milk drinks |
| Lipase | *Candida* spp. | Flavour development in cheese |
| Pectinase | *Aspergillus* spp. | Clearing of wines and fruit juices |
| Protease | *Bacillus subtilis* | Meat tenderizers |
| Pullulanase | *Klebsiella aerogenes* | Soft ice cream manufacture |
| Sucrase | *Saccharomyces* spp. | Confectionery production |

## 30.5  Biotechnology and pharmaceuticals

Since the antibiotic penicillin was first produced on a large scale in the 1940s, there has been a considerable expansion in the use of biotechnology to produce a range of antibiotics, hormones and other pharmaceuticals.

### 30.5.1 Antibiotics

Antibiotics are chemical substances produced by microorganisms which are effective in dilute solution in preventing the spread of other microorganisms. Most inhibit growth rather than kill the microorganisms on which they act. Some, like **penicillin**, are only effective on relatively few pathogens – **narrow spectrum antibiotics**, while others, e.g. **chloramphenicol**, will inhibit the growth of a wide variety of pathogens – **broad spectrum antibiotics**. Although around 5000 antibiotics have been discovered only 100 have proved medically and commercially viable.

Antibiotics are made when growth of the producer organism is slowing down rather than when it is at its maximum. They are therefore secondary metabolites and their production takes longer than for primary metabolites (Fig. 30.4). It also means that continuous fermentation techniques are unsuitable and only batch fermentation can be employed.

In penicillin manufacture, a stirred-tank fermenter is inoculated with a culture of *Penicillium notatum* or *Penicillium chrysogenum* and the fungus is grown under optimum conditions: 24 °C, good oxygen supply, slightly alkaline pH. Penicillin production typically commences after about 30 hours, reaching a maximum at around 4 days. Production ceases after about 6 days, at which point the contents of the fermenter are drained off. As the antibiotic is an extracellular product, the fungal mycelium is filtered off, washed and discarded. The liquid filtrate containing penicillin is chemically extracted and

Penicillin fermentation

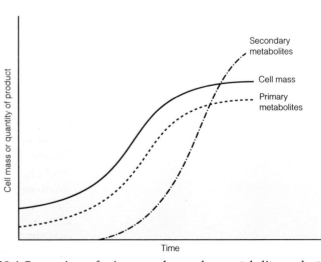

Fig. 30.4 *Comparison of primary and secondary metabolite production*

## BIOLOGY AROUND US

### Biosensors

Biosensors have been devised which enable a quick and accurate measurement of glucose to be made. This is important industrially but also medically, enabling diabetics to monitor their own blood sugar levels. The method used relies on the specificity of the enzyme glucose oxidase, allowing glucose to be assayed in the presence of other sugars.

Glucose oxidase catalyses the conversion of glucose to hydrogen peroxide ($H_2O_2$).

$$\beta\text{-D-Glucose} + O_2 \xrightarrow{\text{Glucose oxidase}} \text{Gluconic acid} + H_2O_2$$

This is coupled to a reaction catalysed by peroxidase and utilising the hydrogen peroxide.

$$\underset{\substack{\text{Colourless} \\ \text{hydrogen donor}}}{DH_2} + H_2O_2 \xrightarrow{\text{Peroxidase}} 2H_2O + \underset{\substack{\text{Coloured} \\ \text{compound}}}{D}$$

The glucose oxidase, peroxidase and the colourless hydrogen donor can be immobilized on a cellulose fibre pad. This forms the basis of 'Clinistix', the glucose dipsticks used by diabetics.

More recently the term biosensor has been used to describe the association of a biomolecule, such as an enzyme, with a transducer which produces an electrical signal in response to a charge in the substrate.

Biosensors are not just used for the quantitative detection of glucose. They have also been devised for pregnancy testing kits (see page 425), to check the freshness of food (there being a correlation between deterioration and the number of microorganisms present) and to detect the presence of pollutants in the environment, as well as for the estimation of many substances, such as urea, ketones and cholesterol, in blood and urine.

purified using solvents to leave a crystalline salt. After sterilization the fermenter is available for the next batch.

The development of resistance to antibiotics by pathogens means there is a continuing need to find new types. The emphasis has moved from searching for new natural antibiotics to the development of new strains using genetic engineering. However, this is not easy. Being secondary metabolites, antibiotics are the product of a long metabolic pathway involving numerous genes. Manipulation of these is complex and difficult. Programmes for enhancing the production rate of existing strains and using random mutation and selection methods to develop new ones, are continually developed. Table 30.3 lists some other antibiotics and their producer organisms.

## BST

The hormone bovine somatotrophin (BST) controls lactation in cows by increasing the number of cells in the mammary glands. When the genetically engineered version is injected into the animals, their milk production can increase by up to 20%. The use of BST was approved by the US Food and Drug Administration (FDA) in November 1993 who declared milk produced from cows given the artificial hormone to be indistinguishable from other milk. Its use is banned in Europe.

Opponents are concerned because the incidence of mastitis among cows given the hormone is 79% higher than normal. They fear that this will lead farmers to use more antibiotics which could stay in the milk and eventually reduce the effectiveness of antibiotics against bacteria that affect humans. Opposition groups have threatened to boycott the milk but the FDA has ruled that it need not carry special labels and neither can other milk simply be declared 'hormone-free'. The introduction of such genetically engineered products without the implementation of strict labelling regulations concerns a number of 'pure food' campaign groups.

TABLE 30.3 **Some antibiotics and their producer organisms**

| Antibiotic | Producer organism | Type of organism |
|---|---|---|
| Penicillin | *Penicillium notatum* | Fungus |
| Griseofulvin | *Penicillium griseofulvum* | Fungus |
| Streptomycin | *Streptomyces griseus* | Actinomycete |
| Chloramphenicol | *Streptomyces venezuelae* | Actinomycete |
| Tetracycline | *Streptomyces aureofaciens* | Actinomycete |
| Colistin | *Bacillus colistinus* | Bacterium |
| Polymyxin B | *Bacillus polymyxa* | Bacterium |

### 30.5.2 Hormones

With the advent of recombinant DNA technology it is now possible to use microorganisms to produce a wide range of hormones which previously had to be extracted from animal tissues. Hormone manufacture using fermentation techniques is relatively straightforward, but the high degree of purity of the final product, which is essential, makes downstream processing a complex process. Ion-exchange, chromatography and protein engineering are some of the techniques employed to provide a high level of purity.

Hormones produced in this way include insulin, used in the treatment of diabetes, and human growth factor which prevents pituitary dwarfism. A number of steroids are also manufactured including cortisone and the sex hormones, testosterone and oestradiol. Others with possible commercial and medical value are relaxin which aids childbirth, and erythropoietin for the treatment of anaemia. Bovine somatotrophin (BST), a hormone administered to cows to increase milk yield, is also in current production.

## 30.6 Biotechnology and fuel production

The rise in oil prices in the early 1970s led to research into alternative means of producing fuel. With only a finite supply of oil available, work continues in this field, accelerated to some extent by the harmful consequences of burning traditional fossil fuels. One method already tried is the fermentation of waste to yield **gasohol** (alcohol) or **biogas** (methane). It may be that in years to come, these fuels will be formed from crops specifically grown for the purpose.

### 30.6.1 Gasohol production

The 1970s rises in oil price hit oil-importing developing countries, such as Brazil, especially hard, and prompted the initiation of the **Brazilian National Alcohol (or Gasohol) Programme**. The concept was simple – namely to use yeasts to ferment Brazil's plentiful supply of sugar cane into alcohol and so create a relatively cheap, renewable home-produced fuel.

The programme began in 1975 and incorporated research into improving sugar cane production as well as fermenter technology. By 1985 sugar cane production had increased by a third, fermentation conversion by 10% and the fermentation time had been reduced by three-quarters. Over 400 distilleries now yield more than $1.2 \times 10^{10}$ dm$^3$ of alcohol annually and all Brazilian cars have been converted to using the fuel, either entirely or mixed with petrol. (Some petrol is added to all alcohol fuels as a disincentive to people drinking them.) It is hoped that by the year 2000 all the country's energy needs will be supplied in this way. What makes the programme so successful in Brazil is that the sugar cane is not only a source of the fermentation substrate, but also a fuel for the distilleries. Once the sugar is extracted from the sugar cane, the fibrous waste, called **bagasse**, can be dried and burnt as a power source for the distillery.

The actual process entails a number of stages:

**1.** Growing and cropping sugar cane.

**2.** Extraction of sugars by crushing and washing the cane.

**3.** The crystallizing out of the sucrose (for sale) leaving a syrup of glucose and fructose called **molasses**.

**4.** Fermentation of the molasses by *Saccharomyces cerevisiae* to yield dilute alcohol.

**5.** Distillation of the dilute alcohol to give pure ethanol, using the waste bagasse as a power source.

The special circumstances in Brazil have doubtless contributed to its success but schemes in some other countries, e.g. Kenya, have been abandoned as uneconomic. Nevertheless, the potential for solving both the problem of diminishing oil supplies and disposal of waste at the same time has its attractions. Waste straw, sawdust, vegetable matter, paper and its associated waste, and other carbohydrates are all possible respiratory substrates although many require enzyme treatment to convert them into glucose before yeast can act upon them.

### 30.6.2 Biogas production

The capacity of naturally occurring microorganisms to decompose wastes can be exploited to produce another useful fuel, methane (biogas). It has the advantage over alcohol (gasohol) production of not requiring complex distillation equipment – indeed, the process is very simple. A container

Biogas generator, Senegal

## PROJECT

Substances are sold which claim to accelerate the production of compost. Investigate these claims by studying the production of biogas by decomposing vegetable matter.

known as a **digester** is filled with appropriate waste (domestic rubbish, sewage or agricultural waste can be used) to which is added a mixture of many bacterial species, e.g. *Methanobacterium* spp. The anaerobic fermentation of these wastes yields methane, which is collected ready for use for cooking, lighting or heating. Small domestic biogas fermenters are common in China and India.

## 30.7 Biotechnology and waste disposal

Sewage farm showing filter beds

In the previous section we saw how microorganisms could be used not only to dispose of wastes but also to yield a useful by-product at the same time. These are not the only ways in which microorganisms are used to dispose of unwanted material; the disposal of sewage, the decomposition of plastics and the breakdown of oil are further examples.

### 30.7.1 Sewage disposal

In a typical sewage filter bed a large variety of microflora are immobilized on layers of coke or stones. Openings above, below and in the sides of the filter, and the spaces between the 'clinker' maintain aerobic conditions. As the effluent trickles down, the action of the microorganisms changes its composition. As a result, the species become stratified vertically in the filter bed. On the surface are numerous mobile protozoa as well as fungi o the genus *Fusarium*. In the upper layers occur *Zoogloea* spp., while *Nitrosomonas* spp., *Nitrobacter* spp. and stalked protozoa are found lower down. Between them, these and other species found in the filter oxidize the many organic substances in the sewage, to largely inorganic chemicals.

Sludge digestion can be carried out either anaerobically or aerobically. In anaerobic digestion the sewage sludge is drained into large digester tanks where obligate anaerobes like *Clostridium* spp. ferment the protein, polysaccharides and lipids of the sludge into acetic acid, carbon dioxide and hydrogen. These products are then acted upon by *Methanobacterium* spp. which form methane (biogas) – a useful fuel, that can be used to power the sewage treatment plant.

Aerobic digestion utilizes a technique known as **activated sludge**. Here the liquid from the primary settlement process is pumped to tanks where it is sparged with air by pumping it through diffusers at the base. Aerobic microflora, including *Zoogloea* spp., *Nitrobacter* spp., *Nitrosomonas* spp., *Pseudomonas* spp., *Beggiatoa* sppp. and others, oxidize the organic components. The liquid is moved to other tanks where the remaining solids settle out in lumps called **flocs** – a process facilitated by bacteria, e.g. *Zoogloea ramigera*. This settled materia can be returned to the aeration tanks for further treatment.

Any solid sludge not decomposed by either of these methods is led into storage lagoons where slow decomposition by anaerobic microorganisms over many years reduces it to a largely inorganic residue. It may otherwise be used for the production of fertilizer.

## 30.8 Biotechnology and agriculture

The rise in global population has led to wider use of biotechnology to increase food production. Two such applications of biotechnology are silage production and the resistance of plants, not just to disease, but also to herbicides used to control weeds.

### 30.8.1 Silage production

Traditionally grass has been preserved for winter use by drying it to make hay, which is then stored. While haymaking is still common, the preservation of grass as silage is now the more usual means of storing grass in Britain.

The energy and protein levels of silage are greater than those of hay, in part because grass for silage is cut early when its nutrient levels are higher. This early harvesting also allows more than one crop to be taken from a given area of land, thus increasing annual yields.

The cut grass is stored immediately either in large plastic coverings or in special containers called silos. Either way, air is excluded so that the grass can be fermented into silage by anaerobic microorganisms. These convert the sugars in the grass to lactic acid whose high acidity prevents the further breakdown of the grass by other microbes.

### 30.8.2 Resistance in plants

For some time now plants have been genetically engineered for their resistance to particular diseases. This has led to better crop yields, at least until the pathogen evolves its own mechanisms of overcoming the resistant gene of the plant.

An alternative use of genetically engineered plants permits farmers to control weeds. The crop plant is manipulated so that it is resistant to the chosen herbicide. When the crop is sprayed, only the vulnerable weeds are destroyed, leaving the resistant crop plant unaffected.

## 30.9 Other products of the biotechnology industry

In addition to all the biotechnological applications of microorganisms already discussed, there is an assortment of other products made in this way. Some of these are given in Table 30.4.

In addition to their products, microorganisms may be utilized directly to human benefit. The nitrogen-fixing bacterium *Rhizobium* spp. lives symbiotically in nodules on the roots of certain plants where it forms nitrogenous compounds of use to its host. The addition of this bacterium to the soil, along with the seeds of the plants utilizing them, ensures inoculation of the crop and a resultant better yield in areas where natural inoculation is unlikely.

False-colour scanning EM of *Escherichia coli* (×8000 approx)

TABLE 30.4 **A range of other commercial substances produced by microorganisms**

| Product | Producer organism | Function of product |
|---|---|---|
| Protease | *Aspergillus oryzae* | Detergent additive |
| | *Bacillus* spp. | Removal of hair from animal hides |
| Butanol and acetone | *Clostridium acetobutylicom* | Solvents |
| Indigo | *Escherichia coli* | Textile dye |
| Xanthan gum | *Xanthomonas campestris* | Thickener used in food, paints and cosmetics |
| Cellulases | *Trichoderma* spp. | Brightener in washing powders |
| Cyanocobalamin (vitamin B$_{12}$) | *Propioni bacterium shermanii* | Food supplement |
| Gellan | *Pseudomonas* spp. | Food thickener |
| Glutamate | *Corynebacterium glutamicum* | Flavour enhancer |
| Streptokinase | *Streptomyces* spp. | Treatment of thrombosis |
| Interferon | *Escherichia coli* | Treatment of viral infections |
| Ergot alkaloids | *Claviceps purpurea* | Vasoconstricter used to treat migraine and in childbirth |
| Cyclosporin | *Cotypocladium inflatum* | Immunosuppressant drug |

The bacterium *Bacillus thuringiensis* produces a protein which is highly toxic to insects. By contaminating the natural food of an insect pest with the bacterium, some control can be effected. The ecological consequences of using such 'natural' pesticides need further investigation but it seems likely that they will be less harmful than their artificial counterparts.

A recent, and controversial, development is the use of the bacterium *Pseudomonas syringae* to form artificial snow at winter holiday resorts. The bacterium, which is sprayed with water on to a fan, has surface properties which act as nuclei for the formation of ice crystals. The fact that this process could cause considerable frost-damage if used on food crops illustrates the risks that attend many biotechnological advances if used wrongly, either by accident or with malice.

## 30.10 Cell, tissue and organ culture

It is not only microorganisms that can be utilized to produce useful substances. Although more difficult to establish, plant and animal cells can also be grown *in vitro* in order to manufacture a variety of products. The culture requirements for eukaryotic cell are far more sophisticated than for prokaryotic cells.

# BIOLOGY AROUND US

## Biological washing powders

The first biological washing powder was manufactured as long ago as 1913 using an extract from the pancreas which contained trypsin. This had very limited success in the alkaline liquids produced by the washing soda containing it. Since then the detergent industry has become the largest single outlet for industrial enzymes. Proteases remove protein stains such as blood, grass, egg and human sweat; lipases digest oily and fatty stains; amylases remove residues of starch substances. Some washing powders also contain a cellulase complex which modifies the fluffy microfibrils which develop when cotton and cotton-mix garments have been washed several times. This has the effect of brightening the colours and softening the fabric as well as removing some dirt particles.

Most of the enzymes are produced extracellularly by bacteria such as *Bacillus subtilis* grown in large-scale fermenters. The bacteria have been genetically engineered to produce enzymes which are stable at a high pH in the presence of phosphates and other detergent ingredients as well as remaining active at temperatures of 60 °C. Subtilisin, a protease, has also had an amino acid residue replaced with an alternative to make the enzyme more resistant to oxidation. During the 1970s the industry suffered a setback when many of the enzymes were shown to produce allergic reactions. This has been solved by producing encapsulated enzymes which are dust-free.

### 30.10.1 Plant cell, tissue and organ culture

The presence of a semi-rigid cell wall around plant cells effectively reduces their ability to divide and grow. For this reason plants retain groups of immature cells which form the only actively growing tissues. These tissues are called **meristems**. If a part of a plant containing a high proportion of meristematic tissue, e.g. bud, root tip or germinating seed, is removed and grown aseptically on a nutrient medium, an undifferentiated mass known as a **callus** frequently develops. Plant hormones – such as auxins, gibberellins and cytokinins (Section 29.2) – a nitrogen and carbohydrate source, as well as vitamins, trace elements and growth regulators need to be present in the nutrient medium. Undifferentiated callus produced in this way is an example of **plant tissue culture**. If the callus is suspended in a liquid nutrient medium and broken up mechanically into individual cells it forms a **plant cell culture**. These can be maintained indefinitely if sub-cultured giving rise to a **cell-line**. If pectinases and cellulases are added to these cultures, the plant cell walls can be removed and the resulting protoplasts can be fused with the protoplasts of different cells to give hybrid cells which can later be grown on into new plant varieties.

**Plant organ culture** is achieved by taking apical shoot tips, sterilizing them and growing them on a nutrient medium containing cytokinin. A cluster of shoots develops, each of which

Anther calluses on agar

# BIOLOGY AROUND US

## Micropropagation

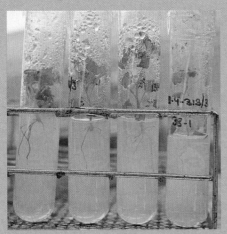

Micropropagation of plants in growing medium

Plant cells are totipotent, that is any differentiated plant cell has the potential to give rise to all the different cells of an adult plant. This is the basis of the tissue culture techniques which form the basis of micropropagation.

Stock plants are kept as pathogen- and pest-free as possible and small pieces are cut (excised) from them. These explants may be pieces of stem tissue, with nodes, flower buds, leaves or tiny sections of shoot tip meristems. The surfaces of the explants are sterilized by using solutions such as dilute sodium hypochlorite and, in aseptic conditions, are transferred to a culture vessel containing nutrients and growth regulators. The medium is usually solidified using a gelling agent, such as agar, to provide a firm matrix for the growing shoots. The vessels are then incubated for 3–9 weeks at 15–30 °C with light for 10–14 hours per day. The new shoots that develop are removed from the explant and subcultured on a new medium. This process is repeated every few weeks so that a few explants can give rise to millions of plants within 1 year. The composition of medium used varies for different varieties. Tissue culture plants must be acclimatized in special greenhouses until they reach marketable size.

Micropropagation is now widely used as an alternative to conventional propagation of many horticultural species (for pot plants, cut flowers and ornamental bulbs) and some agricultural crops such as potatoes and sugar beet. Tissue culture allows the rapid production of large numbers of genetically identical plants, can be used for plant species which are difficult to propagate by traditional methods, helps to eliminate plant diseases, overcomes seasonal restrictions and enables cold storage of large numbers of plants in a small space.

However, there are also some problems. Plants propagated in this way may be genetically unstable or infertile, their chromosomes being structurally altered or their chromosome numbers being unusual. When oil palms produced by micropropagation were introduced to Malaysia in the 1970s they turned out to be sterile. This problem has now been overcome and most oil palms are the result of micropropagation techniques. It is a technology which requires sterile conditions and a well trained labour force and so costs are higher than with traditional propagation methods.

may be grown on into new clusters. This form of micropropagation results in a large quantity of genetically identical individuals.

### 30.10.2 Applications of plant cell, tissue and organ culture

There are two main applications of these forms of culture. The first is the generation of plants for agricultural or horticultural use. Vast numbers of plants can be grown in sterile controlled conditions ensuring a much greater survival rate than would be the case if seeds were planted outdoors. These plants can all be identical if required, thus ensuring a more uniform crop which incorporates desired characteristics. A particular advantage of this form of propagation is that the stock plants, raised as they are in sterile conditions, are completely pathogen-free when planted out, by which time they have developed defence mechanisms against many diseases.

The second application is the manufacture of useful chemicals by plant cultures. To date only one product, shikonin, a dye used in the silk industry and in the treatment of burns, has been produced commercially, but Table 30.5 lists some of the possible applications of plant cell culture once the processes become economically viable.

TABLE 30.5 **Some useful plant chemicals which might be produced using plant cell culture**

| Product | Producer plant | Use of product |
| --- | --- | --- |
| Atropine | Deadly nightshade (*Atropa belladonna*) | Ophthalmic use – dilation of pupil Treatment of certain heart conditions |
| Codeine | Opium poppy (*Papaver somniferum*) | Pain killer |
| Digoxin | Foxglove (*Digitalis* spp.) | Treatment of cardio-vascular complaints |
| Jasmine | Jasmine (*Jasminium* spp.) | Perfume |
| Menthol | Peppermint (*Mentha piperita*) | Food flavouring |
| Quinine | Chinchona tree (*Chinchona ledgeriana*) | Drug used to treat malaria Bitter flavouring in drinks |
| Pyrethrin | Chrysanthemum (*Chrysanthemum* spp.) | Insecticide |

### 30.10.3 Animal cell culture

Only in recent years has it proved possible to culture vertebrate cells on any scale. The process begins by treating the appropriate tissue with a proteolytic enzyme like trypsin in order to separate the cells. These are transferred to an appropriate nutrient medium where they attach themselves to the bottom of the container and divide mitotically to give a monolayer of cells. This is referred to as the **primary culture**. Cells from these can be used to establish secondary cultures but their life span is limited, division often ceasing after 50–100 divisions.

It is possible to make these cultures continue to divide indefinitely by the addition of chemicals or viruses which induce the formation of cancer cells. These cell lines are said to be transformed and are **neoplastic**, i.e they can induce cancer if transplanted into a related species.

# BIOLOGY AROUND US

## Genetically modified organisms (GMOs)

Since the earliest days of farming man has modified crop plants and domesticated animals through selective breeding. This has resulted in crops with higher yields and animals that are more docile and produce meat and milk with a lower fat content. Modern technology allows the alteration of genetic material in a way that does not occur naturally by mating and the desired characteristics are likely to be achieved in a much shorter time. These are **genetically modified organisms**. The potential for applying DNA technology to food production is enormous.

### Genetically modified tomatoes

In order to develop their full flavour tomatoes need to ripen on the vine. However as they ripen they become soft and difficult to harvest and maintain in ideal condition for sale. For this reason they are usually picked while they are still green and allowed to ripen later, with a consequent loss of flavour. Tomatoes soften as a result of the action of the enzyme polygalacturanase which hydrolyses long polymers in the middle lamella into shorter, soluble fragments. If fruit is to ripen without softening the production of this enzyme has to be stopped or reduced. The so-called Flavr Savr tomato produced in America is a GMO in which the gene for the production of polygalacturanase has been 'switched off'. This has been done by using so-called 'antisense' technology. Using *Agrobacterium* as a vector a reversed sequence of the PG (polygalacturanase) gene has been inserted into the cells. This codes for an 'antisense' mRNA strand which binds to the mRNA coding for the enzyme. This results in double-stranded mRNA and prevents transcription of the gene. As a result softening is delayed and the fruit can remain on the vine to ripen. However, production of these tomatoes has not been continued due to problems with disease resistance. Another approach to the problem has been taken in the UK. Bases have been 'cut' from the PG gene so that the cells produce less of the enzyme. The tomatoes develop greater flavour without softening. Approval was given in 1995 for these GM tomatoes to be sold as paste, but not as fresh fruit. The product has a full flavour and is thick; harvesting and processing losses have been reduced.

In both of these examples the genetic modification has been achieved by modifying the plant's own DNA, no 'foreign' DNA has been introduced.

### Herbicide resistant crops

It is claimed that the development of crop plants resistant to particular herbicides will boost yields and reduce the application of costly chemicals. Soya beans which are grown commercially on a huge scale for oil, protein and other ingredients have been genetically modified to be resistant to certain herbicides. The processed GM soya is indistinguishable from normal soya and, because it may be mixed with it, concerns have been expressed by people wishing to avoid GM products. There are further economic, ethical and environmental concerns over herbicide-resistant crops which tend to be produced by the same company that makes the herbicide to which they show resistance. This means the farmer must buy both seed and herbicide from the same manufacturer. The resistance of the crop means that increased levels of herbicide may be applied without damage. There is an environmental risk too because resistance may be passed to wild plant species by cross pollination and new varieties of resistant weed may evolve.

*Pesticide and disease resistance*
Approximately 30% of all genetically modified crops and trees are engineered for pest and disease resistance using toxins derived from naturally occurring biopesticides. Rice suffers from the rice stripe virus (RSV) but the transgenic forms, which have the gene for the virus protein coat introduced, show increased resistance to the virus. However there are some concerns about the long term effects on the environment because of our lack of knowledge about the interactive behaviour of viruses.

Other crops such as maize, have been genetically modified to produce a toxic protein when they are attacked by insect pests. The gene for this toxin has been derived from *Bacillus thuringiensis* and the protein it produces is toxic to a variety of insects, but not to mammals. However, as the use of these 'products' increases resistance to them may build up and populations of 'super pests' may arise.

*Ethical and environmental concerns*
Unlike many scientific inventions or discoveries of the past, genetic engineering has been subject to wide debate as each new product comes on line. For some people the ideas are clear-cut; it is not natural and we should not 'play God'. But not all that is natural is good and harmless and not all that is unnatural is bad and harmful. The issues and arguments are complex and there may be no right or wrong answers. We have already considered some of the possible environmental implications of the release of GMOs. Perhaps it will result in a reduction in the use of harmful pesticides, herbicides and fertilisers and as the world population increases genetic engineering may help to reduce food shortages in developing countries. On the other hand resistance may spread to weeds and insect pests, an animal virus may mutate into one that affects humans and developing countries may not be able to afford the new technology. In the UK there are regulations implementing European Directives to control laboratory experiments, field trials and the commercial use of GMOs. In addition there are extensive risk assessment trials to assess the environmental impact of the release of GMOs.

Many genetically engineered crops contain genes coding for resistance to specific antibiotics. This is so that the success, or otherwise, of modification can be seen by applying the antibiotic to destroy plants without the modified gene. Concern have been expressed that this may spread antibiotic resistance.

As fears continue to be voiced about the spread of GMOs, consumer organisations are demanding that all foods containing GM products should be labelled. Such labelling will not always result in diminished sales, indeed the sale of labelled GM tomato paste in its first two years outstripped the sales of unmodified paste, in some stores.

Consumers need to be provided with appropriate and understandable information so that they can make informed choices. Many people find genetic modification of plants acceptable although others disagree with all genetic modification on the grounds that we should not interfere with nature. There are concerns expressed about the possibility of transferring genes of animal or human origin to other species and how widespread it becomes is likely to be very dependent on consumer acceptance. The UK government set up a committee to consider some ethical issues. They concluded that most Christian and Jewish groups found genetic modification acceptable; Muslims, Sikhs and Hindus have ethical objections to consuming organisms containing copy genes from animals which are the subject of dietary restrictions for their religion; strict vegetarians would object to incorporating copy genes of animal origin in a plant. In addition animal welfare supporters stress that mankind has a moral obligation to care for animals and honour their intrinsic value. There is obviously massive potential for us all to benefit from this new technology which touches all aspects of our lives. Wide-ranging and open discussions should ensure that all concerns can be addressed and new developments are introduced safely.

# 30.11 Questions

A yeast culture, containing initially $18\,000$ cells cm$^{-3}$ and a supply of glucose, was set up in a laboratory fermenter and maintained in a constant temperature waterbath. The glucose concentration, ethanol concentration and pH were monitored over a 24-hour period. The number of yeast cells was estimated at intervals during the experiment.
The results obtained are shown in the graph below.

Changes occurring in a yeast culture over a 20-hour period (as drawn by computer)

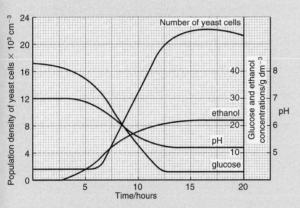

Adapted from *Microbiology and Biotechnology*, Cadogan and Hanks.

(a) Suggest, with a reason, a suitable temperature for the waterbath. *(1 mark)*

(b) (i) Using information from the graph, calculate the mean rate of increase in the number of yeast cells per hour between 6 and 13 hours. *(2 marks)*

    (ii) What is the name given to this phase of growth? *(1 mark)*

(c) Explain the shape of the curves for:
    (i) ethanol; *(2 marks)*
    (ii) glucose. *(2 marks)*

(d) (i) From the graph, state the pH at the beginning and at the end of the experiment. *(1 mark)*

    (ii) Explain precisely the reason for the change in pH. *(2 marks)*

(e) (i) Calculate the percentage of glucose which had been used by the yeast by the end of the experiment. (Show your working.) *(2 marks)*

    (ii) Some glucose remained at the end of the investigation. Suggest one reason to account for this fact. *(1 mark)*

(f) Name one technique which can be used to estimate the numbers of yeast cells. *(1 mark)*

*(Total 15 marks)*

*Oxford June 1997, Paper 41, No. 4*

2. The enzyme amylase can be produced industrially in a fermenter. In one series of experiments, a fermenter was set up to investigate how amylase production by a microorganism is affected by the carbohydrate source. A number of different carbohydrate sources were used and in all the experiments the pH was kept between pH 7 and pH 8. All other conditions were kept constant. Amylase production was measured in arbitrary units. The results are shown in the table below.

| Carbohydrate source | Amylase production /arbitrary units |
|---|---|
| Corn starch | 235 |
| Maltose | 179 |
| Glucose | 52 |
| Sucrose | 17 |
| Lactose | 0 |
| None | 0 |

(a) (i) Describe the effect of the carbohydrate source on the production of amylase by the microorganism. *(3 marks)*

    (ii) Suggest **one** reason for any differences you observe. *(1 mark)*

(b) State **three** commercial uses of amylase. *(3 marks)*

(c) In a further experiment to investigate the effect of different pH values on the production of amylase, only one of the carbohydrate sources was used. The results are shown in the table below.

| pH | Amylase production /arbitrary units |
|---|---|
| 6.0 | 0 |
| 6.5 | 4 |
| 7.0 | 13 |
| 7.5 | 18 |
| 8.0 | 14 |
| 8.5 | 11 |

(i) Suggest which of the carbohydrate sources has been used in this experiment. *(1 mark)*

(ii) Comment on the effect of pH on amylase production *(2 marks)*

(d) Suggest why it may be an advantage to a microorganism to be able to utilize more than a single carbohydrate source. *(2 marks)*

*(Total 12 marks)*

*Edexcel June 1997, B/HB4A, No. 6*

3. (a) Describe a biochemical test which could be used to show that a reducing sugar such as glucose was present in a solution. (*2 marks*)

(b) Enzyme electrodes can be used to measure the concentration of substances in solutions. The diagram shows an enzyme electrode which can be used to measure glucose concentration.

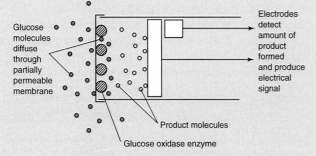

Glucose molecules diffuse through partially permeable membrane

Electrodes detect amount of product formed and produce electrical signal

Product molecules

Glucose oxidase enzyme

Hospitals have to carry out large numbers of tests to measure the amount of glucose present in blood samples. Suggest and explain **two** advantages of using an enzyme electrode rather than the biochemical test you described in part (a) to measure the amount of glucose in a blood sample. (*4 marks*)

Fructose is widely used in the food industry as it is sweeter tasting than glucose. The enzyme glucose isomerase is used to convert glucose to fructose. The table compares some different ways of converting glucose to fructose using glucose isomerase. Arbitrary units have been used.

| Method | Amount of glucose isomerase used | Amount of magnesium salts used | Amount of impurities formed | Cost per tonne of fructose produced |
|---|---|---|---|---|
| **A Batch production** Glucose is mixed with glucose isomerase in solution. At the end of the reaction the fructose is separated. | 180 | 40 | 0.7 | £500 |
| **B Batch production** Glucose is mixed with immobilized glucose isomerase. At the end of the reaction the fructose is separated. | 11 | 40 | 0.2 | £30 |
| **C Continuous production** A stream of glucose solution is passed over immobilized glucose isomerase. Fructose is produced and separated as the process continues. | 2 | 7 | less than 0.1 | £5 |

(c) Explain what is meant by **immobilized** glucose isomerase. (*1 mark*)

(d) Use the data in the table to explain **two** reasons why method **C** is the most economical way of producing fructose from glucose. (*3 marks*)

(e) Explain why methods **A** and **B** use the same amount of magnesium salts but different amounts of glucose isomerase. (*2 marks*)

(f) Glucose isomerase is a thermostable enzyme.
  (i) What is meant by a **thermostable** enzyme? (*1 mark*)
  (ii) Explain why it might be an advantage to use a thermostable enzyme in an industrial process such as the conversion of glucose to fructose. (*2 marks*)

(g) Lipolase is a hydrolase enzyme. Its substrate is triglyceride. What products are formed by the action of lipolase on triglycerides? (*1 mark*)

(h) Lipolase is added to washing powders where it is used to remove lipid stains. The graph shows the effect of different concentrations of lipolase on the removal of lipid stains.

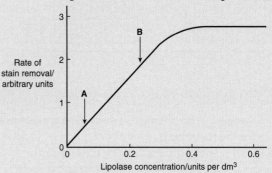

Rate of stain removal/ arbitrary units

Lipolase concentration/units per dm$^3$

  (i) What is the evidence from the graph that the rate of stain removal is limited by enzyme concentration between points **A** and **B**? (*1 mark*)
  (ii) Suggest why there is no further increase in the rate of stain removal with increasing lipolase concentration above 0.4 units per dm$^3$. (*2 marks*)

(j) The graph below shows the effect of temperature on the relative efficiency of two lipid-removing enzymes, lipolase and lipolase ultra.

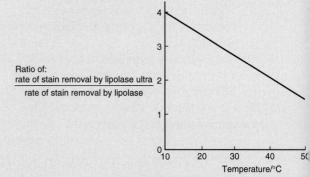

Ratio of: rate of stain removal by lipolase ultra / rate of stain removal by lipolase

Temperature/°C

In Asian countries and the United States, wash temperatures of 10°C to 20°C are common. Giving a reason for your answer, suggest which of lipolase or lipolase ultra would be most suitable for use in washing powders in these countries.                    (1 mark)
(Total 20 marks)

AEB January 1998, Paper 1, No. 4

An experiment was carried out to investigate the efficiency of various antibiotics in destroying a pathogenic bacterium.

Petri dishes of nutrient agar were inoculated with the bacterium using a spreading technique. A paper disc with six different coloured discs attached to it (called Mastring) was then carefully placed on the surface of the agar in each Petri dish. This is shown in the diagram below.

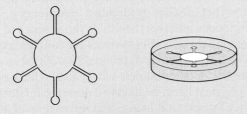

Each disc on the Mastring had previously been dipped into a different antibiotic solution and allowed to dry. The Petri dishes were sealed with adhesive tape, turned upside down and incubated. After 24 hours, the diameter of the clear zone around each disc was measured and used to calculate the area of the clear zone.

The results are given in the table below.

| Antibiotic | Area of clear zone/cm² |
|---|---|
| Chloramphenicol | 9.07 |
| Erythromycin | 4.90 |
| Novobiocin | 3.79 |
| Penicillin G | 0.78 |
| Streptomycin | 0.00 |
| Tetracycline | 2.54 |

Adapted from Freeland, *Investigations in Applied Biology and Biotechnology*.

(a)  (i)  Which antibiotic appeared to be the most effective against the bacterium? Give a reason for your answer?                    (2 marks)
    (ii)  Compare the relative activities of novobiocin and tetracycline in destroying the bacterium.          (2 marks)
(b)  (i)  Describe how the spreading technique is carried out.                    (3 marks)
    (ii)  Why were the Petri dishes sealed with adhesive tape?                    (1 mark)
    (iii)  What was the reason for turning the Petri dishes upside down before placing them in the incubator?  (1 mark)
(c)  Explain why penicillin is produced commercially by batch fermentation, rather than continuous culture.          (2 marks)
(d)  Suggest **two** reasons why commercial yields of penicillin are much greater now than they were when production first started.                    (2 marks)
(Total 13 marks)

ULEAC June 1995, Paper 4A, No. 1

# 31 Human health and disease

## 31.1 Principles of human health

Some scientific terms are relatively easy to define, others are more difficult; 'health' and 'disease' fall into the latter category. Some would suggest that 'disease' is merely a disorder of a system's normal functions and that 'health' is the absence of 'disease'. Can a person whose bodily systems are functioning properly but who feels unhappy or depressed be defined as healthy? Can alcoholics or drug-addicts whose habits have not as yet caused any physical harm be likewise described? Clearly health is more than physical well-being; it involves mental and social well-being as well.

If it is difficult to say what we understand by 'health'; to define 'disease' is even more problematic. It is not so much a single entity as a description of certain symptoms that suggest a pattern of future events. Skill and expertise in accurately predicting these future events is what makes an effective doctor

### 31.1.1 Classification of diseases

Any classification of diseases into groups invariably leads to problems when one attempts to place a specific disease into a single category. This is because, while a number of diseases fit neatly and entirely into one category, some seem to belong to more than one group and yet others combine elements of all types. This being said, six categories are often recognized.

**Infections** – communicable diseases that can be passed on from one individual to another. They are almost always caused by other living organisms, especially microorganisms, e.g. influenza.

**Inherited** – genetic diseases that are inherited from one or other parent, e.g. cystic fibrosis.

**Degenerative** –the result of ageing, or the breakdown of the normal structure of a tissue or organ, e.g. senile dementia.

**Mental** – diseases of the mind, e.g. schizophrenia.

**Human inflicted** – the result of human activities – often one's own, e.g. alcoholism.

**Deficiency** – the result of the absence of one or more essential components of the diet, e.g. rickets.

---

**NOT TO BE CONFUSED**
**3 terms easily mixed up**

**Endemic** refers to a disease found only among a particular group of people or in a local region of the world.

**Epidemic** refers to a disease which occurs in many individuals in a community at the same time.

**Pandemic** refers to a disease that affects many people across the world

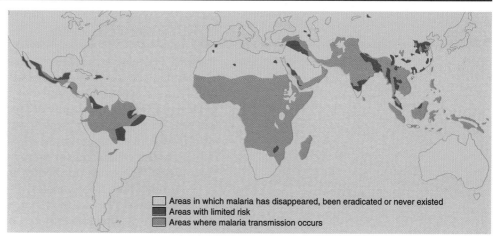

Areas in which malaria has disappeared, been eradicated or never existed
Areas with limited risk
Areas where malaria transmission occurs

Worldwide distribution of malaria

Any disease may be **acute** (it may appear suddenly and be short-lived) or **chronic** (it may develop slowly and persist). It may be the result of environmental influences such as radiation or pollutants or it may have no apparent cause. Some diseases, e.g. coronary heart disease, have a series of 'risk factors', each of which increases the chance of developing the illness. Occupation and life-style often affect the onset of a particular disease.

### 31.1.2 Patterns of disease distribution

The incidence of diseases alters both in time and space. In the nineteenth century, infectious illnesses such as smallpox were very common throughout the world. Thanks to vaccination programmes and other medical advances, smallpox has now been eradicated entirely.

While many infectious diseases, such as malaria and typhoid, are still common in the developing world, they are extremely rare in developed countries; here, deaths from infectious diseases have given way to those caused by heart disease, cancer and accidents. The relative poverty of the developing nations has restricted the extent of medical care, immunization programmes, health education, clean water supplies and communications, all of which could help to reduce the incidence of infectious disease. By contrast, the relative affluence of the developed countries has ensured the control of these diseases, but brought life-styles that include tobacco smoking, reduced exercise as a result of car use, excess alcohol consumption, pollution and overeating. These explain in part the alarming frequency of coronary heart disease, cancers and road accidents in these countries.

The effects and global distribution of a disease such as measles illustrates the differences between the developed and developing world. In developed countries where children are well fed and immunization is common, any occurrence of the disease is normally mild and rarely fatal. In developing countries, malnutrition and the absence of immunization lead to low resistance and high child mortality, especially of those under 2 years of age. Deaths from measles in the UK dropped from over 4000 in 1930 to around 20 a year in recent times, so while it is not in the 20 major causes of death in the UK it is frequently in the top five in developing countries.

# 31.2    Infectious diseases

The human body is an ideal incubator for most microorganisms. It provides a warm environment of constant temperature, a near neutral pH, a constant supply of food and water in nicely balanced proportions for growth, a transport system which efficiently conveys materials to all parts, a ready supply of oxygen, and mechanisms for removing waste materials. Not surprisingly, therefore, our bodies are naturally colonized by a large number of microorganisms, all of which have the capacity to cause disease. The fact that, in most cases, they do not is the result of our considerable armoury of physical and chemical defences. Many microorganisms live more or less permanently in our bodies, benefiting from doing so but doing us no harm. These microorganisms are called **commensals**. Other microorganisms, however, cause disease and these are called **pathogens**. The extent to which the pathogen causes damage is known as **virulence**. For a microorganism to be considered a pathogen it must:

1. Gain entry to the host.

2. Colonize the tissues of the host.

3. Resist the defences of the host.

4. Cause damage to the host tissues.

### 31.2.1 Entry of microorganisms into the body

Entry of pathogens occurs broadly in two ways: via the skin or through natural openings. With its thick, continuous, keratinized layer, the skin is an effective barrier to infection. Microorganisms do not readily adhere to it and can easily be removed as the surface cells are shed or during washing. The acidity of secretions from the sweat and sebaceous glands discourage the growth of microorganisms, and the enzyme lysozyme in tears breaks down bacterial cell walls. Invasion therefore normally only occurs when the skin is broken. Cuts and abrasions may occur as a result of injury or certain skin conditions like eczema. Biting insects such as mosquitoes, lice and fleas, or bites and scratches from animals may also allow entry. In many cases the pathogen is deliberately introduced by the bite rather than by a chance opportunity.

The natural openings of the body make suitable access points for microorganisms. Many infectious diseases are respiratory and, despite a mucus layer, lysozymes, cilia and phagocytic cells at various points in the trachea, bronchi and alveoli, diseases such as influenza, tuberculosis and bronchitis infect via the air inhaled along this route. Food and water may carry the agents of typhoid, dysentery and cholera into the stomach and intestines via the mouth. If they do not succumb to the stomach acid and intestinal enzymes, they may cause disease. The genital and urinary openings may allow microorganisms to enter. Those requiring direct contact for their transference are easily transmitted during sexual intercourse. Examples include the agents of AIDS, syphilis and gonorrhoea.

TABLE 31.1    **Koch's postulates**

| |
|---|
| In 1881, Robert Koch suggested four conditions (postulates) that indicate that a disease is the result of an infectious agent (pathogen). |
| **1**   The causative agent must be present in all cases of the disease but absent in healthy animals |
| **2**   The agent of the disease can be isolated from the diseased animal and can be grown in pure culture. |
| **3**   The disease can be reproduced by inoculating some of the pure culture into healthy animals. |
| **4**   The agent of the disease can be reisolated from the infected animal. |

## 31.2.2 Colonizing the tissues of the host

Pathogens need to fix themselves at the site of their infection. This they achieve through a combination of physical modifications (e.g. the protein spikes of the influenza virus) or chemical means (e.g. adhesive substances in some pneumonia pathogens). Once fixed, multiplication occurs rapidly to increase numbers. The need then is to spread the newly formed pathogens throughout the tissue and/or to other regions of the body. Some microorganisms may produce toxins which cause irritation, and this leads to responses such as scratching, coughing and sneezing which help to spread the infection to unaffected areas. Enzymes produced by some pathogens enable them to penetrate cells and so gradually invade a tissue. Microorganisms may enter the lymphatic system via tissue fluid and so be carried around the body in this way, often entering the blood system and then to all parts of the body. Measles, which initially enters via the respiratory system, is spread in this way, ultimately affecting areas including the skin and the nervous system.

### 31.2.3 Resisting the host's defences

If the skin and mucus linings of the body represent the first line of defence, then the immune responses of the blood and lymphatic system are the second line. Details of how these operate are given in Section 21.3.

Resisting the second line of defence is achieved in a number of ways including:

1. Interfering with the chemotactic attraction of phagocytes for the pathogen (e.g. the tuberculosis bacterium).

2. Resisting ingestion by phagocytes (e.g. plague bacterium).

3. Avoiding digestion once ingested by phagocytes (e.g. leprosy bacterium).

4. Destruction of phagocytes (e.g. staphylococci).

### 31.2.4 Damaging the host

The extent of any damage the pathogen causes and hence the onset of its symptoms is related to the rate at which it multiplies. Pathogens like those causing gastroenteritis divide about every 30 minutes and so produce symptoms within 24 hours of infection. The leprosy bacterium, by contrast, takes up to 3 weeks to divide and so symptoms are not apparent for many months. Some pathogens, e.g. *Salmonella*, will only cause damage if present in very large numbers; others such as the typhoid bacterium cause harm when their numbers are relatively small.

Damage to the host tissues arises as a consequence of one or more of three conditions:

1. **The multiplication of the microorganisms** – Some protozoan infections lead to such a build-up of pathogens that their sheer numbers block the functioning of certain organs. Viruses inhibit the synthesis of DNA, RNA and proteins by the host. The polio virus, for example, prevents nervous stimulation of muscles by this means.

**TABLE 31.2  Comparison of exotoxins and endotoxins produced by microorganisms**

| Exotoxin | Endotoxin |
|---|---|
| Excreted product of cells | Part of cell wall usually released on lysis of cell |
| Primarily produced by gram-positive bacteria, e.g. *Staphylococcus* | Found in cell wall of gram-negative bacteria, e.g. *Salmonella* |
| Most are polypeptides | Lipopolysaccharide complex |
| Unstable at temperatures above 60 °C | Stable for some hours at temperatures above 60 °C |
| Do not produce fever in the host | Produce fever in the host |
| Very toxic | Weakly toxic |
| Stimulates formation of antitoxins | Does not stimulate formation of antitoxins |

629

2. **Toxins from the pathogen** – Most bacterial pathogens produce toxins whose effects are highly diverse. *Clostridium botulinum*, which causes botulism, produces a neurotoxin that is one of the most potent poisons known. The toxin of *Streptococcus pyogenes,* which causes scarlet fever, is a vasodilator, while that of *Corynebacterium diphtheriae*, the diphtheria bacterium, inhibits protein synthesis.

3. **As a result of the immune response** – To enable the host to fight pathogens, the blood supply to the infected area is increased because of vasodilation. This may lead to inflammation and soreness. The immune response can cause rise in temperature and consequent fever. Such symptoms are common in most diseases, including influenza.

### 31.2.5 Acquired Immune Deficiency Syndrome (AIDS)

Having first been diagnosed in 1982 AIDS, unlike most other infectious diseases, is a relative newcomer. Such has been the rapidity of its spread that it is now the leading cause of death among 25–45 year old men in the USA and one-third of all adult in Uganda are infected. The World Health Organization estimates that by the year 2000, up to 40 million people will be infected. AIDS is caused by the **human immunodeficiency virus (HIV)**, a spherical retrovirus whose structure is shown in Fig. 31.1. More details of retroviruses are given in Section 5.2.2.

Once infected with HIV an individual is said to be **HIV positive**, a condition which persists throughout life. As the virus remains dormant for about 8 years, on average, an HIV positive person does not show any symptoms during this period but can act as a carrier, often unwittingly spreading the disease. The virus can be detected in virtually all bodily fluids of an HIV positive individual. However, since it is only in blood, semen or vaginal fluid that the concentration is high, it is usually spread through sexual intercourse, or transfer of infected blood from one person to another – as when drug users share a hypodermic needle – or from mother to baby during childbirth. There is some evidence that HIV can be transmitted from mother to baby across the placenta as well as in breast milk. The transfusion of HIV infected blood has in the past spread AIDS, although blood is now routinely screened to avoid any risk to patients such as haemophiliacs who depend on transfused blood. Faeces, urine, sweat, saliva and tears have such a low incidence of HIV in an infected person that contact with these substances presents only a very remote possibility of contracting AIDS. In any case, the virus quickly dies outside the human body, and therefore even blood, semen and vaginal secretions must be transferred directly. Thus the risk from contaminated clothing, etc., is negligible.

Having entered the blood, HIV infects blood cells carrying CD4 receptors (CD4+ lymphocytes) such as T-helper cells (Section 21.3) to which the virus readily binds. It becomes enclosed within the cell membrane and so its antigens do not stimulate an immune response from the lymphocytes in the blood. Replication of the virus is controlled and it frequently becomes latent. It is months or years later that replication recommences, so that it is on average 8 years before AIDS develops. Most victims then die within 2 years, usually of opportunist pathogens which take advantage of impaired

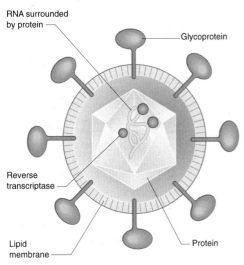

*Fig. 31.1 The AIDS virus*

RNA surrounded by protein

Glycoprotein

Reverse transcriptase

Lipid membrane

Protein

resistance. Oral thrush is often an early symptom, followed by tuberculosis or pneumonia. All AIDS patients lose weight, some develop a skin cancer called Kaposi's sarcoma. Loss of memory and coordination may occur in the late stages of the disease.

There is, as yet, no cure for AIDS. Much effort is being expended in developing a vaccine but progress is hampered by the rapid rate at which HIV mutates, the fact that HIV 'hides' itself within the CD4+ lymphocyte cell membrane, and the risk that a vaccine from attenuated HIV could induce cancers. Furthermore, as AIDS affects almost exclusively humans, there are no suitable animals on which to test new drugs; humans are the only guinea pigs. Current approaches to trying to find a suitable treatment for AIDS involve the development of:

1. Drugs which inhibit HIV.

2. A vaccine to prevent AIDS.

3. Medicines which boost the immune system of AIDS sufferers.

4. Treatments for the other infections which develop in AIDS sufferers.

Despite these efforts preventative measures are, at present, the best means of containing the disease. Education is paramount and much expenditure has been put into informing the population of the risks and how to minimize them. At highest risk are those sharing needles and syringes and those having unprotected anal intercourse. Avoiding contact with the blood of another person (especially by sharing needles) and using condoms for all forms of sexual intercourse are two obvious precautions to take.

Sadly, AIDS still often carries a social stigma which makes some patients feel ostracized and isolated. The disease also raises moral issues about whether HIV positive individuals should be refused insurance or mortgages, or whether others should be required to have an HIV test before being accepted for insurances or mortgages.

### 31.2.6 Influenza

Almost all of us will at some time be infected by the influenza virus. It is therefore sobering to reflect that, what to many of us is just a transient inconvenience, has cost millions of lives this century. The 1918 pandemic alone was estimated to have killed 20 million people worldwide.

The disease primarily affects the respiratory tract and is spread by inhalation of droplets containing the virus which have been expelled during coughing and sneezing of an infected person. The **neuroaminidase** on the virus's surface allows it to liquefy the protective mucus layer of the throat so that the epithelium beneath is exposed. The **haemagglutinin** spikes on the virus's surface then attach to an epithelial cell. The virus penetrates the cell, injecting its RNA. The virus often spreads throughout the respiratory tract causing sore throat, headache and mild fever. Exposure of the epithelium and reduced resistance as a consequence of fighting the infection can lead to complications from other diseases, most notably pneumonia. It is these secondary infections which more often prove fatal, with the very young and the elderly being most vulnerable. The incubation period (the period of time from infection to appearance of symptoms) is normally 1–2 days.

Treatment for influenza entails taking paracetamol or aspirin to relieve the symptoms; antibiotics may be used to help prevent secondary infections (although they do not treat influenza directly). Vulnerable groups can be immunized, although vaccines are only partially effective, immunity is short and there may be side-effects such as a raised temperature. The constantly mutating nature of the virus means that vaccines quickly become ineffective and new ones have to be developed.

### 31.2.7 Tuberculosis

Once a common disease in the UK with up to 40 000 cases a year, tuberculosis (TB) is now relatively rare in developed countries, but remains a major killer elsewhere. Significantly there has been a worrying increase in cases both in the UK and the USA.

*Mycobacterium tuberculosis*, the bacterium causing TB, is rod-shaped and 2–4 $\mu$m long. It may affect almost any human organ, although pulmonary tuberculosis (infection of the lung) is most common. Infection is most frequently from the inhalation of droplets exhaled during coughing by an infected person, although in a healthy individual whose immune system is operating effectively, the bacteria are normally destroyed rapidly. Transmission occurs most readily in damp, overcrowded conditions. Bovine TB can be passed to humans via infected milk. In the UK, pasteurization of milk and the slaughter of infected cattle has eliminated this source of the disease, but it remains a problem elsewhere in the world.

Initial infection is termed **primary TB** and often displays no symptoms. Some bacteria may, however, remain dormant for up to 30 years and then re-emerge as **post-primary TB** in the lungs or elsewhere. Without treatment, the bacteria destroy the lung tissue and cause accumulation of fluid in the pleural cavity between the lungs and the chest wall. Treatment involves the administration of anti-TB drugs for a period of 6 months to ensure its complete eradication. A cocktail of three or four types is given, as there are a number of strains of the bacterium, some resistant to certain drugs.

Prevention of the disease through vaccination has proved the most successful weapon in controlling TB. All children in the UK are routinely tested for their immunity to TB by the injection of a small amount of protein from *Mycobacterium tuberculosis* in what is known as the **Heaf test**. Examination of the injected area some days later may reveal a localized reaction, indicating that the child is already immune. Vaccination of these individuals is unnecessary and dangerous. Those showing no reaction are given the **Bacille Calmette-Guerin (BCG)** vaccine. This is an attenuated (weakened) strain of *Mycobacterium bovis* which causes bovine TB. While this form of mass immunization has been the major reason for the fall in cases of TB in the UK, there is no doubt that improved social conditions have also played a part. Better housing, with less overcrowding and less damp conditions, and better nutrition have reduced the ease with which the disease can be transmitted, until recently. Now there are signs of a resurgence of the disease in some developed countries. In Britain, for example, there were 10 000 more cases of TB between 1987 and 1993 than would have been expected if

## Did you know?

Tuberculosis killed nearly 3 million people worldwide in 1995 – more than in any other year in history.

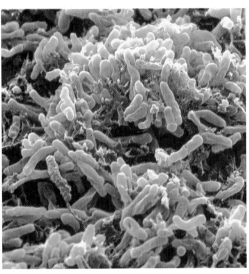

*Mycobacterium tuberculosis* cluster (SEM) (×8500 approx)

## Did you know?

It has been estimated that the bacterium causing tuberculosis resides in the bodies of 2 billion people – more than one-third of all human beings.

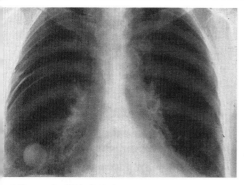

est X-ray of a TB infected person

the previous downward trend of the last 100 years had been maintained. The reasons for this change are complex but include:

1. A greater number of people living 'rough'.

2. More movement of individuals between countries.

3. Reduced immunity levels in some groups, e.g. AIDS sufferers.

4. A larger proportion of elderly, who are more vulnerable, in the population.

5. Greater antibiotic resistance in strains of the bacterium.

Tuberculosis looks set to remain one of the most significant human diseases in years to come and so presents mankind with one of its greatest challenges.

### 31.2.8 Cholera

Until 1817 cholera was thought to be a disease of the Indian sub-continent alone, but a series of pandemics in that year affected many other parts of the world. An English scientist, John Snow, suggested in 1854 that it was a disease spread by water or food but it wasn't until 1883 that Robert Koch isolated the causative agent – the curved rod-shaped bacterium *Vibrio cholerae*. Cholera remains endemic to India and parts of Asia where it kills millions of people each year, with epidemics arising elsewhere from time to time.

Cholera is transmitted by ingestion of water or food contaminated with faecal material containing the pathogen. Such contamination can arise because water is not purified, sewers leak into water supplies, untreated sewage is allowed into watercourses, or organisms, especially shellfish, feed on sewage and are subsequently eaten. Carriers who show no symptoms may unwittingly spread the disease.

The incubation period for cholera can be from 8 hours to 6 days. The most obvious symptom is a watery diarrhoea in which grey liquid stools, called 'rice water', are passed almost unceasingly. This may be accompanied by vomiting. Between them these symptoms can result in immense fluid loss – up to 20 litres a day – causing severe cramps (due to loss of body salts) and eventual collapse. In severe cases death can result within 2 days, but in milder outbreaks or with suitable treatment, complete recovery occurs in 1–3 weeks.

The priority in treatment is to replace water and salts, which may be given orally or in extreme cases intravenously. This is followed by giving antibiotics such as tetracycline to destroy the pathogen. Prevention methods involve proper sanitation and water purification to sever the normal transmission route. Personal hygiene such as washing hands after defecation and not handling food with uncovered hands also contribute. Flies may act as vectors and so preventing them coming into contact with faeces and food is a further preventative measure. Patients with the disease need to be isolated until they are no longer infected, and their faeces and vomit disposed of safely. Vaccination using killed bacteria is partially effective although the length of immunity is short – a mere 6 months.

### 31.2.9 Salmonella

*Salmonella* are a large group of bacteria which can cause a varie of diseases including typhoid, paratyphoid, enteric fever and food poisoning. These infections are collectively called **salmonelloses**. Incidences of food poisoning in the UK have increased in recent years (Fig. 31.2).

Food poisoning by *Salmonella* is characterized by diarrhoea, stomach cramps and vomiting. The incubation period can be as short as 12 hours, but the symptoms normally subside after 2–3 days and recovery is complete. In a few cases, dehydration or blood poisoning (septicaemia) may arise and can, on rare occasions, lead to death. The very young, the elderly or those with reduced immunity are most at risk. Animals, such as turkeys, chickens, pigs and cattle, form a major reservoir of *Salmonella*. If produce from these animals, including eggs and milk, is inadequately cooked before being eaten, food poisonin can result. The faeces of infected humans and domestic pets ma also contain *Salmonella*.

Modern factory farming practices, such as raising poultry in battery houses, can lead to a build-up of *Salmonella* in the animals as a result of their proximity to each other. Farmers use antibiotics and a range of preventative measures to try to conta such outbreaks but it is notoriously difficult to eradicate the bacterium completely. Humans who harbour the bacteria but show no symptoms (human carriers) may also unwittingly spread *Salmonella* infection.

As with all diseases in which diarrhoea is a symptom, treatment entails administering fluid to prevent dehydration. Otherwise it is largely a matter of resting until the symptoms abate. Personal hygiene is important to avoid contaminating other material, especially food, which could transmit infection

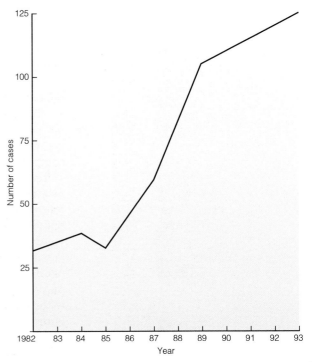

*Fig. 31.2 Cases of food poisoning in England and Wales (1982–93)*

others. Antibiotics can be given but as this encourages the development of strains of *Salmonella* resistant to these drugs, their use is normally reserved for severe cases.

Preventative measures for salmonelloses are centred upon proper hygiene, especially in the preparation and handling of food. In shops and restaurants health regulations control such measures as safe storage and packaging of food, the use of different surfaces for chopping and preparing each type of food, the proper cooking of food, cleaning of utensils and control of flies and rodents. It is equally important to maintain cleanliness and hygiene when dealing with food in the home. Thorough cooking kills *Salmonella* and is essential for animal meat and animal products. Frozen food must be properly thawed and raw and cooked meats should be stored separately. Personal hygiene and control of vermin, especially flies, reduce the risk of infection, as does proper sewage disposal and water purification.

### 31.2.10 Malaria

Malaria is one of the world's oldest and most devastating diseases. It is estimated that 365 million people are currently infected, with a further 2200 million or more at risk from contracting the disease. Up to one million children each year are thought to die from malaria in Africa alone. It is caused by any one of four parasitic protozoan species of which *Plasmodium vivax* and *Plasmodium falciparum* are the most common. Once much more widespread – there were cases in the Kent marshlands as late as the 1930s – it is now mostly confined to the tropics and subtropics.

*Plasmodium* has two different hosts during its life-cycle – humans and mosquitoes of the genus *Anopheles*. The female mosquitoes suck blood prior to laying their eggs and when they bite a human infected with *Plasmodium* they take in the parasite which then continues its life-cycle within the mosquito. When the mosquito later bites another human, the parasite passes in with the insect's saliva. Organisms which transmit diseases from human to human or animal to human are termed **vectors**. An anticoagulant is produced by the mosquito to prevent blood clotting during the feeding.

*Plasmodium* has a complex life-cycle of many stages (Fig. 31.3), but basically the parasite in humans initially invades the liver where it multiplies before releasing vast numbers of one of its stages (**merozoites**) into the bloodstream. Here they invade red blood cells where they further multiply at the expense of the cell. When this new wave of merozoites is released, it is accompanied by a bout of fever in the host. Re-invasion of other red blood cells, multiplication and release occurs about every 2 or 3 days depending on the species and so leads to a similar pattern of fever bouts in the host. Some cells of this stage develop into male and female stages (**gametocytes**) and remain in the blood until taken up by a feeding female mosquito. In the stomach of the mosquito they mature and fertilize, and the resultant zygote burrows through the stomach wall and encysts. From this cyst large numbers of a further stage (**sporozoites**) are released into the mosquito's blood from where they migrate to the salivary glands ready for injection into the next human host.

Mosquito feeding on human

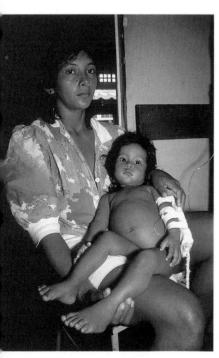

Malaria ward in Brazilian hospital

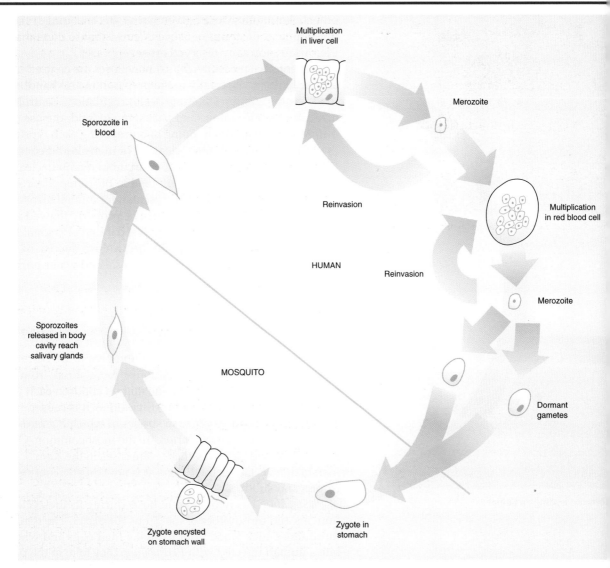

*Fig. 31.3* Plasmodium vivax – *simplified life-cycle*

The incubation period for malaria is 10–14 days. The symptoms recur in cycles which coincide with the release of merozoites and so the frequency varies with each species, e.g. 2 days in the case of *Plasmodium vivax*. The cycle of symptoms normally includes the following sequence:

1. Headache, tiredness, aching and sometimes vomiting.

2. Shivering, feeling of cold which lasts around 2 hours.

3. Sudden rise in body temperature to 40 °C or above, leading to faster heart rate and breathing rate, nausea and fever, lasting about 4 hours.

4. Profuse sweating for between 2 and 4 hours as the body temperature is returned to normal.

If untreated, many bouts of fever may be experienced, leaving the patient anaemic and exhausted. This, coupled with possible blockage or rupture of blood vessels, can cause the death of the patient. People who suffer from sickle-cell anaemia have a higher resistance to malaria than those with normal blood cells. This is discussed fully in Section 10.5.3.

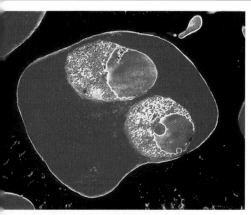

wo *Plasmoduim* merozoites pasrasiting a red blood
ell (EM) (×7000 approx)

Treatment of malaria entails giving anti-malarial drugs such as quinine, chloroquine and quinacrine, often in combination. These drugs have unpleasant side-effects and *Plasmodium* has developed resistance to them in some cases. Its many stages and strains, plus the fact that the parasite is a eukaryotic rather than a prokaryotic cell (see Section 4.1), has made the development of a vaccine very difficult. The latest area of vaccine development has centred on a protein called pfs-25 which attaches itself to the gametocytes prior to them being taken up by the mosquito. The protein seems to prevent the development of sporozoites in the mosquito, breaking the life-cycle of *Plasmodium*. While this treatment does not help the patient directly, if successful it could be used to prevent the disease being transmitted to others.

Prevention of malaria takes a number of forms:

1. Providing drugs which protect against malaria, e.g. proguanil and pyrimethamine.

2. Use of vaccines – difficult and still being developed.

3. Use of insecticides to kill mosquitoes, especially in homes.

4. Use of mosquito nets to prevent biting by mosquitoes during sleep.

5. Drainage of marshes and swamps where mosquitoes breed.

6. Use of insecticides or oil on water where mosquitoes breed, to destroy the larvae before they develop into adults.

7. Use of carnivorous fish to eat mosquito larvae.

Many of the above measures have highly undesirable environmental effects and are, in any case, difficult to implement effectively. This, coupled with the ability of *Plasmodium* to change genetically and so resist drugs and vaccines, has made the control of malaria very difficult. With the disease almost eradicated from developed countries, the impetus to make further developments has lost some of its momentum, and the costs are often beyond the means of the countries in which it is endemic. As a result, the World Health Organization's programme, started in 1955, to eradicate malaria has still a long way to go to achieve its ultimate aim.

### 31.2.11 Athlete's foot

Athlete's foot is caused by the fungus *Tinea pedis*. It is a common infection, especially amongst young adults, which gains its name from the fact that it can be transmitted when the feet are exposed in damp humid conditions, as often arise in changing rooms.

The symptoms include irritation of the skin between the toes, which becomes sodden and peels off. The infection may spread to other parts of the feet and sometimes to the hands also. The irritation is often more acute in summer because sweating exacerbates the condition. The skin can become broken and so lead to secondary infections.

The treatment consists of applying a special fungicide to the infected area, normally in the form of a cream. Other than avoiding areas where the fungus is known to occur, there is little that can be done to prevent the disease, although thorough drying of the feet after bathing, especially between the toes, and the application of talcum powder with a fungicide will help.

## 31.3    Inherited diseases

The considerable advances made in recent years in our understanding of heredity and genetics has improved our ability to recognize and treat inherited disease in a way that was unthinkable only a decade ago. Perhaps, as developed countries overcame many infectious diseases, they became more aware of alternative causes of death, including genetic ones, and focused medical attention on curing these. Certainly our mapping of genes in the human genome now allows us to identify the specific gene or genes which lead to many inherited disorders and, through techniques such as gene therapy, enable us to rectify these. Even where a cure cannot be achieved, amniocentesis and chorionic villus sampling (Biology Around Us on page 244) and genetic counselling (Section 10.7) can be used to allow individuals to make choices in fuller knowledge of the risks involved.

Information on specific inherited disorders is given elsewhere in this book, notably cystic fibrosis (Biology Around Us on page 124), haemophilia and colour blindness (Section 9.4.2), Down's syndrome, Klinefelter's and Turner's syndromes (Section 10.5.5).

## 31.4    Degenerative diseases

Degenerative diseases are the result of the gradual breakdown in the functioning of tissues or organs as a result of deterioration. This deterioration may be the result of ageing, as in the case of some forms of senile dementia, or it may occur much earlier in life, e.g. multiple sclerosis (see Biology Around Us on page 528).

### 31.4.1 Dementia

It is not a new phenomenon that mental faculties may deteriorate with age, but as medical care has considerably increased life expectancy, so the frequency of the disease has increased. Dementia adversely affects memory, intellectual capacity, attention span, personality and motor control. **Alzheimer's disease** is not the natural result of ageing but is due to diminished activity of acetylcholine transferase in the brain. Details of the disease are given in Biology Around Us on page 546.

Other forms of dementia are the result of the ageing process. They may, for example, be the result of **atherosclerosis** which causes a narrowing of arteries due to the hardening and thickening of their walls. The blood supply to the brain can thus be reduced leading to mental deterioration. Thromboses may arise in the vessels, leading to a **stroke**, or the walls may split, resulting in a **cerebral haemorrhage**. Both of these often lead to a sudden, rather than a gradual, onset of dementia.

Treatment for dementia usually consists of making the best use of a patient's remaining faculties. We do not, as yet, have any cure for conditions such as Alzheimer's disease. Much care and patience is required by those looking after the patient,

**Did you know?**

Alzheimer's disease, and other forms of senile dementia, affect around 500 000 people in the UK.

especially as failing memory can make individuals a danger to themselves. It is recent rather than long-term memory which often fails first in cases of dementia. Carers often need much support, guidance and periodic relief from their role, if the task is not to prove harmful to their own health; social services, support groups and voluntary organizations such as Age Concern provide welcome assistance in many cases.

### 31.4.2 Arthritis

Arthritis is the name given to a variety of inflammatory diseases that affect the joints and cause pain and stiffness. They may be the result of a number of factors including old age, injury, infection, genetic influences, gout, cancer, autoimmunity and nervous disease.

**Injury** may damage the smooth articular surface of a joint, especially in the knees, which are particularly vulnerable to damage when playing many sports. **Infection** of the synovial membrane or other joint tissue can also cause arthritis. One form, called **Lyme disease**, is the result of infection by a spirochaete bacterium carried by ticks. **Gout** causes the deposition of uric acid crystals in the joint, which trigger chronic inflammation and tissue damage. **Cancer** may result in tumours which create damage by deranging the anatomy of the joint. More details on cancer are given in Biology Around Us on page 146. **Nervous disease** may cause the joint to become insensitive or result in abnormal muscular movement. Both may cause injury to joints with consequent arthritis.

**Rheumatoid arthritis** is a common disease of joints. In Britain it affects four in 1000 females and one in 1000 males overall but is much more prevalent in the over-65 age-group, affecting 50 in 1000 females and 20 in 1000 males. Although it affects other parts of the body, arthritis begins with inflammation of the synovial membrane of a joint (Fig 31.4). This thickens and becomes filled with white blood cells such as lymphocytes and polymorphs. These begin to attack the cartilage, slowly eroding it away. This misdirection of the body's immune system against its own tissues rather than foreign ones is known as **autoimmunity**. The inflamed tissue releases digestive enzymes

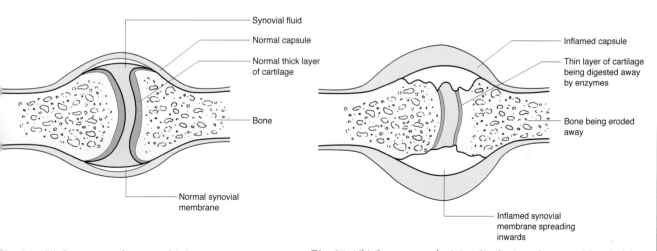

Fig. 31.4(a) Structure of a normal joint

Fig. 31.4(b) Structure of a joint displaying rheumatoid arthritis

which further erode the cartilage. The rate of cartilage destruction is very variable, taking many years in some patients but as little as a few months in others. Ultimately the ends of the bones are left grinding on one another, causing much pain and some bleeding. Tendons may become displaced, and shorter, adding to the deformity and reduced movement of the joint which is characteristic of this condition.

The causes of rheumatoid arthritis are not clearly understood but it is thought that a combination of genetic and environmental factors may initiate the autoimmunity. Because patients with the condition possess abnormal antibodies, the disease can be diagnosed using a blood test and/or X-ray examination.

Treatment of arthritis depends on its cause. Antibiotics are used to treat infection, specific drugs can control gout, while chemotherapy and radiotherapy may alleviate cancers. In the case of rheumatoid arthritis, non-steroid anti-inflammatory drugs (NSAID) such as Voltarol®, Relifex® and Brufen® may be used. Further treatment can involve medicines to block the action of enzymes, immunosuppressive agents and even the use of gold. Despite many years of research and development, an effective cure still eludes us.

## 31.5  Mental illness

The term mental illness covers a broad range of disorders which cause psychological, personality or behavioural symptoms. What constitutes a mental illness may depend upon the 'normal' behaviour of a particular society. What is considered abnormal or deviant in one group might be perfectly acceptable in another. Nor is there a clear distinction between physical and mental disease, each type often displaying symptoms of the other.

**Neuroses** cover personality disorders which often result in an exaggerated or irrational response to the ordinary stresses and demands of life. Behaviour, thought processes, emotions and certain body functions may be influenced. Neuroses include phobic, compulsive, obsessive or hysterical behaviour.

**Psychoses** are mental disorders of a more severe kind which often involve an extensive personality disorder. Disorientation in time and space may occur, hallucinations can be experienced and delusions may arise. One example of a psychosis is **schizophrenia**.

## 31.6  Human inflicted diseases

These are a number of disorders and illnesses which are the direct consequence of an individual's premeditated actions. In some cases, the harmful consequences of the actions are known at the outset; in other cases, the damage only becomes apparent later. Such illnesses include occupational diseases, as well as alcoholism and drug addiction.

### 31.6.1 Effects of tobacco on health

Tobacco smoking is harmful and contributes to the premature death of some 100 000 people each year in the UK. Tobacco smoke is a mixture of chemicals, a number of which interact with each other, multiplying their effects. Carbon monoxide, tar and nicotine have the most influence on health.

**Carbon monoxide** combines easily with the haemoglobin of the blood to form carboxyhaemoglobin. This lowers the oxygen-carrying capacity of the blood because the carbon monoxide is not released at the tissues and so remains permanently attached to haemoglobin, preventing it from carrying oxygen molecules. Regular smokers have around a 5% reduction in the oxygen-carrying capacity of their blood as a result, which leads to breathlessness. Carbon monoxide has also been shown to aggravate angina, a heart condition most often caused by the narrowing of the coronary arteries as a result of atherosclerosis. The growth of the fetus in pregnant women is slowed by the presence of carbon monoxide in the mother's blood.

**Tars** from the burning of tobacco form an aerosol of minute droplets which enter the respiratory pathways causing thickening of their epithelia, leading to chronic bronchitis. The tars can paralyse the cilia lining the trachea and bronchi, preventing them from removing the mucus secreted by the epithelial lining. As a result, dust and germ-laden mucus accumulates in the lungs, leading to infection and damage. The cough, typical of many smokers, is the result of trying to remove this build-up of mucus from the lungs. Most significantly, it is the tars in tobacco smoke which have been shown to cause lung cancer. Heavy smokers have a 25% greater risk of this disease than do non-smokers.

**Nicotine** is quickly absorbed into the blood, taking only around 30 seconds to reach the brain. It stimulates the production of adrenaline by the adrenal glands, leading to increased heart rate and raised blood pressure. Because nicotine makes blood platelets more sticky, it increases the risk of thrombosis in smokers.

Many diseases are caused by tobacco smoking, the most common being coronary heart disease, lung cancer and chronic bronchitis. **Coronary heart disease** results because smoking increases the likelihood of fatty deposits arising on the inner lining of the arteries (atherosclerosis) which cause the lumen to narrow and so restrict the movement of blood through them. Where this narrowing occurs in the coronary artery, it can lead to a heart attack. If the narrowing occurs in the carotid artery, a stroke may be the consequence. There is more than one type of **lung cancer** but bronchial carcinoma is by far the most common. The tars in tobacco smoke may induce the epithelial cells lining the bronchial tubes to become cancerous. If not treated, the tumour may completely disrupt the functioning of the lung, leaving surgical removal as the only effective treatment. A highly persistent cough, blood in the sputum and chest pains are all symptoms of lung cancer. **Chronic bronchitis** is due to the tars in tobacco irritating the epithelial lining of the bronchial tubes, causing it to produce excess mucus. The cilia lining the tubes become damaged and unable to remove this mucus in the usual manner. Only by coughing can the mucus be expelled and

## PROJECT

Is there a relationship between cigarette smoking and lung capacity?

in time this leads to scarring and narrowing of the bronchial tubes, causing breathlessness. Other smoking-related conditions include:

- Emphysema (see Biology Around Us on page 405)
- Cancer of the mouth, throat, bladder and pancreas
- Other cardiovascular diseases
- Peptic ulcers
- Narrowing of blood vessels in limbs
- Damage to the unborn child.

## 31.7 Deficiency diseases

Deficiency diseases are caused by the shortage of some essential nutrient in the diet. Perhaps the most dramatic is **kwashiorkor,** which results from a deficiency of protein in children. Several diseases result from the deficiency of vitamins and minerals. Reduced levels of vitamin C can lead to scurvy, of vitamin D can lead to rickets, while deficiency of iron causes anaemia. More details of these and other deficiency diseases are given in Section 15.2.3.

## 31.8 Protection from disease

Protection from any specific disease depends upon the nature of that disease and, in particular, its cause. Clearly a carefully balanced diet will protect against deficiency diseases. This section deals mainly, but not exclusively, with protection from infectious diseases.

### 31.8.1 Immunity and vaccination

The ability of humans to prevent pathogens establishing themselves on or in their bodies depends largely upon the effectiveness of their immune system. Details of the human immune system are given in Section 21.3.1 and vaccination is dealt with in Section 21.3.3.

### 31.8.2 Antibiotics

Alexander Fleming first discovered penicillin in 1929 and this led to the discovery of many other chemicals produced by microorganisms which inhibit the growth of other microorganisms. These are known as antibiotics and more details of them and their method of production are given in Section 30.5.1.

### 31.8.3 Sterilization and disinfection

Antiseptics and disinfectants are substances used to eliminate or control microorganisms. An **antiseptic** is a substance which is applied to the surface of a tissue or organ (most often the skin) in order to inhibit the growth of potentially pathogenic microorganisms. A **disinfectant** is a substance which destroys all microorganisms, in their vegetative state, which might cause disease. Spore and/or non-pathogenic organisms may not be destroyed. **Sterile** is a term used to denote that the material referred to is completely devoid of any viable form of life.

Sterilization can be achieved by physical or chemical means. A summary of sterilization methods is given in Table 31.1.

### 31.8.4 Diet and exercise

A properly balanced diet not only diminishes the chances of having a deficiency disease but also ensures that the body is in the best condition to protect itself from infection and to combat

ABLE 31.3    **Methods of sterilization**

**PHYSICAL METHODS**

| Method of sterilization | Mechanism by which it operates |
|---|---|
| **Moist heat** | Moist heat at temperatures of 60–80 °C will destroy vegetative microorganisms but not bacterial spores. Boiling in water for up to 6 hours will destroy spores as will heating water to 121 °C in an autoclave for 15 minutes. The heat coagulates macromolecules, especially enzymes. |
| **Dry heat** | Dry heat takes longer to inactivate biological molecules and so 1–2 hours at 160–180 °C is required to kill microorganisms. It is effective through dehydration and oxidation of macromolecules. |
| **Cold** | Temperatures of 2–6 °C will reduce the growth of most microorganisms but not kill them. 0 °C will kill most vegetative forms by the formation of ice crystals, which on warming expand and rupture the cell membrane. Spores, being dry, are not destroyed. |
| **Filtration** | Membrane filters of cellulose esters and other polymers are manufactured with a range of pore sizes. The smallest can trap even the smallest virus. They are useful for sterilizing liquids and gases. |
| **Radiation** | Radiation operates by imparting its energy to molecules in the microorganism and so disrupting them. **Non-ionizing radiation** such as ultra-violet light is absorbed by molecules such as DNA, causing mutation and disrupting protein synthesis. **Ionizing radiation** such as X-rays and gamma rays produce oxidizing ions which break up DNA and other macromolecules. |

**CHEMICAL METHODS**

| Disinfectant group | Mechanism by which it operates |
|---|---|
| **Phenols** | Used by Joseph Lister in 1867. Phenols have high lipid solubility and so disrupt microorganism membranes. |
| **Alcohols** | Ethyl and isopropyl alcohol are effective at concentrations between 50 and 80%. They dissolve lipids from cell membranes causing them to rupture and also cause cell dehydration and protein denaturation. |
| **Halogens** | Chlorine, bromine, fluorine and iodine are strong oxidizing agents. They inactivate proteins by oxidizing –SH groups, causing them to become denatured. Chlorine is used to disinfect swimming pools and drinking water while iodine is used as an antiseptic for skin wounds. |
| **Soaps and detergents** | These primarily work by lowering the surface tension of molecules so that the oily deposits on the skin can mix easily with water and be washed away along with microorganisms. Some act on the cell membrane of microorganisms causing their death. |
| **Alkylating agents** | Alkylating agents, such as formaldehyde, glutaraldehyde and ethylene oxide, act by attaching to ionized –COOH, –NH$_2$ and –SH groups in proteins and nucleic acids, disrupting their structure and killing the microorganisms. |
| **Heavy metals** | Heavy metals such as mercury and silver bind to enzymes and other proteins, causing them to denature. Silver nitrate solution operates in this way. |

any disease that might arise. Such a diet should also ensure that there is no surfeit of a particular food and so prevent disorders such as obesity and alcoholism.

Exercise too can ensure that an individual is less likely to suffer certain diseases and that he/she is also in a better state to combat any illness that is contracted. Exercise reduces the risk of cardiovascular disease such as atherosclerosis and thrombosis. It is helpful in rehabilitation from injuries and can remedy ailments such as asthma. Exercise prevents obesity, especially in conjunction with a balanced diet. Many forms of exercise can be relaxing and so reduce stress, leading to a reduced likelihood of suffering cardiovascular disease and some mental illnesses. By building strength and flexibility in muscles, bones and joints, the chance of injury, e.g. due to falls, is reduced. Exercise is frequently a social activity. Team games can engender qualities of sharing, responsibility, leadership and comradeship amongst others. Alertness can be improved, giving increased awareness to danger and reducing accidents. Being able to perform well and to feel good about oneself can raise confidence and self-esteem and so protect against depression and low self-value which can lead, amongst other things, to drug addiction and crime.

The specific effects of exercise on particular body systems are detailed at various points throughout the book, for example the respiratory system (Section 20.5) and the cardiovascular system (Section 21.5.5).

## 31.9  Detection of disease

There is no question that prevention is better than cure, but experience teaches us that even the best preventative measures sometimes fail and disease occurs. The early detection of any disease considerably increases the chances of it being successfully treated. Modern technology has given the medical profession a formidable array of techniques for providing early warnings of disease and disorders. Screening techniques can be used to examine individuals who are perfectly healthy so that some potentially harmful disease may be detected even before it has produced discernible symptoms. Given that there are not the economic resources, let alone the know-how, to screen everyone for every disease, the process is targeted on the most vulnerable groups for any particular disease, e.g. amniocentesis for pregnant women over 40 years old, who because of their age have a higher risk of bearing children with genetic disorders such as Down's Syndrome. Details of amniocentesis are given in Biology Around Us on page 244. The uses of genetic screening and counselling are discussed in Section 10.7. There are a wide variety of other screening techniques.

### 31.9.1 X-Rays and computerized axial tomography

**X-Rays** are used for body scanning as they penetrate body tissues to a varying degree depending on the density of the tissue. The denser tissues such as bone are resistant to the

# BIOLOGY AROUND US

## Biochemical detection of diabetes

The enzyme glucose oxidase permits an assessment to be made of the amount of glucose in a fluid, even if other sugars are also present – a vital measurement for people suffering from diabetes. Glucose oxidase catalyses the oxidation of glucose to produce gluconic acid and hydrogen peroxide. Biosensors have been developed in which the enzyme is immobilized on a membrane and when it reacts with glucose the product, gluconic acid, causes a change in a transducer which generates electric current. When amplified this can be read on a digital display. The electric current conducted by the acid is proportional to the amount of glucose in the solution.

An alternative approach is to make use of the hydrogen peroxide released by the action of glucose oxidase, coupled with the activity of the enzyme peroxidase. Peroxidase can oxidize a colourless organic compound to a coloured compound using the hydrogen peroxide. The colour given is a measure of the amount of glucose present.

$$\text{Glucose} + \text{Oxygen} \xrightarrow{\text{glucose oxidase}} \text{Gluconic acid} + \text{Hydrogen peroxide}$$

$$\text{Colourless compound} + \text{Hydrogen peroxide} \xrightarrow{\text{peroxidase}} \text{Coloured compound} + \text{Water}$$

Glucose oxidase, peroxidase and the colourless hydrogen donor can be immobilized on a cellulose fibre pad. This is the basis of the sticks, such as 'Clinistix', which enable diabetics to monitor their own blood or urine glucose levels.

passage of X-rays and so give a white image on the X-ray plate as the film is unexposed. Less dense tissues are penetrated and the film becomes dark as it is exposed to the X-rays. These softer tissues can be made visible by introducing into them a fluid material which is opaque to X-rays. For example, the upper region of the intestine can be seen on an X-ray plate if the patient first swallows a suspension of barium sulphate (barium meal). Once the barium is in the stomach/intestine, it resists the penetration of the X-rays and these organs appear white on the X-ray image. The same principle is used in visualizing blood vessels by injecting certain iodine-containing compounds into them.

**Computerized axial tomography (CAT)** involves taking many X-rays from a variety of different angles and combining them into one image. This provides an X-ray 'slice' through the body. By stacking together the images taken at slightly different levels in the body, a fully three-dimensional image can be obtained with the help of a computer. There are two drawbacks to the technique. Firstly, patients are exposed to relatively high levels of X-rays, which increases their risk of developing cancer. Secondly, CAT scans do not provide sharp images of soft tissues.

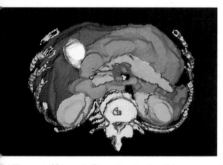

CAT scan of human digestive system

### 31.9.2 Magnetic resonance imaging

The drawbacks encountered with the use of CAT can be overcome using **magnetic resonance imaging (MRI)**. This exploits the fact that 60–70% of the human body is water and water contains hydrogen atoms. When exposed to strong magnetic fields, the nuclei of these hydrogen atoms line up like tiny magnets. If exposed to radio waves of the right frequency, they will resonate and go out of alignment, absorbing energy. By measuring the signal received from different parts of the body, the number of hydrogen nuclei and hence the number of water molecules can be determined. This tells us the relative density of the tissue and allows a computer to construct an image based on this. The need for special rooms to house the equipment and the very sophisticated computer hardware needed make MRI a very expensive technique, but it is especially useful for scanning the brain.

### 31.9.3 Endoscopy

Endoscopy is the examination of the interior of the body through an optical instrument called an **endoscope**. The endoscope may be inserted via natural openings or through specially made incisions. With the use of fibre optics, light can be transmitted to allow the instrument to produce accurate images of internal parts of the body such as the heart, intestines, bladder and joints. The **laparoscope** is a form of endoscope used to examine the abdominal cavity via a small incision just below the naval. It can be used to enable minor operations to be carried out without the need for major invasive surgery.

### 31.9.4 Ultrasound

Rather like light, sound waves can be formed into a beam which is reflected from objects in a way that provides information about their shape. In ultrasound scanning, a beam of high frequency sound (usually 1–10 MHz) is directed into the body. The beam is reflected from internal organs and the pattern of echoes produced is detected by the scanner and transduced into pictures on a screen. The technique can be used to view organs such as the heart, but is especially useful for examination of the fetus during pregnancy. Having rapidly dividing cells, the fetus is especially vulnerable to the mutating effects of X-rays, making this form of examination too dangerous to contemplate. With ultrasound scanning, the size of the fetal head can be determined, giving an accurate estimate of the length of pregnancy so far and hence the likely date of birth. Physical disabilities such as spina bifida or microcephaly are apparent using the technique. Any unusual position of the fetus is also obvious. With this type of information, remedial measures can sometimes be taken or adequate preparations for a difficult birth can be made. Ultrasound is used to guide needles during techniques such as amniocentesis and it also has therapeutic uses because it can be used to generate heat in deep-seated tissues. In this way it may reduce stiffness and pain in joints or be used to treat sports injuries such as hamstring pulls.

# 31.10   Questions

**1.** (a) Give **three** ways by which the virus known as HIV, which causes AIDS, can gain access to the human body. (3 marks)

(b) Suggest ways by which infection by this virus can be avoided. (3 marks)

(c) Briefly explain how HIV infection can lead to death. (3 marks)

(d) Why is it difficult to produce a vaccine against HIV? (2 marks)

(Total 11 marks)

*Oxford March 1997, Paper 42, No. 6*

**2.** The drawing shows the structure of an influenza virus.

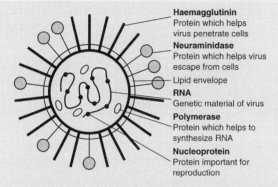

Haemagglutinin
Protein which helps virus penetrate cells

Neuraminidase
Protein which helps virus escape from cells

Lipid envelope

RNA
Genetic material of virus

Polymerase
Protein which helps to synthesize RNA

Nucleoprotein
Protein important for reproduction

(a) Influenza vaccines may be made from parts of viruses. Give **one** part of the virus that would be suitable for making a vaccine. Give a reason for your answer. (2 marks)

(b) In order to provide protection against influenza, it is necessary to vaccinate people with a different vaccine every year. Suggest an explanation for this. (2 marks)

(c) Explain why it is unlikely that influenza affected early human hunter–gatherer groups. (1 mark)

(Total 5 marks)

*AEB Summer 1996, Module Paper 6, No. 3*

**3.** The diagram shows the life-cycle of the malarial parasite, *Plasmodium falciparum*.

(a) (i) What part does the female mosquito play in the transmission of the parasite? (1 mark)

(ii) From the diagram, what is the minimum time which must elapse after infection before a human could infect another mosquito? (1 mark)

(b) Suggest **one** stage in the life-cycle when the parasite would be vulnerable to attack by human antibodies. Give a reason for your answer. (2 marks)

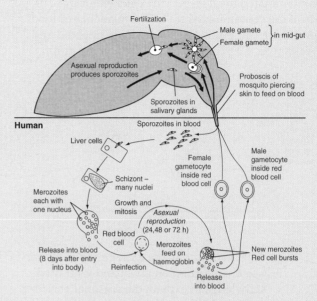

Female *Anopheles* mosquito

Fertilization

Male gamete
Female gamete } in mid-gut

Asexual reproduction produces sporozoites

Proboscis of mosquito piercing skin to feed on blood

Sporozoites in salivary glands

**Human**   Sporozoites in blood

Liver cells

Female gametocyte inside red blood cell

Male gametocyte inside red blood cell

Schizont – many nuclei

Merozoites each with one nucleus

Growth and mitosis

Asexual reproduction (24,48 or 72 h)

Red blood cell

Merozoites feed on haemoglobin

New merozoites Red cell bursts

Release into blood (8 days after entry into body)

Reinfection

Release into blood

(c) The drugs quinine and chloroquine have been used to treat malaria by killing the parasites in the red blood cells. These drugs are now less effective than they used to be. Suggest why. (2 marks)

(d) Recently, a drug called artemisinin has been developed which has proved effective against the malarial parasite. This drug reacts with iron to release a highly reactive iron oxide which is extremely toxic. Suggest why artemisinin is effective against the malarial parasite. (3 marks)

(Total 9 marks)

*AEB Summer 1997, (H. Biology) Paper 1, No. 13*

**4.** Cigarette smoking is considered to be the single greatest cause of preventable and premature death in the United Kingdom. It accounts for about 100 000 deaths each year in Britain; that is about one death in every six which occur.

(a) Briefly explain why smoking:

(i) increases the risk of coronary heart disease and strokes; (2 marks)

(ii) damages the respiratory tract and oxygen transporting mechanism; (2 marks)

(iii) increases the risk to the fetus during pregnancy. (2 marks)

(b) Name **one** other disease which is linked to smoking and explain why smoking will increase the risk of this disease. (2 marks)

(Total 8 marks)

*Oxford March 1997, Paper 42, No. 4*

647

**5.** Mild food poisoning can be caused by a number of different types of bacteria. One such group of bacteria belongs to the genus *Campylobacter*. Humans usually become infected by *Campylobacter* by eating contaminated meat (especially chicken) or by drinking contaminated milk. The incidence of food poisoning caused by *Campylobacter* in England and Wales over a 3-year period is shown in the graph.

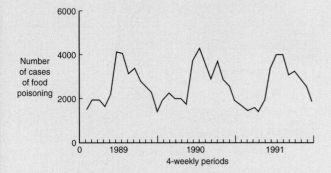

*(a)* What is meant by the term **genus**? *(2 marks)*
*(b)* Use the information given and your own knowledge to explain the seasonal variation in the incidence of food poisoning by *Campylobacter*. *(4 marks)*
*(Total 6 marks)*

*AEB Summer 1996, (H. Biology) Paper 1, No. 14*

**6.** The table below refers to constituents of diet and the effects of deficiencies in the supply of these constituents. Copy and complete the table by writing the appropriate word or words in the empty boxes.

| Constituent of the diet | Effect of deficiency |
|---|---|
| Retinol | |
| | Bleeding from small blood vessels and gums |
| Essential amino acids | |
| Fibre | |
| | Anaemia |

*(Total 5 marks)*

*Edexcel June 1997, B/HB4D, No. 1*

**7.** Chronic bronchitis is more common in the United Kingdom than in any other country in the world.
*(a)* Describe **two** risk factors that could account for the high incidence of chronic bronchitis in the United Kingdom. *(2 marks)*
*(b)* (i) Explain how chronic bronchitis affects the efficiency of breathing. *(3 marks)*
   (ii) The bronchioles (air passages) in the lungs have muscle cells in their walls. The cells are stimulated to contract by acetylcholine produced by nerve endings. The acetylcholine molecules fit into protein receptors on the muscle cell membranes.
Anticholinergic drugs have molecules that fit the same receptors. Explain how these drugs may be useful in the treatment of chronic bronchitis.
*(3 marks)*
*(Total 8 marks)*

*NEAB June 1998, Paper BY08, No. 2*

**8.** *(a)* (i) Describe how the lungs of a patient with emphysema differ from those of a healthy person. *(1 mark)*
   (ii) Explain why the lungs of an emphysema patient cannot supply the body with sufficient oxygen. *(2 marks)*
*(b)* The table shows the results of a study of 83 patients relating the occurrence of black particles in the lungs and emphysema to the number of cigarettes smoked per day.

| | | Number of cigarettes smoked per day | Severity of emphysema/arbitrary scale | | | |
|---|---|---|---|---|---|---|
| | | | 0 | 1 | 2 | 3 |
| Amount of black particles in lungs/ arbitrary scale | 1 | 0 | 11 | 3 | 0 | 1 |
| | | 1–15 | 1 | 5 | 0 | 0 |
| | | 16 or more | 5 | 7 | 3 | 2 |
| | 2 | 0 | 1 | 2 | 1 | 1 |
| | | 1–15 | 1 | 1 | 1 | 0 |
| | | 16 or more | 0 | 7 | 11 | 9 |
| | 3 | 0 | 0 | 0 | 0 | 0 |
| | | 1–15 | 0 | 0 | 0 | 0 |
| | | 16 or more | 0 | 1 | 3 | 6 |

Calculate the percentage of people who smoked 16 or more cigarettes per day who had:
(i) severe emphysema (a value of 3 on the scale): *(1 mark)*
(ii) a large amount of black particles in the lungs (a value of 3 on the scale). *(1 mark)*
*(c)* Some people are genetically unable to produce a protein called $\alpha_1$-antitrypsin. Unless they are provided with this protein they will develop emphysema.
(i) Which **one** of the following techniques would you consider to be of use in detecting inability to produce $\alpha_1$-antitrypsin?
   **A** biochemical test
   **B** endoscopy
   **C** ultrasound
   **D** X-rays

Give the letter of your choice.    (*1 mark*)
(ii)  Suggest why $\alpha_1$-antitrypsin is not given
as a medicine to be swallowed.  (*1 mark*)
(*Total 7 marks*)

NEAB June 1995, BY08, No. 5

*(a)* During a hospital check-up it was found that Mr Binge's liver removed alcohol from his bloodstream at the rate of 9.4 cm³ alcohol per hour. One evening Mr Binge consumed the following drinks.

| Beverage | Measure consumed | Volume of each measure (cm³) | Alcohol content (%) |
|---|---|---|---|
| Beer | 4 cans | 440 | 3.7 |
| White wine | 1 glass | 180 | 8.6 |
| Whisky | 2 glasses | 45 | 40.0 |

Assuming that the entire alcohol content of these beverages was absorbed into Mr Binge's bloodstream, calculate how long it would take for all the alcohol to be removed. Show your working.    (*2 marks*)
*(b)* Suggest **two** different factors that might affect the rate at which alcohol is absorbed from the human gastrointestinal tract.
(*2 marks*)
*(c)* Explain how excessive, long-term consumption of alcohol might adversely affect the following body systems.
(i)  Gastrointestinal tract    (*2 marks*)
(ii)  Nervous system    .    (*2 marks*)
*(d)* The figure shows part of the human airway system and lungs.

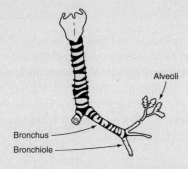

(i)  Goblet cells and ciliated epithelial cells are found lining the bronchioles. Explain how these cells help to protect the lungs.    (*2 marks*)

(ii)  Copy and complete the table below by naming an airway disease that affects each of the labelled regions.
(*3 marks*)

| Name of region | Airway disease |
|---|---|
| Bronchus | |
| Bronchiole | |
| Alveoli | |

*(e)* Inhalers are increasingly used to treat obstructive airway disease. One type of inhaler dispenses measured doses of an involuntary-muscle relaxant such as salbutamol (e.g. ventolin) whereas another type dispenses a corticosteroid such as beclamethosone. Explain the biological role of inhalers such as these in the treatment of obstructive airway disease.
(i)  Involuntary-muscle relaxant
(ii)  Corticosteroid    (*2 marks*)
(*Total 15 marks*)

Oxford & Cambridge June 1996, Unit B7, No. 3

10. An investigation into an outbreak of Salmonella food poisoning in a children's day nursery found that one of the voluntary carers was a carrier of *Salmonella*. The carer did not show any symptoms of the disease and was unaware that she could pass it on. On the day before the outbreak of food poisoning this carer had helped to make ham sandwiches and put ready-prepared rice pudding into dishes. The food had then been covered by cling film and left for 2 hours on a table, ready for tea.
*(a)* (i)  What type of microorganism is responsible for causing Salmonella food poisoning?    (*1 mark*)
(ii)  Explain how this outbreak of food poisoning could have occurred.
(*4 marks*)
*(b)* Suggest how the carer could have been tested to establish whether she was a carrier of *Salmonella*.    (*1 mark*)
(*Total 6 marks*)

NEAB June 1997, Paper BY08, No. 2

# 32     Food, diet and health

Human beings require a constant supply of essential nutrients in balanced proportions in order to maintain themselves in a healthy state. It might therefore be thought that the dietary requirements of all humans are the same – not so. An individual's needs will vary according to size, age, sex, level of activity, state of health and particular personal circumstances, e.g. pregnancy. Even though the requirements of individuals of the same size, age, sex, activity, health and personal circumstances may be the same, the actual diet can differ markedly according to the cultural and economic background of each person as well as their individual beliefs and preferences. Those of us in western Europe with our varied choice of food perhaps too easily forget that in most parts of the world only a few staple foods are available and in many areas even these are lacking in sufficient quantity to sustain the population. Staple foods vary according to the crops grown and these are often determined historically or by climate. Rice is the staple food in South East Asia while maize fulfils this function in Central America. Religious observance may also determine diet to some degree, e.g. Judaism forbids the eating of pork, Hindus are largely vegetarian. Slimmers, vegans and diabetics have their own restricted diets although for very different reasons.

## 32.1     Balanced diet

In humans **carbohydrates** and **fats** are needed in relatively large quantities as sources of energy and **proteins** are needed in large amounts for growth and repair. **Vitamins** and **minerals** are required in much smaller quantities for a variety of specific functions. **Water** is a vital constituent of the diet for many reasons (see Section 32.1.7) and **dietary fibre** (roughage) is necessary for efficient digestion.

### 32.1.1 Energy requirements

The amount of energy in foods is expressed in **joules** although for practical purposes the **kilojoule (kJ)** is a much more convenient unit. Some books and magazines still use the former terms calorie and kilocalorie (one calorie = 4.18 joules and one Calorie (= kilocalorie) = 4.18 kilojoules). To measure the amount of energy in different foods, a given mass is burned in oxygen in an apparatus called a **bomb calorimeter**. The total heat generated gives a measure of the food's energy content which is known as its **calorific value**.

The term which describes the basal metabolic processes needed to keep a human alive is **basal metabolism** and the rate at which energy is used up in maintaining basal metabolism is termed the **basal metabolic rate (BMR)**. It is measured in $kJ\,h^{-1}$ under standard conditions, namely when an individual is completely at rest, lying down in the warmth and at least 12 hours after a meal. Either the amount of heat produced is measured directly or the oxygen uptake (or carbon dioxide output) is measured and from this the energy used can be calculated.

One factor which influences the BMR is body size. As body fat is storage material with a very low metabolic rate, the very variable amounts of fat found in different individuals tends to distort the figures. For this reason the weight of the body excluding fat is normally used as a measure of body size. This is called the **lean body mass**. As women have a higher proportion of body fat than men, as well as being lighter, they have a lower BMR: $251\,kJ\,h^{-1}$ for an average woman (55 kg) compared to $293\,kJ\,h^{-1}$ for an average man (70 Kg). The surface area of the body also affects BMR. The larger the surface area, for any given weight, the greater the heat loss and so the higher the BMR. Age is also a factor. Children have a relatively higher BMR for a given weight than adults (although the actual figure is smaller because of their smaller lean body mass). The maximum BMR occurs at around the age of 20 years diminishing slowly as one ages, e.g. from $293\,kJ\,h^{-1}$ at 20 years old to $259\,kJ\,h^{-1}$ at age 70 years. BMR also increases after taking in food (**diet induced thermogenesis**) as well as with the level of the hormone thyroxine which controls metabolism.

As soon as a person becomes active, the energy requirement increases; the more strenuous the activity the greater the amount of energy needed. Table 32.1 provides examples of the recommended daily energy intake for humans of various ages undertaking various activities.

TABLE 32.1 **Recommended daily intake of energy according to age, activity and sex**

| Age/years | Average body weight/kg | Degree of activity/ circumstances | Energy requirement/kJ | |
|---|---|---|---|---|
| | | | Male | Female |
| 1 | 7 | Average | 3200 | 3200 |
| 5 | 20 | Average | 7500 | 7500 |
| 10 | 30 | Average | 9500 | 9500 |
| 15 | 45 | Average<br>Sedentary | 11 500<br>11 300 | 11 500<br>9000 |
| 25 | 65 (male)<br>55 (female) | Moderately active<br>Very active<br>Sedentary | 12 500<br>15 000<br>11 000 | 9500<br>10 500<br>9000 |
| 50 | 65 (male)<br>55 (female) | Moderately active<br>Very active | 12 000<br>15 000 | 9500<br>10 500 |
| 75 | 63 (male)<br>53 (female) | Sedentary | 9000 | 8000 |
| Any | – | During pregnancy | – | 10 000 |
| Any | – | Breast feeding | – | 11 500 |

## PROJECT

Use a simple calorimeter to investigate the suggestion that low fat cheeses contain less energy than full fat cheeses.

### 32.1.2 Carbohydrates

Details of the chemistry of carbohydrates are given in Chapter 2. Their main function is to provide energy – ideally two-thirds of the total with the remaining third being provided by fats. Sugars and starch are the carbohydrates which provide energy. Sugars are found in most plants in small quantities but are especially concentrated in sugar cane and sugar beet from which the sugar sucrose, is extracted. Foods made from refined sugar are therefore rich in sucrose and these include jams, biscuits and chocolate as well as many sweetened drinks. Honey is rich in another sugar – fructose. Foods rich in starch include bread, porridge and potatoes.

As carbohydrates are the body's main energy source their inclusion in the diet of athletes is clearly important. It has been shown that endurance athletes who eat a diet rich in carbohydrate for 3–4 days, after several days on a normal mixed diet, can increase their glycogen store from 15 g to 25 g for each kg of muscle. This technique is known as **muscle glycogen loading** and is a means of enhancing athletic performance.

Fruits, vegetables and cereal grains are rich in an insoluble carbohydrate called cellulose. While cellulose therefore provides no direct nutritional value, it is no less important as it is the main constituent of **dietary fibre**. Some components of dietary fibre such as hemicellulose can be fermented in the large intestine to yield fatty acids which can be used to provide energy. Dietary fibre is necessary to give bulk to the food so that it can pass efficiently along the alimentary canal. It has also been shown to lower the cholesterol level in the blood. If the diet is low in fibre the risk of certain diseases is increased. These include constipation, appendicitis, heart disease, haemorrhoids, cancer of the colon and diverticular disease.

### 32.1.3 Fats and oils (lipids)

Details of the chemistry and functions of lipids are given in Section 2.6. As fat yields more energy for a given weight than carbohydrate it is the main long-term energy store of the body, but its accumulation can lead to obesity and other health problems. For this reason only about a third of the body's energy requirements should come from fat with the remainder being provided by carbohydrate. Foods rich in fat include meat, milk and milk products such as cream, butter and cheese, margarine and baked products like cakes, pastry and biscuits. Any food which is fried is likely to be rich in fat.

Much attention has been focused on the correlation between a high fat intake in the diet and heart disease. It is always difficult to draw direct relationships between one type of food and the incidence of a specific disease because foods contain a wide variety of substances. In addition factors such as exercise, stress and smoking affect an individual's health and the way food is utilised. It does, however, seem that a high intake of fat, especially saturated fat, is a contributory factor in causing heart disease.

### 32.1.4 Protein

The chemistry of proteins is given in Section 2.7. As a last resort, the body may respire proteins to provide energy, but their main function is as a source of amino acids which are used to

# BIOLOGY AROUND US

## Diseases associated with a low fibre diet

There are a number of diseases of the colon which seem to be linked primarily to eating a diet low in fibre. Fibre adds bulk to food and helps to maintain its normal passage through the alimentary canal by peristalsis. When the diet is low in fibre the segments formed in peristalsis may close completely and build up within them a high pressure. Over the years this tends to push the mucosal lining of the colon into the muscular wall to form balloon-like diverticula often containing faecal material. These diverticula may cause no symptoms and have been found in one third of the population of industrialized countries after middle age. However painful infections may begin in them giving rise to the condition known as **diverticulosis**.

Another disease which develops as a result of a low-fibre diet is **irritable bowel syndrome**. This is characterized by alternating periods of diarrhoea and constipation, by flatulence and a distension of the abdomen. Hard, small stools are passed five or six times a day. It may follow gastroenteritis but often the symptoms appear gradually, usually by the age of 30 and often in teenagers. It is thought to be a stress-related condition since the symptoms worsen in times of anxiety. It seems to result from a lack of coordination in peristalsis so that the waves of contraction become strong and irregular. The symptoms are relieved by increasing the fibre intake although antispasmodic and anti-anxiety drugs may also be used. One-third of all malignant tumours in Western countries are found in the colon and, although there may be a genetic factor involved, the most important factor is thought to be a diet low in fibre. **Cancers of the colon** are rare in Africa and Japan where the intake of dietary fibre is high. If the growth is on the right-hand side it rarely obstructs the colon but it does cause pain, loss of weight, anaemia and fever. Tumours on the left usually cause a blockage leading to pain and distension of the abdomen. Cancers of the colon do not respond well to chemotherapy and so they are removed surgically along with any associated lymph glands. The surgeon then aims to restore the continuity of the colon so that it can function normally. If this is not possible the patient may have a colostomy so that the contents of the large intestine can be voided through the wall of the abdomen into a bag. Four-fifths of people suffering from cancer of the colon make a good recovery.

synthesize new proteins. These proteins are used in metabolism, growth and repair. Of the 20 amino acids needed by humans, 11 can be synthesized by the body and are termed **non-essential amino acids**. The remaining 9 must be provided in the diet and are termed **essential amino acids**. Of these 8 are needed throughout life while one, histidine, is only essential in infancy. The proportions of the 20 amino acids in any protein varies considerably. Clearly proteins with more essential amino acids are of greater value than those with less. More importantly, the proteins with a similar proportion of essential amino acids to the proteins of the human body are of greatest value of all.

Measuring the amount of protein in a food is very difficult and for this reason the amount of nitrogen which is obtained from a protein is used as a more convenient measure. The quality of a protein is measured as its **biological value (BV)**. This is expressed as:

$$\text{Biological value of a protein} = \frac{\text{Nitrogen retained}}{\text{Nitrogen absorbed}} \times 100$$

The amount of nitrogen absorbed by the body is equal to that taken in as food minus that lost in the faeces. The amount retained is equal to that absorbed minus that lost in the urine. We can now express the biological value slightly differently:

$$\text{B.V.} = \frac{\text{Nitrogen intake} - \text{Nitrogen in faeces} - \text{Nitrogen in urine}}{\text{Nitrogen intake} - \text{Nitrogen in faeces}} \times 100$$

The biological value does not take account of how easy it is to digest a protein food. The digestibility of protein is measured as

$$\frac{\text{Nitrogen intake} - \text{Nitrogen in faeces}}{\text{Nitrogen intake}}$$

The digestibility of a protein depends on the nature of the protein, how it is prepared (i.e. the method of cooking) and individual differences in how easily it is broken down.

Foods rich in protein include meat, fish, eggs, milk, cheese, bread, nuts and some vegetables such as peas. Although plant food contains proportionately less protein, a properly balanced vegetable diet can nevertheless provide all essential amino acids. It is only where there is dependence on just one or two plant foods as sources of proteins that malnutrition results. The amount of protein required in the diet varies with age and with differing circumstances, e.g. pregnancy. Table 32.2 gives the recommended values for various groups.

TABLE 32.2  **Recommended daily amount of protein according to age and sex**

| Age (years) | Protein (g) | |
| :---: | :---: | :---: |
| | Females | Males |
| 1 | 27 | 30 |
| 5–6 | 42 | 43 |
| 9–11 | 51 | 56 |
| 15–17 | 53 | 72 |
| 18–34 | 54 | 72 |
| 65–74 | 47 | 60 |
| 75+ | 42 | 54 |
| Pregnancy | 60 | — |
| Lactation | 69 | — |

### 32.1.5 Vitamins

Vitamins are a group of essential organic compounds which are needed in small amounts for normal growth and metabolism. If the diet lacks a particular vitamin, a disorder called a **deficiency** disease results. The vitamins required vary from species to species. Table 32.3 lists those needed in a human diet and the roles they play. Vitamins are normally classified as **water soluble** (vitamins C and the B complex) or **fat soluble** (vitamins A, D, E and K). Whereas excess water-soluble vitamins are simply excreted in urine, fat-soluble vitamins tend to accumulate in fatty tissues of the body, and may even build up to lethal concentrations if taken in excess.

Cooking and storage may affect the vitamin content of food. In the case of vitamin C for example, it is highly soluble in water and therefore food boiled in water quickly loses its vitamin C. In addition it is readily oxidized, especially at higher temperatures, high pHs and in the presence of light. Vitamin C can be broken down by an enzyme found in plant cells, but as the two are kept apart in natural conditions, the vitamin is only affected when the food is cut, dropped or bruised. To maintain the highest level of

TABLE 32.3  **Vitamins required in the human diet**

| Vitamin/name | Fat/water soluble | Major food sources | Function | Deficiency symptoms |
|---|---|---|---|---|
| $A_1$ Retinol | Fat soluble | Liver, vegetables, fruits, dairy foods | Maintains normal epithelial structure. Needed to form visual pigments | Dry skin. Poor night vision |
| $B_1$ Thiamin | Water soluble | Liver, legumes, yeast, wheat and rice germ | Coenzyme in cellular respiration | Nervous disorder called beri-beri. Neuritis and mental disturbances. Heart failure |
| $B_2$ Riboflavin | Water soluble | Liver, yeast, dairy produce | Coenzymes (flavo-proteins) in cellular respiration | Soreness of the tongue and corners of the mouth |
| $B_3$ (pp factor) Niacin | Water soluble | Liver, yeast, wholemeal bread | Coenzyme (NAD) in cellular metabolism | Skin lesions known as pellagra. Diarrhoea |
| $B_5$ Pantothenic acid | Water soluble | Liver, yeast, eggs | Forms part of acetyl coenzyme A in cellular respiration | Neuromotor disorders, fatigue and muscle cramps |
| $B_6$ Pyridoxine | Water soluble | Liver, kidney, fish | Coenzymes in amino acid metabolism | Dermatitis. Nervous disorders |
| $B_{12}$ Cyanocobalamine | Water soluble | Meat, eggs, dairy food | Nucleoprotein (RNA) synthesis. Needed in red blood cell formation | Pernicious anaemia. Malformation of red blood cells |
| Biotin | Water soluble | Liver, yeast. Synthesized by intestinal bacteria | Coenzymes in carboxylation reactions | Dermatitis and muscle pains |
| Folic acid | Water soluble | Liver, vegetables, fish | Nucleoprotein synthesis. Red blood cell synthesis | Anaemia |
| C Ascorbic acid | Water soluble | Citrus fruits, tomatoes, potatoes | Formation of connective tissues, especially collagen fibres | Non-formation of connective tissues. Bleeding gums – scurvy |
| D Calciferol | Fat soluble | Liver, fish oils, dairy produce. Action of sunlight on skin | Absorption and metabolism of calcium and phosphorus, important in formation of teeth and bones | Defective bone formation known as rickets |
| E Tocopherol | Fat soluble | Liver, green vegetables | Function unclear in humans. In rats it prevents haemolysis of red blood cells | Anaemia |
| K Phylloquinone | Fat soluble | Green vegetables. Synthesized by intestinal bacteria | Blood clotting | Failure of blood to clot |

vitamin C, food should therefore be stored in a cool, dark place, prepared with the minimum of cutting or chopping necessary and cooked in the minimum of water for the least possible time.

### 32.1.6 Minerals

The principal minerals required in the human diet, and their sources, are given in Table 32.4

**Calcium** is a particularly important mineral as it is a major component of the skeleton – so much so that, by law, it must be added to all white flour to try to ensure an adequate quantity is available in most people's diet. The absorption of calcium is assisted by vitamin D, without which little would be taken up, and so the consequences of their deficiencies are much the same – namely **rickets** (in children) and **osteomalacia** (in adults). In both cases the bones become soft and weak with the long bones of the legs bending under the body weight as a consequence in the case of rickets. The amount of calcium absorption in women falls around the time of the menopause possibly leading to osteoporosis. Growing children require more calcium than adults as it is needed for growth of bones. The recommended daily intake in children is 600–700 mg, falling to 500 mg in adults. Women need more calcium in the diet during pregnancy and

TABLE 32.4 **Some essential minerals required in the human diet**

| Mineral | Major food source | Function |
|---|---|---|
| **Macronutrients**<br>Calcium ($Ca^{2+}$) | Dairy foods, eggs, green vegetables | Constituent of bones and teeth, needed in blood clotting and muscle contraction. Enzyme activator |
| Chlorine ($Cl^-$) | Table salt | Maintenance of anion/cation balance. Formation of hydrochloric acid |
| Magnesium ($Mg^{2+}$) | Meat, green vegetables | Component of bones and teeth. Enzyme activator |
| Phosphate ($PO_4^{3-}$) | Dairy foods, eggs, meat, vegetables | Constituent of nucleic acids, ATP, phospholipids (in cell membranes), bones and teeth |
| Potassium ($K^+$) | Meat, fruit and vegetables | Needed for nerve and muscle action and in protein synthesis |
| Sodium ($Na^+$) | Table salt, dairy foods, meat, eggs, vegetables | Needed for nerve and muscle action. Maintenance of anion/cation balance |
| Sulphate ($SO_4^{2-}$) | Meat, eggs, dairy foods | Component of proteins and coenzymes |
| **Micronutrients (trace elements)**<br>Cobalt ($Co^{2+}$) | Meat | Component for vitamin $B_{12}$ and needed for the formation of red blood cells |
| Copper ($Cu^{2+}$) | Liver, meat, fish | Constituent of many enzymes. Needed for bone and haemoglobin formation |
| Fluorine ($F^-$) | Many water supplies | Improves resistance to tooth decay |
| Iodine ($I^-$) | Fish, shellfish, iodized salt | Component of the growth hormone, thyroxine |
| Iron ($Fe^{2+}$ or $Fe^{3+}$) | Liver, meat, green vegetables | Constituent of many enzymes, electron carriers, haemoglobin and myoglobin |
| Manganese ($Mn^{2+}$) | Liver, kidney, tea and coffee | Enzyme activator and growth factor in bone development |
| Molybdenum ($Mo^{4+}$) | Liver, kidney, green vegetables | Required by some enzymes |
| Zinc ($Zn^{2+}$) | Liver, fish, shellfish | Enzyme activator, involved in the physiology of insulin |

lactation to satisfy the additional needs of the fetus and new-born. The recommended daily intake for these women therefore rises to 1200 mg.

**Iron** deficiency leads to **anaemia** because it is a component of haemoglobin in red blood cells. Tiredness, lethargy, dizziness and headaches are all symptoms of anaemia as a consequence of less oxygen being carried by the blood. It is the commonest deficiency disease in Britain, although diet is not the only cause. Anaemia is much more common in women, with around 15% in Britain suffering from the disorder, largely because of the loss of iron in the blood during menstruation.

While it is usually a mineral deficiency which adversely affects health, in the case of **salt (sodium chloride)** an excess is more the problem. High salt intake increases blood pressure (hypertension) leading to, or compounding, other cardiovascular diseases.

TABLE 32.5 **Human daily water balance**

| Process | Water uptake /cm$^3$ | Water output /cm$^3$ |
| --- | --- | --- |
| Drinking | 1450 | – |
| In food | 800 | – |
| From respiration | 350 | – |
| In urine | – | 1500 |
| In sweat | – | 600 |
| Evaporation from lungs | – | 400 |
| In faeces | – | 100 |
| TOTAL | 2600 | 2600 |

## Did you know?

The average human in a lifetime consumes 75 tonnes of water, 17 tonnes of carbohydrates, 2.5 tonnes of proteins and 1 tonne of fats.

### 32.1.7 Water

Water makes up 60–70% of the total body weight of humans and serves a wide variety of important functions . Table 32.5 gives the daily water balance in a human not engaged in active work, i.e. there is no excessive sweating.

### 32.1.8 Milk

As milk is the only food received by humans in the period after birth, it follows that it must provide all essential materials for growth and development. In this sense it is a balanced diet in itself. It cannot, however, sustain healthy development indefinitely for these reasons:

1. **It contains little if any iron** – This is no problem to a new-born baby as it accumulates iron from its mother before birth. This store cannot last indefinitely and alternative sources of iron are necessary in later life.

2. **It contains no fibre** – We saw in Section 32.1.2 the necessity of fibre and the problems associated with its long-term absence from the diet.

3. **It contains a high proportion of fat** – For a young, actively growing human this is ideal, but as we grow the energy demand is reduced. This could lead to an increase in weight due to storage of the excess fat and a consequent increased risk of heart disease. For the early years, and as a supplement to the human diet in later life, milk nevertheless plays an invaluable role.

### 32.1.9 Dietary reference values

We have seen throughout this section that the requirement for any particular food depends upon the age, sex and physical condition of an individual. Tables can be constructed which show the **recommended daily amount (RDA)** of each nutrient which any particular group of individuals needs in order to maintain good health. These quantities are also referred to as **dietary reference values (DRV)**.

The values form a measure which can be used to make comparisons of the nutritional intake of different groups. In themselves they do not show whether or not a person is malnourished as individual requirements differ; they are more a type of 'average' requirement for a particular group. An individual with an intake less than the DRV for a particular nutrient will not necessarily suffer any harm as a result, but could be in danger of doing so.

## 32.2  Malnutrition

Good health depends upon the consumption of a diet with the relevant balance of nutrients to suit the sex, age and physical condition of an individual. Too much or too little, in part or total is known as malnutrition and could, in time, lead to ill health. The reasons for malnutrition vary. They can be as a result of disease, e.g. diabetes, a consequence of over-indulgence or due to economic or cultural factors; poor education or a lack of understanding of diet is a common underlying cause. While the members of the more wealthy nations often strive unsuccessfully to reduce their food intake, many of their counterparts in poorer countries struggle equally unsuccessfully to find enough food to survive. While richer nations spend vast sums of money in treating the medical conditions resulting from overeating, people in poorer nations starve for want of a subsistence diet.

### PROJECT

Is there always a relationship between body fat and fitness?

### 32.2.1 Overnutrition

With supermarkets full of food from all over the world and available throughout the year, it is difficult to imagine our ancestors (or indeed those in many countries today) who had to eat what food was available when it was available. Food was often seasonal and long periods might elapse before another meal could be taken. As a result as much food as possible was consumed, some of which was stored to act as an energy source when the external supplies dried up. As this internal store of food added weight to the body, possibly restricting movement, the least heavy type of food – namely fat – was stored. The legacy of this irrefutable logic of evolution is that even when food is readily available we still tend to consume it in quantity, and store it as fat as if we feared that all the supermarkets and local shops were about to go out of business, or close for an extended holiday. As a result a large percentage of people in Britain are overweight increasing their risk of cardiovascular disease, diabetes, certain cancers and gall stones amongst other problems.

The ideal weight for an individual depends upon his/her height. One measure frequently used is the **body mass index (BMI)**. This is the weight (W) in kgs divided by the height ($h$) squared in metres.

$$\text{BMI} = \frac{W}{h^2}$$

A body mass index of between 20 and 25 represents the least risk to health. Where the BMI exceeds 27.5 an individual is said to be **obese**, a condition which presents a considerable risk to health.

The causes of obesity are not just an excessive intake of food, but often a lack of physical exercise which is the best means of 'burning off' some of the energy taken in. There may also be a psychological dimension with eating being increased under conditions of stress, boredom or depression. The range, quantity and variety of food available coupled with aggressive marketing increases the temptation to eat more food than is strictly essential. Many convenience foods which can be consumed rapidly and with no preparation, e.g. crisps, biscuits and soft-drinks, are especially attractive in the increasingly busy and hectic world in which we live. These foods are concentrated forms of energy and do not provide much bulk, and so do not give the feeling of fullness which would depress appetite and prevent more from being eaten.

Reduction in weight is best achieved by a combination of reducing the energy intake in the form of food and increasing energy output through physical exercise. Any slimming diet should ensure that there is an adequate supply of essential minerals and vitamins. The intake of carbohydrate and especially fat should be reduced. It is important not to limit energy intake too drastically – typically a daily consumption of 3500–6500 kJ will be effective in losing weight although much depends on the extent of physical activity. There are dangers in reducing energy intake too rapidly because the body needs time to adjust to changes and the diet may prove too unappetizing to be maintained for long. Such diets can only be endured for a short period and so weight is often put on again equally rapidly once it has been abandoned. Equally any diet which is restricted to only one or two foods cannot provide the full range of essential nutrients and there is a high risk of deficiency diseases arising.

### 32.2.2 Undernutrition

A lack of an adequate quantity of all, or any one, nutrient will adversely affect health. Starvation is the result of a general lack of nutrients of which the absence of adequate protein and energy – **protein energy malnutrition (PEM)** – has the most obvious impact in the form of two conditions, kwashiorkor and marasmus.

**Kwashiorkor** results when there is severe protein deficiency in the diet. This frequently arises where the diet comprises largely one staple food such as cassava or yams, which is low in protein. It is common in young children particularly after weaning because this results in a change from protein-rich milk to a more carbohydrate-based diet. The symptoms are reduced weight, retarded growth, wasting of muscles and fluid in the tissues (oedema); the latter results in the distended abdomen which is so characteristic of this condition. Providing patients with protein, e.g. dried skimmed milk, will rectify the situation temporarily, but long-term solutions depend on an overall improvement of diet by increasing the protein production of those nations where the disease is common.

**Marasmus** has similar causes to kwashiorkor, although there is often also a carbohydrate deficiency. The symptoms include a wizened face, wasted muscles but not the oedema common in kwashiorkor.

# BIOLOGY AROUND US

## Eating disorders

The so called 'slimmers disease' **anorexia nervosa**' largely affects adolescent girls. It is estimated that about 1 in 150 are affected, four times the frequency in adolescent boys. Typical symptoms are a severe loss of weight and a refusal to eat, lack of menstrual periods (**amenorrhoea**) and an abnormal fear of being fat and a desire to be thin. It is relatively rare in Afro-Asian populations but is more frequent in Western cultures which tend to admire and idealize slim people. There is also an above average incidence in social classes I, II and III and in certain groups, like ballet schools, where thinness is considered important.

Anorexics grossly overestimate their own body size, even when they are dangerously underweight. They are often people who feel rather inadequate and attempt to control their own lives by refusing to eat. They may be unable to cope with the challenges of puberty and may come from families who, while appearing united on the surface, also find it difficult to cope with changes.

Anorexia often starts with dieting but the weight loss gets out of control; the sufferer may show a great interest in food but will still refuse to eat. Conflicts often begin in the family and the anorexic undergoes severe personality changes. Treatment for anorexia must be prolonged and recovery is often slow. It is often difficult to get an anorexic to admit that there is a problem and then to agree to treatment but it is vital because sufferers can die of starvation. The most severe cases are usually treated in hospital with a caring but strict regime in which weight gain is rewarded with privileges. Psychotherapy is important to prevent relapse but of the most severe cases only 40% recover fully.

**Bulimia nervosa** is a variant of anorexia, often seen in older girls. Bulimics often have a body weight nearer to normal and may also menstruate. Bulimia is characterized by recurrent episodes of 'binge' eating, frequently on fatty foods or cream cakes. During these spells the sufferer feels a lack of control over eating behaviour. The binges are followed by various methods to prevent weight gain: self-induced vomiting, the use of laxatives or diuretics, strict fasting or vigorous exercise. Such patterns of 'binging' and over-compensating for a high food intake can lead to serious electrolyte imbalances and to recurrent infections. Bulimics are often very strong characters who can become very depressed about their lack of control. They are treated by psychotherapy and by being encouraged to follow strict patterns of eating such as eating at set times and in a particular room and being encouraged to leave something on the plate.

Both anorexia and bulimia are complex conditions with no single cause or cure but perhaps there would be fewer cases if young people were not encouraged to feel that their body shape was so important.

The lack of a single nutrient in the diet leads to specific deficiency diseases. **Vitamin A (retinol)** is essential for the growth and metabolism of cells, for the maintenance of a healthy skin, cornea and mucus membranes and for the formation of rhodopsin (visual purple) a pigment in the retina of the eye. A deficiency of retinol therefore leads to a reduced growth rate in children, **poor night vision** and a condition known as **xerophthalmia**. In extreme cases xerophthalmia causes blocked tear ducts and as a result a dry, inflamed cornea. Prolonged deficiency leads to ulceration of the cornea and blindness.

**Vitamin C (ascorbic acid)** is needed for the formation of collagen, a major component of connective tissues and it also aids the absorption of iron from the intestines. Deficiency of ascorbic acid causes a condition called **scurvy** whose symptoms include bruising and bleeding under the skin, especially around the gums. Wounds and fractures are also slow to heal.

**Iron** is an essential component of the haemoglobin found in red blood cells which carries oxygen around the body. It is also part of the myoglobin molecule which carries oxygen in muscle. A deficiency of iron leads to **anaemia**, the symptoms of which are headaches, dizziness and lethargy.

**Vegetarian diets** are increasingly common for a variety of reasons. Any diet comprising milk, cheese and eggs as well as plant material should provide all the essential nutrients but if the diet is restricted to entirely plant material – **vegan diet** – then greater planning is necessary to ensure that all nutrients are included. Cereals, nuts and pulses are normally necessary to maintain adequate quantities of protein, energy, riboflavin and iron. Even then vitamin $B_{12}$ may be lacking.

## 32.3  Food preservation

Foods provide us with the essential nutrients we need for our survival but as similar nutrients are required by microorganisms our food is equally attractive to them. In order to obtain the nutrients from the food, microorganisms produce enzymes which digest the macromolecules into smaller units which can then diffuse into the microbial cells and as a result the food deteriorates and becomes unfit for human consumption. This is known as **microbial spoilage**. While many of these microorganisms are saprobiontic and cause no direct harm to humans, others such as *Salmonella*, *Listeria* and *Campylobacter* may cause food poisoning.

From the moment food is harvested or slaughtered it is not only subjected to microbial spoilage but also decomposition as a result of natural processes within dead cells. The normal active mechanisms which keep various cellular chemicals separate cease upon death and so reactions occur which result in cells digesting themselves. This is called **autolysis** and is largely the result of enzymes acting upon various components of the cell. While this process is useful to some extent in that it tenderizes meat and ripens fruits, for the most part it spoils food, not only making it unpalatable but also more prone to microbial spoilage.

## PROJECT

**It has been said that fresh fruit juices are 'better for you' than preserved ones.**

Use DCPIP to investigate this claim in respect of vitamin C.

Much food is produced only at one season and needs to be stored if it is to be available at other times of the year. Increasingly the points of food production are a long way from the places where they are consumed and so food must be preserved for some time if both quantity and variety are to be available. The preservation of food depends on being able to prevent both microbial spoilage and autolysis. In the short term blanching or cooking of food destroys the microorganisms and enzymes responsible for spoilage, but long-term preservation requires other mechanisms.

### 32.3.1 Freezing

The multiplication of microorganisms and the rate of reaction of enzymes are both temperature dependent. Chilling or freezing therefore reduces or halts the activities of both microorganisms and enzymes and so prevents food spoilage. Reducing temperatures to the range 0–10 °C is known as **chilling** and slows, but does not prevent, degradation of the food. Most household refrigerators chill food, typically at around 4 °C.

**Freezing** entails lowering the temperature to below 0°C with freezers operating at temperatures down to −20 °C; at this temperature enzyme activity and microbial reproduction ceases. A combination of water being unavailable because it is frozen, the inability to use nutrients/gases and mechanical disruption due to ice crystals results in the death of many microorganisms. Some however survive to resume normal activities once the food has thawed. The ice crystals which destroy microbial cells also disrupt the cells of which food is composed. **Quick-freezing**, in which the food temperature is reduced from 0 °C to −4 °C in less than half an hour, produces smaller ice crystals than slower methods of freezing. These smaller ice crystals cause less disruption of cells, helping to preserve the texture of food once thawed. The main advantages of freezing as a method of food preservation are:

1. Most foods can be frozen.

2. The appearance, flavour and texture of the food is preserved in most cases

3. The nutritive value of the food is preserved.

Briefly immersing certain foods, e.g. fruit and vegetables, in boiling water prior to freezing helps preserve them. This process called **blanching**, kills most microorganisms and denatures enzymes and so reduces spoilage during the cooling and thawing processes. Blanching however, reduces some of the food's vitamin C content.

### 32.3.2 Heat treatment

Heat is frequently used to preserve food because raising the temperature of food to a suitable level will both denature enzymes and kill microorganisms. The higher the temperature, the more effective the process, but the greater the damage to the quality of the food.

**Pasteurization** is a mechanism for extending the shelf-life of food without causing major changes to its flavour or nutrient value. Milk is the food most frequently treated in this way. As

## PROJECT

### Indicators can be used to assess the level of microbial activity in milk.

Use methylene blue or resazurin to investigate the keeping qualities of milk.

the only food provided for young mammals milk contains an ideal balance of nutrients, making it particularly vulnerable to microbial spoilage. Sterilizing milk by heating it to temperatures of around 105–110 °C for about half an hour will effectively destroy microorganisms and preserve the milk for some time. Unfortunately the process affects the flavour and colour of the milk as well as reducing its protein, vitamin C and thiamin content. In pasteurization, the milk is either heated to between 63 °C and 65.5 °C for half an hour or to 71.5 °C for 15 seconds. In both cases the milk is then rapidly cooled to below 10 °C. The adverse effect on flavour, colour and nutritional value is less than with sterilization although the shelf-life of the resulting milk is shorter.

**Canning** uses very high temperatures to destroy not only microorganisms but also their spores, and then the sterile food is sealed in a suitable container to prevent infection by microbes. The containers can be plastic or glass as well as the tinned steel traditionally used. Canning usually involves the following processes:

**1. Preparation** – the food is separated from any inedible material, is washed to reduce the number of microorganisms and chopped into a convenient size as necessary.

**2. Blanching** – the food is immersed in boiling water or steam to inactivate enzymes.

**3. Filling of container** – the cans are filled with the appropriate amount of food and any additional liquor eg. syrup, brine.

**4. Vacuum emptying** – a vacuum is applied to the cans to remove any air.

**5. Sealing** – the cans are automatically sealed.

**6. Sterilisation** – the cans are heated under a pressure to 121°C for varying times depending on the size of the can and the food it contains. This process destroys all microorganisms and their spores.

**7. Cooling** – this occurs slowly to prevent any buckling which could break the seals of the cans.

The high temperature used in the canning process alters the flavour, colour and texture of food. Compare a fresh strawberry for example with those which are canned. The nutritive content is also reduced with proteins, vitamin C and thiamin being especially affected. As heating breaks down the cellular structure, canned foods are more easily digestible and more of the nutrients are released. Macromolecules such as starch and protein are also partly broken down by heating and hence more readily digested.

### 32.3.3 Chemical inhibitors

Any chemical which kills or prevents the reproduction of microorganisms can potentially be used to preserve food as can those chemicals which inhibit the enzymes which cause autolysis. The chemicals used however must be harmless to health as they will be consumed; they must also penetrate the food to be effective and should not render the food unpalatable.

## Did you know?

It has been suggested that the high incidence of stomach cancer in Iceland is due to the large amounts of smoked fish consumed there.

As chemicals which have a direct metabolic effect on microorganisms are likely to be harmful to human metabolism, the inhibitors used to preserve food frequently affect conditions such as osmotic concentration or pH.

Vinegar has long been used as a preservative. As few microorganisms survive in acidic conditions, any substance with a low pH such as vinegar will prevent their growth. The flavour of the food is affected, although it is frequently a matter of taste as to whether this is a detrimental or beneficial change. Lactic, benzoic and sulphurous acids are also used to preserve foods and beverages; these are not always additions to the food, but sometimes a natural product. Yoghurt, for instance, is preserved by the lactic acid produced by the bacteria which convert milk into yoghurt and sauerkraut is cabbage preserved by lactic acid produced by bacteria which ferment it. The addition of salt or sugar to foods creates a solution with a high osmotic potential. As a result water is drawn out of microorganisms in the food and the consequent dehydration kills them. The preservation of jam operates on this principle.

**Curing** of certain meats, e.g. bacon, is achieved by injecting the meat with a mixture of salts (sodium chloride, sodium nitrate, potassium nitrate and potassium polyphosphate) and then immersing it in a solution of the same. The salts inhibit microbial growth as well as imparting a pink colour to the meat.

**Smoking** food entails exposing it to the smoke of certain burning woods over a period of time. Substances in the smoke inhibit microbial growth as well as giving the food a distinctive flavour. Bacon, ham, some cheeses and certain fish can be preserved in this way, mostly as an addition to other methods of preservation.

A number of chemicals have direct antibiotic properties; these include sodium nitrite, sodium metabisulphite, nicin and tylosin. The use of these chemicals is closely regulated by law as they can be toxic to humans in high concentrations. More details on preservatives are given in Section 32.4.1.

### 32.3.4 Dehydration

All microorganisms require water for their growth and reproduction. Equally the enzymes which cause autolysis cannot function without water and so the removal of moisture from food is a highly effective way of preserving it. This is best achieved slowly, otherwise a hard, dry outer layer develops acting as a barrier to the loss of water from the centre. Cereal grains, pulses, fruits, vegetables, meats and milk can all be preserved in this way.

### 32.3.5 Irradiation

Short-wave ionizing radiation such as X-rays or gamma rays can be used to inactivate microorganisms. Although irradiation produces little if any radioactivity in food, there has been consumer resistance to this method of preservation. The process uses gamma rays from radioactive cobalt–60 or caesium-137 or a beam of high energy electrons produced by a linear accelerator. The process is especially effective against insects and other parasites as these are sensitive to relatively low doses; stored grain can therefore be protected from damage by insects in this way. Irradiation can reduce the levels of vitamins such as ascorbic acid and thiamin in food. It does not prevent autolysis, nor will it render harmless those toxins already present from the activities of microorganisms.

### 32.3.6 Food packaging

It is clearly advantageous to health to minimize the amount of direct handling of food and this becomes even more important where the food has been sterilized since any handling will contaminate the food. Even exposure to air will lead to loss of sterility and so packaging of food has become a vital part of food preservation. Packages protect food during storage and transport, from a variety of potentially harmful factors such as mechanical damage, climatic conditions and contamination.

The glass, wood, metal, pottery and paper traditionally used for packaging are giving way to synthetic materials such as plastics, celluloses and polythenes. The advantage of these materials is that they can be easily moulded into a suitable shape. In some cases they can be used to **shrink-wrap** food. Here the air, which contains the oxygen needed by microorganisms, can be largely excluded from around the food, helping to preserve it. Where the wrapping material is impervious to oxygen this is particularly effective. **Vacuum packaging** involves actively removing all the air so that oxidation of the contents cannot occur. This is especially useful in packaging margarines and other fats which are readily oxidized. Where sunlight may also cause deterioration of the food, aluminium foil can be used rather than a transparent plastic. It is virtually impossible to remove all the oxygen as small quantities will be trapped within the food and in any case anaerobic microorganisms may continue to degrade it. Some plastic films have very low permeability to water vapour so that there is hardly any weight loss (as little as 2%) when fruit and vegetables are packed in these. Some cellophane films have up to 8–9% weight loss from their contents due to evaporation of water vapour.

A more recent method of preserving foods in their packages has been to modify the atmosphere in the package. Not only can all oxygen be excluded but the replacement gas may have some other beneficial effect, e.g. it may be used to delay ripening. **Modified atmosphere packaging (MAP)**, as it is called, uses gases which may be divided into three broad categories:

1. **Inert blanketing** – using nitrogen.

2. **Semi-reactive blanketing** – using a combination of nitrogen and carbon dioxide.

3. **Fully-reactive blanketing** – using carbon dioxide alone, or in combination with oxygen.

Nitrogen simply replaces the oxygen and so prevents aerobic microorganisms spoiling the food as well as preventing oxidation. Carbon dioxide can exert a powerful inhibitory effect on the growth of many bacteria and moulds, while the addition of oxygen can inhibit growth of some anaerobic microorganisms. To increase the shelf-life of meat from 2–4 days to 5–8 days, it is recommended that it be wrapped in an atmosphere of 60–85%

> ## PROJECT
>
> Investigate weight loss in packaged foods.

oxygen and 15–40% carbon dioxide. The oxygen helps to retain the desirable bright red appearance of the meat while the carbon dioxide inhibits microbial growth; cream on the other hand is packed with 100% nitrogen as any carbon dioxide confers a sharp taste to it.

# 32.4 Food additives

Substances may be added to food for a number of reasons:

**1.** So that the food will keep longer by preventing autolysis and/or microbial decay – **preservatives.**

**2.** To prevent food deteriorating by becoming oxidized – **antioxidants.**

**3.** To add taste to the food – **flavourings.**

**4.** To improve the natural taste of the food – **flavour-enhancers**

**5.** To make the food appear more attractive – **colourings.**

**6.** As part of the growing or processing of food – **residues**.

There is legal control of all substances added to food and for these purposes they are classified into six groups:

**1.** Preservatives

**2.** Antioxidants

**3.** Emulsifiers and stabilizers

**4.** Colours

**5.** Sweeteners

**6.** Miscellaneous additives

Each additive is given an **E-number** once its use has been permitted within the European Union. In some cases, the addition of substances to food is compulsory by law in Britain. Potassium iodide, for example, is added to common salt to help prevent goitre – a deficiency disease caused by a lack of iodine in the diet. Margarine for home, rather than catering purposes, has to have vitamins A and D added to help prevent rickets and xerophthalmia. The addition of vitamin $B_1$ (thiamin) and vitamin $B_3$ (niacin) to white flour is compulsory, to compensate for the removal of these substances when the germ of the wheat is removed during its production.

### 32.4.1 Preservatives

Certain food additives are designed to prevent autolysis and microbial decomposition so that food can be stored for longer periods and some of these chemicals were discussed in Section 32.3.3. Preservatives have E-numbers from 200 to 90. One common group of preservatives is the **sulphites and metabisulphites** which are salts of sulphur dioxide. As they leave an unpleasant after-taste they are used largely for foods which will be cooked or boiled, e.g. sausages, as this drives off the sulphur dioxide and leaves the taste unaffected. These preservatives also destroy any vitamin B$_1$ (thiamin) in the food. **Sorbic acid** and its salts are effective fungicides and so are used for foods liable to be contaminated by yeasts and moulds, e.g. fruit yoghurts and soft drinks. Meats and cheeses are often preserved by the addition of **sodium and potassium nitrites and nitrates** and illustrate the dilemma of using preservatives. They have a clear beneficial effect in that they are especially effective against *Clostridium botulinum* which causes botulism and, but for the use of these salts many more deaths would have resulted from this cause. On the other hand nitrites react with haemoglobin in the blood and reduce its oxygen-carrying capacity leading to dizziness and headaches. In young babies the condition can be life-threatening. For this reason nitrites and nitrates are not yet permitted in baby foods intended for children under six months of age. In addition, nitrites can combine with amines in the stomach to produce nitrosamines, substances with the potential to cause cancer.

Other preservatives include **benzoates** which are used in beer, jams, fruit pie fillings and salad cream and **propionic acid** which helps prevent moulds developing in bread and other baked products.

### 32.4.2 Antioxidants

Lipids (fats and oils) readily react with oxygen which converts the triglycerides of which they are composed into a variety of aldehydes and ketones. These give the lipids an unpleasant taste and they are said to have become **rancid**. Antioxidants are chemicals which prevent this oxidation process. They have E-numbers between 300 and 322 and include substances such as L-ascorbic acid, tocopherol and lecithins. Apart from their usefulness in preventing rancidity in lipids, antioxidants may be added to certain fruits and vegetables to prevent the browning which can occur due to the effect of a natural enzyme (polyphenol oxidase) which they contain.

### 32.4.3 Flavourings and flavour enhancers

Flavour is clearly an important factor when it comes to choosing food and manufacturers expend large sums in trying to tempt us to sample their 'tasty' products. Only salt, sweet, sour and bitter tastes can be detected by the tongue; much of what we call taste is really smell. Flavourings are therefore normally highly volatile compounds which readily produce an odour which can be detected by the nose. Many flavours added to food are natural substances derived from other foods. These include oils obtained from natural foods such as oranges, limes, lemons, garlic, ginger, clove and thyme. Other, less volatile, extracts used are obtained from a variety of spices and herbs.

Synthetic flavours may be less popular with consumers but are often cheaper and easier to use by manufacturers. These synthetic flavours are frequently very similar in chemical structure to their natural counterparts although their exact compositions are normally kept secret by the manufacturers. With over so many natural and synthetic flavourings currently in use, their control is more problematic than for preservatives and antioxidants.

**PROJECT**

**Lemon juice can prevent sliced apple going brown**

Find out what factors affect the rate of browning in various fruits and vegetables.

**Did you know?**

Over 3000 different flavourings are added to our food.

667

# BIOLOGY AROUND US

## Additives, allergies and ailments

The use of food additives is strictly controlled and they have to undergo rigorous testing before their use is licensed. Although tests must show them to be safe, effective and necessary a small number of people still show adverse reactions to some of them. Some additives have been linked to the behavioural disorder known as **hyperactivity** which most commonly affects children and young people. Sufferers become excited and impulsive with a short attention span. They may become aggressive and antisocial and some show a lack of muscular coordination. The Hyperactive Children's Support Group (HASG) recommends avoidance of a number of additives including many colourings, such as tartrazine (E101), quinoline yellow (E104), cochineal (E120) and ponceau 4R (E124). Also listed as possible risk factors are preservatives such as benzoic acid (E210) and antioxidants like butylated hydroxyanisol (BHA or E320).

Other groups who may possibly risk side-effects are asthmatics and those who are sensitive to aspirin. Different people react to different additives but the list of possible ones to avoid includes the preservative potassium benzoate (E212), the antioxidant propyl gallol (E310) and a number of flavour-enhancers. Monosodium glutamate (E621) causes some people to suffer short-lived effects such as palpitations, chest pain and dizziness. Although there is no evidence for any additives causing cancer in humans some, such as nitrates and nitrites (E249–E252) used as preservatives do cause cancers in rodents and may put humans at risk if they are consumed in large amounts (see Section 32.4.1). Their use is not permitted in baby foods. There are a number of antioxidants whose use causes gastric irritation in sensitive individuals. These include the gallates (E310–E312) and the two closely related chemicals butylated hydroxyanisole (BHA) and butylated hydroxytoluese (BHT) (E320 and E321). These antioxidants have also caused cancer in rats when consumed in high doses and they are banned in baby foods.

**Flavour enhancers** modify the taste of food by seeming to make existing flavours more prominent while themselves being tasteless. Salt and soy sauce have been used as flavour enhancer for many years in China and Japan. It is an ingredient of soy sauce, **monosodium glutamate** which is now the most widely used flavour enhancer; a derivative of the amino acid glutamic acid, it has been commonly used in Chinese cuisine. In large doses monosodium glutamate can cause dizziness, but used sparingly it can enhance the flavour of meats and certain vegetables. It is widely used in canned and dried meats and vegetables as well as in soups.

### 32.4.4 Colourings

Processing of food often results in loss of colour and yet consumers are particularly careful about colour when choosing food. However appetising and palatable it might be, few would

Do you fancy blue bread? How does colour affect our perception of flavour?

choose to buy blue meat! About 50 colourings are permitted and these have E-numbers from 100 to 180. Many are extracts from natural substances, e.g. beta-carotene from carrots, but others such as the azo dye tartrazine are synthetic. Some examples of permitted colours and the foods they are used in are given in Table 32.6.

TABLE 32.6

| Colouring | E-number | Used in |
|---|---|---|
| Curcumin | E100 | Margarine |
| Tartrazine | E102 | Cake mixes, soft drinks |
| Cochineal | E120 | Alcoholic drinks |
| Indigo carmine | E132 | Blancmange, confectionery |
| Chlorophyll | E140 | Canned vegetables, soups |
| Beta-carotene | E160 | Margarine, soft drinks |
| Lutein | E161 | Egg yolks (added to poultry feed to yellow yolks) |
| Anthocyanins | E163 | Yoghurt, soft drinks |
| Titanium dioxide | E171 | Confectionery |

### 32.4.5 Chemical contamination of food due to agricultural practices

Modern agricultural practices involve the addition of a wide range of chemicals to crops and animal feeds and residues from these chemicals sometimes remain in food consumed by humans. We saw in Section 18.6 for example, that pesticides such as DDT can increase in concentration as one moves up the food chain. Where humans form part of a food chain, they are invariably at the top and so at greatest risk from these accumulating residues. Moreover, the residues often build up in one particular tissue where concentrations can become very high. DDT, for example, being fat soluble, accumulates in adipose (fat) tissue and as a consequence many humans possess a higher concentration of DDT in some of their fat than many countries would permit in meat for human consumption.

We also saw in Section 18.5 how nitrates from agricultural fertilizers may run off into lakes and rivers. Drinking water taken from these lakes and rivers, despite purification, may contain levels of nitrate which are dangerous to young children because they react with haemoglobin reducing its oxygen-carrying capacity. Even in adults nitrates can react with amines in the stomach to produce the carcinogenic nitrosamines.

Concerns are also being raised about the use of hormones and antibiotics in the raising of animals for human consumption and the possible health risks they may present. Bovine somatotrophin (BST) is one such hormone.

# 32.5   Questions

**1.** Bovine somatotrophin, BST, is a hormone which, when given to cows, will increase milk production. BST used for this purpose is made by genetic engineering. The process is summarized below:

The BST gene is isolated from the DNA of a cow

↓

The BST gene is inserted into a bacterial cell

↓

The bacterium is cloned and the BST isolated

(*a*) Describe how enzymes may be used to isolate the BST gene from the DNA of a cow and insert this gene into the DNA of a bacterial cell.   (*3 marks*)
(*b*) BST is a protein. Explain why any BST that gets into the cow's milk will be unlikely to have any effect on a human who drinks milk.        (*1 mark*)
(*c*) Suggest why cows that are being treated with BST require extra calcium and protein in their diet.
                                              (*2 marks*)
                                         (*Total 6 marks*)

*NEAB June 1995, Paper BY07, No. 4*

**2.** Distinguish between the members of each of the following pairs.
(*a*) Flavourings and flavour-enhancers        (*2 marks*)
(*b*) Preservatives and antioxidants           (*2 marks*)
                                         (*Total 4 marks*)
*ULEAC 1996, Specimen Paper B/HB4D, No. 3*

**3.** Discuss the advantages and disadvantages of different methods of food packaging.
                                        (*Total 10 marks*)

*ULEAC 1996, Specimen Paper B/HB4D, No. 8*

**4.** The daily food intake of a 30-year-old woman contains 70 g of protein, 70 g of fat and an unknown amount of carbohydrate.
(*a*) Assume energy values per gram are 17 kJ for protein, 37 kJ for fat and 16 kJ for carbohydrate.
    (i) Calculate the maximum energy yield of the fat in the diet.                        (*1 mark*)
    (ii) If the energy needs of the woman are 10 800 kJ per day how much carbohydrate must she consume to be in energy balance? Show your working.             (*3 marks*)
(*b*) (i) Explain the term *essential amino acid*.
                                              (*1 mark*)

(ii) Suggest **one** reason why a person eating an entirely vegetarian diet must usually eat a greater mass and variety of protein per day than a person eating a diet containing animal protein.                        (*1 mark*)
                                         (*Total 6 marks*)

*AEB June 1992, Paper 1, No. 1*

**5.** *Staphylococcus aureus* is a bacterium which produces toxins in foods. These toxins are a common cause of food poisoning. *Staphylococcus aureus* grows aerobically and anaerobically, at an optimum temperature of 37 °C. It is killed at temperatures higher than 55 °C. The toxin it produces is heat-stable and remains active after heating to 100 °C or freezing at −18 °C.
The diagrams below show the sequence of events which led to an outbreak of staphylococcal food poisoning. The outbreak was traced to a manufacturer of processed cold meat.

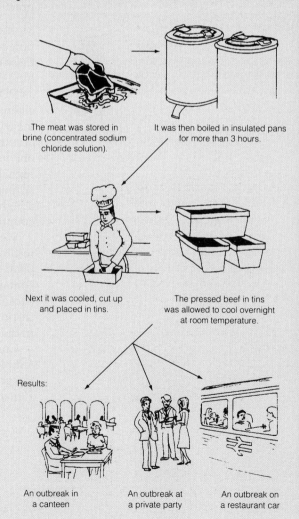

The meat was stored in brine (concentrated sodium chloride solution).

It was then boiled in insulated pans for more than 3 hours.

Next it was cooled, cut up and placed in tins.

The pressed beef in tins was allowed to cool overnight at room temperature.

Results:

An outbreak in a canteen

An outbreak at a private party

An outbreak on a restaurant car

(a) Comment on the biological principles underlying the following procedures:

    (i) storing the meat in brine (concentrated sodium chloride solution) for two days; (*2 marks*)

    (ii) boiling the meat in insulated pans. (*2 marks*)

(b) (i) Suggest the most likely source of contamination of the pressed beef. Explain your reasoning. (*3 marks*)

    (ii) Suggest **three** ways in which the outbreaks of food poisoning could have been avoided. (*3 marks*)

(c) State **two** other sources of microbial contamination of food. (*2 marks*)

(*Total 12 marks*)

*ULEAC June 1993, Paper 4B, No. 2*

Body mass index is given by the equation

$$BMI = \frac{Mass/kg}{(Height/m)^2}$$

The maximum BMI value recommended for good health is 25. A person with a BMI value greater than this is probably overweight.

(a) The table below shows the height and mass of six 18-year-old students.

| Student | Height/m | Mass/kg |
|---|---|---|
| Susan | 1.50 | 54 |
| Nasreen | 1.65 | 71 |
| Rebecca | 1.79 | 77 |
| Chris | 1.82 | 79 |
| Mike | 1.60 | 74 |
| Ashish | 1.68 | 65 |

    (i) Which of these students is/are overweight, according to their body mass indices? Show your reasoning. (*4 marks*)

    (ii) A person is diagnosed as clinically obese if he or she has a body mass 15% or more above the maximum recommended for his or her height. Give the name(s) of any student(s) in the table who would be diagnosed as clinically obese. Show your reasoning. (*3 marks*)

(b) Describe **one** method, other than measurement of body mass, by which a person might be diagnosed as obese. (*2 marks*)

(c) Give **three** reasons why the mean life expectancy of clinically obese people is less than that of people of normal body mass. (*3 marks*)

(*Total 12 marks*)

*ULEAC June 1995, Paper 4B, No. 1*

7. (a) In a study of dietary fibre intake in Denmark, people living in rural areas had a mean intake of 18.0 g per day while those living in cities had a mean intake of 13.2 g per day. Suggest an explanation for the difference in dietary fibre intake between these two groups. (*2 marks*)

(b) Various medical studies have shown that low dietary fibre intake is correlated with a high incidence of constipation and diverticulitis. Explain why it is not possible to say from this evidence that lack of dietary fibre causes constipation and diverticulitis. (*2 marks*)

(*Total 4 marks*)

*NEAB June 1995, Paper BY08, No. 2*

8. In formulating a diet, it is necessary to consider the nutritional value of different component foods.

The *biological value* (BV) of a source of protein is defined as the percentage of absorbed protein that is converted into body protein.

The *digestibility* of a source of protein is a measure of the proportion of that protein which is broken down into amino acids during digestion.

The *net protein utilization* (NPU) is the percentage of protein eaten that is retained by the body. The relationship between the BV, digestibility and NPU is given by the following equation.

$$NPU = BV \times digestibility$$

The BV and NPU values of six different sources of protein are shown in the table below.

| Source of protein | BV value | NPU value |
|---|---|---|
| Egg | 98 | 96 |
| Meat | 80 | 76 |
| Milk | 77 | 71 |
| Soya flour | 70 | 60 |
| Maize | 36 | 31 |
| Gelatin | 9 | 0 |

(a) (i) Calculate the digestibility of egg protein. Show your working. (*2 marks*)

    (ii) The digestibility of soya flour protein is 0.86. Comment on the difference between this figure for soya flour and that calculated for egg protein in (a) (i). (*3 marks*)

(b) The BV of a protein depends on the content of essential amino acids.

    (i) Explain what is meant by the term *essential amino acid*. (*2 marks*)

    (ii) Suggest why gelatin has a BV of 0. (*1 mark*)

    (iii) Suggest why, in the foods given in the table, most animal proteins have a higher BV than the plant proteins. (*2 marks*)

(c) Suggest a reason why protein malnutrition is common in countries where cassava (manioc) is the staple diet. (*2 marks*)

(*Total 12 marks*)

*ULEAC June 1996, Paper B/HB4D, No. 6*

# Further Questions

**1.** For each of the following biotechnological processes, state **two** benefits to society or to the environment:

    (a) the use of biogas digesters;     (*2 marks*)

    (b) the use of DNA probes;     (*2 marks*)

    (c) the production of gasohol.     (*2 marks*)

                        (*Total 6 marks*)

*Oxford June 1997, Paper 41, No. 1*

**2.** An experiment was carried out to investigate water loss from two arthropods, woodlice and caterpillars (of the large white butterfly).

10 woodlice and 10 caterpillars were exposed to a range of temperatures, from 10 °C to 60 °C, in dry air. The evaporation from the surface of each animal was measured in mg of water $cm^{-2}h^{-1}$.

The results are shown in the table below.

| Temperature/°C | Rate of evaporation of water/$mg\,cm^{-2}h^{-1}$ | |
|---|---|---|
| | Woodlice | Caterpillars |
| 10 | 5.0 | 0.0 |
| 20 | 7.5 | 0.0 |
| 30 | 10.0 | 2.0 |
| 40 | 14.5 | 3.5 |
| 50 | 19.0 | 9.0 |
| 60 | 26.0 | 13.5 |

    (a)  (i)  Plot the data on graph paper.   (*5 marks*)

        (ii) From your graph, find the rate of evaporation at 45 °C for each group of arthropods.     (*2 marks*)

    (b) State **two** ways in which the responses of the two arthropods to the different temperatures are similar.     (*2 marks*)

    (c) State **two** ways in which the rate of evaporation from the caterpillars differs from that of the woodlice.     (*2 marks*)

    (d) Comment on these results in relation to adaptations of these arthropods to a terrestrial environment.     (*2 marks*)

                      (*Total 13 marks*)

*Edexcel June 1997, (AS) B5/HB5, No. 1*

**3.** The table at the top of the next column shows part of the genetic code. The position of each base in an mRNA codon may be read from the table to give the abbreviation of the amino acid for which it codes.

    (a) Use the information in this table to give:

        (i)  an mRNA sequence which would code for the amino acid Tyr;   (*1 mark*)

        (ii) a tRNA anticodon for the amino acid His.     (*1 mark*)

| 1st position | 2nd position | | | | 3rd position |
|---|---|---|---|---|---|
| | U | C | A | G | |
| U | Phe | Ser | Tyr | Cys | U |
| | Phe | Ser | Tyr | Cys | C |
| | Leu | Ser | STOP | STOP | A |
| | Leu | Ser | STOP | Trp | G |
| C | Leu | Pro | His | Arg | U |
| | Leu | Pro | His | Arg | C |
| | Leu | Pro | Gln | Arg | A |
| | Leu | Pro | Gln | Arg | G |

    (b) The diagram shows the sequence of bases on part of one strand of a DNA molecule and two mutants of this.

                A A T G G C G A T

    **Mutant 1**   A A G G C G A T

    **Mutant 2**   A A T G G T G A T

        (i)  Give the name of the type of gene mutation in **Mutant 2**.   (*1 mark*)

        (ii) Use the information in the table to explain how each mutation will alter the part of the polypeptide for which this piece of DNA codes.

        **Mutant 1**           (*2 marks*)

        **Mutant 2**           (*2 marks*)

A phage is a virus that attacks bacteria. It consists of length of DNA surrounded by a protein coat. The flow diagram on the next page shows the results of a investigation which provided evidence that DNA was the genetic material.

    (c) Explain why the DNA was labelled with radioactive phosphorus and not nitrogen.     (*1 mark*)

    (d) Use evidence from the flow chart to explain the following:

        (i)  after infection, the phage protein remains outside the bacterial cell;   (*1 mark*)

        (ii) after infection, the phage DNA enters the bacterial cell;     (*1 mark*)

        (iii) DNA is the genetic material.   (*2 marks*)

    (e) Explain why the new generation of phages which emerge from the bacterial cells contain radioactive DNA.     (*3 marks*)

    (f) Three samples of phage DNA were each subjected to a different treatment.

    Sample **A.**   Incubated with the restriction endonuclease *Eco* R1.

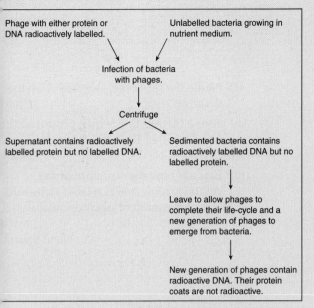

Phage with either protein or DNA radioactively labelled.

Unlabelled bacteria growing in nutrient medium.

Infection of bacteria with phages.

Centrifuge

Supernatant contains radioactively labelled protein but no labelled DNA.

Sedimented bacteria contains radioactively labelled DNA but no labelled protein.

Leave to allow phages to complete their life-cycle and a new generation of phages to emerge from bacteria.

New generation of phages contain radioactive DNA. Their protein coats are not radioactive.

Sample **B**.  Incubated with the restriction endonuclease *Hae* III.

Sample **C**.  Left untreated.

The drawing shows the result of electrophoresis carried out on each of the three samples.

A — DNA incubated with *Eco* R1
B — DNA incubated with *Hae* III
C — Untreated DNA

Explain why:
(i)   the untreated DNA moved the least distance;                    *(1 mark)*
(ii)  the DNA treated with *Eco* R1 produced a different pattern from that obtained for untreated DNA;          *(2 marks)*
(iii) the pattern produced when the DNA was incubated with *Eco* R1 was different from that obtained when it was incubated with *Hae* III.   *(2 marks)*
                    *(Total 20 marks)*

*AEB January 1997, Module Paper 2, No. 4*

**4.** The diagram shows part of a DNA molecule.

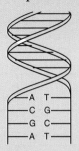

A    T
C    G
G    C
A    T

(a) Describe **two** differences between a DNA molecule and a molecule of tRNA.   *(2 marks)*
(b) Explain how a DNA molecule
    (i)  codes genetic information;      *(3 marks)*
    (ii) is able to produce an exact copy of itself during replication.      *(4 marks)*
(c) Describe how different types of gene mutation may lead to the production of different proteins.      *(4 marks)*
(d) Explain how the frequent use of antibiotics can lead to the evolution of resistant strains of bacteria.      *(4 marks)*
                    *(Quality of language: 3 marks)*
                    *(Total 20 marks)*

*AEB January 1996, Module Paper 2, No. 5*

**5.** In humans the condition of white forelock (a white streak of hair at the front of the head) is caused by a dominant allele, **F**, and it is not sex-linked. A study was made of several couples where only the female partner had a white forelock and was known to be heterozygous for this character. The phenotypes of their offspring were as follows:

| Phenotype of children | Numbers |
|---|---|
| Male, white forelock | 33 |
| Male, normal hair | 23 |
| Female, white forelock | 28 |
| Female, normal hair | 16 |

(a) Showing full genetical details explain why a 1:1:1:1 ratio would be expected in the offspring.      *(2 marks)*
(b) (i)  The chi-squared ($\chi^2$) test can be used to test whether the observed results fit the expectation. In the table at the top of the next page, $E$ represents the number of each phenotype expected and $O$ represents the number actually observed. Copy out and complete the last three columns of the table overleaf.      *(2 marks)*
    (ii) Calculate the value of $\chi^2$ using the formula:

$$\chi^2 = \sum \frac{(O - E)^2}{E}$$
                    *(1 mark)*

| Phenotype | Number observed (O) | Number expected (E) | Difference (O−E) | Difference squared (O−E)$^2$ |
|---|---|---|---|---|
| Male, White forelock | 33 | | | |
| Female, White forelock | 28 | | | |
| Male, Normal hair | 23 | | | |
| Female, Normal hair | 16 | | | |

(iii) Use the following extract from the $\chi^2$ table to decide whether the observed numbers of offspring are significantly different from those expected. Explain how you reached your answer.

(3 marks)

| Degrees of freedom | Probability (p) | | | | | | |
|---|---|---|---|---|---|---|---|
| | 0.90 | 0.50 | 0.20 | 0.10 | 0.05 | 0.02 | 0.01 |
| 1 | 0.02 | 0.46 | 1.64 | 2.71 | 3.84 | 5.41 | 6.64 |
| 2 | 0.21 | 1.39 | 3.22 | 4.61 | 5.99 | 7.82 | 9.21 |
| 3 | 0.58 | 2.37 | 4.64 | 6.25 | 7.82 | 9.84 | 11.34 |
| 4 | 1.06 | 3.36 | 5.99 | 7.78 | 9.49 | 11.67 | 13.28 |

(c) If the condition had been sex-linked, what ratio of offspring would be expected? Show how you arrived at your answer. (2 marks)

(Total 10 marks)

*AEB Summer 1997, (AS H. Biology) Paper 1, No. 12*

**6.** In an investigation, a student tested a number of supermarket desserts.

(a) Copy and complete the table which shows the results of five tests on a 'Caramel Dessert'. (5 marks)

| Test | Result of test | Conclusion |
|---|---|---|
| Iodine in potassium iodide solution added | Pale yellow colour | |
| Boiled with Benedict's or Fehling's solution | Blue colour | |
| Boiled with dilute acid then boiled with Benedict's or Fehling's solution | Brick-red colour | |
| Shaken with ethanol, ethanol decanted into water | White emulsion | |
| Biuret solution added | Lilac colour | |

(b) The drawing at the top of the next column shows part of a cellulose molecule.

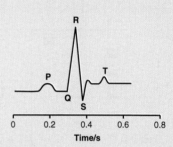

(i) Name the monomer labelled **A** on the diagram. (1 mark)

(ii) Name the reaction which produced the bond labelled **B** on the diagram. (1 mark)

(iii) Explain how the structure of the cellulose molecule is related to its role as a component of plant cell walls. (2 marks)

(Total 9 marks)

*NEAB February 1995, BY1, No.*

**7.** An electrocardiogram (ECG) shows the pattern of electrical activity associated with a heart. The diagram shows a normal ECG for one heart beat.

● **P** represents the electrical activity as it passes over the atria.

● **Q**, **R** and **S** represent the spread of electrical activity over the ventricles.

● **T** indicates the electrical recovery of the ventricles.

(a) Use the diagram to calculate the heart rate. (1 mark)

(b) There is a delay of 0.1 seconds between **P** and **Q**. Explain what causes this delay and why it is important in the functioning of the heart. (3 marks)

(c) What is happening to the flow of blood in the heart during **T**? (1 mark)

(d) The table on the next page shows the volume of blood flowing from the left ventricle to various parts of the body in one minute. The measurements were taken at rest and at various levels of exercise.

(i) What is the cardiac output per minute of this person when undertaking light exercise? (1 mark)

(ii) By what percentage has the blood flow to the skeletal muscle increased from rest to heavy exercise? (1 mark)

| | Volume of blood/cm³ | | |
|---|---|---|---|
| Organ | Rest | Light Exercise | Heavy Exercise |
| Brain | 750 | 750 | 750 |
| Heart muscle | 250 | 350 | 750 |
| Skeletal muscles | 1 200 | 4 500 | 12 500 |
| Skin | 500 | 1 500 | 1 900 |
| Kidney | 1 100 | 400 | 600 |
| Other organs | 2 000 | 2 000 | 1 000 |
| **Total** | 5 800 | 9 500 | 17 500 |

(iii) Use the table and your knowledge to give **three** ways in which this increase is achieved. *(3 marks)*

(e) (i) How is the muscle in the heart supplied with blood? *(1 mark)*

(ii) Why is an increased blood supply to the heart muscle necessary during exercise? *(1 mark)*

(f) The graph shows changes in phosphocreatine concentration in a muscle during and after a period of strenuous exercise.

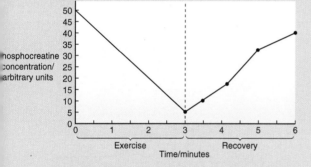

Calculate the mean rate of phosphocreatine consumption over the period of exercise. Show your working. *(2 marks)*

(g) (i) Complete the equation to show the relationship between phosphocreatine and ATP.

ATP + ......... → phosphocreatine + ......... *(1 mark)*

(ii) Explain why the change in phosphocreatine concentration in the period after the completion of exercise is associated with high oxygen consumption. *(3 marks)*

(iii) Suggest how the presence of phosphocreatine is more of an advantage to a sprinter than to a long distance runner. *(2 marks)*

*(Total 20 marks)*

*AEB June 1998, Paper 5, No. 4*

**8.** Primrose flowers exist in two different forms. Some plants have flowers which are 'pin-eyed' while the flowers found on other plants are 'thrum-eyed'. The two types of flowers are shown in the diagram.

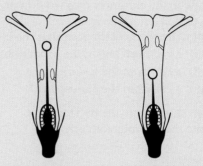

Pin-eyed flower        Thrum-eyed flower

(a) Using information from the diagrams:
(i) describe **two** differences between pin-eyed and thrum-eyed flowers; *(2 marks)*

(ii) give **one** piece of evidence that suggests that primroses are insect-pollinated. *(1 mark)*

(iii) Primrose flowers are normally cross-pollinated. Explain how the different structures of these flowers increases the probability that pin-eyed flowers will be pollinated with pollen from thrum-eyed flowers. *(2 marks)*

(b) Explain why variation is possible among the offspring of plants which:
(i) can only reproduce asexually; *(1 mark)*
(ii) are self-pollinated. *(2 marks)*

Flower type in primroses is determined by a group of genes which are closely linked called a 'supergene'. The letter **b** may be used to represent the group of alleles which determines pin-eyed flowers and **B** used to represent the group of alleles which determines thrum-eyed flowers. Pin-eyed plants are homozygous recessive and thrum-eyed plants are heterozygous for the supergene.

(c) (i) Give a genetical explanation for the fact that populations of primroses usually contain equal numbers of pin-eyed and thrum-eyed plants. *(3 marks)*

(ii) What is meant by genes which are **closely linked**? *(2 marks)*

(d) Occasionally primrose plants are found where the flowers show some of the characteristics of pin-eyed plants and some of the characteristics of thrum-eyed plants. Explain:
(i) how this might occur; *(2 marks)*
(ii) why it occurs only rarely. *(1 mark)*

Wild primroses are diploid and have 22 chromosomes in each somatic cell. Some cultivated varieties are tetraploid and have 44 chromosomes in each somatic cell. A wild primrose was crossed with a tetraploid plant. The wild primrose was chosen as the male parent and the cultivated plant as the female parent.

   (e) How many chromosomes would you expect to find in a nucleus from each of the following parts of the resulting seed:

      (i)  a cell from one of the cotyledons;
      (ii) a cell from the testa;
      (iii) a cell from the endosperm?    (3 marks)

The diagram shows how the two forms of phytochrome may be interconverted.

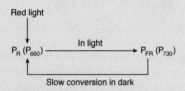

   (f) Use the information in this diagram to explain how exposure to:

      (i)  short-day conditions will lead to flowering in primroses;    (3 marks)
      (ii) long-day conditions will inhibit flowering in these plants.    (2 marks)
                                             (Total 24 marks)

   AEB Summer 1995, Common Paper 2, No. 1

9. The polymerase chain reaction is a technique used by biologists to make large amounts of DNA from very small samples. The process is explained in the diagram.

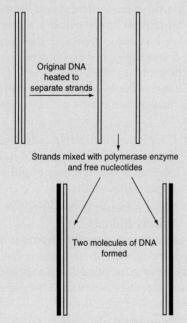

   (a) Explain why the DNA produced in this reaction is exactly the same as the original DNA.    (2 marks)

(b) At the end of the first cycle of this reaction, there will be two molecules of DNA. How many molecules of DNA will there be at the end of five cycles?    (1 mark)

(c) Give **two** ways in which this process differs from transcription.    (2 marks)
                                          (Total 5 marks)

   AEB Summer 1997, Module Paper 2, No.

10. (a) The two-spot ladybird, *Adalia bipunctata*, is a common British beetle. Copy and complete the table classifying *Adalia bipunctata*.

| Kingdom | |
|---|---|
| Phylum | Arthropoda |
|  | Insecta |
|  | Coleoptera |
|  | Coccinellidae |
| Genus |  |
| Species |  |

                                          (3 marks

(b) The diagram shows a food web linking two-spot ladybirds and some of the other insects living on nettle plants.

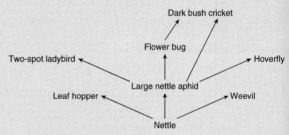

   (i)  Name the trophic level occupied by the two-spot ladybird.    (1 mark

   (ii) The nitrogen contained in the bodies of the insects in this food web becomes available to nettle plants. Describe the part played by bacteria in this process.    (3 marks

   (iii) The table shows the results from an ecological investigation of the organisms in one food chain from this food web.

| Species | Mean mass of organism/g | Population density/ number m$^{-2}$ |
|---|---|---|
| Two-spot ladybird | 0.027 | 21 |
| Large nettle aphid | 0.002 | 5420 |
| Nettle plant | 38.1 | 23 |

For this food chain, use the figures to help you to sketch the shape of:

1.  the pyramid of numbers;
2.  the pyramid of biomass.        *(2 marks)*

*(c)* The drawings in **Figure 1** show two different
varieties of the two-spot ladybird, the normal
red form and a black form. These two
varieties are determined by a single gene
with the allele for black body, **B**, being
dominant to that for red body, **b**.

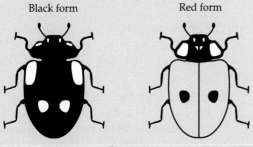

Black form        Red form

Figure 1

The bar chart shows the frequency of the
allele for black body in autumn and spring
samples over a number of years.

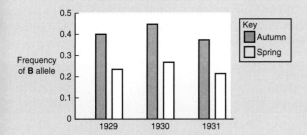

(i)  In the autumn 1929 sample, what was
the frequency of:
1.  the **B** allele;
2.  the **b** allele?        *(1 mark)*
(ii)  Use the Hardy–Weinberg expression to
calculate the expected frequency in the
autumn 1929 sample of:
1.  ladybirds with the genotype **Bb**;
        *(2 marks)*
2.  black ladybirds.        *(2 marks)*

*(d)* Some information about the biology of two-
spot ladybirds is given below.
 ● The two-spot ladybird spends the winter
   as an adult. When the weather gets
   warmer it becomes active and starts to
   feed and breed.
 ● The temperature of the ladybird depends
   on the temperature of its environment.
   The higher the temperature, the more
   active the ladybird.
 ● Temperature sensors placed under the
   wing cases showed that the black areas
   cool down and heat up faster than the red
   areas.

Use this information to explain the seasonal
changes in frequency of the **B** allele shown in
the bar chart.        *(4 marks)*

*(e)* **Figure 2** shows a variety of ladybird which
has very small wings and is unable to fly.

Figure 2

Describe briefly how you could show that
this condition is due to a single pair of alleles
with the allele for wingless, **w**, recessive to
that for normal wings, **W**.        *(2 marks)*
        *(Total 20 marks)*

*AEB Summer 1997, Module Paper 2, No. 4*

**11.** The graph shows changes in the mean diameter of
follicles and corpora lutea in the ovaries of a pig over
a period of 50 days.

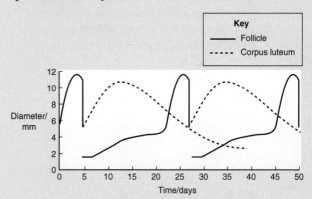

*(a)*   (i)  Explain the changes in follicle size
which took place between days 5 and
27.        *(2 marks)*
   (ii)  Describe the part played by hormones
in producing these changes.        *(3 marks)*
*(b)* Describe **two** pieces of evidence which
suggest that this animal did not become
pregnant over the period of time shown on
the graph.        *(2 marks)*
*(c)* Mark the graph with an arrow (↓) to show
**one** time when you would expect this animal
to be in oestrus.        *(1 mark)*
*(d)* In pigs, the allele for saddleback, **b**, is
recessive to the allele for white, **B**.
Describe, by means of a genetic cross, how
the genotype of a white pig may be
determined.        *(2 marks)*

(e) In an investigation into the timing of ovulation in pigs, a saddleback female was mated with two boars. At the beginning of oestrus, she was mated with a saddleback male; at the end of the same oestrus period she was mated with a pure-breeding white male. All the young were saddleback.

(i) Copy and complete the layout below to give a genetic explanation for the fact that all the young born in this investigation were saddleback.

|  | Male | Female |
|---|---|---|
| Parental phenotypes: | ..................... | ..................... |
| Parental genotypes: | ..................... | ..................... |
| Gametes: | ..................... | ..................... |
| Offspring genotypes: | ..................................... | |
| Offspring phenotypes: | ..................................... | |

(2 marks)

(ii) Explain the importance to a pig farmer of knowing the exact time of ovulation.
(2 marks)

(f) The most reliable sign of oestrus in a pig is the presence of the **standing reflex**. Only when she is in oestrus will a female pig stand with her hind legs held rigid when pressure is applied to her lower back.

(i) Copy and complete the diagram by adding and labelling the structures involved in a spinal reflex such as the one which controls this behaviour.

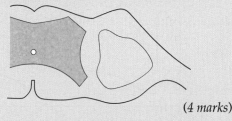

(4 marks)

(ii) Suggest how this reflex might be important in the life of a wild pig.
(2 marks)
(Total 20 marks)

*AEB Summer 1996, Module Paper 4, No. 4*

12. Haemoglobin is an oxygen carrying pigment found in red blood cells. A molecule of haemoglobin consists of an iron-containing haem group and a protein called globin. The diagram at the top of the next column shows how haemoglobin is produced in the human body.

(a) Describe the part played in protein digestion by:
(i) exopeptidases; (2 marks)
(ii) the epithelial cells of the small intestine.
(2 marks)

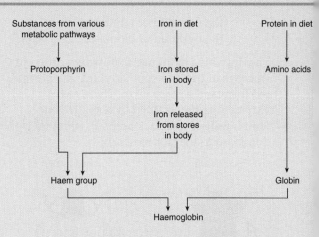

(b) Suggest why the level of protoporphyrin in the red blood cells of people suffering from anaemia may be higher than normal.
(2 marks)

In a study of three groups of women, the mean blood loss during menstruation was measured. Each of the women in group **A** was fitted with a standard intra-uterine device (IUD). Those in group **B** were fitted with an IUD which continually released small amounts of progesterone. Those in group **C** acted as a control. The results are shown in the table.

| Group | Treatment | Mean blood loss during menstruation/cm³ |
|---|---|---|
| A | Standard IUD | 91 |
| B | IUD which releases progesterone | 19 |
| C | Control group | 41 |

(c) Suggest an explanation for each of the following observations:
(i) anaemia is often associated with the use of intra-uterine devices; (1 mark)
(ii) the mean blood loss during menstruation of the women in group **B** was lower than that of the women in the control group. (3 marks)

(d) There are 12.5 g of haemoglobin in 100 cm³ of blood. The iron content of haemoglobin is approximately 0.3%. Calculate the mean amount of iron lost by the women in group **C**. Show your working. (2 marks)

(e) The graph on the next page shows the changes which took place in the haemoglobin concentration of the blood and the total blood volume of a woman during a normal pregnancy.
(i) Suggest an explanation for the change in haemoglobin concentration which took place between weeks 0 and 20.
(2 marks)

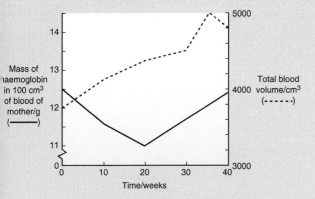

(ii) Explain the advantage of the change in haemoglobin concentration which took place between weeks 20 and 40.

(2 marks)

(f) The drawing shows an electronmicrograph of part of a human placenta.

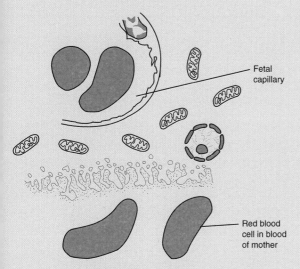

Fetal capillary

Red blood cell in blood of mother

The placenta absorbs iron from the blood of the mother mainly by active transport. Explain how **two** features, visible in the drawing, are adaptations for this function,

(4 marks)

(Total 20 marks)

*AEB June 1998, Paper 6, No. 4*

3. The following diagram shows a series of biochemical reactions in humans together with enzymes that catalyse these reactions and the position of a block which causes albinism, an inherited disease. This disease is caused by a defective form of enzyme B.

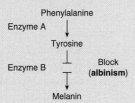

Phenylalanine

Enzyme A

Tyrosine

Enzyme B — Block (albinism)

Melanin

(a) Enzymes are proteins. Name the two steps by which the coded information in DNA is converted into amino acid sequences in enzymes. (2 marks)

(b) Proteins are synthesized in the cytoplasm of a cell. Outline the various processes involved in the synthesis of enzyme A in the cytoplasm of a skin cell making melanin. (5 marks)

(c) In most people enzymes A and B function normally. An altered form of enzyme B prevents tyrosine being converted into melanin. What sort of genetic change would account for this enzyme deficiency? Explain your answer. (2 marks)

(d) From the diagram, how many different gene loci are involved in melanin synthesis from phenylalanine? Explain your answer. (2 marks)

(e) Albinism is recessive. Use the letters **B** and **b** to show the genotypes of (i) albinos and (ii) people with pigmented skin. (2 marks)

(f) Albinos are not able to synthesize melanin. These people have no pigment in their skin and have pink eyes. Suggest how the absence of melanin might affect the reaction of their bodies to sunlight. (1 mark)

(Total 14 marks)

*Oxford & Cambridge June 1997, Unit B2, No. 1*

14. Copy and complete the following table using a tick (✓) if the atoms/structures **could be** present in the molecules indicated and a cross (✗) if the atoms/structures are **not** present in the molecules.

| | Amino acid | DNA | RNA | Mono-saccharides | Phospho-lipids |
|---|---|---|---|---|---|
| Carbon, hydrogen, oxygen | | | | | |
| Nitrogen, sulphur | | | | | |
| Nitrogen, sulphur, phosphorus | | | | | |
| Phosphorus | | | | | |
| Hydrogen bonds | | | | | |
| Glycosidic bonds | | | | | |

(Total 6 marks)

*Oxford February 1997, Paper 1, No. 2*

15. (a) State **three different** roles for ATP in cells. (3 marks)

(b) ATP may be synthesized by both oxidative phosphorylation and photophosphorylation.

(i) State **four** ways in which these two processes differ. (4 marks)

679

    (ii) Outline the mechanism of cyclic
         photophosphorylation.     *(3 marks)*

    (iii) Indicate **three** ways in which cyclic
          photophosphorylation differs from
          non-cyclic photophosphorylation.
                                   *(3 marks)*

*(c)* Explain why anaerobic respiration is
considered to be less efficient than aerobic
respiration.                   *(3 marks)*
                          *(Total 16 marks)*

*Oxford & Cambridge June 1997, Unit B1, No. 1*

**16.** *(a)* The formula below shows two amino acids
      joined together by condensation.

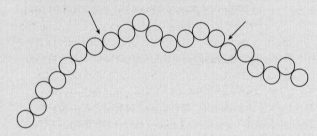

Draw a diagram to show how the molecule
in the formula above could be hydrolysed to
produce two amino acid molecules.  *(2 marks)*

*(b)* The diagram below shows part of a
polypeptide molecule.

Name the type of protein-digesting enzyme
that would hydrolyse the polypeptide at the
points shown by the arrows.      *(1 mark)*

*(c)* Describe **two** ways in which the epithelial
cells lining the ileum are adapted for their
function of absorbing the molecules
produced by digestion.        *(2 marks)*
                           *(Total 5 marks)*

*NEAB June 1997, Paper BY10, No. 3*

# Appendix: The water molecule

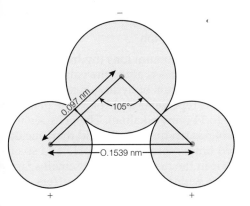

Fig. A.1 Structure of water molecule

Water is the most abundant liquid on earth. It is, however, no ordinary molecule. It possesses some unusual properties as a result of the hydrogen bonds which readily form between its molecules. These properties make water an ideal constituent of living things.

### Structure of the water molecule

The water molecule is made up of two atoms of hydrogen and one of oxygen. Its basic atomic structure is given in Chapter 1, Fig. 1.4. This is a simplified representation for in practice the two hydrogen atoms are closer together, as shown in Fig. A.1. By weight, 99.76% of water molecules consist of $^1H_2^{16}O$; the remainder is made up of various isotopes such as $^2H$ and $^{18}O$. The commonest isotope is deuterium ($^2H$) and when this is incorporated into a water molecule it is known as **heavy water**, as a result of its greater molecular mass. Heavy water may be harmful to living organisms.

### Polarity and hydrogen bonding

The distribution of the charges on a water molecule is unequal. The charge on the hydrogen atoms is slightly positive while that on the oxygen atom is negative (Fig. A.1). Molecules with unevenly distributed charges are said to be **polar**. Attraction of oppositely charged poles of water molecules causes them to group together. The attractive forces form **hydrogen bonds**. Although individual bonds are weak, they collectively form important forces which hold water molecules together. This makes water a much more stable substance than would otherwise be the case.

### Thermal properties

Due to the hydrogen bonds, more energy is required to separate water molecules. It therefore requires more heat than expected to convert liquid water into vapour; thus evaporation of sweat is an effective means of cooling in mammals. For this reason, the boiling point of water is much higher than expected. In the same way, its **specific heat capacity** is abnormally high. More heat is needed to raise the temperature of a given mass of water. Water is heated and cooled more slowly than expected – it in effect buffers sharp temperature changes.

At temperatures of 0 °C and below, water forms the crystalline substance ice. The arrangement of the water molecules in ice makes it less dense than liquid water. As a result, ice will form at the surface of a body of water such as a pond or lake. This insulates the water beneath and thus prevents the whole of the body of water freezing solid. Living organisms can therefore survive beneath the ice providing there is sufficient food and oxygen available. Water has its maximum density at 4°C; above this temperature the additional heat breaks some hydrogen bonds and so the water molecules are less densely compacted.

## Dissociation, pH and buffers

There is a natural tendency for water molecules to dissociate into ions.

$$H_2O \rightleftharpoons H^+ + OH^-$$
water    hydrogen ion    hydroxyl ion

The positively charged hydrogen ions become attached to the slightly negatively charged oxygen atom of another water molecule

$$H^+ + H_2O \rightleftharpoons H_3O^+$$
hydrogen ion    water molecule    oxonium ion

The complete reaction may be summarized thus:

$$2H_2O \rightleftharpoons H_3O^+ + OH^-$$
water    oxonium ion    hydroxyl ion

At 25 °C the concentration of oxonium ions (hydrogen ions) in pure water is $10^{-7}$ mol dm$^{-3}$ and this is given the value of 7 on the **pH scale**. When the concentration of hydrogen ions in a solution is $10^{-3}$ mol dm$^{-3}$ this represents a pH of 3. The pH scale ranges from 1 (very acid) to 14 (very alkaline). The pH scale is logarithmic and so a pH of 6 is ten times more acid than one of pH 7, pH 5 is one hundred times more acid than pH 7 and so on. The pH within most cells is in the range 6.5–8.0. It remains fairly constant because substances within the cells act as **buffers**. Buffer solutions do not appreciably change their pH, despite the addition of small amounts of acids or bases. This is important in cells, because fluctuations in pH could affect the efficiency with which their enzymes work. Apart from dissociating itself, water readily causes the dissociation of other substances. This makes it an excellent solvent.

## Cohesion and surface tension

Cohesion is the tendency of molecules of a substance to attract one another. The magnitude of this attractive force depends upon the mass of the particles and their distance apart. Gases, with their smaller molecular masses, have small cohesive forces. In liquids, the cohesive forces are much greater. Unlike gases, liquids cannot be expanded or compressed to any degree. Hydrogen bonding increases the cohesive forces between water molecules. One effect of these large cohesive forces in water is that the molecules are pulled inwards towards each other, so forming spherical drops rather than spreading out in a layer. The inward pull of the water molecules creates a skin-like layer at the surface. This force is called **surface tension**.

## Adhesion and capillarity

**Adhesion** is the tendency of molecules to be attracted to ones of a different type. Considerable adhesive forces exist between the walls of xylem vessels and the water within them. The magnitude of these forces has been estimated at up to 100 000 kPa. **Capillarity** is also the result of intermolecular forces between various molecules. If one end of an open glass tube is held vertically beneath the surface of water, the liquid can be seen to rise up the tube. The smaller the diameter of the tube the higher it rises. Xylem vessels, with their diameters around 0.02 mm, have considerable capillarity forces which contribute to the movement of water up a plant. Capillarity also plays an important rôle in the upward movement of water in soil.

Pond-skater walking on water

## Did you know?

All living things contain water. A lettuce leaf is 94% water, a human being 60–70% and a pine tree 55%.

# Glossary

**Absorption spectrum** a graph which results from plotting the degree of absorption of light of different wavelengths by a pigment such as chlorophyll

**Acid rain** rain which is more acidic than normal as a result of gases from the atmosphere which have dissolved in it

**Action potential** change which occurs in the charge across the membrane of a neurone when an impulse passes

**Activation energy** energy required to bring about a chemical reaction. The amount of activation energy is lowered by the presence of enzymes

**Active site** a group of amino acids comprising the region of the enzyme into which the substrate fits in order to catalyse a reaction

**Active transport** movement of a substance from a region where it is in a low concentration to a region where it is in a high concentration. This requires the expenditure of energy

**Allele** one form of a gene. For example, the gene for the shape of peas may appear in two forms, or alleles, 'round' and 'wrinkled'

**Allosteric** a term usually applied to enzymes whose shape may be altered by something in the environment. For example, the presence of a molecule other than the substrate

**Alternation of generations** shown by a plant life-cycle in which there are two distinct stages, one having haploid cells and the other diploid cells

**Amniocentesis** a technique for removing a small sample of amniotic fluid containing fetal cells. This can then be used for genetic screening

**Anabolic reaction** an energy-requiring process in which small molecules are combined to make larger ones

**Antagonistic muscles** muscles which occur in pairs; when one contracts the other relaxes

**Antibiotic** a substance produced by one kind of microorganism which inhibits the growth of another

**Antibody** a type of protein produced by lymphocytes in response to the presence of the appropriate antigen

**Anticodon** sequence of three bases on the transfer RNA corresponding to the codon on the messenger RNA

**Antigen** a molecule which triggers an immune response by the lymphocytes

**Apoplastic pathway** pathway through the cell walls and intercellular spaces of a plant

**Artificial insemination** introduction of sperm into the vagina by artificial means

**Atheroma** fatty deposits on the walls of arteries, often associated with high cholesterol levels in the blood

**ATP** (adenosine triphosphate) a molecule produced during respiration which is important in the transfer of energy

**Atrio-ventricular node (AV node)** area of muscle between the atria and the ventricles of the heart. It plays an important role in coordinating the heart beat

**Autonomic nervous system** part of the nervous system controlling the muscles and glands which are not under voluntary control

**Autosome** a chromosome which is not a sex chromosome

**Autotrophic nutrition** a method of nutrition in which the organism uses energy to build up complex organic molecules from simple inorganic substances

**Balanced diet** diet containing all the basic nutrients in the correct proportions for health

**Basal metabolic rate (BMR)** the amount of energy needed to maintain the vital activities of life such as breathing and the beating of the heart

**Batch fermentation** method of growing microorganisms in a fermenter without adding organisms or nutrients during the process. At the end of the procedure the fermenter is emptied and sterilized for re-use

**Biochemical oxygen demand (BOD)** the amount of oxygen removed from a body of water in a given time, usually measured over the course of 5 days at 20°C. The presence of large numbers of bacteria in polluted water increases the BOD

**Biological control** a specific means of limiting the numbers of a pest organism by using its natural predators or parasites

**Biomass** the amount of living material present, normally measured in a specific area for a given time

**Biosensor** equipment which uses biological molecules to measure the levels of certain chemicals

**Biotechnology** using microorganisms and biochemical reactions to produce useful products

683

**Bohr effect**   a term which describes the effect of additional carbon dioxide on the oxygen dissociation curve

**Calvin cycle**   a biochemical pathway which forms part of the light-dependent stage of photosynthesis

**Capillarity**   the ability of water to move up a fine tube

**Capture–recapture method**   a method of estimating the size of a population by catching a number of animals, marking them and then releasing them into the general population. The proportion of marked animals caught in a second sample provides a means of estimating the total size of the population

**Cardiac cycle**   a continuous series of events which make up a heart beat

**Carrier molecule**   a protein on the surface of a cell which helps to transport molecules across the cell membrane

**Carrying capacity**   the maximum population that can be maintained in a particular environment

**Cascade effect**   the way in which a small amount of hormone can cause a target organ to produce a large amount of product

**Catabolism**   chemical reactions involving the breakdown of large molecules

**Cell fractionation**   a technique used to separate cell organelles by breaking up the cell and centrifuging the mixture at various speeds

**Central nervous system**   term used to describe the brain together with the spinal cord

**Climax community**   the organisms that make up the final stage of ecological succession

**Cohesion-tension theory**   provides an explanation for the upward movement of water from the roots to the leaves of a plant

**Commensalism**   a term usually used to describe a nutritional relationship in which one organism benefits and the other is not directly harmed

**Community**   all the living organisms present in an ecosystem at a given time

**Competitive inhibition**   reduction in the rate of an enzyme-controlled reaction caused by a molecule which has a similar shape to the substrate

**Condensation**   chemical reaction in which two molecules are joined with the removal of a molecule of water

**Continuous variation**   variation in which organisms do not fall into distinct categories but there are gradations from one extreme to the other

**Counter-current system**   a mechanism by which the efficiency of exchange between two substances is increased by having them flowing in opposite directions

**Crossing over**   the process whereby a chromatid breaks during meiosis I and rejoins to the chromatid of its homologous chromosome so that their alleles are exchanged

**Deamination**   process by which the amino group is removed from an amino acid

**Deflected succession**   occurs when human activities prevent the climax community being developed in ecological succession

**Denitrification**   conversion of nitrates to atmospheric nitrogen by bacteria

**Dialysis**   method of separating molecules of different sizes. The term is often applied to artificial kidneys which rely on this process

**Diastole**   the stage in the cardiac cycle when the muscles are relaxed and the ventricles fill with blood

**Differentiation**   the process by which cells become specialized for different functions

**Diffusion**   the movement of molecules from a region where they are in a high concentration to one in which their concentration is lower

**Dihybrid cross**   a genetic cross involving two genes which are carried on separate chromosomes

**Diploid**   a description applied to cells whose chromosomes occur in pairs

**Directional selection**   selection which operates toward one extreme in a range of variation

**Discontinuous variation**   variation shown when the characters of organisms fall into distinct categories

**Division of labour**   adaptations of different parts of an organism to carry out particular functions

**Double circulation**   a blood system in which the blood passes through the heart twice for every circulation around the body

**Downstream processing**   the processes which follow the extraction of products from a fermenter

**Ecosystem**   all the living (biotic) and non-living (abiotic) components of a particular area

**Ectotherm**   an organism that uses the environment to regulate its body temperature

**Electron transport system**   a chain of carrier molecules along which electrons pass, releasing energy in the form of ATP as they do so

**Endocytosis**   the inward transport of large molecules through the cell surface membrane

**Epistasis**   when a characteristic is affected by two or more genes which interact with each other

**Essential amino acid**   an amino acid which cannot be synthesized in humans and which therefore must be included in the diet

**Eutrophication**   term applied to an increase in nitrates and phosphates in freshwater lakes and rivers. This may have a marked effect on the environment

**Exocytosis**   the outward movement of materials through the cell surface membrane

**Extracellular digestion**   chemical breakdown of food molecules occurring outside cells

**Facilitated diffusion** diffusion which involves the presence of protein carrier molecules to permit the passage of substances across the cell surface membrane

**Fermentation** a process by which energy is released from large molecules in the absence of oxygen. It produces lactate in animals and carbon dioxide and ethanol in plants and microorganisms

**Fertilization** the fusion of a male gamete and a female gamete to produce a zygote

**Fick's Law** states that the diffusion of a substance across a membrane is directly proportional to the surface area of the membrane and to the difference in concentration on either side, and inversely proportional to the thickness of the membrane

**Fluid mosaic model** a model used to explain the arrangement of phospholipid and protein molecules in a cell membrane

**Food chain** a simplified sequence used to illustrate the flow of energy from one organism to another in a community

**Gametogenesis** the formation of gametes which takes place in the ovaries (oogenesis) and the testes (spermatogenesis)

**Gametophyte** haploid, gamete-producing stage in the life-cycle of a plant

**Gene** a length of DNA on a chromosome normally coding for a specific polypeptide

**Gene mutation (point mutation)** a change to one or more bases in the nuclear DNA of an organism

**Gene pool** the total number of alleles in a particular population at a specific time

**Gene probe** a single strand of DNA which has a base sequence complementary to the gene being identified

**Gene therapy** a means of curing genetic diseases by replacing or masking the effects of a faulty gene

**Genetic engineering** a means of altering the genetic make-up of an organism

**Genetic fingerprinting** a means of distinguishing between different individuals by studying the similarities and differences in parts of their DNA

**Genotype** the genetic make-up of an organism

**Gluconeogenesis** the conversion of non-carbohydrate molecules to glucose

**Glycogenesis** the conversion of glucose to glycogen

**Glycogenolysis** the conversion of glycogen to glucose

**Glycolysis** first part of respiration in which glucose is broken down to two molecules of pyruvate

**Haploid** a term referring to cells which contain only a single copy of each chromosome

**Hardy–Weinberg principle** states that the proportion of dominant and recessive alleles of a particular gene remains the same if certain conditions are met

**Heterotrophic nutrition** a form of feeding in which the organism consumes complex organic material

**Heterozygote** a condition in which the alleles of a particular gene are different

**Homeostasis** the maintenance of more or less constant internal conditions

**Homologous** refers to structures which may have different functions but which have a common evolutionary origin

**Homologous chromosomes** a pair of chromosomes having the same gene loci and which are capable of pairing during meiosis

**Homozygote** a condition in which the alleles of a particular gene are identical

**Hydrolysis** the breaking down of large molecules into smaller ones with the addition of a water molecule

**Hydroponics** a means of growing plants without soil

**Hypothermia** a condition which results from the core body temperature falling below normal

**Hypoxia** a deficiency of oxygen reaching the tissues

**Immunization** an artificial means of producing immunity either by the injection of antibodies (passive immunity) or by inducing the body to produce its own antibodies (active immunity)

**Implantation** the attachment of a developing embryo to the lining of the uterus

*In vitro* refers to experiments carried out outside the living body, for example in test tubes

**Indicator species** an organism whose sensitivity to a particular abiotic factor enables it to be used to indicate the presence or absence of that factor

**Induced fit hypothesis** a variation on the lock and key hypothesis to explain the functioning of enzymes. It supposes that the substrate causes the active site to change shape slightly so that the two fit together perfectly

**Interspecific competition** competition between organisms of different species

**Intraspecific competition** competition between organisms of the same species

**Isotonic** solutions which have the same concentration of solutes as each other.

**Krebs cycle** an important pathway in aerobic respiration involving decarboxylation and oxidation

**Lag phase** stage in the growth of a population where the organisms may increase in size but they do not increase in number

**Light-dependent reaction** stage in photosynthesis in which light energy is required to produce ATP and reduced NADP

**Light-independent reaction**   stage of photosynthesis which does not require light energy and in which carbon dioxide is reduced to form carbohydrate

**Limiting factor**   a variable which limits the rate of a particular reaction

**Linkage**   term used to describe the situation in which two or more genes are found on the same chromosome

**Lock and key hypothesis**   simple model to explain the way in which the active site of the enzyme binds to the substrate to catalyse a reaction

**Log phase**   stage in the growth of a population in which there is a rapid increase in numbers

**Mass flow**   the transport in bulk of substances from one part of an organism to another

**Meiosis**   the type of nuclear division in which the number of chromosomes is halved

**Meristem**   a group of plant cells which are capable of mitotic division to bring about growth

**Metabolic rate**   a measure of the rate of energy release by the body

**Metabolism**   all the chemical processes that take place in living organisms

**Mitosis**   the type of nuclear division in which the daughter cells have the same number of chromosomes as the parent cell

**Monoculture**   term used to describe a large area of land in which only one type of crop is grown

**Multiple alleles**   term used to describe a gene which has more than two possible alleles

**Mutation**   a change in the amount or the arrangement of the genetic material in a cell

**Mutualism**   a nutritional relationship between two species in which both gain some advantage

**Negative feedback**   a series of changes which result in a substance being restored to its normal level – an important part of homeostasis

**Net productivity**   a measure of the rate at which an organism accumulates new body substances

**Niche**   the precise point at which an organism fits into its environment, both in terms of where it lives and what it does

**Nitrification**   the conversion of ammonium compounds to nitrites and nitrates

**Nitrogen fixation**   the incorporation of atmospheric nitrogen gas into organic nitrogen-containing compounds

**Non-disjunction**   the failure of chromosomes to separate properly during meiosis

**Null hypothesis**   a statement based on the assumption that there is no significant difference between two or more sets of experimental results

**Oogenesis**   the process by which female gametes are formed in an animal

**Ornithine cycle**   biochemical pathway in the liver that converts ammonia to urea

**Osmoregulation**   the ability to control the concentration of body fluids

**Oxidation**   a chemical reaction involving the loss of electrons

**Oxidative phosphorylation**   the formation of ATP through the oxidation of hydrogen atoms in the electron transport system

**Oxygen debt**   the amount of oxygen needed to oxidize the lactic acid that accumulates during anaerobic respiration

**Oxygen dissociation curve**   a graph illustrating the relationship between the partial pressure of oxygen and the percentage saturation of haemoglobin with oxygen

**Parasite**   an organism which lives on or in a host organism. The parasite gains a nutritional advantage and the host is harmed in some way

**Parthenocarpy**   fruit development without fertilization

**Partial pressure**   a measure of the amount of a particular gas present in a mixture of gases

**Passive immunity**   may be brought about when antibodies made in the body of one animal are passed to the body of another

**Peptide bond**   the chemical bond formed between two amino acids during a condensation reaction

**Percentage cover**   an ecological term to describe the percentage of ground covered by a particular organism

**Phagocytosis**   a transport mechanism through the cell membrane for large particles

**Phenotype**   the characteristics of an organism resulting from both its genotype and the effects of the environment

**Photolysis**   splitting of the water molecule which occurs during the light-dependent stage of photosynthesis

**Photophosphorylation**   the formation of ATP which occurs during the light-dependent stage of photosynthesis

**Phototropism**   growth movement of a plant organ in response to light, the direction of the response being related to the direction of the stimulus

**Pinocytosis**   the way in which fluids are passed through the cell surface membrane into the cell

**Plankton**   name given to all the microscopic plants and animals which float in the surface layers of open water

**Plasmid**   a small circular piece of DNA found in bacterial cells

**Plasmolysis**   the shrinkage of cytoplasm away from the cell wall which occurs as a plant cell loses water by osmosis

**ollination** the transfer of pollen from the stamen to the stigma

**olygenic inheritance** when a characteristic is controlled by more than one gene. Such characteristics ill show continuous variation

**olymerase chain reaction** a technique used to amplify NA, producing many thousands of identical copies

**olyploidy** the possession of three (triploid) or more ts of chromosomes in a cell

**opulation** a group of individuals of a particular ecies which are capable of interbreeding

**ositive feedback** when a substance varies from its ormal level, processes usually begin to return it to ormal but positive feedback results in further departure om the norm

**ressure potential** as water enters a cell by osmosis it eates a hydrostatic pressure which pushes outwards the cell wall. This is the pressure potential

**rimary structure (of a protein)** the sequence of amino ids which makes up the polypeptides of a protein

**rotandry** when the male parts of a flower mature efore the female parts

**rotogyny** when the female parts of a flower mature efore the male parts

$_{10}$ **(temperature coefficient)** the increase in the rate of reaction when the temperature is increased by 10°C

**uaternary structure (of a protein)** when a protein is ade of more than one polypeptide chain

**ecessive** term used to describe an allele which is only xpressed in the phenotype if two identical alleles are resent

**ecombinant** a cell which contains a different ombination of genes or alleles from that found in its arent cell

**eduction** chemical process involving the gain of ectrons

**efractory period** period during which the membrane f a neurone cannot be depolarized and no new action otential can be initiated

**esolving power** ability to distinguish between two oints that are close together

**espiratory quotient** a measure of the ratio of carbon ioxide evolved by an organism to the oxygen onsumed over a certain period

**esting potential** the difference in electrical charge aintained across the cell membrane of a neurone

**estriction endonucleases** groups of enzymes which e able to cut lengths of DNA at specific points

**etrovirus** a virus which contains the nucleic acid NA but which is able to make a DNA copy of this side a host cell, using reverse transcriptase

**Root pressure** a force generated by the roots of some plants which pushes water and mineral salts up into the xylem

**Saltatory conduction** the way in which nerve impulses 'jump' from node to node along a myelinated neurone

**Saprophyte** an organism which lives on dead or decaying organic matter

**Saturated fatty acids** a fatty acid in which there are no double bonds between the carbon atoms in the hydrocarbon chain

**Second messenger** a molecule found inside a cell which responds to the presence of a hormone outside it by activating a particular enzyme

**Secondary structure (of a protein)** the way in which the chain of amino acids in a protein is folded or coiled

**Selection** a process which results in the best adapted individuals in a population surviving to breed and pass their genes on to the next generation

**Selective breeding** a way of improving a variety of plants or animals by choosing individuals with the desired characteristics and breeding from them

**Semi-conservative replication** the way in which DNA can make exact copies of itself by unwinding the double helix so that each chain acts as a template for the next

**Sex linkage** a characteristic is said to be sex-linked if the genes which determine it are found on the sex chromosomes

**Single circulation** the kind of blood system found in, for example, fish where the blood only passes through the heart once during every circulation of the body

**Sino-atrial node** an area of cardiac muscle in the right atrium which controls and coordinates contraction of the rest of the heart

**Sliding filament hypothesis** a model which explains the way in which skeletal muscle contracts

**Solute potential** the pressure exerted by solute molecules in a solution

**Speciation** the evolution of two or more new species from existing species

**Species** a group of similar organisms which can breed together to produce fertile offspring

**Spermatogenesis** the process of forming male gametes in an animal

**Sporophyte** the diploid spore-producing stage of a plant

**Succession** a community passes through a number of stages from its origin to its climax. The transition from one stage to the next is called succession

**Symplastic pathway** the route taken by substances through the cytoplasm of plant cells

**Systemic insecticide**    a chemical which is absorbed into the tissues of a plant to control a pest

**Systole**    a stage in the cardiac cycle involving contraction of the heart muscle

**Taxis**    the movement of a whole organism towards or away from a stimulus

**Tertiary structure (of a protein)**    the irregular folding of a polypeptide chain in a precise way, determined by the sequence of amino acids of which it is composed

**Test cross**    a cross between an organism of unknown genotype and the relevant homozygous recessive organism

**Thermoregulation**    the processes involved in maintaining a more or less constant body temperature

**Tidal volume**    the volume of air breathed in and out when a person is at rest

**Transamination**    the formation of amino acids by transferring amino groups from an amino acid to another molecule

**Transcription**    the formation of a mRNA molecule from the DNA which makes up a particular gene. It is the first part of protein synthesis

**Translation**    the process whereby the code on a piece of mRNA is converted to a particular sequence of amino acids which will go on to make a polypeptide and ultimately a protein

**Translocation**    the transport of substances from one part of a plant to another

**Transpiration**    evaporation of water from a plant

**Trophic level**    one of the steps in a food chain

**Tropism**    a growth movement of part of a plant in response to a directional stimulus

**True breeding**    an organism which is homozygous for the allele under consideration

**Turgid**    a turgid cell is one that is full of water and has a water potential of zero

**Ultrafiltration**    filtration under pressure. A term often applied to the first stage of urine formation in the kidney

**Ultrasound**    very high frequency sound waves used in medical screening techniques

**Unsaturated fatty acid**    a fatty acid in which the hydrocarbon chain has one or more double bonds between the carbon atoms

**Variation**    differences which exist between living organisms as a result of their genotypes and/or the environment

**Vasoconstriction**    narrowing of the blood vessels

**Vasodilation**    widening of the blood vessels

**Vector**    a carrier. This may refer to something like a plasmid carrying DNA into a cell, or to an organism which carries a parasite to its primary host

**Ventilation**    a mechanism ensuring the exchange of gases across a respiratory surface

**Viability**    the ability of seeds to germinate under suitable conditions

**Vital capacity**    the total volume of air that can be breathed in and out of the lungs during one deep breath

**Water potential**    when water molecules move they exert a pressure on the membrane that surrounds them; this is the water potential. The greater the number of water molecules present, the higher the water potential

**Weed**    any plant growing where it is not wanted

**Wilting**    a condition which occurs when the rate of water loss by transpiration exceeds water uptake by the roots

**X chromosome**    one of the sex chromosomes. Human females have two (XX) and males have one (XY)

**Xerophyte**    a plant adapted to live in dry conditions

**Y chromosome**    one of the sex chromosomes. In humans its presence brings about the development of the testes

**Zygote**    cell formed by the fusion of two gametes

# Index